ENCYCLOPEDIA OF
Twentieth–Century Photography

BOARD OF ADVISORS

Ellen Handy
Art History Faculty, Art Department
City College of New York
New York, New York

Mark Haworth-Booth
Senior Curator of Photographs
Victoria and Albert Museum
London, United Kingdom

Lynn Herbert
Senior Curator
Contemporary Arts Museum
Houston, Texas

Eikoh Hosoe
Photographer and Professor
Tokyo, Japan

John P. Jacob
Director
Photography Curators Resource
Blue Hill, Maine

Deborah Klochko
Director
Ansel Adams Center for Photography
San Francisco, California

Ryszard Kluszczynski
Curator and Writer
Warsaw, Poland

Laura Letinsky
Faculty, Committee on the Visual Arts
University of Chicago
Chicago, Illinois

Asko Mäkelä
Director, Finnish Museum of Photography
Helsinki, Finland

Arthur Ollman
Director and Curator
Museum of Photographic Arts
San Diego, California

Esther G. Parada
Faculty, Art Department, School of Art and Design
University of Illinois
Chicago, Illinois

Ulrich Pohlmann
Director
Münchner Stadtmuseum
München, Germany

Charles Dare Scheips
Archivist
Condé Nast Publications
New York, New York

Charlotte Townsend-Gault
Faculty, Department of Fine Arts
University of British Columbia
Vancouver, Canada

Gary van Wyk
Curator
Axis Gallery
New York, New York

Katherine Ware
Curator of Photographs
Philadelphia Museum of Art
Philadelphia, Pennsylvania

Deborah Willis-Kennedy
Curator
Anacostia Museum and Center for African American History and Culture
Smithsonian Institution
Washington, D.C.

Trudy Wilner Stack
Curator, Historian
Tucson, Arizona

Paul Wombell
Director
The Photographers' Gallery
London, United Kingdom

Tim Wride
Curator of Photography
Los Angeles County Museum of Art
Los Angeles, California

ENCYCLOPEDIA OF

Twentieth-Century Photography

VOLUME 1

A–F

INDEX

Lynne Warren

EDITOR

Routledge

Taylor & Francis Group

New York London

Published in 2006 by
Routledge
Taylor & Francis Group
270 Madison Avenue
New York, NY 10016

Published in Great Britain by
Routledge
Taylor & Francis Group
2 Park Square
Milton Park, Abingdon
Oxon OX14 4RN

Printed in the United States of America on acid-free paper
10 9 8 7 6 5 4 3 2 1

International Standard Book Number-10: 1-57958-393-8 (Hardcover)
International Standard Book Number-13: 978-1-57958-393-4 (Hardcover)
Library of Congress Card Number 2005046287

Library of Congress Cataloging-in-Publication Data

Encyclopedia of twentieth-century photography / Lynne Warren, editor.
p. cm.
Includes bibliographical references and index.
ISBN 1-57958-393-8 (set : alk. paper) -- ISBN 0-415-97665-0 (vol. 1: alk. paper) -- ISBN 0-415-97666-9 (vol. 2 : alk. paper) -- ISBN 0-415-97667-7 (vol. 3 : alk. paper)
Photography, Artistic. I. Title: Encyclopedia of 20th century photography. II. Warren, Lynne.

TR642.E5 2005
770'.9'0403--dc22 2005046287

T&F informa
Taylor & Francis Group is the Academic Division of T&F Informa plc.

Visit the Taylor & Francis Web site at
http://www.taylorandfrancis.com

and the Routledge Web site at
http://www.routledge-ny.com

Contents

Contributors xi

Alphabetical List of Entries xv

Thematic List of Entries xxi

Glossary xxvii

Introduction xxxvii

Entries A to Z 1

Index I1

CONTRIBUTORS

Stuart Alexander
Jenny Allred Redmann
Vangelis Athanassopoulos
Andrew Atkinson
Lane Barden
Suvash Barden
Nancy Barr
Terry Barrett
Anne Barthélemy
Rob Baum
Lili Bezner
Momolina Bhattacharyya
Heather Blaha
Anne Blecksmith
Nancy Breslin
Amanda Brown
Leslie K. Brown
Wolfgang Brueckle
Catherine Burdick
Katherine Bussard
Matthew Butson
R.M. Callender
Michael Carlebach
Justin Carville
Peter Caws
James Charnock
Milan Chlumsky
Vincent Cianni
Yves Clemmen
Alan Cohen
Jill Conner
Leslie Humm Cormier
Andy Crank
Mike Crawford
Isobel Crombie
Cristina Cuevas-Wolf
Thomas Cyril
Lorraine Anne Davis
Scott Davis
Peter Decherney
Anthony DeGeorge
Margaret Denny
Penelope Dixon
Julia Dolan
Donald A. Rosenthal
Petra Dreiser
Erina Duganne
Jeffrey Edelstein

Diana Edkins
Jan Estep
Hannah Feldman
Jane Fletcher
Stacey Fox
Jason Francisco
Daniel Friedman
Maki Fukuoka
John Fuller
Michel Gaboury
Monika Kin Gagnon
William Ganis
Daniella Geo
Christian Gerstheimer
Constance W. Glenn
Renata Golden
Richard Gordon
Sara Greenberger
Kristen Gresh
Kristina Grub
Justin Gustainis
David Eduard Haberstich
Sophie Hackett
Matthias Harder
Lindsay Harris
Janice Hart
Katharina Hausel
Brigitte Hausmann
Richard Haw
Jennifer Headley
Lisa Henry
Scarlett Higgins
Randy Hines
Katherine Hoffman
Ali Hossaini
Kirsten Hoving
Andrew Howe
Richard Howells
Christina Ionescu
Brandi Iryshe
Steven Jacobs
Philippe Jarjat
Karen Jenkins
Martyn Jolly
Birgit Kaufer
Rachel Keith
Jean Kempf
Kay Kenny
Geraldine Kiefer
Laura Kleger
Peter Kloehn
Lilly Koltun
Sabine Kriebel
Yves Laberge
Kimberly Lamm
John H. Lawrence
Susan Laxton
Bob Lazaroff
Peter Le Grand
Danielle F. M. Leenaerts
Marc Leverette
Linda Levitt

Tricia R. Louvar
Sarah Lowe
Darwin Marable
Sara L. Marion
Kelly Maron
Patrick Mathieu
Stacey McCarroll
Jim McDonald
Sarah McDonald
Bruce McKaig
Lambert McLaurin
Julie Mellby
Ara Merjian
Marco Merkli
Johanna Mizgala
Dominic Molon
Stephen Monteiro
Jean-Luc Monterosso
Allison M. Moore
Susan Morgan
Rebecca Morse
John Mraz
Kevin J. Mulhearn
Alla Myzelev
Yasufumi Nakamori
Caryn E. Neumann
Nathalie Neumann
Jennifer Olson-Rudenko
Robert Oventile
Daniel Palmer
J. P. Park
Sara-Jane Parsons
Martin Patrick
Lori Pauli
Nancy Pedri
John Peffer
Michele Penhall
Nuno Pinheiro
Justin Pittas-Giroux
Mark Pohlad
Maren Polte
Luca Prono
Laurel Ptak
Mark Rawlinson
Shirley Read
Kevin Reilly
Melissa Renn
Yolanda Retter
Lyle Rexer
Kate Rhodes
Edward A. Riedinger
Leesa Rittelmann
Claudia Rivers
Jean Robertson
Naomi Rosenblum
Cynthia Elyce Rubin
Mark Rudnicki
Esther Ruelfs
Roberta Russo
Rolf Sachsse
Marisa Sanchez
Manuel Santos

Roger Sayre
Rudolf Scheutle
Elizabeth Schlatter
Franz-Xaver Schlegel
Franziska Schmidt
Jennifer Schneider
Savannah Schroll
Danielle Schwartz
Erin Schwartz
Rebecca Senf
Jeffrey Shantz
Roni Shapira
Carla Rose Shapiro
Nancy Shawcross
Nabeela Sheikh
Scott Sherer
M. Kathryn Shields
Elizabeth Siegel
Christye Sisson
George Slade
Lynn Somers-Davis
Linda Steer
John Stomberg
Ryuji Suzuki
Johan Swinnen
A. Krista Sykes
Blaise Tobia
Susan Todd-Raque
Rebecca Tolley-Stokes
Charlotte Townsend-Gault
Peter Turner
Stijn Van De Vyver
Gary van Wyk
Miriam Voss
Scott Walden
Rachel K. Ward
Grant Warren
Lynne Warren
Shannon Wearing
Max Weintraub
Sarah Wheeler
Elizabeth K. Whiting
Renate Wickens
Brian Winkenweder
Marianne Berger Woods
Kelly Xintaris
Nancy Yakimoski
Shin-Yi Yang
Janet A. Yates
Ronald Young
Stephenie Young
Raul Zamudio
Leon Zimlich
Annalisa Zox-Weaver
Catherine Zuromkis

ALPHABETICAL LIST OF ENTRIES

A

Abbott, Berenice
Abstraction
Adams, Ansel
Adams, Eddie
Adams, Robert
Aerial Photography
Africa: An Overview, Photography in
Africa: Central and West, Photography in
Africa: East and Indian Ocean Islands, Photography in
Africa: North, Photography in
Africa: South and Southern, Photography in
Afterimage
Agitprop
Alpert, Max
An American Place
Appropriation
Araki, Nobuyoshi
Arbus, Diane
Architectural Photography
Archives
Arnold, Eve
Art Institute of Chicago
Artists' Books
Astrophotography
Atget, Eugène
Auerbach, Ellen
Australia, Photography in
Australian Centre for Photography

B

Ballen, Roger
Baltz, Lewis
Barr, Jr., Alfred H.
Barthes, Roland
Bauhaus
Bayer, Herbert
Beaton, Cecil
Becher, Bernd and Hilla
Bellmer, Hans
Berger, John
Berlinische Galerie
Bernhard, Ruth
Beuys, Joseph
Bibliothèque nationale de France
Billingham, Richard
Bischof, Werner
Black Star
Blossfeldt, Karl
Blumenfeld, Erwin
Body Art
Boltanski, Christian
Bourdeau, Robert
Bourke-White, Margaret
Bracketing
Bragaglia, Anton Giulio
Brandt, Bill
Brassaï
Bravo, Manuel Álvarez
Breitenbach, Joseph
Brownie
Bruguière, Francis
Burgin, Victor
Burning-In
Burri, René
Burrows, Larry
Burson, Nancy

C

Cable Release
Cadieux, Geneviève
Cahun, Claude

Callahan, Harry
Calle, Sophie
Camera: 35 mm
Camera: An Overview
Camera: Diana
Camera: Digital
Camera: Disposable
Camera: Instant or Polaroid
Camera Obscura
Camera: Pinhole
Camera: Point and Shoot
Canada, Photography in
Capa, Robert
Caponigro, Paul
Carrillo, Manuel
Cartier-Bresson, Henri
Censorship
Center for Creative Photography
Central America, Photography in
Centre National de la Photographie
Chambi, Martin
Chargesheimer (Hargesheimer, Karl-Heinz)
China and Taiwan, Photography in
Christenberry, William
Clark, Larry
Close, Chuck
Coburn, Alvin Langdon
Cohen, Lynne
Coke, Van Deren
Color Temperature
Color Theory: Natural and Synthetic
Composition
Conceptual Photography
Condé Nast
Connor, Linda
Conservation
Constructed Reality
Contact Printing
Contrast
Coplans, John
Corbis/Bettmann
Corporate Collections
Creative Camera
Crewdson, Gregory
Crime Photography
Cropping
Cunningham, Imogen

D

Dada
Dahl-Wolfe, Louise
Darkroom
Dater, Judy
Davidson, Bruce
de Meyer, Baron Adolph
Deakin, John
DeCarava, Roy
Decisive Moment, The
Deconstruction
Delano, Jack
Depth of Field
Developing Processes
diCorcia, Philip-Lorca
Digital Photography
Dijkstra, Rineke
Discursive Spaces
Documentary Photography
Dodging
Doisneau, Robert
Domon, Ken
Drtikol, František
Duncan, David Douglas
Dye Transfer

E

Eastman Kodak Company
Edgerton, Harold E.
Eggleston, William
Eisenstaedt, Alfred
Elsken, Ed van der
Emulsion
Enlarger
Erfurth, Hugo
Erotic Photography
Erwitt, Elliott
Ethics and Photography
Europe: An Overview, Photography in
Evans, Frederick H.
Evans, Walker
Export, Valie (Waltraud Lehner)
Exposure

F

Family Photography
Fani-Kayode, Rotimi
Farm Security Administration
Fashion Photography
Faucon, Bernard
Faurer, Louis
Feininger, Andreas
Feininger, T. Lux
Feldmann, Hans-Peter
Feminist Photography
Festivals
Film
Film: High-Contrast
Film: Infrared

Filters
Fine Arts Presses
Finsler, Hans
Fischer, Arno
Fischli, Peter and David Weiss
Flaherty, Robert Joseph
Flusser, Vilem
Formalism
Fosso, Samuel
France, Photography in
Franck, Martine
Frank, Robert
Freund, Gisèle
Friends of Photography
Fukase, Masahisa
Fukuda, Miran
Funke, Jaromir
Furuya, Seiichi
Fuss, Adam
Futurism

G

Galleries
Gelpke, Andre
Germany and Austria, Photography in
Gerz, Jochen
Giacomelli, Mario
Gibson, Ralph
Gidal, N. Tim
Gilbert & George
Gilpin, Laura
Gloaguen, Hervé
Gohlke, Frank
Goldin, Nan
Gowin, Emmet
Graham, Dan
Graham, Paul
Grossman, Sid
Group f/64
Gursky, Andreas
Gutmann, John

H

Haas, Ernst
Hahn, Betty
Hajek-Halke, Heinz
Halsman, Philippe
Hamaya, Hiroshi
Hammarskiöld, Hans
Hand Coloring and Hand Toning
Hartmann, Erich
Heartfield, John (Helmut Herzfelde)
Heath, David Martin
Heinecken, Robert
Hellebrand, Nancy
Henderson, Nigel
Henri, Florence
Hers, François
Hilliard, John
Hine, Lewis
Hiro
History of Photography: Nineteenth-Century Foundations
History of Photography: Twentieth-Century Developments
History of Photography: Twentieth-Century Pioneers
History of Photography: Interwar Years
History of Photography: Postwar Era
History of Photography: the 1980s
Höch, Hannah
Horst, Horst P.
Hosoe, Eikoh
Hoyningen-Huene, George
Hurrell, George
Hütte, Axel

I

Image Construction: Perspective
Image Theory: Ideology
Impressionism
Industrial Photography
Infrared Photography
Instant Photography
Institute of Design (New Bauhaus)
Internet and Photography, The
Interpretation
Ishimoto, Yasuhiro
Iturbide, Graciela
Izis (Israel Bidermanas)

J

J. Paul Getty Museum
Jacobi, Lotte
Janah, Sunil
Japan, Photography in
Jones, Harold
Jones, Pirkle
Josephson, Kenneth

K

Karsh, Yousuf
Käsebier, Gertrude
Kawada, Kikuji
Keetman, Peter
Keïta, Seydou

Kertész, André
Kessels, Willy
Kesting, Edmund
Khaldei, Yevgeny (Chaldej, Jewgeni)
Killip, Chris
Klein, Aart
Klein, Astrid
Klein, William
Klett, Mark
Korea, Photography in
Koudelka, Josef
Kozloff, Max
Krauss, Rosalind
Kruger, Barbara
Krull, Germaine

L

Lange, Dorothea
Lartigue, Jacques Henri
Latin America: An Overview, Photography in
Laughlin, Clarence John
Lebeck, Robert
Lee, Russell
Leibovitz, Annie
Lemagny, Jean Claude
Lens
Lerski, Helmar
Levinthal, David
Levi-Strauss, Claude
Levitt, Helen
Levy, Julien
Liberman, Alexander
Library of Congress
Liebling, Jerome
Life Magazine
Light Meter
Lighting and Lighting Equipment
Link, O. Winston
Linked Ring
List, Herbert
Long, Richard
Look
Lüthi, Urs
Lynes, George Platt
Lyon, Danny
Lyons, Nathan

M

Maar, Dora
Madame d'Ora
Magnum Photos
Maison Européenne de la Photographie
Man Ray
Man, Felix H.
Manipulation
Mapplethorpe, Robert
Mark, Mary Ellen
Masking
McBean, Angus
Meatyard, Ralph Eugene
Meiselas, Susan
Messager, Annette
Metzker, Ray K.
Mexico, Photography in
Meyerowitz, Joel
Michals, Duane
Mikhailov, Boris
Miller, Lee
Misrach, Richard
Model, Lisette
Modern Photography
Moderna Museet (Fotografiska Museet)
Modernism
Modotti, Tina
Moholy-Nagy, László
Montage
Morath, Inge
Morimura, Yasumasa
Morris, Wright
Moses, Stefan
Mulas, Ugo
Multiple Exposures and Printing
Muniz, Vik
Munkacsi, Martin
Museum Folkwang
Museum of Modern Art
Museums
Museums: Canada
Museums: Europe
Museums: United States

N

Namuth, Hans
National Geographic
Netherlands, Photography in The
Newhall, Beaumont
Newman, Arnold
Newton, Helmut
Nixon, Nicolas
Non-Silver Processes
Novak, Lorie
Nude Photography

O

Office of War Information
Olsen, Lennart

Optics
Outerbridge, Paul Jr.
Owens, Bill

P

Panoramic Photography
Parr, Martin
Penn, Irving
Peress, Gilles
Periodicals: Historical
Periodicals: Professional
Perspective
Peterhans, Walter
Pfahl, John
Photo Agencies
Photo League
Photo-Secession
Photo-Secessionists
Photogram
Photographic Theory
Photographic "Truth"
Photography and Painting
Photography and Sculpture
Pictorialism
Picture Post
Pierre et Gilles
Pin-Up Photography
Plossu, Bernard
Plowden, David
Polaroid Corporation
Popular Photography
Porter, Eliot
Portraiture
Posterization
Postmodernism
Prince, Richard
Print Processes
Private Collections
Professional Organizations
Propaganda
Public Art Photography

R

Rainer, Arnulf
Rauschenberg, Robert
Ray-Jones, Tony
Renger-Patzsch, Albert
Representation
Representation and Gender
Representation and Race
Riboud, Marc
Rice, Leland
Riefenstahl, Leni
Riis, Jacob
Ritts, Herb
Roh, Franz
Rosler, Martha
Rothstein, Arthur
Royal Photographic Society
Rubinstein, Eva
Ruff, Thomas
Russia and Eastern Europe, Photography in

S

Safelight
Salgado, Sebastião
Salomon, Erich
Sander, August
Sandwiched Negatives
Scanning
Schadeberg, Jürgen
Schmidt, Michael
Schneiders, Toni
Sekula, Allan
Semiotics
Serrano, Andres
Seymour, David "Chim"
Shahn, Ben
Shaikhet, Arkadii
Sheeler, Charles
Sherman, Cindy
Shibata, Toshio
Shore, Stephen
Simpson, Lorna
Singh, Raghubir
Siskind, Aaron
Skoglund, Sandy
Snow, Michael
Snowdon (Anthony Armstrong-Jones)
Social Representation
Socialist Photography
Solarization
Solomon-Godeau, Abigail
Sommer, Frederick
Sontag, Susan
South America, Photography in
Spain and Portugal, Photography in
Spence, Jo
Starn, Doug and Mike
Stedelijk Museum
Steichen, Edward
Steiner, Andre
Stettner, Louis
Stieglitz, Alfred
Stone, Sasha
Strand, Paul
Street Photography

Struth, Thomas
Stryker, Roy
Sudek, Josef
Sugimoto, Hiroshi
Surrealism
Szabo, Stephen
Szarkowski, John
Szilasi, Gabor

T

Tabard, Maurice
Teige, Karel
Teske, Edmund
Tice, George
Tillmans, Wolfgang
Time Exposure
Tokyo Metropolitan Museum of Photography
Toning
Tosani, Patrick
Toscani, Oliviero
Traub, Charles
Tseng Kwong Chi
Turbeville, Deborah
Typology

U

Ubac, Raoul
Uelsmann, Jerry
Ulmann, Doris
Umbo (Otto Umbehr)
Underwater Photography
United States: Midwest, Photography in the
United States: South, Photography in the
Uzzle, Burk

V

Van Vechten, Carl
VanDerZee, James
Vernacular Photography
Victoria and Albert Museum
Virilio, Paul
Virtual Reality
Vishniac, Roman
Visual Anthropology

W

Wall, Jeff
War Photography
Watanabe, Yoshio
Webb, Boyd
Weber, Bruce
Weber, Wolfgang
Wedding Photography
Weegee
Weems, Carrie Mae
Wegman, William
Welpott, Jack
Weston, Edward
White, Clarence
White, Minor
Wiener Aktionismus
Willis-Kennedy, Deborah
Winogrand, Garry
Witkiewicz (Witkacy), Stanislaw Ignacy
Witkin, Joel-Peter
Wojnecki, Stefan
Woodman, Francesca
Worker Photography
Works Progress Administration

X

Xerography

Z

Zero 61 Group
Zwart, Piet

THEMATIC LIST OF ENTRIES

Equipment

Brownie

Cable Release
Camera: 35 mm
Camera: An Overview
Camera: Diana
Camera: Digital
Camera: Disposable
Camera: Instant or Polaroid
Camera Obscura
Camera: Pinhole
Camera: Point and Shoot

Developing Processes

Enlarger

Film
Film: High-Contrast
Film: Infrared
Filters

Lens
Light Meter

Safelight

Institutions, Galleries, and Collections

An American Place
Art Institute of Chicago
Australian Centre for Photography

Bauhaus
Berlinische Galerie
Bibliothèque nationale de France
Black Star

Center for Creative Photography
Centre National de la Photographie
Condé Nast
Corbis/Bettmann
Corporate Collections

Eastman Kodak Company

Farm Security Administration
Friends of Photography

Galleries

Institute of Design (New Bauhaus)

J. Paul Getty Museum

Library of Congress

Magnum Photos
Maison Européenne de la Photographie
Moderna Museet (Fotografiska Museet)
Museum Folkwang
Museum of Modern Art
Museums
Museums: Canada
Museums: Europe
Museums: United States

Office of War Information

Photo Agencies
Photo League
Polaroid Corporation
Private Collections

Royal Photographic Society

Stedelijk Museum

Tokyo Metropolitan Museum of Photography

Victoria and Albert Museum

Works Progress Administration

Persons

Abbott, Berenice
Adams, Ansel
Adams, Eddie
Adams, Robert
Alpert, Max
Araki, Nobuyoshi
Arbus, Diane
Arnold, Eve
Atget, Eugène
Auerbach, Ellen

Ballen, Roger
Baltz, Lewis
Barr, Jr., Alfred H.
Barthes, Roland
Bayer, Herbert
Beaton, Cecil
Becher, Bernd and Hilla
Bellmer, Hans
Berger, John
Bernhard, Ruth
Beuys, Joseph
Billingham, Richard
Bischof, Werner
Blossfeldt, Karl
Blumenfeld, Erwin
Boltanski, Christian
Bourdeau, Robert
Bourke-White, Margaret
Bragaglia, Anton Giulio
Brandt, Bill
Brassaï
Bravo, Manuel Álvarez
Breitenbach, Joseph
Bruguière, Francis
Burgin, Victor
Burri, René
Burrows, Larry
Burson, Nancy

Cadieux, Geneviève
Cahun, Claude
Callahan, Harry
Calle, Sophie
Capa, Robert
Caponigro, Paul
Carrillo, Manuel
Cartier-Bresson, Henri
Chambi, Martin
Chargesheimer (Hargesheimer, Karl-Heinz)
Christenberry, William
Clark, Larry
Close, Chuck
Coburn, Alvin Langdon
Cohen, Lynne
Coke, Van Deren
Connor, Linda
Coplans, John
Crewdson, Gregory
Cunningham, Imogen

Dahl-Wolfe, Louise
Dater, Judy
Davidson, Bruce
de Meyer, Baron Adolph
Deakin, John
DeCarava, Roy
Delano, Jack
diCorcia, Philip-Lorca
Dijkstra, Rineke
Doisneau, Robert
Domon, Ken
Drtikol, František
Duncan, David Douglas

Edgerton, Harold E.
Eggleston, William
Eisenstaedt, Alfred
Elsken, Ed van der
Erfurth, Hugo
Erwitt, Elliott
Evans, Frederick H.
Evans, Walker
Export, Valie (Waltraud Lehner)

Fani-Kayode, Rotimi
Faucon, Bernard
Faurer, Louis
Feininger, Andreas
Feininger, T. Lux
Feldmann, Hans-Peter
Finsler, Hans
Fischer, Arno
Fischli, Peter and David Weiss
Flaherty, Robert Joseph
Flusser, Vilem
Fosso, Samuel

Franck, Martine
Frank, Robert
Freund, Gisèle
Fukase, Masahisa
Fukuda, Miran
Funke, Jaromir
Furuya, Seiichi
Fuss, Adam

Gelpke, Andre
Gerz, Jochen
Giacomelli, Mario
Gibson, Ralph
Gidal, N. Tim
Gilbert & George
Gilpin, Laura
Gloaguen, Hervé
Gohlke, Frank
Goldin, Nan
Gowin, Emmet
Graham, Dan
Graham, Paul
Grossman, Sid
Gursky, Andreas
Gutmann, John

Haas, Ernst
Hahn, Betty
Hajek-Halke, Heinz
Halsman, Philippe
Hamaya, Hiroshi
Hammarskiöld, Hans
Hartmann, Erich
Heartfield, John (Helmut Herzfelde)
Heath, David Martin
Heinecken, Robert
Hellebrand, Nancy
Henderson, Nigel
Henri, Florence
Hers, François
Hilliard, John
Hine, Lewis
Hiro
Höch, Hannah
Horst, Horst P.
Hosoe, Eikoh
Hoyningen-Huene, George
Hurrell, George
Hütte, Axel

Ishimoto, Yasuhiro
Iturbide, Graciela
Izis (Israel Bidermanas)

Jacobi, Lotte
Janah, Sunil
Jones, Harold
Jones, Pirkle
Josephson, Kenneth

Karsh, Yousuf
Käsebier, Gertrude
Kawada, Kikuji
Keetman, Peter
Keïta, Seydou
Kertész, André
Kessels, Willy
Kesting, Edmund
Khaldei, Yevgeny (Chaldej, Jewgeni)
Killip, Chris
Klein, Aart
Klein, Astrid
Klein, William
Klett, Mark
Koudelka, Josef
Kozloff, Max
Krauss, Rosalind
Kruger, Barbara
Krull, Germaine

Lange, Dorothea
Lartigue, Jacques Henri
Laughlin, Clarence John
Lebeck, Robert
Lee, Russell
Leibovitz, Annie
Lemagny, Jean Claude
Lerski, Helmar
Levinthal, David
Levi-Strauss, Claude
Levitt, Helen
Levy, Julien
Liberman, Alexander
Liebling, Jerome
Link, O. Winston
List, Herbert
Long, Richard
Lüthi, Urs
Lynes, George Platt
Lyon, Danny
Lyons, Nathan

Maar, Dora
Madame d'Ora
Man Ray
Man, Felix H.
Mapplethorpe, Robert
Mark, Mary Ellen
McBean, Angus
Meatyard, Ralph Eugene

Meiselas, Susan
Messager, Annette
Metzker, Ray K.
Meyerowitz, Joel
Michals, Duane
Mikhailov, Boris
Miller, Lee
Misrach, Richard
Model, Lisette
Modotti, Tina
Moholy-Nagy, László
Morath, Inge
Morimura, Yasumasa
Morris, Wright
Moses, Stefan
Mulas, Ugo
Muniz, Vik
Munkacsi, Martin

Namuth, Hans
Newhall, Beaumont
Newman, Arnold
Newton, Helmut
Nixon, Nicolas
Novak, Lorie

Olsen, Lennart
Outerbridge, Paul Jr.
Owens, Bill

Parr, Martin
Penn, Irving
Peress, Gilles
Peterhans, Walter
Pfahl, John
Pierre et Gilles
Plossu, Bernard
Plowden, David
Porter, Eliot
Prince, Richard

Rainer, Arnulf
Rauschenberg, Robert
Ray-Jones, Tony
Renger-Patzsch, Albert
Riboud, Marc
Rice, Leland
Riefenstahl, Leni
Riis, Jacob
Ritts, Herb
Roh, Franz
Rosler, Martha
Rothstein, Arthur
Rubinstein, Eva
Ruff, Thomas

Salgado, Sebastião
Salomon, Erich
Sander, August
Schadeberg, Jürgen
Schmidt, Michael
Schneiders, Toni
Sekula, Allan
Serrano, Andres
Seymour, David "Chim"
Shahn, Ben
Shaikhet, Arkadii
Sheeler, Charles
Sherman, Cindy
Shibata, Toshio
Shore, Stephen
Simpson, Lorna
Singh, Raghubir
Siskind, Aaron
Skoglund, Sandy
Snow, Michael
Snowdon (Anthony Armstrong-Jones)
Solomon-Godeau, Abigail
Sommer, Frederick
Sontag, Susan
Spence, Jo
Starn, Doug and Mike
Steichen, Edward
Steiner, Andre
Stettner, Louis
Stieglitz, Alfred
Stone, Sasha
Strand, Paul
Struth, Thomas
Stryker, Roy
Sudek, Josef
Sugimoto, Hiroshi
Szabo, Stephen
Szarkowski, John
Szilasi, Gabor

Tabard, Maurice
Teige, Karel
Teske, Edmund
Tice, George
Tillmans, Wolfgang
Tosani, Patrick
Toscani, Oliviero
Traub, Charles
Tseng Kwong Chi
Turbeville, Deborah

Ubac, Raoul
Uelsmann, Jerry
Ulmann, Doris
Umbo (Otto Umbehr)

Uzzle, Burk

Van Vechten, Carl
VanDerZee, James
Virilio, Paul
Vishniac, Roman

Wall, Jeff
Watanabe, Yoshio
Webb, Boyd
Weber, Bruce
Weber, Wolfgang
Weegee
Weems, Carrie Mae
Wegman, William
Welpott, Jack
Weston, Edward
White, Clarence
White, Minor
Willis-Kennedy, Deborah
Winogrand, Garry
Witkiewicz (Witkacy), Stanislaw Ignacy
Witkin, Joel-Peter
Wojnecki, Stefan
Woodman, Francesca

Zero 61 Group
Zwart, Piet

Publications and Publishers

Afterimage

Creative Camera

Life Magazine
Look

Modern Photography

National Geographic

Periodicals: Historical
Periodicals: Professional
Picture Post
Popular Photography

Regions

Africa: An Overview, Photography in
Africa: Central and West, Photography in
Africa: East and Indian Ocean Islands, Photography in
Africa: North, Photography in
Africa: South and Southern, Photography in
Australia, Photography in

Canada, Photography in
Central America, Photography in
China and Taiwan, Photography in

Europe: An Overview, Photography in

France, Photography in

Germany and Austria, Photography in

Japan, Photography in

Korea, Photography in

Latin America: An Overview, Photography in

Mexico, Photography in

Netherlands, Photography in The

Russia and Eastern Europe, Photography in

South America, Photography in
Spain and Portugal, Photography in

United States: Midwest, Photography in the
United States: South, Photography in the

Topics and Terms

Abstraction
Aerial Photography
Agitprop
Appropriation
Architectural Photography
Archives
Artists' Books
Astrophotography

Body Art
Bracketing
Burning-In

Censorship
Color Temperature
Color Theory: Natural and Synthetic
Composition
Conceptual Photography
Conservation
Constructed Reality
Contact Printing

Contrast
Crime Photography
Cropping

Dada
Darkroom
Decisive Moment, The
Deconstruction
Depth of Field
Digital Photography
Discursive Spaces
Documentary Photography
Dodging
Dye Transfer

Emulsion
Erotic Photography
Ethics and Photography
Exposure

Family Photography
Fashion Photography
Feminist Photography
Festivals
Fine Arts Presses
Formalism
Futurism

Group f/64

Hand Coloring and Hand Toning
History of Photography: Nineteenth-Century Foundations
History of Photography: Twentieth-Century Developments
History of Photography: Twentieth-Century Pioneers
History of Photography: Interwar Years
History of Photography: Postwar Era
History of Photography: the 1980s

Image Construction: Perspective
Image Theory: Ideology
Impressionism
Industrial Photography
Infrared Photography
Instant Photography
Internet and Photography, The
Interpretation

Lighting and Lighting Equipment
Linked Ring

Manipulation
Masking
Modernism
Montage
Multiple Exposures and Printing

Non-Silver Processes
Nude Photography

Optics

Panoramic Photography
Perspective
Photo-Secession
Photo-Secessionists
Photogram
Photographic Theory
Photographic "Truth"
Photography and Painting
Photography and Sculpture
Pictorialism
Pin-Up Photography
Portraiture
Posterization
Postmodernism
Print Processes
Professional Organizations
Propaganda
Public Art Photography

Representation
Representation and Gender
Representation and Race

Sandwiched Negatives
Scanning
Semiotics
Social Representation
Socialist Photography
Solarization
Street Photography
Surrealism

Time Exposure
Toning
Typology

Underwater Photography

Vernacular Photography
Virtual Reality
Visual Anthropology

War Photography
Wedding Photography
Wiener Aktionismus
Worker Photography

Xerography

GLOSSARY

Editor's note: These definitions err on the side of succinctness and are intended to be beginning points for the serious student. An attempt to standardize terminology commonly found in the medium of fine arts photographs that avoids copyrighted term or trade names ("dye-destruction print" in lieu of "Cibachrome" and so on) has been made using guidelines set forth by the J. Paul Getty Institute. In acknowledgment of the increase in collecting vintage prints and the perennial interest in historical processes, many nineteenth century processes and obsolete terms are included.

Cross referencing within the glossary is indicated by italics; encyclopedia entries are indicated by small capitals.

Additive colors The primary colors of red, green and blue which are mixed to form all other colors in photographic reproduction. See entry COLOR THEORY: NATURAL AND SYNTHETIC.

Agfacolor Trade name for a subtractive color film manufactured by the European company Agfa-Gevaert; analogous to Kodachrome and Ansocolor.

Albumen print Prints obtained from a process in wide use during the nineteenth century in which paper is prepared with an albumen emulsion obtained from egg whites and made light sensitive with a silver nitrate solution. See also *Collodion process*; *Dry plate processes*.

Amberlith An orange acetate historically used for masking mechanicals during the process of preparing plates for commercial printing. The area so masked photographs as black to the camera, printing clear on the resulting positive film. See also *Rubylith*.

Ambrotype An image created by the collodion process, historically on glass, which gives the illusion of being positive when placed against a dark backing, often a layer of black lacquer, paper, or velvet. Also see *Ferrotype*.

Anamorphic image An image featuring differing scales of magnification across the picture plane, especially varying along the vertical and horizontal axes, with the result being extreme distortion.

Aniline A rapid-drying oil-based solvent used in the preparation of dyes and inks for photographic applications.

Aniline process A method of making prints directly from line art (drawings) on translucent materials bypassing the need for a negative. Also see *Diazo process*.

Aniline printing See *Flexography*.

Angle of incidence The measurement in degrees in terms of the deviation from the perpendicular of the angle at which light hits a surface.

Angle of view The measurement in degrees of the angle formed by lines projected from the optical center of a lens to the edges of the field of view. This measurement is used to identify lenses and their appropriateness to capture various widths or degrees of actual space in a photographic representation, thus an extreme telephoto lens captures between 6 and 15°; normal lens generally fall in the 40 to 100° range; a "fisheye" wide-angle is 150 to 200° (or more).

Anscocolor Trade name of a subtractive color film manufactured by the European company GAF Corporation.

Anti-halation layer The light absorbing layer in raw stock that prevents reflection of light back into the light-sensitive emulsion, preventing unwanted fogging.

Aristotype Trade name for a variety of non-albumen printing papers which became a general term; largely obsolete in the twentieth century.

Artigue process Variation on the carbon process; largely obsolete in the twentieth century.

GLOSSARY

Aspect ratio The ratio between height and width in photographic applications.

Autochrome One of the first commercially viable color photography techniques using pigments in potato starch fixed by means of varnish and coated with a light sensitive emulsion (orthochromatic gelatin bromide) on a glass plate. Also known as an additive color process color plate. Used most widely between 1900 and 1930.

Autotype A carbon process for making prints from negatives; originally a trade name which became the generic name for prints made with a variety of carbon processes.

Bichromate processes A family of processes, not utilizing silver, to make prints on various grounds by coating them with a colloid, which can be gum arabic, gelatin, or starch, that has been treated to be light sensitive with potassium or ammonium bichromates. Grounds include papers, films, and fabric. Also known as gum-bichromate or dichromate processes. See also entry NON-SILVER PROCESSES.

Black-and-white print See *Gelatin silver print*.

Bleaching The use of various chemicals, including iodine compounds or potassium ferricyanide, to remove the silver from an image.

Bleach-out process A technique for creating a hand drawing from a black and white print in which a drawing is made over a photographic image, which is then bleached completely away.

Bleed An image that runs to the edge of a print or page; "full-bleed" indicates the image goes to all four edges.

Blindstamp An embossed mark, generally colorless and usually outside the image, used to identify the publisher, printer, photographer's studio or photographer. The stamp may be a symbol, initials, or full name and address. Also known as drystamp and chop.

Blueprint An image created via the cyanotype process that results in blue tones, most often used in architectural plans. See *Ozalid process* and *Diazo process*. See also entry NON-SILVER PROCESSES.

Bromoil process A variation of the carbro process in which the silver image of a bromide print is converted to a carbon image and then prepared with oil-based inks for printing.

Bromide print A print created on a black and white paper in which the emulsion contains silver bromide and silver iodide, resulting in a relatively greater sensitivity to light. See entry NON-SILVER PROCESSES.

Bracketing See entry.

Burning-in See entry.

Calotype An early and widely used paper negative process in which the paper was made light sensitive with silver iodide, also called Talbotype after its inventor, W.H.F. Talbot.

Camera obscura See entry.

Carbon processes Name for the family of photographic processes, originating in bichromate technique, accomplished using particles of carbon or colored pigments that includes the *Carbro process*. See also entries NON-SILVER PROCESSES; PRINT PROCESSES.

Carbro process Carbon process of versatility similar to silver processes in that it can be used for enlarged prints, with capabilities to manipulate during both development and enlarging (such as burning and doding), developed from ozotype and ozo processes; name obtained from a combination of *car*bon and *bro*mide. Standardized as assembly process color print. See also *Ozotype* and entries NON-SILVER PROCESSES; PRINT PROCESSES.

Carte-de-visite French for "visiting card"; a mainly mid-nineteenth century phenomenon of small photographs mounted on cards that became widely popular to exchange or distribute.

CCD For charge coupled device, a sensing device found in most digital cameras consisting of a rectangular grid of light sensitive elements that generate an electrical current relative to the amount of light sensed and replacing film.

Celluloid A type of plastic of dubious stability and extreme flammability developed in the mid-nineteenth century; used toward the end of the nineteenth century for the support for photographic emulsion in film manufacture.

Chloro-bromide print Variation of the gelatin silver print wherein the light sensitive material in the emulsion consists of silver chloride and silver bromide; produces a warmer image than the gelatin silver print. See also *Gelatin silver print*.

Chromogenic development Process in which chemical reactions are used to create colors (dyes) in a light sensitive emulsion. See *Chromogenic development print* and as opposed to *Dye destruction process*.

Chromogenic development print Standard generic name for common trade names such as in which a color image is obtained by means of silver halide coupled with cyan, magenta, and yellow dyes. This process is the opposite of the dye destruction process. See also entry PRINT PROCESSES.

Cibachrome Trade name for prints obtained by means of the dye destruction process originated by the British photographic concern Ilford in concert with CIBA AG of Switzerland. Originally 'Cilchrome.' Standardized as dye destruction print. Also less commonly: silver dye bleach process print.

CIE Color System International color system developed by ICI (CIE) using scientific color measurement to standardize color names and the color they describe. See also *ICI (CIE)*.

Circle of confusion The size of the largest open circle which the eye cannot distinguish from a solid dot, used to determine sharpness and thus depth of field. See entry DEPTH OF FIELD.

Cliché-verre A method for reproduction of drawings or painting by photographic means in which glass is coated with an opaque ground that is scratched away and then used as a photographic negative. Also known as *Hyalotype*.

Collage Two-dimensional or bas-relief image created by gluing or pasting together various pieces of images and materials collected from various sources. See also *Montage*.

Collotype Bichromate process for obtaining printed reproductions of photographic imagery invented mid-nineteenth century using plates of glass coated with a layer of adhesive gelatin followed by a layer of gelatin sensitized with potassium bichromate. Used chiefly for commercial printing applications before superseded by offset lithography in early decades of the twentieth century. See entry NON-SILVER PROCESSES.

Color Key Trademark of Pantone Corporation for a color identification system used largely in graphic design and commercial printing applications.

Color temperature See entry.

Composite photographs A photograph created through the combining of two or more individual images to form a whole and generally rephotographed to create a seamless final image, as distinguished from montage.

Contact print See entry CONTACT PRINTING.

Continuous-tone process Any of a family of processes which create an image in which modulations from dark to light are achieved by variations in density of the image-forming substance, most commonly silver in black and white photographs and dyes in color photographs, in relation to the amount of light exposure received. As opposed to *Halftone process*.

Cyanotype A widely used iron-based process deriving from the discovery in 1841–1842 by Sir John Herschel that many iron compounds were in fact light sensitive. A relatively simple and versatile process that produces white images on a blue ground. Also known as the Ferroprussianate process.

Daguerreotype A photographic process invented by L.J.M. Daguerre at the beginnings of photography in 1839 most commonly achieved by a thin film of silver on a copper plate that achieves a grainless, yet relatively fragile image. Largely obsolete by 1860s.

"The Decisive Moment" See entry.

Densitometry The science of measuring the opacity of silver or dye images in films and prints; when standardized these measurements are used to determine a wide range of photographic aspects, including the speed of film; the length of exposure and development, contrast, and so on.

Depth of field See entry.

Depth of focus The area on either side of an image plane of a lens in which the image remains sharp. See *Circle of confusion*.

Developing-out paper The term for a family of photographic papers that require developing after exposure. See also entry PRINT PROCESSES.

Diazo process A method of obtaining color images through the use of diazonium compounds as the light sensitive medium.

Dichromate processes See *Bichromate processes*.

Digital print Any print created through digital means. See also *giclee print* and *inkjet print*.

Dry mounting Process of using heat-activated adhesives to mount photographs.

Dry plate processes Chiefly used to indicate a family of nineteenth century processes that were advances on the wet collodion process in which the light sensitive medium on glass plates or paper was exposed when dried. Also used more expansively to indicate any dry exposure process. See also *Albumen print*; *Wet collodion process*.

Dye bleach See *Bleach*.

Dye coupler Colorless compounds that when activated react with other agents to form dyes whose color depends on the dye coupler molecule. See entries COLOR THEORY: NATURAL AND SYNTHETIC; DEVELOPING PROCESSES.

Dye destruction process Generic name for process that is used by products with such common trade names as Cibachrome in which a color image is obtained by means of bleaching away unnecessary dyes from the emulsion. As opposed to processes that use chromogenic development to create dyes in the emulsion.

Dye destruction print Print made with dye destruction process. Standardized generic equivalent for Cibachrome.

Dye diffusion transfer process color print Print in which the emulsion is composed of multiple layers, including a final backing layer, that together create both the negative and final positive print. Standardized generic equivalent for the Polaroid print, a trademark of the Polaroid Corporation and other systems that create so-called "instant" photographs. See entry INSTANT PHOTOGRAPHY.

Duratrans Trademark of Kodak Company for a large-scale durable transparency generally mounted in lightboxes.

Dye transfer See entry.

Ektachrome Trade name of Kodak Company for a film that produces a positive or transparency (slide).

Emulsion A suspension of light-sensitive materials, generally silver halide crystals, in a support material, generally gelatin.

Etch-bleach process A technique for converting high-contrast images, such as obtained with lith films, to line-art. Also known as and see *Bleach-out process.*

False color image A monochromatic image in which various gradations of tone or densities are assigned arbitrary colors and presented as a color photograph. Generally used in scientific, especially astronomy, applications but also used as an artistic effect.

Ferrotype The generic name of the direct positive process on a metal ground known as Tintype. See *Ambrotype*.

Ferrotyping A process for obtaining a glossy or glazed surface on a photographic print by means of drying the print as in contact with a highly polished surface.

Finlaycolor process A method of full-color imaging by means of screens of specifically spaced elements as opposed to the random, mosaic screen used in the Autochrome process. Used primarily with panchromatic film to create a negative capable of being printed in color.

Film speed The capacity of any given film to record light within a specified timeframe, measured in units known as ASA (after the standardization organization American Standards Association) before 1980 and ISO after 1980. See entry FILM.

Fish-eye lens An extremely wide-angle lens, generally capturing between 140 and 200° (or more) of the angle of view.

Flexichrome process A method of hand coloring in which film is developed so that the exposed gelatin is hardened, allowing the unexposed portions to be washed away. Silver is then removed through bleaching; the remaining hardened emulsion dyed gray to be visible for hand-toning or coloring.

Flexography A process of printing an image using inks onto a nonabsorbent or uneven surface by preparing a negative relief from a photography which is then used to cast a rubber mold that will conform to an irregular surface or can be prepared with inks that will bind to ceramic, plastic or other nonabsorbent surfaces. Also called aniline printing.

Fluorography The recording of images rendered onto a screen in which the screen (as opposed to the object; this is known as fluorescent photography) is illuminated with X-rays.

Focal length A method of determining the basic optical character of a lens by measuring the distance along the optical axis from the rear nodal point (the center or highest point of the lens) to a plane when the camera is set at "infinity" on which an object remains in sharp focus. Also see *angle of view*.

Footcandle A method of measuring the intensity of light. A one candlepower light source emits 12.6 lumens. The amount of illumination is thus measured by the number of lumens falling on a square unit of a specified area such as per square foot or meter. See *lumen*.

Flare Unwanted light that scatters within the lens and can result in loss of contrast in exposed images.

Flash A device for creating a high-intensity light of short duration.

Framing A method used at the time a photograph is taken by which the camera distance and angle of view is used to mark off the edges of the photographic composition. Also the placing of the finished photograph in a frame for final presentation.

Fresson process A method of color printing invented at the turn of the twentieth century in France by Theodore-Henri Fresson that produces an image that is characteristically diffused and subtle, reminiscent of the "pointillism" of Impressionist painting.

Fresnel lens A condenser characterized by a series of concentric rings, each equivalent to a designated section of the curved surface of the lens that maximizes the light output of the lens. Originated by A.J. Fresnel in the early nineteenth century for use in lighthouses; used in photographic applications such as in camera viewing systems and rear-projection systems.

***f*-stop, *f*-number** The aperture settings on a camera. See entries CAMERA: OVERVIEW and LENS.

Fuji-color Trade name of a color negative film manufactured by the Fuji Corporation, Japan.

Gaslight paper A developing-out paper of relatively low light sensitivity used for contact printing in the late nineteenth century. So-called as it was light safe under weak gaslight illumination.

Gelatin silver print Any photographic print achieved using a paper in which silver or its compounds are used as the light sensitive material in a gelatin support, most commonly silver halide crystals but also silver chloride and silver bromide. Also known as black and white print and silver gelatin print. See also *Chloro-bromide print; Emulsion* and also entry PRINT PROCESSES.

Ghosting Any incident of a double-image, but most often used to describe accidental occurrences, such as that which may occur when an electronic flash is used in an exposure with adequate ambient light or to describe the ghostly images that appear in long-exposures typical of early photographic processes where a human would move through the exposure leaving a blur or partial image.

Giclee print A term derived from the French "to spray" adopted in 1990 by Nash Editions to describe fine-art prints produced by digital spray technologies. See also *Digital print* and *Iris print*.

Glazing See *Ferrotyping*.

Gold toning The application of a bath of gold chloride where each silver particle in a gelatin silver print is coated with a layer of gold, rendering a warm tone and increasing the life of the image, as gold is resistant to tarnishing (oxidation).

Grain A description of the measurable, visible characteristics of the light sensitive medium of an emulsion. In unexposed materials, this measures, in silver processes, the undeveloped silver halide crystals; in a developed image, the bits of metallic silver themselves, expressed in a subjective scale of "fine" grain to "coarse" grain. See *Granularity*.

Granularity The measurement of the number of grains per unit of a specified area in an developed image. See *Grain*.

Gray card A standard to determine exposure and used to evaluate color balance in a transparency or print achieved through a gray-coated card that reflects visible wavelengths equally and reflects approximately 18 to 20% of the ambient light that strikes it, these percentages reflecting an averaging of the typical distribution of light and dark in a typical photographic scene.

Gray scale Description of the shades of gray or more accurately, range of tones from black to white in a photographic print.

Guide number A reference number used to calculate exposure when using flash that is not synched to the camera's light meter (automatic). Film speed, *f*-stop setting, flash unit light output, and the distance between the flash and the subject are the four variables used to calculate this number.

Gum-bichromate See *Bichromate processes*.

Gum ozotype process See *Ozotype process*.

Gum print A print made through one of the many *Bichromate processes*.

Halation An effect wherein excess or unwanted exposure is caused by the reflecting of light off the film base back into the emulsion.

Halftone A photographic image obtained by means of a halftone process.

Halftone process Any of a family of processes which create an image by means of tiny dots or lines not visible to the unaided eye. As opposed to continuous-tone process.

Hand coloring See entry HAND COLORING AND HAND TONING.

Hardener A chemical or compound that by reducing the ability of a gelatin medium to absorb water during the developing and/or processing of film or photographic papers allows for a denser and therefore more durable surface on the final product.

Heliography Term used initially by the pioneer of photography Nicéphore Niépce to describe the process in which he was able to make the first permanent photographic images. From the Greek *helios* (sun) and *graphien* (writing).

Heliogravure Alternative French term for photogravure, a mid-nineteenth century photoengraving process made on Nicéphore Niépce's discoveries. See *Photogravure*.

Heliotype A collotype process widely used in commercial printing at the end of the nineteenth century.

High contrast films and papers Photographic products which feature a limited range of gray tones or no gray tones at all. Often known as lith films and papers.

High speed photography Photography undertaken in acknowledgment that there are many physical processes that take place that the unaided human eye cannot resolve, which in its basic definition is photographs made with extremely short exposure times. In general terms, though always evolving, this means photography with exposure times shorter than about 1/1000 of a second that almost always require special techniques, especially in light sources. For some purposes, the definition is shutter speeds beyond what is available on general use 35-mm cameras, commonly 1/4000 of a second, up to trillionths of a second. Pioneered in the nineteenth century by Eadweard Muybridge, to demonstrate the galloping of a horse; in the twentieth century, Harold Edgerton, an inventor of high-speed flash techniques, is considered the "father of high speed photography." See entry HAROLD E. EDGERTON.

Hologram See *Holography*.

Holography A technique for making photographs known as holograms which give the illusion of three dimensions through embedding images in the photographic matrix that change in *parallax* and perspective as the angle from which the image is viewed changes. Holographs are made through the recording of "coherent" light—light which is emitted and follows a single wave pattern known commonly as lasers (as opposed to "incoherent" light—ordinary light which is of varying wavelengths with random phase relations). Holograms were described theoretically in 1947 by Dennis Gabor and became more common as advances in the laser technology needed to realize them were made in the late decades of the twentieth century.

Hyalograph A photograph created by means of etching an image from a negative into glass.

Hyalotype A method of creating positive transparencies used in the mid-nineteenth century primarily for lantern slides. See *Cliché-verre*.

Hydrotype A bichromate process in which the master image is transferred to a ground of moistened paper, allowing the creation of multiple copies.

Hypo Common terminology for hyposulfite of soda, a nineteenth century designation for sodium thiosulfate, used during the developing process for films and papers to fix the image. See also entries DARKROOM; DEVELOPING PROCESSES, FILM.

Hypo eliminator Solution used in the processing of film or paper to neutralize the *hypo*. See also entries DARKROOM; DEVELOPING PROCESSES, FILM.

ICI (CIE) International Commission on Illumination based in France; in French, Commission International de l'Eclairage, an organization that sets photographic standards, most notably a system for scientific color measurement in use worldwide to standardize color names and the color they describe. See also *CIE Color System*.

Imperial print A designation of nineteenth century photography indicating a mount for a photograph measuring 7 × 10 inches that could accommodate a contact print from the most common photographic plate then in use.

Incident light The light falling on any surface, in its various combinations of reflected, absorbed, or transmitted light. See entry LIGHT METERS.

Infinity setting The lens focus setting marked ? indicating the setting for photographing in focus objects at the greatest distance from the camera.

Infrared photography See entry.

Intaglio processes The term for a family of processes in which the image is formed by means of incisions below the surface of the material that is being used as a ground (often metal plates). Most commonly used in photoetching or photoengraving, both in commercial and fine arts applications.

ISO International Standards Organization, which sets a wide variety of standards in various fields; in photography, the designation of film speeds.

Iris print A digital print created using the printing equipment, inks, and papers developed by Iris Graphics of Bedford, Massachusetts but also used as a generic term for inkjet print created for fine arts applications. See also *Digital print* and *Giclee print*.

Ivorytype A photographic print transferred to materials manipulated to mimic ivory, popular in the mid-nineteenth century.

Kallitype A printing process using iron compounds developed at the end of the nineteenth century suitable for printing on paper and fabrics. A simple form of the kallitype is the Vandyke print.

Keystoning The linear distortion in which one end of a rectangle is larger than the other, usually as a result of the camera, when taking a photograph, not being parallel to the subject.

Kodachrome Trade name of Kodak Company for a film using a subtractive process (dye destruction) color film.

Kirlian photography A form of electrophotography named for the Russian couple who first identified it in which film in a metal container is placed in direct contact with the object or subject protected by insulating material. A current is passed through the film, and the pattern of energy as affected by the object or subject is recorded and developed.

Kodacolor Trade name of Kodak Company films.

Kodalith Trade name of Kodak Company's high-contrast films and papers.

Law of reciprocity See *Reciprocity*.

Lens hood Simple shielding device attached to front of lens to prevent flare.

Light box A device for viewing negatives or transparencies by internal illumination through a translucent material or a device for the display of photographic transparencies, especially popular in advertising and late-century fine art photography.

Line art In graphic arts and commercial printing applications, a term for a negative or positive image consisting of only two tones and featuring no modulation, as in a *continuous tone* image. See also *Lith films and papers*.

Lith films and papers High-contrast photographic materials most generally used in photomechanical reproduction, especially commercial graphic arts applications, prior to onset of digital technologies. See also *High contrast films and papers*.

Loupe Manual instrument used for viewing contact sheets, slides, or magnifying sections of full sized prints.

Lumen Unit for the measurement of the radiant energy emitted by a light source.

Lux See *Lumen*.

Microfiche A method by which sheet film is exposed by means of microphotography to create miniaturized images; widely used in the second half of the twentieth century by libraries and other institutions for records storage; made largely obsolete by the digital revolution.

Moiré A pattern created when superimposed line art or dot patterns interact and interfere with one another. Indication of poor registration in mechanical reproduction processes that layer multiple images; also used as a special effect by means of screens or filters.

Montage An assemblage of photographic images; generally distinguished from *collage* in both the restriction to photographic images (as opposed to drawn or three-dimensional elements) as well as the presentation of the final image as a unified whole, often by rephotographing. See entries MONTAGE; MANIPULATION.

Munsell system Standard system in the United States for specifying color in pigments and other opaque colorants.

Negative Any photographic film or print wherein the range of tonalities or color is reversed or the opposite of that of the subject or view photographed.

Negative print A photograph in which the opposite tones or colors from the subject of exposure is presented as a final work, usually for artistic effect.

Noble print Prints made with any of the family of bromoil processes, often featuring hand coloring.

Notch code An identity method used by film manufacturers by means of v-shaped notches incised into the right-hand corner side edge of sheet films.

Offset A photomechanical reproduction created when an image is transferred to a plate photographically, transferred in reverse to a roller, and then printed positively on paper or canvas; most commonly used in commercial printing applications. Also known as offset lithography.

Offset print Print created using offset process.

Orotone process A decorative process consisting of the photographic image being printed first onto glass plates, the silver then toned to a rich brown-gold tone. The glass is backed with a dusting of fine gold pigment.

Orthochromatic Designation for photographic emulsion that is sensitive to ultraviolet, blue, green and several yellow wavelengths but does not record red, allowing the use of a red safelight during the developing process. Also known simply as ortho.

Ostwald system Method of specifying color based on subjective (as opposed to scientific or mathematical) criteria. Often displayed as a cone or other form in which variations of hue affected by additions of white, black, and complementary colors are arranged in logical progressions.

Ozalid process A commercial diazo process developed in the early twentieth century to copy plans and drawings; commonly known as blacklines or brownlines. See also *Diazo process*.

Ozobrome process An improvement on the Ozotype process using a bromide print instead of the gelatin-bichromate sheet.

Ozotype process A carbon process developed at the turn of the twentieth century using a gelatin sheet sensitized with bichromate exposed by contact printing with a negative that is then flattened against a prepared carbon-pigmented tissue that hardens or tans the exposed emulsion. A variation on this process using a gum arabic emulsion is known as the Gum ozotype process.

Palladiotype Variation of the platinum print wherein the light-sensitive element of the emulsion is a compound of palladium, developed in the 1910s due to the prohibitive cost of this process due to the rarity of platinum. See entry NON-SILVER PROCESSES.

Palladium print More common term for the Palladiotype.

Panchromatic Designating an emulsion for which the light sensitivity is essentially equal for all visible light wavelengths.

Parallax The discrepancies in the field of view or coverage resulting from two differing viewpoints.

Paraglyphe A print resulting from a technique which achieves the illusion of low-relief or bas-relief by using a negative image to mask the same image's positive in creating an image which is a synthesis of the two.

Pinatype A bichromate process in which the master image is transferred to a ground of soft gelatin, allowing the creation of multiple copies.

Pixel The smallest discrete component of an image or picture on a television screen, computer monitor, or other electronic display, usually manifesting as a colored dot. In digital photographic processes, a unit of measurement to determine resolution (clarity of detail) of an image.

Photogram See entry.

Photomontage See *Montage.*

Photogalvanography An early bichromate process used in commercial printing to create printing plates from photographs.

Photoglyphy An early bichromate process used to create printing plates from photographs, patented in 1852 by photographic innovator W.H.F. Talbot.

Photogravure A photomechanical process adapting the traditional etching process that revolutionized commercial printing of reproductions in its ability to reproduce the appearance of the continuous tones found in photographs, an advance on photoglyphy. A sheet of bichromate gelatin tissue is adhered, using heat, against a resin-dusted copper plate and contact-printed with a positive transparency, the exposed gelatin hardening and protecting the plate lying beneath it. The unhardened gelatin is then washed away and the plate is processed in an acid bath, the unprotected copper being etched away at various depths. The plate is then inked; the etched areas holding ink to create the dark tones; the protected areas holding no ink and creating the highlights and used to transfer a positive image to paper.

Photolithography Using photographic methods to create the image in the traditional printmaking technique of lithography.

Photomicrography The recording by photographic means of highly magnified images seen through microscopes, most commonly for scientific and medical purposes, but also in fine arts photography.

Photoserigraphy Using photographic methods to create the image in the traditional printmaking technique of silkscreen or serigraphy. Also known as photosilkscreen.

Photostat A registered trademark for a commercial photocopying process using high-contrast that came into common use referring to a duplicate of an original.

Platinotype Patent name for prints created using papers light-sensitized through the use of platinum compounds marketed in the late nineteenth century.

Platinum print Generic term for any photographic paper using platinum and its compounds combined with iron salts as the light-sensitive material and developed in potassium oxalate, notable for its broad range of subtle, silvery-gray tones and for its relative permanency due to the stability of platinum.

Polaroid print See *Dye diffusion transfer process color print.*

Polaroid transfer A technique in which a Polaroid 669 print is soaked in hot water until the top emulsion layer lifts off its backing, allowing it to be transferred to a broad range of surfaces, including nonabsorbent surfaces such as glass. Also known as Polaroid emulsion lift.

Positive Any photographic film or print wherein the range of tonalities or color duplicates those of the subject or view photographed.

Posterization See entry.

Primuline process A diazo process developed at the end of the nineteenth century using the dye Primuline yellow.

Printing-out papers The term given to a family of photographic papers that require no developing after exposure, in which the emulsion of the negative is placed in direct contact with that of the print material, exposing it to light until an image is formed. Also known as photolithic papers. See also entry PRINT PROCESSES.

Radiography X-ray photography used primarily in medical applications.

Resin-Coated paper Photographic papers coated with resin to prevent absorption of developing bath into fibers, thus reducing washing time. Also known as RC Paper, a trademark of the Kodak Company. See also entry PRINT PROCESSES.

Reciprocity Term used to indicate the responses of film or paper to an exposure time plus amount of light (most often through controlling aperture setting), thus a long exposure with a small aperture opening will result in a similar exposure as a short exposure time with a larger aperture opening. Also known as Law of Reciprocity.

Reciprocity failure An effect in which a film's sensitivity to light does not respond under conditions that should achieve mathematical reciprocity, such as in long exposures, or changes from the first exposure to the last exposure in a multiple image and overexposure, underexposure, or color shifts may result in the film. Also known as reciprocity effect.

Recto/verso In describing a photographic print, recto is the image side, verso the back or mount.

Resolution In photochemical processes, the size of the silver or other light sensitive elements in the emulsion; in digital technologies, the amount of detail or clarity offered relative to the number of pixels per square inch of an electronic image.

Retouching The manual manipulation of a photographic print or negative with brushes, airbrushes, pencils, inks, bleaching agents and so on to change details such as removing blemishes or filling in wrinkles in a portrait subject, or to correct defects in the exposure, such as dust spots.

Rubylith A red acetate historically used for masking mechanicals during the process of preparing plates for commercial printing. The area so masked photographs as black to the camera, printing clear on the resulting positive film. See also *Amberlith*.

Sabatier effect See entry SOLARIZATION.

Salted paper print Prints created by means of ordinary writing paper that has been light-sensitized with alternate washes of a solution of common table salt and a bath of silver nitrate; invented by W.H.F. Talbot in 1834 and characterized by a matte finish and a soft image resolution.

Scanner Device used in digital photography to electronically convert a visual (analog) image into digital data. See entry SCANNING.

Selenium print A print that has been toned with selenium which creates a warm tone and increases longevity, a misnomer in that the print is generally a gelatin silver print and the selenium is used only as an enhancement.

Sequencing The placing of photographs to create a narrative, visual message, or pictorial effect; a practice developed especially through scientific photography at the end of the nineteenth century by figures such as Eadweard Muybridge or E.J. Marey, and photojournalism and the photo-essay that emerged in the 1930s. Photographs can be those that exist in sequence as photographed with their inherent narrative, or can be disparate images that through such placement create a narrative, a practice especially explored by fine arts photographers in the postwar decades.

Silver-dye bleach process See *Cibachrome*; *Dye destruction print*.

Silver print Variation of *gelatin silver print*, not preferred usage.

Slide See *Transparency*.

Solarization See entry.

Stroboscope Rapidly firing flash used in high speed photography.

Solio paper A printing-out paper utilizing a gelatin-silver chloride emulsion for amateur use produced by Kodak in the late nineteenth century and used well into the twentieth century.

Spotting Method of retouching, most commonly used to describe the repair of imperfections such as dust spots, scratches to the film's emulsion, and so on by means of specially prepared dyes applied with a brush or pen that are matched to common paper tonalties.

Stereoscope A device for viewing photographs either hand-prepared or made with a stereographic camera that creates the illusion of three dimensions. Also stereograph.

Superimposure A combination of images, usually one atop another, in which aspects from the images are combined into a new image. Images can be superimposed in the camera through various exposure techniques, or created in the darkroom with multiple negatives. See entries MULTIPLE EXPOSURES AND PRINTING and SANDWICHED NEGATIVES.

Synchronization The relationship of timing between the action of the camera shutter and the activation of the flash.

Talbotype A short-lived name for W.H.F. Talbot's calotype process.

Test strip A simple method of judging proper exposure by means of creating a sample image on a strip of photographic paper by masking and then allowing progressively longer exposures. See entry DARKROOM.

Thermal imaging Imaging methods that capture radiant energy (heat) as a visual image, used in surveillance, medical imaging, and other industrial applications. Also known at Thermography.

Time-lapse photography The exposing of a series of images at regular intervals in still or motion picture photography or the multiple exposing of a single image in still photography, most often used to create illusions in motion pictures ("stop action") or record a progressive motion or action, such as a rising sun.

Tinting See *Toning*.

Tomography A technique in radiography (X-ray) to obtain clear imaging by means of rotating the X-ray emitting tube in a specified manner.

Tone-line process Alternative name for *Etch-bleach process* and see *Bleach-out process*.

Toning See entry.

Transparency A positive photographic image on a transparent or translucent support, such as glass or film intended for viewing by a transmitted light source, such as a projector or a light box.

Trichrome carbro process An early form of the modern dye-transfer method in which layers of subtractive color images in carbon pigments are assembled in registration to create a color image, developed in the mid-nineteenth century. Also known as three-color carbro process.

Tripod Common form of support for a camera to allow for steady focusing and shooting, especially during long exposures; generally featuring three adjustable or telescoping legs that allow for set up on varying terrain.

T-stop A lens calibration similar to *f*-stop system that takes into account the variance between lens of differing designs in the amount of light transmitted to the film with particular applications in motion picture photography.

Ultraviolet photography Photography which captures light in the blue-violet end of the spectrum, not visible to the human eye, especially useful in evidence photography, and technical and industrial applications.

Uniform system (U.S.) Early calibration system for exposure settings on a camera, predating the *f*-stop system.

Unique print A photograph so printed or altered that only one original exists.

Van Dyke process A print process utilizing iron compounds which is the most basic form of the kallitype. Also known as brownprint.

Variant Used to describe photographs of a subject or view taken at approximately the same time that feature slight variations in either what appears as subject matter or the orientation or framing of the subject matter. Also prints of the same subject featuring varying exposures, cropping, or toning.

Varnishing Coating prints or negatives with varnishes or shellacs both to provide protection and achieve an even appearance.

Velox Trademark of the Kodak Company for a developing-out contact paper.

Vignetting An effect by which the central image is emphasized in a photographic print usually in a roughly circular or oval form. When unintended, vignetting is caused by an incorrect match between lens and camera format or improper lighting or exposure; when intended by masking the image during exposure or projecting image through a mask in the enlarging process.

Waxed paper negative A variant of the calotype negative.

Wash-off relief process See entry DYE TRANSFER.

Wet collodion process An early photographic process in which glass plates were made light sensitive utilizing a solution of nitrocellulose (gun cotton) in ethyl alcohol and ethyl ether. Exposure was made before the plate solution dried. Also known as the wet plate process.

Woodburytype A bichromate process developed in the mid-nineteenth century that achieves a true continuous tone and exceptionally faithful reproduction to the original through the creation of a relief image from a mold or series of molds.

Xerography See entry.

Zone focusing A method by which the *f*-stop can be selected based on predetermination of where the action or view to be photographed may occur.

Zone system Exposure and developing system developed by Ansel Adams and Fred Archer in the 1930s for black and white photography intended to allow the photographer to previsualize and predetermine exposure settings to achieve richest blacks and fullest range from black to white in any individual photograph, and match this to proper development techniques. Zones, which are conceptual rather than actual view areas, are numbered 0 through IX or in a later refinement, 0 through XI, Roman numerals being used to avoid confusion with *f*-stop numbers. Zone 0, for example, is represented by the maximum black tone obtainable in the individual print, with Zone I being the first discernible gray tone, and so on.

INTRODUCTION

Creating, in one useful, comprehensive publication, an encyclopedia of the history and practice of photography in the twentieth century is a daunting task. In any endeavor, the doing of it often best teaches how it should be done; and not only does the doing perfect the process, it refines the understanding of the subject of the endeavor and focuses the content to be more authoritative. Such is the case, certainly, with the current project.

The ambition of this project was to provide a useful resource of the entire scope of photography in the twentieth century. It was neither to be a definitive technical manual nor a compendium limited to the field's aesthetic achievements, but something more. The aim was to create an encyclopedia that would serve as a resource and a tool for a wide readership of students, researchers, and anyone interested in a scholarly discussion of photography history.

In this we believe it succeeds. The encyclopedia introduces the reader to the history of technical issues that have changed over a hundred-year period. It explains the contributions of photographers and situates their contribution within the history of photography. It defines the concepts, terms, and themes that have evolved over a century. It describes the role of institutions and publications in the shaping of that history. Importantly, the encyclopedia also explains the development of the medium in specific countries and regions around the world—offering a global understanding and a more local perspective of photography history.

This is the main purpose of the encyclopedia, to define the broad outlines and fill in the intimate details of twentieth-century photography. The user will find the large and small of twentieth-century photography. The project gathers information on the most often cited names, terms, concepts, processes, and countries, and it also gives ample attention to those most overlooked. Significantly, it provides the historical and theoretical contexts for understanding each entry so that the expanse of photography history in both its distinct and its partial developments is maintained throughout.

As a resource, the encyclopedia supplies the reader with tools for finding information. Extensive cross-referencing allows the reader insight into the various directions a topic or individual entry may lead: historical, theoretical, or technical. A glossary of terms directs the reader to definitions, describes processes as they were standardized at the end of the century, and gives technical information on photographic terminology, equipment, and accessories. In addition to an alphabetical listing of articles, the articles are also listed by subject to help orient the reader. Subjects are straightforward: equipment; institutions, galleries, and collections; persons; publications and publishers; regions; topics and terms. Each article is signed by the contributing scholar; readers can find a list of contributors in the front matter of volume one. Scholarly references are included at the end of each article so that the interested individual may further explore the topic in more detailed publications. Over 200 illustrations and glossy inserts in each volume will aid the reader's understanding of the articles, but the illustrations are not intended to be the strength of the encyclopedia. This is a work of scholarship, a book intended to be read rather than viewed—we point the readers to resources that contain the thousands of photographs that constitute twentieth-century photography. Finally, the analytical index serves as a critical tool that systematically guides the reader through the contents of the three volumes. The index directs the reader to discussions of sought for information but also allows the reader to explore the contents and discover related items of interest.

While it is hoped that the professional will find the publication as useful as someone approaching photography for the first time, the publication was not intended to take the place of the many fine monographs, textbooks, exhibition catalogues, and websites published for the professional audience that have proliferated in the field at the end of the century. It might be considered a port of entry to the world of twentieth-century photography and photography scholarship.

When this project was conceived, the twentieth century was in its final decade, yet it was not then clear that the arbitrary demarcation of the century as regards photography would be an actual marker as well. The astonishingly rapid rise of digital technologies during the 1990s distinguishes the shape of the medium in the twentieth century in a real way, just as the introduction in 1898 of the mass-use Brownie camera and all its attendant technologies forever wrenched the medium from its nineteenth-century essence as the domain of the dedicated enthusiast, whether professional or amateur. The democratization of the medium certainly seemed to be the main story being told at mid-century, and it may indeed, at further remove, be the overarching feature of the twentieth century. For ironically the digital revolution offers at the same time more and less access—more if one has electricity, a digital camera, and a computer, less if one does not, and many, at the beginning of the twenty-first century, certainly do not. Yet whatever the digital revolution may hold, it seems clear that the obsolescence of the standard photo-chemical processes and the widespread access to the medium they undoubtedly provided will define photography in the new century. Already, in 2005, photo-chemical films and papers have been discontinued or are no longer distributed in the United States; traditional processing labs are vanishing, and items that stocked the traditional darkroom are becoming collectibles, if not landfill.

The encyclopedia had the benefit of the knowledge provided by the distinguished Advisory Board. These individuals freely provided their expertise and advise. The process of selecting the topics and photographers, like anything else, reflects a degree of subjectivity. Yet this subjectivity was tempered by the broad range of experience represented by the Board. Topics were selected to provide snapshots of the entirety of the field utilizing established genres—"fashion photography" or "documentary photography," or obvious entities—"camera" or "Museum of Modern Art." Entries on individuals were more winnowed out than selected. The towering figures are obvious: they fill bookshelves and auction catalogues. But other, lesser known figures of regional importance or photographic innovators were also deemed important to record, and their selection rested on judgment, and to some extent, intuition. The attempt was also to broaden the scope from the United States and Europe, with its long history of photography, to an international one, both in topic discussions and selection of photographers. It goes without saying that many, many other serious, important practitioners of photography and photographic topics and institutions could have been included, yet for the purposes of this publication, we limited the number of entries to 525.

Finally, as tempting as it might have been for the many fine art historians, critics, and writers who authored these essays (and I thank them deeply for their efforts) to come up with original interpretations of photographers' contributions or innovative theoretical stances, the encyclopedia was not intended as an opportunity for scholarship in the form of new interpretations of established figures or revisionary accounts of historical movements.

Conventions and Features

The encyclopedia is arranged alphabetically; spellings of names reflect the most common usage at the end of the century and attempt to use proper diacritical marks in languages which require them. The use of monikers as opposed to given names (i.e. "Weegee" as opposed to Arthur Fellig, or "Madame D'Ora" as opposed to Dora Kallmus) is also based on most common usage. Such "noms-de-photographie" are arranged in the appropriate alphabetical order, with given names included in the entry.

In reference materials, names of institutions are generally given as the full, proper name at the time of the citation. Thus, prior to 1972, it is the George Eastman House; from 1972 onward, the International Museum of Photography and Film, George Eastman House. For the most part, institution names are given in the original language to alleviate confusion about proper translation and ease further research, thus rather than the National Library of France, Bibliothèque nationale de France, and so on.

All entries feature bibliographies or further reading lists. Topics on individuals feature a Capsule Biography for quick reference and a list of Selected Works. Photographers also receive a listing of selected Individual and Group Exhibitions, with as complete information as is available detailing those exhibitions. Websites are occasionally given for governmental agencies, established institutions—especially museums—as well as for some foundations or individual archives. Private websites were generally avoided both to avoid endorsement and the fact that many such websites fail to be maintained over the course of time.

* * *

Although I am a curator of contemporary art, my first love was for photography. I studied it in school and practiced it as a student, taught by photographers who themselves turned out to be "towering figures." As a curator I have organized a number of photography exhibitions, and overseen the collecting of contemporary photography. Yet I am hardly the foremost expert in the field, and thus was truly honored to have been asked to edit this important publication. I hope that my efforts have been equal to expectations.

Lynne Warren
Chicago, Illinois

A

BERENICE ABBOTT

American

Berenice Abbott's accomplishments in the world of photography are wide-ranging and unique. As a photographer, Abbott made important contributions to the art of portraiture, visual documentary, and science photography. As an archivist, she maintained and promoted the work of Eugène Atget for nearly 40 years. Equally, she was an educator, inventor, and an important photographic theorist. She maintained that "the vision of the twentieth century has been created by photography [...] the *picture* has almost replaced the *word* as a means of communication" (Abbott 1951, 42). Likewise, she believed in the ability of the photograph to record the modern world, supplying novel ways of seeing and new truths.

Abbott spent her youth in Columbus and Cleveland before enrolling at Ohio State University in 1917. After only a year at the college, she grew restless and moved to New York. While there, she shared a Greenwich Village apartment with Djuna Barnes, Malcolm Cowley, and Kenneth Burke and worked at the Provincetown Playhouse. Despite what must have been an invigorating experience, Abbott grew disenchanted with America and in 1921 bought a one-way ticket to France.

During her first two years in Paris, Abbott studied sculpture and drawing, yet failed to maintain a steady income. In 1923, she was introduced to the American-born Dada artist Man Ray who was looking for a photographic assistant. Abbott volunteered and was accepted on the spot. Under Man Ray's tutelage, Abbott learned about the darkroom, but by her own admission, nothing about the practicalities of photographic techniques. While vacationing in Amsterdam in 1924, she took her first photographs and her devotion to the medium followed quickly. She began to photograph Paris and gained a sizable reputation. Soon the two photographers suffered an acrimonious split after arts patron Peggy Guggenheim bypassed Man Ray and requested a portrait session with Abbott. Although the relationship ended badly, Abbott would later state that Man Ray "changed my whole life; he was the only person I ever worked for [...] He was a good friend and a fine photographer" (O'Neal 1982, 10).

In 1926, Abbott held her first solo exhibition, established her own studio, and flourished. She worked for *Vogue* magazine, and her clients included artists and writers Jean Cocteau, Max Ernst, André Gide, James Joyce, Claude McKay, and Edna St. Vincent Millay. "To be 'done' by [...] Berenice Abbott," Sylvia Beach once remarked, "meant you rated as someone" (O'Neal 1982, 12). Turning her back on the accepted standards of portrait photography, Abbott sought to dramatize, not flatter or romanticize her subjects. As she stated:

> A portrait can have the most spectacular lighting effect and can be perfect technically, but it fails as a document (which every photograph should be) or as a work of art if it lacks the essential qualities of expression, gesture and attitude peculiar to the sitter [...] Personally I strive for a psychological value, a simple classicism in portraits.
>
> (O'Neal 1982, 13)

In 1929, Abbott returned to New York for a brief visit only to find her former home irrevocably altered. She was fascinated by the city's rapid transformation and decided against returning to Europe. She settled her affairs in Paris and embarked upon one of the most ambitious photographic projects of the twentieth century: to document in a comprehensive and precise manner, the face of modern, changing New York. As she stated in 1932 she sought to dramatize the contrasts of "the old and the new and the bold foreshadowing of the future." Keenly aware of the scope and essential significance of the nascent modernity and urbanization of the city, Abbott desired to "crystallize" its transition in "permanent form" (O'Neal 1982, 16).

Abbott's first New York photographs appeared in *Architectural Record* in May 1930, but during the five years that followed she was unable to procure funding from any of the private and institutional sources she approached. Throughout this period, Abbott supported herself working for such magazines as *Fortune* and *Vanity Fair*. In 1934, the New School for Social Research offered her a job teaching photography. She accepted a one-year contract little knowing that the position would supply her main source of income for many of the next 24 years. This year also witnessed the first major exhibition of Abbott's New York photography. Mounted at the Museum of the City of New York, the show helped raise the profile of Abbott's New York project and greatly contributed towards a successful funding application.

In 1935, Abbott applied for funding to the Federal Arts Project (FAP). In part, her proposal read:

> To photograph NYC means to seek to catch in the sensitive and delicate photographic emulsion the spirit of the metropolis, while remaining true to its essential fact, its hurrying tempo, its congested streets, the past jostling the present. The concern is not with an architectural rendering of detail, the buildings of 1935 overshadowing everything else, but with a synthesis which shows the skyscraper in relation to the less colossal edifices which preceded it [...] it is important that they should be photographed today, not tomorrow; for tomorrow may see many of these exciting and important mementos of eighteenth and nineteenth century New York swept away to make room for new colossi.
>
> (Abbott 1973, 158)

In September 1935, her project—recently entitled *Changing New York*—was accepted by the FAP. Abbott was ranked project supervisor and was awarded funding and a small staff. Consequently, *Changing New York* became an immediate success. The photographs were published in *U.S. Camera*, *Popular Photography*, and the *Coronet*. the *New York Times* and *Life* both did extensive features. In December 1937, the Museum of the City of New York held another hugely successful exhibit; yet by December 1938, Abbott had taken her last project photograph and was demoted to assistant project supervisor. By August 1939, she had no staff at all. After proposing to document the 1939 World's Fair, she was told she could remain on the FAP payroll only as a staff photographer. Choosing independence over employment, Abbott quit the FAP.

In late 1939, Abbott wrote a short memo to herself, the essence of which would occupy her photographic career for most of the next 20 years. Essentially she believed that "we live in a world made by science" and that photography could mediate between (as a "friendly interpreter") science and the layperson in order to articulate and explain how knowledge controls and functions in everyday life (Van Haaften 1989, 58).

Subsequently, Abbott began to experiment with scientific photography and in 1944 she became photo-editor of *Science Illustrated.* Although she quit the magazine two years later, Abbott continued to photograph scientific phenomena and the 1948 textbook *American High School Biology* included many of her illustrations. Her science photography inspired her to develop new photographic equipment, lighting methods, and techniques. In 1947, she incorporated The House of Photography to develop and promote her photographic inventions. Often in financial trouble, the company lasted until 1958, during which time Abbott established four patents.

Abbott continued her science photography in the 1950s, but her reputation, along with her finances, languished until 1957, when the launch of the Russian Sputnik sparked a national obsession with science. Abbott, once again in vogue, was hired by the Physical Science Study Committee of Educational Services (PSSCES) to produce images for a new high school textbook. Her science photographs appeared in national and international magazines, and exhibits of her scientific work were shown in exhibitions around the country. In 1960, Abbott appeared on television in a program called *The Camera Looks at Science*, and the Smithsonian Institution acquired her entire scientific archive. After completing the seminal textbook, *Physics* (1960), Abbott left the PSSCES. She collaborated with Evans G. Valens on a further three scientific books in the 1960s.

Although Abbott's photography is often grouped into three distinct periods—portraits, New York, and science photography—she was equally fascinated by the landscape of America. Under the direction of Henry Russell Hitchcock, Abbott traveled America in 1933 recording the buildings of pre-Civil War America and the work of architect Henry Hobson Richardson. In 1935 she traveled to St. Louis with her friend Elizabeth McCausland, before heading into the Deep South. The resultant photographs anticipate much of the work conducted by Roy Stryker at the Resettlement Administration, although Abbott herself found it extremely difficult to intrude into the lives of people burdened with such poverty. In the 1940s, Abbott briefly worked for Stryker at Standard Oil, but had to withdraw due to poor health. In 1943, Abbott documented the work of the Red Rock Logging Company of California and in 1948 released her second New York book, *Greenwich Village: Today & Yesterday*. In the early 1950s, the photographer conceived a plan to document life along the Route 1 highway. Although she traveled from Kent, Maine to Key West, Florida twice in 1953, and took nearly 400 photographs, the project failed to find a publisher and remains Abbott's most obscure work. By the 1960s, however, Abbott's reputation was in the ascendancy and in 1966 she was given carte blanche to produce a photo-guide to the state of Maine, her recently adopted home. Shunning the standard guidebook images of the state, Abbott pointed her camera inshore and focused on the people and industries that made up everyday life in the state.

Abbott often stated that she had always had to balance two careers: her own and that of Eugène Atget. Abbott was introduced to Atget's photography in 1925 and subsequently befriended the aging photographer. As she later noted, "Atget's photographs somehow spelt photography for me [...] their impact was immediate and tremendous. There was a sudden flash of recognition—the shock of realism unadorned" (Abbott 1964, 1). After Atget's death in 1927, Abbott acquired his complete archive and began to promote his work. On her return to America, Abbott lobbied to have the French photographer's work shown alongside her own and, for 40 years, acted as curator and agent for the Atget file, before finally selling the collection to the Museum of Modern Art in 1968. Moreover she supported the work of numerous other photographers. She endorsed the work of Mathew Brady, William Jackson, Dorothea Lange, Helen Levitt, Lisette Model, Nadar, and Timothy O'Sullivan. In 1939, she helped raise the profile of Lewis Hine by organizing an exhibit of his work at New York's Riverside Museum.

Throughout her life, Abbott wrote about the nature and practice of photography. Much of her thinking is clarified through her long-standing objection to the work and influence of Alfred Steiglitz. Abbott met Steiglitz in 1929 and found him pretentious and condescending. In contrast to Steiglitz as a modernist, Abbott believed there was "poetry in our crazy gadgets, our tools, our architecture" and that photography should fulfill "civic responsibilities": "the photograph may be presented as finely and artistically as possible, but to merit serious consideration, it must be directly connected with the world we live in" (O'Neal 1982, 14, and Abbott 1951, 47). Unlike Stieglitz and his followers of the important "291" Gallery, Abbott saw no connection between painting and photography:

> If a medium is representational by nature of the realistic image formed by the lens, I see no reason why we should stand on our heads to distort that function. On the contrary, we should take hold of that very quality, make use of it, and explore it to the fullest.
>
> (Abbott, "It Has to Walk Alone" 1951, p. 6)

She repudiated the manipulation of images characteristic of avant-gardism and championed realist, that is, documentary content. Photography, she believed, should orient itself towards documentary expression: it should strive towards the real and historical, not the artificial; it should record not imagine. Abbott's photography exemplified her philosophy. For almost 70 years, Abbott sought to capture the changing nature of everyday life. Through it, she forged an aesthetic of modernist realism that reflected the American scene, the medium of photography, and the essence of the twentieth century.

RICHARD HAW

See also: **Atget, Eugène; Architectural Photography; Man Ray; Works Progress Administration**

Biography

Born in Springfield, Ohio, 17 July 1898. Attended Ohio State University, 1917–1918; moved to Paris to study sculpture, 1921. Worked as photographic assistant to Man Ray, 1923–1926; established own portrait studio in Paris and held first solo exhibition, 1926; began to document New York City independently, 1929–1935; traveled with Henry Russell Hitchcock to record pre-Civil War architecture and the work of Henry Hobson Richardson, 1933; began to teach photography at New York's New School for Social Research, 1934; traveled the South with Elizabeth McCausland, 1935; received funding from the Federal Arts Project and worked on the *Changing New York* project, 1935–1939; began science photography, 1940; documented the Red Rock Logging Company in California, 1943; worked as photo editor on *Science Illustrated*, 1944–1946. Published *Greenwich Village: Yesterday & Today* (1949), *Magnet* (1964), *Motion* (1965), *A Portrait of Maine* (1968), *The Attractive Universe* (1969), and *The Red River Photographs* (1979). Incorporated the House of Photography, and established four photographic patents, 1947–1958; began to photograph Route 1 project, 1953; retired from teaching at the New School for Social Research, 1958; worked for the Physical Science Study Committee of Educational Services, 1958–1961. Honorary doctorate from the University of Maine, 1971; honorary doctorate from Smith College, 1973; received the Association of International Photo Art Dealers' award for Outstanding Contribution to the Field of Photography, 1981; honorary doctorate from Ohio State University, 1986; awarded the First International Erice Prize for Photography, 1987; inducted as an Officer in the Legion of Arts and Letters by the French government, 1988. Died in Monson, Maine, 9 December 1991.

Individual Exhibitions

1926 *Portraits Photographiques*; Au Sacre du Printemps; Paris, France
1932 *Berenice Abbott: Portraits*; Julien Levy Gallery; New York, New York
1934 *Photographs for Henry-Russell Hitchcock's Urban Vernacular of the Forties, Fifties and Sixties*; Yale University, New Haven, Connecticut, and traveling
1934 *Photographs of New York City*; Museum of the City of New York; New York, New York
1937 *Changing New York—125 Photographs*; Museum of the City of New York; New York, New York
1947 Galerie de l'Epoque; Paris, France
1950 Akron Art Institute; Akron, Ohio
1951 Art Institute of Chicago; Chicago, Illinois
1953 San Francisco Museum of Modern Art; San Francisco, California
1959 *Science Photographs*; New School for Social Research; New York, New York
1960 *Science Photographs*; Smithsonian Institution; Washington D.C. and traveling
1970 *Berenice Abbott: Photographs*; Museum of Modern Art; New York, New York
1973 Witkin Gallery; New York, New York, and traveling
1976 *Berenice Abbott*; Marlborough Gallery; New York, New York
1977 Treat Gallery; Lewiston, Maine
1979 *Berenice Abbott: The Red River Photographs*; Fine Arts Work Center; Provincetown, Massachusetts
1980 *Berenice Abbott: Documentary Photographs of the 1930s*; The New Gallery of Contemporary Art; Cleveland, Ohio
1982 *Berenice Abbott: The 20s and 30s*; Smithsonian Institution; Washington, D.C., and traveling
1989 *Berenice Abbott, Photographer: A Modern Vision*; New York Public Library; New York, New York
1996 *Berenice Abbott: Portraits, New York Views and Science Photographs*; International Center of Photography; New York, New York
1997 *Berenice Abbott: Changing New York, the Complete WPA Project*; The Museum of the City of New York; New York, New York

Group Exhibitions

1928 *Film und Foto*; Deutsche Werkbund; Stuttgart, Germany
1928 *Avant-Garde*; Salon des Indépendants; Paris, France
1932 *Murals and Photomurals*; Museum of Modern Art; New York, Brooklyn Museum; Brooklyn, New York
1932 *Philadelphia International Salon of Photography*; Ayer Galleries; Philadelphia, Pennsylvania; Albright Art Gallery; Buffalo, New York
1940 *Pageant of Photography*; Golden Gate Exposition; San Francisco, California
1969 *Women, Cameras and Images III*; Smithsonian Institution; Washington, D.C.

Selected Works

Eugène Atget, Paris, France, 1927
Julien Levy, 1927
James Joyce, c. 1928
New York at Night, 1934
Newstand, 32nd Street and Third Avenue, Nov. 19, 1935
Daily News Building; 42nd Street between Second and Third Avenues, Nov. 21, 1935
Canyon: 46th Street and Lexington Avenue, Looking West, 1936
McGraw Hill Building; From 42nd Street and Ninth Avenue looking east, May 25, 1936
Gasoline Station; Tremont Avenue and Dock Street, July 2, 1936
Herald Square, 34th and Broadway, July 16, 1936
Rockefeller Center, from 444 Madison Avenue, 1937
Financial district rooftops: II; Looking southwest from roof of 60 Wall Tower, June 9, 1938
Jacob Heymann Butcher Shop, 345 Sixth Avenue, Manhattan, 1938
Repair Shop, Christopher Street, c. 1946
The Pendulum, c. 1960
Beams of Light Through Glass, c. 1960

Further Reading

Abbott, Berenice. "Eugène Atget." *Creative Art* 5 (1929).

Abbott, Berenice. "Photographer as Artist." *Art Front* 2 (1936).

Abbott, Berenice. *Changing New York*. Text by Elizabeth McCausland. New York: E. P. Dutton, 1939; Reprinted as *New York in the Thirties as Photographed by Berenice Abbott*. New York: Dover, 1973.

Abbott, Berenice. *A Guide to Better Photography*. New York: Crown, 1941, Revised in 1953 as *A New Guide to Better Photography*.

Abbott, Berenice. "Photography at the Crossroads." *Universal Photo Almanac* (1951).

Abbott, Berenice. "It Has to Walk Alone." *Infinity* 7 (1951).

Abbott, Berenice. *The World of Atget*. New York: Horizon Press, 1964.

Berman, Avis. "The Unflinching Eye of Berenice Abbott." *Art News* 80 (1981).

———. "The Pulse of Reality—Berenice Abbott." *Architectural Digest* April (1985).

McCausland, Elizabeth. "The Photography of Berenice Abbott." *Trend* 3 (1935).

———. "Berenice Abbott—Realist." *Photo Arts* 2 (1948).

McEuen, Melissa A. *Seeing America: Women Photographers Between the Wars*. Lexington: University Press of Kentucky, 2000.

O'Neal, Hank. *Berenice Abbott: American Photographer*. New York: McGraw-Hill, 1982.

Raeburn, John. "Culture Morphology and Cultural History in Berenice Abbott's *Changing New York*." *Prospects* 9 (1984).

Steinbach, Alice C. "Berenice Abbott's Point of View." *Art in America* November/December (1976).

Sundell, Michael. "Berenice Abbott's Work in the 1930s." *Prospects* 5 (1980).

Van Haaften, Julia. *Berenice Abbott*. New York: Aperture, 1988.

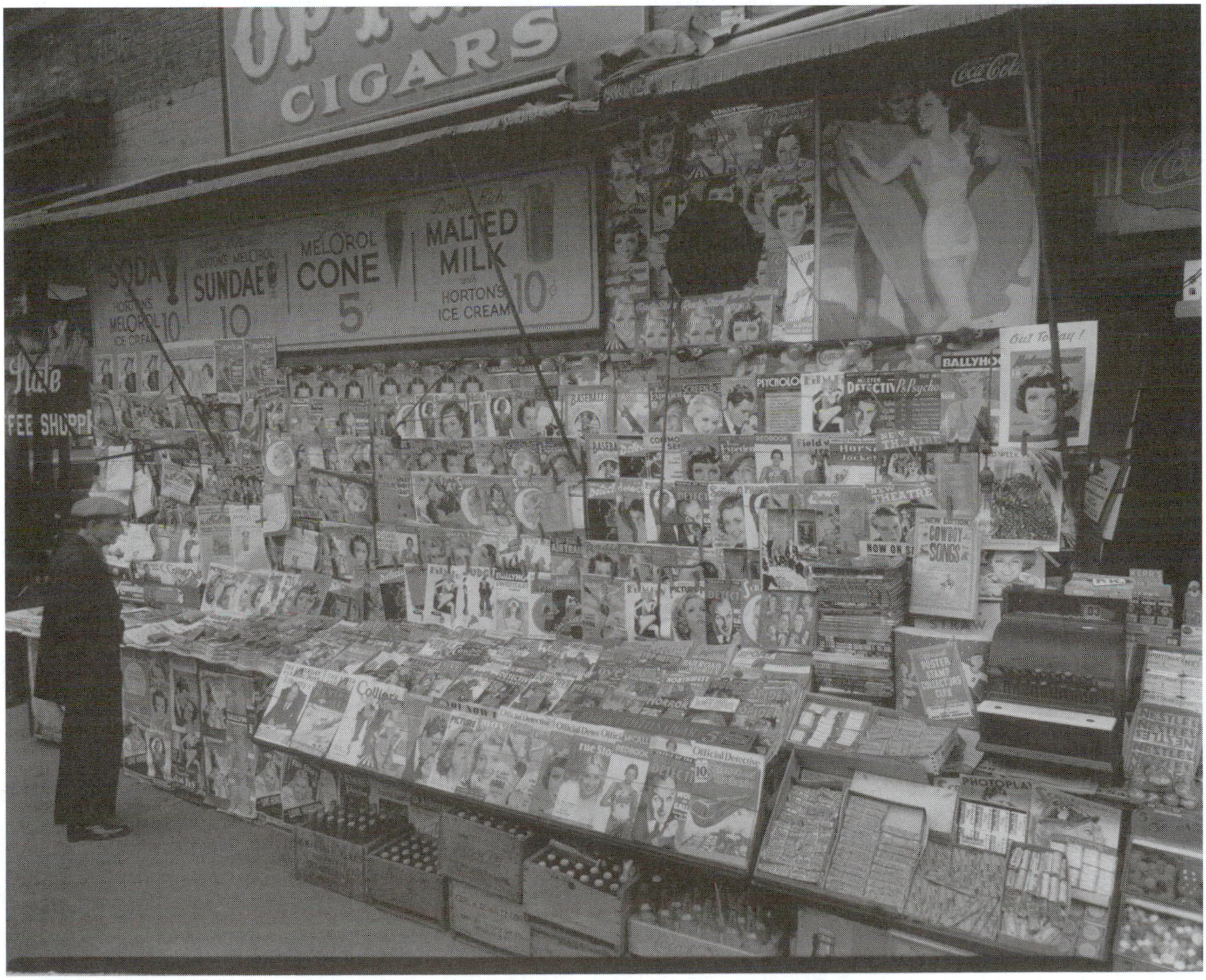

Berenice Abbott, November 19, 1935, Photography Collection, Miriam and Ira D. Wallach Division of Art, Prints and Photographs.
[*© Berenice Abbott/Commerce Graphics Ltd., NYC. The New York Public Library/Art Resource, New York*]

———. *Berenice Abbott, Photographer: A Modern Vision.* New York: New York Public Library, 1989.
———. "Berenice Abbott, American Photographer: A Bio-Bibliography." *Bookman Weekly* (30 January 1995).
Yochelson, Bonnie. *Berenice Abbott: Changing New York, the Complete WPA Project.* New York: The New Press and The Museum of the City of New York, 1997.

ABSTRACTION

Discussions of abstraction in photography may seem to be a paradox as one is accustomed to its function of mechanical reproduction and of its descriptive representation. Yet, the fact that a photograph is difficult to recognize or hardly legible is not incompatible with its technical definition—a luminous print on a photosensitive surface. Whatever its nature is, the photographic image always remains an image or representation of something, even if the photographer uses various processes to make the viewer forget what the image is a representation of. Since its discovery in 1839, photography has served many documentary uses, producing pictures based upon the representational codes of human vision (verism). Nevertheless, from the early twentieth century, many photographers have sought to transcend this use by experimenting and developing an abstract practice of photography.

Origins of Abstraction

The history of photography often converges with that of Modernism in the late nineteenth and early twentieth centuries, chronologically as well as intellectually. The photograph's history was marked in particular by the idea of the specificity and growing autonomy of the medium—the medium's internal logic, principles, and evolution. The earliest abstract paintings emerged around 1910 by Vasily Kandinsky, Kasimir Malevich and others; historians observed almost at the same time the emergence of similar preoccupations among photographers. As early as the beginning of photography from the "photogenic drawings" of William Henry Fox Talbot in the 1830s to the studies of motion by Thomas Eakins and Etienne-Jules Marey (what he termed "chronophotography") in the 1880s, one finds images that could be described as abstract, although they serve scientific and technical purposes over aesthetic goals. It is only by 1908 that the germ of the formalist, stylized processes indicative of modernity emerged in Great Britain with Malcolm Arbuthnot's *The Doorstep* or *The Wheel*; these works revealed his interest in Japanese art with emphases on composition, structure, asymmetry, line, distribution of light and shade. After Arbuthnot, the appearance of deliberately abstract photography occurs in the mid-1910s in America with Paul Stand's *Porch Shadows* or *The Bowls* in 1915, pictures in which he played with forms and masses, composition and close frame. Already three years earlier, a similar work was realized by Alvin Langdon Coburn with his series *New York From Its Pinnacles*, and in particular, *The Octopus*, in which a bird's eye view flattened perspective and generated two-dimensional pattern. Strand would wait until his meeting with Ezra Pound and the Vorticism movement, inspired by the complexities of industrialization and urbanity, to realize between 1916 and 1917 his well-known series *Vortographs*. These works revealed his interest for cubist diffraction of space, and Italian futurism's obsession with dynamism and movement.

Evolution

The tendency towards abstraction in form of the aforementioned photographers illustrates what followed and lingered throughout the twentieth century, that is, the coexistence of two parallel views among American and European modernist photographers. These views included on the one hand, the inheritance of "pure" or "Straight" photographic aesthetic launched by American photographers such as Alfred Stieglitz, Aaron Siskind, and others; and on the other hand, an experimental aesthetic directly derived from the European avant-gardism of László Moholy-Nagy, Alexander Rodchenko, and others.

Straight Photography sought to seize an objective reality made of everyday objects that usually escape the human eye. Without any manipulation and by emphasizing purely photographic processes such as framing, lighting, focus, scale, or viewpoint, the resulting images exploited the pure formalism of flattened and two-dimensional patterns, geometry, and design. This trend was well illustrated in America with Bernard Shea Horne, Max Weber and their students of Clarence H. White School of Photography in the 1910s, in Charles Sheeler's *House Of Doylestown, Staircase* (1917), in Stieglitz's series *Equivalents* in 1923–1931, and in Siskind's later work of the 1930s and 1940s. A related strain of the Americanists' Straight Photography materialized with the New Vision (Neue Sehen) in Germany and Russia whose prominent representatives were Moholy-Nagy (*From the Radio Tower Berlin*, 1928) and Rodschenko (*On The Pavement*, 1928).

Even more experimental or aesthetically radical than the work of the aforementioned Straight photographers was another strain of abstraction that considered photography as an ideal means of plastic expression to build and create new visual codes. Using a diversity of practices such as the photogram, manipulation of light, movement and chemistry, European photographers realized a range of recurrent features that became associated with modernist abstraction. Because the photogram was produced without a camera, the artist could create images from shadows and silhouettes of objects that were placed between the light source and light-sensitive paper or film, thus bypassing the mechanical or technical apparatus in favor of imagination and even surrealism.

At the origins of numerous abstract manipulations, the photogram became one of the most enduring techniques of the century, finding practitioners in Christian Schad as early as 1918, Man Ray in 1921, and Moholy-Nagy in 1922. Exemplifying Dadaist and Constructivist preoccupations, photogram processes allowed the exploration of photography's profound nature by exploiting the play of texture, pattern, transparency, and the duality of positive-negative relationships. The process permitted many possibilities such as experimentation with dematerialization, the interpenetration of forms, distortion and lack of perspective. Various artists such as Theodore Roszak, Georg Zimin, Piet Zwart, and Willy Zielke made photograms in the 1930s; Bronislaw Schlabs, Julien Coulommier, Andrzej Pawlowski, Beksinki and Kurt Wendlandt in the 1940s and 1950s; Lina Kolarova, René Mächler, and Andreas Mulas in the 1970s; Tomy Ceballos, Kare Magnole, Andreas Müller-Pohle, and Floris M. Neusüss have utilized the process in the 1980s.

Equally important among abstract practices, the use of light remains a fundamental principle with the function not only to reveal and make visible, but also to be exploited as a real material. In this respect, several trajectories can be traced, including the pictures of lighted surfaces or volumes in Francis Bruguière's *Light Abstractions* (1919) and Jaromir Funke's *Light Abstraction, Rectangles* in the 1920s. Between the 1930s and the 1950s photographers such as Moholy-Nagy with his *Light Modulator* "machines," Barbara Morgan seized upon luminous flow, whether fixed or in motion, to produce calligraphic expression. More recently in France, Thomas Reaume in the 1980s and Bernard Lanteri in the 1990s have realized luminous and fluid forms that defy the fixed nature of the photographic image.

Movement and blurredness represent another aspect of abstraction in photography. This tendency is illustrated by the works of Italian futurists such as the brothers Arturo and Antonin Bragaglia's photodynamism and aerial photography by Fedele Azari and Filippo Masoero, in addition to the kineticism of German photographers Oskar Schlemmer, Peter Keetman and Otto Steinert in the 1940s–1950s. Generally, these works fit an aesthetic of speed and movement linked to the expressions of the artistic avant-garde of the time. But it is only by the 1950s that an aesthetic of blurredness, movement, and random quality peculiar to photography found expression. As such, it seemed that American William Klein's work was as much a beginning and a major reference for contemporary photographers such as Gerard Dalla-Santa, Frederic Gallier, Hervé Rabot, Patrick Toth, and Müller-Pohle who during the 1980s viewed movement not only as a transcription of the urban world's brutal dynamism but also as a mine of pure form, revealing the visual and tactile qualities of photography (for example, grain).

Finally, choosing to relinquish the optical aspect of the medium, another group of photographers preferred to explore the medium's physical chemistry. Relying on darkroom experimentation and camera-less imagery, photographers explored the abstract qualities possible in chemical experimentation, leading to the specific forms of Edmund Kesting and Chargesheimer in the 1940s, and Stryj Piasecki or Pierre Cordier in the 1950s. Sigmar Polke during the 1970s and Riwan Tromeur during the 1980s have produced a peculiar

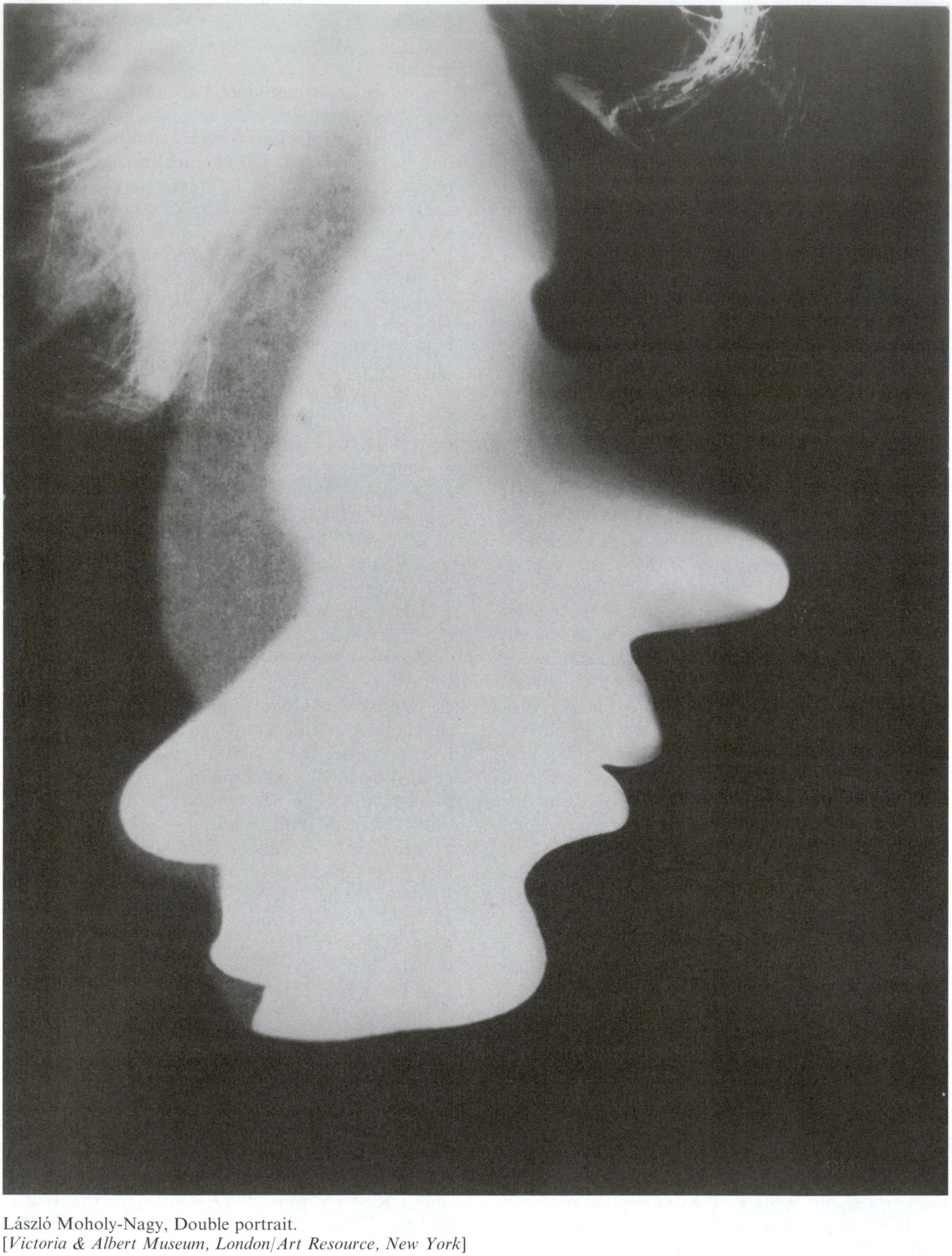

László Moholy-Nagy, Double portrait.
[*Victoria & Albert Museum, London/Art Resource, New York*]

formal vocabulary by altering the very photographic chemical process.

ANNE BARTHELEMY

See also: **Bragaglia, Antonin; Bruguière, Francis; Chargesheimer; Dada; Funke, Jaromir; Modernism; Moholy-Nagy, László; Photogram; Siskind, Aaron; Stieglitz, Alfred; Strand, Paul; Zwart, Piet**

Further Reading

Barrow, T. Hagen, C. Neusüss, F.M. *Experimental Vision. The Evolution of the Photogram Since 1919*. Denver: Denver Art Museum, 1994.

De Sana, J. (dir.) *Abstraction in Contemporary Photography*. Clinton, NY: Emerson Gallery and Richmond, VA: Anderson Gallery, 1989.

Grundberg, Andy. *Photography and Art Interaction Since 1945*. New York: Abbeville Press, Los Angeles County Museum, 1987.

Lyons, Nathan, ed. *Photographers on Photography: A Critical Anthology*. Rochester, NY: 1966.

Phillips, C., ed. *Photography In the Modern Era: European Documents And Critical Writings. 1913–1940*. New York: The Metropolitan Museum of Art and Aperture, 1989.

Szarkowski, John, *Photography Until Now*. New York: Museum of Modern Art, 1989.

Tucker, J.S. *Light Abstraction*. St Louis: University of Missouri, 1980.

Yates, S., dir. *Proto Modern Photography*. Rochester, New York: George Eastman House, 5 December 1992–7 February, 1993.

ANSEL ADAMS

American

Throughout his life, Ansel Adams made monumental contributions as a photographer, teacher, lecturer, conservationist, and writer. He is best known as an undisputed master of straight natural landscape photography. His photographic studies of the American western landscape have gained extraordinary prestige and popularity, partly because he achieved an unsurpassed technical perfection by approaching the medium in a scientifically precise way and insisting on absolute control of the photographic process. According to Adams, an initial and most important constituent of this process is the photographer's visualization of the final product, which involves an intuitive search for meaning, shape, form, texture, and the projection of the image-format on the subject. The image forms in the photographer's mind before the shutter opens. Put in Adams's own words:

> The camera makes an image-record of the object before it. It records the subject in terms of the optical properties of the lens, and the chemical and physical properties of the negative and print. The control of that record lies in the selection by the photographer and in his understanding of the photographic process at his command. The photographer visualizes his conception of the subject as presented in the final print. He achieves the expression of his visualization through his technique—aesthetic, intellectual, and mechanical.
>
> (Adams 1985, 78)

Born in San Francisco in 1902, Adams was interested at an early age in music and was trained to become a concert pianist. At the age of 14, on a family vacation in the Yosemite Valley, he took his first photographs—an experience that would inspire him for the rest of his life. Back in San Francisco, parallel to his education in music, Adams studied photography with a photofinisher. He returned to Yosemite regularly to dedicate himself to photography, exploration, and climbing. In 1920, he formed an association with the Sierra Club (a conservation organization), and in 1928, the year he married Virginia Best, began to work there as an official photographer. His first photographs were strongly influenced by the prevalent pictorialist style, visible in his 1921 *Lodgepole Pines*, a characteristic soft-focus, romantic image. This style would turn quickly into a more "honest" representation of nature. In 1927, Adams's first portfolio was published, *Parmelian Prints of the High Sierras*. After meeting Paul Strand in 1930 and being deeply influenced by his straight approach to the subject, Adams took the decision to devote his life to photography. By working as a commercial photographer, he found a solution that would allow him to support his family and at the same time enable him to pursue the development of his own artistic photographic work.

Although first offered only occasional photographic jobs by private persons and California area companies, Adams gained gradually a reputation and was soon offered jobs across the country by major companies such as the American Telegraph and Telephone Company, *Life* magazine, the American Trust Company, and Eastman Kodak (later in his career).

Adams's first individual exhibition was held in 1931 at the Smithsonian Institution, Washington, D.C., and a year later, his work was exhibited at the M.H. de Young Memorial Museum, San Francisco. In that same year, 1932, he founded the Group f/64 together with Willard Van Dyke, Edward Weston, Imogen Cunningham, Sonia Noskowiak, John Paul Edwards, and Henry Swift. The name f/64 refers to the smallest aperture of the camera lens, a setting that produces the largest field depth and consequently sharply focused and finely detailed images.

The group promoted straight, pure modernistic photography, in contrast to the prevalent sentimental turn-of-the-century pictorialist style. Soft-focus and emotionalism was replaced by emphasis on crystalline sharp form and texture. Frequently, the photographic subjects were chosen deliberately simple, often seen in close-up and creating sometimes abstract designs, as for example in *Burnt Stump and New Grass, 1935; Rose and Driftwood, 1932, Frozen Lake and Cliffs, Surf Sequence* (a sequence of five images), 1932; or *Wood Flame, Tree Detail.* The prints were produced on glossy gelatin silver papers mounted on white board. Filters and only basic printing techniques, such as burning and dodging, were considered acceptable. In fact, Adams used filters often in order to accentuate the structure of clouds against the sky, or in general to darken a blue sky to appear almost completely black on the prints, as for instance in *Monolith, the Face of Half Dome* or *High Country Crags and Moon, Sunrise,* c. 1935.

Despite the clear rules of the Group f/64, Adams did not eschew a certain degree of experimentation, and used a variety of miniature and large-format cameras. After meeting Alfred Stieglitz in 1933, he opened the Ansel Adams Gallery in San Francisco. He published several articles in *Camera Craft* in 1934 and a year later, his first book, *Making a Photograph*, which was received with enthusiasm and assured him a worldwide reputation as a photographer. In many of his publications, Adams promoted the approach of the Group f/64 with passion. The most convincing, tangible, and by the broad public best understood and admired arguments in favor of this approach, however, were undoubtedly Adams's photographic studies of the west coast. They stand as testimony for the power and beauty of straight photography. The sharp images of majestic mountainous landscapes, untouched by mankind, convey a sense of awe and instill respect and a desire for conservation of nature, an aspect that was most important to Adams throughout his life. Famous examples are Adams's *Tenya Lake, Mount Conness, c. 1946; Winter Sunrise, 1944*; or *Moon and Half Dome, 1960*. Adams developed a strong intuition for the exact moment in time where the constellation of sun and clouds, shadow and light would combine to the desired dramatic interplay between strongly textured and planer, flatter elements of the image. Anticipation plays a decisive role in capturing the right moment: "Anticipation is one of the most perplexing capabilities of the mind: projection into future time. Impressive with a single moving object, it is overwhelming when several such objects are considered together and in relation to the environment" (Adams 1985, 78). Examples showing the effect of successfully capturing the right moment are Adams's *Clearing Winter Storm* (1944), or *Mount Williamson* (1944). However, the best example is his most well-known photograph, *Moonrise, Hernandez, New Mexico*, 1941, where, as is often the case, capturing the right moment was a matter of seconds:

> After the first exposure I quickly reversed the 8×10 film holder to make a duplicate negative, for I instinctively knew I had visualized one of those very important images that seem prone to accident or physical defect, but as I pulled out the slide the sunlight left the crosses and the magical moment was gone forever.
>
> (Ansel Adams, 273)

By 1936, Adams had earned such a reputation and impressed Stieglitz so much that an important one-man exhibition of his work was held at An American Place, New York. Adams moved into the Yosemite Valley, taking trips through the Southwest with Edward Weston, Georgia O'Keeffe, and David McAlpin. The resulting photographs were published in 1938 in *Sierra Nevada: The John Muir Trail.* He met Nancy and Beaumont Newhall in New York in 1939, where in the following year, he assisted, together with McAlpin, in the creation of the Department of Photography at the Museum of Modern Art (MoMA).

In an effort to control the photographic process and to be able to record the visual impressions of a specific quantity and quality of light, Adams, with the help of Fred Archer, developed the Zone System in the late 1930s. This tool provides the photographer with a practical, yet scientifically grounded method implementing the conceptual basis of Group f/64. It helps to realize the vision by controlling exposure, development, and printing, and thus enabling the photographer to project the wanted detail, scale, texture, and tone onto the final image. The Zone System is still used today by professional photographers. Each of the 11 zones, ranging from 0 (pure black) to X (pure white) corresponds to a specific ratio between a subject's brightness as measured with a light meter to its density in the negative and hence to its tone in the final print. The Zone System became very popular thanks to Adams's publications and workshops, and soon became the most important form of printmaking.

At the beginning of World War II, Adams went to Washington, D.C., working as a photomuralist for the Department of the Interior. Photographs of a war-time essay for the cause of interned Japanese-Americans were exhibited at MoMA in 1944 under the title *Born Free and Equal.* During the next two years, Adams taught photography at the museum and in 1946 he co-founded one of the first departments of photography at the California School of Fine Arts, later known as the San Francisco Art Institute. In the same year, he obtained a Guggenheim Fellowship to photograph national park locations and monuments. The Fellowship was renewed in 1948, and five productive years of important and creative photographic work followed.

Portfolio 1: In Memory of Alfred Stieglitz was published in 1948 and in the same year, Adams started publishing technical volumes in the *Basic Photo Series.* In 1950, *Portfolio 2: The National Parks and Monuments* was issued. In 1953, he collaborated with Dorothea Lange on a photographic essay on the Mormons in Utah for *Life* magazine and started a photography workshop in Yosemite in 1955. His *Portfolio 3: Yosemite Valley* was published by the Sierra Club in 1960.

Adams moved to Carmel, California in 1962, where he played an important role in the foundation of the Friends of Photography, of which he became president. A year later, the de Young Museum exhibited a retrospective show of his work from 1923–1963 and in 1966, Adams was elected a Fellow of the American Academy of Arts and Sciences. By the late 1960s, Adams had given up active photography and dedicated his time to revising the *Basic Photo Series*, publishing several books containing his life's work, as well as preparing prints for numerous exhibitions. Two years before his death, Adams defined his personal photographic credo in a catalogue for his exhibition *The Unknown Ansel Adams* at The Friends of Photography:

> A great photograph is one that fully expresses what one feels, in the deepest sense, about what is being photographed, and is, thereby, a true manifestation of what one feels about life in its entirety. This visual expression of feeling should be set forth in terms of a simple devotion to the medium. It should be a statement of the greatest clarity and perfection possible under the conditions of its creation and production.
>
> My approach to photography is based on my belief in the vigor and values of the world of nature, in aspects of grandeur and minutiae all about us. I believe in people, in the simpler aspects of human life, in the relation of man to nature. I believe man must be free, both in spirit and society, that he must build strength into himself, affirming the enormous beauty of the world and acquiring the confidence to see and to express his vision. And I believe in photography as one means of expressing this affirmation and of achieving an ultimate happiness and faith.
>
> (Ansel Adams, 235)

Adams died in 1984 in Carmel. Major collections of his work are found in the following institutions: Center for Creative Photography, University of Arizona, Tucson (archives); San Francisco Museum of Modern Art; the M.H. de Young Memorial Museum, San Francisco; Bancroft Library, University of California, Berkeley; MoMA New York; Victoria and Albert Museum, London; Bibliothèque Nationale, Paris.

There are several films dealing with Adams and his work: *Ansel Adams, Photographer*, directed by David Myers in 1957; *Yosemite, Valley of Light*, directed by Tom Thomas in 1957; *Photography: The Incisive Art*, five television films directed by Robert Katz in 1959.

Marco Merkli

See also: **Bibliothèque nationale de France; Center for Creative Photography; Cunningham, Imogen; Friends of Photography; Group f/64; Modernism; Museum of Modern Art; Newhall, Beaumont; Stieglitz, Alfred; Strand, Paul; Victoria and Albert Museum; Weston, Edward**

Biography

Born in San Francisco, California, 20 February 1902. Tutored first privately at home, studies piano at San Francisco Conservatory 1914–1927 and photography with photofinisher Frank Dittman, San Francisco, 1916–1917. Began career as photographer in 1927; worked as commercial photographer 1930–1960; co-founded the Group f.64, San Francisco 1932; co-founded the Photography Department, Museum of Modern Art, New York, 1940; instructor, with Edward Weston, *U.S. Camera* photographic forum, Yosemite Valley, 1940; instructor in Photography, Art Center School, Los Angeles, 1941; photography consultant, Office of War Information, Los Angeles, 1942–1944; instructor in photography MoMA, New York, 1945; founder and instructor, Department of Photography, California School of Fine Arts, San Francisco, 1946; Guggenheim Fellowships 1946 (renewed 1948), 1958; founder and instructor, Ansel Adams Annual Photography Workshops, Yosemite Valley, 1955–1984; member of the board of directors, 1934–1971, and honorary vice-president, 1978–1984, Sierra Club, San Francisco; founder and chairman, Friends of Photography, Carmel, 1967; Conservation Service Award, United States Department of the Interior, 1968; Progress Medal, Photographic Society of America, 1969; Chubb Fellowship, Yale University, New Haven, Connecticut, 1970; participates in creation of the Center for Creative Photography, University of Arizona at Tucson, 1970; United States Presidential Medal of Freedom, 1980; Hasselblad Prize, 1981; Died in Carmel, California, 23 April 1984.

Individual Exhibitions

1928 Sierra Club, San Francisco, California
1931 Smithsonian Institution, Washington, D.C.
1932 M.H. de Young Memorial Museum, San Francisco, California
1934 Albright Art Gallery, Buffalo, New York
Yale University, New Haven, Connecticut
1936 *An American Place*, New York, New York
1938 University of California, Berkeley, California
1939 San Francisco Museum of Art, San Francisco, California
1944 Museum of Modern Art, New York, New York
1946 Santa Barbara Museum, Santa Barbara, California
1950 Pasadena Art Institute, Pasadena, California
1951 Art Institute of Chicago, Chicago, Illinois
1952 International Museum of Photography, Rochester, New York; Smithsonian Institution, Washington, D.C.
1956 Photokina, Cologne, Germany
1956 Limelight Gallery, New York, New York
1961 American Federation of Arts, Carmel, California
1963 *The Eloquent Light*, M.H. de Young Memorial Museum, San Francisco, California (retrospective)
1972 *Recollected Moments*, San Francisco Museum of Modern Art, San Francisco, California, and traveling to Europe and South America
Witkin Gallery, New York, New York
San Francisco Museum of Art, San Francisco, California
1973 Friends of Photography, Carmel, California
1974 *Photographs by Ansel Adams*, Metropolitan Museum of Art, New York, New York and traveling
1967 Center for Creative Photography, University of Arizona, Tucson, Arizona, Victoria and Albert Museum, London, England
1977 Fotografiska Museet, Stockholm, Sweden
1980 *Ansel Adams: Photographs of the American West*, organized by The Friends of Photography for the USICA and circulated through 1983 in India, the Middle East, and Africa
1981 Chrysler Museum of Art, Norfolk, Virginia
1982 *Ansel Adams at An American Place*, San Francisco Museum of Modern Art, San Francisco, California, and traveling
1983 *Ansel Adams: Photographs*, The Friends of Photography, and traveling to Shanghai, Beijing, Hong Kong, and Tokyo
1987 *Ansel Adams: One with Beauty*, M.H. de Young Memorial Museum, San Francisco, California
1997 *Ansel Adams, A Legacy: Masterworks from The Friends of Photography Collection*, and traveling in United States and Japan
2002 *Ansel Adams at 100*, San Francisco Museum of Modern Art, San Francisco, California, and traveling

Group Exhibitions

1932 *Group f/64*, M.H. de Young Memorial Museum, San Francisco
1937 *Photography 1839–1937*, Museum of Modern Art, New York, New York
1944 *Art in Progress*, Museum of Modern Art, New York, New York
1951 *Contemporary Photography*, Contemporary Arts Museum, Houston, Texas
1959 *Photography at Mid-Century*, George Eastman House, Rochester, New York
1963 *The Photographer and the American Landscape*, Museum of Modern Art, New York, New York
1978 *Mirrors and Windows: American Photography since 1960*, Museum of Modern Art, New York, New York, and toured the United States, 1978–1980
1980 *The Imaginary Photo Museum*, Kunsthalle, Cologne, Germany
1985 *American Images*, Barbican Art Gallery, London, England and toured Britain
1987 *Photography and Art 1946–1986*, Los Angeles County Museum of Art, Los Angeles, California

Selected Works

Photographs
Lodgepole Pines, Lyell Fork of the Merced River, Yosemite National Park, 1921
Monolith, the Face of Half Dome, Yosemite National Park, 1927
Rose and Driftwood, San Francisco, 1932
Frozen Lake and Cliffs, Sierra Nevada, Sequoia National Park, California, 1932
Burnt Stump and New Grass, Sierra Nevada, California, 1935
High Country Crags and Moon, Sunrise, Kings Canyon National Park, California, c. 1935
North Dome, Basket Dome, Mount Hoffman, Yosemite, c. 1935
Surf Sequence, San Mateo County Coast, California, 1940
Moonrise, Hernandez, New Mexico, 1941
Winter Sunrise, The Sierra Nevada, from Lone Pine, California, 1944
Clearing Winter Storm, Yosemite National Park, 1944
Mount Williamson, Sierra Nevada, from Manzanar, California, 1944

Tenya Lake, Mount Conness, Yosemite National Park, around 1946
Moon and Half Dome, Yosemite National Park, 1960
Wood Flame, Tree Detail, Yosemite National Park, around 1960
Aspens, Northern New Mexico, 1976

Books of Photographs

Taos Pueblo. Text by Mary Austin. San Francisco: 1930.
Sierra Nevada: The John Muir Trail. Berkeley, CA: 1938.
Michael and Anne in Yosemite Valley. Text by Virginia Adams. New York and London: 1941.
Born Free and Equal: The Story of Loyal Japanese-Americans at Manzanar Relocation Center. New York: 1944.
My Camera in the National Parks. Boston: 1950.
The Islands of Hawaii. Text by Edward Joesting. Honolulu: 1958.
Yosemite Valley. Nancy Newhall, ed. San Francisco: 1959.
These We Inherit: The Parklands of America. San Francisco: 1963.
Fiat Lux: The University of California. Text by Nancy Newhall. New York: 1967.
Ansel Adams: Images 1923–1974. Text by Wallace Stegner. Boston: 1974.
Photographs of the Southwest. Text by Lawrence Clark Powell. Boston: 1976.
The Portfolios of Ansel Adams. Introduction by John Szarkowski. Boston and London: 1977.
Ansel Adams: An Autobiography. With Mary Street Alinder. Boston: 1985.

Technical Books

Making a Photograph. New York and London: 1935.
Basic Photo Series: *Camera and Lens*. New York: 1948 and 1970; *The Negative*. New York: 1948; *The Print*. New York: 1950; *Natural Light Photography*. New

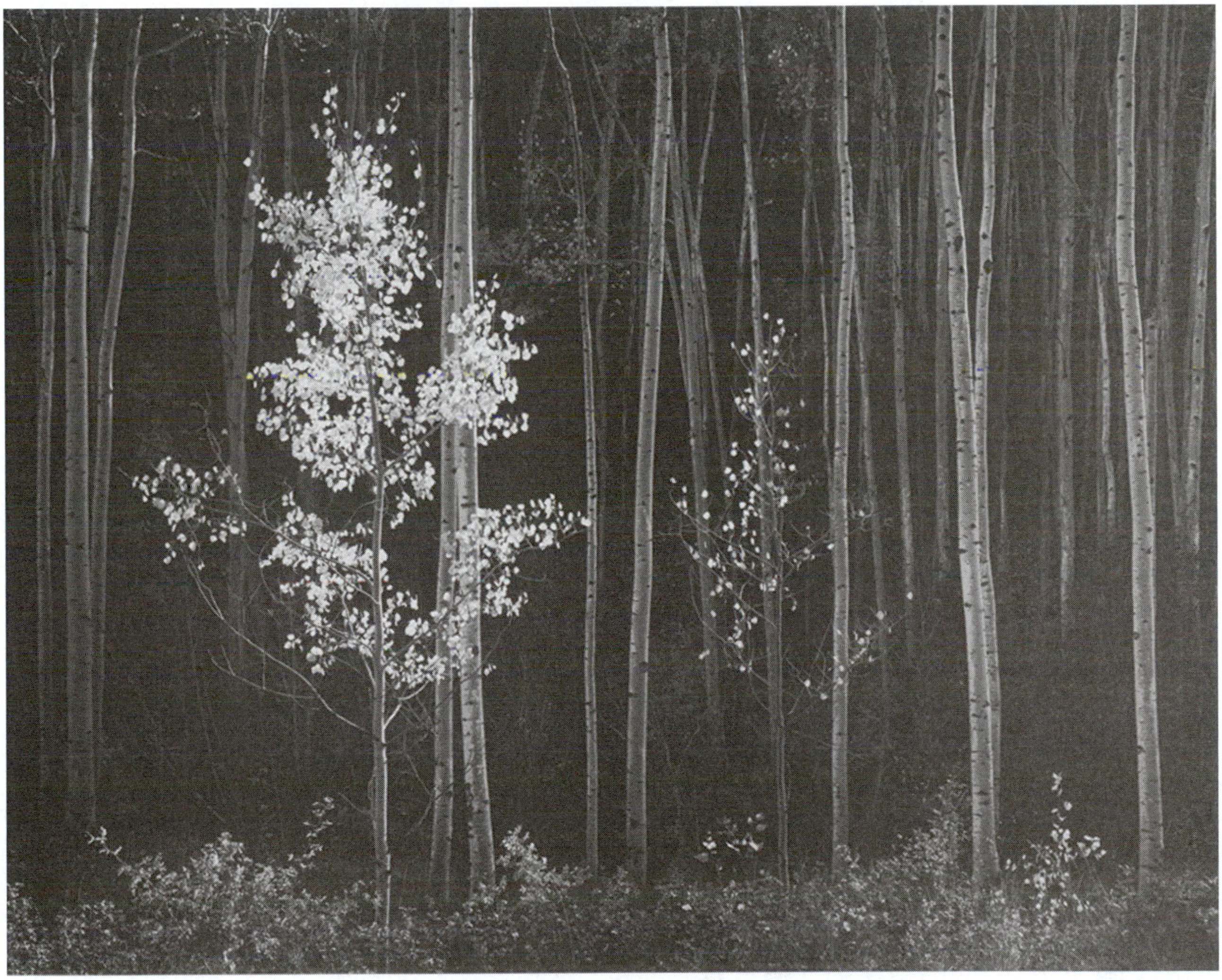

Ansel Adams, Aspens, Northern New Mexico, Print No. 6 from Portfolio VII, 1976, New Mexico, 1958, Gelatin-silver print, 17 ⅞ × 22 ⅝″, Gift of the photographer in honor of David H. McAlpin.
[*Digital Image © The Museum of Modern Art/Licensed by SCALA/Art Resource, NY*]

York: 1952; *Artificial Light Photography*. New York: 1956.
Polaroid Land Photography. Boston: 1979.
The Camera. Boston: 1980.

Further Reading

Alinder, James. *Ansel Adams: 50 Years of Portraits*. Carmel, CA: 1979.
Doty, Robert, ed. *Photography in America*. New York and London: 1974.
Gray, Andrea. *Ansel Adams: An American Place*. Tucson, AZ: 1984.
Newhall, Nancy. *The Eloquent Light*. San Francisco: 1963.
Szarkowski, John. *Looking at Photographs*. New York: 1973.

EDDIE ADAMS

American

A prolific photojournalist, the self-taught Eddie Adams has photographed over 13 wars in the course of a career that has spanned more than 40 years. Although it is specifically these war-related photographs that have earned him international renown as well as hundreds of awards including a 1969 Pulitzer Prize, Adams's oeuvre also includes portraits of numerous American presidents, foreign leaders of state including Pope John Paul II and Fidel Castro, celebrities such as Louis Armstrong and Clint Eastwood, and anonymous figures around the world. Adams's photos have regularly appeared in such newspapers and magazines as *Time*, *Newsweek*, *Life*, *Paris Match*, *Vogue*, *Vanity Fair*, *The New York Times*, and *Stern*, and he has also done commercial, fashion, and advertising photography for numerous corporate and private clients.

Adams is probably best-known through his Pulitzer Prize winning photograph he took in February 1968, while stationed in Saigon as a member of the Associated Press. The image depicts the American-educated and trained Brig. General Nguyen Ngoc Loan (then South Vietnam's National Chief of Police) in the act of executing a Viet Cong prisoner who had just been apprehended for murdering several of Nguyen Ngog Loan's men. Graphic and violent, this photograph was published on the front page of the *New York Times* and, along with the NBC film of the same event, is credited with having provoked the civilian outrage that lead to massive demonstrations against the Vietnam War and quite possibly to President Johnson's decision not to seek reelection. Since then, the image (along with Nick Ut's photograph of a naked girl fleeing her napalmed village) has been reproduced so frequently that it has come to serve as synecdoche for the entire Vietnam War, and stands as Adams's most significant photograph.

The image of the Viet Cong prisoner's execution has also played an important role in the decades-long debate regarding the risks and values of war photography. Without images like this one, some have argued, the horrors of war would remain invisible to the public far away from the fighting and might therefore be taken less seriously. Yet others contest that contemporary war depends on the very possibility of photographic exposure and that egregious acts of violence are committed as a result of this publicity. For instance, it has been argued that Nguyen Ngoc Loan was only interested in publicly assassinating the Viet Cong prisoner because there were AP press corps there to capture the image. For him, the photographic evidence of the execution was meant to teach the Viet Cong what would happen to their forces if caught. In this sense, the image represents a staged event as much as it represents a document of truth, thereby putting into question the unmitigated truth-value of photography.

Adams is also well known for his photographic essay of South Vietnamese refugees entitled *The Boat of No Smiles*. It is often suggested that Congress circulated copies of this series of touching photographs in order to raise support for an amendment to current immigration law that would allow President Carter to allow 200,000 South Vietnamese refugees the right to come to the United States.

Born in Pennsylvania, Adams enlisted in the U. S. Marine Corps during the Korean War. Self-taught in photography, he began working as a photojournalist for the Associated Press in 1961. Assignments in the 1960s and 1970s took him to Vietnam, Cambodia, Africa, and other international hot spots. In the 1980s and 1990s he has served as a special correspondent for *Parade* magazine, shooting numerous covers for that publication. Beginning in 2000, Adams embarked upon a project to travel the world photographing important advocates of human rights. In 2002, he published these photos, along with interviews conducted by Kerry Kennedy Cuomo in a Random House book entitled *Truth to Power: Human Rights Defenders Changing Our World*.

Adams's contribution to twentieth century photography also includes his work at Barnstorm: the Eddie Adams Workshop, a tuition-free training camp he started in Jefferson, New York in 1988. Intended for ambitious student photographers interested in a hands-on opportunity to work with leaders in their field, the workshop has become very prestigious and is notoriously difficult to get into. Its importance in training a new generation of photojournalists will be seen as the twenty-first century unfolds.

HANNAH FELDMAN

See also: **War Photography**

Biography

Born in Pennsylvania. Enlisted in the U.S. Marine Corps during Korean War; began working as a photojournalist for the Associated Press in 1961 and as a Special Correspondent for the AP in 1976. Has also worked for *Time*, the *Philadelphia Bulletin*, and as a Special Correspondent for *Parade*; has published photographs in dozens of other international publications including *Vogue*, *Life*, and *Paris Match*. Established Barnstorm: The Eddie Adams Workshop in 1988. Published first collection of photographs: *Truth to Power: Human Rights Defenders Changing Our World* with Kerry Kennedy Cuomo in 2002. Pulitzer Prize, 1969. National Press Photographer Association's (NPPA) Magazine Photographer of the Year, University of Missouri, 1975. Joseph Sprague Award, 1976. Recipient of hundreds of other awards including the Sigma Delta Chi Distinguished Service Award (three times) and the George Polk Memorial Award.

Selected Works

Saigon, Vietnam, 1968
Coal Miner with Burro, 1970s
Boat of No Smiles, 1977
Fidel Castro, 1980s
Beirut, 1991
Abubacar Sultan of Mozambique, 2001
Truth to Power, 2002

Further Reading

Browning, Michael. "War Photos that Changed History." *Palm Beach Post* (12 May 2004).

NikonNet Lens Behind the Lens. "Eddie Adams: Connecting to the Collective Soul." http://home1.nikonnet.com/nikoncentre/photojournalism/photojournalism-adam.html. (Accessed July 17, 2005).

Pauser, Eric, dir. *466 Ly To Thai Street*. Ikon Films, Sweden, date unknown.

Sontag, Susan. *Regarding the Pain of Others*, New York: Farrar, Strauss and Giroux, 2003.

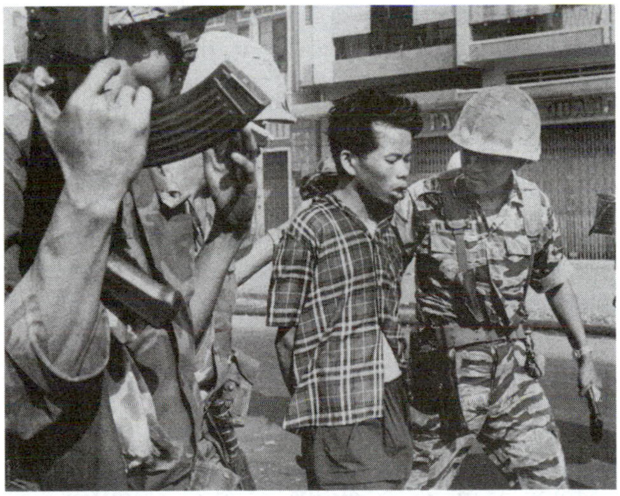

Eddie Adams, Vietcong Arrested, 1968/print 1988, gelatin silver print, 19.0 × 23.8 cm, Gift of The Associated Press. [*Photograph courtesy of George Eastman House, © The Associated Press, Eddie Adams*]

ROBERT ADAMS

American

Photographer Robert Adams has documented the changing American West since the late 1960s. His black and white photographs, along with his significant writings, have explored the complex relationship of humankind to the natural environment. Adams's photographs emphasize the tension that lies between human expansion and nature. His seemingly stark, documentary-style images capture the need for home, the inescapable destruction of the land in western expansion, and the resiliency of nature. These photographs record suburban housing tracks, desolate prairie highways, mountain overlooks, highway exchanges, beaches, and people shopping. Adams seeks out the ordinary and often overlooked, allowing the viewer to question their own place and behavior within society and their natural surroundings.

Adams has always had an interest and love of the land. Some of his earliest and fondest memories are of hiking with his family in the woods. In the 1940s, Adams began to suffer from asthma. This propelled his family to move first to Madison, Wisconsin, and then to Colorado, for his health. While growing up in Colorado in the 1950s, Adams continued to be very active in the outdoors, becoming an Eagle Scout, guide and camp counselor, and working for the U.S. Forest Service. The many natural areas Adams explored as a young man would later become the areas he would see so drastically changed and be compelled to document in his photography.

At age 19 and before going to college, Adams's concern for societal issues led him to consider becoming a minister, as his great-grandfather had been in the Midwest. Although he did not pursue the ministry, his social concerns would be born out through his photography. Adams went on to study English at the University of Redlands in California, graduating in 1959 and later, pursued his Ph.D. in English from the University of Southern California, which he completed in 1965. In 1962, Adams returned to Colorado to teach English at Colorado College in Colorado Springs. He was troubled by the changes that had occurred during his absence. "I came back to Colorado to discover that it had become like California...The places where I had worked, hunted, climbed and run rivers were all being destroyed, and for me the desperate question was, how do I survive?" (Di Grappa 1980).

During his time in Colorado Springs, Adams began to find that through photography he could "say what he wanted to say—which approximated what I felt" (Brooke 1998, 100). With little formal training in photography, Adams would in the late 1960s begin to capture the rapidly changing American West and the people who inhabit it. He wrote of his work in an essay "In the American West is Hope Possible":

> So, when I have the strength to be honest, I do not hope to experience again the space I loved as a child. The loss is the single hardest fact for me to acknowledge in the American decline. How we depended on space, without realizing it—space which made easier a civility with each other, and which made plainer the beauty of light and thus the world.
>
> (Adams 1989, 159)

Adams taught at Colorado College until 1970, when he turned to photography full-time. Important to his early career, Adams met John Szarkowski, director of the department of photography at the Museum of Modern Art (MoMA), in 1969. Szarkowski subsequently bought four of Adams's prints and supported Adams and his new approach to documenting the Western landscape. Adams was included in exhibitions at MoMA in 1970, 1971, and 1973 and throughout his later career. In 1975, he was one of several photographers featured in the important exhibition *New Topographics: Photographs of a Man-Altered Landscape* at the International Museum of Photography at George Eastman House, Rochester, New York. Through this exhibit, he became associated with the "new topographic" photographers, including Lewis Baltz, Joe Deal, Frank Gohlke, and Stephen Shore. These photographers all acknowledged the human existence in nature through their work, in contrast with other "western" photographers such as Ansel Adams (no relation), Imogen Cunningham, and Edward and Brett Weston of Group f/64, whose photographs often reflected a mythical and pristine natural landscape. Robert Adams and others were utilizing the photographic medium to begin defining a new area of social critique.

Adams's inspirations are many. In his writings or in the accompanying text to his work, he regularly quotes poets and writers, including Henry David Thoreau, Edward Abbey, and others. He also cites and discusses painting, sculpture, and architecture as influential to his work. In particular, the German architect Rudolph Schwarz, known for his church designs, has influenced Adams. Beyond the documentary and social context, Adams's photographs have also been critiqued on a formal or aesthetic level. Most notably, his work has been compared to the paintings of American painter Edward Hopper, through his similar use of stark light, lone figures, and a building or element within the broader landscape.

Adams published his first book, *White Churches of the Plains*, in 1970 and proceeded to successfully publish over 20 books over the following 30 years. Included are *The New West: Landscapes Along the Colorado Front Range* (1974), an important early work; *From the Missouri West* (1980), Adams's personal survey of western expansion; *Summer Nights* (1985), which captured the contrasting beauty and solitude of the inhabited suburban landscape; *To Make it Home: Photographs of the American West* (1989); published to coincide with his major retrospective exhibit at the Philadelphia Museum of Art; and *West from the Columbia* (1995), which captures the landscape of the Oregon Coast where Adams and his wife vacationed for years and now live.

Adams's oeuvre extends beyond obvious irony and does not suggest an easy answer to the existential questions it poses. The viewer must come to grips with his or her own position in relation to the future and in relation to landscape and civilization. In sorting out these conflicts, the photographer has written,

> Most of my hopes are for the amelioration of problems—a more conservative pattern of land use, a reduction in air pollution, a more prudent consumption of water, a lessening of animal abuse, a more respectful architecture. When I think about the possibility, however, of a landscape enriched by specific places to which we have responded imaginatively and with deference, I find myself thinking that we might be permitted to call it improved.
>
> (Adams 1989, 163)

JIM MCDONALD

See also: **Adams, Ansel; Baltz, Lewis; Gohlke, Frank; History of Photography: 1980s; Szarkowski, John**

Biography

Born in Orange, New Jersey, 8 May 1937. Attended University of Colorado, 1955; studied English, University of Redlands, California, B.A., 1959; studied English, University of Southern California, Ph.D., 1965. Self-educated in photography. Assistant Professor at Colorado College, Colorado Springs, 1962–1970; editorial assistant at The Colorado Associated University Press, Boulder, 1972. John Simon Guggenheim Memorial Foundation Fellowship, 1973; National Endowment for the Arts Photographer's Fellowship, 1973; Award of Merit, American Association of State and Local History, 1975; National Endowment for the Arts Photographer's Fellowship, 1978; Colorado Governor's Award in the Arts, 1979; John Simon Guggenheim Memorial Foundation Fellowship, 1980; Peer Award from The Friends of Photography, 1983; Charles Pratt Memorial Award, 1987; John D. and Catherine T. MacArthur Foundation Fellow, 1994; Spectrum International Prize for Photography, 1995. Living in Astoria, Oregon.

Selected Individual Exhibitions

1971 *Robert Adams*; Colorado Springs Fine Arts Center, Colorado Springs, Colorado

1976 *Robert Adams*; St. John's College, Santa Fe, New Mexico

1978 *Prairie*; Denver Art Museum, Denver, Colorado

1979 *Prairie*; Museum of Modern Art, New York, New York, and traveling

1980 *From the Missouri West*; Castelli Graphics, New York, New York

1981 *The New West: Photographs by Robert Adams*; Philadelphia Museum of Art, Philadelphia, Pennsylvania

1984 *Our Lives & Our Children: Photographs Taken Near the Rocky Flats Nuclear Weapons Plant*; Moravian College, Bethlehem, Pennsylvania

1986 *Summer Nights*; Denver Art Museum, Denver, Colorado, and traveling

1989 *To Make it Home: Photographs of the American West 1965–1986*, Philadelphia Museum of Art, Philadelphia, Pennsylvania

1991 *Robert Adams*; Photo Gallery International, Tokyo, Japan

1992 *Robert Adams*; Centre d'Art Contemporain, Brussels, Belgium

1993 *At the End of the Colombia River*; Denver Art Museum, Denver, Colorado

1994 *Listening to the River*; Sprengel Museum, Hanover, Germany, and traveling

1995 *West from the Columbia*; Fraenkel Gallery, San Francisco, California

1996 *Our Lives and Our Children*; Musee d'Arte Moderne de St. Etienne, St. Etienne, France

1998 *To the Mouth of the Columbia*; Princeton University, Princeton, New Jersey

2000 *California*; Fraenkel Gallery, San Francisco, California

2001 *Robert Adams: Places—People*; National Museum of Contemporary Art, Oslo, Norway

Reinventing the West: The Photographs of Ansel Adams and Robert Adams; Addison Gallery of American Art, Andover, Massachusetts

Sunlight, Solitude, Democracy, Home...Photographs by

Robert Adams; Douglas F. Cooley Memorial Art Gallery, Reed College, Portland, Oregon
2002 *Robert Adams: Topography of Consequence;* Northwest Museum of Arts and Culture, Spokane, Washington

Selected Group Exhibitions

1970 *New Acquisitions*; Museum of Modern Art, New York, New York
1971 *Photographs by Robert Adams and Emmet Gowin*; Museum of Modern Art, New York, New York
1973 *Landscape/Cityscape: A Selection of Twentieth–Century American Photographers*; Metropolitan Museum of Art, New York, New York
1975 *New Topographics: Photographs of a Man-Altered Landscape*; International Center for Photography at George Eastman House, Rochester, New York
1977 *Contemporary American Photographic Works*; Museum of Fine Arts, Houston, Texas
1978 *Mirrors and Windows: American Photography Since 1960*; Museum of Modern Art, New York, New York
Amerikanische Landschaftsphotographie 1860–1978; Neue Sammlung, Munich, Germany
1979 *Photographie Als Kunst 1879–1979/Kunst Als Photographie 1949–1979*; Tiroler Landmuseum, Innsbruck, Austria
American Images: New Work by Twenty Contemporary Photographers; Corcoran Gallery of Art, Washington, D.C.
1981 *American Landscapes*; Museum of Modern Art, New York, New York
Biennial Exhibition; Whitney Museum of American Art, New York, New York
New Landscapes, Part II; The Friends of Photography, Carmel, California
1982 *20th Century Photographs from the Museum of Modern Art*; The Seibu Museum of Art, Tokyo, Japan
1983 *An Open Land: Photographs of the Midwest, 1852–1982*; Art Institute of Chicago, Chicago, Illinois
Personal Choices; Victoria and Albert Museum, London, England
1984 *Three Americans*; Museum of Modern Art, New York, New York
1985 *Albert Renger-Patzsch/Robert Adams*; Kunstverein Munchen, Munich, Germany
1986 *Artists in Mid-Career*; San Francisco Museum of Modern Art, San Francisco, California
Ansel Adams and American Landscape Photography; Australian National Gallery, Canberra, Australia
1987 *Nuovo Paesaggio Americano/Dialectical Landscapes*; Museo Fortuny, Venice, Italy
Road and Roadside: American Photographs, 1930–1986; Art Institute of Chicago, Chicago, Illinois
1988 *Another Objectivity*; Institute of Contemporary Arts, London, England
1989 *Photography Until Now*; Museum of Modern Art, New York, New York
On the Art of Fixing a Shadow: 150 Years of Photography; National Gallery of Art, Washington, D.C.
Photography Now; Victoria and Albert Museum, London, England
Une Autre Objectivite; Centre National des Arts Plastiques, Paris, France
Decade by Decade; Center for Creative Photography, Tucson, Arizona
The Art of Photography: 1839–1989; Museum of Fine Arts, Houston, Texas
1990 *The Indomitable Spirit*; International Center of Photography at George Eastman House, Rochester, New York
Passages de l'Image; Musee National d'Art Moderne, Paris, France
1991 *Pleasures and Terrors of Domestic Comfort*; Museum of Modern Art, New York, New York
Visions/Revisions; Denver Art Museum, Denver, Colorado
1992 Robert Adams, Wim Wenders: Photographs of the American West; Amerika Haus, Berlin, Germany
A History of Oregon Photography; Portland Art Museum, Portland, Oregon
1993 *Critical Landscapes*; Tokyo Metropolitan Museum of Photography, Tokyo, Japan
1996 *Crossing the Frontier: Photographs of the Developing West, 1849 to the Present*; San Francisco Museum of Modern Art, San Francisco, California
Perpetual Mirage: Photographic Narratives of the Desert West; Whitney Museum of American Art, New York, New York
1997 *Documenta X*; Kassel, Germany
The View from Denver; Denver Art Museum, Denver, Colorado
1998 *Measure of Nature*; Art Institute of Chicago, Chicago, Illinois
Sea Change: The Seascape in Contemporary Photography; Center for Creative Photography, Tucson, Arizona
Waterproof; Belem Cultural Center, Lisbon, Portugal
1999 *The American Century Art and Culture, 1900–2000*; Whitney Museum of American Art, New York, New York
2000 *How You Look At It*; Sprengel Museum, Hannover, Germany
2001 *Settings and Players*; White Cube, London, England
2002 *American Century of Photography: The Hallmark Photographic Collection*; Denver Art Museum, Denver, Colorado

Selected Works

Alameda Avenue, Denver, 1970–1972
Colorado, 1970
Quarried Mesa Top, Pueblo County, Colorado, 1978
Redlands, Looking Toward Los Angeles Across San Timoteo Canyon, San Bernardino, California, 1978
Colorado Springs, Colorado, 1979
Dead Palms, Partially Uprooted, Ontario, California, 1983
Untitled, Berthoud, Colorado, late 1970s
Fort Collins, Colorado, 1980
Longmont, Colorado, 1980
Southwest from the South Jetty, Clatsop County, Oregon, 1990

Further Reading

Adams, Robert. *White Churches of the Plains: Examples from Colorado*. Introduction by Thomas Hornsby Ferril, Boulder, Colorado: Colorado Associated University Press, 1970.
Adams, Robert. *The New West: Landscapes Along the Colorado Front Range*. Foreword by John Szarkowski. Boulder, CO: Colorado Associated University Press, 1974.

Adams, Robert. *From the Missouri West*. New York: Aperture, 1980.
Adams, Robert. *Beauty in Photography: Essays in Defense of Traditional Values*. New York: Aperture, 1981.
Adams, Robert. *Our Lives & Our Children: Photographs Taken Near the Rocky Flats Nuclear Weapons Plant*. New York: Aperture, 1983.
Adams, Robert. "Introduction." In Daniel Wolf, *American Space: Meaning in Nineteenth-Century Landscape Photography*. Middletown, CT: Wesleyan University Press, 1983.
Adams, Robert. *Summer Nights*. New York: Aperture, 1985.
Adams, Robert. *To Make It Home: Photographs of the American West, 1965–1986*. New York: Aperture, 1989.
Adams, Robert. *Why People Photograph: Selected Essays and Reviews*. New York: Aperture, 1994.
Adams, Robert. *West from the Columbia*. New York: Aperture, 1995.
Adams, Robert, Lewis Baltz, Bernd and Hilla Becher, Joe Deal, Frank Gohlke, Nicholas Nixon, John Schott, Stephen Shore, Henry Wessel, Jr. *New Topographics: Photographs of a Man-Altered Landscape*. Rochester, NY: International Center for Photography, 1975.
Brooke, Elizabeth Heilman. "Land Lover." *ARTNEWS* (February 1998).

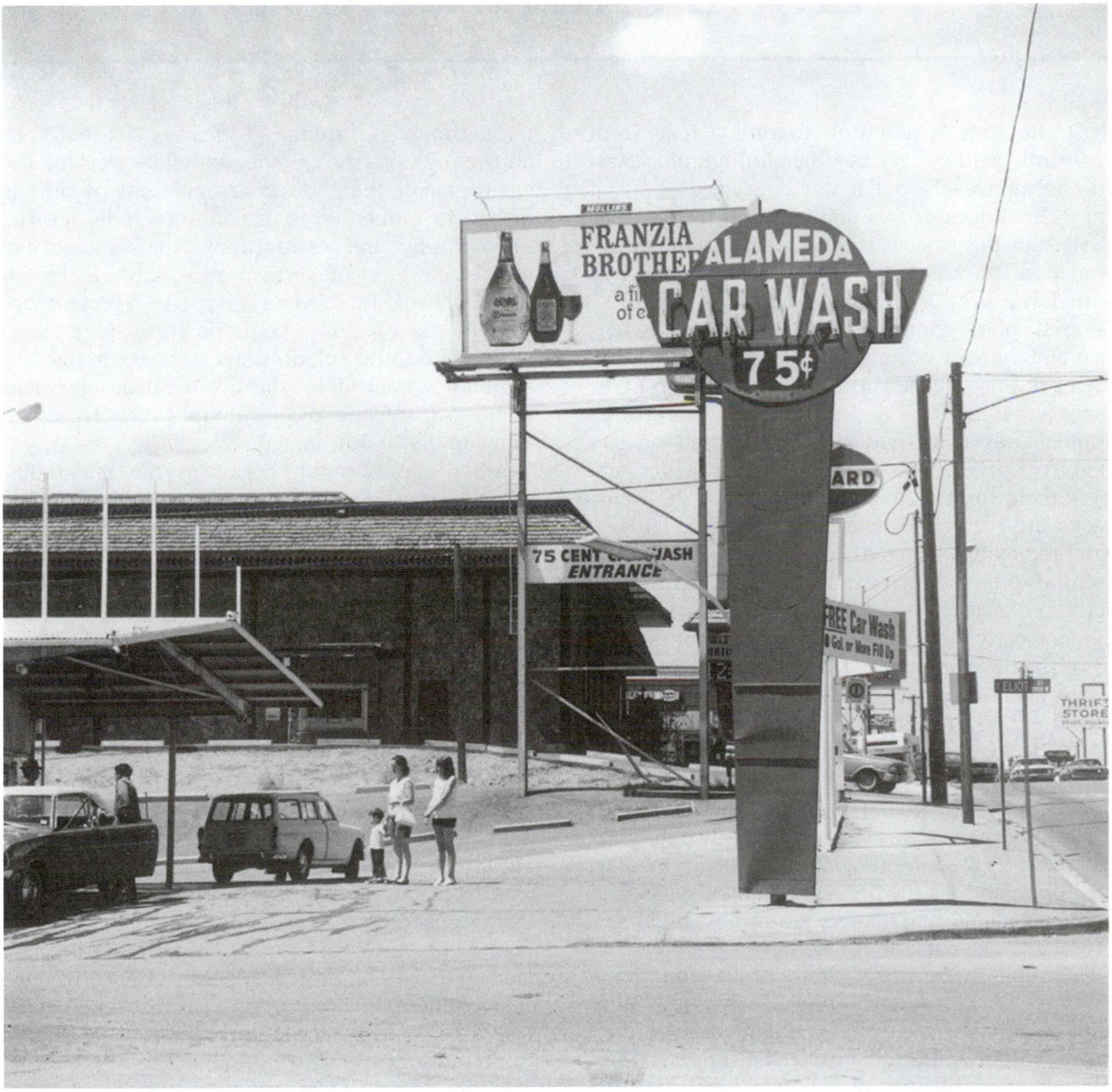

Robert Adams, Alameda Avenue, Denver, 1970-72, The New West, p. 73.
[*Courtesy Fraenkel Gallery, San Francisco*]

Castleberry, May. *Perpetual Mirage: Photographic Narratives of the Desert West.* New York: Whitney Museum of American Art, 1996.
Di Grappa, Carol, ed. *Landscape Theory.* Lustrum Press, New York, 1980.
Fillin-yeh, Susan and Leo Rubinfien. *Sunlight, Solitude, Democracy, Home...Photographs by Robert Adams.* Seattle, WA: University of Washington Press, 2002.
Phillips, Sandra S. *Crossing the Frontier: Photographs of the Developing West, 1849 to the Present.* San Francisco, CA: San Francisco Museum of Modern Art, 1996.
Ratcliff, Carter. *Route 66 Revisited: The New Landscape Photography.* Art in America, January/February, 1976.
Weinberg, Adam D. *Reinventing the West: The Photographs of Ansel Adams and Robert Adams.* Andover, MA: Addison Gallery of American Art, 2001.

AERIAL PHOTOGRAPHY

The technology of aerial photography stems from nineteenth century devices—the photographic camera and air travel—but it was conceived in social and technological forces that began at the dawn of Western civilization. It is thus central to the development of photography, even though it is rarely treated as a subject of commentary.

Aerial photographs offer a geometrically determined view of objects within a given area. The origins of this view lie in the third millennium BCE, when Sumerian priests ruled city-states through estate management and a religion based on sky gods. As conceived at the time, urban deities surveyed their domains from the sky, conveying legitimacy onto the priests, who realized the aerial view with surveying. Since then surveying has been essential to governance, and from it has come geometry and a cascade of geometric disciplines, notably perspectival drawing and classical optics, that led to the development of photography.

The uses of aerial surveys have changed little since the days of Sumer. Every day the infrastructure and citizens of advanced nations are photographed dozens of times by a vast network of cameras based on satellites, aircraft, buildings and poles. These cameras are creating real-time maps of their subjects at scales ranging from the intimate to the global, and, as the first survey maps of Sumer, these automated mapmakers aid in governance of society and the control of resources.

The relation between photographs and maps may not be immediately obvious because most photographs are vertically stratified, that is they reveal the horizontal detail of their subject. However, when the picture plane of a camera is held parallel to the surface of the earth, as in aerial photography, the inherently map-like nature of photography is intuitively obvious. Photographs and maps both reveal the spatial aspects of the environment, that is, the arrangement of objects on a plane in relation to one another. In both aerial photography and cartography, the vantage can offer some level of vertical stratification, the so-called chorographic view, or it can represent objects in their proper geometric form. Our visual intuition on the relationship between maps and cameras is backed by the historical development of the camera and the techniques of perspectival drawing that it automated.

Aerial photography began in the mid-1800s, some thirty years after the advent of photography. In 1858 the pioneering Parisian Nadar took a camera on a series of balloon ascents, and in 1864 he published a book about the experience, *Les Memoires du Geánt*. On the other side of the Atlantic, J. W. Black and Sam King ascended 1,200 feet in a balloon to take a photograph of Boston in 1860. It was war, however, that stimulated the development of aerial photography. Nadar refused his services to Napoleon III in 1859, but commanded the Paris balloon corps during the siege of the early 1870s. By then the American Civil War had established a number of wartime precedents. As the war broke out in 1861 a civilian balloonist inadvertently flew over Confederate states. His report convinced the Union government to support the creation of the U.S. Balloon Corps, which operated until 1863. During that time photographers stationed in tethered balloons created large-scale maps of battlefields that were overlaid with grids to determine troop movements.

In the twentieth century, the prospects of aerial photography improved as did aircraft, cameras, and telemetry. Balloon reconnaissance continued in World War I, but by World War II lighter-than-air craft were replaced by airplanes. Development intensified during the Cold War. In the 1950s high-performance spy planes cruised the stratosphere, but, with the Soviet downing of an American U-2 in 1960, officials on both sides of the conflict realized that orbiting satellites were the safest option. The Soviet Union orbited the first surveillance satellite, but it was rapidly followed by the Corona program of the United States. The first generations of spy satellites ejected bulky containers of film into the atmosphere, but these were replaced by high resolution video signals.

To this day military and intelligence bureaus have been the prime innovators of aerial photography. Every aspect of the medium is subject to constant improvement. Airplanes and spacecraft have been improved, lenses have staggering resolution and digital technology has replaced analog signals. Aerial photography is of such importance that its full capabilities at any given time are a state secret. Surveillance programs were kept hidden for many years, and there is a lag of decades between the collection of military photographs and their release for other uses.

The dominance of the United States at the end of the twentieth century cannot be overstated. The satellites of Russia, France and a few other space-going nations offer little competition to the extensive surveillance network maintained by the United States. During the Cold War aerial imagery mostly served strategic purposes, but the U.S. military is now creating systems that offer live imagery of battlefields from satellite and aircraft, notably the Predator drone used in Serbia, Afghanistan, and Iraq in the last decade of the twentieth century. Building on Civil War technologies, computers overlay battlefield images with an information grid that provides a tactical advantage to combat soldiers.

Aerial photography has also found ample civilian application. Commercial applications include architecture, construction, urban planning and other development schemes, the travel industry, advertising applications of various sorts, publishing, especially in such popular magazines as *National Geographic*, and agriculture. The Aerial Photography Field Office, Farm Service Agency is the primary source of aerial imagery for the U.S. Department of Agriculture, holding over 10 million images from 1955 to the early 2000s in an archive accessible at www.apfo.usda.gov/.

In the scientific realm, multispectral cameras have become essential tools for geographers, oceanographers, ecologists and even archeologists. For instance, an aerial archive of Middle Eastern archeological sites was established in 1978 under the patronage of Crown Prince Hassan bin Talal of Jordan, which consists of over 8,000 photographs and several hundred maps. Aerial photography's application in ecological and conservation efforts has been particularly front and center. Satellite imagery can precisely track large-scale changes in forests, deserts, oceans and other physical phenomena. Some artists have joined scientists in the skies, creating portfolios of merit, including the lush, colorful work of French photojournalist Yann Arthus-Bertrand with his massive "Earth from Above" series. Shown to huge crowds in venues around the world, Arthus-Bertrand's aerial photography has proven to be a useful tool for ecological awareness. He has instigated a worldwide organization to raise awareness of ecological concerns, including a professional organization, Altitude, which features international aerial photographers on its website. Often the reverse can happen, with photographs taken by those who would identify themselves primarily as scientists taking on considerable aesthetic value, such as Bradford Washburn's pioneering aerial views of Alaska's mountains and glaciers, including such starkly beautiful images as *Miles Glacier—Dead Ice at NW Edge*, 1938.

Aerial photography has become ubiquitous in the daily government of urban societies, joining cartography and surveillance as an essential tool of governance. Citizens of industrial nations can be surreptitiously photographed dozens of times a day in low aerial view by government and corporate cameras. Virtually every square meter of land in industrial nations has also been photographed in cartographic perspective from aircraft and satellites at a variety of scales. This visual information has been incorporated into Geographic Information Systems (GIS) that composite photographs with maps, political boundaries, property titles and other data. In most developed countries, private photographers also offer aerial services, often shooting homes or landscapes on commission for a range of clients, often as "portraits" of an individual's or family's property.

Many university libraries collect aerial photographs for historical and research purposes. Notable collections include the University of California, Berkeley; the Fairchild Aerial Photography Collection at Whittier College, Whittier, California, featuring historical views of that state; the Aerial Photography Collection at the University of Oregon Library, featuring some 525,000 aerial photographs of Oregon from 1925 onward; University of

Waterloo Library, Waterloo, Ontario, Canada; and the Aerial Archive of the Institute for Prehistory and Protohistory of the University of Vienna.

Aerial photography is an important genre within fine-arts photography as well. From the austere black and white photography of Hiroshi Hamaya, whose striking photographs of the Himalayan mountains and deserts and wild places around the world gave new views to nature in the 1960s to Emmet Gowin's documentation of post-eruption Mount St. Helens in Washington State in 1980–1986 and more recent examinations of the changes wrought by atomic blast sites and mining of his "Changing the Earth" series, contemporary photographers have created memorable aerial images.

Many nature photographers utilize aerial photography as one of the available vantage points to capture their subjects. Notable in this regard are Indian photographer Subhankar Banerjee with his photographs of the Artic National Wildlife Refuge at the turn of the century. Most modern aerial photography is accomplished through the use of airplanes or helicopters using gyroscopically stabilized cameras, but a significant number of professionals and amateurs use radio-controlled drones or even kites.

Kite aerial photography was in fact pioneered by Chicago self-taught photographer and businessman George R. Lawrence in 1906 to capture extraordinary wide-angle views of the devastation in the aftermath of the San Francisco earthquake. In an era before flight and when the volatile gases used in balloons could be extremely dangerous, thus limiting aerial photography, Lawrence's large-scale views caused an international sensation. Aerial photographer Robert Cameron had devoted his practice to aerial documentations of the major cities and scenic or historic sites of the world in a series of popular books such as *Above London* of 1980 or *Above Yosemite* of 1983.

Aerial photography can also be practiced from vantage points offered by skyscrapers; Margaret Bourke-White's pioneering efforts of the 1930s being notable examples; Oscar Graubner's 1931 photo of her perched atop an ornament of the Chrysler Building at work with her camera is an icon of twentieth century photography. Bourke-White was also a pioneer of capturing the skyscape from an aerial perspective, creating such striking, almost abstract images as *B-36 at High Altitude, Flying over Wichita, Kansas*, 1951. New York City in fact has been photographed 'from above' by numerous photographers, from the well known such as Bourke-White to the lesser known, such as the Hungarian photographer György Lőrinczy who documented the city in the late 1960s.

At the turn of the twenty-first century, much aerial photography was being accomplished through use of digital technology and remote sensing or "the science and art of obtaining information about an object, area, or phenomenon through the analysis of data acquired by a device that is not in contact with the object, area, or phenomenon under investigation" (Lillesand and Kiefer, *Remote Sensing and Image Interpretation*) had become a field within the discipline. As the human eye becomes increasingly removed from direct observation of the physical world, whether in aerial or other photography, the range of images captured and the ability to interpret them will become increasingly complex.

Ali Hossaini

See also: **Bourke-White, Margaret; Gowin, Emmet; Hamaya, Hiroshi; National Geographic; Propaganda; War Photography**

Further Reading

Antenucci, John, Kay Brown, Peter Croswell and Michael Kevany. *Geographic Information Systems: An Introduction to the Technology*. New York: Van Nostrand Rheinhold, 1991.

Evans, Charles. "Air War Over Virginia." *Civil War Times* Oct. (1996): 1–7.

Hossaini, Ali. *Archaeology of the Photograph*. Ann Arbor, MI: UMI Microforms, 1994.

Lillesand, Thomas M. and Ralph W. Kiefer, *Remote Sensing and Image Interpretation*, 3rd ed., New York: John Wiley and Sons, 1994.

MacDonald, D. Air Photography. *Journal of the Optical Society of America* XLIII (4) (1953): 290–298.

Muehrcke, Philip C. and Juliana O. Muehrcke. *Map Use: Reading, Analysis, Interpretation*. Madison, WI: J.P. Publications, 1992.

Peebles, Curtis. *The Corona Project: America's First Spy Satellites*. Annapolis, MD: Naval Institute Press, 1997.

Ray, Sidney F. *The Lens and All Its Jobs*. New York: Focal Press, 1977.

PHOTOGRAPHY IN AFRICA: AN OVERVIEW

Twentieth century photography in Africa encompasses a wide variety of genres and practices. Months after its public invention in 1839, photography was introduced to Egypt, spreading quickly to coastal cities across Africa and more slowly to rural areas and the interior. The first half of the twentieth century saw studio photography practiced by Africans across the continent, although the prohibition against images made photography less popular in Islamic North Africa. At the same time, Europeans documented modern colonialist life in Africa, and European and American ethnographers traveled the continent in order to photograph, classify, and codify "tribal" Africans. These images, along with landscape photography and animal and plant exotica, comprise the genres of photography practiced mostly by Westerners for publications like *National Geographic* and other journals. By the 1950s and especially after the independence of most nations in the 1960s, African photojournalism flourished along with studio portraiture. Some African cultures, like the Yoruba and the Bini, incorporated photography into centuries-old political or religious rituals. In recent decades, photography as a contemporary art practice has also become popular, and photographers with international art world reputations have emerged from Morocco to South Africa, although many African photographers now work from Paris, London, and New York.

Because of the variety of practices that have developed at different times in various regions, many scholars today refer to "photographies" in Africa, emphasizing photography's multiple histories. "Africa" itself here constitutes a geographic definition only, and should not be understood as indicative of a monolithic cultural identity. Aside from the violent oppression of European colonialism and subsequent independence of most nations during the 1960s, which colors the history of all countries except Ethiopia and Liberia, it is difficult to generalize about continent-wide similarities in cultures, politics, histories, traditions, and the influences of modernity, including photography. While some characteristics of photography in Africa certainly bear similarities to photography everywhere, other aspects may appear recognizably West African, Egyptian, or Yoruban, but rarely if ever "African," in that the phrase implies a consistent trait or style that occurs across the continent.

The history of photography in Africa is a burgeoning field, with further research, writing, and critical evaluation still needed in many areas, although much new information has come to light in the past 15 years. Two of South Africa's best known photographers, David Goldblatt and Peter Magubane, published books documenting apartheid as early as the 1970s and 1980s. However, the surge of art world interest in African photography and subsequent publications on the topic can be dated closer to the mid-1990s. Several years after the 1991 exhibit *Africa Explores* at the Museum of African Art in New York anonymously exhibited Malian photographer Seydou Keïta's striking black-and-white studio portraits. Keïta and his compatriot Malick Sidibé were subsequently "discovered" by Andre Magnin, who wrote their monographs. Further solo and group exhibitions, as well as books, journal articles, and catalogues, have since provided valuable new information about individual African photographers as well as common photographic practices in many parts of Africa. In Bamako, Mali, the first biennale exhibiting African photography, *Rencontres de la Photographie Africaine*, was organized in 1994 by the editor of Revue Noire, Simon Njami. Revue Noire has since published the work of a number of African photographers.

Nigerian curator Okwui Enwezor has also been instrumental in bringing African photography and art to a wider public. With Salah Hassan and Olu Oguibe, he founded *Nka: A Journal of Contemporary African Art* out of Cornell University in 1994. Enwezor co-curated the landmark exhibition at the Guggenheim in New York in 1996, *In/sight: African Photographers, 1940 to the Present*, which showcased studio photographers, contemporary artists, and the journalist photography of *Drum*, a popular South African magazine. The exhibition *The Short Century* (2001–2002), also curated by

Enwezor, and its accompanying catalogue, were especially important in bringing awareness of African photography, art, and political history to a wider public. Thanks to these and other efforts, significant research has been published pertaining to photographers and practices in West Africa, and a wide variety of sources can be found on different genres of photography in South Africa, including recent photographic festivals. A smattering of research also covers East Africa, Central Africa, and the islands of the Indian Ocean. Although traditionally considered separate from sub-Saharan Africa in African art and anthropology, some research exists on North Africa as well.

At the same time that photography by Africans is coming to widespread public attention in the West, revisionist histories that critically examine photographs taken by Europeans and Americans of Africans for anthropological and ethnographic purposes are cropping up as exhibitions and books. Such texts use post-colonial and feminist methodologies to analyze and re-situate these photographs, many of which are still in circulation, in the discourses of African art, history, and anthropology, within an understanding of European racism and the hierarchical classificatory systems it generated.

By 1900 colonial rule was strongly established in most African nations, and this vast attempt to reorganize and control African societies and land for European profit was often documented and celebrated by the colonizers through photographs that today appear horrifying in their casual acceptance of European brutalities. Sometimes these photographs fostered nascent European anti-colonialism and reform movements through their dissemination to sympathetic activists. For example, photographs that documented the abuses perpetrated by King Leopold II of Belgium in Congo Free State (now Democratic Republic of the Congo [DRC]) led to widespread condemnation of his behavior in Europe and the United States. As a result, in 1908 the Belgian Parliament annexed Congo Free State, ending the worst of the atrocities. This early example of the use of photojournalism in the fight against colonialism recurred in many countries during the independence struggles of the 1960s, and as late as the 1990s in South Africa, whose rule of apartheid ended in 1994.

The racist political system of apartheid contributed to South Africa's unique position in the history of African photography. Photographs by white South Africans followed the general trend of European photography, but with less interest in radical artistic innovation. Portrait photography became popular among all races, as elsewhere in Africa. However, it is the photography of *Drum*, a popular magazine pitched to black South African life, which has become particularly well-known today for its quality photojournalism as well as its promotion of black self-representation.

Originally aimed toward a European conception of a "tribal" audience, *Drum* was published in 1951 as *The African Drum*, but failed after three issues. After a change in ownership and attitude, *Drum* quickly became a hugely popular magazine depicting the lifestyles, newsworthy events, and social concerns of black South Africans. *Drum*'s celebratory appreciation of township life and investigative reports into socio-political situations provided black South Africans with visual representations of their lives; under the regime of apartheid, *Drum*'s presence was profoundly political. Although *Drum* was unable to overtly protest conditions in South Africa, the magazine's journalists and photographers pushed the constraints of censorship when possible. For example, *Drum* serially published Alan Paton's novel, *Cry the Beloved Country* (1948), which describes the clash between a black minister and a racist white farmer. However, *Drum*'s owner Jim Bailey refused to publish British photo-journalist Ian Berry's shots of the 1960 Sharpeville massacre; when Berry sent the prints to London instead, international outrage erupted.

Drum also contributed to the evolution of a Pan-African sensibility, as offices were eventually opened across sub-Saharan Africa. The first office was opened in Nigeria in 1953 and the second in Ghana a year later. An East African office was established in 1957, and the last office opened in Central Africa in 1966. *Drum* reported on political events outside of South Africa, documenting Nigeria's independence, for example, and the initial meetings of the alliance of the West African Federation.

Aside from photojournalism, many countries established governmental photo agencies either during colonialism or after independence. Congopresse in DRC was one such colonialist organ. Agencies in Madagascar, Angola, and Guinea were introduced under colonialism and changed names and structures after independence. Other post-colonial agencies based on former colonialist organizations include AMAP in Mali and ONICEP in Nigeria. The archives for some of these official agencies are not publicly available; for example, Seydou Keïta's work for the government of Mali has not been released. The types of photography these organizations practiced varied; although most were political, Madagascar's SGM used photography for military and geographic purposes before colonialism, and its post-colonial incarnation, FTM, services tourism.

Although generally agency photographers were allowed and indeed expected to document the political process and government activities in a way that had been illegal before independence, they worked in the service and within the boundaries of the new states' ideologies. Photographic image production, with its accompanying authority in appearing to present "reality," became a way for the new governments to assert their authenticity, but often at the expense of truth. In many countries, the public eventually came to doubt the veracity of official photography, which was often censored by corrupt post-colonial governments.

From the turn of the century until the 1960s, however, commercial black-and-white studio portraiture constituted the most popular and widespread type of photography in sub-Saharan Africa. Although studio photography was introduced by Europeans, Africans began to open their own studios for African clientele as early as the 1880s in some areas. At first only available to the wealthy, who were usually civil servants working for the colonial governments, photography became affordable to the growing middle classes in many parts of Africa by the 1930s. Many photographers learned their trade working in an older photographer's studio, although sometimes soldiers who had fought in Europe during the world wars returned home with cameras and newly learned photographic techniques. The need for identity photos contributed to the proliferation of photographers not only in cities but in rural areas.

Through studio portraits, Africans were able to participate in their own image creation, a practice that acted as a valuable social and cultural resistance to colonialism. The portrait photograph, a collaboration between photographer and subject in the creation of the subject's own self-image, was a particularly apt genre for this re-imaging of photography from an African point of view. Photographic portraiture was seen as modern and embraced for its modernity. Portraits were taken to commemorate special and celebratory occasions, in which the sitters usually posed in their best clothing. Photographs were hung in living rooms, set in photo albums that were shown to guests, or sent back by urban migrants to their rural families. Such photographs were usually made directly from contact prints using box cameras without an enlarger, and so were quite small. Usually a photographer who took over another's studio "inherited" the former owner's negatives as well. Recognizable traits developed in certain areas that appear to show regional photographic practices, like the patterned backdrop or portraits of two sitters in matching clothing in West Africa.

Studio photography remained popular after independence, but the introduction of color labs starting from the late 1960s through the 1980s drastically reduced the number of studios and their ability to survive economically. The new technology appears to have contributed to the decline of the studio photographer and the increased prominence of the itinerant photographer, thus initiating a new aesthetic. Usually young men hoping to make a living without previous training in a studio, the itinerant photographers have been criticized by the older black-and-white studio photographers as lacking in quality.

Few women African photographers have been recognized to date, but Stephen Sprague records women working as studio photographers in Nigeria in the 1970s, and Heike Behrend has documented women practicing photography recently in Mombasa, Kenya. Several women also worked for Guinea's Syli-Photo in the 1960s. Currently, Jo Ractliffe and Penny Siopsis of South Africa, Zarina Bhimji of Uganda, and Lamia Naji of Morocco are working internationally as contemporary art photographers. Other male contemporary art photographers with international reputations today include Zwelethu Mthethwa and Santu Mofokeng of South Africa, Samuel Fosso of Central African Republic, Philip Kwame Apagya of Ghana, and Tahoumi Ennadre of Morocco.

ALLISON MOORE

See also: **Ballen, Roger; Fosso, Samuel; National Geographic; Photography in Africa: Central and West; Photography in Africa: East Africa and Indian Ocean Islands; Photography in Africa: North; Photography in Africa: South and Southern; Portraiture**

Further Reading

Behrend, Heike, and Jean-François Werner, eds. "Photographies and Modernities in Africa." *Visual Anthropology*, v. 14, no. 3, (2001).

Bell, Clare, Okwui Enwezor, Danielle Tilkin, Octavio Zaya, and Olu Oguibe. *In/sight: African Photographers, 1940 to the Present*. New York: Solomon R. Guggenheim Museum, 1996.

Coombes, Anni. *Reinventing Africa*. New Haven: Yale University Press, 1994.

Enwezor, Okwui, ed. *The Short Century: Independence and Liberation Movements in Africa 1945–1994*. Munich: Prestel, 2001.

Fall, N'goné, and Pascal Martin Saint Léon, eds. *Anthology of African and Indian Ocean Photography*. Paris, France: Éditions Revue Noire, 1999.

Geary, Christraud. *In and Out of Focus: Images from Central Africa, 1885–1960*. Washington, D.C.: National

Museum of African Art, Smithsonian Institution & Philip Wilson, Publishers, 2002.
Grundlingh, Kathleen, ed. *Lines of Sight: Perspectives on South African Photography*. Cape Town, South Africa: South African National Gallery, 2001.
Lamunière, Michelle. *You Look Beautiful Like That: The Portrait Photographs of Seydou Keïta and Malick Sidibé*. Cambridge, MA: Harvard University Art Museums, and New Haven, CT, and London: Yale University Press, 2001.
Noorderlicht Photo Festival. *Africa Inside*. Groningen, The Netherlands: Aurora Borealis, 2000.
Sprague, Stephen F. "Yoruba Photography: How the Yoruba See Themselves." In *Photography's Other Histories*. Christopher Pinney and Nicolas Peterson, eds. Durham and London: Duke University Press, 2003; 240–260.
University of Cape Town. *Encounters with Photography: Photographing People in Southern Africa, 1860–1999*. Rondebosch, South Africa: University of Cape Town, 2000.
Wendl, Tobias, and Heike Behrend, eds. *Snap Me One! Studiofotografen in Afrika*. Munich, Germany: Prestel, 1998.

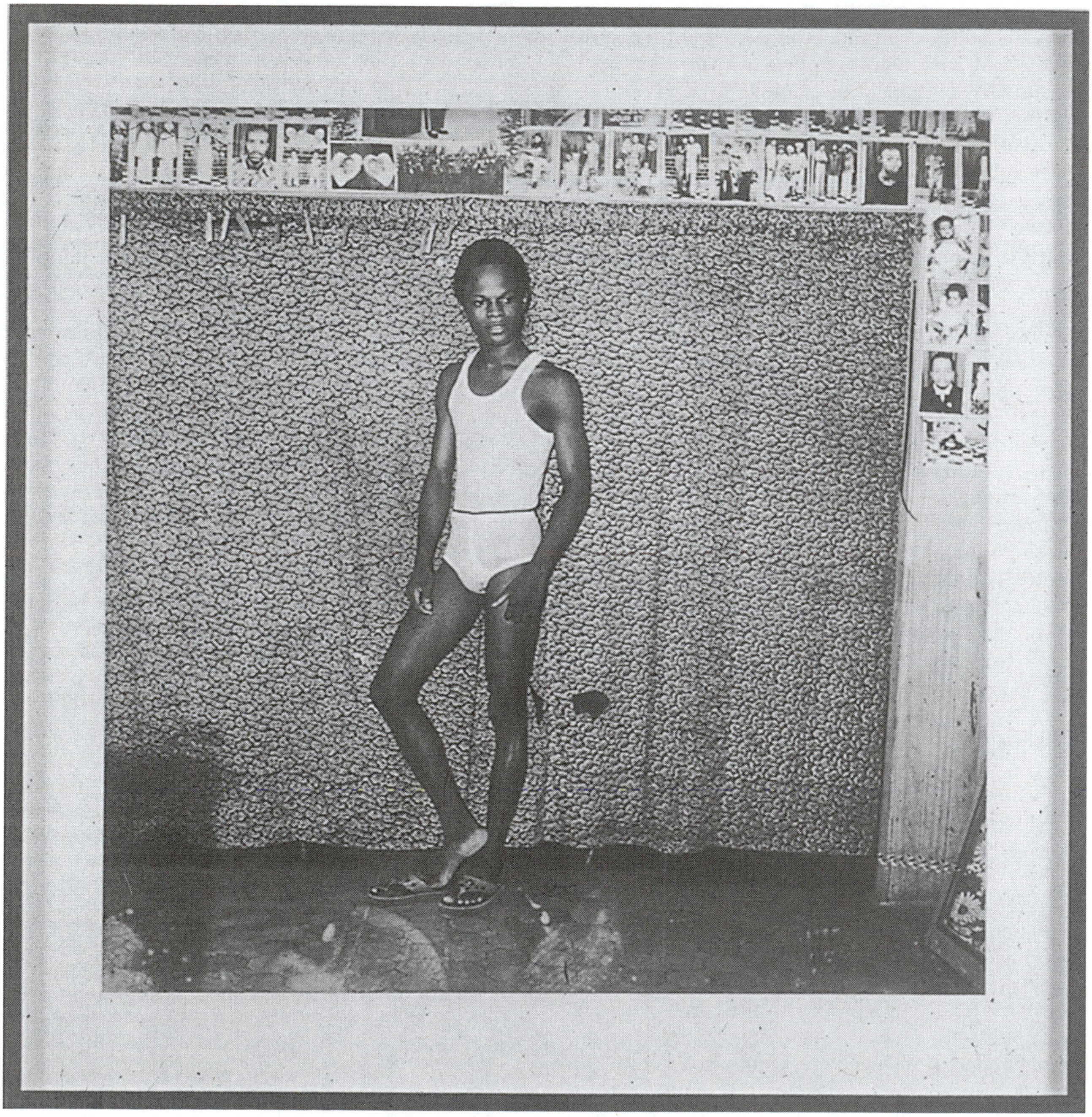

Samuel Fosso, Self Portrait (Maillot, la vie c'est la liberte), 1977, gelatin-silver print.
[*Courtesy of Jack Shainman Gallery, New York*]

PHOTOGRAPHY IN AFRICA: CENTRAL AND WEST

West African portrait photography has garnered much Western attention, spurred by the international fame of Malian Seydou Keïta. Scholars' gazes have also fixed on West and Central Africa's rich history of anthropological photography. Forms of state-sponsored photography and contemporary art practice have likewise elicited interest.

The medium of photography reached Western Africa's coastal towns soon after its invention, and African practitioners were active by the 1860s. The end of the nineteenth century saw the spread of commercial studios from coastal to inland centers. Varying policies by colonial authorities either fostered or impeded the development of indigenous photographers, yielding uneven progress. In the beginning of the twentieth century, studios participated in the international postcard market, supplying images to European publishers and distributing work regionally to Westerners (but rarely to Africans). Several photographers and publishers may be considered as exemplary of those participating from West and Central Africa in this global trade in images. The most important local producer was Frenchman Edmond Fortier, active in Senegal. Fortier's grand project is described by David Prochaska in his *African Arts* article "Fantasia of the Photothéque: French Postcard Views of Colonial Senegal" (1991) as a series of photographic documents, conceptually "filed" as colonial knowledge. Indigenous African studio and postcard photographers active at the beginning of the century include several Sierra Leone Creoles, whose work has been discussed by Vera Viditz-Ward in her article "Studio Photography in Freetown" in *Anthology of African and Indian Ocean Photography* (1999), and Togo's Alex Acolatse, whose career has been sketched by Phillipe David in the *Anthology of African and Indian Ocean Photography* article "Photographer-publishers in Togo" (1999). The thorny question of whether African photographers articulated a different vision than their European counterparts is considered by Christraud Geary in *Delivering Views: Distant Cultures in Early Postcards* (1998), where she offers a nuanced answer, acknowledging both the power of Western conventions and the possibility of a particularly African vision.

Following World War Two, a boom in indigenous portrait studios responded to the needs of a growing African middle class. In the 1940s, Mama and Salla Casset operated studios in Dakar, Senegal, and Seydou Keïta began work in Bamako, Mali. Typically, Keïta's sitters availed themselves of costumes and studio props to project a fashionable, modern appearance. (The fascinating migration of Keïta's work from its Malian context into the canon of Western art photography is explored by Elizabeth Bigham's *African Arts* article, "Issues of Authorship in the Portrait Photographs of Seydou Keita" [1999].) The next generation of portraitists active after national independence, exemplified by Mali's Malick Sidibé and Niger's Philippe Koudjina, eschewed the studio formality of Keïta's work, frequently bringing the camera out-of-doors to photograph the leisure of a burgeoning youth culture. Samuel Fosso, a studio operator in the Central African Republic, has wrought personal statements from studio conventions since the 1970s in a series of theatrical self-portraits. In the 1980s, color photography arrived and studio photographers began to fade from the scene. An exception is Phillip Kwame Apagya who has worked in Shama, Ghana since 1982, relying on elaborate painted backdrops to create imaginative environments for his sitters.

Valuable anthropological studies of portrait photography are now being produced by Western scholars. The integration of photography into Yoruban cultural formations in Nigeria is the subject of Stephen Sprague's groundbreaking article in *African Arts*, "Yoruba Photography: How the Yoruba See Themselves" (1978). Taking the work of Cote d'Ivoire-based Cornélius Yao Azaglo Augustt as an example, Jean-François Werner's article "Photography and Individualization in Contemporary Africa: An Ivoirian Case-study" in *Visual Anthropology* (2001) argues from the ubiquitous identity portrait that photography's centrality in African visuality is derived from association with modern state power. In his article "Self and Accessory in Gambian Studio Photography" in *Visual Anthropology Review* (2000–2001), Liam Buckley, by contrast, discerns common ground in Gambian practice between portrait-making and tailoring—both are forms of surface adornment.

The use of photographs as anthropological and ethnographic documents is another focus of contemporary study. Colonial ethnography was inevitably associated with colonial power, and its photography reveals the uneven relations of power at the heart of this endeavor. On the other hand, Western expeditions often maintained a stock of pictures with which to impress the "natives," unwittingly providing indigenous people with a means of scrutinizing the West even as they are observed. Among the contemporary scholarly works analyzing ethnographic photography are two that treat important expeditions to the Congo before World War One: the efforts of expedition leader Emil Torday and photographer M. W. Hilton Simpson are considered by Jan Vansina in "Photographs of the Sankuru and Kasai River Basin Expedition Undertaken by Emil Torday (1876–1931) and M. W. Hilton Simpson (1881–1936)" (1992), while Herbert Lang's work is discussed by Enid Schildkrout in "The Spectacle of Africa Through the Lens of Herbert Lang: Belgian Congo Photographs, 1909–1915" (1991). The oeuvre of Casimir Zagourski, a Pole active in the Belgian Congo between the wars, whose photography was collected in series entitled *L'Afrique Qui Disparaît*, shows how postcards and albums served as important means of distributing ethnographic images.

Government-sponsored colonial photography projects were often structured through binary oppositions between "civilized" (Europeans or Westernized Africans) and "savage" ("unenlightened" segments of the population). Christraud Geary's *In and out of Focus: Images from Central Africa, 1885–1960* (2002) recounts the long history of colonial image production in the Congo. Circulated in Europe as postcards and through illustrated periodicals like *L'Illustration Congolaise* (1924–1940), photographs were visual propaganda of "the protection and moral development of the natives" only fitfully contested by reformers, whose photographs laid bare the brutality of the colonial regime.

Politically aware African self-representation in the colonial period occurred in images of and by King Njoya of Bamun, Cameroon. Christraud Geary's *Images from Bamum: German Colonial Photography at the Court of King Njoya, Cameroon, West Africa, 1902–1915* (1988) attributes to Njoya an aesthetic and political agenda that he wished to express through portraiture. Earlier exceptions aside, the years immediately following national independence in the 1950s and 1960s saw the greatest flowering of the photographic promotion of African political programs. Official press agencies like Syli-Photo in Guinea, Congopresse in the Democratic Republic of the Congo, and ANIM in Mali, crafted the public personae of the charismatic leaders of the era. Among the many photographers engaged in this effort was Keïta, who toiled for the Malian government from 1962 to 1971. The moment of national independence also saw the efflorescence of independent mass-media, particularly in the form of South Africa-based *Drum* magazine, which published editions in Ghana and Nigeria.

Contemporary artists using photography, often based in Western Africa's diaspora communities in the West, include the late Rotimi Fani-Kayode, who explored, in collaboration with British photographer Alex Hirst, the connection between the body and an identity, which in his case was Black, African, and homosexual. In the 1990s, photography's conjunction of personal experience and historical imagination has been interrogated by Nigerian-born Iké Udé and Ghana-born Godfried Donker, among others.

KEVIN MULHEARN

See also: **Documentary Photography; Fani-Kayode, Rotimi; Fosso, Samuel; Keïta, Seydou; Photography in Africa: An Overview; Portraiture**

Further Reading

Bigham, Elizabeth. "Issues of Authorship in the Portrait Photographs of Seydou Keita." *African Arts* 32 (Spring 1999); 56–57, 94–96.

Buckley, Liam. "Self and Accessory in Gambian Studio Photography." *Visual Anthropology Review* 16 (Fall/Winter 2000–2001); 71–91.

David, Phillipe. "Photographer-publishers in Togo." In *Anthology of African and Indian Ocean Photography*. Paris: Éditions Revue Noire, 1999; 42–47.

Enwezor, Okwui. "A Critical Presence: *Drum* Magazine in Context." *In/sight*. New York: Solomon R. Guggenheim, 1996.

Flash Afrique: Photography from West Africa. Vienna: Kunsthalle Wein, 2001.

Geary, Christraud. *Images from Bamum: German Colonial Photography at the Court of King Njoya, Cameroon, West Africa, 1902–1915*. Washington, DC: Smithsonian Institute Press, 1988.

———. "Missionary Photography: Public and Private Readings." *African Arts* 24 (Fall 1991); 48–59, 98–100.

———. "Different Visions? Postcards from Africa by European and African Photographers and Sponsors." In *Delivering Views: Distant Cultures in Early Postcards*.

Washington, DC: Smithsonian Institute Press, 1998; 147–177.
———. *In and Out of Focus: Images from Central Africa, 1885–1960*. New York: Phillip Wilson Publishers, 2002.
Koudjina, Phillipe. "Phillipe's Nights in Niamey." In *Anthology of African and Indian Ocean Photography*. Paris: Éditions Revue Noire, 1999; 174–177.
Lamore, Jean. "Samuel Fosso." *Nka* 13–14 (Spring/Summer 2001); 34–39.
Lamunière, Michelle. *You Look Beautiful Like That: The Portrait Photographs of Seydou Keïta and Malick Sidibé*. Cambridge, MA: Yale University Press, 2001.
Prochaska, David. "Fantasia of the Photothéque: French Postcard Views of Colonial Senegal." *African Arts* 24 (October 1991); 40–47, 98.
Schildkrout, Enid. "The Spectacle of Africa Through the Lens of Herbert Lang: Belgian Congo Photographs, 1909–1915." *African Arts* 24 (Fall 1991); 70–85, 100.

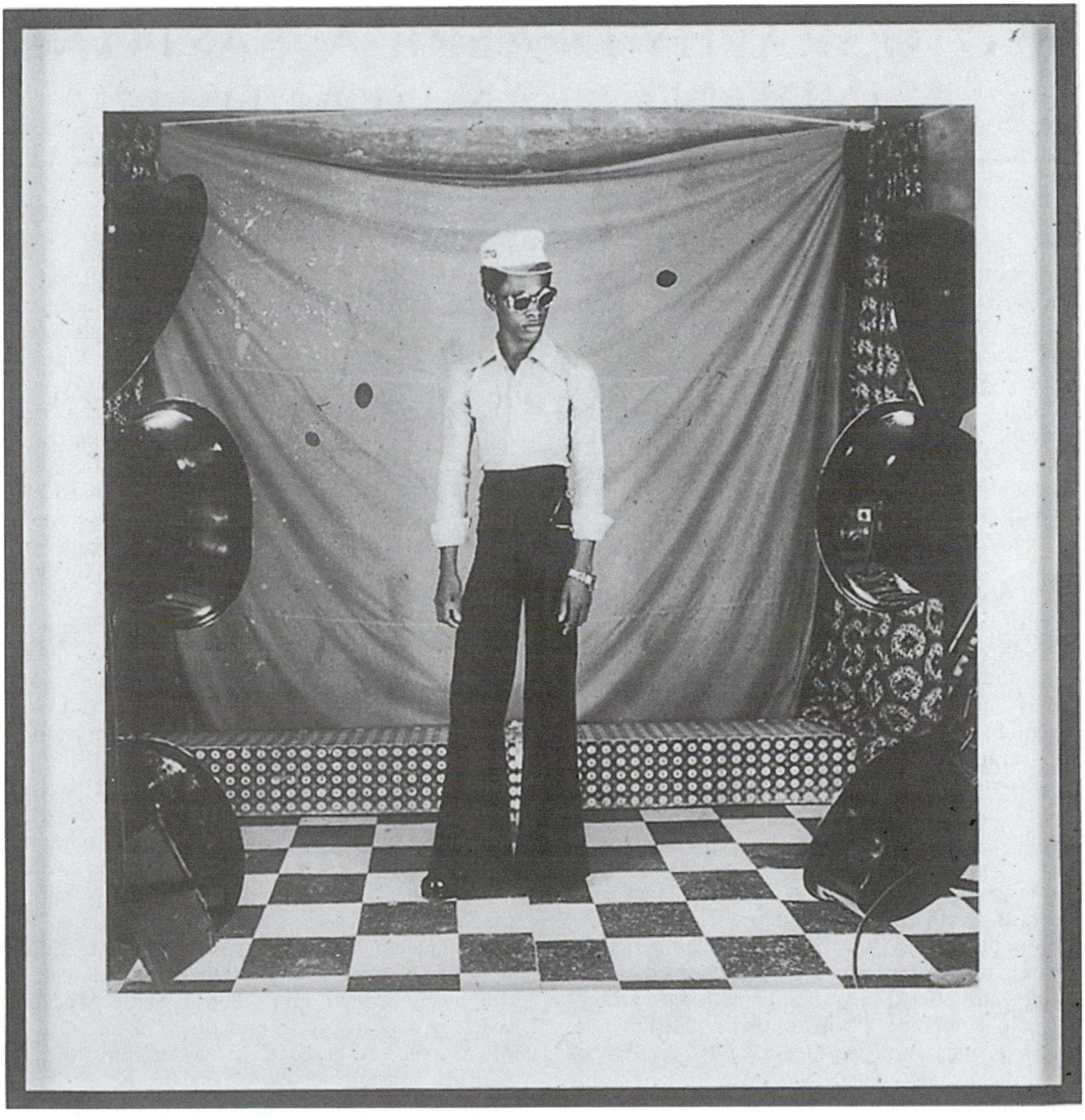

Samuel Fosso, Self Portrait, 1977 gelatin silver print.
[*Courtesy of Jack Shainman Gallery, New York*]

Sprague, Stephen. "Yoruba Photography: How the Yoruba See Themselves." *African Arts* 12 (Fall 1978); 52–59, 107.
Vansina, Jan. "Photographs of the Sankuru and Kasai River Basin Expedition Undertaken by Emil Torday (1876–1931) and M. W. Hilton Simpson (1881–1936)." In *Anthropology and Photography 1860–1920*. New Haven, CT: Yale University Press, 1992; 193–205.
Viditz-Ward, Vera. "Studio Photography in Freetown." In *Anthology of African and Indian Ocean Photography*. Paris: Éditions Revue Noire, 1999; 34–41.
Werner, Jean-François. "Photography and Individualization in Contemporary Africa: An Ivoirian Case-study." *Visual Anthropology* 14 (2001); 251–268.

PHOTOGRAPHY IN AFRICA: EAST AND INDIAN OCEAN ISLANDS

Throughout the twentieth century, the East African photographic images in widest circulation in the West were those related to safaris and disasters. Within the region, portrait photography flourished and became integrated into political life and society. While less known and studied than work from elsewhere in Africa, the region's photographic practices (including those of adjoining Indian Ocean islands) embody a long history and several rich traditions.

With its exotic animal life, East Africa was and is regarded as a natural wonder. As early as the 1850s, Westerners were using photography to scientifically document animals and create mementos of big-game hunts in the present-day nations of Kenya, Tanzania, and Sudan. The telephoto lens and other technical developments of the 1880s and 1890s made possible the prospect of "hunting" with the camera rather than the gun. Pioneering camera adventurer A. Radclyffe Dugmore wrote in 1910 of the challenge of such hunts: "shooting animals is so much easier than photographing them that there is no possible comparison" (226). Typical of works published before 1914, including those by C.G. Shillings and Edward North Buxton, Dugmore's book features 140 photographs, mostly of wild animals. The accompanying text narrates the capture of the photos and offers practical information on arranging and equipping a trip to British East Africa. James Ryan's *Picturing Empire: Photography and the Visualization of the British Empire* (1997) discusses the ideological underpinnings of these early wildlife photo books and places them in the context of the visual construction of British imperialism. Photosafaris remain popular and, despite technological advances, archetypes established by photographers a century ago remain current.

The prominence of East African images in the world news media is, by and large, a development of the last quarter of the twentieth century even though Ethiopian Emper or Haile Sellassie's coronation in 1930 was covered by European illustrated periodicals, and Alfred Eisenstaedt photographed Italy's 1935 invasion of the country. Images of Ethiopia's devastating 1984 famine created one of the century's most significant media events, and the most important documentation was a video produced by South African reporter Michael Buerk and Kenya-based cameraman Mohammed Amin. Amin, who co-founded Nairobi's Camerapix agency in 1969, was one of the region's most active and celebrated photojournalists until his death in 1996. In general, the development of indigenous photojournalism has been limited, though Sébastien Porte's article "The Press in Kenya" (Porte 1999) highlights the against-the-odds dynamism of Kenya's indigenous press photography. Usually, crisis-driven coverage of East African events in the Western media is undertaken by photographers from outside the region: for example, the 1993 famine in Sudan was photographed by South African Kevin Carter and the 1994 Rwandan genocide by Frenchman Gilles Peress. Susan Moeller's article provocatively frames the vital question of whether such coverage in the Western press of East Africa's disasters serves to educate the public or simply inures its viewers to suffering (Moeller 1999).

Photography's political role in the region spans colonial and postcolonial eras. In turn of the century

Mauritius, portrait photographers were engaged to produce identity photographs of Asian and African immigrants, demonstrating English colonial rulers' use of photography for social control. Perhaps the most infamous interaction between colonial authority and photographic representation occurred in Rwanda and Burundi, under German and later Belgian control. Photographs were used to underscore European anthropological theories about racially-based distinctions between indigenous populations: pastoralist Tutsi, a minority ruling elite, and majority, agriculturalist Hutu. Photography provided visual "evidence" for colonial officials and missionaries of the Tutsis' "European" qualities, and thus supported the preservation of Tutsi dominance. After independence, this situation fostered violence that reached an awful apex in the 1994 Rwandan genocide.

Native elites in Madagascar and Ethiopia recognized the political relevance of photographic portraiture. On Madagascar, photography provided a means of self-representation and state building for the rulers of the Merina kingdom before the 1896 French conquest, and the medium's role in public life continued in the colonial and post-colonial eras through official photography agencies FTM and ANTA. In Ethiopia (which survived as an independent state through most of the colonial era) photography played a persistent role in domestic politics. Using images of uncrowned ruler Lij Iyasu, Western scholar Richard Pankhurst pieces together how photographs became weapons in the internal political struggles of early twentieth century Ethiopia in his article "The Political Image: The Impact of the Camera in an Ancient Independent African State" (Pankhurst 1992). After noting a local belief that opposition among the country's Christian nobility to Lij Iyasu was fostered by a now-unknown doctored photograph of the prince in Muslim dress, Pankhurst examines extant authentic portraits of the prince in both Christian and Muslim dress. Pankhurst carries the story forward, discussing the use of faked photographs to discredit Emperor Haile Selassie around the time of his overthrow in 1974.

In East Africa, commercial portrait photography proceeded from the coasts inland. The daguerreotype arrived on Mauritius as early as 1840 and, by 1843, the first photographic studio was established. Joseph Razaka, Madagascar's first indigenous photographer, opened a studio in 1889 that he operated until his death in 1939. Early commercial studios on the mainland coast included those of the Coutinho Brothers and A.C. Gomes and Son, both active in Zanzibar. Englishman William D. Young ran studios in Kenya and was the "official" freelance photographer for the construction of the Uganda railway. In Ethiopia, portrait studios were initially run by Armenians, including the Boyadjians, a dynasty of royal court photographers. At the end of the century, Ethiopian studios were run mostly by indigenous photographers who continued to produce mostly formal, studio-based images for life passages and rituals including weddings and baptisms. Important studio photographers in Ethiopia include Negash Wolde Amanuel and Ato Kebede Guebre Mariam, with photographs taking on deep cultural meaning in the realm of familial relations, rituals, friendships, and courtships. The postcolonial history of this genre and its integration into society has been addressed by Heike Behrend in a series of articles on Kenyan and Ugandan portrait photography, including "A Short History of Photography in Kenya" from *Anthology of African and Indian Ocean Photography* (1999), "Fragmented Visions: Photo Collages by Two Ugandan Photographers" from *Visual Anthropology* (2001), and "Imagined Journeys: The Likoni Ferry Photographers of Mombasa, Kenya" from *Photography's Other Histories* (2003). In these articles, she highlights the contributions of South Asian photographers in Kenya, analyzes the elaborate collage-based practice of two Ugandan portraitists, and discusses the role of backdrops in the work of street photographers in Mombasa, Kenya. These articles situate photography firmly within East African culture as a means of documentation, commemoration, and self-identification. Together, Behrend's articles begin to demonstrate how portrait photographers in East Africa create for their customers a space in images for wish fulfillment and imagination, allowing—through painted backdrops, montage, and composite printing—for patrons to access luxuries, travels, and social relationships which would normally be out of reach.

KEVIN MULHEARN

See also: **Documentary Photography; Peress, Gilles; Photography in Africa: An Overview; Portraiture**

Further Reading

Barnard, Roger. "Camerapix." In *Anthology of African and Indian Ocean Photography*. Paris: Éditions Revue Noire, 1999; 232–235.

Behrend, Heike. "A Short History of Photography in Kenya." In *Anthology of African and Indian Ocean Photography*. Paris: Éditions Revue Noire, 1999; 160–165.

———. "Fragmented Visions: Photo Collages by Two Ugandan Photographers." *Visual Anthropology* 14 (2001); 310–320.

Behrend, Heike. "Imagined Journeys: The Likoni Ferry Photographers of Mombasa, Kenya." In *Photography's Other Histories*. Durham: Duke University Press, 2003; 221–239.

Bréville, Tristan. "*En Route* to India." In *Anthology of African and Indian Ocean Photography*. Paris: Éditions Revue Noire, 1999; 318–325.

Dugmore, A. Radclyffe. *Camera Adventures in the African Wilds*. New York: Doubleday, Page & Company, 1910.

Geary, Christraud. "Views from Outside and Inside: Representation of Madagascar and the Malagasy, 1658–1935." In *Objects as Envoys: Cloth, Imagery, and Diplomacy in Madagascar*. Washington, DC: Smithsonian Institution, 2002.

Izydorczyk, Frédéric. "The Great Island." In *Anthology of African and Indian Ocean Photography*. Paris: Éditions Revue Noire, 1999; 326–349.

Moeller, Susan. *Compassion Fatigue: How the Media Sell Disease, Famine, War and Death*. New York: Routledge, 1999.

Pankhurst, Richard. "The Political Image: The Impact of the Camera in an Ancient Independent African State." In *Anthropology and Photography 1860–1920*. New Haven, CT: Yale University Press, 1992; 234–241.

Pankhurst, Richard, and Denis Gérard. "Court Photographer in Ethiopia." In *Anthology of African and Indian Ocean Photography*. Paris: Éditions Revue Noire, 1999; 118–133.

Porte, Sébastien. "The Press in Kenya." In *Anthology of African and Indian Ocean Photography*. Paris: Éditions Revue Noire, 1999; 224–231.

Ryan, James. *Picturing Empire: Photography and the Visualization of the British Empire*. Chicago: University of Chicago Press, 1997.

PHOTOGRAPHY IN AFRICA: NORTH

North Africa's twentieth century photographic history was shaped primarily by the colonial era and the extended struggle for national liberation. Perhaps because of greater European immigration and integration into the global economy in the nineteenth century, photography by and for the colonial class became quite highly developed in the first half of the twentieth century. Colonization, tourism, and a taste for the Orientalist picturesque fueled the consumption of photographs of North Africa in West.

Colonial authorities in the first half of the twentieth century—French, English, and Italian—deposited photographs in vast archives. Daly and Forbes published images from Britain's Sudan archive and noted that the photographs, taken mainly by officials and tourists but also by commercial photographers and press correspondents, were initially collected in the service of military intelligence. Durand-Evrard and Martini presented photographs from France's Algerian archive alongide other textual and visual documents. Thematically organized around such topics as agriculture, écoles and lycees, and Saharan exploration, their book puts photography in the broader context of the production of colonial knowledge. Of particular interest are surveillance images from secret police files. A related group of identity photographs discussed by Carole Naggar offers the case of shamefully unveiled Berber women, whom Marc Garanger was forced to photograph after being pressed into service as a regimental photographer. These women offer defiant gazes that resist the camera's coercive effects, and Garanger viewed these images' publication in the 1980s as a riposte to France's willful amnesia about the war of 1954–1962. (One might also mention photojournalism of Algeria's conflicts: Magnum photographer Marc Riboud's exemplary coverage of the 1954–1962 war, or photography of the under-covered "dirty war" between the government and Islamist rebels, typified in Algerian photojournalist Hocine's so-called *Madonna of Benthala*, an image of a grieving woman after a 1997 massacre [see Convert].)

The decades before World War One were a golden age for commercial photography of North Africa, a form of photography most widely distributed as postcards. The Koranic injunction against realistic images seems to have impeded the development of native-owned commercial and portrait studios, which were therefore often operated by Europeans and especially Armenians in this period as well as until well into the later decades of the century. Recently, a number of publications have offered country-specific selections of postcards, though unfortunately with poor quality reproductions (See Hébrard and Hébrard, Laronde, and Karmazyn).

Several important commercial studios active in the colonial era should be noted. The Bonfils family, based in Lebanon and Egypt, produced large quantities of photographs in the late nineteenth century that remained in commercial circulation through the early twentieth. Jules Gervais-Courtellmont, a French convert to Islam, published the illustrated magazine *L'Algérie Artistique et Pittoresque* (1890–1892) and created thousands of direct color autochrome plates frequently reproduced in the popular press. Austrian photographer Rudolf Lehnert and German manager Ernst Landrock worked together in Tunis from 1904–1914 and Cairo from 1924–1930, at which time Lehnert returned to work in Tunis alone. Prolific and artistically ambitious, the two produced a broad range of images, including romantic Saharan vistas and erotic portraits, distributed through monographs and as original prints, lithographs, and postcards.

In an important theoretical text on Algerian postcards, Malek Alloula describes the corrosive impact of these mass-produced, erotic postcard images on the society of their colonized subjects. He writes

> Behind this image of Algerian women, probably reproduced in the millions, there is visible the broad outline of one of the figures of the colonial perception of the native. This figure can be essentially defined as the practice of a right of (over)sight that the colonizer arrogates to himself and that is the bearer of multiform violence. The postcard fully partakes in such violence... (5)

Westerners' creation of visual imagery stimulated by a vision of North Africa(ns) as exotic "Other" began well before the period on which Alloula concentrates (1900–1930) and arguably extends to the present. Paul Bowles' recently published "souvenir snapshots" of his life in Tangier, Morocco, ambiguously relate to this tradition, offering a hermetic vision of the author's expatriate existence.

Anthropological and archeological photography represent two varieties of imagery created throughout the twentieth century. In the first category is the work of pioneering Finnish sociologist Edward Westermarck, whose photographs of Morocco in the years before the First World War were made into lantern slides to illustrate his lectures and, intended only as utilitarian documents, were frequently of questionable technical quality. By contrast, the work of Harry Burton was of sufficient aesthetic merit to warrant a 2001 exhibition at the Metropolitan Museum of Art in New York. Burton was an archeological expedition photographer in Egypt for the Metropolitan and for Howard Carter and Lord Carnavon, discoverers of the tomb of Tutankhamen.

The Second World War, fought across North Africa, saw the creation of innumerable photographs, which generally take as their subjects the battling Axis and Allied armies. Unfortunately, these images are usually published in books aimed at aficionados of military history, which reproduce images with little of the context that is of particular interest to art historians.

The early history of artistic photography in North Africa is, of yet, little studied. The first photographic exhibition was held in Egypt in 1923; the second, in 1933, featured 600 photographs by roughly 130 photographers, over half them Egyptian. Contemporary photographers have figured in recent exhibitions of African art in the West. The 1996 exhibition at the Solomon R. Guggenheim Museum in New York, *In/sight: African Photographers, 1940 to the Present*, included, for example, Egyptian Nabil Boutros' documentary images of Cairo's people by night and arresting photographs of the body at moments of birth and death by Tunisia's Touhami Ennadre. Zineb Sedira works in the context of the North African diaspora. Born to Algerian immigrants in Paris, her work deals with cultural assimilation and family identity within North African Muslim society in the West.

Kevin Mulhearn

See also: **Documentary Photography; Photography in Africa: An Overview; Portraiture; Representation and "the Other"**

Further Reading

Alloula, Malek. *The Colonial Harem*. Minneapolis: University of Minnesota Press, 1986.

Bowles, Paul. *Paul Bowles Photographs: How Could I Send a Picture into the Desert?* New York: Scalo, 1994.

Convert, Pascal. "Medea the Algerian." *Art Press* 286 (January 2003); 19–23.

Courtellemont, Guy. "Jules Gervais-Courtellemont (1863–1931): Autochromist." *History of Photography* 20 (Fall 1996); 255–257.

Daly, M.W., and L.E. Forbes. *The Sudan: Photographs from the Sudan Archive, Durham University Library*. Reading, UK: Garnet Publishing, 1994.

Durand-Evrard, Françoise, and Lucienne Martini. *Archives d'Algérie: 1830–1960*. Paris: Hazan, 2003.

Egypt: Dream and Realities. Cairo: Aujourd'hui l'Egypte, 1993.

Evans, Elaine Altman. *Scholars, Scoundrels, and the Sphinx: a Photographic and Archaeological Adventure up the Nile*. Knoxville, TN: McClung Museum, 2000.

Fletcher, David. *Tanks in Camera: Archive Photographs from the Tank Museum, the Western Desert: 1940–1943*. Gloucestershire: Sutton, 1998.

Gabous, Abdelkrim. *La Tunisie des Photographes: 1875–1910*. Tunis: Editions CERES, 1994.

Hébrard, Jean-Louis, and Marie-Claude Hébrard. *L'Algérie Autrefois*. Le Coteau: Horvath, 1990.
Karmazyn, Jean-Claude. *Le Maroc en Cartes Postales: 1900–1920*. Cahors: Publi-fusion, 1994.
Laronde, André. *La Libye à Travers les Cartes Postales: 1900–1940*. Paris: Paris-Méditerranée, 1997.
Lehnert, Rudolf, and Ernst Landrock. *L'Orient d'un Photographe*. Lausanne: Favre, 1987.
Münnich, Ralf. *Panzer in Nord-Afrika: 1941–1943*. Friedberg: Podzun-Pallas-Verlag, 1977.
Naggar, Carole. "The Unveiled: Algerian Women." *Aperture* 199 (Summer 1990).
Suolinna, Kirsti, et al. *Portraying Morocco: Edward Westermarck's Fieldwork and Photographs, 1898–1913*. Åbo: Åbo Akademis Förlag, 2000.

PHOTOGRAPHY IN AFRICA: SOUTH AND SOUTHERN

Photography has been practiced in Southern Africa since the earliest days of the medium. From its earliest years in Africa there has been a tension between the documentary and the artificial uses of photography, a tension which was made more profound due to the pressures of foreign domination and racial classification derived from the colonial period. According to scholar Karel Schoeman , just as they became popular abroad, plate glass images, daguerrotypes, and ambrotypes, as well as paper images were also made in South Africa by private amateur or traveling artists, and by 1846 they were being produced in commercial photography studios. *Cartes-de-visite* were produced by Arthur Green in Cape Town as early as 1861. The conventions for sitters and their attire followed those of Victorian Europe. Also notable for this period were the anthropometric studies of Khoi-San people made by Wilhelm Bleek, whose attention was more directed at aspects of physical description and items of dress of the "natives" than the style of memorial portraiture seen in visiting cards of white subjects. By the 1890s, postcards were also produced in Southern Africa, mostly for tourist consumption. They described scenes from the diamond and gold mining camps, the rise of great cities Cape Town, Durban, Port Elizabeth, and Johannesburg, technological marvels, railroads, the destructiveness and genocide of the Boer War, native "types," and various aspects of the control of native populations by colonial powers and settlers, including images of Africans administering corporal punishment to other Africans. Another early use of photography in Southern Africa, as noted by Patrick Harries, was as propaganda for missionaries, especially "before and after" shots of Christianized and western-clothed Africans. Also, in Mozambique, Harries notes that the anthropologist Henri-Alexandre Junod used photography to present a view of "primitive" Thonga society living "close to nature," in contrast to Europeans in cities who were experiencing the "trauma of industrialization."

By the time of the partition of the African continent among European powers after 1884, thus at the height of the colonial enterprise, European photographic greeting cards had evolved from the chromolithograph trade. These cards, collected in albums, were made as souvenirs of places traveled to in Europe, and also in its colonial outposts. What began as exoticism at home was transferred quickly to an exoticism of the colonial world, and thus it became fashionable among the middle class of Europe and in Africa to collect images of the scenes and types of the "countries of the world." These cards started as lithographic prints, soon included photographic prints, and then went into mass production using the halftone screen process. Christraud Geary notes that by 1900, Sallo Epstein and Company in Johannesburg had become the largest publisher of postal cards in Southern Africa. Epstein and other commercial houses, as well as individual artists, according to Geary, worked along the lines similar to photographers in other African territories. They reproduced similar stereotypes of the "native," such as the solitary warrior male and the seductively arranged, eroticized native female group. Studio portraits of Africans often blurred the edges between factual document and paternalistic fantasy. Interestingly, images of the amaZulu were in especially great demand abroad, because of their nation's famous resistance against European territorial ambitions under leaders like Shaka, Dingane, and Cetshwayo. Virginia Lee-Webb has noted that many nineteenth century images of the amaZulu often were made in-camera using fantasy backdrops, jungle scenes, and staged sittings. South African studio photographers even had boxes of "tribal" props for their sitters to wear and hold.

While in both ethnographic and commercial photography, African people were mostly imagined to be part of the flora of the country, a small number of studios such as H. F. Fine in Johannesburg, Deale in Bloemfontein, and traveling portrait photographers took pictures of petit bourgeois, middle class, and mission-educated black sitters. These images were mostly forgotten in storage rooms and the bottoms of drawers during the apartheid years from 1948–1994, but have recently been unearthed as part of Santu Mofokeng's (1991–2000) conceptual archival project, *The Black Photo Album/Look At Me 1890–1950*. In these portraits, turn of the century black families imagine themselves differently than the authors of the anthropological or studio fantasies of the "natives." They face the camera with dignity and wear Victorian attire.

At the other end of the spectrum was the multi-year, 6000 image documentary project on native "types" by Alfred Martin Duggan-Cronin, a former employee of De Beers Consolidated Mines in Kimberley. His tribal categorizations are random and arbitrary, but his images have the benefit of giving dignity to their subjects and not removing whatever signs of contemporaneousness they wore as everyday garb. His pseudo-ethnological four-volume *The Bantu Tribes of Southern Africa (1928–1954)*, however, would later be used, especially after 1948 by the architects of apartheid like Daniel Malan and Hendrik Verwoerd, as evidence of the "natural" separation of the races and ethnicities. This, they believed, needed to be enforced through strict policing of borders and national legislation to keep African groups distinct from each other and apart from Europeans.

Closer in line with art photography, but equally romanticizing of her subject, were the many portraits of amaNdebele taken by Constance Stuart Larrabee during the 1930s and 1940s. The amaNdebele were a people whose lands had been taken during the nineteenth century and were living scattered on white farms just a short drive north of Stuart's studio in Pretoria. Because of easy access to their homesteads by white weekenders, the amaNdebele have become something of an archetype of pristine native life in South Africa as seen as a whole. For this reason they would later be organized into a "homeland" and a tourist colony by the South African government.

By the 1950s and 1960s, the entrenchment of apartheid was reacted against by the efflorescence of documentary type, series-oriented, photojournalistic photography. Popular white owned, but black oriented and black staffed photo magazines like *Drum* and *Zonk!* devoted themselves to the politics and social life of the day. *Drum* would later be printed in West African and Caribbean editions, thus bringing images of South African life to other parts of Africa during the period of independence. At a time of growing racial animosity, activism by Nelson Mandela and the African National Congress, and government repression, *Drum* featured photographers like Alf Khumalo, Jürgen Schadeburg, Peter Magubane, Ranjith Kally, G.R. Naidoo, and Bob Gosani, giving the first mass exposure to a mixed-race group of outstanding photojournalists.

Black photographers were treated with particular roughness by the authorities. In 1969 Peter Magubane was placed in solitary confinement for two years, and then banned from taking photographs for another five. He later worked for *Time* and has published several major books on the 1976 Soweto student uprising and the revolutionary struggle of the 1980s. His colleague Ernest Cole was less fortunate. Cole's book *House of Bondage*, published in 1967, was a book-length version of the kind of photo essay work seen in *Drum*—the absurdity of pass laws, conditions of black poverty, illegal drinking establishments in the black townships, syncretic religion, the African middle class, and the romance/exile of the "bantu homelands"—but for an international audience. *House of Bondage* was banned in South Africa but copies were circulated underground and Cole's work influenced several subsequent generations of black and white photographers in South Africa. Unable to live in South Africa after the publication of his book, Cole went into exile and eventually died penniless on the streets of Manhattan. The other great master of the serial documentary approach was David Goldblatt who from the 1960s published a number of disturbingly frank portraits in a number of works including *Some Afrikaners Photographed* (1975), and *The Transported of KwaNdebele* (1989). Roger Ballen continued this documentation of Afrikaners in their homes and enacting inexplicable rituals in the

1980s and 1990s, to considerable international acclaim. Goldblatt was also instrumental in the founding of the Market Photography Workshop and as an individual mentor, where a number of young artists of all races, most notably Santu Mofokeng, could get hands-on training and also engage in intellectual discussions about the politics of representation.

The 1970s and 1980s saw the rise of this workshop atmosphere between artists and of social realist "struggle" photography. Still there was a tension regarding the most appropriate subject matter and formal approach among those who hoped to document the struggle and aid the effort to overthrow apartheid in South Africa. This tension can be seen by comparing two books from the 1980s: *South Africa: The Cordoned Heart*, prepared by the Carnegie Inquiry into Poverty and Development in Southern Africa; and *Beyond the Barricades: Popular Resistance in South Africa*, a project by the activist photographic collective Afrapix founded in 1982. *The Cordoned Heart* chronicles the underdevelopment of black South Africa. It contains mostly straightforward domestic scenes and some images of political rallies (it includes a portion of Goldblatt's "Transported"). The only image of the State is at the end: in a photo by Omar Badsha, police appear at the airport to escort a recently released political prisoner. In contrast, *Beyond the Barricades* is by turns more lyrical and more harshly realist, since it includes scenes of the popular unrest and the police violence that permeated South African life during the 1980s. Cops and protesters and banners and blood are everywhere in these images, but there are also sections without images and a text that makes clear that photography, even press photography, was also used by the State as an instrument to surveil and silence. Afrapix members such as Steven Hilton-Barber, Santu Mofokeng, Paul Weinberg, and Guy Tillim, who initially worked together to supply the radical press, workers' organizations, and struggle culture magazines such as *Staffrider* with images at low cost, by the later 1980s began moving away from the starker definitions of struggle photography. Weinberg began photographing the San of the Kalahari, Mofokeng went to look for spiritual sources in Lesotho, and Hilton-Barber showed images of northern Transvaal male circumcision—this last caused great controversy when exhibited in 1990 at the Market Gallery in Johannesburg. Photojournalists were also critical to the exposure of atrocities committed by South African occupying forces in Namibia. Likewise in Mozambique, Ricardo Rangel set up a photography-training institute and archive for anti-colonial work, the Centro de Formacao Fotografica in Maputo.

Just before the first democratic elections in South Africa in 1994 high stakes commercial work was in great demand by foreign press agencies and a number of intrepid photojournalists, including Ken Oosterbroek, Mike Marinovich, Joao Silva, and Ken Carter helped sensationalize the ultraviolence of the transition period. After the elections and the broader access to international exhibitions and other art histories abroad, the 1990s and early 2000s also witnessed the production of more conceptual and experimental approaches to photographic technique including the use of serially arranged compositions (Mofokeng and Abrie Fourie), the grid (Hentie van der Merwe), life-sized color prints (Zwelethu Mthethwa), digital media (Minette Vari), constructed still-life composition (Lien Botha), and solopsistic meditations on the history of the archive of South African photography itself (Senzeni Marasela).

Because of the long history of struggle for representation, there is still a strongly social activist tendency in present photographic practice in Southern Africa, even on the more artistic/conceptual end of the spectrum. Now there are other struggles besides colonialism or apartheid: the problems of overcrowding and urban blight, AIDS, the gay lifestyle, the continuing "stain" of race, and the unifying yet divisive potency of the sacred in everyday life. Artists working with photographic-related processes today are more aware of the alternating perception of the photograph as both artifact and artifice than were their peers during the nineteenth century. Some, such as Andrew Tshabangu, Tracey Rose, Jean Brundrit, Berni Searle, and others, are endeavoring to use this empowering knowledge to address the new demands for representation felt by South Africans in the post-apartheid era.

John M. Peffer

See also: **Ballen, Roger; Documentary Photography; Drum; Photography in Africa: An Overview; Portraiture; Schadeburg, Jürgen**

Further Reading

Van Wyk, Gary. "Drawing a Bead on Blacks: Eastern Cape People Painted by Baines, Shot by Pocock." In South African National Gallery's *Ezakwantu: Beadwork from the Eastern Cape*. Cape Town, South Africa: SANG, 1993.

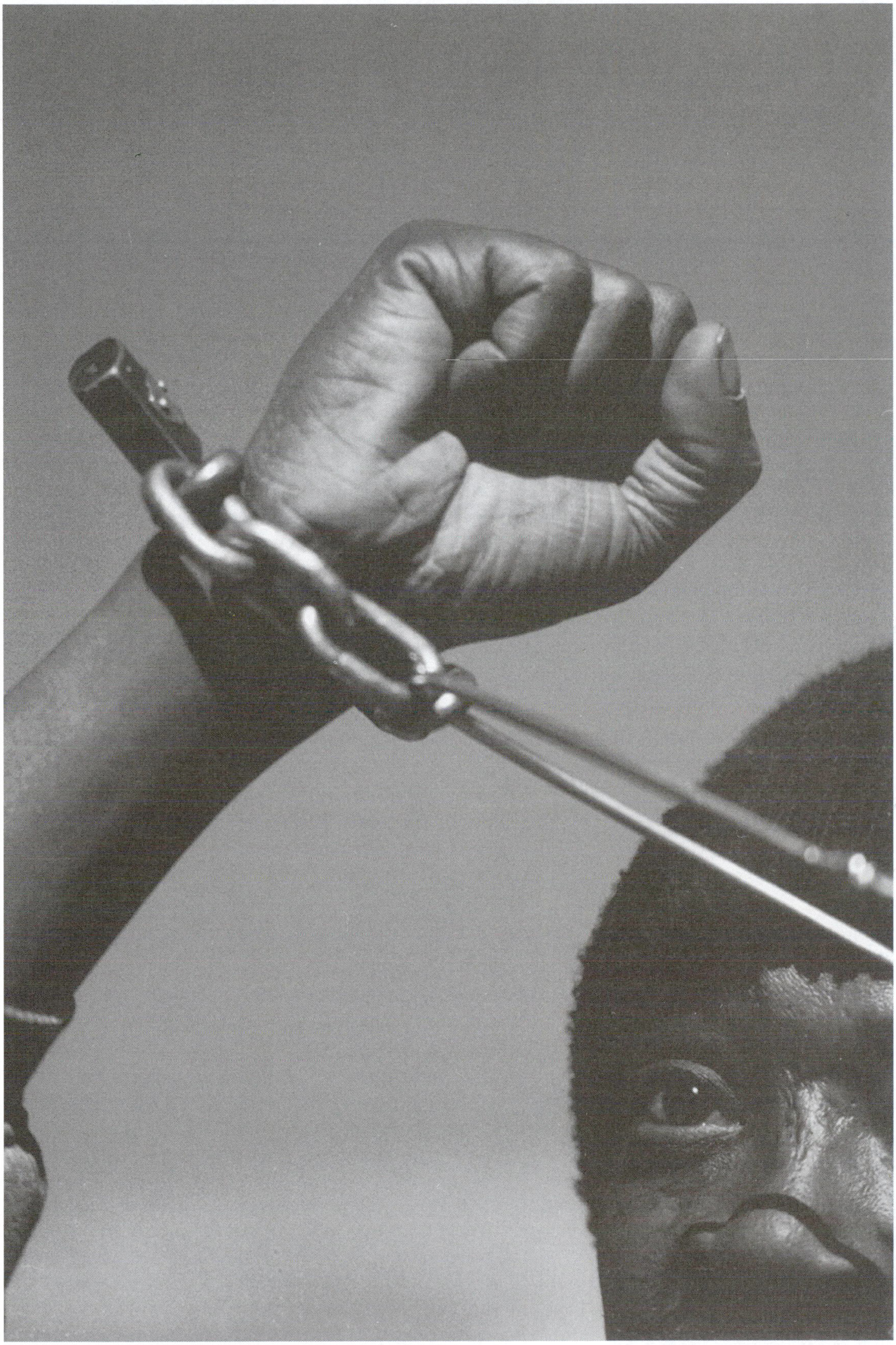

Jodi Bieber, South Africa, Johannesburg, 1996 June 16 Celebration. Apartheid Protest.
[*Jodi Bieber/South Photographs*]

AFTERIMAGE: THE JOURNAL OF MEDIA ARTS AND CULTURAL CRITICISM

Founded in 1969 by the writer, photographer, and curator Nathan Lyons, the Visual Studies Workshop (VSW) in Rochester, New York, was also the birthplace of the well-known journal *Afterimage: The Journal of Media Arts and Cultural Criticism*. *Afterimage* remains the primary journal devoted to a critical understanding of issues in photography and art, despite its unassuming black and white broadsheet format. Since its conception, the journal has taken a radical political stance. *Afterimage* was founded in order to provide a forum for the investigation of the relationships between politics, art and photography. As Grant H. Kester writes in the introduction to the anthology of *Afterimage* essays published in 1998, the questions motivating *Afterimage's* founding were,

> What is the relationship between art production and more direct (or at least more conventionally recognizable) forms of political struggle and protest? What constitutes an activist art practice? And what is the role of criticism, and the critic, in relation to such a practice? (p.1, *Art, Activism, and Oppositionality: Essays from Afterimage*. Durham and London: Duke University Press, [1998]).

The founding of *Afterimage* coincided with burgeoning socio-political critiques of photographic representation promulgated by such scholars as John Tagg, Abigail Solomon-Godeau, Victor Burgin, Rosalind Krauss, and Allan Sekula, influenced by French post-structuralist philosophers such as Michel Foucault and Roland Barthes. *Afterimage's* program was also concurrent with the initial stirrings and subsequent growth of revisionist art history and was part of a general movement towards visual culture studies at large, which included movements to break down barriers between scholarly disciplines.

The VSW began as an experimental, multi-purpose space, incorporating a gallery, archive, library, media center, educational programs and a press for the publication of artists' books as well as *Afterimage*. Lyons founded the VSW after leaving his post as chief curator and assistant director at the George Eastman House's International Museum of Photography (IMP), also located in Rochester, so it is not a coincidence that Rochester has become a nexus of Visual Culture Studies and a hotbed of photographic activity. Graduate students and artists contributed to the workshop's initial and continued efforts, and Joan Lyons was originally in charge of the book publishing section. The organization even had a VSW Book Bus that brought the publications and ideology of the VSW to the citizens of Rochester. Today, the State University of New York (SUNY) College at Brockport offers a Masters of Fine Arts in conjunction with VSW.

The overall goals of the VSW were to create a bridge between theory and practice, in order to provide a more critical and useful understanding of both. Photographic work, so easily reproduced, was also seen as more democratic than other forms of art, in terms of its inexpensiveness and accessibility through circulation. Little institutional support at that time existed either for photographic criticism or for any kind of photography that was not strictly high art. Independent film and video were also fledgling industries and lacked little institutional support, and so the aims of VSW and *Afterimage* were also to provide institutional support and a forum for discussion of these media. Naturally, *Afterimage* has since incorporated discussions and work of digital media as well.

In the 1980s, according to Kester, *Afterimage* focused on the identity of the photographer or writer, at the same time attempting to locate his or her work in the context of political struggle. MFA programs in photography were becoming more widespread, and artists and photographers were trying to incorporate larger political issues into their local practices. Cultural diversity among practitioners was increasing at the same time the so-called "culture wars" that began in 1989 when grants to fund exhibitions of works by Robert Mapplethorpe and Andres Serrano by the

National Endowment for the Arts came under close scrutiny by the political right garnered wide attention. Under editors like Martha Gever, Catherine Lord, and David Trend, *Afterimage* focused on such political and topical issues as AIDS, reproductive rights, racial identity, political organizing, queer theory, sexual difference, patronage in the form of institutional support, audience reception and deconstructing the art world and art and photographic practice. *Afterimage* allowed new, formerly marginalized voices to be heard, and its authors engaged in contemporary debates about new scholarship, canons and practices. In the 1980s *Afterimage* published such important essays as Jan Zita Grover's "Visible Lesions: Images of PWAs" (Vol. 17, summer 1989); Coco Fusco's "Fantasies of Oppositionality" (Vol.16, December 1988) and Lorraine O'Grady's "Olympia's Maid: Reclaiming Black Female Subjectivity" (Vol. 20, summer 1992).

In its early days, *Afterimage* adopted two methodological approaches in order to question photography's aesthetics and to criticize institutional ways of understanding photography. Articles in the journal argued against the then standard mode of viewing art photography as separate from the daily uses of photography; essentially to argue for an inclusion of *all* types of photography in its study and history. The other, interrelated approach was to cross over the boundaries between critic, curator, and artist, creating new personas that incorporated some or all of these aspects, exemplified in Lyons, the founder, who took photographs as well as edited, wrote and curated. A strong interest in vernacular photography and the hope of creating an interdisciplinary field that would embrace popular and visual culture also motivated the early issues of *Afterimage* and continue to inform its ideology today.

Physically, *Afterimage* does not look much different than it did thirty years ago, and its articles remain focused on topical political, theoretical, and social issues, as its subtitle suggests. Current issues are slightly larger and include four more pages than in the past. Currently edited by the French photographer and writer Bruno Chalifour, *Afterimage* devotes 24 pages to photography, video, film, digital media, and art, encompassing issues of craft, methodology, and social criticism alike. The bimonthly journal also includes exhibition and book reviews, a national list of exhibitions including some international venues, a list of internships and grants, editorials and letters to the editor, and usually contains an artist's portfolio of images. *Afterimage* is published internationally and keeps a rotating staff of freelance writers.

Allison Moore

See also: **Barthes, Roland; Burgin, Victor; Krauss, Rosalind; Lyons, Nathan; Photographic Theory; Postmodernism; Sekula, Alan; Solomon-Godeau, Abigail**

Further Reading

Afterimage: The Journal of Media Art and Cultural Criticism published by the Visual Studies Workshop, 31 Prince Street, Rochester NY (1969–present).

Kester, Grant H. ed. *Art, Activism and Oppositionality: Essays from Afterimage*. Durham and London: Duke University Press, 1998.

AGITPROP

The term "agitprop" fuses the first syllables of the two words agitation and propaganda. During the 1920s and 1930s in particular, this term was applied to a brand of Central European Left-wing cultural practice (theater, literature, painting, photography) that sought to propagate Marxist-Leninist ideology at the same time that it aimed to agitate its viewers toward political action. Thus, agitprop was a socially-oriented art form whose aim was simultaneously to re-educate and politically stimulate. The use of the term signified differently depending on the political circumstances in which it was employed. In 1920s Germany, for instance, agitprop cultural practice intended to galvanize a mass audience toward a communist revolution in the context of a capitalist political economy. Therefore, the tone of agitprop art was generally critical of and oppositional toward the governing regime. In the Soviet Union, by contrast, a communist revolution had already occurred in 1917. Therefore, agitprop took on a legitimizing function, designed to further enable the construction of an ideologically-strong socialist state. During the immediate post-revolutionary period in Russia, for instance, agit-trains traversed the countryside while agit-boats docked in harbors. Plastered with pro-Bolshevik images, these mobile agitprop vessels spread the new ideology on the premise that the visual image was the most effective and legible means by which to persuade an often illiterate mass audience.

Photography played a vital role in agitprop culture, not least because it was easily transportable, endlessly reproducible, and possessed a documentary status. As such, a photograph either provided testimony to Soviet industrial and social development, or it asserted capitalist "degeneracy" in the West. In Soviet Russia, the most innovative agitprop photographer was the avant-garde artist Aleksandr Rodchenko. Through the use of extreme camera angles, such as close-up, bird's eye, and worm's eye views, Rodchenko aimed to stimulate the eye and the mind, seeking to produce a fresh vision of a revolutionary society. Furthermore, technological advances in printing methods in the early 1920s, most notably the rotogravure process, allowed for the mass reproduction of both text and photograph on the same page. Thus, the journal *USSR in Construction*, which was published in four languages and distributed to an international readership, photographically documented the major construction projects in the Soviet Union during Joseph Stalin's first and second Five-Year Plans. During this time of accelerated industrialization, the use of dramatic formal elements such as compositionally-assertive diagonals, close-up, and wide-angle views projected the image of dynamism, energy, and industrial prowess that the Soviet State desired to promote abroad. Rodschenko was only one of many contributors to this journal.

In Germany, the mass media empire of Willi Münzenberg, which was loosely affiliated with the Communist International (Comintern), used the photographs as the centerpiece of its agitation and propaganda efforts. Such was the impetus behind the Münzenberg-sponsored *Der Arbeiter-Fotograf* (The Worker-Photographer), a journal founded in 1926 and designed to educate a cadre of amateur proletarian photographers who would generate class-conscious photographs for the revolutionary cause. Similarly, Münzenberg's *Arbeiter Illustrierte Zeitung* (Worker's Illustrated Journal) provided imaginative and socially critical photoreportage on a weekly basis for a broad leftist readership. In this journal, visually and politically compelling photographs were provocatively juxtaposed with incisive text or other photographs in order to activate communist political consciousness. Until the advent of National Socialism in early 1933, the *Arbeiter Illustrierte Zeitung* reached a peak circulation of 500,000, making it the second-most popular illustrated journal in Germany. Exiled to Prague, the journal continued to circulate its revolutionary message until 1938, albeit to a reduced readership of around 12,000.

Photomontage, or the juxtaposition of photographs with text or other photographs, was equally if not more significant as an agitprop device as pure photography. With the cut-and-paste technique of photomontage, it was possible to disassemble and then reassemble the familiarly represented world. The procedure emphasized the artifice of pictorial construction, which, depending on its context, either functioned as a metaphor for the deconstruction of the status quo, or signaled a new society still in the making. Typically, photomontage upset conventional representations of space, accentuating incongruity and spatial instability in order to convey social dynamism and change. Early Soviet photomontage, such as Gustav Klucis' poster design *Electrification of the Entire Country* of 1920, juxtaposed abstract forms drawn from Constructivist aesthetics with photography, thus combining symbols of avant-garde art with technological modernization. Photomontages generated during Stalin's Five-Year Plans featured a more immediately legible pictorial composition, in keeping with intensified propaganda efforts, but still foregrounded emphatic diagonals and a disjunctive syntax. This shift in representation is readily evident in Klucis' 1930 *Male and Female Workers (Let Us Fulfill the Plan of the Great Projects)*, which unifies multiple hands, palm up, into a symbol of the Five-Year plan while it slices across the pictorial surface in a gesture of resolute solidarity.

At the same historical moment, the provocative photomontages of the German artist John Heartfield (pseudonym of Helmut Herzfelde) were featured within the pages and on the front covers of the *Arbeiter Illustrierte Zeitung*. The goal of these photomontages was to seize and politically stimulate the passing gaze in a public sphere saturated by the photographic image. They aimed to reveal the reali-

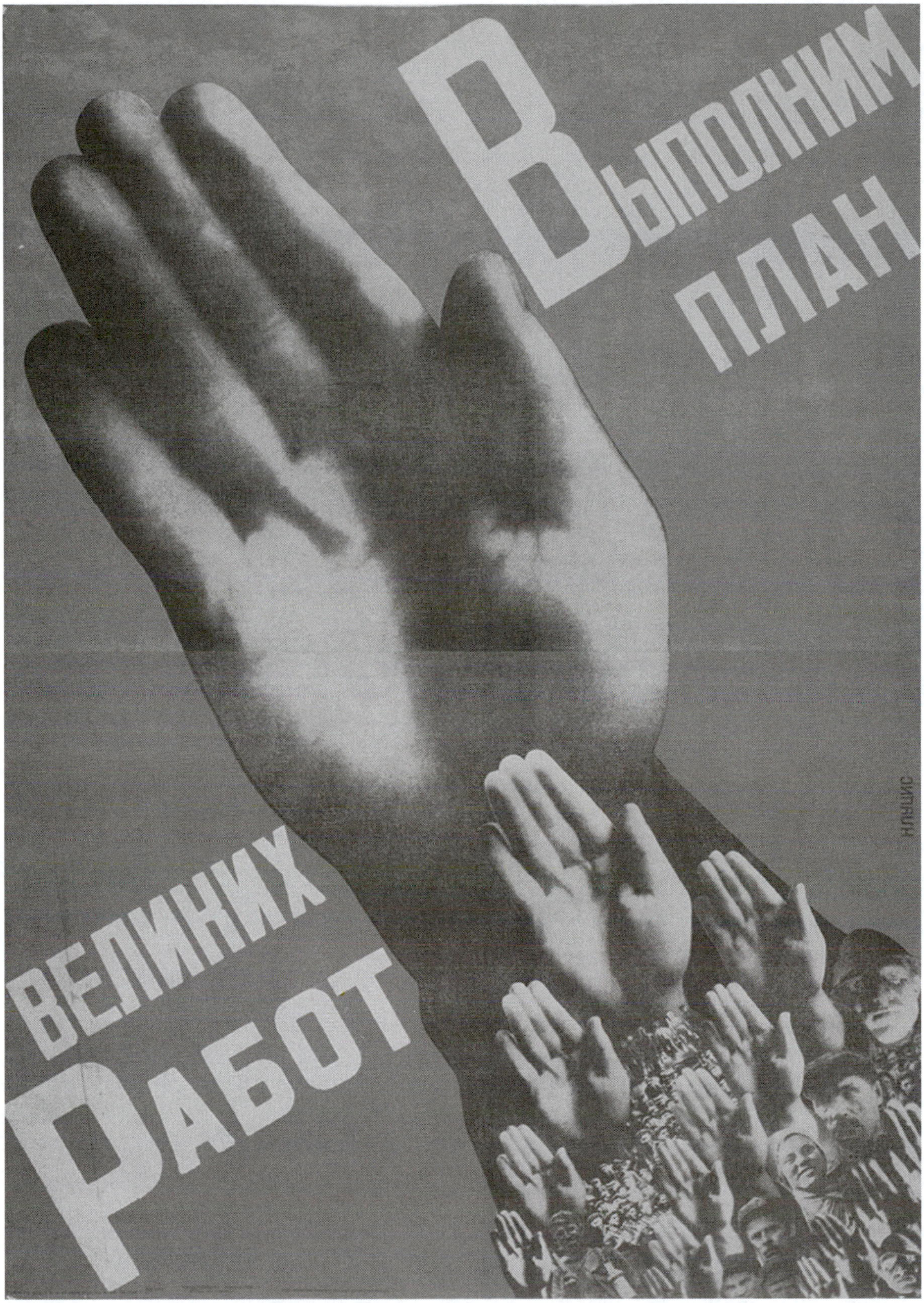

Gustav Klucis, Fulfilled Plan, Great Work, 1930, Lithograph, printed in color, 46 ¾ × 33″, Purchase Fund, Jan Tschichold Collection.
[*Digital Image © The Museum of Modern Art/Licensed by SCALA/Art Resource, New York*]

ties behind appearances, mobilizing the visual machinery of satire, including, as the scholar David Evans points out, metamorphosis, hybridization, anthropomorphism, and metaphors of scale. In Heartfield's 1932 photomontage *The Meaning of the Hitler Salute*, for example, Hitler's arm does not thrust vigorously forth, but flops limply back, palm up, to receive millions of Rentenmarks from the hand of a giant, bloated capitalist standing behind him. "Millions stand behind me," declares the caption—Hitler's own proclamation—while the image reports the true source of Hitler's electoral support.

In photography, the notion of agitprop continued to be redefined in the later half of the twentieth century and has become primarily a tactic within advertising that uses references to the historical practice.

Sabine Kriebel

See also: **Heartfield, John; Image Theory: Ideology; Photography in Europe: Russia and Eastern Europe; Social Representation; Worker Photography**

Further Reading

Ades, Dawn. *Photomontage*. London: Thames and Hudson, 1986.

Buchloh, Benjamin. "From Faktura to Factography," *October* 30, (1984) 82–119.

Evans, David. *John Heartfield, AIZ/VI: 1930-1938*. London: Kent Fine Art, Inc., 1992.

Evans, David and Sylvia Gohl. *Photomontage: a Political Weapon*. London: Gordon Fraser, 1986.

Gaßner, Hubertus, et al., *Gustav Klucis*. Stuttgart: Verlag Gerd Hatje, 1991.

Tupitsyn, Margarita. *The Soviet Photograph: 1924–1927*. New Haven: Yale University Press, 1996.

MAX ALPERT

Russian

Max Alpert was a leading Soviet photographer who helped shaped the modern photo essay through his work as a propagandist of the Soviet state in the 1930s through the 1950s. His documentations of huge state-sponsored projects form a lasting record of Soviet industry and ideology. Although always under the direction of the state to photograph the properly sanctioned material, Alpert brought a stark artistry to all his work, enabling it to survive while much Socialist Realist and propaganda photography has not.

Alpert was born in 1899 in Simferopol in the Crimea (present-day Ukraine). The son of an artisan, at age 15 he was apprenticed to a photographer in Odessa. In 1919 Alpert volunteered for the Red Army. During the 1920s he became a leader of the Red Army's photographic brigade alongside such young photographers as Yevgeny Khaldei. After his demobilization in 1924 he joined the Moscow newspaper *Rabochaya Gazeta* where he worked for four years. Many of his photographs from this period, including *Maxim Gorky's Return from Italy*, were widely published.

Hired by Soviet organ *Pravda* in 1928 he photographed the collectivization of agriculture and construction during the first of Premier Josef Stalin's now infamous Five Year Plans. As part of his coverage of these projects he began to work systematically on developing serial or sequence photography. An important early example includes his series *The Construction of the Magnitogorsk Steelworks Factory* of 1929–1930. Over the years Alpert made repeated visits to the town to document its ongoing development. Among his most noted works was the sequence *Master and Builder* in which Alpert chronicled the career of Viktor Kalmikov, a worker at the Magnitogorsk steel foundry who began as an illiterate mason and became an expert construction worker.

In 1931 Alpert began photographing for the magazine *USSR na stroike* (*USSR in Construction*) contributing to stories directed at foreign audiences. During this time he covered the digging of the Fergana Canal (also known as the Great or Grand Fergana Canal), to draw water for irrigation of cotton crops in the Fergana Valley in present-day Uzbekistan and contributed a series of photos of the hydroelectric plant on the Dnepr River.

In 1931, along with Arkady Shaikhet and Salomon Tulesa, Alpert worked on the picture story *Twenty-Four Hours in the Life of the Filippov Family*. The photo-essay, published as a cover story in the German weekly *Arbeiter Illustrierte Zeitung* to wide praise in Europe and the United States, covered the life of a metal worker in Moscow's Red Proletarian factory. The influential work was critical in establishing the photo essay as a significant photographic genre and was among the most significant photography projects of its time, touring Vienna, Berlin, and Prague as an exhibition in 1931. The project was organized by editor Lazar Mezhericher as a manifestation of his views as expressed in his article "Serial Photography as the Highest Stage of Photographic Propaganda." The three photographers spent four days with the Filippov family, producing around 80 pictures of Nikolai Filippov and his wife and children; of these, 52 were used in the photo essay.

The images depict specific events in the life of what is claimed to be a typical family, each shot presenting an intelligible narrative which adds to the whole. The series begins with portrayals of the Moscow neighborhood in which the Filippovs live. Contrast is made between the Filippov's previous wooden house and their new and comfortable apartment building by including a miniature shot of their former dwelling. The meaning of such juxtapositions is supported with explanatory texts to show the greatly improved living conditions of working families in the new Soviet society.

Following the presentation of the living environment the photographers present a complete portrait of the family members, each identified by name, as they enjoy a morning tea inside their furnished apartment. This introduction prepares viewers to identify family members as they go about their day on the streetcar, in the factory where the father and son work, in the stores where the mother shops, and in the store where the daughter works. Close-ups of joyful and happy family members portrayed the security Soviet workers felt while photos of the factory and commune showed that such security is only possible through the work of the community.

A year later the essay was analyzed thoroughly in *Proletarskoye Foto* in an article that identified the photo essay as a new art form, similar to film. The enormous success of the Filippov essay made photo stories mandatory. Prominent photo stories that followed included Alexandr Rodchenko's White Sea Canal essay in 1933 and Mark Markov-Grinberg's sequence on the coalminer Nikita Izotov in 1934. The essay form as put forth by Alpert and his colleagues had a powerful impact on photography internationally, providing inspiration for *Life* magazine's founding in 1936. It also proved influential on the works produced by the Farm Security Administration in the United States.

Alpert, along with Arkady Shaikhet, led the Union of Russian Proletarian Photographers (ROPF), which formed in the early 1930s. The photojournalists of ROPF repudiated the experimental manipulation of the October group, the avant-garde agitprop artists as exemplified by Rodchenko. In opposition to the startling angles and crops deployed by these photographers, now commonly called the Constructivists, the realists of ROPF urged straightforward reportage. ROPF rejected notions of art for art's sake and argued that photography pursue a purpose. Content rather than style should be the photographer's primary consideration.

Along with Shaikhet, Alpert offered some of the earliest denunciations of the nonrepresentational works and theories of the October Association photographers, including Rodchenko, Boris Ignatovich, and Elizar Langman. This position eventually garnered official support. In 1931, the Central Committee of the Proletarian Cinematographers and Photographers sanctioned the photographic approach presented in *Twenty Four Hours in the Life of the Filippov Family* as the appropriate model for the proletarianization of Soviet photography.

Alpert's work was displayed at the Exhibition of Works by the Masters of Soviet Photo Art in 1935, the last exhibition to show the vitality and diversity of Soviet photography prior to the institutions of socialist realism. Alpert also exhibited in the First All-Union Exhibition of Photo Art at the State Pushkin Museum in Moscow in 1937. This exhibit signified the closing chapter in post-revolution Soviet innovative photography. At the same time Alpert's images were produced not for galleries or museums but for a mass audience.

During World War II Alpert reported for TASS news agency. As with other Soviet photojournalists of The Great Patriotic War (World War II), few of Alpert's wartime photos were ever shown in galleries. Following the war Alpert worked for the Soviet Information Office and the Novosti Press Agency. He died in 1980.

Jeffrey Shantz

See also: **Agitprop; Photography in Europe: Russia and Eastern Europe; Propaganda; Shaikhet, Arkady; Socialist Photography; Worker Photographer**

Biography

Born in 1899 in Simferopol in the Crimea. Relocated to Odessa; apprentice in a photographic studio, 1914. Red Army service, 1919; a leader of the Red Army's photographic brigade, early 1920s. Joined the Moscow newspaper *Rabochaya Gazeta* 1924–1928. Hired by the newspaper *Pravda*, 1928, worked photographing collectivization of agriculture and construction during the first of Stalin's Five Year Plans. Began work for the magazine *USSR na stroike*; work on photo essay *Twenty-Four Hours in the Life of the Filippov Family*, 1931. Involvement in Union of Russian Proletarian Photographers (ROPF), early 1930s. Correspondent for TASS News Agency, 1941–1945. After the war he worked for the Soviet Information Office and Novosti Press Agency. Died 1980.

Selected Works

Magnitogorskii Zavod, 1929
Viktor Kalmikov on the Train to Magnitogorsk, 1929
A Kulak's Cottage Is Given to a Poor Peasant, 1930
Viktor Kalmikov, 1930
Construction of Magnitogarsk Steelworks, 1930
Viktor Kalmikov at Night School, Magnitogorsk, 1931
Twenty-Four Hours in the Life of the Filippov Family, 1931
Elections to the USSR Supreme Soviet, 1936
View of Dnepro-GES Dam, The Ukraine, 1936
Construction of Fergana Canal, 1939
Three Fergana Canal Workers, 1939
The Line of Fergana Canal Workers, 1939
Workers at Sunrise, 1960

Further Reading

Bakshtein, J. "Russian Photography and Its Contexts." *Art Journal* 53 (1994): 43–44.
Bendavid-Val, Leah. *Propaganda and Dreams: Photographing the 1930s in the USSR and the US*. Zurich: Edition Stemmle, 1999.
Carlisle, Olga. "The Aperture of Memory." *Aperture* 116 (1989): 40–45.
Eerikainen, Hannu. "Up from Underground." *Aperture* 116 (1989): 56–67.
Mihailovic, Alexandar. "Armed only with a Camera: An Interview with Dmitri Baltermants." *Aperture* 116 (1989): 2–6.
Mrazkova, Daniela. "Many Nations, Many Voices." *Aperture* 116 (1989): 24–33.
Reid, Susan. "Photography in the Thaw." *Art Journal* 53 (1994): 33–39.
Sartorti, Rosalinde. "No More Heroic Tractors: Subverting the Legacy of Socialist Realism." *Aperture* 116 (1989): 8–16.
Shudakov, Grigori. *20 Soviet Photographers, 1917–1940*. Amsterdam: Fiolet and Draaijer Interphoto, 1990.
Shudakov, Grigori, Olga Suslova, and Lilya Ukhtomskaya. *Pioneers of Soviet Photography*. New York: Thames and Hudson, 1983.
Tupitsyn, Margaret. "Against the Camera, For the Photographic Archive." *Art Journal* 53 (1994): 58–62.
Tupitsyn, Margaret. *The Soviet Photograph, 1924–1937*. New York: Yale University Press, 1994.
Tupitsyn, Victor. "The Sun Without a Muzzle." *Art Journal* 53 (1994): 80–84.
Welchman, J. "The Photograph in Power: Images from the Soviet Union." *Arts Magazine* 64 (1990): 74–78.

AN AMERICAN PLACE

In the aftermath of the catastrophic stock market crash that ushered in the Great Depression, photographer and curator Alfred Stieglitz opened his last gallery in December 1929. Stieglitz's first gallery, The Little Galleries of the Photo-Secession (known as "291" for its location at 291 Fifth Avenue in New York City) had been open from 1903 to 1917, and during those years, Stieglitz had championed photography as a fine art with exhibitions of American and European photographers and painters that provoked questions about the relationship between media and advanced the cause of an avant-garde aesthetic. During the 1920s, Stieglitz's own photographic production had flourished, inspired by his new relationship with painter Georgia O'Keeffe, and he continued to champion the cause of modern art in America with exhibitions he organized at the Anderson Galleries (1921–1925) and The Intimate Gallery (1925–1929), both in New York City. In these years Stieglitz made some of his best-known works, including his photographs of clouds known as *Equivalents* and his vast portrait of O'Keeffe undertaken over two decades. As the 1929 season at The Intimate Gallery came to a close in May, Stieglitz learned that the building would be demolished. Several colleagues felt strongly that he needed to continue his work as a supporter of American art at a new gallery, and photographer Paul Strand and close friend Dorothy Norman raised funds to rent a space at 509 Madison Avenue that Stieglitz dubbed "An American Place." The light-filled space included five rooms, with white or pale grey walls, and a plain, painted cement floor. The gallery opened on December 7 with an exhibition of new watercolors by John Marin.

At An American Place, Stieglitz maintained and refined the same approach to exhibiting art that had informed his work in the earlier spaces. He disavowed any commercial practices including advertising or promoting the gallery to potential customers. The phone number was not listed in the phonebook and one oft-repeated story involved a woman asking Stieglitz where she might find the gallery he ran, and the photographer responding with a dismissive explanation that he did not run any gallery—clearly he felt the confused woman to be unworthy of the kind of intellectual and spiritual sustenance offered by An American Place. Stieglitz did not profit financially from his role at the gallery. Funds from the sale of works of art went directly to support the artists and to pay the rent. During the 1920s and 1930s, Stieglitz focused his attention on an increasingly small group of American artists, rather than the international artists that he had championed from 1903–1917. The limited season of four to five shows annually at An American Place featured regular exhibitions of new work by painters John Marin, Arthur Dove, and Georgia O'Keeffe; other artists supported at the gallery included Charles Demuth, Paul Strand, and Marsden Hartley. With the opening of the Museum of Modern Art (MoMA) just one month earlier than An American Place, Stieglitz anticipated MoMA's preference for the European avant garde and sought to advocate on behalf of the American artists he had supported since the earliest years of their careers.

Only a handful of photographers had exhibitions at An American Place, but their impact was nevertheless significant, and photography remained an essential element of the American modernist aesthetic advanced by Stieglitz. Soon after Julien Levy opened his new gallery in New York devoted to Surrealist art and photography in the fall of 1931, Stieglitz decided to mount a retrospective of his own work. *127 Photographs (1892–1932) by Alfred Stieglitz* was open from February 15 to March 5, 1932, and featured early images of New York and portraits of colleagues such as Marin and Paul Rosenfeld, as well as *Equivalents*, portraits of Dorothy Norman, portraits of O'Keeffe, and new views of the changing skyline in midtown Manhattan as seen from the windows of An American Place and his apartment at the Shelton Hotel. Just one month later, Stieglitz mounted his final exhibition of work by Paul Strand. This show included images from Strand's driftwood series and views of the New Mexico and Colorado landscape. Their friendship of more than fifteen years, however, was strained and Strand saw less and less relevance in the spiritual formalism advocated by his mentor. After handing in his keys to the gallery at the close of his exhibition, Strand would spend the next decade involved with social-realist and documentary filmmaking. Inspired by the rediscovery of some of his old negatives from the 1880s and 1890s, Stieglitz mounted one final exhibition of his own work in December 1934, to coincide with the publication of the collection of essays, *America and Alfred Stieglitz*.

On March 28, 1933, a new young photographer walked into the gallery and presented his work to Stieglitz. After looking through the portfolio, the senior master welcomed Ansel Adams to An American Place. The two photographers maintained a regular correspondence over the next decade, and the West Coast-based photographer made annual visits to New York to meet with Stieglitz. Stieglitz harbored hopes that Adams might take on the mantle of championing American art and photography at An American Place, but the younger artist would not abandon his connection to the Western landscape. Stieglitz presented Adams's work in a solo show at An American Place in the late fall of 1936. The only other solo exhibition of photographs at An American Place featured the work of Eliot Porter. The December 1938 show included black and white wildlife studies and intimate landscapes. Following his experience at An American Place, the naturalist chose to focus exclusively on his photographic career, eventually producing the spectacular color images of nature for which he is best known.

In the final decade of the gallery, before Stieglitz's death in 1946, photographers continued to visit or correspond with Stieglitz in hopes of some acknowledgement from the elder statesman of their field. László Moholy-Nagy, Walker Evans, and Weegee (Arthur Fellig) all made contact with Stieglitz during these years, and for better or worse, each counted the interaction a significant moment in their development. The final seasons of An American Place were devoted to exhibitions of paintings by O'Keeffe, Dove, and Marin.

RACHEL ARAUZ

See also: **Adams, Ansel; Evans, Walker; Levy, Ansel; Modernism; Moholy-Nagy, László; Museum of Modern Art; Porter, Eliot; Stieglitz, Alfred; Strand, Paul; Weegee**

Further Reading

Frank, Waldo, Lewis Mumford, Dorothy Norman, Paul Rosenfeld, and Harold Rugg, eds. *America & Alfred Stieglitz: A Collective Portrait*. New York: The Literary Guild, 1934.

Greenough, Sarah. *Modern Art and America: Alfred Stieglitz and His New York Galleries*. Washington, DC: National Gallery of Art, 2000.

Hoffman, Michael, and Martha Charoudi. "Spirit of An American Place: An Exhibition of Photographs by Alfred Stieglitz," *Philadelphia Museum of Art Bulletin*, 76 (1981) no. 331.

Newhall, Nancy. *From Adams to Stieglitz: Pioneers of Modern Photography*. New York: Aperture, 1989.

Norman, Dorothy. *Alfred Stieglitz: An American Seer*. New York: Aperture, 1990.

Seligmann, Herbert J. *Alfred Stieglitz Talking*. New Haven: Yale University Library, 1966.

Whelan, Richard. *Alfred Stieglitz A Biography*. New York: Little, Brown and Company, 1995.

APPROPRIATION

Appropriation became one of the most confounding and provocative strategies used by artists during—and since—the 1980s. The medium of photography was integral to this method as the most effective tool to enable artists to take possession of, borrow, steal, or otherwise copy existing imagery, whether drawn from the public domain, the works of other artists, or the general cultural context.

Art historical precedents for the late twentieth century strategy of appropriation included French avant-garde artist Marcel Duchamp's decision to exhibit "readymades" such as his signed urinal entitled *Fountain* beginning in 1913, the Dadaist collages and photomontages of Kurt Schwitters and others, Robert Rauschenberg's use of found objects in his "combine" works of the late 1950s, or the Pop Art and Fluxus movements of the early 1960s, both of which frequently incorporated commercial imagery. Certainly Andy Warhol's landmark photo silkscreens depicting multiple representations of Campbell's Soup cans, Coca-Cola bottles, and Hollywood personalities such as Marilyn Monroe became touchstones for later practitioners of appropriation such as American sculptor Jeff Koons.

Among the most notable artists to emerge in the wake of appropriation were Jack Goldstein, Louise Lawler, Sherrie Levine, Richard Prince, and Cindy Sherman. Each of these artists used photographic techniques that played off photography's ability to represent reality and to create multiple originals, and expanded the definition of fine arts photography. Goldstein (re-)presented brief film clips such as the MGM lion's roar shown on a continuous loop, and Prince enlarged and thereby distorted imagery drawn from magazine advertisements featuring the iconic Marlboro cowboy. Levine critiqued the myth of the great Modernist masterwork in her re-photographic works such as the series *After Walker Evans*. Lawler, who also collaborated early on with Levine, became known for her photographs of works of art as they are displayed in public institutions and private homes. Sherman did not appropriate images as such, but uncannily mimicked the general look of 1950s and 1960s Hollywood films in her disarmingly straightforward 35-mm black-and-white series of *Untitled Film Stills*.

Artists such as Levine found support in the writings of critics such as Douglas Crimp and Hal Foster. Crimp, in his remarks as curator of the 1977 exhibition *Pictures*, made the case that artists were now in explicitly Postmodernist territory, having departed from existing Modernist norms: "Those processes of quotation, excerption, framing and staging that constitute the strategies of the work I have been discussing necessitate uncovering strata of representation... underneath each picture there is always another picture." Meanwhile Foster in his analysis of appropriation commented that "this shift in practice entails a shift in position: the artist becomes a manipulator of signs more than a producer of art objects, and the viewer an active reader of messages rather than a passive contemplator of the aesthetic or consumer of the spectacle."

However painters such as Julian Schnabel and David Salle met with strong market support yet were received coolly by those critics largely unsympathetic to a "return to painting" often perceived as uncritical and market-driven. While Schnabel gained initial renown for applying shattered crockery to the canvas and then covering it partially by thick layers of pigment, and also made reference to artists from Caravaggio to Warhol, others relied strongly on photography. In his paintings Salle incorporated both his own photography and found sources ranging from the art historical to the pornographic. The New York East Village painter Mike Bidlo created meticulous copies of the works of Pablo Picasso and other Modern artists, and by the 1990s he was also photographing staged tableaux based upon works such as Edward Manet's *Olympia* and offering his own direct homages to Duchamp's early readymades. Jean-Michel Basquiat also combined spontaneous and exuberant drawing by hand with photo-silkscreened elements from borrowed sources. Jeff Koons embraced his borrowed imagery in the name of a new pseudo-populist aesthetic. In his quest to please his collectors, he oversaw the replication of stuffed animals, liquor decanters, and posed for photographs using the idioms of advertising, publicity shots, and hardcore pornography.

Sigmar Polke and Gerhard Richter and the Russian émigré duo Komar and Melamid responded to their own specific cultural surroundings. Polke and Richter, both raised in the former German Democratic Republic, or East Germany, created works in the mid 1960s under the heading "Capitalist Realism" and both experimented extensively with photography. Polke manipulated and distorted his photographs technically and incorporated them into his large, nonsensical paintings, while Richter made exquisitely rendered paintings from family and found photographs. Komar and Melamid in their SOTS art appropriated and transformed the iconography and stylistic effects of Socialist Realism, yielding aesthetically seductive and critically incisive results.

The subtle and complex feminist critique evident in the works of Levine, Lawler, and Sherman was proclaimed more boldly in the photomontages of former graphic designer Barbara Kruger, which displayed such slogans as "Your Body is a Battleground." "It's a Small World (but not if you have to clean it)," and "Your Gaze Hits the Side of My Face," presented as bold white typographic statements set into red banners laid over large-scale appropriated images. Jenny Holzer also used fragments of everyday speech and received knowledge in her textual works, most characteristically displayed using moving LED display signs. Other contemporary artists such as the American media artists Dennis Adams and Hans Haacke, the Chilean social activist photographer Alfredo Jaar, and Polish-Canadian public art innovator Krzysztof Wodiczko recontextualized documentary images within gallery installations, light boxes, and slide projections in order to offer pointed political commentary particularly during the Reagan era of the mid-1980s.

Appropriation became a characteristic artistic style of the 1980s, but perhaps as with its contemporaneous movements graffiti and neo-expressionism, its power and influence seemed to initially diminish after a period of overexposure. However in a more positive sense appropriation today has become merely one of a range of Postmodernist tools still actively used by contemporary artists in the context of multidisciplinary works. The general ubiquity of technology in the early twenty-first century, and the widespread use of digital replication and repetition in music, advertising, and film, almost ensures the likelihood that the strategy of incorporating borrowed images will continue unabated in the contemporary art world.

MARTIN PATRICK

See also: **Conceptual Photography; Feminist Photography; History of Photography: 6: the 1980s; Krauss, Rosalind; Kruger, Barbara; Modernism; Postmodernism; Prince, Richard; Rauschenberg, Robert; Representation; Sherman, Cindy; Solomon-Godeau, Abigail**

Further Reading

Baudrillard, Jean. *Simulacra and Simulation*. Ann Arbor: University of Michigan Press, 1995.

Bolton, Richard, ed. *The Contest of Meaning: Critical Histories of Photography*. Cambridge, Massachusetts: MIT Press, 1989.

Crimp, Douglas. *On the Museum's Ruins*. Cambridge, Massachusetts: MIT Press, 1993.

Endgame: Reference and Simulation in Recent Painting and Sculpture, Boston: Institute of Contemporary Art/MIT Press, 1986.

Foster, Hal. *Recodings: Art, Spectacle, Cultural Politics*. Seattle: Bay Press, 1985.

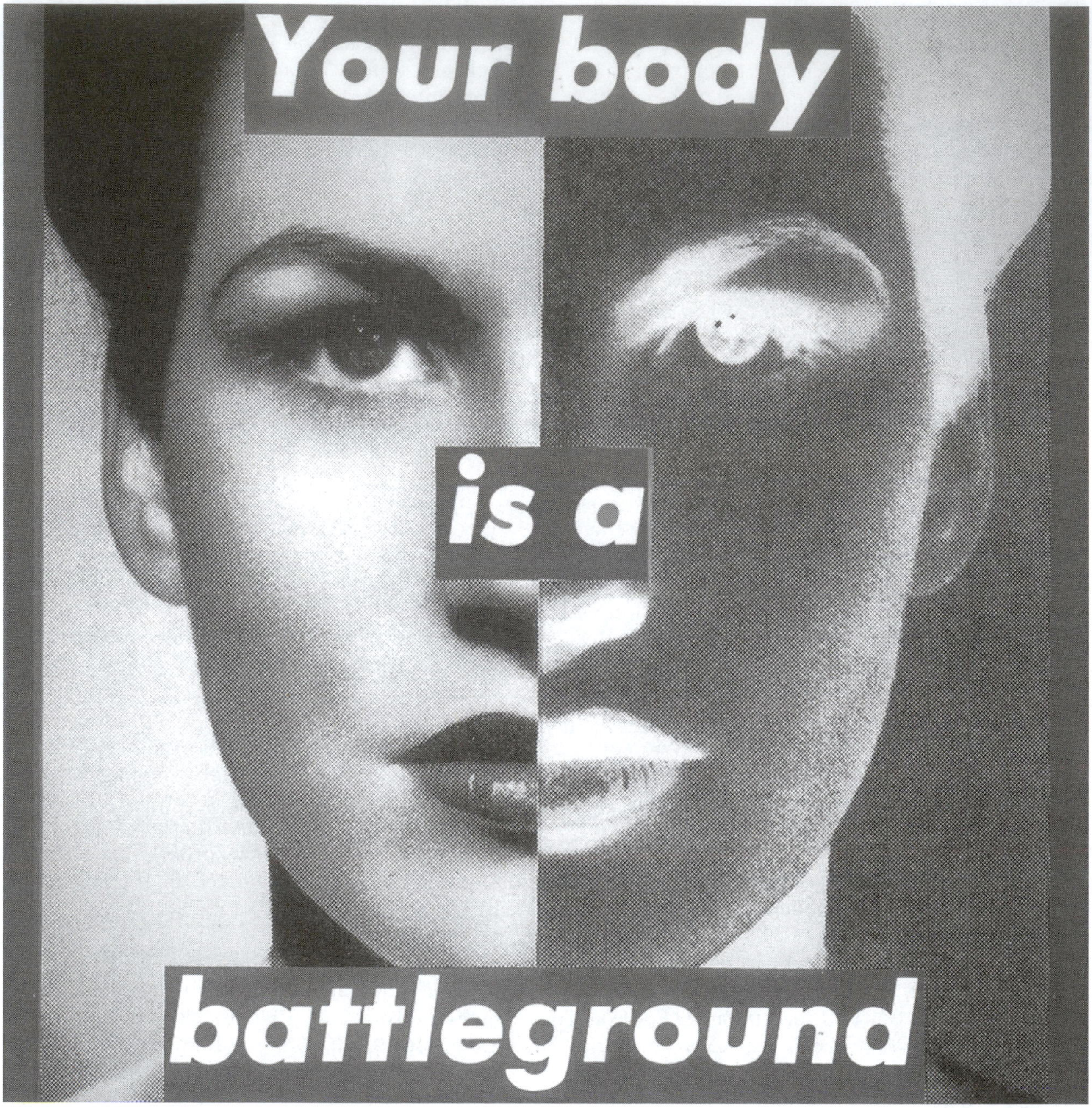

Barbara Kruger, Untitled (your body is a battleground), 1989, photographic silk on vinyl, 112 × 112 ″.
[*BARBARA KRUGER, "Untitled" (Your body is a battleground), 112″ by 112″, photographic silkscreen'vinyl, 1989, © Barbara Kruger. Collection: The Broad Art Foundation, Santa Monica. Courtesy: Mary Boone Gallery, New York*]

Heartney, Eleanor. *Critical Condition: American Culture at the Crossroads*. Cambridge, England: Cambridge University Press, 1997.

Krauss, Rosalind. *The Originality of the Avant-Garde and Other Modernist Myths*. Cambridge, Massachusetts: MIT Press, 1986.

Nagy, Peter, moderator. "From Criticism to Complicity [a discussion with Sherrie Levine, Peter Halley, Jeff Koons, Haim Steinbach, Ashley Bickerton, Philip Taaffe]," *Flash Art*, Summer 1986, 129.

Owens, Craig. *Beyond Recognition: Representation, Power, and Culture*. Berkeley: University of California Press, 1994.

Solomon-Godeau, Abigail. *Photography at the Dock: Essays on Photographic History, Institutions, and Practices.* Minneapolis: University of Minnesota Press, 1994.

Wallis, Brian, ed. *Art after Modernism: Rethinking Representation.* Boston: David R. Godine, 1984.

NOBUYOSHI ARAKI

Japanese

Tokyo-based Japanese photographer Nobuyoshi Araki has gained worldwide notoriety for his candidly erotic pictures. Perhaps the most prolific photographer in the history of the medium, Araki is the author of more than 200 books, and his exhibitions often include thousands of images. A self-styled "photo-maniac," photography is a lifestyle for Araki; he shoots many, sometimes dozens of rolls of film a day. Best known for his voyeuristic, snapshot-style images of women often tied up with ropes (*kinbaku*) and colorful, sensual flowers, Araki has used photography to interpret emotions and experience.

Born in Tokyo, Araki was given a camera at the age of 12 by his father. In 1963, he graduated from the engineering department at Chiba University, majoring in photography and cinema. He went into commercial photography soon after graduating, working at the advertising company Dentsu in 1963. During his nine years there, he also pursued his own projects. In 1964 he received the Taiyo prize for *Satchin* (1963), a black and white photographic series featuring kids from downtown Tokyo, whose title derives from the pet name of a little girl. He exhibited these works and others in his first exhibition in 1965.

In 1970 Araki created the first of his *Xerox photo albums*, which he produced in a limited edition and sent to friends, art critics, and people randomly selected from the phone book. The quality of this early type of photocopy often led to unusual tonal effects in the resulting images. In 1971, he published the privately printed photographic collection *Sentimental Journey (Senchimentaru na tabi)*, in which his personal life, in particular his wedding and honeymoon with Yoko Aoki, was displayed in a diary format. At first glance the images seem to be naïve records but they are in fact staged. *Sentimental Journey* established Araki's reputation, and in 1972 he left Dentsu and became a freelance photographer. Since then, almost all his works have revolved around his own life, and are almost always about the women who are close to him.

Stylistically, Araki has never been a purist. He works in black and white and color, using cibachrome as well as color photocopies for their garishness and artificiality; he uses natural light and hard flash. Araki has also employed many experimental techniques and processes including collage, montage, solarization, and hand-applied color, including paint (one series presents paint dripped onto close-up images of vaginas). He also works with negatives that are damaged or decayed, and scratches into the emulsion on finished prints, such as in a series where he scratched out the genitals on nudes. He juxtaposes snapshots with studio photos, portraits, and street scenes, and still lifes with hardcore pornography. He photographs voraciously, from the female body to food to cats. Araki works primarily with a Pentax 6 × 7 format camera, dating the resulting prints to register them in time; in his ongoing *Tokyo diaries* Araki uses a camera that automatically prints the date on the image. Reflecting the nature of how he shoots, his work is presented and is best understood in the context of the series.

Araki's work is paradoxical in that it is subjective and yet makes no claim to photographic truth; he often appears in scenes containing sexual activity, yet one of his best known images is a self-portrait wearing his recently deceased wife's pink coat, gripping a large black-and-white framed portrait of her. For Araki, an everyday street scene may become transformed into a setting of intimate revelation. Particularly preoccupied with female sexuality, Araki attempts to become more intimate with women through photography, claiming the ropes he uses replicate an embrace. However critics argue that the photographer's objectification of his subject limits if not precludes emotional connection and hence empathy, creating in effect, images void of intimacy. Similarly to Goldin and Joel-Peter Witkin, who also work with erotic imagery, Araki's work seeks to balance the sublime and the obscene; it is at once shocking and mysteriously tender. Over the years, his bold, unabashed photographs have been the object of censorship, especially in his native Japan, a fact that has not diminished his influence. Series have included images of gagged and tied women wearing the traditional dress of the kimono, on *tatami* mats in a *riyokan* (Japanese inn). Although the women are often restrained and silenced, the Japanese art of rope-tying, *kinbaku*, differs from Western style bondage. Araki's images are also heir to the Japanese tradition of erotic art, especially *Shunga*, the erotic painting from the Edo period. They combine ecstasy and death, a passion for life and a melancholy awareness of the finiteness of life.

Flowers have featured in several of Araki's projects of the 1990s and are appropriate subjects for his fusion of eros and death. Araki's photographs make explicit that flowers are reproductive organs and emblems of the consummation of love. However, Araki's flower studies are hardly sentimental; the flowers petals are often painted with garish colors and seem past their prime.

The city of Tokyo is another of Araki's chosen subjects although he claims only an interest in the urban areas he frequents and knows well, such as Shinjuku, Tokyo's entertainment district with its nightclubs, strip joints, and seedy hotels. People often seem sad and lonely in Araki's Tokyo. He claims that "photography is synonymous with what relates to me. I don't go somewhere simply to take photographs."

Araki has edited most of his own books, and has gained a strong and growing following in the United States and Europe. He has formed friendships with other great photo-diarists such as Robert Frank and Nan Goldin, and in 1995 Araki published a book with Goldin (*Tokyo Love*). He has also delved into stylized fashion photography. In 2002, the German publisher Taschen released a lavish tribute to Araki's work—an enormous and unique (numbered and signed) book featuring 1000 images, with a print run of only 2500 copies. In 2003 the photographer published *Araki by Araki: The Photographer's Personal Selection 1963–2002*—the most comprehensive collection of his work, gathering images from each year.

DANIEL PALMER

See also: **Erotic Photography; Goldin, Nan; Photography in Japan**

Biography

Born Tokyo, Japan, May 25 1940. Graduated from Engineering Department of Chiba University with a major in Photography and Filmmaking, 1963. Started work at Dentsu advertising company, 1963. Received prize for *Satchin*, a collection of photographs, 1964. First exhibition, 1965. Privately published *Sentimental Journey*, 1971. Left Dentsu in 1972 to work as a freelancer. Helped found the Workshop School of Photography, 1974. Opened the Nobuyoshi Araki School, 1976. Formed the Araki Limited Stock Company, 1981. Established Photo Clinic, 1982. Established AT Room, 1988. Lives and works in Tokyo, Japan.

Selected Individual Exhibitions

1965 *Satchin and Mabo*, Shinjuku Station Building, Tokyo, Japan
1966 *Subway*, Mitsubishi Denki Gallery, Tokyo, Japan
1967 *Ginza*, Mitsubishi Denki Gallery, Tokyo, Japan
1973 *Flowers in Ruins*, Shimizu Gallery, Tokyo, Japan
1976 *Yoko, My Love*, Nikon Salon, Tokyo, Japan
1984 *A World of Girls*, Zeit-Photo Salon, Tokyo, Japan
1986 *Araki's Tokyo Erotomania Diary*, Zeit-Photo Salon, Tokyo, Japan
1987 *Arakism: 1967–1987*, Zeit-Photo Salon, Tokyo, Japan
1990 *Towards Winter: Tokyo, A City Heading for Death*, Egg Gallery, Tokyo, Japan
Tokyo Lucky Hole, Apt Gallery, Tokyo, Japan
1993 *Erotos*, Parco Gallery, Tokyo, Japan
1995 *Journale Intime*, Fondation Cartier pour l'art contemporain, Paris, France

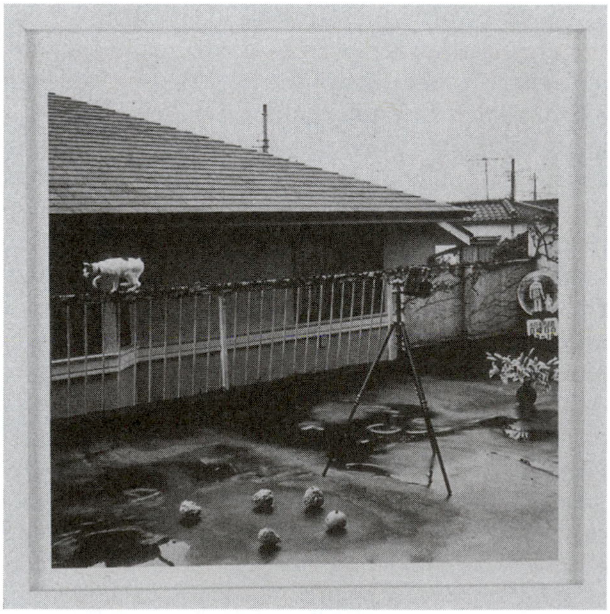

Noboyoshi Araki, Tokyo Cube #102.
[*Collection Museum of Contemporary Art, Chicago, partial and promised gift from the Howard and Donna Stone Collection, Photograph © Museum of Contemporary Art, Chicago, © Nobuyoshi Araki, Courtesy of Yoshiko Isshiki Office*]

1997 *Tokyo Comedy*, Wiener Secession, Vienna, Austria
2000 *Viaggio Sentimentale*, Centro per l'Arte Contemporanea Luigi Pecci, Prato, Italy
2002 *Araki Nobuyoshi: Hana-Jinsei*, Kyoto Museum of Contemporary Art, Kyoto, Japan
2002 *Nobuyoshi Araki: Tokyo Still Life*, Helsinki City Art Museum, Helsinki, Finland

Selected Group Exhibitions

1971 *The 10th Contemporary Art Exhibition of Japan*, Tokyo Metropolitan Art Museum, Tokyo, Japan
Japan *15 Photographers*, The National Museum of Modern Art, Tokyo, Japan
1977 *Neue Fotografie aus Japan*, Graz City Museum, Graz, Austria
1979 *Japan: A Self-Portrait*, International Center of Photography, New York, New York
1989 *Tokyo: A City Perspective*, Tokyo Metropolitan Museum of Photography, Tokyo, Japan
1991 *Japanese Photography in the 1970s*, Tokyo Metropolitan Museum of Photography, Tokyo, Japan
1994 *Liquid Crystal Futures: Contemporary Japanese Photography*, The Fruitmarket Gallery, Edinburgh, Scotland
2001 *Facts of Life: Contemporary Japanese Art*, Hayward Gallery, London, England
Open City: Street Photographs Since 1950, Oxford: Museum of Modern Art Oxford, England

Selected Works (Books)

Satchin, 1963
Sentimental Journey (Senchimentaru na tabi), 1971
The Camera Between Men and Women (Otoko to onna no aida ni wa shashinki ga aru), 1977
Yoko, My Love (Waga'ai Yoko), 1978
Tokyo Elegy (Tokyo ereji), 1981
World of Girls (Shojo sekai), 1984
Tokyo Autumn (Tokyo wa aki), 1984
Tokyo Story, 1989
Towards Winter: Tokyo, A City Heading for Death, 1990
Sentimental Journey/Winter Journey, 1991
Tokyo Love, with Nan Goldin, 1995
Naked Faces, 1996
Obscenities and Strange Black Ink Stories, 1997
Tokyo Luck Hole, 1997
Tokyo Comedy, 1997
Flowers, 1998
Tokyo Nostalgia, 1999
Sentimental Photography, Sentimental Life, 1999

Futher Reading

Araki, Nobuyoshi. *Araki by Araki: The Photographer's Personal Selection 1963–2002*. Tokyo: Kodansha International, 2003.
Araki, Nobuyoshi. *Shikijyo: Sexual Desire*. Text by Jean-Christophe Ammann, Peter Weiermair, and Mario Kramer. Zurich: Edition Stemmle, 1997.
Brougher, Kerry, and Russell Ferguson. *Open City: Street Photographs Since 1950*. Oxford: Museum of Modern Art Oxford, 2001.
Grosenick, Uta, and Burkhard Riemschneider, eds. *Art at the Turn of the Millennium*. Köln: Taschen, 1999.
Sans, Jérôme. "Araki Interviewed by Jérôme Sans." In *Araki*. Zurich: Taschen, 2003.

DIANE ARBUS

American

Diane Arbus, whose singular, often shocking portraits emerged among the most iconic and modern images of the 1960s, famously wrote in 1971, "A photograph is a secret about a secret. The more it tells you the less you know" (Arbus 1971, 64). Although Arbus's quote reveals her skepticism toward the common assumption that photography tells the truth—in other words, that it is a visually accurate medium—her work has nonetheless been linked to the documentary photographic tradition. By the late 1950s American photographers in particular began to register their discontent with the prevailing photographic conventions that focused on formalism or "fine art" aesthetics. Photojournalism—including the role it played in larger cultural upheavals, such as Vietnam, the civil rights and women's movements—emerged as a viable mode of photography. Moreover, the role of the photographer in relation to his or her subject came under scrutiny. Post-World War II figures such as Lee Friedlander, Garry Winogrand, Danny Lyon, Bruce Davidson, and Arbus, among others, pointed their cameras toward the common, everyday, and often ugly realities of urban existence and the individual subject. Their vernacular approach, which actually borrowed from both the fine art and documentary traditions, came to be described as the snapshot aesthetic. These pictures of the so-called "social landscape" were often captured quickly using portable 35-mm cameras, often on the street. They appeared to be casually composed (if at all), incorporating movement and happenstance. Critics and historians of photography such as Nathan Lyons and John Szarkowski attempted to describe this fresh development that brought greater, self-conscious creativity to the objective and socially conscious picture.

A formative exhibition that introduced the notion of social landscape photography was *New Documents: Diane Arbus, Lee Friedlander, Garry Winogrand* (1967), organized by Szarkowski at the Museum of Modern Art in New York. Head of the museum's photography department from 1962 to 1991, Szarkowski's wide-ranging and groundbreaking exhibitions helped place photography within the company of painting and sculpture in the art museum and beyond. *New Documents* heralded a nascent age in a photography that emphasized the pathos and conflicts of modern life presented without editorializing or sentimentalizing but with a critical, observant eye. Szarkowski saw in these three artists a shift in the documentary approach, traced through Walker Evans, which incorporated deeply personal ends. He wrote in the Museum's wall panel, "Their aim has been not to reform life, but to know it. Their work betrays a sympathy—almost an affection—for the imperfections and frailties of society (Szarkowski quoted in *Diane Arbus Revelations* 2003, 51).

Arbus's affinity for imperfection and frailty is today legendary, making her role in this sea-change historically relevant. Yet her oeuvre is also distinct and virtually unique in her generation for its emphasis on portraiture in its classical sense. Unlike the loose and cropped compositions of her peers, who often captured fleeting images and moments, Arbus's photographs relied upon an established relationship of some sort between the sitter and the photographer. In other words, Arbus's process intimately involved the subject, who was usually posed, and always remained cognizant of the photographer's presence. While the pictures may appear candid, they were more often than not painstakingly composed with an emphasis on visual narrative and description. Her talents lie in her uncanny ability to communicate something distinct, private, and mutable about her subjects' personalities, fantasies, or experiences, what she called "the gap between intention and effect" (Arbus 1972, 1–2). Drawn to the power of myth and self-invention, Arbus's titles reflected this interest in telling a story about her subjects: *A family on their lawn one Sunday in Westchester, N. Y.* (1968), *Man at a parade on Fifth Avenue, N.Y.C.* (1969), *A Jewish giant at home with his parents in the Bronx, N.Y.* (1970), and *Child with a toy hand grenade in Central Park, N.Y.C.* (1962). This narrative approach is related to the context in which the images were first seen—primarily in the pages of popular magazines where they appeared as photo essays.

Diane Nemerov Arbus's photographic career began as a commercial one in which she partnered with her husband Allan Arbus. The couple ran a successful commercial studio in New York City, and their work appeared regularly in *Glamour* and other magazines. Diane generally devised the concepts and designed and styled the shots, while Allan worked behind the camera; she learned from him how to develop film and print negatives in the makeshift darkroom that was the couple's bathroom. She simultaneously took her own pictures, using a 35-mm Nikon to photograph people, often those characters she met on the street. The Arbuses worked together from about 1941 to 1956 when Diane quit the business to pursue her own photography fulltime; she pursued editorial assignments in order to pay for more creative, personal work.

In 1959 she earned her first commissioned photo essay, ostensibly about the vagaries of urban life in New York City for *Esquire* magazine. Titled *The Vertical Journey: Six Movements of a Moment Within the Heart of the City*, the portfolio included portraits as disparate as a side-show performer known as *The Jungle Creep*, who appeared in Hubert's Museum of eccentrics in Times Square to an honorary regent in the Washington Heights chapter of the Daughters of the American Revolution. She went on to publish more than 250 pictures in *Harper's Bazaar*, *Esquire*, the *Sunday Times Magazine* of London, and elsewhere. Other photo essays included *The Auguries of Innocence* (*Harper's Bazaar*, December 1963), *The Soothsayers—What's New: The Witch Predicts* (*Glamour*, January and October 1964), and *People Who Think They Look like Other People* (*Nova*, October 1969). Arbus generally wrote extensive text captions for the essays' images. She approached her personal work in much the same manner.

Although Arbus's most famous subjects were outsiders such as transvestites, strippers, carnival performers, nudists, dwarves, and other assorted "freaks," she was equally drawn to the prosaic in subjects as ordinary as children, mothers, couples, old people, and the like. She photographed her subjects in familiar settings: their homes, on the street, in the workplace, in the park. While the environmental setting often provides description as to the sitter's personality or life, it does not distract from the matter at hand, namely the poignancy or intensity of the interaction between Arbus and her subject.

She admired and was influenced by the typologies of August Sander, whose assorted shopkeepers, industrial workers, peasants, artists, as well as social outcasts reflected archetypes the photographer found within his own milieu—Germany in the 1920s and 1930s. She shared with Sander a breadth of iconography and a sympathy with subjects presented without romanticism. Her nearly archeological interest in social mores and milieus is evidenced in her project proposal for a 1963 Guggenheim Grant. Titled *American Rites, Manners and Customs*, she sought to depict a range of social ceremonies, including beauty pageants, games and competitions, costumes, parties, and the like. Arbus called these ceremonies "our symptoms and our moments. I want to save them, for what is ceremonious and curious and commonplace will be legendary" (Arbus quoted in *Diane Arbus Revelations* 41). She won this grant and received a second one from the Guggenheim in 1966. Arbus's photography also bears the influence of her teacher, Austrian-born Lisette Model, who also photographed for *Harper's Bazaar* and whose expressive images monumentalize their human, often quirky, subjects.

In order to achieve sharper, less grainy images, Arbus had abandoned the 35-mm format by 1963 for a wide-angle Rolleiflex and later a Mamiyaflex camera, each of which produced 2-¼" square negatives. A photographer held the 2-¼ cameras at waist-level, looking down, which slowed down the process of picture-making considerably. This format was in keeping with her prolonged portrait sittings. In addition, the wide angle of her first Rolleiflex created a slight warping of the contents of the frame, lending a subtle skewing of the composition that enhanced the psychological effect of the picture. As early as 1965 she began printing her pictures with the irregular, black borders that showed the entire, uncropped negative. These borders (also used in Richard Avedon's portraits) called attention to the fact that the image was constructed on a two-dimensional surface rather than a window-like view to the subject. Typical of the 1960s documentary aesthetic, Arbus's use of the negative borders put stress upon the subjectivity of the photographer and her vision. Arbus's portraits search the *surface* of people, their facades, costumes, eccentricities, and her direct, frontal compositions reflect this. However, penetrating vision often points to a hidden psychology, or at least the traces of the vulnerabilities that lie beneath this surface.

Historians have noted the potency, and discomfort, associated with Arbus's seemingly voyeuristic iconography, especially in relation to the viewer. Arbus was intently aware of the role she played in relation to her subjects, including any responsibility she might have for or to them. Because she recognized that the pictures were the result of an often passionate, emotional investment in her subjects, she was careful to temper this with aesthetic deliberation and dispassion. This complex intertwining of roles—between photographer and subject, photographer and viewer, and subject and viewer—reveals Arbus's masterful understanding of empathy moderated by critical distance (Phillips, *Diane Arbus Revelations* 59). The gravitas of her work, in fact, lay in this acute, triangular relationship linking photographer, subject, and viewer. It represented a rather early understanding of image theory that would later inform much of postmodern photography.

In keeping with Arbus's interest in subcultures, in 1969 she began photographing at a home for the mentally retarded in New Jersey. These images remain mysterious glimpses into the photographer's subjective mindset as well as beautifully poignant representations that seem to waver on the line between what is normal and abnormal. Arbus's care to show her subjects as individuals—without exploitation or editorializing—was reflected in the seriousness of this personal project, for which she had to seek extensive permissions. Most of the photographs from this series were posthumously printed and titled (as *Untitled* images). In her notebooks of the time she detailed the various residents by name, often describing particular interactions on a given day. The work was edited by her daughter Doon Arbus and published in 1995 (Arbus, *Untitled* 1995).

That same year she self-produced a limited edition portfolio of museum-quality prints titled *A Box of Ten Photographs* (dated 1970). The prints were displayed in a minimalist, elegant, clear box that doubled as a framing device, designed by her friend Marvin Israel. The collection of photographs—all of which related to the family—as well as their presentation represented a conscious statement about how she viewed herself as an artist and her photography (Phillips, *Diane Arbus Revelations* 66). The portfolio included several images from *New Documents* and five that had been published in *Artforum*, May 1971. She advertised the sale of the portfolio in *Artforum* magazine; only four sets sold in her lifetime, one to the artist Jasper Johns.

At the time of her death by suicide in 1971 (she had suffered from depression throughout her adult life), Arbus's photography was not widely exhibited in museums and galleries, although it would prove to be instrumental in the artistic reexamination of photography within American museums, where the medium would assume a sure and stable place during Szarkowski's tenure. Although Arbus had serious reservations about displaying her pictures in museum exhibitions, where she feared her intentions might be misunderstood, her work has retained a vital and major place within the history of photography.

LYNN M. SOMERS-DAVIS

See also: **Documentary Photography; Model, Lisette; Street Photography; Szarkowski, John; Winogrand, Garry**

Biography

Born Diane Nemerov, New York City, March 14, 1923 to Gertrude and David Nemerov. Her wealthy family of Russian-Jewish descent owned Russek's, a fashionable Fifth Avenue department store. Married Allan Arbus against parents' wishes in 1941. Brother was Howard Nemerov, Pulitzer-prize winning poet and U.S. Poet Laureate in 1988. Daughter Doon Arbus born 1945; daughter Amy Arbus born in 1954. With husband opened fashion photography studio ("Diane and Allan Arbus"), 1946. Attended first photography course in mid-1950s with Alexey Brodovitch at New School for Social Research, New York City; studied with Lisette Model at the New School, 1956–1958. Quit the business in 1956 to pursue her own work, garnering assignments for *Esquire*, *Harper's Bazaar*, and the London *Sunday Times Magazine*. The Arbuses separated amicably, 1959; that year Diane began keeping notebooks of her writings with ideas for pictures and other interests. By early 1960s discovered Hubert's Museum (flea circus in Times Square) and Club 82 (a female-impersonator club in downtown Manhattan); revisited these sites extensively to photograph. Met Walker Evans through Marvin Israel, 1962. Received first Guggenheim Fellowship for *American Rites, Manners and Customs*, 1963; second Guggenheim Fellowship for *The Interior Landscape*, 1966. Began teaching at Parsons School of Design, New York City. Included in MoMA exhibition *New Documents*, 1967. Hired by John Szarkowski at Museum of Modern Art, New York, to research exhibition on news photography, *From the Picture Press*, 1969–1970. Produced with Marvin Israel a limited edition portfolio of 10 photographs (*A Book of Ten Photographs*), 1969–1970; published *Five Photographs by Diane Arbus*, *Artforum*, May 1971. Taught a private master class at Westbeth, the artists' cooperative housing where she lived, 1971. Died by suicide in her New York City home, July 28, 1971. Subject of posthumous retrospective at Museum of Modern Art, New York, with accompanying monograph *Diane Arbus* (1972).

Individual Exhibitions

Note: Arbus's sparse exhibition history and the relative lack of scholarship on her is due in part to the control The Estate of Diane Arbus has maintained over her work including exhibitions and reproductions of it.

1972 *Diane Arbus*; Museum of Modern Art, New York, New York, and traveling retrospective

2003 *Diane Arbus: Family Albums*; Mount Holyoke College Art Museum, South Hadley, Massachusetts, and traveling

2004 *Diane Arbus Revelations*; San Francisco Museum of Modern Art; San Francisco, California; traveling to Los Angeles County Museum of Art, Los Angeles, California; Museum of Fine Arts, Houston, Texas; Metropolitan Museum of Art, New York, New York; Museum Folkwang, Essen, Germany; Victoria and Albert Museum, London, England; and Walker Art Center, Minneapolis, Minnesota

Selected Group Exhibitions

1955 With Allan Arbus. *The Family of Man*; Museum of Modern Art, New York, New York

1965 *Recent Acquisitions: Photography*; Museum of Modern Art, New York, New York

Invitational Exhibition: 10 American Photographers; School of Fine Arts, University of Wisconsin, Milwaukee, Wisconsin

1967 *New Documents: Diane Arbus, Lee Friedlander, Garry Winogrand*; Museum of Modern Art, New York, New York

1969 *Thirteen Photographers*; Pratt Institute, Brooklyn, New York

Human Concern/Personal Torment: The Grotesque in American Art; Whitney Museum of American Art, New York, New York

New Photography U.S.A.; Museum of Modern Art, New York, New York, and traveling

10 Photographers; U.S. Pavilion, Japan World Exhibition, Osaka, Japan

1971 *Contemporary Photographs I*; Fogg Art Museum, Harvard University, Cambridge, Massachusetts

Venice Biennale, Venice, Italy

1977 *Mirrors and Windows: American Photography since 1960*; Museum of Modern Art, New York, New York

1989 *On the Art of Fixing a Shadow: One Hundred and Fifty Years of Photography*; National Gallery of Art, Washington, D.C., and Art Institute of Chicago, Chicago, Illinois, and traveling to Los Angeles County Museum of Art, Los Angeles, California

Photography Until Now; Museum of Modern Art, New York, New York, and traveling to the Cleveland Museum of Art, Cleveland, Ohio

2003 *Cruel and Tender: The Real in the Twentieth-Century Photograph*; Tate Modern, London, England

Selected Works

Headless Man, N.Y.C., 1961

Child with a toy hand grenade in Central Park, N.Y.C., 1962

A house on a hill, Hollywood, California, 1962

The Junior Interstate Ballroom Dance Champions, Yonkers, N.Y., 1963

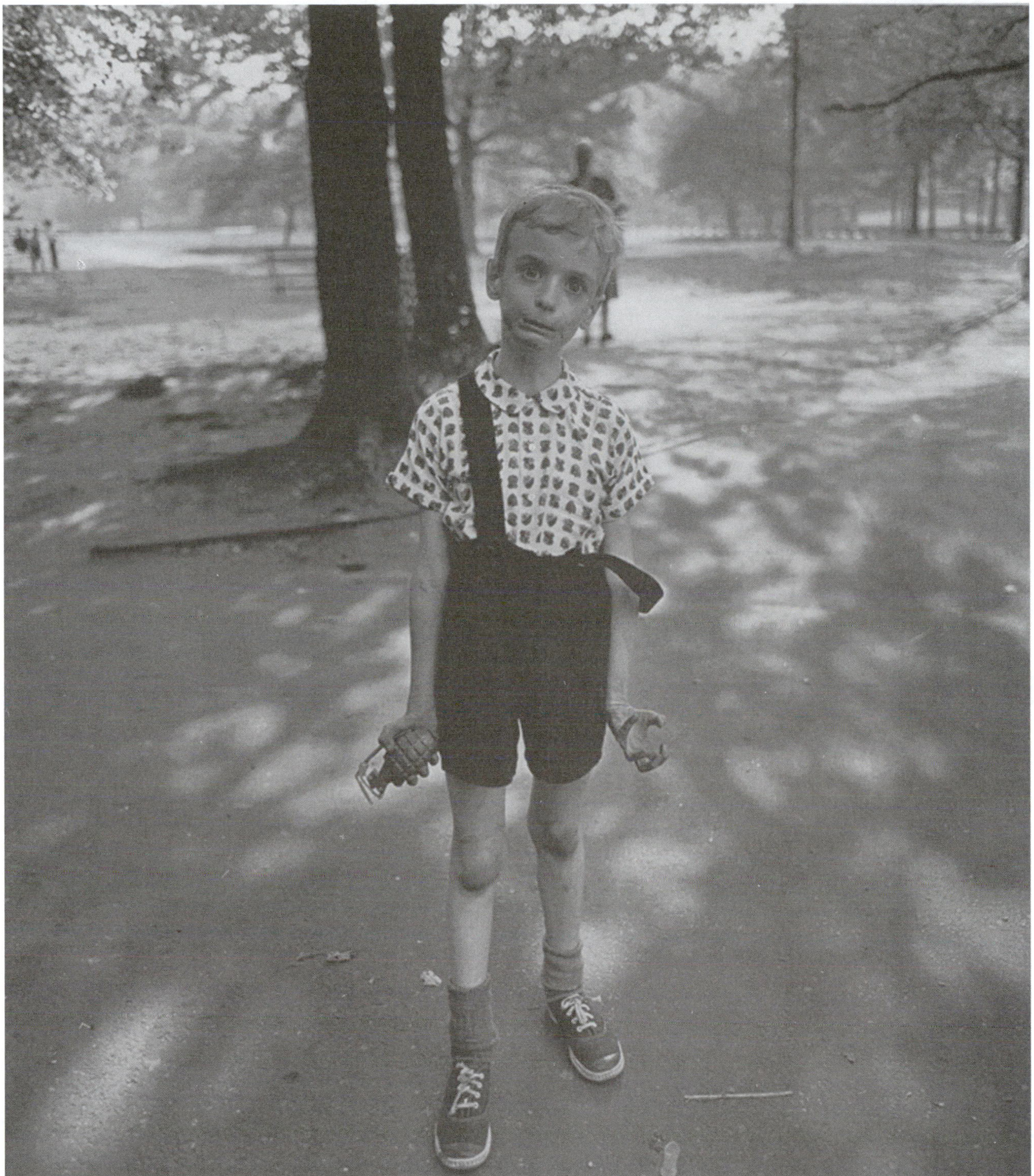

Diane Arbus, Child with toy hand grenade, New York, New York, 1962, Gelatin-silver print, 7 ¼ × 8 ⅜″.
[*Digital Image © The Museum of Modern Art/Licensed by SCALA/Art Resource, NY*]

Teenage couple on Hudson Street, N.Y.C., 1963
A young man in curlers at home on West 20th Street, N.Y.C., 1966
A family on their lawn one Sunday in Westchester, N.Y., 1968
A naked man being a woman, N.Y.C., 1968

Man at a parade on Fifth Avenue, N.Y.C., 1969
A Jewish giant at home with his parents in the Bronx, N.Y., 1970
The King and Queen of a Senior Citizens' Dance, N.Y.C., 1970
Mexican dwarf in his hotel room, N.Y.C., 1970

Further Reading

Arbus, Diane. *Diane Arbus: An Aperture Monograph*. Millerton, New York: Aperture, 1972.

Arbus, Diane. *Diane Arbus: Untitled*. Edited by Doon Arbus and Yolanda Cuomo, afterword by Doon Arbus. Millerton, New York: Aperture, 1995.

Arbus, Diane, and Thomas Southall. *Diane Arbus: Magazine Work*. Edited by Doon Arbus and Marvin Israel. Millerton, New York: Aperture, 1984.

Arbus, Diane. "Five Photographs by Diane Arbus." *Artforum* (May 1971).

Armstrong, Carol. "Biology, Destiny, Photography: Difference According to Diane Arbus." *October* 66 (Fall 1993).

Bosworth, Patricia. *Diane Arbus: A Biography*. New York: Alfred A. Knopf, 1984, reprinted in 1995 by W. W. Norton.

Decarlo, Tessa. "A Fresh Look at Arbus." *Smithsonian* (May 2004).

Diane Arbus Revelations. Essays by Sandra S. Phillips, Neil Selkirk, chronology by Elisabeth Sussman and Doon Arbus, afterword by Doon Arbus, (Exhibition catalogue). San Francisco and New York: San Francisco Museum of Modern Art, Random House, and The Estate of Diane Arbus LLC, 2003.

Goldman, Judith. "Diane Arbus: The Gap Between Intention and Effect." *Art Journal* v. 34, no. 1 (Fall 1974).

Hirsch, Robert. *Seizing the Light: A History of Photography*. New York: McGraw Hill, 2000.

Lee, Anthony. W., and John Pultz. *Diane Arbus: Family Albums*. New Haven and London: Yale University Press, 2003.

Lord, Catherine. "What Becomes a Legend Most: The Short, Sad Career of Diane Arbus: Part I." *Exposure* v. 23, no. 3 (Fall 1985).

Rosenblum, Naomi. *A History of Women Photographers*. New York: Abbeville Press, 2000.

ARCHITECTURAL PHOTOGRAPHY

Architectural Photography is the representation of architecture in images. This includes the depiction of buildings and interiors in photographs, but also comprises the reproduction of designs, the depiction of architectural models, the participation in preservation campaigns, and all forms of journalistic imagery for magazines and newspapers. This genre of photography has wide commercial and industrial application, as well as a long tradition as a fine-arts practice. Architectural Photography is a tool for architects as well as for construction and development companies to advertise their services or product. For industries that manufacture components such as windows, doors, tiles, or drain pipes, the attractive, yet accurate rendering of the items provides a valuable shorthand reference.

Throughout its history, Architectural Photography has been as important in interpreting architectural design as in criticizing political approaches represented in buildings and constructions. Architectural Photography has also shaped architectural design itself through its pedagogical uses. Indeed, since the invention of photography in the mid-nineteenth century, Architectural Photography has been of primary importance to instruct architects-in-training as well as historians and others interested in the field. This included some of the technical derivations of Architectural Photography such as photogrammetry and (aerial) topogrammetic photography.

Architectural Photography may not have been more than just another aspect of the commercial and industrial use of photography if it had not been for the work of Eugène Atget. Atget linked the nineteenth and the twentieth centuries, both in his choice of subjects and in his stylistic approach. A frantic collector of edifices and details, who was especially attentive to situations that ordinarily might be overlooked, within three decades working on his own, he produced a grand oeuvre in Architectural Photography. This treasure trove was not widely known until it was discovered toward the end of Atget's life in the 1920s by the Parisian avant-gardists. The Americans Man Ray and his then-assistant Berenice Abbott were instrumental in bringing Atget's work to the attention of the New York fine arts and publishing world. The latter figure followed Atget's lead by amassing an extraordinary portfolio of architectural photographs of New York in the 1930s. At about the same time Walker Evans contributed his unique, intimate approach to architectural subjects. With Abbott and Evans, a firm tradition of Architectural Photography was established that concentrated on the accumulation of large numbers of images, especially of vernacular architecture. Abbott's example was followed by photographers such as Chicago-based Harold Allen and Clemens Kalischer, whereas Evans found followers throughout the American continent, notably Wright Morris and David Plowden, who used a panoramic camera to capture wide sections of the built environment.

One subgenre within architectural documentation of the late nineteenth and early twentieth centuries had social purposes as well. Before 1900, a number of authors and social reformers had outlined the effects of living conditions on health and criminal activity, and photographers soon took up the cry. Thomas Annan photographed the old closes of Glasgow in the 1860s, Jacob Riis worked for city authorities in New York in the 1890s, and Lewis Hine's seminal photographs of New York City tenements were taken for the Red Cross from 1910 to 1930. The Berliner Hermann Lichte photographed for the Prussian health insurance industry around 1913, and anonymous colleagues were commissioned for similar work in the German cities of Kassel and Heidelberg. Many of these photographs were taken with small format cameras and flash and captured candid images of families living in neglected, rundown tenements in squalor and misery. Most of the architecture shown in these series had been erected in the nineteenth century, and it was the clear intention of both the photographers and their patrons that these buildings were to be dismantled as soon as possible. This application of Architectural Photography thus had the function of destroying the past and making way for future structures. These socially concerned series were part of the emergence of modernism, with Architectural Photography, changing its functions and form as did architecture itself.

In the realm of architectural practice, photography proves that a design has been executed, a building has been erected, or a bridge constructed. This documentation is now an integral part of the business practice of architects. One of the earliest architects to exist on private commissions and run a modern, professional office was the Beaux Arts architect Henry Hobson Richardson of Boston, Massachusetts. He was scrupulous in hiring the best photographers of his time. These images were not only used for covering the walls of his office and impressing prospective clients, but Richardson also arranged to have them reproduced in architectural magazines—at his own cost—in one of the earliest appearances of Architectural Photography as a public relations strategy. The photographs Richardson commissioned focused primarily on the idea of the building, often showing a small but representative detail that best depicted his architectural and design ideas. To accentuate the building itself, when possible, Richardson set his structures on small hills so they had to be approached from a lower level, dominating and further impressing the viewer. He instructed his photographers to duplicate and even accentuate this experience in their photographs, creating portraits of his building more than strict documents.

This method of depiction was taken up and promulgated, somewhat ironically, when the Arts-and-Crafts movement spread through the United Kingdom and Central Europe around 1900. Although architects such as Charles Robert Ashbee, William Richard Lethaby, Mackay Hugh Baillie Scott, and Charles F.A. Voysey rejected any connection to the Beaux Arts school in architecture, they asked their photographers to set up their shots not only utilizing a low viewpoint, but using the raking light available when the sun was low on the horizon early in the morning or late in the day, or by photographing on a day when the sky was filled with dark clouds. It was at this time that Architectural Photography became a profession in its own right, and when some architects themselves took up photography, the two professions merged. Important photographs have been made by architect-photographers. Heinrich Rückwardt of Berlin, published his *Architectural Details* as portfolios in enormous sizes—up to 60 × 80 cm—from 1895 onwards, with a great number of photographers following his lead, each developing a different approach to documenting buildings both new and old.

Among the important architectural photographers around 1900 are Francis B. Johnston and Henry Bedford Lemere, who served as propagandists of the Arts and Crafts movement. Both operated throughout the United Kingdom and had well-known workshops in the vicinity of London. Although there is no typical stylistic approach in their work, it is clear that both leaned more toward the clear and straightforward designs of Charles Rennie Mackintosh than the wealth of detail characteristic of the work of other designers and architects of the era. Instigated by books and reports on English architecture, Italian, French, and German photographers such as Mauricio Lotze, Michel Neurdein, and Waldemar Titzenthaler began to produce portfolios of interesting interiors and other series for the illustrated papers; some of them cooperated with well known architects by providing them not only with pictures of their edifices but with historical material as well. Similar to the work of their English counterparts, the presentation of architecture by these early twentieth century figures was meant to educate and refine the sensibilities of the increasing number of wealthy clients who had made their fortune in the late nineteenth century.

In the years shortly before World War I, modernism made its way to the public via Architectural Photography. European architects such as Le Corbusier, Walter Gropius, and Ludwig Mies van der Rohe had begun their careers at offices like those of Peter Behrens and Theodor Fischer, which featured large archives of photographic material from all kinds of sources. When Le Corbusier traveled to Greece and Italy he took photographs to aid his memory, but when he published his research in several magazine articles and books—thus founding avant-garde architecture—he used existing pictures by photographers such as Fred Boissonas, Arthur Koester, and Hugo Schmoelz. On the other hand, the American architect Frank Lloyd Wright began a close collaboration with the photographer Clarence Fuermann.

In the area of industrial use of Architectural Photography, the Deutsche Werkbund, a congregation of industrialists, architects, designers, artists, and craftsmen founded in 1907, set the parameters for modern object photography by producing catalogues of well-designed pieces shown on white backgrounds under diffuse light—a method of display used throughout the twentieth century. The years following World War I saw the beginnings of so-called straight photography as a fine art, with Architectural Photography playing a large role in this development, along with the conventions that arose around object photography in commercial and industrial applications. Although some American and European fine arts photographers, including Frederick Henry Evans, Alfred Stieglitz, Edward Steichen, and Hugo Henneberg, had used architecture as motifs in their compositions, Architectural Photography was not an important theme in this movement. The careers of Charles Sheeler and Paul Strand, however, placed Architectural Photography front and center in American fine arts photography. Their reference medium was the documentary film, and after finishing their movie about New York in 1921 architecture became their metaphor for both old and modern as well as rural versus urban life: Sheeler's series on Shaker villages as well as Strand's still lifes of metal objects were executed in technically perfect prints and shown as if they were commercial Architectural Photography, elevating it to a fine art.

Different sources in Europe gave birth to similar results. The German Neue Schlichkeit (New Objectivity) was a painting movement emphasizing motifs that had been previously explored in Architectural Photography, and it returned to fine art photography again in the works of Albert Renger-Patzsch, August Sander, and their successors. In France, film had early on acquired the status of a fine art and the realism of French film, as in the work of the director René Clair, infused Architectural Photography into the modern consciousness in its use of settings. The photographer Claude Gravot had his roots in this cross-fertilization; he had worked for Le Corbusier and Robert Mallet-Stevens, the most renowned French film architect in the 1930s. In Belgium, documentary filmmakers such as Joris Ivens provided inspiration for the photography of Willy Kessels and Camille Petry. Only the United Kingdom seemed content with the aesthetic promulgated by the Arts-and-Crafts movement and its influence on the Linked Ring Brotherhood. Frederick Henry Evans, who had done most of his architectural subjects between 1890 and 1910 in England and France, found his successors in Bill C. Clayton, and later in Anthony Ayscough and Edwin Smith. Modernism in British Architectural Photography lies chiefly on the shoulders of Herbert Felton whose immense oeuvre is now one of the main sources of material on 1930s' design.

In the 1930s, Modernism continued to spread throughout the world, Architectural Photography being an important means of dissemination of the ideas of the modern architects who used the camera both for the preparation and the distribution of their work. Architectural Photography received a new quality in the work of Erich Mendelsohn, renowned modernist architect in 1920s Berlin who emigrated in 1933, arriving in San Francisco after a decade in Israel. Mendelsohn had cooperated with photographers like Arthur and Walter Koester but was driven to a collection of photographs showing American grain elevators and industrial sites that were presented by Walter Gropius at an exhibition of the Deutsche Werkbund in 1914. In 1924 he received the commission from one of his clients to photograph and describe modern American architecture and traveled to the United States. The photographs he brought back to Germany were not only interesting in their choice of subjects but as stylistic approaches as well. They subsequently caused a fashion of Americanism in European Architectural Photography strictly connected to Modernism.

By the late 1920s, conventions about how to depict modern architecture had spread throughout Europe. These conventions included depicting the building through an axial or diagonal (45°) orientation on the selected facade, generally in bright early morning or late afternoon sunlight with long and strong shadows that emphasized cubic volumes, or setting the building against a sky dark with cumulus clouds, and presenting the image in a crisp clear print with an overall depth of field and a glossy surface. Another convention was that except for the inclusion of one or two individuals in order to convey the scale of the structure, the pictures were empty of life. Motorcars were banned except when the architect had also designed an automobile, as in the case of Gropius and Le Corbusier. Trees were only allowed without leaves. Preeminent among the architectural photographers of this style were Claude Gravot and André Kertész in France, John Havinden, Francis Yerbury, and the German emigree Walter Nurnberg in the United Kingdom, the Studio Vasari in Italy, the Koester brothers in Berlin, Werner Mantz and Hugo Schmoelz in Cologne, Eduard Wasow in Munich, Otto Lossen in Stuttgart, Albert Renger-Patzsch in Essen, and especially Lucia Moholy in Dessau who, with her series on the new buildings of the Bauhaus, lay down the rules for a strict documentary approach to modern architecture. This modernist convention was propagated in illustrated papers, magazines, books, and most of all, on picture postcards.

Modernism became the global style in architecture, immensely aided by the exhibition, The International Style, at the newly founded Museum of Modern Art in New York in 1932. Organized by the art historian Henry-Russell Hitchcock and the architect Philip Johnson, the exhibition and its accompanying book drew from a wealth of photographic material that showed architecture from all over the world. This new international convention of Architectural Photography was quickly adapted by commercial photography studios, most notably companies such as Hedrich & Blessing in Chicago, Nyholm & Lincoln in New York, and Dell & Wainwright in London. These studios and others presented modern architecture in elegant, technically perfect images ready for publication in the glossy magazines of the day. Modern architecture was the rising star of lifestyle, and Architectural Photography was its medium. Individuals such as Sigurd Fischer and Ralph Steiner in the United States, Roger Schall and Maurice Tabard in France, or Hans Spies, Werner Mantz (both emigrated from Germany), and Jaap d'Oliveira in The Netherlands contributed to this mainstream reporting on quality design and photographic art. And there was Margaret Bourke-White with her huge series on the construction of Rockefeller Center and the Chrysler building in New York as well as the industrial photographs from the Soviet Union where photographers like Alexandr Rodchenko tried to integrate Architectural Photography into their Agitprop work.

The rise of power of the Nazi party in Germany saw the usurping of Modernism and its depiction of architecture as a propaganda tool. The Nazi stylistic approach, best described as an uncanny mixture of classicism and romanticism, saw a number of photographers profiting from their alliance with the regime. Walter Hege and Helga Glassner served as de facto reporters of Germany's historic architectural and social greatness; Otto Eisenschink., Max Krajewski (not to be misindentified as the Bauhaus student of the same name) and Hugo Schmoelz were named *Fotografen der Bewegung* (Photographers of the [Nazi-]Movement). Schmoelz' son Karl-Hugo at the age of 22 received the commission to photograph Nazi architect Albert Speer's gigantic model of Berlin's sweeping transformation. Some photographers were able to continue to integrate modern strategies into their architectural propaganda: Heinrich Heidersberger with his use of infra-red photography to create black skies over industrial buildings and small houses in Northern Germany (which influenced others across Europe) as well as in the work of Jonathan Jonals (Jonals Company) from Denmark and in the night journeys through Paris by Brassaï.

The end of World War II saw numerous new commissions for Architectural Photography in Europe and Japan to document the widespread destruction. Although it was forbidden in several countries—notably the United Kingdom and Germany—amateur photographers even during the war years had documented the substantial losses of their home cities and areas. As well, the Allied forces employed photographic surveillance units to record the damage of structures in detail, both in aerial and in ground-based films and still images. The reaction to these photographs was profound and nongovernmental organizations such as C.A.R.E. were founded to aid the devastated European populations. The destruction of Hiroshima and Nagasaki by atomic bombs dropped by American forces was first captured in aerial photographs. When blow-ups were printed in magazines and newspapers, people had difficulty believing what they saw—a particularly striking example of the power of Architectural Photography to stir individuals to political or social activism. This use of Architectural Photography has become a convention that has persisted to the present day.

The disruptions of emergence of the Nazi regime, World War II, and its immediate aftermath saw exiles and refugees fleeing Europe in the late 1930s, and again in the late 1940s and early 1950s. In architecture, Gropius, Mies van der Rohe, and several other Bauhaus masters founded large architectural offices in the United States, all in need of good advertising photography. Mies became associated with Chicago's New Bauhaus (later Institute of Design) which trained many photographers in the "whole human" philosophy of László Moholy-Nagy, emphasizing industrial, product, and Architectural Photography. These expatriates joined other Europeans, notably Richard Neutra and Rudolf Schindler, who had already emigrated to the Los Angeles area in the 1920s. Neutra, an expert photographer himself, often told the story that in need of a good photographer in the late 1930s, he encountered Julius Shulman. Shulman had no professional training and was told by Neutra how to look at and photograph buildings. Legend or not, it was the beginning of an outstanding career which lasted for half a century. Shulman photographed not only every design by Neutra and Schindler but nearly every modern building in California. Modern American architecture would not have achieved its outstanding international reputation without Shulman's work.

The late 1940s with their postwar reconstruction and improving economies across Europe, Japan, and the United States, gave birth to a number of significant practitioners of Architectural Photography, each individually successful and important in his own country: Ezra Stoller and George Cserna in the United States; Eric de Maré in the United Kingdom; Heinrich Heidersberger, Arthur Pfau, and Karl-Hugo Schmoelz in Germany; Lennart Olson, Erik Hansen, and Carl Gustav Rosenberg in Sweden; Jean-Philippe Charbonnier and Robert Doisneau in France; Eva Besnyö and Cas Oorthuis in The Netherlands; and Studio Vasari and Paolo Monti in Italy, among many others. Important collaborations among photographers and architects began, like the life-long relation between Luis Barragán, Mathias Goeritz, and Armando Salas Portugal in Mexico, the latter being the photographer of both the architect and the sculptor. Some architects were married to photographers whose careers were secondary to those of their husbands: most prominent among them were Binia Bill and Ursula Wolf-Schneider.

The 1950s saw the first cross-over artists in Architectural Photography: writers such as Wright Morris followed Walker Evans, historians Martin Huerlimann and G.E. Kidder Smith were as competent as photographers as they were experts in their fields. Even fine art cross pollinated with Architectural Photography; the Americans Clarence John Laughlin, Jerry Uelsman, and other artists in photography used architecture as the metaphoric base of their ideas. A similar use of architecture is found in European fine art photography of the 1950s, which was further deeply influenced by existentialist philosophy: the Paris stories by the Dutch photographer Ed van der Elsken and the Swiss René Groebli needed the city's streets and places as much as Bill Brandt's perspectives or the work of the German *fotoform* group and Robert Häusser's heroic pictures. The same can be said about the world-wide work of Henri Cartier-Bresson, the New York images of André Kertész, the Spanish series by Inge Morath and W. Eugene Smith, and a number of other photographic journalists whose photographs closely related their subjects to the architectural spaces in which they appeared.

All of these works influenced Architectural Photography by the introduction of the city scape as subject. Whether inspired by writings of theorists like Kevin Lynch, Lewis Mumford, or William Hubbard on the importance of the image of the city, or simply actively involved in cultural movements of arts and literature, photographers such as John Szarkowski, Cervin Robinson, Morley Baer, and others began to document the conglomeration of what had grown within one century of American building, mainly in the big cities. Some, like Evelyn Hofer, returned to their European roots and—by titles like *The Stones of Florence*—even to the Arts-and-Crafts movement. There was also a return to one of the foundations of Architectural Photography: the preservation of monuments. In Chicago, Richard Nickel meticulously recorded every detail of historic buildings as they were being torn down; he paid with his life when part of the building collapsed while he was photographing the demolition of Louis Sullivan's Stock Exchange building. In photographing the demolition of New York's Pennsylvania Station in 1964, Norman McGrath succeeded in bringing back the political sense of building preservation that it had had in the nineteenth century.

Inventories of buildings to be preserved or lost were always politically influenced, but when modernism began to become stale in the late 1960s this field of Architectural Photography rapidly began to grow as a base of citizenship initiatives concerned about the integrity of their neighborhood.

Industrial archeology and oral history both used the camera to establish their methods hitherto seen as irrelevant. Photographers such as Hilla and Bernd Becher collected industrial construction forms; Concept Art groups like the London-based Art & Language (with Victor Burgin) or the Artist Placement Group (with Stuart Brisley) began with large collections of vernacular photography for specific reasons grounded in local contexts but with the space—and thus architecture—as constant background. When in 1975 the European year of building preservation was proclaimed, these initiatives were the first to gain political effort. But preservation still is not always seen as positive by governing forces; photographers such as Xujong, who want to save Beijing's *Hutong* quarters from being torn down, have to fight for decades with their work. Travel photography has also gained from the new interest in old buildings as can be traced in the work of the Swiss photographers Werner Studer and Emil Schulthess.

Urbanism is more than just old and new constructions along the roads and places of a given city, it includes the spirit of an overall layout, which was detected by a number of photographers and artists in the 1960s. Art Sinsabaugh with his large panoramas of motorway crossings and railroad junctions is an urbanist as well as other panoramists: Eugene Omar Goldbeck, Joachim Bonnemaison, and Josef Sudek. Ed Ruscha produced long *leporellos* of simple images taken along roads like Hollywood's Sunset Strip, which inspired architectural theory like Venturi and Rauch's *Learning from Las Vegas* and influenced Pop Art and Conceptual Art alike. Painters like Gerhard Richter began to work from aerial views of city centers by projecting these onto their canvasses. Richard Hamilton and Sigmar Polke had bird's eye views of urban places enlarged to the visibility of printing dots and transferred these images into oil paintings or silk screen prints.

The staleness of architectural modernism only was surpassed by the boredom of Architectural Photography at the same time. Postmodernism was on its way, and it would not have been possible without the influence of fashion and lifestyle photography in the 1970s. Again, this influence was made evident by the preservative character of photography, and large collections of pictures served as depositories for construction details freshly combined by architectural double-coding (Charles Jencks, *The Language of Post-Modern Architecture*, London: Academy Editions [1977]). Manfred Hamm was an important interpreter of industrial heritage and dead technique. Reinhart Wolf began to set New York's skyscrapers' heads, Georgia's framework houses, Spanish *castillos*, and German as well as Japanese vernacular architecture into scenes. Jean-Claude Gautrand and the philosopher Paul Virilio strengthened their interest in bunker archeology along the French Atlantic coast. Gabriele Basilico went along Mediterranean coasts for his series on Italian and French harbors. Richard Pare collected courthouses in the United States; Lewis Baltz recorded industrial construction sites as well as parking lots all over the world; and Stephen Shore concentrated on road crossings.

Frank Gohlke, Joel Meyerowitz, and William Eggleston reduced the concept of their collections to the randomness of their appearance at a certain place, a concept to be followed by a large number of photographers in the early 1980s: Heinrich Riebesehl and Wilhelm Schürmann in Germany, Manfred Willmann in Austria, Luigi Ghirri and Giovanni Chiaramonte in Italy, Tony Ray-Jones and Martin Parr in the United Kingdom, and Jay Ullal in India. Postmodernism formed a full circle when the Japanese photographer Yukio Futagawa began to publish his magazine *Global Architecture* concentrating on the heroic period of modern architecture with the works of Frank Lloyd Wright, Ludwig Mies van der Rohe, Le Corbusier, and others.

In the 1980s photography had become a fine art in itself, established and regarded all over the world. Bernd Becher was awarded an academy professorship, and his Dusseldorf class seemed to be the first one constituting Architectural Photography as an important subclass of photographic art. Although the first generation of his students—Tata Ronkholz, Volker Döhne—followed his example of collecting vernacular or forgotten architectural specimen, the second generation began to make Architectural Photography in itself a theme: closure and distance were the categories to subsume their art now. They form the most renowned group of students from this class: Andreas Gursky, Candida Höfer, Axel Hütte, Thomas Ruff (today Becher's successor on the seat), Thomas Struth, and Petra Wunderlich. The third and last generation no longer regarded even these categories as serious, and only a small number of them still stuck to Architectural Photography: Laurenz Berges, Johannes Bruns, Elger Esser, Jongmyung Lee, Heiner Schilling, and Josef Schulz.

Becher's class had competition from the early 1980s onwards in a group of students forming themselves under difficult conditions of the late-communist Leipzig academy: Rudolf Schäfer,

Max Baumann, Matthias Hoch, Frank-Heinrich Müller, Frank Silberbach, Marion Wenzel, and Thomas Wolf, among others. When the school was reformed in 1991, the interest in Architectural Photography shifted similar to the Becher class from architectural documentation towards the distance between reality and imagery, only Frank Müller, Annett Stuth, and Thilo Kühne stuck to Architectural Photography. As usual in academic training, the Becher class reproduced itself: Thomas Struth and Candida Höfer gained seats in Karlsruhe and inspired students like Mona Breede. A number of other teachers in European and American academies and universities incorporated Architectural Photography more or less willingly into their curricula as was asked by the students.

Some photographers with a background in architecture, sculpture, engineering, or even computer science announced themselves in the late 1980s and early 1990s as the heralds of late modernism or new constructivism in Architectural Photography. Tomas Riehle came from the Düsseldorf academy having studied sculpture, Richard Bryant settled in the United Kingdom after leaving his native South Africa for the United States, Heiner Leiska became one of the best model photographers in the world after a career in computer-aided construction. The German Klaus Kinold and the Austrian Eduard Huber, working in New York, were trained architects but concentrated on photography in their subsequent work. Today, in most architectural departments of design schools, academies, and universities Architectural Photography is an integral part of basic instruction. There still is a large need for good Architectural Photography in magazines, books, and on websites but it is clear to see that the field will have had its days within the next decade.

Virtual Reality had found its way into architecture, and it has crept into the work of model builders, master draftmen, and finally into photography. The results of computer-aided design at the end of the twentieth century finally left the plainness of scattered lines and flat surfaces to become more and more integrated into a form of photomontage. A simple photograph of a site is melded into an image of forthcoming constructions, and in more and more cases it is animated in one form of movement or another. Another development is of similar importance to the future of Architectural Photography: the fame of an architect is no longer dependent on the realization of his buildings. A good presentation at competitions, perfect CAAD visualizations of projects, a book or two with a wealth of text—all lead more to international acclaim rather than the actual building. Architectural Photography has lost its basic function but it is now recognized as fine art.

Rolf Sachsse

See also **Abbott, Berenice; Aerial Photography; Agitprop; Bauhaus; Atget, Eugéne; Becher, Hilla and Bernd; Bourke-White, Margaret; Brandt, Bill; Brassaï; Burgin, Victor; Cartier-Bresson, Henri; Conceptual Photography; Doisneau, Robert; Eggleston, William; van der Elsken, Ed; Evans, Frederick Henry; Evans, Walker; Gohlke, Frank; Gursky, Andreas; Hine, Lewis; Hütte, Axel; Industrial Photography; Kertész, André; Kessels, Willy; Laughlin, Clarence John; Linked Ring Brotherhood; Man Ray; Meyerowitz, Joel; Modernism; Morath, Inge; Morris, Wright; Museum of Modern Art; Olson, Lennart; Parr, Martin; Plowden, David; Propaganda; Ray-Jones, Tony; Renger-Patzsch, Albert; Riis, Jacob; Ruff, Thomas; Sander, August; Sheeler, Charles; Shore, Stephen; Steichen, Edward; Stieglitz, Alfred; Struth, Thomas; Sudek, Joseph; Szarkowski, John; Tabard, Maurice; Uelsman, Jerry; Virtual Reality**

Further Reading

Blau, Eve, and Edward Kaufman, eds. *Architecture and its Image*. Cambridge, MA: MIT Press, 1989.

de Maré, Eric. *Photography and Architecture*. London: Architectural Press, 1961.

Exh. cat. *Images et Imaginaires d'Architecture. Dessin Peinture Photographie Art Graphiques Théâtre Cinéma en Europe Aux XIXe et Xxe Siècles*. Paris: Centre Georges Pompidou, 1984.

Exh. cat. *Moderne Grüße, Architektur der 1920er Jahre auf Bildpostkarten*. Essen: Pomp Verlag, 2001.

Exh. cat. *City Scape East, Topographic Photographs of Eastern Germany*. Stuttgart: Hatje Cantz, 2001.

Jencks, Charles. *The Language of Post-Modern Architecture*. London: Academy Editions, 1977.

Pare, Richard, ed., Exh. cat. *Photography and Architecture 1839–1939*, Montreal: Canadian Centre for Architecture, 1982.

Robinson, Cervin, and Joel Hershman. *Architecture Transformed. A History of the Photography of Buildings from 1839 to the Present*. Cambridge, MA: MIT Press, 1987.

Sachsse, Rolf. *Bild und Bau. Zur Nutzung technischer Medien beim Entwerfen von Architektur, Bauwelt Fundamente 113*. Braunschweig Wiesbaden: Vieweg Verlag, 1997.

Veltri, John. *Architectural Photography*. Garden City, NY: Amphoto, 1974.

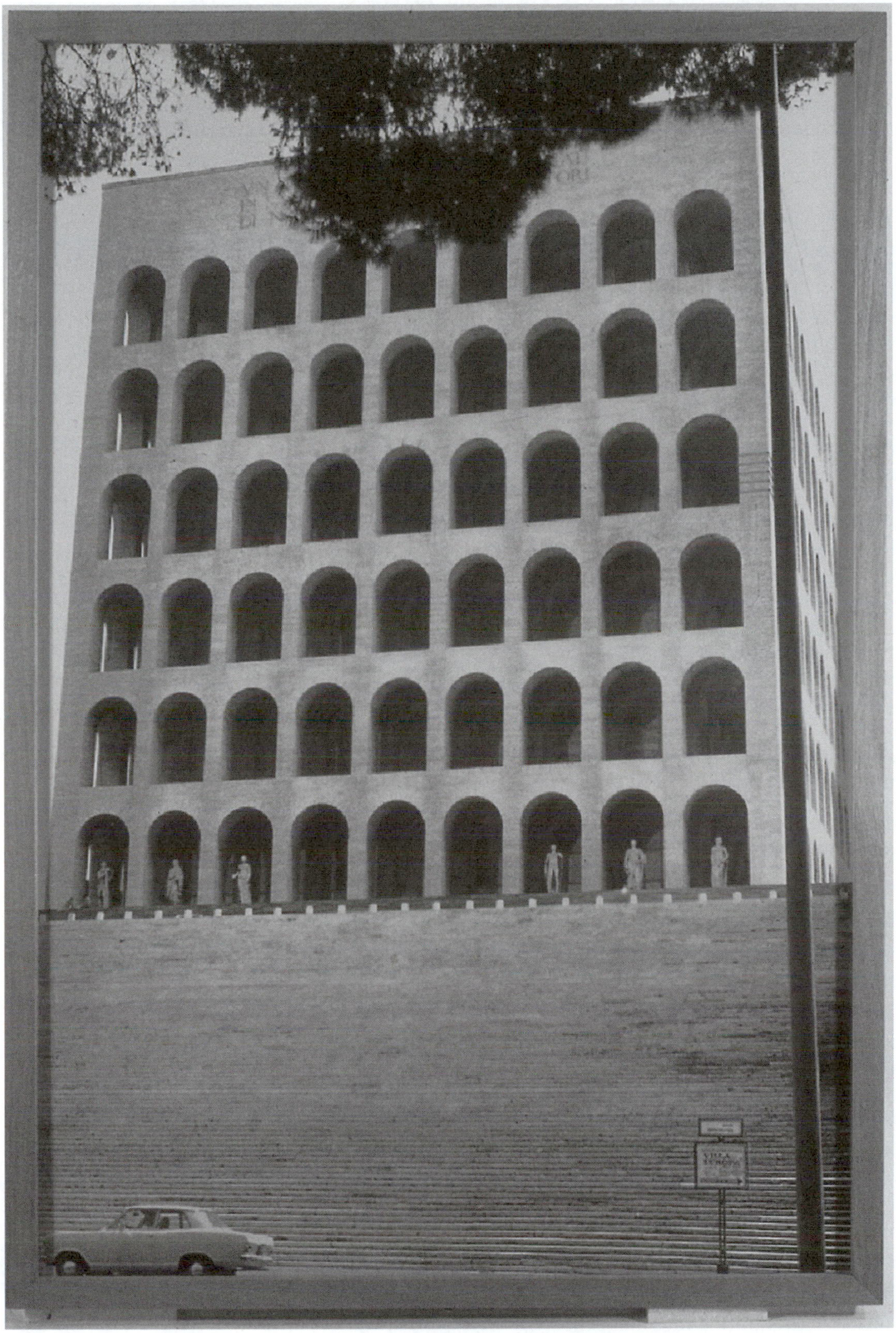

Günther Förg, E.U.R. Palazzo della Civilta, 1985, Gelatin silver print, 71 × 47″
Collection Museum of Contemporary Art, Chicago, Gerald S. Elliott Collection.
[*Photograph © Museum of Contemporary Art, Chicago*]

ARCHIVES

There is considerable confusion surrounding the concept of archives, and even professional archivists exacerbate the problem by employing the word in several ways. The words "archive" and "archives" are used in several different contexts, especially with regard to photographs. "An archive" is classically defined by archivists as the records of a governmental organization or institution, and such a file of records frequently contains photographs. However, by extension the term covers other kinds of collections, including business records, personal papers, and other archival collections. A long, rich tradition governs the manner in which such archives are processed, catalogued and described, stored, and made available for research. Archivists are professional staff responsible for the care of archival collections. The profession is well developed and is represented by a number of organizations in the United States and other countries, such as the Society of American Archivists, formed in 1936. Archival training is offered at various universities, often in history departments and library schools.

Archival, Library, and Museum Traditions

Because this entry concerns photographs in archives and archival collections, it is necessary to compare how photographs are managed in three basic types of repositories. Photographs are found in libraries, museums, and archives. Each type of organization has a distinctive tradition and methodology, although in practice they overlap considerably, with frequent exceptions to general rules. Libraries tend to be item-oriented: the bound book is the unit to be catalogued and tracked, from its shelf location to its circulation to patrons. By extension, the individual photograph in a library file cabinet is analogous to the book as a research or study unit; in practice it may not be individually catalogued—although it presumably would be if time and resources permitted. When possible, libraries may mark each photograph with a code or number which facilitates refiling it in its proper location. In a museum collection, the individual photograph is also the unit to be catalogued, typically according to aesthetic or technological criteria, rather than subject content. In an art museum, emphasis is usually placed upon the photographer, and works by identified artists are stored by the artists' names in alphabetical order. Exceptions may be made for special formats, especially unidentified or unattributed items. Anonymous daguerreotypes, for example, may be stored together. Accepted museum practice requires that each photograph, regardless of its precise storage location, be marked with a unique catalogue number to link it to its individual catalogue record, whether manual or electronic, which will also identify its provenance.

In archives and archival collections, the basic unit to be identified, catalogued, and tracked is a container, such as an approved, acid-free box, and its contents. The container may be filled with dozens or even hundreds of sheets of paper, including materials such as correspondence, financial documents, or photographs, neatly organized in labeled folders. To draw a parallel between library and archival practice, one might think of a box of paper documents in folders as rather like an unbound book Typically, however, the archival document box and its contents will be described in a "finding aid" or "container list" rather than in separate manual catalogue cards or entries in an electronic database.

Archival theory and tradition assume that true archives and most "archival collections," that is, organically created and assembled business and personal papers as well as "artificial" collections of papers and photographs (usually collected from external sources selectively) whether carefully or chaotically, will be processed and handled at the group level, both for theoretical and practical reasons. An archival collection such as the records of a governmental unit is usually retained in its original order, if that order was meaningful. Respect for original order derives from the fact that, in organically formed document collections, the existing order reflects the history and activities of the organization and the arrangement in itself provides information, which might be lost if that order were disrupted or destroyed. Implicit in the rule of retaining original order within a particular group of documents, regardless of the medium or form of the documents (e.g., manuscripts, typescripts, sound recordings, videotapes, photographs), is that the group will not be commingled with other groups; each will retain its separate identity and its provenance will be clearly articulated. These features of archives may be appreciated most vividly by contrasting them with the practices of most libraries, which tend to interfile the components of collections according to subject criteria. Certainly this is true of books, usually arranged by subject according to a classification scheme without regard to provenance. Similarly, libraries that collect photographs for study purposes often interfile them in accordance with subject criteria or a pre-ordained classification system, disregarding photographers and provenance. By contrast, archives do not normally interfile photographs in this manner because of concern for maintaining original order and provenance. It should be noted that many libraries and some archives do not attempt to identify and record photographers.

Photographs in Archives

Since at least the 1970s, many archivists have specialized in photographs, and training is available in university settings and in special workshops. The Society of American Archivists has sponsored courses on the management of photographic collections for many years, but archivists without specialized training are also expected to have at least a rudimentary knowledge of photographs and their physical and documentary characteristics in order to preserve them and make them available for research purposes effectively.

Margery S. Long of the Society of American Archivists wrote:

> Archivists and historians did not always recognize photographs as primary source materials. In the formative years of archives, only written records were regarded as archival and deserving of preservation. Pictorial materials, if they were retained at all, often were removed from the collections of records and manuscripts and assembled in general picture files; the principle of provenance was seldom applied to them. Some archivists designated photographs "miscellaneous ephemera" or "memorabilia" and relegated them to the last boxes in manuscript and archival collections. Some photographs were not even noted in finding aids, but were left in their original location, intermingled with manuscripts, documents, and correspondence. Since photographs often had no identifying information written on them, such undisturbed positions in archival collections were fortunate. Often the only clue to identification for some photographs is their location in files, reports, or diaries, or their proximity to a letter describing the events or naming the persons shown in the photographs.
>
> (Ritzenthaler et al., *Archives & Manuscripts: Administration of Photographic Collections*, Revised edition 1999.)

Attempts to maintain original order can create challenges for archivists, especially with photographs. For example, photographs intimately associated with other types of materials ideally may require a different standard of care and storage environment than the associated papers. Photographs are generally not catalogued individually because they are part of a group, which can be described at the collective level in registers and container lists; this practice, however, implies that the removal of a photograph from its file location for copying, reproduction, or exhibition represents a tracking challenge to ensure that the item eventually can be returned to its proper location. Many photographs are part of a large group, which would be difficult or impractical to catalogue at the item level. A by-product of the increasing interest in all kinds of historic photographs since the 1960s and 1970s is that greater numbers of photographs from archives are being selected for reproduction and other purposes, and greater demand creates challenges for archival methods and assumptions. Some archives have adopted a strategy of selective item-level cataloguing for photographs and other high-demand items on a user-driven basis, since usage frequently begets repeat demand and an increased need for staff to locate individual photographs or information about them; the need to identify image surrogates such as copy negatives and scan files implies item-level cataloguing in spite of the archival protocol for group-level description. Such practice makes the archival repository a more hybrid kind of organization, overlaying archival techniques with library and museum methods. Since photographs frequently embody many layers of meaning—as historical evidence, aesthetic object, and cultural artifact, whether identified and interpreted singly or in groups—a flexible approach to varied modes of access may be advisable. A library, museum, or archival repository can severely limit its options and its services to patrons by attempting to impose a rigid, tradition-bound policy for access to its holdings.

Photographs and other visual materials, no matter how well they function in a group context, ultimately demand some degree of item-level access. While a written document may be referenced, summarized, or quoted without physically removing it from its file location, visual materials occasionally must be removed from their archival context to facilitate forms of "quotation" such as copying, scanning, or public display.

Groups of photographs whose "original order" is deemed not meaningful or absent altogether can be rearranged for the convenience of the archivists and their patrons. This situation often occurs when the original owners or creators of the photographs failed to recognize significant relationships among them or simply never devised a useful filing system. Archivists also deal with materials that are not "archives" in the sense of representing organic organizational records. Such aggregations, often broadly called "manuscript collections," regardless of the precise content, frequently can be rearranged without loss of contextual information. Indeed, many such collections are acquired by archival organizations whose mission is to collect relevant research materials according to specified guidelines from a variety of collectors and sources. Some "archives" are hybrid organizations, fulfilling several distinctive missions. The archives of the Art Institute of Chicago, which hold the business records of the Art Institute, also collect the papers of artists—often including photographs—as well as miscellaneous research materials from a variety of sources.

Archival organizational structures vary widely. Some archival collections are found in libraries, which may or may not include administratively separate archival sub-units. The so-called "special collections" of many libraries often include manuscript collections and photographic files, and collections that are managed in accordance with archival traditions. University libraries typically hold such "special collections," usually including photographic materials.

Archives range in size and scope from the files generated by a small business or an individual professional person (such as a photographer) to the vast holdings of governmental units. The National Archives and Records Administration of the United States preserves the records generated by the many official agencies of the U.S. government. The Still Picture unit of the Special Media Archives Services Division, located in College Park, Maryland, contains millions of photographs, which are made available to serious researchers. The National Archives is perhaps the quintessential archival repository, which helps to set archival standards for the entire profession. The Library of Congress, a separate government entity, is not merely a gigantic library but is a hybrid organization that includes collections of documents that are managed according to archival principles. It serves as a highly influential creator of descriptive standards. Its Machine Readable Cataloguing (MARC) format for cataloguing databases is employed internationally for the cataloguing of books, and has been adapted for the description of archival materials such as photographic collections, at both group and item levels. Museums have tended to avoid the MARC format because of its library orientation.

Photographers' Archives

The life's work of a photographer, containing a variety of forms and media, such as original negatives, transparencies, prints, and professional and personal papers, is often called an archive. A few organizations, most notably the Center for Creative Photography (CCP) at the University of Arizona in Tucson, actively acquire selected photographers' archives, most through donation. Photographer, curator, and educator Harold Jones was the founding Director of the CCP (1975–1977). The CCP holds more archives and individual works by twentieth-century North American photographers than any other museum in the nation. These holdings include a research collection featuring the archives of over 60 photographers—Ansel Adams, Richard Avedon, Lola Alvarez Bravo, Louise Dahl-Wolfe, Robert Heinecken, W. Eugene Smith, and Edward Weston among them. Archives include photographs, negatives, albums, work prints, manuscripts, audio-visual material, contact sheets, correspondence, and memorabilia and have recently been mined as a resource for specialized publications that contextualize photographers' careers within their archives.

Other universities, libraries, historical societies at the regional, state, and municipal levels, and some museums also collect photographers' archives on a limited basis, often because the photographer was an alumnus or former teacher or the work matches a preexisting collection strength. The archives of documentary photographer David Plowden, who attended Yale, is now in the collections of Yale University, for example. Laura Gilpin, famous for her views of the west, has her archive at the Amon Carter Museum in Fort Worth, Texas, known for its Western U.S. collections. Amon Carter also holds Eliot Porter's archives.

Because a photographer's archive can necessitate a heavy investment of space, budget, and staff involvement for processing and preservation, nonprofit historical organizations must be highly selective and are understandably wary of large acquisitions. Art museums, normally devoted to issues such as connoisseurship and the acquisition and management of individual works of art, usually are unable to accommodate entire photographers' archives except very selectively. And often these archives are accessioned along with a gift of a body of the photographer's work suitable for collecting and exhibition, as was the case of a 1997 donation to the Art Institute of Chicago by Irving Penn.

Some museums build collections around an important archive, such as the August Sander Archive in Cologne, which presents exhibitions of other photographers along with holding the seminal German figure's work, or the Berlinische Galerie's acquisition in 1979 of the Hannah Höch Archive of paintings, collages, graphics, and photographs.

At the end of the twentieth century, however, photographers' archives constituted a looming problem; many photographers or their heirs were unable to locate permanent homes for a sudden influx of thousands of negatives, prints, and papers, even on a gift basis, and large aggregations of significant photographs, whether considered works of art or historical documents, went begging for institutional protection, risking eventual dispersal or destruction. A fairly new solution is to set up an independent foundation (often with tax benefits to the estate) to house the archive; a model is the Foundation Henri Cartier-Bresson, inaugurated in 2003. Another is the Lee Miller Archive in East Sussex, England.

Another strategy is to pinpoint a genre or topic that can sustain broader donor interest than a single artist's archive, such as the Women in Photography International Archive, which amasses biographical files, books, and articles on female photographers past and present and as well as photographs taken by women.

Archives have also been increasingly seen as a source of profit. The venerable Bettmann Archive, long the model of a commercial stock photo archive, was acquired at the end of the century by Corbis, founded by Microsoft's Bill Gates to acquire images for digitalizing and distribution via the internet. The Hulton Archive, London, is another large international stock photo archive. Condé Nast publications' inventory of more than one million fashion, celebrity, still-life, and travel photographs and illustrations is housed in the Condé Nast Archive. Traditional photo agencies such as Black Star or Magnum Photos, though clearly commercial concerns, also function as archives.

Artifact Archives

"Archive" also has been used as a generic term for collections without regard to form of material, especially at the George Eastman House in Rochester, New York, thereby introducing an additional element of confusion over the application of the word. Originally Eastman House's holdings of photographs, cameras, and other photographic apparatus, and ephemera were called simply "the collections," but beginning in the 1980s these holdings came to be called "archives," in opposition to the terminology employed by most museums. This apparently coincided with the "PABIR" slogan ("photographic archives belong in Rochester"), which was used in the successful fund-raising and public relations campaign to prevent the contents of the museum from being transferred to the National Museum of American History at the Smithsonian Institution. A distinction is now made between Eastman House curators and archivists: curators collect, organize exhibitions, and perform research, while archivists care for the collections and provide reference services for researchers. Since "archivists" normally deal with papers, photographs, and media such as motion pictures and sound recordings according to the archival traditions previously mentioned, the notion of archivists working with technological and cultural artifacts such as cameras, in the museum item-level tradition, strains the usual definition. On the other hand, in many institutions so-called manuscript collections (including photographs) are entrusted to manuscript "curators" rather than "archivists," even though they utilize archival methodology.

In the broadest possible, if non-traditional, sense, an archive may be construed as any body of original or primary source material maintained as historical evidence for study, so perhaps Eastman House can be forgiven for its extension of the term to cover its collection of "three-dimensional" cultural and technological artifacts. If the original assumption of archivists was that their collections would consist essentially of language materials—documents containing written words and mathematical symbols—it soon became evident that pictorial materials could not logically be excluded. Maps, engineering drawings, hand-rendered illustrations, and photographs—all documentary, historical evidence—are properly the concern of archivists. The distinction between museum collections and archival manuscript collections at times appears arbitrary in terms of the forms of material collected, hinging upon the volumetric versus the flat. Museums, of course, collect both types of objects, so photographs are found in both museums and archives. If the distinguishing feature of archives is their emphasis on groups of objects that bear some internal relationship or association, it seems simplistic and arbitrary to exclude volumetric items merely because the archival tradition assumes flatness.

Conclusion

The essence of museum and archival collections is their emphasis on primary source materials. Conventional libraries collect mass-produced, secondary materials, rather than unique or original items, although most libraries also contain some rare items and some libraries specialize in rarities. Photographic collections in libraries may serve as primary source materials, and they have the advantage of facilitating immediate subject access to materials unrelated by provenance, introducing insights that may not be available in archival, self-selected collections. Photographs often function as primary source materials, although it must be admitted that this is a relative thing. Some photographs, especially photographs of objects that are still extant in approximately the same state as their photographs indicate, may function as secondary source materials. Archives, with their emphasis on aggregates and accumulations of related materials, provide a valuable service for those who require an extensive study of related photographs.

David Haberstich

See also: **Art Institute of Chicago; Black Star; Center for Creative Photography (Tucson); Condé Nast; Conservation; Corbis/Bettmann; Farm Security Administration; Jones, Harold; Library of Congress; Magnum Photos; Museums; Museums: Europe; Museums: United States**

Further Reading

Betz, Elisabeth, comp. *Graphic Materials: Rules for Describing Original Items and Historical Collections*. Washington, DC: Library of Congress, 1980.
Burke, Peter. *Eyewitnessing: The Uses of Images as Historical Evidence*. Ithaca, NY: Cornell University Press, 2001.
Derrida, Jacques. *Archive Fever: A Freudian Impression*. Chicago: University of Chicago Press, 1998.
Eskind, Andrew, and Deborah Barsel. "International Museum of Photography: Conventions for Cataloging Photographs." *Image* 21 (1978), 1–31.
Fox, Michael J., Peter Wilkerson, and Suzanne R. Warren, eds. *Introduction to Archival Organization and Description: Access to Cultural Heritage*. Getty Information Institute, 1998.
Jones, H.G., ed. *Historical Consciousness in the Early Republic: The Origins of State Historical Societies, Museums, and Collections, 1791-1861*, North Carolina Society, 1995.
Muller, S., J.A. Feith, and R. Fruin. *Manual for the Arrangement and Description of Archives*. Trans. of second edition, Arthur H. Leavitt, Chicago: Society of American Archivists, SAA Classics Series, 2003.
Ritzenthaler, Mary Lynn, Gerald J. Munoff, and Margery J. Long. *Archives & Manuscripts: Administration of Photographic Collections*, SAA Basic Manual Series, Chicago: Society of American Archivists, 1984, Revised edition, 1999.
Schellenberg, T.R., *Modern Archives: Principles and Practice*, Chicago: SAA Classics Series, Society of American Archivists, 2003.
Sekula, Allan. "The Body and the Archive." *October* 39 (Winter 1986), 3–64.
Shaw, Renata V. "Picture Organization: Practice and Procedures, Parts 1 and 2." *Special Libraries* 63:10 and 11 (1972): 448–56, 502–06.

EVE ARNOLD

American

Driven by simple curiosity and a love of the unpredictability of photography, Eve Arnold helped shape photojournalism in the latter half of the twentieth century. Part of the Magnum Photos stable, Arnold took still photographs for magazine and newspaper assignments, advertising campaigns, and films. In choosing her photographs, Arnold asked herself if the subject was visual and if words would enhance the picture. Rather than selecting the sensational, Arnold let the subject dictate the treatment, angle of approach, and point of view. Describing her vision, she stated that if a topic interested her then she believed that she could make it interesting to others. Her aim has been to hold a mirror up to the world and make people aware of the human condition.

Arnold became involved in photography in 1943 through a position as a manager at a photo-finishing plant in New Jersey. She began photographing while working at the plant and decided to take a six-week course in photography offered by the influential photography teacher Alexey Brodovitch at New York City's New School for Social Research. Impressed by her pictures of a Harlem fashion show, Brodovitch encouraged Arnold to keep shooting. Some of these photographs were eventually published in a British magazine, which brought her to the attention of Magnum.

Arnold soon took up the profession full-time and capitalized on her status as a woman photographer—still a relatively rare occurrence—by using her female insight and personality to interpret what she photographed. After a disastrous experience in which a hostile writer changed the meaning of Arnold's fashion show photographs, she resolved to get as much control as possible over the words that accompanied her pictures; for Arnold, a photograph without words fell short.

Throughout the 1950s, Arnold concentrated mainly on portraiture, usually undertaken as assignments for magazines or Hollywood film productions. As she became more confident, she began to produce work independently, enjoying both the freedom and the knowledge that if the photographs were of sufficient quality, they would appear in more venues than if they had been tailored to the editorial needs of a particular magazine. Yet she kept the marketplace in mind when selecting her subjects.

Arnold first became associated with Magnum Photos in 1951 and became a full member in 1955. Always interested in improving herself, as she recalled later, Arnold scoured the files at Magnum, especially going over the proof sheets in an effort to understand how other photographers worked. Arnold had begun her career using a $40 Rolleicord camera and had gone on to a Rolleiflex before she discovered that it was very hard to fill the frame of the large square-format pictures these cameras produced. She then changed to the 35-mm format Nikon, in part because it was difficult to get German-made Leicas in the United States after World War II. To move around easily and elicit more from her subjects, Arnold streamlined her equipment early in her career, eschewing motor drives, lights, or tripods, and carrying a minimal amount of gear in a single bag. As Arnold explained in her autobiography, *In Retrospect*, her way of working was a low-key approach based on establishing contact with the subject and using whatever light was available.

For example, when photographing on movie sets, Arnold habitually worked barefooted, seeking to not draw the attention of her subjects, and would stop photographing if noticed. For greater variety Arnold would photograph the same situations in black-and-white and in color; she continued this method until the mid-1970s when the market for monochrome largely disappeared. In her color work, Arnold was inclined to use color as an accent or as part of the overall design and believed that muted color often proved more effective than stark tones.

While Arnold is known for her photographs of Hollywood stars, political figures, and religious leaders, including such notables as Marlene Dietrich, Joan Crawford, Senator Joseph McCarthy, Presidents Richard M. Nixon and Dwight D. Eisenhower, and Malcolm X, she also photographed ordinary people. The photographs for which she is perhaps best known are those of Marilyn Monroe. Unlike those of many celebrity photographers of the 1950s and 1960s, Arnold's photographs are typically candid, unretouched shots, as her portraits of Monroe illustrate. She had a total of six sessions with Monroe, ranging from press conferences to her last film, *The Misfits*. Male photographers generally captured Monroe's sexuality, whereas Arnold portrays a more relaxed star.

In 1961, Arnold began work with the London *Sunday Times* and relocated to England in 1962; she stayed under contract with the *Times* for the next ten years. At this stage in her career, Arnold worked autonomously, originating ideas and handling everything from initial research through to the finished prints. Although she completed difficult assignments such as traveling alone through the mountains of Afghanistan, Arnold never covered armed conflict. Despite her desire to do so, her art director refused to allow her to cover the Vietnam War because of the hazards involved.

Arnold is also known for her 11 books, which she closely oversaw, including volumes that featured Marilyn Monroe and Mikhail Baryshnikov and the American Ballet Theater. From the start of her days as photographer, Arnold had dreamed of shooting in China; a 1979 assignment resulted in the book *In China*. In it Arnold sought to reflect the happiness that most Chinese felt about the approach of industrialization. The pictures brought Arnold her first major solo exhibition at the Brooklyn Museum in 1980.

CARYN E. NEUMANN

Biography

Born in Philadelphia, Pennsylvania in 1913. Began photographing in 1946; took a six-week course in photography with Alexei Brodovitch at New York City's New School

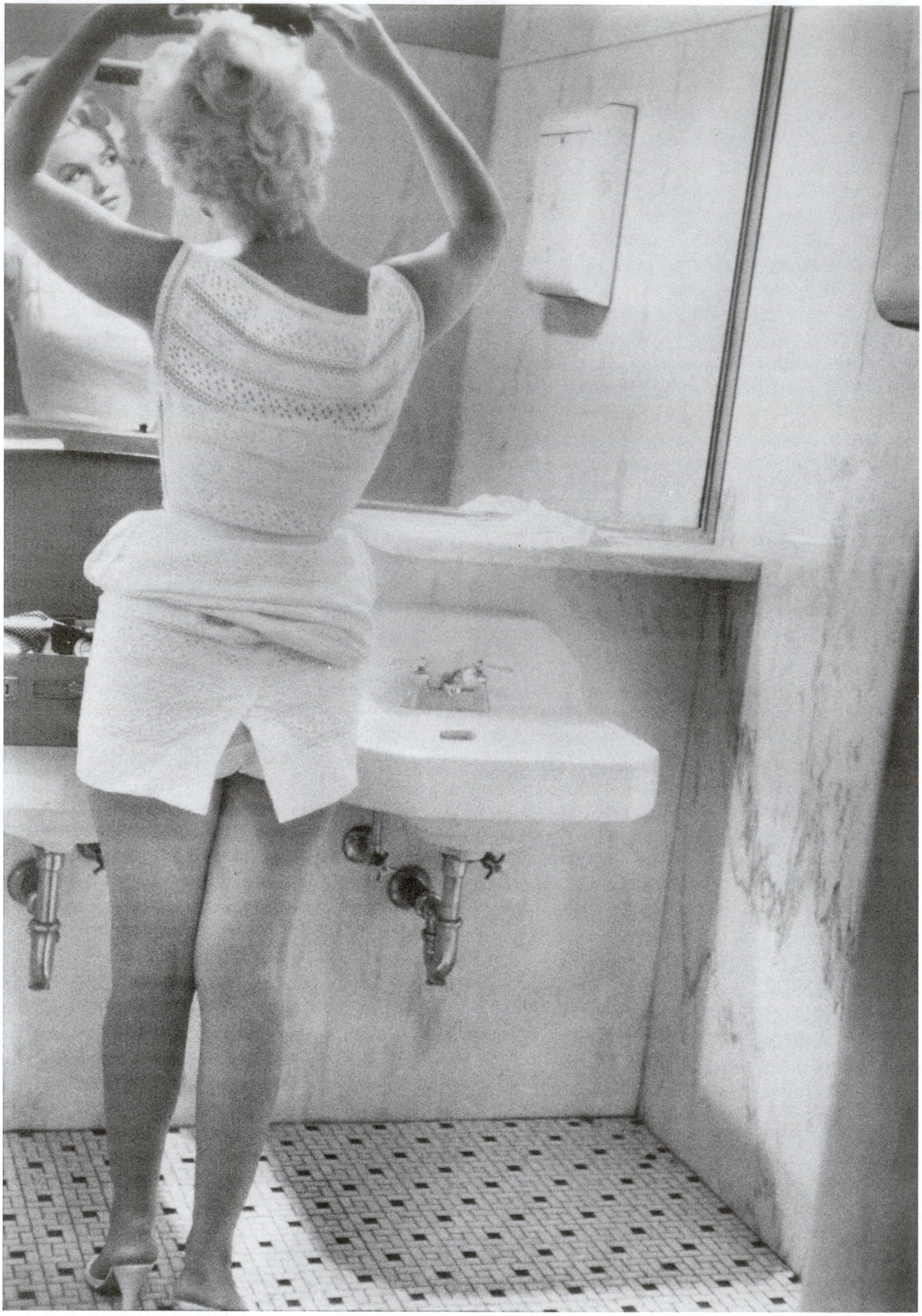

Eve Arnold, Marilyn Monroe—Airport Ladies Room, Chicago, 1955.
[© *Eve Arnold/Magnum Photos*]

for Social Research in 1948; associated with Magnum Photos in 1951; became full member of Magnum in 1955; worked freelance and on assignment for magazines; employed by London *Sunday Times*, 1961–1971; first major solo exhibition at the Brooklyn Museum, 1980; Lifetime Achievement Award from the American Society of Magazine Photographers, 1980; Fellow of the Royal Photographic Society, 1995; elected "Master Photographer" by New York's International Center of Photography, 1995; recipient of the Kraszna-Krausz Book Award for her autobiography *In Retrospect*, 1996; awarded Honorary Degree of Doctor of Science from the University of St. Andrews, Scotland, 1997; awarded Honorary Degree of Doctor of Letters from Staffordshire University, 1997; awarded Honorary Degree of Doctor of Humanities from American International University in London, 1997; appointed member of the Advisory Committee of the National Museum of Photography, Film & Television, 1997. As of 2004 resides in England.

Individual Exhibitions

1980 Brooklyn Museum, Brooklyn, New York
1991 *In Britain*; The National Portrait Gallery, London, England
1995 *In Retrospect*; Barbican, London, England
1995 The National Portrait Galley, Edinburgh, Scotland
1996 The Gallery of Photography, Dublin, Ireland
1996 The Ikon Gallery, Birmingham, England
1997 Castelli Galleries, New York, New York
1997 International Center of Photography, New York, New York
1997 Menil Museum, Houston, Texas
1997 The National Museum of Film, Photography, and Television, Bradford, England

Selected Works

The Unretouched Woman, 1976
Flashback: The 50s, 1978
In China, 1980
In America, 1983
Portrait of a Film: The Making of White Nights, 1985
Marilyn For Ever, 1987
Marilyn Monroe: An Appreciation, 1987
Private View: Inside Baryshnikov's American Ballet Theatre, 1988
All in a Day's Work, 1989
The Great British, 1991
In Retrospect, 1995
Magna Brava: Magnum's Women Photographers, 1999

Further Reading

Eve Arnold: Film Journal. Boomsbury Publishers, 2002.
Eve Arnold in Retrospect. New York: Alfred A. Knopf, 1995.
Brown, Sarah. "Eve Arnold." *British Journal of Photography* (5 January 2000).
Magnum Photos. "Eve Arnold." http://www.magnumphotos.com/portfolio/are/arebio.html (Accessed July 17, 2005).

ART INSTITUTE OF CHICAGO

Chicago in the late nineteenth century experienced a burst of cultural and philanthropic activity as new universities, libraries, theaters, and museums appeared on the landscape. After a series of evolutions under different names, the Art Institute of Chicago was established on Michigan Avenue in 1882. Within about twenty years, the Art Institute was the largest art museum in the country. The museum presently encompasses 400,000 square feet and includes a theater and film center. Home to more than 300,000 works of art in 10 curatorial departments, the museum owns masterpieces by Pablo Picasso, Henri de Toulouse-Lautrec, Georges Seurat, Claude Monet, and Constantin Brancusi.

The School of the Art Institute, founded by a small group of artists in 1866, predates the museum and is presently the largest art school in the country. Another Chicago art school, the Association of Arts and Industries, was established in 1922 to compete with European product design. The Association had hoped to establish a school with a focus on design after attempts to join the School of the Art Institute were unsuccessful. In 1937 the Association invited László Moholy-Nagy to head the new design school. The New Bauhaus: American School of Design was reformed and renamed as the Institute of Design and eventually became part of the Illinois Institute of Technology. In 1950 the Institute of Design became the first American art school to offer a graduate program in photography, conferring its first advanced degrees in 1952. James N. Wood, president of the Art Institute of Chicago from 1980 until 2004, has said, "Ask any photographer with whom he or she trained, and you can probably trace that education back to the Institute of Design." After four years of research, the Art Institute mounted a presentation of the Institute of Design's contribution to American photography titled *Taken by Design: Photographs from the Institute of Design, 1937–1971*. Installed at the Art Institute in 2002, "Taken by Design" traveled to the San Francisco Museum of Modern Art and the Philadelphia Museum of Art in 2003.

As the Art Institute was settling into its new home in the 1880s, photography was just becoming established as an art form in America. The first major photography exhibition in Chicago was held in April 1900, when the Society of Amateur Photographers presented the First Annual Photographic Salon. No American museums had yet established photography departments or programs, although three New York galleries were exhibiting photography in the early 1900s.

Alfred Stieglitz's protégé Julien Levy collected and exhibited photography at his New York gallery from 1931 until 1949. When the Art Institute acquired the Julien Levy Collection in 1975, it encompassed the work of 35 photographers, including Alvin Langdon Coburn, Imogen Cunningham, Lee Miller, László Moholy-Nagy, and Ralph Steiner, in addition to Eugéne Atget's entire collection of photographs and negatives, which Levy had bought in 1927.

Under the direction of Robert B. Harsche, the Art Institute hired a professional curatorial staff in the 1930s, which led to the development of the Department of Prints and Drawings, which in turn generated the photography department. Daniel Catton Rich was named the Art Institute's Director of Fine Arts in 1938, and throughout his tenure provided support for exhibiting and collecting photography, before most other U.S. museums considered photography a fine art medium. Rich met Alfred Stieglitz's muse and painter Georgia O'Keefe in 1929 through Mabel Dodge Luhan, the arts doyenne of Santa Fe, thus cementing a friendship. After Stieglitz's death in 1946, O' Keefe turned to Rich for advice about dispersing Stieglitz's photographs and ultimately donated a major portion of the collection to museum.The memorial exhibition titled *Alfred Stieglitz: His Photographs and His Collection*, which opened in January 1948, included photographs by Edward Steichen, Ansel Adams, Paul Strand, David Hill, Julia Margaret Cameron, and other members of Photo-Secession Group. Rich eventually arranged O'Keeffe's first American solo exhibition.

Hugh Edwards, associate curator of prints and drawings at the Art Institute from 1959 until 1970, was one of the most influential curators of photography in America. Edwards shepherded the nascent photography collection at the Art Institute until it became an officially recognized department. His enthusiasm for street photography was infectious and served as inspiration for Danny Lyon, among others, and ultimately changed what was considered a proper subject for art. He was the first to offer shows to Duane Michaels and the first to exhibit Robert Frank's *The Americans* in 1961.

Edwards established an Art Institute tradition of granting solo exhibitions to photographers early in their careers: André Kertész and Walker Evans in 1946, Ansel Adams and Edward Weston in 1952, Gordon Parks in 1953, and Henri Cartier-Bresson in 1954. An exhibition of photographs by Harry Callahan in 1951 inaugurated the Photography Exhibition Gallery. In 1953 "Photographs in the Peabody Fund" displayed pictorial photographs donated by Mrs. Stuyvesant Peabody expressly for the newly established gallery, which according to an assistant curator was "part hallway, part waiting room." The gallery later became the AIC Gallery of Photography and was launched with an exhibition of work by Frederick Sommer in 1963.

Photography exhibitions at the Art Institute at that time were small by today's standards and organized without accompanying catalogs or checklist documentation. But the department continued to grow with additional gifts and acquisitions, including major donations of works by Paul Strand and more than 200 photographs by Edward Weston. The first color exhibition featured works by Arthur Siegel in 1954; Yasuhiro Ishimoto was the first Japanese photographer exhibited at the museum, in 1960.

The Art Institute continues to bring contemporary photography to Chicago, including shows by Mark Klett, Susan Meiselas, and Raghubir Singh, and a retrospective of the work of Kenneth Josephson in 2000. An exhibition titled *About Face: Photographic Portraits from the Collection* in October 2004, featured recent acquisitions in the Art Institute's collection. Thirty contemporary photographers were represented, including Sally Mann, Nicholas Nixon, Vik Muniz, Cindy Sherman, Nan Goldin, Susan Meiselas, Richard Avedon, Chuck Close, Luis Gonzalez Palma, and Fazal Sheikh.

RENATA GOLDEN

See also: **Museums; United States**

Further Reading

Harris, Neil. *Chicago's Dream, a World's Treasure: The Art Institute of Chicago, 1893 – 1993*. Chicago: Art Institute of Chicago, 1993.

Maxon, John. *The Art Institute of Chicago*. New York, Harry N. Abrams, Inc., 1970.

May, Sally Ruth. *The Art Institute of Chicago: The Essential Guide*. Chicago, The Art Institute of Chicago, 1993.

Travis, David. *Photographs from the Julien Levy Collection: Starting with Atget*. Chicago: The Art Institute of Chicago, 1976.

One Hundred Years at the Art Institute: A Centennial Celebration. Art Institute Museum Studies, Vol. 19, No. 1, (1993).

The Art of Photography: Past and Present. Collection of the Art Institute of Chicago, National Museum of Art, Osaka, Japan, 1984.

ARTISTS' BOOKS

In diverse forms and contexts, artists' books experienced a dynamic presence in the myriad of art movements in the twentieth century. The evolution of artists' books reflects changes in technology as well as social, political, cultural, and economic developments. Artists' books have been made from traditional materials and bookbinding techniques, or radically challenging materials and various methods of compilation or presentation that sidestep bookbinding entirely.

No single definition of an artist's book can be both broad and specific enough to be useful but some book forms can be excluded. Some deluxe editions, letterpress work, handset type, for instance, do not typify the nature of an artist's book. Some artists' books can be mass-produced through xerography or other economical printing methods. In the 1950s, Robert Heinecken printed photographs of highly political or pornographic imagery directly onto the pages of popular magazines that he then placed back on store shelves for sale to an unsuspecting public. Some artists' books exist in limited editions, perhaps produced with the participation of a printer, book center, gallery, or museum exhibition or collection. These efforts have spread in recent years, but remain distinct from books called *livre d'artist*. Some artists' books may be a one-of-a-kind object, but generally the term refers to editioned, mass-distributed materials. Some artists' books entirely avoid material existence and circulate as performance pieces or as part of the World Wide Web.

Some artists' books are "containers of information," the material support being secondary to the expression or contemplation of personal, political, emotional, or social ideas. In other artists' books, the object itself is the principle exploration and can exist in many forms. Artists' books can be bound in traditional, accordion folds, various Japanese bindings, or the book can be otherwise constructed, involving no binding at all. The book may consist of pages, be in scroll form, be kinetic and involve moving parts, or be sculptural and exist for viewing as a 3-D work of art. Some artists alter already bound books.

The growth and intensity of work with artists' books in the twentieth century has several historical references. In 1974, the Grolier Club organized an exhibition and book titled, *The Truthful Lens*, which describes 175 books with original photographs, mostly from the nineteenth century, claiming that a more complete list might number 2,500 titles. Technology changes in the late nineteenth century such as lithography, machine-set type, and the linotype machine, facilitated the mass-production and distribution of books. This activity did not end the practice of more elaborate book making and by the early twentieth century, the mass production of cheaper editions sometimes included the production of a limited number of more elaborate copies.

In the 1920s, Russian Constructionism served as a foundation for the idea of books as art. Art movements such as Dadaism, Surrealism, Expressionism, and Futurism searched not only for new content but for new forms of expression and artists' books were made by Tristan Tzara, Wassily Kandinsky, László Moholy-Nagy.

In the 1930s, Walker Evans established a style often mimicked in subsequent photography books, with the photographs placed on the right-hand page and the left-hand page usually left blank. Many artists' books are constructed with this gallery-in-hand presentation.

In the 1950s, the German-born provocateur Dieter Roth shredded, then boiled paper that he stuffed into animal intestines to make "literary sausages." Considered one of the instigators of the contemporary movement in artists' books, Roth used a variety of found materials, such as overruns from commercial printers, as well as rubberstamping to establish many of the conventions of the field. Another seminal figure is the California painter Ed Ruscha. In the 1960s, Ruscha published *Twenty-six Gasoline Stations* and made clear his intent to explore book art as primary material, not as support for his other explorations in art. Ruscha's books have been highly sought-after, despite their original modest intent to reach a wider audience in expensive, unlimited editions. By the 1980s, book art branched out into the performing arts. In a review on performing arts in the 1990s, British editor Claire MacDonald refers to the theatrical manuscript, describing a new interest in questioning conventional relationships between oral and written texts.

In 1984, in the United States, the National Endowment for the Arts added bookmaking to its categories for funding. This fund was eliminated several years later.

In the last decades of the twentieth century, Great Britain, Europe, Japan, and the United States saw a number of new printing establishments, mixing craft techniques in paper making and book binding. These establishments are sometimes part of a university or art school, sometimes a private institution such as New York City's Center for Book Arts or the Purgatory Pie Press. Book art centers may provide facilities for the production of work as well as funding and an infrastructure to showcase results. In 1965, Stan Bevington set up Coach House Press in Toronto primarily to publish Canadian authors but also to make more craft laden books. Since 1972, under the direction of Joan Lyons, the Visual Studies Workshop in Rochester, New York, has produced more than 200 books, including artists' books as well as critical or historical visual art titles. Other book art centers include the Pacific Center for the Book Arts (California), Printed Matter Bookstore and the Franklin Furnace (New York City), Bookworks (London), Art Metropole (Toronto), Women's Study Workshop (Rosendale, New York). Franklin Furnace, founded in 1976, has pursued an active and often controversial roll in the production and distribution of artistic works not supported by existing artistic organizations. In 1979, Franklin Furnace exhibited work curated by several prominent figures from the art world including Clive Phillpot, whose curating, writing, and other activities made a significant contribution to the book arts in the twentieth century. The Nexus Press (Atlanta) is run by and for photographers who want to publish their own books. In 1976, Chicago Books appeared, inviting six to ten artists a year to produce a book at its facilities. In 1977, the Writer's Center in Bethesda, Maryland, expanded its activities to include the production of artists' books. Pyramid Atlantic, a book art center in Maryland, opened in 1981 under the direction of Helen Fredrick.

Thus, the expansion of funds and facilities for the production of artists' books progressed but diffusion of such objects remained problematic throughout the century. Their singularity often makes them both precious and inaccessible. Sometimes, artists' books can be showcased in traditional venues for books, such as bookstores, coffee houses, reading rooms, or libraries. Sometimes, such objects are best distributed through more traditional art venues such as galleries, museums, and art fairs. Art fairs devoted specifically to books provide fertile ground for artists and collectors to compare otherwise singular isolated works. Pyramid Atlantic hosted half a dozen such book fairs in Washington, DC, in the 1990s. In New York City, the Brooke Alexander Gallery showcased artists' books concurrent to the yearly Armory Show of prints and drawings. By the end of the century, many individuals, universities, and museums began to collect and exhibit artists' books, including the Museum of Modern Art, New York, the Bibliotheque Nationale Paris, France, The School of the Art Institute of Chicago, the Manchester Metropolitan University, and the Carnegie Mellon Libraries, Pittsburgh, Pennsylvania.

Fear that mechanical and digital technological changes throughout the twentieth century would bring an end to the artist's book did not prove true and the book as object remained a leading genre in the art world. Technology advances made desktop publishing an increasingly democratic possibility, supplementing works with precious materials with works available to low-budget projects. By the end of the century, immaterial books existed on the computer screen via the world wide web.

Bruce McKaig

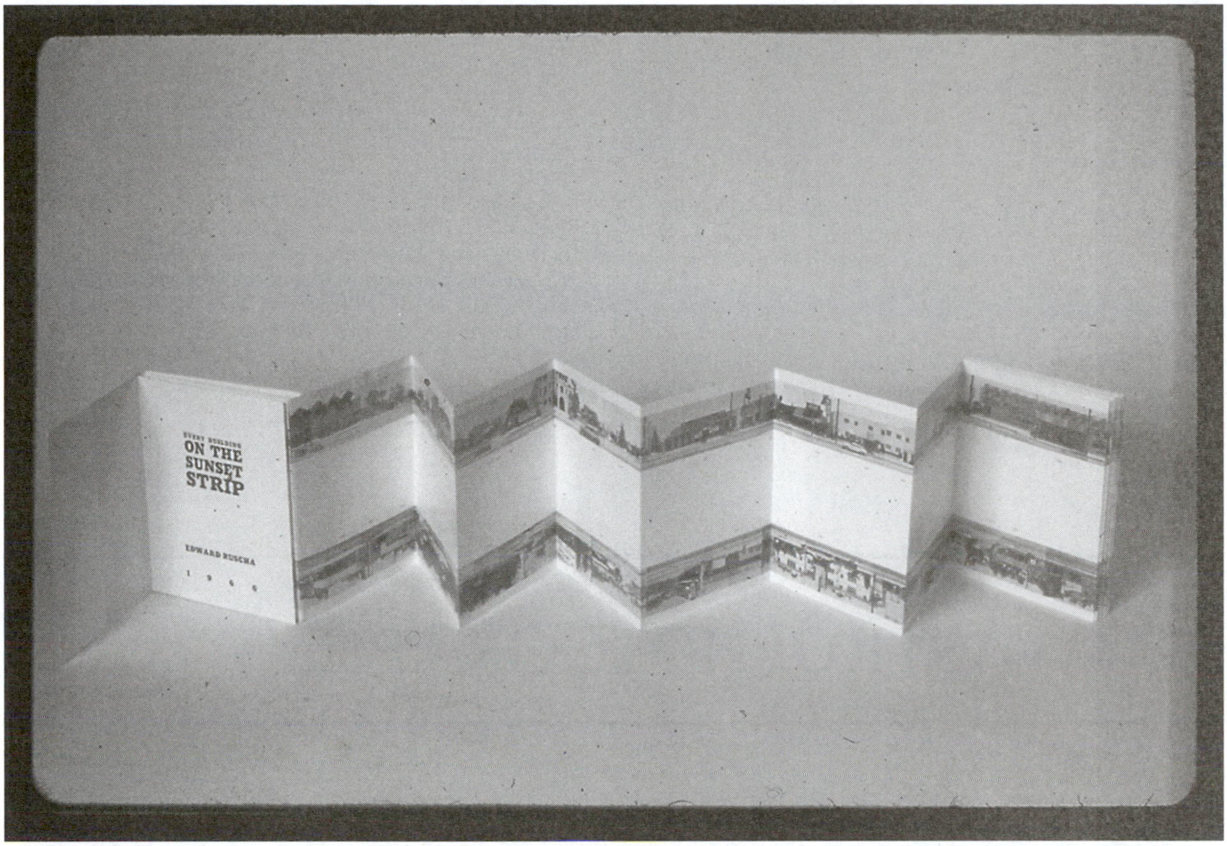

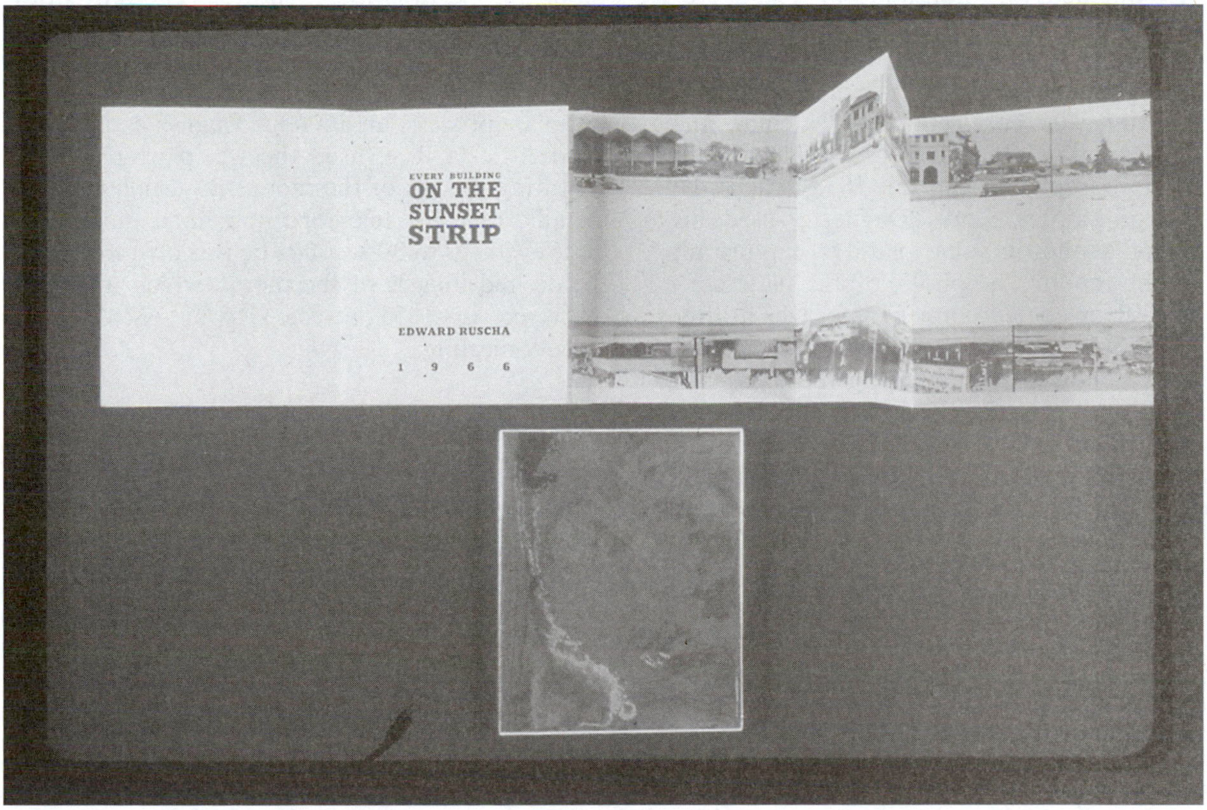

Ed Ruscha, Every Building on The Sunset Strip, 1966, MCA purchase.
[*Photograph © Museum of Contemporary Art, Chicago*]

See also: **Conceptual Photography; Evans, Walker; Moholy-Nagy, László; Museums: United States; The Internet and Photography**

Further Reading

Castleman, Riva. *A Century of Artists Books*. New York City: Museum of Modern Art, 1994.

Drucker, Johanna. *The Century of Artists' Books*. New York City: Granary Books, 1995.

Eaton, Timothy. *Books as Art*. Boca Raton, Florida: Boca Raton Museum of Art, 1991.

Goldschmidt, Lucien, and Naef, Weston. *The Truthful Lens: A Survey of the Photographically Illustrated Book 1844–1914*. New York: The Grolier Club, 1980.

Kenny, Lorraine. "On Artists' Book Publishing." *Afterimage*, vol. 12 (March 1985).

Klima, Stefan. *Artists Books: A Critical Survey of the Literature*. New York: Granary Books, 1998.

Lippard, Lucy. *Six Years: The Dematerialization of the Art Object from 1966 to 1972*. Berkeley: University of California Press, 1997.

Moeglin-Delcroix, Anne. *Esthetique du livre d'artiste 1960–1980*. Paris: Editions Jean-Michel Place, 1997.

Rolo, Jane, and Ian Hunt, eds. *Book Works: A Partial History and Sourcebook*. London: Book Works, 1996.

Trend, David. "At the Margins: Artists' Books in the '80s." *Afterimage*, vol. 13, no. 1 & 2 (1985).

ASTROPHOTOGRAPHY

The night sky has been observed and its movements documented for thousands of years. Numerous symbolic visual paintings and carvings are found around the world as well as manmade solar and lunar calendars. But a true image of a celestial body was as fleeting as catching the moon's reflection in a bucket of water. The history of astrophotography began in 1838 when the French stage painter, Louis Daguerre, used his invention of a photographic plate to capture an image of the moon. The photographic plate consisted of a silver coated copper plate, which after taking a photograph was exposed to vaporized magnesium, followed by immersing the plate into sodium thiosulfate to fix the image and dissolve the unused silver iodide by rinsing the plate with hot water. This process was dubbed the Daguerreotype process. The image of the moon, however, was not very clear.

Wet Collodion Process

The Daguerreotype was used up until 1851, when a new process called Collodion or "Wet Plate" process was invented by a Frenchman named G. Le Gray and introduced by Frederick Scott-Archer. The Collodion process quickly became the preferred process of choice by astrophotographers. Due to the sensitivity of the plate—five to ten times more sensitive than Daguerrotypes—the exposure time was much shorter. The only drawback was that the plate had to be used immediately after it was made.

A year later, following the introduction of the wet plate process, an amateur English astronomer, Warren de la Rue, used the wet plate process in capturing images of the moon. By using a 13-inch metallic reflector telescope and hand moving the plate every 10 to 30 seconds he was able to capture the desired images of the moon, which were later displayed in 1853 at the Royal Astronomical Society meeting.

Dry Emulsions

Another field of study that became intertwined with astrophotography was that of spectroscopy. Scientist realized during the 1880s that the light spectrum emitted by stars and planets contained information about the stars' chemical components. Spectroscopy did not become practical until the invention of the dry plate. In 1871, Dr. R.L. Maddox, an Englishman, produced the first positive dry emulsion plate by using a gelatin rather than using a glass base for the plate. Three years later in 1874, the negative dry emulsion plate was made by Johnston and Bolton. Dry plates could be made and stored until needed as well as being 100 times more sensitive than the wet plates of earlier times. In 1876 the first spectrum of Vega was completed by a spectroscopist, W. Huggins, who also did the first spiral galaxy in 1899. Photography dramatically changed in 1884 when George Eastman once again advanced the art with the invention of the celluloid-based photographic film. But astrophotographers continued to use the glass plates for several reasons, such as film can shrink and warp over time, film is not completely flat all the time, and telescopes at observatories had large focal planes and had no use for the smaller film image frames. However for the backyard astrophotographer and the traveling scientist, the use of Kodak's new roll film was ideal.

Color and CCD

Astrophotography continued to be shot in black and white although the Kodachrome process was marketed in 1935 and color film had been introduced commercially during the 1940s. There was a problem in trying to capture a color image of the heavens because long exposure times resulted in distorted color representation. The sensitivity of the film needed to be increased so the exposure time could be shorter. The Kodak 103a spectroscopic films were still more sensitive than the color film and also the color films were not available in plate form. William Miller of the Mount Wilson and Palomar Observatories was the pioneer of color astrophotogrpahy. The 200-inch Hale reflector telescope at Palomar Observatory was built exclusively for photography. In 1959 Miller used Super Ansochrome, a commercially available reversal type film. Miller gave the film extended exposure time to offset the problem of reciprocity failure due to the film's speed, ASA 100.

Eastman-Kodak solved the problem of low-intensity reciprocity failure. This is where the photosensitive grains of the emulsion do not respond to light in a linear way because water and oxygen molecules become trapped within the emulsion. The answer was hypersensitizing, also known as gas hypering.

In 1969, bubble memory, a new type of computer memory discovered at Bell Labs was made sensitive to light. More sensitive than film, they are stable and can be directly input into a computer. Emulsion based astrophotography was replaced by the introduction of charge-coupled device or CCD sensor. The CCD is a small chip broken up into very small cells. Light traveling through the lens, is reflected by mirrors, then reflected by a prism onto the surface of the CCD detector. CCD is affected by the photons of light when hit. Photons hitting the surface of the CCD knock electrons out of place in the cell. While CCDs were becoming popular, Kodak introduced a new film, Tech Pan in 1980, an emulsion with high contrast and sensitivity that also recorded infared and ultraviolet objects. CCD however, had become the preferred method for astronomy. Most professional observatories now use the CCDs. CCDs were also the choice of NASA for the Mars Pathfinder mission, which upon landing on the Martian surface on July 4, 1997, began to send back very sharp images of the red planet.

The Camera in Space

Astrophotography in the twentieth century literally reached new heights. Now the cameras themselves were actually flying through the very heavens they had earlier captured while attached to telescopes on terra firma. In 1959 the Soviet *Luna 3* probe swung around the moon and captured the first photograph of the moon's far side. Sister probe to *Mariner 3*, *Mariner 4* reached Mars in 1965, and took the first close-up images of the Martian surface. NASA's Apollo missions had the objective of using photography to map the entire lunar surface. Hasselblad cameras were used with both black and white and color film. Several cameras were mounted within the command module while several other that were controlled by the command module were stowed in the scientific instrument module. The voyager space probes during the period of 1979–1980 sent back photographs of the planetary family as they swung by Jupiter and Saturn. The most astonishing photographs of the universe were to come once again from a telescope, but this time the telescope was floating in space. Launched on April 4, 1990 at 12:33:51 UTC, the Hubble Space Telescope began to send back remarkable images of our own galaxy as well as others. A 2.4 m, f/24 Ritchey-Chretien telescope, the Hubble could make observations in visible, near-ultraviolet and new-infared. The imaging and spectroscope of the future is the Next Generation Space Telescope, whose primary mirror diameter is twice that of Hubble's and designed to see the far visible to the mid-infared part of the spectrum.

Camera and Tripod

The most accessible type of astrophotography is that of the camera mounted on a tripod. The camera is mounted on the tripod and the shutter is held open with a trigger release cord. Most 35-mm cameras have a B or bulb setting to do this. This allows the film to be exposed to low levels of evening sky light. A large variety of wide and zoom lenses are incorporated, depending on the object being captured. Star tracking is one of the most common and easiest special effects to accomplish. This is where the shutter is left open for more than 15 seconds, thus letting star trails form on the exposed film.

Piggyback Photography

This is where the camera is connected to a telescope either in a piggyback fashion or hooked up to the eye piece of the telescope via an adapter. Piggyback photography provides the photographer with the ability to "track" the stars. An equatorial mount is used in which the rotational axis of the tracker is aligned with the rotational axis of the earth. This is different from an alt-azimuth mount where the camera is mounted on a vertical swivel so the camera may be aimed at a star during a long exposure. This type of mount produces an image of a star in the middle of the photo as a dot while outlying stars show up as arcs, which elongate the further the stars position from the center. The arcs are a product of field rotation, caused by the camera swivel not being aligned with the rotational axis of the earth.

Autoguided Photography

Two types of auto guiding are popular, the use of an off-axis guider and the use of a separate guiding scope. Professionals usually use a CCD autoguider or a reticle eyepiece. Reticle eyepieces used are either standard or illuminated. With CCD software for personal computers, an amateur astrophotographer with a hybrid telescope/camera can now be hooked up to a personal computer and guided through the night sky.

Stacy Fox

Further Reading

Arnett, Bill. *Planetary Science Spacecraft*. http://seds.lpl.arizona.edu/nineplanets/nineplanets/Spacecraft.html (accessed May 4, 2005).

De Vacouleurs, Gerad. (trans. by R. Wright) *Astronomical Photography, from the Daguerreotype to the Electron Camera*. London: Faber & Faber, 1961.

Kodak, *History of Kodak*. http://www.kodak.com/about kodak/kodakHistory/milestones78-32.html.

Malin, D. "The Developing Art of Star Photography." *New Scientist* 120 (Dec. 17, 1988), 23–28.

Milan, Wil. *The Photographer's Progress: A Short History of Emulsion-Based Deep-Sky Photography*. http://www.astrophotographer.com.

Schirmer, A.F., and S.R. Majewski. *History of Photometric Measurements in Astronomy*. http://www.astro.virginia.edu/~afs5z/photometry.html 1999 (accessed May 4, 2005).

Space Telescope Science Institute. *Hubble Primer*. http://oposite.stci.edu/puinfo/spacecraft/Primer.

EUGÈNE ATGET

French

Although much has been recorded about the lives of photographers and artists who worked in Paris during the late nineteenth and early twentieth centuries, the photographer Eugène Atget is an exception. What little that is known about his life has been laboriously reconstructed; however, the vast amount of work he produced provides a record of his accomplishments as a photographer. Bits of his life have been pieced together from the memories of the few people whom he chose to befriend. These include André Calmettes, actor and motion picture director, Man Ray, photographer, and particularly the American photographer Berenice Abbott who dedicated much of her time to the public recognition of Atget. Although he died virtually unknown and never formally exhibited his work, upon his death Atget left approximately 2000 eight by ten-inch glass plates and almost 10,000 prints.

Orphaned at age five or six, Atget was raised by an uncle. At a young age he signed on as a cabin boy on a steamer bound for Uruguay, and would later exaggerate that he had been on several voyages. As a young man he turned to acting, and around 1886 met the actress Valentine Delafosse-Compagnon who became his lifelong companion, or *amie*, and the two toured minor provincial theaters. Atget's physique and provincial accent kept him from landing anything but undesirable "third" roles, and in 1888 he was dismissed from the theater. Around 1889 he and Valentine moved to Paris where he unsuccessfully tried his hand at painting (some of his paintings were uncovered in his studio upon his death). Sometime during the late 1890s he devoted himself to becoming a self-taught photographer, a technology only about 40 years old. Little is known about how he learned photographic techniques, but Abbott has described his early efforts as taking place in remote gardens where he was able to learn and experiment undisturbed.

Atget's early photographs were taken with the idea of creating study material for artists, and for some years he took pictures of natural images such as landscapes and plants. It is thought that Atget began working as a photographer in 1898, and it is clear that he was soon successful enough to meagerly support himself. The following announcement appeared in the February 1892 issue of *La Revue des Beaux-Arts:*

> We recommend to our readers, M. Atget photographer, 5 Rue de la Pitié (Paris), who has for artists: landscapes, animals, flowers, monuments, documents, foregrounds for artists, reproductions for paintings, will travel. Collections not commercially available.

The hand lettered sign outside his fifth-floor apartment-studio at 31 rue Campagne Première read, "Documents pour Artistes," and it is said that numerous Parisian painters, including Georges Braque, Henri Matisse, and Man Ray were among his customers.

Atget's friend André Calmettes conveyed the photographer's early aspirations, "He already had the ambition of creating a collection of everything artistic and picturesque in and about Paris." Perhaps as early as 1898 Atget decided upon the subject for which he is best known, a systematic record of the streets, storefronts, people, architectural details, and landmarks of old Paris. These works were not commissioned, offering Atget an artistic freedom that was more agreeable to him than his earlier natural studies. He eventually disclosed to Abbott that he did not like taking commissions because "people [do] not know how to see." He allowed himself to seek and capture the endless surprises of Paris, the winding streets, and the old houses, the statues and reflections. His idea was nominally successful and in 1901 he began a series that was overseen by the Bibliothèque historique de la Ville de Paris. The series, titled *La Topographie du Vieux Paris*, was in many ways a continuation of his own documentation of Paris. The concept behind this series, which made it different from Atget's earlier work, was to visually record architectural and historical sites that were about to be demolished, capturing the spirit of a Paris about to disappear.

The photographs of Old Paris by Atget are invaluable as a record of a quickly changing city, which underwent redevelopment at least twice during his lifetime. Napoleon III came to power in 1853, appointing Baron Georges Hausmann as chief administrator to oversee the task of modernizing the city of Paris with the purpose of showcasing it as the center of western culture and modernity. In the process of building parks, widening avenues, and raising new buildings and cathedrals that became known as "Hausmannizaton" many old landmarks were demolished, such as the street and buildings that were the subject of *Cour, rue Beethovan, 9* (1901). Victorien Sardou tipped off Atget as to which Parisian buildings and landmarks were destined for demolition, and Atget managed to visually record many of these sites just before their destruction. The process of modernization again occurred in Paris during the period following World War I when Parisians were concerned with rebuilding their devastated city. Atget himself did little to no photography during the war, but picked his camera back up after the war's conclusion and expanded his subject matter to include the countryside around Paris.

One intriguing aspect of Atget's photos is the ability of the viewer to see historic Paris through the eyes of an artist who insisted on the documentary character of his work. It is this view of his own work that might lead one to suggest that Atget fully realized the historical context in which his images existed and their potential value to future generations.

In 1926, Atget met the young American photographer Berenice Abbott. Abbott's interest in Atget's photography and life has proven to be indispensable. Upon Atget's death in 1927, Abbott purchased a number of his prints, negatives, slides, and papers from André Calmettes, and this collection was purchased in 1968 by the Museum of Modern Art, New York. Abbott photographed Atget only days before his death, and completed biographical writings on his life that have proven to be indispensable to scholars.

Atget captured the contradictions of Paris; the simple beauty of the urban landscape and the elegance of Versailles juxtaposed with the poverty and hard reality of the times. He used various mechanical and compositional techniques in his photography to invite the viewer into the composition. His photographic style did not emulate painting as most photography then did, but instead his experience and facility with the camera allowed him to capture detail and surface texture, heightening the viewer's sense of reality of the subject. The depth of his images and their atmospheric quality also had the effect of drawing the viewer into his photographs. There was anintensity to his work often achieved by juxtaposing the focal point of the image, such as the statue in *Versailles, parc* (1906), against a dark background. His work welcomed the viewer's gaze because he used an eye-level viewpoint almost exclusively, and often created asymmetrical or angled images of his subjects, inviting one to mentally "step toward and move around" his subjects.

Although much of Atget's subject matter is architectural, he also explored human figures as subjects. His studies of people, sometimes casually posed and always naturalistic, represented honest investigations of the working class as they appeared in daily life on the streets of Paris as typified by *Ragpicker, Paris* (1899–1900) and *Street Musicians* (*Joueur d'orgue*, 1899–1900). These images did not generally describe the particular individual, but instead, described their class or occupation through dignified and sensitive renderings. Given the technological limitations of photography at the time, Atget probably posed his figures, asking them to "hold still a moment."

Atget used a simple 18 × 24 cm view camera with a tripod. His methods were considered old fashioned by the end of his own lifetime, requiring him to lug over 40 pounds of equipment including heavy glass plates, bellows camera, and the wooden tripod. The Paris Metro was his preferred means of transportation, and his client lists provide both addresses and the closest metro station. Atget never hired assistants to help him with his equipment, but preferred to work alone.

One of the photographic techniques Atget used that set his images apart from those of other photographers of his day was his use of a rapid rectilinear lens with a short focal length, resulting in a wide lens. This gave his pictures more depth than was fashionable at the time, the result being very different from contemporary styles of painting. He was a so-called "straight" photographer, meaning that he did not crop, trim, or alter the final image by burning or dodging any of his prints in the darkroom. He printed his glass plates by daylight and toned them with gold chloride. Atget relied on nature and instinct, using no artificial light for his interior shots, no light meter, and judging exposure by experience and charts. In 1906 he discovered the "faulty" technique of shooting directly into the sun, a process that reduced detail but increased the atmospheric quality of his images.

Despite suggestions made by the surrealist photographer Man Ray to update the type of paper he used, Atget insisted upon using old fashioned paper that curled and had to be glued onto cardboard, the acid eventually damaging the prints themselves. Because of the processes he chose, particularly the paper selection, many of his works have not survived well. Although Atget rarely dated his works, he did etch numbers into the emulsion, sometimes causing permanent damage to his negatives.

One of the reasons that Atget did not achieve much recognition during his lifetime was that he did not associate with any sort of photographic or artistic groups. He was a dedicated photographer who made little time for friends, clubs, or other social activities. He rose at dawn every day and used the morning hours to photograph in order to avoid traffic and crowds, and in the afternoon he would develop. His kept strict habits in his manners of dress and appetite, was a quiet figure who wore patched clothes and a large overcoat, and lived for 20 years on nothing but bread, milk, and sugar.

Atget's work has been compared with that of both the Cubists and the Surrealists, but it was the Surrealists who took an interest in his photography and looked to him as a pioneer of their movement. Man Ray's exclamation "I discovered him!" adequately describes the enthusiasm the group held for Atget. The Surrealists were interested in publishing Atget's work in their magazines, but he would often only submit his work anonymously, explaining "These are simply documents." The Surrealists found a certain mystery and atmospheric quality in Atget's photographs, particularly in images such as *Avenue des Gobelins, Paris* (1925), *Men's Fashions* (1925), and a myriad of images of shop mannequins and urban ennui. In 1931, Walter Benjamin wrote in his *Small History of Photography*, "Atget's Paris photos are the forerunners of surrealistic photography." The photographer's everyday subjects, his found objects (or what the Surrealists called the *objet trouvé*), and the tiny details hidden in his works fascinated Surrealists as such objects and images were believed to be imbued with psychological meaning and mystical overtones. Painter Salvador Dalí commented upon

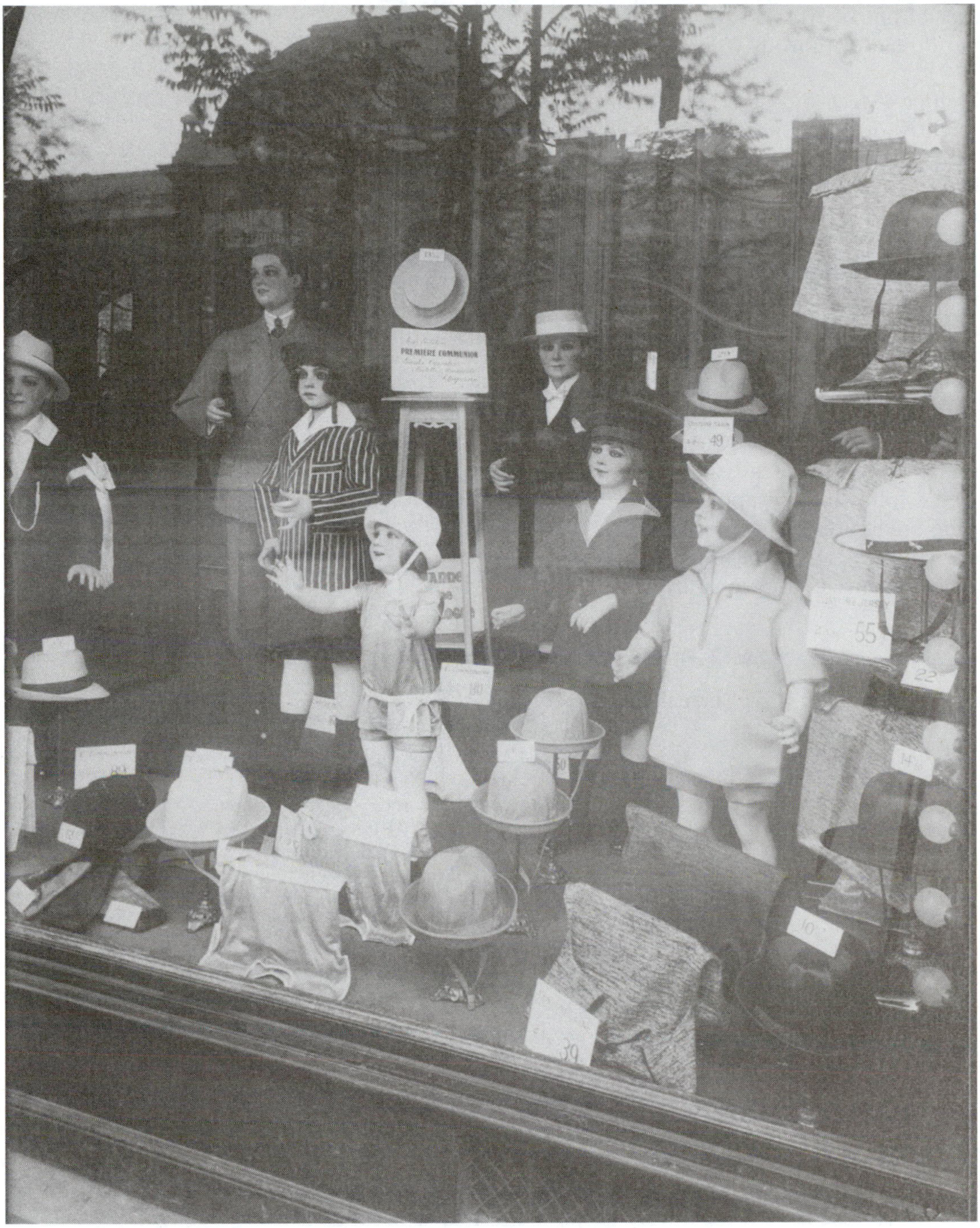

Eugène Atget, Avenue des Gobelins, 1925, silver printing-out paper print, 22.9 × 17.2 cm, ex-collection Man Ray.
[*Photograph courtesy of George Eastman House*]

a detail in a corner of one of Atget's street images, "The reel with no thread clamorously demands to be interpreted."

During his lifetime Atget did not receive the recognition he rightly deserved according to his peers, critics, and photographers who followed in his wake. He died virtually unknown and unpublished in any major photographic publications; he never showed his work in the many Parisian salons. There were several institutions, however, that honored him by purchasing collections of works during his lifetime. These included the Bibliothèque historique de la Ville de Paris, the Bibliothèque nationale, and the library of the Musèe des Arts décoratifs. Despite nominal success during his own lifetime, the work of Atget has been increasingly admired since his death. Calmettes wrote to Abbott the following epitaph for Atget, "May all those who are interested in what he loved so much...still pronounce sometimes his name, which was that of a strong, courageous artist, of an admirable *imagier*."

CATHERINE BURDICK

See also: **Abbott, Berenice; Man Ray; Surrealism**

Biography

Jean Eugène Auguste Atget was born at Libourne, near Bordeaux, France, February 12, 1857. Moved to Paris, 1860s, enrolled in Catholic high school. Enrolled in Conservatory of the French National Theatre, 1879. Returned to Paris around 1889 and began photography around 1898. Self-educated in photography. Sold 100 prints to the Bibliothèque historique de la Ville de Paris, 1899. Began *La Topographie du Vieux Paris*, 1901. Sold 2600 plate glass negatives to the Service Photographique des Monuments Historiques around 1920. Published in *La Révolution surréaliste*, 1926. Died in Montparnasse, August 4, 1927.

Selected Works

La Topographie du Vieux Paris (series)
Street Musicians, 1899–1900 (printed in 1956 by Berenice Abbott from Atget's negative)
Cour, rue Beethovan, 9, 1901
Versailles, coin de parc, 1902
Versailles, parc, 1906
Ragpicker, Paris, 1899–1900
Eclipse, 1911 (printed in 1956 by Berenice Abbott from Atget's negative)
St. Cloud, 1919–1921
226 Boulevard de la Villette, 1921
Avenue des Gobelins, Paris, 1925
Men's Fashions, 1925 (published title *Magasin, avenue des Gobelins*, printed 1956 by Abbott from Atget's negative)
Buttes Chaumont, 1926
Fete de la Villette, 1926
Boulevard de Strasbourg, 1926

Further Reading

Abbot, Berenice. *The World of Atget*. New York: Berkley Publishing Corporation, 1964.
Atget, Eugène. *Atget Paris*. Paris: Hazan, 1992.
Atget, Eugène. *Atget's Gardens: A Selection of Eugène Atget's Garden Photographs*. New York: Doubleday and Company Inc., 1979.
Borcoman, James. *Eugène Atget: 1857–1927*. Ottawa: National Museums of Canada, 1984.
Lemagny, Jean-Claude. *Atget: the Pioneer*. Munich, New York, London: Prestel, 2000.
Szarkowski, John. *Atget*. New York: The Museum of Modern Art and Calloway, 2000.
Trottenberg, Arthur. D., ed. *A Vision of Paris: The Photographs of Eugène Atget, Words of Marcel Proust*. New York: Macmillan Publishing Co., Inc., 1963.

ELLEN AUERBACH

American

Ellen Auerbach founded a pioneering woman-run photography studio in Berlin in the late 1920s and early 1930s, where she created memorable portraiture and advertising photographs. This studio, consisting of Auerbach and her close friend Grete Stern, came to a sudden end with Hitler's rise to power. Throughout her flight from Berlin to Tel Aviv and then to London Auerbach still managed to work as a photographer. In 1937 she immigrated to the United States where she worked as a freelance photographer and then, late in life, as an educator working with children suffering from schizophrenia.

Auerbach's work, along with that of Stern's, focused on the object almost as a sculptural study, concentrating on the essential, revealing her affiliation to Walter Peterhans, with whom she studied privately, and the tenets of the Bauhaus. Auerbach, however, displayed a particular sensitivity to nature and children and conveys what she calls poetically "The third eye": "In my photographic work, I have not only endeavored to record what one sees on the surface, but also to capture the essence that lies beneath the surface of things."

Auerbach studied sculpture at the Badische Landeskunstschule from 1924–1927 and continued her studies at the Academy of Art (Am Weissenhof) in Stuttgart. Her uncle gave Auerbach her first camera (9 × 12 cm) in gratitude for the bust she had made of him. The new artistic possibilities and also a newly found financial independence led Auerbach to discontinue her study of sculpture and take up the study of photography.

In 1929, together with Grete Stern she took classes in photography as a private pupil with Walter Peterhans in Berlin and, aside from these classes, Auerbach was self-taught, although because of her association with Peterhans she is often considered as Bauhaus-trained. Even though the German capital in the 1920s was one of the most interesting places for artists, Auerbach and Stern appeared to have remained isolated from the various photographic circles. Stern had a short contact with the photographer Otto Umbehr, an acquaintance of her brother who advised her to study with Peterhans.

When Peterhans closed his studio to join the Bauhaus staff in Dessau in 1929, Auerbach and Stern acquired it with a small inheritance that Stern had received. They then opened "foto ringl + pit" (a moniker derived from Grete's childhood nickname, and the dancer Pepita Pit, whom Auerbach resembled), the first women-run advertising photo studio in Berlin. The studio specialized in portraiture, still life, advertising photography, and magazine illustration (1931–1933). The studio produced clear and precise images in the spirit of the *Neue Sehen* or new photography that was typical of Berlin photographers of the era. Their work was also notable for its imaginative usage of surrealist motifs and critical humor. Although photographs by ringl + pit appeared in periodicals such as *Gebrauchsgraphik* (*Commercial Art*) and *Cahiers d'art*, as well as *Neue Frauenkleidung und Frauenkultur* (*New Women's Clothing and Women's Culture*), and the firm's advertising clients ranged from manufacturers of hair lotion and cigarettes to distributors of petroleum products, Auerbach and Stern could not make a living with their studio work.

Aside from her commercial efforts, most of Auerbach's photos from this time were the result of a creative interplay with Grete Stern. Their studio was not only a place of work, but also a space of vivid exchange and friendship. To this Auerbach brought sculptural sensibility and Stern brought her graphic design know-how; both photographers signed the works with the studio's name, making it difficult to distinguish authorship. This concentration on the world of objects differed from the contemporary use of the camera as a means to explore urban reality, represented by other photographers of the late Weimar Republic such as Lotte Jacobi and Marianne Breslauer. The ringl + pit studio time allowed Stern and Auerbach to take initiatives and to experiment with various techniques, including montage. They developed alternative representations of women in advertisement, for instance, their famous image *Komol*, and engaged in a playful confusion between "living model and manikin" (e.g., *Petrole Hahn*: the manikin is dressed in an old-fashioned nightgown, while a human hand holds the product).

In 1933 the studio ringl + pit gained international recognition as the two photographers received first prize from the Deuxième Exposition Internationale de la Photographie et du Cinéma in Brussels for its advertising photograph *Komol*, taken to advertise a hair lotion of the same name. But the incipient careers of Auerbach and Stern were soon stymied by Adolph Hitler's rise to power as chancellor in 1933. Her future husband, Walter Auerbach, an active communist, advised the two women of Jewish origin and with left-wing ties to leave Germany permanently.

As Auerbach could not provide the proof of financial independence necessary for emigrating to England as Grete Stern did, at the end of 1933 she emigrated with Walter Auerbach to Tel Aviv, Palestine. She found work with the Jewish National Fund (KKL) and the Women's International Zionist Organization (WIZO), but commissions aimed at promoting a Jewish state in Palestine were far from the photographer's interests.

Together with her friend Liselotte Grschebina and Walter Auerbach, she opened the children's portrait studio "Ishon," or eyeball. Her work in Palestine was radically different than her work done in Berlin. While the ringl + pit pictures could for the most part be considered studio work, which focused on representations of identities, with her emigration such criteria took on a secondary importance. The photographer became an "open window" to the reality of the outside world. After the outbreak of the Abyssinian war in 1936, Auerbach shut down Ishon and visited Grete Stern in London. In the British capital, she met the likes of Bertolt Brecht, also in exile, whom she had the opportunity to photograph. Because Stern was to immigrate to Argentina, Auerbach intended to take over her London studio but was refused the requisite work and residence permits.

In 1937, she married Walter Auerbach and in April they immigrated to the United States, settling in Elkins Park near Philadelphia close to relatives. While Auerbach toured the suburbs of Philadelphia as a baby photographer, both she and her husband worked for the art collection of the Lessing-Rosenwald family in Jenkintown, Pennsylvania. Photographing the prints collection allowed Auerbach to explore even further new photographic procedures, experimenting with infrared and ultra-violet light to reveal restoration work and changes made to prints. During this period the photographer couple also made use of the carbo printing process. She and her husband entered the so-called New York School circles, where Auerbach took a photograph of an as-yet-unknown Willem de Kooning with his wife Elaine.

Auerbach separated from her husband in 1944 and went to New York, where she rented part of the studio belonging to the painter Fairfield Porter, whose brother, Eliot, was also a photographer. As a freelancer, she received commissions from *Time* magazine and *Columbia Masterworks*. In 1946 she traveled to Buenos Aires, where she met Grete Stern for the first time in a decade. In 1946 and 1948 Auerbach made film and photographic studies of babies and small children for the Menninger Foundation, a research institute based in Topeka, Kansas, and produced photographs and two 16-mm films, *Mounting Tension*, about the behavior of infants. In 1953 she traveled extensively to Europe (Greece, Majorca, Germany, and Austria). After a visit to the photographer Eliot Porter in Maine in 1953, she decided to accompany him on a photographic journey to Mexico in the fall of 1955. During this trip, the two photographers collaborated on a large color-photo documentation of Mexican churches, published some 30 years later: *Mexican Churches* (1987), and *Mexican Celebrations* (1990).

In her 60s, Auerbach reinvented herself again, and worked until 1986 with children suffering from learning disabilities. From 1984 on, photography receded into the background. Auerbach died on July 30, 2004 in New York, after having finally received recognition for her important photographic work.

NATHALIE NEUMANN

See also: **History of Photography: Interwar Years; Peterhans, Walter; Photography in Europe: Germany and Austria; Porter, Eliot**

Biography

Born as Ellen Rosenberg on May 20, 1906 in Karlsruhe, Germany, she died on July 30, 2004 in New York City. Studied sculpture at the Karlsruher Kunstakademie (1924–1927) and in Stuttgart (1928), later photography with Walter Peterhans in Berlin (1929). 1930–1932 opened the advertising studio "foto ringl + pit" with Grete Stern, which won first prize at the deuxième Exposition Internationale de la Photographie et du Cinéma (Brusseles) for its advertising photograph *Komol* in 1933. Emigrated in 1933 to Palestine, made a 16-mm movie and opened "Ishon" photo studio. Official photographer for WIZO (Women's International Zionist Organization); joined Stern in London (1936); married Walter Auerbach (1937) and immigrated to the United States. Worked at the Lessing Rosenwald Print Collection in Philadelphia (1937–1944); Freelance photographer in New York City (1945) working for *Time* magazine, *Columbia Masterworks*. 1946, 1953, 1956 extensive travels to Argentina, Greece, Majorca, Germany, and Austria. Worked with Sybille Escolana for the Menninger Foundation, film: *Mounting tension*. Professor at Junior College for Arts and Craft in Trenton (1953). Documented Mexico with Eliot Porter (1955–1956). Traveled extensively, gaining a fascination for esotericism and psychology. From 1965–1984 undertook educational therapy for children at the Educational Institute for Learning and Research in New York.

Individual Exhibitions

1978 *Mexican Church Interiors*, Sander Gallery, Washington, DC
1980 *Images from Mexican Churches* (Porter/Auerbach), Cathedral St. John the Divine, New York, New York
1981 *ringl + pit*, Bauhaus-Archiv, Berlin, Germany
1982 *Ellen Auerbach: pictures after 1934*, Photographers' Gallery, London, United Kingdom
1998 *Die Fotografin Ellen Auerbach, Retrospektive*. Akademie der Künste, Berlin, Germany
2003 *Ellen Auerbach, La Mirada intuitiva*, Lleida: Fondacion "la Caixa," Foundation Centre Social i Cultural (Blondel, 3), Spain

Group Exhibitions

1977 *Künstlerinnen International, Berlin 1877–1977*; Schloss Charlottenburg, Berlin, Germany
1978 *Das experimentelle Photo in Deutschland 1918–1940*, Galerie de Levante, Munich, Germany, and Centre Pompidou, Paris, France

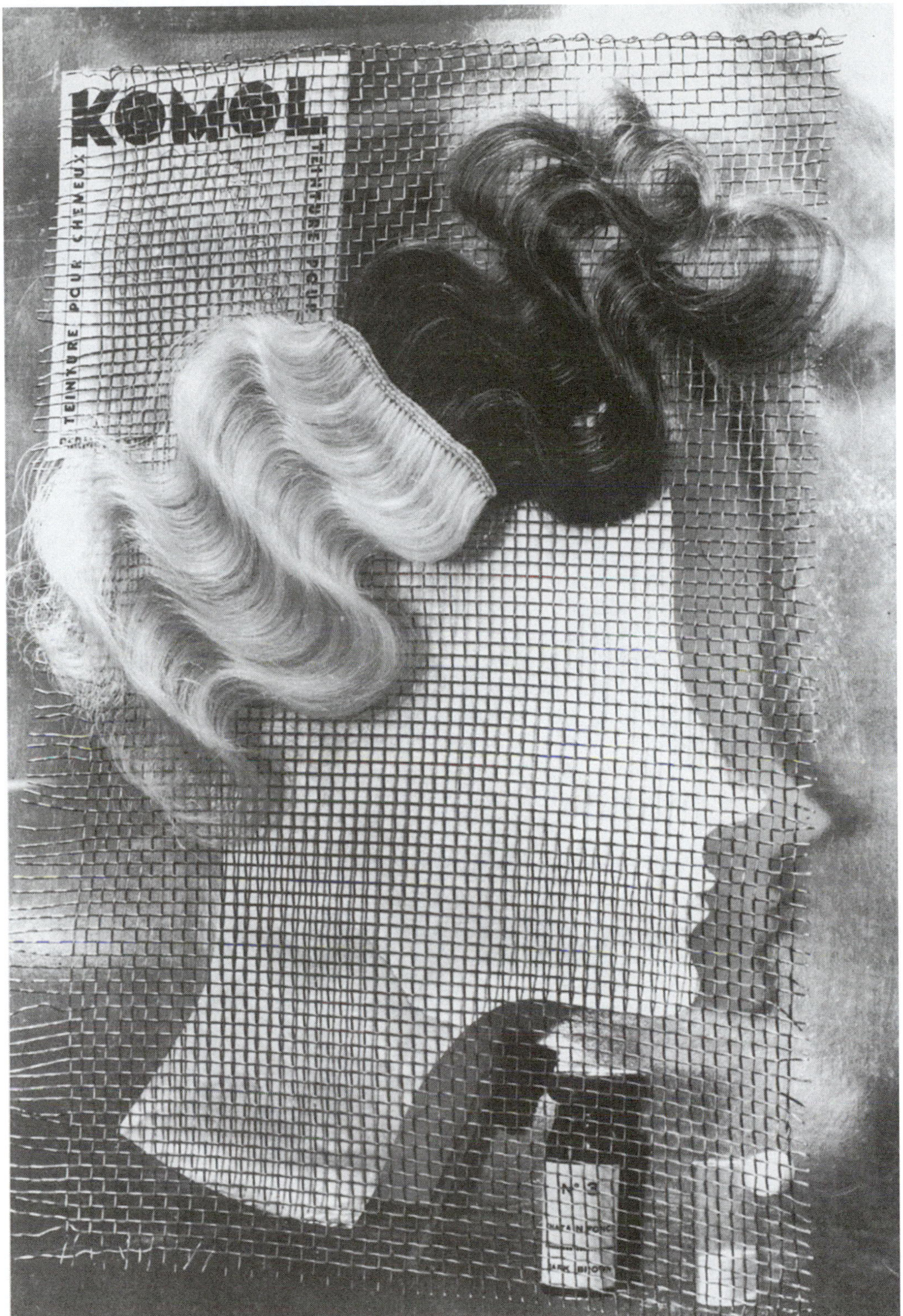

ringl + pit (Grete Stern and Ellen Auerbach), "Pétrole Hahn", Werbefoto, Blatt 8 aus dem Portfolio "Fotografie ringl + pit," Zwölf Fotografien von Grete Stern und Ellen Auerbach, 1929–1933, Sander Gallery Editions, New York 1985 (Mappe IV/XV), 1932/ 1985 Silbergelatinepapier unter Passepartout-karton montiert, 33.5 × 22.2 cm Abzugmaß (HxB); 48.3 × 38.2 cm Passepartout (HxB).
[*Photograph courtesy of Bauhaus-Archiv Berlin, Copyright Ellen Auerbach Estate. Courtesy Robert Mann Gallery*]

1980 *Avant-Garde Photography in Germany, 1919–1939*, San Francisco Museum of Modern Art, San Francisco, California, and traveling
1980 *When Words Fail*, International Center of Photography, New York, New York
1981 *ringl + pit*, Bauhaus-Archiv, Berlin, Germany
1982 *Avant-garde Fotografie in Deutschland, 1919–1939*, Munich, Germany
1983 *Bauhausfotografie*, Institut für Auslandsbeziehungen, Stuttgart, Germany, and traveling
1984 *ringl + pit*, Deutsche Botschaft, Buenos Aires, Argentina
1984 *ringl + pit*, Goethe-Institut, New York, New York
1986 *Photography: a Facet of Modernism*, San Francisco Museum of Modern Art, San Francisco, California
1986 *Photographie und Bauhaus*, Kestner Gesellschaft Hannover, Hannover, Germany
1988 *Experiment Bauhaus*, Bauhaus-Archiv, Berlin, Germany
1988 *Photography Between the Wars*, Metropolitan Museum of Art, New York, New York
1988 *Emigriert: Grete Stern und Ellen Auerbach, Fotografien vor und nach 1933*, Stadtbibliothek Wuppertal, Germany
1989 *Werbefotografie in Deutschland seit den 20er Jahren*, Museum Folkwang, Essen, Germany
1990 *Fotografie am Bauhaus*, Bauhaus-Archiv, Berlin, Germany
1992 *Photography at the Bauhaus, The Information of Modern Aesthetic*, Fotofest, Houston, Texas
1993 *ringl + pit*, Grete Stern und Ellen Auerbach, Museum Folkwang, Essen, traveling to Berlin, Karlsruhe, Dessau, Germany
1997 *Auerbach, Ellen & Anton Stankowski, Zeitgenossen*, Walter-Storms Galerie. Munich, Germany

Further Reading

Bertonati, Emilio. *Das experimentelle Photo in Deutschland 1918–1940*. Munich; 1978.

Dickel, M. and J. F. Oppenheim. *22 Fotografinnen*. Köln: 1983.

Eskildsen, Ute, et al. *Die Fotografin Ellen Auerbach, Retrospektive*. Berlin: Akademie der Künste; Munich: Prestel Verlag, New York: 1998.

Eskildsen, Ute. *ringl + pit: Grete Stern und Ellen Auerbach*. Fotograf. Kabinett, Museum Folkwang, Essen, 1993.

Frowein, Cordula. *Emigriert: Grete Stern und Ellen Auerbach*, Fotografien vor und nach 1933, Stadtbibliothek Wuppertal, Germany, 1988.

Lavin, Maud. *ringl + pit: The Representation of Women in German Advertising (1929–1933)*. In *Idem, Clean New World*. Cambridge, MA: 2001.

Mellor, David. *Germany: The New Photography 1927–1933*. London: Arts Council of Great Britain, 1979.

Morris Hambourg, Maria. "Photography Between the Wars." In *Metropolitan Museum of Art Bulletin*, New York; 1988.

Pierce, Donna. In *Mexican Churches / Eliot Porter & Ellen Auerbach*. Albuquerque: University of New Mexico Press, 1987.

Pierce, Donna, Eliot Porter, and Ellen Auerbach. *Mexican Celebrations*. Albuquerque: University of New Mexico Press, 1990.

Sullivan, Constance. *Women Photographers*. New York: Harry N. Abrams, 1990.

Valdivieso, Mercedes, Inka Graeve Ingelmann, et al. *Ellen Auerbach*. La Mirada intuitiva, Fondacion "la Caixa," Barcelona: 2002.

PHOTOGRAPHY IN AUSTRALIA

Australia is an island continent situated between the Indian and Pacific Oceans to the southeast of Asia. Settled at least 40,000 years ago by Australian Aborigines it was colonized by Britain in 1788. Despite its geographical distance from Europe, news of the invention of photography reached Australia's small free settler population by late 1839 and, two years later, George Goodman took the first known daguerreotypes. The introduction of photography paralleled the establishment and rapid growth of colonial settlement, and the camera became an extremely popular way for European photographers to represent a "new" land and its distinctive features.

By the time Australia became a Federation on 1 January 1901, the practice of photography had developed significantly as a creative process. Along with thriving commercial portrait studios, the turn of the twentieth century saw a dedicated group of photographers committed to promoting the medium as art. Pictorialism, an international photographic movement that originated in Great Britain in the late 1890s, began to gain currency in Australia by the early 1900s and was a dominant style for several decades.

John Kauffmann was one of the country's earliest and finest Pictorialists gaining his first-hand awareness of this soft-focus, aesthetic style from his travels to Great Britain and Europe. While Kauffmann was especially adept at "low-toned" work, fellow Pictorialist Harold Cazneaux helped promote a "higher-keyed" approach. Cazneaux believed sunlight was a key element in helping create a distinctly Australian form of Pictorialism and, as a leading member of the Sydney Camera Circle (founded in 1916), he actively promoted the so-called "Sunshine School." Cazneaux was an influential advocate and theoretician, publishing articles on the aesthetic possibilities and development of photography for the *Australasian Photo-Review* (*AP-R*) and the British publication, *The Photograms of the Year*.

Most Australian Pictorialists were amateurs, producing work for exhibition at local and international salons, but professional photographers also applied this style to their commercial work. Around the turn of the century, for instance, H. Walter Barnett adopted a soft-focus approach in his highly regarded society and celebrity portraiture, and was the only Australian to be offered membership of the prestigious British group, the Brotherhood of the Linked Ring. Other notable professional Pictorialist photographers included Ruth Hollick who specialized in child and social portraiture and was one of a number of Australian women to take up the medium. Commercial photographer and adventurer Frank Hurley applied some of the atmospheric qualities of Pictorialism to very different and dramatic ends when he was employed as official photographer for both Charles Mawson and Sir Ernest Shackleton's various expeditions to Antarctica and to the Australian Imperial Force during World War One.

Pictorialism remained popular with many Australian photographers throughout the 1930s and 1940s. Jack Cato was a major studio photographer whose work extended this by now well-established style to include more modern elements. Cato is also significant as the author of Australia's first history of the medium, *The Story of the Camera in Australia* (1955). However, despite the continuation of Pictorialism it was clear that the creative spirit of the times was changing. As modernism took hold in the arts internationally, a group of avant-garde Australian photographers began to abandon the "fuzzy-wuzzy" look of Pictorialism for an approach that they believed was more in tune with the machine age.

Information concerning modernist photography reached Australia in the 1930s through imported magazines such as *US Camera*, *Das Deutsche Lichtbild*, and *Modern Photography*. Their illustrations had a strong impact on a group of younger Australian practitioners who began to experiment with modernism and Surrealism in their personal and commercial work. Also influential were a small number of modernist photographers who had been forced to migrate to Australia due to the rise of Nazism. Photographers Wolfgang Sievers, Helmut Newton, Margaret Michaelis, and Henry Talbot, all arrived between 1938 and 1940 and brought with them first-hand knowledge of modernist photography.

Max Dupain was one of the most prolific and talented Australian-born photographers of the mid 1930s and 1940s. Along with the impact of modernist photography on his practice he was influenced by popular debates concerning the revitalization of society following World War One. In this interwar period, he produced many photographs that are often critical of modernity as a degenerative force on the body or which—in images such as *The Sunbaker*—suggest the regenerative possibilities of contact with nature, in particular, the Australian beach. Important outlets for Dupain's work in the 1930s were innovative magazines such as *Art in Australia* and *The Home*, which featured a wide variety of creative practice from architecture and fashion to art photography.

Olive Cotton also adopted modernism in her own diverse practice. She developed a distinctive photographic approach to her architectural and commercial subjects but her most enduring interests lay with the natural world. Cotton's sensuous appreciation of nature shows her delight in the ways that light and patterning could play both a compositional and atmospheric role. Another photographer to appreciate the creative possibilities of light was Athol Shmith. A Melbourne-based fashion and commercial photographer, Shmith mixed the clean lines of the modernist style with a seductive Hollywood glamour. His studio work in particular shows his ability to use lighting, darkroom techniques, and hand-coloring to create flawless images of beauty.

In the post-war period a group of Australian photographers began to produce work in the so-called Documentary style. This international movement, with its emphasis on creating clear statements of actuality, made a major impression on Australian photographers including Max Dupain, Axel Poignant, David Moore, Jeff Carter, and David Potts. These practitioners considered the Documentary style well suited to recording how contemporary Australians lived and worked. With a social realist perspective inspired by the Documentary philosophy of Scottish-born filmmaker John Grierson, these photographers focused on the world around them recording a diverse range of subjects from urban poverty to outback life and the Australian interest in sport and the outdoors.

An important source of inspiration for Australian Documentary photographers was the photo-essay, a new format in which writing was combined with images. Local outlets for Documentary work were limited with few magazines offering the opportunity of extended photo-essays. Talented photographers such as the Swiss-born Axel Poignant persisted for a time producing bodies of work that looked at distinctively Australian subjects, such as the natural environment and people living in the outback. He was particularly interested in the lives of Aboriginal people and produced thoughtful series of work in this area often publishing his images in the locally produced *Walkabout* magazine. But despite the success of his book *Piccaninny Walkabout* (1957), Poignant eventually left Australia to find work overseas.

David Moore, probably Australia's best-known photo-journalist, managed to sustain his career by regularly contributing to international journals including *Life*, *Time*, and *Picture Post*. One of Moore's most celebrated images was *Migrants Arriving in Sydney*—a photograph that captures the mixed emotions of joy, anticipation, and anxiety on the faces of those arriving for the first time in Australia. The photograph also summed up a specific moment in social history, when Australia's migration policies were relaxed sufficiently to allow people to settle from a broader range of European countries.

The humanistic approach of Documentary work reached its height internationally with the *Family of Man* exhibition mounted by the Museum of Modern Art in New York in 1955. This exhibition, which included the work of David Moore and Laurence le Guay, toured to Australia in 1959 and was viewed by record crowds. Following the flurry of interest in Documentary practice, the 1960s were a relatively quiet time for creative photography in Australia. An exception was "Group M," a group of committed amateur photographers in Melbourne, including Albert Brown and George Bell, who mounted a series of exhibitions that explored documentary and social realist issues. Mervyn Bishop, Australia's first professional Aboriginal photographer, also made a significant contribution in this period. Bishop began his long career as a press photographer in 1962 with the major daily newspaper, the *Sydney Morning Herald* and was awarded the coveted News Photographer of the Year Award in 1971.

In the 1960s, other Australian professional photographers also continued their work in the fields of fashion, architecture, and industry with one highly significant practitioner being Wolfgang Sievers. Sievers, who had been trained at the Contempora School for Applied Arts in Berlin, arrived in Australia in the late 1930s and applied his experience of modernism to his industrial and architectural assignments. He created many powerful, even theatrical images that often showed the interrelationship of workers and the products of modernity.

In common with many other countries, a new energizing spirit infused Australian photography in the 1970s. A wave of social and political change swept through society and with it a desire for more contemporary means of creative expression. Many artists considered the camera to be a powerful aesthetic tool without the historical "baggage" of other mediums and one that offered a fresh way to express their social, political, and creative concerns.

The surge of interest in photography was met by institutional funding with the Labour government of the time injecting funds into art schools, many of which began to include photography in their curriculum for the first time. This period saw the foundation of collections of photography at public galleries. In 1967, the National Gallery of Victoria established the first separate curatorial Department of Photography in Australia and provided funds for a broadly based collection to be formed. It also began a program of Australian and international photographic exhibitions bringing the medium to the attention of a wide local audience. The Australian National Gallery, Canberra, made its first acquisitions of photographs in 1972 founding the basis for an important, wide-ranging collection; and the Art Gallery of New South Wales, Sydney established its Department of Photography in 1974 and began to build a strong collection. In 1974, the Australian Centre for Contemporary Photography in Sydney opened its doors as a venue for the exhibition, instruction, and promotion of the medium. The 1970s also saw the establishment of commercial galleries that specialized in photography, most notably in Melbourne, and important corporate sponsorship of photography including the Philip Morris Arts Grant.

Documentary photography continued to be popular among artists but was now often used to different ends. Carol Jerrems and Max Pam adopted a collaborative approach in their documentary work based on the consent of their subjects rather than simply "taking" portraits. In their distinct ways, both Jerrems and Pam captured the mood of the times: Jerrems taking portraits of a young Australian urban generation and Pam following the hippie trail to the East and a world of new experiences.

The impact of counter-culture politics and feminism also brought a distinctive range of subject matter to light as the "personal became political." Ruth Maddison was one of a group of photographers who validated the richness of everyday Australian experiences by focusing on the often overlooked rituals of ordinary life, while Sue Ford used her friends as the models for her fascinating study of faces taken a decade apart. Ford's apparently simple photographs reveal the power of photography to show how physical, emotional, and social changes are reflected in a person's face.

The creative uses of photography expanded considerably in the 1970s. The medium began to be absorbed into the "mainstream" art world as conceptual and performance artists started to employ the medium. For body artist Stelarc, photographs were an important creative adjunct to his art events in the 1970s. In a different vein, Jon Rhodes was one of several photographers of the period to address social issues when he used the medium to bring attention to land rights issues for Aboriginal people in the Gove Peninsula in his series, *Just Another Sunrise?* Others, such as John Cato and Les Walking, explored the metaphoric potential of photography. The range of photographic processes similarly expanded in this period. Most photographers still preferred to produce formally composed and finely printed black and white images but some, most notably women photographers, found that hand-coloring added to the creative possibilities of their vision.

The 1980s was a time of diversity in Australian photography. One distinctive aspect of the period was photography by practitioners from non-Anglo-Saxon backgrounds. Takis Christodoulou, for instance, used the documentary approach to create disturbing, almost claustrophobic images suggesting the cultural pressures for contemporary Greek families living in Australia.

However, generally speaking, critical attention was diverted in this period away from the documentary to a different kind of practice influenced by the theories and practices of Postmodernism. This complex international movement proved a powerful invigorating force on contemporary theory, art, and culture. Its influence on photography in Australia was profound, raising fundamental issues concerning the interpretation of images, the nature of reality, and the role of the artist. Critical debate concerning photography flourished and, in 1983, the magazine *Photofile* (published by the Australian Centre for Photography) became an important venue for writing in the field.

In general, post-modern photographers called into question the long-held objectivity of the medium, revealing the partial nature of any photograph through the obviously constructed or "set up" character of their work. Naturalism, so long held to be the foundation of photography, was widely abandoned among Australian photographers in favor of openly declared theatrical fabrications. There was also a shift in the materials used, with black and white, discretely sized documentary photographs being replaced by large-scaled, opulent productions with photographers often reveling in the lush, saturated colors of the Cibachrome or Polaroid processes.

Post-modern photographers frequently questioned cultural truths through the use of allegory, parody, and the montaging of image with text to disrupt the usual interpretation of the photograph. The visual language of popular culture, film, and traditional fine arts, such as painting, were all raided in the process, as were other photographic genres—in particular, glamour, advertising, and surrealist imagery. Photographer and filmmaker Tracey Moffatt's series *Something More* was characteristic of this fertile new area of inspiration for artists. In this influential series, Moffatt borrowed from 1950s B-grade films to create a fevered story of a young woman's search for "something more" in her life. Casting herself in the lead role, Moffatt set her disturbing and sometimes violent narrative in outback Australia, producing images that resemble film stills.

Another characteristic trait of 1980s Australian photography was the appropriation of imagery from various sources. In one of the most notable series of the 1980s, *Bondi: Playground of the Pacific*, Anne Zahalka wittily explored and subverted the mythology and stereotypes that have evolved around this famous stretch of the Australian coast by reworking various Australian artworks. Julie Rrap also drew on art history in her installation *Persona and Shadow*, taking a feminist approach to provoke the viewer to consider how women have been represented in the visual arts, while Fiona Hall created complex tableaux of figures sculpted from sardine cans in her large scale Polaroids illustrating Dante's *The Divine Comedy*.

In 1988, the Bicentennial of the founding of European settlement in Australia offered an opportunity to re-evaluate the country's achievements. Many major art and social histories were published including two major histories of photography: Gael Newton, *Shades of Light: Photography and Australia 1839–1988* and Anne Marie-Willis, *Picturing Australia: A History of Photography*. Another major photographic publication was *After 200 Years*, which contained substantial photo-essays on, or by, contemporary Aboriginal and Islander Australians, and reflected the beginnings of a renaissance in work produced by indigenous photographers.

The advent of New Media in the 1990s prompted fundamental shifts in how photography was understood. With technological advances that allowed the total manipulation of content and style, the connection between the photograph and the real world was severed. As a result, some Australian critics suggested that photography was dead. However, despite their pessimism the "corpse" of photography in fact remained remarkably lively with many concurrent streams of practice evident. Key areas of contemporary photography in the 1990s included an interest in digital technologies, gender issues (including queer art), abstract photography, photograms, and documentary photography.

Patricia Piccinini uses sophisticated new digital technologies to make witty and disturbing comments on genetic engineering. Her seemingly innocuous images of computer generated "life forms" point to one of the major issues of our times: that is, the ability to create and manipulate life. Another technically sophisticated photographer is Bill Henson, who continues to expand on a very successful local and international career begun in the late 1970s, with installations of highly lyrical images essentially concerned with untranslatable emotions. Henson was the first photographer chosen to represent Australia at the Venice Biennale in 1995, a mark both of his standing in the arts community and a sign of the incorporation of photography into wider art practice.

Perhaps in reaction to the overturning of traditional definitions of photography, a number of Australian artists are using various early photographic techniques, such as photograms. Penelope Davis is one photographer who turns the tables on the medium to ironically produce camera-less images of the camera. Anne Ferran has used convict women's clothes to create a series of evocative photograms in which the ghostly qualities of the medium evoke the bodily forms of women whose histories are now otherwise lost.

Another significant aspect of contemporary photography in the 1990s was the re-working of traditional processes and styles, most notably in the area of documentary photography. After years of critical neglect, documentary practices underwent a surge in popularity with a new generation using and extending this way of working to explore the world around them. Two Australian prizes that helped encourage documentary photography among younger practitioners were held in the 1990s: The Felix H. Man Memorial Prize, at the National Gallery of Victoria (1992 and 1993), and the Leica Documentary Photography Award, at the Centre for Contemporary Photography, Melbourne in 1998 (ongoing).

One of the most significant photographic trends of the 1990s, which continues to develop, is the outstanding work produced by Aboriginal and Torres Strait Islander photographers. In a fascinating twist on nineteenth century photography, indigenous photographs are often reconfiguring images of indigenous people taken by European photographers. Leah King-Smith and Brook Andrew, for instance, have both produced powerful bodies of work that quote nineteenth century photography in order to question how Aboriginal people have been depicted and to reassert their own continuing presence.

The work of indigenous artists is one important aspect of the robust contemporary photographic scene in Australia. Despite its relatively small population (around 19 million), the country has a rich photographic tradition and continues to produce many talented photographers. Although Australian practitioners historically have tended to follow broad international trends, the images they produced often showed considerable innovation and experimentation. Some, especially in the early to mid 1900s, sought to create an Australian photographic style based on local conditions and subjects—a desire for distinction that is of less interest among contemporary practitioners whose work is generally "internationalist" in appearance. While photography has a well-established and respected place in Australia's visual arts, knowledge of its practitioners internationally is relatively limited: outside of Tracey Moffatt and Bill Henson, who have well-established international careers, few others are known in any depth. However, as the domination by traditional centers of photography is slowly replaced by a more encompassing and inclusive worldview, it seems likely that the significant and ongoing contributions of Australian photographers will reach wider prominence.

Isobel Crombie

See also: **Australian Centre for Photography; Digital Photography; Documentary Photography; Linked Ring Brotherhood; Pictorialism; Postmodernism; Newton, Helmut**

Further Reading

Cato, Jack. *The Story of the Camera in Australia.* Melbourne: Georgian House, 1955.

Crombie, Isobel, and Sandra Byron. *Twenty Contemporary Australian Photographers: From the Hallmark Cards Australian Photographic Collection*. Melbourne: National Gallery of Victoria, 1990.

Ennis, Helen. *Australian Photography: The 1980s*. Melbourne: Australian National Gallery, 1988.

French, Blair, ed. *Photo Files: An Australian Photography Reader*. Sydney: Power Publications and Australian Centre for Photography, 1999.

Gellatly, Kelly. *Re-Take: Contemporary Aboriginal and Torres Strait Islander Photography*. Canberra: National Gallery of Australia, 1998.

Michael, Linda. *Photography is Dead! Long Live Photography!* Sydney: Museum of Contemporary Art, 1996.

Moore, Catriona. *Indecent Exposures: Twenty Years of Australian Feminist Photography*. Sydney: Allen and Unwin; Power Institute of Fine Arts, 1994.

Newton, Gael. *Silver and Grey: Fifty Years of Australian Photography*. Sydney: Angus and Robertson, 1980.

Newton, Gael. *Shades of Light: Photography and Australia, 1839–1988*. Canberra: Australian National Gallery, 1988.

North, Ian. *A Decade of Australian Photography, 1972–1982: The Philip Morris Arts Grant at the Australian National Gallery, Canberra*. Canberra: Australian National Gallery, 1983.

Taylor, Penny, ed. *After 200 Years: Photographic Essays of Aboriginal and Islander Australia Today*. Canberra: Aboriginal Studies Press, 1988.

Willis, Anne-Marie. *Picturing Australia: A History of Photography*. Sydney: Angus and Robertson, 1988.

AUSTRALIAN CENTRE FOR PHOTOGRAPHY

The Australian Centre for Photography (ACP) is a publicly funded gallery curating exhibitions of Australian and international photography, combined with a workshop offering courses to the public and access to photographic facilities. It also publishes the magazine *Photofile*.

The ACP opened in 1974 and it was very much a child of its time. Interest in photography as a creative art was booming in Australia in the early 1970s. Art museums were establishing departments to collect and exhibit international and Australian photography, art schools were establishing photography departments to turn out graduates in what was then regarded as the hottest new medium, entrepreneurial individuals were opening (mostly short-lived) private photography galleries, and magazine and book publishers were experimenting with (mostly short-lived) publications devoted to the new art form. The boom took off first in Melbourne, but spread to other provincial capitals. This photography boom coincided with a general cultural and social renaissance in Australia, fueled in large part by greatly increased arts funding as a result of the progressive federal government, which had been elected in 1972.

In this climate a small group, led by the important Australian documentary photographer David Moore, successfully applied to the government for funds to set up a 'foundation' for photography. Their initial plans were wildly grand: they conceived of it having a populist, social role (somewhat akin to Edward Steichen's gathering the millions of photographs from which he selected the seminal *The Family of Man* exhibition shown at the Museum of Modern Art, New York, in 1955) as well as a professional role in supporting individual photographers—from giving them direct grants and commissions to collecting their work. But within a year or two of its opening APC had settled into a mode of exhibiting curated shows of photography to an art audience on a gallery/museum model, occasionally touring exhibitions, and offering facilities and courses to the general public in a workshop that was established in 1976.

The ACP has always suffered an uneasy relationship with its shifting and fractious constituency. In its formative years it was resented by some for draining scarce funds away from the other artist-run photography spaces, quasi-commercial photography galleries, and small photography magazines that were springing up and struggling to survive across Australia. This single institution, located in the heart of Australia's largest and wealthiest city, was a natural magnet for accusations of elitism and for being out of touch with "real" photography—whatever that was—since the term covered a constantly changing and expanding range of practices.

The ACP came into its own under the aegis of American museum-based formalism. In its formative years the ACP imported exhibitions by American masters, such as Diane Arbus; and American masters themselves, such as the then Director of the Photography Department of the Museum of Modern Art New York, John Szarkowski, in 1974, and the photographer Lee Friedlander in 1977. However the ACP also began to exhibit and support the first generation of Australian art school graduates, including Carol Jerrems, Bill Henson, and Max Pam. It also began to bring important aspects of Australia's photographic heritage to light, for instance by giving Australia's most important photographer, Max Dupain, his first retrospective in 1975. Olive Cotton, now one of Australia's most loved photographers, was virtually unknown when she held her first retrospective at the ACP in 1985.

Between 1978 and 1982 its director, the U.S. trained Christine Godden, established a new level of museum professionalism in the gallery, and succeeded in moving the ACP to its present location in a busy and fashionable shopping precinct. But during this period the ACP was criticized for perpetuating a so-called "photo ghetto," focusing narrowly on a formalist aesthetic, at a time when camera images were exponentially increasing in quantity, proliferating in format, becoming the central theoretical object of postmodern theories of representation, and forming the lingua franca of contemporary art in general.

From 1982, with Tamara Winikoff as director, the ACP deliberately tried to broaden and connect itself to a wider variety of communities. In 1983 it began to publish *Photofile*, which contained reviews and longer historical, critical, and theoretical articles. The gallery program now often featured community-based and issue oriented exhibitions exemplified by the 'suitcase shows' it toured, which were inspired by the radical socially aware practices of British photographers like Jo Spence.

Photofile was particularly exciting in the mid 1980s, with the critic Geoffrey Batchen as editor, because by then a whole range of sophisticated discourses had taken the photograph as their principal subject, and a new generation of theoretically savvy art school graduates placed the photographic image—if not the idea of photography as an autonomous, historicized, fine art medium—at center stage in Australian art.

During the 1990s, with Denise Robinson as director, this new wave of art school graduates, such as Tracey Moffatt, Anne Zahalka, or Robin Stacey, were all featured in the gallery, which also became an important Sydney Biennale and Sydney Gay and Lesbian Mardis Gras venue. At the same time, however, the Workshop was languishing, *Photofile* was disappearing under a miasma of thick prose and arch imagery, and the ACP was falling into debt.

Much of the tenure of the next director Deborah Ely, appointed in 1992, was involved with successfully negotiating the re-financing and extension of the ACP's building, as well as upgrading and updating the Workshop and revitalizing *Photofile*. The gallery, although closed for refurbishment for long periods, continued the trend of exhibiting work in photographically related, particularly digital, media.

The current director, Alasdair Foster, faces an entirely different climate from the one into which the ACP was born. Photography is no longer a young medium impatiently knocking on the doors of art. As an art practice its edges have long since dissolved into digital media, film, performance, and installation. It is now a pervasive cultural and psychological phenomenon. The ACP is no longer the sole 'foundation' for photography in Australia, it is now just a small part of a vibrant and well established matrix of museums, libraries, galleries, magazines, and art schools across the continent.

MARTYN JOLLY

Further Reading

Australian Centre for Photography Website: *www.acp.au.com* (accessed May 4, 2005).

Ely, Deborah. "The Australian Centre for Photography." *The History of Photography* (Australia Issue) 23 (1999) no. 2.

French, Blair, ed. *Photo Files*. Sydney: The Australian Centre for Photography and Power Publications, 1999.

Newton, Gael. *Shades of Light: Photography and Australia 1839–1988*. Canberra: Australian National Gallery, 1988.

Willis, Anne-Marie. *Picturing Australia: A History of Photography*. Sydney: Angus and Robertson, 1988.

B

ROGER BALLEN

South African

Roger Ballen grew up with an awareness of photography as an art form. His mother, Adrienne Ballen, worked at Magnum Photos from 1963 to 1967, when she founded Photography House, a gallery that showed the work of André Kertész.

In Ballen's first book of photography, *Boyhood* (1977), he describes how his mother's untimely death set him off on a four-year odyssey in search of his own boyhood, a recuperative journey that broadened into one of rediscovering himself. *Boyhood* searches for what is universal in boys: the Tom Sawyerish fantasies and bonding in their play, the stock characters among their peers, the "clown, Romeo, bully, sore sport, hothead, leader, weakling, braggart, tattletale, mope, do-nothing, nice guy, thickhead." Boys in temples, in rags, in motion, in mourning, all are photographed in spontaneous action or posed, often in a way Ballen favors for extracting an essence: compressed between the camera and a wall.

Boyhood took Ballen to South Africa, where he settled in 1982 and married the painter Linda Moross. Armed with a Ph.D. in Mineral Economics, he established a successful career in mining, which took him to remote and depressed parts of the country. Here he photographed the fabric of small towns, or *dorps*—the churches, main streets, stores, signs, and the grain of dilapidating Edwardian columns, railings, and roof ornaments, which suggested to him "a nostalgia for a distant unattainable splendor." In his resulting book, *Dorps: Small Towns of South Africa* (1986), he relates a desire to freeze time, preserving these environments against modernization, much as *Boyhood* had sought to still the innocent timelessness of childhood. But it is the inhabitants and their habitations, particularly the interiors filled with personal mementos, ornaments, and pinups, that loom larger than the towns in *Dorps*. Ballen likens his subjects to the hillfolk of Appalachia, frozen in an earlier era. Their poverty is evident, and the viewer suspects inbreeding in the cramped interiors, scandals in the dirty sheets between the peeling walls. Furthermore, beneath these surfaces lie the ingrained realities of apartheid. These are strictly segregated towns, conservative and racist, parison with American photographers of the rural South during the depression of 1930s, particularly Walker Evans, Margaret Bourke-White, and Dorothea Lange.

The tensions that are subtle in *Dorps* come to the foreground in Ballen's next book, *Platteland: Images from Rural South Africa* (1995). (Platteland is a generic term that means "flatlands" in Afrikaans, and applies to the dreary region of rural plains dotted with *dorps*.) Ballen's introduction to

Platteland clarifies that South Africa's psychosis had now gripped him tighter than earlier, when he was still a relative newcomer. Also, time had not stood still. Between *Dorps* and *Platteland*, the apartheid regime thrashed through the paroxysms of its death throes. First, in the late 1980s, when the government was run by a shadowy clutch of hawks in the military, intelligence, and police forces, the state unleashed a viciously repressive state-of-emergency. When this failed to quash resistance, Nelson Mandela was finally released in 1990, opposition political parties were unbanned, and negotiations began for a new constitution and a democratic election, which was held in 1994. In this transitional phase, the rural areas were particularly tense as conservative whites tried to reverse the changes underfoot, engaging in sabotage and violence against black communities, while reactionary elements in the government simultaneously sponsored terrorism against urban black populations.

In *Platteland*, the poor whites of the region have moved to center stage, assuming a new tragic dimen-

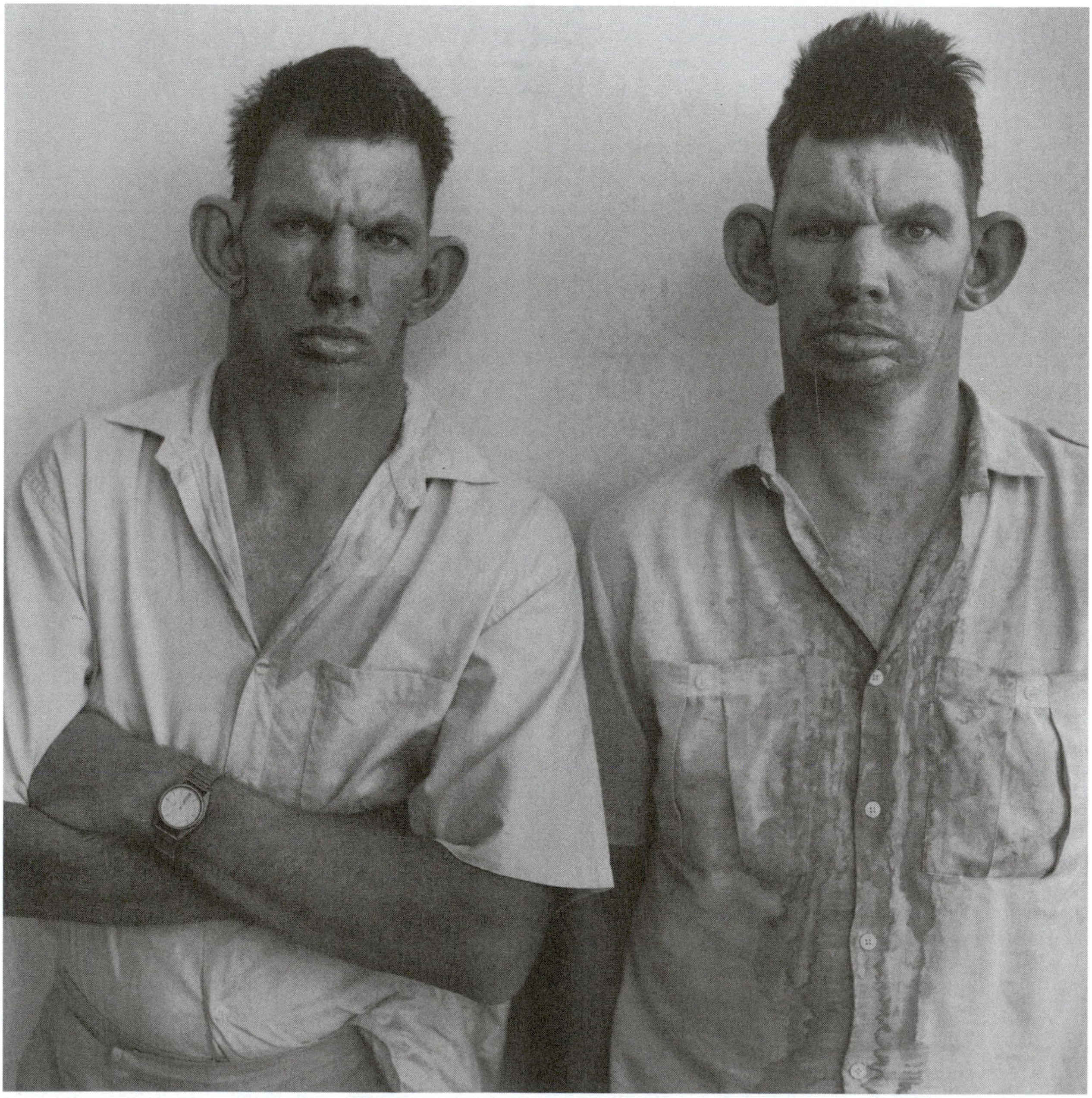

Roger Ballen, Dresie and Casie, twins, Western Transvaal, 1993.
[© *Roger Ballen*]

sion as "ironic archetypes of alienation and immobility, victims of both political forces and personal circumstances, defending themselves against economic deprivation and psychological anguish in a hostile and unyielding environment." They witness the crumbling of a system specifically designed to elevate them over blacks and guarantee them government employment. Experiencing a backlash of increased crime and violence against them, guns are now visible in several homes. A few mixed relationships testify to the legalization of sex between the races.

In *Platteland*, irony stiffens the tension between the subjects' hardscrabble poverty and the sentimentality they attach to pets, pictures, possessions, family life, and toys. So too, between their battered bodies, the dross of their lives, and the gloss of consumer products and the glamour of pin-ups fixed to the wall—along with the subjects' shadows. This disjunction is also evident between the posed and composed subjects and the disarray of their homes, and between the humor some reveal and their sad circumstances.

These are unsettling portraits in which one senses the horror of a horrible era. They are closer to the edgier strain of documentary that gained momentum after the depravity of World War II than to the sympathetic and optimistic humanism of much documentary photography up to and including the 1955 *Family of Man* exhibition. As Ballen remarks, "I believe that humanity is inherently more evil than good and part of my motivation is to force the confrontation of that." Ballen's use of hard flash and the overall grayness of the images, masterfully printed by his friend Dennis da Silva, formally strengthen his association with such photographers as Diane Arbus and, although Ballen's work is formally antithetical to street photography and the snapshot, Weegee and Jacob Riis.

In *Outland* (2001), Ballen's subjects are not passive victims of the lens but expressive actors performing elaborately staged poses. This embroils them, the photographer, and the viewer in the bizarre tragedy of life in which we are all trapped. Graffiti and the wires that dangle haphazardly in these poorly electrified homes animate both moments and surfaces with anxious energy. Where in earlier pictures such elements may have been present by chance, now they are deliberately placed, formal elements that structure the composition and intensify the allusions to Ballen's "universal and metaphorical scenarios." Some actors, too, are familiar subjects returning in varied guises with new props: none of us is ever the same from moment to moment.

Through all of this, as in life, runs the latent charge that flows both in the flux between difference, and within the same. Arguably, it is more in this latter sense, of the diverse motivations that may stir within the self, ranging from the self-hatred of a flagellant to the self-love of a Narcissus, that these pictures hold up before us the mirror of our temporality.

Gary Van Wyk

See also: **Documentary Photography; Photography in Africa: South and Southern**

Biography

Born in New York City in 1950. Settled in 1982 in South Africa and married the painter Linda Moross. With a Ph.D. in Mineral Economics, he established a successful career in mining that took him to many small communities where he photographed the fabric of the land.

LEWIS BALTZ

American

Lewis Baltz is a leading figure in the New Topography movement. His large-scale photographic studies of commercial developments in the United States reflect a detached objectivity. Working within the tradition of the movement's iconography of realism, his photographs of these often minimalist structures comment on and reflect the corrosive destruction of the natural landscape by postwar American development. Baltz began his career photographing in the West and later worked abroad. In the late 1980s he moved away from subjects that formed the New Topographic genre, identified by a seminal 1975 exhibition, and into color and digital photography. A concern with the relationship among power, architecture, and photography unites his work, as does a sense of temporal urgency. A theorist and writer as well as a photographer, Baltz is sought after as an expert on photographic realism and the integrity of the documentary image. Throughout his work he engages critically in issues that are essential to contemporary urbanism and representation.

Born in Newport Beach, California in 1945, Baltz was influenced by the rapid commercial development all around him as he was growing up, as farmland was transformed from landscape into real estate both commerical and residential. After study at the San Francisco Art Institute where he received his B.F.A. in 1969, he attended the Claremont Graduate School where he received his M.F.A. in 1971 and began his well-known series, *The Tract Houses* (1969–1971), 25 images of an estate of newly erected standard houses that depict an architecture where individuality has been eliminated. This series led to Baltz's inclusion in the 1975 exhibition *New Topographics: Photographs of a Man-Altered Landscape*, at the George Eastman House in Rochester, New York, which united major international figures who shared similar photographic viewpoints, including Robert Adams, Stephen Shore, and Bernd and Hilla Becher.

Baltz's next project continued in this genre, detailing the facades of 51 buildings in the second largest industrial park development outside of the Soviet Union in *New Industrial Parks, Irvine California* (1975). The photographs initially seem innocuous but become frustrating with their clean, technically precise images of factories with their impenetrable walls. Baltz also isolates details like openings that are utterly closed, adding a frightening mystery to the series. "You don't know whether they're manufacturing pantyhose or mega death," Baltz explained.

Baltz continued his intensely detailed, multi-pictorial mapping of the alienating effects of commercial development through his prolific black and white studies throughout the 1970s and early 1980s. These photographic documentations, most of which are accompanied by a publication, include *The Tract Houses* (1969–1971), *Maryland* (1976), *Nevada* (1977–1978). *Nevada* strikingly depicts of the wreckage caused by development in the Nevada desert. *Park City* (1980–1981) continues his inquiry into commercial development and includes 102 8×10 inch photographs, documenting the development of the country's largest ski resort and the metamorphosis of a territory, from coal mining area to skiing complex.

In the mid-1980s, Baltz became increasingly interested in the marginal zones of urban planning, open areas where one sees both nature and the presence of industrialization. *San Quentin Point* (1982–1983) for example features 59 photographs of detritus and empty landscape with forensic detail as if investigating a crime scene—a land scraped bare of almost all natural references. In this work, he increasingly moves away from a clear narrative trajectory or moral perspective, and from traditional perspective and realism by isolating details, ridding the land of recognizable markers, and reflecting the disorientation caused by this junked space. *Near Reno* (1986), 14 photographs, also documents a terrain of scattered seemingly meaningless objects. For *Candlestick Point* (1984–1986) Baltz scans a hilly dumping site in a neighborhood of San Francisco. In the late 1980s, he settled in Europe, and began to work in color, often making larger prints for works, leading to muralistic studies of urban surveillance such as *Rule Without Exception* (1991) and in the spectacular *Ronde de Nuit* (1992), 12 large, unframed Cibachrome prints.

His work in the 1990s uses digital photography to further investigate the representational ability of the photograph, juxtaposing various documetnary genres, sometimes even breaking down the image to unrecognizable parts, showing the limitations of photography to reveal truth, for example in the trilogy, *Ronde du Nuit*, *Docile Bodies* (1995), and *Politics of Bacteria* (1995). These works expand his critique of realism and maintain his emphasis on architecture and the architectural qualities of photography while being increasingly interested in science and technology. In his more recent work, he has been inspired by cultural theorists Guy Debord and Michel Foucault and urban theorist Paul Virilio, with their analysis of the politics of space, power, and spectacle in postmodernity. His works are also produced in other media besides photographic installations. *Deaths in Newport* was produced as a book and CD-Rom in 1995 and in many of his projects and productions, especially in the 1990s, Baltz has become directly involved in planning within a city or neighborhood.

Although Baltz remains frequently defined by his inclusion in the New Topography group, he resists easy categorization given the diversity of his work since the 1970s. His work shares concerns shown by other documentarians of urban landscapes including Charles Sheeler, Berenice Abbott, and Walker Evans. Links can also be made with conceptual photographic works of Ed Ruscha in the 1960s. Uniting the work, however, is an inquiry into photography's ability to reveal truth, regardless of quantity or scale of the work, a project not confined to the New Topographic, social documentary, or landscape traditions.

At the Canadian Centre for Architecture in 2002, an exhibition of the *New Industrial Parks, Irvine California* series asserted a relationship between architecture and photography that Baltz has seen since the beginning of his career. Baltz's concept of architecture is that it is the most prominent and enduring material artifact produced by the dialectic of nature and culture, and his practice attempts to formalize this theoretical stance by producing architectural photographic experiences.

DANIELLE SCHWARTZ

See also: **Abbott, Berenice; Adams, Robert; Architectural Photography; Becher, Bernd and Hilla; Evans, Walker; Sheeler, Charles; Shore, Stephen**

Biography

Born in Newport Beach, California, September 12, 1945. San Francisco Art Institute, B.F.A. 1969; Claremont Graduate School, M.F.A. 1971. Begins association with Castelli Graphics, New York, 1971. Part-time Instructor, Pomona College, Claremont, 1970–1971; Visiting Lecturer in Art, University of California, Davis, 1981; Regent's Visitor in Art, University of California, Santa Cruz, 1982; Visiting Artist, Rhode Island School of Design, Providence 1983; Visiting Associate Professor of Art, University of California Riverside and Santa Cruz, and University of Victoria, British Columbia, 1984; Visiting Artist, California Institute of the Arts, Winter 1992 and 1998; Yale University, New Haven, Connecticut, Spring 1992 and 1999; Ecole nationale supérieure des Beaux-arts, Paris, Fall 1992; Hochschule für Gestaltung, Zurich, Switzerland, Fall 1993; Ecole supérieure d'Art et de Design, Reims, France, 1994–1995; Academy of Fine Arts, Helsinki, April, 1995; University of Göteburg, Sweden, 1995; Royal College of Art, London, 1998 and 1999; Visiting Professor, Hochschule für Gestaltung, Offenbach am Main, 1999–2001 Professor, Instituto Universitario di Architecture de Venezia. Recipient of National Endowment for the Arts Fellowship 1973, 1977; John Simon Guggenheim Memorial Fellowship, 1977; Professor of Photography, *European Graduate School* in *Saas-Fee*, Switzerland, 2002. Living in Paris and Zagreb, Croatia.

Individual Exhibitions

1971 Castelli Graphics, New York, New York
1972 George Eastman House, Rochester, New York
1974 Corcoran Gallery of Art, Washington, D.C.
1975 Philadelphia College of Art, Philadelphia, Pennsylvania
University of New Mexico, Albuquerque, New Mexico
1976 Museum of Fine Arts, Houston, Texas, Corcoran Gallery of Art, Washington, D.C., Baltimore Museum of Art, Baltimore, Maryland, La Jolla Museum of Contemporary Art, La Jolla, California
1985 Victoria and Albert Museum, London, England.
1986 Newport Harbor Art Museum, Newport Beach, California
1987 Galerie Espace L'Orient, Paris, France, Tokyo Institute of Polytechnics, Tokyo, Japan
1991 *Rule Without Exception*: P.S. 1, Long Island City, New York
1992 *La Ronde de Nuit*: Seibu Contemporary Art, Tokyo, Japan; Centre Pompidou, Paris, France; Stedelijk Museum, Amsterdam, the Netherlands; Los Angeles County Museum of Art, Los Angeles, California
1995 *Works 1979–1994*: Lousiana Museum of Modern Art, Humlebaek, Denmark
1998 *Lewis Baltz: the Politics of Bacteria, Docile Bodies, Ronde de Nuit*: Museum of Contemporary Art, Los Angeles, California
2002 *Lewis Baltz: Park City, Contemporary Photographs*: Yale University Art Museum, New Haven, Connecticut
New Industrial Parks, Irvine California: Canadian Centre for Architecture, Montreal, Canada
Lewis Baltz: Nevada and Other Photographs: Princeton Art Museum, Princeton, New Jersey

Group Exhibitions

1975 *New Topographics: Photographs of a Man-Altered Landscape*; International Museum of Photography and Film, George Eastman House, Rochester, New York
1977 *La Photographie créatrice au XXe Siecle*; Musée national d'Art Moderne, Centre Georges Pompidou, Paris, France
1978 *Mirrors and Windows: American Photography since 1960*. Museum of Modern Art, New York, New York, and toured the United States, 1978–1980
1979 *American Images*: Cocoran Gallery of Art, Washington, D.C., and traveling to the International Center of Photography, New York, New York; Museum of Fine Arts, Houston, Texas: Minneapolis Institute of Arts, Minneapolis, Minnesota; and Indianapolis Museum of Art, Indianapolis, Indiana, 1980; American Academy, Rome, Italy, 1981
1982 *Slices of Time*: Oakland Art Museum, California, and traveling to the Security Pacific National Bank, Los Angeles, California
1984 *Photography in California 1945–1980*: San Francisco Museum of Modern Art, San Francisco, California, and traveling to the Akron Art Museum, Akron, Ohio; Corcoran Gallery of Art, Washington, D.C.; Los Angeles Municipal Art Gallery, Los Angeles, California; Cornell University, Ithaca, New York; High Museum of Art, Atlanta, Georgia; Museum Folkwang, Essen, Germany; Centre Georges Pompidou, Paris, France; Museum of Photographic Art, San Diego, California
1985 *American Images*: Barbican Art Gallery, London, England, and toured Britain
1986 *The Real Big Picture*: Queens Museum of Art, Queens, New York
1987 *Photographs and Art 1946–1986*: Los Angeles County Museum of Art, Los Angeles, California
1990 *Signs of Life: Process and Materials, 1960–1990*: ICA, Philadelphia, Pennsylvania
1992 *Wasteland*: Rotterdam Biennial III, Rotterdam, the Netherlands
1993 *Critical Landscapes*: Metropolitan Museum of Photography, Tokyo, Japan
1999 *The American Century*: Whitney Museum of American Art, New York, New York
2000 *Visions from America*: Whitney Museum of American Art, New York, New York
2003 *Cruel and Tender: The Real in the Twentieth-century*

Photograph: The Tate Modern, London, England, and the Museum Ludwig, Koln, Germany

Selected Works

The Tract Houses, 1969–1971
The New Industrial Parks Near Irvine, California, 1975
Maryland, 1976
Nevada, 1978
Park City Utah, 1980
San Quentin Point, 1986
Candlestick Point, 1986
Rule Without Exception, 1991
Ronde de Nuit, 1992
Docile Bodies, 1995
Politics of Bacteria, 1995

Further Reading

Baltz, Lewis. *The New Industrial Parks Near Irvine, California*. New York: Castelli Graphics, 1974; 2nd edition Baltz, Lewis. Baltz, Lewis. *The New Industrial Parks Near Irvine, California*, 2nd Edition. Los Angeles: Ram Publications, 2001.
Baltz, Lewis, ed. *Contemporary American Photographic Works*. Houston: Museum of Fine Arts, 1977.
Baltz, Lewis. *Nevada*. New York: Castelli Graphics, 1978.
Baltz, Lewis, and Bernard Lamarche-Vadel. *Lewis Baltz*. Paris: Editions de la Difference, 1993.
Baltz, Lewis, and Gus Blaisdell. *Park City*. Albuquerque: Artspace Press, 1980.
Butler, Connie. *The Politics of Bacteria, Docile Bodies, Ronde de nuit*. Los Angeles: Museum of Contemporary Art and Ram Publications, 1998.

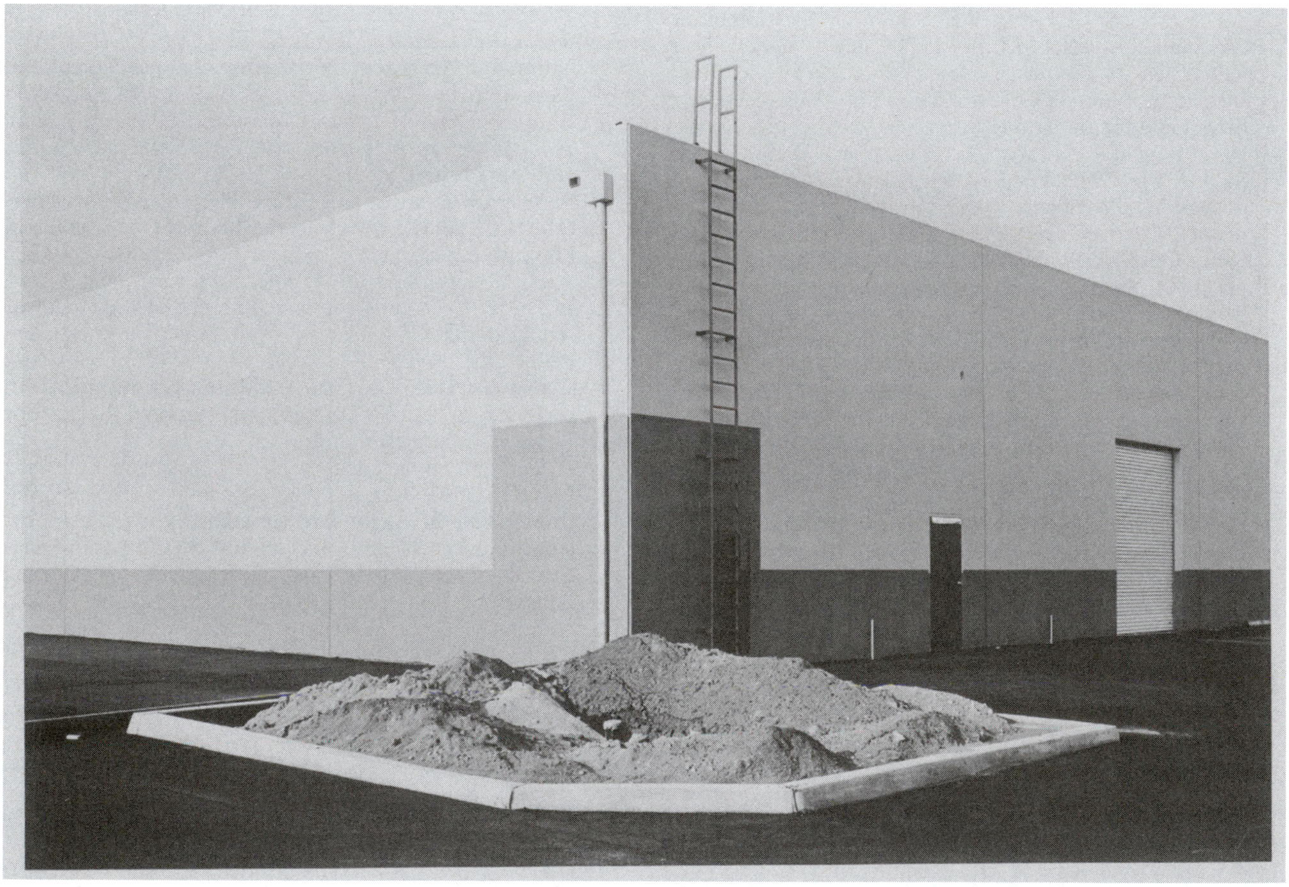

Lewis Baltz, South Corner, Riccar America Company, 3184 Pullman, Costa Mesa, 1974, gelatin silver print, 15.1 × 22.8 cm, Gift of the photographer.
[*Photograph courtesy of George Eastman House,* © *Lewis Baltz*]

Green, J. *American Photography: A Critical History 1945 to the Present*. New York: 1984.
Turrell, Julia Brown, ed. *Lewis Baltz: Rule Without Exception*. Des Moines: Des Moines Art Center, and Albuquerque: University of New Mexico Press, 1991.
Weinberg, Adam, and Lewis Baltz. *The New Industrial Parks Near Irvine, California*. Los Angeles: Ram Publications, 2001.

ALFRED H. BARR, JR.

American

Widely regarded as an eloquent writer on the subject of modern art, Alfred H. Barr Jr. became the first director of the Museum of Modern Art, New York (MoMA) in 1929. This appointment was the product of the labors of the so-called "adamantine ladies," wealthy patrons Abby Rockefeller, Lillie P. Bliss, and Mary Quinn Sullivan, who began planning for the first museum devoted to contemporary art the previous year. After preliminary meetings, the women enlisted the expertise of Harvard University Fogg Art Museum Director Paul J. Sachs, who in turn recommended 27 year-old Barr, a former student from Sachs's famed "museum course" at Harvard.

Though initially Alfred Barr deferred, contending that Sachs himself would make a better inaugural director, Barr was excited at the prospect and ultimately convinced of his own readiness to direct the Museum, which quickly became a reality in the months immediately preceding the devastating stock market crash of 1929. In fact, Barr was both well prepared and well compensated for his newly awarded position, which commanded the then giant salary of $10,000 per year with a $2,500 stipend.

Prior to taking the position for which he is so associated, Barr taught at Vassar College in Poughkeepsie, New York, before going to Europe in 1924. For the 1925–1926 academic year Barr was awarded an associate professorship at Wellesley College in Massachusetts where he taught the first-ever official course in Modern Art, a subject first canonized in the aftermath of the Armory Show of 1913 held at the 69th-regiment armory in New York City. One of the most historic American exhibitions, the Armory Show aroused a great deal of emotion—much of it outrage—for the avant-garde artwork it displayed.

After pioneering the Vassar course in modern art, Barr again headed to Europe. He visited married artists Alexsandr Rodchenko and Varvara Stepanova in Russia and then the Bauhaus in Dessau, Germany, before returning to Vassar with a wider range of reference for modern art scholarship, which would be his lifetime vocation.

Besides being a popular young professor at the women's colleges, Barr was introduced to the American public when he was asked to write an article for *Vanity Fair* magazine based on tests incorporated into his modern art curriculum: his 50-question "Modern Art Questionnaire" was published in August 1927. While Barr noted in the introduction that "there are no spellbinders such as: Name four important artist-photographers whose names begin with St---," the questionnaire included items on Saks Fifth Avenue, James Joyce, and The Barnes Collection of Pennsylvania. This article can be seen against the backdrop of philistine criticism of abstract art. With his penchant for formal analysis, Barr is perceived as having had a one-man mission to convert the public into modern art believers.

Born the eldest son to a prolific Presbyterian preacher's family and reared in Baltimore, Maryland, Barr received his B.A. in 1922 and his M.A. in 1923 from Princeton University in New Jersey. His rigorous and analytical art historical training, largely under the tutelage of Professor Charles Rufus Morey, cultivated his interest in the discipline, and provided an antecedent for the way Barr would configure the institution of the MoMA. While in school, Barr made frequent trips to New York City, where he saw exhibitions of late nineteenth-century French painting at the Metropolitan Museum of Art, consisting of works representative of the seeds of modern art. Barr also visited the 291 Gallery, also known as the Little

Galleries of the Photo-Secession, run by photographer Alfred Stieglitz.

From its beginning the Museum of Modern Art was a major force in contemporary American art, unique in its incorporation of living artists into its program. The first of the seven exhibitions of the first year of the MOMA, consisting of 98 works by French painters, opened at the end of 1929 on the 12th floor of the Heckscher Building on Fifth Avenue in New York. The walls, erected within the extant space under the direction of Barr, were covered in light-hued monk's cloth to provide an appropriate base for the display of modern art. The inaugural exhibitions at MoMA, widely informed by the collections and collecting habits of the museum patrons and trustees, showcased both European and American art, of which the European examples were hugely favored over the American ones.

In 1930, before the full effects of the stock market crash of the previous year and ensuing depression were felt, which in any case had little bearing on families such as the Rockefellers and Blisses, Alfred Barr married Italian Margaret Scolari-Fitzmaurice in Paris at a church on Quay D'Orsay. Marga, or Daisy as Mrs. Barr was also known, spoke many languages and was an indispensable travel partner and general administrator for her husband. From the outset, Barr's role as director was a professorial rather than administrative one, evident in the way he generously compiled summer reading lists for trustees including titles by Thorsten Veblen.

In his introduction to the catalogue for "Art In Our Time, an exhibition to celebrate the tenth anniversary of the Museum of Modern Art and the opening of its new building (11 W. 53rd Street) held at the time of the New York World's Fair, 1939," Barr wrote that MoMA "is a laboratory: in its experiments the public is invited to participate." Barr's concept of the laboratory incorporated an interdisciplinary vision of the museum, which included the establishment of departments of film, photography, design, and architecture.

The first ten years of MoMA constituted Barr's most influential in terms of programming. In 1932, Barr's colleagues and friends, architects Henry-Russell Hitchcock and Philip Johnson, curated the seminal exhibition *Modern Architecture: International Exhibition*, which established the active relationship between the modern and contemporary art. In 1934 Barr mounted the *Machine Art* exhibition showcasing the design collection among other things. Late that same year Dorothy Miller, a talented art historian, began a long tenure at MoMA with an appointment as her friend Alfred Barr's assistant. In 1936, Barr organized one of his most respected shows, *Cubism and Abstract Art*, the catalogue of which contained the famous Barr-authored diagram on *The Development of Abstract Art*.

Photography always played a central role in Barr's modern art and was exhibited as early as 1932. In the mid-1930s Beaumont Newhall, also from Sachs's museum course at the Fogg, was hired as the first MoMA librarian. In addition, he served as official photographer. Newhall told MoMA biographer Russell Lynes:

> Barr had long wanted an exhibition of photographs on a scale with the biggest of the painting exhibitions and given the same importance as had been given them.

With all haste, Newhall and his new wife Nancy were sent by Barr to Europe to get material for the historic *Photography, 1839–1937*, a traveling exhibition of European and American photographic work and equipment. In addition to his formative years as director, Barr's major contribution to the field of modern art came in the form of his volume of writings and his dedication to the permanent collections of MoMA. In 1943, following the 1941 appointment of Nelson A. Rockefeller as museum president and the museum's increased relationship with the U.S. government, Barr was officially dismissed as director, though he never gave up his office on the premises. Five years later, the same year Edward Steichen became the director of Department of Photography, Barr was appointed director of the newly formed Museum Collections department, a post which he held for the next 20 years, building the museum's world-renowned collection until his retirement in 1967.

SARA GREENBERGER

See also: **Modernism; Museum of Modern Art; Newhall, Beaumont; Steichen, Edward; Stieglitz, Alfred**

Biography

Born Alfred Hamilton Barr, Jr. in Detroit, Michigan, 1902. Art History, Princeton, B.A., 1922. Art History, Princeton, M.A., 1923. Attended Harvard University, Art History and Museum Studies, with Paul J. Sachs, 1924. Taught Art History Vassar College, Poughkeepsie, New York, 1924 and Princeton University, Princeton, New Jersey, 1925. Assistant Professor, Wellesley College, Wellesley, Massachusetts, 1925–1927. Director of the Museum of Modern Art, New York, 1929–1943. Director, Museum Collections, Museum of Modern Art, New York 1947–1967. Died in Salisbury, Connecticut, 15 August 1981.

Further Reading

Barr, Alfred H. Jr. and the Museum of Modern Art. *Cubism and Abstract Art*. New York: Museum of Modern Art, 1936.

Barr, Alfred H. Jr., ed. *Fantastic Art, Dada, Surrealism*. New York: Museum of Modern Art, 1936.

Barr, Alfred H. Jr., ed. *Machine Art, March 6 to April 30, 1934*. New York: Museum of Modern Art, 1934.

Barr, Alfred H. Jr. *Painting and Sculpture in the Museum of Modern Art, 1929–1977*. New York: Museum of Modern Art, 1977.

Kantor, Sybil Gordon. *Alfred H. Barr, Jr. and the Intellectual Origins of the Museum of Modern Art*. Cambridge, MA, and London: The MIT Press, 2002.

Lynes, Russell. *Good Old Modern: An Intimate Portrait of the Museum of Modern Art*. New York: Atheneum, 1973.

Marquis, Alice Goldfarb. *Alfred H. Barr Jr.: Missionary for the Modern*. Chicago: Contemporary Books, Inc., 1989.

Sandler, Irving, and Amy Newman, eds. *Defining Modern Art: Selected Writings of Alfred H. Barr, Jr.* New York: Harry N. Abrams, Inc., 1986.

ROLAND BARTHES

French

Until his death in 1980, Roland Barthes' professional writing career spanned more than three decades, during which he sporadically offered commentary about the medium of photography. Most prominent among Barthes' writings on photography are three essays—*The Photographic Message* (1961), *Rhetoric of the Image* (1964), and *The Third Meaning* (1970)—and one book, *Camera Lucida: Reflections on Photography* (1980). Associated at first with the structuralism of Claude Lévi-Strauss) and the semiology of Ferdinand de Saussure, Barthes is also considered a poststructuralist, that is, one of many, such as Michel Foucault and Jacques Derrida, who offer a radical critique of structuralism's faith in the stability of linguistic structures and its capacity to provide the analytical grid by which a new synthesis of all the human sciences could be established. Barthes' writings on photography, therefore, emphasize different issues at different times; all, however, depend on the nomenclature of structuralism and semiology.

In the 1950s Barthes assumed a position that perceived the photographic work as a sign capable of being decoded. A "sign" comprises a "signifier" and a "signified." The signifier is the physical entity, such as a word, used to communicate the signified, the conceptual meaning or message. The relationship between the signifier and signified is arbitrary according to Saussure: there is nothing about a dog that demands that it be called a "dog," and it is, in fact, called "un chien" in French. By the 1960s Barthes deepens his analysis of the structure of communication. In *The Photographic Message* he first posits that the photograph holds a privileged relation to literal reality: it is its perfect *analogon*. He argues that although the photograph is a reduction in proportion, perspective, and color of the object captured on film, it is *not* a transformation (in the mathematical sense of the term). Barthes' structural methodology, therefore, does not fully apply. Although a photographic image may function as a sign (a message that can be decoded), it remains a medium of communication that is not truly arbitrary, the way that language is. He draws two conclusions: the photographic image is a message without code and the photographic message is a continuous message. The working hypothesis, however, of *The Photographic Message* is that the photographic message in press photography is also connoted, and the remainder of the essay articulates the main levels of analysis of photographic connotation, including trick effects, pose, selection of objects or content, photogenia, aestheticism, and accompanying text. All indicate something about how content, composition, or use can be manipulated in the photograph.

In *Rhetoric of the Image*, an essay that focuses on images used in advertising, Barthes repeats his statement that the photograph is a "message without code" or "a continuous message"; he also states that the photograph does not simply convey a consciousness of the object or subject "being-there" (which any copy might provoke), but a consciousness of the thing's "having-been-there." The principal argument of this essay is that the rhetoric of the image comprises three messages: linguistic, denoted, and symbolic (cultural or connoted). It is essentially in explicating the denoted message that Barthes must address the inherent difference between a photograph and, for example, a drawing. At the structural level of denotation the photograph presents an "uncoded" message, while the drawing's message subsists as coded. The literal message of the photograph derives not from a transformation between signifieds and signifiers but from a registration that is mechanical. The registration of a drawing, on the other hand, arises through human intervention.

The Third Meaning concerns the Soviet avant-garde filmmaker Sergei Eisenstein, but the focus of the essay is not the moving pictures that Eisenstein has created but rather the movie stills that have accompanied his works. The first two meanings that Barthes ascribes to the photographic still are (1) informational, which serves the realm of communication and (2) symbolic, which functions on at least four levels—referential, diegetic, Eisensteinian, and historical—and which represents the still's *signification*. Yet to such seemingly complete categories with regard to "meaning" in the photograph, Barthes feels compelled to add a third, for, quite simply, the first and second meanings are "obvious." To the stratification and understanding of meaning Barthes inserts the proposition that something may remain in the analysis of the photographic still that transcends conventional or obvious meaning, something that he cannot be certain is justified or can be generalized. The third meaning possesses a theoretical individuality, and Barthes distinguishes this meaning as "obtuse," that which supplements and cannot be absorbed by intellectual analysis—a meaning both persistent and fugitive, apparent and evasive, and beyond culture, knowledge, and information.

In *Camera Lucida*, a text commissioned by *Cahiers du cinéma*, Barthes offers not only his longest critique on the medium of photography but also his most controversial and compelling. Comprising two parts, Barthes begins by attempting to quantify and qualify the medium's unique essence (its *noeme*). To this end he employs methodological tools and schemata that inform his structural analysis. By Part Two his attempt at an impartial, scientific investigation is fully abandoned for a highly personal reflection on the medium and its *noeme*. He begins this inquiry by looking through family photographs, where he discovers an image of his mother and her brother when they were children (known as the Winter Garden photograph). The power of this one photograph to capture and convey to him the unique individual who was his mother (she had recently died) suggested to Barthes that what distinguishes the photographic medium from any other is its ability to authenticate "that-has-been." He offers as new terms to the critical discussion of the medium *studium* and *punctum*, the former referring to the field of cultural information that a photograph may possess and that is generally available for analysis and the latter referring to the undefinable and varying aspect that overtakes an individual viewer. *Studium* relates to the field of connoted messages articulated in earlier essays; *punctum* can be linked to the obtuse meaning described in *The Third Meaning* but exceeds that notion by Barthes's invocation of the *punctum*'s ability not only to disturb but also to wound. Among the most radical assertions that he makes in *Camera Lucida* is that photography's *noeme* has nothing to do with analogy (a feature it shares with all kinds of representations): the photograph is not a copy of reality but rather an emanation of past reality. Barthes now suggests that to ask whether a photograph is analogical or coded is not a good means of analysis. The book concludes that photography's madness and its ecstasy is its essential link with intractable reality, obliging the viewer to return to the very letter of time.

NANCY M. SHAWCROSS

See also: **Semiotics**

Biography

Born in Cherbourg, France, 12 November 1915. Attended the University of Paris, where he received degrees in classical letters (1939) and grammar and philosophy (1943). Taught at lycées in Biarritz, France (1939), Bayonne, France (1939–1940), Paris, France (1942–1946), at the French Institute, Bucharest, Romania (1948–1949), University of Alexandria, Egypt (1949–1950), and Direction Générale des Affaires Culturelles, Paris (1950–1952); research appointments with the Centre National de la Recherche Scientifique, Paris (1952–1959); director of studies at the École Pratique des Hautes Études, Paris, (1960–1976); visiting professor at Johns Hopkins University, Baltimore (1967–1968); and chair of literary semiology at the Collège de France, Paris (1976–1980). Died in Paris, France, 26 March 1980.

Selected Works

Mythologies, 1957; *Mythologies*, selected and translated by Annette Lavers, 1972

Roland Barthes par Roland Barthes, 1975; *Roland Barthes by Roland Barthes*. Translated by Richard Howard. 1977

La Chambre claire: Note sur la photographie, 1980; *Camera Lucida: Reflections on Photography*. Translated by Richard Howard. 1981

"L'Image" ("Image"). In *L'Obvie et l'obtus: Essais critiques III*. (1982): 9–61; *The Responsibility of Forms: Critical Essays on Music, Art, and Representation*. Translated by Richard Howard. 1985: 3–62

Further Reading

Barthes après Barthes: une actualité en questions: actes du Colloque international de Pau, 22-24 novembre 1990 (Barthes after Barthes: Current Issues, Acts of the Pau International Conference, 22-24 November 1990). Pau, France: Publications de l'université de Pau, 1993.

Knight, Diana, ed. *Critical Essays on Roland Barthes*. New York: G.K. Hall, 2000.

Rabaté, Jean-Michel, ed. *Writing the Image after Roland Barthes*. Philadelphia: University of Pennsylvania Press, 1997.

Rylance, Rick. *Roland Barthes*. New York: Harvester Wheatsheaf, 1994.

Shawcross, Nancy M. *Roland Barthes on Photography: The Critical Tradition in Perspective*. Gainesville: University Press of Florida, 1997.

Stafford, Andy. *Roland Barthes, Phenomenon and Myth: An Intellectual Biography*. Edinburgh: Edinburgh University Press, 1998.

BAUHAUS

The Bauhaus, founded and directed by architect Walter Gropius, is renowned as the landmark German modernist school of the early twentieth century in which the integration of the arts and design with technology was first explored and practiced. The school was composed of workshops in painting, furniture design, typography, and other fine and practical arts courses, each taught by a master. Each Bauhaus student commenced hands-on training with a study of the elements of design common to all modern design endeavors. Established in 1919 and arising out of the combining of two pre-existing schools, the Weimar Art Academy and the Weimar Arts and Crafts School, in Gropius' words the Bauhaus, strove for "unity in diversity" in function, design, and thought and reflected the influence of the Werkbund movement on its founder.

The Werkbund called for integration among the arts and the economic realities of capitalism, and looked favorably upon emerging technologies of the early twentieth century to assist this aim. The Bauhaus was a surprising success at what might seem a utopian aim. Best known for producing well-designed yet practical furniture, household items, including dishware and cutlery, graphic arts, typography, and training teachers, in the area of photography the Bauhaus had a profound and lasting impact.

In the strict sense, photography as an independent medium came rather late to the Bauhaus. It was not introduced into the curriculum of the school until 1929, four years after the establishment of the Dessau Bauhaus (1925–1933) and a full decade after the earlier Weimar school (1919–1925). László Moholy-Nagy, the multi-talented abstract artist and the master of the design foundation course, was the first to recognize the value of photography not only to document the Bauhaus, but as an independent art form. His modern teachings validated the significance of the photograph for generations of Bauhaus students, from Germany to America, first in his teaching, and later via his directorship of the New Bauhaus in Chicago (1936–1938). Number 8 of the famous Bauhausbucher series, *Painting, Photography, Film*, by Moholy-Nagy, is devoted to this medium.

Bauhaus photography tends toward the artistically self-referential: Bauhaus photographers photographed Bauhaus buildings, Bauhaus designs, and Bauhaus personages, including fellow Bauhaus photographers. Though Walter Gropius and the Bauhaus masters repeatedly denied the existence of any "Bauhaus style," Bauhaus photographers nonetheless invented and shared an experimental method that today is readily identifiable. The hallmark of Bauhaus photography and its aesthetic strength is in its abstract qualities. Intense contrasts of blacks and whites, or strongly cast shadows in shades of gray, predominate. The compositions are most often structured by geometry, either the horizontals and verticals of Cubism or De Stijl, or else slashed through via the raking diagonals of Futurism. Like the Bauhaus itself, photography at the school was dominated by a Teutonic coolness of form, an anti-Romantic, New World view, known as *die Neue Sachlichkeit*, or New Objectivity.

The New Objectivity, particularly as expressed by Bauhaus photography, is a world of stark images and abstract white cubic buildings, inhabited by impersonal males and languid females. It is a world of pure Platonic form. Bauhaus masters claimed that their inspirations were to be found not in art photography, but in technology and science. Thus distortions such as scale and angle produced abstract photographs influenced by views the eye could actually encounter only through the technology of a microscope or from an airplane. Even the commonplace objects of everyday life could become abstractions: human hands, for example, could be seen as sculptural abstractions in Bauhaus photographs.

The utilization of technology to create designs free of the strictures of the past was crucial to the Bauhaus. In fact, history courses were not part of the curriculum. Only through removing or reducing the capriciousness of human emotion could a modern purity of design emerge, although paradoxically, the Bauhaus foundation courses stressed hands-on activities through the creation of hand-made objects. The goal was an egalitarian one: to improve the lives of ordinary people. A secondary goal was to introduce new ways of seeing, technology understandably being at the forefront of this endeavor. Purity of image, however, became so important to Bauhaus photographers that technology was in fact eschewed. The direct contact of the subject with the treated paper, removing even the camera from the process of photography, was developed by Moholy-Nagy in the form of the photogram, a photographic image made without the use of a camera (also known as light graphics). Even though the form had been explored earlier by practitioners including Man Ray, the perfection and dissemination of the photogram can be seen as a seminal contribution to photography by the Bauhaus.

Moholy-Nagy was also a sculptor, and the amalgam of his sculptural abstraction with the flat image of the photograph was innovative. His imposition of three-dimensional objects, casting their shadows directly onto the two-dimensional flat surface of the treated photographic paper, created a wholly new formal type of composition. Ambiguous spatial effects are evident in these works, as unidentifiable objects seem to float within the empty space of a black background. One excellent example of such a photogram is found in the collection of the Busch-Reisinger Museum, Harvard University (BR 2004.18). Just as we think we grasp Moholy-Nagy's hard-edged abstraction, however, he astounds us with his sensuous, erotic art photograph of 1927, 'Two Torsos' (1949, 214).

Moholy-Nagy's first wife, Lucia, was also one of the photographic innovators of the Bauhaus. Lucia is renowned for the dramatic architectural portraits of the Gropius-designed white cubic and glass Bauhaus buildings. Her photographs provide the iconic images of the Bauhaus complex, and the visual memories by which the world recalls the Bauhaus. A selection of her documentary architectural photographs, also in the collection of the Busch-Reisinger Museum, attests to Lucia Moholy's formal sense of composition, her abstract love of form, her dramatic vision of architecture devoid of people, her profound stillness (see, for example, BR GA.20.57).

Other masters of the Bauhaus applied photography with varying and interesting perspectives. Typography master Herbert Bayer integrated photographs into his montages for posters, book jackets, and advertisements. The poster Bayer designed for master Marcel Breuer's 'Metallmobel' design exhibition is a classic. T. Lux Feininger contributed an informal use of photography to the Bauhaus repertoire, creating the most naturalistic, snapshot-like pictures of other Bauhaus students and masters, often unexpectedly at play. Documentary portraits of some of the major figures in the history of modernism, who visited the Bauhaus, were made by Bauhaus photographers, including formal pictures of architects Gropius, Mies van der Rohe, and painters Wassily Kandinsky, Paul Klee, Amédée Ozenfant, and El Lissitzky, to name but a few. Photographers associated with the German Bauhaus include Walter Peterhans, Florence Henri, and Ellen Auerbach.

Achievement in photography at the Bauhaus was not restricted to those primarily associated with the medium. Josef Albers, known for his "homage to the square" paintings, created photographs that come the closest of all Bauhaus artists to what can be called art photography, surprising in that they indicate the painting master gave himself a freedom in photography that he denied himself in his primary medium. In a series of abstract landscapes of fields and fences, and views of sea foam on sand, for example, Albers let his camera paint freely.

The great educational experiment came to a close in 1933 when the Bauhaus was closed by the Nazis. Bauhaus photography continues to be valued and appreciated not just for its rigorous aesthetics and design innovations, but as a document of a seminal period in the development of modernism created out of the utopian visions of a handful of artists. The legacy of the Bauhaus continues in photography today through the influence of Moholy-Nagy's Institute of Design (New Bauhaus) and the dozens of teachers who trained there in the mid and late twentieth century.

Leslie Humm Cormier

See also: **Architectural Photography; Auerbach, Ellen; Bayer, Herbert; Feininger, T. Lux; Formalism; Futurism; Henri, Florence; History of Photography: Twentieth-Century Developments; Institute of Design; Lissitzky, El; Manipulation; Modernism; Moholy-Nagy, László; Photography in Europe: Germany and Austria**

Further Reading

Busch-Reisinger Museum, Harvard University Art Museums, Photography Collection, Bauhaus Archives and Gropius Archives. For original images, documentation, and works of Bauhaus design.

Mendelshohn, Harvey L., trans. *Bauhaus Photography*. Cambridge, MA: Massachusetts Institute of Technology Press, 1985.

HERBERT BAYER

Austrian

Herbert Bayer considered himself a painter, but he is recognized as a prolific artist who worked successfully in a variety of media including sculpture, typography, graphic design, and photography. During his long, multifaceted career, he designed furniture and tapestries, executed murals, and was an architect and photographer. Bayer discovered photography in the 1920s while a student at the Bauhaus in Germany. In an atmosphere of experimentation and reverence for industrial society and the machine age, Bayer embraced the camera as a means to create imagery suitable for the modern era. He went on to develop an innovative body of photographs including a series photomontages in addition to a series he called *fotoplastiken* that included still life and geometric objects.

Herbert Bayer was born on April 5, 1900, in Haag am Hausruck, a small village near Salzburg in Northern Austria. As a child he developed an interest in skiing, mountaineering, and drawing. Bayer's interest in art grew throughout his youth, but plans for Bayer to attend art school in Vienna were curtailed by the unexpected death of his father, leaving his family few financial resources. After serving in the military during the last years of World War I, he became the apprentice of artist Georg Schmidthammer of Linz, Austria, in 1920. Bayer designed letterheads, posters, and advertisements. He left Schmidthammer's workshop and settled in Darmstadt, Germany, where he worked for Viennese architect Emmanuel Margold at the Darmstadt Artists Colony.

In Darmstadt, Bayer was trained in the Art Nouveau styles. He became interested in the aesthetic philosophies of Walter Gropius after reading his book *Bauhaus-Manifest*. Gropius had founded the Bauhaus in Weimar, Germany in 1919. He based its curriculum around the principals of the Arts and Crafts movement, specifically the incorporation of art and industry. After an interview with Gropius, Bayer was admitted to the Bauhaus school in 1921. He left Darmstadt moving to Weimar, and for the next four years studied with the school's great professors concentrating on design and typography. He later joined Wassily Kandinsky's mural workshop.

When Bayer completed his studies, he was appointed by Gropius to head the printing and advertising workshops for the school. He moved to Dessau, Germany, where the school had relocated in 1925. Bayer taught graphic design and typography until 1928. He instituted the lowercase alphabet as the style for all Bauhaus printing and founded the now common type style variously called universal or univers. He also designed the signage for the Bauhaus's new building complex, which has become an icon of twentieth century design.

Bayer's earliest exposure to photography was in the 1920s while studying with Bauhaus instructor László Moholy-Nagy. Influenced by many of the innovative visual techniques characteristic of Moholy-Nagy's work, Bayer shot with a handheld camera and favored unusual cropping and composition techniques, including extreme close-ups and angles as well as presenting scenes from unusually high or low vantage points. His work set him at the forefront of avant-garde photography in the early twentieth century.

In 1929 Bayer left the Bauhaus and became the art director of *Vogue* magazine in Berlin. The period marked a distinct change in his approach to photography. Influenced by the surrealist movement and fascinated by the human subconscious, Bayer used the technique of photomontage to create psychologically compelling and fantastic images. In one of his signature images from this period, *Self Portrait*, 1932, Bayer looks into a mirror while removing his arm at the shoulder to his own amazement. This photograph was one of a series for use in a picture story called *Man and Dream*, which was never completed.

Although Bayer's photomontages were reminiscent of work by other surrealist artists, his photographs demonstrated a refined sense of design as a result of his training at the Bauhaus. Through skillful arrangement of objects, composition, and lighting, Bayer exploited the illusionary aspects of the photographic medium recreating otherworldly scenarios for his 1936 series of photographs he called *fotoplastiken*. One of the works, *Metamorphosis*, is regarded as Bayer's most successful treatment of spatial manipulation and symbolism. In the foreground, he arranged basic geometric forms—the sphere, the cone, and the square—that appear to converge upon a distant horizon of sky, clouds, and forest to suggest the sublime contrast of culture and nature or more deeply, the confrontation of reason and emotion.

Bayer fled Nazi Germany and immigrated to the United States in 1938. His career in the arts continued to proliferate. He designed exhibitions at the Museum of Modern Art including *Bauhaus 1919–1928*, *Road to Victory*, *Airways to Peace*, and *Art In Progress*. Following the end of World War II, Bayer was a consultant for the Container Corporation of America, whose president was the visionary executive Walter Paepcke, who had funded the Chicago manifestation of the Bauhaus, and later chaired the corporation's design department. Relocating to Aspen, Colorado in 1946, Bayer became the design consultant for the development of Aspen as a ski resort and cultural center, and was appointed architect for the Aspen Institute of Humanistic Studies, also funded by Paepcke, who had a second residence in the mountain town. Bayer also completed the first recorded "earthwork" environment entitled *Grass Mound* in 1955. From 1966 until his death, Bayer was a design consultant for the Atlantic Richfield Company.

After suffering a heart attack in 1970, Bayer and his wife, Joella, moved their residence from the high elevation of Aspen to Santa Barbara, California, where the artist maintained an active studio until his death in 1985. Herbert Bayer's contributions to the world of art and design are unique and are demonstrated in an outstanding career that touched nearly every field of the arts from architecture to the fine arts, as well as photography and graphic design. During his lifetime, he had over 150 one-man exhibitions and seven traveling museum retrospectives throughout the United States and Europe. Over 100 books, articles, and films exist that deal exclusively with Bayer's extensive creative oeuvre. His work is included in major museums throughout worldwide. In addition, there are substantial archives of his work in the Bauhaus archive in Berlin, Germany, and the Bayer archive at the Denver Art Museum in Colorado.

Nancy Barr

See also: **Bauhaus; Moholy-Nagy, László; Montage; Museum of Modern Art; Photography in Europe: Germany and Austria; Surrealism**

Biography

Born in Haag, Austria, 5 April 1900. Apprenticeship in architecture with G. Schmidthammer, Linz, Austria, 1919. Studied in Darmstadt with Emanuel Margold, 1920. Student at the Bauhaus in Weimar, Germany, 1921–1923. Also studied mural painting with Wassily Kandinsky, 1921. Master at the Bauhaus in Dessau teaching typography, 1925–1928. Art Director at the Dorland Studio, 1928–1938 and at *Vogue*, 1929–1930 in Berlin. Consultant at the Aspen Institute of Humanistic Studies, 1949. Chairman of the department of design of the Container Corporation of America, 1956–1965. Recipient of numerous awards including: the Ambassador's Award for Excellence in London in 1968; the Kulturpreis for photography in Cologne in 1969; and Adalbert Stifter Preis für Bildende Kunste in Austria in 1971. Employed as a consultant in architecture, art, and design by Atlantic Richfield Company, 1965–1985. Appointed Honorary Fellow of the Royal Academy of Fine Art in The Hague in 1975 and of the Hochschule für Kunstlerische und Industrelle Gestalung of Linz, Austria in 1978. Recipient of the Austrian Honor Cross for Art and Science in 1978. Awarded an honorary doctorate of fine arts from the Art Center College of Design in Pasadena, California in 1979. Died in Montecito, California, 30 September 1985.

Individual Exhibitions

1929 Kunstlerbund Marz; Linz, Austria Galerie Povolozky; Paris, France

1931 Bauhaus; Dessau, Germany

1936 Kunstverein; Salzburg, Austria
1937 *Herbert Bayer: Austrian*; London Gallery, London, England
1939 Black Mountain College; Black Mountain, North Carolina
1940 Yale University Gallery of Art; New Haven, Connecticut
1947 *Retrospective: The Way Beyond Art*; Brown University, Providence, Rhode Island, and traveled to Harvard University, Cambridge, Massachusetts; Institute of Design, Chicago, Illinois; Joslyn Art Museum Omaha, Nebraska; Boise Art Museum, Boise, Idaho; Boseman Museum, Boseman, Montana; Portland Art Museum, Portland, Oregon; Seattle Art Museum, Seattle, Washington; San Francisco Museum of Art, San Francisco, California
1955 Aspen Institute for Humanistic Studies; Aspen, Colorado
1956 *Retrospective: Herbert Bayer: 33 Jahres Seines Schaffens*; Germanisches Nationalmuseum, Nuremberg, Germany, and traveled to Die Neue Sammlung, Munich, Germany; Kunstgewerbenmuseum, Zurich, Switzerland; Hochschule fur Bildende Kunste, Berlin, Germany; Stadtisches Museum, Braunschweig, Germany
1958 *Recent Works of Herbert Bayer*; Fort Worth Art Center, Fort Worth, Texas, and traveled to Walker Art Center, Minneapolis, Minnesota; University of Oklahoma, Norman, Oklahoma
1960 Stadtische Kunsthalle; Dusseldorf, GermanyMuseum am Ostwall; Dortmund, Germany
1961 Bauhaus-Archive; Darmstadt, Germany
1962 *Herbert Bayer, Retrospective*; Stadtisches Kunstmuseum, Duisberg, Germany, and traveled to Roswell Museum and Art Center, Roswell, New Mexico; Colorado Springs Fine Arts Center, Colorado Springs, Colorado; The Art Gallery, University of California at Santa Barbara, Santa Barbara, California; La Jolla Museum of Art, La Jolla, California; Joslyn Art Museum, Omaha, Nebraska; Memorial Art Gallery of the University of Rochester, Rochester, New York
1969 University of California, Santa Barbara Art Gallery; Santa Barbara, California
1970 Germanishces Nationalmuseum; Nuremberg, Germany Osterreichisches Museum fur Angewandte Kunst; Vienna, Austria
1973 *Herbert Bayer: Fotografien, Fotomontagen 1926–1937*; Landesbildstelle, Hamburg, Germany *Herbert Bayer: A Total Concept*; Denver Art Museum, Denver, Colorado
1976 *Herbert Bayer: Beispiele aus dem Gesamtwerk 1919–1974*; Die Neue Galerie, Linz, Austria
1978 *Herbert Bayer: Photographs, Paintings, Drawings.* Goethe-Institut, Münich, Germany
1980 *Inaugural Exhibition of the Herbert Bayer Archive*; Denver Art Museum, Denver, Colorado, and traveled to Neue Galerie, Linz, Austria; Galerias Mer-Kup, Mexico City, Mexico
1986 *Herbert Bayer, Kunst und Design in Amerika 1938–1985.* Bauhaus-Archiv, Museum für Gestaltung, Berlin, Germany
1997 *The Aspen Years*; Kent Gallery, New York, New York
1999 *Herbert Bayer: The Total Artist*; Smallworks Gallery, Las Vegas, Nevada
2000 *Herbert Bayer 1900–1985*; Neue Galerie, Linz, Austria

Group Exhibitions

1923 *Kunst and Technik: eine neue Einheit*; Bauhaus und Staatliches Landesmuseum, Weimar, Germany
1929 *Film und Foto: Internationale Ausstellung des Deutschen Werkbundes*; Ausstellungshallen und Königbaulichtspiele, Stuttgart, Germany
1931 *Fotomontage*; Kunstgewerbemuseum Domela-Nieuwenhuis, Cologne, Germany
1932 *Surréalisme*; Julien Levy Gallery, New York, New York
1932 *Modern Photography at Home and Abroad*; Albright Art Gallery, Buffalo, New York
Modern European Photography; Julien Levy Gallery, New York, New York
1936 *Entartete Kunst*; Haus der Deutschen Kunst, Munich, Germany
1951 *Subjektive Fotografie*; Staatlichen Schule für Kunst, Germany
1959 *V Bienal*; Sao Paulo, Brazil
1966 *Les Années 25*; Musée de Art Décoratifs, Paris, France
1967 *50 Jahre Bauhaus*; Württembergische Kunstverein, Stuttgart, Germany
1977 *Diez Grandes Fotografos: Bernice Abbott, Eugène Atget, Diane Arbus, Richard Avedon, Herbert Bayer, Bill Brandt, Brassaï, Robert Frank, Irving Penn, Maurice Tabard*; Museo de Arte Contemporáneo de Caracas, Caracas, Venezuela
1978 *Paris-Berlin 1900–1933*; Centre Georges Pompidou, Paris, France
1979 *Fabricated to be Photographed*; San Francisco Museum of Modern Art, San Francisco, California
1980 *Avant-Garde Photography in Germany 1919–1939*; San Francisco Museum of Modern Art, San Francisco, California
1985 *Self-Portrait: The Photographer's Persona 1840–1985*; Museum of Modern Art, New York, New York
1989 *L'Invention d'un Art*; Centre Georges Pompidou, Paris, France
1992 *A Confrontation with Photography: Photographs Are for Seeing: Herbert Bayer, Philippe Halsman, Roman Vishniac, Edward Weston*; London Regional Art & Historical Museums, London, Ontario

Selected Works

Pont Transbordeur, over Marseilles, 1928
Look into Life, 1931
Self Portrait, 1932
Lonely Metropolitan, 1932
Nature Morte, 1936
Metamorphosis, 1936

CECIL BEATON

British

One of the best-known portrait photographers of the twentieth century, Cecil Beaton was a consummate arbiter of style and elegance. He passionately chronicled women, the social set, celebrities, and many aspects of World War II, documenting these through photography, writings, and illustrations over the course of half a century. Although known chiefly for his photography, he also received great acclaim for his set and costume designs, among them the legendary overstated Ascot hats and gowns for *My Fair Lady* and the beautifully evocative costumes for *Gigi*. Enormously prolific, his artistic roles were extraordinarily varied, however, and complexly interwoven, with style and culture always at the heart of the matter. Beaton intuitively understood the power of the press and media and defined how it could create and celebrate the notion of "celebrity," his own included. The Paris editor of *Vogue* in the 1950s, Bettina Ballard, wrote he was "forever improvising." Philippe Garner of Sotheby's London wrote, "Beaton was an impresario who used fashion to colour the scenario of the play that he made of his life, and in which he himself starred as production photographer and principal player."

Beaton's interest in photography came quite early. While attending Harrow, he received from his parents a folding Kodak No. 3A Autographic, which produced postcard-sized negatives. He started taking pictures of his sisters, Baba and Nancy, dressing them up in various fantastic costumes under the direction of his nanny. He used mirrors or cellophane or painted backdrops to create a theatrical effect, and would pose family members dressed in elegant costumes, as seen in *Baba Beaton: A Symphony in Silver*, 1925. Self-taught in photography, he gradually developed a style of arty, stylized portrait photographs, inspired by such illustrious contemporaries as Baron de Meyer and Edward Steichen, the master fashion photographers of the early twentieth century. The roots of his fantasy of beauty lay in his comfortable Edwardian childhood, while his fashion pictures were constructed with elaborate artifice reflecting a kind of loosely derived, drawing room Surrealism.

Beaton began a career as a portraitist, where he was "taken up" by poet and society figure Edith Sitwell, of whom he took a number of memorable studies, and introduced to high society and the world of high fashion in the late 1920s. His first photographic exhibition, in 1927 in London, was a great success that eventually led to a contract with Condé Nast's *Vogue* magazine. First hired by British *Vogue* as a cartoonist, he soon was photographing for the magazine as well as for the American and French editions. He worked for *Vogue* into the mid-1950s. That Beaton was the sole British exhibitor at the landmark 1929 *Film Foto* exhibition of modernist photography in Stuttgart indicates the consideration given to his earliest work. Beaton first visited the United States in 1929 where he photographed various stars for *Vanity Fair*.

Condé Nast, the irascible publisher of *Vogue*, loved to inspire his photographers by having them compete against each other to see who could create the most striking and exciting fashion photos. Beaton therefore found himself competing against one of the men upon whom he had modeled himself, the well-established Edward Steichen in New York as well as George Hoyningen-Huene in Paris. Although Beaton's style did not change radically from that of his earliest, highly theatrical set-ups, it was refined, and his ability to make his "interesting, alluring, and important people...look stunning," in the words of his biographer Hugo Vickers, was his real key to success. His unique, if eccentric style was richly varied with enough visual references to Surrealism to make the photographs inventive, witty and stylish.

Beaton would pose society women as well as mannequins in the most flamboyant Greek tragedy poses or as if in ecstatic mystical states, such as his 1935 portrait of actress Marlene Dietrich in which she poses as a "mirror image" of a classical bust. In many of his works, his human subjects became elements of an entire decorative tableau. The only stipulation that infringed on Beaton's happiness at *Vogue* was Conde Nast's insistence that he give up his "little" Kodak and replace it with an 8 × 10 camera that would provide the quality of prints the *Vogue* readers expected. The small camera had enabled Beaton to crawl around on ladders and get at things from odd angles, reflecting his belief that amusement, innovation, and shock were essential to fashion. But Beaton adjusted to the larger format, which gave better quality images, and used it consistently except when on travels.

Beaton himself was of as much interest as his photographs. He had turned his back on middle class conventions and entered the aristocratic world of High Bohemia with his wide-brimmed hats, flowing cravats, and natty suits, which became his trademarks. Articulate and creative, he was accepted into many artistic and social circles, including royalty. He served as Wallis Simpson's official photographer at her wedding to the Duke of Windsor in 1937, is credited with helping create the beloved image of the Queen Mother after her husband's ascent to the throne, and photographed in exquisite color the Coronation of Queen Elizabeth in 1953. His color photographs of Elizabeth just before becoming Queen and of the young Princess Margaret are subtle, delicate, and simply beautiful renderings of women. Of Beaton's photographs of the Queen the *Illustrated* noted in 4 November 1950, "It has caught her radiance...that elusive quality of light and fairy book charm surrounding her." His compulsive work habits and discerning eye speeded up the process of trend setting.

Beaton moved easily through the worlds of high-fashion photography, Hollywood, and the theatre, and became a member of the glamorous world of money and celebrity that he flattered with his camera. His love of beauty and glamour worked superbly in the Hollywood of the 1930s, where he created portraits of film stars such as Greta Garbo in somewhat surreal settings.

With the gathering of war in the late 1930s, Beaton's flamboyant style fell somewhat out of favor. During the Second World War, he became a war correspondent for the British Ministry of Information. He was made an official photographer for the Royal Air Force and late in 1942 sent *Vogue* photographs of a burned-out German tank and other eerie "abstractions of destruction" from the North African desert. These photographs were as much an aesthetic exploration as a document. He traveled in the East and was with Lord Mountbatten, the Viceroy of India, in New Delhi.

The experience gained during the war years influenced the style of his portraits, which became less whimsical, more direct. In December 1945 he was reporting on what there was left of French fashion, using the crumbling walls of Paris as a backdrop for models wearing Balmain coats and Bruyere gowns. Beaton said of these shoots

> There have been very great technical difficulties. However, in some cases I think the cutting of electricity and other drawbacks have resulted in our getting some pictures that are outside the usual fashion sphere—in particular, one, of a girl standing in an artist's backyard in a flannel Chinese blouse, in which I tried for some of the lighting of a Corot portrait. I think it one of the best I have ever taken.

Following the war, and still under contract to *Vogue*, Beaton returned to fashion photography, adapting some of the more restrained scenarios (including women dressed in high fashion but surrounded by everyday situations) typical of the "new realism" that was pervasive during this era. But new stars in fashion photography began to emerge in the 1950s, and the photographs of Richard Avedon and Irving Penn made Beaton's pictures seem outdated. His contract with *Vogue* was terminated. The later 1950s and 1960s led to his increased involvement with theater and cinema. Beaton designed the sets and costumes for both *Gigi* and *My Fair Lady* and won Oscars for both. In 1956 he began photographing for *Harper's Bazaar* such personalities as actress Marilyn Monroe, and writers Carson McCullers and Evelyn Waugh. These portraits were more personal and considerably more direct, showing that Beaton's ability to create a great portrait did not lie solely in his talent as a set decorator. He was knighted in 1972. In 1974 he suffered a stroke, and was not able to photograph for several years.

Beaton was unique in the variety of roles he took upon himself. He was not only fashion and celebrity photographer but also a chronicler of twentieth century fashion and a photographic historian whose contributions to these subjects include most notably, *The Glass of Fashion*, published in 1954 and *The Magic Image*, published in 1975 and written in collaboration with Gail Buckland. In it Beaton's pure love and clear understanding of the evolution of photography is eloquently and authoritatively set forth. Beaton's descriptions of individual photographer's contribution to the development of the medium are among the best writings on photography especially by a practicing photographer. He also was a tireless diarist, filling 145 volumes with words and pen and ink sketches from 1922 to 1974. Facing his own mortality, in 1977, Beaton sold his entire archive of over 150,000 photographs, and hundreds of thousands of negatives and transparencies to Sotheby's London, which remains the principal holder of his works. In 1979, however, Beaton began photographing again, and continued to do so until the time of his death.

DIANA EDKINS

See also: **de Meyer, Baron; Fashion Photography Portraiture; Hoyningen-Huene, George; Nast, Condé; Steichen, Edward; Surrealism**

Biography

Born in January 14, 1904, Hampstead, London. Attended Heath Mount School, London: attended St. Cyprian's School, Eastbourne, 1916–1918; entered Harrow School in 1918 and is encouraged in his interests in art by E. Edgerton Hine; St. John's College, Cambridge, 1922 to 1925, leaving without a degree. Publishes theatrical caricatures in *Granta*. Self-taught in photography. Freelance portrait and fashion photography 1926–1930. Photographs Edith Sitwell for the first time in 1926. Starts regular work for British *Vogue*, Visits New York and works for the first time for American Condé Nast. Portrays Hollywood stars for *Vanity Fair*, 1929. Publishes *The Book of Beauty*, November 1930, a mix of society heroines and entertainment stars. Takes lease on Ashcombe House, Wiltshire. 1931–1938 settles into a pattern of trans-Atlantic professional commuting for *Vogue*. 1932 Meets Greta Garbo for first time. 1933 visits Paris meets Cocteau, Christian Berard, and Pavel Tchelitchew and travels to North Africa with fellow *Vogue* fashion photographer and portraitist, George Hoyningen-Huene. 1935 designs costumes and décor for the Walter-Sitwell ballet, The First Shoot. 1938 forced resignation from *Vogue* following his addition of anti-Semitic scribbles on the cover of one of his decorative illustrations. Also completes *Cecil Beaton's New York*. 1940 receives commissions from the British Ministry of Information to photograph Churchill and War Cabinet members. Documents Blitz victims and damage to historic buildings in London. He is re-employed by *Vogue*. 1941 undertakes further official governmental propaganda photography for the Royal Air Force. These images are widely reproduced and later gathered into two books, Air of Glory and Winged Squadrons. 1942 joins the RAF as photographer and documents the Mid East theatre of war in Egypt, Iran, Iraq, Syria, and Jordan.

He turned to stage and costume design in the 1940s and continued through the 1970s. Receives two Academy Awards for *My Fair Lady*, 1965, and one for *Gigi* in 1959. Curates his own retrospective exhibition at the National Portrait Gallery at the behest of its director, Roy Strong. Knighted at Buckingham Palace in 1972, suffers stroke, 1974. *Vogue* commissions to photograph the Paris collections, 1979. Dies January 18, 1980.

Selected Books by Cecil Beaton

Beaton, Cecil. *The Magic Image: The Genius of Photography from 1839 to the Present Day*. London: Weidenfeld and Nicolson, 1973. American edition: Boston: Little, Brown & Company, 1975

Beaton, Cecil. *Cecil Beaton's Diaries 1944–1948 The Happy Years*. London: Weidenfeld & Nicolson, 1972. American edition: *Memoirs of the 40s*. New York: McGraw-Hill, 1972. French edition: *Les Annees Heurreuses*. Paris: Coedition Albin Michel-Opera Mundi, 1972

Beaton, Cecil. *The Best of Beaton*. London: Weidenfeld & Nicolson, 1968

Beaton, Cecil. *Cecil Beaton's Diaries 1939–1944 The Years Between*. London: Weidenfeld & Nicolson, 1965

Beaton, Cecil. *Royal Portraits*. London: Weidenfeld & Nicolson, 1963. American edition: New York: Bobbs Merrill, 1963

Beaton, Cecil. *Images*. London: Weidenfeld & Nicolson, 1963. American edition: New York: Bobbs Merrill, 1963

Beaton, Cecil. *Cecil Beaton's Diaries: 1922–1939, The Wandering Years*. London: Weidenfeld & Nicolson, 1961

Beaton, Cecil. *The Glass of Fashion*. London: Weidenfeld & Nicolson, 1954. American edition: New York: Doubleday, 1954. French edition: *Cinquante Ans d'Elegances et d'Art de Vivre*. Paris; Amiot-Dumont, 1954. Japanese edition: Tokyo: Kern Associates, 1954

Beaton, Cecil. *Photobiography*. London: Odhams, 1951. American edition: New York: Doubleday, 1951

Beaton, Cecil. *Ashcombe*. London: Batsford, 1949

Beaton, Cecil. *Cecil Beaton's India Album*. London: Batsford, 1945

Beaton, Cecil. *Cecil Beaton's Chinese Album*. London: Batsford, 1945

Beaton, Cecil. *Far East*. London: Batsford, 1945

Beaton, Cecil. *British Photographers*. London: Collins, 1944

Beaton, Cecil. *Time Exposure*. With Peter Quennell. London: Batsford, 1941

Beaton, Cecil. *Portrait of New York*. London: Batsford, 1938

Beaton, Cecil. *Cecil Beaton's Scrapbook*. London: Batsford, 1937

Beaton, Cecil. *The Book of Beauty*. London: Duckworth, 1930

Selected Books on Cecil Beaton

Danziger, James. *Beaton*. London: Secker & Warburg, 1980

Garner, Philippe, and David Alan Mellor. *Cecil Beaton*. London: Jonathan Cape, 1994

Mellor, David Alan. *Cecil Beaton*. London: Barbican and Weidenfeld and Nicolson, 1986

Spence, Charles. *Cecil Beaton: Stage and Film Designs*. London: Academy; New York: St. Martin's, 1975

Vickers, Hugo. *Cecil Beaton: A Biography*. New York: Donald I. Fine, Inc., 1985

BERND AND HILLA BECHER

German

The documentary works of Bernd and Hilla Becher contributed substantially to the public recognition of photography as an art form in Germany and are the foundation for much of the acceptance of straight photography in the late twentieth century on a par with painting, sculpture, or other traditional forms. The Bechers are best known for their *Typologien* (*Typologies*), which document the vanishing industrial architecture of the nineteenth and early twentieth centuries. Their series of chiefly black-and-white photographs feature frontal views of factories, blast furnaces, gas storage tanks, cooling towers, tipples, mineheads, water towers, and other industrial structures. Over the years, they have constructed approximately 200 comprehensive documentary collections, each consisting of 50 to 100 images according to each structure's complexity and size. In displaying these photos in exhibitions, the Bechers presented serial arrangements of nine to fifteen photographs, creating grids of imagery. Series include *Zeche Zollern 2*, Dortmund-Bövinghausen; *Zeche Hannibal*, Bochum-Hofstede; and *Gutehoffnungshütte*, Oberhausen. In books, the photographs were published in a distinctly conceived typological design, with each photo the same size and presented in sequence. Among these are *Fachwerkhäuser des Siegener Industriegebietes* (Munich: Schirmer/Mosel, 1977); *Fabrikhallen* (Munich: Schirmer/Mosel, 1994); and *Gasbehälter* (Munich: Schirmer/Mosel, 1993).

The Bechers' collaboration began in 1959 at the Staatliche Kunstakademie (Academy of Art) in Düsseldorf, where Hilla, née Wobeser, was employed in the department of photography. Bernd, who had studied printmaking, painting, and lithography at the Staatliche Kunstakademie Stuttgart from 1953 to 1956, was studying typography at Düsseldorf from 1957 to 1961. Hilla who had had contact with the medium at a very early age through her mother, studied photography until 1961, the year she married Bernd Becher. After finishing school, she completed a three-year photography apprenticeship in her hometown, Potsdam, with Walter Eichgrün, a member of a famous family dynasty of photographers. Her training included architectural photography, a genre that already fascinated her, and she learned the basic principles that would later serve her well in her first collaborative work with Bernd Becher, photographs of the mining complex Alte Burg in the area of Germany called Siegerland.

The Siegerland area was home to Bernd Becher, who was born in the city of Siegen in 1931. The industrial landscape of this ore-rich region, with its iron and steel production and the half-timber construction of the worker housing complexes, became central to the drawings and painting that Bernd undertook upon finishing his training at Stuttgart. But the speed at which change was occurring to this largely nineteenth century architecture, with much of it being dismantled, prompted Becher to move from the time-intensive art of drawing to photography. Although he had initially taken up the camera as an aid in creating his paintings, through photography he could record and thus preserve the industrial landscape in a more efficient manner with more accurate detail.

The Bechers' collaboration is unique in that they share all aspects of making their art, from locating sites, negotiating with property owners and local authorities, setting up the camera to making the exposures and printing the final works. It was as collaborators that they developed the characteristic "Becheresque" visual language, which assumes the frontal focus captures the most objective view possible of their subjects. These straight-on perspectives are taken from an elevated vantage point that avoids as many distractions as possible, and removes elements that could designate a specific place in time. The centered viewpoint presents the subject occupying the middle of the final print, largely filling the picture. The light—always natural—is diffuse and shadowless, as the couple photographs under overcast skies during hours of the day and seasons of the year—spring and fall—that are most amenable to capturing such light. Because most situations they photograph do not permit an isolated view of the individual architectural elements within a complex of industrial structures, the Bechers frequently enlarge details from larger groupings and present them as stand-alone images.

Although the lighting is flat and without strong contrast, the images they capture are unfailingly precise and sharp, which can be attributed to working with a large-format Plaubel plate camera (13 × 18 cm) and utilizing relatively long exposure times—generally 10 to 20 seconds, but occasionally as long as 10 minutes. As a consequence, the structures seem both far and near, appearing three-dimensions and extending out of the picture, but also seeming unapproachable and at a timeless distance from the viewer. This combination of distant absorption and concrete presence of the subject is found historically in the painters, draftsmen, and architects who, for example, sought to memorialize ancient Rome. Like these artists, the Bechers are concerned with preserving the images of buildings threatened with destruction; but, uniquely, the Bechers' work focuses on practical architecture and everyday, useful structures that are choreographed as monuments that should remain arrested in memory. Without, they say, "making relics of old industrial relics," the Bechers would like "to create a nearly perfect chain of distinctly manifested forms" (Becher 1969). They are not concerned with preserving buildings that have lost their economic and social function; rather, they aim to take stock of the passing world of heavy industry and mining—with its blast furnaces, winding towers, silos, factory buildings, gasometers, cooling towers, and workers' housing. Although such vernacular architecture, whose function gave it its form—a form for which engineers and factory operators were largely responsible—has been documented by others in both the nineteenth century and the early years of the twentieth century, the Bechers' approach has proven to be unique. For the Bechers such themes serve as sources for new ideas about photography and contemporary art, whereas in the work of Albert Renger-Patzsch and Werner Mantz in the 1920s, the objective was merely to document. Inspired by the objective, encyclopedic, inventory-like photography of the 1920s (such as August Sander), the Bechers also borrowed elements codified in nineteenth century architectural photography by survey photographers working to preserve historical monuments: central focus, temporal neutrality, elevated vantage point, monochrome, gray sky, and the exclusion of human work and other signs of life.

Another important precursor of the Bechers' work is that of Eugène Atget. Spurred by his personal desire, Atget set out to document old Paris as it was facing rapid change around the turn of the twentieth century. Another antecedent is the work of Karl Blossfeldt. A professor of arts and crafts, Blossfeldt made detailed close-up photos of parts of plants and flowers centered on a neutral, illuminated background. This made them appear concrete and at the same time seem like abstracted ornaments. The origins for Blossfeldt's photo-herbarium can be found in Ernst Haeckel's *Kunstformen der Natur* (1899–1904) or even in the descriptive botany of Carl von Linné and gave rise to the kind of spatial sorting of images adopted by the Bechers. This presentation allows a vivid tableau of the object that, upon multiple viewings, preserves the individual characteristics of various types of things yet creates a typology. An example is the Bechers' presentation of gas storage tanks (*Gas-holders* [Germany, Belgium, France, Britain, United States, 1966–1993]) in a grid five across and three deep, which creates a tableaux of forms: spirals, telescoping shapes, disks, and spheres. Characteristically presented in blocks of nine, twelve, or fifteen photos, the Bechers' clusters of images enable the viewer to register them simultaneously while still giving thorough attention to each individual image.

Bernd Becher describes the path to typological serialization of photos as a personal engagement with the objects, which, when compared, reveal their distinctive character. This process also conveys the regional and national characteristics of certain types of structures (Becher 1999, 2). In addition to photographing in Germany, the Bechers worked in England, Scotland, France, Belgium, Luxembourg, and the United States. Mixing together the topographical and the narrative, the resulting series remove the historical context for the various individual structures, depriving them of their functional associations and presenting them in isolation. By presenting various categories of structures in sets of photographs, most 16 × 12 inches or smaller, their individual architecture is made distinct and their unique aesthetic qualities are revealed at the same time that their similarities can be noted. The place and the name of the industrial plant and the date of the photograph are added as information that ameliorates against the tendency encouraged by this mode of presentation to see these images as pure plastic forms.

The Bechers' critical reception in a purely artistic context began in 1968 with a solo exhibit in the Städtisches Museum in Abteiberg, Mönchengladbach, Germany. This was a year after their participation in the Leverkusen exhibit *Konzeption—Concepti*on dedicated to conceptual art. Co-curator of this exhibit was a gallery owner from Düsseldorf, Konrad Fischer, whose program concentrated heavily on minimal and conceptual art. Through him the Bechers came to know American minimal sculptors Carl Andre and Sol LeWitt, California-based conceptual artist and photographer John Baldessari, and Richard Long, among others. The rhetoric of the static image and the Bechers' interest in typology proved compatible with the existing currents in art, something Carl Andre confirmed in "A Note on Bernd and Hilla Becher" published in the December 1972 issue of *Artforum*, in which he situates the Bechers' grids of anonymous industrial structures within the context of the serial production found in contemporary art of that era. The Bechers' work was also associated with what was called *Spurensicherung* (securing traces), a movement that deals with fragments and traces of history in which artists attend to their private histories and the ever-quickening changes of life. This tendency was explored at the 1972 *Documenta 5*, organized by leading Swiss curator Harald Szeemann, which included works by the Bechers. Under the slogan "individual mythologies," their works were shown together with pictures depicting both private and collective histories. In 1975 they were the only European photographers to participate in the ground-breaking exhibition *New Topographics: Photographs of a Man-Altered Landscape*, at the George Eastman House in Rochester, New York. In the beginning the Bechers framed individual typologies together, but later changed to framing each individual picture. This allowed the construction of images on the wall that is not only larger than a typical painting but has a sculptural presence; in fact their work *Typologien* (*Typologies*) was awarded the prize for sculpture at the 1990 Venice Biennial.

In 1976 Bernd Becher secured a post as professor of photography at his alma mater, the Kunstakademie Düsseldorf. It was the first official photography professorship anywhere in Germany. Because it was legally impossible to grant a couple one position, the professorship went to Bernd, with Hilla also working with students. Among the first were Candida Höfer, Axel Hütte, Andreas Gursky, Thomas Ruff, and Thomas Struth, who have gone on to be highly influential contemporary photographers. The Bechers' teaching methods included familiarizing students with the entirety of art, while expecting them to work systematically and rigorously on a theme of their choice. The Bechers' influence is obvious on the early works of their students, which show a clear, unmanipulated view of nearby surroundings, yet strict typological serialization is found in only a few of the students' works (for example, Thomas Ruff's large-format frontal portraits). Students were also schooled in the meaning of the presentation of their works.

After the first and thoroughly successful generation of Becher students, the success of Jörg Sasse, Boris Becker, Claus Goedicke, Elger Esser, among others, testifies to the Bechers' vision in tapping into the social desire for a language of images that is peaceful, clear, and seemingly objective, and unmanipulated.

In 1996 the Bechers entered into a cooperative relationship with the photography collection of the SK-Stiftung Kultur, Cologne, which focuses on objective documentary photography, to archive and publish their documentation industrial plants and structures.

MAREN POLTE

See also: **Architectural Photography; Atget, Eugène; Documentary Photography; Gursky, Andreas; Hütte, Axel; Photography in Europe: Germany and Austria; Renger-Patzsch, Albert; Ruff, Thomas; Schools of Photography: Europe; Struth, Thomas; Typology**

Biography

Hilla Becher born Hilla Wobeser in 1934 in Potsdam, Germany. Schooling as photographer, 1953–1957; employed as commercial and aerial photographer, 1958–1961. Meets Bernd Becher 1959; employed in the photography department and studied photography at Staatliche Kunstakademie Düsseldorf; marriage to and collaboration with Bernd Becher; 1961.

Bernd Becher born in 1931 in Siegen, Germany; 1947–1950 apprenticeship as decorative painter in Siegen; 1953–1956 studied painting at the Staatliche Kunstakademie Stuttgart; 1957–1961 studied typography at the Staatliche Kunstakademie Düsseldorf; and marriage to Hilla Wobeser; 1961; 1959–1965 photography primarily of Siegen, the Ruhr area, The Netherlands; 1963 beginning of photography of the mining industry in The Ruhr area, cement industry in southern Germany, lime-mining industry in The Netherlands; 1964 beginning photography of the industrial areas of Belgium, France, and Luxembourg; 1965 beginning photography of the mining industry of England, Wales, and Scotland; 1966 stipend in England; 1966–1967 photography in France and Luxembourg; 1968, 1974 photography in the United States; 1970 photography in Belgium; 1990 together they received the Golden Lion, the prize for sculpture at the Forty-fourth Venice Biennial; 1994 awarded the Kaiserrings in Goslar, Germany. Erasmus Prize for European Culture, 2002. Retires as Professor at the Düsseldorf Academy of Art; 1999. They live and work in the town Kaiserswerth near Düsseldorf.

Individual Exhibitions

1963 Galerie Ruth Nohl, Siegen, Germany
1966 Staatliche Kunstakademie, Düsseldorf, Germany
1967 *Industriebauten, 1830–1930*, Die neue Sammlung—Staatliches Museum für angewandte Kunst, Munich, Germany
1968 Städtisches Museum, Abteiberg, Mönchengladbach, Germany
1969 *Anonyme Skulpturen*, Städtische Kunsthalle, Düsseldorf, Germany

1970 Moderna Museet, Stockholm, Sweden
1972 Sonnabend Gallery, New York, New York
International Museum of Photography and Film, George Eastman House, Rochester, New York
1973 Galerie Konrad Fischer, Düsseldorf, Germany
1974–1975 Arts Council of Great Britain, London, England, and traveling
1975 *Fotografien, 1957–1975*, Rheinisches Landesmuseum, Bonn, Germany
1978 Milwaukee Art Center, Milwaukee, Wisconsin
1981 *Bernd und Hilla Becher*, Stedelijk van Abbemuseum, Eindhoven Westfälisches Landesmuseum, Münster, Germany
1985 *Fördertürme*, Museum Folkwang, Essen, Germany, and traveling
1986 Architekturmuseum, Basel, Switzerland
1989 Palais des Beaux-Arts, Brussels, Belgium
1991 Carpenter Center for the Visual Arts, Harvard University, Cambridge, Massachusetts
1994 *Bernd und Hilla Becher: Industriearchitektur*, Kunstsammlung der Ruhr-Universität, Bochum, Germany
1995 *Bernd und Hilla Becher: Typologien*, Westfälisches Landesmuseum, Münster, Germany
1999 *Bergwerke*, Photographische Sammlung, SK-Stiftung Kultur, Cologne, Germany
2001 *Fachwerkhäuser*, Museum für Gegenwartskunst, Siegen, Germany

Group Exhibitions

1969 Städtisches Museum, Leverkusen, Germany
1970 Museum of Modern Art, New York, New York
1971 Städtische Kunsthalle, Düsseldorf, Germany
1972 *Documenta 5*, Kassel, Germany
1974 Art Institute of Chicago, Chicago, Illinois
Photokina, Cologne, Germany
1975 *New Topographics: Photographs of a Man-Altered Landscape*, International Center of Photography and Film, George Eastman House, Rochester, New York
1976 Centre d'Arts Plastique Contemporains, Bordeaux, France
1977 *Documenta 6*, Kassel, Germany
XIV Biennale, São Paulo, Brazil
1978 Louisiana Museum, Humlebaeck, Denmark, and traveling
1981 *Absage an das Einzelbild*, Fotografische Sammlung Museum Folkwang, Essen, Germany
1982 *Documenta 7*, Kassel, Germany
1983 Museum of Modern Art, New York, New York
Solomon R. Guggenheim Museum, New York, New York
1988 Centre National des Arts Plastiques, Paris, France, and traveling
1989–1990 Wilhelm Lehmbruck Museum, Duisburg, Germany
1990 XLIV Biennale, Venice, Italy
The National Museum of Modern Art, Tokyo, Japan
1991 *Aus der Distanz*, Kunstsammlung Nordrhein-Westfalen, Düsseldorf, Germany
1992 *Photographie in der deutschen Gegenwartskunst*, Museum Ludwig, Cologne, Germany, and traveling
Distanz und Nähe, Institut für Auslandsbeziehungen, Stuttgart, Germany
1993 *Deutsche Kunst mit Photographie*, Deutsches Architekturmuseum, Frankfurt, Germany, and traveling
1997 *Vergleichende Konzeptionen*, Photographische Sammlung, SK-Stiftung Kultur, Cologne, Germany
Deutsche Fotografie: Macht eines Mediums, Kunst-und Ausstellungshalle der Bundesrepublik Deutschland, Bonn, Germany
2000 *How You Look at It*, Sprengel Museum, Hannover, Germany, and traveling

Selected Works

Typologie von Fachwerkhäusern, 1959–1974
Zeche Zollern 2, 1977
Fördertürme, 1983
Wassertürme (Water Towers) U.S., 1988
Gasbehälter (Gas-holders) Germany, Belgium, France, Britain, U.S., 1966–1993

Further Reading

Andre, Carl. "A Note on Bernd and Hilla Becher." *Artforum* (Dec. 1972): 59–61.

Becher, Bernd, Hilla Becher, Hans Günther Conrad, and Eberhard G. Neumann. *Zeche Zollern 2: Aufbruch zur modernen Industriearchitektur und Technik: Entstehung und Bedeutung einer Musteranlage in Dortmund um die Jahrhundertwende*. Munich: Prestel-Verlag, 1977.

Becher, Bernd, and Hilla Becher. *Die Architektur der Förder- und Wassertürme. Heinrich Schönberg und Jan Werth, Die technische Entwicklung*, Munich: Prestel-Verlag, 1971.

Becher, Bernd, and Hilla Becher. *Kunst-Zeitung* nr. 2 (January 1969).

Becher, Bernd. *Frankfurter Rundschau Zeit und Bild* (November 6 1999); 2.

Dobbe, Martina. *Bernd und Hilla Becher: Fachwerkhäuser*. Siegen: Museum für Gegenwartskunst, 2001. Herzogenrath, Wulf. ed. *Distanz und Nähe*. Stuttgart: Institut für Auslandsbeziehungen, 1992.

Lange, Susanne, ed. *Vergleichende Konzeptionen*. SK-Stiftung Kultur Köln, Munich: Schirmer/Mosel, 1997.

Lange, Susanne. *Die Industriefotografien von Bernd und Hilla Becher: Eine monographische Untersuchung vor dem Hintergrund entwicklungsgeschichtlicher Zusammenhänge*. Munich: Schirmer/Mosel, 1999.

Rowain, Lothar, and Detlef Bluemler, eds. *Künstler: Kritisches Lexikon der Gegenwartskunst*. 7. Munich: Weltkunst und Bruckmann, 1989.

Steinhauser, Monika, and Kai-Uwe Hemken, eds. *Industriefotografie: Im Spiegel der Tradition*. Kunstgeschichtliches Institut der Ruhr-Universität Bochum, Düsseldorf: Richter, 1994.

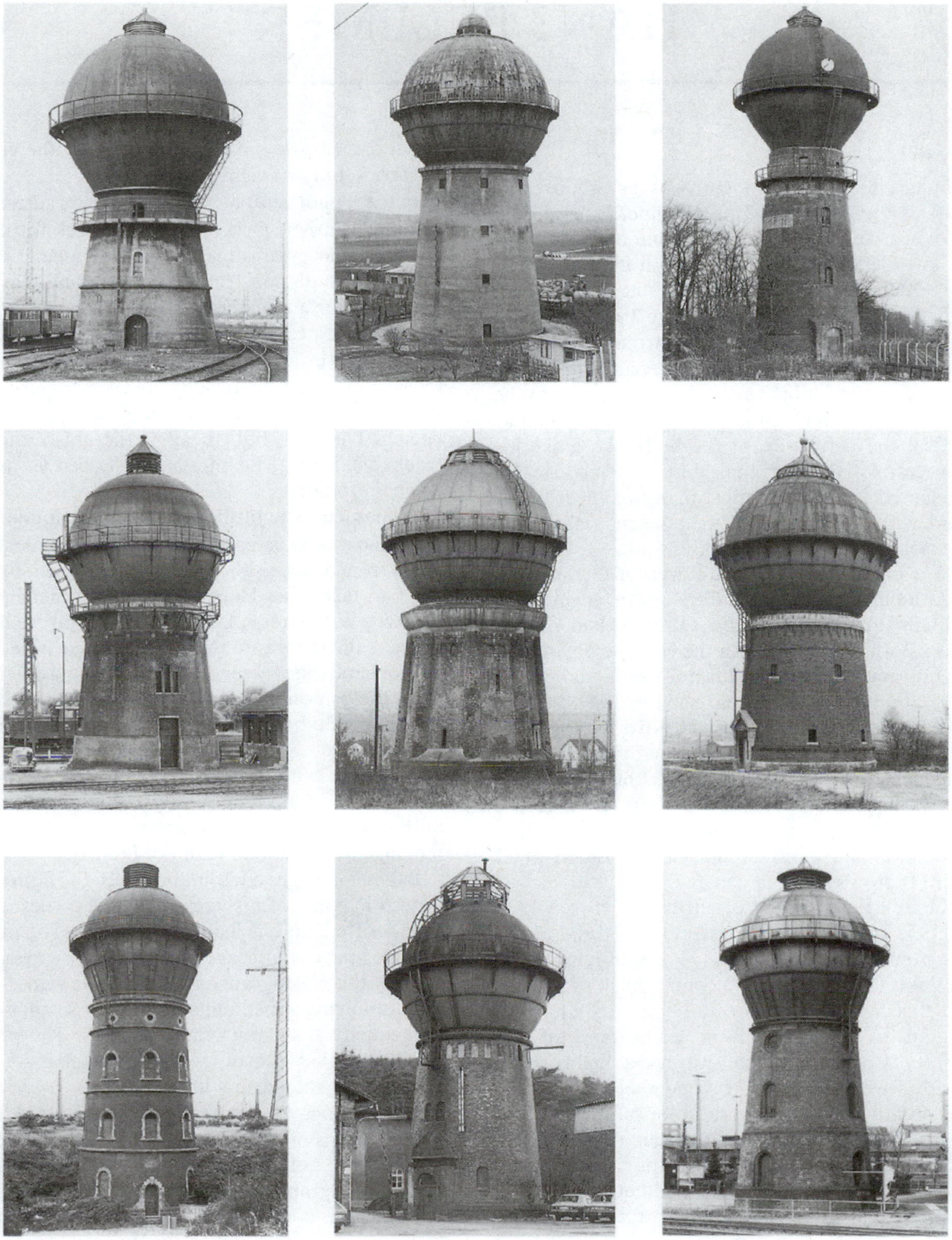

Bernd and Hilla Becher, Water Towers 1965–1982.
[© *Bernd and Hilla Becher. Courtesy Die Photographische Sammlung/SK Stiftung Kultur—August Sander Archiv, Cologne*]

HANS BELLMER

German

Although his primary identity is as a Surrealist draftsman and painter, Hans Bellmer created such a provocative series of images in that of his dolls, he was awarded a singular place in photographic history. Often described as a poet of the erotic obsession, his fetishistic creations have been found by many to be disturbing in their extreme manipulation of the female form. More recent scholarship ties his choice of subject matter to opposition to the rise of Nazism during the late 1920s, which had as its ideal the perfection of the body. To make his photographs, Bellmer built his own models. He augmented his photographs, many of them hand-toned, with prose and published the images and text in various magazines or books.

Born in the Upper Silesian area of Germany in 1902, Bellmer initially studied as an engineer in Berlin in 1924. He met artists Otto Dix and George Grosz, both associated with the German Expressionist movement; they taught him the fundamentals of art and design. After marrying in 1927, he supported himself with an industrial advertising studio, but by 1938, denounced, as were many other artists, as "degenerate," and grieving over the death of his wife, Bellmer left Germany for Paris. Even before his arrival he had made contact with the Surrealists but maintained a rather marginal position amid Andre Breton's circle of artists.

The doll Bellmer first constructed between 1932 and 1933 had a complex genealogy. Toys and objects from his childhood that had been returned to him upon his father's death commingled with other events, such an erotic obsession with a young cousin, and his inspiration by a performance of *The Tales of Hoffman,* which features a lifelike doll. This doll was a metal and wood skeleton covered in plaster that resembled a robot or puppet. But the construction itself was not the object; it existed only through the medium of photography. In his book *Die Puppe* (1934) (The Doll), Bellmer collected 10 selected black and white photographs. Preceding the photographs is a prose poem that details the idea of tearing apart the mannequin and putting it together again. Serving as an aesthetic counterpart to the text, the series of photographs shows the constant shift between construction and deconstruction with no final creation left at the end of the series, only a fragment.

In these photographs the female figure surrenders to the voyeuristic gaze; in the paperback format of the book this gaze is readily made available to all. Bellmer also demonstrates an alternating play between interior and exterior views. The exterior skin fosters the expectation of seeing a natural body, but the sight of the interior, of the constructed elements, reveals a hopeless artificiality; an ever indeterminate shifting between deception and disappointment begins. The doll, both near to the grasp and unreachable, is what Bellmer has described as "an incitement to poetry."

A characteristic of this first construction is what has been called a panorama of the female torso made from a barrel-like structure fitted with objects of "bad taste," as Hans Bellmer's brother has remarked. With stress placed on the left nipple of the mannequin the panorama of the torso is set into motion and one observes it in the figure's navel. With the ostensibly knowing gaze into the recesses of the female body, the viewers own projection is reflected back onto the male and female observer. This kind of panorama of a female torso, however, is never truly realized, but only in the construction's outlines does the idea suggest itself and thus it remains in the viewers realm of fantasy.

Bellmer engages a fascination with the figure that viewed in some of his works raises the question of whether the figure is living or artificial. The photographic image stands as an analog in its capacity to mortify the photographed object while at the same time supplying a medium allegedly possessing more authenticity than any other ever has. The photographed doll is in many ways a confusing creation between art and nature, life and death.

From image to image Bellmer created various combinations of body parts for the doll. They were conceived in potentially limitless combinations and in the photographs of the second doll his combining of body parts continued. In building the second doll in 1935, Bellmer sought to force a greater sense of metamorphosis and volubility. An innovation in this second doll was the torso's ball-and-socket joint—a construction inspired by a wooden jointed puppet. The remarkable characteristic of the second figure was how its two stomachs were placed in mirror-image opposition on the stomach joint that circled the mid-section of the body. Individual limbs were interchangeable. Bellmer then staged the enhanced variability of poses in 100 photographs from 1935 to 1937 that he colored by hand. In 1949, Bellmer published 14 selected images together with accompanying texts and poems from Paul Eluard in the volume titled *Les Jeux de la Poupée*.

The construction of the second doll left open the ways one could read the image of the body, making a kind of "anagram" in Bellmer's sense of the word. The photographs of this second model demonstrate the floating meaning of the body's various parts: the vulva is double in size and is set in place of the mouth, breasts have wandered to the position of the lap, and so this act could go on ad infinitum. No top or bottom of the doll's anatomy is clearly defined. Already in the photographic portraits of the first doll, Bellmer created a being that seemed posed between realities, a principle of crossing boarders that refuted polarization, and Bellmer furthered this principle in the construction of the body of the second doll.

Bellmer's sculptures also focus on the theme of dolls. With a bronze sculpture of the second model (1965) Bellmer released the body of the doll into "reality"—outside the medium of photography. In his sculpture, *La mitrailleuse en état de grace* (1937), Bellmer connected elements of both his doll creations. He fit the mechanical leverages of the robotic looking first doll to the smooth bodily form of the second. In 1972, Bellmer constructed his final mannequin figure, *La demi poupee*, which was not created to be photographed. As the name suggests, this doll had only one arm, one leg, and one breast.

Following the writing of Georges Bataille (*L'histoire de l'oeil*, 1946)—a theme of which is the multiple meanings of sexual signs—Bellmer created photographic series that featured bodies in twisted positions but not featuring the use of a doll. In 1958 the poet Unica Zürn posed for photographs in which the anagrammatic element was raised to a governing principle. The photographs show Zürn's body constricted by wires in a way suggesting the anatomy, much like a doll quilted from an actual body. The automatic generation of biological and artificial body parts also suggests the reproduction process of the photographic medium itself.

After giving up his photographic work with dolls Bellmer turned to graphic art, and these works also focus on variations of composite bodies. Drawing as a medium provided the possibility of interfusing various formations of anatomic parts. Bellmer could now move totally within the world of fiction in contrast to photography. He abandoned the subtle play between the real and the virtual that results from the "believability" inherent in the photographic medium. Bellmer presented his works not only in book form, but also in Surrealist exhibitions (e.g., 1938 in Paris) and in surrealist journals (e.g., in *Minotaure* 1935). In 1972 the first major retrospective of the photographs was mounted in Paris (Centre national d'art contemporain) and for the first time the dolls were also displayed.

Bellmer's works are shown in numerous exhibits. With her representation of artificial body fragments, Cindy Sherman (*Sex Pictures*, 1992) refers directly to Bellmer's creations. Bellmer executes a mediated notion of "female" in two simultaneous ways: in the medium of the doll and in photography. Thus he is of interest to gender studies as well as to discussions of virtual worlds and of body production through gene technologies.

Birgit Käufer

See also: **Erotic Photography; History of Photography: Interwar Years; Photography in Europe: France; Photography in Europe: Germany and Austria; Representation and Gender; Surrealism**

Biography

Born in 1902 in Kattowitz (Oberschlesien). Studied engineering in Berlin, 1923–1924. Broke off his studies to become a graphic artist for book illustrations. A self-taught artist, he had contact with artists such Otto Dix and George Grosz. First trip to Paris, established contacts with the Surrealists, winter 1924–1925. Constructed the first doll and photographed the model, 1932–1933. Constructed second doll, 1935 and photographed the second model, 1935–1937. Moved to Paris, 1938. Detention in southern France with Max Ernst, 1940. Stayed until 1948 in southern France and produced series of graphic artworks. Returned to Paris, 1948. Met the poet and life-long companion Unica Zürn in Berlin, 1953. In the 1960s he produced primarily graphic works. First major retrospective in Centre national d'art contemporain in Paris, 1971. Bellmer died in 1975 in Paris.

Selected Works

Note: The following are titles of Bellmer's original publication of his images; individual images from each series are titled with the series name.

Die Puppe (*The Doll*), 1934
Les Jeux de la Poupée (The Joy of the Doll), 1949
L'Anatomie de l'image (translated to English as *Little Anatomy of the Physical Unconscious*), 1957

Individual Exhibitions

1967 *Hans Bellmer Photographe*; Kestner-Gesellschaft, Hannover, Germany

1970 *Hans Bellmer*; Stedeliijk Museum, Amsterdam, Netherlands
1971 *Hans Bellmer*; Centre national d'art contemporain, Paris, France
1975 *Hans Bellmer*; Museum of Contemporary Art, Chicago, Illinois
1983 *Hans Bellmer Photographie*; Centre Georges Pompidou, Paris, France
1983 *Bellmer Peintures Gouaches Collages*; L'autre Musée, Paris, France
1984 *Hans Bellmer Photographe*; Kestner-Gesellschaft, Hannover, Germany
1999 *Hans Bellmer, Photographs and Drawings from the 30s*; Ubu Gallery, New York, New York; and Galerie Berinson, Berlin, Germany
2001 *Behind Closed Doors: The Art of Hans Bellmer*; International Center of Photography, New York, New York

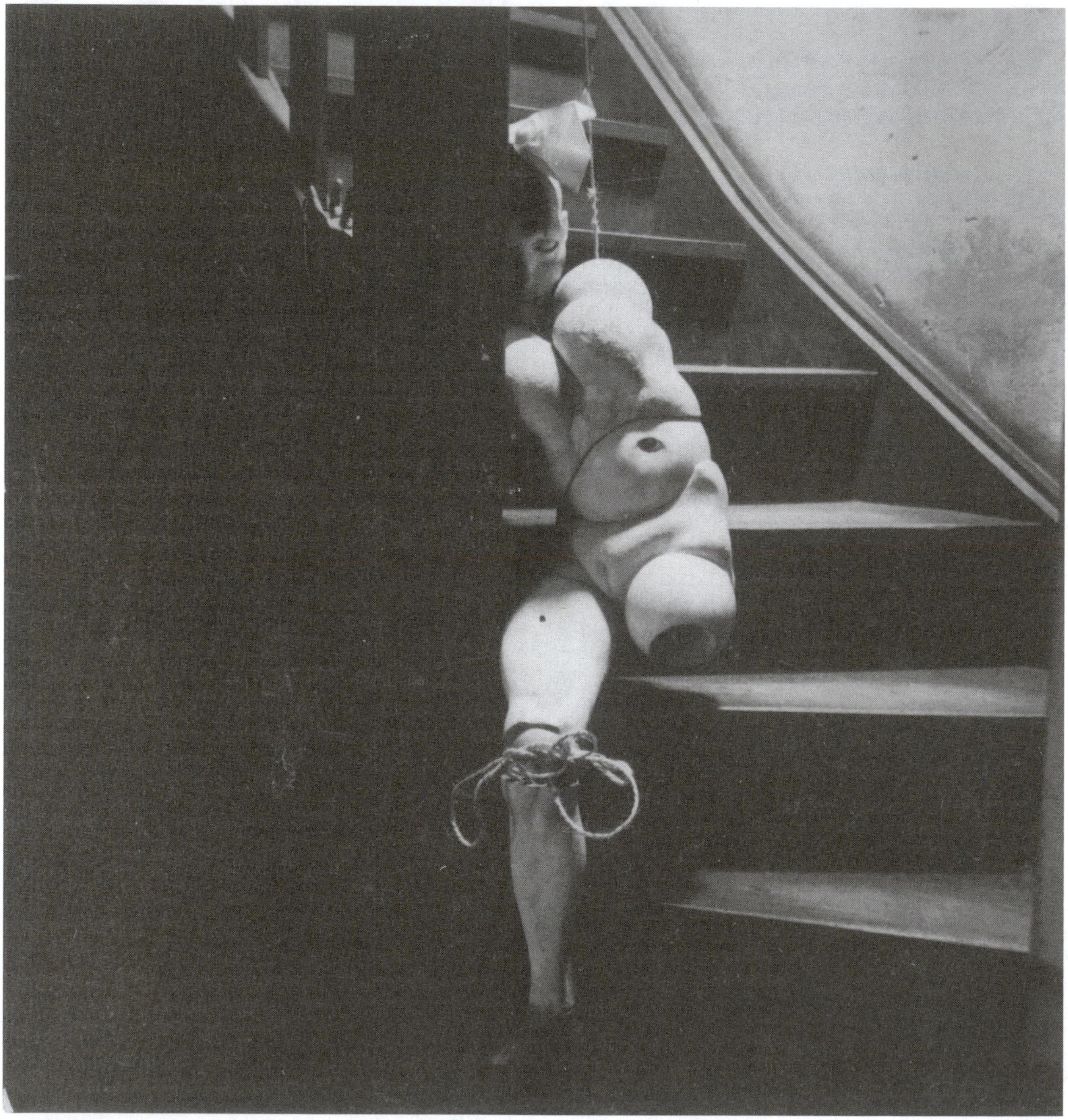

Hans Bellmer, The Joy of the Doll, Page No. 9 of the maquette. Photo: Philippe Migeat.
[*CNAC/MNAM/Dist. Réunion des Musées Nationaux/Art Resource, New York*]

Group Exhibitions

1938 *Exposition Internationale du Surréalisme*; Galerie Beaux-Arts, Paris, France
1985 *L'Amour fou. Photography & Surrealism*; Corcoran Gallery of Art, Washington, D.C., and traveling
1994 *Bunuel! Auge des Jahrhunderts*; Kunst-und Ausstellungshalle der Bundesrepublik Germany, Bonn, Germany
1995 *Féminin/masculin. Le sexe de l'art*; Centre Georges Pompidou, Paris, France
1999 *Puppen Körper Automaten. Phantasmen der Moderne*; Kunstsammlung Nordrhein-Westfalen, Düsseldorf, Germany
2000 *Die verletzte Diva. Hysterie, Körper, Technik in der Kunst des 20. Jahrhunderts*; Kunstverein, München, Germany; and Siemens Kulturprogramm, München, Germany; and Städtische Galerie im Lenbachhaus, München, Germany; and Galerie im Taxispalais, Innsbruck, Austria; and Staatliche Kunsthalle, Baden-Baden, Germany
2000 *Surreale Welten*; Kunsthalle, Hamburg, Germany, and traveled to Von der Heydt-Museum, Wuppertal; Kunsthalle, Tübingen; Neue National Galerie, Berlin, Germany
2000 *Der anagrammtische Körper und seine mediale Konstrukton*; ZKM - Zentrum für Kunst und Medientechnologie, Karlsruhe, Germany

Further Reading

Dourthe, Pierre. *Bellmer. Le Principe de perversion*. Paris: Jean Pierre Faure éditeur, 2000.

Gauthier, Xavière. "Das Werk Bellmers. Die Perversion." In *Surrealismus und Sexualität. Inszenierung der Weiblichkeit*. Edited by Xavière Gauthier; translated by Heiner Noger: Medusa Verlag Wölk + Schmid Berlin, 1980 (Editions Gallimard, Paris 1971).

Gorsen, Peter. "Das Theorem der Puppe." In *Der Körper und seine Sprachen*. Edited by Hans-Jürgen Heinrichs, Frankfurt am Main; Paris: Qumran, 1985.

Gorsen, Peter. "Die Erotik des hermaphroditischen Bildes. Hans Bellmer und die Puppe." In *Sexualästhetik. Grenzformen der Sinnlichkeit im 20. Jahrhundert*. Edited by Peter Gorsen, Reinbek bei Hamburg: Rowolths enzyklopädie, 1987.

Käufer, Birgit. "Hans Bellmer und das Double der Wirklichkeit." In *Surreale Welten*. Edited by Kunsthalle. Hamburg: SKIRA Editore Mailand, 2000.

Krauss, Rosalind, and Jane Livingston. "Corpus delicti." In *L'Amour fou. Photography & Surrealism*. Washington, DC: The Corcoran Gallery of Art, 1985.

Lichtenstein, Therese. *Behind Closed Doors: The Art of Hans Bellmer*. Berkeley: University of California Press, 2001.

Masson, Céline. *La Fabrique de la Poupée chez Hans Bellmer. Le "feure-oeuvre perversif" une étude clinique de'objet*. Paris, Montreal: L'Harmattan, 2000.

Schade, Sigrid. "Hans Bellmer—Die Posen der Puppe." *Kairos* 4, no. 1 and 2 (1989).

Taylor, Sue. *The Anatomy of Anxiety*. Cambridge, MA: MIT Press, 2000.

Taylor, Sue. "Hans Bellmer in the Art Institute of Chicago: The Wandering Libido and the Hysterical Body." In *Museum-Studies* vol. 22, no. 2 (1996).

Webb, Peter, and Robert Short. *Hans Bellmer*. London: Quartet Book, 1985.

JOHN BERGER

British

Painter, novelist, screenwriter, poet, critic, and occasional photographer, John Berger was known initially as the leading member of a group of post-World War II painters dubbed "the Kitchen Sink School" for their commitment to an unvarnished working-class realism. Berger later gained fame as a Marxist-oriented critic for *The New Statesman* and as the author of several novels, including *G*, which won the prestigious Booker Prize in 1972. In the range of his interests and abilities (he has written on topics as different as the life of Pablo Picasso and the writings of the Mexican political activist Subcommandante Marcos), he has few equivalents among English-speaking writers. Unlike his American and European counterparts, he has worked outside a university umbrella. The closest comparison is with the late Michael Ayrton, an English sculptor, essayist, and novelist. In the case of both, their literary careers and recognition gradually usurped their importance as artists, but their experience of art making has given tremendous force and personality to their insights.

Although Berger has always been most attentive to painting and drawing, his interest in photography is longstanding and profound. It has produced numerous essays, four book-length collaborations with the French photographer Jean Mohr, including the seminal *Another Way of Telling* (1982), a commentary in letters on the work of photographer Martine Franck, *Martine Franck: One Day to the Next* (1999), and a stunning revision of his own work, the novella *Once In Europa* (1987/99), which he transformed into a dialogue of text and images with the photographer Patricia Macdonald. In spite of Berger's trenchant criticism of photography—he has famously dubbed it a "quotation of reality" and like Susan Sontag indicted it for robbing us of the ability to remember—he has been compelled by the rich particularity of photographs, especially their ability to convey social, political, physical, and even environmental information. As one who believes deeply in the rootedness of art in its historical and political situation, Berger cannot help celebrating and exploring photography's fundamentally documentary nature.

Berger's reputation as a critic of photography rests largely on three texts: his first collaboration with Jean Mohr, *A Fortunate Man* (1967, as of this writing in its 54th printing), the essay *Why We Look at Photographs* (1978), and another Mohr collaboration, *Another Way of Telling* (1982). His fundamental insight, the ramifications of which he explores in all three writings, is that photography is essentially overdetermined in terms of information and undetermined in terms of meaning. Just as reality per se cannot explain itself, so the images captured by the camera can convey an enormous—indeed, often an uncontrollable—amount of detail but remain ambiguous and always in need of interpretation. To drive this point home, in *Another Way of Telling* Mohr shows to a group of people various photographs he has taken and asks them to explain what they see. In only a few cases do their conjectures approach the original circumstance of the image, and in some instances completely contradict it.

Such ambiguity poses significant problems. First, outside their originating contexts, photographs risk almost complete meaninglessness. So Berger attempts to anchor their interpretation in a visual "grammar" that is little more than the fact of an image's coherence in an instant of time and in space. The "art" of a photograph consists in the complex of correspondences or relationships it frames. These correspondences within an image articulate ideas that include but reach beyond the particulars of the moment. As Berger puts it, "In the expressive photograph, appearances cease to be oracular and become elucidatory." For one so sensitive to the life of photographs with in communities of interpretation, this is a strikingly formalist approach, placing great weight on the graphic and iconographic structures of the image.

Nevertheless, photographic images can be used for any purpose, from propaganda to testimony to advertising, and as soon as a private image, with direct and clear significance to some viewer, becomes severed from this viewing context, it loses its anchor (but not necessarily its poignancy). This suggests another way that photographs can be made to "mean"—as elements of a narrative. Coupling image and text can limit and direct the photograph's waywardness and even restore it as an agent of memory. As Berger puts it in *Why We Look at Photographs*, "A radial system has to be constructed around the photograph so that it may be seen in terms which are simultaneously personal, political, economic, dramatic, everyday and historic."

Berger had already embodied this idea of storytelling in *A Fortunate Man*, his collaboration with Mohr detailing the life of the rural English doctor John Sassall. More narrowly political and psychological than its journalistic predecessors *Let Us Now Praise Famous Men* by James Agee and photographer Walker Evans or the photo stories of W. Eugene Smith for *Life* magazine, Berger's book preserves their traditional relation between image and the explicating, polemical text. Not so *Once In Europa*, his story of love, death, and industrial exploitation in rural France. Here it is the images that comment on, contextualize, and expand the framework of the written story and its characters.

Another Way of Telling takes yet a third approach, eschewing commentary at the end of the book in favor of an extended suite of images, which leave it to the reader to reconstruct a "story" of French peasant life. This follows the line of Berger's didactic and highly successful art history text, *Ways of Seeing* (1972), which provides readers various ways of interrogating art images and objects, and then gives them images to work on. In truth, Berger's photomontages aspire to the condition of cinema, a form that can fully reap the suggestive benefits of juxtaposition, explore the texture of duration and history, and unfold a set of terms for its own interpretation.

Yet in the end, Berger is drawn to the single image as the bearer of existential and historical testimony. Where critic Roland Barthes scans photographs like a visual flaneur, Berger scrutinizes images for their lived realities and fugitive insights. He is at his best as an interpreter, discovering through his responses to what he sees, broader significance, whether in August Sander's image of three country boys in suits or in Paul Strand's photographs. Perhaps what Berger is ultimately seeking is the core of memory within himself, not suppressed but released by the photograph. These encounters provoke him, as he said in a 2002 interview, to "tell the story of being here at this moment in time."

LYLE REXER

See also: **Barthes, Roland; Evans, Walker; Franck, Martine; Image Theory: Ideology; Life; Photographic Theory; Photographic "Truth"; Sander, August; Sontag, Susan; Strand, Paul; Visual Anthropology**

Biography

Born London, November 26, 1926. Educated St. Edward's School, Oxford. Won scholarship to Central School of Art, London, but education interrupted for two year's military service, 1944–1946. Resumed education for three years at Chelsea School of Art, London. Exhibiting painter throughout the late 1940s, 1950s, and 1960s. Writer for weekly *Tribune*. Appointed art critic for the *New Statesman*, 1951, provoking controversy for his Marxist views and defense of realism. First novel, *A Painter of Our Time*, published in 1958 and withdrawn from publication under pressure from the CIA. Throughout the 1960s published poems, novels, criticism, translations, and first photographic collaboration with Jean Mohr. Won Booker Prize in 1972 for novel *G* and donated half the prize money to U.S. radical group Black Panthers. Developed ground-breaking BBC television series on art, *Ways of Seeing*, aired in 1972. Moved permanently to small village in Haut Savoie in the French Alps, 1974. Subsequently collaborated on scripts for three films with director Alain Tanner and published a series of novels on peasant life, *Into Their Labors*. Continues to write articles, essays, poems, and novels.

Further Reading

Berger, John. *The Look of Things*. New York: Viking, 1971.
———. *The Success and Failure of Picasso* New York: Pantheon, 1980 (1965).
———. *About Looking*. New York: Pantheon, 1980.
———. *The Sense of Sight*. New York: Pantheon, 1985.
Berger, John, and Patricia Macdonald. *Once In Europa*. London: Bloomsbury, 1999.
Berger, John, and Jean Mohr. *A Fortunate Man*. New York: Holt, Rinehart and Winston, 1967.
———. *Another Way of Telling*. New York: Pantheon, 1982.
Baker, Kenneth. "Q & A John Berger: The Moment of Truth is Now." *San Francisco Chronicle* (January 6, 2002).

BERLINISCHE GALERIE

On November 21, 1975, the Berlinische Galerie was opened as a private society by fifteen patrons and interested citizens of the city of Berlin, Germany. The society stated

> The Berlinische Galerie is a museum which collects art works and material concerning the artistic and cultural history of Berlin from the fields of visual art, architecture, artistic photography, applied art and design, carrying our research into these and making them available to the public.
>
> (Quoted in Jörn Merkert, "Berlin or the Round Head", in the *Berlinische Galerie visits Dublin*, Dublin 1991, p. 12.)

As the founding director, Eberhard Roters envisioned a museum that would highlight Berlin art history in all fields from 1870 to the present, which no other museum in the city was doing. Such an endeavor in a then divided city was no easy task.

From the beginning there had been financial problems, but Roters' early vision was well targeted and persistent, resulting in an interdisciplinary collection of Berlin art from 1870 to the present that included painting, graphic arts, sculpture, video, photography, architecture, and the archives and papers of various artists. Roters chose to stay in the public eye by mounting changing thematic or monographic exhibits, rather than a permanent exhibition of the growing collection, and by continually announcing new acquisitions. A primary benefactor for the new museum, as for a number of the other Berlin museums was the Foundation Deutsche Klassenlotterie in Berlin.

In 1986 the fledgling museum moved to the prestigious Martin-Gropius Bau, designed by Martin Gropius and constructed in 1881. Designed in a style similar to an Italian Renaissance palace, the building contained beautiful mosaics, reliefs illustrating the different arts and crafts, and crests at various German cities. Left in ruins after World War II, the building was not to reopen until 1981, with minimal alteration, to house large exhibitions. The Berlin Wall stood behind the building. The Galerie used this space until 1997. The building was further renovated for large exhibitions in 1999.

The Galerie then used space in the Lapidarium, once Berlin's pumping station from 1873–1876 and also home to magnificent large sculptures that once decorated the Avenue of Victory in Berlin's *Tiergarten.* The Galerie also sponsored exhibits in different sections of the city of particular significance were its *Längschnitte* (sections) and *Querschnitte* (cross sections) held at Jebenstrasse near the Zoo Station, in space previously used by the Gallery of the Twentieth Century. From February 2002 to April 2003, the Berlinische Galerie sponsored a series of five exhibits, "*Zwischenspiel*" at the Berlin Grundkreditbank. In 2003 the Berlinische Galerie finalized a contract to purchase and renovate a former glass warehouse at 124–128 Jakobstrasse, 10969 Berlin-Kreuzberg, near the Jewish Museum designed by Daniel Liebeskind. Scheduled to open in October 2004, the new Berlinische Galerie space with its wide expanses would be able to mount significant and innovative exhibitions that celebrated and examined the richness of Berlin's art from 1870 to the present. The new museum space would also include a library, study rooms, workshop space for restoration projects, office space, and a restaurant.

Two large initial goals for the Galerie were to bring renewed recognition to those artists who had been termed "entartet" or degenerate under Hitler's rule and to establish respect for contemporary artists. Examples of the Galerie's early exhibits include: Berlin Artists of the Twenties: Feldberg Collection (1978); Art in Berlin from 1960 to the present (1979); Art in Berlin 1930–1960, (1980); George Tappert, A Berlin Expressionist, (1980); Berlin Realism, 1890–1980 (1981); Dada Montage, (1982); Aus Berlin Ernigriert (Artists forced to leave Berlin after 1933), (1983); Berlin at 1900, (1984). Later the Galerie sponsored exhibits including, *Self Portraits of the Twenties* (2004), *Russians in Berlin from the Twenties* (2003), and *Menschen untereinander (Men together): Graphics and Photography 1918–1933*, (2002). A major exhibit that the Galerie mounted with the Pushkin Museum in Moscow was "Berlin-Moscow/ Moscow-Berlin 1900" that was shown in Berlin in the Martin Gropius Bau in 2003.

The museum's collection now includes approximately 7,000 paintings, 1,500 sculptures, 150,000 works on paper, and 250,000 photographs. In addition to its focus on Berlin art, the collection also includes major international works of modern art, such as the avant garde of Eastern Europe. The collection reflects the revolutionary experiments in Expressionism, Dadaism, Constructivism, the Bauhaus, and so on. and the larger historical currents that accompanied two world wars, the social crisis between the wars, the reign of National Socialism, the Cold War, and a divided Germany and Berlin, as well as current trends since the fall of the Berlin Wall.

In 1979 a major acquisition to the permanent collection was the Hannah Höch Archive with its collection of paintings, collages, and graphics. Höch's Dada experiments, her scrapbooks, etc. provide a window on a stimulating and active period of German and European cultural and art history. Celebrating the 100th anniversary of Höch in 1989, the Galerie produced "Hannah Höch—*Eine Lebenscollage*," volume I, containing significant archival material.

The photographic collection is an important part of the museum's holdings. Under the initiative of Janos Frecot, the collection has grown to contain major holdings in the history of photography. The oldest materials are portrait daguerreotypes from various Berlin ateliers in the 1840s. The oldest architectural photographs include images of the magnificent synagogue on Orangienburger Strasse, taken in 1866. Architectural photographs by Max Panckow later in the nineteenth century show new buildings representing the rise of industry and villas in new suburbs of Berlin. Further, one finds images of F. Albert Schwartz, the urban photographer, showing landscape scenes, iron works, and general city views. Heinrich Zille, working between 1900 and 1910, shows a darker side of Berlin, the working class, broken down dwellings, rubbish piles, etc. The fashionable and elite were recorded in the Art Nouveau portraits of Nicola Perscheid, who worked summers in Baden-Baden and winters in Berlin. Experiments with geometry and abstraction in photographs, photo-grams, and photo-montages are seen in the collection's holdings of El Lissitzky, László Moholy-Nagy, and Heinz Hajek-Halke. The great Weimar Republic photojournalist, Erich Salomon, is well represented with glass and film negatives, slides, and vintage prints. One can see, for example, the English prime minister, Ramsay MacDonald in conversation with Albert Einstein, along with Max Planck, and Secretary of State for Foreign Affairs, Julius Curtius, in 1931, or Marlene Dietrich with her daughter in Berlin in 1930. Salomon's illustrated reports on sessions of the Reichstag, on conferences in Berlin, Paris, the Hague, London, Geneva, etc. were greatly respected and widely read. Other photojournalists represented in the collection include: Felix H. Man, Martin Munkacsi,

Erich Comeriner, Fritz Eschen, and Umbo (Otto Umbehr). The great portrait photographers such as Lotte Jacobi, who photographed those involved in the arts and sciences before escaping to the United States, or August Sander, the recorder of a variety of levels of society, are represented here. Experiments in advertising photography such as that of Fritz Brill or Herbert Bayer or the archives of the popular magazine *Volk und Welt* are to be found in the collection.

From 1955 to 1965 Berlin was an important fashion center. Photographs by the Hamburger, F.C. Gundlach present an atmosphere of a city trying to rise out of the ashes of World War II. Michael Schmidt, the founder of the Berlin Werkstatt für Photographie (Photographic Workshop) fostering emerging photographers is represented by his early work such as his *Kreuzberg* and *Wedding* series (1978 and 1980), and from the exhibit *Waffenruhe* (cease-fire).

In 1990 the East-Berlin collection of the photographic history of East Germany was obtained by the Berlinische Galerie. This collection includes approximately 1,500 images by seventy photographers, including work by Sibylle Bergemann, Arno Fischer, Thomas Florschuetz, Helga Paris, Evelyn Richter, and Ulrich Wüst.

The Berlinische Galerie continues to collect in a variety of areas. Its photography is probably one of the strongest aspects of its collections. With its new building, its future appears to promise increased acquisitions, exhibitions, and study areas for Berliners and the world at large, fulfilling much of the vision of its 1975 founders.

KATHERINE HOFFMAN

See also: **Dada; Hajek-Halke, Heinz; Höch, Hannah; Jacobi, Lotte; Lissitzky, El; Museums: Europe; Photography in Europe: Germany and Austria; Schmidt, Michael; Umbo (Umbehr, Otto)**

Further Reading

Dawson, Barbara. *Berlin!: The Berlinische Galerie Art Collection Visits Dublin 1991.* Berlin: Berlinische Galerie, 1991.

Heinrich Zille. *Photograph der Moderne: Verzeichnis des Photographischen Nachlasses.* Berlin: Berlinische Galerie und Munich: Schmirmer/Mosel Verlag, 1995.

Photographie als Photographi: Zehn Jahre Photographische Sammlung 1979–1989. Berlin: Berlinische Galerie, 1989.

Salomon, Erich. *Leica Fotografie 1930–1939.* Berlin: Berlinische Galerie, 1986.

Situation Berlin—Fotografien-Photographs 1953–1960. Berlin: Berlinische Galerie, 2001.

Sprung in der Zeit. *Bewegung und Zeit als Gestaltungsprinzipien in der Photographie.* Berlin: Verlag Ars Nicolai, 1992.

RUTH BERNHARD

German

Ruth Bernhard is known for her "radiant" photographs of female nudes that have been described as "hauntingly sensual but classically reserved." She is also known for her doll images and her meticulous photographs of commonplace objects such as lifesavers, an egg slicer, and a teapot, for which she has been acknowledged as a "a master of the still life genre," by art critic Ilee Kaplan.

Born in Berlin, Bernhard was the daughter of famed poster artist Lucian Bernhard. In 1927 she emmigrated to New York where her father then lived. She learned the rudiments of photography while using an 8 × 10 view camera when she worked briefly at *The Delineator*, a popular woman's magazine. After she was fired for lack of motivation, she began to freelance as a fashion and advertising photographer.

Her first published image was *Lifesavers* (1930). Her still lifes are at times reminiscent of the work of avante-garde photographers associated with the Bauhaus school, for example Hein Gorny's rows of men's collars and Grete Stern's dolls and use of light "as the defining element in the image." Bernhard has said "It's not the object that is beautiful, its the light in which we see it."

In 1934 while on assignment for the *Machine Art* exhibition at the Museum of Modern Art in New York, she photographed her first nude. A visiting friend noticed the large stainless steel bowls she was shooting, and Bernhard asked her to pose in one of them and she agreed. Bernhard produced a series of these photographs, and they soon became her signature images.

Her meeting with Edward Weston in 1935 was a turning point in her life. Inspired by his work, she began to regard photography as art. A year later, she set up a studio in Los Angeles and had her first solo exhibit at bookseller Jake Zeitlin's gallery, which received good reviews. One image was described as "leaves [that] quiver with subtle changes of light that we had never noticed before." Her doll images were the first photographs she took after meeting Edward Weston. This series was made between 1936 and 1939 in Bernhard's Hollywood studio when she made portraits of children. She says she regards the dolls in her photographs as children.

She returned to New York in 1939 and continued working on commercial assignments. Two years later, she sold some of her images of seashells at an exhibit in Florida and produced a series of seashell images that were published in a special edition of *Natural History Magazine*. The influence of Weston was still strong and can be seen if one compares her *Classic Torso* and his *Nude by the Door*.

Bernhard says that she later grew critical of Weston's nudes seeing in his images "his interest in seduction and connection," while her "quest" was "abstraction and sculpture...I wanted to achieve and ideal harmony...with the universal idea of the body as a work of art. I wanted to convey innocence...the innocence of a tiger or a cloud in the sky."

During World War II Bernhard joined the Women's Land Army and spent her time at a working farm in New Jersey. After the war, she returned to California and continued her association with Edward Weston, known for his many love affairs, visiting him at his home in Carmel. She maintains that although there was a mutual romantic attraction, she preferred not to risk the loss of the friendship.

In 1953, she moved to San Francisco where she eventually became part of a circle of photographers that included Ansel Adams and Imogen Cunningham. She began teaching photography in 1966 and throughout the years has felt that her teaching "is more important than my photos." In 1970, the first book containing her images, *The Eternal Body: A Collection of 50 Nudes*, was published. Several years later, she produced two limited edition portofolios: *The Eternal Body* (1976) and *The Gifts of the Commonplace* (1976). Both sold out quickly. During that time, and due to inhaling fumes from a faulty heater, she lost her ability to concentrate for long periods of time, and has made no new negatives since then. In spite of this limitation, Bernhard, now in her 90s, retains her *joi de vivre*. In *Between Art and Life*, she lists eight factors contributing to long life, including "never get used to anything," "hold on to the child in you," and "say 'yes' to life with passion."

While Bernhard has enjoyed acclaim for the sheer artistry of her images, on another level, her photographs of nude women, including women of color, and her relationships with several men, suggest unexamined issues related to gender and ethnic perspectives. The new biography by Margaretta Mitchell is forthcoming about Bernhard's bisexuality. She considered Eveline Phimister, an artist and designer as "the love of her life." Bernhard also maintained long relationships with Edward Weston, an older man, and with a former Tuskegee airman, Price Rice, a younger man. In order for Bernhard's complex aesthetic to be better understood, her work deserves critical examination on levels hitherto ignored.

Yolanda Retter

See also: **Adams, Ansel; Cunningham, Imogen; Weston, Edward**

Biography

Born in Berlin, October 14, 1905. Education at The Akademie der Kunste, Berlin, 1926–1937. Emigrated to the United States, 1927. Career (selective): Freelance photographer, New York, 1927–1935; Los Angeles, 1936–1953; San Francisco since 1953; Instructor: University of California Extension, Berkeley and San Francisco, 1966–1975; Columbia University, New York. Recipient: National Urban League Award, 1961; San Francisco Art Commission, 1984; Cyril Magnin Award, San Francisco, 1994.

Individual Exhibitions

1941 Little Gallery, San Francisco, California
1958 Institute for Public Relations, Mexico City, Mexico
1973 Chicago Center for Contemporary Photography, Chicago, Illinois
1982 Portland Art Museum, Portland, Oregon
1996 The Art Museum, Princeton University, Princeton, New Jersey
2000 Friends of Photography, San Francisco, California

Group Exhibitions

1968 *Light 7*; Massachusetts Institute of Technology, Cambridge, Massachusetts
1975 *Fifty Women of Photography*; San Francisco Museum of Art, San Francisco, California
1984 *Photography in California, 1945–1980*; San Francisco Museum of Art, San Francisco, California
1996 *History of Women Photographers*; New York Public Library, New York, New York

Further Reading

Bernhard, Ruth. *The Eternal Body*. Text by Margaretta Mitchell. San Francisco: Chronicle Books, 1986.

Corinne, Tee. "Ruth Bernhard." In Claude Sommers, ed. *The Gay Lesbian Bisexual Transgender Online Encyclopedia*. Forthcoming.

Kaplan, Ilee, Marina Freeman, and Constance Glenn. *Ruth Bernhard: Known and Unknown*, Long Beach, CA: California State University Art Museum, 1996.

Mitchell, Margaretta. *Ruth Bernhard: Between Art and Life*. Chronicle Books: San Francisco, 2000.

JOSEPH BEUYS

German

Joseph Beuys was not a photographer; however, as a conceptual artist, he exploited the promotional capacity of photographs, using them to document his performances and disseminate his ideas, greatly influencing the development of photography in the 1970s as he influenced virtually every other area of contemporary art practice. Beuys infused his art with his persona, establishing his own image as the central icon in his oeuvre. To achieve this, Beuys consistently wore the same uniform: felt hat, fisherman's vest, white work shirt, blue jeans, and black boots. As a result, Beuys's photographic image registered instant recognition informing the production of startling, compelling images of himself as a political and spiritual leader during the Cold War era. Although Beuys created art in traditional forms, most notably drawings and sculptures, he is best known for his socially-oriented didactic performances and political activities. Photographs recording these events are central to understanding his diverse oeuvre.

Beuys avoided traditional art media and adopted such materials as fat, felt, honey, and other organic substances in a personal symbolism for his theoretically complex work. A tireless promoter of his pedagogical concept, "Social Sculpture," Beuys drew extensively from his life experiences to underscore his central belief that humans are creative beings and that only by harnessing this power could a true democracy be fully realized. Beuys did not remain isolated in the realm of art; he established several political organizations in West Germany, including the German Student Party and the Organization for Direct Democracy through Referendum, and he was a co-founder of the Green Party. These ventures enabled him authentically to fuse art with politics and gain access to a wider audience. Harnessing the propagandistic force of photographs, Beuys infiltrated the political arena to publicize his aesthetic ideology. He famously proclaimed:

> Every human being is an artist who—from his state of freedom—the position of freedom that he experiences at firsthand—learns to determine the other positions in the total artwork of the future social order. Self-determination and participation in the cultural sphere (freedom); in the structuring of laws (democracy); and in the sphere of economics (socialism)."
>
> (Cuoni 1990, 21)

As a young adult, Beuys considered medicine for a profession but was drafted by the German military in 1940. He became a dive-bomber in the Luftwaffe and, in 1943, his plane was shot down in the Crimea. He claimed to have been found, unconscious, by Tartars who smothered his body with animal fat and covered him with felt (animal pelts) to keep him warm. For 12 days, he drifted in and out of consciousness before being found by a search party, ultimately regaining full consciousness in a German hospital. It is unclear if his recounting of this event is fact or the creation of a personal myth; Beuys's hospital records indicate the crash occurred in 1944 and that Russian civilians delivered him to the Germans. In an effort to support his account of this wreck, Beuys provided photographs of (reportedly) his damaged Stutka. Regardless of Beuys's accuracy in recall, this trauma was a key episode that transformed the development of his iconography and aesthetics.

After the war, Beuys studied at the Kunstakademie Düsseldorf with Ewald Mataré, working as Mataré's master student until 1954. Throughout the 1950s, Beuys produced countless works on paper and later claimed that his aesthetic ideology and personal iconography were initially established during this phase. After undergoing a severe depression that lasted several years, Beuys was appointed Professor of Monumental Sculpture at the Kunstakademie in 1961, and, by the mid 1960s, his political convictions were the core of his artistic endeavors. At this time, Beuys cast himself as a modern shaman whose primary mission was to enable the spiritual redemption of the German people after the traumas inflicted by Hitler and the Nazis. Focusing on the student population, Beuys recognized that his greatest skill was as a pedagogue. Most of his performances culminated in prolonged question-and-answer sessions in which he lectured for as long as his audiences would listen.

Participating in several Fluxus—a loose association of performers and Dada-influenced artists-instigators—concerts, Beuys viewed performance art as a means for translating his artistic ideas into theatrical presentations. The initial importance of photography in Beuys's career can be traced to stunning images taken of his performance at a Fluxus event at the Aachen Technical College in 1964. At this concert, Beuys's performance was disrupted by conservative students who stormed the stage, and one of them punched the artist in the nose. Resolute and determined to proceed, Beuys was photographed by Heinrich Riebesehl with his nose bloodied, his right arm raised, his left hand carrying a crucifix, his visage exuding concentration and confidence. This photograph radiates with a resolute power that supercedes the time-based constraints of the performance itself, operating as an art work in its own right. Drawing on this experience, Beuys recognized the power of theater and, just as importantly, the documentary authority of photography.

Shortly thereafter, Beuys began to conceive of performances (*Actions* as he called them), with a keen awareness of how the camera would capture isolated moments. In the following year, Beuys organized an action, entitled *How to Explain Pictures to a Dead Hare*, that occurred on the opening night of his first major solo exhibition at the Galerie Schmela in Düsseldorf in 1965. At this event, Beuys coated his face with honey and gold leaf, presenting himself as a sun god. In his arms, the artist cradled a dead hare. During much of the performance, Beuys sat in a chair, lecturing to the animal. No visitors were allowed in the exhibition space; rather, the public was only allowed to watch the performance through the gallery's front window. Beuys explained his drawings to the dead rabbit, animatedly gesticulating and eventually carrying the corpse throughout the exhibition space. The resulting photos by Ute Klophaus conferred the status of a mythological figure on Beuys. Although the performance occurred long ago, these photographs remain haunting images that underscore Beuys's aesthetic philosophy and the central role of photography in his oeuvre.

After this performance, Beuys consciously recognized that his choice of symbols and the aura of his personae could resonate within photographic images; co-opting the photo as a work of art in its own right, Beuys began to use photographic reproductions as one of numerous resources that promoted his "expanded concept of art." Beuys's 1974 performance, *Coyote: I Like America, America Likes Me*, further implicated this artist's reliance on photographic images. Responsible for producing an installation at the René Block Gallery's inaugural exhibition in New York, Beuys created a week-long action documented by many oft-reproduced photos. In this event, Beuys cohabitated the gallery space with a wild coyote flown in from New Mexico. Beuys intended his interaction with the animal to symbolize a reconciliation between Europe and America.

Beuys's interest in photography was not concerned with technical proficiency. Rather, his approach to the image was to use photos that violated common technical conventions of framing, lighting, and printing. For the traveling exhibition *Arena: What I Would Have Achieved If I Had Been Intelligent*, first shown in Naples in 1972, Beuys selected more than 400 photographs of himself and his art, which were displayed in aluminum containers. Beuys reworked the images, covering them with diverse substances such as wax, grease, honey, and gelatin. Although the photographs documented his prior activities, Beuys's reworking of them created unique works of art. In the following year, Beuys made *Enterprise*, a sculpture in an edition of 24, which incorporated a photograph of Beuys's family watching television. The sculpture consisted of a zinc box with a print of the photograph glued to the lid's interior; the box itself contained a box camera with a round piece of felt covering the lens. Later, Beuys turned to using manipulated photographs to create a series of postcards that promoted his aesthetic ideology. Although best known as a performance and installation artist, Beuys routinely exploited the documentary nature of photographic images to promote his aesthetic theories and political ideology.

BRIAN WINKENWEDER

See also: **Body Art; Conceptual Photography; Postmodernism**

Biography

Born in Krefeld, Germany, 12 May 1921. Served in the German military as a combat pilot and radio operator,

1941–1946. Studied at the Staatliche Künstakademie, Düsseldorf, 1947–1951. Worked as Ewald Mataré's master student, 1952–1954. Professor of Monumental Sculpture, Staatliche Künstakademie, Düsseldorf, 1961–1972. Founded the German Student Party with Johannes Stüttgen, 1967. Founded the Organization for Direct Democracy through Referendum, 1971. Initiated legal proceedings for wrongful dismissal for trespassing from the Staatliche Künstakademie, 1972 (won case 2 March, 1978). Founded the Free International University with Heinrich Böll, 1974. Granted honorary doctorate from Nova Scotia College of Art and Design, 1976. Awarded Lichtwark Prize, Hamburg, 1977. Received Thorn Prikker Plaque of Honor of Krefeld, 1978. Nominated as member of the Akademie des Kunst, Berlin, 1978. Awarded Goslar Art Prize, 1979. Candidate of the Green Party to the European Parliament, 1979. Nominated as member of the Royal Academy of Fine Arts, Stockholm, 1980. Awarded the Wilhelm Lehmbruck Prize, Duisberg, 1986. Died in Düsseldorf, Germany, 23 January 1986.

Individual Exhibitions

1961 *Joseph Beuys*; Das Städtisches Museum Haus Koekkoek, Kleve, Germany
1967 *Beuys*; Städtisches Museum, Mönchengladbach, Germany, and traveling
1968 *Joseph Beuys: Work in the Collection of Karl Ströher*; Neue Pinakothek, Haus der Kunst, Munich, Germany, and traveling
1970 *Block Beuys*; Hessisches Landesmuseum, Darmstadt, Germany
1971 *We Are the Revolution*; Modern Art Agency, Naples, Italy
1972 *Arena*; Modern Art Agency, Naples, Italy, and traveling
1975 *Richtkräfte '74*; René Block Gallery, New York, New York, and traveling
1978 *Joseph Beuys: Drawings and Objects*; Bremerhaven, Germany, and traveling
1979 *Joseph Beuys*; Solomon R. Guggenheim Museum, New York, New York

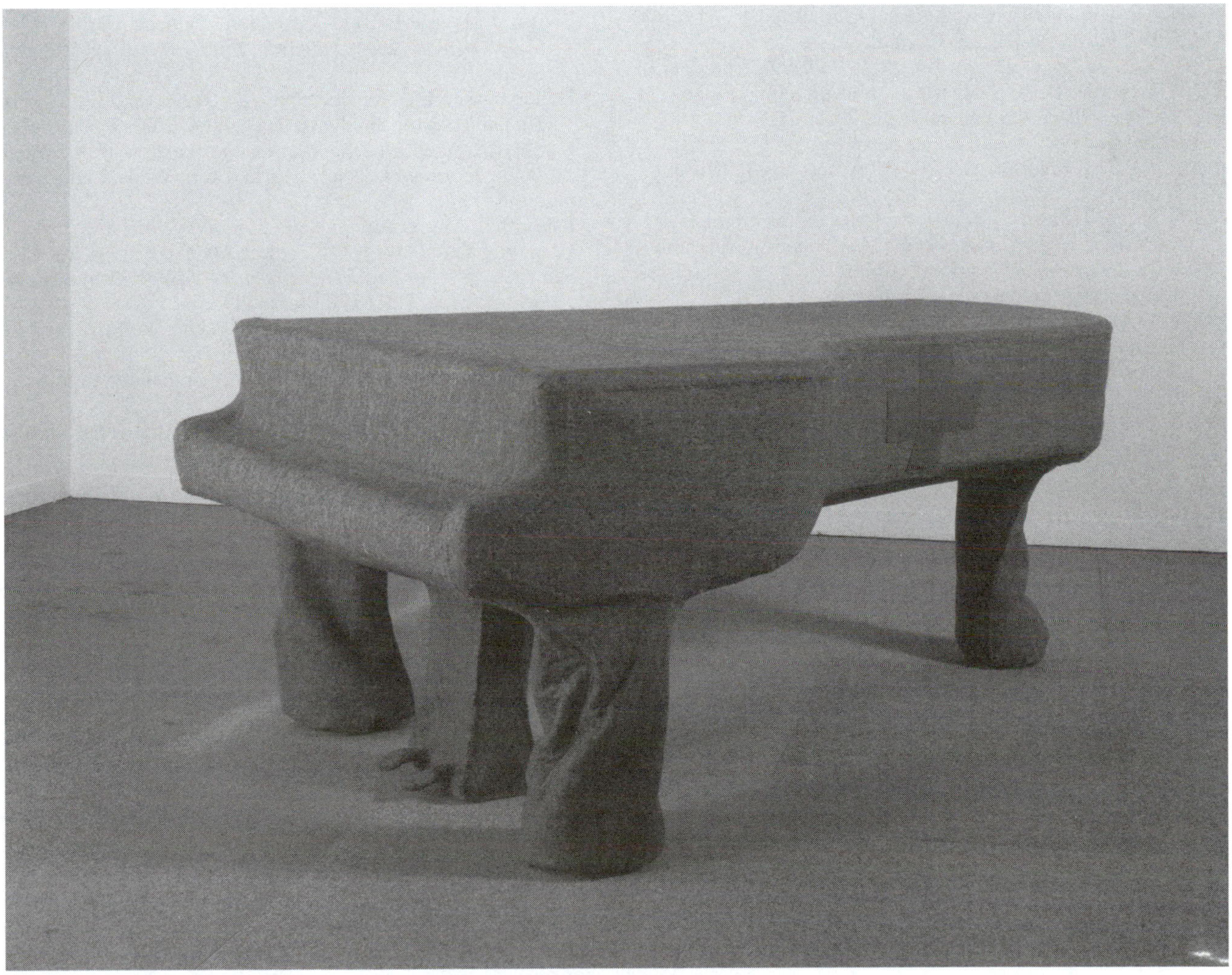

Joseph Beuys, Homogenous Infiltration for Grand Piano (Infiltration homogen für Konzertflügel). Piano covered in felt and fabric.
[CNAC/MNAM/Dist. Réunion des Musées Nationaux/Art Resource, New York © ARS, New York]

1980 *Joseph Beuys: Multiples, 1965–1980*; Düsseldorf, Germany, and traveling
1984 *Joseph Beuys*; Seibu Museum of Art, Tokyo, Japan
1987 *Joseph Beuys*; Dia Arts Foundation, New York, New York
1987 *Beuys on Beuys: Early Works in the van der Grinten Collection*; Ministerium für Bundesangelegenheiten des Landes Nordrhein-Westfalen, Bonn, Germany, and traveling
1987 *Bits and Pieces: A Collection of Work by Joseph Beuys from 1957–1985*; Richard Demarco Gallery, Edinburgh, Scotland, and traveling
1988 *Joseph Beuys: Ideas and Actions*; Hirschl & Adler Modern, New York, New York
1989 *Joseph Beuys: Drawings, Objects and Prints*; Institute for Foreign Cultural Relations, Stuttgart, Germany, and traveling
1990 *Joseph Beuys*; Kestner Gesselschaft, Hannover, Germany, and traveling

Group Exhibitions

1963 *Festum Fluxorum Fluxus*; Düsseldorf, Germany
1964 *Documenta 3*; Kassel, Germany
1964 *Festival for New Art*; Aachen, Germany
1968 *Documenta 4*; Kassel, Germany
1969 *Live in Your Head: When Attitudes Become Form*; Kunsthalle, Bern, Switzerland, and traveling
1972 *Venice Biennale*; Venice, Italy
1972 *Documenta 5*; Kassel, Germany
1972 *Reality, Realism, Reality*; Von der Heydt Museum, Wuppertal, Germany, and traveling
1974 *Art into Society—Society into Art: Seven German Artists*; Institute of Contemporary Art, London, England
1976 *Venice Biennale*; Venice, Italy
1977 *Documenta 6*; Kassel, Germany
1979 *Mataré and his Students*; Academy of Art, Berlin, Germany, and traveling
1980 *Venice Biennale*; Venice, Italy
1982 *Documenta 7*; Kassel, Germany
1985 *Art in West Germany, 1945–1985*; National Gallery, Berlin, Germany
1985 *German Art in the 20th Century, Painting and Sculpture 1905–1985*; Royal Academy of the Arts, London, England, and traveling
1987 *Warhol/Beuys/Polke*; Milwaukee Art Museum, Milwaukee, Wisconsin, and traveling

Selected Works

The Chief, 1964
How to Explain Pictures to a Dead Hare, 1965
The Pack, 1969
Arena, 1970–1972
We Are the Revolution, 1972
Enterprise, 1973
Coyote: I Like America and America Likes Me, 1974
Show Your Wound, 1977

Further Reading

Adriani, Götz, Winfried Konnertz, and Karin Thomas. Translated by Patricia Lech. *Joseph Beuys: Life and Works*. Woodbury, NY: Barron's Educational Series, 1979.
Beuys, Joseph, Manfred Leve, and Eugene Blume. *Leve Sieht Beuys: Block Beuys, Photographs*. Göttingen: Steidl, 2004.
De Dominizio Durini, Lucrezia. *Joseph Beuys: The Image of Humanity*. Milan: Silvana Editoriale, 2001.
Kuoni, Carin, ed. *Energy Plan for the Western Man: Joseph Beuys in America*. New York: Four Walls Eight Windows, 1990.
Rosenthal, Mark. *Joseph Beuys: Actions, Vitrines, Environments*. New Haven, CT: Yale University Press, 2004.
Schirmer, Lothar, ed. *The Essential Joseph Beuys*. Cambridge, MA: The MIT Press, 1997.
Schneede, Uwe. *Joseph Beuys: Dio Aktionen*. Stuttgart: G. Hatje, 1994.
Stachelhaus, Heiner. *Joseph Beuys*. Translated by David Britt. New York: Abbeville Press, 1991.
Tisdall, Caroline. *Joseph Beuys*. New York: Thames and Hudson, 1979.

BIBLIOTHÈQUE NATIONALE DE FRANCE

Starting with royal collections that became national collections after the French Revolution, Bibliothèque nationale de France (BnF or French National Library) has evolved through many forms and locations before its present manifestation, reflecting the evolution of French culture and socio-political structure through the centuries. Today, the BnF is the major national repository of French and international photographic work, and serves as the principal source for many modern French photography exhibitions.

The library's royal collection was transient for the first generations of its existence, until Louis XI

(1461–1483) issued decrees that stabilized the library. Jean-Baptiste Colbert, as Louis XIV's controller and minister of finance, moved some of the royal library contents to rue Vivienne in Paris, which is the present day site for the BnF Richilieux site.

The library continued to expand, and during the twentieth century, faced lack of space for collections, ever more acute problems of conservation, and rapidly increasing demand by readers and researchers. At the end of the century, the need for additional space was addressed by the construction of an additional site for the BnF, consisting of an esplanade and four impressive towers. The public reading rooms in this new Bibliothèque François-Mitterrand at Tolbiac in the 13th arrondissement Paris opened in December 1996, and in October 1998, the opening of the research library finally brought this major project to completion.

The abundant material in the special collections of the BnF—manuscripts, engravings, photographs, maps and plans, music, coins, medals, antiquities, and material on the performing arts—remains within the Richelieu library, to be reorganized with larger stockrooms and reading rooms. All special collections have been reorganized into five departments, including prints and photographs.

It is generally considered that the Cabinet Photographique, or Prints and Photographs Department of the BnF, thusly named in 1976, was founded in 1667, with 120 engravings and drawings from the Abbé de Marolles collection. The department began to receive legal deposit prints in 1638, while successive gifts, bequests, and purchases steadily increased the size and importance of the collection, numbering at the turn of the twentieth century from 2 to 3 million photographs. The department's mission is to conserve images that can be reproduced in multiple copies, and thus photographs are but one of many mediums that are collected.

Dating from a 1537 decree by Francois I, "*depot legal*," or legal deposit, required that all printers and booksellers deposit a copy of any printed matter with the royal library as a legal or copyright deposit. Legal deposit provisions were considerably improved and reinforced in 1925, applying this obligation to both printers and publishers, which was successively extended to cover imported books and other materials including photographs. Thus, with certain stipulations, French photographers are required by law to have a copy of their photographs in the BnF collection. Obviously, the sheer volume of photographic production in France prohibits the democratic application of this law. In practice, the Curator of Photography at the BnF must monitor and solicit work deemed appropriate for the national collection.

Photography has been in the forefront of the collection from an early date, when photographers began voluntarily depositing legal deposit copies in 1851. Most initial attention to photography did not concern itself with the photograph as a work in its own right, but with the photograph only as a subject matter information source. This policy for collecting continued until the 1940s when a growing awareness of the photograph as art allow new approaches to photographic collection and exhibition.

The department holds an impressive collection, including collections of nineteenth century masters, as well as works by Eugène Atget. The work of contemporary photographers is particularly well represented with a collection of 100,000 prints. Chief curator for prints and photographs from 1963–1998, Jean-Claude Lemagny, acquired works by contemporary photographers through donations, purchases, and under the terms of "depot legal." Largely due to his diligent work, the BnF houses one of the most important photography collections in the world. After Lemagny's retirement in 1999, Phillippe Arbaizar was appointed chief curator of photography.

Significant twentieth century acquisitions include 50,000 prints from the Nadar study collection that were purchased in 1949. In 1961, 200,000 prints from four major French press agencies were acquired (Rol, Meurisse, Mondial, SAFARA). The department acquires works from two to three hundred contemporary photographers a year. From 1986 to 1996, for example, the collection grew by over 46,000 photographs. As a library and not a museum collection, the department is able to collect from the general and vast world of photography, building a diverse body of work by both French and international photographers.

The Prints and Photographs department at the BnF has a reading room where original photographs from the collection can be accessed. Staff is available for guidance and, as a matter of library policy, even principle curators are available for consultation to the public on a regular basis. Additionally, works from the collection are exhibited on a regular basis in the Galerie Colbert, Passage Colbert 2 rue Vivienne. Named after the seventeenth century minister who shaped the BnF, the Galerie Colbert has been an experimental exhibition venue, striving to establish an appropriate setting for the exhibition of contemporary photography. The gallery has one wall of windows that face directly onto the Passage Colbert. The exhibitions are accompanied by a text usually written by the Curator of Photography. Photography exhibitions at Galerie

Colbert strive to balance the best qualities of both public and private institutions: free access, impartial selections, and direct contact with the public with freedom of initiative and flexible activities. More than one hundred exhibitions have filled the gallery walls since its inception.

The photography collection at the BnF is often the principal source of images for many major exhibitions. The 1977 exhibition of creative twentieth century photography at the National Museum of Modern Art in the Georges-Pompidou Center was built from the BnF collection. Also, works from the BnF were exhibited at the Pavilion des Arts in 1984 titled, "Creative Photography." The 1994–1995 exhibition and book, *La matiere, l'ombre, et la fiction*, grouped 279 photographs by 104 authors in a major look at works from the collection.

BRUCE MCKAIG

Further Reading

Bibliothèque nationale de France homepage. http://www.bnf.fr/ (accessed May 4, 2005).

Bibliothèque nationale de France, ed."Bonjour Monsieur Lemagny." in *Nouvelles de la photographie*, Paris: 1996.

Delage de Luget, Marion. *Jean-Claude Lemagny, maitre d'oeuvre*, D.E.A. d'Arts Plastique Universite Paris VIII, U.F.R. Arts Plastique, Research Director Francois Soulages, June 2001.

Lemagny, Jean-Claude. *La Matiere, l'ombre, la fiction* (Matter, Shadow, Fiction), Paris: Nathan and the Bibliothèque nationale de France, 1994.

RICHARD BILLINGHAM

British

Richard Billingham does not consider himself strictly a photographer. He began taking snapshot photographs as part of a wider effort to gather preparatory source materials for his paintings when he started his degree in fine art at the University of Sunderland in 1991. Over the course of the next five years, using a simple auto-exposure camera and cheap film, Billingham photographed his family in their council flat home in the Midlands of England. The resulting color images are garish in technique and content. They seem to break all the classic formal rules of photography and suggest amateurism; many images are out of focus, overexposed, haphazardly framed, or display an extremely grainy print quality. But Billingham's candid portraits of his parents, Ray and Liz, his brother Jason, and various family pets, are an intimate and unapologetic depiction of the artist's working class home life. Their amateurism can perhaps be overlooked in light of their honesty.

In this collection of photographs, distressing images of addiction and violence are juxtaposed with captured moments of comedy and tender affection. Ray's alcoholism is a consistent theme. Billingham's grey-haired, gaunt, middle-aged father is pictured in various states of sobriety; falling over, seated next to a vomit-spattered toilet, tucked up in bed with the covers to his chin, or just staring back at the camera through vague, uncertain eyes. Billingham captures his mother's expressive range also. Liz, a large rounded woman with vibrant tattooed arms, is pictured vehemently arguing with Ray, and then joyfully cuddling a tiny kitten. Her presence is felt throughout the home as various feminine knickknacks decorate the grubby walls and furniture of the flat.

Initially Billingham's photographs of his family were not intended for exhibition or to form a cohesive series, and most still remain untitled. But a selection of images was first publicly shown in 1994 in *Who's Looking at the Family?* at the Barbican Art Gallery in London, and from there, Billingham's career quickly flourished. By 1995 his work was being represented by Anthony Reynolds Gallery in London and his first book of photographs, *Ray's a Laugh*, was published in 1996. Overnight the book brought him notoriety and critical acclaim as critics were at odds about the photographs. Admirers applauded his snapshot aesthetic and the vernacular quality of the spontaneous images. They commended his critique of traditional social documentary practices by using gaudy color and avoiding a customary discreet or impartial distance from his subject. In this respect Billingham's work was likened to that of other contemporary British photographers, Martin Parr and Nick Waplington. But other critics accused Billingham of sensationalism. Their polemic revolved around moral questioning and the notion that the work irresponsibly commodified the private reality of the artist's family, providing spectacle for the popular entertainment of others in the style of a reality television show.

It is quite ironic then that the next major public venue for Billingham's work was the controversial show *Sensation; Young British Artists from the Saatchi Collection* in 1997. This group exhibition was likely truly responsible for establishing Richard Billingham's place in the British art scene and launching his international career, with concurrent solo shows in New York, Los Angeles, and Paris. His first major commissioned work came the following year from Artangel (London) in conjunction with the British Broadcasting Corporation. For this assignment Billingham produced *Fishtank* (1998), a 45-minute film comprised of Hi-8 video footage. Rather than a narrative, the piece functions more as a cinematic vignette of the artist's series of family photographs, depicting everyday actions such as Ray feeding the goldfish or Liz playing with her pets.

Fishtank aired to mixed reviews on BBC2 in December 1998. Again, the arguments for and against the power of Billingham's out-of-focus family scenes revolved around the question "is this art or social commentary?" Critics suggested it was difficult for an audience to understand the film because there is no voiceover or introductory narration; a criticism which echoed earlier claims that Billingham's photographs were difficult to understand because they were not captioned like traditional documentary images. Was the artist seriously challenging his audience or merely exploiting his own family and their miserable living conditions? Billingham later made other films in this vein; *Playstation* (1999) features a close-up of his brother hands while playing a video game. His nail-bitten fingers dart over the controls of the game in a mundane, repetitive, yet mesmerizing fashion.

Billingham received further critical attention in 2001 when he was nominated for the Turner Prize, a prestigious annual award given by the Tate Gallery to a British artist for a significant body of work. Billingham was shortlisted on the strength of his major solo exhibition at the Ikon Gallery in Birmingham (2000), which featured his now infamous series of family-based photographs and videos. Although he did not win the prize, he was a notable candidate because it was rare for a photographer to even be nominated. Since then Billingham's more recent work has engaged concerns of landscape aesthetic. Even though he has photographed landscapes since the early 1990s, this component of his work has been largely overshadowed by the controversial family pictures.

Billingham's series of untitled landscapes from 1992–1997 depict semi-urban places; odd forgettable spaces located between rural land and housing estates. But these places were not forgotten by Billingham, who associates these mundane landscapes of derelict playground areas and grassy industrial wastelands with the rites of passage of his boyhood. By contrast, landscape images included in the exhibition *New Pictures* (2003) at Anthony Reynolds Gallery introduced a new perspective of Billingham's longstanding yet overlooked interest in beau-ty and nature. Experimenting with using a medium format camera for the first time, the new photographs depict various natural landscapes where the artist's emphasis is about experiencing a place for the first time, rather than documenting a specific or personal space. Formal concerns of pattern, texture, and space override any apparent social comment Billingham may wish to convey, and this new work is obviously a concerted effort by a young artist trying to expand his range in style and technique.

Sara-Jayne Parsons

See also: **Ethics and Photography; Family Photography; Parr, Martin; Vernacular Photography**

Biography

Born in Birmingham, England, 1970. University of Sunderland, B.A. (Hons) Fine Art, 1991–1994; Felix H. Man Memorial Prize, 1995; The Citibank Private Bank Photography Prize, 1997; Turner Prize Shortlist, Tate Gallery, London, 2001; Glen Dimplex Artist Award Shortlist, IMMA, Dublin, 2001; Sargent Fellowship, British School in Rome, 2002; Prince of Wales Bursary for the Arts, Athens, 2003; ArtSway Residency, New Forest, Hampshire, 2003; Artist in Residence, VIVID, Birmingham, 2004. Living in Stourbridge, England.

Individual Exhibitions

1996 Anthony Reynolds Gallery; London, England
1996 National Museum of Film and Photography; Bradford, England
1996 Portfolio Gallery; Edinburgh, Scotland
1997 Luhring-Augustine; New York, New York
1997 Regen Projects; Los Angeles, California
1997 Galerie Jennifer Flay; Paris, France
1998 Anthony Reynolds Gallery; London, England
1999 Galerie Monica Reitz; Frankfurt am Main, Germany
1999 British School at Rome; Rome, Italy
2000 Ikon Gallery; Birmingham, England and touring to Douglas Hyde Gallery, Dublin, Ireland; Brno House of Arts, Brno, Czech Republic; Hasselbad Centre, Gote-

borg, Nikolaj, Sweden; Copenhagen Contemporary Art Centre, Copenhagen, Denmark
2002 *Fishtank*; Temple Bar; Dublin, Ireland
2003 *New Pictures*; Anthony Reynolds Gallery, London, England; House of Contemporary Arts, Budapest, Hungary
2004 *New Forest*; ArtSway Galleries; Hampshire, England
2004 Sintlukas; Brussels, Belgium

Selected Group Exhibitions

1994 *Who's Looking at the Family?* Barbican Art Gallery, London, England
1996 *New Photography 12*; Museum of Modern Art, New York, New York
1997 *Sensation: Young British Artists from the Saatchi Collection*; The Royal Academy, London, England
1997 *The Citibank Private Bank Photography Prize*; Royal College of Art, London, England
1998 *Wounds. Between Democracy and Redemption in Contemporary Art*; Moderna Museet, Stockholm, Sweden
1999 *Close-Ups-Contemporary Art and Carl Th. Dreyer*; Nikolaj, Copenhagen Contemporary Art Centre, Copenhagen, Denmark
1999 *Common People*; Fondazione Sandretto Re Rebaudengo, Guarene, Venezuela
2000 *Quotidiana*; Castello di Rivoli, Turin, Italy
2001 *Turner Prize Exhibition*; Tate Britain, London, England
2001 *49th Venice Biennale*; Venice, Italy
2002 *Lifesize—International Photography Festival*; National Gallery of Art, Rome, Italy
2003 *Social Strategies: Redefining Social Realism*; University of California, Santa Barbara, California
2003 *Love Over Gold*; Gallery of Modern Art, Glasgow, Scotland
2004 *Stranger than Fiction*; City Art Gallery, Leeds, England
2004 *Tape 291*; 291 Gallery, London, England

Selected Works

* photographs are untitled.
The family photographs (color series), 1990–1996*
The family photographs (black & white series), 1990–1996*
Triptych of Ray, 1991
The landscapes, 1992–1997*
Fishtank, video, 1998
Liz Smoking, video, 1998
Ray in Bed, video, 1999
Playstation, video, 1999
New Pictures (color landscape series), 2003*

Further Reading

Billingham, Richard. *Black Country*. London: The Public, 2004.

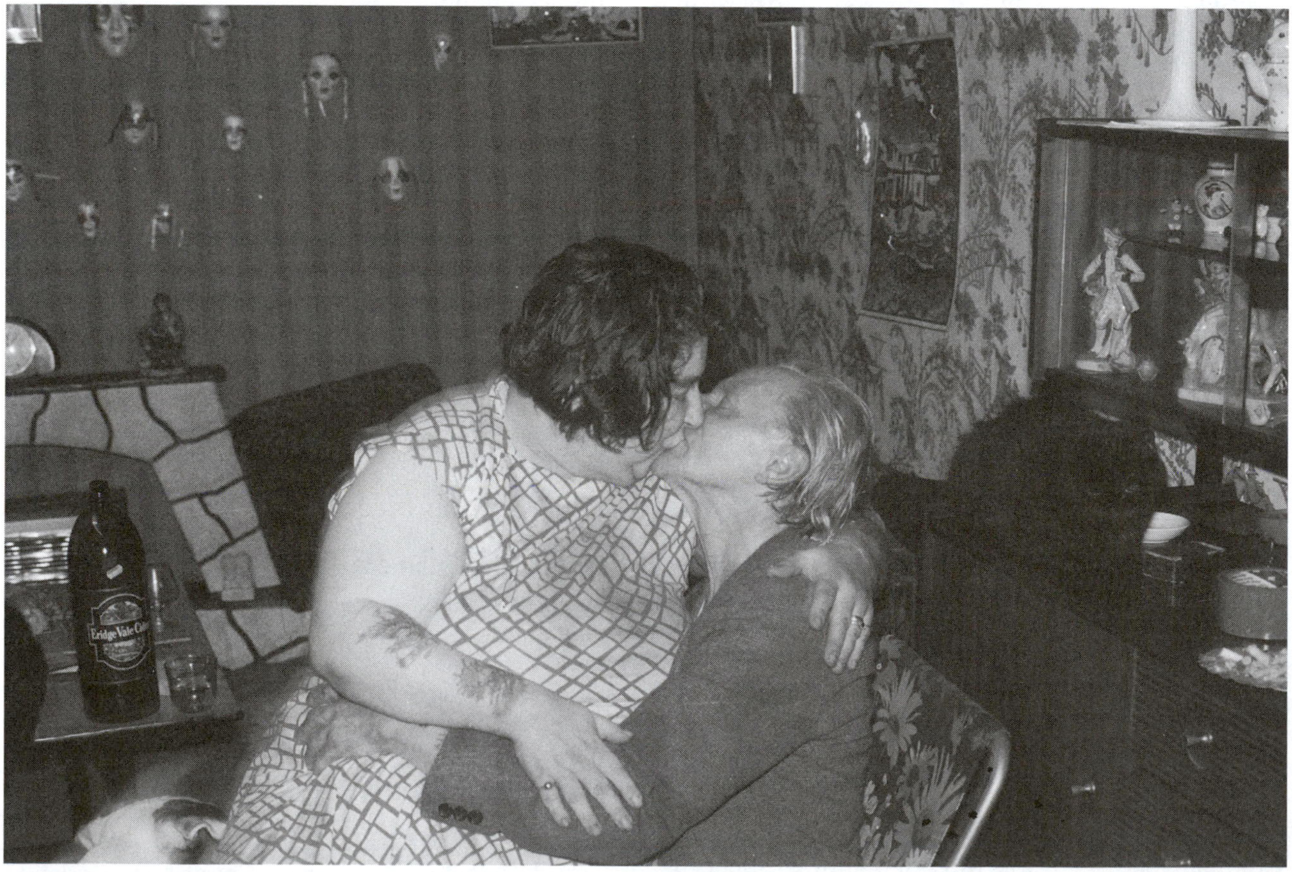

Richard Billingham, Untitled, 1995, original in color.
[*Image courtesy of eyestorm, copyright Richard Billingham*]

Billingham, Richard. *Ray's a Laugh*. Zurich: Scalo, 1996.
Buck, Louisa. "I only make pictures...everything else is a bonus." *Art Monthly* 13 (March 2003).
Colin, Anne, and Charles Penwarden. "Turner Prize 2001: Tate Britain." *Art Press* 277 (March 2002).
Corbetta, Caroline. "Billingham's TV Fishtank." *Flash Art (International Edition)* 32, no. 205 (March/April 1999).
Cork, Richard. "At Home with Ray and Liz." *The Times* (June 9, 2000).
Estep, Jan. "Ha Ha, Ray's a Laugh." *New Art Examiner* 27, no. 1 (September 1999).
Godfrey, Tony. "Birmingham and Dublin: Richard Billingham." *The Burlington Magazine* 142, no. 1170 (September 2000).
Lewis, Jim. "No Place Like Home: The Photographs of Richard Billingham." *Artforum International* 35 (January 1997).
Haworth-Booth, Mark. "Shooting Stars, Richard Billingham." *British Journal of Photography* 17 (January 1996).
Home, Stewart. "Richard Billingham: Ikon Gallery, Birmingham." *Art Monthly* no. 238 (July/August 2000).
Hornby, Nick. "Life Goes On: Richard Billingham." *Modern Painters* 10 (Winter 1997).
Pagel, David. "Family Portraits." *Los Angeles Times* (March 14, 1997).
Richard Billingham. Birmingham: Ikon Gallery, 2000.
Roth, Nancy. "Closeness as Metaphor." *Afterimage* 28, no. 2 (September/October 2000).
Smith, P.C. "Richard Billingham at Luhring Augustine: New York." *Art in America* 85 (May 1997).
Turner, Grady, T. "Richard Billingham: Luhring Augustine." *Flash Art* (May/June 1997).

WERNER BISCHOF

Swiss

Although relatively young when he died, Werner (Werner Adalbert) Bischof was one of the most influential international photojournalists of the period following World War II. His most well-known pictures combine intense observations of his subjects and a technical perfection out of which arises a striking beauty. His documentary photographs especially set a new standard for the genre.

Born in Zurich, April 26, 1916, Bischof was raised in Waldshut, Germany, where he received his basic and secondary education. He returned to Switzerland to attend the Kunstgewerbeschule in Zurich (Zurich School for Applied Arts), where he took a newly established photography course from Hans Finsler, one of the most important advocates of the technically-oriented photography of the German "New Vision" (*Neue Sehen*) school. Under Finsler's influence, Bischof photographed large numbers of plants, shells, and various other subjects in a dispassionate, technical style. After his studies, Bischof worked as an independent designer and photographer in the fields of fashion and advertising in Zurich-Leiten, 1936. In 1938, he took a position at a Zurich publishing house, but also worked as a graphic and interior architectural designer. In 1939, he designed a pavilion for graphic design and worked for the fashion pavilion at the Swiss National Exposition.

During a stay in Paris in the same year, he decided to suspend his photographic activities to concentrate on painting. The beginning of hostilities in 1940 forced his return to Switzerland where he served in the military until 1942 and during this time he returned to photography. In 1942 Bischof began experiments with light and shadow effects, publishing the results in the magazine *Du*. He soon became a regular contributor and began to work as a photojournalist, choosing a path that was basically in opposition to his object-oriented education and experience to date. Artificial arrangements in the studio were left behind. The ravages of war caused him to take up what would become his primary subject: people. His subjects were not spectacular catastrophes or atrocities, but the devastating effects of war both internalized by those who survived it, and expressed by the environments in which they had to survive. Bischof controlled the forcefulness of his statements by use of subtle framing of what might first appear to be casual snapshots. In 1944–1945 Bischof, as a member of the art group Allianz, published his first reportages. During this time his photo essays, *Der Zirkus* (*The Circus*) and *Die Invaliden* (*The Invalids*)—early examples of the form in color—were published. In 1945 after he spent time with Italian partisans who had sought refuge in the Swiss state, Tessin. *Die Flüchtlinge* (*The Refugees*) was a result of this sojourn. He also traveled to France, Germany, and Holland to capture the devastation caused by the war. In his candid photographs Bischof demonstrated that this technique, more than any other type of war photography, is best able to describe the inconceivable consequences of war. In December 1945 and May 1946, some of these pictures appeared in *Du*, shocking many with a photograph showing the mutilated face of a Dutch boy on the title page. There was public consternation at this imagery, and as a result, Bischof's projected book about the consequences of the war was never realized.

After the war Bischof became increasingly involved in the making of photographs and picture stories for the international press. From 1946 to 1948 he worked as a photographer for Schweizer Spende, a Swiss relief organization for war-disabled in Italy, Greece, Austria, and Eastern Europe (Rumania, Hungary, Czechoslovakia, and Poland), then in Finland, Sweden, and Denmark. In 1949 his photos were published in *Du* and in a special edition of *Atlantic*. In 1948 Bischof photographed the Winter Olympics in St. Moritz for *Life* and in 1949 he worked for the British magazines *Picture Post* and *The Observer* following his move to England. In the same year he became a founding member of Magnum Photos, New York and Paris, which with help from other members such as Robert Capa, David "Chim" Seymour, and Henri Cartier-Bresson, became one of the most important organizations of socially engaged photographers in the post WWII period. Trips to Italy, Sardinia, Paris, and Iceland followed. In the Italian magazine *Epoca*, a feature on *Le Piazze d'Italia* (*Italian Plazas*) appeared. For *Life*, in 1951, Bischof photographed probably his most famous reportage, *Famine in Bihar* (Hunger in Bihar), which covered the famine in the Indian province. Stunned by the bitter poverty of the Indian people, he captured striking images without exploiting or sensationalizing his subjects, including, for example, a worm's-eye view photo of a begging mother with a child in her arms. The symbolic communication of pictures such as these were particularly powerful.

From 1951 to 1952, Bischof was sent by *Life* to Tokyo. There he rediscovered himself as an artist, increasingly choosing tranquil, well-balanced compositions that avoided dramatic effects. He reflected on this period of personal transition in his book, *Japan*, which appeared in 1954 and for which he received the Prix Nadar (France) in 1955. Outstanding examples of pictures from this time include *Schlafender Priester im Ryoanji-Tempel* (*Sleeping Priests in the Ryoanji-Temple*), Kyoto, Japan (1951) and *Steinweg durch den Teich im Heiangarten Kyoto* (*Stone Path Through the Pond in the Heian Garden of Kyoto*) (1952). Thus it was with reluctance that he accepted an assignment in Indochina as a war correspondent for *Paris Match*. Doubting more and more the capacity of photojournalism to change society, Bischof had sought independence from magazine work and wanted to remove himself from war correspondence since 1951. He was able to move more toward creating photoessays that depicted the culture and lifestyles of various nations. In Finland, Bischof worked on an international documentary about *Women Today*. That same year he wrote a feature on British Columbia for *Fortune* magazine. Via California and Mexico he and his wife traveled to South America for an extended photo tour.

In 1954 Bischof worked on a photo story in Lima, Peru, and Santiago, Chile, after working for a period in Panama on assignment for *Life*. When his wife returned to Switzerland, Bischof flew to the Inca city, Machu Picchu. Returning to Lima he met the geologist, Ali di Szepessy, who was on an Amazon expedition, and decided to accompany him. On 16 May, 1954, their wrecked car was found in a gully. Just a few days before the accident Werner Bischof's undeniably best known photograph, *Flöte spielender Junge bei Cuzco* (*Boys Playing Flutes in Cuzco*) had appeared. It was a poignant and impressive ending to Bischof's career in which he had been able to reduce situations to their essentials: parents and children, hunger and war, loneliness—all timeless, universal themes. Through the unification of ambitious aesthetics and ethics, Bischof's works have become classics that convey the misery of our world in a dignified and enduring manner.

Franz-Xaver Schlegel

See also: **Capa, Robert; Cartier-Bresson, Henri; Finsler, Hans; Life; Magnum Photos; Picture Post; Seymour, David "Chim"; War Photography**

Biography

Born in Zurich, April 26, 1916. Basic education, 1922–1931. Childhood and youth in Waldshut, Germany. Higher education: studied drawing and sports at a teaching school in Schiers/Graubünden (Switzerland), 1931–1932. Studied at the Kunstgewerbeschule in Zurich (Zurich School for Applied Arts), 1932–1936 under Hans Finsler. From 1936 on, worked as an independent photographer and technical drawer (fashion, advertisement) in Zurich-Letten. Employed by Graphis-Verlag (publishing house), Zurich, 1938. Employee and later chief editor of the newspaper *Du*. Publication of his photos of devastation of war in Europe in the illustrated newspaper *Du*, 1942–1944. War reportages covering France, Germany, The Netherlands, Italy, and Greece, 1945. Official reporter for *Life* at the Winter Olympic Games in St. Moritz,

1948. From this followed further commissions for *Life* as well as for *Fortune, Picture Post, Weekly Illustrated, The Observer, Epoca, Paris Match,* etc. Founding member of Magnum Photos, 1949. Married Rosellina Mandel, 1949; two sons, Marc, 1950 and Daniel, 1954. A co-founder of the Kollegiums Schweizerischen Photographen (Committee of Swiss Photographers), 1951. Photo reports from Europe, The Middle East, and America. Died in a car accident in the Peruvian Andes, the region of Trujillo, May 16, 1954.

Individual Exhibitions

1953 *Menschen im Fernen Osten*; Galerie St. Annahof, Zurich, Switzerland
1955 *Japan*; Art Institute of Chicago, Chicago, Illinois
1956 *Werner Bischof, Retrospektive*; Kunstgewerbeschule Zurich, Switzerland
1957 *Retrospektive Werner Bischof*; Kunstgewerbemuseum Zurich, Switzerland
1960 *Werner Bischof*; Musée des Arts Décoratifs, Paris, France
1966 *Werner Bischof*; Galerie Form, Zurich, Switzerland
1967 *Werner Bischof*; Musée des Arts Décoratifs, Paris, France
1968 *Werner Bischof*; IBM Gallery, New York, New York
1984 *Werner Bischof*; Galerie Municipale du Château d'Eau, Toulouse, France
1986 *Werner Bischof*; Kunsthaus Zurich, Switzerland, and traveling
1988 *Werner Bischof*; Centro de Arte Reina Sofia, Madrid, Spain
1989 *Werner Bischof*; Photoforum Pasquart, Biel, Switzerland
1990 *Werner Bischof*; International Center of Photography, New York, New York
1994 *Werner Bischof (1916–1954)*; New Zealand Centre of Photography, New Zealand
1998 *Werner Bischof: Nach dem Krieg*; Galerie Mangisch, Zurich, Switzerland
2001 *The Compassionate Lens—The Photographs of Werner Bischof 1945–1954*; Bruce Museum, Greenwich, Connecticut
2004 *Werner Bischof—Photographs 1932–1954*; The Minneapolis Institute of Arts, Minneapolis, Minnesota

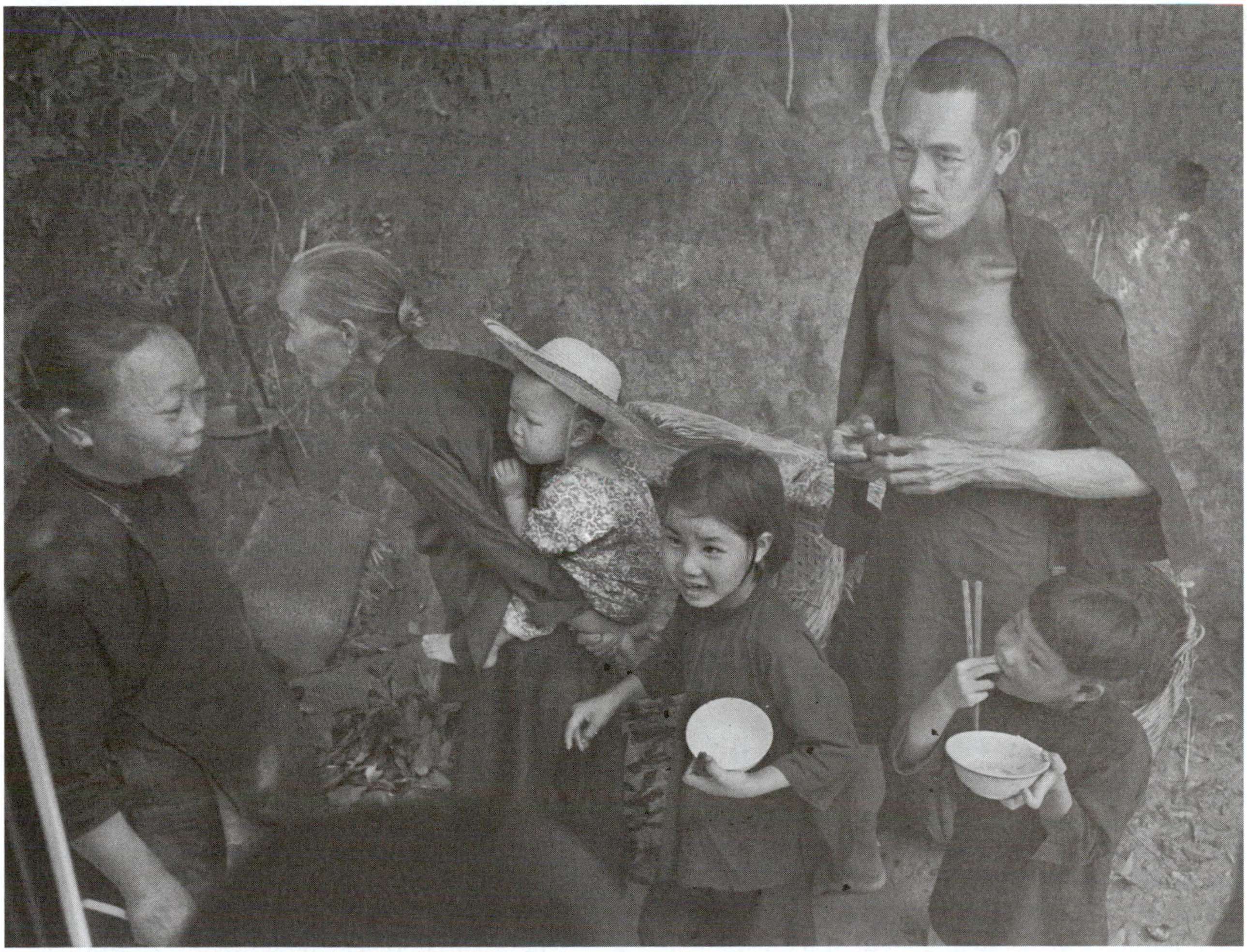

Werner Bischof, Hong-Kong, 1952.
[© *Werner Bischof/Magnum Photos*]

Group Exhibitions

1949 *Photographie in der Schweiz von 1848 bis heute*; Gewerbemuseum, Basel, Switzerland
1955 *The Family of Man*; Museum of Modern Art, New York, New York, and traveling
1959 *10 Years of Photography*; George Eastman House, Rochester, New York
1960 *The World as Seen by Magnum*; Musée des Arts décoratifs, Paris, France
1969 *Photography in the 20th Century*; National Gallery of Canada, Ottawa, Canada, and traveling
1977 *Documenta 6*, Museum Friedericianum; Kassel, Germany
1979 *Photographie als Kunst—Kunst als Photographie 1879–1979*; Tiroler Landesmuseum Ferdinandeum, Innsbruck, Austria
1980 *The Imaginary Photo Museum*; Photokina, Cologne, Germany
1985 *Triennale internationale de la photographie*; Musée d'Art et d'histoire, Fribourg, Switzerland
1990 *Zeitblende—5 Jahrzehnte Magnum-Photographie*; Kunsthaus Zurich, Switzerland
1999 *Patient Planet So Many Worlds*; Auckland City Art Gallery, Auckland, New Zealand

Selected Works

Die Flüchtlinge, 1944
After the War (series), 1945
Weinendes Kind, 1947
Ungarn (series), 1947
Schlafender Priester im Ryoanji-Tempel, Kyoto, Japan, 1951
Bihar, India, 1951
Hungersnot in Madras (series), 1951
Die indische Tänzerin Anali Hora bei der Morgentoilette, 1951
Indochina, 1952
Steinweg durch den Teich im Heiangarten Kyoto, 1952
Flöten spielender Junge bei Cuzco, 1954

Further Reading

Bischof, Rosallina, and P. Schifferli. *Werner Bischof: Querschnitt*. Zurich: Manesse Verlag, 1961.
Bischof, Werner. *Werner Bischof*. Intro. by Claude Roy. London: Thames + Hudson, 1989.
Bischof, Marco, and René Burri. *Werner Bischof*. London: 1990.
British Journal of Photography 138 (1991) no. 6809, v. 28.2. 1991; 16–19.
Bischof, Werner. *After the War*. Washington, DC: Smithsonian Publishers, 1997.
Browne, Turner, and Elaine Partnow, eds. *Macmillan Biographical Encyclopedia of Photographic Artists & Innovators*. New York and London: Collier MacMillan, 1983.
Burri, Rosellina, and René Burri, eds. *Bischof-Burri*. Manuel Gasser, essay.
Capa, Cornell, ed. *The Concerned Photographer*. New York: 1968.
Cookman, Claude. *Werner Bischof—55 Photos*. London, Paris, Berlin: Phaidon Press, 2001.
Die Welt der Camera. Luzern and Frankfurt: 1964.
Farova, Hanna, ed. *The Photographs of Werner Bischof*. Prague: 1964.
Flüeler, Niklaus, and Romeo E. Martinez, eds. *Grosse Photographen unserer Zeit: Werner Bischof*. Luzern: 1973.
Gasser, Manuel. *Werner Bischof Unterwegs*. Zürich: Manesse Verlag, 1957.
Gasser, Manuel. *The World of Werner Bischof: A Photographer's Odyssey*. New York: 1959.
Gasser, Manuel. *24 Photos von Werner Bischof*. Bern: 1946.
Genossenschaftsbund, Migros, ed. *Mutter und Kind*. Zurich: 1949.
Gruber, L. Fritz, ed. *Große Photographen unseres Jahrhunderts*. Berlin: Darmstadt and Wien, 1964.
Gruber, L. Fritz, and Renate, eds. *The Imaginary Photo Museum*. Cologne: 1980.
Guillain, Robert. *Japan*. Paris, Delpire, 1954.
Photo Classics II—Werner Bischof 1916–1954. London: 1971.
Tuñon de Lara, Manuel. *From Incas to Indios* (Photographs by Werner Bischof, Robert Frank and Pierre Verger). New York: 1956.

BLACK STAR

By the mid-1930s, photojournalism in America was firmly established. Editors and publishers used photographs freely, secure in the public's support for newspapers and magazines that used photographs to describe the events of the day. Ironically, the photographers who produced all those pictures, who made illustrated journalism a fact of life in America, received little in the way of either respect or gratitude. Most often, images in the press were run without credit, and those who made the pictures in the first place were routinely characterized as uncouth brutes. To make matters worse, prints and negatives were rarely archived; when newspapers or magazines changed hands or went out of business, or when photographers changed jobs or retired, old negatives and prints were simply thrown away. But all that was about to change, and the Black Star picture agency, founded in New York City in early 1936 was a principle instrument of that change.

The origins of Black Star lay in Europe, especially in Germany. The rise of Adolph Hitler and the Nazis in January 1933 impelled some of Europe's most talented journalists to emigrate to the United States where they had an immediate and profound influence on journalistic practice. Three among them were the founders of Black Star: Ernest Mayer, director of the Mauritius Publishing Company, one of Germany's most successful photo agencies; Kurt Safranski, manager of the legendary Ullstein group of magazines; and Kurt Kornfeld, a literary agent.

As it happened, the three German émigrés arrived just as the world of American magazines was being transformed by publishers such as Henry Luce of Time, Inc. and Mike Cowles of the Des Moines, Iowa *Register* and *Tribune*. Convinced that the public's appetite for the visual mandated a different approach to illustrated journalism, Luce and Cowles were determined to produce national magazines in which the photograph and the photographic essay reigned supreme. Luce won the race to produce America's first large-format picture magazine; the first issue of *Life* hit the newsstands in November 1936. Cowles's *Look* followed in February 1937.

In the year before the publication of the first issue of *Life*, Luce relied on advice and counsel from Black Star, and early editions of the magazine nearly always contained work produced by Black Star photographers. This is hardly surprising since Time, Inc. had agreed to pay Black Star a minimum of $5,000 a year for first refusal rights on all Black Star photographs not taken expressly for other publications. In addition, Luce's company agreed to pay extra to secure first rights on all photographs imported from Europe by the agency.

The phenomenal impact of *Life* and Cowles's *Look* led to a proliferation of photographically-illustrated magazines and to the early success of Black Star. Most of the new picture magazines kept their staffs small, preferring instead to purchase images from agencies like Black Star that had connections with photographers and other agencies around the world. For instance, before the United States went to war in 1941, Black Star had a curious and special arrangement with Deutscher Verlag, the official Nazi news agency. For years, Black Star received photographs of the German army nearly every day in the mail. At *Life* one bureau chief remembered that in the early days the magazine "needed Black Star more than they needed us." And it was not simply access to the occasional exclusive photograph that mattered, for *Life* also "needed their stories for our files, their contacts, their staff for assignments, and their pictures." The relationship between the agency and the magazine was so symbiotic that some of Black Star's most talented photographers—Ralph Crane, Andreas Feininger, Fritz Goro, Walt Sanders, Bill Ray, and Burk Uzzle—eventually joined the staff at *Life*.

While the initial success of Black Star undoubtedly lay in what historian Hendrik Neubauer calls "the enormous appetite which magazines worldwide had for photographs," there is much more to the story. Even in the heyday of the big picture magazines like *Life* and *Look*, the agency sought to widen its client base to include corporate and advertising photography, which is far more remunerative than traditional news and documentary photography. Since the demise of the large-format picture magazines in the 1960s and 1970s, the need to include corporate and advertising photography in the work of the agency is clear, though not universally appreciated. Howard Chapnick, the legendary president of the agency from 1964 to 1989, noted with some frustration that in spite of the "large number of publications using photography," comparatively few have any use for the kind of "extensive documentary picture stories" that were once the mainstay of the business.

Ben Chapnick, Howard's first cousin and successor as president of the agency, concurs. "It is quite apparent to me," he told Hendrik Neubauer, "that without the corporate business and its expansion since 1960," Black Star might have managed to eke out a narrow existence as "a much smaller entity" or ceased to exist altogether. Instead, by recognizing both the necessity and value of producing commercial photography, the agency assures that its photographers will continue to work, even though their journalistic and documentary efforts no longer bring in the kind of income they once did.

Black Star's importance in the history of twentieth-century photography is unquestioned. Beginning with its early association with *Life* magazine, the agency became one of the most important suppliers of news and feature photography to newspapers, magazines, books, and corporations around the world. The photographers represented by the agency were and are at the top of the profession; many, such as W. Eugene Smith, David and Peter Turnley, John Launois, Claus Meyer, and Charles Moore have rightly achieved considerable fame. The approximately 350 men and women now associated with the agency produce a daunting array of work for journalistic and commercial clients worldwide, and Black Star's enormous collection of stock photographs constitutes a stunning visual history of the world since the mid-1930s.

Michael Carlebach

See also: **Archives; Feininger, Andreas; Life Magazine; Look; Uzzle, Burk**

Further Reading

Chapnick, Howard. *Truth Needs No Ally. Inside Photojournalism.* Columbia, MO: University of Missouri Press, 1994.

Neubauer, Hendrik. *Black Star. 60 Years of Photojournalism.* Koln, Germany: Konemann, 1997.

Schuneman, R. Smith, ed. *Photographic Communication. Principles, Problems and Challenges of Photojournalism.* New York: Hastings House, 1972.

Smith, C. Zoe. "Black Star Picture Agency: *Life's* European Connection." *Journalism History* 13, no. 1 (Spring 1986).

KARL BLOSSFELDT

German

Karl Blossfeldt depicted plants by the thousands—in photographs which feature flowers, buds, branched stems, clusters, or seed capsules shot directly from the side, seldom from an overhead view, and rarely from a diagonal perspective. He usually placed the subjects of his photographs against white or grey cardboard, sometimes against a black background. Hardly ever can details of the room be detected. The light for his shots was obtained from a northern window, making it diffuse, yet the light came from the side, creating volume. The technique and processing conditions were simple; only the size of the negative format was more demanding. Nothing should detract from the subject. Blossfeldt produced such pictures for over 30 years and producing them was nothing but work.

This line of work was not his main profession, although his fame today rests on his photographs. Rather, plant photography was part of an all-inclusive whole, a teaching concept. He taught for over 30 years at the *Kunstgewerbeschule* (School of Arts and Crafts) in Berlin. Shortly before his death, when already famous for his photography, he announced his intention to publish his teaching methods, in order to place the images in their right as he saw it. Neither this plan nor that of completing an archive of plant photographs was ever realized. What has remained are bundles of photographs, which have made history on their own, and the memory of a teacher, who—like so many in his field—left no lasting impression outside of his personal sphere. But Karl Blossfeldt's life achievement occupies a firm place in the history of twentieth century photography.

To a certain extent, he had foreseen that he neither would be recognized as a photographer in the style of plant-loving still life painters nor as an artist in his own field, sculpture. He knew that his photographs were part of a straight vision just recently discovered before his first exhibition in 1925, and he hoped that, at least, his photographs would teach people to look more closely at nature, even through art. Two sentences of his rare writings encapsulate all of his ideas:

> But the plant never falls into the sober representation of a mere object; it forms and grows according to logic and function, and, with primeval power, forces everything to the most sublime artistic form....My flower documents should contribute to restoring the relationship to nature. They should reawaken a sense for nature, point out its teeming richness of form, and prompt the viewer to observe for himself the local plant world.
>
> (Blossfeldt 1932, 5)

Born in the Harz Mountains in central Germany, Karl Blossfeldt grew up in the country surrounded by plants and animals, which he enjoyed drawing and modeling. His education included an arts and crafts apprenticeship, a craftmen's scholarship for further education in drawing, and some musical instruction about which sparse biographical sources provide no details. He appears to have wavered between a career as a relief sculptor and that of a singer's rehearser until he was given the task that was to determine his life's work. As a student of the Berlin School of Arts and Crafts he was asked to produce models for drawing classes in accordance with the method of Moritz Meurer, then his teacher. Meurer and six of his students were given a grant to live and work in Rome for six years in order to produce a collection of drawings and models of natural ornaments to be used by Germany's industry. Karl Blossfeldt was one of the two modelers in this party.

Moritz Meurer and his assistants not only collected, drew, and cast botanical specimen in Rome and its outlying regions, but also systematically photographed plants. Shoots were removed from stems, roots cut back and, if necessary, buds opened. The plant types were stuck on a support, mounted before a uniform background, and exposed. In the history of photography the adoption of this method with its roots in painting was a tradition in itself. The first publication of the project was dedicated to a single plant—acanthus (cowparsnip)—and its influence on ancient art; two of its photographs bear Blossfeldt's name. They show the leaf and stem of the acanthus with the characteristic pointed tips and crenature on the head, pictured before a grey background. When the book was published in 1896, Moritz Meurer returned to Berlin and left Blossfeldt without subsidy.

For a time Karl Blossfeldt went through a phase of reorientation, undecided whether to stay in Italy, emigrate to the United States, or assume employment in the German arts and crafts industry. In the end, he chose a position as an assistant teacher for modeling from plants at the Kunstgewerbeschule in Berlin. In 1899 he was elevated to the post of lecturer. Blossfeldt's task in his beginners' classes was essentially that of demonstrating that the best constructions for industrial designs had already been anticipated in nature. So he did, with nearly no change and development until his dismissal in 1930—and as steady as his teaching method was his use of the camera.

In 1925, the Berlin gallerist Karl Nierendorf recognized Karl Blossfeldt and his plant photographs. He immediately realized their similarity to 1920s' avant-garde art, asked Blossfeldt to print a larger number of exhibition photographs, and subsequently prepared their publication in a book. It appeared under the title *Urformen der Kunst* (Basic Forms of Art) in 1926, with a second issue within one year, and was translated into several languages. The great photographic exhibition of 1929, *Film und Foto* in Stuttgart, showed his work with the greatest respect possible. After 1930 there was scarcely a major photo exhibition and nearly no important annual without Blossfeldt's images. In the autumn of 1930, Karl Blossfeldt had reached retirement age and gave up teaching in order to devote himself to the evaluation of his plant archives. His second book of photographs, *Wundergarten der Natur* (*Nature's Wonderful Garden*), was published in the spring of 1932. On December 3, 1932, Karl Blossfeldt died in Berlin.

ROLF SACHSSE

See also: **Photography in Europe: Germany and Austria**

Biography

Born in Schielo, Harz Mountains, Central Germany, June 13, 1865. Apprenticeship as a caster in an art foundry of ironworks at Maegdesprung, Selke Valley, and private music lessons, 1881–1984. Scholarship for drawing courses at the Berlin school for arts and crafts, continued music lessons, 1884–1986. Work as an art caster in Berlin, 1886–1989. Assistant to Moritz Meurer on a design commission for the Prussian Ministry of Trade in Rome, 1890–1997. Assistant to the Director of the Berlin school of arts and crafts, 1898. Lecturer for drawing after nature, 1899–1920, Professor for drawing after nature at the Berlin school for arts and crafts, 1921–1930. As Professor emeritus, work on a theory of drawing after nature and rearranging his photographic material, 1930–1932. Died in Berlin, 3 December 1932.

Individual Exhibitions

1926 *Karl Blossfeldt, Urformen der Kunst*, Galerie Nierendorf, Berlin, Germany
1976 *Karl Blossfeldt, Fotografien 1900–1932*, Rheinisches Landesmuseum, Bonn, Germany
1994 *Karl Blossfeldt*, Städtisches Kunstmuseum, Bonn, Germany, and traveling
1999 *Karl Blossfeldt*, Akademie der Künste, Berlin, Germany, and traveling through Germany, Switzerland, and Austria

Group Exhibitions

1929 *Film und Foto*; Internationale Ausstellung des Deutschen Werkbundes, Stuttgart, Germany, and traveling through Germany, Switzerland, and Austria
1977 *Documenta VI*, Kassel, Germany
1993 *Pantheon der Fotografie des 20*; Jahrhunderts, Kunsthalle der Bundesrepublik, Bonn, Germany
1997 *Deutsche Fotografie, Macht eines Mediums 1870–1970*, Kunsthalle der Bundesrepublik, Bonn, Germany
1999 *Karl Blossfeldt, Silvie + Chèrif Defraoui*; Pflanzenbilder, Wilhelm-Lehmbruck-Museum, Duisburg, Germany
2000 *Die Sprache der Pflanzen*; Kunsthalle, Erfurt, Germany
2000 *Die Natur der Dinge*; Kunstforum NRW, Duesseldorf, Germany
2001 *Karl Blossfeldt and Natascha Borowsky*; SK-Stiftung, Cologne, Germany

Selected Works

Equisetum hyemale, n.d.
Impatiens glandulifera, n.d.
Dipsacus laciniatus, n.d.
Cucurbita, n.d.
Adiantum pedatum, n.d.
Aristolochia clematitis, n.d.
Laserpitum siler, n.d.
Blumenbachia hieronymi (Loasaceae), n.d.

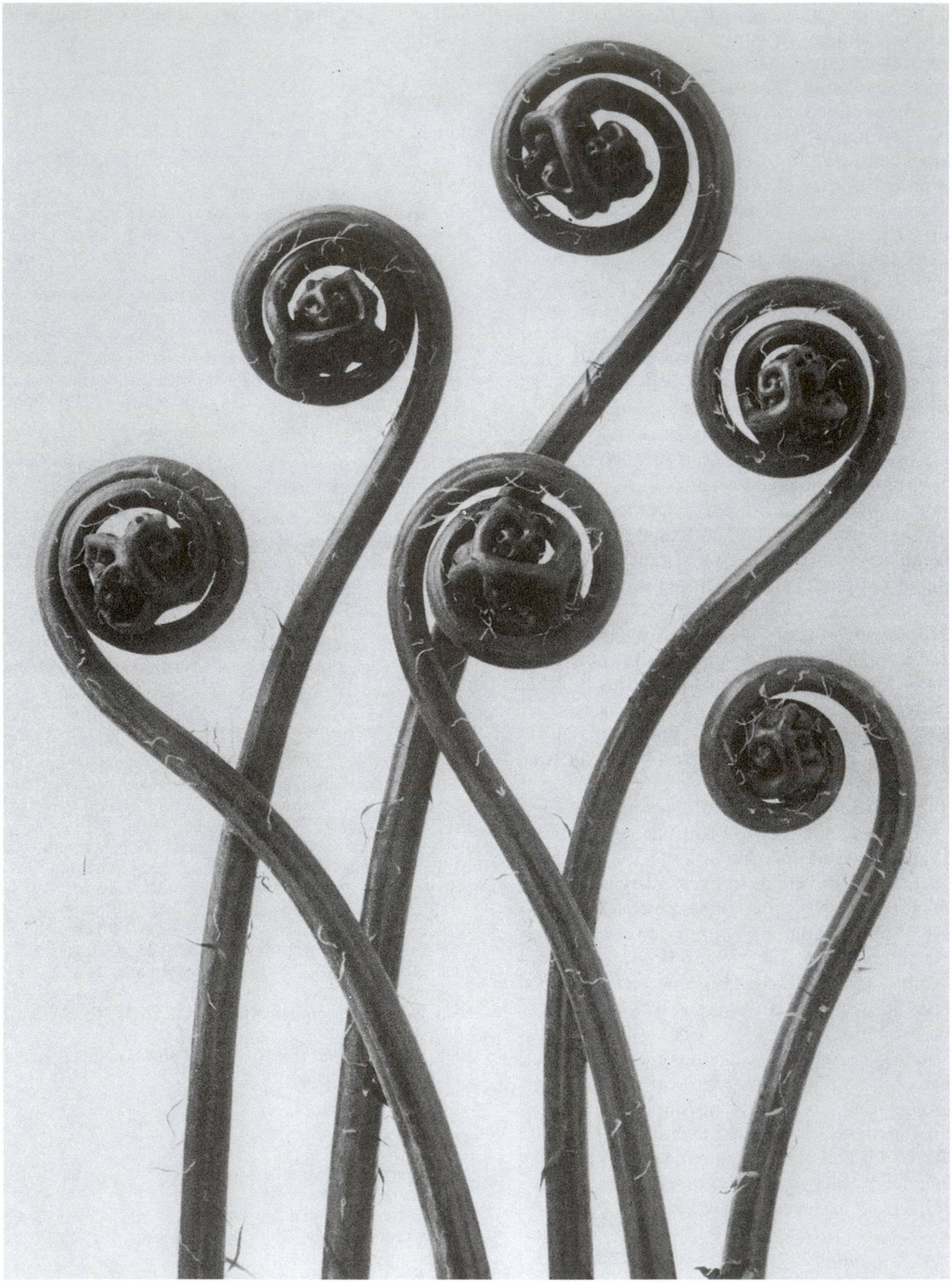

Karl Blossfeldt, Adiantum Pelatum, 1928, Photogravure, 10 × 7 ½″ (25.4 × 19.05 cm), Los Angeles County Museum of Art, Gift of Joyce Essex.
[*Photograph © 2004 Museum Associates/LACMA*]

Further Reading

Blossfeldt, Karl. *Urformen der Kunst*. Berlin: Wasmuth, 1926.
Blossfeldt, Karl. *Wundergarten der Natur*. Berlin: Wasmuth. 1932.
Karl Blossfeldt Photographs 1900–1932. Exhibition catalogue. Bonn: Rheinland Verlag, 1977.
Karl Blossfeldt 1865–1932, Das fotografische Werk. Text by Gert Mattenklott. Munich: Schirmer/Mosel 1981.
Roh, Franz, and Jan Tschichold. *foto-auge photo-eye*. Tübingen: Wasmuth, 1929.
Sachsse, Rolf. *Karl Blossfeldt Photographs*. Köln: Taschen, 1993.
Vergleichende Konzeptionen, August Sander, Karl Blossfeldt, Albert Renger-Patzsch, Bernd und Hilla Becher. Exhibition catalogue. Munich: Schirmer/Mosel 1997.

ERWIN BLUMENFELD

American

In 1921, Erwin Blumenfeld mailed a postcard from Amsterdam with a photograph of his face collaged atop a woman's body and the words "President-Dada-Chaplinist–Charlotin" to poet and Dada founder Tristan Tzara. Tzara and the Berlin Dadaists, to whom Blumenfeld was connected, actively recognized the value of photography and its creative possibilities. Several key members of the group would become innovators of photomontage and an important influence on political propaganda, photojournalism, and advertising photography following World War I. Always true to his Dadaist spirit, Blumenfeld never ceased to experiment in the darkroom, using techniques such as solarization and double-exposures, and created clever, unexpected compositions in his photographs. He would later become one of the most sought-after, highest-paid photographers in the world.

Erwin Blumenfeld was born on January 26, 1897, to an upper-middle class Jewish family in Berlin. His father, Albert Blumenfeld, was a principal partner of Jordan & Blumenfeld, an umbrella manufacturer. The Blumenfelds initially lived a life of bourgeois comfort, and the children were treated to expensive toys as well as regular outings at the theatre and art museums. During a trip to the Kaiser Friedrich Museum, Blumenfeld was deeply affected by the delicately veiled nudes of Sandro Botticelli's *Venus* and Lucas Cranach the Elder's *Lucretia*. As a result of this visit, veiling and female nudity would subsequently become a recurrent theme in his work.

Blumenfeld received his first camera as a gift at age 10 and described this moment as when his "real life started." He shared his enthusiasm with his best friend, Paul Citroen, a Dutch boy he met at school, the rigorous Askanisches Gymnasium in Berlin. The boys commemorated their friendship in a 1910 double self-portrait, which they later re-enacted in 1916 and 1926. Fittingly, the young Blumenfeld was intrigued by reflected images and fascinated by mirrors. In his first self-portrait dressed as Pierrot, he captured simultaneous frontal and profile views of his face using a mirror.

In 1913, Blumenfeld finished his studies and began a three-year apprenticeship for Moses & Schlochauer, a German dressmaker. He abandoned further education due to his father's mental deterioration and consequent death from syphilis that left the family in financial ruin. As he grew disenchanted with the garment industry, Berlin was becoming a dynamic forum for the international avant-garde. Expressionists, Fauvists, Cubists, and Futurists exhibited regularly in the city beginning in 1910; the same year Herwarth Walden's cultural weekly, *Der Sturm*, began publication. In 1915, Blumenfeld and Citroen met Walden, and Citroen became the manager of the *Der Sturm* bookstore in 1916. That same year, Blumenfeld fell in love with Citroen's cousin Lena.

Through Walden, Citroen and Blumenfeld met the founding members of the Berlin Dada movement: George Grosz, Walter Mehring, Wieland Herzfelde, and his brother Helmut Hertzfelde (John Heartfield). In 1917, Citroen was dispatched to Amsterdam as a representative of *Der Sturm*, and

Blumenfeld was drafted in to the German army originally as an ambulance driver and soon after became the bookkeeper for a field brothel. Blumenfeld planned to desert the army while on leave in 1918, only to be reported by his mother and imprisoned. After the war's end, he left Berlin for Amsterdam where he was reunited with Paul and Lena Citroen and declared himself the president of Dada in Holland.

Once in Amsterdam, he sought to establish himself as a Dada artist and created some of his most important collages. He married Lena in 1921, and two years later, he opened The Fox Leather Company, described in his autobiography as: "eaten up by expenses from the day of its birth." At the shop's second location, he discovered a hidden darkroom, where he would master solarization, and asked customers to pose for portraits, sometimes nude, which he displayed in the front window. In 1932, Blumenfeld had his first exhibition as a photographer at the Kunstzaal van Lier. Two years later, Blumenfeld published photographs in the noted French publication, *Photographie*. In 1935, French painter Georges Rouault's daughter Geneviève, a dentist, visited Blumenfeld's shop and agreed to exhibit his work in the waiting room of her office in Paris.

With the hope of becoming a professional photographer, Blumenfeld moved to Paris in 1936. Upon arrival, Geneviève Rouault collected a small group of clients eagerly awaiting sittings, including her father and famed painter Henri Matisse. The portrait business did not prove lucrative, and he set his sights on fashion photography. In the meantime, he accepted advertising commissions and rented a studio in Montparnasse where he continued his own work. In 1937, Blumenfeld published a series of photographs in the first two issues of the prestigious art quarterly, *Verve*. Among these images were several of his accomplished nudes such as *Nude Under Wet Silk*. Later, *Verve's* editors sold 50 of Blumenfeld's images to an American publication, *Coronet*, and the annual *Photographie* continued to prominently feature his photographs.

Although he was well represented in magazines and galleries, work as a fashion photographer remained unattainable until 1938, when he met British photographer Cecil Beaton, who helped him secure a contract at Condé Nast. His first portfolio appeared in the October 1938 issue of French *Vogue*, and the May issue included another 20-page spread, which featured Blumenfeld's legendary photograph of model Lisa Fonssagrives on the edge of the Eiffel Tower. In 1939, *Vogue* did not renew his contract, and as a result, he decided to seek opportunities in New York.

Shortly after arriving in New York, Alexander King promised him work at *Life*, and a meeting with editor Carmel Snow at *Harper's Bazaar* resulted in an immediate, well-paid assignment in Paris. After returning to Paris, he was ordered to report to a French concentration camp in 1940. When it was determined that Blumenfeld had been interned by mistake, he and his family fled to America, only to be detoured and detained again by German forces in Morocco. Rescued by the Hebrew Aid Society, they arrived in New York, and Blumenfeld's arrival was greeted with a rewarding contract from *Harper's Bazaar*.

At *Harper's Bazaar*, Blumenfeld worked with renowned art director Alexey Brodovich and forged a close relationship with photographer Martin Munkacsi. Although *Harper's Bazaar* was an effective showcase for Blumenfeld's work and secured him major advertising contracts with clients such as Helena Rubenstein and Elizabeth Arden, he responded to financial incentives at Condé Nast and returned to *Vogue* in 1944. Art director Alexander Liberman conceded a considerable amount of creative freedom to Blumenfeld and encouraged him to experiment with veiled images, where models were photographed behind ground glass and cellophane or reflected in mirrors, as well as color photography, integrating motifs derived from painting into his work. Liberman appreciated his Dadaist and Surrealist sensibilities and recognized that his carefully composed, surprising images would make impressive covers. He included Blumenfeld's photographs in his book, *The Art and Technique of Color Photography*, published in 1951.

Blumenfeld's contract with *Vogue* ended in 1955; however, he still received advertising commissions from loyal clients and signed with L'Oreal in 1963. Although he was included in two group exhibitions at the Museum of Modern Art, NewYork, in 1947 and the Los Angeles County Museum of Art in 1948, Blumenfeld seldom exhibited in the United States. He dedicated the latter years of his life to composing his autobiography and collecting his best 100 photographs into a book. Of those images, only four are from his work as a fashion photographer. Both works were published posthumously. Erwin Blumenfeld died on a trip to Rome, Italy in 1969.

Anne Blecksmith

See also: **Beaton, Cecil; Condé Nast; Dada; Fashion Photography; Heartfield, John; Liberman, Alexander; Manipulation; Montage; Multiple Exposures and Printing; Munkacsi, Martin; Propaganda; Solarization**

Biography

Born Berlin, Germany, January 26, 1897. Died Rome, Italy, July, 4, 1969. Received secondary school certificate from the Askanisches Gymnasium, 1913. Drafted into German army, 1916–1918. Moves to Amsterdam to join Paul and Lena Citroen, 1918. Marries Lena Citroen, 1921. Opens the Fox Leather Goods Company, 1922. Birth of daughter Lisette, 1922. Birth of son Heinz, 1925. Birth of son Yorick, 1932. Exhibition at the Kunstzaal van Lier, 1932. Moves to Paris, 1936. Exhibition at Galerie Billier, 1936. Photographs published in *Verve*, 1936. First work at French *Vogue*, 1936. Covers Paris fashion for *Harper's Bazaar*, 1939. Moves to New York to work for *Harper's Baazar*, 1941. Joins *Vogue*, 1944.

Individual Exhibitions

1978 *Erwin Blumenfeld*; Witkin Gallery, New York, New York
1988 *Erwin Blumenfeld: Dada Collage and Photography*; Rachel Adler Gallery, New York, New York
1989 *Erwin Blumenfeld*; Museum für Kunsthandwerk und Gewerbe, Hamburg, Germany
1996 *Erwin Blumenfeld: A Fetish for Beauty*; Barbican Art Gallery, London, England

Selected Group Exhibitions

1993 *Paul Citroen and Erwin Blumenfeld*; The Photographers' Gallery, London, England

Selected Works

Momie vivante, 1932
Nude under Wet Silk, c. 1937
Carmen the Model for Rodin's "The Kiss", 1937
Portfolio de Vogue*: La Tour Eiffel*, French *Vogue*, 1939
Nude in Artificial Snow, 1949
Spring Fashions/Do Your Part for the Red Cross, American *Vogue* cover, 1945
1950: Mid-century Fashions, Faces, Ideas, American *Vogue* cover, 1950
In hoc signo vinces, 1967

Further Reading

Blumenfeld, Erwin. *Durch tausendjährige Zeit [Autobiographie]*. Frauenfeld: Huber, 1976; as *Eye to I: Autobiography of a Photographer*. Translated by Mike Mitchell and Brian Murdoch. New York: Thames and Hudson, 1999.
Blumenfeld, Erwin. *Meine 100 Besten Fotos*. Bern: Benteli, 1979. As *My One Hundred Best Photos*. Text by Hendel Teicher, translated by Philippe Garner with an introduction by Maurice Besset. New York: Rizzoli, 1981.
Blumenfeld, Yorick. *The Naked and the Veiled: The Photographic Nudes of Erwin Blumenfeld*. London: Thames and Hudson, 1999.
Ewing, William, and Schinz, Marina. *Blumenfeld: A Fetish for Beauty*. New York: Thames and Hudson, 1999.
Ewing, William. *The Idealizing Vision: The Art of Fashion Photography*. With a preface by Anna Wintour. New York: Aperture Foundation, 1991.
Liberman, Alexander. *The Art and Technique of Color Photography*. New York: Simon and Schuster, 1951.

BODY ART

At the end of the 1960s, artists in the United States and Europe began using their own bodies as the material and instruments of the artistic work. Decades before, actionist elements were already increasingly important, especially under the influence of experimental theater and the reception of the historical avant-garde of the second and third decades of the twentieth century. Hans Namuth's photographs of Jackson Pollock painting his Abstract Expressionist canvases played a key role in this development; these images had a catalyzing influence on artists as different as the French "Art Informel" figures Georges Mathieu (1921–) and Yves Klein (1928–1962), the Japanese Gutai Group, the American "Happenings" artist, Allen Kaprow (1927–), and the Vienna Actionists (Wiener Aktionismus), both on their performance and on their stated doctrines. Body artists pursued the fusion of art and life that was typical of the 1960s and 1970s to its very apex. Practitioners differed considerably and distinguished their use of the body in its social, sexual, cultural, and political meaning. Though the actions or performances usually took place before audiences or in private venues including the studio, photography was an essential component, recording, documenting, and codifying the activity. Although film and video were other important components, it is the still images that have come to stand in for the temporal action, giving Body Art its face to the contemporary art world. Next to the alternately poignant and humorous self-examination of Vito Acconci (1940–) stand the physical and psychic extremes of the Yugoslavian-born Marina Abramovic (1946–), who often performs nude, allowing her body to be slammed, pushed past, or otherwise stressed as in *Rhythm 0*, of 1974, and Chris Burden (1946–), the Californian conceptualist notorious for having himself shot in the arm. Leading contemporary art figure Bruce Nauman (1941–) has learned from modern dance that simple everyday actions can be art; his spouting of a stream of water *Self-Portrait as a Fountain* (1966–1967) in homage to Marcel Duchamp's famous urinal titled *Fountain*, has become an icon of postwar contemporary art. Figures who emerged in the 1980s often explored popular culture, such as Californian Paul McCarthy (1945–) who pushes American popular culture to the limits of good taste with often scatological actions in which individuals wear Santa Claus costumes or Mickey Mouse ears. The Cuban-born Ana Mendieta (1948–1985) and American Dennis Oppenheim (1938–) fuse body and land art, while the Japanese artist Yayoi Kusama (1929–), who lives in the United States, uses her body as a sign of sexual liberation and political protest. Feminism came to the fore in the late 1960s and early 1970s in America with Carolee Schneeman (1939–) in her body-in-motion film and performance works, with Hannah Wilke (1940–1993) in her narcissistic poses and role-playing, and in Europe with Gina Pane (1936–1990) in her acts of auto-aggression, including a famous action in which she sliced her face with a razor blade, *Psyche* of 1974.

A principle in the Vienna Actionism movement, Günther Brus (1938–) reduces the body to its most basic functions; the German Rebecca Horn (1944–) expands it with prosthetic devices; and the Cyprus-born Stelarc (1946–) dreams of a post-biological body. These artists plumb the limits of the body, set free suppressed fears and repressed feelings, and overstep taboos, and the radical, asymbolic corporality of earlier body art raises actions to a legendary, mythic standing. Nevertheless, they were largely forgotten in the 1980s—a decade that favored painting—and were rediscovered in the 1990s.

Critical to their rise, as the body artists always emphasize, were the social and political events of the 1960s. More directly than other genres, body art transported the conflicts and attitudes of the civil rights and protest movements, sexual liberation, feminism, rock and pop culture, the explosion of mass media, and the atmosphere of disruption and violence. Noteworthy in this respect is the great number of women who took part, as well as the fact that body art, was for many artists, such as William Wegman, Dennis Oppenheim, Barry Le Va, Stuart Brisley, Keith Arnett, Valie Export, and Lucas Samaras, only one episode in their lifework.

Critic Willoughby Sharp coined the term "body works" in 1970. He saw in it a variation of conceptual art inasmuch as it followed a firm dramaturgy. European theorists such as Lea Vergine and François Pluchart, who had earlier worked in psychoanalytic interpretation, expanded Sharp's definition.

Body works exist in many variations: as performance and also in the form of photography, film, video, and text. In contrast to other artistic developments directed toward performance, these call for the participation of the public only in a limited way or not at all; to shut out distractions, many artists exclude the public altogether. This restricts the effect of their works; so, in general, to keep the works from falling into oblivion, artists have resorted to using reproductive technologies, which have become immensely important if not absolutely unavoidable as they are in the case of happenings, action art, and land art. Most artists engaging in body art have great appreciation for these art movements; the development and perfection of body art owes much to the possibility of recording and distributing ephemeral artistic experiments. Since the 1960s, recording equipment has become less and less expensive, enabling individual artists to purchase and use it.

Only by recording their works does their art become a product that they can exhibit and market. Instead of the "original," they show exhibits of photos, film stills, and video prints, which are offered to the art market. A famous example is the edition called "Eleven Color Photographs (1966–1967) of Bruce Nauman's, which included *Self-Portrait as a Fountain*. A very few artists with an especially rigid ethos decline to record their works, such as Ulay and (Marina) Abramovic in the early phase of their collaboration; they distrusted the truth of photography and considered marketing their art a commercial excess. This is why the black-and-white photo documentary of their collaborative performances *Relation in Space* (Venice Biennial, 1976) and *Expansion in Time* (Documenta 6, 1977) comes across as simplistic and blurry; only in the 1980s did they begin to allow photo editions of their work. These artists stand against recording was an exception.

To prevent posthumous distortions of his art, Chris Burden allowed his body works to be carefully photographed and, occasionally, filmed, and he controlled their publication. Documenting his start in the 1970s, he released plays in book format, *Chris Burden 71–73* (Los Angeles, 1974). Burden established a prototype for their presentation in which he meticulously communicates his intentions with a photograph and a description of the project. Despite their considerable length, his works can be captured visually in a single moment because they are created from a single situation. From his choice of photographs, Burden shows he has a thorough sense for aestheticizing and dramatizing his works. For *Through the Night Softly* (1973), he crawls fifty feet over broken glass before the eyes of a few passersby; in the photograph he released of the event, the little pieces of glass against a solid black background look like a shimmering starry sky. The photograph of *Doorway to Heaven* (1973) shows the artist with two tense electric wires around his chest, and a flash of electricity makes it look like he is encircled by a halo. Although his pieces are both simple and sensational, Burden became the darling of the mass media that always recognize star potential and report and broadcast the most controversial and risqué experiments. Artists understand just as well how to harness the power of the media for their own goals. For example, in the erotic environments she creates, Yayoi Kusama poses as a pin-up girl both in front of her camera and in front of the press and public, who are informed beforehand.

In explaining his body works, Vito Acconci claims that despite their simplicity, it is necessary to freeze the flow of time, which he does with video—Acconci is considered the founder of Life-Video-Performance—and with Super 8 film, in the same way as Bruce Nauman, Paul McCarthy, Rebecca Horn, and others who prefer video and film to the camera. The sequence of rather simple photographs from, for example, *Conversion II* (1971) is of secondary importance because the photos are taken in such rapid succession that they are difficult to tell apart; a complete, successful, and detailed collection of photographs must convey a precise impression whenever possible. Gina Pane engages in the same practice, though clearly in a more artistic way. Her action art, such as *Azione sentimentale* (1973), plays out in three phases. First she prepares every detail from sketches she has on hand. When she executes her performance, Pane becomes an active photographer and strictly follows her plans and the arrangements prepared in advance. The third part is the precise arrangement of the photographs into a tableau and their exhibition as an installation. The photographic recording and distribution serve Pane as the substance and results of her action art. This understanding of photography's role is shared by many, including Ana Mendieta, who has carefully recorded *Glass on Body* (1972) and *Silueta Series* (1980) in color photographs, and Dennis Oppenheim, who as a rule permits the public to view only recorded documentation of his performances. Among Oppenheim's color photographs is *Reading Position for a Second Degree Burn* (1970), in which he allows the sun to burn his skin except for an area of his chest shaded by a book. Hannah Wilke emphasizes photography in her work for different reasons—she practices body art as a staging of the self before the eye of the camera in, for example, *S. O.S. Starification Object Series* from 1974. *So Help Me Hannah* was from the beginning only a series of photographs that were taken and exhibited at P.S. 1, New York, in 1978. Only afterward did she create a performance out of it that she staged many times between 1979 and 1985. She continued her work until her death, including *Intra-Venus*, a series of photographs of cancer therapy taken by her lifelong partner, Donald Goddard.

The spectrum of photography within body art ranges in varying degrees of ability, from chance snapshots taken by the public and press to professional photography taken by the artist or from the artist's instructions. Among these are also carefully staged and arranged works with an expressive value independent of the performance.

Brigitte Hausmann

See also: **Export, Valie; Feminist Photography; History of Photography: 7: the 1980s; Namuth, Hans; Photography in Europe: Germany and Austria; Rainer, Arnulf; Wegman, William; Wiener Aktionismus**

Further Reading

Abramovic/Ulay: *Relation in Space*, 38. Biennale di Venezia, 1976, in Marina Abramovic, *Artist Body*, Milan: Charta, 1998.

What the Body Cost: Desire, History, and Performance.

L'Art au corps: Le Corps exposé de Man Ray à nos jours. Marseille: Musée d'Art Contemporain, 1996.

Blocker, Jane. *What the Body Cost: Desire, History, and Performance.* Minnesota: University of Minnesota Press, 2004.

Burden, Chris. *Doorway to Heaven.* November 15, 1973, in Paul Schimmel, *Out of Actions: Between Performance and the Object, 1949–1979.* Los Angeles: Museum of Contemporary Art, 1998, p. 96.

Fogle, Douglas, ed. *The Last Picture Show: Artists Using Photography, 1960–1982.* Minnesota: Walker Art Center, 2004.

Goldberg, RoseLee. *Performance: Live Art, 1909 to the Present.* London: Thames and Hudson, 1979.

Hors limites: L'Art et la vie, 1952–1994. Exh. cat. Paris: Centre Georges Pompidou, 1994.

Jones, Amelia. *Body Art/Performing the Subject.* Minneapolis: University of Minnesota Press, 1998.

Krull, Craig. *Action/Performance and the Photograph.* Los Angeles: Turner and Krull Galleries, 1993.

Loeffler, Carl, and Darlene Tong. *Performance Anthology.* San Francisco: Comtemporary Arts Press, 1980.

Pane, Gina. *Azione sentimentale*, 1973, in Valerio Dehò, *Gina Pane: Opere, 1968–1990*, Reggio Emilia: Chiostri di San Domenico, 1998–99, p. 47.

Phelan, Peggy. *Unmarked: The Politics of Performance.* New York and London: Routledge, 1993.
Photography & Performance. Exh. cat. Boston: Photography Resource Center, 1989.
Photography as Performance: Message through Object and Picture. Exh. cat. London: Photographer's Gallery, 1986.
Roth, Moira. *The Amazing Decade: Women and Performance Art in America, 1970–1980.* Los Angeles: Astro Artz, 1983.
Sayre, Henry. *The Object of Performance: The American Avant-Garde Since 1970.* Chicago: University of Chicago Press, 1989.
Schimmel, Paul. *Out of Actions: Between Performance and the Object, 1949–1979.* Los Angeles: Museum of Contemporary Art, 1998.
Schneider, Rebecca. *The Explicit Body in Performance.* New York and London: Routledge, 1997.
Schröder, Johannes Lothar. *Identität Überschreitung/Verwandlung. Happenings, Aktionen und Performances von bildenden Künstlern.* Münster: LIT, 1990.
Sharp, Willoughby. "Body Works," *Avalanche.* no. 1 (Fall 1970) 14–17.
Vergine, Lea. *Body Art and Performance: The Body as Language.* new ed. of *Il corpo come linguaggio: La Body-art e storie simili* (1974), Milan: Skira, 2000.
Wilke, Hannah. *S.O.S. Starification Object Series.* Copyright Estate of Hannah Wilke; New York: Ronald Feldman Fine Arts, 1974.

CHRISTIAN BOLTANSKI

French

Christian Boltanski is not, strictly speaking, a photographer. He frequently describes himself as a painter though he does not utilize pigment and canvas either. He is an artist who works with several mediums and utilizes photography—usually found images—by implementing them into his installation pieces and artists' books. He has remained thematically consistent throughout his career, as the subjects he returns to most often are childhood, absence, and death. His aim has always been to blur the division between art and life, and to touch his viewers on a personal level without being overtly didactic or sentimental.

The artist's biography is somewhat elusive, largely because much of his artwork has involved the propagation of false stories regarding his past. He was born in Paris just two weeks after the city's liberation in 1944. His mother was Catholic and his father was a Jewish-born doctor who converted to Catholicism at a young age. Despite his conversion, Boltanski's father had to feign disappearance during the occupation and hide in a narrow crawlspace in the family apartment. As a child Boltanski felt like an outsider among his peers, and at the age of 11 was allowed to leave school to be instructed by his parents and two older brothers. He did not return to school, and is self-taught as an artist.

The environment of postwar France has continuously influenced the tone and subject matter of Boltanski's work. He began developing his artistic practice in the late 1960s, a time of political and social upheaval culminating with the May 1968 student rebellions. His early projects bear a resemblance to the Arte Povera works in Italy made around the same time. Like many artists of his generation, Boltanski became interested in the dereification and dematerialization of the art object as a means of subverting the art market. Never pledging allegiance to any singular medium, Boltanski embraced a variety of techniques for his early pieces, including mail art, experimental film, ephemeral sculptures, and found objects.

He became particularly interested in creating fictional histories in the guise of autobiography, and told true and untrue stories about his own childhood using visual mediums. Yet the stories he related are not remarkable; he purposely emphasized the most banal possible events and objects in order to convey a sense of universal childhood that any viewer might be able to relate to. His earliest utilization of photography involved inventories of personal objects he associated with his childhood, from vacation snapshots to pictures of old toys. In a 1972 artist's book entitled *Ten Photographic Portraits of Christian Boltanski, 1946–1964*, the artist showed snapshots of 10 different people posed in the same location, arranged in order of age from 2 to 20 years. Each bears a caption identifying the figure as Christian Boltanski, but only the last image is a true portrait of the artist. Boltanski found photography to be particularly useful for these mythmaking projects, since viewers tend to have an automatic trust in the inherent veracity of photographic documents.

Boltanski subsequently became interested in inventing other people's stories, and began rephotographing found snapshots of strangers. In the 1971 project *Photo Album of the Family D., 1939–1964*, he attempted to reassemble such pictures into a linear narrative, knowing he would always fail, since photographs cannot reveal truth as we often expect them to. There is also a somber undertone to Boltanski's found photographs to the extent that they convey a sense of loss and absence. They are images that have been stripped of their original meanings by being separated from their original owners.

In the mid-1980s Boltanski created a series of works entitled *Monuments*, for which he recycled pictures of children's faces, usually re-photographed from school portraits and blown up into blurry, ghostlike visages. The images were installed in darkened rooms, in some instances placed over stacks of rusted tin biscuit boxes, and illuminated by electric bulbs placed around each picture. The effect is of a Catholic shrine with icons illuminated by candles. Though these installations are referred to as monuments, which suggests the commemoration of deceased individuals, it is not the loss of life being mourned but the loss of childhood and of memory. These pieces can also be interpreted as references to the Jews killed in the Holocaust—an event that often haunts Boltanski's installations without being directly invoked. Boltanski's preoccupation with the lost histories of anonymous figures continued in a project entitled *Reserve: The Dead Swiss*, for which he assembled photographs cut from the obituary pages of Swiss newspapers. He specifically chose to memorialize people from Switzerland because they lack a strong cultural or historical association; the neutrality of the Swiss nation thus lends itself to universality.

Crucial to Boltanski's artistic method is a perpetual recycling of images. He not only lifts photographs from mass media and photo albums into his own work, he also lifts images from his own past projects and inserts them into new ones. In 1987 Boltanski created an installation for Documenta 8 entitled *Archive*, which was essentially the sum total of all the portrait images he had ever used for previous projects. Such a practice underlines Boltanski's belief in the fluidity and ephemerality of materials, and disavowal of the notion of the eternal and unique art object.

Boltanski has also been consistently interested in problematizing the notions of good and evil, particularly in relationship to the events of World War II. He has frequently explored the idea that atrocities such as the Holocaust can be committed by anyone, and do not require a supernaturally diabolic impulse—a concept defined by Hannah Arendt as the banality of evil. In his 1995 installation *Menschlich (Humanity)*, Boltanski interspersed the images of Nazis and their victims across a gallery wall, not differentiating between the guilty and innocent. The following year he carried a similar idea into the installation *The Concessions*, which involves images of murderers and their victims projected onto curtains throughout the middle of the gallery. On the walls are hung several photographs of the victims' mutilated bodies, which are covered by curtains but periodically revealed when a fan placed in the room causes these coverings to levitate. Again, the artist does not identify which are criminals and which are victims.

Throughout his career Boltanski has maintained his devotion to impoverished materials, subordinating formal concerns in favor of story and process. He has held fast to the belief that the universality of his message depends on the commonness of his materials and means. He is married to artist-photographer Annette Messager and continues to live and work in Paris.

Shannon Wearing

Biography

Born in Paris, France, 6 September 1944. Artist in Residence, Deutscher Akademischer Austausdienst (D.A.A.D.), Berlin, Germany, 1975; Guest Artist, Harvard University, Cambridge, Massachusetts, 1981. Living in Paris.

Individual Exhibitions

1973 *Les Inventaires*; Staatliche Kunsthalle, Baden-Baden, Germany, and traveling
1978 *Arbeiten: 1968–1978*; Badischer Kunstverein, Karlsruhe, Germany
1979 Sonnabend Gallery; New York
1981 *Compositions*; A.R.C./Musée d'Art Moderne de la Ville de Paris, Paris, France
1984 *Boltanski*; Centre Georges Pompidou, Paris, France
1987 *Le Lycée Chases*; Kunstverein für Rheinland und Westfalen, Düsseldorf, Germany

1988 *Lessons of Darkness*; Museum of Contemporary Art, Chicago, Illinois, and traveling
1989 *Réserves: La Fête de Pourim*; Museum für Gegenwartskunst, Basel, Switzerland
1995 *Menschlich*; Kunsthalle Wien, Vienna, Austria
1996 *Les Concessions*; Galerie Yvon Lambert, Paris, France

Group Exhibitions

1976 *Identité/Identification*; CAPC/Centre d'arts plastiques contemporains, Bordeaux, France, and traveling
1977 Documenta 6; Museum Fridericianum, Kassel, Germany
1980 IXL Biennale di Venezia; Venice, Italy
1981 *Westkunst*; Museen der Stadt Köln, Cologne, Germany
1986 *Lumière: Perception-Projection*; CIAC/Centre international d'art contemporain, Montreal, Canada XLII Biennale di Venezia; Venice, Italy
1987 Documenta 8; Museum Fridericianum, Kassel, Germany
From the Europe of Old; Stedelijk Museum, Amsterdam, The Netherlands
1991 Carnegie International 1991; Carnegie Museum of Art, Pittsburgh, Pennsylvania
1993 XLV Biennale di Venezia; Venice, Italy
1995 *Take Me (I'm Yours)*; Serpentine Gallery, London, England XLVI Biennale di Venezia; Venice, Italy
1997 *Made in France*; Centre Georges Pompidou, Paris, France

Selected Works

Research and Presentation of Everything that Remains of my Childhood, 1944–1950, 1969
Photo Album of the Family D., 1939–1964, 1971

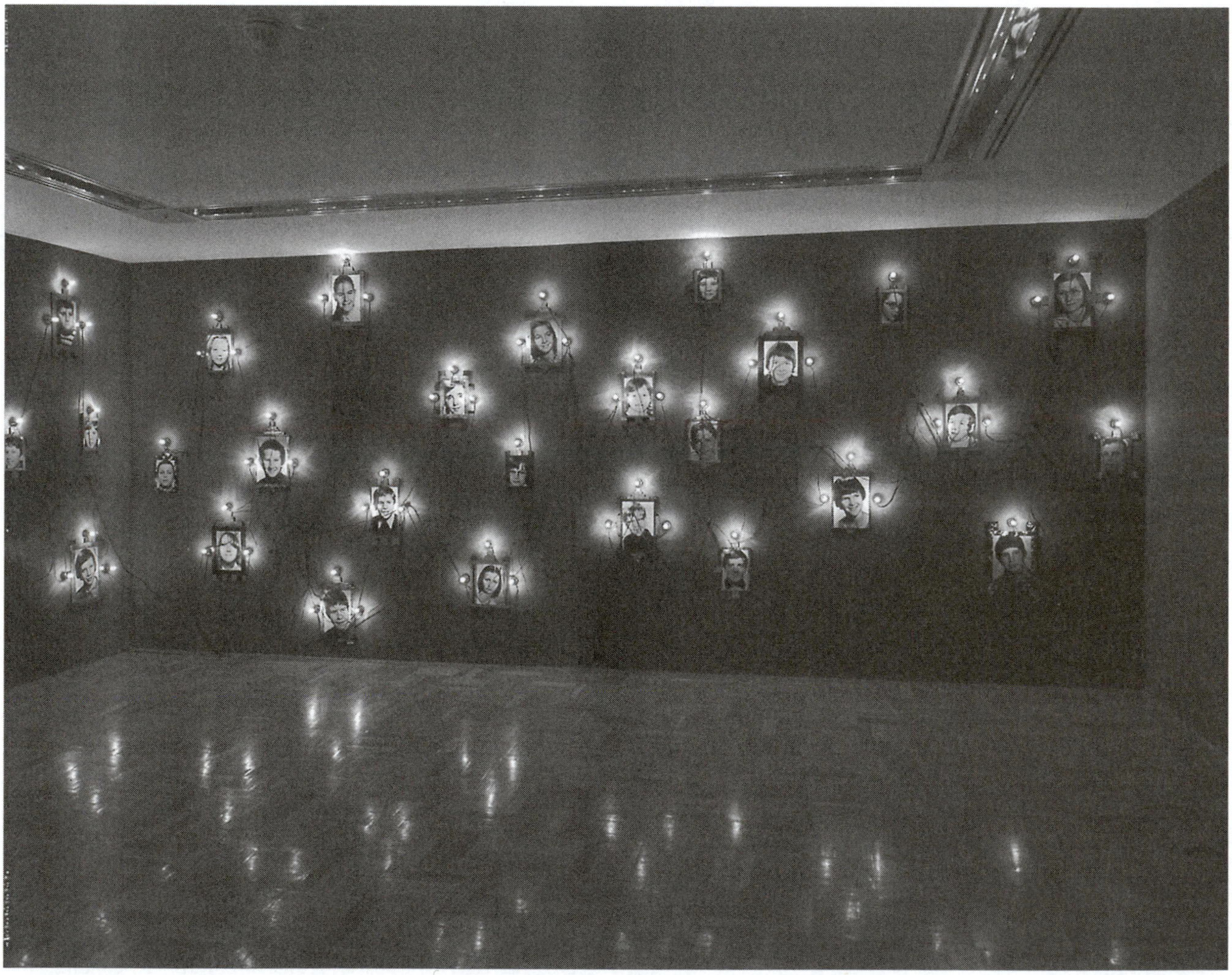

Christian Boltanski, Monument: Les enfants de Dijon (Monument: The Children of Dijon), 1985, Gelatin silver and chromogenic development prints, and light fixtures, Installed dimensions variable. Photographs: 11 × 9 ½″ to 15 ¾″ (27.9 × 24 cm to 40 × 50.2 cm), Collection Museum of Contemporary Art, Chicago, gift of the William J. Hokin Family. [*Photograph © Museum of Contemporary Art, Chicago*]

Ten Photographic Portraits of Christian Boltanski, 1946–1964, 1972
The 62 Members of the Mickey Mouse Club in 1955, 1972
Inventory of Objects that Belonged to a Resident of Oxford, 1973
Photographic Compositions, 1976
Monument: The Children of Dijon, 1985
Archives, 1987
Altar to the Chases High School, 1988
Reserve: The Dead Swiss, 1990
Menschlich (Humanity), 1995
Passion, 1996
The Concessions, 1996

Further Reading

DeRoo, Rebecca. "Christian Boltanski's Memory Images: Remaking French Museums in the Aftermath of '68." *Oxford Art Journal* v. 27 no. 2 (2004): 221–238.

Gumpert, Lynn, and Mary Jane Jacob. *Christian Boltanski: Lessons of Darkness*. Chicago: Museum of Contemporary Art, 1988.

Gumpert, Lynn. *Christian Boltanski*. Paris: Flammarion, 1994.

Marmer, Nancy. "Boltanski: The Uses of Contradiction." *Art in America* v.77 (October 1989): 168–81.

Semin, Didier, Tamar Garb, and Donald Kuspit. *Christian Boltanski*. London: Phaidon, 1997.

Solomon-Godeau, Abigail. "Mourning or Melancholia: Christian Boltanski's *Missing House*." *Oxford Art Journal* v. 21 no. 2 (1998): 1–20.

ROBERT BOURDEAU

Canadian

Since the late 1950s, Robert Bourdeau has been a bridge between modernists of the early twentieth century and contemporary photographers. Pursuing a goal more often associated with Pictorialism (making photographs that evoke timeless feelings in the beholder) with the visual language of modernist formalism, Bourdeau has created a body of work remarkable for its rigorous consistency, both of vision and of craft, and its lasting fascination and beauty.

Bourdeau was born in Kingston, Ontario on November 14, 1931. He lived there with his family until he went to the University of Toronto to study architecture in 1957. He had always been an avid snapshot-taker, but while he studied architecture, he discovered that the photographs he made of structures interested him more than the structures themselves. This would prove to be an enduring interest.

In 1958, Bourdeau left the University of Toronto. He returned to Kingston, and there he came across a back issue of *Aperture* magazine from 1955. The quality and vision of the magazine impressed him. He immediately wrote to then editor Minor White, who was in Rochester, New York, and asked to meet him and to see more issues of *Aperture*. White agreed, and their relationship actively continued in person, through letters and over photographs until 1968.

Bourdeau's correspondence with White, along with his relationship with Paul Strand, whom he met in New York in 1965, formed the backbone of his photographic practice. From White, Bourdeau took an approach to making photographs, what White, and Alfred Stieglitz before him, called "camera work." There is also the concept of the "feeling state," an emotional state reached while photographing.

Bourdeau relates an anecdote where Minor sent him to contemplate *Windowsill Daydreaming*—this was an often-repeated photo reading exercise. After an hour, Bourdeau returned and said, "Minor, now I know what love is all about." White used Bourdeau's quote under that image in his book *Mirrors, Messages, Manifestations*.

From Strand, Bourdeau gleaned an uncompromising commitment to print craft as well as a sense of humanity.

Bourdeau cites no other photographic influences. As his career progressed, he no longer actively engaged with the work of other photographers, in order to focus more clearly on his own vision. He did however find inspiration from a wide range of other artists such as Cézanne, Hopper, Beethoven, and Bach.

He first exhibited in a traveling group show at the National Film Board (now the Canadian Museum of Contemporary Photography) in Ottawa in 1966. In 1980, Bourdeau approached Jane Corkin, a fledgling photography dealer in Toronto, to represent him. As he recalls, Corkin's energy and intelligence immediately impressed him. Their relationship has lasted to this day, and has been instrumental in bringing Bourdeau's photographs to the attention of curators, writers and collectors, nationally and internationally. In 1985, with Corkin taking care of sales and promotion, Bourdeau was able to leave the job as an architectural technologist that he had had since 1960 and was free to devote himself entirely to photography.

During the summer months, Bourdeau travels and makes photographs—he prefers the light of long days—and during the winter, he prints and researches locations for the next summer's forays. He has photographed extensively in Canada and the United States, and in England, Sri Lanka, Ireland, Scotland, Mexico, Costa Rica, on the French-Spanish border, Germany, Luxembourg, and France.

Mary Bourdeau, his wife, an artist in her own right, always accompanies him to help with the equipment and provide a quiet working environment—Bourdeau refers to her as both quartermaster and chief grip—but also his companion. Bourdeau acknowledges that he could never have accomplished what he has without their artistic partnership.

Bourdeau does not set up his camera—an 8″ × 10″ format Kodak Master View he bought in New York for $150 in 1973 (before that he worked in 5″ × 7″ format)—until he has scouted the location and intuited its potential for a successful photograph. He determines the "station point," the point at which the visual, emotional, and spiritual come together and shoots about 40 images, which Bourdeau then wittles down to 15 or so final prints.

A Bourdeau photograph is unmistakable for its print quality—what writer David Livingstone has described as "soft greys, pearly whites and velvety black." Bourdeau has always gold-toned his prints for a subtle warmth and added intimacy, and for its composition, often a loss of scale and heightened texture. His 8″ × 10″ negatives are either contacted or enlarged only slightly: impeccable presentation.

For Bourdeau, the subject of his photographs often becomes secondary to his experience of photographing them, to the transcendence he seeks to achieve while photographing. "The subject itself becomes secondary to greater meanings—a universality, emotional and spatial ambiguities, and a sense of timelessness," he wrote in January 1994. The record of the subject is a by-product of the whole experience. Undeniably, however, there are certain sites Bourdeau has repeatedly sought out to find those transcendent experiences.

When Bourdeau began to photograph, the landscape was all-consuming and he photographed purely in the landscape for 15 to 20 years. In 1979, he traveled to Sri Lanka and Ireland, and began photographing Buddhist, Hindu, Christian, and pre-Christian structures in addition to the landscape, as well as the visual interplay between structure and landscape.

Bourdeau also makes still life photographs—he calls them small landscapes—for example, peaches on a densely floral tapestry, or a field of small white flowers, close-cropped, a tapestry in itself. He has also made many portraits that have never been exhibited.

In 1990, Bourdeau began the most important work of his career to date. He started to photograph abandoned and disused industrial sites—steel plants, coal mines, textile mills, quarries, "secular cathedrals" as he calls them—in Europe and North America, many of which have since been completely dismantled. Of this work he wrote, in July 1998:

> These industrial sites are places that possess a power in which I feel vulnerable, with a sense of ominous stillness and qualities that transcend the specificity of time. These are in a state of transition, transformation and possible transcendence where order and chaos are in perpetual altercation. I must emphasize that this is not a documentary but a photographic and inner quest.

These photographs carry clear threads from such photographers as Margaret Bourke-White, Charles Sheeler, and Germaine Krull. However, they eschew the monumentality and drama of these modernist images, just as they eschew the removed typology of the work of his contemporaries Bernd and Hilla Becher. Instead they carry what novelist Anne Michaels has called an "elegiac" quality. And in that sense, they are more akin to Berenice Abbott's *Changing New York* project, even though Bourdeau's intention is distinct from Abbott's—they are an homage to time passing, to place, and to love. Paradoxically, the *Industrial Sites* photographs are powerful both for their timelessness—an important concept for Bourdeau—but also for their timeliness.

Bourdeau has been the recipient of numerous Canada Council grants, and was elected to the Royal Canadian Academy of Arts (RCA) in 1983. Bourdeau taught photography at the University of

Ottawa from 1980 to 1994. In 1999, he was awarded the Advertising & Design Club of Canada Award for Still Life Photography.

Sophie Hackett

See also: **Abbott, Berenice; Becher, Bernd and Hilla; Bourke-White, Margaret; Krull, Germaine; Sheeler, Charles; Stieglitz, Alfred; Strand, Paul; White, Minor**

Biography

Born in Kingston, Ontario, November 14, 1931. Studied architecture at the University of Toronto in 1957–1958. Marries Mary Eardley in 1961; son Robbie born in 1962 and son Sean born in 1965. Began to photograph after meeting Minor White in Rochester in 1958; from 1958–1968 White becomes a significant influence through correspondence. Meets Paul Strand in New York in 1965. First exhibition in 1966 at National Film Board of Canada (now the Canadian Museum of Contemporary Photography). From 1960 to 1985, works as an architectural technologist. In 1980, Jane Corkin agrees to represent him. Teaches photography at the University of Ottawa from 1980–1994. Pursues photography full-time from 1985. National Gallery of Canada exhibits a retrospective in 1990, the same year he begins his breakthrough series *Industrial Sites*. Lives and works in Ottawa, Ontario.

Individual Exhibitions

1968 Smithsonian Institution, Washington, D.C.
1976 Yajima Gallery, Montreal, Canada
1977 Secession Gallery, Vancouver, Canada
1979 Agnes Etherington Art Centre, Kingston, Canada
1980 *Landscapes*; International Centre of Photography, New York, New York
1981 Jane Corkin Gallery, Toronto, Canada
1981 Art Gallery of Ontario, Toronto, Canada
1983 Galerie Zur Stockeregg, Zurich, Switzerland
1983 Jane Corkin Gallery, Toronto, Canada
1984 The Afterimage Gallery, Dallas, Texas
1985 *Landform & Architecture*; Jane Corkin Gallery, Toronto, Canada
1988 49th Parallel Gallery, New York, New York
1988 Vancouver Art Gallery, Vancouver, Canada
1988 Glenbow Museum, Calgary, Canada
1988 London Regional Gallery, London, Ontario
1988 Edmonton Art Gallery, Edmonton, Canada
1988 Winnipeg Art Gallery, Winnipeg, Canada
1989 Peter Whyte Gallery, Banff, Alberta
1989 Agnes Etherington Art Centre, Kingston, Canada
1990 Beaverbrook Museum, Fredericton, New Brunswick
1990 *Robert Bourdeau, A Retrospective*; National Gallery of Canada, Ottawa, Canada
1992 *Recent Work*; Jane Corkin Gallery, Toronto, Canada
1994 *From Light to Dark*; National Gallery of Canada, Ottawa, Canada
1994 *Recent Work*; Jane Corkin Gallery, Toronto, Canada
1997 *30 Years of Collecting Photographs*; National Gallery of Canada, Ottawa, Canada
1997 The Canadian Embassy, Tokyo, Japan
1997 Galerie Baudoin Lebon, Paris, France
1998 *Industrial Sites: Europe and United States*; Jane Corkin Gallery, Toronto, Canada
1999 *La surface du réel: images*; CIPRA, Briey-en-forêt, France
1999 *Industrial Sites*; Michael Hoppen Galley, London, England
2000 *Industrial Sites*; Edwynn Houk Gallery, New York, New York
2001 *Industrial Sites*; Forum Gallery, Los Angeles, California

Group Exhibitions

1970 *The Photograph as an Object*; Art Gallery of Ontario, Toronto, Canada
1983 *Perceptions*; The Gallery/Stratford, Stratford, Ontario, Canada
1986 *Masterpieces from the Gallery Collection*; Jane Corkin Gallery, Toronto, Canada
1986 *Contemporary Photography*; Watson Gallery, Houston, Texas
1987 *10 Ways of Looking at Landscapes*; Watson Gallery, Houston, Texas
1988-90 *The Meditated Image*; Glenbow Museum, Calgary, Canada
1990 *Is There Life in the Still Life or is Nature Morte?* Watson Gallery, Houston, Texas
1990 *The Landscape: Eight Canadian Photographers*; McMichael Canadian Art Collection, Kleinburg, Ontario, Canada
1990 *Money Matters: A Critical Look at Bank Architecture*; Museum of Fine Arts, Houston, Texas, and traveling
1990–1992 *Children in Photography*; Dalhousie Art Gallery, Halifax, Canada, and traveling
1991 *Four Canadians*; Vision Gallery, San Francisco, California
1993 *Magicians of Light*; National Gallery of Canada, Ottawa, Canada
1993 *Observing Traditions: Contemporary Photographs*; National Gallery of Canada, Ottawa, Canada
1993 *Flora Photographica: The Flower in Photography from 1835 to the Present*; Vancouver Art Gallery, Vancouver, Canada
1999 *Icons and Iconoclasts*; Jane Corkin Gallery, Toronto, Canada
2000 *Building Images: Architecture 1851 to the Present*; Jane Corkin Gallery, Toronto, Canada

Selected Works

Granite quarry, Vermont, 1995
Steel plant, Pennsylvania, 1996
Coal mine, Nord Pas-de-Calais, France, 1998
Steel plant, Luxembourg, 1998
Steel plant, Lorraine, France, 1999

Further Reading

Corkin, Jane, ed. *12 Canadians, Contemporary Canadian Photography*. Toronto: McClelland & Stuart, 1980.
Dault, Gary Michael. "Robert Bourdeau Makes a Photo." *Canadian Art* (Fall 1998).

Enright, Robert. "Getting the Inside Outside: An Interview with Robert Bourdeau."
Robert Bourdeau: Industrial Sites. Toronto: Jane Corkin Gallery. 1998.
Livingstone, David. "More than the Eye Can See." *Maclean's* (December 3, 1979).
Michaels, Anne. "The Station Point—The Photographs of Robert Bourdeau." *Border Crossings.* 1998.
Thomas, Ann. "An Inquiry Into the Aesthetics of Photography." *Arts Canada* (1974).
Thomas, Ann. "Robert Bourdeau: In Praise of the Lucid." *Arts Canada* (1977).
White, Minor. *Mirrors, Messages, Manifestations. Camera.* Switzerland, 1969.
"Memento Mori—Photographs by Robert Bourdeau." *Fortune* (May 29, 2000).
"Robert Bourdeau, Photographer of Transcendental Light." *PhotoLife Magazine* (1992).
"Robert Bourdeau: Industrial Sites." *Queen's Quarterly* 106/1 (Spring 1999).
Wise, Kelly, ed. *The Photographer's Choice.* Dansbury, NH: Addison, 1976.

MARGARET BOURKE-WHITE

American

Bourke-White's career reads as a sequence of milestones and she had a knack of being in the right place at the right time. She knew which genres and styles of photography would sell. She was a risk taker who, once her path of attack was strategized, would not be satisfied until she had attained her objectives. In many instances, these involved taking considerable risk in forcing her cameras and lighting equipment right into the midst of heavy industrial or military action. She herself was an invader in as much as she took pictures of private scenarios, often without asking permission and almost always rearranging the scene for dramatic effect. She was also cognizant of how manipulating her own image as a woman familiar with the inner workings of high executive circles could open doors. Publicity shots she had taken of herself at work—leaning over skyscraper parapets, taking a shot right in the middle of trafficked downtown streets, peering into industrial sites, surrounded by Russian crowds, all posed and costumed in the height of fashion—were arguably as effective as the shots she took in making her name a national byline by 1930 and a national buzzword by the early 1940s.

Bourke-White was a consummate, if not innovative, photographic communicator. Her pictures worked either the "dramatic angle, neutral background, luminous lighting... and subject...to create an idealized picture" or "the chaos of patterns... vibrat[ing] to disturb the viewer" (Puckett 1984, 33). She also excelled in pre-visualizing photos as components of stories. Raw materials—both human and nonhuman—were refined, processed, and ultimately transformed into marketable products.

In 1927 when Bourke-White, aged 23, established a commercial practice as an estate, industrial, and corporate photographer in Cleveland, she was already a skilled marketer and entrepreneur. Educated in public schools in New Jersey, she was encouraged by her parents in science and engineering but excelled in writing, drama, debating, and organizing student activities. She took a photography course at the Clarence H. White School of Photography during her freshman year at Columbia University, New York. After her father died and she was forced to fund her higher education, she freelanced during subsequent student years at the University of Ann Arbor, Michigan. As a senior at Cornell University, Ithica, New York in 1926–1927, she established a small business photographing the campus for the alumni newsletter and marketing prints through various sales outlets. Her competitive edge over John Troy, campus photographer, consisted in unusual angles of view; taking advantage of mood-inducing atmosphere and natural and artificial lighting; composing rhythmic shapes and patterns; and taking multiple exposures and views so as to ensure a marketable "hit." These would be the leitmotifs of her success throughout an adventurous, nonstop globe-trotting career that only Parkinson's disease could terminate. Equally key were the contacts she made with high-placed, influential administrators, professors, and graduates, which percolated into a working familiarity with the upper echelons of the corporate world.

Bourke-White's first major clients were the Otis Steel and Union Trust companies in Cleveland. In 1929 she became a charter and contributing editor of *Fortune* and in 1930 she moved to New York. This led to numerous national and international industrial assignments as well as to major corporate advertising commissions and to the beginning of her association with major publishers. Her corporate and industrial photographs of the late 1920s, followed by her industrial and commercial jobs of the early to mid-1930s, are the most self-consciously styled of her oeuvre, reflecting early twentieth-century corporate ideals and cultures of empire. In her sequence on Cleveland's new union station, the Terminal Tower (1927–1929), the building and its spire became the hub of numerous "imperial" views as she moved in from the distance up to the tower, framed it in massive viaduct arches, positioned it over "mountains of ore" (the title of one image), and geysered it over the curving sluices of parallel railway tracks. Close-up views of the grand lobby breathe heavy, dark, and jewel-like airs of material opulence and spatial grandiloquence. Likewise, in her work for Otis Steel, which the company published in a folio-styled brochure, she moved into and around the blast furnace and featured fiery, molten steel illuminating its vast, murky halls. This early work is indebted to Tonalism and language of pristine Pictorialism as practiced by Clarence White, Alfred Stieglitz, Alvin Langdon Coburn, and Frederick H. Evans. Modernism and Edward Steichen's hard-edged shapes, reflections, and shadows lie behind Bourke-White's NBC photomurals, executed in 1933 for the R.C.A. Building, Radio City, in Rockefeller Center, New York. *Skyscraper* of 1935, commissioned by American Catalin Corporation, and *Bottled Time*, a sequence of work for the Elgin National Watch Company published in *Fortune* in April 1930, exemplify this more abstract, direct-to-upscale-consumer approach.

The mid-1930s, capped by her move from *Fortune* to *Life*, were the time of Bourke-White's maturation as an artist. Not only did she show her work with other photographers of the American avant-garde, but she codified an avant-garde vocabulary of monumental form, high contrast and, most characteristically, closely conjoined, repeated objects, positioned close to the picture plane as freshly minted coinage from the proverbial assembly line. She came into prominence writing for and being written about in leading newspapers and magazines, as an artist, designer, and "trapper" of "the Waves of Sound" (*Vanity Fair* 1978, 26–27). Her credo exulted the glory of "industrial subjects, which are so powerful and sincere and close to the heart of life....because the industrial age which has created them is powerful and art...must hold the germ of that power." (Batchelor, May 10, 1930, MBW Papers). Her status as an independent artist was bolstered by her appropriation of the semantics of advertising and public relations–grandiose, over-achieving, hyperbolic, and massively appealing to the image managers of the American public.

It is widely believed that, due to a change of heart while photographing the Dust Bowl in 1934 for *Fortune*, Bourke-White gave up the glamorous world of advertising and devoted the rest of her career to the human-interest stories she illustrated in *Life* and delineated in her books. These began in the Depression-scourged South and hit their stride in the European theaters of World War II. This generalization is misleading. Although it is true that she did turn to people as her prime subjects and did not court corporate clients after1936, even while freelancing for *Life* from 1940 to 1951, she continued to do advertisements (*Industrial Rayon Corporation, Painesville, Ohio* and *Coiled Rods, Aluminum Company of America*, both 1939). Her work continued to adduce and promise an ideal "American way" predicated on the "world's highest standard of living." Quite possibly her most famous image from the 1930s, featuring a billboard with those exact slogans, is *Flood Victims, Louisville, Kentucky* (1937). The billboard itself was a component of a huge national publicity campaign mounted by the National Association of Manufacturers to stimulate consumption and promote industry. Its message aptly summarizes the message of the voluminous writings and photographs Bourke-White would produce over the next 25 years. Whether the image was military (*Waist Gunners, England*, 1942) or civilian (*Bridge Construction, New York Thruway*, 1954), the glorification of American-fabricated, consumable, and surplus power seared its way into viewers' eyes and minds.

Unlike many of her contemporaries in documentary photography, Bourke-White was not part of the federally funded Farm Security Agency photographic project led by Roy Stryker in the 1930s. Nor did she participate in the Standard Oil of New Jersey-sponsored photography archive amassed under Stryker's direction in the 1940s. These projects were extremely important stages in the evolution of documentary photography as it surveyed the successive landscapes of poverty, prosperity, and an emergent highway culture. This omission comes as some surprise as Bourke-White was the first twentieth-century photographer, after Lewis Hine, to be featured in the third, 1930 edition of *American Economic Life*, an important textbook co-authored by Stryker while he was associated with sociologist Rexford G. Tugwell at Columbia University. Stryker's projects were conceived and executed as sociological studies. They were carefully scripted, long-term experiences in living and picturing poverty. Bourke-White's approach elevated consumption, the individual, and the image of individuality. She not only accepted, but thrived on short deadlines. She vaunted her ability to capture the essence of a story in one or two visits, pre-visualizing it in the "day in the life" of a representative character. She worked for her publishers but continually wrote her own scripts. She was not a sociologist studying human habitats, but a publicist ripping gutsy pictures and good copy.

Bourke-White's strikingly memorable images come from her war and postwar assignments: *Nazi Bombing of Moscow*, 1941; *German Civilians Made to Face Their Nation's Crimes, Buchenwald*, 1945; and the famous *Mohandas Gandhi at His Spinning Wheel, Poona, India*, 1946, among others. However manipulated by her agents, editors, biographers, and herself, behind them reads a real story of nonstop danger and adventure where the photographer justifiably took center stage to get pictures no one else scooped. This story, enscripted in her autobiography, *Portrait of Myself* (1963), became Bourke-White's final milestone. She died in 1971.

Getaldine Wojno Kiefer

See also: **Coburn, Alvin Langdon; Evans, Frederick H.; History of Photography: Twentieth-Century Pioneers; Industrial Photography; Life; Modernism; Pictorialism; Steichen, Edward; Stieglitz, Alfred; White, Clarence**

Biography

Born in New York City, 14 June 1904. Attended Rutgers University, Newark, New Jersey, Columbia University (Clarence H. White School of Photography), New York, University of Michigan, Ann Arbor, Case Western Reserve University, Cleveland, Ohio, Cornell University, Ithaca, New York, 1921–1927. B.A., Cornell University, 1927. Teacher at Cleveland Museum of Natural History, 1925. Located first studio in Cleveland, 1927–1930. Published first photo series in *Trade Winds*, Union Trust Company, 1928. Published first photo portfolio in *Otis Steel, Pioneer*, Otis Steel Company, 1929. Hired by Henry Luce of *Fortune*, 1929. First photographer in that publication with byline, 1930. Moved studio to New York, 1930. Traveled to Germany and Russia, 1930, and again to Russia, 1931. Published *Eyes on Russia* and *USSR Photographs*, 1931 and 1934, respectively. Traveled to Brazil, 1936. Photographed premier cover for *Life* and became *Life* staffer, 1936. Published *You Have Seen Their Faces* with journalist Erskine Caldwell, 1937. Traveled to Spain and Czechoslovakia, 1938. Published *North of the Danube* with Caldwell, 1939. Traveled to England, Rumania, Turkey, Syria, Egypt, 1939–1940. Resigned from *Life*; worked for *PM*, 1940. Returned to *Life* as free-lancer, 1940. Published *Say, Is This the USA?* with Caldwell, 1941. Traveled to China and Soviet Union, 1941. Published *Shooting the Russian War*, 1942. Traveled to England and North Africa, 1942. Traveled to Italy, 1943–1944. Returned to Italy, 1944. Published *They Called It Purple Heart Valley*, 1944. Traveled with Patton's Third Army, 1945. Published *Dear Fatherland, Rest Quietly*, 1946. Traveled in India, photographed Gandhi just before he was assassinated, 1946–1948. Published *Halfway to Freedom*, 1949. Traveled to South Africa, 1949–1950. Resumed staffer appointment at *Life*, 1951. Assigned to Strategic Air Command, 1951. Traveled in Japan and Korea, 1952–1953. Published *A Report of the American Jesuits* with John La Farge, 1956. Published last story for *Life*, 1957. Published *Portrait of Myself*, 1963. Received honorary doctorate from Rutgers University, New Jersey, 1948. Honorary doctorate from University of Michigan, 1951. Retired from *Life*, 1969. Died in Darien, Connecticut, 27 August 1971.

Individual Exhibitions

1929 Little Gallery, Lindner's, Cleveland, Ohio
1931 *An Exhibition of Photographs by Margaret Bourke-White*; Cincinnati Art Museum, Cincinnati, Ohio
1972 *Margaret Bourke-White, Photojournalist*; Andrew Dickson White Museum of Art, Cornell University, Ithaca, New York
1976 *Margaret Bourke-White; The Cleveland Years, 1927–1930*: The New Gallery of Contemporary Art, Cleveland, Ohio
1978 *Margaret Bourke-White: The Deco Lens*; Joe and Emily Lowe Art Gallery, College of Visual and Performing Arts, Syracuse University, Syracuse, New York
1983 *The Humanitarian Vision*; Joe and Emily Lowe Art Gallery, School of Art, College of Visual and Performing Arts, Syracuse University, Syracuse, New York
1988 *Bourke-White*; International Center of Photography, New York, New York, and traveling
1994 *The Arthur Gray Collection: Margaret Bourke-White, Photographs, with an Exhibition of Works by Arthur Gray*; Rachel Davis Fine Arts, Shaker Heights, Ohio
1998 *Power and Paper: Margaret Bourke-White, Modernity, and the Documentary Mode*; Boston University Art Gallery, Boston, Massachusetts
2000 *Steel and Real Estate: Margaret Bourke-White and Corporate Culture in Cleveland, 1927–1929*; College of Wooster Art Museum, Wooster, Ohio
2003 *Margaret Bourke-White: The Photography of Design, 1927–1936*; The Phillips Collection, Washington, D.C.

Group Exhibitions

1928 *May Show*; Cleveland Museum of Art, Cleveland, Ohio
1929 *American Institute of Graphic Arts Sixth Annual Exhibit*; Cleveland Public Library, Cleveland, Ohio
1931 *Margaret Bourke-White, Ralph Steiner, Walker Evans: Photographs by Three Americans*; John Becker Gallery, New York, New York
1934 *Third Detroit Salon of Pictorial Photography*; Detroit, Michigan

1934 Group exhibition in conjunction with *Machine Art* traveling exhibition; The Cleveland Museum of Art, Cleveland, Ohio
1937 *Photography 1839–1937*; Museum of Modern Art, New York, New York
1937 Group exhibition sponsored by Museum of Modern Art; Musée du Jeu de Paume, Paris, France
1985 *A Collective Vision: Clarence H. White and His Students*; University Art Museum, California State University, Long Beach, California, and traveling
1995 *From Icon to Irony: German and American Industrial Photography*; Boston University Art Gallery, Boston, Massachusetts
1996 *Pictorialism into Modernism: The Clarence H. White School of Photography*; The Detroit Institute of Arts, Detroit, Michigan, and traveling

Selected Works

Terminal Tower, Cleveland (series), 1927–1929
Otis Steel Company, Cleveland (series), 1927–1928
Elgin National Watch Company (series), 1930
Chrysler Building, New York City (series), 1931
NBC Photomurals (series), 1933
Airplane for TWA, 1935
Skyscraper, 1935
Fort Peck Dam, 1936
Flood Victims, Louisville, Kentucky, 1937
Nazi Bombing of Moscow, 1941
Waist Gunners, England, 1942
German Civilians Made to Face Their Nation's Crimes, Buchenwald, 1945
Mohandas Gandhi at His Spinning Wheel, Poona, India, 1946
Bridge Construction, New York Thruway, 1954

Further Reading

Batchelor, E.A. "Personal and Confidential: Margaret Bourke-White." *Detroit Saturday Night*, May 10, 1930, MBW Papers.

Bourke-White, Margaret. *Portrait of Myself*. New York: Simon and Schuster, 1963.

Caldwell, Erskine, and Margaret Bourke-White. *You Have Seen Their Faces*. Foreword by Alan Trachtenberg. Athens, GA: University of Georgia Press, 1995.

Callahan, Sean. *Margaret Bourke-White, Photographer*. Boston, New York, Toronto, and London: Little, Brown and Company, 1998.

Callahan, Sean, ed. *The Photographs of Margaret Bourke-White*. New York: New York Graphic Society, 1972.

Dorfman, Elsa. "Elsa Dorfman Photography Reviews: part of http://elsa/photo.net.

Goldberg, Vicki. *Margaret Bourke-White: A Biography*. New York: Harper and Row, 1986.

Grundberg, Andy. "What Was Cubism's Impact?" *The New York Times* (December 13, 1981): D39.

Hurley, F. Jack. *Portrait of a Decade: Roy Stryker and the Development of Documentary Photography in the Thirties*. Baton Rouge: Louisiana State University Press, 1972.

Kozol, Wendy. *Life's America: Family and Nation in Postwar Photojournalism*. Philadelphia: Temple University Press, 1994.

Puckett, John Rogers. *Five Photo-Textual Documentaries from the Great Depression*. Ann Arbor: UMI Research Press, 1984.

Silverman, Jonathan. *For the World to See: The Life of Margaret Bourke-White*. New York: The Viking Press, 1983.

Tedlow, Richard S. *Keeping the Corporate Image; Public Relations and Business, 1900–1950*. Vol. 3 of *Industrial Development and the Social Fabric*. Ed. Glenn Porter. Greenwich, CT: JAI Press Inc., 1979.

Trachtenberg, Alan. *Reading American Photographs: Images as History, Mathew Brady to Walker Evans*. New York: Hill and Wang, 1989.

BRACKETING

Bracketing is a technique by which a photographer tries to ensure that he gets a correct (or desired) exposure for the conditions under which he is shooting. Using a camera's built-in light meter or a separate light meter, the photographer can meter the light around his subject and adjust his camera's shutter speed and aperture settings accordingly for a correct exposure. However, some variables can cause a light meter to recommend an incorrect exposure—for example, if the subject is surrounded by either a very light or a very dark background, or if there is a bright light somewhere in the frame of the shot. In these instances, a light meter will tend to average all present light and recommend a setting that will, in fact, either overexpose (resulting in an image that is too bright and does not have enough dark tones or shadows) or underexpose (resulting in an image that is too dark and does not have enough light tones or highlights) the subject. Both over-and underexposure result in film that has not recorded much discernable information, which will translate to prints or slides that lack detail in the highlights or the shadows. With bracketing, the photographer takes two or more additional shots: one or more slightly overexposed and one or more slightly underexposed. This way, he is more likely to have a correct exposure—with different settings and exposures. Even if the light meter has recommended an exposure that is slightly off, the photographer will have compensated for the possibility of incorrect metering by shooting the additional under- and overexposed shots. Bracketing is most commonly used by studio photographers or with views amenable to fixed equipment or conditions, which allow deliberate shooting; obviously any sort of action photography is not well served by this technique.

Bracketing with film cameras is done in one of two ways: either by adjusting the shutter speed or the lens aperture. Which method is used depends on what the photographer is shooting and what he hopes to accomplish with the image. If the photographer is concerned with maintaining a consistent depth of field, he should adjust the shutter speed when bracketing, rather than the lens aperture. On the other hand, if the photographer is concerned either with capturing or stopping motion, he should adjust the lens aperture rather than the shutter speed. Leaving the ISO consistent with all the shots, the photographer takes one exposure at the recommended settings, then re-sets either the aperture by closing it either one or one-half stop or the shutter speed by increasing it one increment, takes another exposure, and then re-adjusts the aperture by opening it to either one or one-half stop above the original light meter recommendation or the shutter speed by decreasing it one increment from the original recommendation and taking a third exposure. It is important that the under-and overexposed shots are calibrated in relation to the light meter's recommended "correct" exposure. After adjusting the aperture or shutter speed to underexpose a shot, the photographer should adjust the settings not in relation to where they are, but to where they were for the "correct" exposure.

Automatic bracketing is an option on some digital cameras, and if this setting is chosen, the camera will automatically adjust the aperture or shutter speed a pre-set degree above and below the "correct" setting so that the photographer can trip the shutter three times and will record three exposures with the three different settings. Often with digital cameras, the over- and underexposed bracketing exposures have to be taken within a limited time frame before the camera automatically re-sets to the "correct" exposure. With digital photograph manipulation software, a photographer can layer the exposures on top of one another and then use a tool such as an "erase" tool to uncover different exposures in areas of the image. With this type of manipulation, a photographer might be able to combine his preferred exposures of different areas of the image to create a composite image that was not attainable with one combination of aperture and shutter-speed settings.

If the photographer desires, a wider bracket can be achieved by taking more than one overexposed shot and more than one underexposed shot. Generally, it seems that with one overexposed shot and one underexposed shot, the photographer has sufficiently accounted for imperfections in the light metering and will be pleased with one of the three resulting images. Occasionally, even if the recommended setting proves to be correct, the photographer may prefer either the under-or overexposed image for aesthetic reasons.

In film photography, one disadvantage of bracketing is that when a photographer uses this technique, he expects that some of the exposures will be incorrect—so the photographer knowingly "wastes" film. With experience, photographers can become more sure of getting a correct exposure and can reserve bracketing for use only when unsure about an exposure, rather than for every shot. If a photographer wants to be assured that he will get a correct exposure, though, bracketing is a good way to make sure that even if the photographer's light meter is incorrect, he will still be able to get a good image from one of the shots in the bracket.

With digital photography, bracketing is often easier to incorporate into regular practice—since there is no film to waste, unless storage on disk (or other removable media) space is limited, photographers can bracket without reserve. And just as sometimes it is the "incorrect" exposure that gives photographers their best or favorite print or slide image, digital photographers should wait to delete images that they feel are incorrectly exposed until the files have been moved onto a computer. Whether a photographer chooses to manipulate images in a software program or simply choose the best image from those he shot, the ease with which digital media can be erased and re-used makes it easy for photographers to postpone editing decisions until later, rather than trying to edit at the same time that he is shooting.

Bracketing works well as insurance for the photographer. Even if an image can be re-shot, it is much easier to have a variety of exposures to choose from rather than having to rely on a light meter to give a correct reading every time. And if an image cannot be easily re-shot, then bracketing ensures that out of multiple exposures, it is almost guaranteed that one will be correct.

JENNY ALLRED REDMANN

See also: **Camera: An Overview; Camera: Digital; Digital Photography; Exposure; Film; Light Meter**

Further Reading

International Center for Photography: Encyclopedia of Photography. New York: Pound Press (Crown Publishers Inc.), 1984.

McDarrah, Gloria S., Fred W. McDarrah, and Timothy S. McDarrah. *The Photography Encyclopedia*. New York: Schirmer Books, 1999.

Pinkard, Bruce. *The Photographer's Dictionary*. London Associates: BT Badsford, 1982.

ANTON GIULIO BRAGAGLIA

Italian

Among early twentieth-century photographers, perhaps none rivaled Anton Giulio Bragaglia in the crusade—both practical and theoretical—to distinguish photography as an art form. The mystical and metaphysical predilections of Bragaglia's imagery—which Giovanni Lista has called "the first modern revolution in photography"—liberated photography from the rigid cast of a recording machine. Bragaglia's photographic innovations inspired an entire generation of Italian artists—Wanda Wultz and Tato, Ivo Pannaggi and Fortunato Depero among them—to adapt the medium of photography to the expanding contours of Futurist art and activism. On a wider scale, his experiments and expositions anticipated European avant-garde approaches to photography as a fine art in its own right, independent of painting or the cinema.

Born in Frosinone, Italy on February 11, 1890, Anton Giulio entered the seminary at the suggestion of his monsignor uncle, and studied there until 1910, developing a strong interest in literature and archaeology. Thereafter, he dedicated himself to photography with the intention of becoming a journalist, despite his father's opposition. Along with his brother Arturo (1893–1962), Anton Giulio began frequenting the Cines film studios for which his father served as the general manager and lawyer. After buying their first camera in the Campo dei Fiori in Rome, the brothers undertook various kinds of photographic experimentation, using a bedroom in their home as a makeshift studio and darkroom. During the first years of their collaboration (1911–1914), the two brothers signed their photographs with the shared epithet "Bragaglia." Anton Giulio seems to have composed and staged the images, while Arturo served as the technical force behind the pair. The Bragaglias appropriated the fundaments of E.J. Marey's chronophotographs to their own method of "vitalist" expression—a photography of movement that they would come to term *Fotodinamismo*. Of the two brothers, Anton Giulio was by far the more theoretically oriented artist, writing various theses, conducting conferences, and launching manifestos on the development of *Fotodinamismo*.

Late in 1912 the brothers met the Futurist ringleader F.T. Marinetti through the painter Giacomo Balla, and their *Fotodynamismo* was baptized an official branch of the Futurist avant-garde. As an interdisciplinary movement seeking to integrate new forms of art with modern life, Marinetti's Futurism initially embraced photography as an eminently modern vehicle of expression. Anton Giulio became increasingly involved in the Futurist fold, collaborating with painters and poets on numerous projects. The Futurist painter and musician Luigi Russolo, for example, served as Bragaglia's model in the now famous image *Il fumatore* (*The Smoker*) of 1913; sculptors and painters Balla, Umberto Boccioni, Luciano Folgore, and Francesco Pratella would all pose for *fotodinamiche* (*photodynamics*) as well. There also became a certain reciprocity between the Bragaglias' photographic experiments and the early paintings of Balla, and the mutual influences of these works are difficult to sort out. Bragaglia's *The Typist* (1912) or *The Slap* (1913), for example, share much with Balla's paintings of protracted movement, most notably *Dog on a Leash* (1912) and *Girl Running on a Balcony* (1912), revealing a common inspiration in the chronophotographic image.

Yet Anton Giulio actively and emphatically distinguished his *Fotodinamismo* from photography *per se*. Their only affinity, he claimed, was in the shared use of the camera. Despite his obvious and far-reaching debts to Marey, Bragaglia disavowed influence by the French photographer in an attempt to disassociate his images from the technical, mechanical reputation of photography. In his essay *Fotodinamismo futurista* (1911), first published in the Florentine journal *Lacerba* in July 1913, Bragaglia criticized Marey's chronophotography for coldly fragmenting movement rather than "synthesizing" it. For Bragaglia, Marey's positivist experimentations failed to transcend the realm of science; only the rhythmic flux of *Fotodinamismo* could make photography over into an art form. *Fotodinamismo*, Bragaglia argued, transfigured the visual world by deforming it, refracting it—thus creating a new, artistic image that captured something beyond the physical, material world.

"We despise the precise, mechanical, and glacial reproduction of reality," he wrote. "For us this is a negative element, whereas for cinematography and chronophotography it is the very essence." *Fotodinamismo*, he argued, proffered not a dissection of physical and temporal units, but a synthetic flow of sensation turned inside out: "A shout, a tragic pause, a gesture of terror, the entire scene...can be expressed in one single work," declared an ebullient Bragaglia. (Bragaglia 1970, 39).

Like much Futurist discourse, Bragaglia's writings and images vacillate between, on the one hand, a drive to represent movement and action, and on the other, a turning away from external appearances, to "seek the interior essence of things." Mere photography—whether cinematic or chronophotographic or simply descriptive—failed to evince the lyrical and emotive aspects of visual experience. In short, they did not sufficiently "dynamize" (to use a Futurist watchword) the subject.

In this regard, Bragaglia was profoundly influenced, as were many of his contemporaries in Italy and abroad, by the metaphysical theories of the French philosopher Henri Bergson. Bergson's concepts lent to art a renewed purpose of penetrating beyond the material world, beyond quantitative measurements or descriptions. Bergson's championing of intuition over rationalized thought clearly influenced Bragaglia's approach to the photographic image.

> "We are not interested in the precise reconstruction of movement, which has already been broken up and analyzed. We are involved only in the area of movement which produces sensation, the memory of which still palpitates in our awareness."
>
> (Bragaglia 1970, 38)

Fotodinamismo thus willfully incurred dissolution, dematerialization, and interpenetration. The nimbus-like trails of light clinging to Bragaglia's subjects, as in the image *Change of Position* (1911), are meant as signifiers of memory still "palpitating." By flooding their subjects with light and overexposing the photographic plate, the Bragaglia brothers hoped to record not motion, but the psychic and emotional energy underlying it. The spiritual pretensions of *Fotodinamismo* also derived in part from other trends circulating in contemporary art and literature, such as Theosophy and mysticism, and the rarefied geometries of the "fourth dimension." Anton Giulio himself subscribed to various occultist and mediumist theories, and believed that *Fotodinamismo* could reveal invisible and spectral qualities that lurked within matter.

Notwithstanding Bragaglia's invectives against positivism and the "precise reproduction of reality," his own images were, in turn, subjected to a very similar criticism from within Futurist ranks. The eminent Futurist artist and theoretician Umberto Boccioni came to disparage Bragaglia's work, claiming that photography could not be an art form, much less a Futurist one. Boccioni viewed Bragaglia's *photodynamics* as prosaic, cinematographic inventories of movement, for all their pretensions to a poetic rendering of dynamic synthesis. Six Futurist artists published a statement disavowing any affinities between *Fotodinamismo* and Futurist "plastic dynamism." Under pressure from the importunate Boccioni, Marinetti withdrew his support of the Bragaglia brothers towards the middle of 1913. Such polemics not only reveal the nuances of what is often perceived as a monolithic Futurist movement, but also mark a significant chapter in the contentious history of photography as art.

In 1914, Anton Giulio temporarily abandoned photography for experimental novels, but soon collaborated again with Arturo, this time publishing a (notably un-Futurist) study of Roman ruins entitled *Nuova archaeologia romana* (1915). The following year, Bragaglia created his own film company and shot three full-length films. His film *Thaïs* (1916), one of the few Futurist films ever produced and the only Futurist film extant today, featured elaborate, abstract sets by the artist Enrico Prampolini. Despite the originality of Prampolini's sets and Bragaglia's compositions, the film shared little with the theories of *Fotodinamismo* or Futurism. Anton Giulio's exclusive engagement with the cinema was short-lived, in any case.

The trajectory of his career reveals the prominence of photography not only as an aesthetic end in its own right, but also as a supplement to and document of avant-garde performance and experimentation. After founding the Casa d'Arte Bragaglia in Rome in 1918, as well as his own theater company in 1922, Anton Giulio dedicated himself to exhibition promotion, set design, theater production, and continued photographic experiments with *Fotodinamismo*. A tireless writer, he wrote numerous theoretical tracts on the theater and photography throughout the 1920s and 1930s, while participating in many collective exhibitions of Futurist photography. Bragaglia died in Rome in 1960.

Ara H. Merjian

See also: **Futurism; History of Photography: Twentieth-Century Pioneers; Image Theory: Ideology**

Biography

Born in Frosinone, Italy, 11 February 1890. Published the essay *Fotodinamismo futurista* (originally written 1911) on 1 July 1913; published an early book of Futurist photographs, June 1913; published *Nuova Archeologia romana* with Arturo, 1915; founded his own film company, La Novissima, and directed the films *Thaïs*, *Il perfido incanto* (*Wicked Enchantment*), and *Il mio cadavere* (*My Corpse*), and *Dramma in Olimpo* (*Drama in Olympus*), 1916; founded the Casa d'Arte Bragaglia in Rome, 1918; founded the Teatro degli Independenti in Rome, 1922, which he directed until 1936; directed the Teatro delle Arti in Rome until 1943. Died in Rome, 15 July 1960.

Group Exhibitions

1918 *Fotoritratti d'arte*; Casa d'Arte Bragaglia, Rome, Italy
1923 *Prima Esposizione Internazionale di Fotografia, Ottica, e Cinematografia*; Turin, Italy
1925 *Primo Salon Italiano d'Arte Fotografica Internazionale*; Turin, Italy
1928 *Esposizione di Scenografia Cinematografica*; Casa d'Arte Bragaglia, Rome, Italy
1930 *Primo Concorso Fotografico Nazionale di Roma*; Rome, Italy
1931 *Mostra Sperimentale di Fotografia Futurista*; Turin, Italy
1931 *Prima Mostra Fotografica Internazionale*; Milan, Italy
1932 *Mostra Fotografica Futurista di Trieste*; Trieste, Italy
1932 *Prima Biennale Internazionale d'Arte Fotografica*; Rome, Italy
1933 *Sezione Fotografica della Grande Mostra Nazionale Futurista di Roma*; Rome, Italy
1932 *Prima Grande Mostra Nazionale Futurista*; Rome, Italy
1981 *Photographie Futuriste Italienne*; Musée de la Ville, Paris, France
1984 *Fotografia Futurista Italiana*; Museo de Bellas Artes, Bilbao, Spain
1984 *Futurism and Photography*; Hillwood Art Gallery, Long Island University, New York
1985 *I Futuristi e la fotografia: creazione fotografica immagine quotidiana*; Museo Civico d'Arte Contemporanea
2001 *Futurism and Photography*; Estorick Collection of Modern Italian Art, London, England

Selected Works

The Greeting, 1911
The Slap, 1912
The Violincello Player, 1913
The Smoker, 1913
Carpenter Sawing, 1913
Self-portrait, 1913
A Step Forward, 1928
Polyphysiognomic portrait, 1930
Self-caricature, 1932

Further Reading

Bragaglia, Anton Giulio. "Futurist Photodynamism." In *Futurist Manifestos* Umberto Apollonio, ed. New York: The Viking Press, 1970.
Bragaglia, Anton Giulio. *Fotodinamismo Futurista*. Turin: Enaudi, 1970.
Bragaglia, Arturo. "La Fotografia Futurista." *Futurismo* I, no. 7 (23 October 1932).
Celant, Germano. "Futurism and the Occult." *Artforum* no. 5 (January 1981).
Hulten, Pontus, ed. *Futurismo & Futurismi*. Milan: Bompiani, 1986.
Lista, Giovanni. *Futurism and Photography*. London: Merrell Publishers Ltd., 2001.
Lista, Giovanni. "Cinema Futurista." In *A nuova luce: cinema muto italiano*. Bologna: Edizioni Clueb, 2000.
Lista, Giovanni. *Fotografia Futurista Italiana*. Bilbao, Spain: Museo de Bellas Artes de Bilbao, 1984.
Scharf, Aaron. "Marey and Chronophotography." and "A Note on Photography and Futurism." *Artforum* vol. xv, no. 1 (January 1976).
Scimé, Giuliana, ed. *Il laboratorio dei Bragaglia 1911/1932*. Ravenna: Editoriale Essegi, 1986.

BILL BRANDT

British

Often characterized as England's most British photographer, Bill Brandt was in fact born in Hamburg, Germany. He moved to London in 1931, at the age of 27. The fact of his true country of origin and Brandt's own habit of presenting himself as British born, however, cannot obscure his role in the history of British photography. During his long career he produced important work in the genres of social documentary, landscape, the nude, and portrait photography. Brandt committed to England and English society in a profound way, documenting its imposing class structure and the physical landscape as well as making portraits of many of the luminaries of the British arts and letters. His many photography books were noteworthy for the ways in which he contrasted wealth and poverty as well as how he depicted reality mixed with a surrealistic edge.

While he pursued numerous subjects throughout his career, Brandt tended to follow one genre for an extended period before moving on to the next. He first became known as a social documentary photographer in the 1930s. This is when he first published his evocative scenes of both the struggling working class and their privileged counterparts in Edwardian society. Brandt's documentary work coincided with the rise of the picture press in England and consequently, his early photographic series became synonymous with the extremes of British life between the wars. This work was striking for its dark grittiness, a mood that reflected both the political atmosphere and England's economic depression at the time.

After World War II Brandt turned away from reportage. During the second half of his career his photographs were characterized more and more by mystery, experimentation, and a brooding quality that reinvigorated some of photography's oldest and most common genres; landscape, portraiture, and the nude. By the late 1970s Brandt had long been recognized as one of the masters of modern photography. While his work from earlier decades is included in major collections of photography around the world, his last body of work consisting of color photographs of still life's and three-dimensional box-like constructions was little seen or understood. While Brandt explored many genres and processes throughout his life, it is the work of the post-WWII period for which he is best known.

Beginning in the 1930s and continuing through the 1960s Brandt created a distinct photographic language based on dramatic composition, stark lighting, and shadows. The empathy for his working class subjects often found in his social documentary work was slowly replaced by a haunting surrealism and a probing focus on the individual in both his nudes and his portraits of English writers and artists. In addition to having his work published in periodicals like *Picture Post*, *Lilliput*, and in both the British and American editions of *Harper's Bazaar*, Brandt also published his work in photography books. These publications, which include *A Night in London* (1938), *Camera in London* (1948), and *Literary Britain* (1951), and finally *Perspective of Nudes* (1961), are among the most influential photo books of the modern period. Brandt's published works, often focusing on the social interactions of upper and lower classes, reveal powerful narratives, created through the deliberate sequencing and placement of the images throughout each book. Brandt was often cited as an early influence of Robert Frank, whose own book, *The Americans* (1955) became a turning point in American social documentary photography.

Brandt's early childhood was spent in Europe and his early career as a photographer was shaped in large part by his time in Paris, where he was surrounded by the artistic avant-garde, including Man Ray, Brassaï, Eugène Atget, and the work of the Surrealists. Moving permanently to Britain in 1931, the spirit of that country became an important theme.

During World War II Brandt began a series depicting London at night, a series of images that perfectly captured both the eerie beauty of the city and the anxiety that gripped its inhabitants. While the city was under siege, the city's first defense was to extinguish all streetlights, creating an environment that had not existed since the introduction of the gas lamps of the previous century. "The glamorous make-up of the world's largest city faded with the lights," Brandt wrote in *Camera In London* (1948).

Though the city may have lost its shimmering glitter, the shadowy urban nights that he photographed had a graphic allure similar to that of Brassaï's Paris. Brassaï and André Kertész were both early influences on the photographs in both *Camera in London* and *A Night In London* (1938). Work from the latter bears a striking similarity to Brassaï's *Paris de Nuit* (1932). Another assignment during the war, commissioned by the Ministry of Information in 1940, produced one of Brandt's most memorable picture stories; people huddling in improvised bomb shelters in locations throughout the city. At night Brandt visited tube shelters, church crypts, and cellars and photographed these overcrowded spaces with artificial light. The impact of the series owes virtually as much to the strong contrast of light and dark as it does to the difficult subject matter of displaced, fearful families huddled in cold, uncomfortable spaces. Seen together, Brandt's photography during this period records the extremes of life during the war years while simultaneously displaying the innovations in night photography.

The 1940s also saw Brandt turn to portrait commissions as another source of income. He published portraits of poets, writers, painters, and film directors for the next 40 years. In 1941 *Lilliput* magazine published a series of eight portraits that revealed his distinctive approach to this traditional photographic genre. While his portraits captured single subjects usually in their homes, Brandt's vision often turned typical sitting rooms and libraries into strange environments. He avoided isolating the sitter's face or focusing on her or his expression. Still he was able to consistently reveal the intensity of the sitter's character by the juxtaposition of sitter and environment. Subjects such as the painter Francis Bacon and the writer Martin Amis appear lost in their private realities.

While his early documentary works expand the notion of documentary photography as a tool for social change, Brandt's later work reveals his powerful formal inventions. As he branched out from reportage, Brandt began to explore the technical side of the medium and found darkroom work to be more interesting than the act of pressing the shutter. Near the end of World War II Brandt dedicated himself to photographing the female nude. Inspired perhaps by the distorted nudes created by Surrealist photographers via reflections in various materials, Brandt experimented with distorting the female form, the image he produced, however, taking on a disturbing, psychological edge. Posed individually, either in stark English townhouse interiors or on the rocky British coastline, these nude studies stand in sharp contrast to the elegant views of the British aristocracy and the humble tableaux of grimy coal mines of his earlier works. While seemingly grounded in the reality of a figure in a naturalistic setting, these are among Brandt's most surreal images, and can be said to be the photographic equivalent of British artist Henry Moore's abstracted figure sculptures.

Brandt considered the nudes to be the major artistic statement of his photographic career and he continued to focus on it for almost three decades. Unlike virtually all other photographers who employed distortion techniques to highlight the sensual or erotic in their nudes, Brandt seemed interested in avoiding any hint of eroticism. Brandt later noted that the Orson Wells's film *Citizen Kane* deeply influenced the look of these photographs, and it is clear that this cinematic vision is further enhanced by Brandt's use of a wide-angle lens with a fixed focus and no shutter. By using this antiquated equipment he was able to produce images where the human form was wildly distorted and viewed in unrealistically deep perspective. While depicting the female nude, even in distorted forms was not new in visual art, Brandt's extreme formalism was striking and the results were images in which the sexual availability of the sitter was completely erased. In contrast to his earlier work, where the viewer is made to feel like an invisible observer of the photographed scene, the women in Brandt's later work often look directly at the camera meeting the viewer's gaze.

In the 1970s and 1980s, following the nudes, Brandt began to explore entirely new processes. After working for nearly 50 years in traditional black and white photography he began creating three-dimensional collages using rocks and debris found on the beach, and started photographing in color. This late work was personal and experimental. Initially this work seemed to have little apparent relation to his earlier photographic interests, resembling garish, deserted dreamscapes. This abstract work, however, drew heavily on his lifelong interest in Surrealism and points to the early influence of Man Ray's work in the 1920s. Although the collages and color photographs were exhibited in London in the mid 1970s and again 10 years after Brandt's death in 1992, they were never fully embraced by either critics or the public and are seldom included in retrospectives of his work. Brandt's stature as a giant of British and indeed international postwar photography, however, is assured.

LISA HENRY

See also: **Brassaï; Documentary Photography; History of Photography: Interwar Years; History of Photography: Postwar Era; Kertész, André; Man Ray; Nude Photography; Portraiture; Surrealism**

Biography

Born in Hamburg, Germany in 1904. Moved to London in 1931. Died in 1992.

Individual Exhibitions

1938 *London By Night*; Galerie Chasseur d'Images, Paris, France
1948 Museum of Modern Art, New York, New York
1963 George Eastman House, Rochester, New York
1969 Museum of Modern Art, New York, New York, and The Hayward Gallery, London, England, and traveling
1974 The Kinsman Morrison Gallery, London, England
1976 Marlborough Fine Art, London, England Marlborough Gallery, New York, New York
1979 *Perspective of Nudes*; Zeit Foto Salon, Tokyo, Japan Galerie Pule Pia, Antwerp, Belgium
1981 *Retrospective*; Royal Photographic Society, National Center of Photography, Bath, England
Early Photographs; University of Kent Library, Kent, England, and traveling
1982 *Photographs by Bill Brandt 1929–1975*; Art Gallery of Ontario, Ontario, Canada
Bill Brandt: Portraits 1982; The National Portrait Gallery, London, England
1983 *Retrospective*; International Center of Photography, New York, New York
London by Night; The Photographers' Gallery, London, England
1984 De Beyerd Center, Breda, The Netherlands
Philadelphia Museum of Art, Philadelphia, Pennsylvania
Literary Britain; Victoria and Albert Museum, London, England
1986 *Behind The Camera*; Aperture's Burden Gallery, New York. New York
1994 *Retrospective*; Barbican Art Gallery, London, England Centre nationale de la photographie, Paris, France
1999–2000 *Retrospective*; International Center of Photography, New York, New York
2001 *Brandt: Seen & Unseen*; Edwynn Houk Gallery, New York, New York
Retrospective; Museum of Photographic Arts, San Diego, California
Toppers & Cloth Caps; The Special Photographers Gallery, Notting Hill Gate, London, England
2002 *Retrospective*; Monash Galleries, Melbourne, Australia, and National Portrait Gallery, Canberra, Australia
2002–2003 *Bill Brandt: A Retrospective*; Milwaukee Art Museum, Milwaukee, Wisconsin, and Yale Center for British Art, New Haven, Connecticut
2004 *Bill Brandt: A Centenary Retrospective*; Victoria and Albert Museum, London, England

Further Reading

Brandt, Bill. *The English at Home*. Introduction by Raymond Mortimer. London: Batsford, 1936.
———. A Night in London. Paris: Arts et métiers Graphiques; and New York: Charles Scribner's Sons, 1938.
———. *Literary Britain*. Hurtwood Press, 1984.
———. *Perspective of Nudes*. Preface by Lawrence Durrell. Introduction by Chapman Mortimer. London: Bodley Head, 1961.
———. *Bill Brandt: Nudes 1945–1980*. Introduction by Michael Hiley. New York: The New York Graphic Society/Little Brown and Company, 1980.
———. *Photographs, by Bill Brandt*. Introduction by Mark Haworth-Booth. Washington, DC: International Exhibitions Foundation, 1980.
———. *Behind the Camera: Photographs by Bill Brandt*. Mark Haworth-Booth. New York: Aperture, 1985.
Brandt, Bill. *London in the Thirties*. Menston, England: Scolar Press, 1998.
Brandt, Bill, and Mark Haworth-Booth. *The Land: Twentieth Century Landscape Photographs*. Cambridge, MA: Da Capo Press, 1976.
Delany, Paul. *Bill Brandt: A Biography*. Jonathan Cape, 2004.
Jay, Bill. *Bill Brandt: Portraits*. New York: Harry N. Abrams, 1999.
Jay, Bill, and Nigel Warburton. *Brandt: The Photography of Bill Brandt*. London: Thames and Hudson, 1999.
Jeffrey, Ian. *Bill Brandt: Photographs, 1928–1983*. London: Thames and Hudson, 1994.
Ross, Alan. *Portraits (Photography and Film)*. London: Herbert Press, 1990.

BRASSAÏ

Hungarian-French

Brassaï's obsession with the diverse character of social relationships, urban spaces, and the objects and events that often go unnoticed in everyday experience prompted expatriate American novelist Henry Miller to nickname him "The Eye of Paris." Brassaï pursued a style of immediacy and intimacy to bridge the distances between subject matter, artist, and viewer. His landscapes of nighttime monuments and deserted streets and his portraits of both the unknown as well as the most famous artists and writers in mid-century Paris demonstrate photography's ability to bracket references to reality for heightened awareness and interpretation. Brassaï often repeated that his "ambition was always to see an aspect of everyday life as if discovering it for the first time." While best known as a photographer, Brassaï was also a writer and accomplished in drawing, painting, and sculpture.

Brassaï was born Gyula Halász in Brassó, Transylvania, then a part of Hungary. The pseudonym means "a native of Brassó." In 1903–1904, Brassaï's father, a professor of French literature, brought his family to live with him in Paris while he was conducting research at the Sorbonne, and at a young age, Brassaï developed a love of Paris that would remain throughout his life. Brassaï served in the Austro-Hungarian cavalry in World War I and afterwards briefly attended the Academy of Fine Arts in Budapest. In December 1920, after Transylvania became part of Romania under Soviet influence, Brassaï fled to Berlin and began a career as a journalist for Hungarian-language newspapers and magazines. In part to avoid being drafted into the Romanian Army, Brassaï attended the Akademishce Hochschule where he cultivated the image of a rebellious bohemian. In Berlin, Brassaï developed a close friendship with Lajos Tihanyi, a prominent Hungarian painter; met László Moholy-Nagy and modern painters Oskar Kokoschka and Wassily Kandinsky; and read Goethe, whose appreciation of commonplace objects and events would inspire Brassaï's emphasis on seemingly direct depictions of people and places. With runaway inflation in Germany, Brassaï returned to Brassó in late spring 1922 for what would be his last visit to his birthplace.

He arrived in Paris in early 1924 and wandered through the city, being fascinated with the details of the built environment and the lives of the city's inhabitants. Writing for publications in Germany, France, the Netherlands, Great Britain, and the United States, Brassaï first began signing his articles "Gyula Brassaï" to separate the opinion and trivial topics of his journalism from more artistic literary and visual works for which he planned to use the family name "Halász," but by the 1930s, he began to use "Brassaï" exclusively.

Initially disparaging photography as illustration, Brassaï only began collecting old photographs and postcards in 1924, and he did not begin to take his own photographs until the end of 1929 when he could afford to buy a camera, a Voigtländer, and then a Rolleiflex in 1935. With his own photography, Brassaï began to recognize the potential of the medium for detailed observation. Exploring Paris at night, Brassaï focused his attention and his camera on deserted areas, buildings, and monuments and on human interactions at all levels of society from the bourgeoisie to prostitutes, ruffians, and the poor on the fringes of society. In late 1932, this material was published as *Paris after Dark*, with written text by Paul Morand. Offers for exhibitions and magazine assignments followed, and Carmel Snow and Alexey Brodovitch, editors of *Harper's Bazaar*, hired Brassaï to begin a more than twenty-year relationship with the magazine. Working at a time of great popularity for illustrated magazines, Brassaï produced photographs for substantial weekly publications, Surrealist and post-Surrealist journals, fashion magazines, and detective and sexually evocative "*magazines legers*," which were important sources of income for many period photographers and for the promotion of modern photography.

Not until 1976 did Brassaï publish *The Secret Paris of the 30s*. This series explored a range of licit and illicit locations of entertainment and pleasure, ranging from high society to fringe establishments, such as opium parlors, bordellos, and homosexual bars. Combining artistic and documentary interest, though often appearing to be candid journalistic press photography, Brassaï's photographs were made with his subjects' agreement that they would be photographed but without knowledge of when. He conducted research to anticipate action and bought drinks for and gave payment to some of his subjects. Brassaï's interest was not that his images be true but that they be convincing. He did not invent but observed, selected, and developed his ideas. Considering literal translation of an object to be a betrayal of reality, Brassaï pursued imaginative resemblance and representation that was anchored in lived experience and the objective world.

In 1932, Brassaï was asked by Tériade to take photographs of Pablo Picasso, his work, and his studio for the first issue of *Le Minotaure*. Brassaï published over 150 images in the first nine issues of the journal with half of the photographs being portraits of artists and images of their work and their studios. Brassaï worked on portraits of Picasso for four decades and was much stimulated by their association. Picasso's etching on one of Brassaï's negatives inspired his *Transmutations* series. *Conversations avec Picasso* grew from the notes Brassaï began to collect after their first meetings, but not until 1960 and with Picasso's suggestion did these materials become a book. Included are discussions of Picasso's working habits, philosophies, friends and wives, as well as discussion of Brassaï's own work habits and interests. Picasso much appreciated the opportunity through Brassaï to see his own work with "new eyes."

Brassaï also famously photographed the great painter Henri Matisse at work in his studio.

Although often linked with the Surrealists, Brassaï's relationship to Surrealism is complicated. Brassaï did not meet Surrealist major domo André Breton until 1931, and by then, many of Brassaï's friends, including Jacques Prévert, Robert Desnos, and Raymond Queneau had already been expelled from the official movement. Many of Brassaï's images were influenced by Surrealism and were used to express Surrealist ideas, but Brassaï refused to join the movement, and his interest in the physical world was incompatible with Surrealist emphasis on fantastic associations. Like Picasso, Brassaï's images remain based on rational, visible, and mental constructions of the complexity of the world. Brassaï's photography expresses in a two-dimensional discourse the authenticity of the subject of the image.

Graffiti especially inspired Brassaï because of its ancient history and its correspondence to the origins of writing. Over a thirty-year period Brassaï kept careful notebooks and witnessed its changes over time. In regards to graffiti, but useful as a general statement of his philosophy of art, Brassaï explained that a work of art

> stands alone and naked, like a conscript in front of a recruiting board, and it should be allowed to be its own judge. The way it was generated, its genealogy, the ambition or intention that inspired it, none of these has anything to do with its value, and can neither enhance nor reduce it, justify nor destroy it.
>
> (Brassaï, "Images latentes," *L'Intransigeant*, 15 November 1932)

In 1943–1945, when working as a photographer was not possible during the Nazi occupation and with Picasso's encouragement, Brassaï began drawing again, and in 1946, he published, *Trente dessins*, a portfolio consisting mostly of nudes, with a poem by Jacques Prévert written in response to the images. After this publication, again with Picasso's influence, he began to sculpt palm-sized river stones, usually extracting female torsos from them. Later sculptures were larger and made use of other materials, a practice that continued through the early 1970s. Shortly before his death, Brassaï completed *Marcel Proust sous l'emprise de la photographie*, a study of Proust's interest in photography and the role of photography and photographs in *A la récherche du temps perdu*. At the close of the twentieth century, Brassaï's work was receiving considerable scholarly attention, both for his own contributions and his role as part of the Parisian avant-garde of the 1920s and 1930s, one of the most fertile periods of photographic practice of the century.

SCOTT A. SHERER

See also: **History of Photography: Interwar Years; Photography in France; Surrealism**

Biography

Born in Brassó, Transylvania, 1899. Became French citizen in 1947. Died in Beaulieu-sur-Mer, France, 7 July 1984.

Individual Exhibitions

1933 *Brassaï*; Galerie Arts et Métiers Graphiques; Paris
1945 *Brassaï, dessins*; Galerie Renou et Colle; Paris
1954 *Brassaï*; Art Institute of Chicago (traveled to Walker Art Center, Minneapolis, Minnesota; George Eastman House, Rochester, New York; Institute of Art, New Orleans, Louisiana)
1956 *Language of the Wall: Parisian Graffiti Photographed by Brassaï*; The Museum of Modern Art; New York, New York
1958 *Language of the Wall: Parisian Graffiti Photographed by Brassaï*; Institute of Contempoary Arts; London
1963 *Brassaï, photographies, sculptures, gravures*; Bibliothèque Nationale; Paris (traveled to Résidence du Louvre, Menton)
1964 *Les sculptures de Picasso et les photographies de Brassaï*; Galerie Madoura; Cannes, France
1968 *Brassaï*; Museum of Modern Art; New York (traveled to St. Louis Art Museum, Missouri; National Gallery of Victoria, Melbourne; Farmer's Blaxland Gallery, Sidney; Auckland City Art Gallery, Auckland; National Art Gallery, Wellington; Govett-Brewster Art Gallery, New Plymouth, New Zealand; Centro Venezolano Americano, Caracas; Museo de Arte Moderno "La Tertulia," Cali, Colombia; Museo de Arte Moderno de Bogotá, Colombia; Museo de Zea, Medellín, Colombia; Institutio Nacional de Cultura, Lima, Peru; Museo de Arte Contemporanea, São Paulo, Brazil; Museo de Arte Moderna de Bahia, Salvador, El Salvado; Hayden Gallery, Boston)
1973 *Brassaï*; Dartmouth College of Art; Dartmouth, New Hampshire (traveled to Corcoran Gallery of Art, Washington, D.C.; University of Iowa Museum of Art, Iowa; University of California, Berkeley; Winnipeg Art Gallery, Winnipeg; Munson-Williams-Proctor Institute, Museum of Art, Utica, New York; Everson Museum, Syracuse, New York)
1976 *The Secret Paris of the 30s/Le Paris secret des années trente*; Marlborough Gallery; New York and traveling
1979 *Brassaï, Artists and Studios*; Marlborough Gallery; New York and traveling
Brassaï; The Photographers' Gallery, London (traveled to Brewery Arts Center, Kendal; The Scottish Photography Group Gallery, Edinburgh; Tolarno Galleries, Melbourne; Salford University, Salford, Australia)
1987 *Picasso vu par Brassaï*; Musée Picasso, Paris
1988 *Brassaï, Paris le jour, Paris la nuit*; Musée Carnavalet; Paris

Paris tendresse; Galerie de la FNAC; Paris
1993 *Brassaï*; Centre national de la photographie; Paris
Brassaï: del Surrealismo al informalismo; Fundació Antoni Tapies; Barcelona
1998 *Brassaï and Company*; Art Institute of Chicago, Chicago, Illinois
Brassaï: The Eye of Paris; The Museum of Fine Arts; Houston (traveled to The J. Paul Getty Museum, Los Angeles; The National Gallery of Art, Washington, D.C.)

Group Exhibitions

1931 *Photographes d'aujourd'hui*; Libraire-Galerie de la Plume d'Or, Paris, France
1932 *Modern European Photographers*; Julien Levy Gallery, New York, New York
1933 *Groupe annuel des photographes* Galerie de la Pléiade, Paris, France
Exposition internationale de photographie, Palais des Beaux-Arts, Brussels, Belgium
1935 *La photographie contemporaine international*, Musée Rath, Geneva, Switzerland
1936 *Exposition internationale de la photographie*, Musée des Arts Décoratifs, Pavillon de Marsan, Paris, France
1937 *Photography 1839-1937;* Museum of Modern Art, New York, New York
1948 *French Photographers*; The Photo-League, New York
Troisième Salon national de la photographe; Bibliothèque nationale de France, Paris
1951 *Five French Photographers*; Museum of Modern Art, New York, New York
1953 *Post-war European Photography*; Museum of Modern Art, New York, New York
1959 *Photography at Mid-century*, George Eastman House, Rochester, New York
1964 *The Photographer's Eye*; Museum of Modern Art, New York, New York
1976 *One Hundred Master Photographs*; Museum of Modern Art, New York, New York
1977 *Documenta 6*; Museum Fridericianum, Kassel, Germany
1980 *Photographic Surrealism*; Brooklyn Museum of Art, New York
Les realisms 1919-1939; Centre Georges Pompidou, Paris, France
1981 *Paris-Paris: creation en France 1937-1957*; Centre Georges Pompidou, Paris, France
1982 *Counterparts. Form and Emotion in Photography*. The Metropolitan Museum of Art, New York
1985 *L'amour fou. Photography and Surrealism*; Corcoran Gallery of Art; Washington, D.C. (traveled to Centre Georges Pompidou, Paris, France)
1987 *Regards sur Minotaure*; Musée Rath, Geneva, Switzerland
L'oeil du Minotaure, Ubac, Brassaï, Alvarez-Bravo, Bellmer, Man Ray; Galerie Sonia Zanettacci, Geneva, Switzerland
1988 *Une exposition de photographie française à New York*; Centre Georges Pompidou, Paris, France
1989 *The New VisionL Photography between the World Wars*; Metropolitan Museum of Art, New York, New York
1997 *Le Paris des photographes*; Bunkamura, Tokyo, and Suntory Museum, Osaka, Japan

Selected Works

Place de la Concorde on a Rainy Day, 1928
Self-Portrait in an Opium Den, c. 1931
Backstage at the Folies-Bergère, 1932
Girl Playing Snooker, Montmartre, 1932
Large-Scale Object: Cotton, 1932
Lovers in a Café, 1932
La Môme Bijou (alternate title: *Bijoux of Montmarte*), 1932
Le Viaduc d'Auteuil, c. 1932
Chez "Suzy", 1932–1933
Graffiti, c. 1933
Pharmacy, Beaune Hospital, France, 1951

Further Reading

Brassaï. *The Artists of My Life*. New York: Viking Press, and London: Thames & Hudson, 1982; as *Les Artistes de ma vie*, Paris: Denoël, 1982.

———. *Conversations avec Picasso*. Paris: Gallimard, 1964, 1969, 1987, 1997; as *Conversaciones con Picasso*, Madrid: Aguilar, 1966; as *Picasso and Company*, preface by Henry Miller, introduction by Roland Penrose, Garden City and New York: Doubleday, 1966; as *Picasso & Co.*, London: Thames & Hudson, 1967; as *Conversations with Picasso*, preface by Henry Miller, introduction by Pierre Daix, Chicago: University of Chicago Press, 1999.

Brassaï and Henry Miller. *Histoire de Marie*. Paris: Éditions du Pont du Jour, 1949. Arles: Actes Sud, 1997.

———. *Henry Miller: the Paris Years*. trans. by Timothy Bent, New York: Arcade Publishers, 1995.

Brassaï and Pablo Picasso. *Graffiti*. Stuttgart: Belser Verlag, 1960; Paris: Les Éditions du Temps, 1961; preface by Gilberte Brassaï, Paris: Flammarion, 1993. *Letters to My Parents*. trans. by Peter Laki and Barna Kantor. Chicago: University of Chicago Press, 1997.

———. *Marcel Proust sous l'emprise de la photographie*. Paris: Gallimard, 1997.

Brassaï and Paul Morand. *Paris de nuit*. Éditions Arts et Métiers Graphiques, Paris 1933; as *Paris after Dark*, London: Batsford Gallery, 1933; *Nachtliches Paris*, Munich: Schirmer/Mosel Verlag, 1979; Paris: Flammarion, and London: Thames & Hudson, 1987; as *Paris by Night*, New York: Pantheon Books, 1987; *Paris de nuit*, Tokyo: Misuzu Shobo, 1987.

———. *Le Paris secret des années 30*. Paris: Gallimard, 1976; as *The Secret Paris of the 30's*, London: Thames & Hudson, and New York: Pantheon Books, and Frankfurt: S. Fischer, 1976; Tokyo: Misuzu Shobo, 1977.

Berman, Avis. *Smithsonian*, 30, no. 7 (October 1999).

de Montherlant, Henry, D. Aubier, and Brassaï. *Séville en fête*; as *Fest in Seville*, Feldafing: Buchheim-Verlag, 1954; as *Fiesta in Seville*, London: Thames & Hudson, and New York: The Studio and Thomas Y. Crowell, 1956.

Durrell, John and John Szarkowski. *Brassaï*. New York: Museum of Modern Art, 1968.

Sayag, Alain and Annick Lionel-Marie, eds. *Brassaï*. Boston: Bulfinch Press, 2000.

Tucker, Anne Wilkes. *Brassaï: The Eye of Paris*. Houston: Museum of Fine Arts, 1999.

Walker, Ian. *City Gorged with Dreams: Surrealism and Documentary Photography in Interwar Paris*. Manchester: Manchester University Press, 2000.

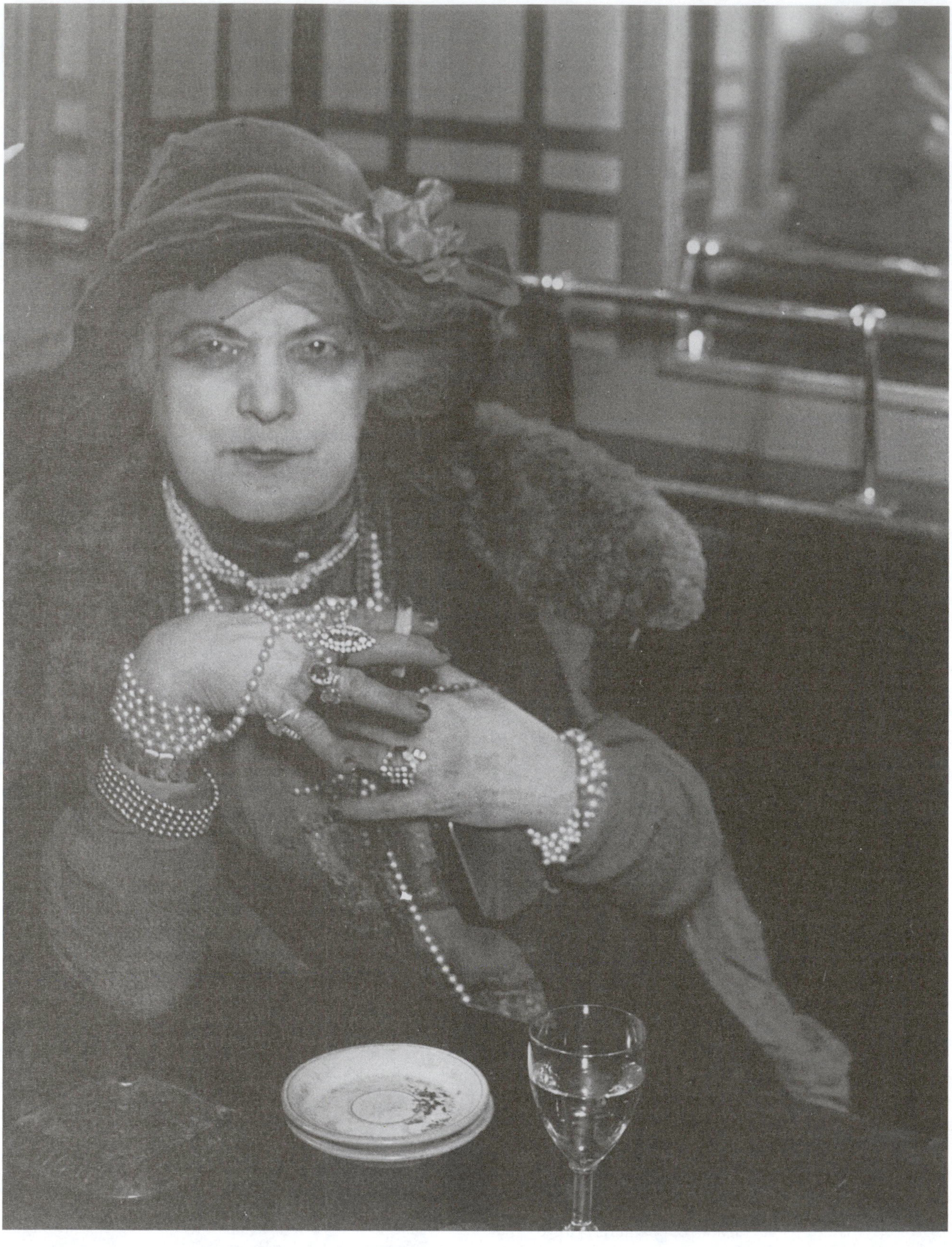

Brassaï (Guyla Halasz), "Bijou" of Montmartre. 1932 or 1933, Gelatin-silver print, 11 ⅞ × 9 ⅛″ (30.2 × 23.2 cm). David H. McAlpin Fund.
[*Digital Image © The Museum of Modern Art/Licensed by SCALA/Art Resource, New York*]

MANUEL ALVAREZ BRAVO

Mexican

Arguably the most renowned photographer of Latin America, Manuel Alvarez Bravo is the cornerstone of this medium in Mexico. When he began photographing in the 1920s and 1930s, artists who constitute a veritable "who's who" of the lens immediately acknowledged his innate capacity: Edward Weston, Tina Modotti, Paul Strand, and Henri Cartier-Bresson. The respect that he engendered was encapsulated in Cartier-Bresson's response when someone likened Alvarez Bravo's imagery to Weston's: "Don't compare them, Manuel is the real artist." Alvarez Bravo's unique eye was such that the founder of surrealism, André Breton, sought him out in 1938 to commission an image for the cover of a surrealist exhibition catalogue. His recognition by such luminaries notwithstanding, Alvarez Bravo had little visibility within the United States prior to the modest 1971 exhibit at the Pasadena Art Museum in California. Subsequent exhibitions at the Corcoran Gallery of Art in Washington D.C. (1978) and San Diego's Museum of Photographic Arts (1990) made Alvarez Bravo a much more familiar figure, and his consecration was assured by the 1997 exhibit at the Museum of Modern Art in New York.

When Alvarez Bravo began photographing in the 1920s, the Mexican Revolution (1910–1917) had unleashed a national search for identity, and the question of what to do with Mexico's inherent exoticism was the burning issue for photographers. Perhaps influenced by his relationship with Weston and Modotti, Alvarez Bravo was the first Mexican photographer to take a militantly anti-picturesque stance, and he achieved international recognition for work that reached creative heights from the late 1920s through the mid-1950s, a period during which he perfected a sophisticated approach to representing his culture. Conscious both of Mexico's otherness and the way in which that has led almost naturally to stereotypical imagery, Alvarez Bravo has always swum counter to the stream of established clichés.

Consider *Sed pública* (*Public Thirst*), the 1934 photo of a boy drinking water from a village well. This image contains all the elements necessary to make it picturesque: a young peasant, dressed in the white clothing typical of his culture, perches on a battered village well to drink the water which flows from it; an adobe wall behind provides texture. But, the light in the image seems to concentrate itself on the foot that juts forward into the frame, a foot that is too particular, too individual to be able to "stand for" the Mexican peasantry, and thus represent their other-worldliness. It is this boy's foot, not a typical peasant's foot, and it goes against the expectations of picturesqueness raised by the other elements, "saving" the image through its very particularity.

A similar tactic can be observed in *Señor de Papantla* (*Man from Papantla*, 1934), where an Indian stands with his back to the wall, facing the camera. Here, as with the image of the boy, the objective elements in the photo would seem to make it picturesque: white peasant clothing, bare feet, and adobe walls, as well as a *sombrero* and bag woven of reeds. But, having awakened our anticipation of the exotic, Alvarez Bravo cuts back against it with an artistry that rejects the facile. The man refuses to dignify the camera by returning its look. It is often felt that the esthetic strategy in which the subject "retorts" the camera's gaze is that which most effectively represents people at their most active, because it negates somewhat the camera's tendency to reduce them to objects. But here, Alvarez Bravo gives us another turn of the screw by presenting us with an Indian who, in looking away, seems to say disparagingly: "Take all the pictures you want, outsider. Who cares what you do?"

Alvarez Bravo's search for *mexicanidad* (Mexicanness) led him to reconfigure national symbols. For example, *Sand and Pines* is an early image from the 1920s that demonstrates that a young Alvarez Bravo was much influenced not only by pictorialism, but also by the then pervasive interest in Japanese art. Infusing international art forms with Mexican meaning, Alvarez Bravo forms the background to his "bonsai" with what is in essence a mini-Popocatepetl, one of the volcanoes that dominate the Valley of Mexico. Another example is the 1927 photo of a rolled-up mattress. Here, he chose not to use the beautifully textured, folkloric *petate* which, woven of wide reeds, provided depth to the still lives created by Modotti and Weston. Instead,

Alvarez Bravo photographed a modern mattress, but with the twist that its bands of shading make it look like the well-known Saltillo *sarapes*. In his recurrent imagery of the maguey cactus we can see his interest in playing with a ubiquitous symbol of Mexican culture; in one photo he "modernizes" the maguey by making it appear as if the central flower stem that sprouts from these plants has been converted into a television antenna.

The politics of Alvarez Bravo are always talked about in relation to his most famous photograph, *Striking Worker, Assassinated, Oaxaca, 1934*. Nonetheless, while it is certainly true that he rejects official nationalism as completely as he does the picturesque, this image is problematic: its meaning is determined by the title ascribed to it, which may have been influenced by Alvarez Bravo's involvement in LEAR (League of Revolutionary Writers and Artists) during the 1930s. It may be argued instead that the politics of Alvarez Bravo—and his search for Mexico's essence—can better be found in the ways he represents the daily life activities of humble people, rather than in overt social commentary. His imagery is a modest, almost transparent portrayal of individuals whom he seems to have "found" within their natural habitats rather than to have "created" through conspicuous visual rhetoric. A very understated esthetic that avoids overt expressivity, Alvarez Bravo's is an all but invisible technique designed to capture anonymous people in ordinary activities, where they are neither romanticized nor sentimentalized. A perfect instance is *La mamá del bolero y el bolero*, an exquisite image from the 1950s in which a mother visits her son to bring him lunch, and eats with him while he rests from his tasks of shining shoes.

Manuel Alvarez Bravo has been a definitive influence on Mexican and Latin American photography. His rejection of the facile, his insistently ambiguous irony, and his redemption of common folk and their daily subsistence have marked a path of high standards for photographers from his area.

John Mraz

See also: **Modotti, Tina; Photography in Latin America: Mexico; Strand, Paul; Weston, Edward**

Biography

Born in Mexico City, 4 February 1902. Attended Catholic school from 1908 to 1914, but left in 1915 to work. Begins to educate self in photography, asking advice from photography suppliers, and learning English by reading the labels on developer bottles. The 1923 arrival of Edward Weston and Tina Modotti in Mexico City is crucial to Alvarez Bravo's development, and he buys his first camera in 1924. Wins first major award in 1931, and decides to pursue photography as full-time career, in part as a still photographer in cinema productions. Meets Andre Breton in 1939, and his work is included in a Paris Surrealist exhibit. In 1942, the Museum of Modern Art (New York) acquired their first works by Alvarez Bravo and, in 1955, his photographs were included in Edward Steichen's *The Family of Man*. During 1959, Alvarez Bravo stopped working in the film industry, and became the photographer of important art books for El Fondo Editorial de la Plástica Mexicana, Mexico City, of which he was a founder. Alvarez Bravo left the Fondo in 1980 to work with the Mexican-based media empire, Televisa, where his collection of photography was exhibited and published in a three-volume set. In 1996, Alvarez Bravo's collection moved to the newly-created Centro Fotográfico Alvarez Bravo in Oaxaca City, Mexico. Bravo died in Mexico City, October 19, 2002.

Selected Individual Exhibitions

1942 *Manuel Alvarez Bravo*; Photo League Gallery, New York, New York

1968 *Manuel Alvarez Bravo: fotografías de 1928–1968*; Palacio de Bellas Artes, Mexico City, Mexico

1971 *Manuel Alvarez Bravo*; Pasadena Art Museum, Pasadena, California, and traveled to The Museum of Modern Art, New Cork, New York; San Francisco Museum of Modern Art, San Francisco, California; George Eastman House, Rochester, New York

1972 *Manuel Alvarez Bravo: 400 fotografías*; Palacio de Bellas Artes, Mexico City, Mexico, and traveled to The Art Institute of Chicago, Chicago, Illinois; Galerie Municipale de Château-d'Eau, Toulouse, France; Musée Nicéphore Niépce, Chalon-sur-Saòne, France; Museo de Bellas Artes, Caracas, Venezuela

1978 *M. Alvarez Bravo*; Corcoran Gallery of Art, Washington D.C.

1983 *Dreams-Visions-Metaphors: The Photographs of Manuel Alvarez Bravo*; Israel Museum, Jerusalem, and traveled to The National Museum of Photography, Film and Television, Bradford, United Kingdom; Museum of Modern Art, Oxford, United Kingdom

1989 *Mucho sol: Manuel Alvarez Bravo*; Palacio de Bellas Artes, Mexico City, Mexico, and traveled to Museo de Bellas Artes, Caracas, Venezuela

1990 *Revelaciones: The Art of Manuel Alvarez Bravo*; Museum of Photographic Arts, San Diego, California, and traveling

1997 *Manuel Alvarez Bravo*; Museum of Modern Art, New York, New York

Selected Group Exhibitions

1935 *Exposición fotografías: Cartier-Bresson, Alvarez Bravo*; Palacio de Bellas Artes, Mexico City, Mexico

1939 *Mexique*; Galerie Renou et Colle, Paris, France

1955 *The Family of Man*; The Museum of Modern Art, New York, New York, and traveling

1964 *The Photographer's Eye*; The Museum of Modern Art, New York, New York

1978 *Imagen histórica de la fotografía en México*; Instituto Nacional de Antropología e Historia, Mexico City, Mexico

1979 *Les invites d'honneur: Manuel Alvarez Bravo (Mexi-*

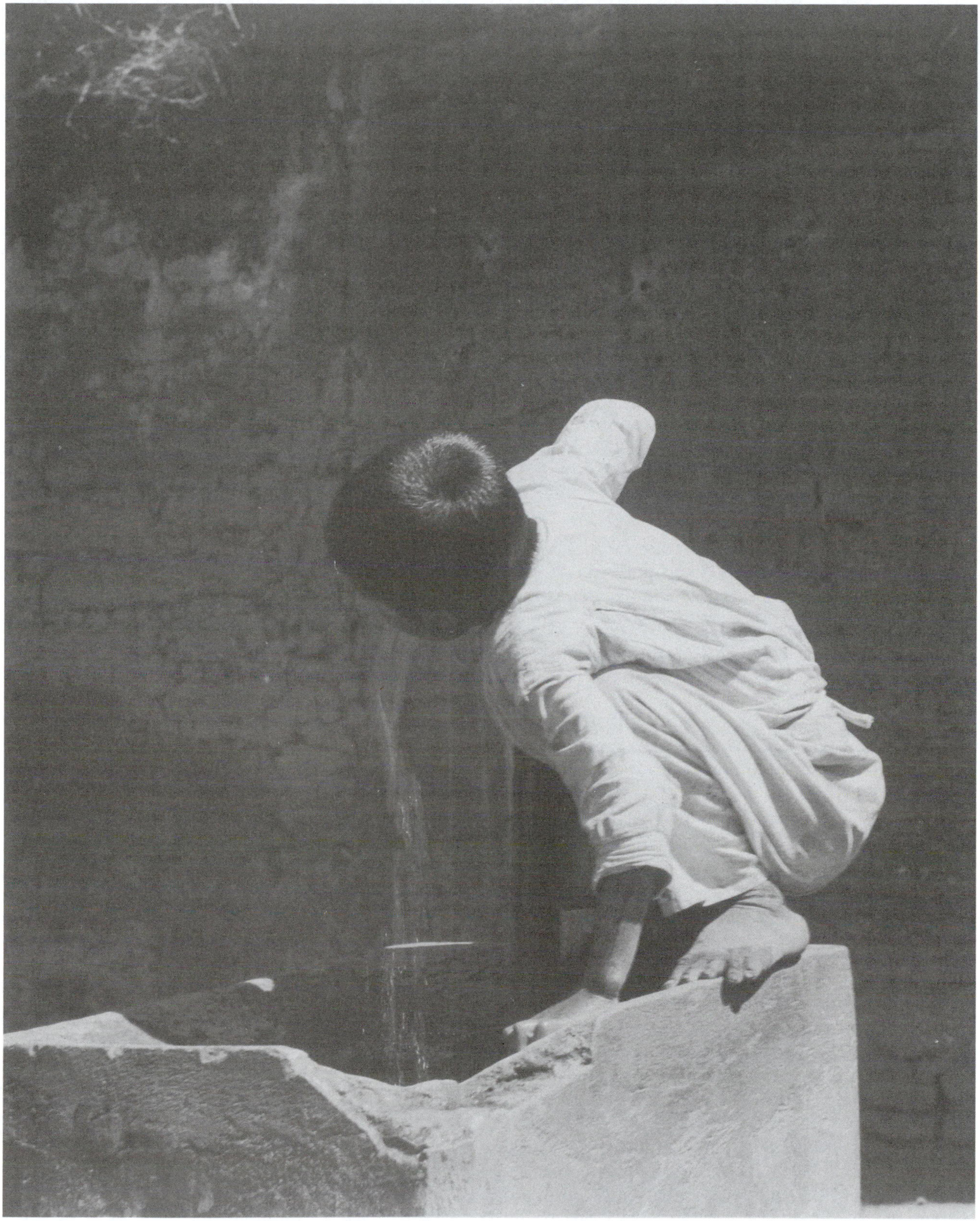

Manuel Alvarez Bravo, Public Thirst (Sed pública), 1933, Gelatin Silver Print.
[© *Colette Alvarez-Urbajtel. Victoria & Albert Museum, London/Art Resource, New York*].

que), Aaron Siskind (USA), et Henri Cartier-Bresson (France); Musée Réattu, Arles, France

1986 *50 años de la exposición de Manuel Alvarez Bravo y Henri Cartier-Bresson*; Palacio de Bellas Artes, Mexico City, New York

1989 *On the Art of Fixing a Shadow: One Hundred and Fifty Years of Photography*; National Gallery of Art, Washington, D.C., and traveled to The Art Institute of Chicago, Chicago, Illinois; Los Angeles County Museum of Art, Los Angeles, California

Selected Works

Arena y pinitos (*Sand and Pines*), 1920s
Peluquero (*Barber*), 1924
Colchón (*Matress*), 1927
Los agachados (*The Bent Ones*), 1934
Sed pública (*Public Thirst or The Public Fountain*), 1934
Señor de Papantla (*Man from Papantla*), 1934
Obrero en huelga, asesinado (*Striking Worker, Assassinated*), 1934
La buena fama durmiendo (*The Good Reputation Sleeping*), 1938
La mamá del bolera y el bolero (*The Mother of the Shoeshine Boy and the Shoeshine Boy*), 1950s

Further Reading

Coleman, A.D. *Manuel Alvarez Bravo: Aperture Masters of Photography*. New York: Aperture, 1987.

del Conde, Teresa. *Mucho sol: Manuel Alvarez Bravo*. Mexico City: Fondo de Cultura Económico, 1989.

Kismaric, Susan. *Manuel Alvarez Bravo*. New York: The Museum of Modern Art, 1997.

Livingstone, Jane. *M. Alvarez Bravo*. Washington D.C.: Corcoran Gallery of Art, 1978.

Luna Córnea. 1 (Issue dedicated to Manuel Alvarez Bravo.) Winter (1992–1993).

Ollman, Arthur, and Nissan Perez. *Revelaciones: The Art of Manuel Alvarez Bravo*. San Diego: Museum of Photographic Arts, 1990.

Paz, Octavio, and Manuel Alvarez Bravo. *Instante y revelación*. Mexico City: Fondo Nacional para Actividades Sociales, 1982.

Perez, Nissan, and Ian Jeffrey. *Dreams-Visions-Metaphors: The Photographs of Manuel Alvarez Bravo*. Jerusalem: Israel Museum, 1983.

Poniatowski, Elena. *Manuel Alvarez Bravo: el artista su obra, sus tiempos*. Mexico City: Banco Nacional de México, 1991.

Scimè, Giuliana. *Manuel Alvarez Bravo*. Barcelona: Orbis, 1994.

Interviews with Manuel Alvarez Bravo

Pacheca, Cristina. "Manuel Alvarez Bravo: La fotografía como el realismo máximo." *La luz de México: entrevistas con pintores y fotógrafos*. Mexico City: Fondo de Cultura Económico, 1995.

Hill, Paul, and Thomas Cooper. "Manuel Alvarez Bravo." *Dialogue with Photography*. Manchester: Cornerhouse Publications, 1979.

JOSEF BREITENBACH

German-American

Josef Breitenbach embraced photography in its entirety as a professional and artistic photographer, collector of historical photography, and instructor of photography. Shaped by the desperation and ingenuity of exile, a passion for photography, and a keen interest to preserve the "other Germany," Breitenbach participated in the creative foment of the refugee artists, intellectuals, and scientists in Paris, France, in the 1930s. His photographs are poetic in the tradition of Eugène Atget and at times, recall the psychological depth of Christian Schad's portraits. Creating disparate bodies of work in Germany, France, and the United States, it was only in the late decades of the twentieth century that his contribution has been fully recognized.

Breitenbach was born into an upper middle-class family of Franconian Jews in Munich on April 3, 1896. Although his parents were newcomers to this Bavarian metropolis, the move to Munich brought upward economic, social, and political mobility. Upon graduating in 1912 from the *Oberrealschule* (modern high school), Breitenbach undertook a commercial apprenticeship, as he would eventually take over the family business, a successful wholesale wine business. He also became an activist in the youth section of the Social Democratic Association, a pacifist organization. In spite of this, Breitenbach was drafted into the army in early 1916, but was discharged for health reasons at the end of the year.

His civilian life resumed and gravitated around the circle of Kurt Eisner, where he met Oskar

Maria Graf and his colleagues Erich Mühsam and Ernst Toller. In 1918, Breitenbach played an active part in the successful November Revolution to overthrow the Bavarian government and became a member of the Provisional Central Workers' Council. Eisner became the first minister-president of the Free State of Bavaria and Breitenbach was given a small post in the new administration as diplomatic courier for the Bavarian embassy in Switzerland. Kurt Eisner was in power for only a few months when his political opponents assassinated him. His death precipitated the proclamation of the "Soviet Republic" by the Bavarian left, and marked the end of Breitenbach's political ambitions.

Breitenbach remained associated with the Social Democratic party in the 1920s, but his life adopted a new focus—family, business, and art. He married Pauline Schmidtbauer in 1918, more than a year after the birth of their son Hans. The marriage ended in divorce in 1926. He took over his father's business in 1922, and it went bankrupt in 1930. It is not clear if this was due to his lack of interest in the business. But what is certain is that the many business trips through Central European wine regions became photographic excursions and led to his study of viniculture, which won the gold medal at the Milan Photography Competition in 1928.

In 1932 Breitenbach opened his own photographic studio and began a steady engagement as stage photographer for the Münchener Kammerspiele (Munich Studio Theater). His portraits of great actors such as Alexander Moissi, Albert Basserman, and Karl Valentin earned him modest artistic recognition and financial success. His promising career, however ended abruptly in the summer of 1933, when the Nazis came to power.

It seems that his life was spared because of a photograph he made of Franz von Papen, Hitler's deputy in the National Socialist government. Legend has it that SS agents visited Breitenbach with the intention of taking him into custody. Breitenbach confronted them with the Papen portrait and the accompanying letter of thanks. Caught off guard by this first-class reference, the SS left Breitenbach to confirm that they had not descended on the wrong person. Breitenbach wasted no time in leaving the country for France. For the National Socialists, the participants in the November Revolution of 1918 were the most hated of opponents. They were decried as "November criminals" and were the victims of the first wave of terror, which liquidated the political opposition. Breitenbach, therefore, was a target of the Nazis more because of his earlier political commitment than his Jewish birth.

Breitenbach found himself in Paris among throngs of artists and intellectuals who formed a network of new alliances referred to as the "other Germany." With his son Hans he took up residence in a Latin Quarter hotel. The series of bureaucratic hurdles that restricted the lives of the exiles made Breitenbach's initial stay in Paris difficult. However, Breitenbach did not arrive as an anonymous person in Paris. The Comité National de Secours aux Réfugiés Allemands Victimes de l'Antisémitisme recommended him on October 10, 1933 to the Police Prefecture. Such protection helped him set up a business. Two months after his arrival in Paris he was invited to show his work in an exhibition of exiled photographers at the Librairie Lipschutz, held from November 20–30, 1933. The exhibition was organized by the Comité Française pour la Protection des Intellectuels Juifs Persécutés, a group of university professors dedicated to assisting exiled Jews in France. After only a year, Breitenbach had established himself as a professional and artistic photographer in Paris. He held his first solo exhibition in Paris at the Galerie de la Pléiade.

During these years Breitenbach experimented with numerous techniques, including multiple printing, solarization, hand-coloring, and bleaching. It was in one area, however, that Breitenbach was a true innovator. In 1937 he began using a process, developed by French botanist Dr. Henri Devaux, to capture in visual form odors from various things such as camphor, cigars, coffee beans, and pine needles. These "odor emanations" resemble his work in photograms, with which he also experimented.

Breitenbach also continued his work in portraiture, shooting the leading figures of the day, including playwright Bertolt Brecht, novelist James Joyce, and painters Vasily Kandinsky and Max Ernst. He was also a beloved teacher of photography, who promised "thorough individual specialist training" in courses of several months or in compact seminars. His most important pupil was Ruth Snowman, who became also his lover and business agent and would aid him in escaping France. It was in 1935 that Breitenbach began to work as a photojournalist, documenting Brecht's theater productions in Paris and the exhibition *Free German Art*, among other events. Although Breitenbach made only a modest living, he received artistic recognition and was accepted into the Société Française de la Photographie in 1938 and the Royal Photographic Society of London 1939, the leading photographic associations of the time.

On September 26, 1938, the seventieth expatriate list announces "the forfeiture of the German citizenship" of Josef Breitenbach; a year later he is interned by the French authorities, his career once again shut down. Breitenbach was released from internment on November 18, 1940 and emigrated to New York, finally ending his long flight from National Socialism.

In the United States Breitenbach worked for a number of magazines including *Fortune* under Walker Evans. The painter Josef Albers invited him to teach at the short-lived but now legendary Black Mountain College, North Carolina, in 1944. Later, he would teach at both the New School for Social Research and Cooper Union in New York, retiring from teaching finally in 1975. He created his last major body of work in Asia on intermittent trips from teaching and under the auspices of the United Nations. After his death in 1984, his archive was donated to the Center for Creative Photography in Tucson, Arizona.

CRISTINA CUEVAS-WOLF

See also: **History of Photography: Interwar Years; Manipulation; Photogram; Portraiture**

Biography

Born in Munich on 3 April, 1896. Attended the *Oberrealschule* (modern high school), graduates in 1912. Completed a commercial apprenticeship, but self-educated in photography. Drafted in early 1916. Active in the November Revolution, 1918; Member of the "Provisional Central Workers' Council." Diplomatic courier for the Bavarian embassy in Switzerland, 1918. Photographic excursions through Central Europe's wine regions, 1920s. Gold medal at the Milan Photography Competition, 1928. Opens his own photographic studio, 1932. Works as stage photographer for the Munchener Kammerspiele (Munich Studio Theater), 1932. Registered as a photographic studio in Paris in September 1934, elected member of the Société Française de la Photographie in 1938 and the Royal Photographic Society of London in 1939. Interned by the French authorities, September 1939; accepted as voluntary "Prestataires," 30 May, 1940. Immigrates to United States, 1941; becomes U.S. citizen 1946. Works for various magazines in New York, early 1940s. Serves as chief of still photography, United Nations Reconstruction Agency, Korea, 1952–1953. Teaches at Black Mountain College, 1944, at both the Cooper Union, 1946–1966 and New School for Social Research, 1949–1975. Died in New York on 7 October, 1984.

Individual Exhibitions

1934 *Portraits, Paysages, Theatre*; Galerie de la Pléiade, Paris, France
1935 Galerie Fernand Nathan, Paris, France
1944 Black Mountain College, Black Mountain, North Carolina
1948–1949 A-D Gallery, New York, New York
1950 *Pictorial Photographs by Josef Breitenbach*; Smithsonian Institute, Washington, D.C. *Portraits and Landscapes by Joseph Breitenbach*; Brooklyn Museum, Brooklyn, New York
1954 *Korea*; Limelight Gallery, New York, New York
1961 New School for Social Research, New York, New York
1965 *Wanderung: 250 Photographien 1930 bis 1965*; Münchner Stadtmuseum, Munich, Germany
2000 *Photographs by Josef Breitenbach*; Fox Talbot Museum, Lacock, United Kingdom
2001 *Photographs by Josef Breitenbach*; Scottish National Portrait Gallery, Edinburgh, Scotland
2001–2002 *Josef Breitenbach, 1896–1984*; *Une Photographie Impure*, Musée Nicéphore Niépce, Chalon-sur-Saône, France

Group Exhibitions

1933 Joint exhibition of exiled photographers, Librarie Lipschutz, Paris, France
1935 *Documents de la vie sociale*; Galerie de la Pléiade, group exhibition of the AEAR (Association des Écrivains et Artistes Révolutionnaires)
1955 *Family of Man*: Museum of Modern Art, New York, New York
1960 *Photography in the Fine Arts II*: Metropolitan Museum of Art, New York, New York
1961 *Photography in the Fine Arts III*: Metropolitan Museum of Art, New York, New York
1961 *Photography in the Fine Arts IV*: Museum of Fine Arts, Boston, Massachusetts

Selected Works

La Tour Eiffel, Paris, 1928
Seefeld in Tirol, 1928
Mr. Josef Schnaffner, Decorateur, Munich, c. 1932
Karl Valentin in "The Bartered Bride," 1933
Max Ernst, Paris, 1938
Graf Vittorio Cerutti and Wife, Paris, 1933–1939
Late Harvest, near Calais, August, 1939
Korea, 1964

Further Reading

Berlanga, Paul, and Stephen Daiter Gallery. *Josef Breitenbach: Munich, Paris, New York*, Chicago: Stephen Daiter Gallery, 2003.
Breitenbach, Josef. *Installation Views of the Exhibition Freie Deutsche Kunst and Two Other Exhibitions*. 1938.
Breitenbach, Josef. *Women of Asia*. New York: The John Day Co., 1968.
Dryansky, Larisa. *Josef Breitenbach*. Paris Chalon-sur-Saône: Amateur; Musée Nicéphore Niépce, 2001.
Holborn, Mark. *Josef Breitenbach, Photographer*. New York: Temple Rock Company, 1986.
Holz, Keith, and Wolfgang Schopf. *Im Auge Des Exils: Joseph Breitenbach Und Die Freie Deutsche Kultur in Paris 1933–1941*. 1. Aufl. ed. Berlin: Aufbau-Verlag, 2001.
Immisch, T. O., Ulrich Pohlmann, and Klaus E. Göltz. Staatliche Galerie Moritzburg, and Münchner Stadtmuseum. Fotomuseum. *Josef Breitenbach: Photographien Zum 100. Geburtstag*. München: Schirmer/Mosel, 1996.
Münchner Stadtmuseum Fotomuseum. *Die Sammlung Josef Breitenbach ZurGeschichte Der Photographie : Eine Ausstellung Im Fotomuseum Des Münchener Stadtmuseums Vom 20. Juli 1979 Bis 9. September 1979*, Exh. cat. München: Münchner Stadtmuseum, 1979.

BROWNIE

The proliferation of amateur snapshot photography and its impact on contemporary society in the twentieth century can be traced to pivotal developments in both camera technology and the marketing of the medium to the masses at the end of the nineteenth century. Entrepreneur George Eastman (1854–1932) began his career in banking but soon turned his budding interest in photography toward professional ends, founding the Eastman Dry Plate Company (later Eastman Kodak Company) in Rochester, New York in 1880. While at the forefront of the manufacture of dry plates in the United States, Eastman realized photography's cumbersome equipment and processing requirements was daunting for potential users and strove to introduce a radically simplified process. Although the paper roll film holder Eastman soon devised (along with other manufacturers) helped to supplant the dry plate negative, the small 'detective' camera he first equipped with this new type of film in 1886 was still too complicated and expensive to achieve broad success in the marketplace. By 1888, Eastman created a new version of the hand-held roll film camera—a small wooden box fitted with a simple lens and loaded with film capable of recording 100 circular images, 2½ inches in diameter. The name Kodak was coined for this latest manifestation of the hand camera—chosen by Eastman for the authoritative look of the word's two letter 'Ks' and for the ease of its pronunciation in various foreign languages. Yet the widespread success of this camera can be attributed to neither its catchy name or even wholly to its innovative film format, but rather to Eastman's groundbreaking marketing of the total photographic endeavor.

In addition to being simple enough that "anybody, man, woman or child, who has sufficient intelligence to point a box straight and press a button" could make successful photographs, the preloaded Kodak camera was returned intact after the exposures were made to the Eastman Company for development and printing and was finally sent back to the customer re-loaded and ready for use (Eastman in Coe and Gates, *The Snapshot Photograph* [1977] page 17). Eastman's ingenious marketing strategy, encapsulated in the company's slogan, "You press the button, we do the rest," and laid the foundation for a widespread democratization of photographic practice in the decades to follow (Ford, *The Story of Popular Photography* [1989] page 62).

Yet the Kodak camera was still relatively expensive—at the cost of $25 in 1888, it was well outside the range of many, and by 1898, the Eastman Company introduced a less expensive, easy-to-operate camera aimed at further broadening the pool of amateur photographers. This simple box camera, called the Brownie, was devised by Frank A. Brownell, who had designed and manufactured cameras for the Eastman Company since 1885 and who would be its chief camera manufacturer until 1907. The Brownie was made of wood and jute board with an imitation leather covering and was equipped with a simple fixed-focus lens and rotary shutter. It was capable of producing successful exposures in relatively strong sunlight with subjects in focus from several feet to around 100 feet. The Brownie had no viewfinder but was marked with V-shaped sight lines on the top of the box which aided, when held at waist level, in aiming the camera toward the subject. The Brownie was pre-loaded with roll film, and yielded six 2¼-inch square images per strip, which could be tracked through a built-in red indexing window. At the cost of $1.00 (film included), the Brownie did indeed satisfy the demand for a markedly less expensive camera accessible to the amateur practitioner. With developing, printing, and mounting of prints equally affordable at $0.40, sales of the Brownie camera soared, reaching more than 100,000 cameras by the end of 1900.

By 1910, approximately one-third of all Americans owned a camera—that many of these were Brownie cameras must be attributed to a significant factor beyond its technical simplicity—namely Eastman Company's deliberate marketing of the new camera to children, both through a barrage of advertisements and in the very naming of the camera itself. Brownie was very much a household word in turn-of-the-century America before becoming the name of Eastman's latest camera. It described a type of small elf culled from popular legend to occupy the pages of author and illustrator Palmer Cox's children's stories. First published in the juvenile magazine, *St. Nicholas*, the brownies were further immortalized in numerous books, each of which bore the same introductory description of these creatures:

> Brownies, like fairies and goblins, are imaginary little sprites, who are supposed to delight in harmless pranks and helpful deeds. They work and sport while weary households sleep, and never allow themselves to be seen by mortal eyes....
>
> (Cox, *The Brownies: Their Book* 1887, n.p.)

This description of the Brownie, when associated with the Eastman's camera, speaks both to common assumptions about the nature of photography as revealing of something of the intangible aspect of the visual world unseen by the naked eye, as well as to its fit with Eastman's targeted users—children. The original 1900 packaging of the Brownie camera featured one of Cox's mischievous creatures playing against a colorful red, yellow, and green background on all four sides of the carton. In addition, these same brownie characters pitched the notion of photographing with the camera as a playful toy in advertisements for the ten years from 1900 to 1910. Ultimately, this manufactured relationship surfaced in one of Cox's own illustrations, which featured his character armed with the camera bearing his name.

In addition to the marketing of the Brownie camera with this popular children's character, Eastman Company also appealed to youth as potential photographers through extensive illustrated advertisements. In fact, it is estimated that images of children, engaged with this new photographic 'toy,' previously known to many of them solely within the formal confines of the portrait studio, comprised more than one-third of all those advertisements produced by the company between 1917 and 1932. Reproduced extensively in popular juvenile magazines of the day such as *St. Nicholas*, *The Youth's Companion*, *American Boy and Boy's Life*, as well as in the professional dealer publication, *Kodak Trade Circular*, such Brownie advertisements were often accompanied by the slogan, "Any Schoolboy or Girl Can Make Good Pictures with the Brownie Camera." Ads produced after 1910 often focused on young boys in particular, targeting their potential for a more sophisticated understanding of the camera's advanced features and capabilities, as opposed to the carefree leisurely practice of the "Kodak Girls" of Eastman's earlier campaigns. Eastman Company expanded upon the marked success of such campaigns with various special promotions such as a Brownie Camera Club. In celebration of the fiftieth anniversary of the founding of the company, Eastman offered young girls and boys a free camera for their twelfth birthday during 1930—specifically, a unique variation of the No. 2 Hawkeye Brownie covered in tan imitation leather and marked with a gold foil anniversary seal. In just a few days in May 1930, approximately 550,000 of these special edition Brownies were distributed to children.

Following the first Brownie introduced to the public in 1900, to the last camera that carried this name, nearly 100 different models were produced. The first variation, simply called the No. 2 Brownie, was introduced in 1901 and varied from the original (thereafter call the No. 1) in several ways. The No. 2 Brownie was equipped with a reflective viewfinder as well as three aperture options and produced $2^1/_4 \times 3^1/_4$-inch images. While this second version of the Brownie cost twice as much as its predecessor, it was extremely popular and served as the model for numerous variations in design produced through the 1950s. In fact, by 1930, the price of the No. 2 Brownie was not prohibitive, representing only 15% of the average weekly wage of Eastman Company's factory employee.

The vastly popular Nos. 1 and 2 Brownies, widely imitated by competing companies in both the United States and abroad, were also produced in an ongoing line by Eastman Company in the coming decades. In Great Britain, George Houghton and Sons devised a version of the Brownie in 1901 called the No. 1 Scout, while the American company ANSCO sold a competing line of cameras bearing the name Buster Brown, beginning in 1906. Those variations of the original Brownie camera produced by Eastman Company included several larger, and more expensive, folding camera models, produced between 1904 and 1926. In 1934, designer Walter Dorwin Teague created the Baby Brownie in a series of smaller models equipped with 127 roll film. The design of the Baby Brownie embodied both newly evolving capabilities in the molding of those plastics used to form the camera body, as well as the sleek, streamline aesthetics of the era. Specialty editions of already existing models were produced throughout the 1930s, including the Boy Scout Brownie (marketed in 1932 and 1933–1934), which featured the insignia of the American Boy Scouts against a geometric design on the camera's front panel as well as a similar model commemorating the World's Fair (marketed in 1939–1940). Other embellishments included Brownie models produced in a range of colors, such as the No. 2 Portrait Brownie. In addition to being outfitted with a special adjustable lens for close-up portraiture, this camera, marketed especially to women, was available in six colors as well as the standard black.

Although Eastman Company's initial advertisements of the Brownie cameras emphasized its perfect suitability for children, such promotion likewise underscored the camera's inherent simplicity for all amateur users, young and old alike, as well as its natural associations with the notions of adventure and imagination. Its removal of the need to understand the technical aspects of photographic processing and printing furthermore helped to introduce the snapshot to a vast array of new practitioners, who produced a myriad of images of family life, travel, leisure, and work, largely marked by an informal spontaneity as yet unseen in the history of the medium. A new element of the everyday entered into photography's vernacular, which stood in opposition to both the rare occasion of the family portrait and the elevated concerns of the photographic artist.

Yet the snapshot's thorough saturation in contemporary popular culture, with its origins in these turn-of-the-century amateur practitioners, has been met with both chagrin and critical interest. While considered far outside the purview of the art establishment by some, the last few decades have likewise seen the snapshot made the subject of scholarly attention and museum exhibition, while the simple aesthetic potential of the Brownie camera has been utilized by artists such as photographer William Christenberry.

Karen Jenkins

See also: **Camera: Point and Shoot; Eastman Kodak Company; Vernacular Photography**

Further Reading

Coe, Brian. *Kodak Cameras: The First Hundred Years*. Hove, East Sussex: Hove Foto Books, 1988.

Coe, Brian and Paul Gates. *The Snapshot Photograph: The Rise of Popular Photography 1888–1939*. London: Ash & Grant, Ltd., 1977.

Cox, Palmer. *The Brownies: Their Book*. New York: Appleton-Century-Crofts, Inc., 1887.

Ford, Colin, ed. *The Story of Popular Photography*. North Pomfret, Vermont: Trafalgar Square Publishing, 1989.

Lothrop, Jr., Eaton S. *A Century of Cameras: From the Collection of the International Museum of Photography at George Eastman House*. New York: Morgan & Morgan, Inc./Dobbs Ferry, 1973.

West, Nancy Martha. "Operated by Any School Boy or Girl: The Marketing of the Brownie Camera." In *Kodak and the Lens of Nostalgia*. Charlottesville & London: University Press of Virginia, 2000.

FRANCIS JOSEPH BRUGUIÈRE

American

Francis Bruguière produced some of the most avant-garde photography experiments of the early twentieth century. Always drawn to the abstract, Bruguière blended the sharp lines of modernism with a passion for darkroom effects. Until he found his own voice, however, Bruguière's first explorations were in a more traditional vein and thus largely neglected in the photographic canon today. Perhaps this censure was also due to Bruguière's frequent collaborations combined with his late involvement with one of the premiere movements to establish photography as a fine art, Alfred Stieglitz's Photo-Secession. Nevertheless, Bruguière forged a unique vision that did not end with the demise of Stieglitz's group, but began after it.

Bruguière was born to parents of French and Spanish heritage in 1879 in San Francisco, California. From a wealthy background, he attended a private school in the East and toured Europe. In 1901, he met and married Eliza Jones, a Broadway actress, who bore him a son three years later. In 1905, Bruguière visited New York. Instead of being drawn to the enigmatic Stieglitz, as many Photo-Secessionists were, he was instead drawn to Frank Eugene. Originally a painter, Eugene was known for incorporating liberal handwork into his negatives and prints and was often criticized for his extreme techniques. At Eugene's encouragement, Bruguière began to investigate photography as an art form and opened a studio in 1906. The two remained friends and corresponded for the rest of their lives.

Typical of the aesthetics and subject matter of Pictorialists, misty scenes of nudes comprised Bruguière's early work. In 1915, Bruguière and the Bay Area Photo-Secessionist Anne Brigman curated the photography section of the Panama-Pacific Exposition in San Francisco. It was not shown in the Palace of Fine Arts, where one could see Impressionist and Post-Impressionist masters, leading his fellow Photo-Secessionists to boycott. Despite becoming a Photo-Secessionist in 1905, Bruguière remained on the outskirts of the movement geographically and philosophically, allying himself with more minor members. He exhibited only once at the Photo-Secession gallery "291" in New York and contributed only one photograph to its journal, *Camera Work*—one issue before Stieglitz stopped its production in 1917.

Bruguière moved to New York in 1919 and immediately began to investigate a more "modern" aesthetic. There he opened a studio and began photographing for *Vogue*, *Harper's Bazaar*, and *Vanity Fair*. Bruguière also engrossed himself in the theatre, becoming the official photographer for the New York Theatre Guild (1919–1927). It was during a photography session for *Harper's Bazaar* that he met Rosalinde Fuller, the British actress who would become his model and mistress for the rest of his life.

In 1923, Bruguière discovered Sebastian Droste, a young German dancer, and began a daring film project titled *The Way*. Droste and Fuller were the sole actors in this drama, an early example of surrealistic leanings in America. Scenes of *The Way* included jarring multiple exposures, "film-noir-esque" lighting, and eerie heavy makeup. Bruguière intended *The Way* to concern "(the) thoughts if people who imagine rather than act realities. The main idea is that of a man who seeks happiness. From the beginning of his Pilgrimage to the end, he lives in a world of dreams." Unfortunately, Droste died in 1925 and the film was never finished; it survives only in Bruguière's posed still photographs.

Using techniques developed to light the stage, Bruguière began to explore issues of time and space by photographing cut paper. Although Bruguière's experiments recall cubist interests in abstract form, his primary goal was to allude to motion. This theme was further developed when he photographed Thomas Wilfred's "color organ," or clavilux, in 1921. An outgrowth of an interest in "synaesthesia," or the crossing of the senses, color organs allowed people to "see" compositions of light from a keyboard. Bruguière saw in these performances a popular turn-of-the-century notion—the fourth dimension. He wrote: "that is the effect I have long wanted to give. The effect of movement in the eye of the beholder, though the object itself was absolutely stationary when photographed."

In 1928, Bruguière moved to London and became acquainted with two men with whom he would later collaborate: critic Oswell Blakeston and graphic designer E. McKnight Kauffer. Bruguière produced several books in which photographs were integrated with, and sometimes stood in for, text: Lancelot Sieveking's *Beyond this Point* (1929) and Blakeston's *Few Are Chosen* (1931). With Kauffer, Bruguière created novel advertisements that combined photographs, text, and surrealistic imagery for Shell Oil, the British Postal Service, and Charnaux Corset Company.

Perhaps the epitome of Bruguière's blending of various media can be seen in his collaboration with Blakeston on England's first abstract film, *Light Rhythms* (1930). This film exists today only in description and notation as the original was destroyed in World War II. Arranged into movements and accompanied by a piano score, Bruguière's cut paper abstractions were lit by moving lights in pre-arranged sequences. In later investigations into cinematic effects, Bruguière photographed New York buildings at severe angles for a never-finished film he dubbed *Pseudomorphic*.

During the 1930s and 1940s, Bruguière occupied himself with further variations on photographic processes, including solarization and the cliché-verre. Both of these processes do not necessarily rely on an object or even a camera to produce their effects. The strange almost aura-like results of solarization, popularized by Man Ray in the 1920s, are created by exposing a print to light during the development process and engage chance, a topic of interest to the Surrealists.

In 1937, Bruguière was commissioned to design the entrance to the British Pavilion at the Paris Exposition, covering the 50-foot-high walls with large photomurals. Shortly after the exposition, Bruguière moved to the country to devote time to painting. Due to poor health, he returned to London where he began an unfinished autobiography. Before his death in 1945, Bruguière explored C. G. Jung, mandalas, and Eastern philosophies. His multi-disciplinary acumen—ranging from theater, music, film, to graphic design—prefigured a type of artistic activity that was to become more common later in the century, especially with the artists of the postmodern era. His legacy, however, can be seen in the abstract work of later photographers such as Frederick Sommer and Carl Chiarenza.

LESLIE K. BROWN

See also: **Abstraction; Modernism; Photo Secession; Photo Secessionists; Solarization; Sommer, Frederick; Stieglitz, Alfred**

Biography

Born in San Francisco, California, 16 October 1879. Attended boarding school and toured Europe. Studied with Photo-Secessionist Frank Eugene in New York and met Alfred Stieglitz, New York, 1905. Opened a photography studio, San Francisco, California, 1906. Employed as the official photographer for the New York Theatre Guild, 1919–1927; photographed for *Vanity Fair*, *Harper's Bazaar*, and *Vogue*; collaborated on advertisements with E. McKnight Kauffer for Shell Oil, the British Postal Service, and Charnaux Corset Company; designed gateway to the British Pavilion for the Paris Exposition, 1937. Substantial collections reside at at the International Museum of Photography and Film at the George Eastman House, Rochester, New York, the Center for Creative Photography, Tucson, Arizona, J. Paul Getty Museum, Los Angeles, California, and the Oakland Museum of Art, Oakland, California. Died in London and was buried in Middleton Cheney, England, 8 May 1945.

Individual Exhibitions

1916 *Francis Bruguière*; Paul Elder Art Room, San Francisco, California
1927 *Photographs and Paintings by Francis Bruguière*; The Art Center, New York, New York
1929 *Photographic Designs by Francis Bruguière*; The Warren Gallery, London, England
1977 *Bruguière*: *Announcing a Witkin Gallery Portfolio*; The Witkin Gallery, New York, New York

Group Exhibitions

1910 *International Exhibition of Pictorial Photography*; Albright Knox Gallery, Buffalo, New York
1915 *Pan-Pacific International Exposition*; San Francisco, California
1929 *Film und Foto*; Deutsche Werkbund, Stuttgart, Germany
1933 *Francis Bruguière in Collaboration with E. McKnight Kauffer*; Lund, Humphries Galleries, London, England
1937 *Photography 1839–1937*; Museum of Modern Art, New York, New York
1960 *The Sense of Abstraction in Contemporary Photography*; Museum of Modern Art, New York, New York
1976 *Photographs from the Julien Levy Collection*; Art Institute of Chicago, Chicago, Illinois
1979 *Photography Rediscovered: American Photographs, 1900–1930*; Whitney Museum of American Art, New York, New York; and The Art Institute of Chicago, Chicago, Illinois
1981 *Cubism and American Photography, 1910–1930*; Sterling and Francine Clark Art Institute, Williamstown, Massachusetts, and traveling
1997 *The Friends of Anne Brigman: Bay Area Pictorialists, 1900–1925*; Santa Barbara Museum of Art, Santa Barbara, California, and traveling

Selected Works

Portrait of Frank Eugene, 1905
A Portrait, Camera Work, 1916
Thomas Wilfred's Color Organ Projections, 1922
Stage Model for Norman Bel Geddes's set design for The Divine Comedy, c. 1924
The Way, series, 1923–1925
Cut Paper Abstractions, series, c. 1927
Light Rhythms, series, 1930
Advertisement by E. McKnight Kauffer and Bruguière for Charnaux Corset Company, c. 1932

Further Reading

Benedict, Burton. *Anthropology of a World's Fair: San Francisco's Panama-Pacific International Exposition of 1915*. Berkeley, CA: Lowie Museum of Anthropology and Scholar Press, 1985.
Bruguière, Francis. *San Francisco*. San Francisco, CA: H.S. Crocker, Co., 1918.
Bruguière, Francis, and Oswell Blaketon. *Few Are Chosen: Studies in the Theatrical Lighting of Life's Theatre*. London: Eric Partridge Ltd. at the Scholartis Press, 1931.
Enyeart, James. *Bruguière: His Photographs and His Life*. New York: Alfred A. Knopf, 1977.
Enyeart, James L. With reminiscence by Rosalinde Fuller. *Bruguiere: Announcing a Witkin Gallery Portfolio*. New York: Witkin Gallery, 1977.
Henderson, Linda Dalrymple. "Mysticism, Romanticism, and the Fourth Dimension." In *The Spiritual in Art: Abstract Painting, 1890–1985*. Organized by Maurice Tuchman and edited by Edward Weisberger. Los Angeles, CA: Abbeville Press, 1986.
Homer, Willian Innes. *Alfred Stieglitz and the Photo-Secession*. Boston: New York Graphic Society, and Little, Brown and Company, 1983.
Moritz, William. "Abstract Film and Color Music." In *The Spiritual in Art: Abstract Painting, 1890–1985*. Organized by Maurice Tuchman and edited by Edward Weisberger. Los Angeles, CA: Abbeville Press, 1986.
Sieveking, Lancelot de Giberne. *Beyond this Point*. London: Duckworth, 1929.
Sterling, George. *The Evanescent City*. San Francisco, CA: A.M. Robertson, 1915.
Young, Stark. "The Color Organ." *Theatre Arts Magazine* 6 (January 1922): 20–32.
Vandamm, Florence. *The Vandamm Collection: Theater Photographs from the Studios of Florence Vandamm and Francis Joseph Bruguière from 1915–1960 in the New York Public Library, Library and Museum of Performing Arts*. Teaneck, NJ: Somerset House, 1980.

VICTOR BURGIN

English

Equally known for his theoretical writings and for his artworks, Victor Burgin has had a profound impact on photography since the late 1960s. Comprising photography, text, video, and critical writing, his creative practice challenges traditional dualistic categories, operating in the in-between spaces between art and theory, image and text, photography and film, narrative and coincidence, inner and outer realms, psychic and social realities. As Maya Deren did for American avant-garde film, as Joseph Kosuth did for early conceptual art, and as Allan Kaprow did for happenings—artists who were impassioned advocates for their particular media, art histories, and conceptual positions—Burgin has extensively contextualized the ideas and concerns fueling his work. In the process he has staunchly defended the relevance of photographic images to contemporary society. He has done this on two fronts: in terms of the hidden ideologies images represent from the point of view of social, economic, and gendered institutions, and in terms of the way the psychological unconscious fuels our subjective projections onto what we see in the world around us.

Burgin's interests have moved from the semiotics of Roland Barthes to the class consciousness of Karl Marx and Louis Althusser to the psychoanalytic theories of Sigmund Freud and Jacques Lacan, along the way including feminism, film theory, postmodernism, and cultural studies. Often giving a very close reading of his influences, Burgin finds in each of these theorists language that articulates the complexities of interpretation and meaning, with a methodological focus on demystifying social phenomena—sign, image, class, and sex respectively—formerly assumed to be fixed and natural. Burgin's genius is to apply these theories and methods to the task of denaturalizing photography, which also suffers from essentialist assumptions about its truth-value. Throughout all of his investigations is a persistent questioning of the way social institutions and personal experiences mediate photographs, an emphasis on the connotative, rhetorical meanings of photographic images that belie their obvious empirical, denotative meanings.

A few key pieces early on lay Burgin's theoretical, aesthetic groundwork. *Photopath* (1967), first presented in the landmark exhibition *When Attitudes Become Form*, presents a row of photographs of a hardwood floor laid out exactly to match the areas photographed underneath them; the subtle one-to-one displacement, however, briefly confuses the real and the imaged, suggesting the faint ghosting of memory on the actual event. In *Performative Narrative* (1971), nearly identical images of an office desk are paired with 16 different text narratives. The slight differences in both are governed by a strict set of binary possibilities: file folder open or closed, desk chair pushed in or out, events described closer or farther in time, closer or farther in space. The systematic exploration of these possibilities contrasts sharply with the more evocative connotations of the scenes, as the emotional resonance of the photographs shifts depending on who we think took the photo, whose experience we think it captures, and how all those involved relate to one another. The street poster *Possession* (1976), initially posted throughout the city center of Newcastle upon Tyne, England, appropriates the visual rhetoric of mass media but with a linguistic twist; while the image shows a conventionally beautiful couple embracing, relying similar to advertising on the appeal of the image to draw a passerby's glance, the text questions the status quo distribution of wealth and property. Rather than convince us of the accuracy of the camera's reportage, these early photographic projects ask viewers to become critically aware of our own contribution to creating meaning for the images at hand.

One consequence of denaturalizing photography is that all perception can then be understood to arise out of a complicated intermingling of factual, cultural, and psychological associations. In Burgin's more recent work, which includes video portraits of New York, London, Paris, Weimar, and Berlin, and a collection of essays titled *In/Different Spaces: Place and Memory in Visual Culture* (1996), the experience of place becomes the subject of this critical analysis. For example, *Venise* (1993) explores the Mediterranean port city of Marseilles, but is juxtaposed with footage of San Francisco. A voice-over narration that tells the story of *Vertigo* and its dual manifestations in Alfred Hitchcock's film set in California and the original novel set in Paris and Marseilles. Other elements add to this layered doubling to emphasize the theme of migration: colonial imagery from a 1936 French film, North African music on the soundtrack. As the multi-threaded videos suggest, even while walking the streets the real and the imagined are hopelessly confounded by past experiences of other cities, memories of other times, snippets of literary, historical, and filmic representations, and our own idiosyncratic needs and wants. For Burgin, the object of our gaze, much as the object of our love, is never what we think it is; we never see something purely but always filtered through a network of prior recollections and desires. This explains in part the complexity of Burgin's video work: the open-ended narratives, the repetitions and patterns that provide structural support in lieu of a singular storyline, the tendency to appropriate other films and other artworks into his imagery, the shifting authorial voice of its speakers. As in his writings, Burgin quotes many other artists and authors in his artwork: Edward Hopper's *Office at Night*, Edouard Manet's *Olympia*, Johann Wolfgang von Goethe's *Elective Affinities*, Freud's case histories, E.T.A. Hoffman's *Gradiva*, Hitchcock's films, the personal letters of Friedrich Nietzsche and Lou Salome, the correspondences between Freud and his collaborator Sandor Ferenzi. By putting his images in a complex stream of other images, culled together through the peculiarities of his own imagination, Burgin defeats the single point of view of the isolated photograph. He allows photography to work around its own limits, or rather, its material, analogue basis, to begin to represent the harder-to-show subjective side of meaning.

In artists' books and exhibition catalogues such as *Between* (1986), *Some Cities* (1996), and *Victor Burgin* (2001) from his retrospective in Barcelona, Burgin has generously shared a detailed view of his motivating preoccupations. While such articulation should not be taken as narrowly definitive of the work—the work itself being more robust than what the artist has to say about it—it gives a rare chance to understand in depth one artist's relationship to his chosen profession. Those who love photography are fortunate to have such a record at our disposal.

JAN ESTEP

See also: **Artists Books; Barthes, Roland; Conceptual Photography; Interpretation; Photographic "Truth"; Postmodernism; Representation; Semiotics**

Biography

Born in Sheffield, England, 1941. Attended Royal College of Art, London, A.R.C.A (1st Class), 1965; Yale University, New Haven, M.F.A., 1967; Professor Emeritus of History of Consciousness, University of California, Santa Cruz; Millard Professor of Fine Art, Goldsmiths College, University of London. US/UK Bicentennial Arts Exchange Fellowship, Berlin, 1976–1977; Deutscher Akademischer Austauschdienst (DAAD) Fellowship, Berlin, 1978–1979. Allocation de recherché et de séjour, Ministère de la Culture et de la Communication, Délégation aux Arts Plastiques (vidéo et nouvelles technologies de l'image), Paris, 1991. Living in London and Paris.

Individual Exhibitions

1977 *Victor Burgin*; Stedelijk van Abbemuseum, Eindhoven, Netherlands
1979 *Zoo*; DAAD Gallery, Berlin, Germany
1986 *Office at Night*; Renaissance Society at the University of Chicago, Chicago, Illinois
1986 *Danaïdes/Dames*; Massachusetts Institute of Technology, Albert and Vera List Visual Arts Center, Cambridge, Massachusetts
1986 *Between*; Institute of Contemporary Arts, London, England
1991 *Passages*; Musée d'art moderne Villeneuve d'Ascq, Villeneuve d'Ascq, France
1993 *Family Romance*; Center for Research in Contemporary Art, University of Texas at Arlington, Texas
1997 *Szerelmes Levelek/Love Letters*; Mücsarnok Museum, Budapest, Hungary
1998 *Case History*; Yerba Buena Center for the Arts, San Francisco, California
1999 *Lichtung*; Weimar 99 Cultural Festival, Weimar, Germany
2000 *Nietzsche's Paris*; Architectural Association Gallery, London, England
2001 *Victor Burgin*; Fundació Antoni Tàpies, Barcelona, Spain
2002 *Listen to Britain*; Arnolfini, Bristol, England
2003 *Victor Burgin*; LisboaPhoto 2003 Festival, Cordoaria Nacional, Torreão Nascente, Lisbon, Portugal

Group Exhibitions

1969 *When Attitudes Become Form*; Institute of Contemporary Art, London, England
1970 *Information*; Museum of Modern Art, New York, New York
1971 *Guggenheim International Exhibition*; Solomon R. Guggenheim Museum, New York, New York
1972 *Documenta 5*; Museum Fredericianum and Neue Galerie, Kassel, Germany
1972 *36 Biennale de Venezia*; Venice, Italy
1980 *The Third Biennale of Sydney*; The Art Gallery of New South Wales, Sydney, Australia
1987 *Difference: On Sexuality and Representation*; The New Museum of Contemporary Art, New York, New York; The Renaissance Society at the University of Chicago, Chicago, Illinois; Institute of Contemporary Arts, London, England
1987 *The Turner Prize*; Tate Gallery, London, England
1989 *On the Art of Fixing a Shadow: One Hundred and Fifty Years of Photography*; Art Institute of Chicago, Chicago, Illinois; National Gallery of Art, Washington, D.C.; and traveling to Los Angeles County Art Museum, Los Angeles, California

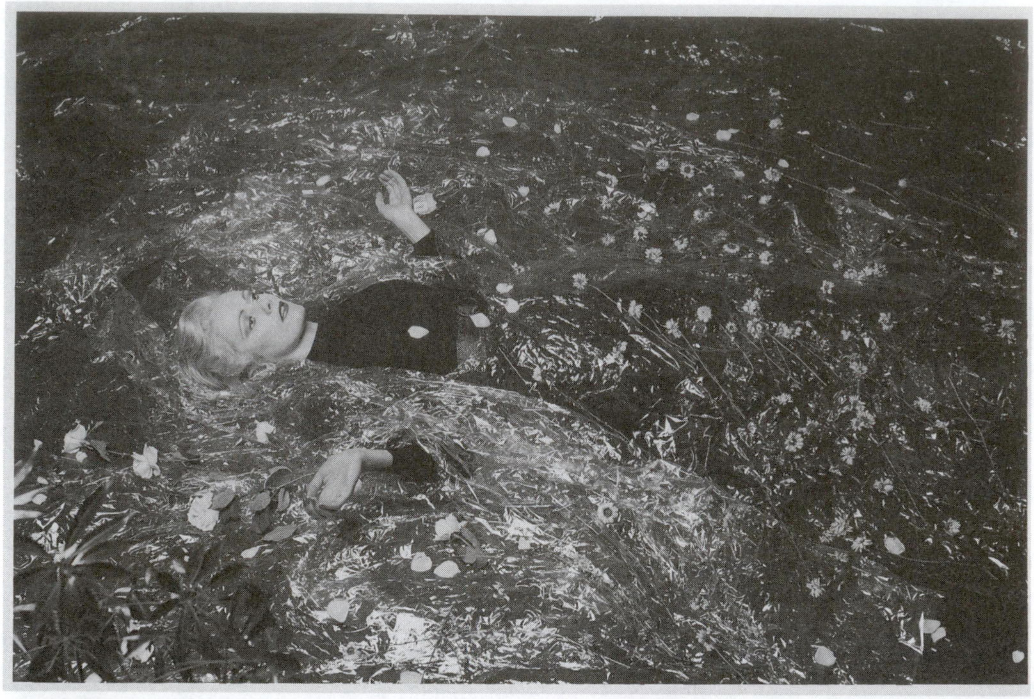

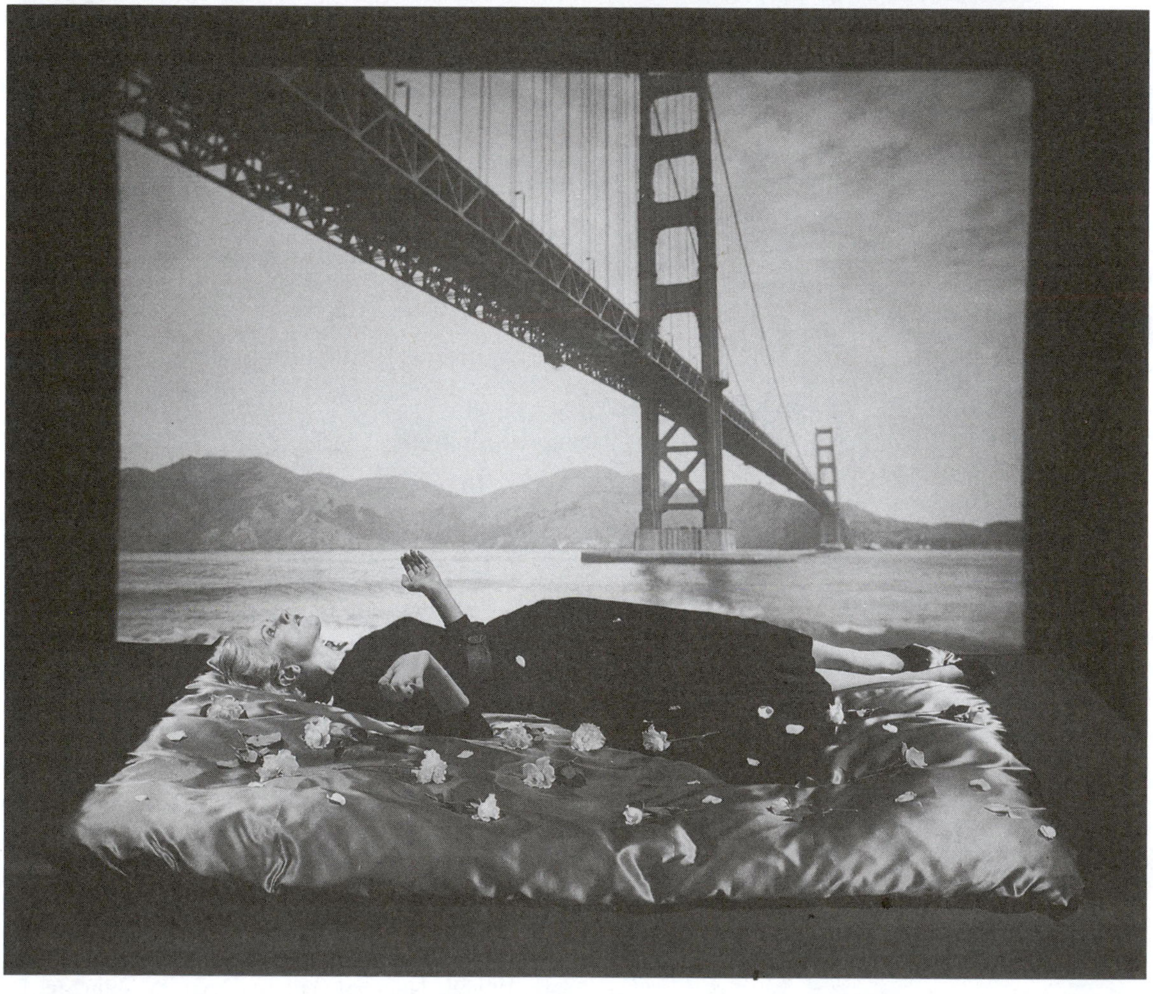

Victor Burgin, The Bridge, 1984, detail from seven section photo-text installation.
[*Reproduced with permission of the artist*]

1989 *The Art of Photography: 1839–1989*; Museum of Fine Arts, Houston, Texas; Royal Academy of Art, London, England; Ministry of Culture of the Soviet Union, Moscow; National Gallery of Australia, Canberra, Australia
1995 *1965–1975: Reconsidering the Object of Art*; Museum of Contemporary Art/The Temporary Contemporary, Los Angeles, California
1996 *Hall of Mirrors: Art and Film Since 1945*; The Museum of Contemporary Art/The Temporary Contemporary, Los Angeles, California
1996 *Face à l'Histoire 1933–1966: L'artiste moderne face à l'événement historique*; Centre Georges Pompidou, Paris, France
2000 *Media/Metaphor*; 46th Corcoran Biennial, Corcoran Gallery of Art, Washington, D.C.

Selected Works

Assemblée dans un Parc, 2004
Listen to Britain, 2002
Watergate, 2000
Nietzsche's Paris, 1999–2000
Lichtung, 1998–1989
Love Stories #2, 1996
Venise, 1993
Office at Night, 1985–1986
The Bridge, 1984
Gradiva, 1982
US 77, 1977
Possession, 1976
Performative Narrative, 1971
Room, 1970
Photopath, 1967

Selected Publications

Exhibition catalogues

Burgin, Victor, Stephen Bann, Peter Osborne, Françoise Parfait, and Catsou Roberts. *Relocating*. Bristol: Arnolfini, 2002.

Burgin, Victor, Norman Bryson, Nuria Enguita Mayo, Francette Pacteau, and Peter Wollen. *Victor Burgin*. Barcelona: Fundació Antoni Tàpies, 2001.

Burgin, Victor, and Anthony Vidler. *Shadowed*. London: Architectural Association, 2000.

Burgin, Victor. *Passages*. Lille: Musée d'art moderne de la Communaté Urbaine de Lille, Villeneuve d'Ascq, 1991.

Burgin, Victor. *Between*. London: ICA, and Oxford and New York: Basil Blackwell, 1986.

Burgin, Victor. *Victor Burgin*. Eindhoven: Stedelijk van Abbemuseum, 1977.

Theoretical Writings

Burgin, Victor. *The Remembered Film*. London: Reaktion Books, 2004.

Burgin, Victor. *In/Different Spaces: Place and Memory in Visual Culture*. Berkeley and Los Angeles: University of California Press, 1996.

Burgin, Victor. *The End of Art Theory: Criticism and Postmodernity*. London: Macmillan Press; and Basingstoke, and New Jersey: Humanities Press International, 1986.

Burgin, Victor, James Donald, and Cora Kaplan, eds. *Formations of Fantasy*. London: Methuen, 1986.

Burgin, Victor, ed. *Thinking Photography*. London and Basingstoke: The Macmillan Press Ltd.; and New Jersey: Humanities Press International, 1982.

Artists' Books

Burgin, Victor. *Some Cities*. Berkeley and Los Angeles: University of California Press; and London: Reaktion Books, 1996.

Burgin, Victor. *Venise*. London: Black Dog Publishing, 1997.

Burgin, Victor. *Family*. New York: Lapp Princess Press and Printer Matter, 1977.

Burgin, Victor. *Work and Commentary*. London: Latimer, 1973.

BURNING-IN

Burning-in is a darkroom technique employed by photographers to fine-tune the tone and shadows in one or more areas of a print by adding more light to those areas than the rest of the image receives. Once a photographer has determined how long his exposure should be and has made a print at that exposure time, he might decide that there are areas of the print that are too light, but that increasing the overall exposure time would make most of the print too dark. Burning-in allows him to add more light only to selected areas of the print while still maintaining the original exposure time for the rest of the image. Burning-in is often used to darken areas that are too light so that, hopefully, more information from the negative will show up on the final print.

It is important to remember that burning-in occurs after the initial exposure time and is the addition of light to specific areas of the print. While burning-in can be a helpful technique, overuse of burning-in can create areas that are grey and murky, and can decrease contrast, especially in black and white prints. Burning-in requires practice, and the added "burning" time changes with each negative printed.

Burning-in an area on an image can be done with or without a specific "burning-in" tool. Some photographers prefer to use their hands, held together in such a way that there is a small hole between the hands or fingers through which light can pass. In some ways, this is easier than using a burning-in tool with a static opening, because the size of the hole a photographer's hands are making can be changed during the burning-in time and is infinitely variable. A burning-in tool is usually a piece of opaque board with a small hole cut or torn somewhere near the middle of the board. The tool (whether board or hands) is then held between the light and the easel, and is moved rapidly back and forth to create a small "spotlight" or light directed onto the image in the area that needs additional light. The rapid back-and-forth movement creates a feathered effect that ensures that the burned-in area will blend with the surrounding areas and with the rest of the image. If the burning-in tool remains static, the area of added light will stand out from the rest of the image with clearly-defined borders.

Once a photographer has determined that an area needs to be burned-in, he places an unexposed piece of photographic paper into the easel and exposes it for the already-determined length of time. Then, without moving either the easel or the enlarger, and without changing the aperture setting, he turns back on the enlarger lamp to add more light to selected areas. This is most easily done with a foot pedal, as that allows the photographer to have both hands free to cover the image and only allow light to fall in the selected area. However, a foot pedal is not necessary, and burning-in can be accomplished with any kind of timing device. It is important that nothing be moved before or during the burning-in, as re-exposing areas of the image after movement will cause blurring on the final image—so not only should the photographer be sure not to move anything before adding light, he should also be careful not to bump the enlarger or the lens with his burning-in tool while making the exposure.

The time needed to burn-in areas agreeably can vary widely. Since burning-in occurs after the initial exposure time, burning-in times are almost limitless. If desired, the photographer can make a test strip in the area that needs to be burned-in, taking as his starting time the overall exposure time and increasing the time from there. Once satisfied with the tone of the area on the test strip, the photographer can make a full-sized print and burn-in the area for the amount of time indicated by the test strip. The photographer can also use trial and error to determine how much additional time an area needs, making educated guesses based on each print he attempts.

Obviously, past a certain point, continued light in an area of a print will turn that area black. This can be used to the photographer's advantage if he is interested in creating, for instance, an artificial vignetted-edged effect—here, the photographer would burn-in each edge for a sufficient amount of time to turn the edge black, making sure to feather the edges into the rest of the print. Using this technique, the photographer can change the appearance of the format he is printing, such as by burning-in the edges to a circular or oval shape.

Burning-in can also be used to create other visual effects in the darkroom. Just as edges of burned-in areas are softened by moving the burning-in tool for the duration of the additional exposure, hard edges can be created by holding a piece of opaque paper with a specifically cut out area stationary between the light and the easel. While most photographers want any burned-in areas of their prints to blend into the non-burned-in areas, there are certainly ways to play with the obviousness of burning-in. Burning-in can be helpful in evening out tones in prints made from uneven or thick negatives, the additional light often bringing out information that did not come through in the initial exposure.

Most digital image manipulation software includes a variable-sized burning-in tool, which can be moved across the image to darken certain areas. However, it often seems that digital burning-in quickly de-saturates and muddies colors, rendering them less vivid than non-burned-in areas. While it can be a useful tool, burning-in seems best used sparingly and in small areas, both digitally and in traditional darkrooms.

JENNY ALLRED REDMANN

See also: **Darkroom; Dodging; Enlarger; Exposure; Manipulation**

Further Reading

The Focal Encyclopedia of Photography. New York: Focal Press Ltd. (McGraw-Hill Book Co.), 1969.

International Center for Photography: Encyclopedia of Photography. New York: Pound Press (Crown Publishers Inc.), 1984.

McDarrah, Gloria S., Fred W. McDarrah, and Timothy S. McDarrah. *The Photography Encyclopedia*. New York: Schirmer Books, 1999.

Swedland, Charles. *Photography: A Handbook of History, Materials, and Processes*. Atlanta: Holt, Rinehard and Winston, Inc., 1974.

RENÉ BURRI

Swiss

The work of René Burri continued the tradition of engaged, documentary photography in the second half of the twentieth century. Traveling with his camera to a myriad of places around the world, he is one of the most important representatives of "live photography." Born in 1933 in Zurich, Burri was educated at the Kunstgewerbeschule in Zurich (Zurich School for Applied Arts) between 1949–1953. His teachers included Johannes Itten who taught elements and color instruction and Hans Finsler who taught photography. Burri's initial interest was in film. While still at the Kunstgewerbeschule, Burri received a scholarship to create a documentary about his school. In 1953, he also served as camera assistant to Ernst A. Heininger for the Disney film, *Switzerland*. His interest in film continued throughout his life, and in 1964 Burri was a founding member of Magnum Films.

After military service, Burri began to work with his 35-mm Leica. Through the intervention of his friend, Werner Bischof, who also motivated him to continue developing his style, Burri's coverage of deaf-mute children at the Zurich Institute for Musical and Rhythmic Education appeared in *Life* magazine (it was previously printed in *Science et Vie*). This began a significant career in international photojournalism with world travels and numerous photographs published in *Look*, *Fortune*, *Paris-Match*, *Twen*, *Stern*, *Geo*, *The New York Times*, and *The Sunday Times*. Many of his best-known series, however, appeared in the Swiss magazine *Du*, including *Gauchos* of 1959 and a series on famed architect Le Corbusier.

Through Werner Bischof, Burri had become acquainted in 1955 with Magnum Photos and its founder Henri Cartier-Bresson. Bresson became a friend and, following Hans Finsler, Burri's second great teacher. Whereas Finsler taught him to view things in an austere manner, emphasizing graphics, Burri was able, via Cartier-Bresson, to confirm his ideas about photojournalism, that it should be humane and has a moral obligation to inform. The combination of these divergent tendencies is significant. Burri is at base a storyteller, for whom photographic composition always plays an important role. Even in the shots that sometimes appear to be fortuitous, a specific moment can be found in which elements such as the cropping, camera angle, composition, and lighting harmonize with the content. Such pictures, therefore, sometimes appear to be constructed.

> I am conscious of my great facility in constructing images, that probably comes from my knowledge and experience of graphic arts. But technique should never impose itself, know-how should never be distracting. The means are made to clarify the end, not to obscure it.
>
> (Burri 1984)

Portraits of artists such as *Pablo Picasso* (1957 and 1960), *Alberto Giacometti* (1960), and actress *Ingrid Bergman* (1960) or the icon-like portrait of revolutionary *Che Guevara* (1963) with a cigar analyze the character of the sitter despite the fortuity of the foreground. With these portraits Burri demonstrates a pronounced knowledge of human nature, proving himself to be a meticulous observer, who understands how to concentrate and imbue the sum of his impressions into single, empathetic photographs. Burri described his procedure as follows:

> There are a few ground rules: The photographer is the clown. With his camera, he can induce something that a journalist cannot. Although a person can tell a journalist everything, a camera can cause the subject to be suddenly confronted with himself. To create intimacy without being perceived is crucial, but not always possible. Some people become too affected by the scene. Everyone is vain, but some can transpose it better than others. Only a very few manage to conceal the vulnerable places.
>
> (Ulmer 1999)

In 1962 *Die Deutschen* (*The Germans*), Burri's first book, was published by Robert Delpire with a forward by French cultural theorist Jean Beaudrillard. In this photoseries Burri explored his mother's nasince the end of the 1950s. On the one hand, he analyzed himself in a sort of critical search for his identity in the former Germany of his mother's time. Following the tradition set by Henri Cartier-Bresson with *Die Europäer* (*The European*), 1950–1955 and his fellow Swiss, Robert Frank with *Die Amerikaner* (*The Americans*) 1954–1958, Burri's photographs received considerable acclaim, while the book itself (now a collector's item) was not a commercial success. His second book, *Gauchos*, with a text by famed Argentinean author Jorge Luis Borges, appeared in 1968.

He achieved more success with his aerial cityscapes in Brazil such as *Sao Paulo* (1960). Using a bird's eye view of the city center, which flattens the architecture, and shooting for dramatic contrasts of both light and geometric and organic forms, a breathtaking panorama is presented that emphasizes the anonymity of the city and the alienation of its human residents, who are depicted as tiny silhouettes.

Idyllic places are rarely depicted in Burri's pictures. Similarly, illustrated confirmations of clichés about places and countries are also rare. Rather, in his photographs he explores national identities through documenting the living history while connecting it with the past, especially evident in such series as *Terre de Guerre* and *In Search of the Holy Land*, which depict war zones, to his Argentinean *Gauchos* and *Amerikanscher Traum: Photographien aus der Welt der NASA und des Pentagon* series. Burri succeeds in depicting a world wherein common human concerns are emphasized while the unique qualities of particular places are captured.

International contracts sent Burri to Czechoslovakia in 1955, France and Libya in 1957, the Middle East and Egypt during the 1956 Suez Canal crisis and the 1967 Six-Day-War, South America for numerous assignments, Korea and Japan in 1961, Vietnam during the Vietnam War in 1963, and China in 1964 among many other places. These trips resulted in photoseries and books such as *Nasser's Egypt* (1958), *Fidel Castro's Cuba* (1963), *The New Petrol Kings* (1974), *A Day in the Life of America* (1974), *Searchers for Gold, Brazil* (1977), *Palestinian Fighters* (1979), and *A Day in the Life of Australia—March 6, 1981* (1981).

Burri most characteristically works in black and white, although he also worked with color since 1976. Parallel to his work in photography, Burri also produced films for advertisement and industry that include *The Physical Face of China* (1965), *Three Villages of China* (1965), *The Industrial Revolution* (1965), *Jerusalem* (1967), *What's It All About?* (1967) —with this film he won the New York International Film and Television Festival Award in 1967—*Jerusalem After the Six-Day-War* (1967), *The Two Faces of China* (1968), *Bracia Si, Uomini No* (1970, with Peter Ammann), *Xerox in Concert* (1971, with Philipp Gittelmann), *Jean Tinguely* (1972), and *Indian Summer* (1973).

Franz-Xaver Schlegel

See also: **Bischof, Werner; Cartier-Bresson, Henri; Finsler, Hans; Life; Look; Magnum Photos; Portraiture**

Biography

Born in Zurich, Switzerland, April 9, 1933. Studied at the Kunstgewerbeschule in Zurich (Zurich School for Applied Arts), 1949–1953. Basic courses from Johannes Itten; Photography from Hans Finsler and Alfred Willimann. From 1953 on active as a photojournalist and published first photo reports. Served in the military and bought his first Leica in 1954. Set up studio with Walter Binder, 1954. In 1955, a photographer for Josef Müller-Brockmann; became an independent photographer. Member of the photo agency Magnum, associated in 1955. In 1956, correspondent in New York and Paris. In 1959 became a full member of Magnum and in 1964, a founding member of Magnum Films. President of Magnum France, vice president of Magnum in Europe, and opened the Magnum Gallery in 1982 together with Bruno Barbey. Married Rosellina Bischof in 1963 and had two children: Yasmine and Oliver. Became Art Director of the *Schweizer Illustrierte* in 1988. Honors: International Film and Television Festival Award, New York, 1967; Dr. Erich-Salomon-Preis der Deutschen Gesellschaft für Photographie (DGPh) (Dr. Erich Salomon Award for the German Society of Photography) in Cologne, 1988; and was named Chevalier d'Ordre des Arts et des Lettres by the French Minister of Culture, 1991. René Burri has remarried and lives in Zurich and Paris.

Individual Exhibitions

1965 *China*; Galerie Form, Zurich, Switzerland
1967 *Selected Works*; The Art Institute of Chicago, Chicago, Illinois
1971 *Selected Works*; Galerie Rencontre, Paris, France
1972 *René Burri*; Raffi Photo Gallery, New York, New York
1972 *René Burri*; Galleria Il Diaframma, Milan, Italy
1980 *Die Deutschen*; Folkwang Museum, Essen, Germany
1983 *Antologica*; Kunsthaus, Zurich, Switzerland
1984 *One World*; Kunsthaus, Zurich, Switzerland, and traveling
1984 *René Burri*; Musée de l'Elysée, Lausanne, Switzerland
1984 *René Burri*; Palais de Tokyo, Japan, Centre national de la photographie, Paris, France
1997 *René Burri*; Galerie Argus Fotokunst, Berlin, Germany
1998 *Die Deutschen*; Photokina, Cologne, Germany, and traveling
1998 *77 Strange Situations*; Villa Tobler, Zurich, Switzerland
2004 *René Burri: Photographs*; Maison Européenne de la Photographie, Paris, France, and traveling

Group Exhibitions

1960 *European Photography*; Museum of Modern Art, New York, New York
1960 *The World as Seen by Magnum*; Takashimaya Department Store, Tokyo, Japan, and traveling
Photography of the Twentieth Century; George Eastman House, Rochester, New York
1965 Musée Réattu, Arles, France *10 fotografos*; Havana, Cuba
1967 *Photography in the Twentieth Century*; National Gallery of Canada, Ottawa, Canada, and traveling
1972 *Behind the Great Wall of China*; The Metropolitan Museum of Art, New York, New York, and traveling

1974 *Photographie in der Schweiz von 1840 bis heute/ Photographie Suisse depuis 1840 à nos jours*; Kunsthaus Zurich, Zurich, Switzerland, and traveling
1977 *Concerning Photography*; The Photographers' Gallery, London, England, and traveling
1979 *Images des hommes*; Brussels, Belgium
1980 *The Imaginary Photo Museum*; Photokina, Cologne, Germany
1981 *Magnum Paris*; Palais du Luxembourg, Paris, France
1982 *Photojournalism 1960–1980*; Stedelijk Museum, Amsterdam, the Netherlands
Terre de guerre; Galerie Magnum, Paris, France
1984 *Sammlung Gruber*; Museum Ludwig, Cologne, Germany
Swiss Photography from 1840 until Today; Pro Helvetia Foundation, Zurich, Switzerland, and traveling
1986 *Von Photographen gesehen: Alberto Giacometti*; Bündner Kunstmuseum, Chur, Germany
1990 *Dialogue avec Le Corbusier*; Harthof, Basel, Switzerland
1999 *China: Fifty Years Inside the People's Republic*; Asia Society, New York, New York
2001 *Magic Moments II*; Landesvertretung Rheinland-Pfalz, Berlin, Germany, and traveling

Selected Works

Deaf-mute children (series), 1955
The Suez-Crisis (series), 1956
Pablo Picasso, 1957
Ingrid Bergman, 1957
Nasser's Egypt (series), 1958
Argentine Gaucho (series), 1959
Le Corbusier, 1960
Che Guevara, 1963
Lotosblüten im See im Sommerpalast bei Peking, 1964
A Day in the Life of America (series), 1974
The New Petrol Kings (series), 1974
Searchers for Gold, Brazil (series), 1977
Palestinan Fighters (series), 1979
The Impossible Mirror (series), 1998
Blind Indifference (series), 1998

Further Reading

Auer, Michèle, and Michel Auer. *Encyclopédie Internationale des Photographes de 1839 à Nos Jours/ Photographers Encyclopedia International 1839 to the Present*. Hermance (CH): 1985.

Bayer, Jonathan, ed., *Concerning Photography*. London: The Photographer's Gallery, 1977.

Billeter, Erika, ed. *Das Selbstportrait im Zeitalter der Photographie*. Bern: 1985.

Browne, Turner, Elaine Partnow, eds. *Macmillan Biographical Encyclopedia of Photographic Artists & Innovators*. New York and London: Collier MacMillan, 1983.

Burri, René. *Die Deutschen*. Zurich: 1962.

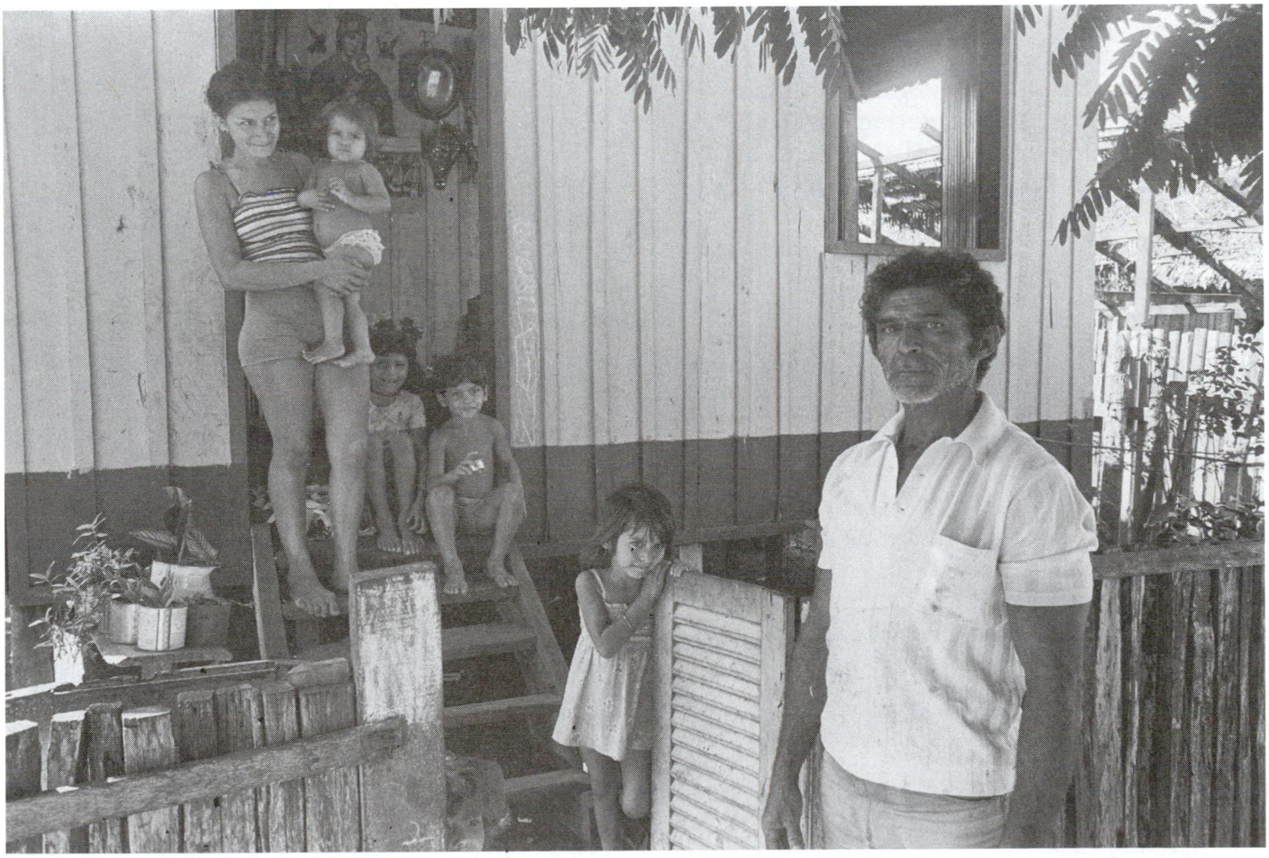

René Burri, Amazonas, Brazil, 1977.
[© *René Burri/Magnum Photos*]

Burri, René, and Michael Koetzle. *René Burri: Photographs*. London: Phaidon Press, 2003.
Fabian, Rainer, and Hans Christian Adam. *Bilder vom Krieg*. Hamburg: 1983; English: *Images of War: 130 Years of War Photography*. London: New English Library, 1985.
Gruber, L. Fritz, and Renate, eds., *The Imaginary Photo Museum*. New York: Harmony Books, 1981.
Guillain, Robert, Francois Meilleau, and Pierre Landy. *Le Japon que j'aime*. (Photographs by René Burri). Paris: 1965.
Hara, Hiromu, Ihei Kimura, eds. *Photography of the World '60*. Tokyo and New York: 1960.
Loetscher, Hugo. *Swiss Photography from 1840 until Today*. Zurich: 1984.
Lyons, Nathan. *Photography in the Twentieth Century*. New York: 1967.
Magnaguagno, Guido. *René Burri: One World. Fotografien und Collagen 1950–1983*. Bern: 1984.
Szarkowski, John, ed. *The Photographer's Eye*. New York: Little Brown & Co., 1966.
Stephan, Peter, ed. *Fotografie! Das 20. Jahrhundert*. Munich: 1999.
Ulmer, Brigitte. *Der Fotograf ist meistens ein Clown* (*The Photographer is Usually a Clown*). In *Tagesanzeiger* (Zurich) 26 Juni 1999.

LARRY BURROWS

British

Shot by shot, story by story, Larry Burrows developed an enduring vision of the war in Vietnam, where he photographed for nine years from 1962 until his presumed death under fire in a helicopter on the Vietnam-Laos border in 1971. In the process, Burrows developed his reputation as one of the preeminent photojournalists of the twentieth century. Working for *Life* magazine, Burrows created remarkable photo essays in both black-and-white and color that chronicle the escalating involvement of the United States in Vietnam, from advisers to full combatants after 1965, and the emotional and physical toll of the war on Vietnamese and Americans alike. Besides the powerful legacy of his Vietnam photographs, Burrows photographed a range of other subjects across several continents in his 25-year career.

Born Henry Leslie Burrows in London in 1926 to working class parents (his father was a truck driver for the railroad, his mother was a housewife), Burrows never attended college. He honed his craft through a lengthy apprenticeship, first as a darkroom assistant at Keystone Photographic Agency in London in 1941, then getting a job in 1942, at age 16, as a photographic laboratory technician in *Life* magazine's London bureau. Rejected by the military because of his poor eyesight, Burrows served in the Home Guard during World War II and experienced the blitz firsthand. He worked in *Life*'s lab until 1945, other than for a period during 1944 when he was conscripted by the government to work in the British coal mines in support of the war effort. His duties at *Life* ranged from fetching tea and coffee for people in the office to processing film and printing photographs taken by some of the legendary combat photographers of World War II, including Robert Capa.

Burrows' professional career as a photographer began in 1945. He was a freelance photographer from 1945–1961, often under contract to *Life*. In this period, he photographed more than 700 assignments, working mainly in Europe, the Middle East, and Africa, although he also went to India, Pakistan, and the United States. His varied subjects included celebrities such as novelist Ernest Hemingway, shots at bullfights in France and Spain, politicians such as Winston Churchill, violent conflicts in Lebanon and the Congo, and archaeological excavations. In this period Burrows also worked on a project photographing great artworks in Europe for reproduction in *Life*, an experience that honed his sensitivity to pictorial composition and taught him to understand and use color like an artist, as a means to create emotion and bring out the nuances of a visual story.

In 1961 Burrows became a *Life* staff photographer, based in Hong Kong, a position he held until his death in 1971. Although Vietnam subsumed much of his time during the last 10 years of his life, he also produced photo essays on subjects in places from India to New Zealand, photographing the architectural wonders of India's Taj Mahal and Cambodia's Angkor Wat, the beauty of New Guinea's birds of paradise, Emperor Hirohito of Japan and Prince Sihanouk of Cambodia, the 1964 Olympic Games, a historical piece on the British East India Company, and the 1970 cyclone in the Ganges Delta in what was then East Pakistan.

In 1962 Burrows went to Vietnam for the first time. The war was a small story in 1962 as far as the United States was concerned: President Kennedy had only recently sent American soldiers as advisers to the South Vietnamese Army, with no commitment of combat troops. Burrows, then 36, grasped at once that Vietnam had the potential of an epic story. According to David Halberstam in his introduction to *Larry Burrows: Vietnam* (2002), Vietnam "was the assignment [Burrows] had always wanted....He was drawn to it by both its elemental humanity and its parallel cruelty and violence, and by the fact that it lent itself so well to what he wanted to do—the magazine photo spread." Burrows used the essay format brilliantly to tell compelling stories, including his first long Vietnam feature in *Life*, titled *In Color: The Vicious Fighting in Vietnam, We Wade Deeper into Jungle War*, a 14-page story with a foldout cover published on January 25, 1963, which helped convey to Americans the quality of that cruel civil war fought by small bands of soldiers in the countryside, pitting Vietnamese against Vietnamese. In this and subsequent essays, Burrows demonstrated his pioneering understanding of when and how to use color effectively for war photography, showing human dramas against landscapes of often stunning beauty.

Burrows had the advantage over press photographers working for daily newspapers, who worked on tight deadlines, of having time to conceptualize and develop a story, often spending months immersing himself intellectually and visually in a long photo essay. Press photographers in Vietnam had extraordinary freedom of access to combat zones, and Burrows was fearless about getting close to the action. Stories abound about his courage and dedication, including strapping himself to the open doorway of an airplane to shoot photos for his 1966 essay, *The Air War*.

A chronological survey of Burrows's Vietnam photo essays demonstrates his intellectual grasp of the important trends of the ever-escalating war, with its terribly mounting violence and evolving psychological texture. *One Ride with Yankee Papa 13*, a spread of 22 photographs published in *Life* on April 16, 1965, chronicled a dangerous helicopter mission during which marines attempted to rescue wounded comrades, one of whom died. Focusing in particular on a young crew chief, Burrows's photo story conveyed the soldier's emotional journey in the course of the mission from grinning newcomer to devastated veteran. *Operation Prairie*, published on October 28, 1966, documented a bloody six-month Marine infantry campaign that took a devastating toll in U.S. casualties. One photo from that story, *Reaching Out* (during the aftermath of taking hill 484, South Vietnam), which shows bandaged soldiers covered in mud, is one of Burrows's most frequently reproduced photos. Although Burrows said he began working in Vietnam with leanings as a hawk, his ten-page photo essay, *Vietnam: A Degree of Disillusion*, published on September 19, 1969, expressed, Burrows wrote in one of his captions, "a degree of disillusion and demoralization in the Army and the population that surprised and shocked me."

On February 10, 1971, as the invasion of Laos was imminent, Burrows and four other combat photographers—Kent Potter, Keizaburo Shimamoto, Henri Huet, and Tu Vu—rode aboard a South Vietnamese helicopter that was shot down by antiaircraft guns along the Vietnam-Laos border. Burrows, who was 44 years old, left behind his wife Vicky, son Russell, and daughter Deborah. Twenty-seven years later, in 1998, an American search and recovery team excavated the crash site in Laos, recovering pieces of film and a Leica camera that most likely had belonged to Burrows.

JEAN ROBERTSON

See also: **Capa, Robert; Life Magazine; War Photography**

Biography

Born in London, England, 22 May 1926. Self-educated in photography. Darkroom assistant, Keystone Photographic Agency, London, 1941; Photographic laboratory technician, *Life* Magazine, London, 1942–1945; conscripted into British coal mines during World War II, 1945; freelance photographer, mostly under contract to *Life* magazine, working primarily in Europe, the Middle East, and Africa, 1945–1961; *Life* staff photographer, based in Hong Kong, with responsibility for an area from India to New Zealand, including Vietnam, 1961–1971. Three-time winner of the Overseas Press Club's Robert Capa Gold Medal; awarded British Press Pictures of the Year, 1965, 1966; awarded the World Press Photo, The Hague, 1966; named Magazine Photographer of the Year by the National Press Photographers' Association (NPPA), 1967; recipient of the Order of Iron Mike (US Marine Corps), 1967. Missing, presumed dead, Laos, 10 February, 1971.

Individual Exhibitions

1998 *Larry Burrows at War: Vietnam 1961–1972*; Laurence Miller Gallery, New York, New York

Selected Group Exhibitions

1987 *Realities Revisited: 15 British Photographers*; Centre Saidye Bronfman; Montreal, Quebec, Canada
1989 *Eyes of Time: Photojournalism in America*; International Center of Photography, George Eastman House; Rochester, New York, and traveling
2003 *Oases: Group Exhibition*; Laurence Miller Gallery, New York, New York

Selected Works (Photo essays published in Life)

Marines Move into Lebanon, 1958
In Color: The Vicious Fighting in Vietnam, We Wade Deeper into Jungle War, 1962–1963, *Life*
One Ride with Yankee Papa 13, 1965
Birds of Paradise, 1965
The Air War, 1966
Marines Blunt the Invasion from the North, 1966
Operation Prairie, 1966
Vietnam: A Degree of Disillusion, 1969

Further Reading

Burrows, Larry. *Larry Burrows, Compassionate Photographer*. New York: Time Incorporated, 1972.
Burrows, Larry. *Larry Burrows: Vietnam*. Introduction by David Halberstam. New York: Alfred A. Knopf, 2002.
Page, Tim, and Horst Faas. *Requiem: By the Photographers Who Died in Vietnam and Indochina*. New York: Random House, 1997.
Pyle, Richard, and Horst Faas. *Lost Over Laos: A True Story of Tragedy, Mystery, and Friendship*. New York: Da Capo Press, 2003.

NANCY BURSON

American

The works of Nancy Burson have earned a place within the history of postmodern photography largely as images that challenge the viewer's perception of visual reality, normality, beauty, and often, abject ugliness. While Burson's portraits share surface similarities with the works of Diane Arbus and Ralph Eugene Meatyard from the previous two decades, they are more directly related to conceptual photography as well as being emblematic of contemporary experiments with digital photography, exploring techniques of manipulation, simulation, and reproduction. However, Burson has always moved omnivorously among photographic media and approaches, and her work is difficult to classify.

Burson's oeuvre can be roughly organized into three phases: her early work (1979 to 1991) dealt with fantasy or surreal faces. These computer-generated works included composite imagery, aged portraits, and digitally manipulated faces that resulted in bizarre and sometimes frightening anomalies. Examples include *Warhead I*, a computer-generated "portrait" composed of media images of world leaders based on quantities of nuclear arsenals of each country. The composite image is 55% of Ronald Reagan, 45% of Leonid Brezhnev, and less than 1% each of British Prime Minister Margaret Thatcher, French President François Mitterrand, and Chinese leader Deng Xiaoping. The work is presented as a full frontal portrait in a format similar to a mug shot, without background. The second phase of her work—made between 1991 and 1995—includes "straight" photographic portraits of what Burson calls "special faces," namely persons whose features have been deformed or marred by disease or other natural abnormalities. The third phase (1996 to the present) includes disparate images that combine straight and manipulated technologies, among these, color Polaroids of "faith healers" (the *Healing* series), and collaborative projects that meld art with science and technology, including *The Human Race Machine* (2000), an interactive installation that allows a viewer to picture himself or herself as a different race or an amalgam of races.

In 1968, shortly after a move to New York City from Denver (where Burson had studied painting at Colorado Women's College), she viewed an exhibition at the Museum of Modern Art that signaled a turning point in her career. *The Machine as Seen at the End of the Mechanical Age* traversed six centuries of historical intersections between art and technology with a particular emphasis on technological art of the 1960s. Burson was thus inspired to conceive an interactive ageing machine, an installation that would allow a viewer to age himself or herself with the aid of a computer. In 1976, the Massachusetts Institute of Technology's Architecture Machine Group (today the MIT Media Laboratory) adopted Burson's project. However, it would take several years for the technology to advance in order for Burson and her collaborators to realize *The Age Machine*. In 1981, the artist and engineer Thomas Schneider jointly received a patent for "The Method and Apparatus for Producing an Image of a Person's Face at a Different Age," which has been subsequently used by the United States government, including the FBI, to locate missing children based on the computer-generated photographs of what they would look like if they had been "aged." Reflective of her ongoing investigations about the self and the myriad representations of identity, sameness, and difference, Burson continued to refine the technology with the aid of computer scientists David Kramlich and Richard Carling. In 1990, Kramlich and Burson presented *The Age Machine* at MIT, an interactive computer station whereby a viewer could sit at a console and scan an image of his or her face, input some data, and within seconds the machine would create a speculative portrait of the sitter 25 years in the future.

Burson relied on this collaboration to create a number of arresting "portraits," or composite pictures in which the structure or features of numerous individuals are blended in the creation of a hybrid, a person who only exists in fantasy or virtual reality. Examples of these include a series of *Untitled* color Polaroids of subjects whose warped features appear partly human, partly alien. Other composites that meld faces of different races, ages, and sexes, as well as media images of celebrities and politicians, result in sometimes eerie, sometimes humorous visages that blur the line between the universal and the particular, self and other. Although some viewers might interpret Burson's composites as simply bizarre or voyeuristic—fodder for a circus sideshow—the artist believes that they represent a relevant curiosity about identity, selfhood, and the truth of the photograph. According to curator Dana Friis-Hansen, "plotting gut instincts about the self and human nature against the mechanics and metaphors of technology led Burson to her considerable achievement: a humanizing technology" (Friis-Hansen, 1990, 8).

Moreover, her work reveals connections not only to the massive history of portraiture but to the history of physiognomy (the study of personality traits based upon facial characteristics), as well as phrenology, a nineteenth-century pseudoscience that purported to establish links between cranial and facial structure and intelligence and racial superiority. While Burson's composites engage with or perhaps echo this history, they do not claim to define or make statements about the aforementioned races or "types" as her historical antecedents did. Rather, Burson is drawn to the question of whether seeing can be equated with believing and whether visual perception can effectively communicate reality. Never one to assume that seeing *is* simply believing, Burson's photography has continually sought to explore the imagistic, the psychological, and the spiritual aspects of the visual world.

After spending approximately 15 years on the forefront of digital and computer technology in order to create her fantastical faces, Burson then turned to a more traditional approach to the medium. She began shooting "straight" portraits of subjects—adults and children—whose faces were deformed by various diseases such as cancer or genetic abnormalities. In effect the photographer turned from digitally altered faces to those that had been biologically altered, if not permanently marred. Burson explained that her interest in photographing children with Apert syndrome and other craniofacial disorders was spurred by her own pregnancy in 1989. Preoccupied with the possibility of genetic deformities, as a prelude to the straight works, she began to produce composite "portraits" based on images she found in medical casebooks. These *Untitled* images from the late 1980s are meant to be read as ambiguous representations of genetic disorder based on multiple images, rather than a specific individual visage. When she turned to flesh and blood rather than virtual subjects, the photographer reexamined the blurry notion of photographic truth (essentially asking, "Does the camera lie?") but also forced the viewer to recognize his or her preconceived notions about Burson's difficult subjects. The result is that the viewer is caught up in the artist's own vision as the camera captures the sometimes stark and grotesque faces of the deformed.

Apert syndrome, an extremely rare and random genetic disorder, affects and deforms the bones of one's head, hands, and feet. Subjects with the syndrome often have overly tall or asymmetrical skulls, sunken features, and webbed hands and feet. Burson's first subject of this kind was Nathaniel, the young son of a friend, Jeanne McDermott. One mother's painful recognition that the world might never accept her son based on his appearance spurred McDermott to ask Burson to photograph him. She desired other people to see a different vision of her beloved child, one in which his humanity would connect rather than differentiate him from others. McDermott wrote in *Nancy Burson: Faces*:

> So deeply embedded is our experience of the visual world with what we see from the moment of birth, that vision never was and never will be a mechanistic process of recording reality 'just as it is.' This is particularly true when it comes to faces. According to studies, within the first five seconds of meeting someone, we make up our minds about a person's character and moral nature based largely on how we see his face.
>
> (Burson and McDermott 1993, n.p.)

Burson echoes this notion in her claim that her faces are mirrors for the viewer, reflecting one's projections and ideas in sometimes startling ways. The untitled series was made with a plastic Diana camera, a simple child's camera that results in square negatives and blurry images, as aperture and focus cannot be manipulated. These snapshot images communicate a poignancy and beauty that brazenly confronts the taboo of looking at the "other" among us. Burson's images of sufferers of Apert syndrome do not shy away from the reality of her subjects' deformities, but they also do not fetishize them. Rather, these images reflect a warmth and tenderness without resorting to sentimentalizing or editorializing. The hazy gray tones, close-up point of view, tight cropping, and seemingly haphazard compositions endow these pictures with an air of mystery and surrealism while also capturing the everyday or snapshot aesthetic. She followed this series in 1994–1995 with 24 × 20-inch color Polaroids of faces altered by cancer, reconstructive surgery, and prosthetics.

Since 1996 Burson has created photographs that echo her investigations into science and technology, often returning to the computer-generated image. In 1997–1998 she photographed androgynous men and women in a series called *He/She*. The sex of the sitter is not made clear to the viewer (all of the Polaroids are untitled) as Burson specifically sought faces that blurred conventionally masculine and feminine features. Burson writes

> My goal is to emphasize the commonality of people rather than their differences or separateness....the series intentionally challenges the individual's notion of self-perception, by allowing viewers to see beyond superficial sexual differences to our common humanity.
>
> (Artist's Statement 2004)

The artist's focus on universality and humanity more closely aligns her work with modern (rather than postmodern) theories of the self. In addition, the *He/She* portraits do not present these ideas in any didactic way, but rather function on a purely aesthetic level.

As part of a series titled *Pictures of Health*, Burson teamed with Russian scientist Konstantin Korotkov in 2000 to photograph the "aura" emitted through a person's fingertips using a Gas Discharge Visualization camera. The camera—used in Europe and Russia for diagnostic purposes—records energy fields, or auras. Two of these works that Burson describes as "aural fingerprints," titled *The Difference Between Negative and Positive Thought* and *The Difference Between Love and Anger*, were made from the hands of hands-on healers who generated a wide range of emotional states within themselves. Burson then photographically "mapped" a range of auras based on the emotional temperature, as it were, of the healer. Other recent, related works made in collaboration with geneticists at the National Cancer Institute include images of healthy and unhealthy DNA. The images are created as scanned electron microscope photographs that Burson outputs as Iris prints.

Lynn M. Somers-Davis

See also: **Arbus, Diane; Camera: Diana; Conceptual Photography; Digital Photography; History of Photography: the 1980s; Manipulation**

Biography

Born in St. Louis, Missouri in 1948; currently lives and works in New York City. Raised in the Midwest; studied painting at Colorado Women's College in Denver, CO, 1966–1968; subsequently moved to New York, NY. Visiting professor at Harvard University, Cambridge, MA, and adjunct professor at New York University. Collaborated with Creative Time and the Lower Manhattan Cultural Council completing several important public art projects including the billboard *There's No Gene For Race* and the poster/postcard project *Focus on Peace* (2000). The *Focus on Peace* project distributed 30,000 postcards and 7,000 posters around the site of the World Trade Center to coincide with the anniversary of 9/11.

Individual Exhibitions

1974 *Nancy Burson*; Bertha Urdang Gallery, New York, New York

1977 *Nancy Burson*; Hal Bromm Gallery, New York, New York

1978 *Nancy Burson*; C. W. Post College, Long Island University, Brookville, New York

1985 *Nancy Burson*; International Center of Photography, New York, New York

Nancy Burson; Institute of Contemporary Art, Boston, Massachusetts

1986 *Nancy Burson*; Chrysler Museum, Norfolk, Virginia

1987 *Nancy Burson*; Torino Fotographia, Turin, Italy

1990 *Nancy Burson: The Age Machine and Composite Portraits*; M.I.T. List Visual Arts Center, Cambridge, Massachusetts, traveled to Museum of Contemporary Photography, Columbia College, Chicago, Illinois; Jayne H. Baum Gallery, New York, New York

1991 *Nancy Burson*; Galerie Michèle Chomette, Paris, France
1992 *Faces*; Contemporary Arts Museum, Houston, Texas; traveled to Denver Art Museum, Denver, Colorado; Center for the Fine Arts, Miami, Florida; Contemporary Arts Center, New Orleans, Louisiana
Nancy Burson and David Kramlich: The Age Machine; New Museum of Contemporary Art, New York, New York
1993 *Nancy Burson*; Jayne H. Baum Gallery, New York, New York
University of Rhode Island, Fine Arts Center Galleries, Kingston, Rhode Island
1996 *Nancy Burson: Volte-Face*; Espace Van Gogh; Rencontres Internationales de la photographie, Arles, France
1997 *Nancy Burson*; Museum of Contemporary Photography, Chicago, Illinois
1998 *Nancy Burson: Portraits*; Forum for Contemporary Art, St. Louis, Missouri
2000 *There's No Gene for Race* (billboard); Creative Time, New York, New York
2002 *Focus on Peace: A project of Lower Manhattan Cultural Council in Partnership with Creative Time*; New York, New York
Seeing and Believing: The Art of Nancy Burson; Grey Art Gallery, New York New York; traveled to Blaffer Gallery, Houston, Texas; Weatherspoon
Museum, University of North Carolina, Greensboro, North Carolina; PhotoEspana, Madrid, Spain

Group Exhibitions

1985 *Identity*; Palais de Tokyo, Paris, France
1987 *Fake*; New Museum of Contemporary Art, New York, New York
1988 *Fabrications: Staged, Altered, and Appropriated Photographs*; Carpenter Center, Harvard University, Cambridge, Massachusetts
The Spiral of Artificiality; Hallswalls Contemporary Arts Center, Buffalo, New York
1989 *Image World: Art and Media Culture*; Whitney Museum of American Art, New York, New York *The Photography of Invention: American Pictures of the 1980s*; Smithsonian Institution, National Museum of American Art, Washington, D.C.; Museum of Contemporary Art, Chicago, Illinois; Walker Art Center, Minneapolis, Minnesota
Photography Now; Victoria and Albert Museum, London, England
1990 *The Indomitable Spirit*; International Center of Photography, New York, New York: Los Angeles Municipal Art Gallery, Los Angeles, California; Sotheby's, New York, New York
1991 *Power: Its Myths, Icons and Structures in American Culture, 1961–1991*; Indianapolis Museum of Art, Indianapolis, Indiana; Virginia Museum of Fine Arts, Richmond, Virginia; Akron Art Museum, Akron, Ohio
1992 *In Vitro: De Les Mitologies de la Fertilitat als Limits de la Ciencia*; Fundació Joan Miro, Barcelona, Spain
1994 *Elvis + Marilyn: 2 x IMMORTAL*; Institute of Contemporary Arts, Boston, Massachusetts, and traveling
Metamorphoses: Photography in the Electronic Age; Museum at the Fashion Institute of Technology, New York, New York, and traveling
Body and Soul: Contemporary Art and Healing; DeCordova Museum and Sculpture Park, Lincoln, Massachusetts
1995 *Photography After Photography: Memory and Representation in the Digital Age*; Aktionsforum Ptraterinsel, Munich, Germany, and traveling
1996 *Counterculture: Alternative Information from the Underground Press to the Internet*; Exit Art, New York, New York
1997 *The Nineties: A Family of Man?*; Forum d'Art Contemporain, Casino Luxembourg
In the Realm of Phantoms, Photographs of the Invisible; Museum Abteiberg, Mönchengladbach, Germany; Kunstalle Krems, Austria; and Fotomuseum Winterthur, Switzerland
1998 *In Your Face*; Warhol Museum, Pittsburgh, Pennsylvania
In Visible Light, Photography and Classification in Art, Science, and the Everyday; Museum of Modern Art, Oxford, England
1999 *Ghost in the Shell*: *Photography and the Human Soul, 1850–2000*; Los Angeles County Museum of Art, Los Angeles, California
2000 *Le Siècle du corps: Photographies 1900–2000*; Musée de L'Elysée, Lausanne, Switzerland
The Human Race Machine; London Millennium Dome, London, England
2002 *photoGENEsis: Opus*; Santa Barbara Museum of Art, Santa Barbara, California
The Other Face: Metamorphosis of the Photographic Portrait: Deutsches Museum, Munich, Germany
Time Framed; Nederlands Foto Instituut, Rotterdam, The Netherlands
2003 *Only Skin Deep: Changing Visions of the American Self*; International Center of Photography, New York, New York
Geometry of the Face; Royal Library, National Museum of Photography, Copenhagen, Denmark
Suture: An Exhibition of "Medical Photographs"; Stephen Bulger Gallery, Toronto, Ontario, Canada
White: Whiteness and Race in Contemporary Art; Center for Art and Visual Culture, University of Maryland, Baltimore, Maryland

Selected Works

First Beauty Composite, 1982
Warhead I (55% Reagan, 45% Brezhnev, less than 1% each of Thatcher, Mitterand, and Deng), 1982
Mankind (Oriental, Caucasian, and Black, weighted according to current population statistics), 1983–1985
Etan Patz Update (Age 6 to Age 13), 1984
Untitled series (portraits of persons with Apert Syndrome), early 1990s
Aged Barbie, 1994

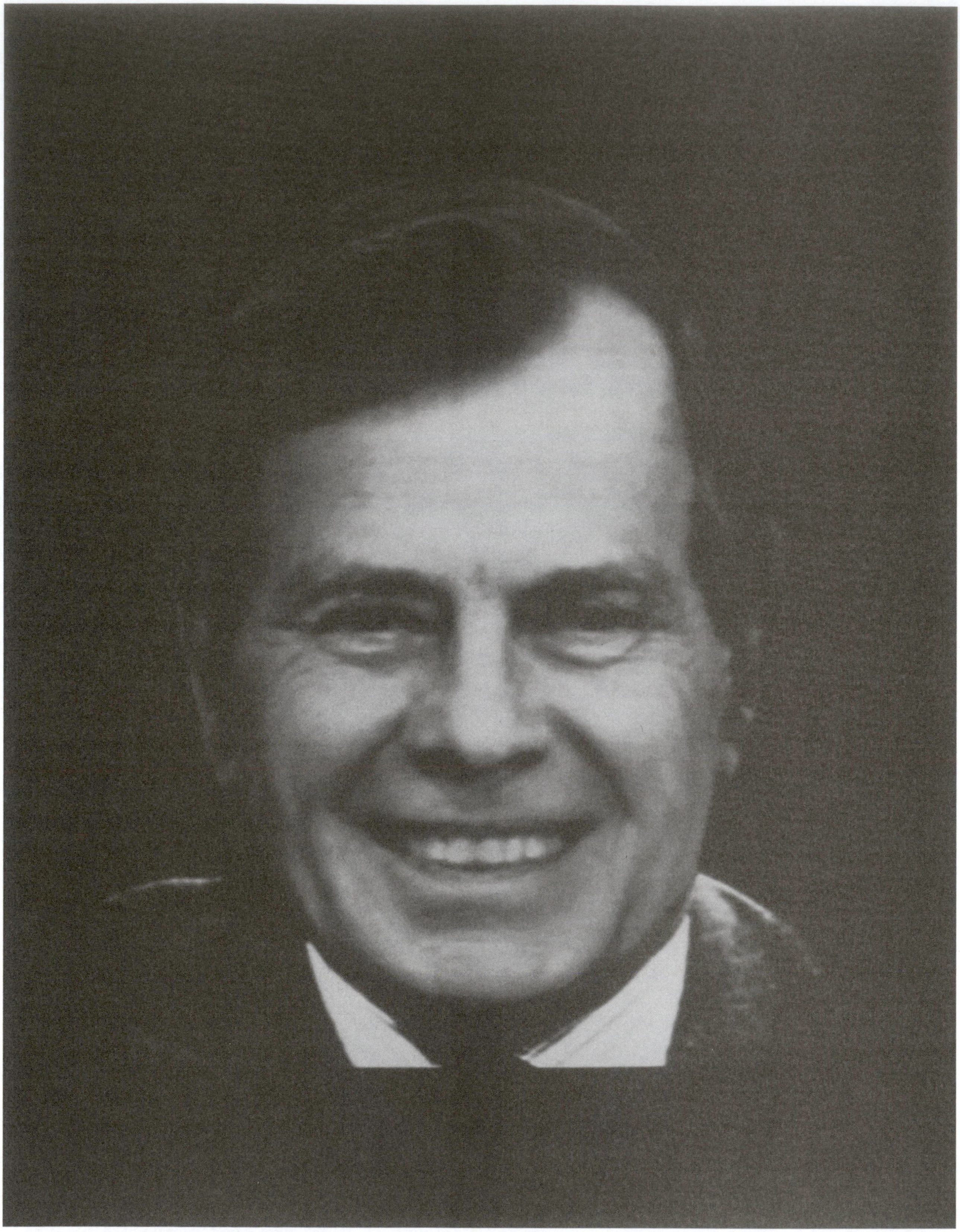

Nancy Burson, The President (second version), 1988, Polaroid print on paper, original in color.
[*Smithsonian American Art Museum, Washington, DC/Art Resource, New York*]

Untitled series (portraits of persons with craniofacial disorders), 1994–1995
He/She series, 1996–1997
Untitled (*Guys Who Look Like Jesus* series), 2000
Healing series, c. 1996–2001
The Difference Between Negative and Positive Thought, 2000
The Difference Between Love and Anger, 2000

Further Reading

Atkins, Robert, and Thomas Sokolowski. *From Media to Metaphor: Art About AIDS*. New York: Independent Curators Inc., 1991.

Burson, Nancy, with Jeanne McDermott. *Faces: Nancy Burson*. Santa Fe, NM: Twin Palms Publishers, 1993.

———. "Love and Death." *World Art* 13 (1996); 84.

Burson, Nancy, with Michael L. Sand, Lynn Gumpert, and Terrie Sultan. *Seeing and Believing: The Art of Nancy Burson*. Santa Fe, NM: Twin Palms Publishers, 2002.

Burson, Nancy, with Richard Carling, and David Kramlich. *Composites: Computer Generated Portraits*. New York: William Morrow, Beech Tree Press, 1986.

Dery, Mark. "Fast Forward: Art Goes High Tech." *ARTnews* 92 (February 1992); 74–83.

Friis-Hansen, Dana. *Nancy Burson: The Age Machine and Composite Portraits*. Exh. cat. Cambridge, MA.: MIT Press, 1990.

Grundberg, Andy. *Crisis of the Real: Writings on Photography 1974–1989*. New York: Aperture, 1990.

Haworth-Booth, Mark. *Photography Now*. Exh. cat. London: Dirk Nishen, 1989.

Heiferman, Marvin, Lisa Phillips, and John G. Hanhardt. *Image World: Art and Media Culture*. Exh. cat. New York: Whitney Museum of American Art, 1989.

Herbert, Lynn. *Faces: Nancy Burson*. Exh. cat. Houston: Contemporary Arts Museum, 1992.

Hirsch, Robert. *Seizing the Light: A History of Photography*. New York: McGraw Hill, 2000.

C

CABLE RELEASE

A cable release is a device that allows the camera shutter to be remotely activated. Seen in practical terms, the device allows the photographer to be "hands-off," because even the almost undetectable movement caused by the body's pulse can be enough to blur the image in a shot with the camera. In technical terms, a cable release is a plunger that the photographer grasps, a cable, and a pin or some device to trigger the camera shutter.

Yet the cable release can be useful in other applications in which the photographer wants to be away from the camera while taking the picture. The cable can be of various lengths, and is most widely used in animal and nature photography where the photographer may need to screen himself or herself separately from view, apart from the camera set-up; candid photography, where the photographer's presence fixed to the camera may dampen spontaneity; children's photography, where the subject may need to be actively distracted by the photographer, and in instances when the photographer wants to appear in the picture.

Professional studio photographers employ cable releases routinely if engagement by the photographer carrying on a conversation with the subject leads to better portraits, less squirming or movement by the subject, and may permit the subject to be more natural and relaxed. The use of large-format cameras, where the parameters of the scene are set by ducking the head under a light-dampening blanket, historically used in studio portraiture, certainly can be seen as inhibiting a natural response in a subject. In nature photography, some means of being away from the camera is often essential a camera being much easier to hide than a person. Cable releases attached to trip wires where the photographer is nowhere in the area have also been increasingly used in remote locations where sitting for hours awaiting a shy or nocturnal animal is simply not practical.

A variation on the conventional mechanical system featured in most cable releases is the use of an air bulb to trigger the device that then clicks the shutter. Some feel this is more gentle, reliable and dependable. The air bulb is attached by a tube to a piston that is moved by the increase in air pressure that occurs when the bulb is squeezed. This motion in turn then triggers the cable release socket on the camera to trip the camera shutter. Typically the fixed mechanical cable release is short and places the photographer near the camera. The tube on the air or bulb release sort of system may be longer, at times up to 20 feet, allowing the photographer to be further away. It also can be released by foot pressure, freeing up both hands for gesturing or otherwise communicating with the subject.

In many modern cameras the cable release is electronic. The plunger is a button that is powered by the power source for the camera, the cable is wire, and the shutter is triggered by the electrical impulse from the plunger. Many modern cameras do not have mechanical sockets for the straightforward cable release; they depend entirely on the electrical system. Other modern external release systems are able to entirely dispense with the cable. A beam of microwaves, light, or radio waves replaces it. No different a change than from the old cable connected television remote to the more modern one that allows much more movement and convenience. Cameras, like many other devices in the modern world, have become wireless.

Each of these devices has its application. In most medium format and large format photography, it is simply convenient to use a mechanical cable release whether the camera is handheld or attached to a tripod. In the case of large format, it is almost always the case that the camera is on a tripod. To go to the trouble of the larger format, the tripod, and then to hand trip the shutter is simply a contradiction.

In the case of studio photography where there may be elaborate lighting setups firing a number of the lights, synchronization of these lights more often than not requires some form of cable release. There are combinations of slaves and triggers that are operated by light, radio frequency, or microwaves that make these setups possible and manageable. This is moving toward the elaborate iteration of the cable release, but the intent is the same—coordination of various pieces of equipment and removal of the photographer's hand from the camera.

In photography such as macro-photography, product photography, or other close-up requirements in which extreme sharpness is important, it is critical that the release of the shutter be as smooth as possible. Thus, to reduce blur, some sort of cable shutter release system is essential. Simple mechanical cable releases are inexpensive and are an affordable way in which to improve the ability to get an optimal exposure. They do jam, bend, and otherwise occasionally fail, and like all camera gear, cable releases should be packed and cared for gently. Air releases are usually marginally more expensive but remain one of the more affordable of all photo accessories. Electronic cables are considerably more expensive, and the wireless systems even more so, and each photographer's requirements will dictate the type of equipment best suited to his or her needs.

It is also important when selecting a camera that one thinks about what sort of work will be done with it and whether or not a cable release system will be required, for there are some cameras that are not equipped with any attachment point for any sort of external release mechanism. There are instructions for homemade cable releases that can be found in books and on the internet that may help if one is confronted with this sort of problem, although it is best avoided.

Lambert McLaurin

See also: **Camera: An Overview; Time Exposure**

GENEVIÈVE CADIEUX

Canadian

The extraordinary force of Geneviève Cadieux's work derives from the visual coherence and breadth with which her often very large creations repeatedly bring corporeal intimacy and absorptive anxiety into an inescapably public forum. They engulf and destabilize the viewer through simultaneous attraction and repulsion, while concurrently calling into play multiple resonances around both aesthetic and social issues. Born in Montreal in 1955 but raised in Ottawa where she obtained a BA with a specialisation in visual arts from the University of Ottawa, she sometimes referred to the influence which her father's repertory cinema had upon her tendency to visualize her works in large-screen filmic format, or as installations in often darkened rooms. For example, in the early installation *Voices of Reason/Voices of Madness*, 1983, as much as in the recent video *Paramour*, 1998–1999, the viewer is offered close-ups of female heads during an endlessly repeated fragmentary event, pregnant with an implied narrative of psychic torment. In the first work, the viewer steps before a color slide projection of a woman's head with only the eyes lighted, staring at the opposite wall, where another woman's head, in a black-and-white projection, gradually dissolves into a milky focus and an anguished expression. Suddenly, the viewer is shocked by a loud shot, and the face gradually returns to focus, to begin again. In the second, the woman anxiously asks again and again, "Haven't you ever loved a woman? Haven't you ever desired a woman? Not once, not for a single moment? Never, ever?" to be answered each time by a male voice from behind the viewer, "No, never."

However, Cadieux's work cannot be enlisted to feminism, as almost any label tends to oversimplify the range and depth of her references. The woman's questions in *Paramour*, for example, are derived from a text of Marguerite Duras, an appropriation of literary sources which Cadieux had previously displayed in *La Blessure d'une cicatrice ou Les Anges* (*The Wound of a Scar or The Angels*), 1987. In that large diptych, the left panel contained a painted image of Le Petit Prince, hero of Saint-Exupéry's famous children's book, his features effaced and with the inscription below "Voilà le meilleur portrait que plus tard, j'ai réussi à faire de lui" [Here is the best portrait that I was later able to make of him], while the right panel reproduced one of the most famous of the *Storyville Portraits* by E.J. Bellocq—a prostitute seen from the rear, her head scratched out in the emulsion. In Cadieux's work, she seems to be drawing a butterfly on the wall. This juxtaposition, taken from two volumes collected by Cadieux in what she called her "archives," combined and amended both literary and visual sources in a duality which problematized portraiture and identity through metaphors of inadequacy and scarring, and the conflation of child, prostitute, and angel. That Cadieux was suggesting an implicit damage or disability when contemplating the sensitive self seems confirmed by another work which also used the Petit Prince quotation, *A fleur de peau* (*On Edge* or *Skin Deep*), 1987. There, the left panel of the diptych reproduced the quotation in Braille, while the right was a clouded mirror; a blind viewer would not see a reflection in the mirror, while a sighted viewer would not understand the Braille unaided, and neither could easily decode the fragmentary or elusive view of self, based as much on suggestible memory as on immediate experience, into which they were being drawn.

These examples also foreground two other defining formal features of Cadieux's work—its multi-media range, including a crucial use of often punning titles, and its intimate focus on bodily damage or enlargement as an evocative mechanism. She frequently uses blown-up scars or parts of the body or skin contextualized by positioning with landscape or architectural elements. For example, the instability of meaning in titles such as *La Fêlure, au choeur des corps*, recalls the postmodern insistence on language games, and is matched with the surreal juxtaposition of two giant lips kissing between two healed scars. This intense interest in the body's pleasures and the marks of corporeal pain, linked to a size which engenders a sense of both overwhelming force and of powerless voyeurism, reflects other postmodern fascinations. This work, constructed at room size and displayed as Canada's contribution at the *Venice Biennale* of 1990, confirmed Cadieux's international stature. She has been exhibited extensively in 13 countries in Europe as well as in Canada, the United States, Japan, Brazil, and Australia, and she has taught in France (1993–1994, 1996), Spain (1997), and in the United States (1998) as well as Canada. Together with some other Canadians such as Jeff Wall and Evergon, she helped to define and influence a tendency among young Canadian art photographers to use large color photographic imagery to construct ironic or surreal worlds.

However, no other Canadian has so effortlessly moved between sculpture, painting, photography, and video formats, appropriations, installations with sound, and classic references to diptych, triptych, and serial forms, all often connected to landscapes, interior or exterior architecture or specific sites. She came to photography later in her artistic training, underlining that, fundamentally, the presence of the artist is felt in her works more in the concept, which determines medium and form, than in the physical mark. This allows her to roam between a very precise realism (e.g., *Elle*, 1993, a cast of her mother's arm) and an evocative abstraction. The texture of the pores of the skin in many of her works can seem indistinguishable from the grain of photographic emulsion, an effect she admits is deliberate. She also calls upon a range of previous classical genres, from nudes to portraiture to landscape, set within a range of social contexts, from medicine to technology; but they are created usually for a museum space which can tolerate and assimilate the works according to that oxymoron, conventional avant-gardist criteria. In portraiture, already referred to above, she has made deft use of her own family members to explore by suggestion themes of attraction and alienation, and of aging. In three of her most well-known works, *Hear Me With Your Eyes* of 1989, *Family Portrait* of 1991, and *La Voie lactée* of 1992, she has used, respectively, her actress sister in a triptych which revealed her at two intense moments some 10 years apart; an installation of three large free-standing lightboxes featuring enigmatic details of her father, mother, and sister turned away from each other at the corners of a triangle; and a billboard-size view of her mother's lush mouth installed on the roof of the Musée d'art contemporarin in Montreal. Except for *Family Portrait*, these works are not, at first, evident as portrait statements; nonetheless, their effectiveness depends on the viewer's sense of identification with the physical and psychological presence, even the suffering, of another which underlies the impact of portraiture.

Cadieux's work has also been likened to pornography (e.g., *Loin de moi, et près du lointain [Far From Me, Near to the Distance]* 1993, a photograph showing a flaccid penis) although the only work to be censored to date is *Blue Fear*, which contrasted an older man's naked back set against a pair of large staring eyes. This work so disturbed the older citizens of Plymouth, England, that, in 1992, the work was rejected for exhibition; notably, it was to have been installed on Plymouth Hoe, a seaside recreational site, not in a museum. However, the body does fascinate her, very like photographic emulsion, which is also sensitive and which makes a record; it is like the body which ages and, in Cadieux's words, "qui enregistre le temps, la peau qui enregistre les blessures" [and which records time, skin which records wounds].

LILLY KOLTUN

See also: **Conceptual Photography; Photography in Canada; Postmodernism; Wall, Jeff**

Biography

Born in Montreal, Canada, 17 July 1955. Obtained a BA with specialization in visual arts from the University of Ottawa, Canada in 1977. In 1993, won a Deutscher Akademischer Austauschdienst to work in Berlin for some months; over 1993–94, was artist in residence at the École nationale supérieure des beaux-arts in Paris, France; in 1996, taught at the École d'art de Grenoble in France; in 1997 at the Universitat Politècnica de València in Spain; and in 1998 at the College of Architecture and the Arts, University of Illinois, Chicago. Lives in Montreal, Canada, and teaches fine art there at Concordia University.

Individual Exhibitions

1977 Saw Gallery; Ottawa, Canada

1981 Galerie France Morin; Montreal, Canada

1982 *Works by Geneviève Cadieux*; Agnes Etherington Art Centre, Queen's University; Kingston, Canada; and The Gallery Stratford, Stratford, Canada

1988 *Geneviève Cadieux*; The Power Plant; Toronto, Canada

1990 *Canada XLIV Biennale di Venezia: Geneviève Cadieux*; Canadian Pavilion; Venice, Italy

1991 *Geneviève Cadieux*; Centre d'art contemporain de Genève; Geneva, Switzerland
Kent Fine Art; New York

1992 *Geneviève Cadieux*; Institute of Contemporary Art; London, England
Geneviève Cadieux; Institute of Contemporary Art; Amsterdam, Netherlands
Geneviève Cadieux; Musée départemental d'art contemporain de Rochechouart; Rochechouart, France
Roppongi Square installation, organized by Sagacho Exhibit Space; Tokyo, Japan

1993 *Geneviève Cadieux*; Centre d'art contemporain de Montréal; Montreal, Canada

1994 *Geneviève Cadieux*; Bonner Kunstverein; Bonn, Germany
Geneviève Cadieux; Museum van Hedendaagse Kunst Antwerpen (MUHKA); Antwerp, Belgium
Geneviève Cadieux; Nouveau Musée/Institut d'Art contemporain; Villeurbanne, France

1995 *Body Currents*; Cleveland Center for Contemporary Art; Cleveland, Ohio
Angles Gallery; Santa Monica, California; and Pittsburgh Center for the Arts; Pittsburgh, Pennsylvania (1996)
Geneviève Cadieux; Tate Gallery; London, England

1997 *Geneviève Cadieux*; Kunstforeningen; Copenhagen, Denmark
Stephen Friedman Gallery; London, England

1998 Galleria S.A.L.E.S.; Rome, Italy
Miami Art Museum; Miami, Florida

1999 *Geneviève Cadieux*; Morris and Helen Belkin Art Gallery, University of British Columbia; Vancouver, Canada

2000 *Geneviève Cadieux*; Americas Society, New York
Beaverbrook Art Gallery; Fredericton, Canada
Geneviève Cadieux; Musée des beaux-arts de Montréal; Canada
Geneviève Cadieux; Art Gallery of Hamilton; Canada

2001 Trafic, FRAC Haute-Normandie; Sotteville-lès-Rouen, France
Galerie Nathalie Obadia; Paris, France

Group Exhibitions

1978 *Cadieux, Duchow, Erskine, Flomen, June*; Galerie Optica; Montreal, Canada

1984 *Avant-scène de l'imaginaire/Theatre of the Imagination*; Musée des beaux-arts de Montréal, Canada

1985 *Aurora Borealis*; Centre international d'art contemporain de Montréal; Montreal, Canada

1987 *XIXth Bienal Internacional de Sao Paulo: Ruidos Do Norte/Northern Noises/Résonances boréales*; organized by the Winnipeg Art Gallery, Canada; Sao Paulo, Brazil

Elementa Naturæ; Musée d'art contemporain de Montréal; Montreal, Canada

1988 *Enchantment and Disturbance*; The Power Plant; Toronto, Canada

La Ruse historique: l'art à Montréal/The Historical Ruse: Art in Montreal; The Power Plant; Toronto, Canada

VIIth Biennale of Sydney: From the Southern Cross: A View of World Art c. 1940–1988; Art Gallery of New South Wales & Pier 2/3; Walsh Bay, Sydney, Australia; National Gallery of Victoria, Melbourne, Australia

1990 *VIIIth Biennale of Sydney: The Readymade Boomerang: Certain Relations in 20th Century Art*; Art Gallery of New South Wales; Sydney, Australia

New Works for Different Places: TSWA Four Cities Project; organised by TSWA for four venues in U.K. (censored in Plymouth, England)

Passage de l'image; Musée national d'art moderne; Centre Georges Pompidou, Paris; Fundació Caixa de Pensions, Barcelona, Spain (1991); Wexner Center for the Visual Arts, Ohio State University, Columbus, U.S. A. (1991); San Francisco Museum of Modern Art, San Francisco, California (1992)

XLIV Biennale di Venezia; Venice, Italy

1991 *Crossroads*; Art Gallery of York University; Toronto, Canada

Outer Space, organised by South Bank Centre, London at Laing Art Gallery, Newcastle-upon-Tyne, England; Ferens Art Gallery, Hull, England; Camden Arts Centre, London, England; Arnolfini Art Gallery, Bristol, England

The Interrupted Life; New Museum of Contemporary Art; New York

1993 *1M = C.299792458'S*; San Sebastian; Spain

Das Bild des Körpers; Frankfurter Kunstverein; Frankfurt am Main, Germany

Passageworks; Rooseum Center for Contemporary Art; Malmö, Sweden

1994 *Cocido y crudo*; Museo Nacional, Centro de Arte Reina Sofia; Madrid, Spain

1995 *Presence: Recent Portraits*; Angles Gallery; Santa Monica, California

Large Bodies; Pace Magill Gallery; New York

Spirits on the Crossing: Travellers to/from Nowhere - Contemporary Art in Canada 1980-94; Setagaya Art Museum; Tokyo, Japan; and National Museum of Modern Art; Kyoto, Japan; Hokkaido Museum of Modern Art; Sapporo, Japan

1996 *Corps étrangers*; National Gallery of Canada; Ottawa, Canada

Fotografische Momenten; Museum van Hedendaagse Kunst; Ghent, Belgium

Happy End; Kunsthalle Düsseldorf; Düsseldorf, Germany

1997 *From Here to There*; Fundaçao Calouste Gulbenkian, Centro de Arte Moderna José de Azeredo Perdigao; Lisbon, Portugal; and Centro Portugues de Fotografia; Porto, Portugal (1998)

Objectif corps; Musée des beaux-arts de Montréal; Montréal, Quebec

1998 *Voices*; Witte de With; Rotterdam, Netherlands; and Fundació Joan Miró; Barcelona, Spain; Le Fresnoy, studio national des arts contemporains; Tourcoing, France (1999)

Disidentico, maschile femminile e altro, produced by the Centre International Mostre, Rome, Italy at Palazzo Branciforte; Palermo, Italy; and Museo di Castelnuovo; Naples, Italy

1999 *Billboards. Art on the Road*; Massachusettes Museum of Contemporary Art; North Adams, Massachusetts

The Time of Our Lives; New Museum of Contemporary Art; New York

2000 *The Bigger Picture: Contemporary Photography Reconsidered*; Art Gallery of Ontario, Toronto, Canada

2001 *Elusive Paradise. The Millennium Prize*; National Gallery of Canada; Ottawa, Canada

Selected Works

Séquence no. 6, 1980
Illusion no. 6, 1981
Voices of Reason/Voices of Madness, 1983
The Shoe at Right Seems Much Too Large, 1986
La Blessure d'une cicatrice ou Les Anges (or The Wound of a Scar or The Angels), 1987
Nature morte aux arbres et au ballon, 1987
Trou de mémoire, la beauté inattendue (or Memory Gap, the Unexpected Beauty), 1988
Storyville Portraits—Le Petit Prince, Montreal, Canada: Galerie Oboro et Galerie René
Blouin, 1988 (editor of artist's book, in 60 copies)
Hear Me With Your Eyes, 1989
Blue Fear, 1990
Portrait de famille (or Family Portrait), 1991
Le corps du ciel, 1992
La voie lactée, 1992
Loin de moi, et près du lointain (or Far From Me, Near to the Distance), 1993
Elle, 1993
Tears, 1995
Juillet 94, 1995
Souffle, 1996
La mer et l'enfant, 1997
Elle et lui (avec main de femme), 1997
Vague, 1997
Paramour, 1998–1999
Dilectio, 1999
Pour un oui, pour un nom, 2000

Further Reading

[Interview with Geneviève Cadieux, December 1987] *Geneviève Cadieux*. Toronto: Power Plant, 1988.

Déry, Louise, and Didier Prioul. *Geneviève Cadieux*. Quebec, Canada: Musée du Québec and Rome: Galleria S.A. L.E.S., 1998.

Gale, Peggy. "Skin Deep, The Beauty and Resonance of Geneviève Cadieux's Installations Come From Her Mixing of Memory with Desire." *Canadian Art*, vol. 7, no. 1, Spring 1990: 58–65.

Godmer, Gilles, and Jacinto Lageira. *Geneviève Cadieux*. Montreal, Canada: Musée d'art contemporain de Montréal, 1993.

Papineau, Jean. "Geneviève Cadieux, Écrans de réflexion, une interview de Jean Papineau." *Parachute* 56, (Oct., Nov., Dec., 1989): 20–22.

Pearson, Gary, Jürgen Brockmann, and Michael Haerdter. *Hotel on Fire*. Kelowna, B.C.: Kelowna Art Gallery, 1997.

Pohlen, Annelie, and Jan Foncé. *Geneviève Cadieu.*, Bonn, Germany: Bonner Kunstverein, and Antwep, Belgium: Museum van Hedendaagse Kunst Antwerpen, 1994.
Pontbriand, Chantal. *Geneviève Cadieux: Canada XLIVéme Biennale de Venezi.*, Montreal, Canada: Les Éditions *Parachute* and Musée des beaux-arts du Montréal, 1990.
Pontbriand, Chantal, Laurence Louppe, and Scott Watson. *Geneviève Cadieux.* Vancouver: Morris and Helen Belkin Art Gallery and Musée des beaux-arts de Montréal, 1999.
Prévost, Jean-Marc. *Geneviève Cadieux.* Limoges, France: Musée départemental d'art contemporain de Rochechouart, 1992.
St-Gelais, Thérèse. "Geneviève Cadieux, le regard et le visible." *Parachute*, 51: 4–10.
Tarantino, Michael. "Geneviève Cadieux Close Up." *Artforum* vol. XXVIII, no. 8, (April 1990): 160–64.
Viau, René. "Geneviève Cadieux, entre regards et desires." *Vie des arts* vol. 38, no. 150, (Spring 1993): 20–24.

CLAUDE CAHUN

French

In the mid-1980s, during the time of gender and identity debates, Claude Cahun(Lucy Schwob), a prominent figure of the Parisian avant-garde, was rediscovered. Her works created photographic productions of personal identity, in which the self-taught photographer thematized gender and identity in playful engagement with masks and role-playing. For feminist theory, which held self-representation as a central theme, Claude Cahun became an interesting case study. She seemed to anticipate the questions raised by prominent feminist author Judith Butler about the influence of sexuality and development on identity and the problem of the social and sexual normalization of individuals. Accordingly, she was routinely connected to the postmodern strategies of self-production promoted by such artists as Cindy Sherman.

The theme of self-production followed Claude Cahun through all her artistic works in various media. She resisted specializing her artistic activity and worked as a poet, essayist, literary critic, translator, actor, and political activist. The growing reception of her works in the 1980s was concentrated primarily on her photography, however, which was in addition to language the most essential medium of her artistic expression.

The central works of this French artist were self-representations, made between 1912 and 1953, that portrayed her in ever-changing roles. Self-enlightenment was not her obsession; rather, she was interested in the production of possible identities, the ambiguity of gender, and the desire and play with masquerade and alienation. She assumed the role of the dandy and dressed like a sailor and as a weight lifter; there are also many photographs of her as the Buddha. She displayed herself in a young girl's costume, with her blond hair falling in her face, or as a little girl with knitted sweater and close-cut hair. In the years 1917 to 1929, she most often posed facing the camera in front of a temporary, tightly pulled sheet, and peered with a fixed gaze back at the viewer that challenged him to position himself opposite her. The unsettling effect of her portraits results from the uncertainty of identity that we try to resolve by relying on biological gender distinctions in the photographs. In her confusing play with these identity constructions, Cahun demonstrates the impossibility of locating a fixed, stable definition of self.

In her frontal portraits, she harkens back to the statuary form of bourgeois studio portraits; she deploys in the background a tightly pulled cloth sheet, a citation from nineteenth-century portrait photography. She worked with mirrors and doubling effects—techniques used by the surrealists and by the photographer Florence Henri as their central method of self-representation. A truly radical artist, she paid no heed to the conventions of female beauty and the limits of her body. In *Frontière humaine* (Human frontier), a distorted enlargement that appeared in the surrealist journal *Bifur* in 1930, her head mutates into a grotesque, vertically stretched, anamorphic image of a skull. In another doubling montage, she presents herself as Siamese twins.

In her most important book, *Aveux non avenus* (*Unavowed Confessions* 1930), autobiographical text fragments, dream sequences, and aphorisms appear next to photomontages that were created with her partner, Suzanne Malherbe (alias Marcel Moore). In it she writes:

> I've spent my solitary hours disguising my soul. The masks were so perfect that whenever they crossed paths along the great square of my conscience they did not recognize each other. Tempted by their comic ugliness, I tried on the worst instincts; I adopted, I raised in me young monsters. But the makeup I had used could not be washed away. I scrubbed myself to remove the skin. And my soul, like a face flayed alive, no longer had a human form.

Born Lucy Schob in 1894, the daughter of the publisher Maurice Schwob in Nantes, France, Cahun grew up in an intellectual Jewish bourgeois family. Her grandfather and then her father published the regional newspaper *Le Phare de la Loire*, and her uncle Marcel Schwob was the founder of the prestigious newspaper *Mercure de France* and also a symbolist writer who had an early influence. After studies in Nantes and Oxford, England, in 1914 Cahun studied philology and philosophy at the Sorbonne, Paris, and published her first article, "Vues et visions," in *Mercure de France* under the pseudonym Claude Courlis; after adopting a number of other pseudonyms, including Daniel Douglas, she began calling herself the gender-ambiguous Claude Cahun in 1917, and began her lifetime relationship with her stepsister Suzanne Malherbe in 1919. Their apartment in Montparnasse became a meeting place of Paris bohemians.

Malherbe was a frequent collaborator as well; between 1929 and 1930, they created ten photo collages that divided the accompanying text into panels. This work reached back into a bank of self-portraits that Cahun used as a sort of self-reference. In these collages, she is working through the fragmentation of the body—mostly faces, but often hands, arms, legs, and eyes—that float in the black visual space. The collaboration between Malherbe and Cahun also allegedly extended to many self-portraits in which Malherbe operated the shutter release.

That Cahun's work circles around the issue of self-identity was surely influenced by the fact that the patriarchal structure of society did not provide a role for a lesbian Jew. The typical role of the female artist in surrealism was that of model, muse, and lover of male artists. However, in the lesbian subculture of Paris in the 1920s, Cahun found support and also a forum for her works, which to that point in her life had never been exhibited. She became friends with the writers and editors Adrienne Monnier, proprietor of the bookstore La Maison des Amis des Livres, a favorite meeting place for the Parisian literary community, and Sylvia Beach, a prominent lesbian expatriate and owner of the English-language Paris bookstore Shakespeare and Company.

The 1930s led to increased politicization of Cahun's art, and she entered public life as an activist. In 1932, she met André Breton and, alarmed by the growing fascist movement, joined for a short while L'Association des Écrivains et Artistes Révolutionnaires (AEAR), a group of revolutionary artists. After a disagreement in 1933 between the organization and the surrealists, whose art was deemed in conflict with the aesthetic line of the Communist International, she left the group and formulated her critique of it in "Les Paris sont ouverts" (translated as Place Your Bets The Parises are Open; 1934). Here, she warned that blind party loyalty would impoverish poetry. In the same year, she became a member of the antifascist political coalition Contre-Attaque, founded by Georges Bataille and André Breton. In the 1930s, she maintained loose contact with the surrealists and signed onto most of their declarations.

During her collaboration with the surrealists in the mid-1930s, she produced works that she exhibited in 1936 as part of the Exposition surréaliste d'objets in Paris and London. In conjunction with this, she published the text "Prenez garde aux objets domestiques" (Beware of Household Objects) in *Cahiers d'Art*. She also created a series of surrealist objects by assembling photographic tableaux, in which numerous artificial human substitutes, such as mannequins, marionettes, and dolls self-made from newspaper, were arranged on a surface with everyday objects. She created the series *Poupée*, which displayed a soldier made from the newspaper *L'Humanité*, the central organ of the French Communist Party, and critically reflected on the position of the Communist Party during the Spanish Civil War. She staged another series with wooden marionettes that she arranged in a scene beneath a glass bell jar.

In 1937, to escape the looming Nazi threat, she moved with Malherbe to the Isle of Jersey, England; she illustrated a collection of poetry for children by Lise Deharme, *Le Coeur de Pic* (*Pic's Heart*), with still-life photographs resembling tableaux. During the Nazi occupation of France, Cahun and Malherbe were suspected of spreading antifascist propaganda and in 1944 were imprisoned, condemned to death, and remained in a prison until liberated by the Allies in 1945; unfortunately, most of Cahun's works were destroyed during the war.

ESTHER RUELFS

See also: **Feminist Photography; Henri, Florence; History of Photography: Interwar Years; Manipulation; Montage; Photography in France; Representation and Gender; Sherman, Cindy; Surrealism**

Biography

Born Lucy Renée Mathilde Schwob in Nantes, France, October 25, 1894; Schooled in Nantes. Father remarried, 1906, bringing stepsister Suzanne Malherbe into the household. Studied in Oxford, 1907–08; created her first photographic self-portraits in 1912; began study of philology and philosophy at the Sorbonne, 1914; published "Héroïnes," translation of Havelock Ellis's *Study of Social Psychology*, 1925; worked as an actress in Pierre Albert-Birot's experimental theater, Le Plateau, 1929; met André Breton, 1932, joined L'Association des Écrivains et Artistes Révolutionnaires, which she left in 1933 after a disagreement between the organization and the surrealists. Joined the antifascist political coalition Contre-Attaque, 1934; participated in *Exposition surréaliste d'objets* in Paris and London, 1936; moved with Malherbe to the Isle of Jersey, England, 1937. Died in Saint-Hélier, Jersey, on December 8, 1954.

Individual Exhibitions

1980 *Claude Cahun*; Galerie Claude Givaudan; Geneva
1992 *Claude Cahun*; Zabriskie Gallery; New York
Claude Cahun, 1894–1954: Photographies des années 20 et 30; Galerie Zabriskie; Paris
1993 *Claude Cahun and Suzanne Malherbe*; The Jersey Museum; Saint-Hélier, Jersey
1995 *Claude Cahun, 1894–1954*; Musée d'Art Moderne de la Ville de Paris Galerie Berggruen; Paris
1997 *Claude Cahun—Selbstdarstellungen*; Kunstverein München, and traveling

Group Exhibitions

1985 *L'Amour fou: Photography and Surrealism*; Corcoran Gallery of Art; Washington, D.C.
Explosante fixe: Photographie et surréalisme; Musée National d'Art Moderne, Centre Georges Pompidou; Paris
1991 *Paris des années trente: Le Surréalisme et le livre*; Galerie Zabriskie; Paris, and traveling
1992 *Photographie et sculpture*; Centre National de la Photographie; Paris
1994 *Mise en scène: Claude Cahun, Tacita Dean, Virginia Nimarkoh*; Institute of Contemporary Arts; London
Le Rêve d'une ville: Nantes et le surréalisme; Musée des Beaux-Arts; Nantes
Feminin—Masculin; Musée National d'Art Moderne, Centre Georges Pompidou; Paris
1996 *Inside the Visible*; Institute of Contemporary Art; Boston, Massachusetts
Rrose Is a Rrose Is a Rrose: Gender Performance in Photography; Solomon R. Guggenheim Museum; New York, New York
1997 *Double Vie—Double Vue*; Fondation Cartier; Paris
Claude Cahun; Ginza Artspace, Fondation Shiseido; Tokyo
Floating Images of Women in Art History: From the Birth of the Feminism Toward the Dissolution of the Gender; Tochigi Prefectural Museum
El rostro velado; Sala de Exposiciones Koldo Mitxelena; San Sebastián
1998 *Mirror Images: Women, Surrealism, and Self-Representation*; MIT, List Visual Arts Center; Cambridge, Massachusetts and traveling

Selected Works

Self-Portrait, c. 1928
Self-Portrait, c. 1929
Frontière humaine (Human frontier), from *Bifur*, no. 5, 1930
Self-Portrait, from Bifur, no. 5, 1930
Humanité Figure (Poupée), 1936

Further Reading

Ander, Heike, and Dirk Snauwaert, eds. *Claude Cahun: Bilder*. Munich: Schirmer/Mosel, 1997.
Blessing, Jennifer, ed. *Rrose Is a Rrose Is a Rrose: Gender Performance in Photography*. New York: Guggenheim Museum Publications, 1997.
Chadwick, Whitney, ed. *Mirror Images: Women, Surrealism, and Self-Representation*. Cambridge, Mass.: MIT Press, 1998.
Claude Cahun: Photographe: Musée d'Art Moderne de la Ville de Paris. Paris: Jean-Michel Place, 1995.
De Zegher, M. Catherine, ed. *Inside the Visible: An elliptical traverse of 20th century art in, of, and from the feminine*. Cambridge, Massachusetts: The MIT Press, 1996.
Leperlier, François, *Claude Cahun. L'Écart et la metamorphose*. Paris: Jean-Michel Place, 1992.
Dean, Tacita, and Virginia Nimarkoh. *Mise en scène: Claude Cahun*. London: Institute of Contemporary Arts, 1994.
Monahan, Laurie J. "Claude Cahuns radikale Transformationen." *Texte zur Kunst* 3, no. 11 (Sept. 1993): 101–109.
Sykora, Katharina. *Unheimliche Paarungen. Androidenfaszination und Geschlecht in der Fotografie*. Cologne: Verlag der Buchhandlung Walter König, 1999.

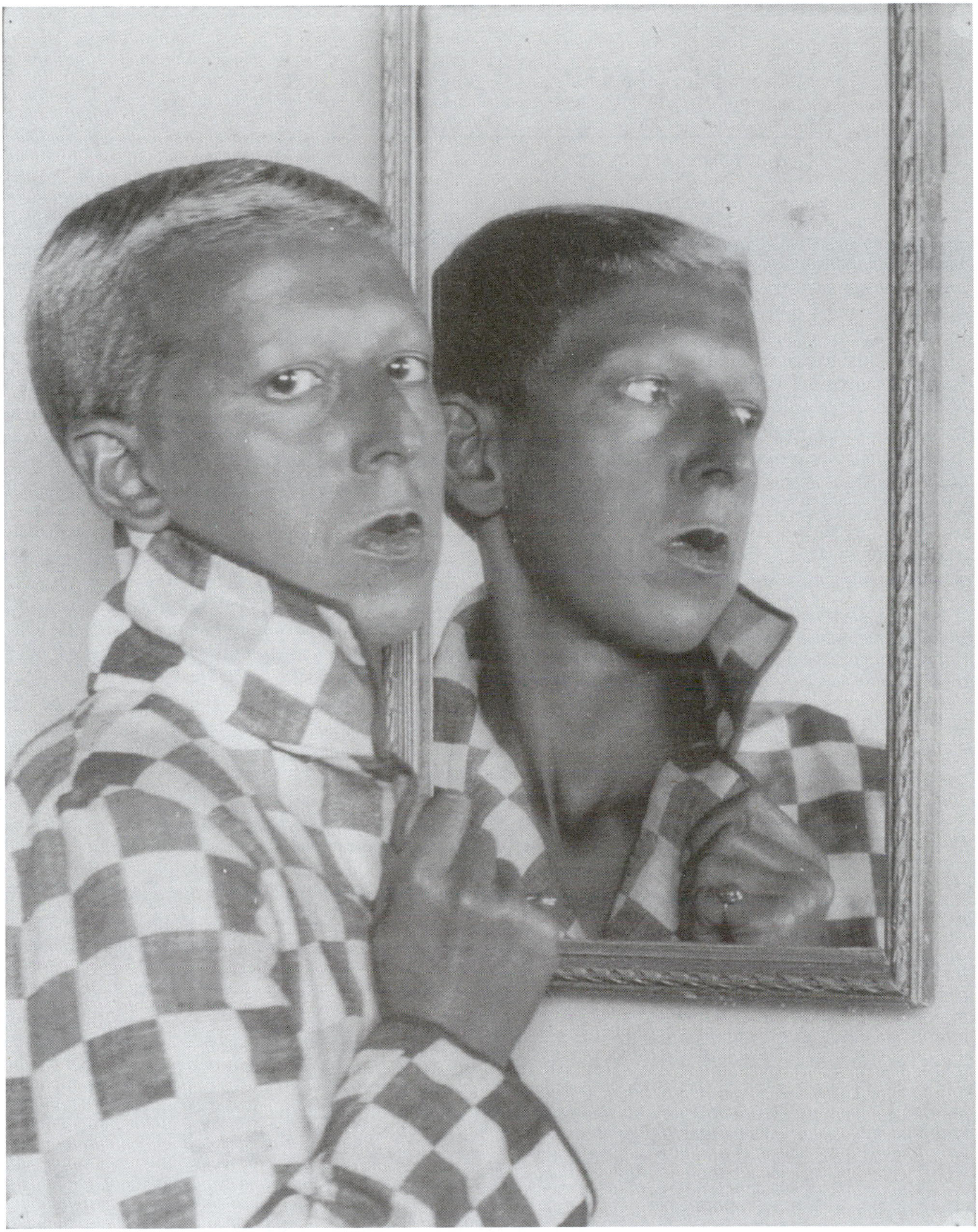

Claude Cahun, Self-portrait, 1928.
[*Réunion des Muséees Nationaux/Art Resource, New York*]

HARRY CALLAHAN

American

Harry Callahan joined the premier ranks of American photographers almost from the beginning of his career in the mid 1940s. By the time he was included in the popular 1955 exhibition *The Family of Man* at the Museum of Modern Art, New York (MoMA), his restless experimentation, always at the service of capturing the human and natural landscape and presenting it to further his values and expressive purposes, had made him one of the most important figures in twentieth-century photography. No matter his subject—and most often it was the stuff of ordinary life—Callahan infused his photographs with emotion and quiet elegance. He was also eloquent in speaking of his vision:

> You must start with a concept, with the idea that there is much more to the subject than meets the unaided eye. The subject is all-important. And I experiment with various techniques to help me see things differently from the way I saw them before. That is seeing photographically, and when you see photographically, you really see.
>
> (Greenough 184)

Born in Detroit in 1912 to a middle-class family, Callahan studied chemical engineering and then business at Michigan State College from 1934 to 1936. After completing his formal education, he worked as a shipping clerk for the Chrysler Motor Parts Corporation. In 1936, he married Eleanor Knapp, who would later serve as the subject of many of his most enduring photographs. It was about this time that Callahan developed an interest in photography through a photo club at his workplace; he purchased his first camera, a Rolleicord 120, in 1938. After attending a 1941 Detroit Photo Guild workshop taught by the landscape photographer Ansel Adams, Callahan began to devote himself seriously to photography. During 1944–1945, he worked as a processor in the General Motors Corporation photo lab.

Aside from his attendance of photo club lectures, Callahan was self-taught. A seminal episode in this education was a 1945 trip to New York that he described as a "personal fellowship" where he met many of the established photographers—including Lisette Model, Berenice Abbott, Minor White, and Paul Strand—and art curators of the day. Two major career developments occurred in the late 1940s: in 1946, he was hired by László Moholy-Nagy, then director of the "New Bauhaus"—the Institute of Design (ID) in Chicago—as an instructor in photography; and he began his long friendship with Edward Steichen, director of the department of photography at MoMA. Callahan was included in numerous group and solo exhibitions at MoMA in the 1940s and 1950s, introducing his work widely to the photography community.

Relocating to Chicago from Detroit in 1946, Callahan spent the next 15 years teaching at ID and shooting some of his best-known photographs. He served as head of ID's Light Workshop (the photography department) beginning in 1949, after the resignation of his old Detroit Camera Club colleague Arthur Siegel. He held this position until 1961, when he left Chicago to assume the chairmanship of the photography department of the Rhode Island School of Design (RISD) in Providence. He held this position until 1973, although he stayed on as a professor until 1977.

Callahan was an influential instructor and a role model for countless students, many of whom would become important photographers in their own right, including Yasuhiro Ishimoto and Kenneth Josephson. His personal innovations and experimentations had a deep impact on ID's photography program, and his legacy to this now-legendary institution included hiring Aaron Siskind in 1951. Although the Bauhaus curriculum at ID emphasized the study of light (which Callahan expressed in photographs that featured tracings of a flashlight beam created by moving his camera), his assignments often included projects that took his students into the streets of Chicago to record the interaction of architecture and the human figure with the raking light and shadows the urban infrastructure could create. Candid studies of people going about their business, their anonymity paradoxically revelatory, were typical of both Callahan and his ID students and have formed a school of photography celebrated in such exhibitions as *Light and Vision: Photography at the School of Design* and *When Aaron Met Harry: Chicago Photography 1946–1971*. Callahan's famous 1950 series of close-ups of anonymous women shoppers in Chicago began a strain of photography that captured average people and celebrated their individuality; Lee Friedlander and Garry Winogrand perfected this style in the 1960s and 1970s, and it is sustained into the new century by photographers such as Beat Struli.

During Callahan's short formative period, he was influenced by the intimate and contemplative nature studies by Adams; the European Modernism exemplified by the Hungarian Moholy-Nagy; and the aesthetic purity of Alfred Stieglitz, the legendary photographer and curator. By the late 1940s, Callahan had forged a style of his own at the service of a clearly articulated goal, which was to be able to express his life and his observations about life through his photography. Thus, it is not surprising that prevalent in Callahan's work are elegant portraits of his wife Eleanor and daughter Barbara, who was born in 1950. These posed yet strikingly intimate works include views of Eleanor in the streets of Chicago, such as *Eleanor, Chicago, 1953*, and the iconic studies of Eleanor nude in the confines of the domestic interior, such as *Eleanor, Chicago, 1948*, and his 8-inch by 10-inch view camera "snapshots" of Eleanor and Barbara going about their daily lives. At the same time, Callahan continued the tradition of Moholy-Nagy in his formalism and experimentation with the photographic medium, although, rather paradoxically, these photographs also are intense and highly personal. Many of his experiments involve layered images, distortion, or manipulations of focus and contrast, such as *Collage, Chicago, 1957*, which features hundreds of clippings from magazines. Callahan had known the architect Mies van der Rohe when they were on the ID faculty together, and van der Rohe's predilections for simplified form that was also generalized and abstract mirrored his own. Influenced by van der Rohe, Callahan created a series of multiple exposures of architectural subjects typified by *Chicago* (ca. 1948).

Throughout his career, Callahan photographed the natural landscape, including brooding, Minimalist beach scenes taken in Cape Cod, Massachusetts, and textural nature studies of leaves, grasses, tree branches, and twigs, such as the elegantly minimal studies of plant stems against a white background, such as *Detroit* (ca. 1947), which mimics the creases and lines of the nude female body of *Eleanor* (1947). These works have a strong sense of abstraction, and taken together with his more experimental multiple-exposure photographs, show his familiarity with painterly issues and the influence of painter friends and colleagues such as Hugo Weber (a fellow ID teacher) and Robert Motherwell, whom he met when he taught a summer session at Black Mountain College in North Carolina.

Although he is often thought of as a photographer of the figure or the cityscape and landscape, Callahan also dealt with popular culture and the mass media. Some of his earliest work photographed neon signs, transforming them with camera movements into expressive bursts of light. Especially in the 1960s, perhaps reacting to the general climate of sweeping social and political change in the United States, Callahan focused on cultural imagery, superimposing images taken from television with images of pedestrians, which contrasted the powerful, carefully constructed media images with the mundane reality of everyday life. This strain in Callahan's work, although not as well known, prefigures much of the "image scavenging," or appropriation, practiced by many artists of the 1980s to the turn of the century, including Barbara Kruger and Richard Prince.

Although Callahan experimented with color from the beginning of his career, his photographs of the 1950s and 1960s were generally in black and white; color came to the fore in 1977 in architectural and landscape studies that featured intense, yet low-key, color. Callahan continued his photographic explorations throughout his long career, returning in the 1990s to subjects that he first explored in the 1950s: landscape and street scenes featuring raking light that abstracts the image.

Callahan was influenced by his travels, including a year-long trip to Europe in 1957, which was funded by a grant from the Graham Foundation. This sojourn in Aix-en-Provence, France, produced his well-known works of double-exposure images of Eleanor and the landscape of Provence. A 1963 trip to Mexico was followed by extensive travels in Europe, South America, the South Pacific, Australia, New Zealand, Japan, and China. He was honored with a retrospective at MoMA in 1976 and a traveling retrospective organized by the National Gallery of Art in Washington, DC, in 1996. His photographs have been exhibited internationally and are included in the collections of virtually every photography museum and photography department within general museums. A variety of magazines published his photographs, including *Life, Newsweek, The New York Times* and *The Chicago Tribune* magazines, *U.S. Camera, Aperture*, and *Harper's Bazaar*.

Lynne Warren

See also: **Adams, Ansel; Institute of Design; Moholy-Nagy, László; Museum of Modern Art; Siskind, Aaron; Steichen, Edward**

Biography

Born in Detroit, Michigan, 22 October 1912. Attended Michigan State College but was self-educated in photography. Instructor in photography at the Institute of Design (ID), Chicago, 1946–49; head of ID's Light Workshop (the photography department), 1949–61; instructor for summer course at Black Mountain College, Black Mountain, North Carolina, 1951; Chairman of the Photography Department, 1961–73, and Professor of Photography at the Rhode Island School of Design, Providence, Rhode Island, 1961–77. Graham Foundation award for Advanced Studies in Fine Arts, 1956; Governor's Award for Excellence in the Arts, Providence, Rhode Island, 1969; John Simon Guggenheim Memorial Foundation Fellowship, 1972; elected Fellow of American Academy of Arts and Sciences, Boston, 1979; recipient of first Distinguished Career in Photography award from the Friends of Photography, Carmel, California, 1981; Brandeis Creative Arts Medal, 1985. Died in Atlanta, Georgia, 15 March 1999.

Individual Exhibitions

1947 *Harry Callahan*; 750 Studio Gallery; Chicago, Illinois
1951 *Photographs by Harry Callahan*; Art Institute of Chicago; Chicago, Illinois
1956 *Harry Callahan*; Kansas City Art Institute; Kansas City, Kansas
1958 *Harry Callahan Exhibition*; George Eastman House; Rochester, New York
1964 *Photographs: Harry Callahan*; Hallmark Gallery; New York and traveling
1972 *Harry Callahan: The City*; George Eastman House; Rochester, New York, and traveling
1976 *Callahan*; Museum of Modern Art; New York, and traveling
1978 *Harry Callahan: 38th Venice Biennial 1978*; United States Pavilion; Venice, Italy
1979 *Harry Callahan: Photographs in Color/The Years 1946–1978*; Center for Creative Photography; University of Arizona, Tucson, and traveling
1983 *The Photography of Harry Callahan, 1941–1982*; Seibu Museum of Art; Tokyo
1984 *Eleanor and Barbara: Photographs by Harry Callahan*; Art Institute of Chicago and traveling
1985 *Harry Callahan: Retrospective 1941–1982*; Ffotogallery; Cardiff, Wales, and traveling
1996 *Harry Callahan*; National Gallery of Art; Washington, DC, and traveling

Group Exhibitions

1948 *In and Out of Focus*; Museum of Modern Art; New York, New York
1950 *Four Photographers: Lisette Model, Bill Brandt, Ted Croner, Harry Callahan*; Museum of Modern Art; New York
1951 *Abstraction in Photography*; Museum of Modern Art; New York
1953 *Contemporary Photography*; National Museum of Modern Art; Tokyo, Japan
1955 *The Family of Man*; Museum of Modern Art; New York, and traveling
1955 *Subjektive Fotografia 2*; Staatlichen Schule für Kunst und Handwerk; Saarbrucken, Germany
1956 *American Artists Paint the City*; United States Pavilion, 28th Biennial; Venice, Italy
1962 *Photographs by Harry Callahan and Robert Frank*; Museum of Modern Art; New York, and traveling
1968 *Photographs in the Twentieth Century*; National Gallery of Canada; Ottawa, Ontario (organized by George Eastman House), and traveling
1974 *Landscape/Cityscape: A Selection of Twentieth-Century American Photographs*; Metropolitan Museum of Art; New York, New York
1980 *The New Vision: Forty Years of Photography at the Institute of Design*; Light Gallery; New York, New York
1983 *Harry Callahan and His Students: A Study in Influence*; Georgia State University Art Gallery; Atlanta, Georgia
1987 *Photography and Art: Interactions Since 1946*; Los Angeles County Museum of Art; Los Angeles, California
1989 *On the Art of Fixing a Shadow: One Hundred and Fifty Years of Photography*; National Gallery of Art; Washington, DC, The Art Institute of Chicago, Chicago, Illinois, and Los Angeles Country Museum of Art, Los Angeles, California
1993 *Light and Vision: Photography at the School of Design in Chicago, 1937–1952*; Banning and Associates; New York
1996 *When Aaron Met Harry: Chicago Photography 1946–1971*; The Museum of Contemporary Photography, Chicago

Selected Works

Detroit, ca. 1947
Eleanor, 1947
Eleanor, Chicago, 1948, 1948
Chicago, ca. 1948
Eleanor, Chicago, 1953, 1953
Collage, Chicago, 1957, 1957
Water's Edge, 1980

Further Reading

Butler, Susan. *Harry Callahan: Retrospective 1941–1982*. Cardiff, Wales: Ffotogallery, 1985.
Greenough, Sally. *Harry Callahan*. Washington: National Gallery of Art, 1996.
Kennedy, Anne, and Nicholas Callaway, eds. *Eleanor: Photographs by Harry Callahan*. Carmel, California: Friends of Photography, 1984.
Maholy-Nagy, László. *Malerei, Photographie, Film*, Munich, 1925 as *The Bauhaus, Weimar, Dessau, Berlin*, Chicago by Hans M. Wingler. Cambridge: MIT Press, 1969.
Martin, Gordon, and Aaron Siskind, eds. *The Multiple Image: Photographs by Harry Callahan*. Chicago: Institute of Design, Illinois Institute of Technology, 1961.
Paul, Sherman. *Harry Callahan*. New York: The Museum of Modern Art, 1967.
Traub, Charles, ed. *The New Vision: Forty Years of Photography at the Institute of Design*. Millerton, New York: Aperture, 1982.
Szarkowski, John. *Callahan*. Millerton, New York: Aperture, 1976.

SOPHIE CALLE

French

Sophie Calle produces unique, even idiosyncratic, works at the intersection of performance, photography, and literature. She continually thwarts expectations by radically transforming her artistic methodology for almost every new project. Although Calle works within the lineage of conceptual art, at times recalling the earlier tactics of American conceptual artists of the 1960s and '70s Vito Acconci (surveillance) or Douglas Huebler (mapping), she always places herself in the midst of her practice, as personal narratives unfold within the varying structural contexts of gallery installations, photographic books, and video documentation.

Calle was born in Paris, France, 9 October 1953. Her parents divorced when she was only three years old. She was an introverted child who read avidly. Calle's father, a doctor, collected contemporary art including examples of Pop Art by the Americans Roy Lichtenstein, and Andy Warhol and the French painter Martial Raysse. Calle was heavily influenced by the turbulent politics of the late 1960s and has recalled, "At 15, I was a militant." At the age of 18, Calle traveled to Lebanon and witnessed the Palestinian struggles firsthand. After her initial sojourn abroad, she returned to likewise witness struggles in Paris between assorted factions of activists, and she involved herself with a group which assisted women in obtaining free contraception and abortion (then illegal in France) on demand. Throughout a seven-year period during the 1970s, Calle spent much of her time traveling abroad, including Canada, Mexico, and the United States.

In 1979, Calle asked 29 different friends and acquaintances to sleep in her bed for eight-hour stretches during a one-week long period, and her resulting documentation culminated in a work called *The Sleepers*. Subsequently, Calle created *Venetian Suite*, which begins with the statement:

> At the end of January 1981, on the streets of Paris, I followed a man whom I lost sight of a few minutes later in the crowd. That very evening, quite by chance, he was introduced to me at an opening. During the course of our conversation, he told me he was planning an imminent trip to Venice. I decided to follow him.

In *The Hotel*, while working as a chambermaid, Calle made clandestine photographs of the guests' belongings. In 1983, she called phone numbers taken from a lost address book, and then published documentation of her communications each day that August in the newspaper *Libération*. Such elaborate stunts and clever games have become a hallmark of her creative approach.

In *The Blind* (1986) one of Calle's most poignant pieces, she interviewed people who were born blind, querying them about their ideas of beauty. In the resulting works, Calle grouped photographic portraits of the interviewees along with their statements ("White must be the color of purity. I'm told white is beautiful. So I think it's beautiful. But even if it weren't beautiful, it would be the same thing.") and an image taken by the artist. A similar instance of physical absence coupled with verbal description is exemplified by the series *Last Seen* (1991), in which Calle solicited comments from museum employees about "missing" works which then were on loan or had been stolen. The remarks shared with Calle ranged widely from being vague and speculative, to at times poetic or exacting in nature ("I don't remember it at all. Except, I remember there was a guy with a top hat and maybe a mustache/I remember a predominant russet tone apart from the pale rose colored face and hands").

Calle's projects have incorporated both social and personal contexts. In *Exquisite Pain* (1984–2003), Calle displayed 92 photographs and recounted a three-month period she spent in Japan as a student, and the subsequent and painful end of a romantic relationship. The photographs are stamped in red to record the artist's countdown "...DAYS TO UNHAPPINESS." The second part of the exhibition is devoted to images evoking and texts recording the period after Calle's lover fails to appear at their designated meeting place, a hotel room in New Delhi. Here, Calle places a diaristic description of her own angst alongside the responses of others to the question "When have you suffered the most?" The 2003 video *Unfinished* (and an accompanying group of photographs) documents Calle's attempts to create a work using footage and photographs appropriated from the cameras installed in automatic teller machines. In dealing with the visual records of daily financial transactions, she pondered the various ways by which she could realize a work drawn from this material. The images in turn seemed to thwart Calle's efforts, and the artist ended up with a work that she declared "unfinished."

Collaboration has played a large role in many of Calle's projects. In 1992, Calle co-directed a feature-length video with the American photographer Greg Shepherd entitled *No Sex Last Night (Double Blind)*, which documented their road trip taken in a Cadillac from New York to California. Each used a separate camera to record the journey and their increasingly tense relations. For the exhibition *Double Game*, Calle worked with the writer Paul Auster, who had previously created a fictional character based on Calle who appeared in his 1992 novel *Leviathan*. Both also share an interest in private detectives, as Calle hired one to trace her steps in the 1981 work, *The Shadow*, and Auster's acclaimed *New York Trilogy* (1985–86) reworks the conventions of the detective novel. Calle later asked Auster if he would conjure another character for her to "inhabit" herself, and inspire works for the artist to then "create." The two have communicated back and forth in this way, blurring the edges between fantasy and reality.

Calle often merges realms of fact and fiction in her diverse body of work, creating a third compelling entity, which combines her voice or text, along with a series of images in accordance with a theme. She tends to spy on other participants, both willing and unwilling, and equally to reveal in calculated fashion more and more aspects of her own private (and public) identity. This frequently results in an effect resembling a mirage, hallucination, or hall of mirrors, as Calle departs from the exactitude of photographic facts and instead favors the poetic character of spoken truths.

MARTIN PATRICK

See also: **Photography in France; Representation and Gender**

Biography

Born in Paris, France, 9 October 1953. Lives and works in Paris and New York.

Individual Exhibitions

1980 *The Bronx*; Fashion Moda Gallery; New York, New York
1981 *The Sleepers*; Galerie Canon; Geneva, Switzerland
1983 *The Hotel*; Galerie Chantal Crousel; Paris, France
1986 *The Blind*; Galerie Crousel-Hussenot; Paris, France
1989 *Sophie Calle, A Survey*; Fred Hoffman Gallery; Los Angeles, California
1990 *The Tombs*; Galeria La Maquina Espanola; Seville, Spain
1991 *Sophie Calle, à suivre…*; ARC Musée d'Art Moderne de la Ville de Paris; Paris, France
1993 *Last Seen*; Leo Castelli Gallery; New York, New York
Sophie Calle: Proofs; Hood Museum of Art; Dartmouth College, Hanover, New Hampshire
1994 *Absence*; Galerie Chantal Crousel; Paris, France
1995 *Proofs*; University Art Museum, University of California; Santa Barbara, California
The Detachment; Galerie Arndt & Partner; Berlin, Germany
1997 *Suite vénetienne*; White Cube; London, England
1998 *Doubles Jeux*; Centre national de la photographie; Paris, France
The Birthday Ceremony; Tate Gallery; London, England
1999 *Souvenirs de Berlin-Est*; Musée d'art moderne et contemporain; Strasbourg. France
Appointment; Freud Museum; London, England
2000 *Die wahren Geschichten der Sophie Calle*; Museum Fridericianum; Kassel, Germany
2002 *Sophie Calle*; Sprengel Museum; Hannover, Germany
2003 *M'as-tu-vue*; Musée national d'art moderne; Georges Centre Pompidou, Paris, France

Group Exhibitions

1980 *XI Biennale de Paris. Manifestation internationale des jeunes artistes*; Musée d'Art Moderne de la Ville de Paris; Paris, France
1981 *Autoportraits photographiques, 1898–1981*; Centre Georges Pompidou; Paris, France
1982 *Du Livre*; Musée des Beaux-Arts; Rouen, France
1983 *Il n'y a pas à proprement parler une histoire…*; Maison de la culture; Rennes, France
1984 *Photographie contemporaine en France*; Centre Georges Pompidou; Paris, France
1985 *Kunst mit Eigen-Sinn*; Museum moderner Kunst; Vienna, Austria
1988 *Beyond the Image. FotoFest '88*; Houston Center for Photography; Houston, Texas
1989 *Culture Medium*; International Center of Photography; New York, New York
Tenir l'image à distance; Musée d'art contemporain; Montreal, Canada
L'invention d'un art; Centre Pompidou; Paris, France
1990 *The Ready-made Boomerang*; Sydney Biennale; Sydney, Australia
Seven Obsessions; Whitechapel Art Gallery; London, England
Images in Transition: Photographic Representation Towards the 90s; National Museum of Modern Art, Kyoto/National Museum of Modern Art; Tokyo, Japan
1991 *Dislocations*; Museum of Modern Art; New York, New York
1992 *Doubletake: Collective Memory and Contemporary Art*; Hayward Gallery; London, England
1993 *Whitney Biennial*; Whitney Museum of American Art; New York, New York
1995 *Féminin/Masculin. Le sexe de l'art*; Centre Georges Pompidou; Paris, France
1996 *Passions privées*; Musée d'Art Moderne de la Ville de Paris; Paris, France

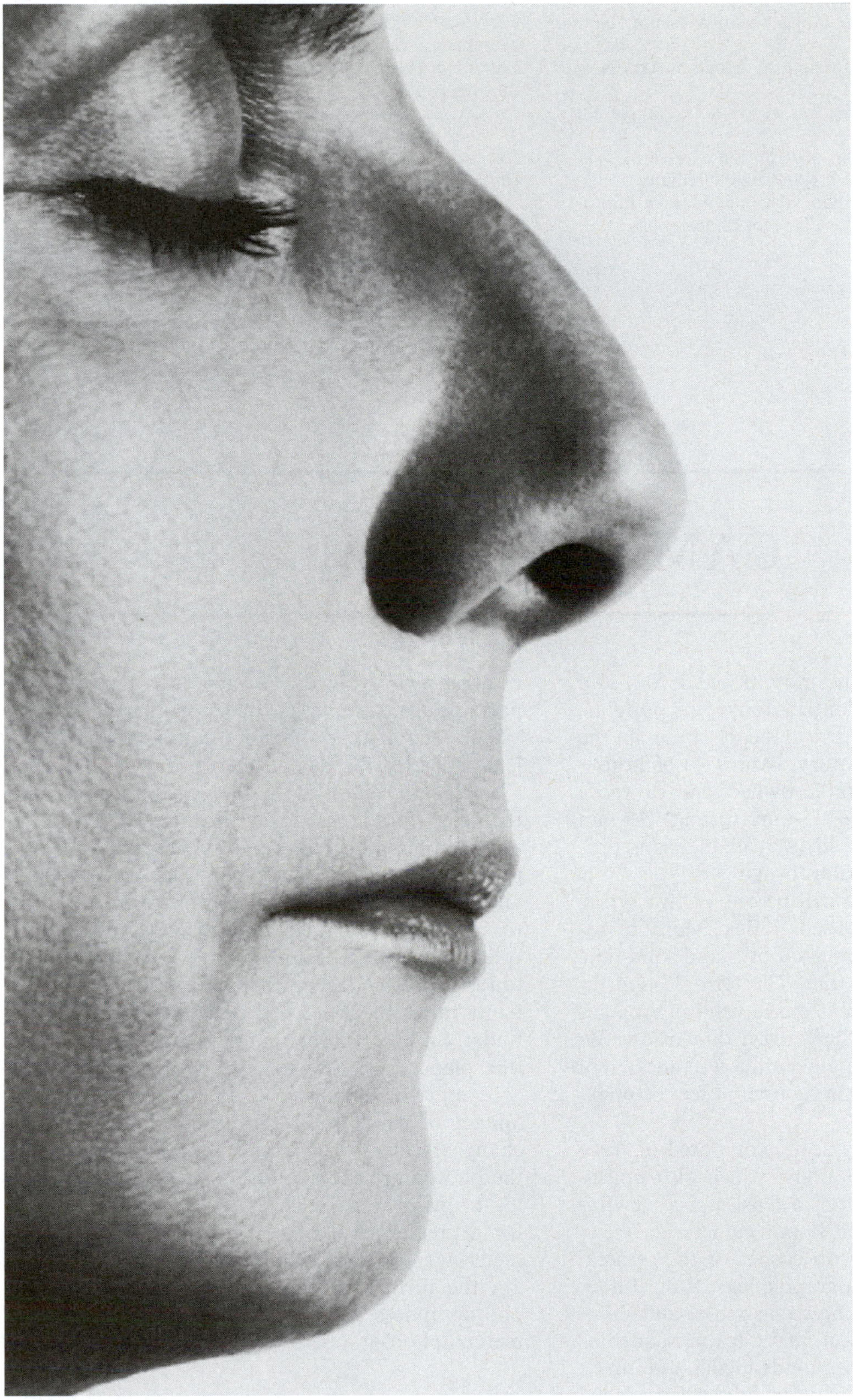

Sophie Calle, Autobiographies (The Plastic Surgery), 2000, gelatin silver print with text panel print: 67 × 47″ (170.2 × 119.38 cm) text panel: 19 ¾ × 19 ¾″ (50.2 × 50.2 cm) Edition of 5 French, 5 English.
[*Courtesy Paula Cooper Gallery, New York*]

1998 *Premises*; Solomon R. Guggenheim Museum; New York, New York
1999 *Museum as Muse*; Museum of Modern Art; New York, New York
2000 *L'empire du temps. Mythes et création*; Musée du Louvre; Paris, France
2001 *CTRL [Space]: Rhetorics of Surveillance from Bentham to Big Brother*; ZKM; Karlsruhe, Germany
2003 *The Furtive Gaze*; Museum of Contemporary Photography, Columbia College; Chicago, Illinois

Selected Works

The Sleepers, 1979
Venetian Suite, 1980
The Hotel, 1981
The Address Book,1983
The Blind, 1986
Last Seen, 1991
No Sex Last Night, 1992
Memories of East Berlin, 1996
Exquisite Pain, 1984–2003
Unfinished, 2003

Further Reading

Calle, Sophie. *M'as-tu vue*. Munich: Prestel, 2003.
———. *Doubles-Jeux*. Arles: Actes Sud, 1998.
Sophie Calle. Hannover: Sprengel Museum, 2002.

CAMERA: 35 MM

The 35-mm format is the most popular film and camera format today. Contributing to its popularity are its small compact size and ease of use. At the end of the twentieth century, over 90% of households in the United States owned one or more cameras, most of these 35-mm format. 35-mm film is inexpensive and widely available, as is processing of this versatile film format.

A 35-mm film camera can be one of two types: a rangefinder or a single-lens reflex. Many of today's popular "point–and-shoot" and one-time use cameras use 35-mm film. The term 35-mm directly relates to the film size; the resulting images on film are 35-mm in the longest dimension. 35-mm film is a roll film, meaning it comes in a light-tight canister containing several feet of unexposed film.

A 35-mm camera is typically composed of three main parts: a light-tight body, which also houses the light meter and shutter, a lens, and a viewfinder. In a rangefinder-type 35-mm camera, the viewfinder is located in the top corner of the camera, independent of the photographic lens. Rangefinder 35-mm cameras, also known as point-and-shoot cameras, typically have automatic features, such as automatic film loading, auto-advancing, automatic exposure, and built-in flash that fires when needed to boost exposure. Other features often found on this type of camera are zoom lenses, date/time imprinting, and advanced flash features such as fill-flash and red-eye reduction. Point-and-shoot cameras have evolved to a camera that is extremely portable, easy to use, and relatively inexpensive.

The second type of 35-mm camera, the single-lens-reflex (SLR), has an incorporated viewfinder. The camera lens is both the viewfinder lens and the lens that is used to photograph with. The image enters the lens, and is reflected off of a mirror up to the viewfinder. The viewfinder of an SLR is composed of several mirrors and prisms to brighten the image and display it in proper orientation to the subject. When the shutter button is depressed, the mirror swings out of the way, temporarily blocking the view through the viewfinder, and allows the image to travel back to the film plane.

35-mm SLRs have the advantage over point-and-shoot cameras in that they allow for interchangeable lenses. The lens is modular, allowing the photographer to choose a specific lens according to his or her needs. SLRs also typically allow for a greater level of control over exposure and metering. For these reasons, 35-mm SLR cameras are the format of choice for many professional photographers, such as photojournalists and commercial photographers.

Camera Components

Body

The camera body is simply a light tight box that houses the film. Inside the camera body is the film advance system. The film advance is designed to pull the film across the film plane (where the image will be formed). Once the photograph is made, the film advances the distance of one frame, or individual picture area. In many point-and-shoot cameras, advancing the film is done automatically. Once the shutter is closed, a motor winds the film to the next frame to ready the camera for the next exposure. In a manual SLR, advancing the film is done with a film advance lever. Motor drives can be added to SLRs to automatically advance the film. Some SLRs come with an integrated motor drive.

The body also houses the shutter. A shutter is a device used to regulate the amount of time light is permitted to strike the film. The shutter is one of two controls used to regulate exposure. Shutters in 35-mm cameras are typically of the focal plane variety, meaning they are located directly in front of the film, or focal plane. These shutters are composed of either a set of cloth slit curtains or metal leaves. The shutter speed is created by the curtains or leaves moving in sequence, exposing the film from side to side or top to bottom. The speed is dependent on how fast the traveling slit moves across the film.

Shutter speeds can range from 1 second to as fast as 1/400 of a second. A standard shutter speed range is: 1 sec (slowest), 1/2, 1/4, 1/8, 1/15, 1/30, 1/60, 1/125, 1/250, 1/500, 1/1000 (fastest). Increments of these speeds are typically double the time, or half the time, depending on the direction. For example, changing the shutter speed from 1/60 to 1/30 doubles the amount of light striking the film, where as changing from a 1/60 to 1/125 cuts the amount of exposure in half. One of these increments is typically known as a stop.

In addition to determining the amount of time light is allowed to strike the film, shutter speeds are also responsible for capturing motion. A long shutter speed will blur motion; a short shutter speed will capture it sharply.

In order for the camera to evaluate the amount of light the film needs to make an exposure, it needs a light meter. Virtually all modern 35-mm cameras have built-in light meters, and depending on the camera, the light meter can either set the exposure controls automatically, or give the photographer a guideline of what the exposure needs to be, allowing for various effects.

Lens

The purpose of the lens is to focus the image on the film plane. Depending on the camera, this focusing can take place manually, by rotating the lens collar, or automatically, in the case of auto focus lenses and cameras. Auto focus lenses work via infrared or ultrasonic sensors that determine subject distance and then set the lens accordingly.

The lens contains the second key element in exposure control, the aperture. The aperture is an iris-like device set inside the lens to control the amount of light that reaches the shutter. The aperture is controlled either automatically through the in-camera light meter, or manually through a series of increments. These increments are called f/stops. A typical f/stop range is as follows: f/2.8 (widest opening), f/4, f/5.6, f/8, f/11, f/16, f/22 (smallest opening). F/stops control how much of an opening there is inside the blades of the aperture. Each increment is half or double the next or last, respectively. For example, changing the aperture from f/11 to f/16 will halve the amount of exposure, while changing from f/11 to f/8 will double it.

Aperture also controls depth-of-field, or the amount of focus in an image. The smaller the aperture opening (higher number), the greater the amount of depth of field there will be in an image. For example, a small aperture would allow a person in a field to be focused as well as the field behind them. A wider aperture (smaller number) would mean the person was sharp, but the field would drop out of focus.

Lens types

Most camera lenses have fixed focal lengths, typically measured in millimeters. A "normal" lens is considered to mimic the average field of view of the human eye, or 50 degrees of view if you are looking straight ahead. To mimic this field of view, a "normal" lens must be equal to the physical diagonal of the film format being used. In the case of 35-mm, this measurement equals approximately 50-mm.

Short focal length lenses are any lenses that are shorter than normal focal length. A 28-mm lens would be considered a short focal length lens for 35-mm format. The shorter the focal length of the lens, the wider angle of view it provides. A 28-mm offers a 75° field of view when on a 35-mm camera. For this reason, short focal length lenses are often known as wide-angle lenses.

Long focal length lenses are any lenses that typically have an angle of view of 35° or less. In a 35-mm, these would be any lenses that are 80-mm or more in focal length. Long focal length lenses enlarge the subject as they narrow the field of view. Within this category are telephoto lenses, which are specially designed long-focal length lenses that magnify the subject to a greater degree than the focal length would normally determine.

Zoom lenses are lenses of varying focal length. They are labeled as a range, e.g., 28–80 mm. The purpose of the zoom lens is to replace multiple focal lengths with a single lens. However, visual quality will almost always fall short when compared to a fixed focal length lens.

Macro lenses are lenses of normal or longer focal lengths that are designed to focus at a much closer range. This allows the lens to be within inches of the subject for much greater subject magnification than conventional lenses. Macro lenses are also optically corrected to focus critically in high magnification.

Exposure

The shutter speed and aperture needed to capture a given photographic image depend largely on the sensitivity of the film. In the earliest days of photography, film was considered to be "slow"—it was not unusual to have to make an exposure of several hours to get any kind of information on film. Modern films are now so efficient photographers are able to capture images in fractions of a second, provided a properly sensitive film is used. Film sensitivity, or speed, is measured in terms of ISO (International Standards Organization). The higher the ISO, the more sensitive the film, where as lower numbers represent films that are not as sensitive, or "fast."

Film speed will dictate the shutter speed and aperture needed to make a good exposure. The camera's internal light meter evaluates the amount of light in a scene. In a manual camera, it will then give the photographer its recommendation as to the shutter and aperture settings to use based on the film's ISO. Many modern cameras set the ISO automatically by scanning an electronic code located on the film canister.

These settings, once determined by the meter, are interchangeable to a point. For example, if the camera recommends that the exposure should be $^1/_{60}$ @ f/8, the photographer has several choices. Shutter speed and aperture share a reciprocal relationship. If the photographer wants more depth of field than f/8 will him, he could use f/11. However, since he has now cut the amount of light striking the film in half, he must compensate by lengthening the time. His final exposure could be $^1/_{30}$ @ f/11, which would produce exactly the same amount of density as his original light meter reading.

Metering Systems

Light meters in all cameras are based on an average. The light meter assumes that the scene will have equal light areas, dark areas, and midtones. This assumption averages out to a characteristic known as middle gray, or 18% gray. The light meter places anything the camera is aimed at in this value. The most common metering system is to simply average all of the subject reflectance that is inside the viewfinder. This system is known as averaging.

However, since not all scenes can or should be averaged to 18% gray, more advanced 35-mm SLR systems allow metering choices. Center-weighted metering places the meter's emphasis in the center of the frame. Matrix metering is based on a grid that is based on a series of typical lighting situations, such as a bright sky on the top of the frame, and darker land at the bottom. The camera then tries to automatically compensate among choices on the grid. Spot metering, the most precise method, allows the photographer to specify a point in the photograph that they would like to be 18% gray, or take readings off of a highlight and a shadow and average the two.

Accessories

Accessories for 35-mm are widely available because of the format's widespread popularity. In addition to interchangeable lenses, flashes, tripods, filters, motor drives, bellows, cable releases, a number of other accessories are available for the novice all the way up to the advanced professional.

Flashes

Many 35-mm point-and-shoot cameras have built-in flashes, as do some 35-mm SLR cameras. SLR cameras also offer the choice of additional external flashes, usually connected to the camera via a top slot called a hot shoe, or into a plug via a synchronization cord. Depending on the camera, photographers can employ an additional electronic flash that has a light sensor located on the flash itself, or one that is more advanced and can work with the camera's meter to shut the built-in flash off at the proper time. These systems are dedicated and automatic, or TTL (through-the-lens) systems, respectively.

Tripods

A sturdy tripod allows a photographer greater freedom when using slower shutter speeds. Tripods can be made of wood, though most common commercial tripods are composed of lightweight metal.

Filters

Filters are used over the lens to either create or negate a particular visual effect. Filters can also be used to block out a particular color or wavelength of light, as in UV filters. Color correction filters can correct a colorcast in a scene, while specialized filters can create images with starbursts around lights or other specialized effects.

CHRISTYE SISSON

See also: **Camera: An Overview; Camera: Pinhole Camera; Camera Obscura; Exposure; Film; Lens; Point-and-Shoot**

Further Reading

Adams, Ansel. *The Camera (Book I)*. Boston: Little Brown & Co., 1995.

Kemp, Gregg. *The Pinhole FAQ*. http://www.pinhole.com/resources/FAQ/ (accessed 19 June 2001).

Kingslake, Rudolf. *Optics in Photography*. SPIE (International Society for Optical Engineers). © 2000 The Society of Photo-Optical Instrumentation Engineers.

Langford, Michael. *Basic Photography*. New York: Focal Press, 2000.

London, Barbara, and John Upton. *Photography*. (7th ed.) New York: Prentice Hall, 1998.

Schaefer, John. *An Ansel Adams Guide: Basic Techniques of Photography, Book 1*. Boston: Little Brown & Co., 1992.

Stroebel, Leslie D., ed. *Basic Photographic Materials and Processes*. New York: Focal Press, 2000.

Wilgus, Jack and Beverly Wilgus. *The Magic Mirror of Life: a search for camera obscura rooms*. http://brightbytes.com/cosite/collection.html (accessed May 5, 2005).

CAMERA: AN OVERVIEW

The camera is in large part responsible for shaping the cultural landscape of the past one hundred years. A camera enables its user to seize a moment in time and capture it on film or as digital information. The camera's final product, the photograph, allows anyone to become an eyewitness to these captured moments, whether 'real' or manufactured. The pervasiveness of photography in world culture is a direct result of advancement in camera technology and manufacture. Modern cameras are portable and precise, though their origins date back to ancient times.

Camera Obscura

The predecessor of the modern camera is the camera obscura ("dark room" in Latin). The camera obscura was often a darkened room, with a small hole in a window covering. Through the hole, an image of life outside the window was projected on to an opposite parallel wall, upside down. This principle had been known in early Chinese, Arabic, and Greek cultures.

The basic concept behind the camera obscura, and all cameras, is that light travels in a straight line. When light rays reflected off of a subject pass through a hole, they cross and reform. The hole acts as a point of projection for the image. Any ray of light that passes through the hole will hit the focus plane (the wall) at a particular point. Any other ray of light, again being reflected off of the initial subject, will intersect at a different point. These multiple points, when reassembled on the focus plane, form the image. The distance from the hole to the focus plane determines the final size of the image.

The discovery of photography in 1827 by Joseph Niépce and his partner, Louis Daguerre, fostered the birth of the modern camera. In fact, Daguerre used camera obscura in many of his early photographic attempts, but soon employed more portable cameras such as pinhole and simple lens cameras.

Pinhole cameras

Pinhole cameras consist of a light-tight box or container with at least two parallel surfaces, with a small hole in one of those surfaces. The primary difference between pinhole cameras and camera obscura is that pinhole cameras use some type of light-sensitive material (film or photographic paper) to capture the image and make it permanent. Pinhole cameras can be made out of almost any container that can be made to be light tight.

Pinhole cameras, though still in use today, present some drawbacks, although some photographers exploit these characteristics for aesthetic ends. Images generated by pinhole cameras are fuzzy and lack detail. Optics, and, finally, complex lenses began to be used in place of the hole in a pinhole camera, allowing an image to be focused on the image plane.

The simple camera

A simple camera consists of three basic parts: a light-tight container, or body, a lens, and an image plane, that is, a place for film or other light sensitive material to be placed to receive the projected image. Modern cameras also include viewfinders to aim and compose the image, a shutter and aperture to control the light reaching the film, and a light meter to determine the amount of light needed to create the image. Modern photography often integrates these systems so that the user is often not aware of the inner workings of the camera.

Camera types can be divided into several categories, most notably by their viewing/lens systems.

View Cameras

The earliest lens camera type, the view camera, is still used today. The view camera body consists of two standards (front and rear) that provide a support system for a flexible length of bellows. The bellows are an accordion-folded length of stiff, light-tight material that extends between the standards. The front standard of a view camera holds the lens board, which contains a view camera lens. A view camera lens contains all of the exposure controls for the camera, including the aperture and shutter speed. View cameras do not have light meters. The rear standard houses the ground glass, the image plane of the view camera. The image is focused on the ground glass with the help of a dark cloth draped over the back of the camera and the photographer. The film is then inserted in front of the ground glass before taking the photograph.

Older view cameras used glass or metal plates coated with photographic emulsions as their light-sensitive material. Many early photographic processes, including Daguerrotypes and Tintypes were done with view cameras. Modern view cameras use sheet film, squares of film cut to fit the size format of the camera. The most popular view camera size today is 4×5, that is, utilizing film that is 4×5 inches, though cameras utilizing 8×10 inch film are still used. Film sheets are loaded in complete darkness in sheet film holders specially designed to be light tight. Once inserted into the view camera, the dark slide protecting the film is removed so that the film can be exposed in the camera. Each film holder contains two sheets of film when loaded. View cameras can also use instant film, such as Polaroid, with a special film holder.

Sheet film presents with the advantages of excellent clarity and resolution, but also is slow to load and inconvenient to shoot quickly. As technological advances in photographic materials allowed for shorter exposure times and flexible films, many photographers wished for cameras that could be used more quickly as well. Roll-film cameras were developed to support burgeoning fields such as photojournalism, allowing photographers to capture images seconds apart. Film was made into long strips, or rolls, to allow for more speed and spontaneity in photography.

Rangefinder Cameras

The dilemma with view cameras is that the viewing system and the image capture system are one and the same. The rangefinder camera attempts to solve that problem by providing a separate "composition" finder, either mounted on top or inside the camera, to allow the photographer to more spontaneously choose and frame their subject.

Many of the first consumer-level cameras were rangefinder cameras developed by George Eastman of Eastman Kodak Company. The Kodak "Brownie," a box camera with roll film already loaded, had a viewfinder in the top corner of the box. No more than a channel blocked off by clear glass, the viewfinder nonetheless allowed users to "point and shoot."

The rangefinder viewing system remains popular today. The advantage of rangefinder cameras is that they are among the quietest and smoothest systems available, with no mirror to jar the image upon exposure. Rangefinder cameras are what are commonly referred to as today's "point and shoot" cameras.

Rangefinder cameras are made for both 35-mm roll film and medium format roll films.

Twin Lens Reflex

The term "reflex" in both twin lens reflex and single lens reflex cameras refers to the use of a mirror to reflect the composed image to the viewfinder. The mirror in a twin lens reflex sits directly behind the upper viewing lens, while the lower lens of the camera is responsible for transmitting the image to film.

The mirror sets the image right side-up, but like any mirrored image, the image is reversed left-to-right. The image is projected on a ground glass surface in the viewfinder for focusing and composition. Since the two lenses are mounted as one piece, any focusing that takes place for the viewing lens is mimicked in the photographic lens. The viewfinder in a twin-lens reflex camera is most often a waist-level finder, meaning the image is projected to the ground glass mounted to the top of the camera. In order to easily see the image in the ground glass, the photographer must hold the camera at waist-level. The ground glass image is typically shielded for viewing by a set of metal leaves that form a box around the ground glass.

Twin lens reflex cameras are typically made for medium format roll films.

Single Lens Reflex

The most common modern camera type is the single lens reflex camera. In a single lens reflex camera, both viewing and photography takes place through a single lens. A mirror deflects the image coming through the lens and sends it to the prism for viewing and composition. The prism of a single-lens reflex camera is made up of a series of mirrors and lenses to brighten the image and orient it properly for the viewer. When the shutter button is depressed, the mirror swings out of the way to allow the image to travel back to the film. Although the most popular example of a single lens reflex camera is 35-mm roll film format, most professional grade medium format cameras today are also single lens reflex.

Light Control

Exposure

Exposure is the amount of light needed to form an image on film or other light sensitive materials. In the early stages of photography, it was not uncommon to require several minutes of exposure to form an image. Technological advances in film sensitivity and characteristics have reduced this time to fractions of a second.

There are many different levels of sensitivity available in today's modern films. Film sensitivity, often referred to as film speed, is measured in terms of ISO (International Standards Organization). The higher the ISO number, the more sensitive the film is, and the less light it will need to make a proper exposure. The lower the film speed, the more light it will need to obtain a proper exposure. For example, a film with an ISO of 800 will allow the photographer to capture images with shorter exposures than will a film with a speed of 400. ISO numbers correspond to their sensitivity; ISO 400 film needs twice as much light to make the same exposure as ISO 800 film.

Light Meters

In order to determine how much light is needed for an exposure, a photographer must use a light meter. Light meters are most often integrated into the camera system, either informing the photographer of the proper exposure for that film and scene, or setting that exposure automatically. In order for the light meter in the camera to function properly, the meter must know the sensitivity, or ISO, of the film being used. Many modern film manufacturers mark the film canister with an electronically read code, called a DX code, so that a DX-code enabled camera can automatically set the meter to the proper ISO.

Shutter and Aperture

Once the amount of exposure has been determined, cameras employ two controls to obtain that exposure, shutter and aperture. The shutter is a device inside the camera that controls the amount of time that the film is exposed to light. Because of today's high film speeds, shutters must travel very quickly, exposing the film in fractions of a second. A typical shutter speed range could be from 1/2000 of a second all the way up to one second. Many cameras set shutter speed in increments so that each speed is twice or half the one next to it. For example, the next speed up from 1/500 of a second would be 1/1000 (half the amount of time), and the next down would be 1/250 (twice the amount of time). These increments are commonly referred to as stops. Most commonly, shutters are located inside the camera body directly in front of the film. These types of shutters are called focal plane shutters, and are usually constructed of a series of cloth curtains or metal leaves. Less common is the leaf shutter, typically found in view cameras and professional grade medium format cameras. A leaf shutter is constructed of lightweight metal in a circular, iris-like fashion.

The other camera control used to control exposure is the aperture. Located in the lens, the aperture is an iris-like device that is set to permit a certain amount of light. When the blades of the aperture are closed down, a very small hole is created for light to pass through. When the blades of the aperture are opened up, a larger hole is created, therefore allowing more light to pass through. Openings of aperture are measured in f/stops, which are based on the area of the opening. A typical range of f/stops on a lens may span from f/2 (wide opening) to f/22 (very small opening). Like shutter speeds, apertures are also most often set in increments to the power of two. For example, an aperture of f/8 lets in twice the amount of light as f/11.

Aperture and shutter speed share an inverse relationship. Each controls a different aspect of the image. If the goal is to capture fast motion, a faster shutter speed is needed. In order to achieve that fast speed, it is usually necessary to open up the aperture to compensate for the short shutter speed. Likewise, smaller apertures allow for a great amount of depth of field. Depth of field is what allows the photographer to control the amount of focus in the image. For example, if someone is photographing a flower with a mountain range for a background, they could have both in focus if they use a very small aperture, such as f/22 or f/32. However, since these f/stops constitute very small openings, a longer shutter speed is usually required to make up for the exposure lost by closing down the aperture.

CHRISTYE SISSON

See also: **Brownie; Camera: 35 mm; Camera: Diana; Camera Obscura; Camera: Pinhole; Camera: Point-and-Shoot; Eastman Kodak Company; Exposure; Lens; Light Meter**

Further Reading

Adams, Ansel. *The Camera (Book 1)*. Boston: Little Brown & Co., 1995.

Kemp, Gregg. *The Pinhole FAQ*. (Accessed 19 June 2001). *http://www.pinhole.com/resources/FAQ/*.

Kingslake, Rudolf. *Optics in Photography*. SPIE (International Society for Optical Engineers). © 2000 The Society of Photo-Optical Instrumentation Engineers.

Langford, Michael. *Basic Photography*. Boston: Focal Press, 2000.

Leggat, Robert, Ph.D. *A History of Photography: From its Beginnings until the 1920s. http://www.rleggat.com/photohistory/index.html* (accessed May 5, 2005).

London, Barbara, and John Upton. *Photography*. (7th ed.) New York: Prentice Hall. 1998.

Schaefer, John. *An Ansel Adams Guide: Basic Techniques of Photography, Book 1*. Boston: Little Brown & Co., 1992.

Stroebel, Leslie D., ed. *Basic Photographic Materials and Processes*. Boston: Focal Press, 2000.

Wilgus, Jack and Beverly Wilgus. *The Magic Mirror of Life: a search for camera obscura rooms. http://brightbytes.com/cosite/collection.html* (accessed May 5, 2005).

CAMERA: DIANA

The Diana Camera is a plastic "toy" camera that contemporary photographers have embraced for its simplicity and unique quality of image. The camera was manufactured by the Great Wall Plastic Factory of Kowloon, Hong Kong, beginning sometime in the early 1960s through reportedly the early 1970s. It was imported to the United States by the Power Sales Company of Willow Grove, Pennsylvania, and only sold by the gross (twelve dozen), with a price ranging from one to three dollars each. Though Diana is the best known brand name, the camera was marketed under other names including Anny, Arrow, Arrow Flash, Asiana, Banier, Banner, Colorflash Deluxe, Debonair, Diana Deluxe, Diane F, Dionne F2, Dories, Flocon RF, Hi-Flash, Justen, Lina, Lina S, Mark L, MegoMatic, Merit Mirage, Pnanx Photon 120, Pioneer, Raleigh, Reliance, Rosko, Rover, See, Shakeys, Stellar, Stellar Flash, Tina, Traceflex, Truview, Valiant, Windsor, Zip, and Zodiac. Two cameras that are currently being manufactured are popular successors to the Diana, the Chinese-made Holga and the Russian-made LOMO.

Technically, the Diana camera has a plastic body, light blue and black, and a plastic lens. The standard model has a single shutter speed that, because of its inexpensive nature, varies in speed from 1/30 to 5/8 of a second. Other models have a B (bulb) setting, and the F model even has a built-in flash. Included on all models are three aperture settings, illustrated by drawings: sunny (f-16), sun with clouds (f-6.3), and cloudy (f-4.5). The camera also allows for limited manual focusing with three settings: 4 to 6 feet, 6 to 12 feet, and 12 feet to infinity. The camera uses 120 film, making sixteen exposures that are approximately 2 × 2 inches. The film is manually advanced. A frame count can be viewed through a red window on the back of the camera. It is often recommended that the body of the camera be taped with black electrical tape along the seams to avoid light leaks.

For many photographers, the very nature of the camera, a plastic toy, allows them a spontaneity that they may not have with more sophisticated and technical equipment. Through its friendly appearance, it allows photographers an ease in which to approach subjects and shoot pictures, especially portraiture. The photographer embraces and is challenged by the serendipitous nature of the resulting work. The light leaks, along with the shape of the negative, the distortion of the plastic lens, and the fact that the lens is not color-corrected all lend an element of surprise to the final image. Often the images come out blurred and distorted, achieving a dream-like, surreal quality.

The use of the camera by students and professionals in the United States dates to the late 1960s. Early milestones include photographer Nancy Rexroth's portfolio of images included in "The Snapshot" issue of *Aperture* in 1974. Her 1977 book entitled *Iowa* included Diana images that were autobiographical of the artist's childhood and furthered her reputation as a serious photographer who used the Diana camera. Another early project that familiarized photographers with the camera came in the late 1970s when photographer Mark Schwartz, for a project entitled *We Do the Rest*, sent several hundred Diana cameras to United States photographers, asking them to shoot the film and return the camera with exposed film intact. In 1980, David Featherstone organized *The Diana Show* for the Friends of Photography in Carmel, California. Featuring the work of 43 photographers, the exhibit and accompanying catalogue and essay were important firsts in highlighting the Diana camera.

The Diana camera and its successors continue to be used by amateur and professional photographers in the fields of fine art, commercial photography, and photojournalism. In the early 1990s, artist Nancy Burson, best known for her digitized composite portrait photographs, used the Diana camera to photograph children with craniofacial condition, a rare disfiguring disorder. Burson used the camera to create subjective, softly focused portraits in sharp contrast to more sterile, clinical portraits. Using the contemporary Holga camera, award-winning photojournalist David Burnett captured unique and powerful images of American political candidates on the 2000 presidential campaign trail.

The idiosyncrasies of the Diana camera are its legacy, allowing photographers to capture images and express themselves in unique and unpredictable ways.

Jim McDonald

See also: **Burson, Nancy; Camera; Vernacular Photography**

Further Reading

Busselle, Rebecca. "A Defining Reality: The Photographs of Nancy Burson," *Aperture*, No. 136, Summer (1994).

Burson, Nancy. *Faces*. Santa Fe, NM: Twin Palm Publishers, 1993.

Featherstone, David. *The Diana Show: Pictures Through a Plastic Lens*. Carmel, California: Friends of Photography, 1980.

Greene, Jonathan, ed. "The Snapshot." *Aperture* 19:1, Millerton, NY: Aperture, 1974.

Malcolm, Janet. *Diana & Nikon*. Boston: David R. Godine, Publisher, Inc., 1980.

Rexroth, Nancy. *Iowa*. Albany, Ohio: Violet Press, 1977.

Van Riper, Frank. "Dr. Burnett's Magic Box." *Washington Post* (July 6, 2001).

Van Riper, Frank. "Holga's (now-Unblinking) Plastic Eye." *Washington Post* (January 3, 2002).

CAMERA: DIGITAL

At the end of the twentieth century, digital cameras were rapidly becoming the norm in many fields of photography. Film photography struggled to compete not in terms of quality, where it remains superior for most photographers, but in the transformations of use that the digital camera has enabled. Digital cameras can be quite diverse in form and function but there are two principle technologies that, while not common to all digital cameras, will serve to distinguish them from their conventional film based counterparts. These are the sensor and the storage system both of which are akin to a "digital film."

The Charge-Coupled Device (CCD) was invented in 1969–1970 making it the first digital sensor array. The array consists of a horizontal and vertical grid of light sensitive elements that convert light into electricity, and which can then be converted into digital data by an analog-to-digital converter (ADC). Each of the elements of an array is called a pixel—a word corrupted from "picture element." During the 1970s it was common to have an array of several hundred pixels across by several hundred deep. By the 1980s an array was developed by Kodak that was 1,500 pixels by 1,000. This totals 1.5 million pixels marking the first step into measuring the resolution of camera images in megapixels (one million pixels is a megapixel). Other forms of more recent sensor device include the Complementary Metal Oxide Semiconductor (CMOS) which, for example, Canon Inc., uses and the Junction Field Effect Transistor (JFET) which Nikon employs.

However, to say that the camera is collecting so many megapixels of information can be misleading. In order for a sensor to capture color it has to filter out the light so that it is reading only one color at a time. Digital cameras function through capturing red green and blue light independently by placing a color filter in front of each element. The most typical arrangement of these Color Filter Arrays (CFAs) is the Bayer grid developed by Kodak. This consists of a 2 × 2 grid which contains two green pixels and one each of red and blue. Because only half of the green pixels are really captured and a quarter of the blue and red, a process called demosaicing was developed to interpolate the missing color information. This results in a slight blurring occurring in images that use the CFA system. The Bayer grid is not the only system; Sony Corporation has developed another grid system not based upon red, green, and blue (RGB) but upon cyan, yellow, magenta, and green filters, and Fuji film corporation has developed a CCD that uses a grid system at a 45° angle which, they claim, gives better data for demosaicing. They have also developed a system that captures at two different sensitivities in order to increase dynamic range. Foveon Inc. makes a CMOS chip that uses three layers of sensors to capture full color data at every location. However, this sensor has a lower sensitivity than CFA systems because the light has to pass through three layers of sensors.

Another method of capturing full color data is to capture the RGB data in three passes. This is how most large format cameras with digital backs work. They scan the subject line by line, three times over in single color in order to create a full color composite in the host computer to which the back is tethered. The disadvantage of this is time: it can take several minutes to "shoot" an image rendering any moving subject unsuitable; the advantage is that the quality is unparalleled as full color information is captured for every pixel.

For digital backs the images are stored on the host computer's hard drive although for the majority of cameras this is not the case. There are various forms of storage that retain the information created. Currently, the most common of these is a Secure Digital card (SD) a card with a tiny form factor (1" × 1⅓") and so is suitable for use in compact digital cameras. Most commonly used in digital single lens reflex (SLR) digital cameras is the CompactFlash (CF) form factor, which is the size of a matchbook. This comes in two differing forms where the type II is slightly thicker than the type I. CF Type I stores the information in flash memory—a nonvolatile form of memory where power is not needed to maintain the information—and the type II form factor is used most often with a Microdrive, which is a small hard drive. Microdrives are slightly slower than flash media but are available in larger capacities. There are several other forms of memory; however, these two are the principal types.

Although the memory and the sensor array are the two distinguishing features of the digital camera, probably the most significant feature is in its connectivity to other digital systems: it sits much more readily within the workflow of the digitized publishing environment such as newspapers; because of specialized imaging needs, it is employed in areas such as astronomy; and, with the rise of the personal computer, a mass market for digital cameras has become a reality.

Astronomy demonstrated the first benefits of using digital technology in the mid-to late 1970s where because of their sensitivity to individual photons digital sensors provided images that conventional film was unable to capture. In 1981 Sony introduced the first digital camera with the Mavica (MAgnetic VIdeo CAmera), the original still video camera. Still video cameras are video cameras that capture single shots as photographs, which is the system still used in the majority of compact digital cameras but not in SLRs. Soon after this, in 1984, photojournalism conspicuously embraced digital cameras enabling shots to be taken at the Olympics in Los Angeles and sent to Japan across phone lines for publication within 30 minutes. Through the mid-1980s all the major camera manufacturers began to market digital cameras aimed at professional users, although the image quality of these early cameras was really quite poor by contemporary film standards. In 1986, Canon produced its RC701 still video camera, Kodak developed its milestone 1.5 megapixel digital sensor, and Nikon produced a digital camera prototype. In 1987 Kodak introduced its Still Video System, which included a printer, storage system, and camera. All of these cameras were prohibitively expensive for anyone bar professional users, but towards the end of the decade, cameras that were aimed at the nascent consumer market were developed, most notably the Logitech Fotoman. Naturally, to bring the price down the image quality that had been steadily becoming finer was reduced for this line of cameras (the Fotoman had a resolution of 640 × 480 pixels).

Also at this time digital studio cameras were being developed that had improved image quality but were tethered to a computer. At the beginning of the 1990s this evolved into high resolution cameras that took the form of the digital back. The digital back utilizes a pre-existing camera, replacing the film holder with a sensor. These have the advantage of using existing camera parts, most notably the camera body and optics. This principle is also used in digital SLRs. In 1992 Kodak paired with Nikon Inc. to produce the first digital SLR, the DCS200, which became the benchmark for digital cameras as that time. Rather than using a video feed that was captured in still frames, it used Nikon's optics and camera integrated with Kodak's sensors producing an image that was four times as fine as the standard still video camera. Kodak and Nikon's collaboration led the digital camera revolution for the next few years, until Nikon produced its own camera and Kodak teamed up with Canon in 1995. As the decade progressed smaller and cheaper sensors provided the consumer market with viable prices that could capture enough detail to satisfy amateur photographers. At the time of writing the high end of the consumer market has reached eight megapixels and the professional SLR cameras have reached 12 to 14 megapixels, although this figure will undoubtedly increase for some time to come.

Andrew Atkinson

Further Reading

Allenbach, Jan P., ed. *The Journal of Electronic Imaging*. The Society of Imaging and Technology (IS&T) and International Society for Optical Engineering (SPIE), 2004.

Blouke, Morley M., John Canosa, and Nitin Sampat, eds. *Sensors and Camera Systems for Scientific, Industrial, and Digital Photography Applications V*. International Society for Optical Engineering (SPIE), 2004.

Lister, Martin. *The Photographic Image in Digital Culture*. London: Routledge, 1998.

Manovich, Lev. *The Language of New Media*. Cambridge, Massachusetts: MIT Press, 2001.

Mitchell, William J. *The Reconfigured Eye: Visual Truth in the Post-Photographic Era*. Cambridge, Massachusetts: MIT Press, 1992.

Von Amelunxen, Hubertus. *Photography After Photography*. Munich: G&B Arts, 1996.

CAMERA: DISPOSABLE

The basic concept behind a disposable camera is a very simple one. Consumers buy a camera the same way they buy a roll of film, and send the camera to process. Film companies are able to sell cameras instead of films. These cameras with film should be very simple and cheap, providing "good enough" quality picture, meeting the needs of those not willing to spend the money on a "real" camera, or to learn some basic concepts of photography. However, the concept proved to be so successful that disposable cameras have seen their way into art photographers hands, seeking a simple "non-technically driven" way of making pictures, or into other serious photographers' bags as a cheap camera to use in harsh environment.

Even if a disposable camera was already in production in 1887 and the first Kodak camera was in concept, if not in price, close to a disposable camera, it was in the late 1980s that the modern disposable camera appeared in the world market. The idea is the same behind disposable razors, bottles, or almost everything in modern society, use and dispose of. It was a sign of the times when resources and environmental consciousness were less developed. The modern disposable camera with its very good technical quality and low price was only possible with modern plastic production technologies, modern optic design, allowing for a fair quality in single elements lens design, and above all to modern film technology with high speed, fine grain, and a large exposure latitude, allowing for good results with a fixed exposure lense.

From a marketing point of view, these cameras are addressed to a public who did not want or is not able to afford a sophisticated camera, with its price, bulk, weight, and technical needs. Children and travelers are the main market targets. These cameras are promoted also as a mean to preserve the "real cameras" from dangerous environments like sand, sea, or snow.

The first modern disposable camera introduced by Fuji in 1986 used the then current 110 film format; it was unable to give a good enough technical quality. However, a year later, the ever-present 35-mm film found its way into a disposable camera, the Fuji Quick-Snap, allowing surprisingly good technical quality. The two key elements for this quality are a simple (usually single element) lens of good quality and a film with wide exposure latitude, particularly in overexposure.

The first disposable cameras were just a cheap and simple way of getting pictures, but soon manufacturers saw increased potential in these humble cameras, and all film manufacturers started producing them. Beach or snow use were among the main concerns of their consumers, so, new models appeared enclosed in a plastic box capable of getting the camera under water, if not to a deep dive, at least to 10 feet. There was even a complete underwater housing made to take a disposable into deeper waters. Panoramic, or pseudo-panoramic, was a fashion of the 1990s made possible by the use of disposable cameras with a wider lens (24 mm or even 17 mm) and a film gate keeping the wide part of 35-mm film (36 mm), but reducing the smallest dimension of the film from 24 mm to 12 mm. This format was also used in compact auto-focus cameras and even in SLRs, but most tried it first with a disposable camera. The telephoto disposable camera was not a big success, but manufacturers kept trying a useful concept for them, and in the summer of 2001 Ferrania introduced a new model using mirrors in the light path to keep with the small size. With a plastic body with some cardboard printed external parts, they were also a good promotional tool for companies and events, making them a favorite for a cheap camera collection.

The modern revival of black and white photography led to the disposable black and white camera using traditional film or modern films based in color negative film technology, and able to be developed in the ever present "one hour lab." Konica even started producing their black and white chromogenic film first for use in disposables and only then sold it as a separate film. Even instant photography went into disposable, with the added difficulty of the price of some camera parts, mainly the rollers needed to develop the film.

The APS format launched in 1996 was supposed to be a revolution in disposable cameras. The basic idea of reducing the film frame, as it was more than adequate for the small prints most costumers wanted, was that it could be applied to the disposable camera market. Cameras could be made smaller with shorter lens and greater depth of field (useful in fixed focus cameras). The panoramic format could be used in the same camera along with the two other APS formats. Most important was the idea that the newer APS disposable cameras could give a start to the changes in photo-finishing business needed to adopt the new format. As with most things in this format, things actually were not up to what was expected and APS seems to represent only a small part of the single use camera market, even if these new cameras are smaller and, sometimes, pretty.

Disposables did not meet the same success in every market. Japan seems to be the place where the concept met a higher success, with a series of accessories, including motor drives and optical complements, available for disposables. The current shift towards digital seems to have cooled down the disposable market; however, disposable camera image quality is still much better than cheap digital cameras can achieve.

The term disposable is not a very accurate one. The cameras are not actually disposed of, most of its parts are reused or recycled. The terms "ready to photograph" or "single use camera" seem more accurate. The unpublicized fact that the cameras are user re-loadable and quite simple technically led to its use in school projects, making it a cheap way of getting a large number of simple and good quality cameras; it has also found favor in some kinds of art photography where technology is to be kept as simple as possible.

NUNO PINHEIRO

See also: **Camera: An Overview**

Further Reading

Lothrop, Eaton S., Jr. Unearthed: single-use camera! *Popular Photography*, March 1998, 9.

CAMERA: INSTANT OR POLAROID

The term instant is applied to a camera that produces photographs developed by the means of the chemical products it has enclosed with the film medium. These developers are released via the simple mechanical process of passing the film packet through rollers that spread the chemicals over the exposed image as it leaves the camera. These rollers characterize all instant cameras and serve to quickly distinguish them from other camera types. Atypical as well is the fact that instant photography has been dominated by a single manufacturer, and the history of instant photography is inseparable from that of the Polaroid Corporation. In fact, the word "Polaroid" is widely used when referring to an instant camera. The instant camera is most widely used as a consumer product, but it also has applications as a professional tool—to make quick proofs when shooting with other cameras, and has been in the later part of the twentieth century an important genre in fine art photography.

Invented by Edwin Land in 1947, this process was first made available to the general public in 1948 by the Polaroid Company. Touted as "one-step" photography, the Polaroid Land Camera produced a 3¼ × 4¼" dry print and sold for the relatively costly price of $89.95. These first cameras used a film not too different from the roll film foldings currently in use: a paper negative that offset the image onto a sheet of sensitized photographic paper were sealed together in a rolled packet. A two-roller mechanism smashed and spread the developer chemicals across this packet and the sensitized papers inside. After exposing the image, the film was separated from the camera. The finished picture was then separated from the negative a few seconds later and the negative discarded.

This new invention was an immediate success. A long succession of new and improved cameras was introduced. They used three series of roll film: type 40 in the first and most sophisticated type 95, 95A, 95b, 100, 110, 110A, and 120, among other models; type 30 and type 20 used on cheaper models and mostly plastic-bodied cameras like the J33 and Swinger models. As none of these films is available these cameras are not usable, unless converted to the still current pack films.

The first films available for use were sepia, but soon came black and white, higher speed black and white, high contrast materials for scientific applications, and positive/negative with a proof print and a usable negative.

In 1963, Polaroid introduced the second generation of cameras. They use the still current type 100/600 peel apart pack film, in several types of black and white and in 75 ASA/ISO color. These were plastic-bodied, box-like cameras, and more sophisticated folding models with differences in body material (plastic or metal) lens design and construction, the presence and type of rangefinders, or timers. There were four successive series the 100, 200, 300, and 400, with no important differences among each series. The series 100 was introduced in 1963 and had six models, the range increased with each series until the 300 series from 1969 had 11 models. Consumer products had an electronic shutter, the first introduced in a mass-produced camera, auto exposure, and needed a hard to find battery. There were manual exposure models, the 180, 185, 190, and the 195; they are sold for high prices in the used market. A new limited production version of these is currently on sale, but it is produced by NPC. Some of the consumer models were a huge success with production numbers up to 1,000,000. However, there were simpler and cheaper plastic bodied models: Colorpack, Memory Maker, Minute Maker. They all have automatic exposure, some had fixed focus lens, while others had some simplified devices to help focus. Some used the smaller type 80 film (Square Shooter). Their prices ranged from around $25 to $45. The Pack film range included also the BigShot, a long focus, fixed-focus, fixed exposure model dedicated to portrait, famous as being used by Andy Warhol; a new range of plastic folding cameras in production until the late nineties (EE-100; Reporter; Propack); the Mamiya based and built 600 and 600 SE, the latter with 75-127- and 150-mm, interchangable lens, and some special cameras dedicated to macro-work. Still in production are Portrait and Passport models with two and four lens, providing two and four images in one single frame.

In 1972, there was an easier way to use instant photography, the new SX70 camera used the first integral film system. There was no need to pull the film from the camera as it had a small motor, powered by the battery in the film pack, to eject the film. The SX70 camera was a folding SLR, not much larger than the pictures it produced. It featured electronic control and electric film ejection. The image was unreversed on film by means of a mirror, the film was parallel to the bottom of the camera, and not to the lens plane. The first model finished in brown leather and brushed metal was an example of good design, from a time most industrial design is bound to be forgotten. The variations of the original SX70 had little more than different colors, black metal with brown leatherette, chromed metal with black leatherette, and even white and gold models. Except for the non-reflex model 3 the technical differences were small.

In 1978, Konica had just introduced the first auto-focus camera, and the SX70 evolved to auto-focus, which was accomplished by adding a sonar auto-focus module on its top. It allowed focusing in complete darkness, a feature stressed by Polaroid advertising. Most auto-focus Polaroid cameras still use this auto-focus system.

SX70s were expensive ($180 in 1972), so the same principle of reversing the image with a mirror was applied to rigid plastic bodied models, the most popular in the United States was the Onestep, which in 1977 became the best-selling camera in the world; it remained so for four years. It was followed by other models some including sonar auto-focus. Art photographers still use these discontinued models as SX70/Time Zero film allows for manipulation not possible with more modern integral films.

Most post-SX70 Polaroid cameras and films are based on this concept. The 600 series cameras use the same size of film but with a speed of ISO 640 instead of ISO 150. With minor adaptations, it is possible to use SX70/Time Zero in these cameras, as this film is not suited for manipulations and SX70 cameras are no longer produced. Most cameras using type 600 film are technically similar simple plastic cameras. However there is a large number of different models, some appealing to a children/youth market, using cartoon (Taz, Barbie) or music characters (Spice Girls), making this film the most popular in the Polaroid range. The current models are different from former models as they are of the folding type, similar in aesthetics to the Spectra/Image range described below. The most capable cameras of these series the 1980s 680 and the more recent 690, are no more than sonar auto-focus SX70s with built-in flash and metering systems able to deal with the faster film. Other current Polaroid film systems are the Spectra/Image system, which works in a similar way but is a bit wider, and led to a more advanced, although non-reflex, camera line, backs to scientific instruments and computer printers. This range originally had four folding cameras, three of which share the same body: the 125 mm, 3 elements F10 lens called Quintic and an unusual focus system consisting of a segmented arc-shaped center element, which swings on a pivot to adjust focus. (Spectra/Image; Spectra/Image 2 Spectra/Image Pro) and another, ProCam, with a more rugged construction, folds sideways and has a wider lens, said to be of better quality. To extend the possibilities of Spectra/Image cameras, Polaroid produced ingenious close-up accessories, some particularly suited to police work. A recent variation of the Spectra/Image is the 1200 series folding cameras using 12 pictures per pack, instead of 10, but with backwards compatibility with earlier Spectra/Image film packs. There are a few current models in this range, including one with an LCD viewfinder.

In 1993, trying to produce a smaller and cheaper film, Polaroid launched the Captiva/Vision series with a concept closer to the original SX70, a folding reflex, with a compartment to keep the ejected picture. It was not a success, but the film type was kept for the the Joycam, a very simple cheap camera that does not have a motor to eject the picture. This film type was also used in the Popshots an ill-fated adventure in the single-use camera market.

The I zone, earlier marketed as Xiao by a Japanese toy maker, uses a smaller film, close to a 35-mm frame in a 110 look alike camera, with bright colors and cartoon characters appealing to a very young public. There is also a scanner dedicated to Izone photographs, a film/digital camera combo, and a camera with a FM radio. In the United States Polaroid also markets the

Mio camera, which seems to be no more than a repackaged Fuji Instax 10 or 20.

For the most part of these more than 50 years, Polaroid was almost alone in the instant photography market even if some companies produced cameras compatible with Polaroid films. Kodak tried to compete with his own line of cameras and films in the late 1970s. All ended with lawsuits and courts ruling Kodak out of this market. In the late 1990s Fuji started producing instant films for the professional market usable on Polaroid cameras and film backs, and later, consumer cameras and films.

In the beginning of the digital era, instant photography seemed to have little reason for existence, and Polaroid faced a very difficult situation, the expert photographer targeted by earlier models and even SX70 seemed to be left out, and current consumer Polaroid cameras aimed at the lower end of the market. Polaroid also marketed low-end conventional film and digital cameras. However the professional/scientific uses of instant photography were still provided as from its beginnings. Polaroid has a commitment to serious photographers, producing cameras, backs, and films for proofing and as a final photograph. Art photographers are using some forms of Polaroid process in the intended and unintended ways. Collectors appreciate the large variety of models (around 275, not counting color variations) and their availability. Polaroid owns some 20 × 24" cameras, which can be rented from their studios in some European and North American cities. The pictures some photographers produced with them are among the most prized of modern photography.

Nuno Pinheiro

See also: **Polaroid Corporation**

Further Reading

Innovation Imagination, 50 Years of Polaroid Photography. New York; Harry N. Abrams, 1999.

Polaroid Guide to Instant Image: Creative Uses of Polaroid Film, Waltham, MA: Polaroid Corporation, 1992. *www.polaroid.com* (accessed August 11, 2005).

CAMERA OBSCURA

The camera obscura existed long before photography itself. In fact, there would be no photography without it. The name literally translates from Latin to mean "dark room." The moniker, however, is a bit misleading, as it leaves out the most crucial element of the camera obscura: a small hole through which light can enter the darkened chamber.

No one invented the camera obscura; it is a naturally occurring optical phenomenon. Like Plato's cave, in which projected shadows are an allegory for reality, the camera obscura projects real life, in full color and movement, onto a two-dimensional wall or screen to be observed and contemplated. Light enters a darkened enclosure through an aperture such as a small hole or a glass lens, projecting an inverted image onto an opposite wall or screen. The science that allows this to occur is simple. Light travels in straight lines. When entering a small hole, rather than scattering, light will only pass through in an organized manner. Thus, light reflected off of a flag atop a flagpole will pass through the aperture and hit the lower part of the back wall or screen. Whereas light bouncing off the base of the pole will end up at the top of the projected image.

In essence, a camera obscura is simply a camera without film. It dates back centuries before light sensitive materials were developed. The first recorded observations of the phenomenon are attributed to the Chinese philosopher Mo-Ti in the fifth century BC. Aristotle (384–322 BC) took note of this process while observing light filtering between the leaves of trees and projecting crescent shaped images of the eclipsed sun on the ground. He also took note that the smaller the hole, the sharper the image appeared.

Although it was probably a principle known by contemporary scholars at the time, the first account of the camera obscura itself dates back to the Arabian scholar Alhazen (Abu Ali al-Hasan Ibn al-Haitham) (c. 965–1039). In 1490 Leonardo da Vinci clearly described the camera obscura which he called *oculus artificialis* in reference to its commonalties with the eye. He also suggested overcoming the problem of the reversed image by projecting it on a sheet of thin paper and viewing it from behind.

The person most often credited, though incorrectly, with developing the camera obscura is the sixteenth century Neapolitan scientist, Giovanni Battista Della Porta. This is because the camera obscura was described in detail in his book, *Magiae Naturalis*, one of the best known works on popular science from that time. Della Porta was the first to describe camera obscura as an aid to artists attempting to draw from life. Though he was not the first to do so, he took advantage of developments to the camera obscura, such as the use of an optical lens instead of a simple hole, which brightened and sharpened the image. He also used a mirror, which, by reflecting the image, corrected its earlier reversal. Della Porta created theatrical pageants that took place directly outside the darkened room, with sets and costumed characters. Once his audience's eyes adjusted to the darkness of the room, what they saw was truly cinematic. Projected before them was a drama acted out by miniature two-dimensional characters. They were in awe. Those who disbelieved Della Porta's explanation of the illusion even accused him of sorcery.

As the camera obscura became more popular, it took new forms. Rather than a specially constructed permanent room or building: smaller, more portable versions were made. Some were small rooms light enough to be carried on rails by two men, like a sedan chair. The astronomer Johann Kepler, who actually coined the phrase "camera obscura," had a portable tent camera that he used when making a topographical survey of Upper Austria in the 1620s.

Very tiny versions were also developed. One was inset into the stem of a goblet. Through the use of a small mirror, an image was projected onto the surface of the wine (white), so that the host could keep an eye on his guests: arguably the predecessor to the modern day surveillance camera. The most popular version of the camera obscura, however, was just small enough for a person to carry under one arm. These had a frosted glass or translucent screen onto which the image was projected (much like a view camera), eliminating the need to be in an enclosed room.

Many seventeenth and eighteenth century artists were interested in the camera obscura's ability to essentially replicate, though monocularly, human vision. It helped them to achieve perfection on difficult to render perspectives. Notables among these artists were Jan Vermeer (1632–1675) and Canaletto (1697–1768). The extent to which they used the camera to create their precise paintings remains controversial to this day.

At this point the camera obscura was essentially the prototype for the modern camera. The only change needed was a way to load it with film. Both Nicéphore Niépce and William Henry Fox Talbot used camera obscuras to expose their various light sensitive materials and produce the first photographs. With this, a major shift in the camera's role in the world occurred. A light and chemical reaction took the place of the artist's pencil. Instead of being an instrument for observing, and possibly drawing a subject, an act still somewhat subjective, it became instead a recorder of a "truth": the creator of a subject itself.

Camera obscuras live on today. Around the world there still exist some walk-in camera obscuras whose function is both entertainment, observation (most of these are in areas of splendid views), and education. Some contemporary artists, such as Ann Hamilton, Vera Lutter, and Abelardo Morell still create work using the phenomenon.

But the camera obscura's true descendant is the modern camera. Be it film or digital, large format or movie camera, the basic structure and concept of the camera has remained the same through the centuries: a light-tight box into which light, admitted through an opening, strikes a parallel surface and projects an image. Unlike in centuries past however, the image, no longer fleeting, can now be kept intact.

Roger Sayre

See also: **Camera: Overview; Photographic "Truth"**

Further Readings

Fish, Peter. "The Magic of the Great Camera Obscura." *Sunset* February 1997, 14.

Gernsheim, Helmut, and Allison Gernsheim. *The History of Photography 1685–1914*. New York: McGraw-Hill, 1969.

Hockney, David. *Secret Knowledge: Rediscovering the Lost Techniques of the Old Masters*. London: Thames and Hudson, 2001.

Sinnott, Roger W. "A 6-Inch Camera Obscura." *Sky and Telescope* January 1997, 96.

Steadman, Philip. *Vermeer's Camera*. Oxford University Press, 2001.

Surdin; V. and M. Kartashev. "Light in a Dark Room." *Quantum* July/August 1999, 40.

CAMERA: PINHOLE

Pinhole photography is photography in its most basic form, involving no optical or electronic elements, working with only a light proof container and a tiny hole. The container can be made from cardboard, wood, metal, plastics, almost anything the photographer's imagination can suggest. In the 1980s, Jeff Guess (American) used his mouth as a pinhole camera. Inside a pinhole camera, either a piece of photo paper or photo film can be placed to record the image. The film or paper can be black and white, color, Polaroid, or hand-sensitized materials. The pinhole opening can be made directly into the container or from other materials such as aluminum shim attached to the container. The shutter can be closed and opened by a simple piece of black tape or more sophisticated mechanical devices. The pinhole camera can be any size, from tiny 35-mm film containers, to a shoe box, lunch box, or trashcan size, to an entire room or building. In the 1990s, Patricia Gabas (French) and Andre Kertzenblatz (French) built a pinhole cabin large enough for several people to fit inside and put it on the back of a truck, a mobile pinhole camera, literally a *camera obscura*, or dark room.

Without the pinhole opening, ambient light striking a piece of photo paper or film cannot represent a scene because light rays, traveling in straight lines, are sending information from any particular point to all directions at once. This excessive information cannot reproduce on photo paper a recognizable image. A piece of photo paper that has been held up to a chair and developed looks exactly like a piece of photo paper held up to a lamp and developed—only the scattered light will be captured and the picture will feature only gray tones. This chaotic quality of light can be structured by forcing the light to travel through a tiny hole. A tiny hole blocks most light rays, transmitting light from a particular point in one, as opposed to, multiple directions. The projected image is upside down but otherwise recognizable. When properly directed light strikes a photographic piece of paper or film, the projected image can be recorded as a photograph.

The phenomena of pinhole, or camera obscura, was understood and exploited well before the advent of photography. In China, Mo Ti (c. 4000 B.C.) describes how light traveling in a straight line, like an arrow, projects a recognizable image. Egyptian scholar Hassan ibn Hassan (c. 1000) describes the use of a pinhole device to observe an eclipse of the sun. Other historical references to pinhole include Aristotle (384–322 B.C.), Francis Bacon (c. 1267), and Leonardo Da Vinci (1452–1519).

Some of the historical activity with pinhole images has been scientific, such as observing eclipses, measuring time, or researching the qualities of light. Some of the activity has been educational, such as workshops or classes where people make and use their own pinhole camera, exploring firsthand the phenomena of orderly light and photography. Some of the historical activity has been in the art world. In the fifteenth century, painters used camera obscura devices to help sketch and paint with perspective. The camera obscura device was a light tight space or container with a small opening pointed at the scene to be sketched or painted. Light traveling through the hole projected the scene onto paper or other support to be traced by the artist. With the advent of photography in the nineteenth century, Sir David Brewster (1856) coined the word pinhole and is the first to have made pinhole photographs. Use of pinhole cameras fell out of use in the early part of the twentieth century. In the 1960s and 1970s, there was a revival of many alternative photographic processes and through the end of the twentieth century, pinhole photography surfaced in the arena of contemporary art.

There are several particular qualities to pinhole photographs, such as long exposures, infinite depth of field, more or less refined resolution, angles of view, possible distortions, and multiple exposures. Without the use of optical glass elements, the projected image is relatively dim and thus exposure times are often necessarily lengthy and can last from a few seconds to several days. Exposure times will vary according to the amount of available light, the size of the pinhole, and the sensitivity of the film or paper being exposed; the more available light and the larger the size of the pinhole, the shorter the exposure time. A smaller opening makes for relatively longer exposure times, but has better resolution than large openings, producing a more refined reproduction of detail. The greater the distance between the pinhole opening and the photo paper or film (the focal plane), the less refined the resulting image. This distance also affects the angle of view. When the pinhole opening and the photo paper or film are relatively close to each other, the resulting angle of view is somewhat wide-angle, becoming more and more telephoto as the hole and paper are farther and farther apart. It is commonly thought that lenses are responsible for improved visual resolution but in fact the principal difference between pinhole and lens photography has to do with intensity not quality of light. In lens photography, the use of optical elements concentrates multiple light rays, intensifying the projected light and shortening exposure times. In both pinhole and lens photography, the visual resolution is more a factor of the size of the opening than the use of a lens. Moreover, a lens imposes the need to focus, whereas a pinhole photograph has infinite depth of field; all objects close or far from the pinhole camera will be reproduced in equal focus. A flat piece of photo paper or film placed directly across from the pinhole opening can reproduce a scene with little visual distortion, or diverse distortions are possible by bending or curving the photo paper or film. Multiple exposures are facilitated by the typically long exposure times and mechanical simplicity of most pinhole cameras.

At the end of the twentieth century, pinhole photography was a well-published topic, a common part of many educational programs, and exhibited in major museums as well as commercial galleries, community centers, and libraries.

BRUCE MCKAIG

See also: **Camera Obscura; Lens**

Further Reading

Gernsheim, Alison, and Helmut Gernsheim. *The History of Photography*. New York: McGraw-Hill, 1969.

International Center of Photography. *Encyclopedia of Photography*. New York: Pound Press/Crown Publishers, 1984.

Renner, Eric. *Pinhole Photography: Rediscovering a Historic Technique*. Boston: Focal Press, 1995.

Shull, Jim. *The Hole Thing*. New York: Morgan & Morgan, 1974.

Smith, Lauren. *The Visionary Pinhole*. USA: Peregrine Smith, 1985.

CAMERA: POINT AND SHOOT

The 35-mm film cameras known familiarly as "point and shoots" are not your (Great) Grandma's Brownie. They are smart, sophisticated, and snap-shot easy miniaturizations of the classic rangefinder cameras, scaled down to a viewing screen to guide the eye and an interior circuitry that automatically measures light and distance. In the hands of a photographer who understands their parameters, a simple model with a good lens can take photographs indistinguishable from their larger and more complicated cousins, the single lens reflex (SLR) and rangefinder cameras.

It took more than a hundred years of invention to perfect cameras as small, sharp, and nearly foolproof as the contemporary snap shot camera. Miniaturization, however, was a goal from the beginnings of photographic research. Henry Fox Talbot, one of photography's founding fathers, realized early on in his experiments with light that tiny cameras with lenses of short focal lengths (the distance between the aperture and the sensitized plate) would concentrate the light in a small area and lead to shorter exposures. Nicknamed "mousetraps" by his wife, some of the little boxes fitted with microscope lenses measured only two–and-a-half inches square. Unfortunately, enlargers had yet to be invented, and the tiny images were dismissed by Fox Talbot as looking like the work "of some Lilliputian artist."

The first functioning roll film camera small enough to take on a picnic was George Eastman's brilliant invention, the Kodak No. 1, introduced in 1888. It was a simple box camera less than seven inches long and four inches wide, with a set shutter speed of $1/25$ of a second and a fixed focus lens that managed a reasonably sharp picture eight feet or more away from its subject. It came with the instructions "You Press the Button, We Do the

Rest" and a preloaded roll of film that recorded 100 images. Film and unopened camera were sent back to the factory in Rochester for processing. It was the beginning of the family snap shot, and its simplicity made the camera a household item.

The Kodak Brownie followed in 1900, along with a host of competing manufacturers of small cameras for the amateur market. It was another 25 years, however, before the development of a 35-mm precision camera capable of sharp focus, variable shutter speeds, and low light exposures. This camera, the Leica, was introduced by Oskar Barnack, head of the experimental department at the E. Leitz German Optical Works in 1925.

Following World War II, color film and the large choice of small, easy to load and use cameras put a modern camera on everyone's wish list, but the rangefinder 35-mm and the increasingly popular single lens reflex 35-mm cameras, introduced shortly after the war, still presented technical challenges to most amateur photographers.

Auto-exposure was the first breakthrough. Built-in light meter systems coupled with electronically controlled shutters set the shutter speed, depending on the photographer's choice of aperture. In 1977 Konica introduced the first 35-mm compact camera with auto-focus and auto-exposure. By the 1990s easy to load film handling, automatic film speed settings, automatic end of the roll rewind, dedicated flash units, zoom lenses, and ultra light-weight compact designs for 35-mm point-and-shoot cameras dominated the amateur market.

Depending on the camera model, there are two systems of auto-focus to choose from: passive or active. In the active system, a beam of light, usually infrared, is emitted from a small opening near the lens and provides the lens with the distance from the subject (as determined by the object in the center of the viewing screen) to the camera. The lens automatically adjusts the focus. This is an effective system in low light, or on a foggy day, but if the subject is behind glass or the beam strikes falling snow, the system fails to focus on the subject.

In a passive system, used frequently on point and shoot cameras with zoom lenses and on auto-focus SLRs, sensors are located behind the lens. These sensors measure both horizontal and vertical bands of the subject and can be more accurate, particularly in a landscape situation. They depend on contrast to work properly. Therefore, a single tone or color (for instance, a field of snow) will be difficult, if not impossible to focus. In some more expensive point and shoots, an active "assist beam" is available for these situations.

In these fully automated cameras, the auto-exposure and the auto-focus function together when the subject is placed in the center of the viewing screen and the shutter is pressed half way down. Light meter sensors, located on the body of the read the areas from several "zones" in the image. These meters average the exposures of the different zones to match an eighteen percent gray card, but generally give greater priority to the center of the viewing screen. Known as center-weighted, this kind of meter is good for subjects in a landscape or backlit (light falling on the subject is less that the light behind the subject).

Some center-weighted meters are balanced with additional metering systems, such as spot meters. Spot meters measure very specific areas, rather than averaging the entire image. Usually, there is a mode or a combination of modes to press to utilize this type of metering.

Continuing to press halfway down on the shutter locks in focus and exposure. This allows the photographer the opportunity to adjust exposure and arrange the composition by moving the camera to a different angle or view. Warning lights indicate if there are problems with these functions.

The lenses on these cameras are "fixed," that is, they are not removable. The range of lens choices, however, continues to grow, with zoom lenses a top consumer choice. These little multifocal lens generally range from from wide-angle 35-mm to the telephoto 145-mm, or higher. A shortcoming of these lens is an aperture range that is rather limited and difficult to use in low light situations. Small but powerful built-in dedicated flash units have been developed to ameliorate this limitation. They can be quickly employed as fill-flash for backlit subjects on a sunny day or as full flash in low light situations. Many of these cameras also come with a night mode or slow sync flash. In this mode, the flash goes off and the shutter remains open, often for as long as a second, to record the ambient light.

A large choice of films and film speeds are available for 35-mm point and shoots. APS point and shoots, however, are far more limited. Film is easily dropped in and speed is read from the DX code on the canister. If the code does not function, these cameras default to a film speed of ISO 100. The film automatically rewinds after the last shot. The ease of these cameras, their low cost, and their precision functions have once again put cameras in the hands of amateurs, just as George Eastman's Kodak No. 1 did in 1888.

KAY KENNY

See also: **Camera: 35 mm; Camera: An Overview; Exposure; Film; Lens**

Further Reading

Coe, Brian. *Cameras: From Daguerreotypes to Instant Pictures*. New York: Crown, 1978.

Eastman Kodak Company, eds. *Kodak's Guide to 35 mm Photography*. Rochester, New York: Eastman Kodak Company, 2000.

Eastman Kodak Company, eds. *The Joy of Photography*. Rochester, New York: Eastman Kodak Company, 1991.

Hedgecoe, John. *The Book of Photography*. New York: Alfred A. Knopf, 1990.

Langford, Michael. *Story of Photography*. 2nd ed. Boston: Focal Press, 2000.

Langford, Michael. *Langford's 35 mm Handbook*. 3rd ed. New York: Alfred A. Knopf, 1993.

London, Barbara, and John Upton. *Photography*. 7th ed. Upper Saddle River, NJ: Prentice Hall, 1998.

The Camera. rev. ed. Alexandria, Virginia: Time-Life Inc., 1981. Time-Life, Library of Photography.

PHOTOGRAPHY IN CANADA

Canada emerged in 1867 when the francophone Lower Canada and anglophone Upper Canada nations, containing almost equal populations, were united, creating a country of vast landscapes and contrasting seasons that makes up the second largest sovereignty in the world after Russia. Canada has offered to photographers and explorers countless exceptional locales and phenomenon.

In the beginning of the twentieth century, Canada's population was concentrated in the eastern provinces, mainly Ontario and Québec, the largest city until the 1960s being Montréal. In the late decades of the century, most of the Canadian population became concentrated in the southern parts of the country, which had some 30 million inhabitants at the end of 2001. The Canadian North, covering half of the country, remains a virtual desert of snow and ice, immortalized by the pioneering ethnographic works of Robert J. Flaherty as early at 1910.

In photography, as in many other areas, Canada's culture and history tend to be overshadowed by that of the United States. America's dominance in the northern hemisphere has resulted in many stereotypes and myths about Canada, with many Americans knowing Canada only for few famous pictures, such as the panoramic perspective of the Niagara Falls. Yet Canada has great depth and breadth of photographic imagery which has both shaped and disseminated its culture, some of the best known being views of the spectacular and historic Quebec City, which was selected by UNESCO to appear on its prestigious "World Heritage List." The magnificent Château Frontenac atop Cap-Diamant and dating from 1893 is perhaps the most photographed hotel in the world.

Unfortunate stereotypes perhaps still linger, as a comprehensive history of Canadian photography has yet to be written. Chief among those who have explored aspects of Canadian photographic history are Professor Michel Lessard, who has written extensively about the origins and evolution of visual arts in Canada. He founded the "Atelier de recherche sur l'image photographique" (ARIP), at the Université du Québec à Montréal (UQAM). Yet it is clear that photographs and photographers were always popular in all regions of Canada. Prior to 1914, for instance, there were some 700 professional photographers, men and women, owning studios just in the St. Lawrence Valley (including Montréal, Québec City, and many villages) (Lessard, 1986). That amazing number tripled in the three following decades. One should add to this number countless amateur photographers across Canada's 10 provinces.

The history of Canadian photography in the twentieth century, however, can be roughly divided into two main categories: that which celebrates the few photographers who were aligned with the aims of the Canadian establishment, and that of the numerous unrecognized photographers, portraitists, and anonymous amateurs who showed a more comprehensive vision of Canadian diversity. The "official" photographers provided images of an urban, expanding colonial country, often depicting only the anglophone élite, even in French majority regions. The workaday professionals and countless amateur photographers, on the other hand, depicted rural peoples and their lives, as well as the urban proletarians who constituted the francophone majority. (According to art historian Louise Désy, who surveyed phone directories from the end of the nineteenth century, 80 percent of the St. Lawrence Valley photographers were francophones [Désy 1984]). These two versions of the history of Canadian photography, the colonial point of view reifying anglophone artists and the post-colonial perspectives that recall the English dominance over the francophone population although lingering to the present, perhaps obscure other histories.

In a country as vast as Canada, photographic postcards proved a useful means of diffusing images that contributed to the social construction of typical Canadian scenes and folkways. Yet it was only from December 9, 1897 that the Canadian government authorized private enterprises to produce and sell illustrated postcards in Canada (Beauregard, 2005). The first postcards available most often represented typical Canadian monuments or neutral images (flowers, children, animals, a lady, lovers). Yet a number of these postcards were produced and printed in foreign countries using photographs originally conceived by the Studios Livernois (Québec City) or by Notman and Son (Montréal), without ever mentioning the source or the author (Poitras 1990). A golden age of the postcard occurred in Canada between 1905 and 1915, and interest in this period supports the collecting of old postcards and clubs for collectors, such as the "Club des cartophiles québécois." Author Jacques Poitras wrote two fine books about the emergence of postcards in Canada (Poitras 1986, 1990).

Canadian photography in the early twentieth century was very much the continuation of the tradition initiated during the nineteenth century, with some respected photographers and famous institutions, such as the studios and galleries founded by William Notman (1826–1891) in Montréal, or the studios of J. Ernest Livernois (1851–1933) and his rival, Louis-Prudent Vallée (1837–1905) in Québec City, pursuing their work and experiments. For instance, since the 1880s, Louis-Prudent Vallée specialized in the stereoscopy, showing panoramic views of Québec City, and that lucrative commerce carried on during the first decades of the twentieth century. The tintype was certainly the most popular type of photographic image in Canada until the end of the 1920s (Lessard 1987).

Some historians considered William Notman (1826–1891) as the most influential photographer in Canada at the end of nineteenth century. Born in Scotland, he came to Montréal in 1856, after studying fine arts in Glasgow. William Notman innovated when his studio on Rue Bleury, Montréal, offered colorized photographs beginning in 1857. His three sons, W. McFarlane Notman (1857–1913), George Notman (1868–1921), and Charles F. Notman (1870–1955), continued their father's enterprise in the beginning of twentieth century. An international corporation of studios and laboratories, Notman and Sons had branches in four Canadian provinces, (in Toronto, Ottawa, Halifax, St. John) and in the United States (in Boston and New York City). At the turn of twentieth century, when funds were needed to finance the construction of the Canadian National Railway and the Canadian National Railway towards the west side of the country, their epic photographs of the Canadian West landscapes contributed to give a positive image of these wild regions of Alberta, Saskatchewan, and Manitoba.

The Studios Livernois in old Québec City was one of the longest-lived institutions in the history of Canadian photography, and the most important laboratory of photographers in Québec City from 1854 to 1974. It began as a family enterprise, la Maison Livernois, founded by Jules Isaïe Benoit de Livernois (1830–1865), known as J.B. Livernois. His son, J. Ernest Livernois (1851–1933), took charge of the commerce a few years after the premature death of his father. In 1910, J. Ernest Livernois opened a three-floor store and a studio on the Rue de la Fabrique, near the City Hall in Québec City. An artist and businessman, J. E. Livernois diversified his commercial activities to include laboratory services, official portraits, death-cards, business cards, photo-albums, and postcards. His son, Jules Livernois (1877–1952), pursued the family enterprise for the third generation, before being succeeded by his sons Victor and Maurice Livernois. But the Studio Livernois was not just a family affair; collaborators included photographers Thaddée Lebel, Georges Landry, André Laberge, Nazaire Dufour, Alexandre Fauchon, Fernand Lamontagne, and Livernois' cousin Émile Pelchat, who was also a photographer (Lessard, 1986). The enterprise was synonymous with quality, style, and distinction. But after 120 years of artistic presence in Québec City, the Livernois Studio closed its doors in 1974, and the whole enterprise ceased its activities in 1979, leaving a legacy of more than 200,000 photographs.

Among other notable photographers, the five members of the Pinsonneault family had studios in smaller towns: in Saint-Jean (Québec), Trois-Rivières, Victoriaville, Sherbrooke.

Sidney Carter (1880–1956) was one of the earliest and certainly most talented of the amateur photographers at the turn of the century who worked toward the recognition of photography as an art form in Canada. Largely unknown today, he created striking images in a Pictorialist style, including self-portraits and a portrait of writer Rudyard Kipling.

Although most Canadian photographers were born in either Québec or Ontario, some of the most celebrated artists in the history of Canadian photography were immigrants, such as the Scottish-born William Notman. Two notable examples in the twentieth century are Chow Dong Hoy and Yousuf Karsh.

A Canadian of Chinese descent who was born in Guangdong, Chow Dong Hoy (1883–1973) had many jobs before adopting photography as a profession, after he emigrated to Quesnel, Canada, in 1902. Between 1909 and 1920, Chow Dong Hoy took some 1,500 photographs of Chinese who had come to British Columbia as workers. Many Chinese workers and gold miners and prospectors engaged Chow Dong Hoy to make their portraits to be sent to far-away families. During this same period, Chow Dong Hoy also photographed with his Kodak model "A" camera Aboriginal nations including the Carriers and the Chilcotins, who were living in West Canada, near Barkerville, British Columbia. He later opened a general store and gradually abandoned photography. Although he also made many portraits of notable Canadians and European immigrants, Chow Dong Hoy is now cherished for his photographs of Natives and Chinese-Canadians. After being more or less forgotten for some decades, an exhibition (*First Son—Portraits by C.D. Hoy*) was dedicated to him by the McCord Museum of Canadian History in Montreal (Moosang 1999).

Possibly the most renowned Canadian photographer of the mid twentieth century is Yousuf Karsh (1908–2002), an Armenian born in Mardin, Turkey, who was forced to leave his country in 1922. After a short stay in Syria, he arrived in Sherbrooke (Québec), in 1924. There, Karsh learned to be a photographer with his uncle, George Nakash, who was already established as a respected photographer-portraitist in Sherbrooke. But Karsh wanted to learn more about his new profession and went to work for a few years in Boston, Massachusetts with photographer John H. Garo, who specialized in portraits of celebrities. Back in Canada, Karsh established himself in Ottawa (Ontario) from 1932, and he soon became the most respected photographer for his official portraits, until his retirement in 1992. Almost every official visitor of the Canadian government—foreign leaders, kings and queens, actresses, and even the Pope— was photographed by Karsh, who had a studio in the Château Laurier, an elegant hotel near the Ottawa Parliament. He made many albums and luxurious books of his most prestigious photographs.

Most of his collection of some 11,000 portraits of celebrities (including Canada's foremost politicians, artists and leaders, and also Winston Churchill) were acquired by the National Archives in Ottawa. After selling his archives, Karsh returned to Boston in 1997 and stayed there until his death, on July 13, 2002. His younger brother, Malak Karsh (1915–2001), was also a photographer who emigrated to Canada in 1937. Like his brother, he made official portraits for the government of Canada; one of his pictures of the Ottawa Parliament once appeared on the one dollar bill. Since he worked with his brother, and to avoid confusion, he signed his portraits only with his first name, "Malak."

Another distinguished Canadian portraitist was Roloff Beny (1924–1984), who in particular achieved an international reputation for his lavishly produced photo books. His photographs, a large mass of which were donated to the National Archives of Canada following his death, record the leading figures in the worlds of dance, opera, music, literature, cinema, theatre, fashion, and politics of the latter half of the twentieth century. One of his best-known images is a 1959 portrait of Canadian pianist Glenn Gould.

Sam Tata, born in 1911 to Indian parents in Shanghai, practiced social documentary photography in China and in the late 1940s with Henri Cartier-Bresson, documented the final years of Mahatma Gandhi's India. After chronicling the establishment of communism in China during the 1950s, he emigrated to Canada in 1956, where he became a notable portraitist, especially of Canada's literary movement of the 1960s and '70s, shooting well-received portraits of Canadian poet and songwriter Leonard Cohen and many others.

Foreign photographers had a significant influence upon the perception of Canada. Many Americans, for instance, had their first encounter with Canada through the pages of *Vogue* magazine. A young photographer from New York City, Lida Moser, went to Montréal in 1950 to prepare a series of articles about Canada. Fluent in French, she met the two most important specialists of the Canadian heritage at that time, novelist Félix-Antoine Savard and folklorist Luc Lacoursière, both professors from Université Laval in Québec City, who helped her to discover rural Québec. Moser also visited Québec City and Montréal (Moser, 1982), shooting landscapes that previously had been mostly unknown to most Canadians, much less Americans. She also made portraits of most of the important Canadian artists and intellectuals of the era, including painter Alfred Pellan, poet Alain Grandbois, actor Pierre Dagenais, novelist Roger Lemelin, and maestro Wilfrid Pelletier. Lida Moser was so delighted with her experience of Canada that she returned in December 1950 to make another series of photographs, for *Look* magazine.

Legendary photographer Henri Cartier-Bresson visited Québec in 1965, and some of his photographs were included in a montage for Rex Tasker and Wolf Koenig's documentary film *Le Québec vu par Cartier-Bresson* (NFB, 1969).

Some respected foreign photographers came to Canada to establish themselves: Pierre Gaudard emigrated from France in 1952; Sam Tata came from Hong Kong in 1956; Gabor Szilasi came from Hungary in 1959; George Zimbel left the United States for Canada in 1971 (Hanna, in Dessureault, 2000).

Canadian-born photographers of importance of this period include Michel Lambeth (1923–1977). A published author, he is known for his in-depth portrait of Toronto of the 1950s, and he was a leading photojournalist during the 1960s. Lambeth also amassed an important historical collection that featured anonymous photographers' shots of Toronto from the early years of the century. Arnaud Maggs, born in 1926 in Montréal, emerged via the important 1977 exhibition *7 Canadian Photographers* at the National Film Board. He had had a successful career as a fashion photographer and graphic designer, and began his photographic career as a portraitist. He is best known for works consisting of materials he collects and photographs, including death notices, factory records, or public signs arranged in grids of dozens of images.

John Max, born in 1936, also took up fine-arts concerns at a time when most Quebec-based photographers were focusing on photojournalistic or social documentary subject matter. In the 1960s, he worked with subjective, autobiographical topics in striking black-and-white photographs that prefigured the turn towards more personal work at the end of the eighties in Canada. After a sojourn in Japan in the 1970s, he returned to Canada to undeserved obscurity. His oeuvre includes a striking two-part portrait of his colleague Sam Tata.

If the Canadian Natives and Inuit were often the subjects of ethnographic or "exotic" photographs, instituted early on by the popularity of Robert Flaherty's images, some also contributed as photographers themselves, mostly towards the end of the twentieth century. A pioneer among Native photographers is George Johnston, a Tlingit Indian hunter, trapper, and entrepreneur, who took many photographs of the Yukon's Natives before 1940. His contribution is memorialized by the naming of an exhibition hall after him, the George Johnston Museum in Yukon.

In the latter half of the twentieth century, most Canadian Native photographers worked in cities in Ontario. Among those Native artists are Jeffrey M. Thomas, born in Buffalo, New York, in 1956, a member of the Onondaga tribe of Six Nations, Ontario; and Barry Ace, born on Manitoulin Island in 1958, an Anishnabe (Ojibwa) of the West Bay First Nation. Both are self-taught artists. Among other notable Native photographers are Greg Hill, an installation, multimedia, performance artist and photographer, whose work explores his Rotinonhsyonni (Iroquoian) identity; and Greg Staats (Mohawk) born in Brantford, Ontario in 1963. Raised on the Six Nations Reserve near Brantford Ontario, Greg Staats is currently based in Toronto. All of them have participated in exhibitions in Canada and in Canadian embassies abroad.

Among Native women photographers from Canada are Mary Anne Barkhouse, a graduate of the Ontario College of Art who was born in Vancouver in 1961, a member of the Nimpkish Kwakiutl nation; and Métis artist Rosalie Favell, a digital photo artist and printmaker as well as a scholar. Rosalie Favell obtained a BFA from the Ryerson Polytechnical Institute and an MFA from the University of New Mexico; she was born in Winnipeg, Manitoba in 1958. Also a graduate of the Ontario College of Art, filmmaker and photographer Shelley Niro, born in Niagara Falls, New York, in 1954, is a member of the Mohawk Nation, Iroquois

Confederacy, Turtle Clan of the Kanien'kehaka, from the Six Nations Reserve.

These photographers participated in an important exhibition, *Emergence from the Shadow: First Peoples' Photographic Perspectives*, held in 1999 at the Art Gallery of the First Peoples Hall of the Canadian Museum of Civilization.

Created in 1939, the National Film Board of Canada (NFB), a governmental institution that specialized in short films, documentaries, animation, and experimental films, has had an extraordinary impact upon the development photography in Canada as well as making Canada an important center internationally in filmmaking. Although primarily an organization to support filmmaking, many innovations came from the various important NFB directors including Norman McLaren, Michel Brault, and Claude Jutra. A documentary directed by Jean-Claude Labrecque, *60 Cycles* (1965), for instance, was the first film to use a 1,000-mm lens in an opening shot that remains famous: a group of cyclists is shown riding towards the camera with the impression that they are not even moving due to the long focal length of this particular lens.

The most original contribution from Canadian filmmakers to the world history of motion pictures was certainly the creation of "Cinéma direct" at the end of the 1950's, which had an influence on U. S. and European documentary directors such as Don Alan Pennebaker and Jean Rouch. Among these cameramen was Michel Brault, who borrowed the spontaneous approach of Henri Cartier-Bresson when filming. Brault is known for his use of wide-angle lenses in lieu of shooting from a distance. Among his best examples are *Les Raquetteurs* (co-directed with Gilles Groulx, 1958) and *Pour la suite du monde* (co-directed with Pierre Perrault, 1963). Brault's aesthetic innovation helped assure a place for francophone directors at the NFB, something that had been more or less denied before 1960, although French-speaking directors were required to submit their projects in English until the mid-sixties.

Through the following decades, those associated with the NFB pursued various explorations into documentary, animation, and some fiction as well, sometimes mixing genres in a single film. *J. A. Martin photographe* (1976)—a feature film that pays tribute to the itinerant photographers who historically traveled to isolated villages, or to factories and hotels, to do portraits of groups, workers, families, and individuals—may have been inspired by a photographer from Nicolet, Québec, named Philias Coulombe. Directed by Jean Beaudin from a script by Marcel Sabourin (who also played the leading role), it was produced by the National Film Board of Canada and gained actress Monique Mercure (who played the photographer's wife) a prize at the Cannes Film Festival.

A unique organization, the National Film Board of Canada has contributed to the creation and conservation of some of the most important collections of images of Canada. Today, a part of that visual heritage is held at the Canadian Museum of Contemporary Photography in Ottawa.

During the two world conflicts in twentieth century, Canada participated along with England and the Allies, and war photography is therefore an important portion of the archives kept by the Canadian Army and veterans. Many cameramen from the National Film Board of Canada were sent abroad to film stock footage for newsreels. The War Museum in Ottawa owns an extensive collection of such materials. A 1973 exhibition catalogue, *Relentless Verit: Canadian Military Photographers Since 1885* edited by Peter Robertson traces a history of Canadian involvement in various actions and wars through the eyes of soldier-photographers, beginning with a documentation of the troops of the Yukon Field Force embarking for Klondike in 1898. The Canadian presence during the South African War in Durban in 1902 as photographed by Henry Joseph Woodside (1858–1929) is featured along with photographs of Canadian soldiers and peacekeepers on the battlefields in Belgium, France and elsewhere in 1917 during World War I and during the World War II years.

Compared to other countries, relatively few books showing the Canadian landscape and urbanscape were published prior to the 1980s. That genre emerged and blossomed when photographers sought to publish the photographs that they exhibited in galleries and Canadian embassies. Mia and Klaus glorified various natural sites in a series of books, such as *Canada* (Mia & Klaus, with Roch Carrier, 1986). Eugen Kedl produced many photography books focusing on Canadian cities and heritage. Known for his ability to catch the sunlight at dawn, photographer Claudel Huot took hundreds of images from Québec City over several decades in which he magnified the lateral lightning of sunrise on urban walls. One of his most striking books, *Québec, ville de lumières* (with a text by Michel Lessard), was published in French and English. Toronto-born artist Bill

Vazan (b. 1933) had a more conceptual approach but remains a main figure in the Land Art movement; he does not limit his subjects and sites to Canada, however.

A number of remarkable illustrated books were published during the second half of twentieth century. Jean Bruchési wrote *Le Canada* (1952) for the famous French publisher, Fernand Nathan, with 131 splendid black-and-white photographs from various sources, including cities, landscapes, famous sites, Natives, and reproductions of paintings in museums. Art books and exhibition catalogues for most of the postwar era remained the chief source of photographic illustrated books, published by many museums. Patrick Altman (born in Paris, France in 1950) made a notable career specializing in reproductions of paintings and works of art.

Perhaps because of the size of Canada and the vast empty landscapes of the north, aerial photography has been frequently employed. Beginning very early on for the genre, from the mid-1920s, W.E. Edwards in Québec City produced aerial photographs of the region; the Fairchild Aerial Surveys Co. in Grand-Mère (Québec) also produced aerial views during the same period.

Provincial governments photographed almost every section of the country from the air. Pierre Lahoud has been particularly active in this area, both as an aerial photographer himself and an historian. His first book, *Québec à Ciel ouvert* (1987), included a short history of the beginning of aerial photography in Canada, with Compagnie aérienne franco-canadienne, an affiliate of Compagnie aérienne française, a French corporation. Lahoud points out that after the cessation of hostilities from World War I in 1919, many combat pilots became private and commercial pilots, hiring themselves out to photographers. Their hydroplanes flew over the Province of Québec from 1920 until 1933 (Lahoud, 1987). And as part of the burgeoning worldwide interest in aerial photography at the end of the century, Lahoud edited his own works into a lavish book with a text by geographer Henri Dorion titled *Le Québec vu du ciel: Au rythme des saisons* (2001), which was also translated in English. Through various viewpoints and angles, vertical and oblique, Lahoud illustrates the magnificence of the Canadian landscape. As a sign of its popularity, the original French version was named "Favorite Book of the Year" in a vote made by the users of Québec City's public library, in the year of its publication. There exist numerous examples of aerial photography of places such as Halifax, Québec City, Ottawa, Toronto, Niagara Falls, Saskatoon, Vancouver, and Victoria. Some of these views were published in a predecessor to Lahoud's widely popular compilation in 1957 by the Canadian publisher, Leméac—*La Province de Québec*, with 141 héliogravures taken by various photographers.

While the natural and built landscapes of Canada have served as primary sources of subject matter for Canadian photographers, another major area of interest is sports. As do many Americans and Europeans, Canadians love sports, and they consider hockey their national sport. Many Canadian newspapers dedicate their third page to sports, making this a major outlet for sports photography. One of the most memorable events of the twentieth century, the competition between an all-star Canadian team and the Russian Army team in 1972, was celebrated in a book titled *Twenty-seven Days in September* (McFarlane 1973).

If illustrated books were always popular in Canada, they usually concentrated on the present, showing the country as it is at any particular moment in time. In the mid 1990's, the Government of Québec's publisher, Les Publications du Québec, created an ongoing series, *Aux limites de la mémoire*, of 11 thematic albums dedicated to vintage photographs of Québec, most before 1960 and some from the early twentieth century. The books focus on specific themes: *Naviguer sur le Fleuve au temps passé 1860–1960* (Franck, 2000) is about sailing; *La Vie Rurale 1866–1953* (2001) about farms and farmers; *Au Rythme du train 1859–1970* (Reford, 2002) features railroad engines, and construction of railroads, bridges, a train trestle, and train accidents. The most recent in the series *Quartiers ouvriers d'autrefois. 1850–1950* (Sicotte, 2004) depicts workers, factories, and working-class neighborhoods. Each title includes almost 200 photographs with detailed comments, year, archival references. An overarching theme is worker photography: the series presents farm employees, blue-collar workers, male and female workers, and even children and aged workers. *Aux limites de la mémoire* had a wide distribution in bookstores, with each title selling more than 7000 copies, an impressive number for art books in Canada; some of those books were accompanied by a traveling photography exhibition.

This concept of exploring history through archival photography was followed by another series produced by a private publisher, GID. Focusing on specific regions and their local history, and using vintage photographs from both private and public archives, titles include *La Côte-du-Sud: Belle à croquer* (Hébert, 2003) and *Les Îles-de-la-Madeleine* (Roy, 2004). These works and others draw in part from the numerous public archives of photographs in Canada, the most important being the National Archive in Ottawa, the Archives Nationales du Québec (in Québec City and Montréal), the archives of the National Film Board of Canada, in Montréal, and the archives of the Cinémathèque québécoise, in Montréal. Important collections of photographs can also be found at The Canadian Museum of Contemporary Photography in Ottawa, at the McCord Museum in Montréal, in newspaper archives, and in those of many religious institutions. The Canadian Press Photo Archives, for example, holds more than 85,000 images taken by Canadian photojournalists.

The decades at the end of the twentieth century made many Canadians aware of the artistic possibilities of photography. In fact, it is contemporary photography that made a whole generation of art enthusiasts care about visual arts. *Confluence: Contemporary Canadian Photography*, by Martha Hanna, Director of the Canadian Museum of Contemporary Photography, summarizes the contribution of some of Canada's most interesting artist-photographers. It includes works by such leading figures as Michael Snow, Lynne Cohen, Geneviève Cadieux, Geoffrey James, and Jeff Wall, all of whom have achieved recognition beyond Canadian borders.

One of Canada's most famous experimental artists abroad, Michael Snow has produced multidisciplinary works which have been an inspiration for many English-Canadian artists. Filmmaker, visual artist, composer, he has produced notable photographic works and art videos since the early 1960's. An example of his complex, theoretically-based work is *Manifestation* (1999), a life-sized self portrait, in which Snow mixes a plastic lamination of a color ink-jet photograph with spray paint, black paper, and a mirror. This unusual photograph can be seen as a new take on a previous work, *Authorization* (1969); both works are in the collection National Gallery of Canada, in Ottawa.

Among contemporary photographers, there are those who practice more traditional types of photographic representation, such as Clara Gutsche, who in her *The Convent Series* showed respectfully the everyday life of cloistered nuns during the 1990s. Edward Burtynsky, born in St. Catherines, Ontario in 1955, is a leading photojournalist and environmental photographer who has made an international reputation with his large-scale, color photographs of mines, quarries, recycling yards from Canada and the United States, ship-dismantling facilities in Bangladesh, and a documentation of the Three Gorges project in China titled *Before the Flood*.

At the end of the twentieth century, Montréal attracted photographers from all horizons—Lynne Cohen (born in Wisconsin), Bertrand Carrière (born in Ontario), Raymonde April (born in Moncton, New Brunswick)—all of whom gained international reputations. Among other notable Canadian artists and contemporary photographers are Patrick Altman (born in France, in 1950), Geneviève Cadieux (born in Montréal in 1955), and Charles Gagnon, Thaddeus Holownia, Geoffrey James (born in 1942, in St. Asaph, Wales), Ken Lum, Diana Thorneycroft, Jeff Wall, (born in 1946, near Vancouver, British Columbia), Ian Wallace, and Jin-Me Yoon. Many of them share a common taste for abstraction and formal research. Many of these photographers were first seen in the prestigious biennial exposition *Mois de la Photo* in Montréal. Since 1989, this event has celebrated current trends in photography in Canada and abroad, with exhibitions, events, festivals, conferences, and workshops.

Many of the most active Canadian photographers both at home and abroad exemplify the most advanced of emerging international trends. Experiences in so-called "rephotography," a type of appropriation, were explored by Andrzej Maciejewski in his book, *After Notman* (2003). The photographs made by William Notman, his sons, and associates between 1890 and 1911 and were taken again by photographer Andrzej Maciejewski (b. 1959), using the same lens format, respecting the angle and viewpoint of original from almost a century removed. Most photographs concentrate on Montréal and give striking examples of the urbanization and modernization that have occurred in most North American cities.

Another book using rephotography created a parallel between old and recent photographs of sites located in Québec City. Written by historian Jean Provencher, with new versions of old photographs made by Jocelyn Paquet, *Québec, les images témoignent* (2001) also includes photographic postcards from the early twentieth century.

Research into holography has also been a common concern of advanced Canadian photographers. Marie-Andrée Cossette, a professor at Université Laval, has specialized in holography since 1976. She was the first scholar worldwide to author a fine arts master's thesis on the topic. As an artist, she exhibited her holograms in Canadian galleries and at the Massachusetts Institute of Technology (MIT) in Cambridge, where she was part of the research team at the Spatial Imaging Group, and taught at the MIT Media Laboratory, in 1987. Among her works are *Barcelona 1982*, a holograph which refers to Gaudi's magnificent unfinished church, La Sagrada Familia, and another tribute to Catalonian art, *Hommage to Dali*, which acknowledges famed Surrealist painter Salvador Dali's own fascination with holograms beginning in the early sixties.

Copy Art, or Xerography, is another arena in which Canadian artists have made pioneering efforts. In Montréal, the Centre Copie-Art was created by artist Jacques Charbonneau; its establishment was influenced by the underground research from Europe and the United States in the 1970s. The center, between 1982 and 2000, promoted new forms of visual research using the photocopier machine and related processes. There were two exhibition rooms, a workshop, a library, plus many photocopying machines and printers, including from a (at that time) rare color photocopier. Many experimental artists gathered from all parts of Canada to create multidisciplinary works, at times combining photography and Xerography. Although it closed in 2000, the Centre Copie-Art was an inspiration for other copy-art centers such as the Centre Canon de Paris in France, the Müseo international de Electrografia (MIDE) in Cuenca, Spain, and the Museum für Fotocopie in Germany.

Experiments in copy art were made in other cities as well. In Québec City, Yves Laberge made many generations of photocopies from a single black-and-white photograph to compare the many stages and the deconstruction of shapes and lines in an exhibition titled *La photocopie: le non-souci du detail* held at the Laval University Library in 1987. As explained in the exhibition catalogue, using a Canon photocopier, an original photograph was photocopied, and the photocopy was then photocopied again, and the new one photocopied once more, each generation being different from the previous and from the following until the forms and lines so apparent in the initial image literally disappeared. Laberge dubbed the process "regeneration."

Advanced, experimental photography has also flourished on the coasts of Canada. On the west coast, a highly conceptual photography has flourished at Simon Fraser University and the University of British Columbia, around the pioneering efforts of Vancouver native Jeff Wall, who taught at both institutions for a number of years. On the east coast, the Nova Scotia College of Art and Design, Halifax, has also trained generations of artists using photography as part of their contemporary art efforts.

Canada also has hosted great numbers of active professional, commercial, and amateur photographers, many associated with camera guilds or clubs. One of the largest is the Canadian Association for Photographic Art/L'Association canadienne d'art photographique, which was formed in 1998 by two venerable associations: the Colour Photographic Association of Canada (founded 1947 in Toronto), and the National Association for Photographic Art (NAPA) founded in 1967 by photographers interested in advancing the practice of black-and-white photography. NAPA published the magazines *Xerography* and *Fotoflash*. The Photographic Guild of Nova Scotia, founded in 1947, also serves as an organization for professional, commercial, and amateur photographers, offering conferences, competitions, and other professional services. Active photo clubs flourish in virtually every major Canadian city, including Calgary, Edmunton, Hamilton, Kingston, Regina, and Victoria, with many members continuing to capture and celebrate the natural beauty of Canada and its towns, cities, and diverse citizenry.

Yves Laberge

See also: **Aerial Photography; Appropriation; Cadieux, Geneviève; Cohen, Lynne; Conceptual Photography; Karsh, Yousuf; Museums: Canada; Periodicals: Professional; Snow, Michael; Szilasi, Gabor; Wall, Jeff ; War Photography; Worker Photography; Xerography**

Further Reading

Books

La Province de Québec. Montréal; Leméac: 1957.

Beauregard, Yves. "Les cartes postales." *Cap-aux-Diamants. Revue d'histoire du Québec*. Québec City, N° 80, (Hiver 2005): 8.

Christopher, Robert J. "Through Canada's Northland: The Arctic Photography of Robert J. Flaherty." In J.C.H. King and Henrietta Lidchi (eds.), *Imaging the Arctic*. Seattle and Vancouver: University of Washington Press and UBC Press, 1998. 181–189.

Franck, Alain. *Naviguer sur le Fleuve au temps passé 1860–1960*. Québec: Les Publications du Québec, 2000.

Greenhill, Ralph, and Andrew Birrell. *Canadian Photography 1839–1920*. Toronto : Coach House Press, 1979.

Hanna, Martha. "Avant-propos." In Dessureault, Pierre (ed.), *Exchanging Views: Québec 1939–1978*. Ottawa: The Canadian Museum of Contemporary Photography, 2000.
Hanna, Martha, ed. *Confluence: Contemporary Canadian Photography/La photographie contemporaine canadienne*. Ottawa; Canadian Museum of Contemporary Photography, and The National Gallery of Canada, 2003.
Hébert, Yves. *La Côte-du-Sud. Belle à croquer*. Québec: Éditions GID, 2003.
Huot, Claudel, with Michel Lessard. *Quebec, City of Lights*. Trans. from *Québec. Ville de Lumières*. Montréal: Éditions de l'Homme, 2001.
James, Geoffrey, et al. *Thirteen essays on Photography*. Ottawa: The Canadian Museum of Contemporary Photography, 1990.
Karsh, Yousuf, with texts by John Fisher. *Canada, as seen by the camera of Yousuf Karsh and described in words by John Fisher*. Toronto : Thomas Allen, 1960.
Leclerc, Paul-André, and Jacques Saint-Pierre. *La Vie Rurale 1866–1953*. Québec: Les Publications du Québec, 2001.
Lahoud, Pierre, with Claude Paulette and Michel Tremblay. *Québec à ciel ouvert*. Montréal: Libre Expression, 1987.
Lahoud, Pierre, with Henri Dorion (texts). *Quebec from the Air. From Season to Season*. Trans. from *Le Québec vu du ciel: Au rythme des saisons*. Montréal: Éditions de l'Homme, 2001.
Lessard, Michel. *Histoire de la photographie au Québec*. Montréal: Atelier de recherche sur l'image photographique, 1986.
Lessard, Michel. *La photo s'expose: 150 ans de photographie à Québec*. Québec: Musée du Québec, 1987.
Lessard, Michel. *Les Livernois photographes*. Québec: Musée du Québec, 1987.
Maciejewski, Andrzej. *After Notman. Montreal Views—A Century Apart*. Buffalo: Willowdale and Montreal: Firefly Books and McCord Museum, 2003.
McFarlane, John, and Brian Pickel. *Twenty-seven Days in September*. Toronto: Hockey Canada and Prosport, 1973.
Mia & Klaus, with a text by Roch Carrier. *Canada*. Translated by Sheila Fischman. Montréal: Libre Expression, 1986.
Moosang, Faith. *First Son: Portraits by C.D. Hoy*. Vancouver: Presentation House Gallery, 1999.
Moser, Lida, with a presentation by Roch Carrier. *Québec à l'été 1950*. Montréal: Libre Expression, 1982.
Ouvrard, Hélène. *J.A. Martin photographe*. Montréal: Art Global, 1999.
Poitras, Jacques. *La carte postale québécoise: une aventure photographique*. Montréal: Éditions Broquet, 1990.
Poitras, Jacques. *Les Dessus et les Dessous de la carte postale*. Saint-Laurent: Musée d'art de Saint-Laurent, 1986.
Provencher, Jean, with Jocelyn Paquet. *Québec, les images témoignent*. Québec: Sylvain Harvey et Commission de la Capitale Nationale, 2001.
Reford, Alexander. *Au Rythme du train 1859–1970*. Québec: Les Publications du Québec, 2002.
Robertson, Peter. *Relentless Verity. Canadian Military Photographers Since 1885*. Québec and Ottawa: Les Presses de l'Université Laval, The Public Archives of Canada Series, 1973.
Roy, Caroline. *Les Îles-de-la-Madeleine*. Québec: Éditions GID, 2004.
Sicotte, Anne-Marie. *Quartiers ouvriers d'autrefois. 1850–1950*. Québec: Les Publications du Québec, 2004.

Catalogues

Cadieux, Geneviève. *Geneviève Cadieux*. Vancouver : Morris and Helen Belkin Art Gallery, 1999.
Gascon, France, ed. *Clara Gutsche: La série des couvents—The Convent Series*. Joliette, Musée d'art de Joliette, 1998.
Karsh, Yousuf. *Karsh, a fifty-year retrospective*. London: Secker & Warburg, 1983.
Karsh, Yousuf. *Karsh: American legends: photographs and Commentary*. Toronto and Boston: Little, Brown, 1992.
Laberge, Yves. *La photocopie: le non-souci du detail*. Québec City, Yves Laberge, 1987.

ROBERT CAPA

Hungarian-American

Perhaps the greatest war photographer ever, Hungarian-born Robert Capa covered five wars in 18 years, during which time he took some of the most enduring images of war ever captured on film. Guided by his own maxim "...if your pictures aren't good enough, you're not close enough," Capa achieved an immediacy and intimacy in his photographs that revolutionized the way wars were documented. His keen eye and preference for small format cameras yielded a signature style that combined a rigorous formal composition with a snapshot's dramatic impact and sense of documentary authenticity, which resulted in compelling and candid images that gave concrete visual expression to war and its effects. A pacifist and anti-war advocate, Capa spent much of his life and ultimately died photographing the human and sometimes inhuman face of the world's conflicts.

Robert Capa was born Endre Friedmann on October 22, 1913 in Budapest, Hungary, the second of three sons born to Dezsö and Julia Friedmann. Capa became politically and socially conscious at an early age, due in part to his contact with the artist, poet and Socialist Lajos Kassak, whom Capa met in 1929. Kassak exposed the young Capa to the photographic work of several Hungarian-born social documentary photographers, as well as the important images coming out of America at the time by the more famous reformer-photographers Jacob Riis and Lewis Hine. Looking to combine his dual interests in politics and literature, Capa soon aspired to a career in journalism. He also adopted many of Kassak's reform-minded political beliefs and sympathies as his own, and by the age of 17 he had already participated in several local demonstrations and marches protesting governmental policies.

Capa's burgeoning political activism led to his more radical participation in local protests and other forms of political agitation in Budapest against what he viewed to be a repressive Hungarian government. His enthusiasm for reform also led him to meet briefly with a recruiter for the Hungarian Communist Party, and while Capa decided not to join the communist organization, his contact with one of its members resulted in his arrest and eventual expulsion from Hungary in the summer of 1931. Thus, Capa left his hometown of Budapest to pursue a degree in journalism at the Deutsche Hochschule für Politik in Berlin, Germany.

Arriving in Berlin with minimal resources, Capa fatefully took a job as a darkroom assistant at Dephot, a photographic agency that at the time represented a number of important photojournalists. Dephot's director, Simon Guttmann, took a liking to Capa and eventually lent him an old 35-mm Leica camera to use and allowed him to cover minor local events for the agency. The Leica was a small, unobtrusive camera well suited for the close-range candid photo-reportage that interested Capa, and for which he would soon become famous. He received his first significant assignment as a photojournalist in November, 1932, when his superiors at Dephot sent to him Copenhagen, Denmark to cover a speech being given there by the exiled revolutionary Leon Trotsky. Able to smuggle his inconspicuous Leica into the stadium and position himself near to where Trotsky was speaking, Capa clandestinely snapped a series of photographs that superbly captured the energy of the impassioned Russian orator and the drama of the moment, so much so that Berlin's *Der Welt Spiegel* devoted a full page to Capa's photographs.

With the rise to power of Adolf Hitler in early 1933, Capa, being both Jewish and a political activist, left Berlin. He eventually settled in Paris, where sometime during the spring of 1934 and after a difficult period living in near poverty Capa met fellow Hungarian André Kertész, a successful art photographer and photojournalist whose work regularly appeared in the French magazine *Vu*. Kertész helped the young Capa by loaning him money, finding him work, and teaching him about photography. It was also in Paris around this time that Capa befriended David Szymin and Henri Cartier-Bresson, two young photographers with whom Capa would develop lifelong personal and professional relationships. Cultivating both his photographic skills and professional contacts through this growing network of photographer friends in Paris, Capa finally began to make a name for himself as a photojournalist, initially through a series of well-received photographs for the Paris paper *Regards*, chronicling the political marches and strikes associated with the leftist Popular Front campaign leading up to the 1936 elections.

In the summer of that year, Capa took the first of several trips to Spain with his companion Gerda Taro to cover the civil war that had recently erupted there. Using primarily his Leica, Capa produced a highly regarded series of photographs documenting the fighting that was taking place in northeastern and southern Spain. And it was in the south near the town of Córdoba that Capa snapped one of the most iconic photographs ever taken: his famous image of a Spanish Republican soldier at the precise moment of his death. This and other photographs by Capa from the Spanish front were featured in a number of large-circulation newspapers and prestigious magazines in France and Britain, and the American magazine *Life* published a series of his images that documented the siege of Madrid and the plight of its inhabitants. Capa's acclaimed photographs of the Spanish Civil War heralded his arrival as a premier photojournalist onto the world stage, and upon his return to Paris he published a book of his and Taro's photographs from Spain titled *Death in the Making*, which he dedicated to Taro, who had died while covering the conflict.

In 1938, the now famous Capa went to China with filmmaker Joris Ivens to photograph another war: the Japanese invasion of China. Capa covered the Sino-Japanese war for six months and once again produced graphic, straightforward visual testimonies of war and its effects on a local populace. His sought-after images appeared in *Life* and elsewhere, and his photographs documenting the Japanese aerial bombardment of the Chinese city of Hankou rank among his most successful.

Upon his return to Europe, Capa worked on a number of miscellaneous assignments, most notably in a piece on orphanages in Biarritz, France, an in-depth assignment on the Tour de France bicycle race for the French magazine *Match*, and a series of stories documenting the working class and the unemployed in and around Antwerp, Belgium. In 1940, he spent several months in Mexico covering the political rallies and usually violent protests leading up to that country's presidential elections. With the outbreak of World War II, Capa worked on a number of assignments devoted to the Allied war effort for news outlets on both sides of the Atlantic, but worked primarily in England for *Collier's* magazine and then as a European correspondent for *Life*. His photographs of London during the Blitz accompanied the text for a book published in 1941 titled *The Battle of Waterloo Bridge*, which documented the resiliency of working-class Londoners during and after the extensive aerial bombardment of the city by the Germans. During the late spring and summer of 1943, Capa covered the Allied campaigns in North Africa and Sicily led by General George S. Patton, and he spent the remainder of that year documenting the Allied advance at various battlefronts throughout mainland Italy, including the liberation of Naples and the fighting around Anzio. On the historic occasion of D-Day on June 6, 1944, Capa accompanied the first wave of American troops landing at Omaha Beach on the Normandy coast of France, snapping some of the most memorable and iconic photographs of World War II while in the water and on the beach during the chaotic opening moments of the liberation of France. To document the Allied landing at Omaha Beach, Capa had with him two 35-mm Contax cameras and a Rolleiflex, and while a majority of the photographs for which he risked his life that day were accidentally either destroyed or damaged in a darkroom mishap back in England, those that survived—including his famous image of soldiers wading ashore from their landing crafts—appeared in *Life* magazine and were hailed as the finest taken of the invasion.

From the beaches of Normandy, Capa went on to cover the Allied troop advances through to the liberation of Paris in August 1944, for which he accompanied the French 2nd Armored Division into the capitol. In Paris, he documented the delirium of the newly liberated inhabitants and their assistance with the elimination of pockets of German resistance by the liberating forces. After the liberation of Paris, Capa went on to cover the fighting that winter in the Ardennes—which would become known as the Battle of the Bulge—where he took a number of dramatic photographs of German soldiers surrendering to allied forces. He also parachuted into Germany with American troops in 1945 and was on hand to photograph the key Allied victories at Leipzig, Nuremberg, and Berlin. As with every conflict that he covered, during World War II Capa focused his lens not only on soldiers and the front-line action, but also on the local population and the war's impact on them, often capturing telling moments in the expressions and gestures of those around him. Throughout the war, Capa's images of both soldiers and civilians appeared regularly in *Life* and *Collier's* in America and in the *Weekly Illustrated* in Britain. For his efforts during the war, Capa, along with 20 other World War II correspondents, received the United States Medal of Freedom in 1947.

Soon after the war, Capa became an American citizen and in 1946 spent several months in Los Angeles, California, during which time he wrote his war memoirs, titled *Slightly Out of Focus,* and briefly aspired to become a director-producer. In 1947, he collaborated with his old friends Cartier-Bresson and Szymin (who now went by David Seymour and his nom-de-plume "Chim"), as well as George Rodger and William Vandivert to found the international photographic agency Magnum Photos. Living primarily in Paris by now, Capa devoted himself to Magnum, overseeing operations at the cooperative's New York and Paris offices and assisting the agency's young photographers.

In addition to running Magnum, during the late 1940s Capa collaborated on a number of travel books, including one documenting a month-long trip that he had taken with John Steinbeck to the Soviet Union in 1947. Also, in May 1948 Capa took the first of three trips to Israel, where he covered the fledgling country's declaration of independence and the ensuing war with its Arab neighbors for *Illustrated.* On his two subsequent trips to Israel, Capa concentrated his lens on the flood of refugees arriving in and around Haifa, photographing their living conditions in the immigrant camps established to process and temporarily accommodate them.

During the first few years of the 1950s, Capa avoided most political assignments, and instead spent much of his time in Paris working at Magnum and writing a series of lighthearted travel articles for *Holiday* magazine. In the spring of 1954, he went to Japan to shoot a photographic series for Mainichi Press on children, a subject that had interested Capa throughout his career during times of both war and peace. Indeed, many of Capa's images of children from throughout his career achieve the same sense of immediacy and intimacy that has become the hallmark of his more acclaimed battlefield images.

Capa's six-week assignment in Japan lasted only three, however, as *Life*, in need of an emergency replacement photographer, sent him to cover the war in what was then known as French Indochina. Soon after arriving in the capitol of Hanoi, he left for Laos to photograph the release of French soldiers captured by the Viet Minh during their historic victory at Dienbienphu. Capa then returned to Hanoi, where he spent several days photographing the inhabitants of the city and their daily routines. On May 25, Capa accompanied a French convoy on a mission to evacuate two outposts, documenting the soldiers' slow advance through the hostile countryside of the Red River delta. While apparently maneuvering to photograph a column of soldiers as they advanced across a meadow Capa, with Contax camera in hand, stepped on a land mine and was killed almost instantly.

Days after his death, the French military awarded Capa one of its highest honors, the Croix de Guerre with Palm. In 1955, the Overseas Press Club and *Life* magazine jointly established the annual Robert Capa Gold Medal Award awarded to photojournalists exhibiting extraordinary courage and enterprise while working abroad. In 1958, Robert's brother Cornell Capa and mother Julia Friedmann, along with David Seymour's sister, created The Robert Capa-David Seymour Photographic Foundation in Israel. Eight years later, in 1966, the Werner Bischof-Robert Capa-David Seymour Photographic Memorial Fund was established to celebrate and support the work of these and other photojournalists, which in 1974 evolved into the International Center of Photography in New York City. In 1976, Capa was inducted into the International Photography Hall of Fame and Museum.

MAX WEINTRAUB

See also: **Cartier-Bresson, Henri; Kertész, André; Life; Magnum Photos; Seymour, David "Chim"; War Photography**

Biography

Born Endre Friedmann in Budapest, Hungary, October 22 1913. Worked at photographic agency Dephot, photographed Leon Trotsky speech, 1932; covered Popular Front political campaign, 1936; took first of several trips to Spain to cover civil war, 1936; traveled to China to cover Japanese Invasion, 1938; worked on miscellaneous assignments for *Life* magazine in United States and Mexico 1939; collaborated with writer Diana Forbes-Robertson on *The Battle of Waterloo Bridge*, 1941. Covered Allied campaigns in North Africa and Italy, 1943; landed with Allied forces on D-Day at Omaha Beach on Normandy coast of France; covered liberation of Paris and Battle of the Bulge, 1944; documented liberation of Germany, 1945; published *Slightly Out of Focus*, 1946. Founded Magnum agency with Henri Cartier-Bresson and others, 1947; took first of three trips to Israel to cover Israeli struggle for independence and Arab-Israeli war, 1948; 1948–1954, wrote for *Holiday* in Paris, continued working at Magnum; collaborated with several writers on travel projects. Worked in Japan on project for Mainichi Press, went to Indochina for *Life*, documenting French withdrawal from Dienbienphu, 1954. Killed by land mine in northern Vietnam, 1954.

Individual Exhibitions

1952 *On Picasso*; Museum of Modern Art; New York, New York
1960 *Robert Capa: War Photographs*; Smithsonian Institution; Washington, D.C.
1964 *Images of War*; Smithsonian Institution; Washington, D.C.
1980 *Robert Capa*; Tokyo, Japan
1985 *Robert Capa, Photographs*; International Center of Photography; New York, New York
1987 *Sala Parpallo*; Valencia, Spain
1997 *Robert Capa: Photographs*; Philadelphia Museum of Art; Philadelphia, Pennsylvania
1999 *Robert Capa: Photographies*; Musee d'Art Americain; Giverny, France
2002 *Robert Capa: Israel 1948–1950*

Selected Group Exhibitions

1951 *Memorable Life Photographs*; Museum of Modern Art; New York, New York
1955 *The Family of Man*; Museum of Modern Art; New York, New York
1960 *The World as Seen by Magnum Photographers*; Smithsonian Institution; Washington, D.C.
1969 *Israel: The Reality*; Jewish Museum; New York, New York
1972 *Behind the Great Wall of China*; Metropolitan Museum of Art; New York, New York
1973 *Looking at Photographs*; Museum of Modern Art; New York, New York

1974 *The Classics of Documentary Photography*; International Center of Photography; New York, New York
1981 *Spain 1936–1939*; International Center of Photography; New York, New York
1986 *No Pasaran! Photographs and Posters of the Spanish Civil War*; Arnolfini Gallery; Bristol, England
1990 *Robert Capa and Cornell Capa: Brothers in Photography*; Fuji Art Museum; Tokyo, Japan
1998 *Photographers Made in Hungary*; Hungarian Museum of Photography; Kecskemét, Hungary
2004 *WWII Photographic Perspectives*; Smithsonian Institution; Washington, D.C.

Selected Works

Leon Trotsky Lecturing, November 27, 1932
Loyalist Militiaman at the Moment of Death, Cerro Murriano, September 5, 1936
Coal Miners, Borinage region, Belgium, November 1937
After an Air Raid, Hankow, China, July 1938
The Tour de France in Pleyben, July 1939
American Landing on Omaha Beach, D-Day, June 6, 1944
French Woman who had a Baby by a German Soldier, August 1944
American Soldier Capturing a German Near Bastogne, Belgium, December 1944
Death of an American Soldier, Leipzig, April 18, 1945
Pablo Picasso and Françoise Gilot, Golfe-Juan, August 1948
Sha'ar Ha'aliya Immigrant Transit Camp, Haifa, 1950
Child at Train Station, Tokyo, April 1954
On the Road from Namdinh to Thaibinh, Indochina, May 25, 1954

Further Reading

Kershow, Alex. *Blood and Champagne: The Life And Times of Robert Capa*. New York: St. Martin's Press, 2003.
Whelan, Richard. *Robert Capa: The Definitive Collection*. New York: Phaidon, 2001.
Aizpúrua, Juan P. Fusi, Catherine Coleman, and Richard Whelan. *Heart of Spain: Robert Capa's Photographs of the Spanish Civil War*. New York: Aperture, 1999.
Capa, Cornell, and Richard Whelan, eds. *Robert Capa: Photographs*. New York: Aperture, 1996.
Capa, Cornell, and Richard Whelan, eds. *Children of War, Children of Peace: Photographs by Robert Capa*. Boston: Bulfinch Press, 1991.
Whelan, Richard. *Robert Capa: A Biography*. London: Faber and Faber, 1985.

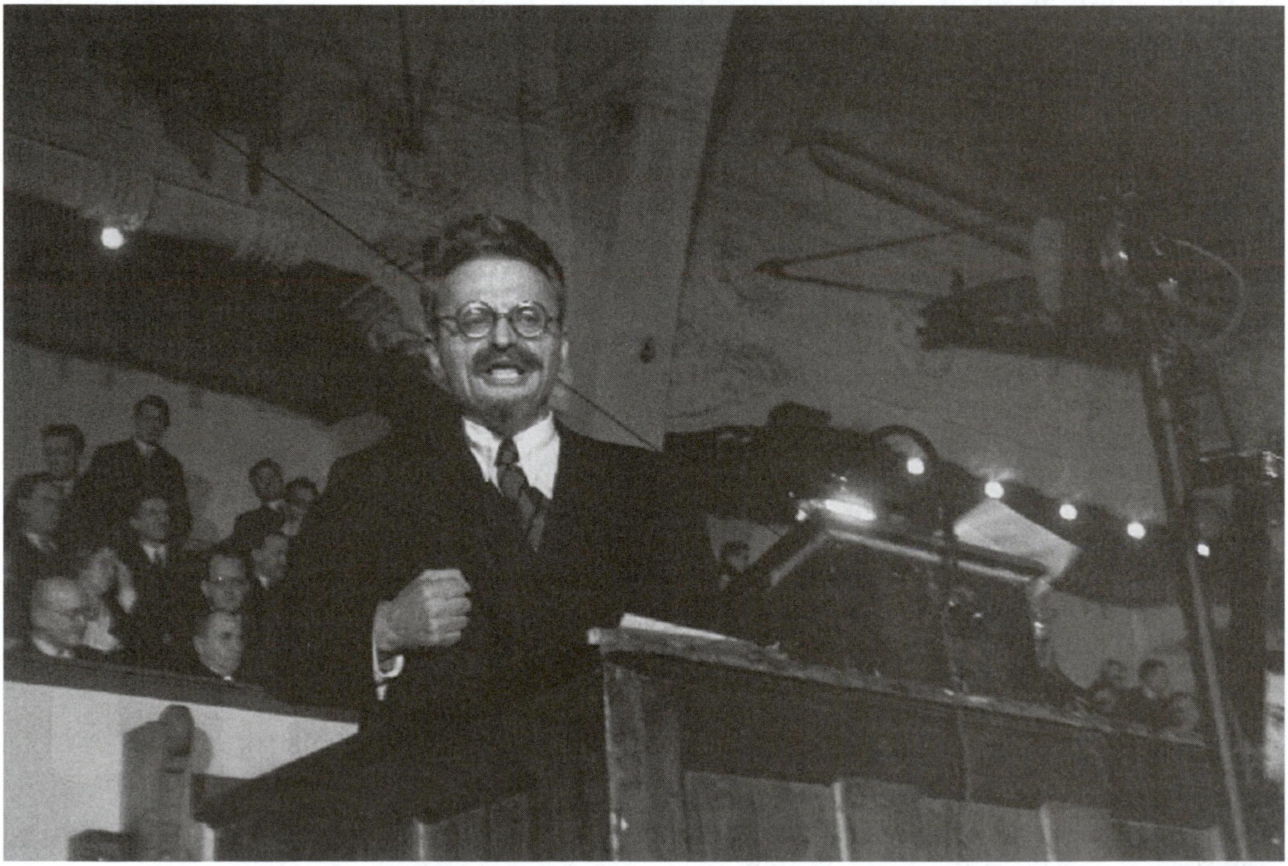

Robert Capa, Leon Trotsky Lecturing, November 27, 1932.
[© *Cornell Capa Photos by Robert Capa © 2001/Magnum Photos*]

PAUL CAPONIGRO

American

In the essence of his work, Paul Caponigro belongs to a long-standing strand of American photography practiced by figures such as nineteenth-century landscape master Carleton E. Watkins, Edward Weston, Laura Gilpin, and William Clift (1944-), who have been drawn, almost mystically, to the power of the natural landscape. Caponigro's subjects are the landscape and still life in all of their manifestations—from close-ups of a sunflower or an apple to a Connecticut rock wall, or light simply reflected in the water, or the megalithic stone monuments of Northern Europe such as Stonehenge, Avebury, and Carnac. Caponigro has also famously captured sublime and enigmatic running white deer, the gardens and temples of Japan, the Arch of Reefert Church, Glendalough, Ireland, the consecrated places of the American Indian in the West, and the great buttes of Utah and New Mexico. At the root of Caponigro's photography is his concern for man's history and awareness of what forces lie around him. In his best work, he reveals nature's delicate balance through simplified forms and formations that have been skillfully observed and meticulously printed. The power of observation and a deft control of his craft have been key elements to Caponigro's contribution to the modern definition of the language of photography.

Paul Caponigro's sensitivity to place and his understanding of the quality of light and how it affects place have enabled him to produce images that are simultaneously remarkably quiet and powerfully resonant. This distinctive strength arises from his masterful darkroom technique in which he is willing to allow each negative to dictate the specific process by which it will be developed and on which papers it will be printed.

Caponigro typically tones his prints so that they contain a subtle but rich gradation of tone so that he might capture "the elusive image of nature's subtle realms."

Paul Caponigro also writes passionately about photography and his work:

> ...of all my photographs the ones that have the most meaning for me are those I was moved to make from a certain vantage point, at a certain moment and no other, and for which I did not draw on my abilities to fabricate a picture, composition-wise or otherwise. You might say that I was taken in. Who or what takes one to a vantage point or moves one at a certain moment is a mystery to me. I have always felt that after such experiences that there was more than myself involved. It is not chance. It happens often.
>
> (*Paul Caponigro*, a monograph 1971)

Early and enduring influences on Caponigro were the lives, vision, and work of Ansel Adams, Edward Weston, Minor White, and Northwest Coast painter Morris Graves. Ansel Adams' sharply focused and highly skilled craftsmanship set a standard for Caponigro to emulate; Minor White's psychological and spiritual approach to photography informed his life-long concern with the mystical and spiritual dimensions of landscape and still life photography, a viewpoint that was very influential on others of Caponigro's generation as well. Early on in his career, Caponigro visited an exhibition by Morris Graves in San Francisco. Graves' paintings of symbolic animals and ritual objects presented a mythical dimension connected to nature yet parallel and apart from it. These paintings influenced by Eastern brush painting and Native American art were a catalyst for Caponigro. Caponigro creates pictures that are immediate; however, he is constantly engaged in the effort to reveal something other—something that is not immediately visible, tangible, or legible. He has conducted a survey of the material world, conducted, over a lifetime, with such metaphysical fidelity that it transcends the need for explanation.

DIANA EDKINS

Biography

Born in Boston, Massachusetts, December 7, 1932. Studied piano, College of Music, Boston University, 1950–1951. Drafted into the army and served as a photographer from 1953–1955; stationed in San Francisco, where he became acquainted with the West Coast photographers Ansel Adams and Minor White. Apprenticed in a commercial photographic concern, 1952. Studied with Benjamin Chin and Alfred W. Richter in San Francisco, 1956, and with Minor White at Rochester Institute of Technology, Rochester, New York in 1957–1958. First solo exhibition, George Eastman House in Rochester, New York in 1958. Assisted Minor White with summer photographic workshops, 1959. Instructor and lecturer in photography at colleges and other centers in the

United States from 1960 until the present. Helped found the Association of Heliographers and their Gallery Archive in New York, 1963. Married Eleanor Morris in 1964. Two Guggenheim Fellowships, in the British Isles in 1966 and Japan in 1975. Exhibition at The Museum of Modern Art, New York in 1968. National Endowment for the Arts Photography Fellowship in 1975 and 1982. Moved to Santa Fe, New Mexico in 1973. Arts Council of Great Britain Grant, 1978; Peer Award, Friends of Photography, Carmel, California, 1983; Annual Governor's Award, New Mexico, 1984. Moved to Maine in the early 1990s and has taught extensively throughout the United States at universities and workshops.

Selected Exhibitions

1985 *Paul Caponigro*; Cincinnati Art Museum; Cincinnati, Ohio

Le Forme della Natura; Fondazione Italiana per la Fotografia; Torino, Italia

1987 *The Implicit Image*; San Francisco Museum of Modern Art; San Francisco

Facets of Modernism; San Francisco Museum of Art; San Francisco

Paul Caponigro; National Museum of Modern Art; Kyoto, Japan

Paul Caponigro; Museum of Fine Art, Museum of New Mexico; Santa Fe

Legacy of Light; Polaroid Corporation; Cambridge, Massachusetts

Photography and Art; Los Angeles County Museum of Art

1988 *Paul Caponigro*; Museum of Contemporary Photography; Columbia College, Chicago Illinois

Photography Speaks; Chrysler Museum; Norfolk, Virginia

Megaliths; Spencer Museum of Art; University of Kansas, Lawrence

Master Photographs from "Photography in the Fine Arts" Exhibitions from 1959–1987; International Center of Photography; New York

Paul Caponigro; Shoto Museum of Art; Tokyo

1995 *Canyonland Visions*; Amon Carter Museum; Fort Worth, Texas

1996 *Meditations in Light*; The Farnsworth Art Museum; Rockland, Maine and traveling

1998 *Meditations in Light*; Art Museum of Southeast Texas, Beaumont, Texas

2002 *New England Days*; Portland Museum of Art, Portland, Oregon

2003 *Le Forme della Natura*; Galleria Civica di Modena; Italia

Le Forme della Natura; Fandazione Italiana per la Fotografia; Torino, Italia

Monographs

Paul Caponigro: Le Forme della Natura. Italy: Nepente, 2003.

New England Days: Photographs by Paul Caponigro. Portland, Maine: The Portland Museum of Art, 2002.

Paul Caponigro: Meditation in Light. Rockland, ME: The Morris Press, 1996.

Paul Caponigro: The Voice of the Print. Portland, ME: Muse Press, 1994.

Paul Caponigro: Masterworks From Forty Years. Carmel, CA: Photography West Graphics, Inc., 1993.

Paul Caponigro: Seasons. New York: New York Graphic Society, 1988.

Paul Caponigro: Megaliths. New York: Little Brown and Company, 1986.

Paul Caponigro: Photography: 25 Years. Introduction by Peter C. Bunnell. Edited By D.W. Mellor. Exhibition catalog for the Photography Gallery, Philadelphia, Pa. and The Weston Gallery, Carmel, CA, 1981.

Paul Caponigro. Landscape. New York: McGraw Hill, 1975.

Sunflower. New York, 1974.

Paul Caponigro. Millerton, New York: Aperature, 1967, revised edition 1972.

The Music of Willem Nyland. New York, 1963, 1964.

Further Reading

Brown, Bruce. *Photographing Maine:1840–2000*. Rockport: Center for Maine Contemporary Art, Maine Coasts Artists, 2000.

Bunnell, Peter C. *Photography at Princeton: Celebrating Twenty-Five Years of Collections and Teaching the History of Photography*. Princeton: The Art Museum, Princeton University, 1998.

Caponigro, Paul. Millerton, New York: Aperture, Inc., 1972.

Fulton, Marianne. *The Wise Silence: Photography by Paul Caponigro*. New York: New York Graphic Society Books and Boston: Little Brown and Company, 1983.

Hawkins, Gerald S. *Stonehenge Decoded*. New York: Dell Publishing Company, 1965.

Hill, Paul, and Thomas Cooper. *Dialogue with Photography*. London and New York: 1979.

Szarkowski, John. *Mirrors and Windows: American Photography since 1960*. New York: Museum of Modern Art, 1978.

Szarkowski, John. *Photographie Nouvelle des Etats-Unis*. Paris, 1969.

Szarkowski, John. *The Photographer's Eye*. New York: Museum of Modern Art, 1966.

Szarkowski, John. *The Photographer and the American Landscape*. New York: Museum of Modern Art, New York, 1963.

Witkin, Lee D., and Barbara London. *The Photograph Collector's Guide*. Boston: New York Graphic Society, 1979.

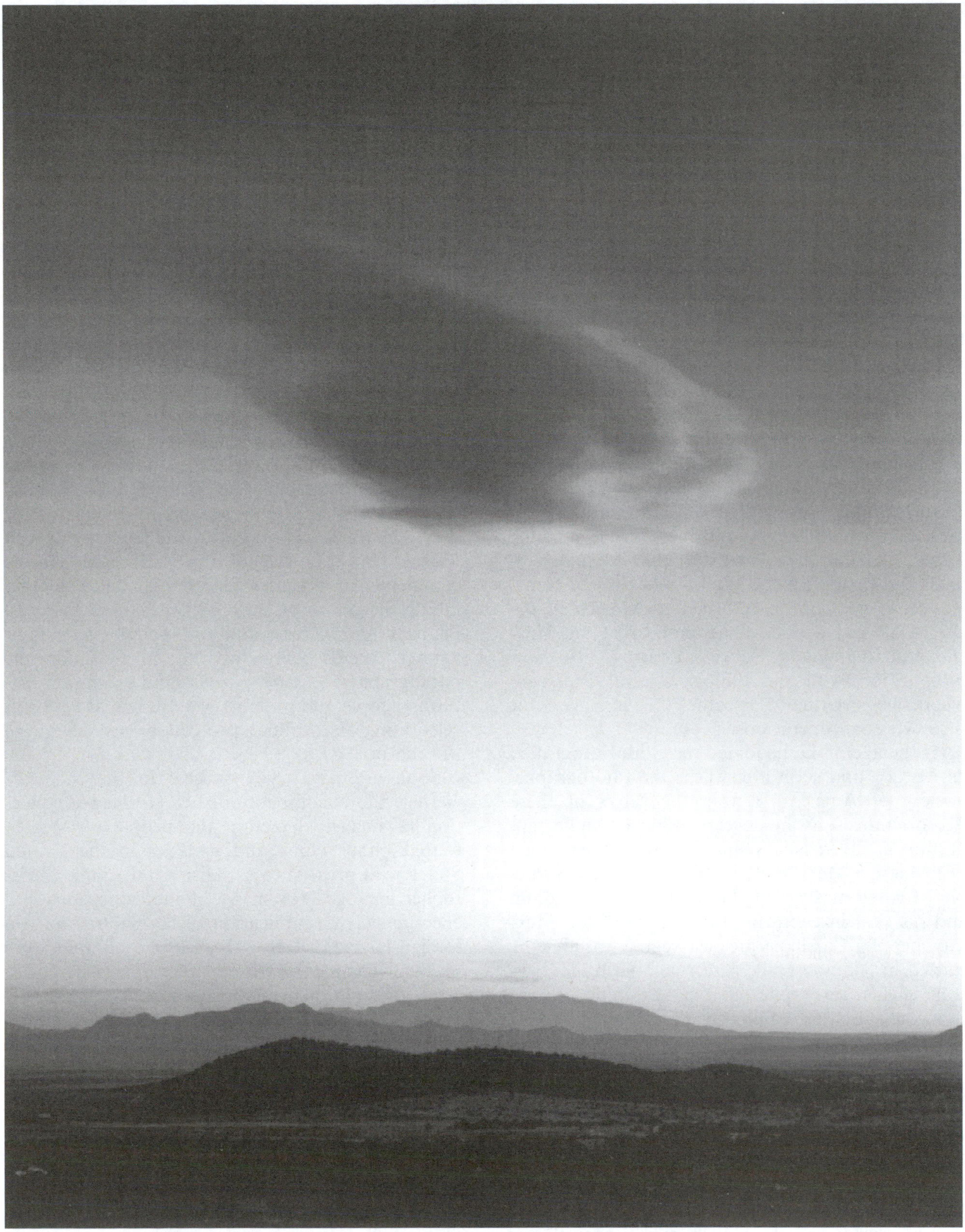

Paul Caponigro, Cloud, San Sebastian, New Mexico, 1982, printed later, Gelatin silver print. [© *Paul Caponigro. Courtesy of the Fogg Art Museum, Harvard University Art Museums, Anonymous loan in honor of Carl Chiarenza. Allan Macintyre.* © *2004 President and Fellows of Harvard College*]

MANUEL CARRILLO

Mexican

Born in Mexico City at the home of his grandparents on January 17, 1906, Carrillo was the son of an important Mexican family with roots in the northern state of Chihuahua. His grandfather, Lauro Carrillo, was a close ally of Mexican dictator Porfirio Díaz, and an uncle, Adolfo Ruiz Cortines, served as President of Mexico from 1952 to 1958. Manuel Carrillo attended several private schools in Mexico and worked briefly in the fledgling Mexican film industry before moving to the United States at the age of 17. In the United States, he worked at a variety of odd jobs, mostly in Chicago and New York, washing dishes, teaching dance at the Arthur Murray Studios, and finally for the Wall Street firm of Neuss Hesslein and Co. He returned to Mexico at the age of 24 and worked for a pioneer of the Mexican tourist industry, Alberto L. Bravo. He later took a job with the Illinois Central Railroad, where he eventually became the manager for their Mexican operations.

At the age of 49, he joined the Club Fotográfico de México and soon afterwards the Photographic Society of America. Within the ranks of these two organizations, he developed his art and a reputation as an artistic genius. He was often called "El Maestro Mexicano" or "El Fotógrafo del Pueblo" for his mastery of the photographic medium and his skill in capturing the essence of the Mexican people. Carrillo's greatest regret was that he started his photographic career so late in life. Several of his early photographic exhibitions were sponsored by his employer, the Illinois Central Railroad, and one of his best-known photographs is *Garrotero de Nonoalco*, a photo of a railroad employee on smoke-shrouded tracks near Mexico City.

His first exhibition, *Mi Pueblo*, opened at the Club Fotográfico de México in 1958, where he had previously participated in several group exhibitions. From the time he joined the organization in 1955, he was active with the group; he won many awards, and the club named a special trophy for him in 1982 that honored its master photographers, and in 1985 it also named an exhibition gallery for him. A version of the *Mi Pueblo* exhibition was displayed at the Chicago Public Library in 1960 and was viewed by an estimated 100,000 visitors.

In 1966, he entered a print entitled *Dog on his Master's Grave* in a *Saturday Review* photography contest. He won first prize in the monochrome category—out of 149,000 entries—and the photo was published in the January, 1967 issue. This award and Carrillo's evocative photographs soon brought him international fame. Many of Carrillo's photographs depict animals, reflecting a long interest in animal rights and animal protection efforts. One of his best-known photographs shows a mass of street dogs, many emaciated, as they wait for food from a private feeding effort in Mexico City. The focus is not sharp, and Carrillo commented in an interview that he had difficulty taking the photo because of the tears in his eyes. Pictures of children and old people with their animal friends were favorite subjects for the photographer. *Los Inseparables*, an exhibition featuring people and animals, was shown at an event celebrating the animal protection law passed in Mexico in 1981.

Soon after his 1967 success in the *Saturday Review* photo competition, his *Mi Pueblo* collection of images depicting the people of Mexico toured photo clubs and galleries in the United States with great success. His friend Frank Christopher arranged for many of the exhibitions and encouraged the publication of his photographs in foreign magazines. In 1970, his photographs were selected for an exhibition at the Palacio de Bellas Artes (the national art museum) in Mexico City, and a few years later they represented Mexico in a tour of the Federal Republic of Germany. Since 1975, his work has been exhibited in 20 different countries in Europe, Asia, and North and South America. In 1980, he was honored at a meeting of the Photographic Society of America and was made an honorary citizen of El Paso. Also in 1980, his work was the subject of a feature in *Photozoom* magazine.

By 1988, Carrillo's work had been seen in 209 individual exhibitions and 27 group exhibitions in Mexico, the United States, and countries around the world. His work has been published in a variety of photographic anthologies and journals. *Manuel Carrillo: Fotografías de Mexico*, published by Juan Salinas Cortés in 1989, captured 225 of Carrillo's best works.

Although some criticize Carrillo's work as being sentimental, his emotional connection to his work often adds dimension to his documentation of everyday life in traditional Mexico. The bulk of Carrillo's photographs were taken from the mid 1950s through the late 1970s, but his choice of subject matter gives the photographs a timeless quality. Children at play, market scenes, and men at work and leisure show the activities of a broad spectrum of Mexican society. Melissa Carrillo (no relation to Manuel), who created an on-line exhibition on Manuel Carrillo's work for the Smithsonian Institution's website, describes his work as an expression of post-revolutionary nationalism, and notes that Carrillo often expressed pride in his country. As Robert Tilendis said in his description of Carrillo's work:

> Carrillo has concentrated on the people and places of Mexico in his work. His photographs are readily identifiable with that county, with a specificity that, rather than diminishing their meaning, adds to their scope. His mastery of photographic technique and of the elements of composition combines with a sensitivity to the nuances of human feeling to produce a series of images rich in associations.

Manuel Carrillo did his own developing and printing, but he always concentrated on the image itself and its composition rather than darkroom manipulation. The images look deceptively simple and straightforward, and they often give the impression of happy coincidences, but Carrillo often waited hours for the right light or effect of shadows. He always used natural light and never used a flash or zoom lens. According to a 1982 interview, he generally produced 6×6 cm negatives, preferring his Rolleiflex or Mamiyaflex cameras; all of his best-known work is in black-and-white. He also had a 35-mm Nikon that he used for color transparencies (most often for portraits, glamour photos, or landscapes) and a Hasselblad, which he used infrequently for wide-angle photography. The Mexico City earthquake of 1985 virtually destroyed his darkroom; he also lost some of his negatives and much of his photographic equipment. This personal disaster led him to look for a home for his photographs in the United States.

Carrillo died on 20 January, 1989, leaving behind an important artistic legacy. His works are held by many private collections, universities, and museums, including the Victoria and Albert Museum in London, the Museum of Modern Art in New York City, the Center for Creative Photography in Tucson, the Museum of Contemporary Art in Chicago, and at least 30 other museums. He maintained close ties with friends in El Paso, a city where his family had lived for a time during the Mexican Revolution and where he received medical treatment in the 1980s. In 1991, the University of Texas at El Paso purchased Carrillo's photographs and papers from his widow, and the collection is now housed in the C. L. Sonnichsen Special Collections Department of the University Library. A virtual museum of his work is available at http://latino.si.edu/virtualgallery/manuelcarrillo/mccode.htm.

Claudia Rivers

See also: **Photography in Mexico**

Biography

Born in Mexico City, 17 January 1906. Attended various schools including the Mexican Military Academy before moving to the United States at the age of 17. He worked at a series of odd jobs in New York. Returned to Mexico at the age of 24. Worked the Consolidated Railroad and Pullman Tourism Service and later for the Illinois Central Railroad from 1934–1966. Married Consuelo Cadena in 1955. Joined the Club Fotográfico de México and the Photographic Society of America in 1955. Honored in Great Britain in 1966 as one of six outstanding foreign photographers by the Photographic Yearbook; won a grand prize for international photography in Bucharest, Rumania in 1981. In 1980, he was honored by the Photographic Society of America and made an honorary citizen of El Paso. Died in Mexico City, 20 January 1989.

Individual Exhibitions

1958 *Mi Pueblo*; Club Fotográfico de México; Mexico City, Mexico
1960 *Mi Pueblo*; Chicago Public Library; Chicago, Illinois
1962 *Manuel Carrillo*; Panamerican Union; Washington, D.C.
1970 *Fotografías de Manuel Carrillo*; Palacio de Bellas Artes; Mexico City, Mexico
1978 *The Photographs of Manuel Carrillo*; The Gilbert Gallery; Chicago, Illinois
1981 *Los inseparables*; Infonavit; Mexico City, Mexico
1981 *La Obra Fotográfica de Manuel Carrillo*; Galería Alvarez Bravo; Mexico City, Mexico
1981 *Manuel Carrillo*; Galeria de Arti Fotografica; Bucharest, Rumania
1986 *Manuel Carrillo*; The Silver Image; Seattle, Washington
1998 *Manuel Carrillo's Mexico*; Centennial Museum; University of Texas at El Paso; El Paso, Texas
1999 *Mexico! Photographs by Manuel Carrillo*; Muscarelle Museum of Art; Williamsburg, Virginia
2000 *Revealing Personal Identity: The Indigenous Vision of Manuel Carrillo*; Smithsonian Center for Latino Initiatives Virtual Gallery; Washington, D.C.

Selected Group Exhibitions

1974 *México y los Mexicanos*; Federal Republic of Germany; various sites
1977 *El Animal en la Cultura*; Centro de Arte Moderno; Guadalajara, Jalisco, Mexico
1982 *Photo-club de Bordeaux 90e Anniversaire*; Salon International d'Art Photographique; Bordeaux, France
1988 *100 Años de Fotografía Indigenista*; Museo de Culturas Populares; Mexico City, Mexico
2002 *Río de Luz:* Wittliff Gallery of Southwestern & Mexican Photography; San Marcos, Texas

Selected Works

(Note: Manuel Carrillo's photos were not titled, but he gave them short descriptions and reference numbers in his own classification system, and these descriptions have been used in lieu of titles.)
Don Trini, (*#1532*) Guanajuato, 1955
Rebozo al aire, (#520) Oaxaca, 1958
Garrotero de Nonoalco, (#1549) Distrito Federal, ca. 1958
Enferma en la banco, Guanajuato, 1960
Viejita, callejón, sombras piramidales, (# 1164) Guanajuato, 1960
Perro sobre tumba, (#5004) Mexico City, 1966
Cruz—sombra humana, Hidalgo, 1973
Asilo de perros callejeros, (#5085) Mexico City, n.d.
Beisbol, perro al fondo, (#147) Jalisco, n.d.
Pescador envuelto en redes, (# 1637) Veracruz, n.d.
Pulquería de Toluca, (#5001) Edo. de México, n.d.

Further Reading

Carrillo, Manuel. Interview. El Paso: Institute of Oral History, 31 May, 1982.
Carrillo, Manuel. *Manuel Carrillo: fotografias de Mexico*. Mexico, D.F.: Juan E. Salinas Cortes, 1987.
"Manuel Carrillo." In *Zoom* (American edition), 1984.
Mi Pueblo: Manuel Carrillo, Obra Fotográfica. Mexico, D. F.: Sindicato de Trabajadores INFONAVIT, 1980.
Of People and Places: the Floyd and Josephine Segel Collection of Photography. Milwaukee, WI: Milwaukee Art Museum, 1987. 72–75.
Old, Joe. "The Eye of Manuel Carrillo." *Nova: The Magazine of the University of Texas at El Paso* (Spring, 1992).
Quarm, Joan. "Photographer Captures Nature of People." *The El Paso Herald-Post* (Saturday, Oct. 17, 1976).

HENRI CARTIER-BRESSON

French

One of the giants of twentieth-century photography, Henri Cartier-Bresson might also be said to be the seminal figure of the postwar era, both for his own achievements and for the wide influence of his humanist photographic sensibility. Described by *The New York Times* as "the archetype of the itinerant photojournalist," he was also a succinct portraitist, capturing newsworthy personalities such as sculptor Alberto Giacometti, writer Jean-Paul Sartre, and Indian leader Mahatma Gandhi in what were to become signature portraits. He was a photographic visionary who co-founded the now-legendary photo agency Magnum Photos and pioneered the concept of "the decisive moment."

Well-illustrated by the 1932 work *Behind Saint-Lazare Station, Paris, France*, which shows a man leaping in the midst of a flooded street, captured in the split-second before his heel will hit the skin of water, Cartier-Bresson's unique photographic sensibility put forth the idea of "the decisive moment"—the exactly proper moment when any particular set of occurrences as observed through the frame of the lens will cohere to become the best possible photograph, balanced in composition and other formal elements and capturing a photographic reality that freezes and thus abstracts the "real world." Cartier-Bresson often described his philosophy thus:

> To take a photograph is to hold one's breath when all faculties converge in a face of fleeing reality. It is at that moment that mastering an image becomes a great physical and intellectual joy.
>
> (HCB Foundation website)

What distinguishes Cartier-Bresson's vision from the many other photographers who strove to capture ideal moments, often instead perpetuating clichés, however, was his ability to pre-visualize and pre-edit the image so that it would be rich and resonant, not merely capturing a suspended instant. The famous Saint-Lazare railway station photograph is filled with remarkable, even uncanny detail.

Posters in the midground reiterate the leaping figure and his reflection in the water; the man has propelled himself off a ladder-like structure that mimics railway track, and so on. Cartier-Bresson was seldom accused of the "lucky shot" culled from numerous exposures, however, for he was famous for shooting judiciously, often exposing only a few frames during events, when other photojournalists would shoot many rolls.

Henri Cartier-Bresson was born in Chanteloup, Seine-et-Marne, on August 22, 1908, the oldest of five children. His father was a textile manufacturer of considerable wealth, yet the household was run as would be one of modest means to the point that as a boy Cartier-Bresson had little idea of the family's resources, which included extensive land holdings in Normandy where he would summer. He was educated in Paris at the Lycée Condorcet, where he read avidly, but received no formal photographic training. His introduction to the medium as a potential career was through seeing photographs by Martin Munkacsi as a teenager, which impressed him with their beauty and possibility. He did, however, study painting in 1927–28 under André Lhote, who had been an early practitioner of Cubism; it was Lhote who Cartier-Bresson claimed taught him everything he knew about photography through his training to observe closely and imaginatively and learn from art history. He was also deeply impressed by the works of the Surrealist artists who were then beginning to dominate the Parisian art world. He studied English literature and art at Cambridge University in London until his induction into the French Army in 1930. Upon his discharge, filled with the poetry and literature and looking for adventure, he was off to the French colony of Côte d'Ivoire to hunt. It was here he first took photographs using a Brownie that he had been given as a gift, and the pursuit of shooting game as a metaphor for shooting photographs, which he often used in his writing and speaking about the medium, also arose. He contracted blackwater fever, however, and almost died. The photographs he took were also lost. Returning to Marseilles to recuperate, he acquired his first professional camera, a Leica, which he used to photograph in earnest when he had occasion to travel the continent with friends. His first exhibition was in Madrid; however, by 1935 he was in New York, where he exhibited at the Julien Levy Gallery. While in New York, he met Paul Strand, who at that time was making films. Inspired by Strand, when he returned to France Cartier-Bresson secured the position of a second assistant on Jean Renoir's *A Day in the Country* and *The Rules of the Game*. He was also involved in a propaganda film the famous director made for the French Communist Party that denounced France's prominent families in France, Cartier-Bresson's own among them. Cartier-Bresson did not join the Communist Party, but he harbored a life-long sympathy for oppressed and demoralized lower classes, which was often reflected in his choice of subject matter.

In 1940, with the German invasion of France, Cartier-Bresson, a corporal in the Army's Film and Photo Unit, was captured. He spent a total of almost three years in prisoner-of-war camps, escaping twice and being recaptured and returned to hard labor, which he later claimed had been a helpful lesson. On his third escape attempt, in 1943, he succeeded, and he hid on a farm in Touraine until he secured false papers that allowed him to travel in France, where he once again took up photographing as a member of the Resistance. He established a photo division within the French underground to document the German occupation as well as their eventual retreat, an experience which surely shaped his ideas about the photo agency, Magnum, when it was established in 1947, and photographed such notables as artists Henri Matisse, Pablo Picasso, and Georges Braque. Following France's liberation in 1944, the United States Office of War Information hired Cartier-Bresson to direct a film about the homecoming of French prisoners and deportees.

Upon completing this well-received film, *The Return*, Cartier-Bresson traveled once again to New York City, where a retrospective at the Museum of Modern Art, conceived as a tribute on the belief that he had been killed in the war, had been planned. He was thus able to work on his own "posthumous" exhibition, and he took time as well to travel around the United States, taking such signature images as *Harlem, Easter Sunday*, 1947, which shows a lovely African American woman wearing a satin-flower filled hat framed within the architectural details of a modest brick structure, which join with the forms of the hat to create an even more elaborate chapeaux.

Returning to Paris in 1947, he learned that his associates Robert Capa, David Seymour (Chim), William Vandivert, and George Rodger, had laid plans for a cooperative photo agency with offices in New York, Paris, and other world capitals. Dubbed Magnum Photos, the organizing group named Cartier-Bresson to their board of directors, knowing that he was like minded and aware of his considerable prestige. He was tapped to be in charge of Far

Eastern assignments; and his insistence on small format cameras, no auxiliary equipment such as flash, tripods, or telephoto lens and the integrity of the frame as photographed—no darkroom manipulation—became the gold standard for postwar photojournalism as well as being highly influential on fine arts photography.

Thus the late 1940s saw Cartier-Bresson's rise as an international photojournalist. For Magnum he traveled to the China, India—where he photographed Gandhi literally minutes before he was assassinated—and Indonesia, photographing political events and the people in their streets and homes. Extraordinary "decisive moments" were captured, such as *Gold Sale, Shanghai, China* of 1949, which shows a human "rope": Chinese peasants with their arms braided and intertwined, binding themselves, as it were, at the stoop of a building. Taken during the communist takeover of China in 1948–49 this remarkable composition captures a run on a bank selling gold; the crowd is not controlled by any authority, but by its own essence of panic and agitation in the face of huge events.

By 1952, Cartier-Bresson, back in Europe, was finally receiving wide recognition in his home country. His first book, *Images à la sauvette* (with its English title of "The Decisive Moment,") with cover art by Matisse, was published. He began a long collaboration with eminent fine arts publisher Robert Delpire, including a book on Balinese theatre, *Les Danses à Bali*, featuring text by Antonin Artaud. His book *Les Européens*, with cover art by painter Joan Miró, was published as well; and in 1955, he received his first exhibition in France at the Louvre.

The 1960s were again a period of intense international travel. He returned to Mexico, where he had made one of his first photographic forays as part of an ethnographic team in the early 1930s. On assignment for *Life* magazine, he traveled to Cuba during a time of high tension between that country and the United States. He visited Japan and once again traveled to India. In 1966, Cartier-Bresson terminated his relationship with Magnum Photos, claiming he had stayed with the agency "two years too long" and admitting to detractors that perhaps he had said all he had to say through photography. Although he took on occasional commissions, such as one from the IBM Corporation, *Man and Machine*, he turned once again to his early passion for painting and drawing. After divorcing his wife of 30 years, the Javanese dancer Ratna Mohini, he married the Magnum photographer Martine Franck in 1970. After 1974, he photographed very little, and then often secretly, which he had perfected during his long career as a photojournalist working with a small camera that he would often further minimize by covering with black tape any metal parts which might reflect light and catch the eye.

Coinciding with a 2003 retrospective of his work at the Bibliothèque nationale de France, and shortly before his 95th birthday, Cartier-Bresson, along with his wife Martine Frank and their daughter, inaugurated the Henri Cartier-Bresson Foundation, which they had conceived several years earlier to "preserve and share the legacy of his work." Housed in an historic atelier in Paris, the Foundation archives Cartier-Bresson's vintage prints and contact sheets, as well as publications, rare books, albums, posters, exhibition invitations, and films and videos that document the photographer's career. The HCB Foundation also bestows an award named after Cartier-Bresson, organizes and circulates exhibitions featuring his work, and maintains a comprehensive website available at www.henricartierbresson.org. Magnum Photos also distributes Cartier-Bresson photographs. Henri Cartier-Bresson died in the south of France on 5 August 2004.

LYNNE WARREN

See also: **Capa, Robert; Franck, Martine; History of Photography: Interwar Years; Magnum Photos; Photography in France; Seymour, David "Chim"**

Biography

Born Chanteloup, Seine-et-Marne, 22 August 1908. Educated Lycée Condorcet, Paris and studies painting with André Lhote, 1927–28; no formal photographic training. Studied English literature and art at Cambridge University, London, 1928–29; inducted into French Army, 1930. Traveled in Africa, 1931, European continent, 1932. First exhibition in Madrid, 1932; New York, 1933. Prisoner-of-war, 1940–43; member MN PGD organization of the French underground, 1943–44. Co-founded Magnum Photos, 1947; worked in Far East, 1948–1952, Cuba, 1963; Japan, 1965; left Magnum in 1966. Traveled in USSR, 1972–73. Married Martine Franck, 1970. Largely ceased photographing after 1974. Numerous awards, including Overseas Press Club of America, 1948, 1954, 1960, 1964; Prix de la Société Français de Photographie, 1959; the Culture Prize, Deutsche Gesellschaft für Photographie, 1975; Hasselblad Award, 1982. Died in Céreste, Alpes-de-Haute-Provence, France, 3 August 2004.

Selected Work

(Note that HCB did not formally title works, and works may appear under various titles.)

Behind Saint-Lazare Station, Paris, France, 1932 (also known as *Place de l'Europe*)

Spanish Morocco, 1933

Valencia, Spain, 1933
Calle Cuauhtemoctzin, Mexico City, 1934 (also known as *Prostitutes in the Calle Cuauhtemoctzin*)
Sunday on the Banks of the River Marne, France, 1938
Dessau: Exposing a Gestapo Informer (also known as *Exposing a stool pigeon for the Gestapo in a displaced persons camp)*, 1945
Jean-Paul Sartre on the Pont des Arts, 1946
Harlem, Easter Sunday, 1947 (also known as *Easter Parade*)
Eunuch of the Imperial Court, Beijing, China, 1948
Gold Sale, Shanghai, China, 1949
Rome, Italy, 1951
Athens, Greece, 1953
Near Burgos, Spain, 1953
Rue Mouffetard, Paris, 1954
Sunbather, Peter and Paul Fortress, Leningrad, USSR, 1973

Individual Exhibitions

1933 Julien Levy Gallery; New York, New York
1947 *The Photographs of Henri Cartier-Bresson*; Museum of Modern Art; New York, New York
1952 Institute of Contemporary Art; London, England
1954 *Photographs by Henri Cartier-Bresson*; Art Institute of Chicago; Chicago, Illinois
1955 Pavillon de Marsan de Louvre; Paris, France
1965 *Henri Cartier-Bresson*; Asahi Gallery; Tokyo, Japan and traveling worldwide
1970 *On France*; Grand Palais; Paris, France and traveling worldwide
1974 *Apropos USSR: Henri Cartier-Bresson*; International Center of Photography; New York, New York
1976 *Glimpses of America: 1945–1975, by Henri Cartier-Bresson*; International Center of Photography; New York, New York
1979 *Henri Cartier-Bresson: Photographer*; International Center of Photography; New York, New York and traveling
1981 *Henri Cartier-Bresson*; Musée d'Art moderne de la Ville de Paris; Paris, France
1985 *Henri Cartier-Bresson*; Museo de Arte Moderno de Mexico; Mexico City, Mexico
Henri Cartier-Bresson: A Half-Century of Portraits; International Center of Photography; New York, New York
Henri Cartier-Bresson en Inde; Centre national de la photographie, Palais de Tokyo; Paris, France
1987 *Henri Cartier-Bresson: The Early Work*; Museum of Modern Art; New York, New York
1988 *The Reluctant Photographer: Henri Cartier-Bresson*; International Center of Photography; New York, New York
Henri Cartier-Bresson In India; International Center of Photography; New York, New York
1994 *Henri Cartier-Bresson: Homage*; International Center of Photography; New York, New York
1997 *De Européenne*; Maison Européenne de la Photography; Paris, France
1998 *Tête à Tête: Portraits by Henri Cartier-Bresson*; Smithsonian Institution National Portrait Gallery; Washington, DC

Group Exhibitions

1935 *Documentary and Anti-Graphic*; Julien Levy Gallery; New York, New York
1951 *Five French Photographers: Brassaï, Cartier-Bresson, Doisneau, Izis, Ronis*; Museum of Modern Art; New York, New York
1972 *Behind the Great Wall of China: Photographs from 1870 to the Present*; Metropolitan Museum; New York, New York
1977 *Concerning Photography*; The Photographers' Gallery; London, England
1984 *In Our Time: The World as Seen by Magnum Photographers*; International Museum of Photography and Film, George Eastman House; Rochester, New York and traveling worldwide
Subjektive Fotografie, Images of the 50's; Museum Folkwang; Essen, Germany (traveled to the San Francisco Museum of Modern Art; San Francisco, California)
1989 *On the Art of Fixing a Shadow: One Hundred and Fifty Years of Photography*; National Gallery of Art; Washington D.C. and Art Institute of Chicago; Chicago, Illinois (and traveled to Los Angeles County Museum of Art; Los Angeles, California)
Photography Until Now; Museum of Modern Art; New York, New York (traveled to the Cleveland Museum of Art; Cleveland, Ohio)
Magnum Founders: Robert Capa, Henri Cartier-Bresson, George Rodger, and David Seymour Chim, 1931–1986; International Center of Photography; New York, New York

Further Reading

Arbaizar, Philippe, et al. *Henri Cartier-Bresson: The Man, the Image and the World: A Retrospective*. Reissue edition. London: Thames & Hudson, 2003.
Cartier-Bresson, Henri. *The Decisive Moment*. Cover by Henri Matisse. New York: Simon & Schuster, 1952.
———. *Les Danses à Bali*. Texts by Antonin Artaud and Béryl de Zoete. Paris: Delpire, 1954.
———. *Henri Cartier-Bresson: Photoportraits*. Preface by Andre Pieyre de Mandiargues. London: Thames & Hudson, 1985.
———. *Henri Cartier-Bresson: Photographer*. Foreword by Yves Bonnefoy. Boston: Little, Brown and Co., 1981.
———. *Henri Cartier-Bresson in India*. Foreword by Satyajit Ray, introduction by Yves Veguard. London: Thames + Hudson, 1987.
———. *Henri Cartier-Bresson (Aperture Masters of Photography)*. Millerton, NY: Aperture, 1997.
———. *Europeans*. introduction by Jean Clair. Boston: Bulfinch Press, Little, Brown and Co., 1998.
———. *Tête à Tête*. Introduction by E. H. Grombrich. Boston: Bulfinch Press, Little Brown and Co., 1998.
———. *A Propos de Paris*. Texts by Vera Feyder and André Pieyre, reprint edition. Boston: Bulfinch Press, Little Brown and Co., 1998.
———. *The Mind's Eye: Writings on Photography and Photographers*. Millerton, NY: Aperture, 1999.
Galassi, Peter. *Henri Cartier-Bresson: The Early Work*. New York and Boston: New York Graphic Society Books/Little, Brown and Co., 1987.
Kirsten, Lincoln and Beaumont Newhall. *The Photographs of Henri Cartier-Bresson*. New York: Museum of Modern Art, 1947.
Orsenna, Erik, and Henri Cartier-Bresson. *Henri Cartier-Bresson: City and Landscapes*. Boston: Bulfinch Press, Little Brown and Co., 2001.

CENSORSHIP

Censorship, in its broadest sense, can be used to indicate the suppression and restriction of written and visual materials on a variety grounds, be they socio-political, economic, moral, or aesthetic. The forms taken by censors are similarly diverse, and can include racial, ethnic, or religious groups, government agencies, social organizations, corporations, educational institutions, even the creator of a work in question. Beyond these vague parameters, however, censorship resists more precise definition, mainly due to the vast multiplicity of agendas to which a censor may subscribe. For some, censorship may be used as a protective measure against an existing verbal or visual assault; for others, it may function as a preemptive strike against an individual or faction who is construed as a threat to the larger group. Regardless of the specific circumstances, censorship is fundamentally about control, and having that power acknowledged both internally and externally.

That censorship has been so prevalent insofar as photography is concerned is due in large part to the nature of the medium, as photographic prints can be easily reproduced and then disseminated over great distances, whereas paintings and sculpture are difficult and time-consuming to reproduce, and are generally viewed in the context of a gallery or museum. Moreover, the apparent naturalism and assumed objectivity of the photographic image—as opposed to one that is hand-drawn—has contributed greatly to the notion that photography is a considerably more dangerous and volatile medium. This is perhaps best exemplified by a trial in New Zealand in 1917, which found a photograph of Giorgione's painting *Sleeping Venus* hanging in a shop window to be "indecent." Due to pressure from the United States Postal Service's policing of nudity in photographs, Eastman Kodak established a private censorship operation in 1949.

Times of war are especially prone to censorship, as governments have often sought to use photographic media to fashion an acceptable view of conflict for the civilian population. American journalists of the First and Second World Wars were subject to the regulatory influence of military censors, who sought to protect the general populace from viewing graphic images of dead and wounded soldiers. The extensive censorship of media images by the United States government during wartime was partially alleviated by the development of the wire services in the 1930s, which enabled news services such as the Associated Press to send images quickly over telephone wires. While the conflicts from Vietnam through to the more recent campaigns in the Middle East continue to be understood mostly through televised news reports, it is often isolated images that circumvent censors and elicit powerful reactions from civilians. Further complicating this issue is the use of the largely unregulated Internet for the dissemination of digital photographs, which will have an enormous effect on the methods of control and management of information in the future.

The thriving avant garde around the Bauhaus in Dessau and Berlin was squashed by the rising tide of Nazism in Germany, which resulted in the closing of the school and the threatening of its instructors. As often is the case, results of censorship can be unpredictable. The fleeing from censorship and oppression by such figures as László Moholy-Nagy or Herbert Bayer brought them productively to the United States, where their work had even greater influence. Decades of tight governmental control in China, which allowed only certain subject matter as suitable for photographing, resulted in a veritable flood of creativity in the field once censorship was relaxed in the 1990s.

Censorship of photography as an instrument of political and social control has also been used to stifle perceived internal conflicts, most notably during the Cold War in the United States, which saw the government exert its enormous influence against the threat of communism by disbanding organizations judged to be subversive. The crusade against what were considered identifiably communistic tendencies in modern art led to the 1947 blacklisting of The Photo League, a group of mainly left-leaning photographers who published a newsletter, *Photo Notes*. The Photo League counted amongst its members some of the most influential figures in American photography, including Lewis Hine, Paul Strand, Walter Rosenblum, Ansel Adams, Edward Weston, W. Eugene Smith, Lisette Model, as well as other photographers formerly employed by the Farm Security Administration (FSA) of the Works Progress Administration (WPA). German photographer Hans Haacke was met with similar disapproval not by the government, but by the Solomon R. Guggenheim Museum in New York, for producing an exhibit in 1971 consisting of photographs of tenement apartments in New York City, revealing through the accompanying text the owners and mortgage holders of each property, all of which was public record. The exhibition was canceled and the curator was fired, despite Haacke's agreement to remove the names from the wall labels. In this circumstance, the gravity of the apparently innocent photographs of buildings is not implicit in the images themselves, but rather in the context in which the artist seeks for us to understand them.

Yet historically, the key objectionable image has been the human body, and controversy ensues when the body portrayed questions the moral standards of sexuality, or more specifically, heterosexuality. Whether presented clothed or nude, in war or at home, in groups or in isolation, the human body is constantly viewed and scrutinized according to a society's value system.

An early example of both political and sexual censoring occurred with the work of Minor White (1908–1976), who began his photography career in the late 1930s. An example of a self-censoring artist in his early years, White omitted overt references to his homosexuality. A veteran of the U.S. Army, White worked and experienced great success for many years within the acceptable limits of his medium. His first experience with censorship occurred when White developed more personal work that was accompanied by his poetry. In the immediate post-World War II era, San Francisco's Palace of the Legion of Honor refused to allow the poetry to join White's photographs; it was deemed both too personal and lacking in patriotism. In the late 1940s and early 1950s, White photographed male nude subjects that were not sexually explicit or outwardly homosexual. Bound by his self-censorship, these works were not shown at the time. However, many of these works were eventually exhibited in 1989. While homoerotic or homosexual depiction became more acceptable toward the end of the century, homosexual content was at the center of one of the most volatile censorship battles of the century.

The most pervasive and publicized appearance of censorship in the late decades of the century was the outcry against photographs deemed to be of "obscene," "indecent," or otherwise distasteful subject matter, generally relating to prurient or anti-religious (typically anti-Christian) themes. Most notable amongst examples of this genre are the exhibitions by Andres Serrano and Robert Mapplethorpe in the late 1980s, both of which erupted in a firestorm of controversy. Serrano, whose *Piss Christ* of 1987 presented a plastic crucifix submerged in a jar of urine, was targeted by irate members of Congress and the religious right, who condemned the photograph as offensive and overtly anti-Catholic. A series of graphic images of erotic homosexual activity and nude children in Mapplethorpe's 1989 touring exhibition *The Perfect Moment* resulted in the cancellation of the show at the Corcoran Gallery of Art, in Washington, DC, followed by the arrest and indictment (and subsequent acquittal) of Dennis Barrie, the Director of the Contemporary Art Center in Cincinnati, who rebuffed an order by the county prosecutor to remove seven of the photographs. The maelstrom caused by these artists was due not only to the perceived unsuitability of the subjects of these photographs, but that the artists and/or the exhibiting institutions were funded by grants from the National Endowment for the Arts (NEA), which rekindled the continuing debate about the purpose of and selection process for government grants for the arts. While the media fanfare surrounding the Serrano and Mapplethorpe cases have made them the most notorious instances, scores of photographers have been met with both successful and unsuccessful attempts at censorship that have been decidedly less visible. For example, works by Alice Sims, Sally Mann, and Jock Sturges, have been cited for indecency for their use of nude or seemingly abused children.

Bradley C. Bailey

See also: **Erotic Photography; Ethics and Photography; Farm Security Administration; Mapplethorpe, Robert; Photo League; Propaganda; Representation and Gender; Serrano, Andres; Socialist Photography; War Photography; Works Progress Administration**

Further Reading

Bezner, Lili Corbus. *Photography and Politics: From the New Deal to the Cold War*. Baltimore and London: Johns Hopkins University Press, 1999.

Bolton, Richard, ed. *Culture Wars: Documents from the Recent Controversies in the Arts*. New York: New Press, 1992.

Dubin, Steven C. *Arresting Images: Impolitic Art and Uncivil Actions*. London and New York: Routledge, 1992.

Foerstel, Herbert N. *Free Expression and Censorship in America: An Encyclopedia*. Westport, Connecticut and London: Greenwood Press, 1997.

Haacke, Hans. "To All Interested Parties." in *Modern Art in the USA: Issues and Controversies of the Twentieth Century*, edited by Patricia Hills. Upper Saddle River, New Jersey: Prentice Hall, 2001.

Heins, Marjorie. *Sex, Sin, and Blasphemy: A Guide to America's Censorship War*. New York: New Press, 1993.

Hoffman, Barbara, and Robert Storr, eds. "Censorship I" and "Censorship II." *Art Journal* 50, nos. 3 and 4 (1991).

Hull, Mary E. *Censorship in America: A Reference Handbook*. Santa Barbara, Denver, and Oxford: ABC-CLIO, 1999.

Meyer, Richard. *Outlaw Representation: Censorship and Homosexuality in Twentieth-Century American Art*. New York and Oxford: Oxford University Press, 2002.

Roeder, George H, Jr. *The Censored War: American Visual Experience During World War Two*. New Haven and London: Yale University Press, 1993.

Steiner, Wendy. *The Scandal of Pleasure: Art in An Age of Fundamentalism*. Chicago and London: University of Chicago Press, 1995.

Wallis, Brian, Marianne Weems, and Philip Yenawine, eds. *Art Matters: How the Culture Wars Changed America*. New York: New York University Press, 1999.

CENTER FOR CREATIVE PHOTOGRAPHY

The Center for Creative Photography (CCP) in Tucson, Arizona, in the United States is an archive, museum and library dedicated to preserving, exhibiting, and promoting the study of creative photography in its broad diversity. It is a repository for the lifetime records and photographs of more than sixty photographers and photographic institutions. It promotes interest in photography by hosting exhibitions drawn from its collections, by exhibiting the work of contemporary photographers organized by its curatorial staff, and by serving as host to traveling exhibitions organized by other institutions. The CCP maintains and circulates an extensive library of books and other publications by and about photographers in its collections and about the greatly diverse range of photographic activity in the history of photography.

A unit of the University of Arizona Library, the CCP was founded in 1975 by then University President John P. Schaefer and photographer Ansel Adams when Schaefer approached Adams and suggested the University of Arizona as an eventual home for Adams' archive. From that initial idea the CCP has evolved to become a major institution supporting the study of the history of photography by offering both the products of a photographers' career and the archival materials documenting the conditions in which that work was created.

The CCP opened in 1975 under the direction of Harold Jones, founding director of Light Gallery in New York. James Enyeart, director of the Friends of Photography, in Carmel, California, became director of the CCP in 1977 when Jones left to found the photography program at the University of Arizona's department of art. Enyeart directed the CCP for more than ten years, further developing its collections and leading the campaign to provide the Center with a permanent home in a state-of-the-art building on the University campus; he left the CCP in 1989 to become director of the International Museum of Photography and Film, George Eastman House in Rochester, New York. Terence Pitts, who had been librarian and later curator under Jones and Enyeart, served as director of the CCP from 1990 to 2000. In August 2003 Douglas R. Nickel, a graduate of Princeton University and formerly curator of photography at the San Francisco Museum of Modern Art, was appointed director of the CCP.

The CCP became a reality when the five founding archives of Ansel Adams, Wynn Bullock, Harry Callahan, Aaron Siskind and Frederick Sommer were received in Tucson in 1975. When the CCP celebrated its twenty-fifth anniversary in 2000 its Research Center held the lifetime archives of over 50 photographers and many smaller collections. In addition to those already cited, the CCP holds archives or significant manuscript collections from the photographers Edward Weston, Dean Brown, Dorothy Norman, Paul Strand and Garry Winogrand, educators Laura Volkerding and Robert Heinecken, fashion photographers Louise Dahl-Wolfe and Richard Avedon, pictorialists William Mortensen and Adolf Fassbender, photographer, educator and theorist Henry Holmes Smith, photojournalists W. Eugene Smith and Dan Weiner, the critics and historians A. D. Coleman, Beaumont Newhall and Nancy Newhall, archives from such collective photographic undertakings as the Espejo and the Water in the West projects, records from the Limelight and Witkin photographic galleries and from the Society for Photographic Education, and materials from many other sources.

Many of the collections are related, yielding to researchers a more complex view of a photographer's work and life, and the web of relations between them and others, than a single archive may on its own. For example, the Edward Weston archive, which contains a wealth of material from the photographer himself—including correspondence, manuscripts of his daybooks, negatives, memorabilia and other materials—is further complemented by the Center's additional holdings of archival materials from Weston's friends and associates Johan Hagemeyer, Sonya Noskowiak, and numerous other small collections.

Although photograph collections at the CCP are predominantly twentieth century and from the United States, nineteenth century photography and work of an international scope are also represented. The Center holds more than 60,000 exhibition quality prints by more than 2,000 photographers in its print collection. Some photographers at the CCP are represented by the largest public collections of their work held anywhere. In addition to work by photographers whose archives are held at the center, the print collection includes important bodies of work by David Levinthal, William Christenberry, Tseng Kwong Chi, Todd Webb, Josef Breitenbach, Lee Friedlander, Andreas Feininger, Arthur Tress, and Marion Post Wolcott.

Since its founding in 1975 the CCP has presented more than 280 exhibitions, many of them traveling to other institution, including foreign venues in 12 countries. A record of exhibitions between 1975 and 1995 at the Center is detailed in *Exhibiting Photography: Twenty Years at the Center for Creative Photography* (1996).

The CCP has an extensive record of publishing the results of research within its collections in its journal *Center for Creative Photography* (later renamed *The Archive*). Issues of the journal have often been devoted to scholarly essays about particular bodies of work in the CCP collections, have provided extensive illustrations of work not previously published or little known and self-reflexively have addressed the matter of study in archives itself. A series of scholarly bibliographies provide access to publications and writings by and about photographers in the collection; these include *W. Eugene Smith: a Chronological Bibliography, 1934–1980* (1981) and *A. D. Coleman: A Bibliography of His Writings on Photography from 1968 to 1995* (2000). Other publications include monographs such as *Solomon's Temple: The European Building-Crafts Legacy* (1996) by Laura Volkerding, retrospectives such as *Reconstruction: The Art of William Christenberry* (1996), collections of essays, as in *Henry Holmes Smith: Collected Writings 1935–1985* (1986), an appraisal of photography in the twentieth century United States on the occasion of the medium's 150th anniversary in *Decade by Decade: Twentieth-Century American Photography* (1989), and the extensive catalog *Edward Weston: Photographs: From the Collection of the Center for Creative Photography* (1992). *Original Sources: Art and Archives at the Center for Creative Photography* (2002) provides a guide to the collections of the CCP.

Since 1991 the Ansel Adams Research Fellowship has provided scholars with the opportunity to research in the Center's archives, print collections and library. The Adams Fellowship is provided twice annually with the support of Polaroid Corporation. Through the auspices of the Center's education department visitors are provided the opportunity to see collection holdings not on exhibition through the print viewing program.

The CCP's department of rights and reproductions administers the copyright to work by numerous photographers whose archives are held in the Center's collections. These include Lola Alvarez Bravo, Louise Dahl-Wolfe, Adolf Fassbender, John Gutmann, Otto Hagel, Hansel Mieth, Hans Namuth, Dorothy Norman, Mickey Pallas, Peter Stackpole, Laura Volkerding, Edward Weston and Max Yavno.

LEON E. ZIMLICH

See also: **Adams, Ansel; Archives; Callahan, Harry; Museums: United States; Siskind, Aaron; Sommer, Frederick**

Further Reading

Conger, Amy. *Edward Weston: Photographs: From the Collection of the Center for Creative Photography*. Tucson: Center for Creative Photography, University of Arizona, 1992.

Enyeart, James, and Nancy Solomon, eds. *Henry Holmes Smith: Collected Writings 1935–1985*, Tucson: Center for Creative Photography, University of Arizona, 1986.

Enyeart, James, ed. *Decade by Decade: Twentieth-Century American Photography from the Collection of the Center for Creative Photography*. Boston: Bulfinch Press, Little, Brown and Company, 1989.

"Exhibiting Photography: Twenty Years at the Center for Creative Photography." *The Archive*, no. 32 (19 Sommer, Frederick 96).

Johnson, William. *W. Eugene Smith: A Chronological Bibliography, 1934–1980*. Bibliography Series, no. 1, Tucson: Center for Creative Photography, University of Arizona, 1981.

"Labyrinths: Essays on Using Archives." *The Archive*, no. 23 (1986).

Rule, Amy, and Nancy Solomon, eds. *Original Sources: Art and Archives at the Center for Creative Photography*. Tucson: Center for Creative Photography, University of Arizona, 2002.

Solomon, Nancy, ed. *A. D. Coleman: A Bibliography of His Writings on Photography from 1968 to 1995*. Tucson: Center for Creative Photography, University of Arizona, 2000.

Stack, Trudy Wilner. *Reconstruction: The Art of William Christenberry*. Jackson, MS: University Press of Mississippi, Center for Creative Photography, 1996.

Volkerding, Laura. *Solomon's Temple: The European Building-Crafts Legacy*. edited by James Alinder, Tucson: Center for Creative Photography, University of Arizona, 1996.

PHOTOGRAPHY IN CENTRAL AMERICA

This entry addresses twentieth-century photography in the continental countries of Guatemala, Honduras, El Salvador, Costa Rica, Nicaragua, Panama, and the island of Cuba, with additional references to other Caribbean countries. A description of some Central American photographers and their explorations and work in photography follows a brief look at historical references and principal themes to twentieth-century photography in Central America.

Photography arrived in Central America soon after its invention. Pioneer photographers in Central American countries include: O. Salvin (1861) and E. Muybridge (1870) in Costa Rica; J. Washington (1841) and Bennet (1842) in the Dominican Republic; R. Alexander (1852), Charney (1859), and W. Bradley (1859) in El Salvador; W. Helsby (1844), Osbert Salvin (1861) in Guatemala; W. Bradley (1859), O. Salvin (1861) in Honduras; A. Molina (1856), E. Mestre (1858) in Nicaragua; E. Muybridge (1870), Timothy O'Sullivan (1870) in Panama; J. Washington (1840), Antonio Rezzonico (1841), Halsey (1841), R.W. Hoit (1841), J.de J. Quintiliano (1855), Molina (1855), Esteban Mestre (1856), Francisco Serrano (1857), C.M. Suarez Arango (1859), Encarnacion Irastegui (1859), and Francisca Madero (1859) in Cuba.

Professional photographers have been active in Central America throughout the twentieth century, including photographers specializing in studio portraiture, journalists specializing in reportage and documentation, and artists using the medium as expression for its own sake. Photography was also present in rural areas of Central America, many towns and villages having their own studio photographer. Through the end of the century, it was common that itinerate photographers traveled from town to town selling their services, in some cases utilizing ingenious ways to make the craft of photography a mobile business. Some photographers used handmade cameras large enough for tiny trays of chemistry inside. The camera produces a paper negative that is developed then rephotographed for the positive image, a 30-minute process from exposure to damp but finished photograph.

For most of the twentieth century, little information is available on photography in Central America, and drawing broad conclusions from the available information is problematic for several reasons. First, Maria Cristina Orive from Argentina describes part of the problem as a heretofore excessively commercial and colonialist market dominated by large foreign firms such that even in their own countries many do not know what has been achieved, exhibited or published. Secondly, much of the available information is about Latin America in general but not necessarily involving Central American photographers or organizations. The large photo colloquia and their accompanying exhibitions in the 1970s and 1980s, starting with *Primer Coloquio Latinoamericano de Fotografía* held in Mexico City in 1978, united hundreds of photographers from Latin America, but few exhibiting artists were from Central American countries. Thirdly, available information comes from two principal sources, either the work of an indigenous researcher with more intimate knowledge of the subject but perhaps with relatively limited research tools, or the visiting researcher from Europe or the United States working with a variety of resources but through foreign eyes. Fidel Castro once commented that non-Latin American curators have enjoyed the luxury of traveling around from country to country for a first-hand look. Many European and US writers on photography make a critical distinction between art photography and social or political works. This distinction may be too arbitrary to impose on Central American photography. Finally, authors on Central American photography describe a plethora of perspectives that fail to blend into one coherent regional identity. Robert Levine in *Windows on Latin American* writes that "the rise of photographic reportage to document social injustice in Europe and the US in the 1880s did not happen in Latin America," whereas Cuban author and photographer Maria Eugenia Haya (Marucha) describes early Latin American work that does demonstrate photography as a tool for social witness.

Even if the literature were more complete, defining a single Central American photographic identity would be a dubious undertaking. For one thing, there is a diversity of cultures and histories in the region. Some countries have relatively small indigenous populations, like Costa Rica; in others the majority is indigenous, like Guatemala. Despite the relative geographical proximity, certain activities and movements are contained and not dispersed in the region. Moreover, some examples of photography from Central America reflect universal, not regional, aspects of photography. In his introduction to the exhibition catalogue *Images of Silence*, João Clemente Baena Soares describes Latin American photography: "The fusion of elements of fantasy and reality has produced a tangible, at times magical, presence in the printed image that the artist-photographer presents to the onlooker." The sentence is both direct and poetic, but it describes photography from around the world. Author and curator Belgica Rodriguez writes, "In Latin America, no one aesthetic or stylistic line predominates."

Many writers are emphatic about the myth of a single homogenous Latin American identity. Relative scarcity of information results in limited conclusions that may reflect research more than reality. Yet there are many commonalties among these neighboring countries, such as historical links to European colonialism; political, social, and economic influences from the United States; the predominance of Spanish as an official language; or the struggles for political stability and independence. Some authors cite the presence of political and social themes as specific to Central American twentieth-century photography, although these themes are also richly explored in other parts of the world. Other authors refer to specific aesthetics, such as high contrast, but again these aesthetics are also found elsewhere in much photography.

Much of the current literature has exposed the mythical interpretations of Latin American photography, a myth summarized by Jorge Gutierrez as "a continent laden with exoticism...between misery, the machete and the gun, filled with lovely but dangerous romanticism." This new awareness follows several events. Although some factors held photographic exploration back in the region (including unstable political regimes, sporadic economic performances, and cultural attitudes about photography's role in society), by the 1990s, situations had progressed to the point that ideas and modes in Central American photography were similar to those in Europe or the United States. The available information makes it clear that the quality and intensity of exploration in photography in Central America keeps pace with other regions of the world. In 1981, El Consejo Mexicana de Fotografia published *Libros Fotograficos de Autores Latinoamericanos,* listing over two thousand titles of photography books by Latin American authors since 1961.

By the end of the century, this exploration was not contained to the world of photojournalism or social and political documentation. A gradual decline over the twentieth century in labor and art agency sponsorship of documentary photography lessened the presence of such photojournalism. The art world sometimes exhibited work previously destined for the media and did so through the end of the century, but with a concurrent increase in art photography.

In the last decades of the twentieth century, more unified photography projects took root, providing context and structure for a look at photography in the region. In Mexico City in 1977, Pedro Meyer guided the Consejo Mexicano de Fotografia, undertaking numerous exhibitions and publications, receiving financial support from the Instituto Nacional de Belles Artes (National Institute of Fine Arts). This activity led to the first of three colloquia on Latin American photography. *Primer Coloquio Latinoamericano de Fotgrafia* held in Mexico City in 1978, which produced a traveling exhibition titled *Hecho en Latinoamérica*. The colloquia each consisted of three days of presentations by guest speakers, various workshops, and a coordinated program of exhibitions with the *Hecho en Latinoamerica* exhibition as its centerpiece. Participation was principally from convocation with little additional curatorial work. The conference inspired representatives from many Latin American countries, including the Central American countries of Costa Rica, Cuba, Guatemala, Honduras, Panama, and Puerto Rico, to found the short-lived Latin American Council of Photography.

The second colloquium, in 1981, was also in Mexico City. In a presentation at this colloquium, U.S. critic Max Kozloff described a "distinctive aura" to Latin American work, both from subject matter and aesthetics. Giuliana Scime from Italy heatedly pointed out that all such criteria could be equally applied to European photography. The program for these colloquia states the following about how photography might contribute to changes in Latin America: "By producing a photograph whose most beautiful incarnation is fulfilled by faithfully showing the face of a mestizo continent that is willing to attain justice for everyone—this being the supreme creative feat."

The *Coloquio Latinoamericano de Fotografia*, the third Hecho en Latinoamerica colloquium and exhibition, was held in 1984 in Havana, Cuba. In addition to the presentations and exhibitions similar to the previous colloquia, Hecho III sponsored a Latin American and Caribbean photography competition at Cuba's Casa de las Americas. La Casa de las Americas has sponsored various cultural activities since its inception in 1959, but, at Pedro Meyer's suggestion, 1984 was the first year photography was included in their activities. Awards were given to Cuban photographers Raul Corrales, Mario Garcia Joya, Rogelio Lopez Marin, and Rigoberto Romero, as well as Puerto Rican photographer Hector Mendez Caratina and Pedro Valtierra from Mexico. The Third Latin American Photography Colloquium was attended by over 400 participants from Latin America, the United States, and Europe. The Cuban dictator Fidel Castro made a surprise visit and presentation during the day's events.

The Hecho colloquia received some criticism for their structure and agenda. Argentinean photographer and publisher Sara Facio criticized the colloquia's "exclusively leftist orientation," especially for the restrictive criteria for the photo competition that required work to reflect the "contemporary reality" in the region. This process selected works that may or may not represent photography overall. Some photographers choose not to even submit. Furthermore, residents of countries under the most restrictive dictatorships were not able to submit at all. In an effort to bring to the forefront of the world's attention the photographic activity of the region, these colloquia proposed a basically socialistic, humanistic mode of photography, despite the fact that many regional photographers chose not to work this way. In promoting such work, the colloquia continued to support the deeply entrenched notion that documentary photography is the natural expression for third-world countries.

The *Hecho en Latinoamerica* colloquia, however, also received praise for some of their accomplishments. They provided a new structure for Latin American photographers to communicate. Prior to these events, many regional photographers had no structure to enable them to be in touch with or even aware of each other's work. Also, the events united sufficient examples of quality work to end the misconception that photography in Latin America is in any way backward or limited. By the third colloquium, there seemed to be a more concentrated effort on the technical and aesthetic preparation of the photographs themselves and their presentation. Finally, these colloquia helped solidify a desire for additional primary research on Latin American photography. American photography and professor at the University of Illinois, Chicago, Esther Parada writes of the potential danger to hoping for social change via stereotyped images of protest, but describes nonetheless a significant public impact of the *Hecho* exhibitions and publications. Despite these criticisms and the fact that most Latin American participants did not come from Central American countries, these colloquia significantly raised regional and global awareness and curiosity about the area, spurring further research and activities both in Latin American countries and around the world.

The Zurich exhibition of *Fotografia Lateinamerika von 1860 bis huete* at the Zurich Kunsthaus in 1981 was curated by non-Latin American researchers. This work traveled widely in Europe with a catalogue in German, eventually translated into Spanish. This was the first comprehensive exhibition of Latin American photography, the result of extensive curatorial work. Similar to the Hecho en Latinoamerica colloquia, most photographers in this exhibition and book are not from Central American countries.

Images of Silence was an exhibition that originated in the United States with more than 60 photographers, each represented by two photographs, from all countries of the hemisphere, showing works that demonstrate both the technical and aesthetic vitality of photography. Photographers in this project were selected by a team of curators from Latin American countries, including the following from Central American countries: Jerry Craig (Jamaica), Alexandra Cummins (Barbados), Magdalena Granadino de Lima (El Salvador), Rosario Murillo (Nicaragua), Jose Antonio Perez Ruiz (Puerto Rico), Marianne Tolentino (Dominican Republic), and Virginia Vargas (Costa Rica). The photographs examine recent paths photography has taken in the region, leaning on artistic endeavors more than social or political documentation. After exhibition in Washington, DC at the Museum of Modern Art of Latin America, part of the Organization of American States, the work traveled to New York and Puerto Rico.

Originally a series of exhibitions for Fotofest 1992 in Houston, Texas, *Images and Memory* became a traveling show with Independent Curators Inc and finally a book in 1998. *Images and Memory* looks at Latin American photography via three criteria: artistic merit, associations with important directions in the history of photographic art in the region, and intentional connection to important aspects of regional history and culture. The book contains material on several Central American photographers, with lucid texts about Latin American photography through the century. The authors are very frank about the lack of information available for some countries, or for the entire region between 1950 and 1980. Nonetheless, the presentation makes a bold argument for the dynamic photographic activity in the region.

As well as several major exhibitions, the end of the decade saw the rise of several cultural institutions devoted to Latin American art. The aforementioned Museum of Modern Art of Latin America exhibits as well as publishes on diverse subjects including photography from Central America. In Paris, La Maison de l'Amerique Latine is a cultural center that hosts conferences, exhibitions, workshops, and it also publishes materials on diverse aspects of Latin American life, politics, and culture.

The following descriptions of Central American photographers, organized by country, is far from complete. It provides a springboard for individual analysis and reflection on twentieth-century photography in Central America.

Cuba has a rich history of photography, especially well documented following the 1959 revolution, and in art photography in the 1980s and 90s. Photographers such as Augutin Victor Casasola and his work on the Mexican Revolution established the tradition of epic photography early in the century in Latin America, and this tradition was richly exploited in the Cuban context. Photography became an international tool for political messages, and the bearded face of Castro became an international icon. The Cuban national sense of identity developed within Cuba's political stance and position in the world, particularly vis-à-vis the U.S. policy of isolation. Many photographers documented the revolutionary aspects of the day, such as Alberto Korda, whose photograph of Ernesto Che Guevara converted that revolutionary figure into an international icon. Photography was appropriated for revolutionary importance, though some photographers produced slightly different bodies of work, such as Tito Alvarez or Mario Garcia Joya. Twentieth-century Cuban photographers include Alberto Diaz Gutierrez (Korda). Born in Havana in 1928, Korda has lived and worked with photography in Havana since 1956. In 1959, he was named Fidel Castro's official photographer, and his *Guerrillero Heroica* is a major publication in the history of photography. Cuban photographer Mario Del Rosario (Mayito), born in 1938, worked as an artist with various agencies and exhibited as well as curated exhibitions in Cuba, Europe, and America. Another Cuban photographer, Ramon Grandal, born in 1950 in Havana, has been a professional photographer since 1970, exhibiting internationally and working for the journal *Revolucion y Cultura*. M. Eugenia Haya Jimenez (Marucha), born in Havana in 1944, participated as a photographer and a writer in many exhibitions and publications, especially in the last 15 years of the century. Marucha was widely published internationally, including *La Fotografia Cubana en el Siglo XIX* (Cuban Photography in the XIX Century). Marucha died in Havana in 1991. Finally, Cuban photographer Gilda Perez, born in 1954 in Havana, exhibited widely and worked for the review *Revolucion*.

Guatemala also has a rich history of photography, though less a part of the international political scene than Cuba. The Japanese photographer Juan Jose de Jesus Yas (1844–1917) operated a formal portrait studio producing numerous portraits of priests. In the 1880s, Yas traveled in Central America, eventually studied with two Guatemalan photographers, and set up his own photo studio in Guatemala City in 1890 before moving to Antigua.

Jose Domingo Noriega, born in 1885 in Guatemala, lived and worked with Yas, exhibiting his work. Photographs and information about both Yas and Noriega appear in a publication called *La Antigua Guatemala, J.J. Yas y J. D. Noriega* (La Azotea). Maria Cristina Orive, born 1931 in Antigua, studied in the United States and Paris, where she lived for 15 years. In 1973, Orive moved to Buenos Aires and with Sara Facio founded La Azotea, an editorial foundation for Latin American photography. Diego Molina, born in Guatemala in 1949, authored numerous books and articles, and traveled and exhibited in India, Norway, China, El Salvador, Japan, and Uruguay. Molina was also a photography professor. Born in Guatemala, Ricardo Mata, studied and trained in the United States and exhibited his photography, which received many awards. Daniel Hernandez, born in Guatemala, worked in the last decades of the century, both as a photojournalist for Associated Press International and as a fine art photographer.

Guatemalan photographer Luis Gonzalez Palma, born in 1957, lived and worked in Guatemala, Paris, and Argentina. Palma's art photography, including three-dimensional works incorporating photography and other media, was widely exhibited and published. One of the most exhibited of Central American artists, his works express tragic legacies of the impact of colonialism on indigenous peoples and their cultures. By abandoning all pretense of documentation and ignoring demands for authenticity, he explores deeper levels of political messages through artistic manipulation. His tearing, taping, and nailing of some of his imagery emphasize the fact that these images are not representations of the world but are objects in the world. Palma's work was exhibited at the Art Institute of Chicago, the Havana biannual, the Museo de Belles Artes, Mexico City, and the Museum of Contemporary Hispanic Art New York City.

In Honduras, Max Hernandez, was born in Tegucigalpa in 1958, and studied in Central America and Europe. Hernandez exhibited internationally and worked as a photojournalist in Honduras.

Nicaraguan Claudia Gordillo, born 1954 in Managua, studied photography in Rome, exhibited internationally, and worked for the newspaper *Barricada*. Gordillo published the book *Nicaragua; una decada de revolucion* (1991). Leonardo Barreto, Director of the National Center for Photography in Managua, studied photography in Nicaragua, Europe, and the United States. Barreto worked for the press *Barricada* and *La Prensa*. Rossana, Lacayo, born in Managua in 1958, studied in Nicaragua and the United States, and worked as a photographer for the Minister of Culture. Since 1980, Lacayo directed 15 documentaries with the Nicaraguan Institute of Film, and she exhibited internationally, including at the Museum of Modern Art, New York, and was awarded the1984 National prize for Photography in Nicaragua.

In Panama, Sandra Eleta, born in Panama City in 1942, worked freelance and exhibited widely, after studying photography in the United States. Eleta published *Portobelo* in 1982.

In El Salvador, examples of photographic activity range from the political arena to the world of fine art. During the 1980–92 civil war, photographs by members of popular organizations, labor movements, combatants, artists, journalists—mostly Salvadorian—were collected into an archive, using documentary photography to chronicle a political moment. The creators of this work were participants in the events. The growing archive of images, titled *In the Eye of the Beholder*, was kept mobile for safety, names of photographers often omitted for privacy. At the end of war in 1992, the archive contained 80,000 negatives. American Katy Lyle worked for years with Salvadorans to organize and protect this archive and to house this work, establishing the Museo de la Palabra y la Imagen/Museum of the Word and the Image in San Salvador. Other examples of photography in El Salvador come from the art world. Maria Teresa Diaz Colocho, born in San Salvador in 1960, studied photography in the United States and exhibited widely. Muriel Hasbun, born in 1961, studied photography in the United States. Hasbun's work was exhibited internationally, and she taught photography in Washington, DC at the Corcoran College of Art and Design. Hasbun, whose parents were involved in photography and the arts, grew up in El Salvador confronting an eclectic personal heritage and a violent national agenda. Her photography draws from intense elements of her personal and political environment. These photographs do not simply document her identity: they shape it.

In the Dominican Republic, Wilfredo Garcia, born in 1935, first studied photography in Puerto Rico. Garcia's work was widely exhibited and received many awards. He was a professor of photography and founder of such groups as Jueves 68 and Fotogrupo. Domingo Batista, born in Santiago de los Caballeros in 1946, began his art career in 1969 with the group Jueves 68. Batista received many national and international awards, including first place in photography at the XV Biennial of Fine Arts in the Dominican Republic in 1981. He was also widely published, and he co-authored *Ten Years of Dominican Photography*, published in 1978. Mariano Hernandez, born in Jimani in 1954, studied photography in 1978 at the UASD of Santo Domingo, was a founding member of Fotogrupo, and exhibited throughout Central America.

Costa Rican Victoria Cabezas Green, born in San Jose in 1950, studied photography in the United States at the Pratt Institute in New York. Green exhibited and taught in Costa Rica. After studying photography, Giorgio Timm, born in Esparza Costa Rica in 1947, worked and exhibited his photography in Costa Rica and abroad.

In Barbados, Ronnie Carrington, born in Barbados in 1949, trained in New York was active as a photographer and in video and television production in Barbados and other Caribbean countries. Tony Lynch, born in Barbados in 1946, studied in the Caribbean and New York and was a freelance photojournalist who was also very active with photo clubs.

In Puerto Rico, Frieda, Medin Ojeda, born in San Juan in 1949, was educated in the United States and Puerto Rico. Ojeda worked as a freelance photographer and was widely published and internationally exhibited. She also worked in filmmaking and installations. Finally, Victor Vazquez, born in San Juan, studied sociology and psychology, and worked internationally as a self-employed photographer.

In Jamaica, Owen Minott, born in Jamaica in 1925, was influenced by Amador Packer. Minott received many awards and exhibited in Jamaica. At the end of the century, Cecil Norman Ward, born in Jamaica in1984, studied in Canada, traveled and worked in Kenya, then freelanced with art, photography, and architecture in Jamaica.

Though far from complete, this list illustrates the dynamic and eclectic complexities concerning twentieth-century photography in Central America. Many photographers are working within the worlds of both journalism and art, or by combing art photography and art education. By the late 1990s, the increasing popularity of web galleries provided some Central American photographers with opportunities to showcase their work without the more expensive and cumbersome channels of traditional exhibition or publication activity. Perdo Meyer presents the work of international and many Central American photographers on the web site *Zonezero*.

In 2001, a meeting of the Popular Culture Association and the 5th Congress of the Americas in Mexico City solicited presentations on photography in Mexico, Latin and Central America, and the Caribbean, citing photography as one of the most primary of common denominators between cultures worldwide, noting that much of the intense national and cultural struggles for identity in twentieth-century Central America have been recorded on film.

Bruce McKaig

See also: **Archives; Documentary Photography; Kozloff, Max; Photography in Latin America: An Overview; Photography in Mexico; Portraiture; Propaganda; Socialist Photography**

Further Reading

Billeter, Erika. *Fotografia Lateinamerika—1860 bis huete*. Zurich: Kunsthaus Zurich, 1981. (Fotografia latinoamericana, desde 1860 hasta nuestros dias. Madrid: El Viso, 1981).

Billeter, Erika. *Canto a la realidad: Fotografia Latinoamericana 1860–1993*. Madrid, Casa de America: Lunwerg Editores, SA, 1993.

Cagan, Steve. "Made in Latin America." *Afterimage* vol. 15 no. 1 (1987).

Gutierrez, Ramon. *Bibliografia sobre Historia de la fotografia en la America Latina*. Rio de Janeiro: FUNARTE, 1997.

Levine, Robert M. Ed., *Windows on Latin America*. Coral Gables Florida: North-South Center, University of Miami, 1987.

Museum of Modern Art in Latin America,. OAS, *Images of Silence: Photography from Latin America and the Caribbean in the 80s*. Washington DC: OAS, 1989.

Parada, Esther. "Notes on Latin American Photography." *Afterimage* vol. 9 nos. 1 & 2 (summer 1981).

Polo, Miguel Angel Yanez. *Fotografia Latinoamericana: Tendencias Actuales*. La Rabida (Huelva) 1991.

Ramney, Edward. "Recent Latin American Photography Books." *Latin American Research Review*, vol. 26 no. 3 (1991).

Rosenblum Naomi. "Changes Below the Border." *Afterimage*, vol. 15 no. 1 (summer 1987).

Rosenblum, Naomi. *A World History of Photography*. New York: Abbeville Press, 1997.

Watriss, Wendy, and Lois Parkinson Zamora, eds. *Image and Memory: Photography from Latin America, 1866–1994*. Austin: University of Texas Press, 1998.

www.zonezero.com. Zonezero from analog to digital photography.

www.lib.usc.edu/retter/pelatam1.html. History of Latin American Photography homepage.

www.mal217.org/. La Maison de l'Amerique Latine Paris. France homepage.

CENTRE NATIONALE DE LA PHOTOGRAPHIE

The Centre national de la photographie (CNP) in Paris, France, is a cultural institution subsidized by the Ministry of Culture and Communication (Délégation aux Arts Plastiques). The mission of the CNP is the promotion of contemporary photography and the support of young talent through in-house and off-site exhibitions, the publication of catalogues and a journal, educational and cultural activities, and the co-production of video works.

The CNP was created in 1982 at the initiative of the Minister of Culture. The first CNP exhibition entitled Moins Trente, Under Thirty, established a link with young artists and has since become a biannual event. Until 1984, the CNP sponsored exhibitions at various sites in Paris. Beginning in 1984 to 1993, the CNP organized 180 exhibitions, which were held at the Palais de Tokyo museum in Paris. The Palais de Tokyo, the largest exhibition space in the world devoted on a permanent basis to photography, was previously housed in the Museum of Modern Art. Since 1993, the CNP has held its exhibitions at the Hotel Salomon Rothschild, in the 8th arrondissment, the same address serving for administrative offices and other cultural activities. Additional exhibitions are regularly organized to travel throughout France and abroad, from Italy to China and other countries. Exhibitions have been organized around themes, such as "Botanica," "Images Indiennes," "La Tour Eiffel," or retrospectives of the work of notable photographers such as Eugène Atget, Robert Capa or introducing the photographic works by those not primarily known as photographers, such as the writer Lewis Carroll (Charles Dodgson). Yet many exhibitions introduce new artists: in the late 1990s solo exhibitions mounted by CNP included the Germans Anna and Bernhard Blume, the French Sophie Calle and Pascal Convert, Russian Boris Mikhailov, Australian Tracey Moffatt, and the Japanese Ryuji Miyamoto and Mariko Mori.

As well as exhibitions, the CNP successfully launched a publication called "Photo Poche," or pocket book. These hand-size and inexpensive publications provide affordable and diverse access to works by various photographers or themes in photography. The first two publications were on the nineteenth century figure Nadar and Henri Cartier-Bresson. Subsequent publications have addressed Jacques-Henri Lartigue and the American Farm Securities Administration photography project. Eighty-five different titles had been published by 1999 and the book is now also published in Great Britain and the United States.

The CNP has also been active in audiovisual productions, providing an additional and highly unique link between work in photography and the general public. These audiovisual products exist in several formats. The CNP and Garance coproduced 170 mini films directed by Agnes Varda called *One Minute for One Image*. Each film is commentary on a particular photograph and they were distributed via television. The photographer William Klein suggested an audiovisual product on photographers analyzing their own work by means of their contact sheets or work prints. This series is called *Contacts* and includes thirteen-minute productions on photographers such as Robert Doisneau, Don McCullin, Elliott Erwitt, Raymond Depardon and Klein himself. Since 1997, the series has branched out thematically to look at photographers' work in ways other than through contact sheets. These films are available on videocassettes or DVDs.

Since 1983, the biannual Moins Trente is a source of funds and recognition for young artists. Since 1989, the CNP also sponsors the richly endowed Grand Prix International Henri-Cartier Bresson (HCB Award) for creation at a higher level.

Robert Delpire was the first director of the CNP, serving from 1982 until the autumn of 1986. Since 1986, Regis Durand has been director. Laurence Brun, working under both directors, has been responsible for meeting with artists and providing other cultural services such as guided tours or educational activities. In 1996, the CNP's mission was redefined by the Delegation of Plastic Arts under the Minister of Culture to specialize in the support of young artists in the exploration of works clustering around photography, thus including video, digital, and installations as well as conceptual photography.

Durand has an academic background in the arts and experience as an art critic. He has published several books, including *Habiter l'image – essais sur la photogrpahie 1990–1994* and *Le Temps de l'image – essais sur les conditions d'une histoire des formes photographiques 1995*. Before assuming the directorship of the CNP, Durand worked under the Minister of Culture and handled artistic direction for the Printemps du Cahors, an annual contemporary art and photography event in France since 1990 with dozens of international participants and over 100,000 visitors each year. As director of the CNP, Durand curated the exhibitions *Biannual of the Image*, *Paris 98* and *Chronicles from outside and other hypothesis*, presented at the Recontres internationales de la Photographie at Arles in the summer of 2000.

Durand describes his vision for the CNP as follows:

> It seems necessary more than ever that artists have access to other tools of production and post-production, more flexible and less burdensome tools. This is the role of art centers and this is how the CNP functions, in a specific field of activity, namely that of the contemporary image, looking at explorations where photography, video, digital and cinemagraphic works coexist. The CNP accepts as its mission the challenge of accompanying and exhibiting the work of artists exploring image in a vast sense of the word image. Photography is neither art nor non-art. Approached in certain ways, photography can reveal information, journalism, documentation. Approached in other ways, photography desperately seeks to be identified with other arts. Photography becomes true creation only when it plays with certain particular photographic qualities, qualities applied to a specific project, notably in its aptitude to produce an image transformed and reflected from the real and at the same time, inventing new forms. This is why photography persists as a remarkable tool for creation, inseparable today from the mobile world of other forms of images.

Bruce McKaig

See also: **Atget, Eugène; Calle, Sophie; Capa, Robert; Cartier-Bresson, Henri; Doisneau, Robert; Erwitt, Elliott; Farm Securities Administration; Klein, William; Lartigue, Jacques-Henri; Mikhailov, Boris**

Further Reading

Le Centre National de la Photographie homepage. *www.cnp-photographie.com/*.

Centre National de la Photographie, 1981–1991 *Vous avez dit culture?...*(1981–1991 Did you say culture?...), Paris: CNP 1992.

Durand, Regis. Habiter l'image – essais sur la photogrpahie 1990–1994. *Paris: Marval, 1994.*

Durand, Regis. *Le Temps de l'image – essais sur les conditions d'une histoire des formes photographiques 1995.*

Larousse/CNRS Editions, *Dictionaire des politiques culturelles de la france depuis 1959*, Paris: Larousse, 2001.

MARTÍN CHAMBI

Peruvian

Few Latin American photographers are more recognized for their technique and artistry than the Peruvian Martín Chambi. In his work, Peruvian society and Inca culture of the first half of the twentieth century still live. As Eugène Atget is to Paris and its streets, so is Chambi to Cuzco and its Inca haunts.

Chambi was born in Coaza in 1891 in an Andean village in southern Peru, near Lake Titicaca. Of Indian descent and raised in poverty, as a boy he joined his father in working for the British Santo Domingo Mining Company. Young Martín attached himself to the company's photographer-surveyor. Fascinated by the man's equipment, the boy bore it for him over the wide and hilly terrain of the mining company's interests. At an early age, therefore, Chambi became familiar with the basic operations of a camera, its placement, angles, and views, and the photos that emerged from it after the magic intermingling in darkness of plates and chemicals.

Some time in his late teens, around 1908, he went to live in Arequipa, possibly to pursue secondary education; but he also became the apprentice of the noted photographer, Max T. Vargas. Remaining with him for almost a decade, Chambi became progressively more skilled in photography. Belonging to a prominent family, Vargas was a noted photographer of Arequipa society, skilled at producing flattering images of his social peers. He was also a good teacher, and Chambi rose to become virtually his partner. Chambi attempted, unsuccessfully, to establish a branch of the Vargas studio in La Paz, Bolivia.

Marrying in 1917, Chambi struck out on his own that same year to establish a studio in Sicuani. In 1920, he moved to Cuzco, briefly setting up with another former apprentice of Vargas. Eventually, he established his own studio, settling on Calle Marqués, a location that soon became the most noted photographer's establishment in the city.

Like Vargas, he cultivated and appealed to an upper-middle-class clientele. However, as someone of Indian descent, he was totally alien to their society. He viewed his clientele sympathetically yet with the insight of an outsider. His individual and group portraits along with his pictures of weddings, parties, and social gatherings have come to bear rich testimony to the world of Cuzco elites in the early twentieth century.

In the best of this work, he captures the dignity and integrity of individuals as reflected in the features of their faces, the cast of their eyes, the posture of their bodies, and the character of their surroundings. For example, he captured the serene innocence and assurance of a socialite bride on the grand stairway of the family mansion. The white train of her gown flows luxuriously down the steps while above her rise richly carved banisters mounting to a mezzanine arched by a canopy of stained-glass roof. Nevertheless, in another portrait, in which he so carefully captured the flamboyance of a fashionably dressed belle, one wonders if he could not also have been quietly yet suitably ambiguously amused at the extravagance of his "newly rich" clients.

Chambi's artistic legacy lies even more so in the work he developed out of doors, with haunting, memorable views of Cuzco, Indian culture, and the Andes mountains. Two factors supported Chambi in his ability to capture the value and dignity of this environment. He was buoyed by the professional respect he had achieved in his society. In addition, he had come to live in a city that was at the center of a revival of indigenous Peruvian pride.

In 1924, the Peruvian political leader, Víctor Raúl Haya de la Torre, living in exile in Mexico City under the protection of the Mexican Revolution, founded the *Alianza Popular Revolucionaria Americana* (APRA—American Revolutionary Popular Alliance). This party believed that the Indian races and the mystical force of their history would be the basis for developing Latin America, which it referred to as Indo America. In 1931, Haya de la Torre returned to Peru, finally able to bring his Aprista doctrine to his native land. In the early thirties, this movement, especially in Cuzco, had cultural, social, and political recuperations still vibrant today in Peru.

Although politically indifferent, Chambi acquired growing respect for his own native roots; he was increasingly absorbed into and articulated the movement that promoted appreciation of indigenous culture. He was an active member of groups in Cuzco that brought together journalists, teachers, literary figures, artists, and other photographers. Gathering in homes, cafes, or taverns, they extolled the value of native culture.

Imbued with a sense of his professional worth and cultural identity, Chambi became an exceptionally effective photographer. He photographed Cuzco with meditative reflections on the aged, subdued dignity of the city's ancient structures. With ineffable sympathy and touching respect, he memorialized itinerant Indian musicians, jovial vendors, and hollow-cheeked street urchins. Among the first to photograph the newly rediscovered (1911) ruins of Machu Picchu, he captured the tenacious ingenuity of its structures nestled in the breathtaking sweep and evanescent mists of the Andes.

Much still needs to be studied regarding the technical achievements and aesthetic components of Chambi's genius. He seems primarily to have used German or English cameras and supplies. Little as yet, though, has been written regarding his photographing habits or developing techniques. How he achieved the singular chiaroscuro (modeling of volume by depicting light and shade by contrasting them boldly) effects that give such nuance, subtlety, depth, and richness to his pictures has not been closely analyzed. A project to catalogue and preserve the tens of thousands of glass plate negatives began in the late seventies under a team headed by Edward Ranney in conjunction with Víctor and Julia Chambi, two of the photographer's children, supported by the Earthwatch Foundation of Belmont, Massachusetts.

The most productive years of Chambi's career spanned nearly a quarter century, from the mid-twenties to the fifties. The earthquake of 1950 that devastated so much of Cuzco and its society also ruptured his career, and his life was increasingly unsettled with age and illness. Although respected in the latter years of his life, it was primarily in Peru where he received recognition. It has been in the years since his death in 1973 that his reputation has reached its international renown. Much as Machu Pichu, its photographer too has come to receive the attentive curiosity and respect of the world.

EDWARD A. RIEDINGER

Biography

Born in Coaza, Peru, November 5, 1891. Worked for Santo Domingo Mining Co. and is camera-bearer for English photographer, 1900–190?. Moved to Arequipa, becoming apprentice and then assistant to photographer, Max T. Vargas (father of Alberto Vargas, creator in the United States of the glamour photographs, *Vargas Girls*), 1908–1917. Married Manuela López Viza, 1917; two sons, four daughters. Moved family to Sicuani, opening own studio, 1917. Moved to Cuzco, 1920, which became permanent residence. Opened third studio in Cuzco, on Calle Marqués, which became his permanent one, 1925. Eldest son, Víctor, became his assistant, 1933. Photographs published in *Cuzco histórico* ("Historical Cuzco") by Rafael Larco Hoyle, 1934. Supported founding of the Instituto Americano de Arte (American Institute of Art), in Cuzco, 1937. Survived earthquake of 1950, extensively photographing it. Declining health and photographic work in following years. Named patron of the first national Peruvian publicity campaign for the promotion of professional photographers, 1971. Died in Cuzco, September 13, 1973.

Individual Exhibitions

1927 Bolivia Grand Hotel, Lima, Peru
1936 Traveling exhibition, Santiago, Viña del Mar, Puerto Montt, Osorno, Chile

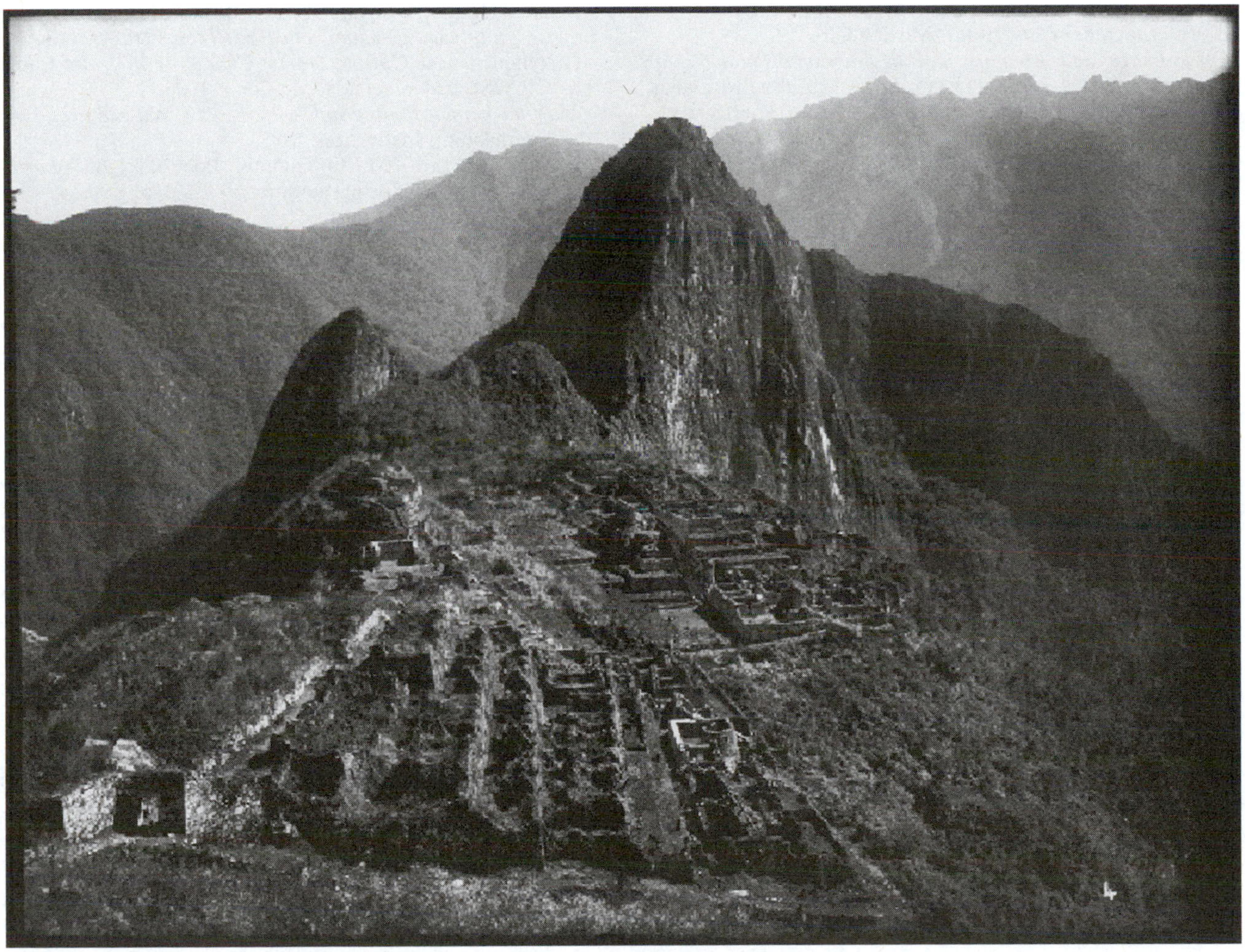

Martín Chambi, Ciudadela de Machu Picchu, Cusco 1925, placa de vidrio, 13 × 18 cm.
[*Courtesy of Julia Chambi López y Teo Allain Chambi, Archivo Fotográfico Martín Chambi, Cusco, Perú*]

1958 Fiftieth Anniversary as a Photographer, Cuzco, Peru
1966 *Cuzco, Yesterday and Today*; Capilla de San Juan de Dios, Cuzco, Peru
1969 *Photographs of Peru*; Instituto Peruano de Cultura Hispánica, Lima, Peru
1979 University of New Mexico Art Museum, Albuquerque; Museum of Modern Art, New York and traveling
1990 Fine Arts Circle, Madrid, Spain
1991 *Centenary of the Birth of Martín Chambi*; Museo de la Nacion, Lima and traveling
1992 *Peruvian Photography, 1900–1930*; FotoFest, Houston, Texas
1993 Centre national de la photographie, Paris, France

Group Exhibitions

1921 Agricultural and Industrial Exhibition, Arequipa
1934 Fourth Centenary of Cuzco, Cuzco, Perus
1981–82 *Latin American Photography, 1860 to the Present*; Kunsthaus, Zürich, Switzerland, and traveling to Madrid, Spain, and Rotterdam, The Netherlands
1984 Third Colloquium of Latin American Photography, Museo Nacional de Bellas Artes, Havana, Cuba
1992 *Two Great Figures of Latin American Photography: Martín Chambi and Sebastião Salgado*; XIX Festival Internacional Cervantino, Mexico City
1994 *Image and Memory, Latin American Photography*; Akron Art Museum, Akron, Ohio, traveling to Dallas, Texas; Sacramento, California; Ponce, Puerto Rico; Miami, Scranton, New Jersey, and New York
1994 *Visions of Modernity*; The Americas Society, New York

Selected Works

Dos Gigantes Cuzqueños, 1917
Ciudadela de Macchu Pichu, 1925
Danzarin de la Diablada, Puno, 1925
Calle Mantas, esquina Plaza de Armas, Cuzco, 1927
Self Portrait (Studio), Cuzco, 1928
Fiesta familiar, Cuzco, 1930
Campesino y nevado Qoyllor Riti, Cuzco, 1934
Merienda de campesinos y nevado Ausangate, Ocongate, Cuzco, 1934

Further Reading

Camp, Roderic. "Martín Chambi: Photographer of the Andes." *Latin American Research Review* 13:2 (1978): 223–228.
———. "Martín Chambi: Pioneer Photographer of Peru." *Américas* 30:3 (March 1978): 5–10.
Castro Ramírez, Fernando. *Martín Chambi, de Coaza al MOMA*. Lima: Centro de Estúdios de Investigación de Fotografía, 1989.
Harris, Andy, and Paul Yale. *Martín Chambi y los herederos de los Incas*. Berwick Universal Pictures, 1986, 16 mm, 50 minutes.
Heredia, Jorge. "Martín Chambi: Breve Revisión Histórica," *http:www.geocities.com/Paris/Lights/8039/rev1.htm.*
Huayhuaca, José Carlos. *Martín Chambi, Fotógrafo*. Lima: CICOSUL, Universidad de Lima, 1993.
Martín Chambi, Photographs, 1920–1950. Washington, DC: Smithsonian Institution, 1993.
Ranney, Edward. "Martín Chambi: Poet of Light." *Earthwatch News* 1 (Spring-Summer 1979): 3–6.

CHARGESHEIMER

German

Chargesheimer (Hargesheimer, Karl-Heinz) is one of Germany's most important photographers of the post-World War II period.Through his advertising photography, portraiture, photo-essay books, and experimental photography, he created a far-ranging and important body of work at mid-century. He was a multi-talented artist who throughout his life expressed himself as a graphic designer, a set designer, theater director, and a sculptor, but for whom photography was both a means of documentation and a favorite artistic medium.

Chargesheimer was born Karl-Heinz Hargesheimer on May 19, 1924, in Cologne, Germany. From 1942–1944 he studied photography, sculpture, and graphic design at the Werkkunstschule in Cologne and later at the Bayerische Staatslehranstalt fuer Lichtbildwesen. Only after 1948 did he adopt "Chargesheimer" as his artist's name. In 1949 he began a beneficial, lifetime association with Cologne collector L. Fritz Gruber who invited him to exhibit in the first *Photo-Kino* exhibition as well as every second year thereafter. He taught photography at the Bikla School for Photography and Film in Dusseldorf, Germany, from 1950–1955, and afterward began his work as a commercial photographer and photojournalist.

Chargesheimer's early photography shows the influence of *Art Informel*, a movement that focuses on abstraction and spontaneity and is aligned with the international movement known as Subjective Photography, which stressed the personal interpretation of otherwise 'realistic' imagery to create subjective works of art. Along with photographers such as Arno Jansen and Edmund Kesting, Chargesheimer exhibited in the 1951 and 1954 *Subjektive Photographie* exhibitions organized by Otto Steinert in Saarbrücken, Germany. Chargesheimer's use of the *Subjektive* aesthetic, or utterly realistic beauty, can be seen in his experimental, abstract work, such as *Play* of 1950 and in his advertising photography, such as *Ford Taunus*, 1960, an automobile atop its reflection off the wet pavement is a typical example of his interpretation of an everyday subject. Chargesheimer described his intentions this way: "I want to show the world as it is, our world in all its harshness, its strangeness, its serenity and its beauty, yes its beauty" (Albus Volker 1997, p. 149–150).

The photo-essay books Chargesheimer published, nine of 12 between the years 1957–1961, dominate his 20-year career. His books were composed primarily of black and white photographs with a brief text accompaniment by authors such as Heinrich Böll and G. Ramsegger. Because many felt that he portrayed the cities and people of Germany's Rhineland area in a negative light, his books evoked strong reactions both pro and con. L. Fritz Gruber described Chargesheimer as a photographer who "possessed a seemingly uncanny ability to capture the personalities of prominent people, and to capture events, landscapes, and buildings as well as the life and emptiness of cities with precise verisimilitude." (Gruber 1982, p. 15).

Chargesheimer was also a portrait photographer known for his close-up portrayals of stars and celebrities such as jazz artists Billy Holiday, Josephine Baker, Louis Armstrong, Ella Fitzgerald, German Chancellor Willy Brandt, and others. One of Chargesheimer's best known photographic portraits is that of German Chancellor, *Konrad Adenauer*, 1954, taken the same year the first television broadcasts were made in Germany.

Reinhold Misselbeck, Curator of Photography and Video at Museum Ludwig, Cologne and one of the leading authorities on Chargesheimer's work, refers to Chargesheimer's photographic approach as the "the opposite of Henri Cartier-Bresson's." (Misselbeck 1983, p. 7.) Misselbeck points out that when photographing in the street, Chargesheimer did not photograph "decisive moments" like Cartier-Bresson, but instead portrayed his subjects as performers in a sort of photographic theater. To bring his interests in photography and the theater closer together, Chargesheimer began working as a theater designer, director and set-builder in cities throughout Germany after 1961 and then produced the photo-essay *Theater-Theater*, in 1967 with behind the scenes shots of rehearsals, make-up rooms, and costume making.

Less known, though, are Chargesheimer's camera-less experiments in the darkroom, which from 1948–1953 included gelatin silver paintings, or light graphics (photograms) that he created without knowledge of similar work by Man Ray or László Moholy-Nagy. Chargesheimer returned to his darkroom experiments in the 1960s, and in the 1990s a catalogue of these experimental photographs were published, making this work more widely available.

The range of Chargesheimer's work can be grasped by comparing his first book *Cologne Intime*, 1957, to his last, *Cologne 5:30 AM*, 1970. In *Cologne Intime*, we see the local *Stadtsbürger* (citizens of Cologne) and the inner city up-close and personal at festivals and at home through the lens of one of the city's native sons, a city and people Chargesheimer knew and loved. In contrast, in *Cologne 5:30 AM*, Chargesheimer shows a cold and alienating city, the results of modern public works. By photographing concrete highways, street signs, and public housing high rises devoid of people, he shows us how much his hometown had changed and indirectly how much this depressed him. In 1995 Cologne photographer Wolfgang Vollmer retraced Chargesheimer's steps and photographed the exact same locations, which can now be found in the book *Cologne 1970/1995*.

Numerous articles were published about him during his lifetime by German, Italian, and English magazines, journals, and newspapers such as: *Die Welt*, *Neue Post*, *Stern*, and *Der Spiegel*. In 1968 Chargesheimer was the recipient of the Kulturpreis der Deutschen Gesellschaft für Photographie and since 1986 the city of Cologne has given a prize titled "Chargesheimer Preis der Stadt Köln" to an emerging photographer from Cologne who works in photography, film, or video. Additionally, in 1970 he was awarded the Karl-Ernst-Osthaus Prize by the City of Hagen, West Germany.

Chargesheimer died on New Year's Eve, 1971 in Cologne, Germany. Since his death, the more than 30,000 negatives he made are being reevaluated, researched, and investigated, and he has been included in a number of exhibitions as his place among the post-war, European avant-garde continues to be reassessed.

Christian Gerstheimer

See also: **Architectural Photography; Cartier-Bresson, Henri; Kesting, Edmund; Man Ray; Moholy-Nagy, László; Photogram; Photography in Germany and Austria**

Biography

Born Cologne, Germany, May 19, 1924. Studied photography at the Werkkunstschule, Cologne, 1942–1944. Taught Photography at The Bikla School of Photography and Film in Düseldorf, 1950–1955; Free-lance photojournalist, after 1952; Stage designer, director and photographer for theaters in Cologne, Bonn, Hamburg, Hannover, Vienna, Braunschweig and Kassel, 1961–1967; Organizes the exhibition *10 Years of World Press Photo*, 1966; Kulturpreis der Deutschen Gesellschaft fuer Photographie, 1968; Karl-Ernst-Osthaus Prize, Hagen, West Germany, 1970. Died in Cologne on New Year's Eve, December 31, 1971.

Individual Exhibitions

1956 Cologne Kunstverein, Cologne, Germany
1958 Galerie Seidee, Hannover, Germany
1971 *Meditationsmuehlen (Meditation Mills)*, Cologne Kunstverein, Cologne, Germany
1972 *Hommage á Chargesheimer*, Kunstverein, Cologne, Germany
1976 *Chargesheimer: Lichtgraphiken, Lichtplastiken*, Wilhelm-Hack-Museum and Staedtische Kunstsammlungen, Ludwigshafen, West Germany
1978 Sander Gallery, Washington D.C., U.S.A.
1980 *Unter Krahnenbaumen*, Museum Folkwang, Essen, Germany
1981 *Chargesheimer 1924–1972: Fotografien*, Goethe-Institut, Munich and traveling
1983 *Chargesheimer: Photographien 1949–1970*, Museum Ludwig Cologne, Germany
1989 *Chargesheimer-Personlich (In Person)*, Museum Ludwig, Cologne, Germany
1990 *Chargesheimer: 1924–1971*, Cologne, Germany
1994 *Chargesheimer-Chaos Form Archform*, Museum Ludwig, Cologne, Germany
1997 *Chargesheimer, Menschen wie diese: Photographien aus den 50er Jahren*, Suermondt-Ludwig-Museum, Aachen, Germany

Group Exhibitions

1949 *Photo-Kino*, Cologne, Germany, (and every two years through 1980)
1951 *Subjektive Photographie*, Staatliche Schule für Kunst und Handwerk, Saarbrücken, Germany
1954 *Subjektive Photographie 2*, Saarbrücken, Germany
1969 *Kunst als Spiel/Spiel als Kunst*, Kunsthalle, Recklinghausen, West Germany
1977 *Fotografische Künstlerbildnisse*, Museum Ludwig, Cologne, Germany
1979 *Deutsche Fotographie Nach 1945 (German Photography After 1945)*, Kasseler Kunstverein, Kassel Germany
1997 *Positionen Künstlerischer Photographie in Deutschland seit 1945 (Positions of Artistic Photography in Germany Since 1945)*, Berlinische Galerie, Martin-Gropius-Bau, Berlin, Germany
1998 *Signaturen des Sichtbaren- Ein Jahrhundert der Fotographie in Deutschland (Signature of the Visible- A Century of Photography in Germany)*, Galerie am Fischmarkt, Erfurt, Germany
1999 *Augenblick und Endlichkeit- Das von der Fotografie gepragte Jahrhundert, (Instant and Finite- A Century Shaped by Photography)*, Museum Ludwig, Cologne, Germany
2000 *Kinder des 20. Jahrhunderts: Malerei, Skulptur, Fotografie*, Mittelrhein Museum, Koblenz, Germany
2001 *Pathos der Sachlichkeit: Industrielandschaft in Meisterwerken der Fotografie: (The Pathos of Objectivity: Industrial Landscapes in Masterpieces of Photography)*, Ludwig Galerie Schloβ Oberhausen, Oberhausen, Germany
Subjektive Fotografie: Der Deutschen Beitrag (Subjective Photography: The German Contribution), Institut für Auslandsbeziehungen, Institute for Foreign Cultural Relations, Stuttgart, Germany

Selected Works

Ruins, 1947
Musical Reflection (gelatin silver print painting) (Wagner), 1949
Dr. Konrad Adenauer, 1954
Kleines Mädchen mit Holzroller, 1955
Im Ruehrgebiet, Fussballplatz, 1958
Ford Taunus, 1960
Untitled (gelatin silver print painting), around 1962
North-South Routes, 1969

Further Reading

Chargesheimer: Lichtgraphiken, Lichtplastiken, Wilhelm-Hack-Museum, Ludwigshafen, Germany, 1976.
Chargesheimer Persoenlich (In Person), Museum Ludwig, Cologne, 1989.
Albus, Volker. "Up and Running: Industrial Products and Advertising," in *Deutsche Fotografie. Macht eines Mediums 1870–1970*, Bramsche, Germany: Rasch, 1997, as *German Photography 1870–1970 Power of a Medium*, edited by Klaus Honnef, Rolf Sachsse, and Karin Thomas, Cologne, Germany: DuMont Buchverlag, 1997.
Böhmer, Sylvia. *Chargesheimer, Menschen wie diese: Photographien aus den 50er Jahren*, Aachen: Suermondt-Ludwig Museum, 1997.
Gruber, Renate and L. Fritz Gruber. *Das Imaginäre Photo-Museum*, Köln: DuMont Buchverlag, 1981; as *The Imaginary Photomuseum*, translated by Michael Rollof, New York: Harmony Books, 1982.
Honnef, Klaus. "From Reality to Art Photography between profession and abstraction," in *Deutsche Fotografie. Macht eines Mediums 1870–1970*, Bramsche, Germany: Rasch, 1997, as *German Photography 1870–1970*

Power of a Medium, edited by Klaus Honnef, Rolf Sachsse, and Karin Thomas, Cologne, Germany: DuMont Buchverlag, 1997.

Misselbeck, Reinhold, ed. *Chargesheimer: Schoene Ruinen (Beautiful Ruins)*. Cologne: Weinand, 1994.

———. *Chargesheimer: Photographien 1949–1970*. Cologne: Kiepenheuer & Witsch, 1983.

———. "Chargesheimer." in *Icons of Photography: The 20th Century*, edited by Peter Stepan, Munich: Prestel Verlag, 1999.

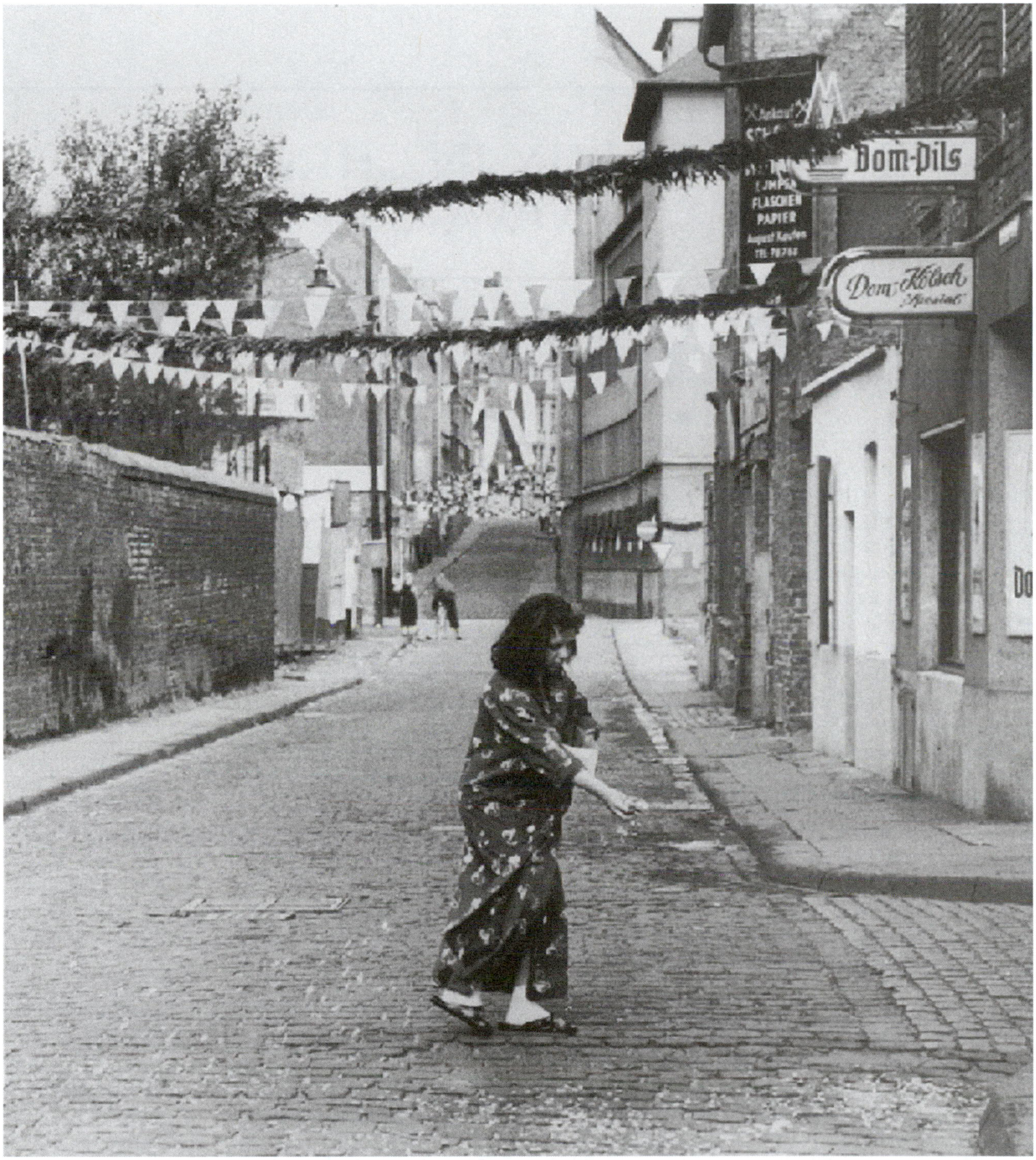

Chargesheimer, "Ohne Titel" from book: "Unter Krahnenbäumen," 1958.
[*Owner: Museum Ludwig, Köln, F 1980/386, Photo credit: Rheinisches Bildarchiv Köln*]

———. "Chargesheimer." *The Dictionary of Art*, edited by Jane Turner, New York: Grove's Dictionaries Inc., 476–477, vol. 6, 1996.
———. "Chargesheimer und Vollmer." *Cologne 1970–1995*, Cologne, Germany: Bachem, 1995.
Solbrig, Anke. "Chargesheimer." *European Photography*, no. 57, vol. 16, Spring 1995.
Weiss, Evelyn. "Chargesheimer." in *Contemporary Photographers*, edited by George Walsh, Colin Naylor, and Michael Held, New York: St. Martin's Press, 1982.
The Chargesheimer Gesellschaft (Society). *http://www.chargesheimer.de.*

PHOTOGRAPHY IN CHINA AND TAIWAN

Photography in China

Photography arrived in China in the 1860s with Western photographers who mostly made portraits. One of the most well-known of these photographers is Milton Miller, an American who owned a photo studio in Hong Kong. He had taken formal portraits of Cantonese merchants, Mandarins, and their families in the early 1860s. The other is the Scottish photographer John Thomson (1837–1921), who owned a photo studio in Hong Kong. Unlike Miller's motifs, his were peasants and workers—the underclass of the late 1860s and early 1870s.

Studios run by Western photographers provided Chinese photographers with practical training and produced some photographers of note. Afong Lai and Mee Cheng were active during this period, and both managed to turn their interest to commercial advantage. Ah Fong was active from the 1860s to 1880s, and in 1937 in Shanghai he published a photo album entitled *The Sino-Japanese Hostilities*, presenting 110 black-and-white photographs, seen primarily as historical documents. Some of his landscapes, however, express aesthetic qualities reminiscent of traditional Chinese painting. Mee Cheung identified himself as a "High Class Photographer," clearly referring to fine-arts aspirations, and is known for his documentary snapshot-style photographs.

As the nineteenth century progressed and the West became more and more fascinated with the country, its culture and art forms, China attracted numerous Western amateur and professional photographers. Most were interested in capturing images of historical importance. The Italian Felice Beato, also known for his later work in Japan, photographed landscapes and battle scenes in the 1860s. Englishman Thomas Childe completed a series of photographs of Beijing and its environments in the early 1870s. During the first two decades of the twentieth century, however, Western photographers were discouraged and then banned from taking photographs in China. Some of the few that exist were taken by a young boy, Walter J. Bronson, shooting surreptitiously as he traveled about China with his family. M.E. Alonso was a photographer for the Wulsin Expedition to Northwest China in 1923, sponsored in part by the National Geographic Society, which brought some of the first photographs made of these territories to the West. Donald Mennie, a British merchant, shot landscapes in a pictorialist style in the 1920s. In 1926 in Shanghai he published a photo album entitled *The Grandeur of the Gorges*, in which he presented his 50 photographic studies of the Yangtze River, along with 12 hand-colored prints. He had previously published the portfolios *The Pageant of Peking* and *Chin—North and South.*

Documentary Photography in China After 1911

In 1925, China was swept by the May 30th Movement, an anti-imperialist movement in protest against the massacre of the Chinese people by the British police in Shanghai on that date. This movement had a great impact on how Western influence was received but also formally introduced modern photography, especially photojournalism, to China, and later shaped the development of photography in the 1930s, as Mao Zedong and the Communit Revolution shaped the history of China.

CHEN Wanli is the most influential photographer during this period of time. He started his study of photography in 1919, coming from a background in medicine. He was concerned with photographic composition and the photographer's artistic interpretation of motifs. His work *The Forbidden City in the Year of 1924* is regarded as the first documentary photography in China. In this series of photos, he documents the scenes of the last emperor of the Chin dynasty, banished from the Forbidden City. In 1928, he selected some photographs from this series and published them as a photographic album through a Shanghai bookstore. His *Dafengji* (1924) is the first photography album created by an individual photographer in China and includes 12 photographs selected from his solo exhibition in Guan Shen in 1924. These photos depict landscape and still life according to the traditional Chinese aesthetic. The photographs express the abstract and pictorial quality of motifs, rather than any realistic association. For him, the art of photography is to express the color of Chinese art and to further develop its characteristics. *Dafengji* was created to reflect upon this understanding of photography. *The Journal to the West*, 1925, is an album that presents photographs he took during his visit to Tun Wong with American anthropologists. He shot over 300 photos, using motifs of desert and rural costume.

Chen was also a leading member of the photographers' association in China. In 1923, and in conjunction with WU Yuzhuo and WU Jix, he organized the first photographic association for amateurs. This group was commonly known as the *Guang* (literally meaning light) *Association*. From 1924 to 1927, the association actively held group exhibitions to display its members' works. In 1928 and 1929, those works were published in two volumes of yearbooks, the first of their kind in China.

LIU Bannong (1891–1934) was well known as a poet and scholar of language, literature, and education, and also as a promoter of the May 30th Movement. In photography, he was the leading exponent of theories on photography in China. He had studied in Britain and France and completed a PhD in literature. He had learned photography during his study in Paris in the early 1920's, and he joined *Guang Association* in 1926, becoming very active in the photographic field. He was editor of two photographic yearbook volumes. He also translated photographic essays in Chinese. In 1927, he published *Talking about Photography*, which summarizes his views about photography. The book was publicly distributed and became very influential. One of his arguments in the book tries to show that photography is a type of art, and then to emphasize the principles of aesthetics in photography, such as composition, lighting, and tonality. He promoted photography as a means of expression and creation, and his ideas remain influential today.

LONG Chin-san (also Jinshan; 1892–1995) was born in Zhejiang province in China and died in Taipei. Between 1903 and 1906, he was trained in Chinese ink painting and later photography in a high school in Shanghai. He had been working for newspaper publishers in China and is regarded as the first photojournalist in China. In 1911, he took a job in an advertising department at a newspaper publisher in Shanghai, where he could observe photography at close hand. Between 1926 and 1937, he worked as a photographer for the Shanghai *Times*.

In 1928, Long Chin-san, together with HU Boxiang (1896–1989), HUANG Baohui, HUANG Zhengyu, and ZHANG Zhenhuo, founded the *China Photography Society* in Shanghai, one of the earliest photographic associations in south China and the most influential nation-wide photography organization in China. Long was a leading photographer in Shanghai during the time. In March, 1926, he had a solo exhibition, which inspired other photographers to hold photographic exhibitions. In 1930, he lectured on photography at Nanyang High School, a girls' school in Shanghai, and this perhaps encouraged the spreading of formal education in photography throughout China. After World War II, Long moved to Taiwan and by 1961 was creating montage pictorial photography.

Social Documentary and Reportage Photography During Anti-Japanese War and Civil War in the 1930s

Photography during the rise of China's Communist Party is associated with reportage photography around motifs of war and portraits of Communist leaders. In 1937, SA Fe joined the Communist Eighth Route Army, and two years later he established a propaganda department to develop reportage photography for the Party. This department initiated photojournalism in the Party. In 1938, SU Jing held the first workshop on photojournalism to train Party photographers. An alternate way of training photography was to apply the age-old master-disciple system to young photographers. Photographic training was intended to achieve two goals: to educate photographers in using the medium for the promotion of the significance of the revolution, and to teach photographers to master basic darkroom skills.

It was also during this period that a number of pictorial newspapers emerged to report the war to the public. The Communist Party saw these newspapers as propaganda tools, and in 1942, it established its own illustrated newspaper to present photojournalism that extolled the successes of the Eighth Route Army. After the establishment of the People's Republic of China in 1949, pictorial newspapers and magazines retained their role in the promotion of the Party and its ideals. Two important pictorial magazines, *China Pictorial* and *China Reconstructs*, were published, providing an outlet for social documentary and reportage photography.

WU Yinxian (1900–1994) was the most active and well-known photographer who favorably addressed Communist concerns. He was popular for his socialist and realist style in documenting the history of China's Communists. He was concerned with the form and technique of lighting to dramatize his visual motifs. His early works focused primarily on the miserable lives of marginal and low-class subjects confronted by the social and political changes in the 1920s and 1930s. He later developed photographic education programs for the Red Army. He had joined the Party in 1938, and in 1939 he published a book called *The Knowledge of Photography*, a textbook for Communist photographers. One of his best-known works, *Dr. Bai Qiuen* (1939), documents outdoor surgery on a Communist solider. This photo expresses the dignity of Dr. Bai who, during attempts to save the solider, seems not to care at all about the danger of the ongoing war. Dr. Bai was a foreigner, but his bravery symbolizes his strong commitment to the revolution. After the establishment of People's Republic of China in 1949, Wu Yinxian focused on developing film education in China.

XU Xiaobing (1916–) and HOU Bo (1924–) are a married couple well known for their portraits of Communist leaders and significant ceremonies in the history of the Party, from the 1930s to 1950s. They are especially famous for depicting Chairman Mao, Hou Bo having been Mao's personal photographer from approximately 1949 to 1961. Though primarily a filmmaker, one of Xu Xiaobing's portraits of Mao is a profile view of him facing an adoring audience. This photo later became an exemplary work for photographers to show their leader's openness toward the public. Xu studied photography in a film company in Shanghai. Later, he joined the Party and served as a photojournalist, documenting on film the early history of Party. After 1949, he was active in documenting important national ceremonies and events. Hou's photo of the ceremonial founding of the PRC in Tiananmen Square records the most significant single moment of the history of the PRC, and her studio portraits of Mao became the basis for the well-known painted, poster, and banner images of Mao that were ubiquitous during this time.

It is not an exaggeration to say there was no "personal" photography in China at this time. Cameras were rare commodities and used only for official purposes: identification, documentation of state projects and leaders, and propaganda as China rebuilt its war-torn nation and emerged into modernity.

It is, however, important to point out the significance of SUN Mingjing's works during this period. Sun was an amateur photographer, and his photography has been lesser known until rather recently. Sun was significant for the establishment and development of film education in China. He had learned film and photography from American missionaries. As a scientist and engineer in the service of the Party, he conducted numerous field trips in China to research the state of industrial manufacturing. He took over a thousand photos and shot documentary films during these trips. Some of those photographs are important for reporting the social conditions during the time, and also for preserving historical moments of this era. Yet some of the photos also express Sun's concerns with the symbolism and aesthetics of photography that were disavowed by social documentary and reportage photography. One photograph depicts a scene in which a city is ravaged by a plague of locusts; Sun uses the locusts to symbolize the invading Japanese army. (The word "locust" in Chinese is euphonically similar to the translation of "Japanese army.") Another photograph depicts rows of young nude teachers, silhouetted against the sunrise performing physical excises. The symbolism of wartime patriotic struggle is obvious from the fact that, in Chinese, the translations of the phrases "against the sunrise" and "against Japan" are exactly the same, as well as the fact that the projected shadows of these men form a pattern that suggests Japan's wartime flag. Sun Mingjing, unique in Chinese social documentary and reportage photography, addressed photography with the idea of transfiguring accepted motifs into symbolic images.

As there was for all intents and purposes no fine-arts expression of photography in the People's Republic, the Cultural Revolution, occurring between 1966 and 1976, had little impact on the field. Although intellectuals, artists, and other cultural elites were persecuted, not allowed to practice their disciplines, interned, and even killed, greatly affecting the study and practice of art, music, and literature, the impact on photography was indirect, with the result being that as reforms were put into place in the late 1970s and into the 1980s, photography for the first time was taken seriously as an artistic medium, following the models of the West. Photographers for the first time could adapt an identity as creative individuals and look at their output as expressive of their individual personalities. Landscape photography, nature studies, expressive portraiture, and even social and veiled political commentary began to be practiced. Documentary photography, however, still dominated.

Several well-known Western photographers created important bodies of work in China in the second half of the century, notably Henri Cartier-Bresson. His wide-ranging documentation was published by Robert Delpire in 1955. Robert Capa, Marc Riboud, and René Burri also undertook important series.

Documentary Photography in the Late 1980s

In the late 1980's, documentary photography emerged to become pervasive in China. HAN Lei and LIU Zheng (1969–) are two examples of photographers engaged in this type of photography. They often took pictures of marginal people—laborers and others of the lower classes who were confronted with the dramatic change of their lifestyle and social status due to China's process of Western modernization. These photographers traveled in order to select their motifs, and they continued to document these motifs for a long period of time. Liu Zheng's series *The Chinese* is considered a pioneering body of images in that they depicted groups and individuals from all walks of life in actual pursuits as opposed to staged, propagandist depictions of Communist Party social programs. Liu Zheng has continued to produce important bodies of work, including his series of lush color tableaux, *Four Beauties*, which presents the lives of four fabled historical women.

CHEN Changfen is an important landscape photographer of this period. He began his career as a professional photographer in 1959. He was selected by *Time* magazine as one of 10 eminent photographers in the history of photography. He is well known for his landscape photography of the Great Wall, a motif that he has been fascinated with and involved in since 1959. In his photographs, he successfully combines the aesthetics of photography and ancient Chinese monuments.

Contemporary Photography After the Mid-1990s

After the mid 1990s, with the increasingly affluence and globalization of the country, photography became widespread in China. It also came to dominate contemporary art practice in China, now eagerly sought after by Western art aficionados. Photography during this period, however, was engaged in by artists who had training in visual art, rather than photography, leading to an open and experimental style. The availability of digital photography was another vital factor that stimulated the development of contemporary photography. The domestic market for photography was further sparked by the rapid ascendancy of Chinese manufacturers of photographic equipment, especially digital cameras, in the 1990s.

QIU Zhijie (1969–) is one of the pioneers of contemporary photography. In his early works, he depicts middle class people's lives in relation to livelihood and lifestyle. Some photographers studied photography abroad and also worked abroad. The early works of XING Danwen (1967–) deal with the Cultural Revolution in a reportage perspective. In her later works, she became interested in China's global issues on E-trash and urban transformation. RONG Rong (1968–) lived and studied photography in Japan in the mid 1990's. He was interested in documentary photography in his early career. Later, he took self-portraits, sometimes with his wife, using ruined buildings and sublime landscapes as his surroundings.

The rapid transformation of China in social, political, cultural, and economic domains came to the lens of these artists' cameras during this period of time. YANG Yong was interested in depicting the city in its various facets. He preferred to take snapshots for his motifs. HONG Hao (1965–) is another Chinese artist looking to the West and interested in set-up photography. In his works, facsimiles of advertising photographs in which he appears as a suave model selling Western luxuries and lifestyles, Hong Ho creates scenes that signify the dream-like world of the middle class in China. A typical work is *Hello, Mr. Hong* of 1998. HAI Bo's (1962–) photographs address the issues of family and his own cultural identity in relation to the socialist meaning of family. He often used historical photographs as the material for creating new works. In *Them*, 1999, he reassembled a number of women wearing drab Maoist garb who had been captured in an official black-and-white group portrait from 1973 to photograph them in exactly the same configuration, but in color wearing Western-style dresses.

The use of historical motifs also underlies the work of ZHUANG Hui, who orchestrates large group portraits of schools, factories, and other institutions in the style of official photography of earlier eras. WANG Qingsong mines the entire span of Chinese history in ambitious, panoramic works that assembled dozens of models in elaborate tableaux, often with the intent of pointing out or satirizing modernization; in the work *Look Up, Look Up*, 2000, a group of people wearing unflattering clothes and hairdos in the latest styles stand gazing up at an oversized bottle of Coca-Cola.

HONG Lei (1960–) is known for his photographic appropriation of Chinese landscape paintings. He found the exact scene that a Chinese painter depicted and took a photo based on the exact aesthetic and visual effect that the painting conveys. ZHAO Bandi (1966–) uses digital techniques to create photos in which his own images, an artificial panda, and texts that are reminiscent of propaganda posters and advertisements, have been incorporated.

Photography in China only recently became connected to international trends. And it was only at the end of the century that photography become a formal major in art colleges. At the end of the century as well, international photography exhibitions began to be held in China, bringing prominent international artists, curators, and critics who displayed their work and lectured there. The CourtYard Gallery and Red Gate Gallery in Beijing, established by Westerners, have been important private institutions for the promotion of Chinese contemporary photography and art. Local artists using photography and video, which had become extremely popular at the end of the century, had increasing opportunities to show their works abroad, especially in Europe, and have become concerned with China's global issues. Seminal traveling exhibitions organized by the Kunstmuseum, Wolfsburg, Germany, and the International Center of Photography, New York circulated at the turn of the century.

Important internationally focused Chinese contemporary photographers include WENG Fen (1961–). Weng Fen's series of large-scale color works entitled *Wall Straddle*, 2001, depicts young girls in school uniforms sitting across crumbling, trash-strewn walls and looking in the distance at modern skylines. His interpretation of China's urban development relies on symbolism—as if in these photos the girls foretell the future of globalized China. CHEN Lingyang is an emerging female photographer whose works are concerned with the female body and female identity related to the image of city. *Twelve Moon Flowers*, 1999–2000, depicts female genitals in a poetic fashion, as the viewer sees their relation to twelve flowers. XIANG Liqing (1973–) montages hundreds of images of high-rise buildings to create colorful, large-scale tableaux that comment on the anonymity of modern urban society. YANG Zhenzhong (1968–) satirizes contemporary Chinese family life and family policy with his portraits of squawking roosters, hens, and chicks that stand in for husbands and wives, fathers, mothers, and children in his *Family Fortunes, Lucky Family* series of the mid-1990s. Important expatriate Chinese photographers include ZHANG Huan (1965–), known primarily for performances that test the limits of his bodily endurance; he also directs performances documented with large-scale color photographs, such as a shot of Chinese men half-immersed in a body of water, titled *To Raise the Water Level in a Fishpond* of 1997.

Photography in Taiwan

Photography appears in Taiwan arguably as early as 1871, when the Scottish photographer John Thomson (1837–1921) visited what was then called the island of Formosa, during his travels in China from 1868–1872. Thomson is known for his ambitious photo album of portrait photography on Chinese workers and peasants, published in England in 1893/4 as *Illustrations of China and Its People*. He appears to be the first photographer to do landscape photography and portraits of aboriginals in Taiwan.

Other photographers during this period of time were Christian priests who lived and worked in Taiwan. They often took portrait photographs of native inhabitants.

Document and Realist Photography from 1895 to 1948 during Taiwan's Colonial Period under Japanese Occupation

Photography in Taiwan during this period of time was heavily influenced by the Japanese. Documentary photography was widespread, although mainly used by Japanese anthropologists, scholars, and reporters during the early period of the Japanese Occupation (1895–1920), as cameras were mostly considered research tools for field work in the newly-acquired colony. Portraiture was the other popular type of photography. As a colonized island under the Japanese, Taiwan was under heavy restriction. The local Taiwanese could not afford to purchase cameras and photographic equipment that Japanese and a few British companies carried. Even so, Taiwan natives were not allowed to acquire negatives or experiment with chemicals or other photographic materials.

The difficult conditions did not entirely prevent the use of photography, however. Japanese photographers and reporters based in Taiwan ran the photo studios and shops, but also offered a few photographic classes to introduce the functions of cameras and basic darkroom techniques to the native population. This was undertaken for commercial reasons to keep up with the demand for portrait and documentary photographs, and there was no formal or professional education in photography in the schools. The master-disciple system was thus strongly relied upon in the commercial photography studios. SHR Chiang and LIN Tsao were two important figures who emerged amidst these conditions. They were trained in the master-disciple system, and they later established their own commercial studios. In 1901, Shr Chiang set up the first studio that was owned and run by Taiwanese natives called *Duplicated Me Photo Shop* which existed until 1946. Around the same time, Lin Tsao (1881–1953) inherited a studio from his teacher Mirimoto, a Japanese reporter based in Taiwan. He renamed this concern *Lin Photo Shop*. Shr Chiang, Lin Tsao, and others who set up shops were largely patronized by Japanese officials to record their activities and to report propaganda events.

PENG Ruei-lin stands out as an exceptional photographer of this era. Like his predecessors, he ran a photo shop to support himself. Unlike them, he had received formal training in photography from a Tokyo professional school in the 1920s. This training made a considerable difference in his approach to the medium. He experimented with various techniques in color photography in 1930 and infrared photography in 1933. While both of these areas had been discovered and discussed by Western photographers, they were little known in Taiwan. Peng Ruei-lin's experimentation illustrates how, even in artistic isolation, he was able to use a camera for artistic creation and to attempt to create aesthetic effects. Yet, Peng Ruei-lin's significance was not widely recognized by other native photographers, and his concerns did not enter the mainstream understanding of photography in Taiwan. He taught classes continuously from 1933 to 1937 in his photo shop, with many of his students becoming key figures in photography after the Japanese departure from the island.

TENG Nan-kuang (1907–1971), CHANG Tsai (1916–1994), and LEE Ming-diao (1922–) were the most active and influential photographers during the late colonial period and Sino-Japanese War from 1934 to 1948. They have been called the "Three Swordsmen of Taiwanese Photography" to identity their roles as strong promoters of photography in Taiwan, especially during the 1950s. Stylistically their photographs are reminiscent of Japanese realism in documentary photography, where the dominance of the realist style leaves little room for photographers' individual creations. Yet , unlike the early documentary photography of Taiwan, so influenced by the Japanese style, the works of these three figures create a more humanistic sense and express each photographer's concern and individual awareness of Taiwan. Traveling all over Taiwan, Teng Nan-kuang, Chang Tsai, and Lee Ming-diao captured images that showed their interest in early Taiwan's rural culture, religious rituals, and social conditions. Teng's best-known work is a series of so-called tea ladies. Shooting candid portraits of the ladies at work. Chang traveled to Orchid Island, an isolated island away from Taiwan, and painstakingly photographed aboriginals in great detail near Jade Mountain, Taiwan's the highest elevation capturing his motifs in a straightforward and direct way. Lee is known for photographs of rural life and the traditions rooted in Han Chinese culture. While qualifing as documentary photographers or photojournalists, the Three Swordsmen were not primarily motivated by commercial or political intentions as were their early Taiwanese counterparts, and their works went a long way to encourage native photographers to reassess the aesthetic potential of the medium.

The Three Swordsmen also helped shape the environment of photography in Taiwan. Teng set up networking and a photographic association, and enhanced formal education on photography in schools. In 1953, he was a co-founder, with LONG Chin-san, of the Chinese Photography Association, the first association for professional photographers. (See below) This association helps gather photographers, exchange knowledge, and nurture the public's understanding of the aesthetic dimension of photography. In 1964, Teng founded the Taiwan Photographic Society, with the dual aim of disavowing the motifs of salon photography and of promoting modern photography in Taiwan. (See below: "Photography in Taiwan in the 1960s and 1970s.") Chang initiated photography classes in professional training schools. Lee published the first professional photographic magazine in Taiwan, which was distributed through photo shops. The magazine published the texts of updated theories and concepts about photography.

Montage Pictorial Photography after World War II

LONG Chin-san (1892–1995) was a leading photographer and an influential promoter of photography in Mainland China and Taiwan, having moved to Taiwan from Mainland China after World War II. Long is regarded as one of the earliest pioneers in photography from the early 1900's and one of the most active photographers in Mainland China. His photographic experiences in China distinguished his works, conceptually and stylistically, from that of other Taiwanese photographers. Unlike those photographers trained in Japan and Taiwan, Long's concern with photography pays attention to both the techniques and aesthetic dimensions of photography. His early training in Chinese ink painting contributed to his understanding and skill in the artistic elements of photography.

In 1961, Long took up a unique photographic practice known as montage pictorial photography. Montage pictorial photography was groundbreaking in the history of photography since it applied photographic techniques to express the aesthetic of Chinese ink painting. The basic concept of montage pictorial photography is to create a black-and-white photograph, based on the classic theory of Chinese ink painting (commonly known as "the six principles of painting"). For Long, photography was capable of presenting the beauty and aesthetic of traditional Chinese art and culture, with two factors determining whether a photograph could be considered art: artistic composition and a significant message embedded in the work—important criteria in all works of art. For Long, positing a scene in a traditional Chinese painting is not unlike composition in photography, even though in painting, an artist can adjust the positions of compositional elements, whereas a photographer is restricted by the mechanical eye. Through photographic techniques, a photographer can resolve this problem.

The process of making a photograph characterized as montage pictorial photography is complex: it includes planning motifs, making the images, planning the layout of the images, collaging negatives through techniques in the darkroom, including multiple exposures, among others. Although Western photographers have, since the 1920s, employed darkroom techniques that achieve image overlap similar to Long's concept of composition, Long's montage pictorial photography depends on the unique considerations of Chinese painting principles.

The Scenery of Lake and Mountain is now generally regarded as Long's most typical "compositional" picture. A landscape compiled by shots of an old man sitting in a pavilion, amid rocks and pine trees, a boat, villages and a lake, the composition depicts a narrative typical of a traditional Chinese landscape. The space created in the photograph dismisses the principle of three-point perspective, with the gradated tonal effects in the photograph also reminiscent of a Chinese ink painting.

Intentional Photography and Modern Photography in the 1960s and 1970s

In contrast to the Salon style and pictorial photography advocated by Long Chin-san, a few styles have emerged that feature what is termed Intentional photography and other modern styles.

KE Shi-jie (1929–) is among the most important photographers who have worked on Intentional photography. In his early works, he shot a series of portraits and landscapes and was concerned with the personal traits and aesthetic quality of his motifs. Later, he went to New York and became a commercial photographer. Quitting his job, he then spent several years, in the late 1970s and early 1980s, traveling the world and photographing. The works that resulted are abstract, featuring dream-like scenery appearing to be influenced by Surrealism, emphasizeing the tonality of the shadows. His best-known works include *Living Tao*, *Still Vision*, *Dancing Brushes*, *Embrace Tiger*, and *Return to the Mountain*. Other Intentionalist photographers are HSIEH Chun-teh (1949–) and Denial LEE. They emphasize the photographer's interpretation of his subject, rather than simply reporting or documenting it, and they are concerned with the elements of color, shape, composition, and contrast in their works.

The modern photography movement in Taiwan began around 1965 and lasted for around ten years. It is important to note the American influence on Taiwanese photography during this period. After World War II, the U.S. army established bases on the island. Taiwan shed Japanese influence, and absorbed American culture and art, motivating photographers and shaping the development of photography. Key figures in this development are JANG Jao-tang, HU Yung, Hsieh Chun-de among others, who used wide-angle lenses to create distorted images, favored high contrast between light and dark, a rough grain, and blurry or out-of-focus images. This tendency did not pervade the entire photographic field in Taiwan, but rather was confined to a group of photographers who held joint exhibitions. One of these was in 1969 and presented the works of eight photographers active in this movement. Ambitious photographers made a number of attempts to increase the awareness of modern trends in photography. A photographic festival was dedicated to modern photography in 1966. Two important magazines began publication: *Photo Century* in 1970 and *Modern Photography* in 1976.

Riding the wave of this cultural change, V-10 was a photography group founded in 1971. It aimed to promote discussion among the modern art, photography, and visual media. The founding members included JOU Dung-guo, Hu Yung, NING Ming-shen, GUO Ying-shen, JANG Guo-shiung, Jang Jao-tang, JUNG Ling, YE Jeng-liang, LUNG Sz-liang, SHIE Jen-ji; and by 1973 the group expanded to include HUANG Yung-sung, Shie Chuen-de, JANG Tan-li, LIU Chen-tzuo, LI Chi-hua, WU Wen-tao. None of them continued to be full-time independent photographers, working instead for newspapers, TV stations, advertising companies, and filmmakers. Some of the founding members had participated in experimental theater and film. Their photographs were frequently published in *Photo Century*, an important magazine for modern photography in Taiwan. While not sharing a unified aesthetic principle, these photographers participated in several group shows in the 1970s.

Reportage Photography from the 1970s to 1990s

Despite the efforts of some photographers, photography in Taiwan was dominated by photojournalism the mid 1970s and 1980s. The development of this style is associated with several political events of the period, a tumultuous period of political and international relations. In 1971, Taiwan was forced out of the United Nations, and in the same year, Japan's government took possession of a small island which both Taiwan and Mainland China claimed as theirs. The sovereignty of Taiwan, threatened by absorption into China, became a critical issue that provoked the awareness of photographers and artists; they sought to identify and preserve Taiwan's culture, society, and people. Photography in Taiwan during those 20 years thus developed into a style of social realism, which was prevalent in photography magazines, popular magazines, and newspapers.

It is important to point out that several photographers had started to work in a reportage style in the 1960s, particularly JANG Shr-shian, CHENG Shang-his, and HSU Ching-po.

Cheng Shang-his was a leading reportage photographer who worked for three important magazines. After its publications, his *Story of the Hung Ye Baseball Team* was regarded as one of the early examples of reportage photography in Taiwan. Another of his well-known works is *The Series of Jilung* (1960–1965) which records the change in his hometown. He was inspired by his teacher, Chang Tsai, and he used a snapshot style with simple and straightforward compositions in capturing his subjects. His student, JANG Jao-tung, later became a very active and important reportage photographer, and in 1965 the two held a two-man show dedicated to modern photography.

The emergence of several photography magazines and newspapers was essential to advocate and popularize the style, allowing serious photojournalists to emerge, including WANG Xhin, LIANG Jeng-jiu, and LIU Chen-hsiang.

Echo magazine was first published in 1971; it aimed to introduce Chinese culture and create cultural exchange between the West and the East. In 1978, the magazine dispensed with its English version and instead launched a version in Chinese that featured a special issue on Chinese photography. It encouraged interest in reportage on the motifs of Taiwanese culture, and exclusively displayed their works, including those of HUANG Yung-sung and JUNG I-jong. The aim of these reportage photographers was to discover the neglected arenas of life in Taiwan, and they played a pioneering role in this wide-spread cultural phenomenon, which also attracted the contribution of novelists and other artists. These photographers were also involved in organizational and editorial works.

In 1973, GAO Shin-jiang, the editor of the section of Art and Literature in *The Times* in Taiwan, devoted several columns to reportage photography. This was the first newspaper in Taiwan to strongly advocate photojournalists and present their various documentations on Taiwanese culture and Taiwanese minorities.

In 1985, the novelist CHENG Yin-jen published a magazine called *Renjian*—literally, "the world that human beings live"— which specialized in text and images for an intellectual Taiwanese audience. This magazine sought to characterize reportage photography as humanistic and truthful, dedicated to providing critical insight into what had become an overwhelmingly materialistic culture and consumer society. The magazine did not focus exclusively on Taiwan, but also covered, among other issues, Ethiopia's critical problem of hunger. Although the magazine ran for just four issues, ending in 1989, it nonetheless served, along with other publications, to foster the emergence and development of reportage photography in the 1980s.

The cover photo of the launch issue of *Renjian* was GUAN Shiao-rung's "Bachrmen," from his series on Orchid Island aboriginals. Guan Shiao-rung exclusively photographed on this island for almost 10 years, moving there to live, his work veering more towards an ethnographic documentary. Later, he helped found an aboriginal foundation and was even personally involved in aboriginal protests in the 1990s. In "Bachrmen," he documented a community of aboriginals who, drawn by its low cost of living, had illegally inhabited this place.

JUNG I-jong, another active photojournalist, was trained as a printmaker in wood cut technique; an active editor and writer, he had no professional training in photography. *Man and Land* (1974–1986) was his first work of reportage, inspired by his memories of youth and its implications on his adult life. *Taipei Tumor* focuses on the city of Taipei, depicting its rapid and chaotic development. *Szu Chin* (1980–1985) records the rural Taipei preserved community for aboriginals. Motivated by his experiences growing up near this area and his encounter with a mysterious saying about this community. and influenced by Henri Cartier-Bresson's concept of "the decisive moment," Jung utilizes a snapshot style in this series. In 1992, he founded *Photographers*, which introduced international photography to Taiwan and vice versa. The magazine has been an essential source for aspiring photographers to understand the works of the masters. He has also published numerous books on photography, which benefit those both in Taiwan and Mainland China.

Female photographers are less common in Taiwan than Mainland China, WANG Shin being the first woman photographer dedicated primarily to reportage. She studied photography in Japan and worked on a series of photographs about a violent incident in an aboriginal community during the Japanese occupation of Taiwan.

Taiwan has also seen an exodus as some photographers left the island to study and work in America.

Contemporary Photography in Connection with Digital Technology in the 1990s

Daniel Lee (1945–) relocated to Philadelphia, Pennsylvania to study photography and film in 1970, after his college training in oil painting. He then worked for a decade at a commercial studio in New York. In the early 1990s, he entered into the field of digital photography. Today, he is hailed as one of the pioneering photographers in the world, and his early works have inspired many Taiwanese to experiment with digital photography.

Motivated by the emergence of new technologies in everyday life, Lee views the use of digital imaging tools as a way to have more freedom in selecting subjects, expressing his concept, and controlling the outcome.

He created his first series with digital means in 1993. Entitled *Manimals*—a word combining the words man and animal—in this series of 12 riveting yet disturbing images Lee accentuates various human features to evoke an animal's to create the 12 animal signs of the ancient Chinese Zodiac associated with birth years, such as "1949—Year of the Ox." The concepts of Lee's works are associated with Buddhism and Taoism, and the cycles of life and reincarnation of the religious beliefs which he encountered during his life in Taiwan. He is also interested in Darwin's theory of evolution. Other of his works include *108 Windows* (1996–2003), *Origin* (1999–2001) and *Judgement* (2002). *Origin* refers to the origin of the human being as proposed by Charles Darwin. The concept of *Judgement* was taken from Taoist folklore about the underworld. In this myth, each individual is presented to the judge of the court in the underworld after death. This work is associated with the cycle of life and reincarnation.

Contemporary Photography in Taiwan

As in the People's Republic, digital photography and video are popular contemporary art forms

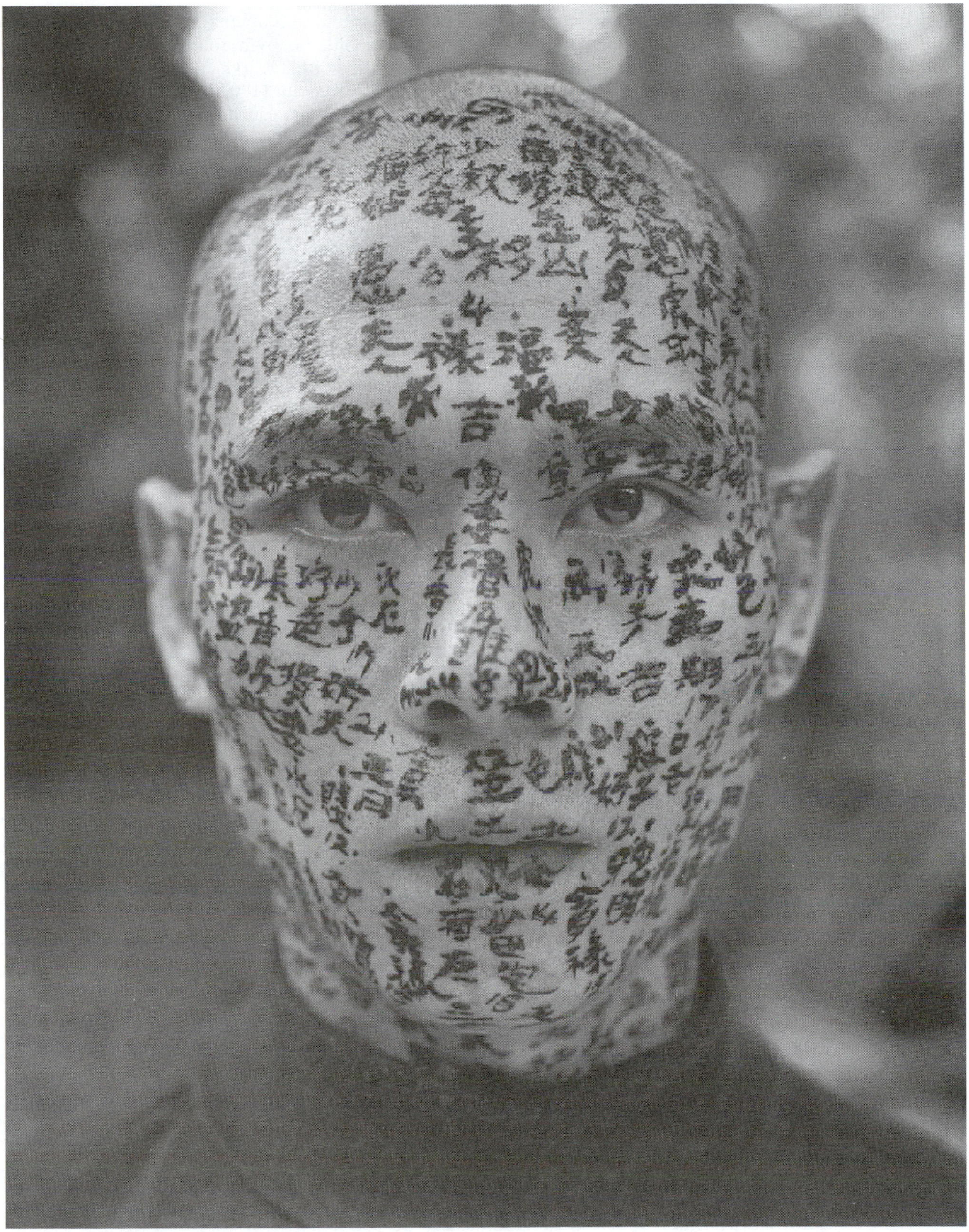

Zhang Huan, from Family Tree, 2000, C-Print, 40 × 50″.
[*Courtesy of the artist and Aura Gallery*]

in Taiwan. CHEN Chieh-jen (1960–) is interested in violent events that occurred in modern Chinese history, depicting his interpretations of the Japanese invasion of China in the 1930s. Using digital techniques to mimic historical photographs that depict horrific acts, including decapitations, Chen Chieh-jen is concerned with the issues of body, national identity, and political power. His works, in their depiction of the life cycle and the afterlife, are also inspired by notions of Chinese Taoism.

HUNG Tung-lu (1968–) is interested in cyber culture and figures that represent this culture in Taiwan and Japan, creating figures based entirely on his imagination through digital techniques which deal with what human beings might become in the advancing cyber culture. He has explored answers to this question in Buddhist tenets and incorporates the idea of nirvana into his cyber creations, which are holographic in nature and mounted in light boxes. WU Tien-chang (1956–) uses digital photography to mimic posters that might be found in Shanghai, incorporating aspects of ancient Chinese myth, folklore, and Taoism into the narrative of his works.

CHEN Shun-chu (1963–) is concerned with the concept of family. He has taken portraits of his family members and others since 1992 and has accumulated hundreds of photos. In his works, he addresses social relations and their connection to the concept of family, and expanding this concept, to the idea of home.

YAO Jui-chung (1969–) a pioneer of Taiwanese contemporary photography, remains a leading photographer. He is also very active in the curatorial field and is known for his critical writing on the contemporary art and photography of Taiwan. In an early photographic series, he made upside-down self-portraits as a parody of Taiwan's national identity in relation to China. He is also interested in landscape that is ruined or abandoned in Taiwan, and the issues of cultural identity generated by these landscapes.

SHIN-YI YANG

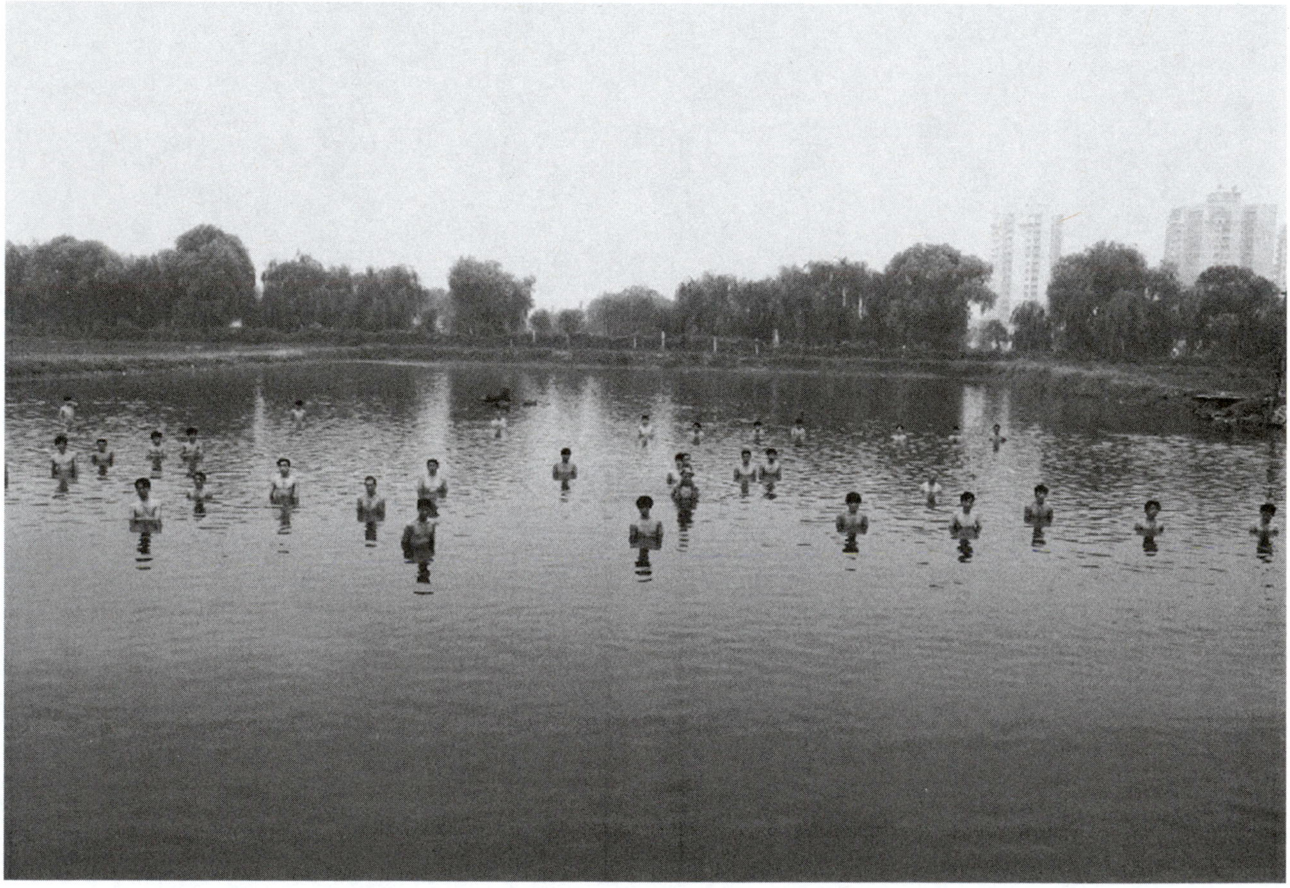

Zhang Huan, To Raise the Water level in a Fishpond, 1997, Performance, Beijing, China. Original in color. [*Courtesy of the artist and Aura Gallery*]

See also: **Documentary Photography; Photography in Japan; Portraiture; Socialist Photography; War Photography**

Further Reading

Cameron, Nigel, ed. *The Face of China, 1860–1912 As Seen by Photographers & Travelers*. Millerton, New York: Aperature, 1978.

Capa, Cornell, ed. *Behind the Great Wall of China: Photographs from 1870 to the Present*. Greenwich, Connecticut and New York: New York Graphic Society and Metropolitan Museum of Art, 1972.

Tuyl, Gijs van, Annelie Lütgens, and Karen Smith. *The Chinese*, Wolfsburg. Germany: Kunstmuseum Wolfsburg, 2004.

Wu Changyun, ed. *1957–2000, An Anthology of Chinese Photography*. Beijing, 2003.

Wu Hung, ed. *The First Guangzhou Triennial. Reinterpretation: A Decade of Experimental Chinese Art 1990–200*. Guangzhou, China: Gaungdong Museum of Art, 2002.

Wu Hung, ed. *Between Past and Future. New Photography and Video from Chin*, New York: International Center of Photography, 2004, and traveling.

WILLIAM CHRISTENBERRY

American

Among the most significant post-World War II color photographers, William Christenberry came upon photography nearly by accident. He began his career as a painter, earning a fine arts degree in 1959 from the University of Alabama in Tuscaloosa, where he was born and raised. At the urging of his instructor, Mel Price, Christenberry traveled to New York City in 1958, where he quickly became enamored of the energetic, avant-garde canvasses of the Abstract Expressionists, namely painters Willem de Kooning and Arshile Gorky. He was later drawn towards the iconic works of Pop artists Claes Oldenburg and Jim Dine, as well as others who incorporated signage into their work. These artists encouraged him to consider the vernacular—the materials of everyday life—as an appropriate subject for his art. He was increasingly drawn to representation in his paintings; and upon his move to Memphis, Tennessee for a teaching position the following year, Christenberry began using an old Kodak Brownie camera as a tool to record the colors, shapes, and forms of his native landscape. On a practical level, the camera's casual, instantaneous, 3 × 5″ drugstore prints functioned as preliminary sketches for paintings; but they also served as a repository for memories of a distant time and place that the artist would collect and nurture over the years.

In 1960, a seminal moment occurred in which Christenberry discovered the Depression-era *Let Us Now Praise Famous Men* (1941) with its text by James Agee and photographs by Walker Evans. Originally commissioned for publication in *Fortune* magazine, the now-classic work, chronicled the landscape and milieu that Christenberry knew so well: Hale County, Alabama, the heart of the South's Black Belt region known for its cotton and slave plantations. In 1936, coincidentally the year of Christenberry's birth, *Fortune* had sent the two men in search of a story, and they returned with an opus. Evans's stark and yet elegiac pictures of the sharecropper families he came to know, their homes, and routines of daily life have since been identified with a modern, documentary style of photography. By refusing to sentimentalize his subjects, he instead presented them with a quiet dignity. Christenberry was captivated by Evans's images as well as Agee's text, which reminded him of another inspiration, that of the Southern literature of William Faulkner and Eudora Welty. Still shooting the Brownie images as studies for painted works, it was not until Christenberry met Evans in October 1961 that he decided to turn his attention to photography as an endpoint.

Evans, then an editor at *Fortune*, helped Christenberry obtain a job as a picture file clerk at Time-Life and remained a close friend until the elder photographer's death in 1975. Evans found the young Christenberry's Brownie prints to have a purity of vision, breathtaking candor, and a poetic quality unlike most color photography, which he found "vulgar" (Southall 1990). Evans strongly encouraged Christenberry to continue with photography. In 1968, Christenberry, using *Let Us Now Praise Famous Men* as a guide, sojourned to Hale County to re-photograph the sites that Evans had memorialized 32 years earlier. He has continued to make the annual pilgrimage ever since.

Christenberry photographed exclusively with the Brownie until 1977, when he turned to the more professional and technically daunting large-format, 8 × 10″ Deardorff view camera. The simplicity of the Brownie format freed the photographer from technical concerns, allowing him to focus on the immediacy of his subject matter and achieve an impressionistic, snapshot aesthetic. The elaborate view camera, which had to be carefully positioned, each frame laboriously composed, resulted in an entirely different but equally beautiful image. The variability of aperture and focus allowed for a fine-grained negative with precise, crisp detail. Christenberry retained his frank, frontal compositions, although the camera's depth of field required him to stand at a greater distance from his subject, thereby incorporating more of the space surrounding buildings (Southall 1990). He has continued to use both photographic formats to achieve different ends.

While the younger photographer shared some of his predecessor's concerns for capturing the poetic qualities of time and place that characterized rural Alabama, he was not simply recreating or quoting Evans's vision. Christenberry felt a deep personal relationship to Evans's and Agee's work based on his childhood experiences and intimate knowledge of the places and even the distant relatives of the families the two men visited. However, Christenberry desired his pictures to imbue something of the losses of past, as well as speak to the present and the renewal of the South, all while encapsulating the regions rich textures and mysteries. Perhaps because his works achieve such a formal purity in their direct compositions, clear contours, and colors, they evoke timelessness or the slow passage of time rather than simply nostalgia. In fact, Trudy Wilner Stack has described the photographer's intention as a reconstruction and discovery of his own impressions alongside those of modernism's prodigies, namely his wide-ranging artistic and literary influences (Stack 1996).

It is noteworthy that Christenberry was never drawn to the languid antebellum mansions, many of which remained in the Hale County environs. Under his watchful eye, Christenberry's subject matter—the Palmist Building, the Green Warehouse, Sprott Church, the cotton gin of Havana Junction, the humble, gravelly gravesites of Hale County—seems to come alive with a vibrant energy, despite the fact that most of these sites have been long abandoned as relics of their oft-troubled past. In fact, the 20-mile radius that comprises Christenberry's focus has remained virtually unchanged since Evans's time (Southall 1990). Although one might expect strip malls, billboards, neon signs, and the other outcroppings of postwar development to have long since invaded and taken over, no McDonald's or its like exists in Hale County. In Christenberry's photographs, the old buildings and landscapes seem to mythically reappear—year after year—as they are inextricably intertwined with Christenberry's memories and the viewers' own associations. Past and present are thus married in these lyrical portraits of the American Deep South. Metaphorically speaking, the images reference life cycles and suggest the residue of human existence, despite the fact that the human figure rarely appears. According to Rebecca Walker, "Courageously, methodically, he [Christenberry] documents one hundred little deaths as the houses and roads and general stores of his childhood change form and face and, eventually, disappear" (Reynolds and Walker 1996).

As an illustration of his working process, consider *Kudzu and House, Tuscaloosa County, Alabama* (1989), a structure that he photographed over a 13-year period. The kudzu, a fast-creeping green vine that grows over much of the Southeast, had nearly engulfed the modest tenant's shack on a hill in 1990. Then, one year later, Christenberry returned, fully expecting the house to be buried under the persistent vines; however, the kudzu had been cut back. And in 1992, the structure had been razed, preparing the reddened, virgin land for something else. His 1991 and 1992 photographs of the site document this narrative. In relation to this and other subjects, Christenberry has spoken of a desire to "possess" his subjects (the buildings in particular), to make material and tactile what is fleeting and evanescent. Alongside his photographs, he has continued to make paintings and small, free-standing sculptures of the various buildings he visits. He memorialized the "kudzu shack" two years later with such a sculpture.

Christenberry's iconography finds form in many media, including paintings and drawings collaged with found objects, sculptural reincarnations of the photographed sites, as well as the more troubling mixed-media installation known as *The Klan Room*, begun in 1962. He has spoken about his desire to memorialize the fullest history of his Southern roots, a place rife with conflicts between good and evil, black and white, rich and poor. In part due to the influence of the Civil Rights movement but also as a means of grappling with his more personal experiences as a Southerner, Christenberry began to look at the Ku Klux Klan in Hale County and use its rhetoric of hate and violence as a means of offering a white man's critique of Southern racism. In 1963, he began making sculptures of Klan figures from G.I. Joe action figures who wore the sumptuously colored satin robes of their group. The dolls were often situated in pairs or groups within built architectural tableaux, and then photographed. Over 40 years later, the sculptures have become part of an ongoing installation comprising over 300 objects and images. Cognizant of the discomfort with which many viewers and even his fellow artists have viewed this body of work, Christenberry insists that *The Klan Room* is a vital part of his oeuvre, stating that "there are times when an artist must examine and reveal such strange and secret brutality" (Christenberry quoted in Stack 1996).

As a consummate photographer of the South—Christenberry has never photographed in Washington, D.C., where he has lived since 1968—he shares with his peers William Eggleston, Emmet Gowin, and others the desire to capture the essence of a culture as he both recognizes and yet transcends its stereotypes. Christenberry is both a part of and a critic of the tradition, the landscape, and the culture of the South, its myths and realities. Although often associated with a regionalist perspective (sometimes pejoratively) Christenberry's photography succeeds in finding the universal within a highly personal language of symbols and signs.

LYNN M. SOMERS-DAVIS

See also: **Brownie; Documentary Photography; Eggleston, William; Evans, Walker; Gowin, Emmet; Photography in the United States: the South**

Biography

Born November 5, 1936 in Tuscaloosa, Alabama. Earned MA, University of Alabama, Tuscaloosa, Alabama, 1959; BA, University of Alabama, Tuscaloosa, Alabama, 1958. Traveled to New York City for the first time, 1958–59 where he saw Abstract Expressionist work; moved to New York, 1961; left to teach in Memphis one year later. Married Sandra Deane, August 19, 1967; the couple moved from Memphis to Washington, D.C., 1968. That same year began annual sojourns to Hale County, Alabama and its environs (for the next three decades) inspired by the work and friendship of Walker Evans. Had first solo show in New York's Zabriskie Gallery of photography and sculpture, 1976; first solo show in Washington, D.C. at Sander Gallery, 1977. Associate and then Professor of Art, The Corcoran School of Art, Washington, D.C., 1968 to present; Assistant and then Associate Professor of Art, Memphis State University, Memphis, Tennessee, 1962–68; Instructor of Art, University of Alabama, Tuscaloosa, Alabama, 1959–61. Selected awards and honors include: Doctor of Humane Letters (Honorary), University of Alabama, Tuscaloosa, Alabama, 1998; The University of Memphis Distinguished Achievement Award in Memory of Elvis Presley, Memphis, Tennessee, 1996; Art Matters Grant, New York, New York, 1994; Educator of the Year, Society for Photographic Education, 1995; Yale University Summer School of Art and Music, Visiting Artist, Norfolk, Connecticut, 1993; Yale University Summer School of Art and Music, Visiting Artist, Norfolk, Connecticut, 1991; Eudora Welty Professor of Southern Studies, Millsaps College, Jackson, Mississippi, 1991; The Alabama Prize, Alabama, 1989; John Simon Guggenheim Memorial Fellowship, 1984.

Individual Exhibitions

1961 University of Alabama Gallery of Art; Tuscaloosa, Alabama

1963 Memphis State University Gallery of Art; Memphis, Tennessee

1967 Mary Chilton Gallery; Memphis, Tennessee

1972 University of Maryland; Baltimore County, Maryland

1973 The Corcoran Gallery of Art; Washington, D.C.

The Baltimore Museum of Art; Baltimore, Maryland

Photographs by William Christenberry; The Octagon House, American Institute of Architects; Washington, D.C.

1979 The Montgomery Museum of Fine Arts; Montgomery, Alabama

The Corcoran Gallery of Art; Washington, D.C.

1982 Atlanta Gallery of Photography; Atlanta, Georgia

1983 *William Christenberry, Southern Views*; The Corcoran Gallery of Art; Washington, D.C.

Southern Views; Huntsville Museum of Art; Huntsville, Alabama

1987 *William Christenberry, Photographs and Sculpture*; Southwest Craft Center; San Antonio, Texas

William Christenberry, Southern Monuments, Northlight; Arizona State University; Tempe, Arizona

1989 The Montgomery Museum of Fine Arts; Montgomery, Alabama

1990 *Southern Exposure*; Cranbrook Academy of Arts Museum; Bloomfield Hills, Michigan

1990 *Dream Buildings and Other New Work*; Middendorf Gallery; Washington, D.C.

William Christenberry; Center for Cultural Arts; Gadsden, Alabama

1991 *Thirty by Forty Photographs*; Middendorf Gallery; Washington, D.C.

William Christenberry, Southern Views, Galveston Arts Center, Galveston, Texas

1995 Pace/MacGill Gallery; New York

1996 *Christenberry*: *Reconstruction*; Center for Creative Photography; Tucson, Arizona and the University of Arizona Museum of Art; Contemporary Arts Center, New Orleans, Louisiana

William Christenberry, The Early Years, 1954–1968; Morris Museum of Art; Augusta, Georgia

1997 The Phillips Collection; Washington, D.C.
2001 *Selected Works*; Hemphill Fine Arts; Washington, D.C.
William Christenberry: Sculpture, Photographs, and Drawings; Pace/MacGill Gallery; New York, New York

Selected Group Exhibitions

1977 *Bill Christenberry—Walker Evans—Photographs*; Longwood Gallery, Massachusetts College of Art; Boston
1978 *The Presence of Walker Evans*; Institute of Contemporary Art; Boston, Massachusetts
1979 *American Photography of the Seventies*; Art Institute of Chicago; Chicago, Illinois
Fotographie in Alltag Amerikas; Das Kunstgewerbemuseum; Zurich, Switzerland
1982 *Color as Form: A History of Color Photography*; International Museum of Photography, George Eastman House; Rochester, New York
1983 *Southern Fictions*; Contemporary Arts Museum; Houston, Texas
1985 *American Images: Photography, 1945–1980*; Barbican Art Gallery; London
Color Roots—William Eggleston—William Christenberry; The Burden Gallery, Aperture Foundation; New York
1987 *10 Photographes Americains Contemporains*; Galerie Zabriskie; Paris
Legacy of Light; International Center of Photography; New York
1989 *The Blues Aesthetic: Black Culture and Modernism*; Washington Project for the Arts; Washington, D.C.
New Southern Photography: Between Myth and Reality; The Burden Gallery, Aperture Foundation; New York
The Photography of Invention: American Pictures of the 1980s; National Museum of American Art, Smithsonian Institution; Washington, D.C.; Museum of Contemporary Art, Chicago, Illinois; Walker Art Center, Minneapolis, Minnesota
Deep South; 20th Recontres Internationales de la Photographie d'Arles; France
1990 *Of Time and Place: Walker Evans and William Christenberry*; Amon Carter Museum, Fort Worth; Wichita Art Museum, Kansas; Portland Museum of Art, Maine; and The Friends of Photography, San Francisco
Walker Evans, Amerika: Bilder aus den Jahren der Depression; Lenbachhaus Städtische Galerie; Munich, Germany
1991 *Motion and Document, Sequence and Time: Eadweard Muybridge and Contemporary American Photography*; Addison Gallery of Art, Phillips Academy; Andover, Massachusetts
1994 *An American Century of Photography: From Dry-Plate to Digital, The Hallmark Photographic Collection*; Nelson-Atkins Museum of Art; Kansas City and traveling
American Studies; The Art Forum Praterinsel; Munich, Germany
Duchamp's Leg; Walker Art Center; Minneapolis, Minnesota
House and Home: Spirits of the South: Max Belcher, Beverly Buchanan, and William Christenberry; Addison Gallery of American Art, Phillips Academy; Andover, Massachusetts; Georgia Museum of Art, University of Georgia, Athens; Morris Museum of Art, Augusta, Georgia; Duke University Museum of Art, Durham, North Carolina; Tampa Museum of Art, Florida
Worlds in a Box, organized by the South Bank Centre, for the Arts Council of Great Britain, London (touring)
1995 *Alabama Impact: Contemporary Artists with Alabama Ties*; Mobile Museum of Art; Mobile, Alabama
Civil Rights Now; Southeastern Center for Contemporary Art; Winston-Salem, North Carolina (traveling)
The Insistent Subject: Photographing Time and Again; The Museum of Contemporary Photography; Columbia College, Chicago, Illinois

Selected Works

Side of Palmist Building, Havana Junction, Alabama, 1961
House, near Marion, Alabama, 1964
Church, Sprott, Alabama, 1971
Church between Greensboro and Marion, Alabama, 1973
Country Store with Gasoline Pumps, Emelle, Alabama, 1974
Child's Grave with Rosebuds, Hale County, Alabama, 1975
Gourd Tree, Pickens County, Alabama, 1979
Kudzu with Storm Cloud, near Akron, Alabama, 1981
The Bar-B-Q Inn, Greensboro, Alabama, 1981
Red Building in Forest, Hale County, Alabama, 1983
Otis and Willie Mae Hicks' Store, outside Greensboro, Alabama, 1987
Southern Monument XVI, 1983-1986, 1987
Kudzu and House, Tuscaloosa County, Alabama, 1989
Sign, near Carrollton, Mississippi, 1991
Providence Church, Perry County, Alabama, 1993

Further Reading

Brownlee, Peter J. "Interview with William Christenberry." *The Southern Quarterly* 32 (1994): 89–94.
Christenberry, William. *Southern Photographs*. Millerton, New York: Aperture Inc. 1983.
Christenberry, William, et al, *In Response to Place: Photographs from the Nature Conservancy's Last Great Places*. Foreword by Terry Tempest Williams, and essay by Andy Grundberg. Boston: Little, Brown, 2001.
Christenberry, William, Max Belcher, and Beverly Buchanan. *House and Home: Spirits of the South*, with essays by Rebecca Walker and Jock Reynolds. Andover, Massachusetts: Addison Gallery of American Art, 1994.
Gruber, J. Richard. *William Christenberry: The Early Years, 1954–1968*. Tuscaloosa: University of Alabama Press, 1998.
Gruber, Rick, and Heather Lustfelt. *William Christenberry: The Constructions and Related Drawings, 1961–1968*. (Exhibition Catalogue). Kansas City: University of Missouri–Kansas City Gallery of Art, 1997.

Hopps, Walter. "William Christenberry: Clan Dolls." *Grand Street* 11 (Winter 1993): 81–95.
Kalinovska, Milena. *William Christenberry: Changing Landscape – The Source Revisited* (Exhibition Catalogue). Washington, D.C.: The Kreeger Museum, 2001.
Lange, Susanne, Claudia Schubert, and Allan Tullos. *William Christenberry: Disappearing Places*. Dusseldorf, Germany: Richter Verlag, 2001.
Simmons, Steve. "William Christenberry: Exploring His Southern Heritage." *View Camera* 6, (May–June 1993): 4–9.
Southall, Thomas. *Of Time and Place: Walker Evans and William Christenberry*. San Francisco and Fort Worth: The Friends of Photography and the Amon Carter Museum, 1990.
Stack, Trudy Wilner, and Allen Tullos. *Christenberry Reconstruction: The Art of William Christenberry*. Jackson, Mississippi and Tucson, Arizona: University Press of Mississippi and the Center for Creative Photography, University of Arizona, 1996.
Weil, Rex. "William Christenberry, Nancy Drysdale." *ArtNews* 94, April 1995: 151.

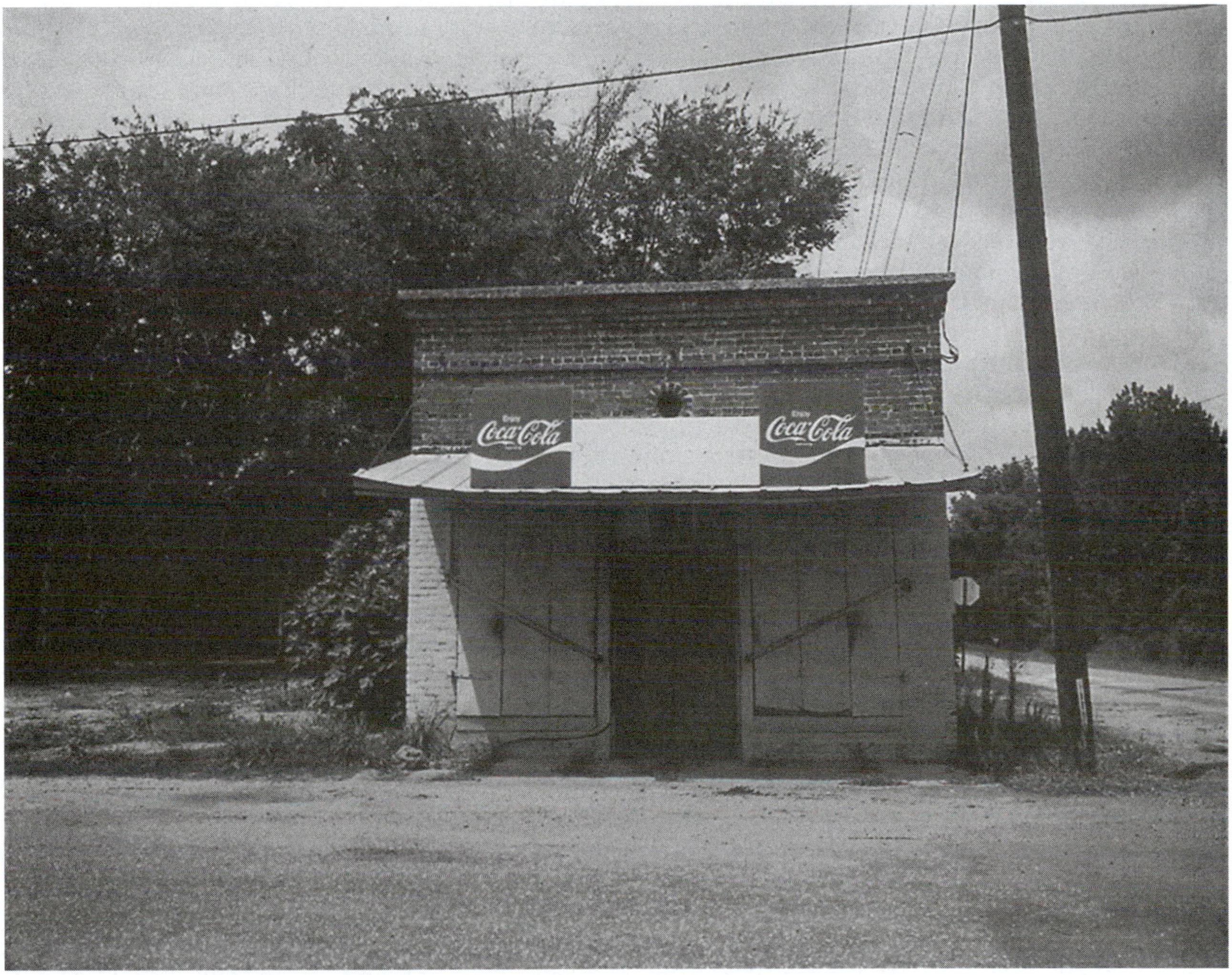

William Christenberry, The Bar-B-Q Inn, Greensboro, Alabama, 1981. Original in color.
[*Courtesy of Pace/MacGill Gallery*]

LARRY CLARK

American

Larry Clark first came to prominence in the New York art world with the publication of *Tulsa* (1971), a collection of graphic photographs of Clark and his friends hanging out, using drugs, having sex, and playing with guns in the homes and suburbs of that Midwestern city. As a photographer and filmmaker, Clark has concentrated his energies on themes of adolescent angst, self-destruction, physical violence, masculine aggression, raw sexuality, and drug culture. Inspired by the conventions of documentary and the immediacy of montage, Clark either records or creates intimate situations that indict the viewer's voyeuristic fascination with the potential for violence in human subjectivity and with the interactions that linger beyond normative veneers. Clark may be criticized for condoning, exploiting, or enabling destructive activities and for sympathy with white masculine excess, but Clark maintains that his work presents cautionary moral tales of under-explored social and cultural dysfunction and marginalization. Clark's work provokes much discussion, often as a result of censorship, regarding the psychic and physical character of adolescence and widespread unease, silence, and blindness about the tensions in adolescent and adult-adolescent relationships.

Clark began his career as a photographer assisting his mother's business, going door-to-door as a baby portrait photographer in his hometown of Tulsa, Oklahoma. At 18, Clark enrolled in a commercial photography school in Milwaukee, Wisconsin. Influenced by students at a nearby art school and the work of W. Eugene Smith, Clark began to think of his medium as being able to present complex information and narrative. Clark's friends in Tulsa had long been accustomed to seeing him with a camera, and Clark began to photograph unsanitized aspects of adolescence in white suburbia. Alluding to the formal and autobiographical conventions of documentary and using a 35-mm camera, a wide-angle lens, and existing light sources, *Tulsa* records graphic scenes of sex, violence, and drug use in youth culture as naturalized activity. Drafted in 1964, Clark was in the army through 1966, serving in Vietnam, and he then traveled throughout the Unites States, with periods living in New York and New Mexico. In 1971, he met Danny Seymour, who had worked with Robert Frank, and Seymour was inspired to finance *Tulsa.* Clark received a National Endowment for the Arts $5000 "Imprimatur of Excellence" grant for his work on *Tulsa*, but after multiple arrests and convictions due to drug and alcohol abuse, violent acts, and the shooting of a friend during a dispute, Clark served a 19-month term in a maximum security prison, beginning in 1976. *Tulsa*, the first book published by Ralph Gibson's Lustrum fine arts press, became a milestone of photography in the second half of the twentieth century.

Teenage Lust (1983) is more sexual, disturbing, and much more autobiographical than *Tulsa*, with images of adolescents living on the edge without fear of violence, dying, and death, and with photographs that directly locate Clark's experience within the context of his work. Clark confronts his viewers with images of youth culture in self-destruction, and critics have charged that these images of teen lust and sex often normalize male aggression and its unpleasant consequences.

Reflecting Clark's enduring obsession with teenagers and sexuality, *The Perfect Childhood* (1993) examines the influence of mass media on teenagers. *Larry Clark, 1992* (1992), Clark's first photo-essay in color, consists of portraits that emphasize teenage male sexuality and autoerotic play with guns.

As a filmmaker, Clark continues his interest in chronicling the confusion, desire, rage, inhumanity, and potential tenderness that animate human relationships. In narratives dedicated to a realistic imperative, untrained or amateur actors and convincing scenes of physical and sexual violence hint at the flaws in human character, and they challenge cultural veneers regarding the conflicts of adolescence. Clark's films have been banned from many venues because they challenge cultural taboos with images of adolescent nudity, sexuality, self-destruction, and brutality.

Clark's first feature film, *Kids* (1995), continues themes of masculine aggression and drug activity, and features a male protagonist who pursues the sexual conquest of female virgins. The film follows 24 hours of a group of young New Yorkers in their daily activities of hanging out, skateboarding, doing drugs, being violent, and having sex. The film's narrative is propelled by one of the girl's learning that she is HIV-positive and looking for the boy who seduced and infected her. Clark commissioned the screenplay from Harmony Korine, who was a skateboarder in his last year of high school when he met Clark. Shot in a *vérité* style with mostly untrained actors, *Kids*, reflects Clark's desire to make "the great American teenage movie, like the great American novel." *Kids* won the Golden Palm award at Cannes Film Festival.

Clark's second feature film, *Another Day in Paradise* (1998), is a grim coming-of-age story, set in the 1970s. Based on a novel by ex-convict Eddie Little, the story concerns the conflict between a life of drugs and crime and the desire for family as two aging junkies mentor two young lovers. The everyday life of heroin users with its inherent violence appears almost ancillary to the ordinary pursuit for strong interpersonal relationships. *Bully* (2001), is based on the book *Bully: A True Story of High School Revenge* by Jim Schutze. The film retells the story of an actual murder of a high school bully by a group of high school friends in Hollywood, Florida, in 1993. *Ken Park* (2002), co-directed with Ed Lachman, takes place in suburban Visalia, California. The film focuses on four teenagers and the adults in their lives and exposes the difficult sexual longings and fears that underlie their self-identity, and many aspects of their relationships become vehicles for expression of subconscious emotional responses. The explicit depiction of sexual practice and sexualized violence juxtaposed against normative social veneers suggests insight into the darker aspects of human character.

SCOTT SHERER

See also: **Censorship**

Biography

Born Tulsa, Oklahoma, 1943. Commercial photography training, Layton School of Art Milwaukee, Wisconsin, 1961. Served U.S. Army 1964–66. National Endowment for the Arts Grant, 1973. Lives and works in New York City.

Individual Exhibitions

1971 San Francisco Art Institute; San Francisco, California
1975 International Museum of Photography and Film, George Eastman House; Rochester, New York
1986 Fotografiska Museet; Stockholm, Sweden
1999 *Larry Clark*; Gröninger Museum; Grönginen, Netherlands (traveled to Galerie Max Hetzler, Berlin, and Galeri Kamel Mennour, Paris)

Selected Group Exhibitions

1981 *Whitney Biennial*; The Whitney Museum of American Art; New York, New York
1985 *American Images 1945–80*; Barbican Art Gallery; London, England
1986 The Museum of Contemporary Art; Los Angeles, California
1992 *American Documents in the Fringe*; Tokyo Metropolitan Museum of Photography; Tokyo, Japan
1995 *Feminin-Masculine: le sexe de l'art*; Centre Georges Pompidou; Paris, France
1996 Wiener Secession; Vienna (traveled to The Photographers' Gallery, London, and Milwaukee Art Museum, Milwaukee, Wisconsin)

Selected Works

Tulsa; New York, 1971
Teenage Lust; New York: Larry Clark, 1983
Larry Clark, 1992; New York: Thea Westreich, 1992
The Perfect Childhood, New York and Zurich: Scalo, 1993
Kids; New York: Grove Press, 1995
Kids; Shining Excalibur Films, 95 minutes, 1995
Another Day in Paradise; Trimark Pictures, 101 minutes, 1998
Heroin; New York: Power House Cultural Entertainment, March 1999
Larry Clark; Groningen, Netherlands: Groninger Museum, 1999
Bully; Lions Gate Films, 112 minutes, 2001
Ken Park; Cinea, 96 minutes, 2002

Further Reading

Chang, Chris. "Larry Clark's Just a Guy Who Can't Say No. Can You?" *Film Comment*, 38, no. 5 (Sept./Oct. 2002).

Doherty, Tom. "Clueless kids." *Cineast*, 21, no. 4 (December 1995).

Giroux, Henry. "Media Panics and the War Against 'Kids': Larry Clark and the Politics of Diminished Hopes." In *Breaking in to the movies: film and the culture of politics*. Malden, Massachusetts: Blackwell Publishers, 2002.

Hooks, Bell. "White Light." *Sight and Sound* 6, no. 5 (May 1996).

Muñoz, José Esteban. "Rough boy trade: queer desire/straight identity in the photography of Larry Clark." In *The Passionate Camera: Photography and Bodies of Desire*, edited by Deborah Bright. London and New York: Routledge, 1998.

Savage, Jon. "Now Larry Clark's Kids." *Sight and Sound* 6, no. 5 (May 1996).

Schrader, Paul. "Babes in the hood." *Artforum International* 33, no. 9 (May 1995).

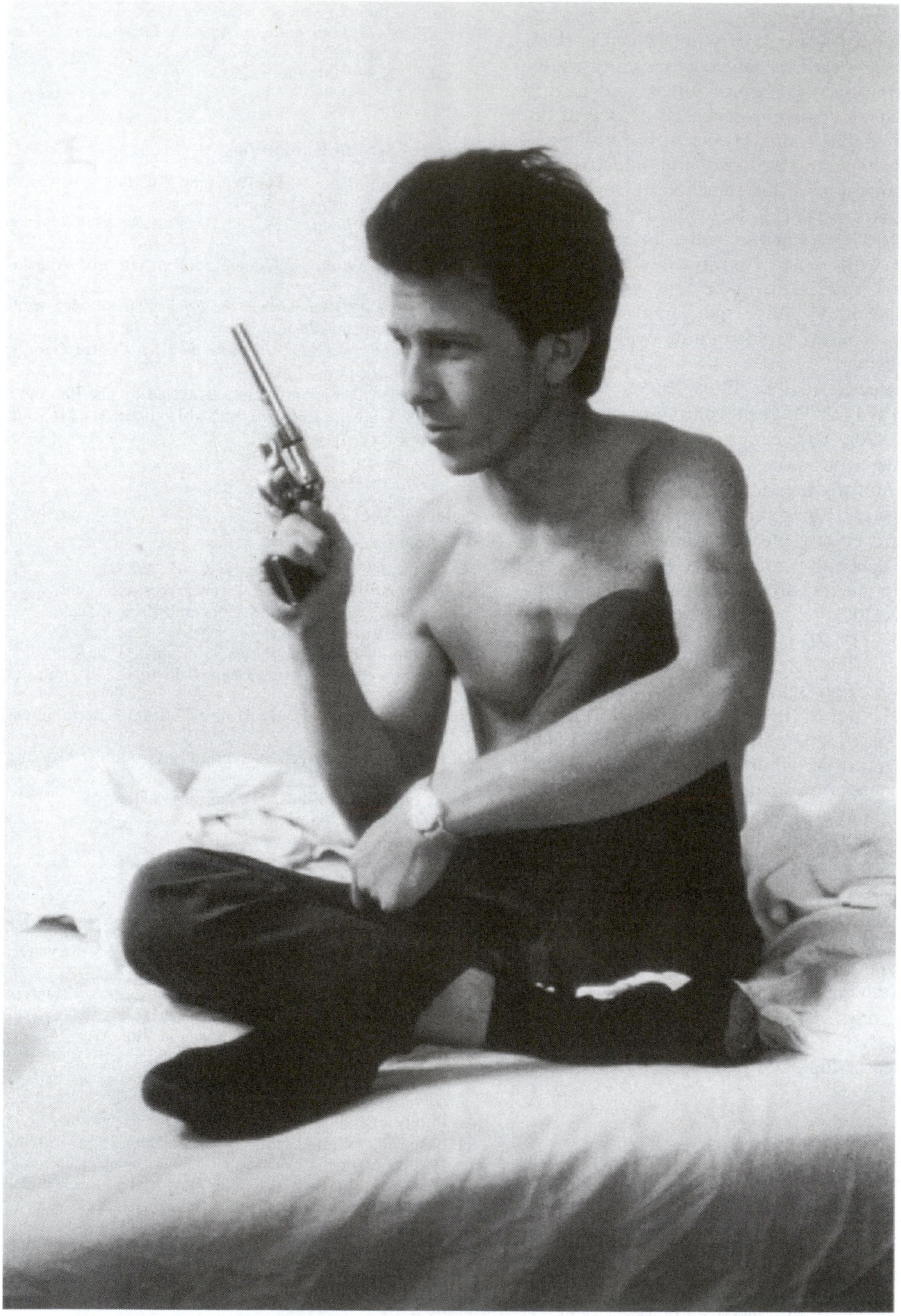

Larry Clark, Tulsa Portofolio, 1972, Gelatin Silver Print,Edition of 10.
[© *Courtesy of the artist and Luhring Augustine, New York*]

CHUCK CLOSE

American

Although recognized primarily as a painter, Chuck Close has also been a photographer since college. Photography is integral to his paintings and prints; his photographs are in turn influenced by his approaches to painting.

Close is best known for iconic portraits that are often more than eight feet high. They begin as photographs that he takes with a 20 × 24 Polaroid camera. He overlays the photo with a penciled grid on a sheet of acetate, which he uses to transfer the image in a process he calls "knitting." Each square in the grid contains a mark that is subtly different from the others and is intriguing for its pattern and value. But when the viewer shifts perspective from the individual mark to the entire painting, the marks meld into a synergistic whole as they begin to define a human face. Close's *oeuvre* can be viewed in the same way: the subject matter varies little—always head and shoulders of a family member, friend, or fellow artist—yet when viewed as a whole paints a much bigger picture.

Close first studied photography in the early 1960s after attending Yale University's summer art program. A methodical artist who admits to being a "control freak," Close earned a B.F.A. and an M.F.A. with highest honors from the Yale University School of Art. There he studied with Philip Guston and Robert Rauschenberg. His classmates included realist painters Rackstraw Downes and Janet Fish, and conceptual and minimalist artists Richard Serra and Nancy Graves, who later became subjects of his portraits. "The trouble is, if it looks like art, it must look like someone else's art or it wouldn't look like art," he has said, referring to early influences that he imitated briefly. "When I met De Kooning I said, 'How do you do? My name is Chuck Close. I'm the person who's made almost as many De Koonings as you've made."

Close says that he used photography to answer questions such as what it means to make a representational painting after the invention of photography. The important distinction of post-war American art, according to Close, was the "sense of overallness" expressed in a painting by Jackson Pollock or Frank Stella. He intended to apply that sense to portraiture by making every feature as important as the next—to make the mustache hairs as important as the eyes. "The camera is not aware of what it is looking at. It just gets it all down," he has said.

His portraits are simultaneously confrontational and coolly distant. The large format of the Polaroid image and the grand scale of his prints and paintings create tension between the artificiality of the flat surface and what the viewer eventually recognizes as a human face. By keeping the subject matter consistent, he minimizes the variables, heightening that friction between style and content. He chooses his enormous scale to accentuate the physical characteristics, lighting and posing his subjects not to flatter them but to introduce interesting details. "Every viewer enters the work through the shared humanity of looking in a mirror, or looking at the faces of loved ones, no matter how much art historical baggage they bring," he explains. Ignoring the emotional aspects of the human face, he heightens its impersonal nature by discouraging any suggestion of expression and by using only the first names of his models in the titles. He refers to his portraits simply as "heads."

At first, he worked from found photographs; by 1966, he was making paintings based on photographs he had taken himself. In 1975, Close moved to the 20 × 24 Polaroid format because its immediacy generated dialogue with his models and allowed him to make changes as he worked. This interaction let him "slowly sneak up on what I wanted rather than having to predetermine what it was." The incremental process of responding to and modifying the existing is formalized in a technique he began using in his paintings in the 1970s. Instead of mixing his colors on the palette, Close replicates the dye-transfer process of building images by applying thin layers of magenta, cyan, and yellow directly on the canvas. He then applies "corrections" to achieve his desired result, discovering the color through the process.

He does, however, acknowledge that his portraits are of real people. "When someone lends me their image ... they don't know what I'm going to do with it, they have no control over it, they're not paying for it, so they can't ask for their nose to be straightened. It requires some bravery and generosity on their part."

In December 1988, Close suffered a rupture to a congenitally weak spinal artery. A violent seizure left him paralyzed from the neck down. After months of physical therapy, he regained limited movement in his arms and now paints with a brush Velcro-strapped to his hand. He also continues to explore photography.

In 1996, Close began working with printmaker David Adamson to produce a series of portraits as digital IRIS prints for the Pace/MacGill Gallery in New York. Close also collaborated with Jerry Spagnoli in 1999 to update the daguerreotype process. For two years, Close photographed a score of musicians and artists, including himself, for a handmade book that includes poems by Bob Holman. Adamson scanned the daguerreotypes and made digital prints for the limited-edition series of 75 books titled *A Couple of Ways of Doing Something*, completed in 2003.

Although art critics of the 1970s grouped Close with the nascent Photorealists, the narrow label inadequately describes the scope of his work. The distinguishing characteristic of Photorealism is its reliance on the camera to produce work that is veristic yet hand wrought. Close chafes at the label "realist" because he feels the artificiality of the work deserves equal weight. As an artist who deliberately shows his hand, Close reveals the magic in an attempt to differentiate between illusion and reality. Demystifying the process, according to Close, is the truth behind realism.

Renata Golden

Biography

Born Charles Thomas Close in Monroe, Washington, July 5, 1940. University of Washington, B.A., magna cum laude, 1964. Attended Yale Summer School of Music and Art, Norfolk, CT, 1961. Graduated from Yale University School of Art and Architecture, B.F.A., 1963 and M.F.A., 1964, both with highest honors. Received numerous honorary degrees and honored by many cultural institutions throughout the United States. Awarded Fulbright Grant to study work of Gustav Klimt and Egon Schiele in Vienna, Austria, 1964–65. Taught painting and photography in the Department of Art at the University of Massachusetts, 1965–67; at the School of Visual Arts in New York, 1967–71; and at New York University, 1970–73. Taught summer school at the University of Seattle, 1970 and the Yale Summer School of Art and Music, 1971 and 1972. Awarded National Endowment for the Arts Fellowship, 1973; Skowhegan Medal for Painting, 1991; University of Washington Alumnus Summa Laude Dignatus, 1997; National Medal of Arts and National Humanities Medal Award, 2000. Disabled by a spinal blood clot in 1988. Lives and works in New York City and Long Island.

Solo Exhibitions

1982 *Chuck Close Photographs*; California Museum of Photography; University of California, Riverside, CA; University Art Museum, UC Berkeley, CA

1985 *Chuck Close: Photographs*; Pace/MacGill Gallery; New York, NY

1985 *Chuck Close: Large Scale Photographs*; Fraenkel Gallery; San Francisco, CA

1987 *Chuck Close: Polaroids*; Aldrich Museum of Contemporary Art; Ridgefield, CT

1988 *Chuck Close: Prints and Photographs*; Pace Editions; New York, NY

1989 *Chuck Close*; Art Institute of Chicago; Chicago, IL, (traveled to the Friends of Photography, Ansel Adams Center, San Francisco)

1996 *Chuck Close: Photographic Portraits*; Pace/MacGill Gallery; New York, NY

1998 *Chuck Close*; The Museum of Modern Art; New York, NY

Group Exhibitions

1981 *Seven Photorealists from New York Collections*; The Solomon R. Guggenheim Museum; New York, NY

1982 *Momentbild: Kunstlerphotographie*; Kestner-Gesellschaft; Hanover, Germany

1983 *Photographic Visions by Martha Alf, Chuck Close, Robert Cumming, David Hockney, Robert Rauschenberg, Ed Ruscha*; Los Angeles Center for Photographic Studies; Los Angeles, CA

1985–86 *Self Portrait: The Photographer's Persona, 1840–1985*; Museum of Modern Art, New York, NY

1986 *50 Years of Modern Color Photography*; Cologne, Germany

1986 *Viewpoint: The Artist as Photographer*; New Jersey Center for the Visual Arts; Summit, NJ

1997 *Photorealists*; Savannah College of Art and Design; Savannah, GA

1999 *Photorealism/Periphery*; Museum of Art Brigham Young University; Provo, UT

2000 The *Persistence of Photography in American Portraiture*; Yale University Art Gallery; New Haven, CT

2003 *New to View: Recent Acquisitions in Photography*; Art Institute of Chicago; Chicago, IL

2004 *Speaking With Hands: Photographs from the Buhl Collection*; Solomon R. Guggenheim Museum; New York, NY

2004 *Printed Light — Photographic Vision and the Modern Print*; National Gallery of Australia; Parkes, Canberra

Selected Works

Philip Glass (working photograph for painting), 1969

Self-Portrait/Composite/Nine Parts, composite Polaroid photograph, 1979

Self-Portrait (3 Parts), Polaroid photograph, 1980

Lucas, 1993

Lorna I, digital ink jet print on kozo paper, 1996

Elton, ink jet print mounted on aluminum, 2000
Self-Portrait, 2002

Further Reading

Clay, John. "Finding the Color World: An Interview with Chuck Close." http://www.artzar.com/content/close/index.html.

Coleman, A.D. "From Today Painting is Dead." *Camera 35* 18, no. 5, (July 1974): 34.

Dyckes, William. "The Photo as Subject: The Paintings and Drawings of Chuck Close." *Arts Magazine* (February, 1974).

Grundberg, Andy. "Blurring the Lines—Dots?—Between Camera and Brush." *The New York Times*, October 16, 1988: 35.

Kramer, Hilton. "Chuck Close's Break with Photography." *The New York Times*, April 19, 1981.

Meisel, Louis K. *Photo-Realism*. New York: Harry N. Abrams, Inc., 1980.

Naef, Weston. *New Trends from the Gallery of World Photography Series*. Japan: Shueisha Publishing Co., 1983.

Princeton University lectures. "Chuck Close, Eminent painter and printmaker." October 9, 2003, http://www.princeton.edu/WebMedia/lectures/.

Nemser, Cindy. "An Interview with Chuck Close." *Artforum* (January 1970): 51–55.

Solomon, Deborah. "The Persistence of the Portraitist." *The New York Times Magazine*, Feb. 1, 1998: 24.

Storr, Robert. *Chuck Close*, with essays by Kirk Varnedoe and Deborah Wye. New York: The Museum of Modern Art, 1998.

Tully, Judd. "Interview with Chuck Close." Smithsonian *Archives of American Art*, 1987, http://artarchives.si.edu/oralhist/close87.htm.

Vaizey, Marina. *The Artist as Photographer*. New York: Holt, Rinehart and Winston, 1982.

Art Institute of Chicago in collaboration with The Friends of Photography, text by Colin Westerbeck. *Chuck Close*. Chicago: The Art Institute of Chicago, 1988.

ALVIN LANGDON COBURN

British

Although mostly known today for his month-long venture into abstract photography in 1917, Alvin Langdon Coburn left a broader contribution to the medium's history. Almost a generation younger than his mentors, Coburn seemed to straddle the various "camps" that desired to realize photography as a fine art circa 1900: Alfred Stieglitz's Photo-Secession in New York as well as those associated with his distant cousin F. Holland Day in Boston and London. Nicknamed the "Hustler," Coburn forged connections to Symbolist, Aesthetic, and Arts and Crafts proponents. Although Coburn seemed destined to make a name in photography after receiving his first camera when he was eight, his career was actually quite brief. He essentially abandoned photography in 1919, devoting the rest of his life to esoteric practices. Nevertheless, Coburn's complex career was a virtual cross-section of early-twentieth-century culture.

Born in 1882 into an old Boston family, Coburn was a determined and privileged child from the outset. His father died when he was seven, leaving him and his very ambitious mother with a substantial inheritance. A year after exhibiting in a Boston studio at the age of 15, he was introduced to Day, who would serve as his guide in photography. When he was 18, Coburn showed nine prints in Day's monumental exhibition, *New School of American Photography*, and helped to hang it at the Royal Photographic Society. While in London, he met a host of important photographers, including Edward Steichen and Frederick H. Evans. After the showing, Day and Coburn transported the work to the Photo-Club de Paris. Once again, Day presented his protégé to notable figures, including Robert Demachy and Frank Eugene, who were masters at gum printing. Variations on this process, which mimicked the tonal effects of impressionistic painting, would become Coburn's preferred photographic method.

Following further European travels, Coburn opened a portrait studio on New York's Fifth Avenue in 1902, not far from what become the headquarters of the Photo-Secession. There, he reestablished contact with Stieglitz and Steichen. He also met the mother figure of the Photo-Secession, Gertrude Käsebier, and worked in her portrait studio. Over the course of Coburn's association with the Photo-Secession, he was granted four issues of their journal *Camera Work* and two one-man shows at their gallery 291, also known as the Little Galleries of the Photo-Secession. Coburn boasted in his autobiography that at the age of 21, he had been elected to "two of the most advanced and artistically conscious groups of internationally-known photographers": the Photo-Secession and the Linked Ring Brotherhood of England.

Perhaps at Käsebier's suggestion, Coburn attended Arthur Wesley Dow's summer school at Ipswich, Massachusetts in 1902 and 1903. Dow, one of the best art teachers in America at the time, had published the great manual *Composition* in 1899, which would run into 20 editions over 40 years. Dow emphasized the Japanese concept of notan—a delicate balance of light and dark tones. Especially fascinated by wood-block printing, Dow had been assistant curator to Ernest Fenollosa in the Boston Museum of Fine Arts's Department of Chinese and Japanese Art. Dow was extremely accepting of photography in his curriculum. Often compared to the painter James McNeill Whistler, Coburn incorporated these oriental tenets into his strikingly balanced arrangements.

In 1904, Coburn persuaded the editor of New York's *Metropolitan Magazine* to commission him to photograph prominent British writers and artists. His first target was George Bernard Shaw, a successful playwright and dabbler in photography. The two became fast friends, and Shaw posed for over 50 sittings, declaring Coburn "one of the most accomplished and sensitive artists now living." Among his other sitters were the poets and authors Edward Carpenter, George Meredith, and G. K. Chesterton. Coburn later broadened his scope to include other intellectuals from other countries, eventually collecting the visages into a book, *Men of Mark* (1913). This was followed by *More Men of Mark* (1922) and his never-finished *Musicians of Mark*.

The Arts and Crafts' ideals of craftsmanship and the blending of all arts played large roles in Coburn's work. In 1904, he went to study with Frank Brangwyn, an English painter and printmaker who had trained with William Morris. Coburn later became a specialist in photogravure—a type of photomechanical reproduction that complimented Pictorial photography's soft tone—and he hand-pulled most of his own images. Coburn's numerous publication credits included his own books, *London* (1909), *New York* (1910), and *Moor Park* (1913), as well as illustrations for some of the leading writers of the day: Maurice Maeterlinck's *The Intelligence of Flowers* (1907), Henry James's *The Novels and Tales of Henry James* (1907–09; 24 volumes), and H.G. Wells's *The Door in the Wall and Other Stories* (1911).

Coburn always enjoyed experimenting in photography, whether it was mixing gum printing with platinum papers, using a specially designed soft-focus lens, or learning the first color photography process, autochrome, from Steichen in 1907. He also photographed from bold angles, such as in a view from the Metropolitan Tower "The Octopus" (1912), making the ordinary seem foreign in its convergence of lines and shapes. In 1916, Coburn was introduced to writer Ezra Pound and artist Wyndham Lewis, two important figures in England's Vorticist movement. Using three mirrors bound together, Coburn photographed Pound and bits of wood and crystal to produce enigmatic images that mimicked mineral formations or cubist renditions of light. Coburn produced his *Vortographs* in January 1917 and exhibited them in February, ending his stint into purely non-objective photography.

Coburn retired to North Wales with his wife for a life of freemasonry, mysticism, Eastern thought, goat raising, pianola playing, and painting. Coburn's interest in spiritual concerns can be seen as an outgrowth of his Symbolist leanings. Indeed, as he later explained, "The greatest artists have always had a spiritual background." In 1932, Coburn became a naturalized British citizen, making official what had been his residence for over 20 years. In 1966, he worked with photography collectors Helmut and Alison Gernsheim to complete an autobiography, thus bookmaking became his career. Before his photographic calling ended, Coburn was acquainted with, and influenced by, a veritable "who's who" of international arts and literary circles.

Leslie K. Brown

See also: **Evans, Frederick H.; History of Photography: Twentieth-Century Pioneers; Käsebier, Gertrude; Linked Ring; Non-Silver Processes; Photo-Secession; Photo-Secessionists; Pictorialism; Portraiture; Steichen, Edward; Stieglitz, Alfred**

Biography

Born in Boston, Massachusetts, 11 June 1882. Attended Arthur Wesley Dow's Summer School of Art, Ipswich, Massachusetts, 1902 and 1903; studied with Frank Brangwyn at his London art school, 1904; studied photogravure at London County Council School of Photo-Engraving, 1906. Opened studio in New York, 1903–06; worked in Gertrude Käsebier's portrait studio, 1903–04. Invited to join the Photo-Secession, New York, 1902; elected to Linked Ring Brotherhood, England, 1903. Major holdings of his work are housed at the International Museum of Photography and Film at the George Eastman House, Rochester, New York; the Harry Ransom Humanities Research Center at the University of Texas at Austin; and the Royal Photographic Society, England. Died in Rhos-on-Sea, North Wales, 23 November 1966.

Individual Exhibitions

1903 Camera Club of New York; New York
1906 Royal Photographic Society; England
1906 Liverpool Amateur Photographic Association; Liverpool, England
1907 Little Galleries of the Photo-Secession; New York
1909 Little Galleries of the Photo-Secession, New York
1917 Show of Vortograph photographs and paintings, Goupil Gallery; New York
1924 Royal Photographic Society; England
1962 University of Reading; Reading, England
1978 *Alvin Langdon Coburn*; George Eastman House; Rochester, New York, and traveling
1982 *Alvin Langdon Coburn, Man of Mark 1882–1966: Centenary Exhibition*, The Royal Photographic Society and The National Centre of Photography; England
1983 *Alvin Langdon Coburn: London/New York, 1909–1910*; International Center of Photography, New York
1987 *Alvin Langdon Coburn: A Retrospective*; Haverford Comfort Gallery, Harverford, College; Harverford, Pennsylvania, and traveling
1998 *Alvin Langdon Coburn*; Photokina, Römisch-Germanisches Museum; Cologne, Germany
1999 *Alvin Langdon Coburn*; George Eastman House, Rochester, New York

Group Exhibitions

1900 *New School of American Photography*; Royal Photographic Society; England; and Photo Club-de Paris; Paris, France
1910 *International Exhibition of Pictorial Photography*; Albright Knox Gallery; Buffalo, New York
1915 *American Pictorial Photography*; Syracuse University; Syracuse, New York
1937 *Photography, 1839–1937*; Museum of Modern Art, New York
1978 *The Collection of Alfred Stieglitz: Fifty Pioneers of Modern Photography*; Metropolitan Museum of Art, New York
1978 *Pictorial Photography in Britain, 1900–1920*; Arts Council of Great Britain, and traveling
1979 *Photography Rediscovered: American Photographs, 1900–1930*; Whitney Museum of American Art; New York; and Art Institute of Chicago; Chicago, Illinois
1981 *Cubism and American Photography, 1910–1930*; Sterling and Francine Clark Art Institute; Williamstown, Massachusetts, and traveling
1983 *Alfred Stieglitz and the Photo-Secession*; Currier Gallery of Art; Manchester, New Hampshire, and traveling
1997 *Alvin Langdon Coburn and H.G. Wells: The Photographer and the Novelist, A Unique Collection of Photographs and Letters from the University Library's H.G. Wells Collection*; Krannert Art Museum; University of Illinois at Urbana-Champaign; Urbana-Champaign, Illinois

Selected Works

The Bridge–Ipswich, 1903
Regent's Canal, London, 1904
Shadows and Reflections, Venice, 1905
Le Penseur (George Bernard Shaw), 1906
Spider Webs, 1906
Notre Dame, 1906
William Butler Yeats, 1908
The Copper Plate Press, self-portrait, 1908
Wapping, Plate X from *London*, 1909
The Great Temple, Grand Canyon, 1911
The Octopus, New York, 1912
Vortograph of Ezra Pound, 1916
Vortographs, series, 1917

Further Reading

Coburn, Alvin Langdon, with an essay by Hilaire Belloc. *London*. London: Duckworth & Co., and New York: Brentano's, 1909.
Coburn, Alvin Langdon with a foreword by H. G. Wells. *New York*. London: Duckworth & Co., and New York: Brentano's, 1910.
Coburn, Alvin Langdon. *Men of Mark*. London: Duckworth & Co., and New York: Mitchell Kennerley, 1913.
Coburn, Alvin Langdon and Nancy Newhall. *A Portfolio of Sixteen Photographs by Alvin Langdon Coburn*. Rochester, New York: George Eastman House, 1962.
Coburn, Alvin Langdon, and edited by Helmut and Alison Gernsheim. *Alvin Langdon Coburn, Photographer: An Autobiography with Over 70 Reproductions of His Works*. New York: Dover Publications Inc., 1966.
Cork, Richard. *Vorticism and Abstract Art in the First Machine Age*. London: G. Frasier and Berkeley: University of California, 1976.
Homer, Willian Innes. *Alfred Stieglitz and the Photo-Secession*. Boston: New York Graphic Society, and Little, Brown and Company, 1983.
Maeterlinck, Maurice. *The Intelligence of Flower*. New York: Dodd, Mead & Company, 1907.
Naef, Weston. *The Collection of Alfred Stieglitz: Fifty Pioneers of Modern Photography*. New York: Metropolitan Museum of Art and Viking Press, 1978.
Steinorth, Karl, editor with essay by Nancy Newhall and texts by Anthony Bannon. *Alvin Langdon Coburn: Photographs 1900–1924*. Zürich and New York: Edition Stemmle, 1998.
Weaver, Mike. *Alvin Langdon Coburn: Symbolist Photographer, 1882–1966, Beyond the Craft*. New York: Aperture Foundation, 1986.
Zinnes, Harriet. *Ezra Pound and the Visual Arts*. New York: New Directions, 1981.

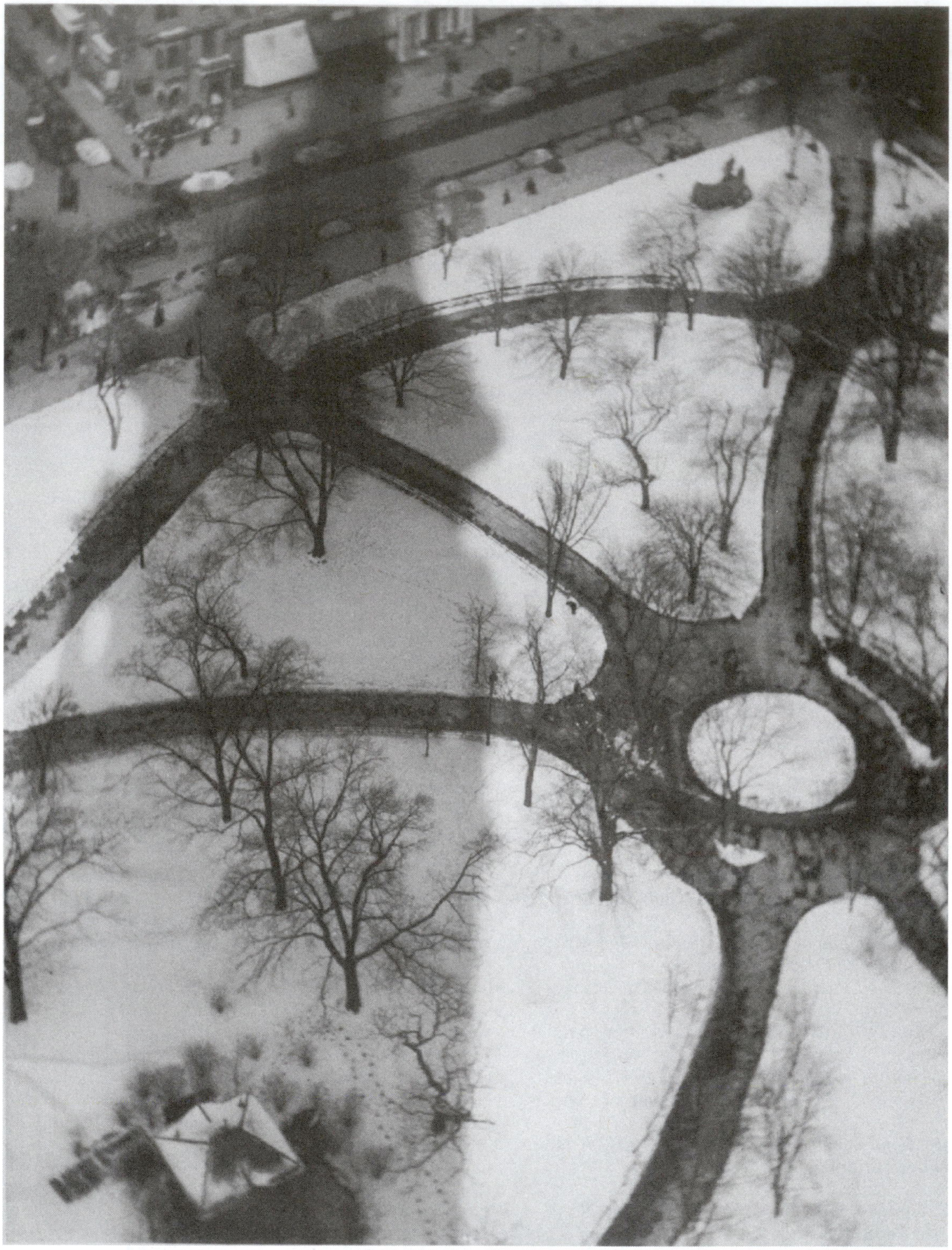

Alvin Langdon Coburn, The Octopus, 1912, gelatin silver print, 20.6 × 15.7 cm, Gift of Alvin Langdon Coburn.
[*Photograph courtesy of George Eastman House*]

LYNNE COHEN

Canadian

Lynne Cohen is one of contemporary art's strongest practitioners of a vein of photography that descends from observers of the social landscape such as Eugène Atget and Walker Evans and has modern-day lineage in the New Topographic photographers of the 1970s. She photographs interiors with a signature impassive style, subtly underlining the dark absurdity of our built environments and the social forces at work within. Cohen titles her photographs with broad descriptions of the type of space in the photograph, elevating the rooms depicted from specific sites to metaphors for larger social relations. Cohen's early work investigated domestic and accessible communal spaces, such as living rooms, beauty salons, and party rooms. Her subject matter has evolved to primarily include spaces implicated in the regulation and structuring of society and its citizens: restricted-access communal or institutional spaces such as men's clubs, classrooms, laboratories, and observation rooms. The ominous nature of these places inflects the more neutral sites included in her later work, such as halls and spas. While the idea of architecture and built space embodying social power structures and codes is commonly linked to the influential theorist Michel Foucault, Cohen herself has declared more of an affinity to the French slapstick writer/director/actor Jacques Tati. In Cohen's photographs, social critique is subtle, served with a healthy side of black humor.

Lynne Cohen was born in 1944 in Racine, Wisconsin, and she has resided in Canada since 1973. She studied art at the University of Wisconsin, Madison, graduating in 1967, with further study at the University of London's Slade School of Art. It was after receiving a Master's degree in 1969 and working in sculpture, printmaking, and conceptual processes that Cohen began making photographs in 1971. Minimalism and Pop Art were strong early influences, and Cohen was drawn to interior spaces as a kind of Duchampian readymade, both banal and extraordinary. Her mature career interests manifested themselves early on in printmaking projects that incorporated tracings from mail-order catalogs of everyday objects and environments. Her long-lasting fascination with the banal was evident in the early project *Front and Back*, a 1972 16-mm film created in collaboration with Andrew Lugg that utilized found postcards of terribly ordinary places, juxtaposing the images and the actual text written by anonymous travelers. While Cohen considered projects such as resituating everyday household objects and furniture into a gallery setting, she settled into photography as the most direct medium for accessing the social and political questions that interested her.

The desire for directness and precision led Cohen to work with a large-format view camera, making both 5 × 7 inch negatives and 8 × 10 inch negatives. She continues to work with the 8 × 10 inch camera to this day, a choice that imparts her photographs with a clarity of detail and depth of focus field that are greater than possible with the unaided human eye. This heightening of perception contributes to the overall project of her photographs: to force a viewer to notice the strangeness at the core of everyday spaces and objects. This peculiarity is so pronounced that her work has been mistaken to be constructed or set up, although Cohen always photographs real, "found" places and does not make any significant alterations to the scene before photographing. Her signature frontal, deadpan, symmetrical, wide-angle style was developed early on as a means of achieving the most apparently neutral view possible, and it has remained remarkably constant through to her present work. This style contributes to the atmosphere of a stage set that pervades most of her images, a feeling enhanced by the absence of any people despite the spaces' evident functionality. Objects become stand-ins for bodies. This happens concretely in the paper targets of human forms found in many of the photographs of shooting ranges, or the outlines of bodies demonstrating the proper use of the space in *Model Living Room*, 1976. Human interaction is also introduced more allusively, such as by the trope of two chairs facing each other standing in for human interaction, which is found in *Recreation Room*, 1971, and *Laboratory*, 1983.

For most of her career Cohen has elected to not date her photographs, and although her photographs can now be found with dates, many of those were assigned retroactively and approximately while working on her book *No Man's Land* (2001) in order to create a traditional chronology. Unlike many photographers, Cohen does not work on series in the conventional sense. Rather, she collects images in a long-term accumulative process. Her images are titled with the type of space depicted (e.g., *Police School*, *Observation Room*, *Library*, and *War Game*). She photographs these rooms as she gains access to them, often a complicated and protracted process, particularly with the institutional spaces. She pursues photographing a type of room as long as her interest remains high, which is often decades. While her photographs are dependent on found, actual things in the world, Cohen is hardly a strict documentarian—collectively, the images are placeless, timeless, and un-situated in any real-world context.

Cohen began her photographic work in black and white and did not begin to make color pictures until the late 1990s. Her early prints were contact printed at the size of the negative, encouraging an intimate viewing experience. In the mid-1980s, she began to enlarge the images, initially to 16 × 20 inches and later as large as 30 × 40 and 40 × 50 inches. She decided early in her career to closely control the framing of her work, thus avoiding the possibility of a gallery or museum framing her photographs with materials that did not reinforce interpretive possibilities. From this point forward, Cohen framed her black-and-white pictures with colored Formica frames as a way of introducing a set of associations carried by color into a particular black-and-white scene. The use of Formica, an inexpensive plastic laminate popular in home and institutional decorating since the 1950s, gives a tactile presence to many of the surfaces depicted within the flat plane of the photograph. Cohen uses the same material to frame her color photographs, using a more limited palette of grays.

Initially arriving in Canada to teach, Cohen is considered one of that country's leading photographers. She has taught at universities and art schools in both countries for as long as she has worked as a photographer and held numerous artist residencies and workshops which have extended her international influence. Cohen's pictures are not rooted in any one nation, but in the modern human experience.

LAURA KLEGER

See also: **Photography in Canada**

Biography

Born in Racine, Wisconsin, 3 July 1944. Attended University of Wisconsin, Madison, 1962–64, 1965–67, B.S. in Fine Arts and Art Education, 1967; Slade School of Art, University of London, England, 1964–65; Eastern Michigan University, Ypsilanti, M.A., 1969. Taught at Eastern Michigan University, Ypsilanti, 1969–73; School of the Art Institute of Chicago, 1984; University of Ottawa, Ontario, Canada, 1974–present. Artist in Residence, Light Work, Syracuse University, Syracuse, New York, 1988, 1995; Centre d'Art Contemporain de Guérigny, France, 1991; Ecole des Beaux-Arts de Bordeaux, France, 1993, 1994, 1996, 1999; Ecole des Beaux-Arts de Paris, France, 1993; Ecole Nationale de la photographie, Arles, France, 1995; Nova Scotia College of Art and Design, 1996; Wexner Center for the Arts, Columbus, Ohio, 1996; Museum voor Fotografie, Antwerp, Belgium, 1998; Academie Sint Joost, Breda, Netherlands, 1999, 2000; Nationaal Hoger Instituut voor Schone Kunsten, Antwerp, Belgium, 2000, 2001, 2002; Bemis Center for Contemporary Arts, Omaha, Nebraska, 2001; Internationalen Sommerakademie für Bildene Kunst, Salzburg, Vienna, 2002, 2004. Awards received include: Logan Award, Art Institute of Chicago 1967; Ontario Arts Council, various awards, 1978–94; Canada Council, various awards, 1975–2003; Ontario Arts Council Senior Arts Grant, 1985, 1993, 2001; Canada Council Senior Arts Grant, 1986, 1989, 1997, 2002; Canada Council Victor Martyn Lynch-Staunton Award, 1991; National Magazine Awards, Canada, Gold award, 2001. Resides in Montréal, Canada.

Individual Exhibitions

1973 A Space Gallery; Toronto, Ontario, Canada
1975 ASA Gallery, University of New Mexico; Albuquerque, New MexicoYajima Gallery; Montréal, Québec, Canada
1978 Carpenter Center for Visual Arts, Harvard University; Cambridge, Massachusetts
Futuric Scientific Place and Other Spaces; International Center of Photography; New York
1979 *Lynne Cohen*; Light Work Gallery; Syracuse, New York
1983 Brown University; Providence, Rhode Island
1984 *Nonfictions*; Nova Scotia College of Art and Design; Halifax, Nova Scotia, Canada
1986 *Matters of Fact*; Gallery 49th Parallel; New York
1988 Art Gallery of Windsor; Windsor, Ontario, Canada, Galerie Samia Saouma; Paris, France
Interim Art; London, England
1989 Museum für Gestaltung; Zurich, Switzerland
Occupied Territory; Art 45; Montréal, Québec, Canada
Sweger Konst; Stockholm, Sweden
1990 *D'un art l'autre*; Galerie Samia Saouma; Paris, France
Galerie Gokelaere & Janssen; Brussels, Belgium

Owens Art Gallery, Mount Allison University; Sackville, New Brunswick, Canada
1991 Mackenzie Art Gallery; Regina, Saskatchewan, Canada
1992 Anderson Gallery, Virginia Commonwealth University; Richmond, Virginia
Art Gallery of York University; Toronto, Ontario, Canada
Chinati Foundation; Marfa, Texas
L'Endroit du décor; F.R.A.C.; Limousin, Limoges, France (travelled to Hôtel des arts, Paris, Framce)
Half Truths; Carleton University; Ottawa, Ontario, Canada
1993 *Fort d'art actuel*; Galerie Rodolphe Janssen; Brussels, Belgium
1994 *Incriminating Evidence*; Louise Spence Gallery; Toronto, Ontario, Canada
1995 Galerie Rodolphe Janssen; Brussels, Belgium
1996 *Plus vrai que nature*; Galerie des Archives; Paris, France
1998 *Lynne Cohen*; Museum voor Fotografie; Antwerp, Belgium
2000 *Espais*; Galeria Visor; Valencia, Spain
Centro de Fotografía, Universidad de Salamanca; Salamanca, Spain
2001 Galeria Fucares; Madrid, Spain
Dalhousie Art Gallery; Halifax, Nova Scotia
Signs of Life; Galería des Àngels; Barcelona, Spain
2001 *No Man's Land: The Photographs of Lynne Cohen*; National Gallery of Canada; Ottawa, Ontario, Canada and Musée de l'Elysée; Lausanne, Switzerland
2002 National Gallery of Canada; Ottawa, Ontario, Canada Fotohof; Salzburg, Austria
2003 *Image/Imatge*; Orthez, France
Musée de l'Elysée; Lausanne, Switzerland

Group Exhibitions

1973 *Photography: Midwest Invitational*; Walker Art Center; Minneapolis, Minnesota
1974 *American Moods*; Whitney Museum of American Art; New York, New York
1975 *Exposure: Canadian Contemporary Photographers*; National Film Board of Canada; Ottawa, Ontario, Canada
1976 *The Photographers' Choice*; Witkin Gallery; New York, New York, University of New Mexico Art Museum; Albuquerque, New Mexico
1977 *Rooms*; Museum of Modern Art; New York, New York
1978 *Silences et Stridences: Lynne Cohen/Robert Walker*; Galerie Delpire; Paris, France
1979 CEPA Gallery; Buffalo, New York
1980 *The Magical Eye*; National Gallery of Canada; Ottawa, Ontario, Canada
1981 *Suite, Serie, Sequence*; Le Centre Cultural Graslin; Nantes, France
Points of View; Musée des Beaux-Arts à Montreal; Montréal, Québec, Canada
Les Choix de l'Oeil; Musée d'Art Contemporain; Montréal, Québec, Canada
1982 *New Vintage*; The Photographers' Gallery; Saskatoon, Saskatchewan, Canada
1983 *Latitudes and Parallels: Focus on Contemporary Canadian Photography*; Winnipeg Art Gallery; Winnipeg, Manitoba, Canada
1984 *Seeing People, Seeing Space: Contemporary Photography from Ontario, Canada*; The Photographers' Gallery; London, England
La Photographie Creatif; Bibliothèque nationale de Paris, Pavillion des Arts; Paris, France
Responding to Photography; Art Gallery of Ontario; Toronto, Ontario, Canada
1985 *Environments Here and Now: Three Contemporary Photographers, Lynne Cohen, Robert Del Tredici, Karen Smiley*; National Gallery of Canada; Ottawa, Ontario, Canada
1989 *Photography Now*; Victoria and Albert Museum; London, England
150 Years of Photography; Manes Galley; Prague, Czechoslovakia
1990 *Living Evidence: Lynne Cohen and Roger Mertin*; Presentation House Gallery; Vancouver, British Columbia, Canada
1991 *Typologies: A Photographic Dialogue*; Newport Harbor Art Museum; Newport Beach, California (traveled to Akron Art Museum, Akron, Ohio; The Corcoran Art Museum, Washington, D.C.; San Francisco Museum of Modern Art, San Francisco, California)
Un-Natural Traces: Contemporary Art from Canada; Barbican Art Gallery; London, England
L'Effet de Réel; Galerie Art & Essai, Université de Rennes; Rennes, France
1992 *Beyond Glory: Re-presenting Terrorism*; Maryland Institute College of Art; Baltimore, Maryland
Photography Without Apology; Emily Carr College of Art and Design; Vancouver, British Columbia, Canada
1993 *Magicians of Light*; National Gallery of Canada, Ottawa, Ontario
1996 *Passions Privées*; Musée d'Art Moderne de la ville de Paris; Paris, France
1997 *Evidence: Photography and Site*; Wexner Center for the Arts; Columbus, Ohio
1998 *Le Donné, le fictive*; Centre national de la photographie; Paris, France
The Light Factory; Charlotte, North Carolina
Photography's Multiple Roles: Art, Document, Market, Science; Museum of Contemporary Photography, Columbia College; Chicago, Illinois
2000 *Le Siècle du Corps*; Musée de l'Elysée; Lausanne, Switzerland
2002 Oberösterreichischen Landesmuseum; Linz, Austria
Musée des Beaux-Arts de Rouen; Rouen, France
2003 *Confluence: Contemporary Canadian Photography*; Canadian Museum of Contemporary Photography; Ottawa, Ontario, Canada

Selected Works

Recreation Room, 1971
Model Living Room, 1976
Men's Club, c. 1977
Laboratory, 1983
Classroom, mid-1980s
Spa, 1994
Laboratory, 1999

Further Reading

Bremner, Ann, ed. *Evidence: Photography and Site*, Columbus, Ohio: Wexner Center for the Arts, 1997.

Cohen, Lynne. *L'Endroit du décor/Lost and Found.* Limoges, France and Paris: Fonds regionals d'art contemporain Limousin and Hôtel des arts, 1992.

Ewing, William, ed. *Occupied Territory.* New York: Aperture, 1987.

Felshin, Nina. *No Laughing Matter.* New York: Independent Curators, 1991.

Freidus, Marc. *Typologies: Nine Contemporary Photographers.* Newport Beach, California, and New York: Newport Harbor Art Museum and Rizzoli, 1991.

Hall, Gary, et al, *Public Exposures: One Decade of Contemporary Canadian Photography, 1980–1990.* Toronto: Toronto Photographer's Workshop, 1990.

Hanna, Martha. *Confluence: Contemporary Canadian Photography.* Ottawa, Ontario: Canadian Museum of Contemporary Photography, 2003.

Museum of Contemporary Photography. *Photography's Multiple Roles: Art, Document, Market, Science.* Chicago: Museum of Contemporary Photography, Columbia College, Chicago, 1998.

Phillips, Carol Corey. "Speaking Through Silence: Female Voice in the Photography of Nina Raginsky, Clara Gutsche, and Lynne Cohen." In *Thirteen Essays on Photography.* Ottawa, Ontario: Canadian Museum of Contemporary Photography, 1990.

Robbins, Mark. *On the Table.* Columbus, Ohio: Wexner Center for the Arts, 1999.

Thomas, Ann. *No Man's Land: The Photography of Lynne Cohen.* New York: Thames and Hudson, 2001.

VAN DEREN COKE

American

Van Deren Coke has contributed to the fine art of photography as an educator, editor, writer, collector, curator, historian, and photographer. From his days as a graduate student in art history at Indiana University, where his selected topic of the influences of photography on nineteenth-century painting was rejected by his thesis committee because "the subject did not exist," to his position of director of the department of photography at the San Francisco Museum of Modern Art, where he championed unknown, controversial artists, Coke helped carve photography's place as a fine art.

Coke taught the fledgling field of creative photography at a number of schools, including the University of Florida in 1958, Arizona State University in 1961 and again from 1988–1991, and St. Martin's School of Art in London in 1968. In 1962, he was appointed director of the art museum at the University of New Mexico, where he began collecting photographs for the museum's permanent collection, and the next year he began the university's creative photography department. After Beaumont Newhall joined the faculty in 1971, UNM became the first school in the country to offer a Ph.D. in photo history.

Coke said he created the UNM graduate program in photography to acquaint students with photography as a means of self-expression on a par with painting, sculpture, and printmaking. It was designed, he said, to "open students to an understanding of the responsibilities of the creative person and what was expected from one who seriously practiced photography as an art and a means of philosophic communication." His students have included Ralph Meatyard, Meridel Rubenstein, and Harold Jones. Curators of a 1991 group exhibition titled *Patterns of Influence: Teacher/Student Relationships in American Photography Since 1945* at the Center for Creative Photography in Tucson, Arizona, said, "Coke's students are not limited to those who have attended the universities where he has taught but can be counted as anyone who attended an exhibition he organized or read a book he wrote."

Coke left UNM to take Beaumont Newhall's place as director of the George Eastman House in Rochester, New York, when Newhall decided to retire. An old friend of Newhall's, Coke began his duties at the Eastman House in 1970 to be trained during Newhall's final year as director. After visiting the Southwest, Newhall changed his mind about remaining in Rochester after retirement, and at Coke's suggestion and Nancy Newhall's urging, he joined the faculty at UNM in 1971, where, by special agreement, Coke was still regarded as a part-time lecturer.

Coke was initially greeted enthusiastically by the board of trustees at Eastman House. Newly independent of Eastman Kodak Company, the museum was growing rapidly. The board hoped that Coke's business and management experience as president of his family's hardware company in Kentucky, where he worked from the time he was discharged from the US Navy at the end of World War II until he began graduate school in 1954, would help them survive as an independent arts institution. As director, however, Coke soon discovered that Kodak still had significant control of Eastman House and did not agree with his vision of the museum as a prominent center of fine art photography. Coke resigned the position in 1972. His legacy was a name change to the International Museum of Photography and Film at George Eastman House, and during his tenure, photo conservation procedures were researched and initiated. He also revived *Image* magazine, an Eastman House publication, after a six-year hiatus.

Coke returned to UNM as chairman of the art department and remained until 1979, when he was hired as director of the department of photography at the San Francisco Museum of Modern Art. Coke mounted many innovative shows in San Francisco that explored the new directions that the medium was taking. In 1985, he curated *Behind the Eyes: Eight German Artists*, the first American exhibition of photography by contemporary German artists who also worked in other media. In 1983, he gave former student Joel-Peter Witkin his first solo exhibition in a major American museum. The same year, Coke also mounted the first in-depth show of Edward Weston's Mexico photos.

Coke had first met Weston in the summer of 1938, when as a teenager he drove his father's Ford from Lexington, Kentucky to Carmel, California to meet his idol. Ten years later, still under Weston's influence as a photographer, Coke studied art in San Miguel de Allende, Mexico. Coke's photographs tend toward the surreal; he was described in a 1992 review in the *New York Times* as "an idiosyncratic photographer with a morbid eye." He experimented with "flashing prints" that involved darkroom manipulation in the 1970s before returning to straight Cibachromes in the 1980s. He demonstrated an interest in photographs that pushed the traditional limits of the medium; "but after finding it," he has said, "I got tired of looking for things that were strange." His students, however, give testament to his enthusiasm for blurring the lines between photography and other media.

"I always court enigma," Coke has said, adding that he believes enigma is the essence of art. His photographs have been exhibited internationally, and he has championed the fine art of photography in books published in Europe, Central America, Hawaii, and the American Southwest. He has written text to accompany catalogues, both of photo shows he has curated and as a guest contributor, and has compiled and edited essays on diverse subjects relating to photography as fine art. A book of his own photography, *Secular and Sacred: Photographs of Mexico*, has been published.

Coke remained at the San Francisco Museum of Modern Art until 1987, when he retired to Santa Fe. He died on July 11, 2004.

Renata Golden

See also: **Meatyard, Ralph; Newhall, Beaumont; Schools of Photography: United States; Weston, Edward**

Biography

Born Frank Van Deren Coke in Lexington, Kentucky on July 4, 1921. Had taken courses in sculpture and design as a boy; received a degree in history and art history at the University of Kentucky, Lexington in 1942. Studied photography with Nicholas Haz in 1939; at the Clarence White School of Photography in New York in 1940; and with Ansel Adams in 1952 and 1955. Worked in the wholesale hardware distributing business founded by his grandfather, Van Deren, in the 1940s. Served as a naval officer during World War II, returned to family business after discharge and resigned as company president in 1954. Received MFA in art history and sculpture from Indiana University, Bloomington in 1958. Assistant professor of photography and photo history at the University of Florida, 1958–1961; assistant professor of photography and photo history at Arizona State University, Tempe, in 1961–1962. Appointed director of the art museum at the University of New Mexico (UNM), Albuquerque in 1962. Served as art museum director and professor of art until 1966 and again from 1973–1979; chairman of the UNM Department of Art 1962–1970. From 1970–1972 served first as deputy director and then director of the International Museum of Photography and Film, the George Eastman House, Rochester, New York. Director of Photography at the San Francisco Museum of Modern Art, 1979–1987. Received the Photography International Award, 1955, 1956, 1957; International Prize, *U.S. Camera*, 1957, 1958, 1960. John Simon Guggenheim Fellowship, 1975; Senior Fulbright scholar, Elam School of Fine Arts, University of Aukland, New Zealand, 1989. Awarded the E. Leitz, Inc. Medal of Excellence "Educator of the Year Award," 1988; Distinguished Career in Photography award from the Friends of Photography in San Francisco, 1992. Gallery in his name dedicated at the University of New Mexico, Albuquerque in 1986. Retired to Santa Fe, New Mexico in 1987. Died Albuquerque, New Mexico 11 July 2004.

Individual Exhibitions

1940 University of Kentucky; Lexington, Kentucky
1961 George Eastman House; Rochester, New York
1975 Galerie Die Brucke, Vienna; Galerie Nagel; West Berlin
1976 *Van Deren Coke*; Susan Spiritus Gallery; Newport Beach, California
1977 *Van Deren Coke*; School of Art and Architecture, University of Southwestern Louisiana; Lafayette, Louisiana
1981 *Retrospective*; University of New Mexico; Albuquerque, New Mexico
1985 Instituto Nacional de Bellas Artes; San Miguel de Allende; Mexico
1991 *Streets of Mexico*; University of New Mexico Art Museum; Albuquerque, New Mexico, and traveling
1993 *Van Deren Coke*; Vision Gallery; San Francisco, California
1997 *50 Years of Photography*; Howard Greenberg Gallery; New York, NewYork

Group Exhibitions

1957 A Photographer's Gallery; New York (with Ralph Meatyard)
1962 *Les Grands Photographes de Notres Temps*; Versailles, France
1973 *Light and Lens*; Hudson River Museum; Yonkers, New York
1992 *Patterns of Influence: Teacher/Student Relationships in American Photography Since 1945*; Center for Creative Photography, University of Arizona; Tucson, Arizona
2000 *Florida Photogenesis: The Works of Creative/Experimental Photographers in Florida*; Florida State Museum of Fine Arts; Tallahassee, Florida

Selected Works

Brett Weston, 1950
Homage to Derain, 1968
Homage to the Dada Constructivists (from the New Mexico Portfolio), 1975

Further Reading

Coke, Van Deren, ed. *One Hundred Years of Photography History: Essays in Honor of Beaumont Newhall.* Albuquerque, New Mexico: University of New Mexico Press, 1975.
Coke, Van Deren. Introductory essay, *Fabricated to be Photographe*. San Francisco: San Francisco Museum of Modern Art, 1979.
Coke, Van Deren. Preface, *Photography: A Facet of Modernism*. San Francisco: San Francisco Museum of Modern Art, 1986.

COLOR TEMPERATURE

Color temperature is the overall measure of the coloration of light. A glowing filament emits this temperature in most light sources from the center of the light bulb. The color of light is dependent upon the temperature of the heated filament, and the range of color temperature moves from low intensity, which is red, through yellow, white, and blue at the highest and most intense setting. This temperature and corresponding color difference is measured on the Kelvin scale, a scale similar to the Fahrenheit or Celsius scales but with 273 degrees added to the Celsius temperature range. On the Kelvin scale, absolute zero is placed at 0°K and the freezing point of water is 273°K.

The color temperature of skylight (bright blue sky) is 11,000°K, an electronic flash 6,000°K, daylight 5,000°K, a flash bulb 4,000°K, a photo floodlight 3,200°K, a household or tungsten light bulb 2,800°K, and candlelight 1,900°K. The more intense the light source and higher the amount of heat, the cooler and bluer the color cast of the light that is produced from the light source. The lower the intensity of the light source and amount of heat produced, the redder the color cast. This goes against common sense notions of hotter objects having a redder color and cooler objects having a bluer tone because the intensity measured is that of heat and light rather than object and its color hue. Two types of film are available for photographing in all light sources: tungsten film, which is 3,200°K and daylight film, which is 5,500°K. These two types of film provide color balance options that match the colorcast of the light to an appropriate range in the film used for photographing in that type of light. Using filters on the camera to adjust and color balance can also be used instead of changing the film color temperature to make color-cast corrections.

Daylight film is the most widely used film for photographing indoors and outdoors. It is color balanced for skylight, daylight, and most types of on-camera and off-camera flash units. It is balanced for high heat and intensity on the Kelvin scale, and when used in tungsten light that is lower in heat and intensity, it will produce a blue cast in photographic images. Tungsten film is used for photographing indoors with household or tungsten lights or with photoflood lamps, and is available in two types: Type A and Type B. Type A is balanced for the 3,400°K photoflood lamp, which is the standard lamp, and Type B is balanced for the 3,200°K photoflood lamp. As tungsten film is balanced for low heat and intensity on the Kelvin scale, when used with daylight and flash units it will produce a red cast in photographic images.

Digital cameras, which use CCD sensors (charged-coupled device) and thus do not offer the photographer a choice of tungsten or daylight film, have settings for either daylight or tungsten light. The digital photographer must manually "white balance" the camera or set the camera to check the color cast of the light source or set the sensors to balance automatically. This procedure is called white balancing because the tone white is checked for neutrality in the camera: if the whites of an image have an orange or blue cast, the camera is incorrectly white balanced and must be calibrated to the light color temperature. Often there is a combination of both indoor tungsten light and outdoor daylight or photographic flash lighting, and the most abundant light source will be chosen for calibration purposes.

Fluorescent light is an anomaly in color balance because it does not fit into the red or blue range of the Kelvin temperature scale. Fluorescent tubes emit a discontinuous spectrum, which randomly varies the intensity of colors, and fluorescent tubes are not standardized to a specific color balance or cast but produce a number of slightly varying color shades. Filters can help correct the green cast generally characteristic of fluorescent lights, and a magenta filter (30M) will block the green color cast from the film or digital sensors when placed on a camera lens. Filters can also be used to color balance daylight and tungsten light with the opposite type of film. To correct the red color cast made when using daylight film in tungsten light, a blue filter (80A) will absorb the red light and balance the resulting scene. Tungsten film used in daylight can be balanced with a yellow filter (85B) and this will absorb the blue light and maintain the neutral white in the image. Images that are incorrectly color balanced can also be corrected through manipulating color printing processes and digital software such as Adobe Photoshop, but these changes are often labor-intensive and difficult. Correcting improper color balance in color slide film is not possible after the film has been exposed and processed because the transparency is the final product, unlike photographic negatives and digital files that are manipulated in the traditional or digital darkroom.

Color and white balance is important when taking photographs to accurately reproduce the color of a specific scene, but can also be used for creative and artistic purposes. The cool blue color cast created when tungsten film is used in daylight is utilized by fine art and fashion photographers, and the warm interior light produced by daylight film in tungsten light is often manipulated by photographers who are capturing architectural or interior shots. The color casts present in reversing the standard film and lighting specifications are not the only creative changes that are used to manipulate the quality of light. Natural daylight changes color as the day progresses, and daylight balanced color film is the most accurate when used between ten in the morning and three in the afternoon, the most neutral time for natural daylight and the color temperature closest to daylight balanced film (daylight at noon is balanced to 5,000°K.) In the early morning the colors of daylight have a cool cast and less saturation, and in the late afternoon and evening daylight is characterized by warm, saturated hues.

JENNIFER HEADLEY

See also: **Color Theory: Natural and Synthetic; Digital Photography; Film; Filters; Lighting and Lighting Equipment**

Further Reading

Folts, James A., Ronald P. Lovell, and Fred C. Zwahlen, Jr. *Handbook of Photography*. Albany, NY: Delmar Thompson Learning, 2002.

Glendinning, Peter. *Color Photography: History, Theory, and Darkroom Technique*. Upper Saddle River, NJ: Prentice Hall, 1985.

Hedgecoe, John. *The Art of Color Photography*. London: Octopus Publishing Group Ltd., 1984.

Hirsch, Robert. *Exploring Color Photography*. New York: McGraw-Hill, 1996.

Horenstein, Henry. *Color Photography: A Working Manual*. New York: Little, Brown, and Company, 1997.

Hunt, R.W.G. *The Reproduction of Color*. London: Fountain Press Ltd., 2004.

Kendra, Erika. *Color Companion for the Digital Artist*. Upper Saddle River, NJ: Prentice Hall, 2004.

COLOR THEORY: NATURAL AND SYNTHETIC

Photographic color theory is based on light and specific colors of light in the visible spectrum, which combine together to form what we call white light. Color can be broken down further into three elements: hue (the wavelength of color), saturation (the intensity of color), and value (the lightness or darkness of a color, sometimes also referred to as brightness). These components make up all photographic light. Black and white photography records light based only on value or brightness, and color photography records light based on two color sets: the additive primaries and the subtractive primaries. These sets are groupings of color that register in the human eye and on the surface of photographic materials. These two color groupings, when mixed together, make up all of the color combinations in photographic imaging.

The color wheel is made up of six colors, and red, green, and blue are placed directly inverse of cyan, magenta, and yellow. The additive primaries are red, green, and blue (also called RGB colors), and when mixed together form white light. The subtractive primaries are cyan (bluish-green), magenta (purplish-pink), and yellow (also called CMY primaries), and when mixed together form black or the absence of light. The six colors in the photographic process create a color wheel with complementary pairs: blue and yellow, green and magenta, and cyan and red. On the color wheel, a triangle is created by both the RGB primaries and the CMY primaries as they are spaced alternately in the six color slots of the color wheel. Mixing the colors on either side of that hue creates each color in the wheel: for example, mixing green and blue creates cyan. These three-color pairs are linked through all traditional film and digital photographic processes. Each set of three primaries can form all six colors, and the additive primaries are used when taking a picture and affect the film, while the subtractive primaries are used for color printing. This is also true in digital imaging: the RGB primaries are used when reproducing color with light, such as a computer screen or television. The CMY primaries are used for printing with the addition of black.

Early color experimentation consisted of photographic material sensitive to red, green, and blue light. Antoine and Louise Lumière invented the Autochrome process in 1907, based on additive color theory. They covered a glass plate with potato starch grains sensitive to three layers of color: red-orange, green, and violet. When light passed through the glass, it was recorded on emulsion sensitive to only the specific color of the potato starch grain that the light passed through and its corresponding wavelength. This created a color transparency, but the process was labor-intensive and unstable. The subtractive color process was introduced into film with the invention of the Kodachrome process in 1935, developed by Eastman Kodak and Leopold Mannes. This process was popular with professional photographers for advertising and portraits, and rarely used by consumers because of its technical sophistication and expense. The consumer photographic market and fine art photography relied heavily on black and white film and developing until the 1970s, when color film was significantly improved by manufacturers such as Eastman Kodak and Fuji. Aesthetic photographic history also changes in the late 1960s as photography is combined with other mediums such as silkscreen, and color is more readily accepted as a vehicle for photographic artists from the 1970s to the present.

Kodachrome film was made up of three layers of emulsion on the film, each sensitive to red, green, and blue light. This process was the origin of all subsequent color film. Color film has three layers of emulsion, each sensitive to one-third of the spectrum (red, green, and blue). When the film is exposed, a latent image is created on each layer and the development process of color film produces a multi-layered negative.

The development process of color film creates the colors in the negative or positive image, negative if the film is to be used to create a photographic print; positive if the film is to serve as a slide or larger-format transparency. Color developing of film occurs when the developing agent is added to the film and dye couplers are activated for each color layer: the area sensitive to red light forms a cyan image, the area sensitive to green light forms a magenta image, and the area sensitive to blue light forms a yellow image. These three layers are then bleached to remove excess silver, and a color composite of all three subtractive hues is formed in the film emulsion. This process is similar in photographic paper and both positive and negative color film. The most widely used process for color negative film is Kodak's C-41, which produces a chromogenic color negative created by dye couplers. Color transparency film has a step that reverses the color process and the tonal range of the film. The standard process for transparency film is Kodak's E-6, but Kodachrome film is processed is a slightly different manner, Kodak's K-14 process.

Color film is affected by exposure, and over- or underexposing slides or positive as well as negative film will change the saturation and value of color. Transparency or slide film has less exposure latitude than negative film, and is affected more by exposure variations. Overexposing slide film will desaturate and lighten the colors in the image, while underexposing slide film will saturate and darken the color range of the image. Color negative film has greater exposure latitude than transparency film, and quality color prints can be produced from under-and overexposed negatives that display little difference in hue and saturation from that of a properly exposed negative. Different film types and brands can also skew color balance, and some films produce a warm tone while others lean more to the cool side of the color spectrum. Color is also affected by film speed. Fast films have less saturation, color contrast, and smoothness than slower color films. Graininess is also an issue with fast film and this texture increases as the film's speed (also known as ISO and ASA) increases. Slow color film has a richer color palette, smoother color forms, and a higher contrast than high-speed film.

Color printing is also a subtractive process. A negative is placed in a color enlarging head, and light is projected through the image onto photographic paper. The filter set of a color enlarging head allows for different amounts of cyan, magenta, and yellow to be adjusted for color balance. The strength of each filter is indicated by its density: the higher the filter number the denser the filter and the less light permeating through that filter. Color balance is achieved by adjusting the filter pack on an enlarger to create an image with neutral shadow and highlight areas. Viewing filters are useful for assessing color balance in color prints and are available in sets of six colors with varying densities for viewing color prints from transparencies and negatives. The subtractive primaries are the only colors used for printing because they make up the rest of the color scale and also merge to form black or the absence of light. In color darkroom printing, yellow is a combination of red and green, magenta is a combination of red and blue, and cyan is a combination of green and blue. Thus, the subtractive printing process in the darkroom allows for all six colors in the photographic spectrum to be created in color prints from negatives or transparencies. Color prints from negatives are often called chromogenic color prints and use a RA-4 color process, and color prints from transparencies use similar processes called Type R, R-3000, or Ilfachrome (formerly Cibachrome). Printing from transparencies produces a higher contrast image with more color saturation than printing from color negatives. Additional color printing processes used in the color darkroom include dye diffusion and dye sublimation prints. Color photographic paper has a variety of qualities, and the paper type instead of the filter pack used in black and white printing affects the contrast range of color paper. Papers are available in a range of subdued to bright and saturated tones, and the photographer can choose the type of paper needed based on his subject matter and vision. By combining color film types and printing papers, a vast color range is available for photographers.

Digital imaging follows a similar process utilizing the additive and subtractive primary colors. The additive primaries correspond to the CCD (charged-coupled device) sensors in a digital camera or scanner and the subtractive primaries, with the added color black, are used for printing digital images. Digital cameras and scanners have CCD sensors that each register red, green, or blue through a grid of translucent image elements. A combination of these three colors will create any of the 256 color possibilities available on a digital screen or computer monitor. RGB colors are transferred to a binary number that is associated with a specific pixel or picture element for each piece of the scanned document or image area, and along with binary information on brightness, value, and tonal range are reassembled by a computer to make a digital picture. The individual red, green, and blue areas are seen together on the screen on a monitor and have a similar breakdown in television broadcasts. Editing digital images with software such as Adobe PhotoShop usually takes place in two color spaces or modes of calibration: RGB mode (red, green, and blue) and CMYK mode (cyan, magenta, and yellow.) CMYK mode is often called process color because black (represented by K) is added to the printer pack. Black is abbreviated by K, which stands for key color, because it is the tone by which all other colors are aligned in the printing press.

Individual color layers called channels make up each mode with the appropriate color breakdown and these channels are displayed as layers of color in a digital imaging program. RGB mode is used for viewing images on the screen, and digital information is captured in this mode through a scanner or digital camera. Most scanners and digital cameras use CCD sensors sensitive to red, green, and blue, but a drum scanner is also capable of creating a digital composite with PMT (photo multiplier tubes) that record more information than traditional CCD film sensors. CMYK mode is used for printing and mimics the cyan, magenta, and yellow tones projected through an enlarger by a filter pack in traditional darkroom color methods. However, in CMYK mode the color black is added because combining cyan, magenta, and yellow does not produce a true black with inkjet pigments. Color balance in digital imaging is also done by using three color pairs in the same manner as traditional darkroom methods: yellow and blue, green and magenta, and cyan and red are all linked together and manipulate the overall color of a digital image. Hue, saturation, lightness or brightness, and exposure can also be manipulated through advanced imaging software applications.

Color in photography is used for a variety of purposes, including emotional and symbolic reasons and has an effect on the viewer's perception of an image. Color is subjective and arbitrary in many photographic images, and seeing a specific color or group of color hues can affect the mood and composition of an image. Juxtaposing color combinations can also change the reception of specific hues and neutral areas of white or black can take on a colorcast: if a green object is placed next to a white area in a photograph, the white area will take on some of the green hue of the adjacent space. The amount of white and black in an image can also alter how the brightness of specific colors are perceived, and brightness is often an arbitrary and subjective interpretation which is also influence by the type of light in which an image is viewed. The amount of perceived difference in adjacent colors is called color contrast, and is often separate from an individual color's value. Warm colors, which range in the spectrum from red to yellow, and cool colors that range from green to purple or violet, are called analogous hues. Analogous hues are also seen as having similar qualities, and when used together in a color image lower that image's overall color contrast.

JENNIFER HEADLEY

See also: **Digital Photography; Dye Transfer**

Further Reading

Ciaglia, Joseph. *Introduction to Digital Photography*. Upper Saddle River, New Jersey: Prentice Hall, 2002.

Glendinning, Peter. *Color Photography: History, Theory, and Darkroom Technique*. Upper Saddle River, New Jersey: Prentice Hall, 1985.

Hedgecoe, John. *The Art of Color Photography*. London: Octopus Publishing Group Ltd., 1984.

Hirsch, Robert. *Exploring Color Photography*. 1992.

Horenstein, Henry. *Color Photography: A Working Manual*. New York: McGraw-Hill, 1997.

Kendra, Erika. *Color Companion for the Digital Artist*. Upper Saddle River, New Jersey: Prentice Hall, 2004.

COMPOSITION

Successful composition in a photograph depends on a set of finely tuned responses to an image captured in a moment of time in a format predetermined by the choice of film and equipment. How well a photographer engages the viewer's attention in the image by setting up camera angle, distance, and placement of objects in a film frame is based on the photographer's understanding of the elements of good design. These elements work together to create a harmonious and effective composition that captures both the intent of the photographer's vision and the viewer's imagination.

These elements: placement, line, shape, texture, pattern, scale, perspective, focus, color, contrast, and balance follow basic rules. A deep understanding these rules is the basis of good composition and the intuited speed of a "photographer's eye."

The Rule of Thirds

This is a traditional rule for placement. The picture frame is divided into horizontal and vertical thirds and the subjects and subordinate elements of the picture are grouped near the intersections of those horizontal and vertical section lines. In landscapes, for instance, the horizon line would appear in the top third or bottom third of the image area. If there is an additional subject, such as a tree or house, it would be placed left or right of center, on the vertical thirds intersection.

Lines

Lines are often invisible connections made by the eye to different points in the picture. They often define shapes such as squares or triangles. They can direct the eye far into the scene and establish distance and a sense of depth in an otherwise flat, two-dimensional plane. Lines also establish links between near and distant areas and help direct the viewer's gaze towards an important element in the photograph. Placing an object or the subject near the camera, but off to the side of receding lines adds a strong dynamic to the image. Lines can underscore movement or stability in a scene. For instance: diagonal lines add motion or drama, parallel or perpendicular lines create a sense of serenity or classic stability, curved lines indicate grace. However, lines, such as a road or a fence, that run parallel to the picture plane can set a different mood by creating a sense of distance and isolation from the subject.

Shape

The basic outline of an area, sometimes subtle, defined only by the intersection of lines, (as in the spaces between tree limbs) or more clearly by the light falling on an object (such as the limbs of the trees) is the first element recognized by the viewer. Shapes are the basic building blocks of an image. Isolating a shape by moving in close and photographing it can create a striking, graphic image. Juxtaposing shapes can create patterns, a sense of scale or distance, and add texture or even tension to an image. The repetition of shapes, through similarly shaped objects or the spaces around them, can reinforce an image or resonate the underlying photographic vision.

Planes

The surface upon which the subject lies is referred to as the picture plane. It is the point of visual contact between the viewer and the picture. Lines, shape, and contrast define planes. For instance, receding mountains are defined by their planes of fading color or contrast. Angled and intersecting planes, such as in aerial photographs, with their vast network of patterns and intersecting lines can provide stunning views. Planes also define perspective.

Perspective

In a two-dimensional picture, perspective can express the depth and vastness of a three-dimensional scene, by establishing the scale and distance of the objects in the scene. The pictorial elements of framing, scale, planes, line, and tonal range (the degree of contrast between light and dark areas) can provide a sense of depth to a photographic image.

Framing

The frame of the image is formed by the edges of the film. Framing is a device that forms a frame within that frame, or using an object or shadow to create a visual direction for the viewer. Overhanging branches in the foreground of a blank sky can help to highlight a distant horizon. The contrast between the near objects and the distant subject can help to establish distance. Following the gaze of a person or an animal in the foreground towards a distant point or the prime subject is another framing device. Using archways and portals to surround an object is an effective means of drawing attention to it. Selective focus, through the choice of lens and aperture can also frame a subject by sharpening the focus on the subject in an unfocused environment.

Scale

Similar to framing is the general use of objects in the foreground as subjects for scale to measure the background or relative size of the subject and to create a sense of distance.

Gaze

Faces and, especially, eyes always lead the viewer through the picture. We will follow the gaze, whether it is human or animal. The eyes do not have to be in focus to follow their gaze, but if the subject is human or animal, focus is critical around the eye area. Another magnet in a photograph are words. They draw the viewer's gaze almost as effectively as faces and eyes. However, they will not redirect the gaze unless carefully placed within the image as elements of pattern or texture.

Strong contrast in black and white, and opposite colors (such as green and red) create tension and drama in a photograph. When photographing in color, look to see where bright or opposite colors are in the image. They will pull the viewer's eye and are one of the most powerful forces in a composition.

Lighting

The color of the light, its direction, and contrast are all part of the elements of design. Motion and blur, sharpness and vantage point are also devices used in the elements of design.

Balance

A completely balanced, harmonious composition can be very easy to view, but ultimately boring and just as easy to dismiss. Understanding the elements of design and using them to insert drama, asymmetry, tension, point of view, mystery, and emotional resonance will draw the viewer's gaze again and again. If the image has a powerful impact, try analyzing the elements of design within its frame.

Kay Kenney

See also: **Image Construction: Perspective**

Further Reading

Eastman Kodak Company, eds. *The Joy of Photography*. Rochester, New York: Eastman Kodak Company, 1991.

Eastman Kodak Company, eds. *How to Take Good Pictures*. Rochester, New York: Eastman Kodak Company, 1995.

Hedgecoe, John. *The Book of Photography*. New York: Alfred A. Knopf, 1990.

Hirsch, Robert. *Exploring Color Photography*. 3rd ed. Dubuque, Iowa: Brown and Benchmark, 1997.

Langford, Michael. *Basic Photography*. 7th ed., Boston: Focal Press, 2000.

London, Barbara, and John Upton. *Photography*. 7th ed. Upper Saddle River, New Jersey: Prentice Hall, 1997.

CONCEPTUAL PHOTOGRAPHY

Conceptual photography places singular emphasis on the idea or message conveyed by a photographic image, rather than on conventional issues of aesthetics or narrative as they have traditionally been applied to photography. This approach to the photographic image privileges its status as a method of documentation, drawing upon its singular ability to faithfully reproduce elements of the world around us. It developed in the mid-1960s as a result of artists' interest in deemphasizing the work of art as an object and foregrounding its function as a method of communication. Conceptual photography often employs the use of text and/or the serial presentation of images to articulate a particular premise or make a specific statement. Ironically, the use of the documentary potential of the photograph in conceptual photography has resulted in its acceptance and current ubiquity in the fine arts.

In the early 1960s, artists began to question the material basis of the work of art. The paintings of Andy Warhol and Robert Rauschenberg introduced a level of distance from the artist's physical involvement with the work of art to create a more pictorial continuation of Marcel Duchamp's critique of art's objecthood. These works used photographic reproductions of everything from astronauts, street scenes, and art works to celebrity icons such as Elvis Presley, John F. Kennedy, and Marilyn Monroe to suggest the growing mediation of everyday life by popular culture. In Germany, Bernd and Hilla Becher resurrected the use of photography as typology perfected in the 1920s and 1930s by such photographers as August Sander and Albert Renger-Patzsch, presenting works that examined the similarities and differences between particular architectural forms. Joseph Kosuth's *One and Three Chairs*, 1965, incorporated a photograph of a chair placed alongside a textual description of the chair and the chair itself, demonstrating how photography might be utilized in a work of art not for its own sake but in the service of the articulation of a philosophical principle or ideal. This understanding of the photographic medium as a documentary means towards the expression of a concept, as an infinitely reproducible (and therefore somewhat "dematerialized") image that resisted the status of a precious art object, characterizes conceptual photography.

Conceptual photography flourished in the 1960s, beginning with Ed Ruscha's seminal photo-based books *Twenty-six Gasoline Stations*, 1963, and *Some Los Angeles Apartments*, 1965, now recognized as progenitors of the artists' books genre, and continuing with Dan Graham's photograph and text-based work *Homes for America*, 1965–1970. These works privileged photography's more basic and essential properties to focus on everyday forms of architecture as mere categorical types in the world rather than evoking their individual particularities. Artists such as Bruce Nauman, Douglas Huebler, Jan Dibbets, and Ger Van Elk employed the photograph towards a different end, creating situations to be documented by the camera towards the expression of ideas about the body and its role in the work of art or the changes that occur within a given situation over a certain period of time. The photograph's ability to record a performance, a given sequence of events, or a linear progression of time or space, resulted in its becoming a central medium for conceptual art practice.

Other conceptual artists approached the circulation of the photograph in popular culture as a means of further distancing the work of art from material production and locating it within a wider cultural sphere. John Baldessari's montage works of the late 1960s and early 1970s, for example, employed images culled from film stills that were arranged to create clever and at times humorous relationships between various cinematic icons or situations. Baldessari also combined banal photographic images with text in his dry, ironic paintings of the 1960s, which contained deadpan observations on everyday life. Many of Gerhard Richter's paintings employ specific photographs as source material, such as his haunting series *Eight Student Nurses*, 1966, (using the portraits of the eight young women slain by Richard Speck in 1965) or *48 Portraits*, 1972, consisting of portraits of prominent composers, writers, scientists, and intellectuals from the late-nineteenth to the mid-twentieth century.

In the early 1970s, conceptual artists such as Vito Acconci, Chris Burden, Gilbert and George, William Wegman, and Bruce Connor focused on performances in the studio, the gallery, and in the expanded field of the world outside, using photography and video to capture these activities. This work often focused on the body in terms of its limits and endurance, its presence as a sexual signifier, and its general role in society. Acconci's *Stretch*, 1969, for example, employs text and photographs taken from the positions described in the text to create a sense of the body's position and physicality even though one never sees the artist himself. Other artists from the 1960s and 1970s, such as Robert Smithson, Richard Long, Hamish Fulton, and Lothar Baumgarten used documentary photography to record their conceptual projects, which concentrated on their personal interactions with the environment. The resulting photographs served to bring the art that was experienced or created in the natural world into the cultural setting of the gallery or museum.

At roughly the same time, a number of women artists used photography to explore identity and female issues and greatly added to the expansion of the notion of photography, notably the Austrian performance and body artist Valie Export, and American performance and video artists Hannah Wilke, Eleanor Antin, Martha Rosler, Adrian Piper, and Cuban-American sculptor Ana Mendieta.

Towards the end of the 1970s, the influence of feminist theory and poststructuralist philosophy began to make its presence felt in the work of artists such as the Americans Cindy Sherman, Richard Prince, and Sherrie Levine, and Canadian Jeff Wall. These artists followed their 1960s predecessors in viewing the photographic image not as a precious object, but as a cultural "text" which they would re-frame and re-contextualize to make incisive observations about how the mass media and cultural production constructs our sense of reality. Sherman's landmark 1977 series *Untitled Film Stills* and Wall's photographic lightboxes address the pervasive impact of cinema on our view of everyday life in their presentation of seemingly "real" scenes, which have been staged for the camera through the kind of meticulous preparation and direction characteristic of mainstream filmmaking. Levine, Prince, and other artists such as Americans Barbara Kruger, Louise Lawler, and Annette Lemieux appropriated pre-existing images from commercial and art culture, furthering Duchamp's radical use of ready-mades by extending this idea into the world of images. Levine was especially notorious for her "rephotographing" in 1981 of iconic Depression-era Farm Security Administration images by Walker Evans that were identical in every way to the originals except that they had been photographed from book reproductions and titled "*After Walker Evans*."

The emergence of artists such as Thomas Struth, Thomas Ruff, Candida Höfer, and Andreas Gursky from Germany in the early-to-mid 1980s marked an important shift in the conceptual photograph in terms of subject matter and formal appearance. The artists of this generation had all been students of the Bechers and focused on such time-honored subjects as architecture, everyday people, and landscape. They distinguished themselves through their combination of the rigorous precision and clarity of their mentors and the seductive visual presence of painters such as Richter and Sigmar Polke. Struth's images of crowded museum interiors, Ruff's immense head-shots of ordinary German people, and Gursky's technically dazzling images of crowds, landscapes, and built structures transformed the conceptual photograph into a genre that could at once present images taken to impart a specific meaning while retaining a painterly sense of composition.

Conceptual photography in the late 1980s and early 1990s took the visual style and idea-based intent of the genre to address political issues of gender, race, and sexual identity. Artists such as Americans Glenn Ligon, Catherine Opie, Lorna Simpson, Cuban-American Felix Gonzalez-Torres, and the Canadian collective General Idea often used photography to make provocative, confrontational work about topics that ranged from hard-core gay subcultures, to the position of African-Americans in contemporary society, to the ongoing crisis resulting from the spread of the AIDS virus. Other artists during this period, such as the Americans Cindy Bernard, Sharon Lockhart, and Christopher Williams and English video artist Gillian Wearing, synthesized the interests in documentation, performance, popular culture, sequential presentation, and rigorously aesthetic composition, which have characterized the progression of conceptual photography from its inception in the 1960s. Lockhart's 1994 series *Auditions*, for example, presents a series of five images of young children embracing for a "first kiss" in a scene taken from the end of Francois Truffaut's 1976 film *L'Argent Poche* (*Small Change*.) The work combines the documentation of a "performance," an inquiry into the cinematic process and experience, and a use of serial presentation to define the children's acts categorically as "auditions" in a way that brings the histories of the conceptual photograph together in a single work. Her complication of this history, and the subsequent reinterpretations of the conceptual photograph by younger artists into the present day, demonstrates how multifaceted the use of photography in idea-based work has become since its beginnings in the early 1960s.

Dominic Molon

See also: **Artists' Books; Becher, Bernd and Hilla; Export, Valie; Feminist Photography; Graham, Dan; Gursky, Andreas; Kruger, Barbara; Photographic "Truth"; Photography and Painting; Postmodernism; Prince, Richard; Rauschenberg, Robert; Renger-Patzsch, Albert; Representation and Gender; Representation and Race; Ruff, Thomas; Sander, August; Sherman, Cindy; Simpson, Lorna; Struth, Thomas; Wall, Jeff**

Further Reading

Alberro, Alexander, and Blake Stimson, eds. *Conceptual Art: A Critical Anthology*. Cambridge, Massachusetts: MIT Press, 1999.

L'art Conceptuel, une perspective, exhibition catalogue, Paris: Musée d'art Moderne de la Ville de Paris, 1989.

Battcock, Gregory, ed. *Idea Art: A Critical Anthology*. New York: E.P. Dutton and Co., 1973.

Goldstein, Ann, and Anne Rorimer, eds. *Reconsidering the Object of Art: 1965–1975*. exhibition catalogue. Museum of Contemporary Art, Los Angeles, and Cambridge, Massachusetts: MIT Press, 1995.

Information, exhibition catalogue, New York: The Museum of Modern Art, 1970.

Lippard, Lucy R. *Six Years: The Dematerialization of the Art Object from 1966 to 1972*. New York: Praeger, 1973.

Meyer, Ursula. *Conceptual Art*. New York: E.P. Dutton and Co., 1972.

Morgan, Robert C. *Conceptual Art: An American Perspective*. Jefferson, North Carolina: McFarland and Co., 1994.

Wiehager, Renate, ed. *Photography as Concept/Fotographie als Handlung*. exhibition catalogue, "4. Internationale Foto-Triennale, Esslingen," Ostfildern, Germany: Cantz Verlag, 1998.

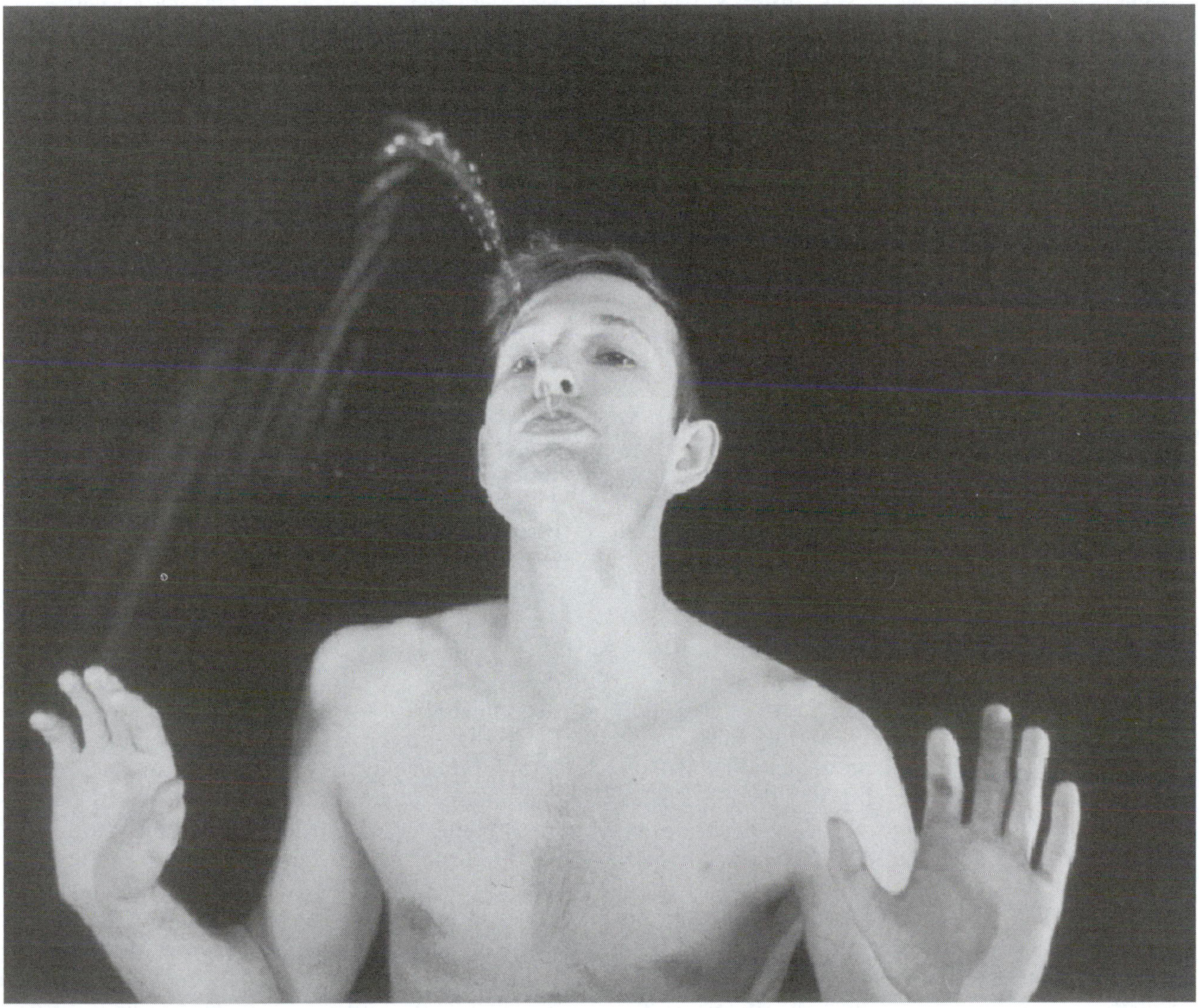

Bruce Nauman, Self-Portrait as a Fountain (from the portfolio Eleven Color Photographs), 1966–1967/70, Collection Museum of Contemporary Art, Chicago, Gerald S. Elliott Collection. Original in color.
[*Photograph © Museum of Contemporary Art, Chicago*]

CONDÉ NAST

After emerging as the brainchild of New York publisher Condé Montrose Nast (1873–1942) in the early 1900s, by the end of the century Condé Nast Publications became one of the largest consumer magazine companies in the world. Its earliest publications, *Vogue* and *Vanity Fair*, were among the first to use studio and portrait photography as illustrations. The rise of fashion and product photography, as well as its evolving marriage with graphic design, also influenced the aesthetics and production of images appearing in media and advertising. Condé Nast has been credited with pioneering the editorial format of fashion and lifestyle periodicals, as well as launching and promoting the careers of numerous prominent photographers from the United States and abroad.

The publishing empire known as Condé Nast established its name on the newsstand in 1909, when Nast acquired The Vogue Company and began revamping *Vogue* magazine, which had debuted as a New York society weekly in December 1892. *Vogue* remained the company's flagship publication as Nast purchased *Dress* and *Vanity Fair* (initially merged then shortened to *Vanity Fair*) in 1913, and *House & Garden* in 1915. In 1922, Nast renamed the company Condé Nast Publications, and five years later, it went public. *Glamour of Hollywood* (renamed *Glamour*) joined the Condé Nast magazine roster in 1939, and by 2000, more than a dozen new titles appeared, including: *Allure*, *Architectural Digest*, *Bon Appétit*, *Bride's*, *Condé Nast Traveler*, *Details*, *Gourmet*, *Gentleman's Quarterly* (renamed *GQ*), *Lucky*, *Mademoiselle*, *Self*, *The New Yorker*, *W*, and *Wired*.

Born in New York and raised in the Midwest, Condé Nast studied math and philosophy at Georgetown University, then went on to receive a law degree from Washington University in St. Louis. Through a highly successful stint as the advertising and business manager for *Collier's Weekly* in New York from 1900–1907, Nast created and refined what became his blueprint for marketing and positioning periodicals in an increasingly competitive marketplace. While targeting circulation to an audience of consumers willing to pay more for magazines featuring color covers and double-page layouts, he aggressively pursued high-end advertisers to fill out more and more pages, thereby maximizing revenue with each new issue. With Nast at the helm as the new publisher of *Vogue*, the magazine's readership expanded from 30,000 in 1910 to 100,000 in 1918.

As Edna Woolman Chase became the *Vogue* editor-in-chief in 1914, she worked closely with Nast throughout its transformation into an internationally visible, fashion-focused, photo-illustrated monthly. Chase's influential tenure with the magazine lasted from 1895 until her retirement in 1952, at the age of 75. The editor-in-chief post of American *Vogue* was subsequently held by Jessica Daves (1952–1962), Diana Vreeland (1963–1971), Grace Mirabella (1971–1988), and Anna Wintour (1988–) In 1916, *Vogue* became the first magazine to spawn international editions, which were published in each country's official language. British *Vogue* debuted in 1916, Spanish *Vogue* in 1918, French *Vogue* in 1920, and German *Vogue* in 1928. Since then, *Vogue* has launched editions elsewhere, including Australia, Brazil, Greece, Italy, Mexico, Russia, Japan, Korea, and Taiwan.

In 1913, Paris-born photographer Adolph de Meyer signed on to contribute exclusively to *Vogue* and *Vanity Fair*, in what was deemed the most generous contract of its kind at the time. In the mid-1920s, *Vogue* opened a photo studio in Paris that served as the source for most of its photographic illustrations. European and American photographers alike brought their artistic concerns to the nascent field of fashion photography. Avant-garde approaches to portraiture, lighting, and composition began to eclipse the tenets of Pictorialism. From the 1920s to the 1930s, the work of photographers such as de Meyer, Horst P. Horst, André Kertész, Man Ray, and Edward Steichen made it into to the pages of *Vogue*, by way of the magazine's Paris studio.

Early on, Nast shaped the visual resonance of his fledgling periodicals by approving each photograph for publication. His affinity for and commitment to the photographic medium was further exemplified in a *Vanity Fair* series on modern photographers, which ran in the early 1920s under the art direction of Heyworth Campbell. On the editorial side, *Vogue* fashion editor Carmel Snow worked collaboratively with photographers like Steichen, who became the chief photographer for *Vogue* and *Vanity Fair* in 1923. Steichen created the first color photograph to appear on a *Vogue* cover in 1932, and Nast hired Horst for the New York edition of *Vogue* that same year. Nast soon began replacing fashion drawings on the covers with photo-illustrations.

One of his favorite artists was John Rawlings, who shot more than 200 cover photographs for *Vogue* and *Glamour* from the mid-1930s up until the 1960s.

Vanity Fair also began bringing a wide audience to photographers who went on to become well-known, as editor Frank Crowninshield published work by Gertrude Käsebier, Alfred Stieglitz, and Clarence White in 1915. Seven years later, Paul Outerbridge, Jr., Steichen, and others produced still-life shots for the magazine. Cecil Beaton, Anton Bruehl, and George Hoyningen-Huene, already established photographers, also began shooting for *Vanity Fair*. Nast's magazines began regularly commissioning fashion, lifestyle, and portrait photography by women in the field in the 1920s, when German photographer Antonie "Toni" von Horn began shooting for *Vanity Fair* and *Vogue* in New York. Von Horn officially joined the Condé Nast staff in 1930. Photographers such as Toni Frissell in the 1930s, Frances McLaughlin Gill in the 1940s, and Diane Arbus and Karen Radkai in the 1950s, created their earliest published work for *Glamour*, *Vogue*, and *Vanity Fair*.

Early on, the Condé Nast publications integrated photography, typography, and editorial themes into a boldly influential blend of content and imagery. As art directors began directly hiring photographers, the fusion of color photography and glossy magazine pages fueled their experimentation with publication layout and design. After joining the company as the art director of *Vanity Fair* in 1929 and *Vogue* the following year, Mehemed Fehmy Agha established a stylistic preference for larger photographs over other illustrations, such as line drawings. As a stable of photographers became an editorial necessity and grew for each magazine under the Condé Nast umbrella, *Glamour* art director Cipe Pineles hired photographers such as Cornell Capa and Herbert Matter. Alexander Liberman, who began as the *Vogue* art director in 1941 and was later the Condé Nast editorial director from 1962 until 1994, brought in Richard Avedon, Gordon Parks, William Klein, Helmut Newton, and Irving Penn.

Penn was initially an art director at *Vogue* and later became a still life and fashion photographer for the magazine, from 1950 onward. His voluminous body of work has been highlighted in museum exhibitions, as many arts institutions began showing the work of fashion photographers in the 1970s. In 1977, a touring exhibition called *The History of Fashion Photography* opened at the International Museum of Photography at the George Eastman House in Rochester, New York. For the next year, the show traveled to large venues within the United States, including the San Francisco Museum of Modern Art. In 1985, the Victoria and Albert Museum in London held the exhibition *Shots of Style*, curated by *Vogue* and *Glamour* photographer David Bailey. Seven years later, *On the Edge: Images from 100 Years of Vogue* opened at the New York Public Library.

After an acquisition by S.I. Newhouse in 1959, the Condé Nast magazines became part of Advance Publications, Inc., one of the largest media conglomerates in the United States. The company launched CondéNet, the Internet counterpart to its magazine group, in 1994. *Vogue* became the first Condé Nast magazine with a parallel Web site in 1999. The site transformed into Style.com, along with content from *W* magazine, in 2000. Condé Nast also has established an archive of thousands of images from its magazines, spanning nearly a century of fashion, celebrity, candid, still-life, and travel photography. By the time the entire collection is catalogued, more than one million photographs and illustrations will reside in the Condé Nast Archive.

KELLY XINTARIS

See also: **Archives; Beaton, Cecil; de Meyer, Adolph; Fashion Photography; Horst, Horst P; Liberman, Alexander; Lighting; Newton, Helmut; Portraiture**

Further Reading

Campbell, Heyworth. *Modern Masters of Photography, Series 1: Pictorialists*. New York: Galleon Press, 1937.

Derrick, Robin, and Robin Muir. *Unseen Vogue: The Secret History of Fashion Photography*. London: Little Brown UK Ltd., 2002.

Devlin, Polly. *Vogue Book of Fashion Photography*. London: Thames and Hudson, and New York: Simon & Schuster, 1979.

Hulick, Diana Emery, and Joseph Marshall. *Photography–1900 to the Present*. Upper Saddle River, New Jersey: Prentice-Hall, 1998.

Hurlburt, Allen. *Photo/Graphic Design: The Interaction of Design and Photography*. New York: Watson-Guptill Publications, 1983.

Neff, Terry Ann R., ed. *Photography's Multiple Roles: Art, Document, Market, Science*. New York: The Museum of Contemporary Photography in association with Distributed Art Publishers, Inc., 1998.

Packer, William. *Art of Vogue Covers: 1909–1940*. New York: Harmony Books, 1980; and New York: Random House Value Publishing, 1988.

Seebohm, Caroline. *The Man Who Was Vogue: The Life and Times of Condé Nast*. New York: The Viking Press, 1982.

LINDA CONNOR

American

Depictions of landscape are usually interpreted in the United States within the framework of manifest destiny, which declares human dominion over the dense and bountiful wilderness. Since the late 1960s, however, Linda Connor has been the main female photographer redirecting these views of landscape. Her photography makes reference to the spiritual and symbolic in a manner that overrides American notions of land ownership. Rarely working in a series or sequences, her individual works are worldly and engage in a touristic attraction that ultimately belies the experience of the religious pilgrimage. Trips taken to the American West, India, Turkey, and Hawaii materialize photographically as rare proof of the necessity of preserving the phenomenon of the natural world.

During the 1960s and 1970s, as conceptual art was on the rise, a number of photographers migrated to the Southwest, where they began to redefine photography's visual role within the fine arts and larger culture. Earthworks such as Robert Smithson's *Spiral Jetty*, Great Salt Lake, Utah (1970) influenced conservationist sympathies towards the natural environment and generated new practices in the visual arts, including developing the notion of pilgrimage as a fine-arts experience. Known mostly through photography, earthworks depended heavily upon such documentation.

Within the larger sphere of society, in places like Arizona, Utah, California, and New Mexico, where modern subdivisions intersected desert environments, awkward change accompanied the growth of cities such as Albuquerque. No longer standing in for the divine or the sublime, contemporary photographers of the landscape captured instead deformity, an overtaking of nature for corporate and urban development. Gathered in the famed exhibition organized by William Jenkins, *New Topographics* (1975), photographers (among them Lewis Baltz, Robert Adams, Nicholas Nixon, and Joe Deal) exhibited a new breed of itinerant photographers far removed from the heroic recording of nature's grandeur accomplished by nineteenth-century figures such as Timothy O'Sullivan and others. This is the historical background against which Linda Connor emerged, and bridging these two tendencies, she worked in a style not easily grouped with others. While her photographs insinuate a mythology that is symbiotic with New Topographics photographers' ideals of conserving geological areas, her images tend to be strikingly personal and evocative. Her influence extends to the success of students, including Larry Sultan, William Mebane, and Anthony Aziz, as well as the founding of PhotoAlliance, a member organization based in San Francisco that encourages artistic production and collecting.

Born in New York in 1944, an adopted child, which informs her later work, Connor studied at Rhode Island School of Design with Harry Callahan and moved to Chicago to study under Aaron Siskind and Arthur Siegal, receiving a Master of Science degree from the Institute of Design at Illinois Institute of Technology in 1969. Since then, Connor has resided in San Francisco, and she teaches at San Francisco Art Institute. Although she studied with Callahan and Siskind, known for their crisp, highly detailed styles, Connor predominantly uses a soft-focus lens (sometimes mentioned as a family heirloom) and a view camera. Her 8 × 10 inch negatives are contact printed onto printing out paper and exposed by the sun. Her photographs thus harken back to the early years of the century both in the method of taking the image as well in their look, which attempts to duplicate that of the platinum print, rich in silver and sepia tones. Lights and darks are not in strong contrast; gray tonalities soften white and black areas.

Rebecca Solnit writes of the notion of the oblique portrait, Connor's ability to materialize spiritual energy to get to the invisible—the energy that reveals a truth, either in the form of ritual offerings, physical environments, or through human activity. In this regard, Connor's work is often compared to the poetic photography of Frederick Sommer. The all-over field of Sommer's eccentric landscapes, often shot in close-up details, creates a similar surreal tonal atmosphere.

Whereas earlier work was mostly romantic, collaging dream-like vignettes in exterior environments to invoke a type of reverie, from the late 1970s onward her work shifted to capturing the petroglyphs and other Native American spiritual sites of the West and Southwest. *Great Gallery, Horseshoe Canyon, Utah* (1982), *Dots and Hands, Fourteen Window Ruin, Utah* (1987), or *Petroglyphs, Sears Point, Arizona* (1985) insinuate the physiological relationship between human existence and nature, which became Connor's main subject. The photographs are reminders of the ancient and continuing life forces that underlie contemporary experience. Images of overlaid and intertwined hands, "Family" (1988) and "My Hand with My Mother's" (1987), are from the same period, a period in which she found her birth family.

Working more in the vein of her colleague Mark Klett, with whom she published a 1986 portfolio *Nepal*, and his Rephotographic Project, Connor's projects such as *Critical Mass* (1993), which tied the New Mexican birthplace of the atomic bomb, Los Alamos, to the landscape of the Pueblo Indians or the National Endowment for the Arts-funded photographic survey *Marks and Measures: Pictographs and Petroglyphs in a Modern Art Context* (1988) stress the effects of human incursion upon natural landmarks.

Entwined Buddha, Ayuthaya, Thailand (1988), one of her best-known images, demonstrates this tendency in Connor's work. Her titles typically read as anthropological notations where subject and location are inseparable because the two are more than just related; together, they are evidence of the human (endeavor) projected as nature incarnate. *Petroglyphs and Star Trials, Sonora, Mexico* (1991) is demonstrative in this regard. A long exposure from a stationary angle causes a streaked star pattern. Light and lens supply the frame of her camera, which is a material space for gathering this information, these spiritual and unifying truths that Connor's Buddhist training underscores.

Photographer Jack Welpott once stated that the definition of self in nature is within the bounds of the universe, necessarily transforming many landscape photographers into philosophers. Connor's trip to India in 1979 and later trips to Nepal, Taiwan, and Hawaii, reveal such religious longings. Initially arriving in India as an observer, Connor was intrigued by yogin religion and their common practices. Aware that Connor is but a visitor to most of the sites she photographs, her work may seem to reflect the romantic leanings of nineteenth-century photography seen in the work of Felix Teynard, Gustave Le Gray, or Johnathan Greene. Most of her photographs, however, are about the modern traveler in search of religious grounding, the reason for the pilgrimage being enlightenment or the search for the sacred, which is not necessarily revealed by the photographer. Her photographs capture these sites as potent moments for significant experience rather than merely securing the picturesque.

Connor's cosmological and spiritual interests are conflated in the 1997 work *The Heavens*, shown at the San Francisco Art Institute. The exhibition included five glass-plate negatives of lunar solar eclipses taken between 1893 and 1922 from the archive of the University of California's Lick Observator in San Jose that Connor reprinted, original scratches and handwritten notations intact. These vintage works were flanked by a series of diptychs—prints of astronomical occurrences juxtaposed by photographs of religious figures photographed by Connor. Egypt, Tahiti, Chile, the United States, Zimbabwe, and France were cited as locations, but *The Heavens* emphasized cosmic relationships rather than the exotic. Linda Connor provides the best summation:

> Our minds seem to be wired for some kind of beliefs or rituals, or superstitions, some way of formulating experience that is far greater than we can deal with. To mitigate that experience, we ritualize it into forms that we can relate to. And my form is photography.
>
> (Webster 1992, 5)

SARA L. MARION

See also: **Adams, Robert; Baltz, Lewis; Institute of Design; Klett, Mark; Nixon, Nicholas; Sommer, Frederick**

Biography

Born 1944, New York City, New York. Bachelor of Fine Arts, Rhode Island School of Design, 1967; Master of Science, Institute of Design at the Institute of Technology, 1969. Professor of Photography, San Francisco Art

Institute, 1969–Present. Received National Endowment for the Arts Individual Artist Grant, 1976/1988; the John Simon Guggenheim Memorial Foundation Fellowship, 1979; Friends of Photography Photographer of the Year Award, 1986; Individual Artists Grant, Marin Arts Council, 1987; Charles Pratt Memorial Foundation Award, 1988; Cypress Award, Center for Photographic Art, 1994; Life Time Achievement Award, Marin Arts Council, 1996; Best Contemporary Monograph for *On Music of the Spheres*, Photo-Eye, Santa Fe, New Mexico; Flintridge Foundation Award for Visual Artists, 2001. Trustee for Friends of Photography, San Francisco, California; Founding member PhotoAlliance, San Francisco, California.

Solo Exhibitions

1973 *Linda Connor*; Light Gallery; New York, New York
1977 *Linda Connor*; M. H. de Young Memorial Museum; San Francisco, California
1982 *Linda Connor*; The Corcoran Gallery of Art; Washington, D.C.
1987 *Linda Connor*; Falkirk Cultural Center; San Rafael, California
1988 *Linda Connor*; Art Institute of Chicago; Chicago, Illinois
1990 *Linda Connor: Spiral Journey, Photographs 1967–1990*; The Museum of Contemporary Photography, Columbia College; Chicago, Illinois
1992 *Earthly Constellations*; San Francisco Museum of Modern Art; San Francisco, California; Museum of Photographic Arts, San Diego, Calfornia; Contemporary Museum of Art, Honolulu, Hawaii; National Museum of American Art, Washington, D.C.; Jocelyn Museum, Omaha, Nebraska; International Center of Photography, George Eastman House, Rochester, New York
Linda Connor and Harry Callahan; Light Factory; Charlotte, North Carolina
1996 *Stones of Faith, Stones of Peace*; The Jewish Museum; San Francisco, California
Linda Connor, Diptychs; Photo-Eye Gallery; Santa Fe, New Mexico

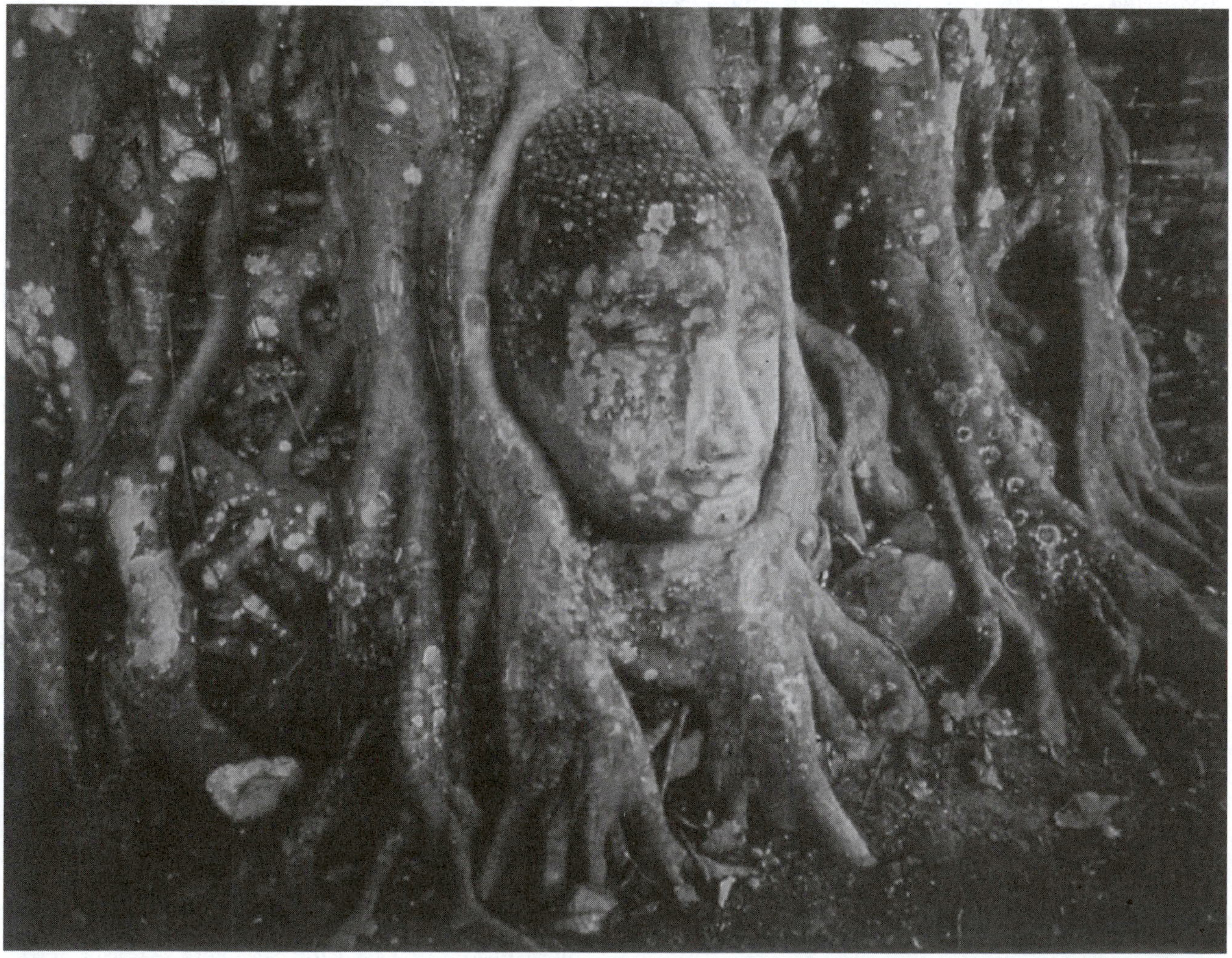

Linda Connor, Entwined Buddha, Ruuthaya, Thailand, 1988.
[*Courtesy Haines Gallery, San Francisco, California*]

Visits; Light Works; Syracuse, New York
1998 *The 7th Annual Lifework Award: Linda Connor*; Falkirk Cultural Center; San Rafael, California
1998/1996 *The Heavens*, San Francisco Art Institute; San Francisco, California; G. Gibson Gallery, Seattle, Washington

Group Exhibitions

1971 *Figure in Landscape*; George Eastman House; Rochester, New York
1977 *Mirrors and Windows: American Photography since 1960*; Museum of Modern Art; New York, New York
1982 *Form, Freud, and Feeling*; San Francisco Museum of Modern Art; San Francisco, California
American Images—New Work by Twenty Contemporary Photographers: 1979–1981; Corcoran Gallery of Art; Washington, D.C. and International Center of Photography; New York, New York
1992 *Mexico Through Foreign Eyes*; Museo Contemporaneo; Rufino Tamayo, Mexico City, Mexico; International Center of Photography; New York, New York; Armand Hammer Museum of Art and Cultural Center, UCLA; Los Angeles, California
1995 *An American Century of Photography: From Dry-Plate to Digital, The Hallmark Photographic Collection*; International Center of Photography Midtown; New York, New York
1998 *Israel Through American Eyes: A Century of Photography*; Skirball Cultural Center; Los Angeles, California
Degrees of Stillness: Photographs from the Manfred Heiting Collection; August Sander Archive; Cologne, Germany
Photography's Multiple Roles: Art, Document, Market, Science; Museum of Contemporary Photography; Columbia College, Chicago, Illinois
1999 *India*; SEPIA International, Inc. and the Alkazi Collection of Photography; New York, New York
Photographie in Una Collezione Privata; Galleria Gottardo, Museo Cantonale d'Arte; Lugano, Italy
2000 *Beyond Boundaries: Contemporary Photography in California*; University Art Museum, California State University; Long Beach, California; Santa Barbara Con-

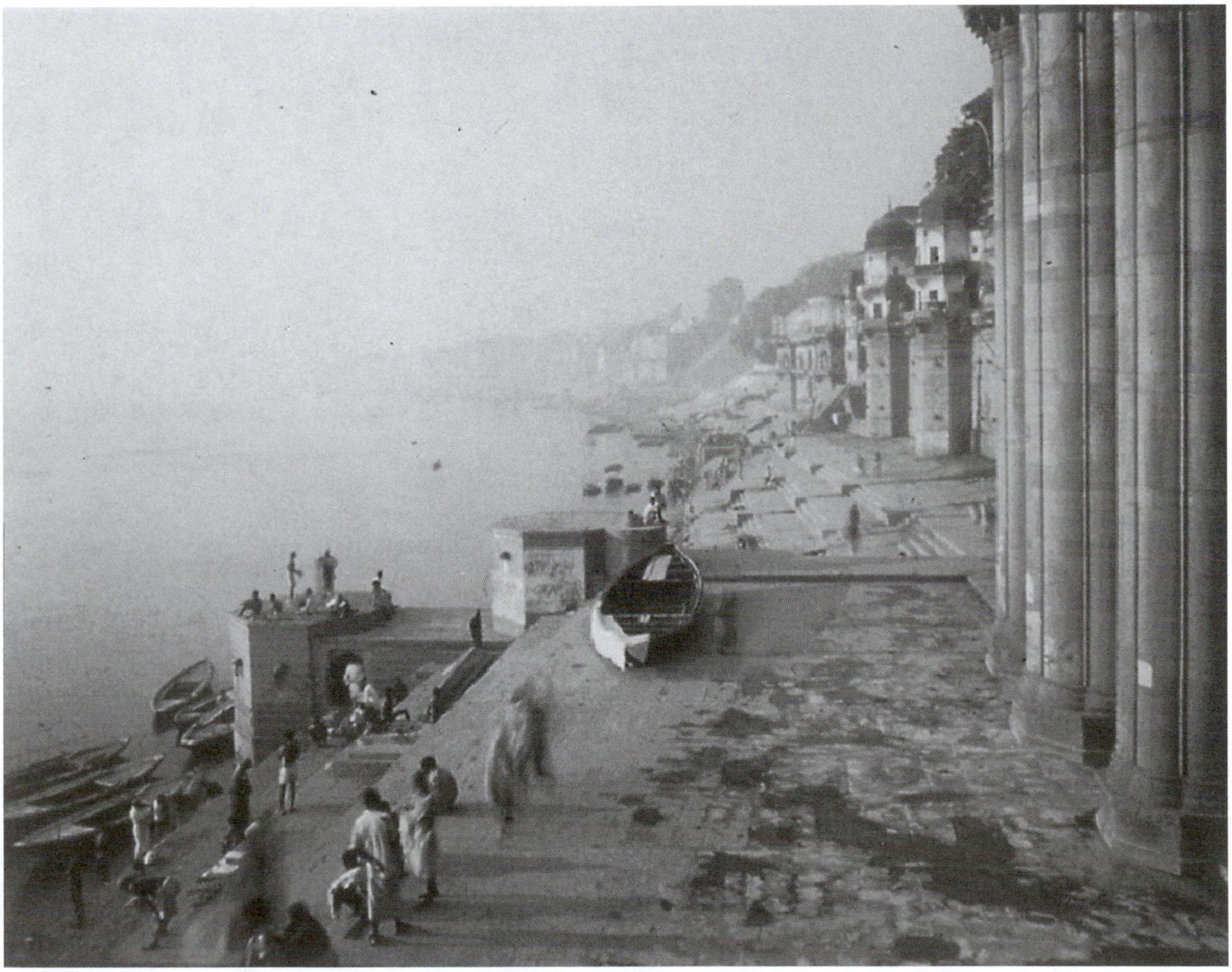

Linda Connor, Banares, India, 1979.
[*Courtesy Haines Gallery, San Francisco, California*]

temporary Arts Museum; Santa Barbara, California; Ansel Adams/Friends of Photography Center; San Francisco, California

2002 *Night Skies and Imaginary Coordinates: The Artist as Navigator*; Palo Alto Art Center; Palo Alto, California

Selected Work

Confirmation, Chicago, 1968
Banares, India, 1979
Petroglyphs, Sears Point, Arizona, 1985
Kapo Kohe Lele, Ancient Ceremonial Cave for Pele, Goddess of the Volcano, Puna, Hawaii, 1986
Entwined Buddha, Ayuthaya, Thailand, 1988
My Hand with My Mother's, 1987
Stones, Kau Desert, Hawaii, 1991
Petroglyphs and Star Trials, Sonora, Mexico, 1991
April 16, 1893 (eclipse), 1995–6
Dots and Hands, Fourteen Window Ruin, Utah, 1987
The Heavens, 1997

Further Reading

Connor, Linda. *Marks in Place: Contemporary Responses to Rock Art*. Albuquerque: University of New Mexico Press, 1988.

———. *Solos: Photographs by Linda Connor*. Millerton, New York: Aperion Workshops Inc., 1990.

———. *Luminance*. Carmel, California: Center for Photographic Arts and Woodrose Publishing, Carmel, California, 1994.

———. *On Music of the Spheres*, essay by Charles Simic. New York City and East Hampton, New York: Whitney Museum of American Art and Glenn Horowitz Booksellers, 1996.

———. *Visits*. Syracuse, New York: Robert Menschel Photography, 1996.

Bright, Deborah. "The Machine in the Garden Revisited: American Environmentalism and Photographic Aesthetics," *Art Journal*, vol. 5, no. 2 (Summer 1992): 60–71.

Davis, Keith and Polly Schaafsma. *Marks in Place: Contemporary Responses to Rock Art*. Albuquerque: University of New Mexico Press, 1988.

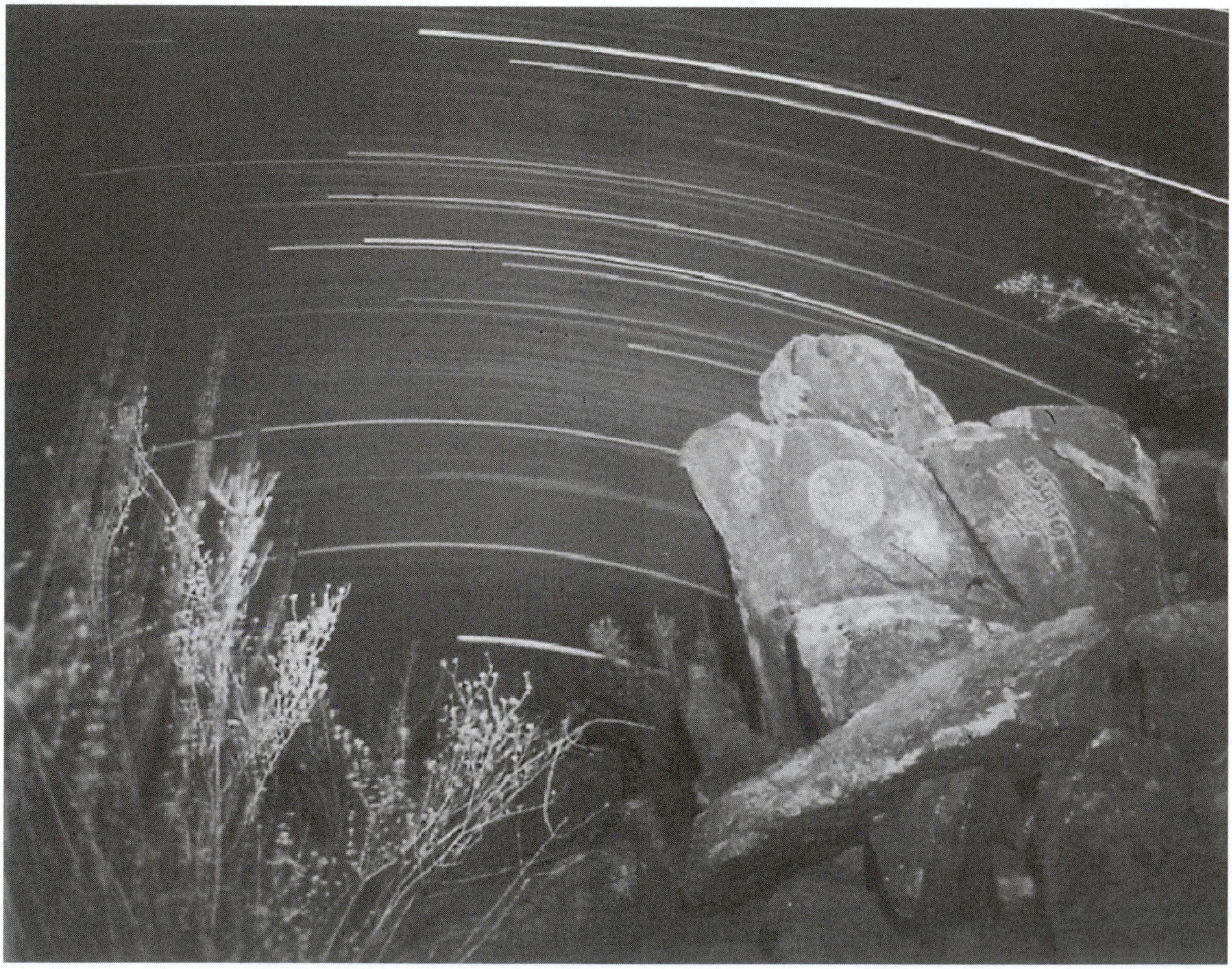

Linda Connor, Petroglyphs and Star Trials, Sonora, Mexico, 1991.
[*Courtesy Haines Gallery, San Francisco, California*]

Galkagger, Chris, and David Hamilton. *The Photographic Vision: Landscape and Cityscape*, series #15, producer Sandra Ostertag, produced by Coast Community College District in Cooperation with Hokt/Dryden/Saunders College, published by Coast Telecourses, Fountain Valley, California: video recording, 29 min, sd, col, 1/400 in., 1984.
Miller-Clark, Denise, and Rebecca Solnit. *Linda Connor: Spiral Journey, Photographs 1967–1990*. Chicago: Museum of Contemporary Photography, Columbia College, 1990.
Solnit, Rebecca. "Unsettling the West: Contemporary American Landscape Photography." *Creative Camera* [London], (December/January 1993): 12–23.
Webster, Mary Hull. "A Conversation with Linda Connor." *Artweek*, vol. 23, no. 30 (December 17, 1992): 4–5.

CONSERVATION

Since its invention in 1839, photography has been practiced using numerous techniques and processes, some of which lasted for many decades and some that survived only for a brief period. Photography has become so commonplace that it is easy to take it for granted and treat photographs casually and with little respect. Whether one is looking after holiday snaps, caring for professional photographs, or working as a professional conservator in charge of historical material there are important considerations for prolonging the life of images and preventing unnecessary deterioration. Some of the most basic and effective methods of preserving images are often the most obvious and the most often overlooked: namely correct handling, good housekeeping, and proper storage.

Photographic materials consist of complex physical and chemical structures, each of which reacts differently to temperature, humidity, environment, and handling. Conservation procedures must take into account all these factors, and knowledge of the image type—platinum print, silver gelatin, and so on—and its particular physical and chemical make-up is essential.

In general terms the conservation of photographs, whether amateur or professional, is problematic and conservation treatment should only be undertaken by a qualified conservator. While some companies offer restoration services for old photographs, these services are generally pointed at the amateur market and should be engaged with caution. Restoration is not conservation. Restoration techniques often use powerful oxidizing agents and extremes of pH in the form of reprocessing, refixing, bleaching, and redevelopment. These processes are irreversible, introduce contaminants, and can permanently damage the image.

Photographs are made up of three main layers: the base; the light sensitive image forming material; and the medium or matrix used to bind the light sensitive material to the base. Together, the light sensitive material and binder make up the emulsion, named after the fluid nineteenth century photographers used to coat glass and metal plates. The most common bases in use in the twentieth century are glass, plastic, and paper, with paper being standard for prints. For negatives glass was in widespread usage from 1851 until the 1950s, although flexible bases for film were introduced as early as the 1880s.

Today the most usual emulsion consists of gelatin with silver as the basis for the most common light sensitive compound, including dyes and filters for color materials, but others include platinum, iron, and carbon. Some processes are identifiable with the naked eye or under a microscope, but professional advice from a trained conservator is the safest course of action. Incorrect identification and treatment can make the problem worse and even destroy the object being conserved.

Common Conservation Problems

Exposure to Light

The processes of developing and fixing have a direct effect on the permanence and durability of the finished image, whether in the form of a negative or the finished print. As inadequate fixing will leave the image prone to deterioration from exposure to light, correct processing is the first step in good conservation practice. Even so nearly all photographs continue to be light sensitive to some degree and prolonged exposure will eventually fade or selectively darken the image (some color processes will even deteriorate in the dark). This must be taken into account when exposing negatives, viewing transparencies, and displaying prints. The brightness of light, the length of time the image is exposed, and the type of light can all have an adverse affect. Brightness and duration are related as prolonged exposure in low lighting can be as harmful as a brief flash of bright light. Sunlight contains the most damaging type of light in the form of ultraviolet (UV) rays. These should be filtered out where possible and tungsten lamps are preferable for display and exhibition. Resin or plastic coated prints are more susceptible to light than archivally processed fiber prints. In order to maximize the life of a black and white print, illumination at 50 lux is recommended during display; there should be a maximum intensity of no more than 100 lux. Color photographs are particularly vulnerable to light and are ideally illuminated at 30 lux and never more than at 70 lux. Light meters should be used to check ambient light levels. In museum and gallery settings light levels are strictly controlled, and the length of time photographs are on view carefully observed.

Transparencies in the form of slides can fade after only 10 minutes in a projector, and it is advisable to preserve the original by using good quality duplicates for viewing.

Heat and Moisture

Heat and moisture both affect photographic materials. Too much moisture in the air can produce chemical changes in the emulsion and encourage the growth of mould—too little can cause emulsions, and papers and plastics to become brittle, flake, and crack. High temperatures also promote chemical changes, particularly in color film. Again there is a link between moisture content of the air, known as relative humidity (RH) and temperature. A stable RH of 20% to 50%, (20% to 30% for color stock) is most desirable combined with a consistent temperature of no more than 21 C, and even lower (8–12 C) for color, but any reduction is helpful. Fluctuations in temperature and RH are extremely damaging as they constantly stress the materials and maintaining a stable environment is essential. Cold storage, including freezing, is increasingly used for preserving photographs. The photographs are placed in tightly sealed bags or containers to avoid fluctuations in RH. When taken out of cold storage the package should be left at room temperature to acclimatize before opening to prevent condensation forming in the cold image surface. However this is only really suitable for photographs that are not often accessed.

Collections should be checked for signs of deterioration. Once every five years is appropriate, more often in the case of nitrocellulose film stock. Things to check are: physical damage including tears, cracks, and flaking emulsion: chemical changes such as discoloration and pungent odors: and environmental problems from air pollution, mould, and insect or rodent attack. Damaged items should be stored separately until treated, as mould and gases and pollutants from chemical changes can quickly spread to adjacent images. Temperature and relative humidity should also be carefully and regularly monitored.

Handling

One of the most overlooked, and yet simplest, aspects of preservation is correct handling. In an ideal world photographs would never be handled at all. Obviously this is impractical but a general goal should be a reduction in the handling of both negatives and prints. As fingerprints leave perspiration and oily stains that can permanently mark the image and also cause chemical changes in the emulsion, it is recommended that photographs and negatives be handled with clean hands and preferably lint free cotton gloves. The emulsion surface should be avoided (in negatives the emulsion is the shiny side) and prints should be supported with two hands. Transparent plastic sleeves allow prints and transparencies to be viewed while safely protecting them from direct contact.

Prints should never be rolled as this puts a strain on the emulsion. Conversely attempts to to unroll and flatten rolled or curled prints should be avoided, as this can cause the surface to crack or wrinkle. If prints or negatives are stuck together attempts to separate them should be left to the conservator, as should flattening curled prints.

Although historically, many fine art photographers sign their works in ink directly on the photograph, generally it is preferable to keep ink pens, especially felt tip and other water based inks, away from photographs. Ideally any information should be written on the mount or enclosure. If it is necessary write on the back of the print, a soft pencil should be used, and care taken not to mar the print. Paperclips, pins, rubber bands, and pressure sensitive tape should never be used. They can only result in physical damage, rust stains, chemical damage from sulfides in the rubber, and staining from glue residues.

Housekeeping

Good housekeeping is also essential in preventing deterioration. Work areas should be kept clean and dust free as dust can cause scratches on the surface of film and prints. Cover work surfaces with newsprint, which can be replaced when it becomes dirty. Use a soft brush or a vacuum with the nozzle covered with gauze for dusting storage areas. Do not use cleaning agents and solvents—they contain harmful chemicals, and wet cleaning such as mopping can cause fluctuations in humidity levels. Obviously do not place photographs near heat sources such as radiators and pipes. Freshly painted or varnished surfaces can give off harmful peroxides for up to two or three weeks and all but the very latest photocopiers and laser printers emit ozone and should be kept away from photographic materials. Food and drink should never be allowed near photographs—an accident is destined to happen! Even nicotine from cigarette smoke can cause staining.

Storage

Poor storage of negatives and prints is the most common cause of deterioration. Prints, transparencies, and negatives should be stored separately and good quality archival storage materials should be used. Paper should be impurity free and unbuffered, i.e., pH neutral, (pHoton and Silversafe are recommended brands). Some papers and cards are described as 'acid free' but still contain alkalines, which can damage photographs. Polyester is the best material for plastic enclosures, but uncoated polypropylene and high-density polythene are acceptable, cheaper alternatives. Polyvinyl chloride (PVC) should be avoided as it contains plasticizers that can migrate to the object. For similar reasons do not use coated, translucent, or opaque plastics. Despite their long tradition as a photographic storage medium, glassine sleeves are not suitable.

Polyester and conservation papers are available as sheets, rolls, and ready-made sleeves and envelopes. Hanging files, museum card boxes, and conservation ring binders make good storage systems, especially for prints, roll film, and transparencies. Cabinets should be made from baked enamel or anodized aluminum finish. Boxes and cabinets made from new wood or freshly painted or varnished wood should be avoided.

Ideally, prints should be stored in transparent sleeves, with unbuffered board if extra support is required, and then placed in folders or museum card boxes. Plastic sleeves should not be used where the emulsion is fragile or flaking, or there is extensive mould damage or images have been hand colored. Platinum prints should be stored flat in archival boxes.

Glass negatives are most at risk from physical damage resulting in chipping, cracking, breakages, and scratches. The plates should be wrapped in pH neutral conservation paper and stored in museum board boxes vertically along their long edge, adding a board separator every fifth plate to give support. Plates larger than 12 × 10 inches are best stored horizontally, at no more than four per box to prevent the weight crushing the bottom plate. The original wooden boxes for storing lantern slides are usually fine, but do check the condition of the box and its lining material.

Cellulose nitrate film base, invented by the Eastman Kodak Company in the 1880s was quickly copied by others and allowed the development of sheet, roll, and cine film. It was in turn replaced by cellulose acetate and later, polyester supports. Nitrate and acetate bases are both prone to serious chemical deterioration and should be checked regularly for signs of deterioration, as this can quickly spread to affect the entire collection.

Nitrate film stock is the most notorious. Introduced in the 1880s it was in use until the 1950s (although still manufactured abroad in 1960s). It breaks down into harmful and dangerous elements that are very acidic and can fade silver, soften the gelatin emulsion, and rust film cans. Nitrate film is also combustible and gives off highly toxic fumes, a by-product of which is oxygen, making fires difficult to extinguish. In the early days of cinema there were many fatal fires in theatres when the nitrate cine film ignited in the projector. The first stage of deterioration can be seen as an amber brown staining, the film then softens and becomes tacky, producing gas bubbles and gives off a 'sweet' odor before the film finally breaks down into combustible powder. Some nitrate can be easily identified by the word "Nitrate" along the edge of the negative but this is by no means conclusive. If nitrate film is suspected, a conservator should be engaged to test a small sample—nitrate film will sink in trichloroethylene. Deteriorating nitrate film should be handled under a fume hood or wearing a respirator. Cold storage in a flameproof lab freezer in a paper enclosure is ideal but be aware that, due to its combustible and toxic nature, storage of nitrate film often invalidates insurance policies. Nitrate film stock is best copied under supervision and either destroyed through the fire department or local authority or stored off-site in specialist facilities.

Cellulose acetate film, sometimes known as safety film, was introduced in the early 1930s to replace flammable cellulose nitrate stock. It does not burn easily, however, warmth and moisture cause chemical breakdown producing acetic acid with its telltale vinegary smell, known as "vinegar syndrome." The film base becomes brittle and starts to shrink while the gelatin layer is softened but remains otherwise unchanged and the two start to separate, causing reticulation—channeling and bubbling in the emulsion layer. For small amounts of film stock or particularly important images a professional conservator can remove the emulsion layer and transfer it to a new support, thus saving the image. However prevention is better than cure—low temperatures and recommended RH levels should be maintained and negatives kept away from acids, especially those found in unsuitable enclosures. Material that is deteriorating should be removed for treatment as vinegar syndrome can rapidly spread to adjacent negatives.

Polyester supports are the most physically and chemically durable—in fact the emulsion is more likely to degrade—and simple to identify. Sandwich the image between two linear polarizing filters (available from camera shops) at right angles to one another. Polyester film produces a "rainbow" effect similar to oil on water but acetate film does not.

Film based negatives most often take the form of single sheets in various sizes or strips, cut into lengths of 4–6 frames. Storing negatives together in a single envelope or box can cause scratches and should be avoided. Negatives should be stored in suitable paper or plastic enclosures, with the exception of nitrate film stock. As there is a danger that toxic gases can be trapped in plastic sleeves, speeding up the process of deterioration, paper enclosures are preferable. Dampness in the air can be trapped as moisture when sleeving negatives, and care should be taken that this procedure is carried out when the relative humidity is low.

Color Photographs and Negatives

Modern color photography was introduced in the 1930s although earlier experiments, mainly in additive processes, have been developed in the nineteenth century. With the exception of the dye transfer, color photographic materials are more sensitive to high RH and temperature than black and white photographs. Color materials are also generally more susceptible to damage during handling and lint-free cotton gloves should always be worn, with the image protected by plastic sleeves for both casual viewing and storage. Hanging file systems are ideal for transparencies as long as the cabinets are not packed too tightly.

Mounts and Albums

People have lovingly mounted their print collections in albums from the earliest days of photography. Historically albums can be viewed as an integral part of the photographic object and should be treated with equal respect as the photographs they house. Acid free tissue paper can be interleaved between pages to protect images on adjacent leaves, but take care that this does not put additional strain on the binding. The album should be wrapped in conservation paper and stored flat in a museum board box. Albums should not be stacked on top of one another, as the pressure will damage the lowest album. Neither is storing upright on a bookshelf ideal as clasps and raised decorative work can cause scratching and abrasion to adjacent albums. Use a cradle to support the album and prevent damage to the spine when viewing. Most commercially available modern albums are not suitable for storing photographs, especially the type with plastic adhesive sheets, PVC sleeves, or acidic boards. Only conservation photo-corners and hinges should be used for mounting prints.

Conclusion

All of the above are essential in the prevention of deterioration of photographic objects, however, it is inevitable that objects will require treatment at some stage. A qualified conservator should always be consulted before treatment is carried out. Surface dirt can be removed using a soft brush, however, remember that dry cleaning is abrasive and can result in scratches and image loss. If absolutely necessary a Mars Staedtler rubber can be used gently to remove dirt from the surrounds and support, but do not attempt to clean the image surface in this way, especially with processes such as platinum prints where there is no binding layer. The housewife's tip of using bread is definitely not recommended as bread contains damaging oils. Wet cleaning processes should be approached with caution. Silver-based images deteriorate in moist atmosphere and gelatin emulsions become sticky. Because of this mounts often have to be removed dry; however, this destroys the mount, which can be an integral part of the object. Alcohol based cleaning is also suspect as the gelatin emulsion can swell. Professional film cleaning fluids are available and can be used carefully with a swab to gently remove dirt. Tears and rips in prints can be repaired with conservation tape, which should always be applied to the back of the picture. Pressure sensitive tapes such as Sellotape or Scotch brand "magic"should be avoided, as they will become brittle with age and leave brown stains that can be virtually impossible to remove. Retouching vintage prints is controversial on ethical grounds, and pigments used in retouching can cause damage from sulfur and other contaminants.

Good processing, a stable environment, and conservation standard storage materials are essential aids for the preservation of photographic objects, supported by common sense, careful handling, and respect. Observation of these rules can ensure that modern photographs should last long after the lifetime of the originator with little recourse to the professional conservator, and will greatly reduce the deterioration of older images until a conservator can assess them. Conservation of photographic images is now entering a new phase with the introduction of digital media. In some cases the image does not exist outside of the computer's hard drive or other storage medium such as CD-ROM or memory cards, until the image is digitally printed. Technical advances mean that both hardware and software quickly become out of date and valuable images may not be retrievable if stored in older formats. In general terms the good conservation practices already mentioned should be followed. CDs should be stored in stable, cool, dark, dry, dust free conditions away from UV radiation, in acid free sleeves. They should be handled with lint-free gloves, avoiding touching the information carrying surface, and cleaned with a lint free cloth from the middle outwards. However only time will tell how stable these 'new' image carrying devices are, and the longevity of digital inks and papers, and only trial and error by the conservator will lead to good care and conservation practices.

Sarah McDonald

See also: **Darkroom; Developing Processes; Film; Non-Silver Processes; Toning**

Further Reading

Ball, Stephen, Susie Clark and Peter Winsor. *The Care of Photographic Materials & Related Media.* London: Museums & Galleries Commission, 1998.

Clark, Susie. *Photographic Conservation.* London: National Preservation Office, 1989.

Gill A.T. *Photographic Processes.* Information Sheet 21, London: Museums Association, 1978.

Hendriks, Klaus B. *Fundamentals of Photographic Conservation: A Study Guide.* Toronto: National Archives of Canada and Lugus Publications, 1986.

McCormack-Goodhart, M.H. "The Allowable Temperature and Humidity Range for Safe Use and Storage of Photographic Materials." in *The Journal of the Society of Archivists*, vol. 17, no. 1.

Museums & Galleries Commission. *Standards in the Museum Care of Photographic Collections.* London: MGC, 1996.

Public Record Office. *An Introduction to Nineteenth and Early Twentieth Century Photographic Processes*, London: PRO.

Rempel, Siegrfried. *The Care of Black and White Photographic Collections: Identification of Processes.* Ottawa: Canadian Conservation Institute, 1979.

Rempel, Siegrfried. *The Care of Photographs.* USA: Nick Lyons Books, 1987.

Swan, A. *The Care and Conservation of Photographic Material.* London: Crafts Council, 1981.

CONSTRUCTED REALITY

Generally, there are two types of constructed realities: those that are fabricated and photographs, which are the result of photographing a specifically constructed stage. Fabricated imagery is produced by techniques like combination printing, montage, and photomontage to invent a scene or event that never existed or took place. "Set-up" or staged photography, also referred to as *tableaux* or directorial photography, involves the artist creating a 'reality' or 'stage' upon which they organize and arrange subjects and/or props in a particular way for the intention of photographing it. While all photographs are set up or produced in some manner, a key distinguishing feature of fabricated and staged images is the reason for the construction: to express the artist's subjective experiences rather than producing objective photographic documents of the world.

There are many historical (nineteenth century) precedents for the both the staged and fabricated image. Julia Margaret Cameron (British, 1815–1879), as part of her leisure activities, staged and photographed specific events, moments, and characters based upon religious, literary, poetic, and mythological sources. She became the director and producer of her images in various ways: creating costumes for her sitters (such as fashioning angel wings from paper), selecting and arranging props, and using dramatic lighting to heighten the theatricality of her tableaux.

In addition to constructing the final image, other photographers, such as Oscar Gustave Rejlander (Swedish, active in England; 1813–1875) fabricated their realities through combination printing where many different negatives were used to produce a photograph of an imaginary event. In *The Two Ways of Life* (1857), Rejlander used as many as 30 negatives layered in his combination print to depict the Victorian notion regarding the choices between good and evil. Henry Peach Robinson (British; 1830–1901), on the other hand, only used five negatives in *Fading Away* (1858) to create a romantic notion of a young woman upon her deathbed. These techniques were particularly evocative of a pictorialist approach that pursued painterly aims in the service of photography.

Early commercial studios, such as the William Notman Studio, offered their patrons a unique type of image in addition to standard portraiture—those created by collage and photomontage. During the 1860s, the Notman studios, whose headquarters were in Montréal (with studios in Toronto, Ottawa, St. John, Halifax, and Boston), became well known for their ambitious indoor studio images that reconstructed winter activities. Dressed in the appropriate attire, clients were positioned in front of elaborately painted backdrops and posed with props to stage sledding, skating, and hunting scenes. Additionally, Notman studios also created complex group scenes consisting of many people participating in, for example, huge skating parties. With a preconceived idea of the final image that was worked out in sketches, separate photographs of people arranged in particular groupings were taken in his studio, and through combination printing and/or collage, an image of an event that never took place was fabricated.

During the twentieth century, artists and scholars increasingly questioned and challenged traditional photographic practices. Photographers were viewed as more than mediators of the material world, they were constructors of it. Their goal was not limited to making literal translation of the world, capturing the "decisive moment" on film to produce artistic images displaying nature's beauty, or providing documents that supplied information, evidence, or proof. Rather, it was argued that photographs were directly connected to the political, the psychological, and ideology among other aspects of the social world. Photographs were interpreted as a form of representation rather than valued only for their verisimilitude.

In various ways during the first half of the twentieth century, artists used photography to challenge its very definition as well as how their viewers perceived photographs. Disruptions to the image can be seen in the work of Russian Constructivist El Lissitzky, notably *The Constructor* (1924) where a photographic self-portrait is combined with images of the tools, diagrams, and lettering related to architectural design. From the title and the imagery, the man depicted seems to be the creator of his own image rather than simply having his portrait taken. The Dadaists, believing that modern society was essentially irrational thus its art should be equally irrational, used photography in ways that challenged traditional and conventional definitions and uses of photography, including the way that photographs were taken. Rejecting the use of a camera, film, and traditional photographic working methods, Man Ray created "Rayographs" (also known as photograms) arranging objects on photographic paper that were exposed to light. The resulting images were nonrepresentational and characterized by spatial and visual ambiguity. German Dadaist John Heartfield selected and arranged pre-existing photographs into new and specific narratives. His photomontages were accompanied by scathing captions that satirized Nazi Germany as they raised leftist political consciousness.

Since the early twentieth century, particular schools of artists have used staged and fabricated photography within various genres such as portraiture, landscape, still life, and reportage photography. Within these genres, they have addressed various social concerns including issues of gender, class, race, and history. Although staged, manipulated, and artificial images fell out of favor among many modernist photographers at mid-century, others continued to acknowledge its creative uses. Since the 1960s and to the end of the century, staged photography was resurrected by numerous influential and disparate artists who exploited in particular the political and social uses of this approach.

In contemporary art circles of the 1960s and 1970s, staged photography became a common, at times even preferred working method. Artists turned to creating their subject matter for different reasons: this type of photography provided more time and control to compose the image and make the necessary technical and aesthetic decisions. Additionally artists could enhance the initial image by re-working the elements upon the stage and re-photographing the set. Another reason for using this approach is linked to the aesthetic: staged photographs revealed the ways the image can be un-true, highlighted the constructed and even relative nature of reality and photographic "truth." Revealing and incorporating the artifice of photography and photographs, and using it as an important element to express the artistic message, the photograph is no longer an authorless text, to use the language of philosophers Roland Barthes or Claude Levi-Strauss. By highlighting artifice, artists can create their own narratives and realities based upon their personal experiences drawn from any number of sources including memories, fantasies, and politics, as well as in relation to (or reaction against) external influences such as history, economics, patriarchy, and so forth. Staged (and fabricated) images thus challenge photographic realism, conventions, genres, or disrupt how photography is perceived and interpreted.

To foreground the artifice, clues are incorporated within the pictorial frame to signal the photo is a product of the photographer-artist's imagination. Although this can be accomplished in a variety of ways several techniques predominate. Some photographers allow the signs of the medium, including the equipment or signs of the camera, remain in the image. Having the studio lights, extension cords, or backdrops visible and a part of the photographic composition reveals how the image is technically produced. Conventionally, evidence of the photographic production is disguised or hidden because exposing the production interrupts the seamless realism expected from photographs. A second way to challenge photographic realism is the artist's treatment of the subject matter: having the image somehow defy the laws governing the universe (such as time, space, and gravity), the improbability hence incredulity of the photo is made apparent. Third, distortions or inconsistencies in scale or volume, playing with horizon lines, the use of unconventional camera angles and perspectives, or cropping the subject matter in a way that inhibits immediate understanding of the imagery prevents the audience from quickly and easily recognizing specific objects. Such ambiguous or obscure imagery places demands upon the viewer: it requires him or her to use imagination to formulate meanings rather than looking to the photograph for information or answers. It should also be mentioned that the context in which the final photograph is viewed (in an art gallery or in a fine art photography book) also contributes to interpreting it as constructed for a specific purpose.

Although various characteristics of the staged photograph are available to the contemporary photography, it is not necessary that all of the aforementioned be present in each image. Furthermore, these elements can be used in an overt or subtle manner; for example, the viewer knows that Sandy Skoglund has constructed her sets prior to be photographed. In *Fox Games* (1989), all the elements in the restaurant (walls, tables, chairs, bread loaves, etc.) are painted in the same monotone gray, which signals that the restaurant itself is not part of the viewer's phenomenal or optical reality. However, it is the many brightly colored red foxes running, walking, or hopping into the frame that simply look unnatural even though they were modeled on actual foxes, but even more from their coloring. From this, the audience quickly recognizes the constructed nature of the image. On the other hand, the work of Jeff Wall uses a subtler approach to his tableau, and sometimes it is difficult to discern his tampering. In the images he made without the use of digital technology, such as *Untangling* (1994), the photo appears more like a snapshot of a garage worker untangling huge blue ropes rather than an obviously constructed image. However, Wall's working method is based on constructing a theatre with all the necessary props and people in place before he captures the decisive moment.

One way that staged photography has been used to comment on its use within scientific circles is found in the work of American artist Patrick Nagatani. Using the field journals of Japanese archeologist Ryoichi, Nagatani created *Excavations*, (2001) in which he stages an archeological dig. The viewers are given glimpses of the top of Volkswagen "Beetle" cars as they are unearthed at Xi'an, Necroplis of Mt. Li', Shanxi Province, China 1988. Nagatani's series uses photography and constructed realities to draw attention to our perception that historical time is linear.

Working in a similar way, Spanish artists Joan Fontcuberta and Pere Formiguera devise species of fauna and flora, and using scientific documentation such as field notes in conjunction with photographic documents, the artists present the fake plants and animals in a scientific manner—even going so far as to exhibit the 'evidence' in museums or museum-like settings. In this 'mockumentary,' trust in written evidence supported by photographic documents is challenged.

Tableaux photography has also been used to draw attention to contemporary political issues, as in the work of the Canadian team, Carole Conde and Karl Beveridge, whose collaboration extends to working directly with unions and community groups. Working with nuclear plant workers to produce their 1985–1986 series *No Immediate Threat*, Conde and Beveridge challenge society's notion that nuclear energy is a safe and clean energy source. In carefully arranged tableaux in which every prop and gesture is meaningful, they articulate the problems of nuclear energy, and bring to the fore the health problems that these plant workers face.

Staged photography has also proven effective for dealing with issues of gender. In her *Tourism* series (1983), Laurie Simmons uses small toy figures of females set against projections of tourist attractions such as the Tower of Pisa, Stonehenge, and the Parthenon. These stiff plastic figures remain outside of the surface of the "picture perfect" images and this is analogous to the place of women in relation to culture.

Cindy Sherman and many other artists, turn the camera upon their own body within a staged environment. Sherman's early black and white *Film Stills* (1977–1980), quote various female stereotypes from B-movies through costume, posing, and stylization. Sherman shoots the sometimes grainy, filmic images against specific backdrops (outdoors or projected images) that reference already existed cultural images. In these recreations, she draws attention to the female stereotypes in popular film, television, and advertising.

Swiss artists Peter Fischli and David Weiss have been working together since 1979. Among their collaborations, they have created *Wurstseries* (*Sausage series*), which uses a small scale tableaux to recreate and reinvent scenes from everyday life. In *The Accident* (1980), they have used cardboard, cigarette butts, and cold cuts to stage a "car" accident between two sausages complete with "human" victims in the form of cigarette butts. While the content is humorous, the accident scene provides a darker comment on disasters caused by humans.

Other contemporary artists who have worked with constructed reality in photography include Jo Ann Callis (American), Lorna Simpson (American), Carrie Mae Weems (American), Sarah Charlesworth (American), Boyd Webb (British), Evergon (Canadian), Brenda Francis Pelkey (Canadian), Janieta Eyre (Canadian), Diana Thorneycroft (Canadian), Holly King (Canadian), Yasumasa Morimura (Japanese), William Wegman (American), Lucas Samaras (American), and Pierre et Gilles (French).

Although constructing a "reality" enables artists to manipulate photographic elements to create specific readings while simultaneously drawing attention to their role in this production, equally significant is the final form of the photograph. The translation of the installation/stage from its three-dimensional form into the two-dimensional photograph creates new understandings and interpretations of the elements and relationships displayed within the image. The conversion of the actual into the photographic turns the environment and/or actions into photographic codes and conventions, that is, into a visual language that is interpreted in a different manner than if one was viewing the set-up or set *in situ*. The transformation from the actual elements into the pictorial is key for artists: understanding the ways in which a photographed object, relationship, or action can be interpreted by viewers allows artists to arrange the elements to position the audience to create certain understandings. Artists, as manipulators of these representational codes, are able to create and express subjective information. It should be noted that the fabricated pieces or installations were important only insofar as they served the artist's purposes, that is, for the production of a photograph. Many artists dismantle their constructions after the photo shoot because it was the image and not the installation that was considered the final art work to be exhibited in galleries.

Nancy Yakimoski

See also: **Barthes, Roland; Conceptual Photography; Deconstruction; et Gilles, Pierre; Fischli, Peter and Weiss, David; Heartfield, John; History of Photography: the 1980s; Levi-Strauss, Claude; Lissitzky, El; Man Ray; Manipulation; Photogram; Photographic "Truth"; Postmodernism; Representation; Sherman, Cindy; Simpson, Lorna; Skoglund, Sandy; "The Decisive Moment"; Wall, Jeff; Webb, Boyd: Morimura, Yasumasa; Weems, Carrie Mae**

Further reading

Bradley, Randy. "The Staged Photograph." *Blackflash*, vol. 7, no. 1, Spr. 1989: 13.

Dines, Elaine K. *Anxious Interiors, An Exhibition of Tableau Photography and Sculpture*. Laguna Beach, CA: Laguna Beach Museum of Art, 1984.

Goldwater, Marge. "Sandy Skoglund," *Cross-References; Sculpture into Photography*. Minneapolis, MN: Walker Art Center, 1987.

Lemagny, Jean-Claude and André Rouillé, eds. "The Fabricated Image." *A History of Photography, Social and Cultural Perspectives*, trans. by Janet Lloyd. Cambridge: Cambridge University Press, 1987: 221; 224–5.

Ratcliff, Carter. "Tableau Photography: From Mayall to Rodan; Its Roots and Its Reason." *Picture*, issue 18, September 1981: 4–47.

Town, Elke. *Subjects & Subject Matter*. London, ON: London Regional Art Gallery, 1985.

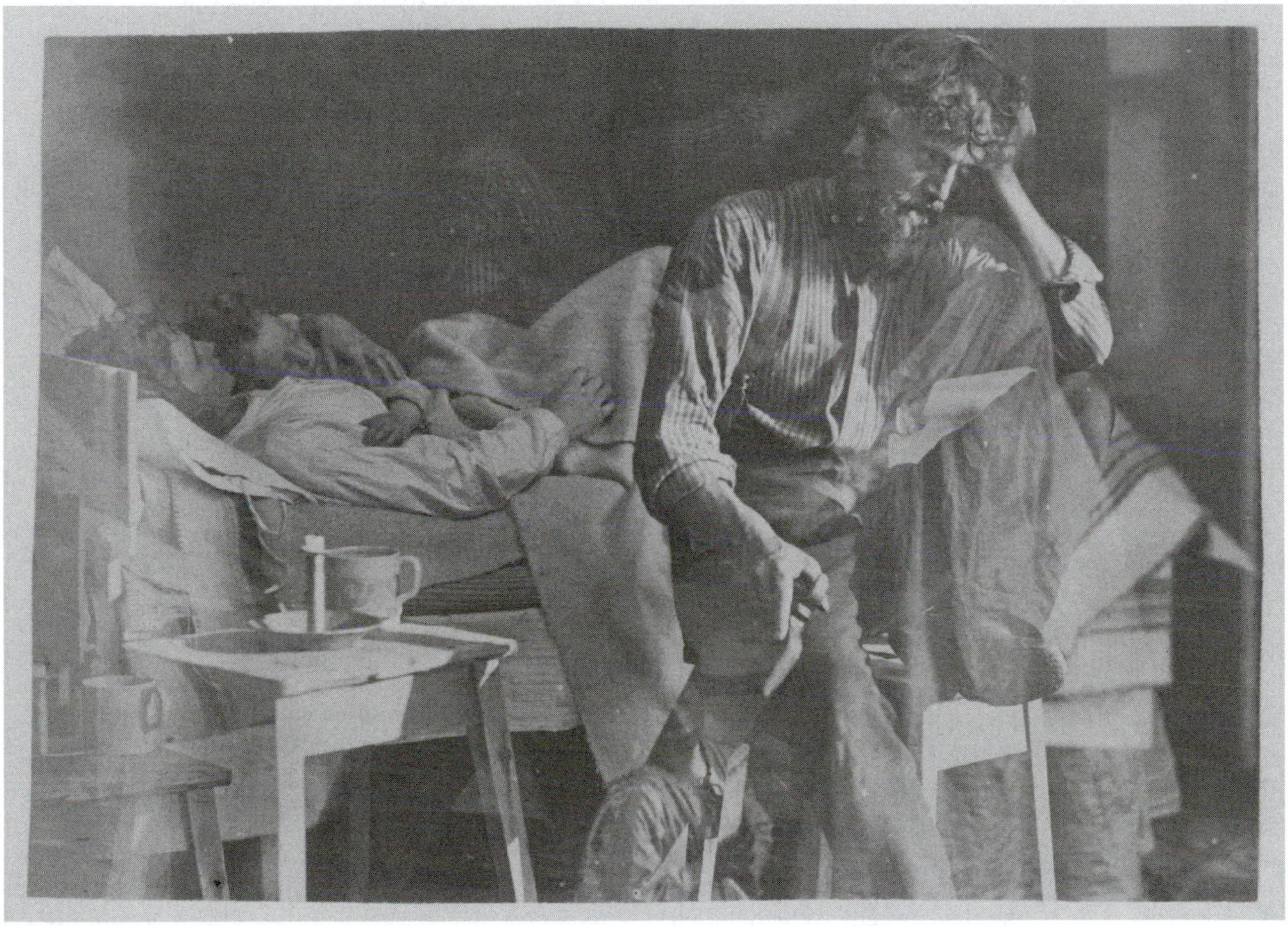

Oscar Rejlander, Hard Times, ca. 1860, albumen print, Museum Purchase, ex-collection A. E. Marshall.
[*Photograph courtesy of George Eastman House*]

CONTACT PRINTING

A contact print is a print made from positioning a negative in direct emulsion-to-emulsion contact with the photographic paper rather than projecting the negative via an enlarger. This process creates a print that is the same size as the negative. While this might seem, at first, only applicable to being used with large- and some medium-format negatives, there are ways to get an enlarged film negative even from 35-mm or smaller negatives. Both film and paper negatives (thus called even though a positive print can be used to make contact prints) can be used to create contact prints. Contact prints can go through many generations, with each iteration being manipulated or modified between prints.

Contact prints can be made with or without a specific "printing frame" easel. Printing frames are used to hold the negatives firmly against the photographic paper. They are built so that the top side is clear (either plastic or glass), and the base side is opaque. One can accomplish the same result by simply placing the unprocessed photographic paper on the base of the easel and then pressing the negative to it with a heavy piece of smooth glass. In either case, the negative-and-paper stack is then exposed to white light to make the print. One should make sure that the white light is uniformly distributed over the entirety of the photographic paper to ensure consistency in exposure across the whole sheet.

Just like other darkroom uses of unprocessed photographic paper, the paper needs to be handled carefully to avoid fogging or otherwise prematurely exposing it to light. When using black and white paper, a red or orange photographic safelight can be utilized to allow the photographer to see and move around in the darkroom while setting up a contact print. While admittedly limited, the sight allowed by the use of a safelight can help a photographer ensure that his negative-and-unprocessed-paper sandwich is set up neatly. Lowering the top piece of glass must be done carefully so as to avoid disrupting the arrangement of negative and paper.

When making contact prints, one can utilize test strips, which are small strips of photographic paper exposed for different lengths of time in easily-remembered intervals, processed, and examined in order to determine the best exposure time for the print. In order to make a test strip, the negative is positioned on top of a small strip of unprocessed photographic paper. Shielding most of the strip with something opaque (often, a piece of heavy cardboard or opaque plastic), the unprotected small portion of one end of the strip is exposed to light for a short amount of time (say, two or three seconds). The process is then methodically repeated by moving the opaque shield along the length of the strip as it is exposed in consistent increments of time. The test strip is then developed for approximately the same amount of time judged necessary to develop the final print. At the end of the developing process and after it has been "fixed," the test strip can be examined under white light to see which exposure time is most desirable to produce the final print. Test-strips are invaluable for allowing the photographer to make an educated guess as to what the correct exposure time for the overall print might be both in making contact prints and in creating enlarged prints as well.

Common Uses for Contact Printing

Most photographers first become acquainted with contact printing when making a contact (or "proof") sheet of film negatives in order to have a better notion of what the images look like in order to choose which ones to print. This is accomplished by cutting the roll of exposed negatives into manageable lengths (photographic suppliers offer a variety of negative-holding sheets or sleeves, which often require the negatives to be cut into strips of between three and seven frames for insertion) and then placing these negatives together directly atop a piece of photographic paper. If contact printing is regularly used to make proof sheets, after one establishes the best position and exposure time, this same position and time can often be used for subsequent sheets without the need to make test strips each time, especially if the negatives are consistent.

Proof sheets offer a number of advantages. They are especially helpful in cataloging images. Since the film negatives are laid emulsion-side down onto the unprocessed photographic paper, the information that identifies frame number and film type come out right-side up on the print, which aids in their usefulness as categorizing tools. As well they allow the photographer to use a loupe or magnifying glass to examine the images for focus, composition, and contrast. Proof sheets can also function as a medium for note-taking by photographers, who often mark on the sheets to designate negatives chosen for enlargement or indicate cropping.

Contact printing for final photographic prints is most often practiced with large format negatives, usually 8 × 10 inch or larger. The resulting prints are extremely detailed and maintain a much higher degree of faithfulness to the negative than enlarged-negative prints do. Also, since the negatives are not being enlarged at all, the prints do not show any of the graininess that can result from over-enlarging a small negative. Many associated with the f/64 group in the 1920s and 1930s, including Ansel Adams and Edward Weston, used contact printing to create their photographs; in the late twentieth-century, Sally Mann and Emmet Gowin are among many using the technique. Smaller view camera formats, including 5 × 7 inch and 4 × 5 inch, are also occasionally contact printed to create the final work. And while contact-printing 35-mm negatives might seem foolish or gimmicky, the amount of detail available in even such a small print is remarkable.

Contact printing can also be done with paper negatives—which are often, actually, positive prints. This method of achieving the final presentation image is common with pinhole photography. Just as with film negatives, the paper negative is pressed emulsion-to-emulsion with the unprocessed photographic paper, and the resulting sandwich is exposed to white light. Sometimes, the paper negative is dampened before being pressed to the unprocessed photographic paper. Doing so and then squeegeeing it against the unprocessed paper helps ensure good contact across the whole area of the print. When the negative and the unprocessed paper are not in good contact, areas of blurry soft-focus and loss of detail will occur.

When a contact print is made from a paper negative, each successive generation of the film-negative print will show degradation, much like successive generations of photocopies. This can be used to the photographer's advantage, as it can be interesting to experiment with the loss of detail and areas of soft focus that can occur with contact printing with paper negatives. Also, the first generation of paper-negative contact prints is most often negative prints, since they are usually made from a paper positive. If a positive print is desired, another contact print would need to be made to turn the image positive again.

Contact printing with paper negatives can also be a way to manipulate photographs without permanently altering the negative itself. One could make a positive print (with either an enlarged or a contact-printed negative) and then draw, paint, scratch, or otherwise manipulate the print. If this paper is then used to make a contact print, those manipulations will transfer to the new print, which may itself then be manipulated and used to create another contact print. It is interesting to see the differences in opacity of pigments. Often, what appears to be a similar shade of black as the black parts of a black-and-white image will, when contact printed, turn out to be much more opaque than the rest of the black area, resulting in a very noticeable white border or outline on the new print.

Limitations of Contact Printing

Contact printing has a number of limitations. A significant drawback is that, since the negative is in direct contact with the unprocessed photographic paper, the photographer is very limited in his ability to selectively expose areas of the print through such darkroom techniques as dodging and burning-in. It is possible to work in a limited way with dodging and burning tools, but their usefulness is reduced by the fact that the negative and positive are in direct contact with one another. Dodging and burning are especially difficult when using paper negatives to make contact prints. Given that most photographic paper is too thick to see through from the back, it is very hard to dodge or burn a specific area of an image except through trial and error. Paper-negative contact prints are also unaffected by colored filters intended to increase or decrease contrast in black and white photography.

Another drawback with paper-negative contact printing is that some photographic papers come printed with the logo of the manufacturer across the back of the paper. This logo, like the image on the front of the paper, will transfer to the non-processed photographic paper once the sandwich is exposed to white light, and will appear on the final print if used as a paper negative.

A third limitation is that photographers making contact prints cannot easily crop the image because the entire negative is pressed onto the unprocessed photographic paper. It is possible to construct some sort of mask to block out areas of the image deemed unnecessary to the final print, but it is much more difficult to crop with contact printing than it is with regular projected/enlarged negative printing.

Contact Printing and Alternative Processes

Contact-printing techniques are used in some alternative-processing photographic techniques, such as gum bichromate printing. In gum bichromate printing, a sheet of otherwise non-photographic paper (or other surface, such as cloth) is coated with a photo-sensitive emulsion of gum arabic and ammonium or potassium bichromate and then exposed to the sun (or other source of white light). Since no type of projector is used, gum bichromate prints are made as contact prints with negatives the same size as the desired final prints.

If one does not have access to a large-format camera, but would still like to use large negatives for contact printing (especially for use in alternative processes like gum bichromate printing), a small- or medium-format negative can be enlarged onto sheet film (such as Ortho or Kodalith films), which is them processed in regular (though often much more-diluted) paper developer and chemistry. After processing, the film's emulsion is, like regular black and white negatives, black and clear. Rather than the unexposed areas remaining white, as they do on black and white photographic paper, the unexposed areas on Ortho film rinse to clear in the developer. Since the first-generation Ortho film print is usually a positive print (since it is achieved by enlarging a negative), a photographer who is interested in ultimately having a positive end-product contact print will first need to make a contact print with Ortho-on-Ortho to achieve a large-size negative. This large sheet film, which can be gotten fairly reasonably-priced in sizes up to 20″ × 24″, is an affordable halfway-point for photographers interested in working with contact prints with film negatives, but who do not have access to a large-format camera.

A photographer can use contact-printing techniques to make prints from things other than negatives or photographic positives; he can, for instance, contact-print anything that is fairly translucent, such as other papers or vellums. Opaque black (or other dark-colored) ink on those surfaces will appear white on the contact print.

JENNY ALLRED REDMANN

See also: **Burning-In; Darkroom; Dodging; Manipulation; Safelight**

Further Reading

International Center of Photography Encyclopedia of Photography. New York: Crown Publishers, Inc., 1984.

CONTRAST

If it were not for contrast, our visual world would be blank. It is the difference between the color and shade of two things that allows us to separate one from the other. One can regard this as positive versus negative space, changes in tone, or extent of color separation, and the appearance of simple texture. In photography this works out to offer three opportunities to address contrast. The first is that of subject brightness and the degree of change of this brightness across the area being photographed. The second opportunity comes with the negative. Negative contrast can be controlled by changes in exposure and development as well as other more specialized techniques like masking, chemical reducing, or chemical intensification. Print contrast and the techniques of printing give the third opportunity to influence contrast. This is a complex field and a specialty unto itself. Here one deals with the entire array of darkroom techniques that vary from choice of paper, paper grade, color filtration, light filtration, and a host of specialized "salvage" procedures.

When one views a picture, painting, drawing, sculpture, or whatever the eye is initially drawn to the area of sharpest contrast. Some might say to the brightest area, but there may not be a bright area only an area of relatively sharp contrast. After seeing this, then one moves the eyes about and views the remainder of the subject. It is paramount that the photographer not be drawn to the sharpest contrast in the subject to the exclusion of the background and the other details in the periphery of the photograph. It is often these aspects, which determine the range of contrasts throughout the image, that are essential to consider when exposing the film. The range of contrasts helps determine shape, location, and texture of the various things in the field of the photograph, and is as important in color photography as it is in black and white.

The negative contrast is influenced by the range of tones in the subject being photographed as well as the development of the film. Altering developers and altering the development time are both straightforward methods of changing negative contrast. The speed of the film, that is its sensitivity to light, and its brand also influence both contrast and sharpness of image. Some films produce more grain in the image than others, and the presence of this grain may reduce both sharpness and apparent contrast. The various densities throughout the negative determine the overall contrast of the negative. These can be seen and estimated by eye or they can be measured using a transmission densitometer. The negative is the opposite of the print (the positive), so the lightest area of the negative produces the darkest area of the print. The darkest area of the negative is the most exposed and thusly produces the brightest highlight area in the print. A low contrast negative will have a short or small density range between the highlights and the shadows. It will typically have a sort of flat look and print gray appearing highlights and shadows unless special attention is given in printing. A negative with a large or long density range will conversely print with dark shadows and very light highlights producing a "high-key" image. If the average density range negative is printed, it will appear with bright, detail-containing highlights, and dark shadows without either appearing in extremes. Unless one is doing research, really enjoys testing film and chemistry, or is working in alternative processes using a densitometer is rarely necessary. Most photographers deal with these issues visually and intuitively.

Photographic print paper contains in the emulsion the elements that determine its contrast. Photo paper may be obtained both in fixed grades of contrast or as variable-contrast paper, variable-contrast papers being more widely available in the late twentieth century than are fixed grade papers. Variable contrast papers depend upon the use of filters or variations in the mixture of colored light being beamed through the negative to expose the print. The filters are typically numbered in a fashion as to approximate the various paper grades. Each photographer must work out the nature of their system, as all of the factors that determine the final output are variables. The enlarger light source, the type or brand of printing paper, the particular set of filters, and the chemical developing process all affect the final print contrast.

The changing of filters or the color of transmitted light is the way in which print contrast is adjusted. There are parts of the paper's emulsion that are sensitive to green light and others that are sensitive to blue light. By changing the amount of blue in the light with filters or by adjusting the light source, silver particles attached to these various dyes are variably activated and different contrasts print during development.

The presence or absence of contrast is what gives a photograph its character and its ability to interest or move the viewer. Highlights without any contrast are just stark whites, often simply the color of the printing paper. As small areas of contrast appear, they impart detail into the highlights and this sense of texture or something being there is, more often than not, desirable. As more color or tone appears, the mid-tones appear and various shapes can be seen. These shapes or objects are defined by the contrast between them and surrounding items. The shadows are the dark areas. The print areas without any contrast are maximum black. The darkest shadows are those that are just discernible from total or maximum black. It is the beginning of contrast that creates this separation and as contrast increases, detail appears in the shadows. As with starting with the highlights, one moves toward the mid-tones so that from darkest gray to more medium gray, shadows appear, again imparting detail, shape, and content to the photographic image.

Finding a style is just that. Deciding what contrast a photograph should contain depends upon the tastes of the photographer, the purpose for which the photo will be used, and the methods employed to produce the photo. Currently there is a huge transition to electronic or digital photography, which allows for contrast adjustment, hue and saturation changes, and brightness or darkness to be infinitely altered by computer. This should be seen as a new and powerful tool, just as the advent of variable contrast paper must have seemed to those darkroom technicians limited to one grade of paper.

Regardless of the techniques employed to create and adjust the contrast and tonality of the print, awareness of contrast and how it affects the viewer is essential. Whether in color printing, black and white printing, alternative process printing, or in digital printing the attractiveness and beauty of the final product will rest on contrast and how it is employed.

LAMBERT MCLAURIN

See also: **Darkroom; Digital Photography; Emulsion; Film; Film: High-Contrast; Filters**

JOHN COPLANS

American

After a long and influential career as a writer, curator, and founding editor of *Artforum* and *dialogue* art magazines, John Coplans turned to the medium of photography in the early 1980s to create a series of stark, nude self-portraits. He continued to photograph himself in the decades following his sixtieth birthday. His photographic work has become an integral part of contemporary discourse on the subject of the human body in art, culture, and society.

Born on a visit to London by his South African parents in 1920, Coplans was schooled in Cape Town and Johannesburg. He dropped out of high school and made his way to England, where at the age of 18 he volunteered for military service, becoming a pilot in 1939 at the outbreak of World War II. After suffering a head injury, he volunteered for ground duty in 1940 and was stationed in Africa and later Burma and India. His military career continued with three years in Ethiopia and leading African troops as an infantry captain. Coplans lived and fought alongside the African soldiers, learning to speak Swahili and acclimating to the customs and traditions of their culture. Later in his life, he would cite these experiences as contributing to his attaining what he described as a sublime understanding of humanity. But when the war ended, he was a young man of 26 who found that his eight years spent in the military had robbed him of his youth and any trace of a formal education.

Coplans turned to artistic endeavors in postwar London and took up painting. After seeing an exhibition of contemporary American painting at the Tate Gallery in 1956, he came to the conclusion that artistic innovation in Europe had stalled. Coplans relocated to the United States in 1960, moving first to New York and then to San Francisco. In America, he would embark on a multifaceted career as a painter, museum director, art critic, and writer.

While living in San Francisco, Coplans painted, exhibited, and taught, but critical neglect of the West Coast art scene led him in 1962 to co-found *Artforum* magazine, which was to become in the 1970s the premier contemporary art journal. Eventually, he abandoned his career as a painter, and moved to Southern California accepting an appointment as the Director of the art gallery at the University of California, Irvine in 1965 and later Senior Curator of the Pasadena Art Museum in 1967. He was an integral part of the group around the now-legendary Ferus Gallery that introduced the emerging group of Los Angeles-based artists including Ed Ruscha. He also taught at the California College of Arts and Crafts and the Chouinard Art Institute, and he wrote for numerous art journals. In his role as a curator, he organized the first museum exhibitions of work by Roy Lichtenstein, Richard Serra, Judy Chicago, and Andy Warhol. His book on this latter figure is a classic of contemporary art scholarship. He also published monographs on contemporary artists, including Ellsworth Kelly, Donald Judd, and Roy Lichtenstein.

In 1971, Coplans took up the mantle of Editor-in Chief at the magazine he'd founded, *Artforum*, which had relocated to New York City. Working at the publication during what might be termed its Postminimalist phase, he published seminal essays by critics and scholars including Rosalind Krauss, Max Kozloff, and Annette Michelson. Dismissal from the magazine in 1976 led Coplans to a position in the Midwest as director of the Akron Art Institute, Ohio, an appointment he held from 1977 to 1979. While he mounted a variety of exhibitions featuring the work of major contemporary artists, in an attempt to appeal to the region's working class audience, Coplans exhibited forms not thought of at that time as suitable material for exhibition in art museums, including Amish quilts and antique jukeboxes.

As he had done in California, Coplans saw the need to establish a forum for artists, curators, and art critics in the Midwest to discuss and promote their work and exhibitions, particularly the work of regional artists. He founded the Midwest arts magazine, *Dialogue*, with the help of artist Don Harvey, who was gallery director at the University of Akron. Coplans asked museums, arts centers, and universities with galleries to publish essays and reviews of their exhibitions in *dialogue*. The publication gave curators an opportunity to write about regional artists who were not covered by major east- and west-coast publications.

Coplans' interest in photography expanded in the 1970s. Earlier in his career, he had rediscovered the work of nineteenth-century landscape photographer Carleton Watkins, becoming an avid collector and promoter of his work. Coplans' continuing interest in photography led him to organize several exhibitions in addition to teaching himself about the technical aspects of the medium with some assistance from his friend Lee Friedlander. He organized the first American exhibitions of John Heartfield's photomontages and of sculptor Constantin Brancusi's photographs, and organized a retrospective of Weegee's photography for the International Center of Photography, New York in 1978. Coplans jettisoned his writing and curatorial career to exclusively pursue the art of photography. His last critical essay about the work of Philip Guston was published in 1980.

By the early 1980s, Coplans had turned to the subject for which he is best known: his own body. With the help of an assistant, Coplans creates compositions featuring large-scale, close-in shots—of his hands, fingers, and feet, back, and so on (but never his head)—that set such formal properties as line, surface, texture, and shape front and center. These qualities can be seen in an early work entitled *Self-Portrait (Feet, Frontal)*, 1984, from his first group of photographs published under the title *A Body of Work* in 1987. Coplans would further explore the formal qualities of the human figure, and he often revealed the body's abstract qualities as well as the sheer mass and weight of the figure as seen in *Self-Portrait (Torso Front)*, both from 1984.

Coplans, however, transcends the mere formal investigation of the human form in his photographs. He presents his body as a subject that is timeless, simultaneously subverting the Western art tradition of the nude as the embodiment of beauty and youth. Coplans' *Self-Portrait (Frieze No. 4, Three Panels)*, 1994, includes nine separate photographs that present an overview of his body from shoulder to knee, in three different angles, right side, back side, left side. Coplans presents his own physical topography in an attempt to reveal humankind in its most primal sense. He noted:

> I got the idea that my body was everybody's body. Like my genes were the genes of the whole human race, shared with them.... My photographs became raceless and timeless and about the whole of human beings. It's not (just) about the exterior. It's also about the genetic past of mankind and what we share together.

The images also pose critical questions about social reactions to age, and Coplans commented:

> The principal thing is the question of how our culture views age: that old is ugly. Just think of Rodin, how he dealt with people of all ages. I have the feeling that I'm alive, I have a body...I can make it extremely interesting. That keeps me alive and vital. It's a kind of process of energizing myself by my belief that the classical tradition of art that we've inherited from the Greeks is a load of bullshit.

After a career as a writer, curator, and editor, Coplans, in later life, evolved into photography and focused on the commonality of the human form, shared by all. By greatly enlarging only one portion of the human body surface in his photographs, he emphasized the similarities shared by everyone, rather than their distinctions (such as the face). Coplans developed this technique to de-emphasize youth, (in particular) beauty, race, and the prevailing idea of perfection by never photographing the entire body. In his pictures, Coplans expressed his beliefs that a detailed picture of himself was really a picture of every human, all joined together by shared genetics, with age not a significant factor.

Nancy Barr

See also: **Heartfield, John; Krauss, Rosalind; Nude Photography; Weegee**

Biography

Born London, England, 24 June 1920; raised in South Africa with frequent trips to England. Served in the British Armed Forces, 1938–46. Moved to San Francisco, California, 1960. Co-founder *Artforum* magazine, 1962. Appointed Director of the art gallery at the University of California, Irvine, 1965, and Senior Curator of the Pasadena Art Museum, 1967. Moved to New York City and became Editor-in Chief of *Artforum* 1971. Recepient of the Frank Jewitt Mather award of the College Art Association, 1974. Moved to Akron, Ohio, after accepting position as Director of the Akron Art Museum, and founded the Midwest arts magazine *Dialogue*, 1978. Recipient of three National Endowment for the Arts fellowships, 1975, 1980, 1992. Awarded two John Simon Guggenheim Memorial fellowships 1969, 1985. Recipient of Officier de l'Ordre des Arts et des Lettres, 2001. Died in August 2003.

Individual Exhibitions

1981 *John Coplans: Recent Portraits*; Art Institute of Chicago; Chicago, Illinois

1982 *John Coplans: Recent Photographs*; New Gallery of Contemporary Art; Cleveland, Ohio

1984 *John Coplans: Photographs*; Emily H. Davis Gallery, The University of Akron; Akron, Ohio

1985 Clarence Kennedy Gallery; Cambridge, Massachusetts

John Coplans: Photographs, 1980–85; The Fine Arts Gallery, University of California; Irvine, California

John Coplans: Photographer; Madison Art Center; Madison, Wisconsin

1986 *John Coplans: Photographies*; Musée du Nouveau Monde; La Rochelle, France

1988 *A Body of Work: Photographs by John Coplans*; San Francisco Museum of Modern Art; San Francisco, California (traveled to Museum of Modern Art, New York, New York; University of Missouri Art Gallery, Kansas City, Missouri; Art Institute of Chicago; Chicago, Illinois [1989])

A Body of Work: Photographs by John Coplans; Sala de Exposiciones de la Fundacion "la Caixa,"; Barcelona, Spain

John Coplans: Autoportraits; Centre de Kerpape, Ploemeur, Rencontres Photographiques en Bretagne; Bretagne, France

1989 *John Coplans: Mains*; Salon d'Angle de la Régionale des Affaires Culturelles; Nantes, France (traveled to Abbaye de Bouchemaine, Angers, France; Centre d'Art Passages, Troyes, France)

John Coplans: Autoportrait, 1984–89; Musée de la Vielle Charité'; Marseille, France

1990 *Self-Portraits*: Frankfurter Kunstverein; Frankfurt, Germany

John Coplans: Self-Portraits, Hand and Foot; Museum Boymans-van Beuningen; Rotterdam, The Netherlands

1991 *John Coplans: Self Portraits*; Matrix Gallery, Wadsworth Atheneum; Hartford, Connecticut

John Coplans; Joseloff Gallery, University of Hartford; Hartford, Connecticut

1992 *John Coplans: A Retrospective*; Gulbenkian Foundation; Lisbon, Portugal

1994 *Self-Portraits*; Musée National d'Art Moderne, Centre Georges Pompidou; Paris, France

1998 *John Coplans: Retrospective*; P.S.1 Contemporary Art Center; Long Island City, New York

1998 Paco das Artes; Sao Paulo, Brazil

1999 National Galleries; Edinburgh, Scotland

Group Exhibitions

1982 *Counterparts: Form and Emotion in Photography*; The Metropolitan Museum of Art; New York, New York

Lichtbildnisse: Das Portrat in der Fotografie; Rheinischen Landesmuseum; Bonn, Germany

1983 *Whitney Biennial Exhibition*; Whitney Museum of American Art; New York, New York

1984 *Face to Face: Recent Portrait Photography*; Institute of Contemporary Art; Philadelphia, Pennsylvania

1985 *Self-Portrait: The Photographer's Persona 1840–1985*; Museum of Modern Art; New York, New York

Nude, Naked, Stripped; Hayden Gallery, List Visual Arts Center, Massachusetts Institute of Technology; Cambridge, Massachusetts

1986 *Staging the Self*; National Portrait Gallery; London, England (traveled to Plymouth Arts Center, Plymouth, England (1987); John Hansard Gallery, Southampton, England (1987); Ikon Gallery, Birmingham, England (1987)).

1987 *The Other Man: Representations of Masculinity*; New Museum of Contemporary Art; New York, New York

The Body Politic: Representations of Sexuality; Photographers' Gallery, London, England (traveled to Impressions Gallery, York, England; Triangle Media Center, Birmingham, England)

1988 *First Person Singular: Self Portrait Photography, 1840–1987*; The High Museum of Art at Georgia-Pacific Center; Atlanta, Georgia

Le Corps Figuré II; Fondation Nationale de la Photographie; Lyon, France

The Second Israeli Photography Biennale, 1988; Mishkan Le Omanut Museum of Art; Ein Harod, Israel

1989 *The Photography of Invention: American Pictures of the 1980s*; National Museum of American Art; Washington, D.C. and traveling

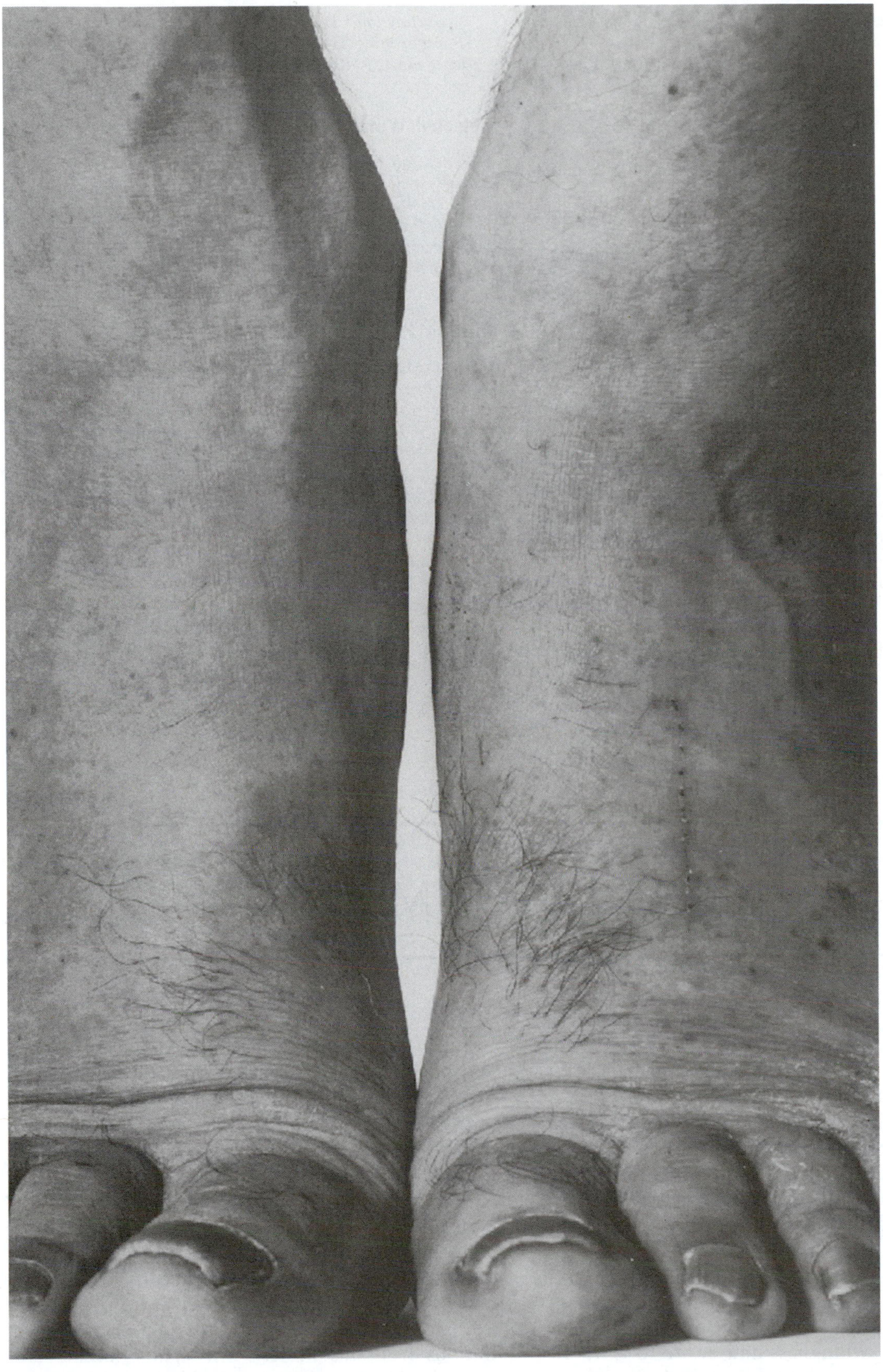

John Coplans, Self Portrait: Feet Frontal, 1984.
[*Tate Gallery, London/Art Resource, New York*]

Prospect Photographie; Frankfurter Kunstverien; Frankfurt, Germany

1990 *The Indomitable Spirit*; International Center of Photography; New York, New York

Body Language: The Figure of Art in Our Time; Rose Art Museum, Brandeis University; Waltham, Massachusetts

1991 *Whitney Biennial Exhibition*; The Whitney Museum of American Art; New York, New York

John Coplans/Chrystele Lerisse; Cardinaux; Chatellerault, France

The Physical Self; Museum Boymans-van-Beuningen; Rotterdam, The Netherlands

1992 *Persona*; Museum of Photographic Arts; San Diego, California

De la curiosité: Petite Anatomie d'un regard; Dazibao, Centre de Photographies Actuelles; Montreal, Canada

Le Portrait dans l'art contemporain, 1945–1992; Musée d'Art Moderne et d'Art Contemporain; Nice, France

Medaljens Bakside: Pirouettes; Lillehammer Art Museum; Lillehamer, Norway

1995 *Rites of Passage*; Tate Gallery; London, England

1996 *Prospect 96: Photography in Contemporary Art*; Schirn Kunsthalle Frankfurt and the Frankfurter Kunstverein; Frankfurt, Germany

Une Aventure Contemporaine, la Photographie (1955–1995); La Maison Européenne de la Photographie; Paris, France

Gender—Beyond Memory; Tokyo Metropolitan Museum of Photography; Tokyo, Japan

2000 *Missing Link - Menschen-Bilder in der Fotografie*; Kunstmuseum; Bern, Germany

Surface and Depth: Trends in Contemporary Portrait Photography; Hood Museum of Art, Dartmouth College; Dartmouth, New Hampshire

Selected Works

Self-Portrait (Feet, Frontal), 1984
Self-Portrait (Torso Front), 1984
Foot, Dark Sole, 1989
Self Portrait Upside Down #1, 1992
Self-Portrait (Frieze No. 4, Three Panels), 1994
Self-Portrait: Hand, Palm, 1999

Further Reading

Chevrier, Jean-François and Jorge Molder. *John Coplans: A Retrospective*. Lisbon: Gulbenkian Foundation, 1992.

Coplans, John, *A Body*. New York: Powerhouse Books, 2002.

———. *A Body of Work*. New York: Printed Matter, 1987.

———. *Hand*. New York: Galerie Lelong, 1988.

———. *Foot*. New York: Galerie Lelong, 1989.

———. *John Coplans: A Self Portrait 1984–99*. Edinburg, Scotland: National Gallery of Modern Art, Dean Gallery, 1999.

Coplans, John, and Jean-François Chevrier. *A Self-Portrait: John Coplans 1984–97*. Long Island City, New York: P.S.1 Contemporary Art Center; D.A.P./Distributed Art Publishers, 1997.

Coplans, John, and Melinda Wortz. *John Coplans: Photographs, 1980–1985*. Irvine, California: Fine Arts Gallery, University of California, Irvine, 1985.

Morgan, Stuart. *Provocations: Writings by John Coplans*. New York: Powerhouse Books, 2001.

CORBIS/BETTMANN

Otto Ludwig Bettmann was born on October 15, 1903 in Leipzig, Germany to Hans and Charlotte Bettmann. His father was an orthopedic surgeon in Leipzig with his own clinic and his mother was from a prominent and well-to-do Jewish family. As members of the educated upper class, both parents were part of the intelligentsia of Leipzig. Raised in a heady atmosphere of science, music, and the arts, Otto and his older brother Ernst were surrounded by affluence and a dedication to learning in which they thrived.

Early on, Otto Bettmann showed a keen interest in academics and a willingness and desire to learn. A somewhat precocious child, he studied piano with Fraulein Schutze, a well-respected music teacher, and sang in the St. Thomas's Boys Choir, focusing on the intricate and precise works of J. S. Bach, an interest that persisted throughout his lifetime.

With Leipzig at the center of the European book trade, Otto's father began collecting rare books, eventually amassing a wide-ranging collection of books, manuscripts, and ephemera. Exposed at a young age to the illustrations found in the pages of his father's books, Otto showed an early proclivity in understanding the illustration as narrative. At the age of thirteen he salvaged discarded medical illustrations from his father's wastepaper basket and created a hand-made, one-of-a-kind 'art book' that he presented to his father on his birthday. This tendency developed into a visual acuity organized with Bachian precision that later served as the basis for Bettmann's career as the well-tempered conductor of a repository of imagery.

At the age of 20 Bettmann enrolled in Leipzig University and majored in cultural history and art. In Germany at that time it was accepted practice to travel from university to university to study under important professors. With this intent, Bettmann travelled to Freiberg where he studied palaeontology, history and philosophy under Edmund Husserl, the famous theorist and proponent of phenomenology; the study of the psychic awareness that accompanies experience and that is the source of all meaning for the individual. Bettmann would admit to never understanding Husserl's teachings then or later.

Bettmann received his Ph.D. in 1927 at the age of 24 from the University of Leipzig for his dissertation *The Development of Professional Ideals in the Book Trade of the Eighteenth Century* (1927). After travelling to England, France, and Italy to pursue his post-doctoral work, he was offered employment with the music publisher C.F. Peters, still in business today. At C.F. Peters he was in charge of maintaining the music archive that, to Bettmann's delight, held many original scores and manuscripts by some of Europe's greatest composers.

He traveled to Berlin, which was then at the height of the modernist movement. Enthralled with the city and its flourishing cultural life, Bettmann was determined to return there to live. In 1932 after receiving a diploma in Library Sciences from the University of Leipzig, he was offered and accepted the post of Rare-Book Librarian at the Prussian State Art Library in Berlin. Once there, he mounted a popular exhibit entitled *The Book in Art* (1933). Organizing and mounting the exhibition gave him the idea of a picture archive organized by subject. He soon began taking 35 mm photographs of the paintings, prints, and illustrations from the rare books that were part of the Library's extensive collection.

In 1934, with Hitler's rise to power, all Jews that held state jobs were relieved of their posts. At the instigation of relatives in Cincinnati who offered to sponsor him, Bettmann decided to immigrate to America. He left Germany with two steamer trunks of the images he had been collecting and a vague idea of being able to do something with such a collection. On November 8, 1935 Bettmann, with his background in the arts and his Ph.D., was welcomed by the immigration authorities in New York City.

With $200.00 from his Ohio relatives, Bettmann rented a one-bedroom apartment and began seeking and acquiring more images. He was very impressed with the accessibility of the New York Public Library system and began searching through the various libraries' holdings throughout the city in search of more imagery. His arrival in the United States had coincided with the rise of the picture magazines such as *Life* and *Look*. Although an academic by training, his enthusiasm for collecting images and disseminating them gave him the impetus to become an imagery entrepreneur. By literally 'pounding the pavement' with the images he had brought with him and collected since his arrival he began peddling his wares door-to-door. He soon received his first commission to supply 300 photographs for a book titled *The History of the World in Pictures* (circa 1937). Bettmann continued to add images to his archive by photographing old copies of *Harper's* and other magazines and by salvaging images from street vendors, flea markets, and used booksellers.

Bettmann had a 'grand plan' that gave shape to the archive as it was growing. He needed, above all, to develop a retrieval system for the images that he had, and to be able to edit pictures before he collected them, rather than after. His discerning eye, his acquaintance with the past, his awareness of the present, his thoughts on the future, and his Bach-like sense of organization allowed him to analyze images and place them within a context that could be easily accessed. Bettmann gathered a myriad of images, and not only straight photographs, but photographs of graphics from printed sources. He developed a multiple cross-referencing system so that they could be quickly retrieved for different uses when the occasions arose. By being aware of the present and the developing fads of the future, Bettmann was able to anticipate what images would be called for and have them in the archive ready to be extrapolated. His aim was to provide needed imagery to his clients within 24 hours of their request and charged a sliding fee-scale. His business flourished because he filled a niche even as the niche was developing. Using his uncanny sense of what was needed in the commercial world of visuals, his archive developed the niche as much as the niche developed his archive.

In 1936 he met his soon-to-be wife Anne Gray, a widow with three children, who complemented his professorial aura with her all-American forthrightness and practicality. They remained happily married until her death, just short of their fiftieth wedding anniversary in 1988.

Once the archive was on its feet and Bettmann had staff that understood its complexities and could access it to its fullest potential, he was able to pursue in tandem his academic interests. He began to write more frequently and collaborate in publishing books. Because his mind was subject-oriented, he had always wanted to publish books that were subject-image oriented, and in the course of his lifetime he wrote, compiled, or contributed to 13 major publications.

Bettmann collected both singular images and entire archives. In 1967, Bettmann purchased the Gendreau Collection of Americana. In 1972 he bought the famous Underwood and Underwood Collection of negatives and prints from 1900 to World War II. By 1980 the Bettmann Archive housed over two million images for commercial and academic use.

Bettmann often purchased rare books just to photograph the contents. As he was not a rare book collector, he would then sell them on. In this capacity, he made the acquaintance of H.P. Krause, the famous rare-book dealer in New York who, in the late 1950s offered to buy Bettmann's entire archive. Bettmann at that time was not ready to sell, but he remembered the offer years later when he was considering retirement. Bettmann decided to accept the offer and in 1981 the Bettmann picture archive was acquired by the now Krause-Thompson Archive. By 1984 Krause-Thompson had also acquired the picture archives of the press agencies United Press International (UPI) and Reuters, bringing the number of collective images in the archive into the millions.

After the sale, Bettmann and his wife moved to Boca Raton, Florida, where Bettmann held an adjunct professorship at Florida Atlantic University for several years. At the age of 89 he became the rare-book librarian at FAU's newly constructed S.E. Wimberly Library. In 1992 he published his autobiography *Bettmann: the Picture Man* (1992), and in 1995 published his biography of Bach entitled *Johann Sebastian Bach, As His World knew Him* (1995).

Otto Bettmann died on May 3, 1998. The research files and manuscripts of his last years form the Bettmann Collection and are found in the Special Collections/Archives at the S.E. Wimberly Library at Florida Atlantic University and relate primarily to his tenure at FAU (1978–1996).

In the 1980s, with Microsoft Corporation consuming digitalized images for its software, Bill Gates founded Corbis, now an international picture agency with offices in New York, Los Angeles, Chicago, London, Paris, Düsseldorf, Vienna, Hong Kong, Kuala Lumpur, and Tokyo. The intent was to capture the globalization of advertising markets using digital imagery. Corbis wanted to provide an agency that offered creative professionals such as filmmakers, publishers, advertisers, and designers, easy access to a wealth of images.

Corbis has access to many outside picture sources and partners itself with individual photographers, image companies, museums, and archives. For film footage Corbis works with Paramount Pictures, Metro-Goldwyn-Mayer, Sharpshooters, CNN, ESPN, Hearst Entertainment, Northeast Historic Film, and Universal Newsreel in addition to several sports-media companies. For illustrations they are partnered with Images.com and QA digital; and for fine art, Alinari, Christie's, the Louis K. Meisel Gallery, Inc., Archivo Iconiografico, S.A., the Philadelphia Museum of Art, the National Gallery in London, the State Hermitage, Russia, and the Brett Weston Archive.

In the mid 1990s Corbis acquired the news agency archives of Sygma, Saba, the celebrity archive 'Outline,' and other smaller photo-journalist archives, stock-houses, and photo agencies. In 1995, Corbis acquired the Thomas/Krause Archive with its holdings from UPI, Reuters, and the famed Bettmann Archive, bringing the Corbis image bank to approximately 70 million. As well, Corbis has access through various agreements, to the Hulton-Deutsche Collection, Newsport, Condé Nast Archive, Brand X, and Image 100, the last two holding royalty-free imagery.

The acquisition of the historic Bettmann Archive brought with it, however, the problem of preservation, and in some cases, emergency preservation. Many of the 11 million physical objects housed in antiquated buildings with fluctuating temperatures, acid based filing materials, and water-damage were in danger of disappearing.

All photographic materials are organically based and biodegradable. At the turn of the twentieth century, gelatin, carrying light-sensitized silver, was used to produce individual glass plate negatives, which were the standard form of negative making. Gelatin is still the vehicle for the light-sensitive chemical used in both film and paper. George Eastman, in his entrepreneurial enthusiasm, wanted to simplify the picture making process for the amateur picture maker, and put a camera in everyone's hand by developing a flexible film. His success resulted in tremendous stores of photographs that accumulated in the twentieth century. However, the materials he used for the flexible film base were cellulose nitrate (first marketed in 1889 and very unstable) then cellulose diacetate, more stable than its predecessor but still biodegradable and most recently, a polyester base film. With the development of colour photography, the impermanence of the colour dyes became an additional issue.

Corbis contracted Henry Wilhelm, the world-renowned photographic conservation expert and the author of *The Permanence and Care of Color Photographs, Traditional and Digital Color Prints, Color Negatives, Slides and Motion Pictures* (1993). Wilhelm produced a 21-page rescue report that advised minus 4 degrees Fahrenheit storage in order to slow the deterioration and extend the life of the material an estimated 5,000 years.

Meanwhile, 65 miles north of Pittsburgh there was an underground storage facility located more than 200 feet below the surface of the earth. Iron Mountain had been a thousand-acre mine supplying limestone to the steel industry. In 1950 it was opened as a storage facility utilizing 30 acres of storage connected by more than twenty miles of passageways. At this writing it is the largest commercially owned underground storage facility in the world and the largest privately owned sub-zero vault.

In 2002, 18 refrigerated trucks were used to transport the entire Bettmann Archive to Iron Mountain to much furor and relief from the opposing camps. On one side were researchers who felt that they would no longer be able to easily access the physical objects or browse through the files. On the other side were conservationists and preservationists who were relieved that the treasure-trove, which spanned virtually the entire visual history of the twentieth century, would be saved for future generations. According to long-time employees at the Bettmann Archive, however, researchers never had had direct access to the files. Files were brought to them by experienced staff who knew where to find and correctly re-file them. This aspect has not changed, and people wishing to do physical picture research are welcome to submit their search requests before visiting the Corbis underground vaults where a staff person will deliver the originals.

The original intent of Bettmann was the commercial licensing of reproduction images for profit and this has not changed, it has only become larger in scope and digitized. Interestingly, the staff at the Bettmann Archive have researched the number of hits made at the archive and noted that of the 7.5 million images (plus 3.5 million duplicates) only 100,000 images had been pulled from the files to be looked at and only 75,000 had been licensed for use.

From 1997 until the move in 2002, the Corbis staff searched the archive for those images most in danger in order to scan and then vault them. In addition, of the negatives and photographs not in immediate danger, decisions were made about which images should be scanned for historical interest as well as which images might likely be selected in the relatively near future. These images include those that might become 'newsworthy,' such as those likely to die during the upcoming decade, or political figures likely be pushed into the news. With this in mind, 1.3 million images were slated to be digitized with, at the end of the century 225,000 already scanned, catalogued, and filed for instant retrieval.

The images are preserved through digital processes that lend the highest resolution and reproduction capabilities. Once the image or negative is scanned, the digital product is cleaned up, coded, catalogued, and electronically stored. As a library is only as good as its cataloguing system, a catalogue system had to be developed that had a sophisticated cross-referencing system, much like the one Bettmann himself had developed. This problem, however, was minor compared to the problem of "forward migration." As software becomes obsolete, the digital files must be translated into the next generation of software and to keep up with the development of hardware.

In addition to preserving images, Corbis is also attempting to identify the photographers, the subjects, and the events depicted. Corbis has a contact point on their website for people who may be able to identify themselves, the event, or the people in the photographs. Corbis will then add that information to the image.

Corbis has tried to achieve globally what Otto Bettmann achieved nationally—a source for images and the insight and foresight to know what images might be appropriate for which clients' needs. To access the Bettmann Archive or the image bank at Corbis, one need only log onto www.Corbis.com. If a professional has additional needs, Corbis also employs designers and consultants who are available 24 hours a day to assist clients in obtaining the right images and the rights to use those images.

Lorraine Anne Davis

See also: **Archives; Conservation; Digital Photography; Visual Anthropology**

Further Reading

Battiata, Mary. "Can the Photos of the 20th Century be Saved?" *The Washington Post Magazine*, May 18, 2003.

Bettmann, Otto L. *Bettmann the Picture Man*. Gainsville, Florida: University of Gainsville Press, 1992.

Bettmann, Otto L. *The Good Old Days–They Were Terrible*. New York: Random House, 1974.

Bettmann, Otto L. *The Bettmann Archive Picture History of the World: The Story of Western Civilization Retold in 4460 Pictures*. New York: Random House, 1978.

Corbis website: http://www.corbis.com (accessed May 6, 2005).

CORPORATE COLLECTIONS

The collecting of photographs began with the invention of the medium. In addition to individual collectors, museums and institutions soon added photographs to their collections and the first "corporate" collections were begun in France when the *Commission des Monuments historiques* formed the *Missions héliographique* in 1851 to photograph buildings and monuments. Baron James de Rothchild then commissioned photographs to be taken along the route of his new railway line between Paris and Boulogne in 1855.

With the constant formation of new companies, it follows that new art collections are forming in the corporate world. Corporations have been collecting art almost as long as there have been corporations, with a recent increase in collections that include photography. Most collections of the late decades of the twentieth century unlike collections of the past, made their acquisitions with the help of curators and art consultants rather than relying on the taste of the president or chief officer of the company. These collections, therefore, are more likely to reflect the ideas and image of the company, becoming an extension of and buttress to the corporation's identity. In the 1980s and 1990s especially, corporations became very savvy about art, with many companies investing in contemporary artists and new ideas to position themselves as forward-looking companies, to provide a stimulating work environment, and as an investment. Perhaps the best-known corporate collection is that of the Kodak company, which was established as the George Eastman House as a public museum now known as the International Museum of Photography and Film in Rochester, New York.

A comprehensive compilation of corporate collections around the world would be impossible; the following is a selection of the better known North American corporate collections. It should be noted, however, that there are many other corporations around the globe which have interesting collections that include photographs, many of which can be found in the *International Directory of Corporate Art Collections*. Other corporate collections include the archives of such publications as *The New York Times, Condé Nast* and *Time-Life*, among others.

The 7-Eleven Collection

The Southland Corporation in California acquired photographs beginning in the early 1980s in conjunction with other works on paper to furnish a new corporate headquarters. The collection eventually grew to over 2,500 prints by the time Southland was bought out by the 7-Eleven Corporation and the active collecting of art was no longer a primary focus. Most of the photographs were placed in storage and are occasionally loaned to museum exhibitions. A decision was made by the company to decrease its holdings by selling a selection of works at auction. One hundred twenty-six lots of photographs were offered at Sotheby's New York in April 2000, totaling $3.6 million with 90% finding buyers. Some of the artists included in the collection were Eugène Atget, Margaret Bourke-White, and André Kertész.

Gilman Paper Company Collection

In 1974 Howard Gilman of the Gilman Paper Company decided to collect and exhibit art in his new Manhattan office. He hired a former curator from the Museum of Modern Art, Pierre Apraxine, to bring his expertise to the collection. Although photography is the strongest part of the collection, the collection is not exclusively photography. Gilman and Apraxine began the collection with contemporary photographs including those of Robert Frank. The collection then began to work backwards, acquiring more historical works, such as those of Eugène Atget, and nineteenth-century figures Carleton Watkins and Henry Fox Talbot. The company's initial objective, "to make a small selection of photographs that would acknowledge photography's place among other art forms" (*Photographs from the Collection of the Gilman Paper Company*, p. 15) was soon eclipsed by a grander vision.

The collection currently holds over 5,000 images and photographic albums, many of them unique objects. In 1993 a major traveling exhibition, accompanied by a lavish book highlighting the collection, was held at the Metropolitan Museum of Art in New York. In 1997, the Howard Gilman Gallery of the Metropolitan Museum was opened and now holds annual exhibitions showcasing parts of the Gilman collection. The company is no longer actively collecting, but the collection is available for viewing by appointment.

Hallmark Photographic Collection

One of the first corporations to collect only photographs is the Hallmark greeting card company. The Hallmark Photographic Collection began in 1964 with the acquisition of 141 prints by Harry Callahan and currently includes more than 5,000 works by almost 900 artists. The Hallmark Collection is a span of American photography, with vintage works dating back to the late 1880s continuing to the present day. Although there is a focus on older processes, such as daguerreotypes, albumen prints, and salt prints, the many contemporary artists represented provide examples of more contemporary processes included as well. Some of the artists that are showcased in the collection are André Kertész, Dorothea Lange, Ralph Eugene Meatyard, and Todd Webb. The collection is still actively acquiring works.

The company has organized and financed many traveling exhibitions over the last 25 years, including the 1994 blockbuster, *An American Century of Photography: From Dry-Plate to Digital, The Hallmark Photographic Collection*, which originated at the Nelson-Atkins Museum of Art, Kansas City, and has printed numerous books and catalogues under the leadership of long-time curator Keith Davis. The collection is presently held at the Hallmark Headquarters building in Kansas City, Missouri. More information on the collection is available at their website: *www.hallmark.com.*

JP Morgan Chase Collection

David Rockefeller, president of the Chase Manhattan Bank, began collecting art in 1959. Corporate art collecting at the time was a relatively new concept. His idea was to adorn the Bank's headquarters with the work of contemporary artists. After over 40 years of collecting, as well as six corporate mergers, the company now has a broad international collection with over 20,000 works housed in over 350 locations. The collection consists of many different media with about 20% of the collection comprising photography. Contemporary artists include such well known names in photography as Cindy Sherman and Lorna Simpson. The collection has been shown in such institutions as the Milwaukee Art Museum, the Walker Art Center in Minneapolis and the Center for the Fine Arts in Miami. More information on the collection is available at their website: *www.jpmorganchase.com.*

LaSalle National Bank Collection

One of the first corporate collections to specialize in collecting photography was LaSalle National Bank, beginning in 1967. Its stated mission is to enrich the lives of those people who visit the bank as well as those who work there. The collection has tried to cover the history of the medium and consists of many important photographers from the early roots of photography, from Henry Fox Talbot to the present with photographers emerging in the 1980s and 1990s, such as Thomas Struth. Some of the important photographers in the collection include Alfred Stieglitz, Walker Evans, and Harry Callahan, among many others. In addition to many important historical photographers, the collection also supports photographers living and working in the Chicago area, including virtually all of the figures associated with the Institute of Design, as well as Dutch artists (due to the affiliation with a Dutch parent company, ABN AMRO). The collection was originally put together with the help of Beaumont and Nancy Newhall as well as the photographer and historian Joel Snyder. The collection has been published in books that highlight various strengths of the collection. More information on the collection is available at their website: *www.lasalle.com*.

Microsoft Collection

The computer giant Microsoft began collecting art in 1987, when the company only occupied six buildings in Redmond, Washington. Today the collection represents mostly contemporary artists in many different media. Microsoft began collecting art to put in their offices to represent the idea of a contemporary corporation, as well as to educate customers and employees. The collection currently holds over 4,000 works (not including the over 20 million photographic images purchased as part of the Bettmann Archives by Corbis) and is housed in more than 90 buildings throughout North America. As the company continues to grow, so does the collection. The collection currently holds over 750 photographs by more than 200 artists, approximately 20% of the entire collection.

The photographs in the collection are all twentieth-century and with an emphasis on post-war and contemporary photographers, and represent a broad range of photographic media, such as photomontages, digital prints, and photo transfers. Some of the artists represented include Cindy Sherman, Laura Larson, Eva Schlegel, and Louis Stettner. There are many American artists, as well as artists from around the world, including Mexico, China, Brazil, Cuba, and Japan. Works from the collection are often loaned to institutions, such as the Art Museum at the University of Washington, and the collection is shown in many traveling exhibitions. In addition to exhibitions, the company also hosts educational programs for the general public. More information on the collection is available at their website: *www.microsoft.com*.

The Polaroid Collection

Polaroid began hiring photographers to test their new instant films in the late 1940s, beginning with Ansel Adams. The company trusted that the opinions of artists would give a point of view from the field, rather than the lab. In the 1950s and 1960s, many more photographers were hired in addition to Adams, including Paul Caponigro, William Clift, John Benson, and Nick Dean. In the late 1960s, the company began acquiring the works that the photographers made during the field tests. Simultaneously, in Europe, the company was acquiring the works of David Bailey, Sarah Moon, Helmut Newton, and Josef Sudek, beginning the International Polaroid Collection.

The two separate collections were combined in 1990 and the complete collection now holds more than 23,000 images by over 1,000 different artists, and is the most diversified collection of original Polaroid instant images. The collection is housed in Waltham, Massachusetts, and many of the works have been added to the permanent archives of such museums as La Maison Européenne de la Photographie in Paris and Le Musée de l'Elysée in Lausanne, Switzerland.

The company continues to give grants to artists to test its films in exchange for providing images to the collection. Under the supervision of long-time curator Barbara Hitchcok, parts of the collection are frequently exhibited around the world, and the corporation produces books and catalogues on its collection and artists represented in the collection. More information on the collection is available at their website: *www.polaroid.com*.

Safeco Collection

Safeco, an insurance company, began collecting art for their Pacific Northwest offices in 1973. Their idea was to enrich the workplace while supporting local artists. The collection focuses on contemporary art with a strong local presence and holds over 2,600 works located in over 70 offices in Washington and across the United States. Within the collection is a significant holding of over 500 photographs by 100 artists. The photography collection is quite diverse, having works by many well known artists like Eliot Porter, Berenice Abbott, and Imogen Cunningham, and also including well-regarded Northwest regional artists such as Marsha Burns and Arthur Aubry. The collection also has several early works, including the work by Myra Albert Wiggens, which dates back to 1898. More information on the collection is available at their website: *www.safeco.com*.

Seagram Collection

The Seagram Company began collecting art in the late 1950s after their landmark building was erected on Park Avenue in Manhattan. Phyllis Lambert, daughter of Samuel Bronfman, the founder of the company, along with photographer Richard Pare, were the principal curators of the collection until the 1980s. In 1972, they began collecting photography. The collection as a whole was put together to adorn the building's executive offices, lounges, and the Four Seasons bar in its Grill Room. Ms. Lambert had the idea to collect pieces of artwork that the average person, not involved in the art world, could appreciate. The photography collection held works by over 130 artists, including Walker Evans, Garry Winogrand, Berenice Abbott, Weegee, and Robert Frank. The theme of American urban life was apparent in the collection. The complete collection had a total of 2,500 works, of which there were over 700 photographs. When the Seagram Company was acquired by the Vivendi Company in 2000, the entire collection went to auction in 2003, and 100% of the photographs were sold. The total sale price of the photography collection came to over $2.8 million.

PENELOPE DIXON

See also: **Archives; Polaroid Corporation**

Further Reading

Apraxine, Pierre. *Photographs from the Collection of the Gilman Paper Company*. New York: White Oaks Press, 1985.

Apraxine, Pierre. *The Waking Dream: Photography's First Century: Selections from the Gilman Paper Company Collection*. New York: Abrams, 1993.

Davis, Keith F. *An American Century of Photography: From Dry-Plate to Digital: The Hallmark Photographic Collection*. New York: Abrams, 1995.

Hitchcock, Barbara. *Emerging Bodies: Nudes from the Polaroid Collection*. Germany: Edition Stemmle, 2000.

Homans, Kathy. *Art at Work: Forty Years of the JP Morgan Chase Collection*. Mississippi: Meridian Printing, 2000.

Howarth, Shirley Reiff. *International Directory of Corporate Art Collections, 2003–2004*. New York: ArtNews Associates, 2004.

Klein, Michael. "Microsoft's Vibrant Pallet." *Diversity Journal*, No. 3, Vol. 3 (2001).

CREATIVE CAMERA

In Britain, photography was not established as a distinct artistic medium until the late 1980s. Technical leanings and camera club alliances still dominated photographic interests in Britain during the twentieth century that printed magazines struggled to overcome. Photography was still succumbing to editorial influences and the social commentary that a printed photograph could offer. *Creative Camera* (London) closed its operation in 2000. Founded in 1966, the magazine was the foremost magazine that demonstrated concern about photography's artistic discourse, which placed Britain in an international debate about photography's progression since World War II.

In 1966, the original magazine *Camera Owner* was bought and redeveloped as *Creative Camera Owner* and then as *Creative Camera*, changing its title to suit a readership with interests diversified from the technical magazine's roots and to establish a site for artistic innovations in British photography. Colin Osman was the second editor after Bill Jay's founding, beginning his tenure in 1968 and leading the magazine's mission until roughly 1986. Located originally on Charles Dicken's Doughty Street *Creative Camera* established a three-dimensional presence, offering a gallery site and bookstore for its book-order company that mirrored the magazine's spreads. Coo Press Limited distributed *Creative Camera* to an international readership and later purchased Mansfield Books International, enlarging *Creative Camera's* mail-order business to one of the largest book holdings in photography during the late 1960s and early 1970s.

In addition to the mail-order section, the magazine also functioned as a gallery guide and open forum. The front page was Osman's editorial voice, which addressed issues raised about the production of the magazine or responded to letters to the editor. In crisis and reconstruction since the end of the Churchill era, Britain searched for an identity that the legacy of World War II provided, which was mainly through photographic war communication. A public consciousness aware that the war era was the beginning of an unknown start was reflected in public projects such as the Mass Observation project beginning in 1937. The *7 Up* film series (1962), and *The Family* (1974) were media-related searches intended to question Britain's postwar social and economic developments. The Realist Movement sparked by France's Cinema Verité also echoed this need for identity politics to hit the heart of local interests. Magazines were a central distribution point supported by the thoughts of editors who witnessed much of this public forum. Photography proved crucial. Osman was dedicated to reinterpreting this role for the negotiation of photography's artistic value.

Initially resembling a published newsletter in design with a signature broad-bordered silver cover, *Creative Camera* stood apart from other publications aimed at the fine-arts photography audience such as *Camerawork*, *Aperture*, and *History of Photography*. Spreads featured aspiring British photographers, but many of the photographers were not of international repute and the magazine struggled against international politics of quality. Funding was an additional struggle given its mission to disclaim a technical practice in favor of artistic directions. Still trying to abate commercial aesthetics, the magazine struggled for innovative advertising that could support its artistic aims. Sponsorship rested mostly on subscriptions, individual contributions, gallery and museum announcements, and its mail-order business. Articles were separated from spreads and varied from press releases to commentaries from the editorial staff and internationally written responses about developments in photography and exhibitions.

The photography of Bill Brandt, which was shown by Museum of Modern Art, New York curator John Szarkowski in a landmark exhibition at London's Hayward Gallery (1970) and traveled throughout England, proved inspirational for two decades of photography that *Creative Camera* featured. Among the published artists, Chris Killip and Martin Parr emerged as the most prolific. Straight photography was the main aesthetic among British photographers, causing *Creative Camera* to align in the 1970s with Szarkowski's famous curatorial vision for a defining emphasis of twentieth century photography. His book, *The Photographer's Eye* (1966) and probably his closing exhibition at MoMA, *Photography Until Now* (1989), established modern photography's appeal as having a critical eye that was wholly pluralistic by being unfettered by societal distinctions. The magazine also reflected other areas of interest. In England, nineteenth-century photography was renewed in collections such as the Victoria and Albert Museum's collection during the 1970s and was part of the quest to examine photography's artistic dimensions. As a result, articles in *Creative Camera* about William Henry Fox Talbot and Julia Margaret Cameron were keenly anticipated. The popularity of American photographers Diane Arbus, Garry Winogrand, and Lee Friedlander initiated a second modernist style of straight photography that assuaged aesthetics with a kind of street smarts that matched the grain and "stylistic grit" of Bill Brandt's legacy and became another following for many photographers displayed in *Creative Camera's* pages.

One of the main issues working against the magazine's success was the separation between the magazine's articles and photographs. *Creative Camera's* readership rose and fell with changes in critical thought. The magazine's editorial bent was initially shaped by ideas based on Henri Cartier-Bresson's aesthetic of "the decisive moment." A synthesis of the theories of John Tagg and Szarkowski about societal systems then dominated the magazine, which was followed with notions based on Victor Burgin's *Thinking Photography* (1982) and French philosophical concerns revolving around deconstruction and semiotics. Burgin's highly influential conceptual photography and writing, as distributed through *Creative Camera* and other venues, inspired a new generation of artists who found their consciousness diversified by greater immigration into England, which readdressed Britain's colonial roots.

Rather than featuring genres like landscape or street life, or the focusing on black and white photography, in the pages of *Creative Camera* artists such as American James Casebere, known for his deserted interiors, Rineke Djikstra, Ratimi Fani-Kyode, and Uganda-born Zarina Bhimji grew in critical importance. Changes in social politics in general allowed the full effects of Burginian and Foucaultian ideas to take affect upon the magazine by 1986, when Colin Osman negotiated his resignation in exchange for full revenue support by The Arts Council of Great Britain. Redesign of the magazine included transferring decisions from the editorial staff to a board of directors. Selected critics—Ian Jeffrey, Jo Spence, Rebecca Solnit, and Geoffrey Batchen—exemplified this shift in editorial perspectives to supplant newsboard aesthetics. By the 1990s, *Creative Camera* resembled more general art world publications like *Art in America* with its leading critical edge.

Creative Camera honored its founding mission its last issue: the February/March 2000 was a sourcebook for photographers. The basic question that had shaped the magazine's history still persisted: How to represent British art photography. Mark Durden's February/March 1998 article "Defining the Moment" reveals that despite the changing opinion, the magazine's subscription base was still true to British photographic traditions. Conceptual and contemporary practices pinned theoretical multimedia practices against straight art photography. The latter was still difficult to define, as explored in articles written by photography critic and professor, David Green. An open forum for debate to the end of its funding reliance, exhibitions such as the Victoria and Albert's *British Photography: Into the 1990s* (1988) and Museum of Modern Art's *British Photography from the Thatcher Years* (1990) paid homage to *Creative Camera's* participation in attempts to decipher the question. David Brittain, the final editor, rechristened the magazine as *DPICT* after its close, which aimed to increase critical influence.

Ultimately, the evidential question for its readership was "what is art photography?" given the succession of movements, theory, attention to certain types of artists, the question of social use, and changes in technology that *Creative Camera* had championed. Both questions proved amorphous. Discourse and discussion over the photograph as object was still the main topic fueling *DPICT* until its closing in 2002. A cumulative book, *Creative Camera: Thirty Years of Writing* (1999), edited by Brittain, is a demonstrative publication voicing significant British perspectives on such questions.

Sarah L. Marion

See also: **Burgin, Victor; Cartier-Bresson, Henri; Killip, Chris; Parr, Martin; Spence, Jo; Szarkowski, John**

Further Reading

British Photography: Towards a Bigger Picture. New York: Aperture Foundation, Inc., 1988.

Brittain, David, ed. *Creative Camera: Thirty Years of Writing*. Manchester and New York: University of Manchester Press, 1999.

Kismaric, Susan. *British Photography from the Thatcher Years*. New York: Museum of Modern Art, 1990.

Osman, Colin and Peter Turner. *Creative Camera International Yearbook*. London: Coo Press Limited, 1975–1978.

GREGORY CREWDSON

American

Gregory Crewdson came to the forefront in photography during the 1990s. His photographs—richly detailed yet uncanny color images of American suburbia—build on a tradition of documentary photography that looks closely at quotidian events in the lives of ordinary people. Intrigued by the tension that exists between domesticity and nature, Crewdson transforms his real, suburban settings into entirely fictional worlds, creating single moments in an absurd, fantastic narrative revealing the hidden underbelly of everyday life. "Photography...is not at all about an exact representation of the truth," Crewdson has said, "but is rather a dramatization of something which ought to have remained hidden" (Moody, 2002).

Born in Brooklyn, New York in 1962, Crewdson first learned of Freudian analysis from his father, a psychologist who conducted sessions with his patients at home. As a child, Crewdson would overhear fragments of these conversations through the floorboards in the living room, inventing entire stories based on excerpts of people's dreams, an experience that would later prove essential to Crewdson's use of narrative in photography. It was Crewdson's father who first introduced his son to the medium, taking him to see the 1972 retrospective exhibition of Diane Arbus at the Museum of Modern Art. Arbus' photographs of New York City, which she explored as both familiar and foreign territory, and her use of the camera to challenge preconceived ideas of the city's reality made a lasting impression on Crewdson and helped shape his concept of photographic truth.

As an art student at State University of New York at Purchase from 1981 to 1985, Crewdson studied photography in a suburban community, an environment that would later serve as the focal point for the majority of his images. During this period, he worked at *Aperture* magazine and did an internship at the Daniel Wolf Gallery in Manhattan. It was at this point that he met Joel Sternfeld, whose photographs of the American landscape he greatly admired, along with those of William Eggleston, Robert Frank, and the paintings of Edward Hopper.

Like these artists, Crewdson developed his aesthetic and artistic technique in response to place. A primary source of inspiration is the natural landscape of western Massachusetts where his family purchased a tract of land on which to build a log cabin when he was a teenager. This area of pristine terrain, which lies adjacent to towns of vinyl siding and subdivisions, has served as a retreat for Crewdson throughout his career. It has also provided him with a model of American life in which an ideal nature collides with ever-encroaching urban blight.

Crewdson first began to photograph suburban life while working on his Master of Fine Arts thesis at Yale University between 1986 and 1988, asking local residents from the nearby town of Lee, Massachusetts to participate in a series of theatrically composed genre scenes. Crewdson orchestrated disquieting, ambiguous situations located within his subjects' homes, with the aim of capturing a furtive moment that usually goes unnoticed.

Crewdson acknowledges that this split second, what he calls "the uncanny aspect of the photograph," is fleeting (Moody 2002). To capture this moment, Crewdson needed to gain greater control over the arrangement and lighting of his compositions. In the late 1980s, he abandoned real life situations to create still-lifes and dioramas of natural environments, which he built in his studio and then photographed. Crewdson tightened his focus to feature animals and birds as the protagonists in these vivid, color photographs, which he titled the *Natural Wonder* series (1989), thus creating startling scenes of macabre moments in the underbrush.

The use of minutely detailed, constructed environments, staged events, and theatrical lighting to reveal the unknown aspects of his subjects' lives recurs throughout Crewdson's work. Crewdson cites numerous film directors and several films among his strongest influences. These include David Cronenberg, David Lynch, and Alfred Hitchcock, whose 1958 psychological thriller *Vertigo,* together with Steven Spielberg's paranormal film, *Close Encounters of the Third Kind* (1977), stimulated Crewdson's interest in combining everyday reality with the extraordinary. Often compared to a movie director himself, Crewdson presents a complete yet ambiguous narrative within one photograph, condensing an entire movie into a single frame.

In the late 1970s, Cindy Sherman began taking a series of photographs in which she re-created the promotional stills from Hollywood B-movies. Photographing herself as an actress, a housewife, a prostitute and the like, she created new archetypes from well-honed film stereotypes. In the 1990s, photographers like Crewdson and Jeff Wall expanded on Sherman's concept, creating extensive and elaborate staged tableaux in which they too created a new fiction by subjecting ordinary North American life to intense scrutiny.

Crewdson regularly works with crews of 30 or more production assistants and technicians to fabricate intricate sets and lighting designs, often installed within a rural, suburban environment. In the *Twilght* series (1998–2002), for example, which includes 40 large-format, untitled photographs, Crewdson transformed a quiet neighborhood street lined with 1950s-style houses into a bustling film set. Photographed at the twilight hour, when both natural and artificial lights are available, these pictures present a hybrid space that is at once real and invented.

Despite the enormous scope of his productions, Crewdson's carefully composed scenes and controlled lighting recall the intricate arrangements of early photographic still lifes. In nineteenth century daguerreotypes, for example, objects were positioned with a scientific sensitivity to depth of field and the play of light and shadow within a composition. Crewdson maintains this traditional approach to photography but magnifies it to the largest possible scale. In this way, he turns the real world into a fictional stage, creating complex images of a choreographed reality. As a professor of photography at Yale University since 1994, Crewdson has profoundly influenced a group of artists who combine documentary photography with fictional, staged elements. Crewdson summarizes his aesthetic vision as follows: "In part I see what I'm doing as exploring the American psyche through the American vernacular landscape" (Grant, 2004). Rather than passively observe the world and record the reality he encounters, Crewdson actively creates a world as he imagines it and photographs it for us to see.

Lindsay Harris

See also: **Conceptual Photography; Constructed Reality; Documentary Photography**

Biography

Born in Brooklyn, New York, 26 September 1962. Attended State University of New York, Purchase, B.A., 1985; studied photography at Yale University, New Haven, Connecticut, M.F.A., 1988. Teaching positions include State University of New York, Purchase, New York, 1988–93; Sarah Lawrence College, Bronxville, New York, 1990; Cooper Union, New York, 1990–93; Vassar College, Poughkeepsie, New York, 1993; Yale University, New Haven, Connecticut, 1994 to present. Received The Aaron Siskind Fellowship, 1991; Visual Artists Fellowship from National Endowment for the Arts, 1992. Resides in New York City.

Individual Exhibitions

1988 Yale University Art Gallery; New Haven, Connecticut
1991 BlumHelman Warehouse; New York (traveled to Portland School of Art, Portland, Maine; Ruth Bloom Gallery, Los Angeles, California)
1992 Houston Center for Photography; Houston, Texas
1993 Feigen Gallery; Chicago, Illinois
1994 Palm Beach Community College Museum of Art; Palm Beach, Florida
1995 Galleri Charlotte Lund; Stockholm, Sweden
Les Images du Plaisir, Frac des Pays de la Loire, Galerie des Carmes; La Flèche, France Jay Jopling / White Cube; London
1996 Ginza Artspace, Shiseido Co.; Tokyo, Japan
1997 Cleveland Center for Contemporary Art; Cleveland, Ohio
1998 Espacio Uno, Museo Nacional, Centro de Arte Reina Sofia; Madrid, Spain (traveled to Salamanca in 1999)

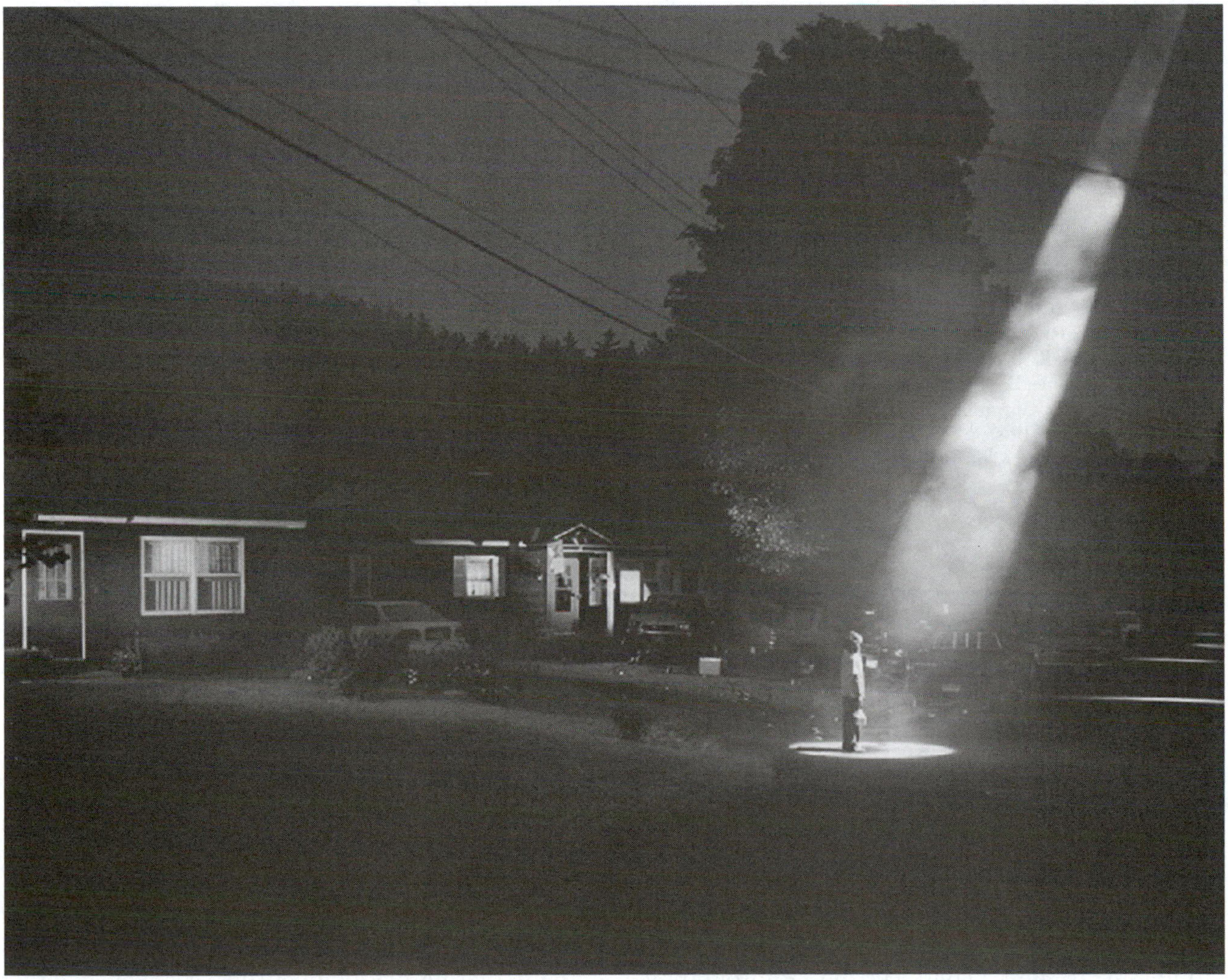

Gregory Crewdson, Untitled (beer dream), 1998, C-print. Original in color.
[© *Courtesy of the artist and Luhring Augustine, New York*]

1999 *Surreal Suburbia*; John Michael Kohler Art Center; Sheboygan, Wisconsin
Twilight; Emily Tsingou Gallery; London
2000 *Gregory Crewdson: Disturbed Nature*; Charles H. Scott Gallery, Emily Carr Institute of Art; Vancouver, Canada
2001 *Gregory Crewdson: Photographs*; SITE Santa Fe; Santa Fe, New Mexico
2002 Luhring Augustine Gallery; New York
2003 *Gregory Crewdson: Photographs*; Mass MoCA; North Adams, Massachusetts

Group Exhibitions

1991 *Pleasures and Terrors in Domestic Comfort*; The Museum of Modern Art; New York
1994 *Recent Photography Acquisitions: Selections from the Permanent Collection*; Whitney Museum of American Art; New York
New Work, New Directions 2; Los Angeles County Museum of Art; Los Angeles, California
1995 *La Belle et La Bête*; Musée d'Art Moderne de la Ville de Paris; Paris, France
1996 *Everything That's Interesting is New*; The Dakis Joannou Collection, organized by the DESTE Foundation. Athens School of Fine Arts, "The Factory;" Athens, Greece
1997 *Gothic*; Institute of Contemporary Art; Boston, Massachusetts
1997 *Kwangju Biennale*; Kwangju, South Korea
1998 *Where: Allegories of Site in Contemporary Art*; Whitney Museum of American Art; New York
1999 *Making it Real*, a traveling exhibition organized and circulated by the Independent Curator's International, New York. Traveled from 1997–99 to the Aldrich Museum of Contemporary Art, Ridgefield, Connecticut; Reykjavik Municipal Art Museum, Reykjavik, Iceland; Portland Museum of Art, Portland, Maine; Bayly Art Museum, University of Virginia, Charlottesville, Virginia; Bakalar Gallery, Massachusetts College of Art, Boston, Massachusetts; Emerson Gallery, Hamilton College, Clinton, New York
2000 *Open Ends: Sets and Situations*; Museum of Modern Art, New York
2001 *Settings and Players: Theatrical Ambiguity in American Photography*, White Cube, London; City Gallery of Prague, Czechoslovakia

Selected Works

Natural Wonder series, 1989
hover [sic] series, 1996
Twilight series, 1998–2002
Dream House series, 2002

Further Reading

Dompierre, Louise. "Gregory Crewdson." In *Digital Gardens: A World in Mutation*. Toronto: The Power Plant Contemporary Art Gallery, 1996.
Feaster, Felicia. "Interview with Gregory Crewdson." *Art Papers* (September/October 1996): 8–13.
Galassi, Peter. *Pleasures and Terrors in Domestic Comfort*. New York: The Museum of Modern Art, 1991.
Goldberg, Vicki. "How Worshippers, Too, Can Denature Nature." *The New York Times*, September 8, 2000.
Grant, Annette. "Lights, Camera, Stand Really Still: On the Set with Gregory Crewdson." *The New York Times*, May 30, 2004.
Harris, Melissa. "Our Town." *Aperture* (Spring 1992): cover.
Homes, A. M. "Dream of Life." *Artforum* (April 1993): 70–3.
Moody, Rick. *Twilight*. New York: Harry N. Abrams, Inc., 2002.
———. Darcey Steinke, Joyce Carol Oates, and Bradford Morrow. *hover*. San Francisco: Artspace Books, 1998.
Paini, Dominique, and Guy Cogeval, eds. *Fatal Coincidences, Hitchcock and Art*, Montreal: Montreal Museum of Fine Arts, 2000.
Steinke, Darcey, and Bradford Morrow. *Gregory Crewdson: Dream of Life*. Spain: Ediciones Universidad de Salamanca, 1999.

CRIME PHOTOGRAPHY

On April 20, 1865, "Wanted" posters were put up all over the United States. Unlike the illustrated ones of the old west, these particular "Wanted" posters featured the photographs of John Wilkes Booth and his two supposed partners in crime, John Surratt and David Harold. Photography, still a fairly new science, had entered the realm of criminal investigation in the 1840s, but the photographs of John Wilkes Booth brought a national legitimacy to this new form of investigation. Since that time, photography has continued to play a key role in the recording, processing, and prosecuting of criminal activity. There are many different types of crime photography, all of which serve some functional purpose, aiding in the gathering or documenting of evidence either for testimony, records, or for later investigation. There is a distinct division between the actual genesis of the crime photograph (photographs which are usually taken at the scene of the crime) and the analysis of the photograph (often conducted at highly specialized laboratories).

Perhaps the most common sub-area in criminal photography is the standard "crime scene photograph." From murder to much less serious crimes, investigators typically take photographs in order to aid later investigation. Photographs are used to reconstruct crime scenes at later dates; it is therefore vital that each object even tangentially related to the crime be photographed by itself (a close-up, frame-filling shot), but also in its spatial relationships to the other objects in the crime scene. If this "completeness of scene" is accomplished, when presenting evidence to judges or juries, two groups who did not benefit from witnessing the original crime scene, a prosecutor can either focus on the minutia of the criminal case by showing a picture of the isolated object (such as the murder weapon), or by giving an impression of the scene as a whole. A general philosophy adhered to by most careful criminal photographers is that of thoroughness. For instance, in the case of a murder, the dead body is certainly photographed, but there are other possible clues that could aid the investigators and are therefore just as important to photograph, such as footprints, potential murder weapons, or parts of the room that have clearly been tampered with. A traffic investigator working for the highway patrol does not just take pictures of the accident, but also looks for indicator signs to photograph, such as skid marks and broken glass. Typically, crime scene photographers are tremendously thorough, presenting every possible angle of the scene. The power of an investigator to recall will never be perfect, and it is impossible for a jury to completely picture how a crime scene would look without some form of visual aid. Therefore, many rolls of film are typically exposed, ensuring that absolutely everything of potential importance be portrayed from every possible angle.

In cases of foul play, after the initial crime scene photographs are taken, another arm of criminal photography comes into play: the autopsy record. Autopsies are typically documented in several different ways, one of which remains the photograph. All autopsies are photographed, but this is particularly true of ones where homicide is suspected. The coroner searches for potential causes of death, taking photographs of any exterior markings (bruises) or interior markings (punctured organs) that seem suspicious or may suggest a potential cause of death. Just as with crime scene photographers, coroners attempt to collect as much evidence as possible by using photographs, which could also become valuable evidence in court. Victims of crime need not always die in order to have their body photographed, however. In cases of sexual, spousal, or child abuse, various regions of the body that were struck or violated are photographed by specialized police photographers, again in order to ensure a record of the crime, which can be used as evidence at a later date.

A final type of crime photography is surveillance. In 1924, the Federal Bureau of Investigation (FBI) was formed, and J. Edgar Hoover was placed at its helm. Within a decade, the FBI had become a large and powerful force in American crime prevention, due in large part to the freedom of action Hoover was accorded. A large part of Hoover's success was due to his everyday and widespread use of surveillance, a style of investigation that sought to analyze the criminal before he struck. Hoover's personal philosophy of "overkill" when it came to surveillance filtered down through the FBI ranks. Files on suspected criminals often contained pages or pieces of evidence numbering in the thousands. A large component of these substantial files was the photographs, which derived from almost constant surveillance of suspected wrongdoers. If a potential criminal was under surveillance by the FBI, every aspect of that person's life was captured on film, including every place he went and every person he met with. This form of documentation was extreme, but it laid the cornerstone for the contemporary "stakeout," which is used by many different law enforcement agencies. Again, thoroughness is encouraged, as there is no predicting when the important event that needs to be photographed might occur. Surveillance is an arm of photography that takes place before the key event, in anticipation that the camera can be used to capture more than just the aftermath of the crime, but the actual crime itself.

Not all crime photography is conducted by employees of law enforcement agencies, however. There is quite a rich tradition of private photographers who "ambulance chase," who tune their radios to police frequencies hoping to arrive at crime scenes in time to take photographs. Some of the more renowned photographers of all time, such as Weegee, have done their best and most famous work within the field of crime photography. And some of the more shocking and disturbing photographs of all time fall within this genre, including photographs of the murder scenes of Dutch Schultz, the St. Valentine's Day Massacre, the Black Dahlia, and Malcolm X, to name a few.

Andrew Howe

See also: **Weegee**

Further Reading

Ehrlich, S. G., and Leland V. Jones. *Photographic Evidence: The Preparation and Use of Photographs in Civil and Criminal Cases*. London: MacLaren, 1967.

Harrison, Wilson R. *Suspect Documents: Their Scientific Examination*. London: Maxwell, 1996.

Murphy, Burt. *Police and Crime Photography*. New York: Vernon, 1960.

Phillips, Sandra, Mark Haworth-Booth, and Carol Squiers. *Police Pictures: The Photograph as Evidence*. San Francisco: Chronicle, 1997.

Runyon, Esther L. *Photographic Evidence*. New York: Carlton, 1991.

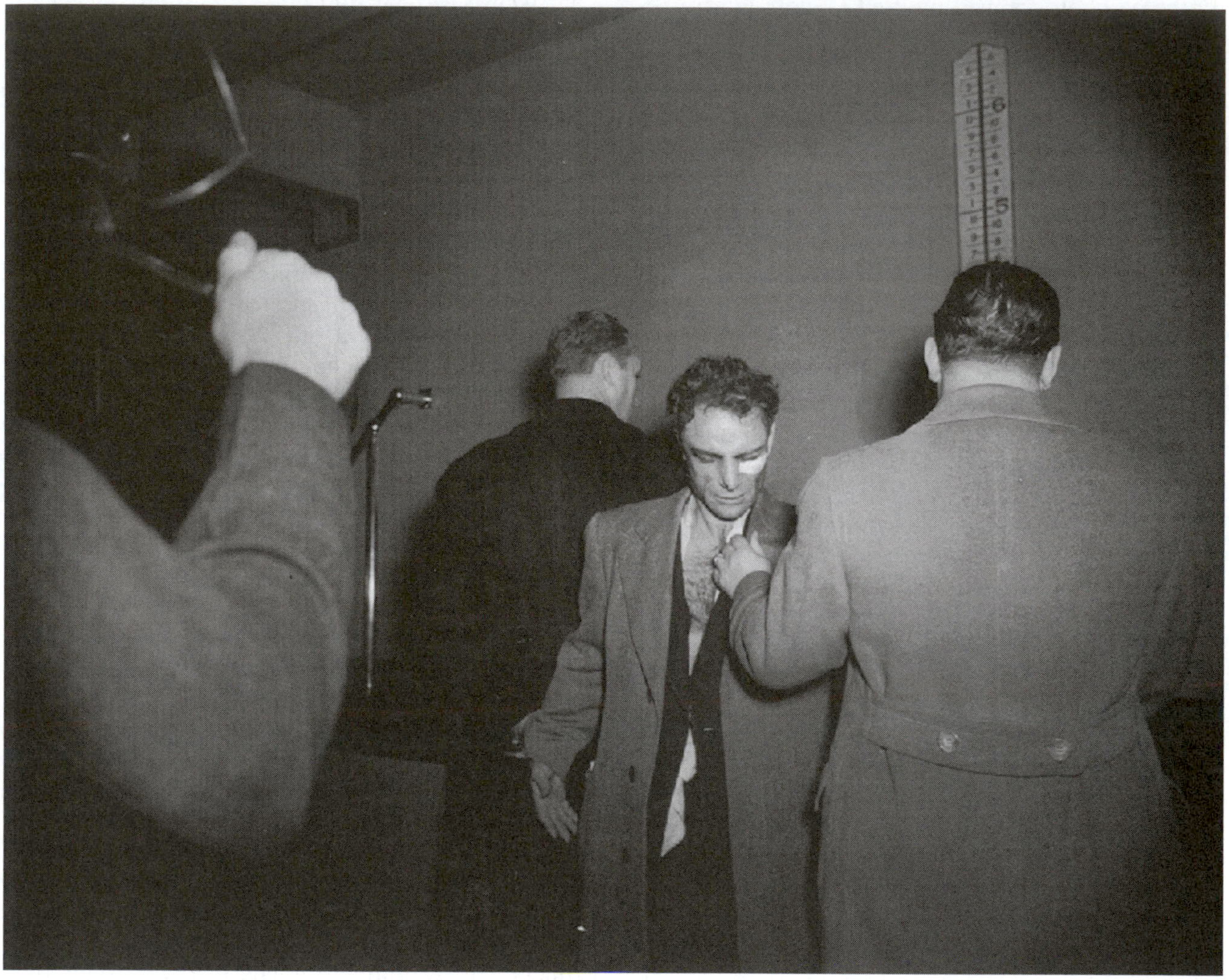

Weegee, Booked on suspicion of killing a policeman, Anthony Esposito, Accused "Cop Killer"
January 16, 1941, gelatin silver print.
[*Weegee (Arthur Felig)/Getty Images*]

CROPPING

Cropping is a technique for focusing the eye upon any particular image by means of reduction. The term is commonly used to describe the removal of extraneous visual data (such as unnecessary background or individuals) from photographs or other kinds of images. Often cropping eliminates partial and extra images not germane to the composition, visuals that cannot be fully read or contextually understood (i.e., any out-of-frame, blurry, or rogue image).

Cropping can be as simple as rounding- or squaring-off corners, or can require cutting and shaping images into other forms. In journalism cropping is one technique of "layout and design" involving, as in traditional newspaper layout, the carefully measured addition of strips of black line delineated by width. The layout technician creates columns, boxes, large and small headers, or simply white space, usually in order to market page space, demarcate advertisements, and draw readers' attention to image or text.

Cropping is also a technique used for building and maintaining scrapbooks, or "scrapbooking," where photos often assume the fanciful shapes of circles, stars, and hearts, or project-specific shapes such as teddy-bears for a baby album, and horse shapes for an equestrienne's album. Aiding in the shaping process, templates include squares, rectangles, circles, triangles, hearts, stars, bells, dolls, and animals. Paper piercing patterns, stamps, mattes, and scraps may add information or provide pure decoration by coordinating colours that help to "bring out" or emphasise an element for aesthetic effect. Scrapbookers select photos, determine what constitutes suitable background, what is unimportant and how best to display the desired image by cutting. Background is important as it may provide useful contextual information, particularly if creating an album as an historical record.

Traditionally, cropping was achieved by means of scalpel, Exacto-blade, razor blade, paper-trimmer, *guillotine*, scissors, paper trimmer, box cutter, punch, or some other sharp cutting tool. Nowadays, cropping is accomplished virtually prior to its concrete appearance on paper. Many of these tools are still used professionally in print journalism and advertising. Nowadays cropping is as likely to be thought of as the virtual correction or alteration to an image prior to its concrete or material appearance; computer software programs perform this kind of operation. Thus page-cropping abilities are to be found in Adobe Acrobat, Adobe Photoshop, PageMaker, and other software publishing programs. Many scanners (machines dedicated to "reading" texts as images or symbols, and transporting them onto computers as binary data) have built-in capabilities of automatic image-cropping.

One of the newer associations with cropping occurs in online editing. Microsoft Picture IQ$^{(TM)}$, a product of software giant Microsoft, allows fades, morphs, texturizing, artistic auto-rendering, and 3D, in addition to the removal of red-eye glare from flashbulbs, scratches, wrinkles, and other unwanted marks on the image. Picture IQ$^{(TM)}$ PhotoTools$^{(TM)}$ Version 2.0, a set of online photo editing and enhancement tools, is a product of global digital imaging network company PhotoChannel Networks Inc. PhotoTools$^{(TM)}$ integrates online advances with cropping controls as well as the standard controls for brightness, contrast, and the omnipresent "clip art" catalogue for illustrating straight text. In addition to permitting cropping changes to the image online (without the interim step of adjusting composition with another software platform), this program enables users to "undo," removing changes made. (For instance, when using the justifiably popular Adobe Photoshop to combine images one might enable the program by clipping a TIFF image before importing it into QuarkXPress.) This adds a degree of flexibility not found in all photo composer packages. According to the industry's news release (Seattle Times, 7 Feb. 2001), PhotoIQ features include user controlled "freeform" cropping, one click cropping to industry-standard print-aspect ratios, red-eye removal, online clipart, customized user interface skins, and addition of photo card templates, borders, and clipart. Most photographic platforms now offer "one-click" cropping, making images even more ephemeral. Other methods for image cropping are found in digital imaging map programs.

Cropping originally concentrated on placing the primary image in a central position, either in the middle of the frame or in the "golden triangle" classically perceived as an aesthetically strong position, clearly adhering to classical concepts of painting, especially portraiture, architectural design, and sculptural technique. A general principle for the use of space is that it should not occupy more than a third of the photo. Under the influence of graphic design and advertising, and the quickly changing visual bytes of cable television, in particular MTV, cropping techniques have altered radically. Cropping has become an art form in itself, drawing attention to an artist's method and personality, and is now widely accepted as a means of delivering a postmodern point of view with any image. Dislodging the image from a hierarchically powerful position in the centre of any given frame, the desired image might be cropped so severely that the subject (for instance, a person's face) is only partially revealed, dominated by the matrix, or removed altogether.

Roy Baum

See also: **Architectural Photography; Composition**

IMOGEN CUNNINGHAM

American

Imogen Cunningham's photography spans 70 years of the twentieth century during which photography became the new way of seeing and interpreting the world. As a master photographer whose compelling portraits of diverse personalities such as Herbert Hoover and Martha Graham appeared in *Vanity Fair* and *Aperture*, she was not interested in developing a philosophy or theory of photography, but was an extremely talented and innovative female artist who strove to search for reality through her lens. Her involvement with her art is reflected in her prolific portfolio, which displays her important role in the history of twentieth-century photography.

Cunningham was born on April 12, 1883 in Portland, Oregon. During her youth, her parents nurtured her artistic talents by paying for summer art lessons. Her interests turned toward photography, and she began experimenting while studying chemistry at the University of Washington in Seattle in 1903. Although there was no official photography department, she learned chemistry as a basis for further study of photography. In 1905, she began experimenting with a 4 × 5 inch format camera that she ordered from a mail order correspondence school. She made her first portraits in 1906—one of which was her own nude body in a field on the university campus, "Self-Portrait" (1906). To pay for her expenses, she worked as a secretary and made slides for botanists. Her father continued to encourage her, and he built a darkroom for her in a woodshed in which the only light was a candle in a red box. She graduated in 1907 with a major in chemistry; her thesis was entitled "The Scientific Development of Photography." She then worked for two years for Edward S. Curtis, known for his photographic study *The North American Indian*; from him she learned platinum printing techniques and how to retouch negatives.

Two events that led her to focus on photography as a career occurred between 1907 and 1910. The first was an article she read in April 1907 about the work of New York photographer Gertrude Käsebier in a periodical called *The Craftsman*. Käsebier's studies of mother and child deeply moved Cunningham, and the article's point that photography could capture an emotional moment—that it was more than just a scientific chemical process—affected the young artist immensely. The second event was a trip she took to Dresden in the fall of 1909 after receiving a fellowship from her university sorority. In Germany, she studied with photo chemist Robert Luther at the Technische Hochschule and viewed the *International Photographic Exposition* where she had her first chance to view some of the best European and American photographic art of the time. Although she took few photographs on her travels, she was inspired by the great museums of Europe and by the artists that she came into contact with in Paris and London. After a stop in New York, she returned to Seattle in September 1910, opened a portrait studio, and began to exhibit her work, which was often portraits of close friends.

As a female photographer, Cunningham took some risks early in her photographic career. One risk was her avid interest in nude photography in an era in America still suffering from the conservatism of the Victorian era. In support of the idea of the modern, independent female, she also published an article called "Photography as a Profession for Women" in her sorority's journal *The Arrow* in 1913 in which she urged women to develop their own style in photography and other professions rather than merely trying to copy what men were doing. This conviction—risky for its time—she held throughout her life.

One of the most notable influences on her work during this early formative period was the art she viewed in the avant-garde periodical *Camera Work* published by Alfred Stieglitz. In this quarterly, she was introduced to many of the new young, experimental photographers that Cunningham would later come to know personally. Although Stieglitx discontinued publishing *Camera Work* in 1917, and she never made it into the journal herself, the type of photographic work illustrated—the beginnings of the clean, modern style—influenced her work throughout the 1920s and 1930s. In addition to *Camera Work*, *Vanity Fair* also drew her attention during her mid-teens with its progressive studies of nudes and its pages portraying avant-garde culture.

In 1914, her first solo exhibition was displayed at the Brooklyn Institute of Arts and Sciences. In February the following year, she married Seattle etcher Roi Partridge, with whom she had corresponded by letter for two years while he was in Europe studying art. When the war forced him to return to the United States, he became Cunningham's husband and model. Their first son, Gryffyd, was born in December of that same year. The following year, she published what was then considered a risqué nude photograph of her husband in the Christmas issue of Seattle's *The Town Crier*.

The family moved to San Francisco in 1917, where Cunningham gave birth to twin sons Rondal and Padraic; she spent the next few years with her three young children, restricting herself to photographing close friends, family, and the plants in her garden, which would be a focal point of her experimental work throughout the 1920s.

She returned to commercial portraiture in 1921 after her family moved to Oakland and her husband took a teaching position at Mills College. During these years, she and Partridge became part of a group of artists that included Edward Weston, Dorothea Lange, and Anne Brigman. Cunningham stretched her artistic horizon toward avant-garde experimentalism; and, like many other young artists, she was greatly influenced by publications such as *Vanity Fair*'s October 1922 issue which included Man Ray's now infamous portrait of the Marchesa Casati. This double exposure influenced Cunningham's portraiture and turned her focus to more abstract details apparent in photographs such as *Two Callas* (1929). She was also affected by Marcel Duchamp's famous Dada painting *Nude Descending a Staircase (No. 2)*.

By the end of the 1920s, her works were routinely made as double-exposures, and she experimented with different techniques, using plants and portraiture as her subjects. She also continued her studies of the nude—often using her husband Partridge and three children as models.

The end of the decade was punctuated by a local exhibition at the Berkeley Art Museum, in which she showed works from her plants series, and, more importantly, by her participation in the seminal *Film und Foto* exhibition in Stuttgart, Germany, in which she displayed 10 prints of what have become some of her best-known photographs, including studies of fleshy, spiky agave, aloe plants, and calla lillies.

In the 1930s and 1940s, Cunningham moved away from the close-up, sharply focused studies of plants and avant-garde experimentalism of the 20s toward celebrity portraiture and then street photography. In 1931, she exhibited at the M.H. de Young Memorial Museum, and after two photographs of the dancer Martha Graham were published in the December 1931 issue of *Vanity Fair*, the editors asked her to take assignments photographing personalities including actors Spencer Tracy, Cary Grant, Joan Blondell, and James Cagney, and President Herbert Hoover. She divorced Partridge in 1934 and moved to New York for a short time to shoot more for *Vanity Fair* including photographs of President Franklin Delano Roosevelt's mother, Mrs. James Roosevelt, but she soon returned to California to her to be closer to her sons. She continued her portraiture, which included such varied personalities as the writer Gertrude Stein, Mexican painter Frida Kahlo, and writer Upton Sinclair, who was then seeking the California governorship.

She joined Group f/64, organized by Willard Van Dyke in 1932 and including Edward Weston and Ansel Adams as members. This group was a very casual gathering of members primarily interested in realism and truth in their work. This aim is reflected in the name Group f/64, which represents the aperture setting on a camera which yields both the most depth and the sharpest focus. In the late 1930s, she began what would become a later life focus on street photography as her work shifted to subject matter concentrating more on the social circumstances of America in the mid-century and the civil strife of the postwar years in the urban and rural centers.

Cunningham opened her own studio on Green Street in San Francisco in 1947, and for the next 13 years her work was exhibited across America as she continued taking street photographs when not hired to take portraits. In these postwar years, she began teaching intermittently at the California School of Fine Arts (San Francisco Art Institute). At this time, she befriended Lisette Model, a photographer for *Harper's Bazaar*, who greatly influenced her portraiture. Together, the two women searched for radical and unusual imagery in the backstreets of San Francisco. Unlike Model's often unforgiving and stark photography, Cunningham's images reveal a mutual respect between her and her subjects, often the homeless or the downtrodden who inhabited San Francisco's seedier neighborhoods.

By the 1960s, Cunningham was running a portrait gallery, teaching portrait classes and photographing the beat generation and flower children in the Bay area. In her work at this time, Cunningham not only reveals the everyday life of this counterculture, but also considers the role of interracial relationships in the time of segregation, as demonstrated by a photograph of a couple in a San Francisco cafe in *Coffee Gallery, San Francisco* (1960). This same year, she was recognized by The International Museum of Photography and Film at the George Eastman House in Rochester, New York, which purchased a collection of her work. She used the money to travel and photograph in Western and Eastern Europe.

In 1964, Minor White devoted an entire winter issue of *Aperture* to her work and reproduced 44 images from her early work and several new portraits. She was elected a fellow of the National Academy of Arts and Sciences in 1967, and near the end of the decade she was awarded an honorary Doctor of Fine Arts by the California College of Arts and Crafts in Oakland.

In 1973, Cunningham turned 90, and these last years seemed to have been the busiest in her life. She received a Guggenheim fellowship to reprint her early glass plate negatives, was given a major exhibition at New York's Metropolitan Museum of Art, and was declared Artist of the Year by the San Francisco Art Commission. During the last year of her life, she made a guest appearance on Johnny Carson's *Tonight Show*, and CBS produced a documentary celebrating her work and life.

Although she became a celebrity, she still worked, and her last and perhaps most intriguing project was a series of work called *After Ninety*, which was a study of the lives of nonagenarians. For this project about old age, she re-photographed people from her own past, including her ex-husband, Roi Partridge, and Ansel Adams. The most moving portraits in this last series are her intimate portraits of women such as *Irene "Bobbie" Libarry 3* (1976)—a nude of a former carnival woman whose entire body had been tattooed—and melancholy studies of the inhabitants of convalescence homes and convents, such as the pensive woman depicted in *Woman in Convalescent Center, Berkeley* (1975). Cunningham died on June 23rd, 1976 at the age of 96 in San Francisco while still working on this final project.

STEPHENIE YOUNG

See also: **Group f/64; Käsebier, Gertrude; Lange, Dorothea; Man Ray; Model, Lisette; Pictorialism; Stieglitz, Alfred; Street Photography; Weston, Edward**

Biography

Born in Portland, Oregon, 1883. 1903–1907 attended University of Washington, Seattle; 1909 studied in Dresden; 1907–9 worked in the Seattle portrait studio of Edward S. Curtis; 1918 worked in San Francisco studio of Francis Bruguière; 1921 resumed commercial portrait business; 1931–1934 photographed for *Vanity Fair*; c. 1940 began working for *Sunset* magazine. Taught at the California School of Fine Arts, San Francisco (San Francisco Art Institute) 1947–1950 and 1965–1967; 1968 taught summer session at Humboldt State College; 1973 taught at San Francisco Art Institute. Awarded fellowship to the Technische Hochschule, Dresden 1909; elected fellow of the American Academy of Arts and Sciences 1967; received honorary Doctor of Fine Arts degree from the California College of Arts and Crafts 1968; Guggenheim Fellowship 1970; declared "Artist of the Year" by The San Francisco Art Commission, 1973; created the Imogen Cunningham Trust 1975. KRON-TV documentary 1952; appeared on the *Tonight Show* 1976; CBS documentary 1976. Died on 23 June 1976.

Individual Exhibitions

1912 *Imogen Cunningham*; Brooklyn Institute of Arts and Sciences; New York

1932 *Imogen Cunningham*; Los Angeles County Museum; Los Angeles, California
1935 *Imogen Cunningham*; Dallas Art Museum; Dallas, Texas
1936 *Imogen Cunningham*; E.B. Crocker Art Gallery; Sacramento, California
1951 *Imogen Cunningham*; San Francisco Museum of Art; San Francisco, California
1953 *Imogen Cunningham*; Mills College; Oakland, California
1956 *Imogen Cunningham*; Cincinnati Museum of Art; Cincinnati, Ohio; Limelight Gallery; New York
1957 *Imogen Cunningham*; Oakland Art Museum; Oakland, California
1959 *Imogen Cunningham*; Oakland Public Museum; Oakland, California
1961 *Imogen Cunningham*; George Eastman House; Rochester, New York
1964 *Imogen Cunningham*; San Francisco Museum of Art; San Francisco, California
1965 *Imogen Cunningham*; Henry Gallery, University of Washington; Seattle, Washington
1967 *Imogen Cunningham*; Stanford Art Gallery, Stanford University; Palo Alto, California
1968 *Imogen Cunningham*; California College of Arts and Crafts Gallery; Oakland, California
North Beach and the Haight-Ashbury; from *Rolling Renaissance Group Show*; Focus Gallery; San Francisco, California
1969 *Women, Cameras, and Images I*; Hall of Photography, Museum of History and Technology, Smithsonian Institution; Washington, D.C.
1970 *Imogen Cunningham*; M.H. de Young Memorial Museum; San Francisco, California; Seattle Art Museum; Seattle, Washington
1971 *Imogen Cunningham*; Friends of Photography Gallery; Carmel, California
The San Francisco Art Institute; San Francisco, California
1973 Metropolitan Museum of Art, New York
1983 *A Centennial Selection*, California Academy of Arts and Sciences; San Francisco and traveling

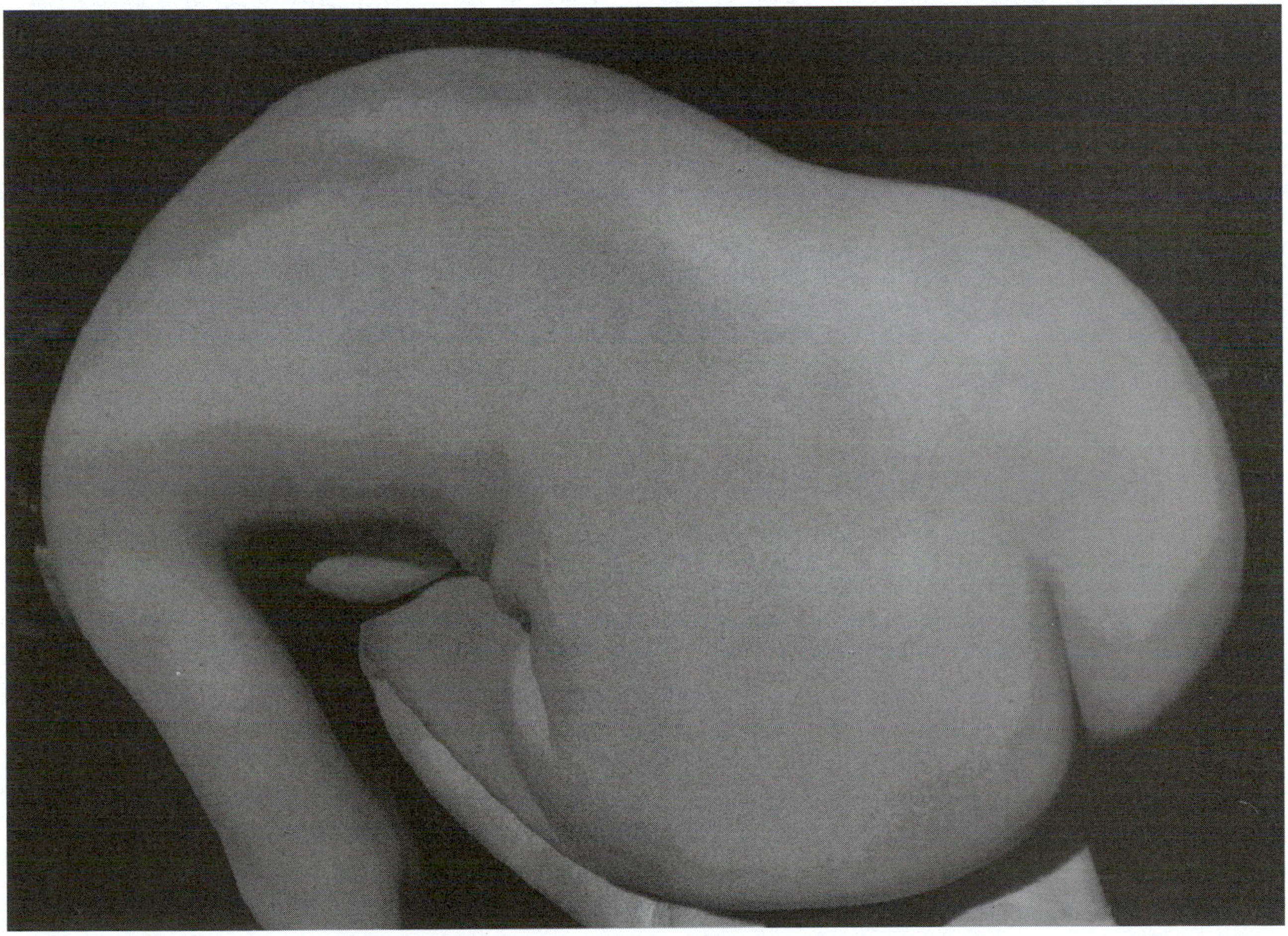

Imogen Cunningham, Nude, 1932, Gelatin silver print, 6 ⅝ × 9 ⅜″, Gift of Albert M. Bender.
[*Digital Image © The Museum of Modern Art/Licensed by SCALA/Art Resource, NY, Reprinted by permission of The Imogen Cunningham Trust*]

Selected Group Exhibitions

1929 *Film und Foto*; Deutscher Werkbund; Stuttgart, Germany
1932 *Group f/64*; M.H. de Young Memorial Museum; San Francisco, California
1937 *Photography 1839–1937*; Museum of Modern Art; New York
1940 *A Pageant of Photography*; Golden Gate International Exposition; San Francisco, California
1954 *Perceptions*; San Francisco Museum of Art; San Francisco, California
1955 *San Francisco Weekend*; Bay Area Photographers Show; San Francisco, California
1959 *Photography at Mid-Century*; George Eastman House, Rochester; New York
1960 *The Photograph as Poetry*; Pasadena Art Museum; Pasadena, California
1970 *Platinum Prints*; Friends of Photography Gallery; Carmel, California
1972 *The Multiple Image*; Massachusetts Institute of Technology; Cambridge
1973 *Images of Imogen: 1903–73*; Focus Gallery; San Francisco

Selected Works

Self-Portrait, 1906
Family on the Beach, 1910
Twins by the Window, 1919
Two Callas, 1929
Nude, 1932
Herbert Hoover with His Dog, 1935
Alfred Stieglitz, Photographer, at His Desk, 1934
Theodore Roethke, Poet, 1959
Coffee Gallery, San Francisco, 1960
A Man Ray Version of Man Ray, 1961
Irene "Bobbie" Libarry 3, 1976

Further Reading

After Ninety, Imogen Cunningham. Seattle: University of Washington Press, 1977.
Dater, Judy. *Imogen Cunningham: A Portrait*. Boston: New York Graphic Society, 1979.
Imogen Cunningham: Photographs. Seattle: University of Washington Press, 1970.
Imogen! Imogen Cunningham Photographs 1910–1973. Introduction by Margery Mann. Seattle: University of Washington Press, 1974.
Lorenz, Richard. *Imogen Cunningham: Flora*. Boston: Bulfinch Press, 1996.
Lorenz, Richard. *Imogen Cunningham: Ideas without End, A Life in Photographs*. San Francisco: Chronicle Books, 1993.
Lorenz, Richard. *Imogen Cunningham: The Modernist Years*. Tokyo: Treville, 1993.
Lorenz, Richard. *Imogen Cunningham: Portraiture*. Boston: Bulfinch Press, 1997.
Rule, Amy, ed. *Imogen Cunningham: Selected Texts and Bibliograph*, Essay by Richard Lorenz. Oxford: Clio Press, 1992.

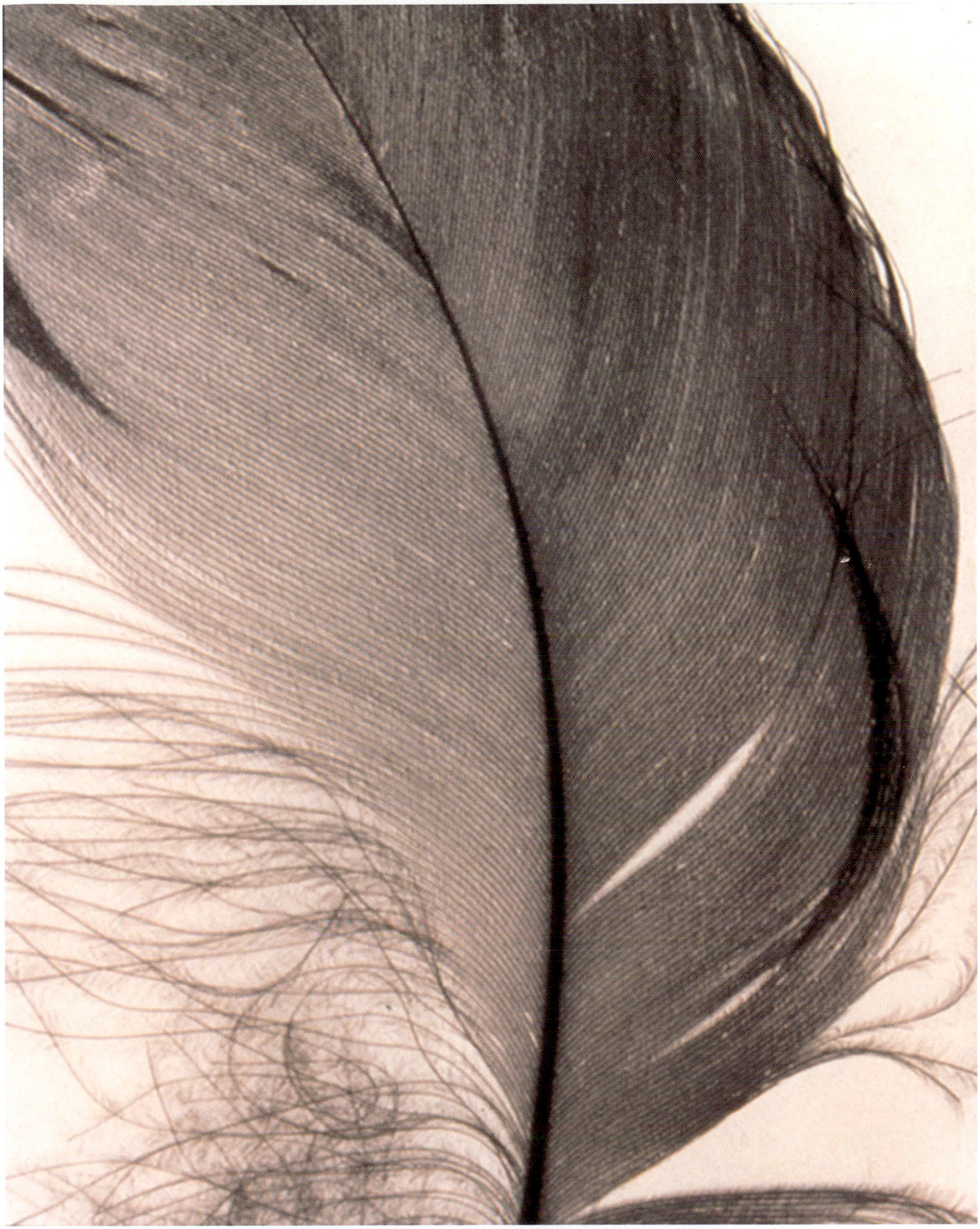

Andreas Feininger, Feather, circa 1956, Gelatin silver print, image: 12½ × 10″.

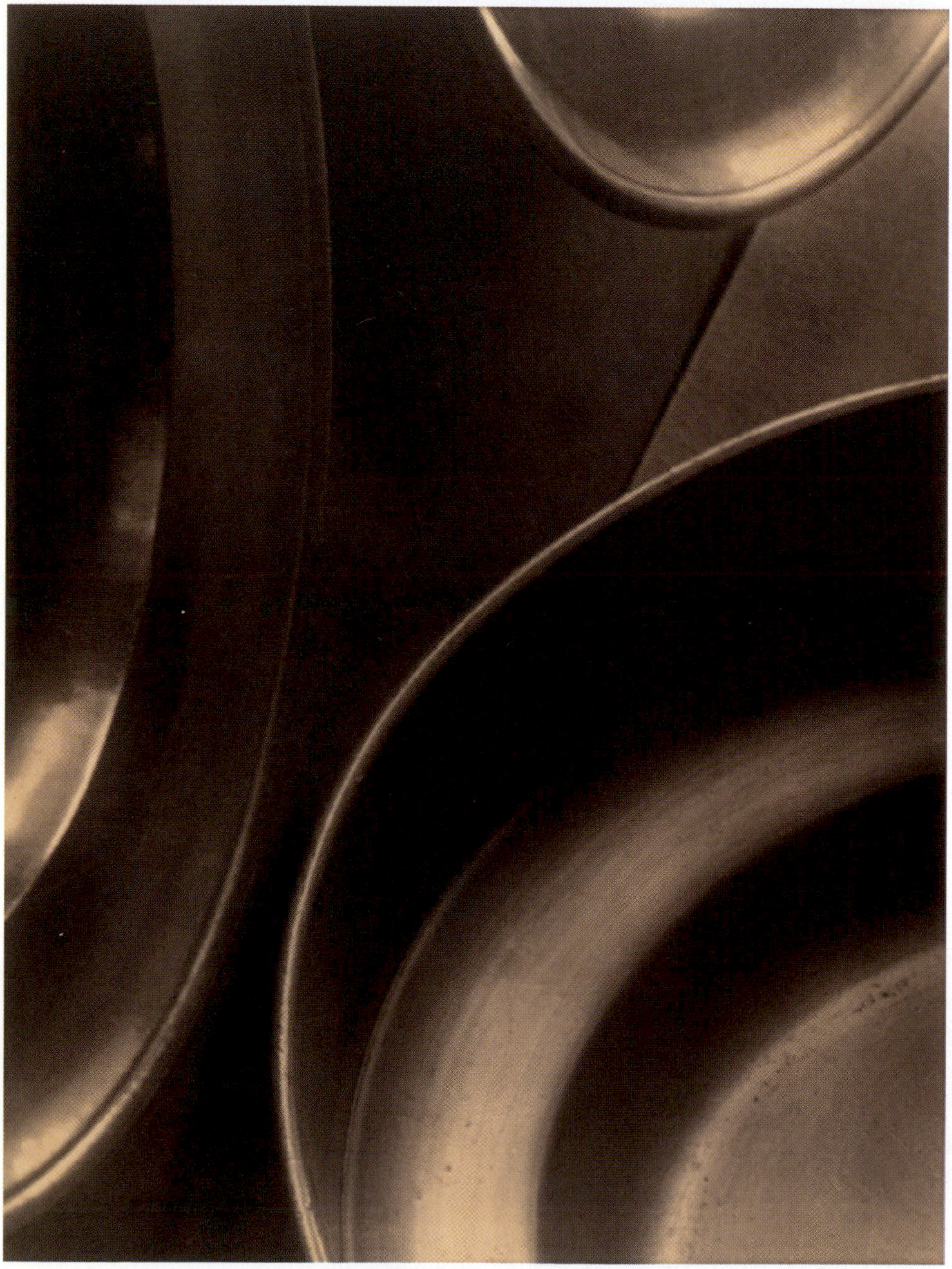

Jaromír Funke, Still life (plates), 1923, Photo: Jean-Claude Planchet.
[*CNAC/MNAM/Dist. Réunion des Musées Nationaux/Art Resource, New York*]

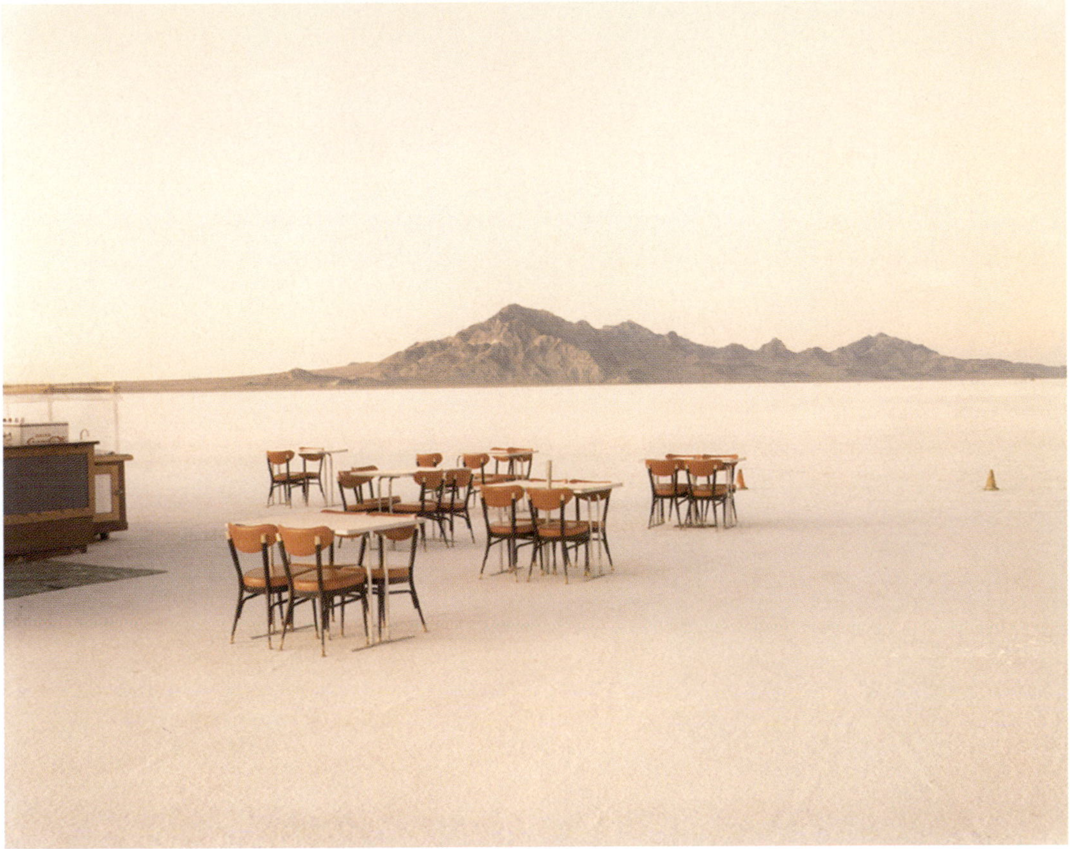

Richard Misrach, Outdoor Dining, Bonneville Salt Flats, 1992, Crimes and Splendor, p. 159.
[*Courtesy Fraenkel Gallery, San Francisco*]

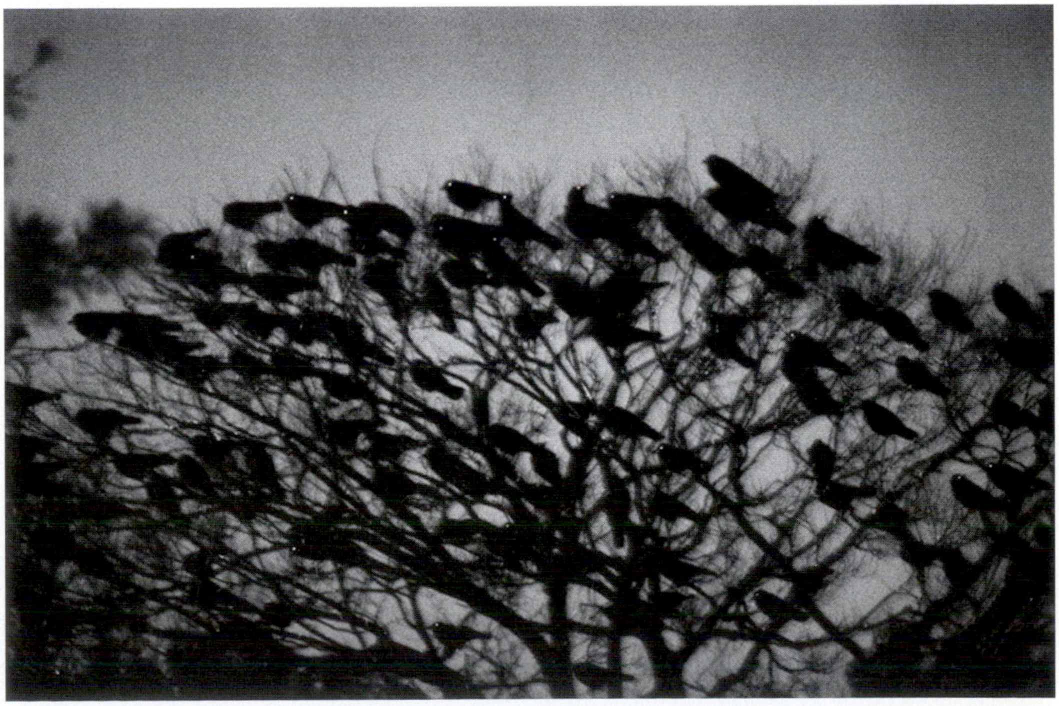

Masahisa Fukase, Kanazawa, 1977.
[*Copyright Masahisa Fukase Estate. Courtesy Robert Mann Gallery*]

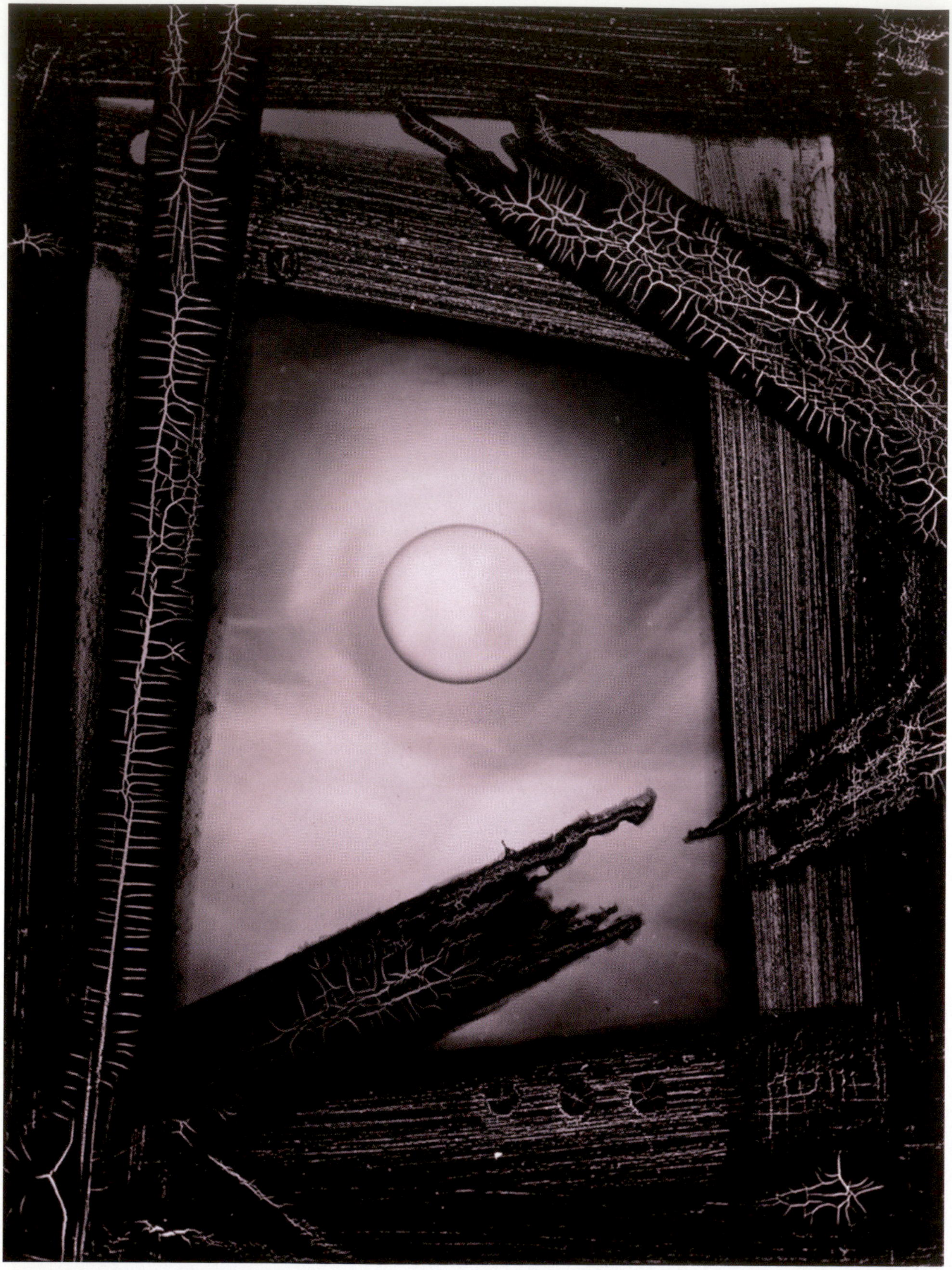

Heinz Hajek-Halke, Ohne Titel, 1950–1968, Photo: Georges Meguerditchian.
[*CNAC/MNAM/Dist. Réunion des Musées Nationaux/Art Resource, New York*]

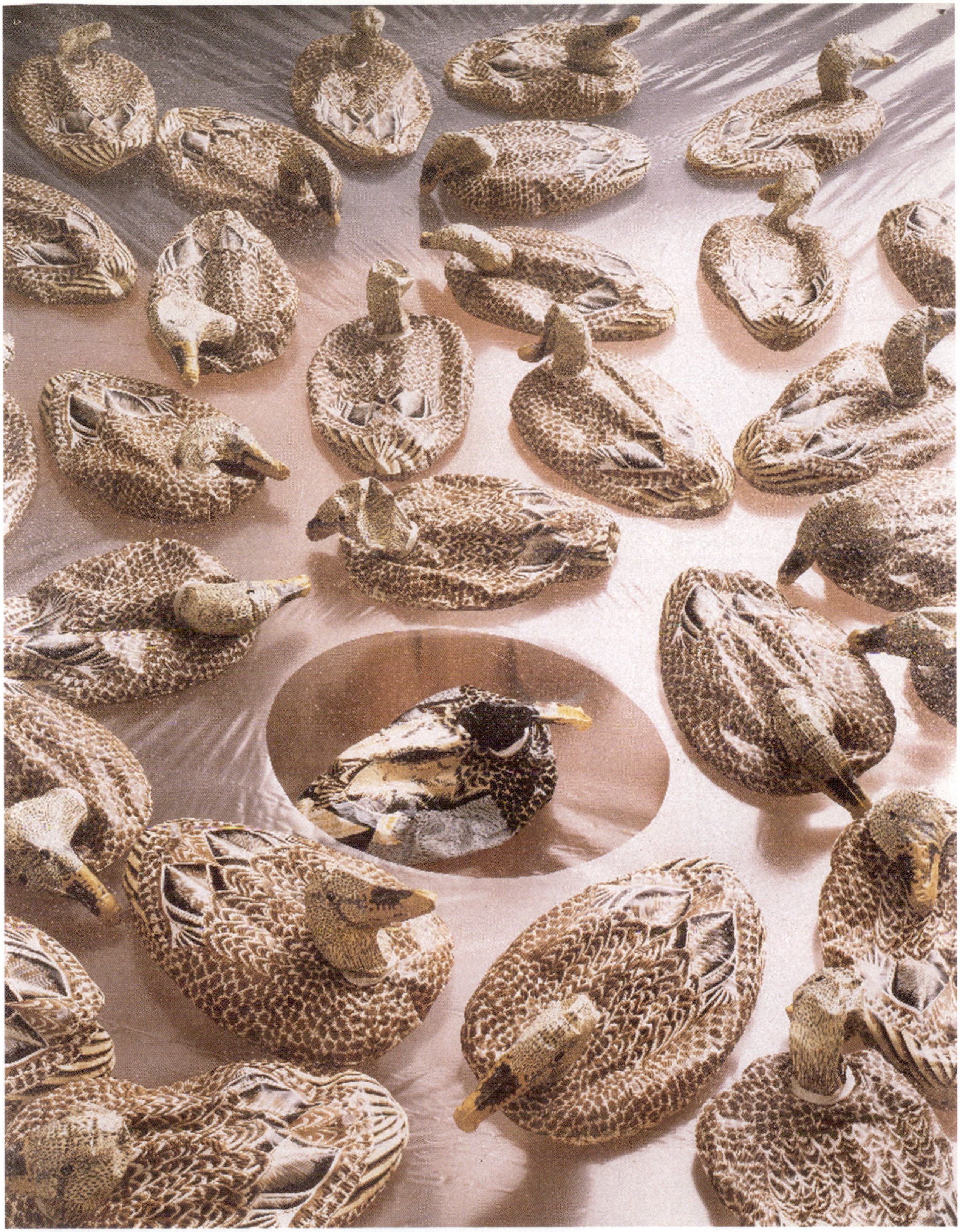

Boyd Webb, Placebo, 1989, Cibachrome photograph.
[*National Gallery of Victoria, Purchased through the Art Foundation of Victoria with assistance of The Herald and Weekly Times Limited, Fellow 1990 © Boyd Webb. Reproduced with permission of the artist*]

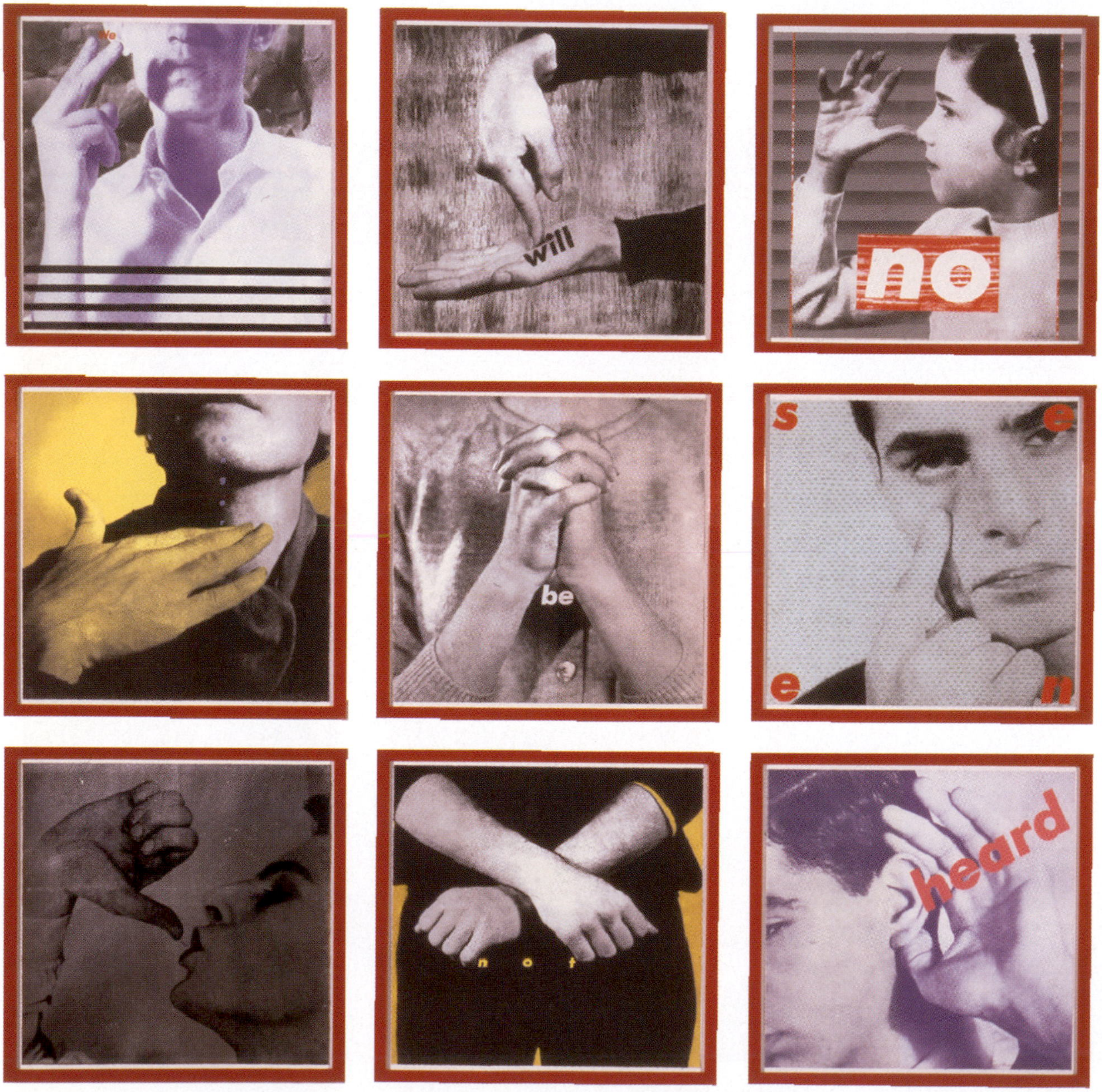

Barbara Kruger, Untitled (We will no longer be seen and not heard), 1985, Lithograph on papersupport, 9 panels, each: 520 × 520 mm.
[*Tate Gallery, London/Art Resource, New York*]

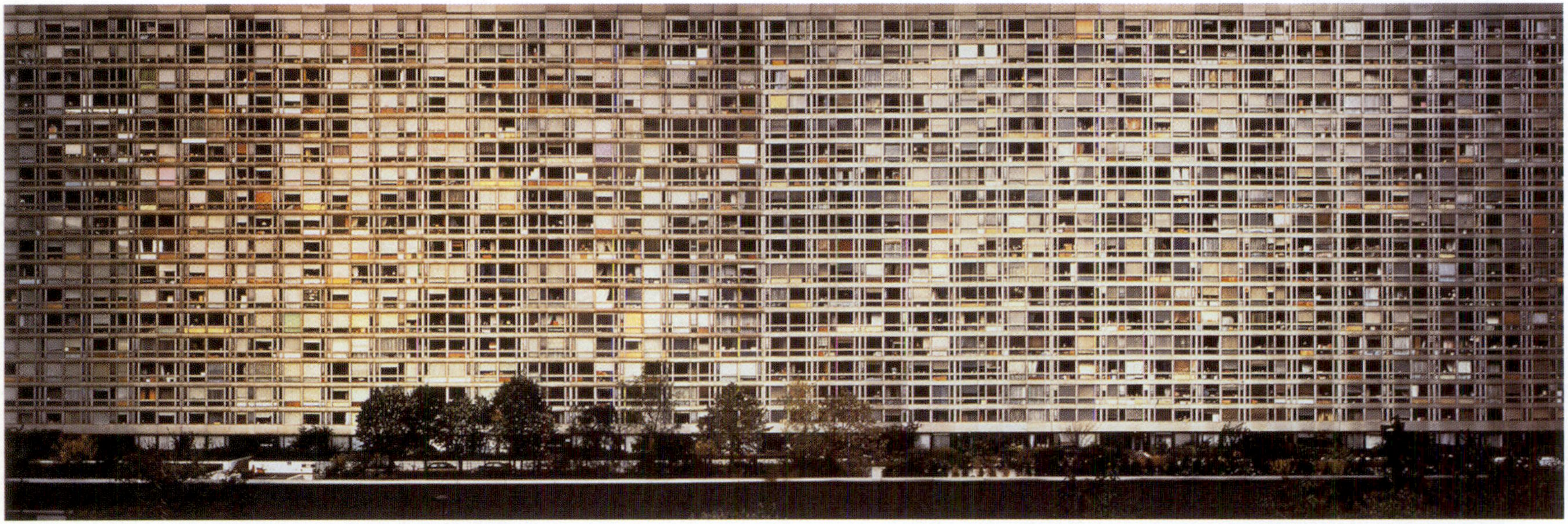

Andrea Gursky, Paris, Montparnasse, 1993.
[*Tate Gallery, London/Art Resource, New York*]

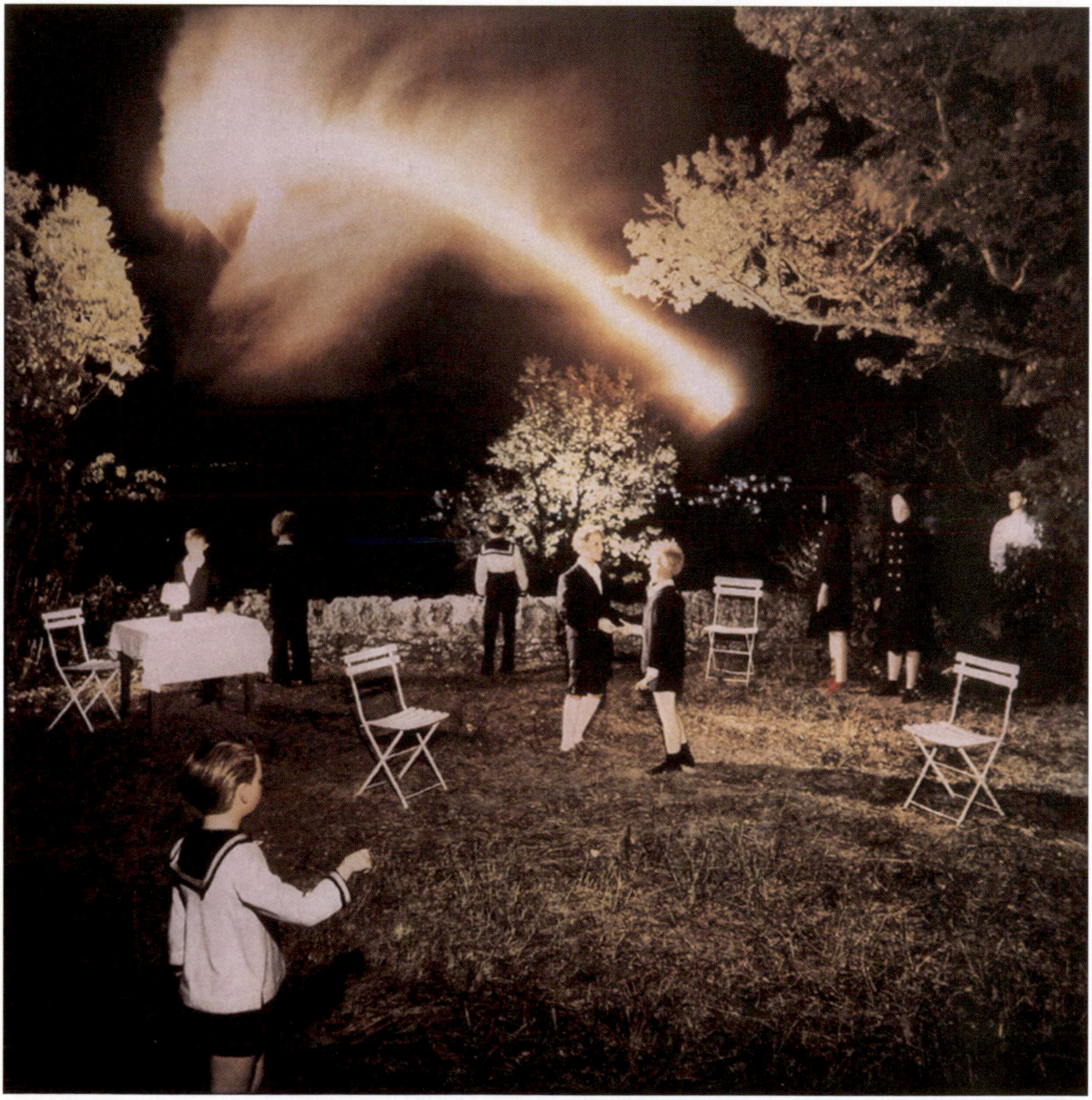

Bernard Faucon, The Comet, 1982.
[*CNAC/MNAM/Dist. Réunion des Musées Nationaux/Art Resource, New York*]

D

DADA

Dada was a visual and literary arts movement known for promoting an anti-art agenda that began in Zurich, Switzerland, during World War I. However, there were many independent Dada groups in other cities, particularly Berlin, Paris and New York. In 1916, Hugo Ball and Emmy Hennings founded the Cabaret Voltaire in Zurich and quickly attracted the participation of Richard Huelsenbeck, Tristan Tzara, Hans Arp, Marcel Janco, and Hans Richter. Later that year, a periodical sharing the name, *Cabaret Voltaire*, published the first use of the term Dada. Huelsenbeck claimed that the term was selected by the random act of stabbing a dictionary with a knife and adopting the pierced word. Tzara emphasized the term's polyglot appeal in his "Dada Manifesto 1918":

> We read in papers that the negroes of the Kroo race call the tail of the sacred cow: DADA. A cube, and a mother, in a certain region of Italy, are called: DADA. The word for a hobby-horse, a children's nurse, a double affirmative in Russian and Romanian, is also: DADA.
>
> (Huelsenbeck 123)

At its essence, Dada initiated an anti-art aesthetic. The dehumanizing violence of World War I forced these artists to question the rationalism of European culture and call for a radical revolution, informed by both Anarchism and Communism. Expressing revulsion with socio-political ideologies that justify reactionary nationalism and rampant materialism, Dada artists sought to shock the bourgeoisie by questioning the values and motives of dominant social institutions. To accomplish these goals, many Dadaists experimented with photographic materials and processes.

In 1917, Christian Schad, associated with Dada in Zurich, used photomechanical materials to contest conventional art-making strategies. By placing variously textured materials onto photosensitive paper and exposing the arrangements to light, Schad made cameraless images that defied artistic conventions. These art works embraced chance and recalled the sudden shifts in scale and abrupt juxtapositions associated with Cubist and Futurist collages. Tzara, who acquired many of these works, named them "Schadographs," which exemplifies the Dadaists' penchant for word play; the term is both a homophone for "shadowgraph," a process used by William Henry Fox Talbot, and an echo of the German word "schaden," which means damaged and thereby epitomizes the group's despair (Marien 247).

The Berlin Dada group, more than other manifestations of Dada, embraced the technique of montage. By cutting, arranging, and pasting fragments of photographs published in magazines and newspapers, artists such as Hannah Höch, Raoul Hausmann, John Heartfield, and George Grosz illustrated the pace of the machine age and the uncertainties of modernity. Using mass-produced images in a technique borrowed from folk traditions—recombinations of photo fragments in family albums is a custom that began in the 19th century—the Berlin Dadaists undermined the aura of aesthetic elitism. These artists hoped that their startling compositions of fragments of reality would provoke responses from spectators inured by mass media's propagandistic use of photographs.

Claims for the origins of this art form were hotly debated: Hausmann and Höch claimed to have been inspired by a composite image of the Kaiser and his ancestors they saw in 1918; Heartfield and Grosz asserted they began making photomontages on postcards they sent from the warfront in 1915 and 1916; the Russian constructivist George Klutsis also claimed to invent the form. Regardless of who first used cut photographs in their art, the technique clearly resonated with numerous artists seeking ways to effectively critique social institutions. By bringing together disparate photographic shards, the Berlin Dada Group conveyed distortions in time and space that defined the modern city. Given that photographs expose the immediate and fragmentary nature of urban life, photomontages enabled practitioners to produce satirical social commentaries rich with sardonic irony. Although Hausmann and Grosz both produced compelling photomontages, the works of Heartfield and Höch have received the greatest scholarly attention.

John Heartfield created photomontages to counter the veil of veracity ascribed to photographs: "I found out how you can fool people with photos" (Pachnicke, 14). Heartfield's photomontages were used by the Malik Verlag, his brother Wieland Hertzfeld's publishing house. The earliest of these was "Everyone his own Football," the cover image for the first issue of *Illustrierte Halbmonatsschrift*. Published in 1919, the cover included images of German political figures arranged on a paper fan below the caption "Who's the Prettiest of them All?" Heartfield quickly dispensed with this straightfoward approach and adopted a more sophisticated technique during the 1920s and 1930s. From 1929–1939, Heartfield contributed 237 full-page photomontages to *Workers' Illustrated Newspaper*, a Communist publication. These images were sharply critical of Hitler and the National Socialist party as typified by works such as *Adolf, the Superman: Swallows Gold and Spouts Junk* (1932), which uses a photo of Hitler speaking at a political rally with an image of gold coins delineating his esophagus and stomach; in *Hurray, the Butter is All Gone!* (1935) Heartfield depicts a German family eating a bicycle in a dining room wallpapered with the swastika emblem and a portrait of Hitler looming in the corner. Heartfield did not take photographs himself, but used images from newspapers, magazines, books, and photograph archives and occasionally had photographs taken when he could not find an image that met specific needs.

Hannah Höch's photomontages were more intuitive and startling in their random shifts in scale and eclectic assortment of source material. She sought to reveal the superficiality of the images she used by suggesting possible alternative realities. Höch's photomontages challenged the seductive surface of photographic reality and thereby the status quo of the bourgeoisie. Her *Cut with the Kitchen Knife Dada through the Last Weimar Beer Belly Cultural Epoch of Germany* (1919–1920) typifies this effort. The image, far larger than most photomontages, is densely packed with images of political leaders, athletes, Dada artists, and leading cultural figures, including Albert Einstein. Consistent with Höch's concerns regarding women's rights, females are granted prominent roles. For instance, an exotic dancer tickles Wilhelm II under the chin, and the central figure around which the composition oscillates is an amalgamation of a dancer's body and Käthe Kollwitz's face, which has been pierced by a spear. The playfulness of the dancing body adjacent to the pain implied by the penetrating spear exemplifies a dialectic between hostility and joy that resonates throughout Höch's work. In an effort to liberate women from their limited societal roles, Höch's work often juxtaposes fashionably dressed females with machinery to achieve a metonymic effect, whereby women are presented as something other than a sexual object, mother, or wife (Lavin 19–22). From 1924 to 1934, Höch worked on *From an Ethnographic Museum*, which combined images from German ethnographic collections with contemporary women. Although Höch was not critical of contemporary ethnographic attitudes, she used these images to continue her critique of European gender definitions.

The New York and Parisian Dada groups also used photography, if not photomontage, specifically. Notable among these artists were Man Ray and Marcel Duchamp. In 1921, these two figures met in New York and collaborated on the only issue of *New York Dada*. The cover depicted a perfume bottle to which a photograph by Man Ray of Duchamp dressed as his female altar ego Rose Sélavy had been affixed. The magazine was a commercial failure and both men went to Paris in the same year to work alongside other Dada artists. The Paris Group included many who went on to establish Surrealism, notably André Breton, Louis Aragon, Frances Picabia, and Max Ernst. While in Paris, Man Ray adopted a cameraless practice similar to Christian Schad's "Schadographs" in the early 1920s. However, unlike Schad, Man Ray used three-dimensional objects to produce his "Rayographs," or photograms. These works typify the Dada spirit by effecting an unexpected dialectical synthesis between abstraction and figuration.

Man Ray later was associated with Surrealism, whereas Duchamp continued exploring chance operations typifying Dada anti-art irreverence. In this effort, Duchamp created numerous enigmatic self-portraits. One such image showed the artist's face covered in shaving cream arranged to suggest the beard and horns of a satyr. This photograph was montaged with a photographic detail of a roulette table to create thirty fake 500 franc bonds. These "bonds," described as "artificial drawings" by Duchamp, were issued in an elaborate, half-joke, half-serious effort to win money gambling at Monte Carlo (1924). Such works illustrate many of the strategies and techniques of Dada. The photomontaged "bonds" were attempts to destabilize and undermine the status quo upon which the bourgeoisie's social dominance relied. Although Dada's anti-art efforts were short-lived, their influence persists to this day.

Brian Winkenweder

See also: **Futurism; Heartfield, John; History of Photography: Interwar Years; Höch, Hannah; Manipulation; Man Ray; Montage; Photogram; Surrealism**

Further Reading

Foster, Stephen, ed. *Crisis and the Arts: The History of Dada*. New York: G.K. Hall, 1996.

Gale, Matthew. *Dada & Surrealism*. London: Phaidon, 1997.

Hays, K. Michael. "Photomontage and Its Audiences, Berlin Circa 1922." *Harvard Architectural Review* (1988): 19–31.

Huelsenbeck, Richard, ed. *The Dada Almanac (1920)*. Malcom Green, English edition, London: Atlas Press, 1992.

Lavin, Maud. *Cut with the Kitchen Knife: The Weimar Photomontages of Hannah Höch*. New Haven: Yale University Press, 1993.

Marien, Mary Warner. *Photography: A Cultural History*. New York: Prentice, 2002.

Pachnicke, Peter and Klaus Honnef, eds. *John Heartfield*. New York: Abrams, 1992.

Pegrum, Mark. *Challenging Modernity: Dada between Modern and Postmodern*. New York: Bergahn Books, 2000.

Rubin, William, ed. *Dada, Surrealism and their Heritage*. New York: Museum of Modern Art, 1968.

Teitelbaum, Matthew, ed. *Montage and Modern Life, 1919–1942*. Cambridge: The MIT Press, 1992.

LOUISE DAHL-WOLFE

American

When Louise Dahl-Wolfe joined the ranks of *Harper's Bazaar* in 1936—a professional association that would last 22 years—fashion photography was still a fledgling field. At the turn of the century, publishers had only begun to realize the benefits of magazines geared towards women. The lavishly illustrated monthlies were equally slow to accept photographs in their pages. Moreover, of the handful of commercial photographers who focused on fashion at the time—from Baron de Meyer, Edward Steichen, and George Hoyningen-Huene to Horst P. Horst—there were few women. During her long career, Dahl-Wolfe recorded highly modern visions of feminine apparel and, by extension, sophisticated glimpses into society's mores at a time when the role of the "American woman" was undergoing radical change.

The youngest of three daughters, Dahl-Wolfe was born in Alameda, California in 1895. Believing it was lucky to have initials that spelled a word, her mother named her Louise Emma Augusta Dahl. The Dahls had come to America from Norway in 1872. A marine engineer, Dahl-Wolfe's father had taken her to shipyards, fostering in her a sense of adventure and the knowledge that there was no place a woman couldn't go. Desiring to be an artist from an early age, Dahl-Wolfe was urged by her sister to attend the

San Francisco Institute of Art. Beginning in 1914 and over the next six years, Dahl-Wolfe studied drawing, anatomy, design, and painting—subjects that would form the foundation for her subsequent career in photography. She learned the nuances of color arrangement, which she later put to use in her work with Kodachrome, one of the first commercially available color films. Her studies with the figure would also pay off, helping her to realize how the body's form behaves beneath clothes.

During the early twentieth century, California was undergoing a cultural renaissance and San Francisco was its epicenter. Besides a cadre of fellow Californian painters, Dahl-Wolfe was exposed to masters such as Pablo Picasso and Henri Matisse at the 1915 Panama-Pacific International Exposition held in San Francisco. A year later, she attended a performance of the experimental Ballets Russes, featuring sets by Picasso, Georges Braque, and Andre Derain, music of Claude Debussy and Igor Stravinsky, and choreography by Vaslav Nijinsky. This fertile cross-disciplinary climate seemed to foster in Dahl-Wolfe an appreciation of all art forms that would later manifest itself in her work: she posed models in front of avant-garde artworks and the leading visual, performing, and literary artists—including Isamu Noguchi, Jean Cocteau, and Colette—numbered among her portrait sitters.

It was in 1921, however, that Dahl-Wolfe was first introduced to the power of photography as an art form. She had been working as an electric sign designer when a friend introduced her to Anne Brigman, a photographer whom had been a member of Alfred Steiglitz's Photo Secession. Dahl-Wolfe visited Brigman's Oakland studio and was "bowled over" by Brigman's daring images of nude female figures posed in harmony with nature. Subsequently, Dahl-Wolfe and a few other art students made their own "Anne Brigmans" using a Brownie box camera.

Inspired, Dahl-Wolfe practiced photography whenever and wherever she could, even producing a makeshift enlarger from a Ghiradelli chocolate box as well as a darkroom light powered by a Ford Model A car battery. She wandered the streets of San Francisco with photojournalist Consuela Kanaga, meeting other Bay Area photographers of import, including Francis Bruguière, Dorothea Lange, and Edward Weston. Some of her best training involved photographing store models from a friend's showroom. "Those girls were at least forty years of age," she wrote in her autobiography *A Photographer's Scrapbook* (1984), "I practiced lighting on them, to get them to look chic, elegant, beautiful, and yet natural—and that took work."

In 1923, Dahl-Wolfe left for New York to study interior design and architecture, returning to work in a California decorating firm. At Kanaga's insistence following her mother's death, Dahl-Wolfe left for an excursion abroad. While in North Africa, she spotted Tennessee sculptor Meyer (Mike) Wolfe from a train window and was immediately enamored. The couple wed a year later and spent time in the Great Smoky Mountains. Some of Dahl-Wolfe's most moving portraits were taken during her time in Tennessee, including *Mrs. Ramsey—Tennessee Mountain Woman* (her first published photograph in 1933 in *Vanity Fair*) and sensitive images of African-Americans. Indeed, her observant portraits of Nashville self-taught sculptor William Edmondson helped him to secure a 1937 exhibition at the Museum of Modern Art, New York, as the first African-American to have a solo show at that institution.

While other designers and photographers translated the machine aesthetic into fashion or sought to capture Greek statues anew, Dahl-Wolfe preferred to show active women who paralleled the increasing freedom they (and she) found in society; what was dubbed the "New Woman" in public became the "New Look" in fashion. Together with her husband, Dahl-Wolfe created sets that she wove into daring, sometimes surrealistic, compositions. At the same time women were leaving the home and entering into the workforce, Dahl-Wolfe also pioneered the practice of photographing in exotic locales, including Guatemala, Cuba, Brazil, and Spain.

Throughout her career, Dahl-Wolfe repeatedly turned down offers to work for *Vanity Fair* and *Condé Nast*, accepting only *Harper's Bazaar's* situations because it offered her the freedom to work in her own studio. In fact, when a newly hired art director peered through her viewfinder to check on a shot in 1958, she promptly quit, retiring altogether in 1960. All told, *Harper's Bazaar* published over 600 of her photographs, plus the 86 that graced their covers. Nonetheless, Dahl-Wolfe never believed photography to be equal to painting. "Photography's not a fine art," she explained, "though you can use it to interpret in artistic ways....Some people are just better at it than others." Dahl-Wolfe certainly was; she was the living example of the daring forthright women she captured with her camera. As Richard Avedon, the leader of the next generation of fashion photographers, put it, "She was the bar we all measured ourselves against."

Leslie K. Brown

See also: **Brownie; Bruguière, Francis; de Meyer, Baron; Fashion Photography; Horst, Horst P.; Hoyningen-Huene, George; Lange, Dorothea; Museum of Modern Art; Nast, Condè; Photo Secession; Steichen, Edward; Stieglitz, Alfred; Weston, Edward**

Biography

Born in Alameda, California, 19 November 1895. Attended San Francisco Institute of Art, studying design and color with Rudolph Shaeffer, painting with Frank Van Sloan, 1914–1920; studied interior decoration, design, and architecture, New York, 1923. Worked as electric sign designer, California; assistant to Beth Armstrong of Armstrong, Carter, and Kenyon, San Francisco, 1924; photographed food for *Woman's Home Companion* and fashion for Saks Fifth Avenue, New York, 1933; staff photographer for *Harper's Bazaar* 1936–1958; freelanced for *Sports Illustrated* 1957–1960 and *Vogue*, 1959; retired from photography, 1960. Major holdings of work are at the Center for Creative Photography, Tucson, Arizona; National Museum of Women in the Arts, Washington, D.C.; and Cheekwood Museum of Art, Nashville, Tennessee. Died in Allendale, New Jersey, 11 December 1989.

Individual Exhibitions

1980 *The Fashion Photography of Louise Dahl-Wolfe*; Cheekwood Fine Arts Center, Nashville, Tennessee
1984 *Louise Dahl-Wolfe*; Cheekwood Fine Arts Center, Nashville, Tennessee
Louise Dahl-Wolfe; Staley-Wise Gallery, New York, New York
1985 *Louise Dahl-Wolfe: A 90th Birthday Salute*; Museum of Contemporary Photography, Chicago, Illinois
1987 *Louise Dahl-Wolfe: A Retrospective Exhibition*; National Museum of Women in the Arts, Washington, D.C.
1994 *Louise Dahl-Wolfe: The Harper's Bazaar Portraits 1938–1958*; Society of the Four Arts, Palm Beach, Florida
2000 *Louise Dahl-Wolfe: The American Image*; Fashion Institute of Technology, New York, New York, and the Center for Creative Photography, Tucson, Arizona

Group Exhibitions

1937 *Photography: 1839–1937*; Museum of Modern Art, New York, New York
1955 *Louise Dahl-Wolfe and Meyer Wolfe*; Southern Vermont Art Center, Manchester, Vermont
Fashion: Seven Decades; Hofstra University, Hempstead, New York
1965 *Louise Dahl-Wolfe: Photographs/Meyer Wolfe: Sculpture and Drawings*; County Art Gallery, Long Island, New York
1975 *Women of Photography, An Historical Survey*; San Francisco Museum of Modern Art, San Francisco, California
1977 *The History of Fashion Photography*; International Museum of Photography and Film, George Eastman House, Rochester, New York (traveled to San Francisco Museum of Art, California, Cincinnati Art Institute, Ohio, Museum of Fine Arts, St. Petersburg, Florida)
1979 *Recollections: Ten Women of Photography*; International Center of Photography, New York, New York
1979 *Fashion Photographs*; Cheekwood, the Botanical Gardens and Fine Arts Center, Nashville, Tennessee
1982 *Color as Form: The History of Color Photography*; International Museum of Photography and Film, George Eastman House, Rochester, New York and the Corcoran Gallery of Art, Washington, D.C.
1983 *Louise Dahl-Wolfe and Paul Outerbridge*; Grey Art Gallery, New York, New York
1984 *Style: An Exhibition of Fashion Photographs*; Vision Gallery, Boston, Massachusetts
1986 *Fifty Years of Modern Color Photography*; Photokina, Cologne, Germany
1993 *A Second Look: Women Photographers from the Collections of the HRHRC*; Harry Ransom Humanities Research Center, University of Texas, Austin, Texas
1999 *The Art of William Edmondson*; Cheekwood Museum of Art, Nashville, Tennessee, and traveling

Selected Works

Mrs. Ramsey—Tennessee Mountain Woman, 1931, published in *Vanity Fair*, 1933
William Edmondson, Sculptor, 1933
Night Bathing, Harper's Bazaar, June 1939
Lauren Bacall for the American Red Cross Donor Service, Cover of Harper's Bazaar, March 1943
Cover, Harper's Bazaar, September 1949
Suzy Parker in Christian Dior Hat, 1950, published in *Harper's Bazaar*, April 1953
Colette, 1951

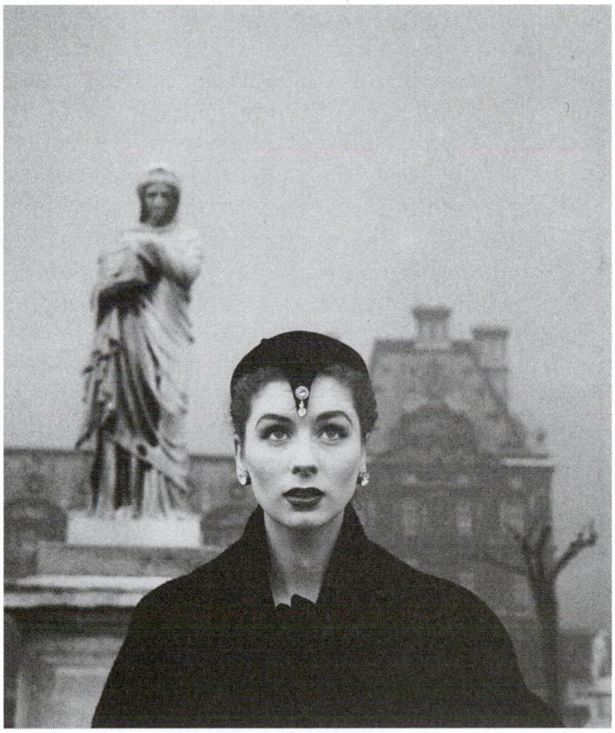

Louise Dahl-Wolfe, Suzy Parker in Christian Dior Hat, Tuileries, Paris, 1950, Gelatin silver print.
[*Collection Center for Creative Photography, The University of Arizona © 1998 Arizona Board of Regents*]

Isamu Noguchi, 1955
Jean Cocteau, 1955

Further Reading

Dahl-Wolfe, Louise. *Louise Dahl-Wolfe: A Photographer's Scrapbook*. New York: St. Martin's/Marek, 1984.
Edmonson, William. *The Art of William Edmondson*. Foreward by Robert Farris Thompson. Jackson, MS: University of Mississippi Press and Cheekwood Museum of Art, 1999.
Euclaire, Sally. *Louise Dahl-Wolfe: A Retrospective Exhibition*. Washington, DC: National Museum of Women in the Arts, 1987.
The Fashion Photography of Louise Dahl-Wolfe. Nashville: Cheekwood Fine Arts Center, 1980.
Fonssagrives, Lisa. *Three Decades of Fashion Photography*. London: Thames + Hudson, 1996.
Goldberg, Vicki, and Nan Richardson. *Louise Dahl-Wolfe: The American Image*. New York: Harry N. Abrams, 2000.
Hall-Duncan, Nancy. *The History of Fashion Photography*. New York: International Museum of Photography and Alpine Book Co., 1979.
Mann, Margery, and Ann Noggle. *Women of Photography: An Historical Survey*. San Francisco: San Francisco Museum of Art, 1975.
Mitchell, Margaretta K. *Recollections: Ten Women of Photography*. New York: Viking, 1979.
Rosenblum, Naomi. *A History of Women Photographers*. New York: Abbeville Press, 1994.
Steele, Valerie. *Fifty Years of Fashion: New Look to Now*. Hew Haven and London: Yale University Press, 1997.
Trahey, Jane, ed. *Harper's Bazaar: One Hundred Years of the American Female*. New York: Random House, 1967.

DARKROOM

Film photography's science is about the interplay of light, emulsion, and chemicals working in unison, with the aid of the human hand and eye, to create a masterful print ready for framing and mounting. To understand the history of photography it is also important to grasp the craft and science behind creating a photography print from negative film. Yet at the end of the twentieth century, many were bidding farewell to photography's traditional darkroom techniques, welcoming the world of digital photography and its computerized darkroom.

The darkroom is the setting for two processes: developing film and printing and developing photographs. The pleasure that can be experienced in producing—from start to finish—a perfect negative and a perfect photographic print is one that has driven photographers since the medium's inception. Some photographers, like Ansel Adams, earned a reputation as being obsessive about creating the perfect photographic print and preached technical perfection as the highest form of photographic artistry, creating systems (the zone system) and a school (Group f/64) dedicated to the pursuit of photographic perfection.

There are of course opportunities for myriad frustrations in the darkroom as well and a wide range of practices that reflect photographer's relationships to the darkroom can be noted. Many professional photographers specialize in shooting film only, send to commercial laboratories for development, and supervise the printing of their photographs by the same labs or by an assistant. Some gladly give over the developing of film to commercial labs, yet create their own prints in the darkroom.

Even if one is never going to use a darkroom, in order to understand and appreciate all facets of photography, it is helpful to understand basic darkroom equipment and how this equipment is utilized. If one is a photographer, it is essential knowledge. Setting up a darkroom comes with no short supply of equipment or expense. Film processing and print processing require specialized equipment and spaces. Chemical mixing, film processing, the creation of proof sheets, the enlarging process, and print processing, fixing, drying, and finally, mounting are the steps required to turn the exposed film into a finished photograph.

Film Processing

A pitch-black closet or space is needed to process film. This space cannot be penetrated by even the smallest amount of light or undeveloped film will be ruined. Even a safelight suitable for print processing offers too much illumination and will wreak havoc on unprocessed film.

Traditional black-and-white film processing requires a sink with a faucet, processing tanks for roll film, trays for sheet film, timers (with a second hand), thermometers for the processing tanks, chemicals, sponges, scissors, a negative carrier, a squeegee, and a drying cabinet. To develop roll film, a bottle opener is generally used to open the film cartridge. In complete darkness, the photographer carefully and gently extracts the film and rolls it onto a reel, which fits inside a light-tight processing tank. The reel is a small stainless steel spiral. Hand placement is very important to avoid scratches or fingerprints on the negative, and the film must be touching only along its sprocket hole edges when transferring from cartridge to steel reel. The film should rest as smoothly as its original position within the cartridge, as lumps in the film will be developed irregularly by the developing agent. Black streaks, blotches, rows of spaced marks, transparent negatives, and streaks indicate problems when the developer touched (or did not touch) the film. These problems may also indicate that light reached the negative during the loading, light leaked in the developing tank, the temperature of the developer was miscalculated, or the film was not left in the developer for the proper length of time. Student photographers practice loading a roll of old negative film onto the reel in daylight until the motion and task become easier.

After transfer to the reel, the film is inserted into the sealed, lightproof development tank. The film developer generally provides instructions regarding chemical ratios, the number of times to agitate the tank, and the amount of time in each stage of development, none of which is strictly standard. For example, a photographed subject might lend itself nicely to cross processing for intensity of contrast. "Cross processing" is the use of color slide film chemicals to develop negative film and vice versa. So called "push processing" is used for overexposed or underexposed film, increasing graininess and contrast, and decreasing details in shadows. "Pull processing" intentionally overexposes the film to bring out details in the dark areas. Cross, push, and pull processing are experimental techniques to consider once one is confident in processing film. After processing with the developer, it is discarded and the film is washed with water introduced into the tank until all developer has been removed. Sheet film is similarly processed, using trays instead of tanks.

Upon the completion of film processing, the negatives are no longer light-sensitive and generally are placed in a dust-free cabinet to dry, with roll films weighted to prevent curling. Once the negatives are dry, a light box and a loupe are helpful to decipher the quality of the negatives. "Thin" negatives with little detail indicate that the film was underexposed, underdeveloped, or both; "thick" negatives with dense areas of blackness and few fully transparent (white) areas indicate the film was overexposed, overdeveloped, or both. Recognizing the quality of the negative suggests adjustments available through further darkroom techniques to create the optimum print from that negative. Roll negatives are traditionally cut into strips of five or six frames and stored in archival sleeves (traditionally waxed paper, which has been supplanted by plastic), then placed in an indexed book of some sort. Larger format films are also stored in archival sleeves.

Print Processing

During the print process, light projected through the negative film strikes the surface of the light-sensitive photographic paper, most commonly silver bromide and gelatin. The simplest way to make a print, however, is by direct exposure to light, which results in a photogram. Most photographs, however, result from the transfer of the image on a negative to the photographic paper, either through direct contact (contact printing) or enlargement, which requires a relatively complicated piece of equipment that combines changeable lenses with a built-in light source.

Yet no matter what method is used to expose the photographic paper, the developing process is consistent: the exposed paper is placed in a bath where the chemicals react with the silvers in the papers, producing patterns of light and dark that must be stabilized with further chemical treatments.

Most darkrooms for processing prints are painted white to reveal chemical stains, which show up as brownish, indicating areas that have been contaminated. Ideally a darkroom has both hot and cold running water, good ventilation, a minimum of natural light, and electricity, although many a fine photograph was created under less than optimal darkroom conditions, including many early photographs, which were developed literally "in the field." Black paper is generally sufficient to block out light remnants and light leakage can easily be accessed by standing in the darkroom for about five minutes. Many photographers work at night if light control is a problem. For the home darkroom, while bathrooms or kitchens provide many of the necessary features, these areas should be avoided for obvious health reasons: the chemicals used in traditional photography can be toxic if not properly handled, are corrosive, and emit fumes. A properly ventilated darkroom continuously extracts fumes and brings in dust-free air, has proper plumbing to handle the corrosive chemicals, and stands apart from everyday activities to prevent contamination.

Most home and all professional darkrooms feature "dry" and "wet" areas. The dry area of the darkroom ideally is dust-free and contains the enlarger, timer, paper trimmer, and cabinet for negatives and paper storage. The wet area houses the mixed chemicals, including developer, stop bath, fixer and toners, water, various trays, a sink, and drying racks.

For print processing, the entire darkroom can be illuminated with the safelight. This light is generally a red or a low-wattage amber filtered bulb, which relies on the fact that most photographic papers are not sensitive to this end of the light spectrum. Yet any safelight too close to photographic paper will fog it to some degree, and papers left exposed for prolonged time periods will also fog.

When working with film, most photographers' first step is to create contact or proof sheets, which provide a one-to-one record of the image on the negatives. Specialized holders are available to flatten the negatives against a glass frame into which is inserted a sheet of photo paper; the holder is then placed under the light of the enlarger. A short burst of light from the enlarger exposes the paper, which then is processed. The contact sheet is not only used to better judge which frames are best to be printed, but provides a record of the exposed film.

When working with films that require enlargement (generally 35 mm and 2 ¼ and 4 × 5 formats, although any film can be enlarged), the negative is inserted into a holder, which is placed between the enlarger's light source, a large lens called a condenser that focuses or diffuses the light, and its interchangeable lens with an aperture to control sharpness and depth-of-field. The photographic paper is generally placed in an easel frame, which holds the paper flat, preventing distortion of the image as it is projected through the enlarger. Many modern enlargers have built-in timers, or an independent timer is coordinated with the manual switching on and off of the light source. Many photographers use trip strips where a piece of paper is exposed in increasingly longer settings through the same negative in order to determine the optimal exposure for the final print.

Enlargers traditionally have been manufactured as "diffuser" or "condenser" enlargers. The diffuser enlarger spreads the light more evenly across the negative; hence, the contrast is not as apparent. A diffuser enlarger is used to make color prints, but offers satisfactory black and white capabilities, whereas the condenser enlarger offers excellent capability for sharp, high contrast images. The condenser enlarger focuses the light, directing it straight through the negative to the lens. Among the enlarger's capabilities is changing the distance between the lens and the paper and thus controlling the size of the final image. A sharp, well-exposed negative allows a greater range of size of the final print, yet even a perfectly-exposed negative becomes "softer" as the distance between the negative and the photographic paper is increased.

As well, during the enlargement exposure, dodging, burning-in, and cropping can be employed. The aperture of the enlarger can be set at a smaller opening requiring a longer light exposure, and thus allowing further manipulation of the amount of light falling on any given area of the photo paper.

All manner of specialized filters and screens to create specialized effects may also be employed, such as filters that increase contrast or provide textures (such as "stone-washed") or patterns (such as "herringbone"). Fogging or solarization can also be affected before the paper has been further processed.

After the paper has been exposed, it is "fixed" generally in a bath of commonly called "hypo" that stops the developing process by dissolving any remaining sensitive silver from the print. Some photographers use a stop bath between the developer and fixer. The stop bath neutralizes the developing agent. Advanced darkroom printmakers often mix their own chemicals for effects rather than adhere to the prepackaged instructions. Darkroom photography is about experimenting with the science of light and chemical reactions.

As these chemicals break down in the light they must be stored in tightly sealed and lightproof plastic jugs. Disposal of used or unneeded photographic chemicals should be done with extreme care. Kodak offers helpful information on its web site.

Once the print is chemically processed, it must be carefully washed to remove all traces of the various chemicals in which it has been bathed. Further manipulation by toning agents may be employed while the print is still wet. While some of these effects are strictly aesthetic, some, like gold-toning, increase the final print's archival qualities. The print is then dried in a dust-free environment.

The color darkroom follows the same basic procedures, with added attention on the variety of chemicals used, their optimal specific temperatures and use of filters to achieve and modulate the color. Commercial darkrooms feature all processes in fully automated systems, which generally allow for less intervention for various artistic effects.

TRICIA LOUVAR

See also: **Adams, Ansel; Burning-in; Conservation; Contact Printing; Cropping; Developing Processes; Digital Photography; Dodging; Dye Transfer; Exposure; Film; Filters; Group f/64; Hand Coloring and Hand Toning; Image Construction: Perspective; Manipulation; Non-Silver Processes; Photogram; Print Processes; Safelight; Sandwiched Negatives; Solarization**

Further Reading

Adams, Ansel. *The Print*. Boston: Bulfinch, 1995.
Anchell, Steve and Bill Troop. *The Film Developing Cookbook*. New York: Focal Press, 1998.
Curtin, Dennis, Joe DeMaio, and Roberta Worth. *The New Darkroom Handbook*. 2nd ed., New York: Focal Press, 1997.
Grimm, Tom. *The Basic Darkroom Book*. 3rd ed. New York: Plume, 1999.
Kodak. *Kodak Black & White Darkroom Dataguide*, 6th ed. Rochester, New York: Silver Pixel, 2001.
Langford, Michael. *The Darkroom Handbook*. New York: Alfred A. Knopf, 1984.

JUDY DATER

American

Judy Dater's career in photography as an artist and teacher spans nearly 40 years. Beginning with black-and-white portraits in the 1960s, Dater's work has richly evolved alongside the changing technologies of photography. Although primarily known for nude portraiture, Dater's work inherently defies narrow classification due to the complexity and range of her subjects, the emphasis she places on the photographic event itself, and the mental exchanges between artist and subject. These aspects of physical and psychological dialogues turn the traditional posing of portrait photography into an event or performance that is memorialized in the photograph. Throughout the 1960s and 1970s, Dater's cutting-edge style and impulse for an image to act as something or someone, rather than to merely represent it, led to comparisons to artists such as Diane Arbus and Richard Avedon.

Born in Hollywood, California in 1941 to a middle-class family, Dater's exposure to image and performance in Hollywood coincided with her father's work as a movie theater owner. To pursue her interest in the arts, Dater attended the University of California, Los Angeles as a student of drawing and painting in 1959. Three years later, she transferred to San Francisco State University where she studied under photographer Jack Welpott, and by 1966, Dater graduated with a master's degree in photography. Welpott and Dater worked very closely together, and in 1964, Welpott introduced Dater to Imogen Cunningham, a photographer noted for her pioneering male nudes. Cunningham would prove to be a singular inspiration in Dater's life and work. During this period of study, Dater had her first exhibition at the Aardvark Gallery and Bindery in San Francisco, where her nude portraits addressed America's questioning of cultural values and norms in the 1960s.

Dater's work gained widespread recognition following her 1972 exhibition at the Witkin Gallery in New York. The open and direct confrontation or relationship between Dater and the subjects of her portraits bore evidence that her work inspired reactions. The nude portraits expressed personal confrontations and an intense self-awareness that led Dater to expand her understanding of the portrait, and she began a quest to further expose the psychological aspects of her subjects. Two of her most recognizable photographs include several characteristic elements of Dater's work. In *Twinka* (1970), a photograph of the model Twinka Theibaud, the image implies that the nude in the sheer dress has been caught in some sort of urgent exchange with the camera. Dater also photographed the woman whom she most admired, Imogen Cunningham, as one of her subjects in *Imogen and Twinka* (1974). This photograph documents the tenuous relationship between artist (Cunningham) and nude subject (Twinka) as the model hesitantly peeks out from behind a tree, encountering or confronting the photographer.

In 1971, Dater and Welpott married, and their professional and personal lives intertwined further with their most significant collaboration: the 1975 publication of photographs, *Women and Other Visions*. This collaboration occurred amidst the 1970s feminist movement and culminated in a series of photographs of women taken by both Dater and Welpott. This event resulted in identifying the differences between the two artists' styles and effects on their nude subjects, read specifically in the sociosexual context of the time. Dater deduced that when she was the photographer, the female subjects emitted a certain self-realization. Focusing vigilantly on the photo shoot's time and place, Dater selected the photograph's precise moment while also carefully observing her subjects' expressions and body language. She aimed to reveal an inner emotion in her women sitters; an image that could invoke what the sitter felt about her relationship to the photographer. This project reinforced that Dater's style focused on the psychological elements of a portrait rather than the aesthetics or singularity of the subject. The clothes, environment, face, and body appeared to disconnect with the subject's inner psyche. Dater's interest in the action of revealing reduced the body to a part, rather than the whole, of the image. This implied that the whole could not be viewed without acknowledging the exchange between the viewer and the subject.

In contrast, the women of Welpott's photographs have been described as noticeably aware of their bodies. For Dater, this self-awareness reduced the possibility of expressing psychological elements that do not stem from the sexual or sensual. Welpott's subjects appeared to project an image of themselves, rather than exposing the reality of themselves.

After divorcing Welpott in 1977, Dater began exploring the use of color photography. Her first color photographs were taken during a trip to Egypt between 1979 and 1980. The resulting images placed emphasis on the aesthetics of color and contrast in relationship to the subject's psyche. The images from this period included many of daily life and landscape, while others are portraits of surprising depth in Dater's exchanges with unfamiliar faces. While focusing on the changes that color photography brought to her work, Dater continued to draw inner emotion from her spontaneous encounters with Egyptian subjects.

The 1980s welcomed strong recognition for Dater throughout the United States and Europe. Her consistent inquiry into the elements of performance and character studies continued to broaden her body of work. She moved to New Mexico in 1980 with her partner, artist Sam Samore, and began looking at herself as a subject, developing works that portrayed herself as a variety of female archetypes. Like Cindy Sherman, Dater's self-portraits examined the full embodiment of social stereotypes, acknowledging the body's role in social exchanges. The series of photographs from 1982 includes *Ms. Clingfree* as the sexy housewife, *Leopard Woman* as the carnal vamp, and *The Magician* as the woman who works miracles. Studying these female archetypes, Dater engaged in an exchange of control as both the photographer and as the subject. Dater performed in a self-designed environment, offering her body and character only as much as, or possibly as far as, the camera and photographer would allow. Other self-portraits depict a nude Dater, returning to the idea that the body is only a part, not the whole, of any exchange, event, or environment. Her nude self-portrait sequence, also from 1982, shows Dater's body as an active object among the desert landscape of New Mexico, recalling the earth performances of artist Ana Mendieta. In acknowledging the complex psychological elements of self-realization and the relationship between photographer and subject, Dater produced photographs of unshakable character. In 1983, she returned to San Francisco and continued exploring new technologies of photography. In 1996, Dater toured the world for her 30-year retrospective, *Cycles*.

Heather Blaha

See also: **Cunningham, Imogen; Nude Photography; Portraiture; Welpott, Jack**

Biography

Born in Hollywood, California, 21 June 1941. Studied drawing and painting at University of California, Los Angeles, 1959–1963; Studied photography at San Francisco State University, 1963–1966; Received MA in Photography, 1966. Instructor at University of California Extension, San Francisco, 1966–1974; Instructor at San Francisco Art Institute, 1974–1978; Guest Instructor at Kansas City Art Institute, 1985; Instructor at International Center of Photography, New York, 1987–1990; Instructor at San Francisco Art Institute, 1992–1994; Instructor at University of California Extension, San Francisco, 1996–1997; Instructor at San Jose City College, San Jose, California, 1996–1997. Dorothea Lange Award, Oakland Museum, Oakland, California, 1974. Associated with Witkin Gallery, New York, early 1970s. National Endowment for the Arts, Individual Artist Grant, 1976; Guggenheim Fellowship, 1978; Marin Arts Council Individual Artist Grant,

1987; National Endowment for the Arts, Individual Artist Grant, 1988. Lives and works in San Francisco Bay area.

Individual Exhibitions

1965 Aardvark Gallery; San Francisco, California
1972 Witkin Gallery; New York, New York
1973 George Eastman House; Rochester, New York (with Jack Welpott)
1975 Spectrum Gallery; Tucson, Arizona
Silver Image Gallery; Seattle, Washington
1976 Musée Réattu; Arles, France (with Jack Welpott)
1979 G. Ray Hawkins Gallery; Los Angeles, California
1982 Lightworks/Film in the Cities; St. Paul, Minnesota
Kathleen Ewing Gallery; Washington, D.C.
1984 *Portraits of Disabled Artists*; San Francisco Museum of Modern Art, San Francisco, California
1986 *Judy Dater*; Webster University, St. Louis, Missouri, Victor Hasselblad Aktiebolag Gallery; Göteborg, Sweden
1988 *The Spirit of Woman: Judy Dater Photographs*; Albin O. Kuhn Library and Gallery, University of Maryland, Baltimore County, Maryland
Recent and Rarely Seen Photographs: Judy Dater; Images Gallery, Cincinnati, Ohio
1989 *Judy Dater: New Works*; Blatant Image/Silver Eye, Pittsburgh, Pennsylvania
1990 Options Gallery; Odessa College, Odessa, Texas
1991 *Judy Dater Photography*; Stockton State College Art Gallery, Pomona, California
1992 *Cycles*; Matsuya Department Store, Ginza, Tokyo, Japan
1993 *Judy Dater: Photographs & Installations 1988–1992*; Smith Andersen Gallery, Palo Alto, California
1994 *Cycles*; Galeries Arlesiennes, Arles, France
Cycles; International Center of Photography, New York, New York
1996 *Judy Dater Photographs*; Fotogaleria del Teatro General San Martin, Buenos Aires, Argentina
Judy Dater: A Selected Survey; California College of Arts and Crafts, Oakland

Group Exhibitions

1969 *Vision and Expression*; George Eastman House, Rochester, New York
1970 *California Photographers 1970*; Pasadena Art Museum, Pasadena, California
Being Without Clothes; Massachusetts Institute of Technology, Cambridge, Massachusetts
1972 *Photographic Portraits*; Moore College of Art, Philadelphia, Pennsylvania
Photographs of Women; Museum of Modern Art, New York, New York
1974 *Photography in America*; Whitney Museum of American Art, New York, New York
Private Realities: Recent American Photography; Museum of Fine Arts, Boston, Massachusetts
1975 *Women of Photography: An Historical Survey*; San Francisco Museum of Modern Art, San Francisco, California
1977 *Great West: Real/Ideal*; University of Colorado, Boulder, Colorado
1978 *Forty American Photographers*; Crocker Art Museum, Sacramento, California
Mirrors and Windows: American Photography since 1960; Museum of Modern Art, New York, New York
Tusen Och en Bild; Moderna Museet, Stockholm, Sweden
1985 *Self as Subject*; Honolulu Academy of Arts, Honolulu, Hawaii
The Nude in Photography; Stadtmuseum, Munich, Germany
Attitudes: Photography in the Seventies; Santa Barbara Museum of Art, Santa Barbara, California
1986 *Staging the Self: Self-Portrait Photography 1840s–1980s*; National Portrait Gallery, London, England
1988 *Behold the Man: The Male Nude in Photography*; Stills Gallery, Edinburgh, Scotland
1990 *Suburban Home Life: Tracking the American Dream*; Whitney Museum of American Art, New York, New York
1991 *Exploring the Unknown Self: Self-Portraits of Contemporary Women*; Tokyo Metropolitan Museum of Photography, Tokyo, Japan
1994 *Portrait of My Mother*; Institute Francais d'Ecosse, Edinburgh, Scotland and Institute Francais du Royaume-Uni, London, England
NUDE; Spiral Hall, Tokyo, Japan
1996 *A History of Women Photographers*; The New York Public Library, New York, New York
Fields of Vision: Women in Photography; Albin O. Kuhn Library and Gallery, University of Maryland, Baltimore, Maryland

Selected Works

Maggie Wells, Painter, 1970
Twinka Thiebaud, Actor, Model, Writer, 1970
Imogen and Twinka, 1974
Pepsi Stand and Pyramid, 1979
Ms. Clingfree, 1982
Leopard Woman, 1982
The Magician, 1982
Self-Portrait Sequence, No. 3, 1982

Further Reading

Dater, Judy and Carolyn Coman. *Body & Soul: Ten American Women*. Lawrence Hill Books, 1988.
Dater, Judy. *Cycles*. Pasadena: Curatorial Assistance, Inc., 1994.
Dater, Judy. *Imogen Cunningham: A Portrait*. Boston: New York Graphic Society, 1979.
Enyeart, James L. *Judy Dater: Twenty Years*. Tucson: The University of Arizona Press, 1986.
Senti, Richard. "Masters of Photography: The Many Faces of Judy Dater." *Darkroom Photography* 5:7 (November 1983): 22–25, 27–31.
Smith, Henry Holmes. *Women and Other Visions: Photographs by Judy Dater and Jack Welpott*. Dobbs Ferry, NY: Morgan & Morgan, 1975.
Sobieszek, Robert A. "Ms.: Portraits of Women by Judy Dater and Jack Welpott." *Image* 16:1 (March 1973): 11–12.

BRUCE DAVIDSON

American

Although *Life* had already published Bruce Davidson's work, his position within the photography world truly solidified with the publication of four of his photographs in the June 1960 issue of *Esquire* under the title "Brooklyn Minority Report" and supplemented with an essay by novelist Norman Mailer. Through this work, Davidson revealed his early interest in the photo-essay as well as his use of photography to intimately study a group of people from the "inside." Both themes have continued to preoccupy him throughout his photographic career.

Motivated both by his disillusionment with photojournalism and his desire to move beyond Robert Frank's seminal book *The Americans*, in the summer of 1959 Davidson turned to a group of "troubled" youth in Brooklyn as a means of making a new photographic statement. With the help of a social worker, he contacted a gang of teenagers who called themselves "the Jokers" and whose "rumbles" frequently appeared in the newspaper headlines. For 11 months, the gang members agreed to let Davidson photograph their daily lives, and the resulting images provide both an intimate portrait of the teenagers as well as a probing examination of the restlessness and alienation of youth culture in 1950s America. Davidson explains:

> What I was photographing was not the gang, but a sense of isolation and tensions within teenagers.... I never felt a separation between myself and what I was photographing because I was really down to the feeling. But that doesn't mean that I didn't feel guilty because I could go home to a motel and they were sleeping on the ground. I just never felt apart. With the gang, I was in the same mood as they were.
>
> (Livingston 330)

Born in Oak Park, a suburb of Chicago, in 1933 to a Jewish family of Polish origins, Davidson developed an early interest in photography; he owned a Brownie camera and had a rudimentary darkroom set up by the age of ten. In high school, he continued to involve himself with photography, working weekends and summers as a stock boy in a camera shop and later as an apprentice to a commercial photographer. In 1951, Davidson entered Rochester Institute of Technology where he studied under Ralph Hattersley. In 1955, he decided to pursue graduate studies at Yale University, studying philosophy, painting, and photography under graphic designer Herbert Matter, photographer and designer Alexey Brodovitch, and painter Josef Albers. A class project at Yale led to his first publication in *Life*, "Tension in the Dressing Room," which Davidson photographed at one of the Yale football games and submitted to the editors at *Life*. The photo-essay appeared in the October 31, 1955 issue.

After one semester at Yale, the U.S. Army posted Davidson to Supreme Headquarters Allied Powers in Europe, just outside Paris. Working as a photographer for the army gave Davidson the opportunity to spend many weekends in Paris, and he soon befriended the widow of the impressionist painter Leon Fauché, a contemporary of Paul Gauguin, Henri de Toulouse-Lautrec, and Pierre-Auguste Renoir. For this project, Davidson devoted weekend after weekend photographing Madame Fauché while she walked to the market or sat in her garret surrounded by her husband's paintings. The images became the subject of his second photographic essay entitled "The Widow of Montmartre," published in *Esquire* in 1958. In Paris, Davidson also met Henri Cartier-Bresson whose work he had been introduced to while at Rochester and who would become not only his mentor but also a personal friend.

In 1957, the army discharged Davidson and he returned to New York to begin working as a freelance photographer for *Life*. In 1958, Magnum Photos offered him an associate membership and a year later he became a full member. He liked the open atmosphere of Magnum much better than the magazine industry, and, in 1961, he accepted an assignment given to him through Magnum by *The New York Times* to cover the Freedom Riders in the South. As a result of this job, Davidson began a documentary project on the Civil Rights movement, and, in 1962, he received a Guggenheim Fellowship to assist him with his work. John Szarkowski at the Museum of Modern Art included photographs from the project in a 1966 one-man exhibition, and they were also included in *The Negro American* (1966), a collection of essays dealing with the situation of African-Americans in the United States.

Davidson's interest in the position of African Americans continued with his project *East 100th Street*, a photographic work that explored one city block of Spanish Harlem. He began the two-year project in 1966 using a large format 4 × 5 inch view camera mounted on a tripod instead of a hand-held camera in order to avoid being perceived as an "intruder" who seized images without interacting with his subjects. For the project he made over 1,000 negatives and in March 1968, *Du* published a portfolio with a text by Davidson. On August 15, 1969, *Life* published a four-page spread on the project. Davidson chose the block largely for its reputation of being one of the worst blocks in the city, and, since its inception, the project has elicited a great deal of controversy. Critics such as A. D. Coleman accused Davidson of exploiting a repressed subculture while supporters like Hilton Kramer praised him for elevating his subject matter to the status of high art. In 1970, the Museum of Modern Art held an exhibition featuring 43 photographs from the project.

Having photographed "inner space" in his *East 100th Street* project, in 1980, Davidson began to document "underground space" through his color photographs of the New York subway, and from 1991–1995 he worked on a project of "open space" with his photographs of New York's Central Park shot with a panoramic camera. Although most of Davidson's work centers on human isolation, *Portraits*, published in 1999, focuses on a diverse range of celebrities, many of whom Davidson photographed while on assignment for magazines and newspapers.

Photography, however, was not the only medium to attract Davidson. From the late 1960s until the mid-1970s Davidson turned to filmmaking, shooting documentaries *Living off the Land* (1969) and *Zoo Doctor* (1971) as well as a fiction film, *Nightmare and Mrs. Pupko's Beard* (1972), based on short stories of Nobel Laureate Isaac Bashevis Singer. Davidson continues to practice photography today, and, although he prefers to work on personal projects, occasionally he still accepts commercial assignments.

ERINA DUGANNE

See also: **Cartier-Bresson, Henri; Documentary Photography; Life Magazine; Magnum Photos; Street Photography**

Biography

Born Oak Lawn, Illinois 5 September 1933. Studied photography with Ralph Hattersley at Rochester Institute of Technology, New York, 1951–1954; studied painting, philosophy, and photography under Herbert Matter, Alexey Brodovitch, and Josef Albers at Yale University, New Haven, 1955. Served in United States Army, 1955–1957; freelance photographer for *Life*, *Réalities*, *Du*, *Esquire*, *Queen*, *Look*, *Vogue*, and member of Magnum Photos since 1958; photography instructor, School of Visual Arts, New York, 1964. Received John Simon Guggenheim Memorial Fellowship, 1962; National Endowment for the Arts grant, 1967, 1970; American Film Institute grant, 1970, 1972; A.F.I. prize, 1971. Living in New York.

Individual Exhibitions

1965 Art Institute of Chicago, Chicago, Illinois
International Museum of Photography, George Eastman House, Rochester, New York
San Francisco Museum of Modern Art, San Francisco, California
1966 Museum of Modern Art, New York, New York
Moderna Museet, Stockholm, Sweden
1970 *East 100th Street: Photographs by Bruce Davidson*; Museum of Modern Art, New York, New York
1971 San Francisco Museum of Modern Art, San Francisco, California
1976 Addison Gallery, Andover, Massachusetts
1979 FNAC Gallery, Paris, France
Galerie Delpire, Paris, France
Galerie Fiolet, Amsterdam, Netherlands
1982 Douglas Kenyon Gallery, Chicago, Illinois
1983 *New York Subway Color*; International Center of Photography, New York, New York
1997 *Bruce Davidson: American Photographs*; Edwynn Houk Gallery, New York, New York
1998 *Bruce Davidson: The Brooklyn Gang, 1959*; International Center of Photography, New York, New York

Group Exhibitions

1959 *Photography at Mid Century*; George Eastman House, Rochester, New York
1960 *The World as Seen by Magnum*; Takashimaya Department Store, Tokyo, Japan and traveling
1962 *Ideas in Images*; American Federation of Arts, New York, New York, and traveling
1966 *Contemporary Photography Since 1950*; George Eastman House, Rochester, New York
Toward a Social Landscape: Contemporary Photographers; George Eastman House, Rochester, New York
1967 *12 Photographers of the American Social Landscape*; Rose Art Museum, Brandeis University, Boston, Massachusetts
1973 *The Concerned Photographer 2*; Israel Museum, Jerusalem and traveling
1974 *Photography in America*; Whitney Museum of American Art, New York, New York
1977 *Concerning Photography*; The Photographers' Gallery, London (traveled to Spectro Workshop, Newcastle-upon-Tyne, England)
1980 *The Imaginary Photo Museum*; Kunsthalle, Cologne, Germany
1982 *Color as Form*; International Museum of Photography, George Eastman House, Rochester, New York

1985 *American Images 1945–1950*; Barbican Art Gallery, London, England, and traveling
1986 *New York School, Photographs, 1935–1963, Part III*; Corcoran Gallery of Art, Washington, D.C.
1989 *On the Art of Fixing a Shadow: One Hundred and Fifty Years of Photography*; National Gallery of Art, Washington, D.C., and Art Institute of Chicago, Chicago, Illinois (traveled to Los Angeles County Museum of Art, Los Angeles, California)
1991 *Appearances: Fashion Photography Since 1945*; Victoria and Albert Museum, London, England
2000 *Reflections in a Glass Eye: Works from the International Center of Photography Collection*; International Center of Photography, New York, New York

Selected Works

Negro American; 1966
East 100th Street; 1970
Subsistence U.S.A., 1970
Photographing Children; 1973
Bruce Davidson: Photographs; 1979
New York Subway; 1986
Central Park; 1995
Bruce Davidson: The Brooklyn Gang, 1959; 1959
Portraits, 1999

Further Reading

Capa, Cornett, ed. *The Concerned Photographer 2*. New York: Grossman Publishers, 1972.
Coleman, A.D. *Light Readings: A Photography Critic's Writings 1968–1978*. New York: Oxford University Press, 1979.
Doty, Robert, ed. *Photography in America*. New York: Random House, 1974.
Green, Jonathan. "East 100th Street." *Aperture* no. 16 (1971).
Harbutt, Charles, and Lee Jones. *America in Crisis: Photographs for Magnum*. New York: Holt, 1969.
Harrison, Martin. *Appearances: Fashion Photography Since 1945*. London: Jonathan Cape, 1991.
Lassiter, Ken. "A Conversation with Bruce Davidson." *Photographer's Forum* (November 1996).
Livingston, Jane. *The New York School: Photographs, 1936–1963*. New York: Stewart, Tabori & Chang, 1992.
Mailer, Norman. "Brooklyn Minority Report." *Esquire* (June 1960).
Szarkowski, John. *Mirrors and Windows: American Photography Since 1960*. New York: Museum of Modern Art, 1978.
Turner, Peter, and John Benton-Harris, eds. *American Images: Photography 1945–1980*. Harmondsworth: Penguin Books and New York: Viking Penguin, 1985.

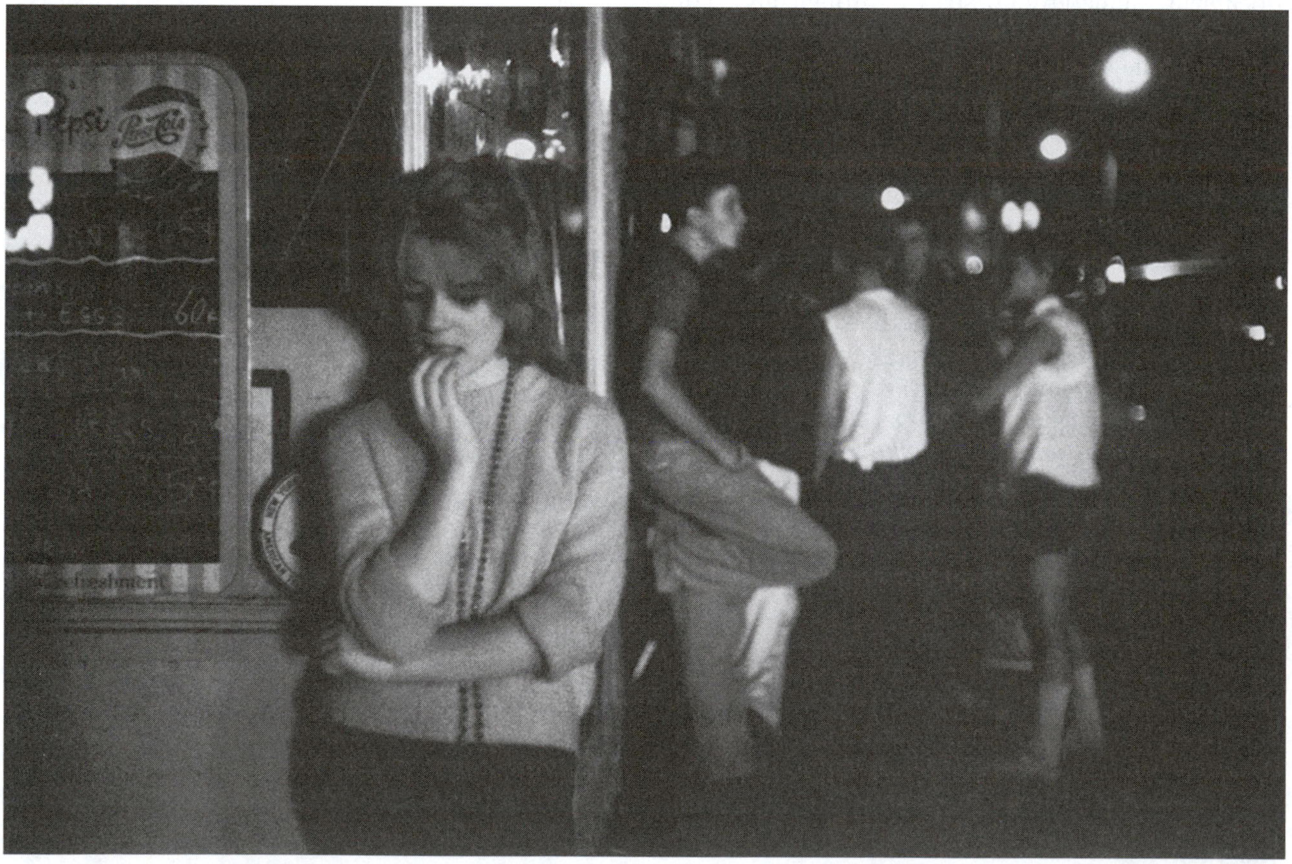

Bruce Davidson, Brooklyn Gang, New York City, 1959.
[© *Bruce Davidson/Magnum Photos*]

BARON ADOLPH DE MEYER

American, born French

Adolph (or Adolf) de Meyer, first a highly influential Pictorialist photographer, later a renowned fashion photographer, magazine editor, and tastemaker, cultivated an enigmatic persona. Many details of his life are obscure because he deliberately fabricated them. He even varied the style and spelling of his name, augmenting the uncertainties about his unusual life. According to the memoirs of the painter Jacques-Émile Blanche, Adolf Meyer was born in the Paris suburb of Auteuil of a Jewish mother and a Scottish father named Watson. Others said the father was German and that the family name was Von Meyer; alternatively, Cecil Beaton claimed that de Meyer was born in Austria. Yet other sources suggested a Finnish lineage. The 1905 *Who's Who* states that Adolf Edward Sigismond de Meyer, a baron of the kingdom of Saxony, was born in Paris, the son of Adolphus Meyer and Adele Watson. In a 1915 interview, de Meyer claimed that his father was Russian.

Adolf Meyer-Watson was raised in Paris by his mother, then studied in Germany at a time when photography was being energized both by technical advances and an increasingly dynamic and sophisticated artistry, on view in photographic salons and exhibitions. As a young man he was deeply inspired by the lifestyle and work of the painter James McNeill Whistler, and became accepted into high society largely because of his personal beauty, style, and manners and was both an example of and an exponent of the cult of beauty. Some have observed similarities between de Meyer and Marcel Proust's fictional Swann, in being both half-Jewish and a member of "cafe society" whose devotion to the "chic" was almost a religion. Panache, glamour, chic, and snobbery were born in a changing society in which aristocrats, artists, and celebrities intermingled.

De Meyer gained entry to the British royal circle (and photographed King Edward VII and his family), largely through his wife Olga Caracciolo, whom he married in either 1896, 1897, or possibly 1899, and who was the godchild of the king—if not also his illegitimate daughter. De Meyer's marriage to Olga was reputedly unconsummated and platonic; he may in fact have been encouraged to marry because, in the wake of the Oscar Wilde scandal and the Dreyfus affair, he sought to disguise his homosexuality and his Jewish background, both of which had become unpopular and risky liabilities. Olga's mother was the Duchessa de Caracciolo and it was thought that the Prince of Wales, who became King Edward VII, was her father, as they were often seen together. De Meyer was granted the title of baron by the King of Saxony so that he and Olga could attend the coronation of Edward as members of the nobility.

Olga inspired him to learn from some of the great painters, and he was especially influenced by the Symbolists. The de Meyers were wealthy, sophisticated members of café society who had homes in Paris, London, Constantinople, Venice, and eventually New York City. Olga had been preceded as de Meyer's patron, favorite model, and close friend by Constance Gladys, Lady de Grey, who had helped introduce him to London society.

In 1898, de Meyer joined the Linked Ring Brotherhood. Beginning in 1903, he exhibited at their London Salon. Eventually he became bored with the group and helped form the Vienna Secession. During these formative years he enjoyed the friendships of a number of important photographers, especially Edward Steichen and Gertrude Käsebier, and it appears that the latter had a significant influence on his work. Other photographic friends included Frances Benjamin Johnston and Alvin Langdon Coburn. He corresponded with Alfred Stieglitz, and they enjoyed an intellectual and artistic intimacy.

In a 1906 letter to Alfred Stieglitz he insisted on showing his work only in solo rather than group exhibitions. Stieglitz published some of his work as photogravures in *Camera Work*, and reproductions of his color Autochromes could be found in *The Studio*. In 1909, after years of letters and business interaction, the two finally met. Although he had been praised by Cecil Beaton for his soft-focus Pictorialism, he told Stieglitz that he believed in "straight" photography, especially in the form of platinum and silver prints. Although he was briefly fascinated with the Autochrome process shortly after its 1907 introduction and exhibited his work in the new medium, he lost interest by 1909 and returned to his silver and platinum imagery.

After King Edward died in 1910, the de Meyers began to make a transition. No longer just a society photographer, he emerged as a fine photographic craftsman, a skilled and highly paid professional. He was both a Symbolist and an Orientalist. He photographed ballet, one of his favorite subjects, and helped bring the Ballets Russes to England in 1911, where he photographed the great dancer Nijinsky.

In 1916 an astrologer gave the couple new names—Mhahra for her, Gayne for him, so sometimes he styled himself as Baron Gayne de Meyer.

When World War I broke out, de Meyer's German title meant that remaining in England would lead to his internment as a prisoner of war, so the couple emigrated to the United States, where Condé Nast had offered him a post as photographer for his magazines *Vogue* and *Vanity Fair*. Much of his fashion work was highly original and innovative, and he influenced other fashion photographers, as well as avant-garde artists like Man Ray.

De Meyer was staff photographer for *Vogue* and *Vanity Fair* magazines from 1913–1922; he also began writing editorials for *Vogue* in 1915. In 1922 he joined *Vogue*'s competitor *Harper's Bazaar* and put his distinctive imprint on the magazine until 1929. He not only had revolutionized fashion photography through his magazine work, but modified the look and format of the magazines themselves. Although he had greatly influenced other fashion photographers, the prevailing style of fashion photography was rapidly changing in the 1930s, taking on a more hard-edged realism, and his style, which had never really escaped soft-focus Pictorialism, became obsolescent.

The baron's photographs helped "establish" women in society. He photographed celebrities in a high-key, soft-focus style, which won him great notoriety. His pictures of Olga are elegant but superficial. Arthur Ollman wrote that "for de Meyer, Olga was a religious icon, an image of perfection, existing on a different plane, a transcendant goddess." She died in 1930.

After Olga's death, de Meyer felt free to move to Hollywood with his heir and lover, Ernst. He destroyed most of his original prints before he left Europe in 1938, but these casualties did not include his portraits of Olga. When preparing a 1940 retrospective at the home of actor Edward G. Robinson, however, he could locate only 40 prints. In 1988, however, the photography dealer G. Ray Hawkins bought a trunk containing de Meyer's belongings and discovered a trove of unpublished photographs of Olga.

In his final years de Meyer abandoned photography, and tried his hand unsuccessfully at writing, leaving behind unpublished novels, plays, and memoirs, but he never recaptured the brilliance of his years as both a photographer and guru of fashion and taste. He died of coronary thrombosis in Los Angeles in 1946. His obituary in the Los Angeles *Times* did not even mention his profession as a photographer.

David Haberstich

See also: **Beaton, Cecil; Condé Nast; Fashion Photography; Linked Ring; Pictorialism; Portraiture; Stieglitz, Alfred**

Biography

Parentage obscure, possibly born in Paris suburb of Auteuil or in Paris, 1868. Raised as Adolf Meyer-Watson in Paris by his mother; studied in Germany but largely self-taught as a photographer. Married Olga Caracciolo in either 1896, 1897, or 1899 and through her connections gained entry to the British royal circle and photographed King Edward VII and his family. Granted the title of baron by the King of Saxony. Joins Linked Ring Brotherhood, 1898. Emigrated to United States, 1913; worked for Condé Nast. Staff photographer for *Vogue* and *Vanity Fair*, 1913–1922. Worked for *Harper's Bazaar*, 1922–1929. Made portraits of wife Olga until her death in 1930; relocated to Hollywood but abandoned photography. Died of coronary thrombosis in Los Angeles, 1946.

Solo Exhibitions

1909 *Photographs in color and monochrome*; The Little Galleries of the Photo-Seccession (291), New York, New York
1909 National Arts Club, New York, New York
1911–1912 Photographs; 291, New York, New York
1976–1977 *An Exhibition of Photographs by Baron Adolf De Meyer*; Helios, New York, New York
1994–1995 *A Singular Elegance: The Photographs of Baron Adolph De Meyer*; International Center of Photography Midtown, New York, New York

Group Exhibitions

1900 *New School of American Photography*; Royal Photographic Society, England; and Photo Club-de Paris, Paris, France
1907 *Photographs by Baron A. De Meyer and George H. Seeley*; The Little Galleries of the Photo-Seccession (291), New York, New York
1910 *International Exhibition of Pictorial Photography*; Albright Art Gallery, Buffalo, New York.
1911 *Modern Photographs*; Newark Museum, Newark, New Jersey
2000 *The Model Wife*; Museum of Photographic Arts, San Diego, California

Selected Works

Baroness Olga de Meyer, c. 1900
Water Lilies, 1906
Alfred Stieglitz, c. 1910–1920
Marchesa Luisa Casati, 1912
Mrs. Harry Payne Whitney, c. 1912
Vaslav Nijinsky as the Favorite Slave in "Scheherazade," 1916
Helen Lee Worthing, 1920
Josephine Baker, 1925–1926

Further Reading

Brandau, Robert, ed. *De Meyer*. New York: Knopf, 1976.
De Meyer, Baron Adolf. *Adolf, L'Après-midi d'un faune: Vaslav Nijinsky, 1912 / Thirty-three Photographs by Baron Adolf de Meyer*. With an essay by Jennifer Dunning and contributions by Richard Buckle and Ann Hutchinson Guest. New York: Dance Horizons, 1983.
———. *A Singular Elegance: The Photographs of Baron Adolph de Meyer*. Dedication by John Szarkowski; introduction by Willis Hartshorn; essay by Anne Ehrenkranz. San Francisco: Chronicle Books in association with International Center of Photography, 1994.
Hawkins, G. Ray, ed. *Of Passions and Tenderness: Portraits of Olga by Baron de Meyer*. Essay by Alexandra Anderson-Spivy. Marina del Rey: Graystone Books, 1992.
Ollman, Arthur. *The Model Wife*. Boston: Little Brown and Company, 1999.

JOHN DEAKIN

British

The British photographer John Deakin died in relative obscurity at age 60 in 1972. His work was likely to have been forgotten if not for exhibitions and books assembled posthumously from the prints and negatives (many of them in very poor condition) left scattered with various archives, collections, friends, and clients. Since his death his importance as a photographer has been recognized and championed for two distinct reasons. The content of his work has been acknowledged as a perfect illustration of a time and place within British cultural history; the postwar 1940s and 1950s of artistic, bohemian London, while the stark, realist style of his photographs are now admired for their directness in execution and for the frank portrayal of his subjects, while still holding within their bleakness a cruel beauty. Coming from a tradition where photographers complemented their sitters, still at times airbrushing towards perfection, John Deakin reveled in portraying life as monochromatic, blemished, and very real.

He was born on May 8, 1912 in Cheshire. His parents had recently moved from Liverpool to be nearer his father's workplace in a soap factory. Not much is known or recorded about Deakin's early life. Later he was to embellish or fabricate the details of his formative years, often referring to himself as "the slum boy from Liverpool." However, records show him to have been an excellent student at his grammar school, his behavior exemplary as well as being a keen swimmer whose chosen career was to join his father in the factory. Instead, by the time he was 18 he had moved to Dublin where he had a succession of jobs including window dressing and possibly a stint in the theatre as well as undertaking some art education. His first passion was for painting which he pursued on moving to London in the early 1930s hoping to make a career as an artist. A wealthy American collector, Arthur Jeffries, became his benefactor and the two traveled widely for several years to the United States, Europe, South America, and the South Seas, allowing Deakin the chance to live in relative luxury, paint, and eventually exhibit in London in 1938.

Deakin started to photograph in the late 1930s while living in Paris. At the outbreak of war he enlisted in the British army as a photographer and was stationed in Cairo, Syria, Malta, Palestine, and Lebanon, rising to the rank of Lieutenant. He enjoyed his military service and returned to London after the war starting his career as a photographer. He opened a studio shooting portraits for *Tatler* and *Lilliput* magazines but achieved little success. Again he drifted until his documentary work, notably his photographs of Paris, came to the attention of British *Vogue*'s editor Audrey Withers who offered him the position of staff photographer in July 1947. His work was divided between fashion, which he did not enjoy and portraiture, in which he was to excel. His photographs were direct and demanded attention through their unadorned simplicity. In most cases the contrast of the print increased the severity of his images. Deakin was entering his busiest and most creative period as a photographer though personally and health-wise he was starting a slow decline. His heavy drinking had inevitably led to alcoholism and he had thrown himself fully into London's Soho drinking culture, frequenting the bars and clubs populated by the artists, writers, musicians, and actors of the day as well as members of the vice and criminal fraternity. His list of friends (or often just acquaintances) included important painters such as Lucien Freud, John Minton, and importantly, Francis Bacon. Though defended by Withers, Deakin was not a popular member of the *Vogue* staff. His drunkenness, rudeness, and lack of regard for *Vogue* equipment led to his dismissal in 1949, after only 14 months' work. However, again he opened a studio, worked for various magazines, and had his first book, *London Today*, published, documenting his impressions of the city. Withers employed him once more in 1951, and he managed to stay with *Vogue* for three years concentrating on portraiture and documentary work, having shown little aptitude or admiration for fashion. His first commission on his return was to photograph Picasso and for the next three years he continued to photograph artists and celebrities.

In retrospect Deakin is now seen as a chronicler of Soho's artistic life of the late 1940s and early 1950s. He stopped photographing sometime in the early 1960s. He had become increasingly unreliable as his health deteriorated, and returned to painting in his last years. Though diagnosed with lung cancer, he continued to travel, accompanying Francis Bacon to the painter's retrospective exhibition in Paris in 1971. His links and friendship with Bacon were one constant in his life. Photographs were important to Bacon as a visual reference and inspiration for his work and he often employed Deakin to provide this source material, having a great admiration for the brutal qualities of the photographers work. John Deakin died of heart failure in May 1972, having been sent by Bacon to Brighton on the South Coast of England to recuperate from his last visit to hospital.

Deakin had originally wanted to be a painter and had died with little regard and care for his photographic work. When his first posthumous exhibition, *The Salvage of a Photographer*, was shown at the Victoria and Albert Museum in London in 1984, prints were selected from the little he had left to his friend, the art historian Bruce Bernard. The next year his archive of prints and negatives at *Vogue* was rediscovered, many frayed and damaged. When his work was next exhibited in 1996 at the National Portrait Gallery in London, these two collections were augmented by the creased, paint-spattered prints found within Francis Bacon's studio. The condition of these prints had not detracted from the content; indeed some critics have seen their deterioration and heritage as a supplement to their aesthetic value and given a new importance to the photography of John Deakin.

Mike Crawford

Biography

Born in England, 18 May 1912. Lived and worked in Dublin, early 1930s before moving to London. Traveling during mid-1930s. Starts to photograph while living in Paris, 1939. Serves as photographer in the British Army during World War II, 1939–1945. Staff photographer for British *Vogue*, 1947–1948. Second employment with British *Vogue*, 1951–1954. Died in Brighton, England, May 1972.

Individual Exhibitions

1938 Mayor Gallery; London, England, (Paintings)
1956 St. Georges Gallery; London, England (Paintings)
1956 *John Deakin's Paris*; Daniel Archer Bookshop, London, England
1956 *John Deakin's Rome*; Daniel Archer Bookshop, London, England
1962 *Collages by John Deakin*; Museum Street Gallery, London, England
1984 *The Salvage of a Photographer*; Victoria & Albert Museum, London, England, (Posthumous)
1996 *Photographs*; National Portrait Gallery, London, England

Further Reading

Deakin, John. *London Today*. London. Saturn Press, 1949.
Farson, Daniel. *Sacred Monsters*. London: Bloomsbury, 1988.
Farson, Daniel. *The Gilded Gutter Life of Francis Bacon*. London: Century, 1993.
Muir, Robin. "John Deakin." In *Photographs*. London: Schirmer/Mosel, 1996.
The Salvage of a Photographer. Exh. cat. London: Victoria and Albert Museum, 1984.

ROY DECARAVA

American

Personal expression shapes the modernist photography of Roy DeCarava. Raised in Harlem in the 1920s, the Harlem Renaissance—a period that called for the self-representation of the Black experience—profoundly influenced his photographs. By the early 1950s, DeCarava produced such poignant prints as *Graduation* (1949) and *Man Coming Up Subway Stairs* (1952), photographs that characterize his humanity and aptitude for juxtaposition. Their vitality aligned him early in his career with important figures in American photography, leading to inclusion in such monumental exhibitions as *The Family of Man* (1955), organized at the Museum of Modern Art (MoMA) by Edward Steichen. His inclusion exemplifies DeCarava's work as an overall expression of the human experience, told through the lives of New York's city laborers and the glimpses of life that are often taken for granted when passing through the urban landscape.

When discussing his work, DeCarava confronts the dilemma of categorization:

> The major definition has been that I am a documentary photographer, and then...I became a people's photographer, and then I became a street photographer, and then I became a jazz photographer and oh, yes, I mustn't forget, I am a black photographer...and there is nothing wrong with any of those definitions. The only trouble is that I need all of them to define myself.
>
> (Blue c. 1984)

In postwar America, focus on city living and advancements in the hand-held camera created a rise in photographic consciousness and the phenomena called "street photography." Attention shifted from the war's aftermath to changes witnessed on America's urban streets. Photographers Robert Frank, Helen Levitt, and Lisette Model grew to acclaim during the 1950s for this instantaneous snapshot that presented the fringe of American culture. For DeCarava, his urban vision was inspired by personal concerns to dignify his community, but also by the technical challenge of a given situation. Similar to Henri Cartier-Bresson, DeCarava was the man on the street, responding to the conditions of his environment. He used the camera's mechanics to evoke particular responses to light and shadow. With suspended manipulation, his images allow for unfocused passages, as in *Coltrane on Soprano* (1963), where the camera's shutter has remained open long enough to capture the instrument in a blur from John Coltrane's rhythmic playing. Yet he also created strikingly intimate views of everyday family life, couples dancing in a kitchen, a father holding his baby.

DeCarava was born in 1919. His mother emigrated from Jamaica to New York during the Great Migration and raised her only son during a period when economic depression effected the optimism of the Harlem Renaissance. Despite the hardships, he attended lower Manhattan's Textile High School where his exposure to Vincent Van Gogh taught him expressionism, which he later applied to photography. In 1938, he entered the Cooper Union School of Art and studied painting and printmaking. He later transferred to the Harlem Community Center in 1940, a dynamic location for young African-American artists. His return to Harlem included participation in the Works Progress Administration's workshops and introduced him to painters Romare Bearden, Jacob Lawrence, Norman Lewis, and Charles White.

Initially DeCarava experimented with photography's formal abilities to crop and provide light contrasts to inform his silkscreens. By 1949, DeCarava solely fixed his camera, loaded with black and white film, on the streets of Harlem. In 1950, gallerist Mark Perper offered him a solo exhibition and introduced him to Homer Page, a seasoned technician and protégé of Edward Steichen. Page taught DeCarava to print with less contrast and to use a narrower range of blacks in favor of gray tonalities to enhance spatial relationships and evoke stronger expression. As a result, defined whites are separated from shadows to enhance the subject. *Hallway* (1953), one of his most acclaimed images, exploits these tonalities in favor of symbolic meaning. The range of grays contrast the softened glare of the single light bulb dangling in a narrow hallway, communicating the housing situation that many people emigrating to urban cities encountered. Page introduced him to Steichen, head of MoMA's Department of Photography, who purchased three of DeCarava's prints for the collection. In 1952, Steichen sponsored DeCarava's receipt of the John Simon Guggenheim Memorial Fellowship, the first received by an African-American. The fellowship allowed him to work full-time as a photographer, resulting in the completion of some of his most renowned images.

The documentary aesthetic is often used to describe DeCarava's style, but his publications of photographic stories about the independent rhythms of cultural communities reveal his poetic interests. *The Sweet Flypaper of Life* (1955) is an international phenomenon in this regard. Published in English, German, and Czech languages, the book merged DeCarava's photographs and their characteristic straightforward, descriptive titles with Langston Hughes' fictional narrative that related issues of family, marriage, and individual experience in 1950s' Harlem. During a time when integration occupied the Supreme Court, DeCarava's images embodied a revolutionary spirit. During the 1950s, DeCarava also began the project of photographing the legendary figures of jazz and bebop, including Count Basie, Duke Ellington, Billie Holiday, Thelonius Monk, Elvin Jones, and Ornette Coleman. As an active participant, he saw jazz and his photography as improvisation—something you do all at once and that melds looking with listening. DeCarava envisioned this series as an intermeshing of prose and image bearing the title *The Sound I Saw: Improvisations on a Jazz Theme (*1962, 2001). The project first materialized in 1983 as an exhibition organized by the Studio Museum in Harlem and was later completed as a publication in 2001 through Phaidon Press.

During the Civil Rights Movement, DeCarava traveled to the March on Washington. Photographs such as *Mississippi Freedom Marcher, Washington, D.C.* (1963) demonstrate that despite the momentous event, capturing human promise rather than documentation was the main subject. As an activist, DeCarava was most vocal during the controversy of the New York Metropolitan Museum of Art's 1969 exhibition *Harlem on My Mind* (1969). The exhibition aimed to represent Harlem through documents and photographic enlargements yet included few African-American artists. Although he was asked to participate, DeCarava declined and wrote a statement in *Popular Photography*, voicing his concerns over misrepresentation and the lack of foresight in presenting photography.

Regardless of racial opposition, DeCarava pioneered organizations throughout his career. From 1955 to 1957, he opened A Photographer's Gallery, one of the first photography galleries in New York City. Exhibited artists included Ralph Eugene Meatyard, Minor White, Van Deren Coke, Harry Callahan, and Berenice Abbott. In 1958, he began work as a freelance photographer for magazines such as *Sports Illustrated*, *Good Housekeeping*, and *Scientific American* and on film and television sets as a still photographer. In 1960, the actor Harry Belafonte produced a CBS television series "New York 19," which used DeCarava's expressionistic images to connect segments of the hour-long program. By the 1970s DeCarava's public presence influenced many younger black artists. He served on the board of American Society of Magazine Photographers, which fostered the Committee to End Discrimination Against Black Photographers. Frustrations with the committee led to the spearheading of the Kamoinge Workshop. The group effort opened a gallery on 125th Street in Harlem. This photography consortium provided an atmosphere of discussion and opportunity by producing group seminars and portfolios. Photography critic A. D. Coleman supported DeCarava for his mentoring and ability to surpass the exclusion that many non-White photographers received during the 1970s.

After his marriage to art historian Sherry Turner in 1971 DeCarava's work included domestic themes and botanicals. In 1975, DeCarava created his first major body of work taken outside of New York City when the Corcoran Gallery of Art in Washington, D.C. sponsored *The Nation's Capital in Photographs*, a series of solo exhibitions based on commissions. In 1981, the Friends of Photography in Carmel, California, mounted *Roy DeCarava, Photographs*, an important exhibition that highlighted Turner's archival research of her husband's work. The exhibition catalogue serves as a monograph and includes her authoritative essay, "Celebrations." The Museum of Modern Art organized, to international acclaim, the photographer's next major exhibition, *Roy DeCarava: A Retrospective* in 1996. DeCarava's editorial photographs, however, were excluded from this survey, which had the result that even greater interest focused on his contributions to and influence on commercial photography. Today, DeCarava's visions of urban communities are seen as foundational to the work of contemporary photographers such as Carrie Mae Weems and Nikki S. Lee. Production of his photographs are managed by Sherri Turner DeCarava, who presides as Executive Director of The DeCarava Foundation and The DeCarava Archive, which holds reproduction rights to his work. Since 1975, DeCarava has taught full-time at Hunter College of the City University of New York and currently teaches as a Distinguished Professor of Photography.

SARA MARION

See also: **History of Photography: Postwar Era; History of Photography: Twentieth-Century Pioneers; Street Photography; Weems, Carrie Mae; Works Progress Administration**

Biography

Born in New York City, New York 1919. Attended Cooper Union School of Art, 1938–1940; Harlem Community Art Center, 1940–1942. Worked as sign painter and display artist, New York, 1936–1937; Technical draftsman, New York 1939–1942; Commercial artist and illustrator, 1944–1958; Freelance Photographer, New York, 1959–1968, 1975 to present; Adjunct Professor of Photography at Cooper Union Institute, New York, 1969–1972; Associate Professor of Art, Cooper Union Institute, 1975–1978; Professor of Art at Hunter College of the City University of New York, New York, 1975–1988; Distinguished Professor of Art at Hunter College, City University of New York, 1988 to present. Awarded John Simon Guggenheim Memorial Fellowship 1952–1953; Benin Creative Photography Award, 1972; Artistic and Cultural Achievement Award, Community Museum of Brooklyn, New York, 1979; American Society for Magazine Photographers, 1983; Distinguished Career Photography Award, Friends of Photography, 1991; Special Citation for Photographic Journalism, American Society of Magazine Photographers, 1991. Honorary Doctorates from Rhode Island Institute of Fine Arts, 1985; Maryland Institute, 1986; Wesleyan University, 1992. Established The DeCarava Archives and The DeCarava Foundation, New York.

Individual Exhibitions

1947 *Roy DeCarava*; Serigraph Galleries, New York, New York
1950 Forty-Fourth Street Gallery; New York, New York
1951 Countee Cullen Branch; The New York Public Library, New York, New York
1954 *People of Harlem*; The Little Gallery, Hudson Park Branch, The New York Public Library, New York, New York
1956 Camera Club of New York; New York, New York
1969 *Through Black Eyes: Photographs by Roy DeCarava*; The Studio Museum in Harlem, New York, New York
1970 *Roy DeCarava, Photographer*; Sheldon Memorial Art Gallery, University of Nebraska, Lincoln, Nebraska
1975 *Roy DeCarava: Photographs*; Museum of Fine Arts, Houston, Texas
1976 *The Nation's Capital in Photographs, 1976: Roy DeCarava*; Corcoran Gallery of Art, Washington, D.C.
1981 *Roy DeCarava, Photographs*; Friends of Photography, Carmel, California
1985 *The Sound I Saw: The Jazz Photographs of Roy DeCarava*; The Studio Museum in Harlem, New York, New York
1987 *Roy DeCarava: Between Time*; Museum of Photographic Arts, San Diego, California
1988 *Roy DeCarava*; The Photographers' Gallery, London, England
Fotografier av Årstider Roy DeCarava; Fotografiska Museet in Moderna Museet, Stockholm, Sweden
Black Photography in America: Roy DeCarava, "To Paris"; Pavillon des Arts, Paris, France
1990 *Roy DeCarava: Recent Photographs*; Witkin Gallery, New York, New York
1996 *Roy DeCarava: A Retrospective*; Museum of Modern Art, New York, New York

Group Exhibitions

1953 *Always the Young Stranger*; Museum of Modern Art, New York, New York
1955 *The Family of Man*; Museum of Modern Art, New York, New York, and traveling
1956 *Five Photographers: Harry Callahan, Roy DeCarava, Scott Hyde, Leon Levinstein, and Victor Obsatz*; A Photographer's Gallery, New York, New York
1959 *Photography in the Fine Arts*; Metropolitan Museum of Art, New York, New York
1964 *Photographs by the Kamoinge Workshop*; Kamoinge Workshop Gallery, New York, New York
The Photographer's Eye; Museum of Modern Art, New York, New York
An Exhibition of Work by the John Simon Guggenheim Fellows of Photography; Philadelphia College of Art, Philadelphia, Pennsylvania
1967 *Photography in the Twentieth Century*; George Eastman House, Rochester, New York
1974 *Photography in America*; Whitney Museum of American Art, New York, New York
1980 *Photography of the Fifties: An American Perspective*; Center for Creative Photography, University of Arizona, Tucson, Arizona
1983 *A Century of Black Photographers, 1840–1960*; Museum of Art, Rhode Island School of Design, Providence, Rhode Island, and traveling
1990 *Photography Until Now*; Museum of Modern Art, New York, New York
1994 *American Photography 1890–1965 from the Museum of Modern Art*; Museum of Modern Art, New York, New York
2001 *Open City: Street Photographs, 1950–2000*; Museum of Modern Art, Oxford, United Kingdom

Selected Works

Graduation, 1949
Man Coming Up Subway Stairs, 1952
David, 1952
Woman and Children at Intersection, 1952
Sun and Shade, 1952
Hallway, 1953
White Line, 1960
Coltrane on Soprano, 1963
Three Men With Hand Trucks, 1963
Mississippi Freedom Marcher, Washington, D.C., 1963
Pepsi, 1963
Boy, Man and Graffiti, 1966
Curtains and Light, 1987

Further Reading

Blue, Caroll. Conversations with Roy DeCarava. Narrator Alex Haley. New York: The Television Laboratory at WNET Thirteen, distributed by First Run Features, 1984, vhs, col and b/w, ½ in., 28 min.

Coleman, A. D. "This Person Passing Through." *Camera and Darkroom*, v. 14 n. 12 (December 1992): 32–41.
DeCarava, Roy. *Roy DeCarava, Photographs*. Carmel, CA: Friends of Photography, 1981.
DeCarava, Roy. *The Sound I Saw: Improvisations on a Jazz Theme*. London and New York: Phaidon Press, 2001.
DeCarava, Roy. *Roy DeCarava: Photographs*. Exh. cat. Houston: The Museum of Fine Arts Boston, 1976.
DeCarava, Roy, and Langston Hughes. *The Sweet Flypaper of Life*. New York: Simon and Schuster, 1955. Reprint Editions: Hill and Wang, 1967; Howard University Press, 1984. In German: *Harlem-story: Der söße Leim des Lebens*. Munich: Edition Langewiesche-Brandt, 1956. In Czech with minor revisions: "*Sladká mucholapka zivota*." In *Svetová literatura* (Prague), n. 5 (1958).
Edwards, Susan. "Roy DeCarava." *History of Photography* v. 21 (Summer 1997): 173–174.
Isé, Claude. "A Conversation with Roy DeCarava." *Artweek* v. 28 (January 1997): 23–24.
Kozloff, Max. "Time Stands Still." *Artforum International* v. 34 (May 1996): 78–83.
Rachleff, Melissa. "The Sounds He Saw: The Photography of Roy DeCarava." *Afterimage* v. 24 (January–February 1997): 15–17.
Roy DeCarava: A Retrospective. New York: Museum of Modern Art, 1996.
Stange, Maren. "Illusion Complete Within Itself, Roy DeCarava, Photographer." *Yale Journal of Criticism* v. 9 n. 1 (Spring 1996): 63–92.
Storr, Robert. "Roy DeCarava." *Art in America* v. 71, n. 8 (September 1983): 174.

THE DECISIVE MOMENT

Unlike many terms in the history of photography, the decisive moment has a clear definition and a precise origin. Most surprising is that the coining of the term occurred so late. It comes from the enormously influential book by Henri Cartier-Bresson, *The Decisive Moment*, published by Simon and Schuster in 1952. In the text he defined the term succinctly thus, "To me, photography is the simultaneous recognition, in a fraction of a second, of the significance of an event as well as of a precise organization of forms which give that event its proper expression."

In a sense, every successful photograph is a decisive moment, from the first photograph made in 1822, reportedly a three-day-long exposure, to images made in the burst of a strobe light in a thousandth of a second in the 1930s. All are records of a particular moment in time. But implicit in the definition is that the photographer is capturing subjects in motion. Such images have been made since Daguerre's 1842 daguerreotype of a man having his boots polished on a busy Paris boulevard. By the 1860s, instantaneous photographs were being made regularly. In the early twentieth century, there were photographers such as André Kertész, active since 1912, who like Cartier-Bresson after him, used a small handheld camera loaded with fast plates or sensitive film to capture life on the move and usually in geometric compositions.

The term became a convenient handle for the kind of photography that Henri Cartier-Bresson had been practicing since 1929, which had been called variously over the years, "poetic accident," "anti-graphic photography," and "fleeting moments." But in the context of the book filled with Cartier-Bresson's own photography there is the further implication that "the decisive moment' is not only of perfect arrangements of peak moments with a strong underlying geometry but the final image is also printed full negative without cropping.

It would be two decades before Henri Cartier-Bresson would define in writing the type of photography that he and his colleagues had been doing all those years. His work gained notice in the 1930s and was exhibited at the Julien Levy Gallery in New York. The young curator of photography, Beaumont Newhall, befriended Cartier-Bresson at that time and later published the first collection of his work in the catalogue for his exhibition at the Museum of Modern Art in New York in 1947. Newhall wanted to publish a book of his friend's photographs. In a letter from Beaumont Newhall to Henri Cartier-Bresson dated 29 October 1949 he wrote,

> I am thinking of doing a new book, to be called "Fleeting Image," which will deal entirely with what you so aptly call slices of 1/100 of a second.... I would like to use a good many of your things [photographs] to develop the thesis.

In another letter from BN to HCB dated 10 February 1951: "I haven't forgotten, and neither has [Richard] Simon, about our plans for a book." Richard Simon of Simon and Schuster, also an amateur photographer, collaborated with the art critic and publisher, Teriade, to realize the book. Teriade was a long-time friend and supporter of Cartier-Bresson. In the late 1930s, he had planned to publish a book of photographs by Cartier-Bresson and several other photographers including Brassaï and André Kertész but the war made it impossible. In 1952, with the assistance of Marguerite Lang, Teriade compiled the photographs, prepared the layout, and published the book in Paris in a style and format similar to his deluxe art review, *Verve*. With the book in preparation, Teriade and Simon pushed Cartier-Bresson to put down in words his approach to photography. That lucid text has been nearly as influential as the photographs in the book.

In formulating his ideas, Cartier-Bresson drew on his studies in the 1920s with the cubist painter and theorist, Andre Lhote, who stressed the balance of compositions based on the golden section. He was also inspired by Maurice Tabard's texts on geometric composition in photography.

This book of photographs and its text had an immediate and far-reaching impact on numerous photographers ranging from Elliott Erwitt to William Eggleston. The book was reviewed by such disparate artists as Walker Evans and Aaron Siskind. In addition to being one of the most important influences on photography for decades, "the decisive moment" quickly became something to react against as well. After Cartier-Bresson's book, the next most important and influential publication of the mid-twentieth century was Robert Frank's *The Americans*. It is filled with images that, in opposition to Cartier-Bresson's, might be characterized as random moments, non-events depicted in ways that seem off-balance. Horizon lines are tilted, figures are cut off at the edges of the frame or partially obscured by objects in the picture. The world appears to be glanced at quickly and without artifice. Frank believed that "the decisive moment' was an artificial way of seeing, that perfect arrangements of peak moments were removed from real life and were in some way dishonest. He said, "I don't want that in photography, the world moves very rapidly and not necessarily in perfect images." There are some skeptics who say that the only "decisive moment" occurs when the time comes to decide which one of the many exposures to make into the finished print. This term and the book's title owe their distinctive name to the fact that the original title selected for the simultaneous French publication of the book, *Images la sauvette*, is impossible to translate adequately into English. According to Cartier-Bresson it is roughly equivalent to, "Images on the Sly." Richard Simon of Simon and Schuster derived the English title for the book from the quote from Cardinal de Retz that Cartier-Bresson selected to be placed on the page before the beginning of his text: "There is nothing in this world that does not have a decisive moment."

Stuart Alexander

Further Reading

Assouline, Pierre. *Cartier-Bresson: L'oeil du si cle*. Paris: Editions Plon, 1999.

Cartier-Bresson, Henri. *Images la sauvette*. Paris: Editions Verve, 1952; as *The Decisive Moment*, New York: Simon & Schuster, 1952.

Henri Cartier-Bresson: The Man, the Image & the World, London: Thames & Hudson, 2004.

Hofstadter, Dan. "Profiles: Stealing a March on the World—I," *New Yorker*, 65, no. 36 (23 October 1989) 59–93.

Hofstadter, Dan. "Profiles: Stealing a March on the World—II." *New Yorker*, 65, no. 37 (30 October 1989) 49–73.

"Photography and Time." in *The Art of Photography*. New York: Time-Life Books, 1971, 112.

DECONSTRUCTION

Over the last four decades, the term deconstruction has infiltrated academic fields, notably philosophy and literary criticism. Deconstructive thinking has partially transformed architectural practice, theological inquiry, and popular culture. The thinker responsible for the term, Jacques Derrida, argues that deconstruction occurs in the works of Karl Marx, Friedrich Nietzsche, and the myriad writers

Derrida queries to establish that deconstruction has been happening since and before Plato. For Derrida, deconstruction is simply what happens. This essay discusses three thinkers, Jacques Derrida (b. 1930), Roland Barthes (1915–1980), and Jean Baudrillard (b. 1929), to introduce some ways deconstruction intersects photography.

The Photographic Text

Deconstruction intersects photography when one recognizes photos as texts. How are photos texts? Looking at a photo constitutes an act of reading. Photos solicit interpretations. A caption accompanying a photo attempts to direct reading toward a specific interpretation in part because interpretations might occur other than the interpretation the caption's author intends, even if the author is the photographer herself or himself. A photographer's intention might irrevocably control a photo's interpretation if, rather than texts, photos were windows opening upon existence. Neither does the reader's intention control the photographic text's interpretation. The illusion of such control requires the reader to ignore a photo's singular textuality.

One might argue that Ansel Adams's *El Capitan, Merced River, Clouds, Yosemite Valley* (c. 1952), requires little if any interpretation since the photo simply presents sublime nature: a spectacular cliff face towering in the background, clouds floating high to the distant horizon, and a turbulent river crossing the foreground. But such an argument forgets that the concept "nature" occurs in a nature/culture opposition laden with philosophical assumptions. The account of nature as a hallowed presence unpolluted by culture constitutes one such assumption. The impression that Adams's photo gives of presenting nature bears witness to an irreducibly textual effect: the persuasiveness of the nature/culture opposition.

Deconstruction involves the dismantling of major conceptual oppositions like the nature/culture opposition. In Adams's photo one reads an account of nature tied to the nature/culture opposition. Yet in reading the photo, when one remarks such an account's cultural specificity, the nature/culture opposition begins to dismantle. Adams's use of black and white film to conjure the impression of a starkly pristine natural landscape emerges as a cultural enterprise informed by a certain kind of preservationist environmentalism. Destabilizing the nature/culture opposition it evokes, the photo opens readers to questions that the nature/culture opposition muffles. This opposition supports narrating Yosemite Valley as a healing refuge free of urban stresses. Of course, tourists experience Yosemite Valley as such a refuge only by way of the tourist industry's urbanizing interventions: roads, public toilets, tour buses, a supermarket, a hotel, and so on. In deconstructing the nature/culture opposition, the photo moves one to ask: How can one's desire for the landscape to which the photo refers avoid being the desire for the consumer object Yosemite Valley threatens to become?

Deconstruction: A Variety of Postmodernism?

Redefining philosophical systems, political circumstances, and cultural artifacts (photographs, for example) as irreducibly textual is a postmodern gesture. Is deconstruction a variety of postmodernism? A leading scholar of deconstruction, Christopher Norris, argues against confusing Derrida's rigorous engagement with philosophical tradition for what Norris calls postmodernism. For Norris, postmodernism's irresponsible relativism flees from the duty to make ethical and political distinctions and decisions. As Norris correctly points out, rather than voiding ethical and political decisions, Derrida elaborates their intricate conditions of occurrence, however daunting and complex Derrida shows those conditions to be. Derrida insists on rethinking the European Enlightenment; on Norris's reading, postmodernism urges the Enlightenment's abandonment. For Norris, postmodernists are pursuing a questionable aesthetic rather than anything comparable to what Derrida calls deconstruction.

Norris's partition of deconstruction from postmodernism has some validity. But photography's crossing from modernism to postmodernism does entail deconstructive processes. One relevant comparison would be between Walker Evans's *Brooklyn Bridge, New York City* (c. 1929) and David Hockney's photo-collage *Brooklyn Bridge, November 28 1982* (1982). Both photographers took advantage of the pedestrian walkway that centrally traverses the bridge. The walkway allows the camera's lens to follow the unexpectedly thin suspension cables as they sweep gracefully from the photographer's standpoint to their convergence at one of the bridge's monumentally solid Gothic-arched towers.

Influenced by Alfred Stieglitz's photographic aesthetic of Pictorialism, Evans aspires to a high-art image of an icon of American modernity celebrated as such by Joseph Stella's paintings *The Voice of the City of New York Interpreted: The Bridge* (1920–1922) and *Brooklyn Bridge: Night* (1922). Evans's photo depicts the walkway scene Stella's paintings investigate. Evans produced his photo to be an illustration for his friend Hart Crane's poem *The Bridge* (1930). In Stella's, Evans's, and Crane's wake, Georgia O'Keeffe's modernist painting *Brooklyn Bridge* (1948) also offers a stylized rendition of the walkway perspective.

Evans helped to make the Brooklyn Bridge a must-see artwork. Amateur photographers often seek out the walkway scene inspired by Evans's photograph, by O'Keeffe's painting, or by popular images based on such modernist works. Countless visitors have meandered the walkway, snapped photos capturing a shot similar to Evans's, and framed their Brooklyn Bridge photographs for display in homes and offices worldwide. The frisson of "art" these framed snapshots provide amateur photographers stems from yet deconstructs the modernist aura Evans, Stella, Crane, and O'Keeffe gave the Brooklyn Bridge. However inadvertently, tourist photography quotes the Evans's photo, displacing it from the context of modernism to various contexts that open the walkway scene to divergent interpretations. In the process, the opposition between elite and popular culture deconstructs, raising questions concerning the sociopolitical values embedded in the distinction between "high" and "low" art. Postmodernism embraces the playful iteration of modernist works for democratized enjoyment.

Postmodern photographers investigate the modernist legacy in experimenting with and questioning representation. The postmodernism of *Brooklyn Bridge, November 28 1982* embraces amateur photography's deconstructive effects on Evans's photo. Hockney quotes the Brooklyn Bridge's modernist photographic representation in the idiom of casual tourist photography to produce an artistically ambitious work available to a popular audience. Standing on the walkway approximately where Evans stood, Hockney took dozens of photos: of the cables, of the tower, of the walkway, and of his own feet on the walkway. After having these "snaps" developed at a one-hour processing shop such as amateur photographers use, Hockney then assembled the photos into a collage. This "joiner," as Hockney calls his photo collages, evokes time and space, argues Hockney, in ways a single photo cannot but that a painting can. *Brooklyn Bridge, November 28 1982* playfully deploys the amateur iteration of Evans's modernist gesture while enacting Pictorialism's postmodern return.

Postmodernism and deconstruction do overlap in questioning representation. This questioning can have serious ethical and political implications. Cindy Sherman and Barbara Kruger are two photographers who make the postmodern inquiry into representation sharply political. Sherman and Kruger mimic and satirize the representational conventions of painting, film, advertising, pornography, and fashion photography to interrogate issues of gender, power, and exploitation. But one would be mistaken to think that Sherman and Kruger are merely suggesting that justice demands more benign representations of women. These photographers implicitly raise a more difficult issue: How is one to evaluate the category "representation" itself?

Derrida: Representation's Deconstruction

Is representation a value-neutral category? For Derrida, "representation" bears questionable philosophical assumptions that inform troublesome institutional practices. Rather than calling photographs representations, one should welcome representation's deconstruction.

The definition of representation as the recovery of presence emerges from "Western" philosophical tradition's dominant self-understanding. This tradition would found itself on a presence. Philosophy has claimed, among other entities, the good, spirit, and the human as foundational presences. (Notice that these presences assume their opposites: evil, matter, and the animal.) Philosophical texts want to recover a foundational presence for readers. When these texts ask, "See what I mean?," they are claiming to have represented a presence. Philosophy defines the text as a sign representing a presence that controls the sign's meaning. Paul, for example, knows Christ as the presence that controls what Paul's Letter to the Romans means.

For philosophy, one finally leaves signs behind in retrieving a presence that one sees, intuits, or knows. Knowledge arrives the moment reading ends. This is the "See what I mean?" moment. In this moment, signs recover a presence uncontaminated by signs. Signs, argues philosophy, are detours on the way to the full presence (say, of spirit) that is knowledge's origin and goal.

Philosophy grasps foundational presences as answers to the question: What is being? Philosophy's various answers to this question tend to conflate being with presence, yielding what Derrida calls the "metaphysics of presence." This metaphysics inheres in philosophy's understanding of language as representation. But Derrida finds that philosophical texts question this representational assumption in dismantling philosophy's binary oppositions. A metaphysic's coherence depends on an opposition that favors one term at the other's expense. To function as a founding presence, spirit must exclude matter. The spirit/matter binary defines spirit in opposition to matter while privileging spirit over matter. Additional oppositions include soul versus body and male versus female.

Such binaries deconstruct when the opposed entities turn out to contaminate each other. When humanity includes animal traits and animals merit an ethical consideration previously reserved for humans, the human/animal binary has undergone deconstruction. Deconstructing the oppositions they posit, texts release the abject terms from subordination to the privileged terms and so redefine both. As the human/animal opposition deconstructs, humanity's relation to animals will never be the same.

In deconstructing themselves, philosophical texts undercut presence's foundational status. Presence emerges as interminably contaminated by representation, deconstructing the presence/representation opposition. When this opposition deconstructs, the sign becomes presence's trace. And presence reconfigures as a trace woven into a textual fabric that presence neither founds, controls, nor escapes. Rather than merely representing being as presence, traces refer to an alterity or otherness irreducible to presence and so unavailable for representation.

For the presence/representation binary, the only possible referent is presence. This binary's logic precludes reference to otherness, rendering alterity unthinkable. This whitening out of alterity's traces reduces others to the same, a homogenization that facilitates such institutional violence as "racial" profiling. Another example: In defining singular others as a presence's mutually substitutable representations, many but certainly not all "multiculturalisms" homogenize those others in the name of "diversity." A violence at work in educational, governmental, and corporate institutions seeking to know, govern, and manage "the diverse" profitably, such homogenizing reduction is virtually inescapable yet always deconstructable.

Understanding photographs through the presence/representation binary risks collaborating with such violence and closing thought to otherness. The trace underscores deconstruction's political implications. Photos refer to alterity in deconstructing representation. Reading photographs as singular others' traces, Barthes and Baudrillard dismantle representational assumptions about photography in quite distinct ways.

"Punctum": Roland Barthes on the Trace

Roland Barthes's *Camera Lucida: Reflections on Photography* (1981) specifies how reading photographs with sensitivity to the trace departs from representational reading. Barthes describes his initial "'ontological' desire" to know what photography is (3). This philosophical craving seeks a foundational presence, an ontological basis, on which to ground knowledge of photography. But Barthes recounts how his "'ontological' desire [...] to learn at all costs what Photography was 'in itself'" gave way to the traces marking the photos he found intriguing (3).

Unthinkable in representational terms, these traces prompt Barthes to ask: "why mightn't there be, somehow, a new science for each object? A *mathesis singularis* (and no longer *universalis*)?" (8). Deconstructing "'ontological' desire," Barthes argues that to do justice to the singular trace of alterity marking a photo, one must invent a singular science. Barthes invents such a science to read what he calls the *Winter Garden Photograph*, a photo of Barthes's mother. Barthes relates how this photo "achieved for [him], utopically, *the impossible science of the unique being*" (71) . With this "*impossible science*," the irreplaceable otherness to which the *Winter Garden Photograph* refers becomes thinkable.

In *Camera Lucida* Barthes names the trace a photo's "*punctum*" and distinguishes it from the photo's "*studium*" (26–27) . The category *studium* defines photographs through a presence/representation binary. The *studium* entails any photographic content thinkable in representational terms. Reducing a photo to its *studium* reads the photo as a sign that represents a presence. For example, ethnographers read photos as representing "ethnicity." One can exchange any photo one reads as representing ethnicity for any other such photo in that one reads them all as representing substitutable instances of the same presence: being Irish, being Jewish, and so on. One homogenizes singular others in knowing them through the predicates that constitute one's answer to the question, for example: "What is Chicano being?" A general science of ethnographic photography may be inseparable from a representational understanding of photographs and the concomitant reduction of others to the same.

Barthes's "*impossible science of the unique being*" reads a photo as irreplaceable in that its utterly singular *punctum* evades representation's homogenizing logic. To read a photo's *punctum* may be impossible, but deconstruction traverses impossibility. As Derrida's *The Deaths of Roland Barthes* (2001) underlines, deconstruction happens in *Camera Lucida* as the other's impossible haunting of the same. A singularity's trace, the *punctum* is nowhere photographable in a photo's *studium*, yet the *punctum* supplements and mobilizes every element of the *studium*. The border between *punctum* and *studium* deconstructs even as the *punctum* remains heterogeneous to and breaches the *studium*'s representational closure. *Camera Lucida* marvelously demonstrates how, in representation's deconstruction, otherness becomes thinkable as otherness.

Jean Baudrillard: Hyperreality and the Trace

In the late 1960s, influenced by Marx, Baudrillard published sociological analyses of post-1945 consumer society. Baudrillard's analyses define objects, rather than commodities' producers, as sociological inquiry's locus. These objects form a "system of commodities" that is also a "system of signs" (Gane, Jean Baudrillard, 12). This concern with "the object" continues in Baudrillard's later writings but mutates dramatically in the 1970s as Baudrillard investigates contemporary societies characterized by global information technologies, biological cloning, and "reality" TV shows.

Baudrillard describes pre-modern societies as having engaged in symbolic exchanges characterized by semantic ambivalence and excessive, wasteful expenditure. The potlatch ceremony of the native peoples of North America's Pacific coast is an example. In contrast, Baudrillard correlates modern political economy with a subject-centered definition of reality as the representable. What one calls the real, Baudrillard argues, is largely European modernity's invention. For example, the gaze of Renaissance perspective "realized" the object in cleansing it of any symbolic dimension. Modernity relentlessly pursues the world's realization or objectification. The enchanting birds medieval hunting manuals depict become real in John James Audubon's disenchanted ornithological illustrations. While yielding exploitable knowledge, the real, the objective, is what the subject's gaze masters as representable. The real is an object's modern representational simulation, but in postmodern society the simulation of the real virtually subsumes reality.

In effect, Baudrillard understands the uneasy feeling that "if X is not on television X does not exist" as implying the following paradoxical answer to philosophy's "what is being?" question: what is the simulation of the real. Already an aggressive "take" on the object, reality now collapses into a hyperreality more real than reality. Digital photographic simulations of Audubon's illustrations posted on the World Wide Web are hyperreal. Digitalization can cleanse marks of deterioration and enhance faded colors to produce a virtual replica of each illustration more real than any of them. If science takes the crow's genome to encode the crow's biological reality, the digital mapping of that genome renders it hyperreal. Modifying DNA to conform to digitally "perfected" model genomes, biologists may soon clone birds whose defining antecedents are hyperreal simulations. Even time itself becomes hyperreal. What cable news shows and high-tech military command centers call "real time" is a hyperreal co-presence that simulates a reality one never encounters in reality: One will never simultaneously be in Washington D.C., London, and Baghdad.

In simulating objects as more than real "virtual" realities, the hyperreal constitutes an almost "perfect crime." This crime attempts the world's complete and final realization as a hyperreality free of (reference to) otherness. Fortunately, the crime is never perfect: Singular traces of otherness remain. In the photo, Baudrillard finds a trace of the object's singular alterity that marks the disconcertingly smooth and claustrophobic hyperreal.

Photos register the object's singularity in bypassing the representational subject's imposition of an objective meaning. Objects do not pose themselves to meet the composing eye's expectations. Photography may give one a glimpse of the object when no one is looking at or objectifying it, suggesting one's disappearance as a subject and one's release from subjective identity's boundaries. Rather than simulating time or movement, the photo, unlike film, video, or computer animation, allows for an "objectality" distinct from subject-centered "objectivity." "Objectality" deconstructs the subject/object binary while seducing us into the vitally illusionary play of a world disillusioned by reality's hyperreal simulation.

For Baudrillard, by insisting on an aesthetic "vision" or a moralistic documentary purpose, photographers retreat from photography's seductive potential and impose a signification onto the photo. Baudrillard is himself a photographer, and several galleries have exhibited his photos. These photos tend to be of things or city scenes exhibiting their "objectality." For example, Baudrillard's *Covered by Hoarfrost* series includes color close-ups of a car coated with hoarfrost and backlit by the early morning sunlight glowing through the windshield and front window with tree trunks and branches in the background. Each photo lingers over the unique pattern of light and color that the chaotic variations in the frost's thickness and texture produce. With the windshield and windows covered with frost, the car is a useless object. In this uselessness, the car's "objectality" emerges.

ROBERT S. OVENTLE

See also: **Barthes, Roland; Conceptual Photography; Interpretation; Modernism; Postmodernism; Representation; Representation and Gender; Semiotics**

Further Reading

Barthes, Roland. *La chambre claire: note sur la photographie.* Paris: Seuil, 1980; as *Camera Lucida: Reflections on Photography*, translated by Richard Howard, London: Flamingo, and New York: Hill and Wang, 1981.

Batchen, Geoffrey. *Burning with Desire: The Conception of Photography*. London and Cambridge, Massachusetts: MIT Press, 1997.

Baudrillard, Jean. *Fotografien, Photographies, Photographs: 1985–1998*. edited by Peter Weibel, translated by Susanne Baumann et al., Ostfildern-Ruit, Germany: Hatje Cantz Publishers, 1999.

Bennington, Geoffrey, and Jacques Derrida. *Jacques Derrida.* Paris: Seuil, 1991; as *Jacques Derrida*, translated by Geoffrey Bennington, Chicago and London: University of Chicago Press, 1993; 2nd edition, 1999.

Caputo, John D., ed. *Deconstruction in a Nutshell: A Conversation with Jacques Derrida.* New York: Fordham University Press, 1997.

Derrida, Jacques. "Les morts de Roland Barthes." in *Psyché: Inventions de l'autre*, Paris: Galilée, 1987; as "The Deaths of Roland Barthes," translated by Pascale-Anne Braul and Michael Naas, in Derrida, Jacques, *The Work of Mourning*, edited by Pascale-Anne Braul and Michael Naas, Chicago and London: University of Chicago Press, 2001.

Gane, Mike. *Jean Baudrillard: In Radical Uncertainty*. London and Sterling, Virginia: Pluto Press, 2000.

McQuillan, Martin, ed. *Deconstruction: A Reader*. New York: Routledge, 2000.

Phillips, David. "Photo-Logos: Photography and Deconstruction." in *The Subjects of Art History: Historical Objects in Contemporary Perspectives*, edited by Mark A. Cheetham, Michael Ann Holly, and Keith Moxey, Cambridge and New York: Cambridge University Press, 1998.

Norris, Christopher. *Deconstruction and the "Unfinished Project of Modernity."* New York: Routledge, 2000.

Plissart, Marie-Françoise. *Droit de regardes, avec un lecture de Jacques Derrida*, Paris: Minuit, 1985; as Derrida, Jacques, *Right of Inspection, photographs by Marie-Françoise Plissart*, translated by David Wills, New York: The Monacelli Press, 1998.

Zurbrugg, Nicholas, ed. *Jean Baudrillard: Art and Artifact*. London and Thousand Oaks, California: Sage, 1997.

JACK DELANO

American

Jack Delano (1914–1997) was a documentary photographer who photographed social and economic conditions for the Farm Security Administration (FSA) through the 1930s, but later moved to Puerto Rico where he became a major postwar visual artist, working in illustration, photography, and film and as a composer. His photographic body throughout his career exemplify the FSA mission to use photography to make a social argument, to inform and educate, using the conventions of that documentary vision but also expanding them stylistically and thematically.

Schooled as a classical musician and as a fine artist, Delano's first photographic study of coal miners in Schuylkill County, Pennsylvania, for the Works Progress Administration (WPA) reflects his earliest attempt at critical engagement with his photographic subjects. He became intimately involved in their lives and lived in the miner's homes and was thus able to photograph with compassion rather than detached objectivity. He knew about being an outsider from his experience as an immigrant born in the Ukraine and raised in Philadelphia where he learned to be "Americanized" including changing his name. This powerful exhibition, informed by the aesthetic values of the popular front highlighting the achievement of workers, was acclaimed by many, including photographer Paul Strand, and led to his hiring by Roy Stryker for the coveted job of staff photographer for the Historical Division in 1939. There, Delano worked closely with his wife Irene whom he married shortly after starting to work for the FSA until 1942. Irene assisted him with shooting scripts, making contact with subjects, and was a lifelong collaborator and artist in her own right.

Delano's work for the FSA was prolific, often focusing on workers' lives and detailing both work and leisure, expressing the mission of the FSA to create a repository of images of American life. His assignments included migrant workers, Portuguese fishermen in Rhode Island, Scandinavian communities in Minnesota, tobacco farmers in Connecticut, displaced persons as a result of the construction of military facilities and public works during World War II, industrialization in the Virgin Islands, and the economic conditions in Puerto Rico. Following the dictates of Roy Stryker, who provided photographers with shooting scripts, Delano also expanded and focused on racial injustice, a major theme in his work. For instance, his photographic study of the residents of Green County, Georgia, for sociologist Arthur F. Raper's *Tenants of the Almighty* feature rare images of inmates in Greene County jail, who while told to dance and sing for the photographer are also portrayed with dignity rather than exoticism or ridicule.

Delano sought to garner respect for his photographic subjects by highlighting their humanity through composition, framing, and careful lighting; he formed a relationship with the subjects rather than "stealing their image," and finally, included aspects of the person's material culture. His striking frontal portraits of families, workers, and farmers are shot from low angles to convey a sense of power or framing the subject against the sky. When asked, Delano cited Ben Shahn and Walker Evans as two influences on his work: Shahn for his artistic composition and Evans for his crisp attention to detail. Like other FSA photographers, Delano did not develop or print his own film; thus framing, composition, and lighting at the time of exposure were essential to the photographic narrative he constructed. Other influences on Delano's practice were formed during a Guggenheim Fellowship to Europe in 1946, which exposed Delano to religious iconography, some aspects of which found their way into his photographs. Some of his photographs have, for instance, a triptych-like composition or a strong internal narrative, made vivid by depth of field and the equal lighting of background and foreground. This strong depth of field was achieved by using various kinds of lighting, natural and artificial, including the use of bulbs in lamps.

Delano openly defended his decision to pose his subjects since photography was never neutral and always involved a number of decisions, large and small. Indeed, Delano carefully set up pictures, arranging family members, lighting the scene—often towards creating a sense of naturalism. In some of his photographs he created a feeling of deliberate appeal to the viewer for sympathy or understanding by directing his subject's gaze at the viewer, for example, in the photograph of a preacher and his wife, *Greene County Georgia.* Delano did not feel that this technique detracted from the documentary value of the photograph. Rather, he felt that framing the photograph and attention to composition was an aspect of truth telling. A photograph of Polish tobacco farmers (1940) laughing has been accused of being posed, but Delano argues that he was not posing them rather he was interacting with them. He also used mirrors in unusual ways, such as to expand the visual horizon, as in his photograph at a Thanksgiving dinner (1940).

Working mostly with a 35 mm and occasionally with an 8 × 10 camera, Delano wanted foreground and background to be produced with equal clarity, to view the subject most fully in their environment for which he used a medium shot. He often chose photographs that had vivid singular elements, which could express a universal and shared meaning regardless of the social background of the viewer. Delano's concern with the reception of the image began with his first exhibition of coal miners in which he refused to use frames. He then expanded through his later television and film productions in which reception among the working people whose lives were captured was part of his political project towards the inclusion of people who had been historically marginalized. Although often shooting in black and white, on his assignment to document Puerto Rican sugar growers, he used the newly developed Kodachrome color transparency film.

An effort towards racial and cultural equality underpinned his work in Puerto Rico where he lived and served as director of the Puerto Rican government's radio and television network following the war and Puerto Rico's new status as a Commonwealth.

Delano was active in the country's arts and cultural programs, and is considered a major cultural figure. Specifically, Delano's photographs were used as part of a broad program for social reform enacted by Luis Muñoz Marín, the first elected governor of Puerto Rico. Delano's photographic series of the public mourning of the 1980 funeral of Marín is important as a private and public tribute. In 1998, Delano was honored with the first major retrospective of his work, *The Art of Jack Delano*, a traveling exhibition organized by the Smithsonian Institution accompanied by the publication of his autobiography, *Photographic Memories.*

Danielle Schwartz

See also: **Documentary Photography; Evans, Walker; Farm Security Administration; History of Photography: Interwar Years; Lange, Dorothea; Lee, Russell; Office of War Information; Representation and Race; Rothstein, Arthur; Shahn, Ben; Social Representation; Stryker, Roy; Works Progress Administration**

Biography

Born Jack Ovcharov near Kiev, Russia, 1 August 1914; emigrated to the United States in 1923; naturalized 1928; adopted the name "Delano" 1940. Educated at the Settlement Music School, Philadelphia, 1925–1933; Central High School, Philadelphia, 1928–1932; Pennsylvania Academy of Fine Arts, Philadelphia 1932–1937; photographer with the Works Progress Administration (WPA) Project, New York, 1936–1937; freelance photographer working mainly for the United Fund, New York, 1939–1940; FSA staff photographer 1939–1943; Office of War Information, 1942–1945; director/producer for educational film services, 1946–1952; program director for the education television station in San Juan, 1957–1964, general manager of TV and radio service of Puerto Rico, 1964–1969. Cresson fellowship, 1936–1937. Awards: John Simon Guggenheim Memorial Fellowship, 1946, 1960; UNESCO fellowship to study educational techniques used by television stations in Asia and Europe to see how they could be applied to Puerto Rico, 1961; National Endwoment for the Humanities Grant in 1979; Composers Award Institute of Puerto Rican Culture, 1984. Died in Puerto Rico, August 1997.

Individual Exhibitions

1938 *Anthracite Coal Miners*; Pennsylvania Railroad Station Gallery, Philadelphia, Pennsylvania
1977 Sonnabend Gallery; New York, New York
1978 Art Students' League; San Juan Puerto Rico
1984 Daytona Beach Community College; Daytona Beach, Florida
1986 *Before and After: The FSA*; Daytona Beach Community College, Daytona Beach, Florida (with Arthur Rothstein and Marion Post Wolcott)
1998 *The Art of Jack Delano*; traveling exhibition organized by the Smithsonian Institution, Washington, D.C., and traveling to Rafael Carrion Pacheco Exhibit Hall, Old San Juan, Puerto Rico; Smithsonian Institution, Washington D.C.; El Museo del Barrio, New York, New York; Chicago Cultural Center, Chicago, Illinois; Orlando City Hall Public Art Program, Orlando, Florida; New Jersey State Museum, Trenton, New Jersey

Selected Group Exhibitions

1955 *The Family of Man*; Museum of Modern Art, New York, New York, and world tour
1962 *The Bitter Years*; Museum of Modern Art, New York, New York
1976 *FSA Photographers*; Witkin Gallery, New York, New York
1977 *Documenta 6*; Kassel, West Germany
1978 *Work*; Fine Arts Museums of San Francisco, San Francisco, California
1979 F.S.A; les Annees Ameres de l'Amerique en Crise, *1935–1942*, Centre Georges Pompidou, Paris, France, and traveled to Galerie Municipale du Château d'Eau, Toulouse, France
1981 *Farbe im Photo*; Josef-Haubrich-Kunsthalle, Colgone, Germany
1982 *Floods of Light*; The Photographers' Gallery, London, England
2004 *Changes: 50 Years of Transformation in Puerto Rican Life*; Casa de la culture, Chicago, Illinois

Selected Works

Mr. And Mrs. Andrew Lyman, Polish tobacco farmers and FSA clients, Windsor Locks, Connecticut, September 1940
Pumpkin pies and Thanksgiving dinner at the house of M. Timothy Levy Crouch, a Rogaine Quaker, Ledyard, Connecticut, November 1940
A preacher and his wife, who lived in a converted schoolhouse with their two grandchildren. Heard County, Georgia, April 1941
In the home of an FSA borrower, Greene County, Georgia, June 1941
The family of Russell Tombs moving out of their home, which was in the area being taken over by the army, Caroline County, Virginia, June 1941
A farm laborer's widow living on a Farm Security Administration project near Manatí, Puerto Rico, 1941
Boy in sugarcane fields bringing lunch to his father. Guánica, Puerto Rico, 1942

Further Reading

Delano, Jack. *Photographic Memories: The Autobiography of Jack Delano*. Washington, DC: Smithsonian Institution Press, 1997.
———. *Jack Delano, Photographic Memories*. Introduction by Sally Stein. Washington, DC: Smithsonian Institution Press, 1997.
———. *Puerto Rico Mio: Four Decades of Change*. Washington, DC: Smithsonian Institution Press, 1990.
———. *El dia que el Pueblo se despidio de Munoz marin*. Carolina, Puerto Rico: Borinquen Litheographers Corporation for Fundacion Luis Muoz Marin, 1987.
Doud, Richard K. "Interview with Jack and Irene Delano." June 12, 1965. Smithsonian Archives of American Art Oral History Collection, Washington, D.C.
Lauria-Perricelli, Antonio. "Images and Contradictions: DIVEDCO's Portrayals of Puerto Rican Life." *Centro* 3, no 1 (Winter 1990–1991): 92–96.
Raper, Arthur F. *Tenants of the Almighty, FSA Photographs by Jack Delano*. New York: MacMillan Company, 1943.
Stein, Stein. "FSA Color." In *Modern Photography* (New York) January 1979.
Stryker, Roy, and Nancy Wood. *In This Proud Land: America 1935–1943, As Seen in the FSA Photographs*. New York: Galahad Books, 1973.

DEPTH OF FIELD

Depth of field refers to the area of critical sharpness within a photographic image. A lens can only focus on one area in an image at a time, and this area is also called the zone of focus and refers to the distance between the closest and farthest parts of an image that are reasonably sharp. Depth of field varies because of a number of factors such as the size of the aperture, the distance between the camera and the subject, and the focal length of the lens. Depth of field is used for creative control and allows the photographer to manipulate the area of focus in a photographic image to a small area of selective focus, a large area of overall sharpness, and any amount in between these two extremes.

A mechanism inside the lens called a diaphragm creates an opening in its center named the aperture, and the diaphragm allows the aperture to change in size creating a variety of aperture settings. The aperture setting is the most influential over depth of field; the larger the aperture in the lens the lower the area of critical sharpness, and the smaller the aperture in the lens the larger the area of critical sharpness. Aperture sizes on most lenses progress through a set of numbers called F-stops, which are numerical values for the opening's area and move from the largest to the smallest in a sequence: f/1.0, f/1.4, f/2, f/2.8, f/4, f/5.6, f/8, f/11, f/16, f/22, f/32, f/64. Setting the aperture at the largest opening is sometimes called "shooting wide open," and the phrase "stopping down" is used to indicate the opening in the lens becoming smaller. If a lens has a variable focal length or a zoom function, the widest aperture may also vary as the focal length of the lens changes. On a darkroom enlarger, the aperture setting of the lens will also affect depth of field in a photographic print. If a print requires more overall sharpness, using a smaller aperture on the enlarger lens will increase the sharpness of the photographic print slightly, while using a large aperture on the darkroom enlarging lens limits the overall range of sharpness projected through the image.

The aperture affects depth of field in a photograph through the formation of small, round image elements called circles of confusion. These circles of confusion are created as light passes through the opening in a lens, and their size is dependent upon the aperture setting. A larger aperture will form big circles of confusion, and a small aperture will create small individual image elements. Thus, using a small F-stop will create an image made up of small circles of confusion, and using a large F-stop will create an image area made of large circles of confusion. The smaller the circles of confusion, the sharper an image will appear on the photograph. The area in the image that is the sharpest is called the plane of critical focus, and depth of field is measured out from this plane. The larger the area on either side of the plane of critical focus, the wider the degree of sharpness; a large area of depth of field is referred to as wide, and a small area of depth of field is called shallow.

Depth of field can also be controlled by the focal length of a lens and the distance between the subject and the lens. A lens with a longer focal length such as a telephoto will condense space and produce a shallow depth of field, while a lens with a short focal length such as a wide angle or fisheye will produce an image with a wide depth of field. As the focal length of a lens increases in a telephoto lens, the magnification of the image will also increase and result in more image distortion that decreases depth of field. A wide angle lens has a very small amount of magnification and thus creates a minimum amount of distortion in the image, resulting in a wider depth of field. The distance between the subject and the lens will also affect depth of field: The farther the object is from the camera lens, the wider the depth of field. As an object moves away from a camera lens, the overall image area is increased and this allows for a larger area of sharpness in the image. The closer an object is to the lens, the shallower the depth of field.

Depth of field can be determined in a number of ways on a camera, such as using the depth of field scale on a lens, utilizing a depth of field preview function if it is available, and setting the focal distance of the subject through zone focusing or hyperfocal focusing on the lens. A depth of field scale is often placed on manual lenses, and will show the area of sharpness relative to the aperture chosen for an image. Many cameras include a depth of field preview function or show the area of critical sharpness through the lens and the viewfinder of the camera as the aperture, focal length, and distance to subject vary. Zone focusing sets the area of depth of field relative to the needed sharpness of a subject and the image composition in advance of shooting the picture, while hyperfocal focusing sets the focus of the lens on the hyperfocal distance (the minimum focal distance that will allow infinity to remain sharp in the image.) Selective focusing and manipulating depth of field is used in all photographic imagery to direct the impact of an image's visual composition and theme. Limiting depth of field to a shallow area will isolate a subject from a background, and using a wide depth of field will emphasize the entire image area. Photojournalists and landscape photographers generally exercise extreme control over depth of field in their genres. Digital darkroom tools such as Adobe Photoshop can also alter the appearance of sharpness in an image through manipulation tools that increase or decrease image sharpness in selective areas.

JENNIFER HEADLEY

See also: **Camera: An Overview; Enlarger; Lens**

Further Reading

Adams, Ansel. *The Camera*. New York: Little, Brown, and Company, 1991.

Horenstein, Henry. *Black and White Photography: A Basic Manual*. New York: Little, Brown, and Company, 1983.

Folts, James A., Ronald P. Lovell, and Fred C. Zwahlen, Jr. *Handbook of Photography*. Albany, NY: Delmar Thompson Learning, 2002.

Horenstein, Henry and Russell Hart. *Photography*. Upper Saddle River, NJ: Prentice Hall, 2001.

London, Barbara, John Upton, Ken Kobré, and Betsy Brill. *Photography*. Upper Saddle River, NJ: Prentice Hall, 2002.

Warren, Bruce. *Photography*. Albany, NY: Delmar Thompson Learning, 2002.

Wildi, Ernest. *Photographic Lenses*. Amherst, MA: Amherst Media, 2001.

DEVELOPING PROCESSES

Overview

In order to make visible, stable images, exposed silver-gelatin plates, films, and papers must be processed through the use of various chemical solutions. Most consumer grade prints and fine art prints are made by the negative–positive system; a negative film or plate is exposed in a camera and processed to yield a negative image. This negative image is exposed onto printing paper by contact printing (1:1 size) or projection (enlargement). The exposed paper is processed in a procedure analogous to the film processing but typically with a separate set of chemicals. This printing process reverses the tonal scale again to yield a final positive image.

Processing of black-and-white negative plates, films, and printing papers is generally a sequence of five steps consisting of (1) develop, (2) stop, (3) fix, (4) wash, and (5) dry, but a number of auxiliary treatments may be added. The development step is where a visible image is developed from the invisible latent image contained in films and papers. Stop bath is used to arrest the development process as well as minimize the developer carryover to the next step. The fixing process removes unexposed and undeveloped parts of photosensitive silver halide from the negative and papers, thereby making the material insensitive to further light exposure. The fixed material is washed to remove the processing chemicals, and then dried for storage.

In silver-gelatin processes, when an individual silver halide crystal (0.1 to 3 μm diameter in size) in the sensitized layer of the photographic material (film or paper) is exposed to light, a tiny speck of metallic silver (photolytic silver) is created, called a latent image center. This speck can be as small as a few silver atoms and is not visible. The latent image is made visible or developed in the development step. Individual developed silver grains contain up to several billion silver atoms. Thus, development is a chemical amplification process with a gain factor on the order of a few billion.

On the other hand, there is a class of silver-gelatin material where development is not used. This is the printing out process (POP, which also stands for print out paper), which is extremely slow contact printing material, mainly used in the early years of silver gelatin photography. In POP, the visible image is formed entirely by photolytic silver, and therefore the exposure must be much more intense and prolonged in order to create grains of metallic silver that are large enough to form a visible image without chemical amplification.

It is obvious, by comparing the developed out process and printing out process, that the development process is a major technological advance that greatly improved photographic sensitivity. Together with the various sensitizing techniques introduced to silver-gelatin emulsions and improved optics, increased overall photographic sensitivity in the twentieth century enabled the photographing of a far wider range of subjects, such as fast moving objects and dimly lit scenes.

History of Developing Processes

Development is an electrochemical reduction process, where a silver ion gains an electron from a reducing agent, to deposit metallic silver selectively on exposed crystals having a latent image center. Historically, the silver ions were supplied from the developer solution, as in William Henry Fox Talbot's developer for the calotype. Calotype developer consisted of a solution of gallic acid fortified with silver nitrate. Silver ions are reduced by the gallic acid, and the metallic silver was deposited on the latent image to form a visible image. This type of developer is called "solution physical developer," which is very slow working and gives slow photographic speed, and therefore is rarely used in current practice. In modern developers, silver ions are supplied from within the silver halide crystals. This type of developer is called "direct developer" or "chemical developer." These two modes of development are not mutually exclusive, and in fact, solution physical development occurs to limited extents in many modern developer solutions, which predominantly use chemical development. Readers are warned that the terms "physical," "direct," and "chemical" are misleading.

Pyrogallol developer, introduced for the wet collodion process in the 1850s, had been used as a part of physical developer in acidic solutions, but it also started the era of direct development when J. Burgess recommended the alkaline developer pyrogallol in ammonia in 1973. This was soon adapted to development of silver gelatin dry plates, thus entering the years of chemical development.

The decade of the 1880s saw the first surge of intense searching for new developing compounds, with many compounds being introduced as developing agents. Developing agents are chemical reductants, but useful developers must have certain electrochemical properties as well so that the developer can act selectively on exposed crystals. In 1880, Abney introduced hydroquinone developer, and Eder and Toth catechol developer. They were followed by *p*-aminophenol and *p*-phenylenediamine by Andersen in 1888, Eikonogen (1-amino-2-naphthol-6-sulfonic acid) by Andersen in 1889, Amidol (2,4-diaminophenol) by Andersen and Bogisch in 1891, Glycin (N-methyl-*p*-hydroxyphenylglycine) by Bogisch and Metol (N-methyl-*p*-aminophenol) by Bogisch and Hauff, both in 1891. These developing agents gave images of varying speeds and contrasts. The way images emerged in the developing plates also varied. In hydroquinone developers, the highlights emerged first and grew in density, while midtone and shadow areas after considerable lag slowly appeared. On the other hand, in Metol developers, shadows and highlights appeared almost simultaneously and grew in density together. Since various developing agents worked differently, many solutions were formulated with different agents for diverse applications.

As early as 1889, a developer solution containing two developing agents was formulated. It is quoted by Levenson (1991) that Henry J. Newton reported that he had added hydroquinone to an Eikonogen developer to boost the highlight density. His developer offered the best of both agents. Shortly after, developers of Metol-hydroquinone (MQ) combination were formulated, and it was noted that the MQ developer was more active than the sum of Metol and hydroquinone activities when used alone. There were several speculative explanations and partial proofs for this "superadditive" phenomenon, but convincing proof had to wait for Levenson's work in the late 1940s, indicating that the image is developed by Metol, and the reacted Metol is regenerated to become active again by hydroquinone, demonstrating the "regeneration theory" of superadditive development. However, without waiting for the science, various empirical data were gathered and practical MQ developers were made. One of the most important MQ developers is the Eastman fine grain (D–76) developer by Capstaff in 1926, which remains one of the most important black-and-white film developers today. The MQ combination was found to be very effective, versatile, and capable of producing high image quality, so that most other agents were made obsolete or spared for special purpose applications, with an exception described next.

Another wave of new developing agents came after the discovery of Phenidone (1-phenyl-3-pyrazolidone) by Kendal in 1940. Various chemical derivatives of Phenidone, as well as other compounds containing a similar heterocyclic ring structure were studied. Phenidone is much more potent than Metol and more rapid in developing images when combined with hydroquinone. The combination of Phenidone and hydroquinone is called the PQ system. It was also less susceptible to accumulation of free bromide ions, a development reaction byproduct that retards further development when used in typical fine grain film developers. These advantages of Phenidone improved several aspects of the development process, especially in volume processing plants, once this compound became commercially available in 1953. Also, since Phenidone is used in such a small quantity, it enabled formulation of packaged developer concentrates, which are ready to use by simply diluting with water. However, original Phenidone (also called Phenidone A) was relatively unstable in alkaline solutions. Thus Phenidone B (4-methyl-1-phenyl-3-pyrazolidone) and Dimezone (4,4-dimethyl-1-phenyl-3-pyrazolidone) were introduced. These compounds solved the instability problem but they had a new shortcoming of not being very soluble in water. Ultimately, Dimezone S (4-hydroxymethyl-4-methyl-1-phenyl-3-pyrazolidone) was introduced, which solved both the stability problem in alkaline solutions and the solubility problem in aqueous solutions. In today's commercial developers supplied as liquid concentrates, Dimezone S is commonly used in a superadditive combination with hydroquinone, with PQ and MQ developer systems covering the majority of black-and-white film and print developers in contemporary use.

Another developing agent from the 1880s that is of current importance is *p*-phenylenediamine. Chemical derivatives of this agent are used in developers for color photography. When exposed silver halide crystals are developed with these agents, the developing agent is oxidized. An oxidized developing agent reacts with a dye coupler to form a dye *in situ*. Dye couplers are usually colorless, but when reacted with oxidized forms of *p*-phenylenediamines, they form dyes whose color depends on the dye coupler molecule. In other words, dye coupler provides one-half of a dye molecule, and *p*-phenylenediamines the other half; the developing reactions of the exposed crystals combine the two halves. The developed metallic silver is then removed, and the resulting image consists of the color dyes. This is the major difference of chromogenic (color) development from black-and-white development.

Practical chemical developer solutions usually contain developing agent(s), an alkaline agent, and a preservative. Many developers also contain an antifogging agent. The alkaline agent in early use was ammonia solution, but it was prone to inconsistent results, and was replaced with more stable agents such as hydroxides, carbonates, and borates. Carbonates and borates form an effective buffering system in the pH ranges commonly used for developer solutions. Early chemical developers lacked a preservative and had short useful lives. Berkeley introduced sodium sulfite to the developer solution in 1882, which prolonged the useful life of the developer. Sulfite in various forms, including sodium sulfite itself, is extensively used in modern developer solutions. Developers of high developing power often cause fogging that does not appear in developers of lesser powers. This type of fog was suppressed by bromide added to the developer solution. The effect of bromide in developer was studied from the very early days of sensitometric investigation of silver-gelatin materials, and it remains one of the most frequently used antifogging agents today, along with newer agents such as benzotriazoles and 1-phenyl-5-mercaptotetrazole.

With numerous developing agents discovered, and many variables associated with them, a great many developer formulae were concocted and published for pictorial negatives and prints. It is conceivable that each new developer was hoped to improve the image quality, photographic speed, tonal range of the developed image, graininess, and perhaps other aspects of the image quality, as seen in all kinds of advantages claimed for the formulae. However, as photographic scientists and engineers accumulated knowledge and experience, it was realized that the entire range of developer solutions could be formulated with a few standard developing agents (Metol, Phenidone, and hydroquinone) and a few common agents. Today, pictorial photographic films and papers are manufactured to exacting photographic properties and technical specifications, to be processed in one of the standard developers. Modifying some properties of modern material through adjusting the developer formulation is possible only with often unacceptable costs in other aspects of the image quality.

As well, the technical requirement for developers changed over time as photography innovated with both photographic processes as well as equipment, particularly in advances in the camera. In the early years of dry plate photography taken with large-format view cameras, the negatives were printed on papers of generally low contrasts, by contact printing, or with low magnification factors. Therefore, high contrast negatives were preferred and graininess was unimportant. However, when high-contrast print emulsions became common, especially in combination with the 35 mm film format, a low contrast developer with improved fine grain quality became necessary. Eastman D–76 fine grain developer of Capstaff, previously mentioned in relation to the MQ developer, appeared just at the time this need was realized. Another important requirement was a developer suitable for consistent processing of a large volume of materials, especially in the processing of motion pictures.

Most amateur processing chemicals are used only once, but this practice is wasteful; a number of alternative processing technologies were developed. While small amounts of developing agents are consumed in the process, loss of the agent can easily be supplemented. The main cause of diminished activity in repeatedly used developer solution thus is accumulation of a development reaction byproduct, free bromide ions, and it is the removal of byproducts that presented a major challenge in reusable developers. In the early years of motion picture processing, two-bath development was studied, where the first bath contained developing agent and the second bath, alkaline buffer with no developing agent. The idea is that the film emulsion absorbs the developing agent in the first bath, and the actual development is activated in the second bath, where the byproduct is released. Since the film is not fully developed in the first bath, this more costly solution can be used repeatedly, while the second bath, could be inexpensively replaced.

Although the two-bath development technique yields acceptable results, it provides a limited range of contrast control. The more preferred technique is to replenish the working bath of the developer. The replenishing solution is designed to maintain a stable pH value and other critical parameters of the developer bath as well. The replenishing technique was a major improvement, but later, minilab machine processing increased the pressure to further reduce the amount of waste solution. A later technology takes part of the working developer bath and removes free bromide ions from it by an ion exchange resin, and puts the rejuvenated solution back into the bath, together with a small quantity of the replenishing solution to supplement for the spent agents, greatly reducing the amount of waste solution. This was very important for the convenience of machine operation as well as the cost of proper disposal of industrial waste solutions.

Stop Bath, Fixing, and Subsequent Handling

Following development, the film or paper is usually immersed in an acid stop bath to acidify the adsorbed solution, thereby rapidly arresting the development reaction. In machine processing, adsorbed developer solution is sometimes removed by a squeegee. In small scale darkrooms, this process is sometimes substituted with a plain water rinse. Despite its name, the stop bath does not literally end the development process. Its most important role is to prevent the developer from being carried over to the fixing bath.

The developed and stopped material is then fixed. The fixing bath contains thiosulfate, which dissolves undeveloped silver halide crystals. In black-and-white processing, acid fixer is traditionally used to minimize the risk of dichroic fog caused by developer carryover. Alum hardener is often added to the fixing bath to minimize the risk of emulsion damage while handling the wet material. However, modern films and papers have generally much more durable coating layers than the time these acid hardening fixers were designed, and therefore hardener is optional and often unnecessary in manual processing. Some fixing solutions are based on sodium thiosulfate and others, ammonium thiosulfate, or a combination of sodium thiosulfate and ammonium chloride. Those that contain an ammonium salt are called "rapid fixer" because they fix materials faster than traditional sodium salt. (Thiosulfates, especially sodium thiosulfate is often called "hypo" but this is a misnomer.)

Each time it is employed, the fixing reaction uses up a small amount of thiosulfate and releases silver-thiosulfate complex ions. The solution becomes exhausted when an excessive amount of silver accumulates in the solution. As in the case of enabling developer to be reused, it is the removal of the silver that is the focus of regenerating fixing bath. There are several practical methods in use for processing on various scales, but because silver is rather precious, methods that maximize its recovery and minimize the volume of waste solution are in widespread use in commercial photofinishing.

After successful fixing of the photographic image, the material must be thoroughly washed because high levels of residual thiosulfate is detrimental to the life of the photograph. The washing time necessary to achieve a level of residual thiosulfate that enables very long life expectancy varies widely, depending on the material, the fixer formula, and the washing water. Impermeable support materials such as polyester film and resin-coated paper can be sufficiently washed in a few minutes of running water. However, traditional fiber-based prints adsorb thiosulfate ions rather stubbornly in both their fibers and sizing materials, and adequate washing requires much longer time. Therefore, fiber-based prints are usually treated with a washing aid, which is a buffered sulfite solution, which accelerates desorption of thiosulfate by an ion exchange mechanism.

In the past, a "hypo eliminator" formula containing peroxide was recommended. This treatment chemically destroys thiosulfate to a harmless form, but this solution is no longer recommended because the treatment is now known to be harmful to the image. Since the necessary washing time to produce prints with good permanence is variable, it is recommended to run a quality control test in each darkroom. One test for residual thiosulfate is called "silver nitrate test" and is facile and sensitive enough for most purposes. The test should be run at regular intervals, emphasising whenever the new printing paper, fixing solution, or washing water is introduced to the darkroom.

In past decades, conservation scientists or conservators found problems with the permanence of silver-gelatin prints and microfilms that had been properly processed and washed. The problems were attributable to improper storage and display conditions. Silver-gelatin materials enjoy very long life expectancy if they are properly processed, washed, and stored. Good storage conditions require low temperature, low humidity, and absence of environmental pollutants and other oxidizing agents, including those from the storage container materials, such as cardboard, wood, adhesives, and paints. The image is also susceptible to pollutants from industrial exhaust and oxidizing agents from the atmosphere, such as ozone. While it is difficult enough to keep valued photographs under ideal storage conditions, it is virtually impossible if the desire is to have easy access to them or indeed if they are displayed.

In order to make the image more permanent in less than ideal conditions, toning treatments of prints have been found to be effective. In particular, treatment with polysulfide toners (such as Kodak Brown Toner) is convenient as well as inexpensive and has been found to be highly protective in a number of studies. Prints should be toned after fixing and washing. Prints must be thoroughly washed again after toning to remove the toning solution, because residual toner is also detrimental to the image. Although polysulfide toned images have increased stability, proper storage conditions remain the key factor in a photographic print's longevity.

Environmental Concerns

Concerns for preserving the environment have also been raised in recent decades. Volume processors use efficient processing methods where waste solution is minimized, which is important in terms of minimizing chemical waste and the cost of disposal treatment. On the other hand, attempts were made to reduce environmental impacts from the effluents of small-scale darkrooms, which are discharged directly into municipal sewer systems, by replacing the rather harmful hydroxybenzene compounds (developing agents such as hydroquinone, catechol, and pyrogallol) with harmless ascorbic acid and its isomers. The developing action of ascorbic acid was known in the early 1930s and it was one of the preferred developing agents among modern researchers studying the mechanisms of development. It was known, however, to be difficult to make practical, robust developer solutions using ascorbic acid. Environmental awareness re-directed attention to these harmless compounds (ascorbic acid is in fact vitamin C), and attempts to use ascorbates are seen in patent literature for a range of applications from low contrast, fine grain film developers to high contrast medical imaging. Major manufacturers sold developers that employed ascorbates in place of hydroquinone in PQ developer systems. However at the beginning of the twenty-first century, this effort has lost importance as most standard solutions already have low environmental loads and most amateur, commercial, medical, and scientific photographers and photojournalists have rapidly migrated to digital imaging technology, leaving only a small population of fine art photographers in the world of traditional, wet-processed materials.

There are many ways to look at the developing processes and their history. It is important to note that many darkroom manuals and photography textbooks contain technical errors and repeat outdated misconceptions; interested readers are encouraged to consult original research publications and review articles written by experts in a particular branch of developing processes. Coote (1982) is a darkroom manual rather rich in technical aspects. Mitchell (1984) is an introductory textbook of photography as a general science class at college level. At a more technical level, Keller (1993) and Locker (1996) are encyclopedia sections giving concise accounts of the photographic process. Haist (1979) is a comprehensive book on the chemistry of photographic processing. Sturge (1977) and Proudfoot (1997) are handbooks for those interested in technical aspects of photography. The newer edition of Sturge (1977) has a considerably different content from the seventh edition. James (1977) is a highly specialized technical reference book for photographic chemists. Levenson's papers give overviews of development reactions with emphasis on superadditivity, for which he made major contributions. Historiography of key technologies and applications in silver gelatin emulsions and processing is one area of void in literature. Jacobson (1991) gives an overview of the progress of the photographic process. Eder (1945) is a book on the history of photography by one of the early active contributors to the silver-gelatin process. Baier (1964) is another comprehensive book on the same topic. Early history is also described in older editions of Neblette (1930). Mees (1961) is a book describing the history of photographic research at Kodak Research Laboratories.

RYUJI SUZUKI

See also: **Camera: An Overview; Conservation; Darkroom; Film; Non-Silver Processes; Print Processes; Toning**

Further Reading

Baier, W. *A Source Book of Photographic History (Quellendarstellungen zur geschichte der fotografie)*. Germany: Veb Fotokinoverlag Halle, London: Focal Press, 1964. (all editions in German).

Coote. *Monochrome Darkroom Practice*. Boston: Focal Press, 1982.

Eder, J. M. *History of Photography*. 4th ed. New York: Columbia University Press, 1945.

Haist, G. *Modern Photographic Processing*. Vol 1 and Vol 2. New York: Wiley, 1979.

James, T. H. *The Theory of Photographic Process*. 4th ed. New York: Macmillan Publishing Co., London: Collier Macmillan Publishers, 1977.

Jacobson, R. E. "Photographic Processes—1890 to the Present Day." *J. Photogr. Sci.*, 39 (1991) 70–76.

Keller, K. ed. *Science and Technology of Photography*. Weinheim, Germany: VCH Verlagsgesellschaft, New York: VCH Publishers, 1993. (The content of this book forms a part of Ullmann's encyclopedia of industrial chemistry.)

Levenson, G. I. P. "Superadditive Developers." *Photogr. Sci. Engr*. 13 (1969) 299–311.

Levenson, G. I. P. "Development of the Latent Image." *J. Photogr. Sci.* 39 (1991) 63–69.

Locker, D. J. *Photography*. In: Kirk-Othmer Encyclopedia of Chemical Technology. 1996.

Mees, C. E. K. *From Dry Plates to Ektachrome Film*. New York: Ziff-Davis Publishing Company, 1961.

Mitchell, E. N. *Photographic Science*. New York: Wiley, 1984.

Neblette, C. B. *Photography: Its Principle and Practice*. 2nd ed. New York: Van Nostrand Company, 1930.

Proudfoot, C. N., ed. *Handbook of Photographic Science and Engineering*. 2nd ed. The Society for Imaging Science and Technology, 1997.

Sturge, J. M., ed. *Neblette's Handbook of Photography and Reprography*, 7th ed. New York: Van Nostrand Reinhold, 1977.

PHILIP-LORCA diCORCIA

American

New York-based Philip-Lorca diCorcia became an essential photographer on the international scene in a few short years in the 1990s. He emerged in the 1980s as conceptual photography had become a significant genre in contemporary photography with pictures that provided an interesting late-century look on the long-standing fiction–reality dialectic that characterizes photography. His work requires careful attention: At first glance his color pictures seem ordinary, not unlike snapshots or amateur efforts. People seem fixed in banality, suspended in their actions, and expressive of stereotypes or cultural prejudices. A closer look, however, reveals clues left by the artist that indicate this is not a captured slice of life, but a well-thought-through scenario, carefully set up and composed both before the shot is taken and during the process of shooting.

His earliest work was based on his family experience; his best-known early photograph, *Mario*, 1978, was carefully staged by diCorcia and the forlorn young man looking into the refrigerator is in fact his brother. This photo was part of diCorcia's *Family and Friends* series, a fictional "documentary."

diCorcia moved to New York in 1984 to pursue commercial work, including fashion and advertising photography, which do not diverge greatly from his fine-arts work. A 1993 exhibition curated by John Szarkoski at the Museum of Modern Art (MoMA) heralded his international career.

The photographic universe of diCorcia is in tension between microcosm and macrocosm, the private and public worlds where what seems familiar may not be, and where what seems intimate may, in fact, be artifice. His collection entitled *A Storybook Life* (consisting of pictures taken between 1975 and 1999 presented as a group in 2003) can be read as a retrospective tracing his career in 76 images. Those portrayed are engaged in trivial or everyday activities: a father with his daughter, a cook, a woman laying down on a bed, a man leaning on his elbow on a car door, having a discussion with the female driver. diCorcia, however, makes his subjects appear singular by his treatment of the scene. The woman who cooks seems removed from the reality of what she is doing; her gestures are suspended, the knife in her right hand, food in the other. Artificial and natural lighting is combined, blurring the photograph as a straightforward document a skill developed by diCorcia in his commercial work. The seemingly naturalistic but highly planned set up places his subjects inside a story, albeit an ambivalent or shifting narrative. With this method and the resulting image diCorcia proposes a new approach to Henri Cartier-Bresson's "decisive moment."

In his series *Hollywood* (1990–1992), composed of 20 handsome and haunting ektacolor prints, diCorcia chose those who have dropped out of mainstream society as photographic topics, including male prostitutes, drag queens, and drug addicts found on California's Sunset Boulevard and Santa Monica sidewalks. For this series, diCorcia initially chose sites (streets, motels, restaurant), planned the set up and the lighting, and then sought out models. These models are in the final work identified by their name or nickname, their age, and their hometown, and become "merchandise" in the strict sense of the word because diCorcia also added to the title the amount paid to the model, as in *Eddie Anderson; 21 Years Old; Houston, Texas; $20*, 1990–1992. Unlike Nan Goldin or Jack Pierson, who incidentally were his classmates at the School of the Museum of Fine Arts, his pictures place each human being in solitude pregnant with a dramatic intensity. Yet diCorcia's working method was in fact subversive, for he paid his models from a grant he received from the National Endowment for the Arts, which at that time had set guidelines in reaction to the controversies that had erupted around Robert Mapplethorpe. diCorcia explained:

> I started to think about that particular project in response to social antipathy towards gays and homosexuals at the end of the 80s and to a generally conservative backlash against that aspect of society. ...I was given a government grant on condition my work did not go against moral values. I protested by indicating in the legends how much I had paid the hustlers using money from this government grant.

The series *Two Hours*, composed of 11 large-scale images taken at the same location on the streets of La Havane, and the series *Streetwork*, depict passersby. But diCorcia does not so much take pictures of individuals as he focuses on a new species, the inhabitants of the street. The people photographed by diCorcia are strange hybrid beings characterized by their stereotypical humanity, like the businessman with his newspaper under the arm, umbrella in one hand and mobile phone in the other, yet becoming unreal archetypes that are barely recognizable as real humans. As always, diCorcia's shooting technique accentuates the fictional character of these photographic sequences. In these series the camera is placed level with the ground instead of at eye level, and he uses flash to augment the natural lighting. The mournful unreality of fiction that infuses his work expresses the alienation and dislocation of contemporary urban life in the United States and around the world.

THOMAS CYRIL

Biography

Born 1953 in Hartford, Connecticut. Attended University of Hartford early 1970s; School of the Museum of Fine Arts, Boston, Massachusetts, Diploma, 1975; Post Graduate Certificate, 1976; Yale University, New Haven, M.F.A., 1979. Relocated to New York City; freelance magazine photographer, 1984–present day, shooting for *Esquire*, *Fortune*, *W*, and *Details*. *Strangers* series, shown at Museum of Modern Art, 1993. Recipient Artist Fellowship, National Endowment for the Arts Fellowship, 1980, 1986, 1989; John Simon Guggenheim Memorial Fellowship, 1987. Visiting Critic, Yale University. Living in New York.

Individual Exhibitions

1985 *Philip-Lorca diCorcia, Fotographies*; Zeus Arts, Milan, Italy

1991 *Philip-Lorca diCorcia*; The Photographers' Gallery, London, England

1993 *Philip-Lorca diCorcia: Strangers*; Museum of Modern Art, New York, New York

Philip-Lorca diCorcia: Strangers and Others; Galeria Palmira Suso, Lisbon, Portugal

1994 *Portraits of America*; Nikon Salon, Tokyo, Japan

1995 *Art & Public*; Geneva, Switzerland

1996 *Street work*; PaceWildensteinMacGill, New York, New York

1997 *Philip-Lorca diCorcia, Hustler/Street work*; Museo National Centro de Arte Reina Sofia, Madrid, and University of Salamanca, Salamanca, Spain

Streetwork; Galerie Almine Rech, Paris, France

1999 *Philip-Lorca diCorcia*; Art Space Ginza, Tokyo, Japan

2000 Galeria OMR; Mexico City, Mexico

2001 Galerie Almine Rech; Paris, France

2004 *Philip-Lorca diCorcia*; Centre national de la photographie de Paris, France

Group Exhibitions

1985 *Seduction: Working Photographs*; White Columns, New York, New York
Contemporary Photography VI; Fogg Art Museum, Harvard University, Cambridge, Massachusetts
1987 *Arrangements for the Camera: A View of Contemporary Photography*; Baltimore Museum of Art, Baltimore, Maryland
New Photography 2; Museum of Modern Art, New York, New York
1990 *Witnesses: Against Our Vanishing*; Artists Space, New York, New York
1991 *Pleasures and Terrors of Domestic Comfort*; Museum of Modern Art, New York, New York
1993 *Under Age: Photographs of Children*; San Francisco Museum of Modern Art, San Francisco, California
Prospect 93; Frankfurter Kunstverein and Schirn Kunsthalle, Frankfurt, Germany
1995 *International Foto Triennale*; Galerie der Stadt Esslingen, Esslingen, Germany
1997 *Whitney Biennial Exhibition*; Whitney Museum of American Art, New York, New York
1998 *Emotions and Relations*; Hamburger Kunsthalle, Hamburg, Germany
Tell Me a Story: Narration in Contemporary Painting and Photography; Centre National d'Art contemporain de Grenoble, Grenoble, Switzerland
1999 *In the City*; Exposition au FRAC Haute-Normandie, Rouen, France
2000 *Hybrid*; Fotomuseum Winterthur, Winterthur, Switzerland
The Shape of the World / The End of the World; Comune di milano, Milan, Italy
2001 *Instant City: fotographia e metropoli*; Centro per l'Arte Contemporanea Luigi Pecci Prato, Italy
Setting and Players: Theatrical Ambiguity in American Photography; White Cube, London, England
2002 *Chic Clicks: Creativity and Commerce in Contemporary Fashion Photography*; Institute of Contemporary Art, Boston, Massachusetts
2003 *Strangers: The First ICP Triennial of Photography and Video*; International Center of Photography, New York, New York
Cruel and Tender: The Real in the Twentieth-Century Photograph; Tate Modern, London, England

Selected Works

Mario, 1978
A Storybook Life, series, 1975–1999
Hollywood, series, 1990–1992
Eddie Anderson; 21 Years Old; Houston, Texas; $20, 1990–1992
Streetwork, 1993–1997
Two Hours, 1999
Heads, 2000

Further Reading

Bond, Henry. "Philip-Lorca diCorcia's Virtual Reality." *Creative Camera* no. 309 (April/May 1991).
Bruce, Chris. *After Art: Rethinking 150 Years of Photography*. Seattle: Henry Art Gallery, 1994.
Galassi, Peter. *Philip-Lorca diCorcia*. New York: Museum of Modern Art and Harry N. Abrams, Inc, 1995.
Galassi, Peter. *Pleasures and Terrors of Domestic Comfort*. New York: Museum of Modern Art, 1991.
Georges, Alice Rose, Abigail Heyman, and Ethan Hoffman, eds. *Flesh and Blood: Photographer' Images of Their Own Families*. New York: Picture Project, Inc., 1992.
Grundberg, Andy. "Looking at Television." In *Acceptable Entertainment*. Paul Laster and Renee Riccardo, eds. New York: Independent Curators, Inc., 1988.
Rian, Jeff. *Œil à gages: Philip-Lorca diCorcia*. Paris: Almine Rech Edition, 2001.
Stack, Trudy Wilner, and William Tolan. *Family Matters: An Exhibition of Works by Sally Mann, Vince Leo, Melissa Shook and Philip-Lorca diCorcia*. Tempe, AZ: Northlight Gallery, Arizona State University, 1993.
Yamagishi, Koko. "Philip-Lorca diCorcia, Portraits of Contemporary Americans." *Deja-vu* No. 15 (1993).

DIGITAL PHOTOGRAPHY

"Digital photography" is a widely used term for the various computer-based technologies being employed to substitute for some or all of the chemical-based technologies of traditional photography. The term "digital imaging" is sometimes used interchangeably with "digital photography" but it has a broader meaning, extending to images of non-photographic origination. An even broader term for the use of the computer with visual materials is "computer graphics."

Digital photography encompasses both direct "digital capture"—that is, the recording of photographic images by a camera employing an electronic sensor and digital data storage rather than film—and indirect "digital conversion" through the scanning of film-based photographic images or existing prints. Once created—by either method—digital image files (computer data that represent a photographic image) may be easily modified, duplicated, transmitted, displayed on screen, or "output" to printed form by a wide variety of means. Some of the printing technologies used within digital photography are fully digital themselves (computer-driven printers such as dye-sublimation or inkjet, or even mass-production offset) and some are hybrids (using computer-driven lasers, for example, to expose standard photographic printing paper that must then be chemically developed).

Traditional photographic technologies are now often referred to as "analog" to distinguish them from those that are "digital." Analog recordings retain a physical relationship to the phenomena they record; the densities of film are proportional to the intensities of light that produced them in the same way that the grooves of a record emulate sound waves. Digital recordings, on the other hand—whether of light or of sound—maintain no analogous relationship to what they represent. An image is translated by the digital camera or scanner into a series of numbers (ones and zeros). To again become intelligible to human senses, digital data must be converted back into analog form; this happens as it is being displayed on a monitor or being printed.

In traditional photography, millions of microscopic grains of silver halide molecules dispersed through a film's emulsion respond proportionally to the intensity of light striking them. In digital photography, millions of microscopic sensors in a grid respond proportionally to the intensity of light striking them. The sensitivity of either a film or a digital capture system may be expressed as an ISO (International Standards Organization) rating; this is a fixed value in the case of film but can be user-adjustable in digital cameras. Generally, the higher the ISO rating of a film, the higher its visible "graininess." As the ISO rating of a digital sensor is increased, its "noisiness" generally increases. After film has been exposed, no visible image exists; a pattern of changed energy states in the silver halides, known as a "latent image," must be chemically developed for the image to be revealed. Neither does a visible image exist in a digital sensor after it has been exposed; it is created through sets of calculations—or algorithms—performed within the circuitry of the camera or in a separate computer. After an image has been created using film, the image continues to reside in the film itself as a unique deposit of silver and/or dyes. After an image has been created by a digital imaging system, it is "written" as a digital image file to some form of digital storage and may be identically reproduced at will.

A digital image is defined by the number of "pixels" (picture elements) that make it up and the numerical value for the brightness of each pixel (or three numerical values in the case of a typical "RGB" color image—one for red, one for green, and one for blue). A five "megapixel" digital camera (five million total sensing elements), for example, will typically produce an image file 2560 pixels by 1920 pixels. In the case of a standard monochrome—or "grayscale"—image, each pixel will be assigned one of 256 possible levels of brightness (represented by numbers from 0, which signifies absolute black, to 255, which signifies absolute white) and the image file will use approximately 5 Mb (megabytes) of computer memory. In the case of a standard RGB color image, there are three brightness values per pixel, each expressed as a number between 0 and 255 (yielding 16.7 million possible color variations at each pixel) and the image file will use approximately 15 Mb of memory. Many digital imaging devices can record an even higher number of tonal variations at each pixel, which may be helpful when photographing scenes of great contrast, but, currently, only 256 variations per pixel are used for screen display. It is worth noting that a higher density of pixels will generally produce an image of higher resolution, but there are other factors affecting image quality, just as in analog photography. Two different five-megapixel cameras may yield very different results, depending upon lens quality and the amount of noise and digital artifacts caused by the sensor and related electronics. To put digital resolution in a traditional photographic context: the largest truly "photo-realistic" color print that could be produced from an RGB image file created by a five-megapixel camera would be about 8 × 10 inches.

One additional technical consideration is that of file formats. A digital image file, to be readable by more than just one computer, must be written to storage using widely agreed-upon protocols, or "formats." The most universal file formats for digital images are PICT (from "picture") and TIFF ("tagged image file format"). Also very popular—virtually ubiquitous—is the JPEG format (named for the "Joint Picture Experts Group" that developed it). JPEG files differ from most PICT or TIFF files in that they are significantly "compressed." They take up less space in storage media and transmit more quickly across networks. Compression is achieved by using special algorithms to find patterns within images whose compact definitions can substitute for a full pixel-by-pixel description. To decompress images, reverse algorithms are used to reestablish the original pixel structure. Because some of the original detail will be lost in this cycle—and some unwanted image "artifacts" generated—JPEG is counted as a "lossy" compression scheme (in comparison with the more moderate, but "lossless" compression schemes used in other formats). In general, as higher compression is employed, more loss occurs.

History

Digital photography has its roots in wire-service image transmission (a precursor to "fax" technology originating in the 1920s), television (which first used electronic sensors to interpret a lens-formed light-based image), in unmanned space exploration (for which computer technologies were developed that could allow for the conversion of visual data into digital form both for visual enhancement and for its transmission over long distances with frequent interruptions), in satellite espionage photography (requiring extensive image enhancement) and in medical imaging (which developed technologies for interpretation and storage of complex visual data). The first crude computer-controlled image scanners were developed in the mid-1950s. NASA introduced digital image processing in the 1960s and transmission in the 1970s. The monitor screen became the primary computer control interface in the 1970s and was enhanced by graphical user interfaces in the early 1980s. The Associated Press wire service introduced its AP Electronic Darkroom—a digitally-based image transmission and storage system—in 1978. These all set the stage for the rapid development of digital imaging technologies during the 1980s and 1990s.

The first major photographically-based technology to become virtually entirely digital was that of mass-production offset printing. By the late 1980s, the vast majority of photographic illustrations appearing in books and magazines were being created by computer-controlled technologies rather than by traditional photo-process halftone plates. Large, powerful industrial computers, drum scanners and printing equipment were able to handle the daunting challenge of creating, handling, and outputting millions of bits of digital visual information well before home computer systems could do so.

Photojournalism was also at the forefront of the switch to digital technologies. The relatively low resolution requirements for newspaper photographs allowed digital capture technologies to be adopted earlier than in photographic fields with expectations of higher image quality. Simultaneously, the press's needs for rapid transmission and distribution of images encouraged development of digital transmission systems. By the early 1990s, the marriage of digital capture and portable, satellite-based digital transmission allowed a newspaper to put a photograph on its front page less than an hour after a photojournalist had taken it in a remote part of the world. Things moved so rapidly in the industry that most major U.S. newspapers were closing their darkrooms by the late 1990s (the *Vancouver Sun* describes itself as the first to go all-digital, in 1995).

At the broader consumer level, two major milestones would be the 1984 introduction of the Apple Macintosh system—which brought a visually-oriented computer to many desktops (usually equipped with a graphically flexible though low-resolution printer)—and the 1990 release of the first version of Adobe Photoshop, the most powerful among a number of early "digital darkroom" programs. Photoshop would, in subsequent releases, go on to become the standard in digital photography software.

On the "capture" side of the developing technologies, Sony introduced its first "Mavica" electronic still video camera in 1981. It wasn't technically "digital" since it used an "analog" video mini-disk recording system, but it heralded the move towards filmless photography. Most major camera manufacturers developed extensive still video photographic systems through the 1980s; these were precursors to truly digital systems. In 1986, Eastman Kodak introduced the first megapixel image recording sensor (incorporating one million individual sensing elements); in 1991 they released the first professional-level digital SLR, the DCS-100, incorporating a 1.3 megapixel sensor into a Nikon-built camera body. The compact Dycam 1 of 1990 was the first truly digital consumer market camera; it could store 32 compressed images in its 1 Mb of internal RAM and then transfer the images to a computer.

These technologies offered interesting insights into the near future, but desktop computing power and the quality of scanners and printers remained far from truly photographic. For anything approaching professional photographic quality, the early 1990s still demanded expensive computer hardware (such as Kodak's half-million-dollar Premier System that came complete with a high quality drum scanner, film writer and mini-computer workstation, and was a relative bargain at the time).

Despite the initial limitations, many artist-photographers had begun experimenting with computer technologies in the early 1980s. Some worked with consumer-level equipment, "grabbing" low-resolution images from video cameras, processing them on low-cost but graphically capable Commodore and Atari computers and printing them on "dot matrix" printers. Others, such as Nancy Burson, obtained access to programmers and high-power academic computers, and began creating truly photographic-looking work, often with interesting conceptual aspects. One of her pieces, *Mankind*, 1983, blended the faces of typical individuals of each of the world's major "races" in proportion to that race's portion of the world's population. The resulting—quite believable—face, looked most strongly Asiatic, but had distinguishable traits of each race.

In 1991, an Eastman Kodak/Apple Computer partnership created the Center for Creative Imaging in Camden, Maine, where many artists went to learn the nascent technologies—and even occasionally get access to a Premier System workstation—until its closing in 1994. Nash Editions, founded in 1990 by musician/photographer Graham Nash and his associate Mac Holbert, with the help of expert printmaker Jack Duganne, modified Iris inkjet printers, originally designed for commercial print-industry proofing, for use as high quality fine-art photo printers. Printing options for photographic artists working digitally began to expand exponentially.

By the mid-1990s, desktop computers were beginning to have enough processing power, memory, and storage to accommodate truly photographic images of moderate size. Desktop scanners and printers were greatly improved and were becoming available at prices affordable to individual photographers (photo-resolution "dye-sublimation" printers, for example, came to be priced under $10,000). In 1992, Kodak introduced its hybrid "Photo CD" technology that would allow photographers to have film images scanned at relatively high quality and low cost and returned to them—up to one hundred per disk—on the same kind of recording media that had previously been used primarily for music. Also being developed were systems for digital image "color management" that would allow some control over the accuracy of digitized color information and its consistency through the various stages of the digital photography process (capture, manipulation, storage/transmission, and presentation).

During roughly the same period, professional-quality scanning backs capable of near-film resolution and color fidelity had been developed for use on view cameras. Their application was limited, however, to subject matter that remained perfectly still for several minutes at a time, and the camera had to remain tethered to a computer. The same was generally true for digital-capture backs developed for medium-format studio cameras. Some very high-end digital SLR cameras could capture instantaneous images acceptable for reproduction in newspapers, even magazines; Kodak's DCS-460, introduced in 1995, raised the image-resolution bar for self-contained camera systems to 6 megapixels. These high-quality digital camera technologies remained very expensive, however, and subject to rapid obsolescence.

One artist who quickly adopted emerging large-format digital capabilities was Stephen Johnson, who married a 4 × 5 inch field camera with a scanning back, a laptop computer, and a van, and took to the back country, updating Ansel Adams's practice for the digital age. Johnson eventually received official recognition from the National Parks Service and engaged in a five-year documentation of the parks system, from 1994–1999, using increasingly capable digital equipment whenever it became available.

On the professional/commercial side of photography, one of the areas to embrace digital techniques both in the studio and post-capture was that of fashion and glamour. This area had always relied heavily upon highly-staged photo shoots and heavy retouching of images to improve the perfection of its illusions of beauty. Digital technologies made it possible to put less effort into the initial staging, since the images could be easily manipulated in post-production, and made perfection—or even hyper perfection—in the final image more fully attainable. Their contemporary use is typified in the work of Patrick Demarchelier and David LaChapelle, who often push their fashion images into the realm of visual fantasy.

Through the rest of the decade, digital imaging equipment became increasingly powerful and increasingly affordable. Computer processing speed—crucial for the massive calculations required in handling high resolution images—doubled roughly every eighteen months (a pattern predicted by the well known "Moore's Law" in 1964). The other components of digital imaging systems—from cameras and scanners through computer workstations and storage media, to monitors and printers—kept up a similar pace of improvement. The standard for quality amateur-level digital cameras moved from "VGA" resolution (roughly one-third megapixel) to one megapixel, to two megapixel, to three megapixel. Professional instant-capture systems (for medium-format studio cameras) approached 20 megapixels and view-camera scan backs approached 100 megapixels. Inkjet printers were developed using increasingly smaller dots and more colors of ink, essentially matching analog photo printing methods. "Writeable" CDs became a common medium of digital image storage and exchange; other kinds of portable storage media evolved from 44 Mb Syquest cartridges to 2 Gb (gigabyte) JAZ cartridges.

One of the qualitative changes that the digital age has brought to photography is that of the mass distribution of images by electronic, rather than print, means. Initially, CD-ROMs were popular, but the rapidly increasing transmission speed of the Internet soon made the WorldWide Web the dominant mode. Mosaic, developed at the University of Illinois and publicly released in 1993, was the first Web "browser" capable of displaying photographic images; subsequent browsers featured increasingly sophisticated image capabilities. Within just a few years, Web-based photographic displays, galleries, auctions, and so on, were quite common.

The first widely acclaimed exhibition of digital fine-art photography was "Iterations: The New Image." Curated by Timothy Druckery and Charles Stainback, it was mounted in 1993 at Montage '93 (an "International Festival of the Image") in Rochester, New York, and in 1994 at the International Center of Photography in New York City. Included among its artists were MANUAL (a collaboration between Ed Hill and Suzanne Bloom), Michael Brodsky, Carol Flax, Esther Parada, Jim Pomeroy and several others. 1994 also saw the launching of the exhibition *Metamorphoses: Photography in the Electronic Age*, curated by the Aperture Foundation and including Barbara Kasten, Peter Campus, David Byrne, Pedro Meyer and Nancy Burson, among others. It opened at the Fashion Institute of Technology in New York City and then traveled in the United States to Houston, Tampa, Philadelphia, and San Jose, and then to Helsinki, Finland, and several other venues. These exhibitions featured images that displayed considerable digital manipulation. By the end of the decade, virtually all large-scale color photographic prints being displayed in galleries or museums were digitally produced. Sometimes the images were obviously manipulated (Patrick Nagatani, Aziz + Cucher); sometimes the possibility of manipulation lurked just below the surface (Jeff Wall, Andreas Gursky). Often, however, the digital nature of the print wasn't an issue at all, as digital technologies were increasingly seen as simply another means of producing "photographs."

Concerns raised by digital photography

Along with the easy duplication and distribution made possible by digital imaging technologies and the Internet came serious concerns about property rights. While no traditional photographer would freely distribute his or her negatives, the digital files being made widely accessible, especially if they were of high resolution, could be seen as "source code" for endless digital copies and even for unauthorized prints. Although there have been ongoing revisions of copyright law and other efforts to protect the authors of images (and other creative materials) in the digital era, these have not been fully successful. Other steps that have been taken include restricting the resolution of digitally distributed images to levels well below the quality of the originals and embedding theoretically unremovable data within image files ("watermarks"—both visible and invisible) that would clearly indicate authorship.

An even more serious concern associated with digital photographic technologies—arising virtually at their inception—has been that of veracity. While traditional photographs have always been susceptible to a variety of manipulations that could distort or modify their apparent meaning, photography has, by and large, enjoyed the popular assumption of truthfulness. On the other hand, digital imaging technologies are widely known for facilitating virtually effortless and undetectable manipulation of the image. In the most extreme case—that of digitally captured photographs—there is not even the equivalent of the original negative to which there might be recourse in the case of claimed manipulation.

Through the 1980s, a number of infamous cases of photographic manipulation came to public attention, including the moving of the Giza Pyramids in a *National Geographic* cover photo, the implied presence of two celebrity actors in one room in a *Newsweek* image when in fact they were photographed separately in New York and Los Angeles, and the placing of one celebrity's head on another's body in a cover photo of *T.V. Guide*. In each of these cases, the publication claimed that the context of use did not imply—and therefore did not require—careful adherence to visual truthfulness. Significant movements arose, often involving photojournalists, news organizations, and public interest groups, seeking to establish clear guidelines for permissible use of image manipulation in the media. The importance of maintaining "truthfulness" as a quality of the documentary image was widely endorsed. Several European countries adopted laws requiring that clearly distinguishable symbols signifying "montage" accompany all significantly manipulated photographs. Despite these movements and regulations, however, actual practice continues to be problematic—no presumption can now be made that any magazine cover image or image in an advertisement has not been manipulated. Even with "editorial" photographs, many cases of manipulation continue to be revealed.

A third area of concern in digital photography has been image permanence. Many digital printing technologies were never designed to produce anything but short-lived products. Early inkjet color prints often faded in a matter of months, to the disappointment of their producers. The printing technologies have matured substantially so that many digitally produced prints can now be expected to last at least as long as their traditional photographic counterparts, if they are kept under the right conditions. (Ink-based prints, especially, tend to be more susceptible to moisture, ultraviolet light, and environmental contaminants than are traditional silver-based photographs). Related to image permanence is the issue of data permanence and accessibility. Many digital image files encoded earlier in the development of digital photography are unreadable by current computers, and this trend towards obsolescence of file formats and storage-media technologies is likely to continue. In addition, the storage media are susceptible to eventual physical degradation, even breakdown. These are problems that the still-young practice of digital photography will have to solve.

In 2003, for the first time, more digital cameras than film cameras were sold in the world, and Eastman Kodak announced that it would no longer engage in film research. It appears that almost all photography will soon be fully or partially digital photography.

Blaise Tobia

See also: **Burson, Nancy; Camera: Digital; Developing Processes; Film; Gursky, Andreas; Photographic "Truth"; Wall, Jeff**

Further Reading

Aaland, Mikkel, and Rudolf Berger. *Digital Photography*. New York: Random House, 1992.

Amelunxen, Hubertus, et al., eds. *Photography after Photography: Memory and Representation in the Digital Age*. Munich: G&B Arts, 1996.

Ciaglia, Joseph. *Introduction to Digital Photography*. Upper Saddle River: Prentice Hall, 2002.

Coleman, A D. *The Digital Evolution: Visual Communication in the Electronic Age, Essays, Lectures and Interviews 1967–1998*, Tucson, Arizona: Nazraeli Press, 1998.

Cope, Peter., *The Digital Photographer's Pocket Encyclopedia*. Silver Pixel Press, 2002.

Druckery, Timothy, ed. *Iterations: The New Image*. New York: International Center of Photography, 1993.

Mitchell, William J. *The Reconfigured Eye: Visual Truth in the Post-Photographic Era*. Cambridge, MA: MIT Press, 1992.

Ritchin, Fred. *In Our Own Image: The Coming Revolution in Photography*. Millerlon, New York: Aperture, 1990.

Metamorphoses: Photography in the Electronic Age. Aperture #136, 1994.

RINEKE DIJKSTRA

Dutch

Rineke Dijkstra's *Beaches* (1992–1996) comprise large-scale, color portraits of adolescents standing in front of the sea. Dijkstra began the project in the Netherlands, and continued to photograph in a variety of locations: America, Belgium, Britain, Croatia, Poland, and the Ukraine. The contrast between her American and European subjects is subtle and poignant. The differences that distinguish the young people are manifested in their clothing, their expressions, and their body language. For each photograph, Dijkstra provides a location and a date, and these confirm our suspicions and cultural stereotypes; the Eastern European children have less fashionable clothes, the American kids are better groomed and more practiced at posing like models. Nevertheless, what is most striking about these portraits is that, despite the obvious differences in appearance among the adolescents, they are united through their self-conscious concentration on the camera/photographer. They share in the feelings of vulnerability that accompany such exposure. A photograph made at Hilton Head Island, South Carolina in 1992, depicts a young American in a peach-colored bikini. Her hair is long, blonde, and streaked. Her plump body is smoothly tanned. Her eyes are a deep blue. Everything is how it should be and, yet, her brow is furrowed as if the effort of looking perfect, or the worry of not, takes the pleasure out of life.

It is the tension between self-consciousness and inadvertent self-exposure that characterizes all Dijkstra's portraits: whether they are still photographs or (derived from) videos. Comparisons are often made between Dijkstra's practice and that of Diane Arbus. In an interview with Jessica Morgan (2001), and paraphrasing Arbus's famous statement, Dijkstra claims that she works in "the gap between intention and effect." In fact, Dijkstra's photographic practice acts as a textbook demonstration of Roland Barthes' description of photographic portraiture in *Camera Lucida* (1982). He refers to four competing "image-repertoires" that "intersect," "oppose," and "distort" each other: the person the subject thinks she or he is, the person the subject wants others to think she or he is, the person the photographer thinks the subject is, the person the photographer wants to make use of in his or her art. Each of Dijkstra's portraits is borne out of this intersection of expectations and desire. The significance of this observation is that it refutes a criticism that has been leveled at her portraiture: that her photographs exploit people's powerlessness. On the contrary, what Barthes' point, and Dijkstra's images, reveal is the necessary reciprocity of the gaze in the posed portrait. Photographer and subject confront each other, and it need not be antagonistic or disempowering. Dijkstra's portraits are insightful and empathetic. Hers is not a brutal stare, but a penetrating one. Unlike Thomas Ruff's photographs of young people, which deliberately emphasize surface details over psychological states, Dijkstra tries to get "beneath the skin" of her subjects.

A regularly cited influence on Dijkstra's practice is the German photographer August Sander. Like Sander, Dijkstra photographs types. In addition to the adolescents in *Beaches*, she has photographed bullfighters, new mothers, school children, disco-goers, and soldiers. In doing so, she sets up a further tension: that of the relationship between the general (category) and the specific (individual).

Take, for example, her *New Mothers*, begun in the 1990s. The young women in Dikjstra's portraits share a look of bemused wonder. They hold their babies protectively against their naked bodies. They behave in comparable ways. And, yet, the series of full-length photographs clearly marks each woman's individuality: different body shapes, different facial characteristics, different hairstyles. It is worth noting, here, that in stark contrast to the de-sexualized, idealized nude of western painting, Dijkstra's women are uncompromisingly corporeal. In *Tecla, Amsterdam, Netherlands, May 16, 1994*, a trickle of fresh, red blood runs down the women's left leg. In *Saskia, Harderwijk, Netherlands, March 16, 1994*, the woman's caesarean scar is painfully apparent. The mothers' commonality and dissimilarity are emphasized formally by the locations in which they pose. Though each place is similar in terms of its neutrality (a plain wall and an uncarpeted floor), the details vary noticeably: wood, linoleum, tiles, an electrical socket, a light switch, the cropped edge of a doorframe.

As with *New Mothers*, Dijkstra's four head-and-shoulder portraits of bullfighters (1994) insist upon the comparative and contrasting signifiers of the individual within a category. Photographed immediately after a fight, with ripped clothes, bruised bodies, and blood-splattered faces, the matadors exhibit an intensity of emotion akin to the young women with babies: a mixture of bewilderment and self-containment.

In 1995, Dijkstra began making video-recordings at clubs in and around Amsterdam, and sometimes in collaboration with Gerald van der Kaap. *Buzz Club/Mysteryworld* (1996–1997) contrasts two venues, a disco in Liverpool, England, and a techno-club in Zandaam, Netherlands. Dijkstra recorded the adolescents against a white background, in a storage cupboard, from where the music was still audible. The effect was to isolate the teenagers from the chaos and noise of the dance floor, without totally altering their mood. Her subjects smoke, drink, and kiss. They move their bodies to the music and play up to the camera. The video, which lasts 26 minutes and is played on two screens, juxtaposes the venues and the types of young people who attend them. Deliberately selecting adolescents who conform to peer groups, Dijkstra demonstrates national and gendere stereotypes, while encouraging her subjects to differentiate themselves from the crowd. In another video piece, *Annemiek* (1997), a young blonde teenager with braces on her teeth, mouths along to a pop song. The video plays on a loop.

The visible oscillation between Annemiek's self-absorption and self-consciousness, in front of the camera, is what makes the work so compelling.

Rineke Dijkstra has exhibited widely in Europe and the United States. She has won several awards that cross the different photographic genres, including the Epica Award for Best European Advertising Photography in 1991 and the Citibank Private Bank Photography Prize in 1998.

JANE FLETCHER

See also: **Photography in The Netherlands; Portraiture; Sander, August; Social Representation**

Biography

Born in Sittard, Netherlands, 1959. Studied Gerrit Rietveld Academie, Amsterdam, Netherlands, 1981–1986; worked as a commercial photographer. Awards: Kodak Awards Netherlands, 1987; Epica Award for Best European Advertising Photography, 1991; Art Encouragement Award Amstelveen, 1993; Werner Mantz Award, 1994; The Citibank Private Bank Photography Prize, 1999.

Individual Exhibitions

1994 *Rineke Dijkstra*; Kunstaanmoedigingsprijs, Amstelveen, Netherlands
1995 *Time Festival: Rineke Dijkstra*; Museum van Hedendaagse Kunst, Ghent, Netherlands
1997 *Location*; The Photographers' Gallery London, United Kingdom
1998 *About the World*; Sprengel Museum, Hannover, Germany
1998 *Menschenbilder*; Museum Folkwang Essen and Galerie der Hochschule für Grafik und Buchkunst, Leipzig, Germany
1999 *The Buzzclub, Liverpool, UK/Mysteryworld, Zaandam, NL*; MACBA Barcelona, Spain
1999 *Annemiek*; Anthony d'Offay Gallery, London, United Kingdom
2001 *Rineke Dijkstra: Portraits*; Institute of Contemporary Art, Boston, Massachusetts
2001 *The French Foreign Legion*; Galerie Jan Mot, Bruxelles, Belgium
2001 *Israel Portraits*; Herzliya Museum of Art, Herzliya, Israel
2004 *Rineke Dijkstra: Historias*; PhotoEspana 2004, Madrid, Spain

Group Exhibitions

1993 *Every Child is Made of Marble*; Beurs van Berlage/Bloom Gallery, Amsterdam, Netherlands
1995 *The European Face*; Talbot Rice Gallery, Edinburgh, United Kingdom
1996 *Prospect 96*; Schirn Kunsthalle, Frankfurt am Main, Germany
1996 *100 Fotos uit dee Collectie*; Stedelijk Museum, Amsterdam, Netherlands
1996 *Colorrealismea: Rineke Dijkstra, Wolfgang Tillmans, Inez van Lamsweerde, Nan Goldin*; Galleria Photology, Milan, Italy
1997 *New Photography 13*; Museum of Modern Art, New York, New York
1997 *Photowork(s) in Progress/Constructing Identity*; Nederlands Fotomuseum, Rotterdam, Netherlands
1998 *Global Vision, New Art From the 90s, Part III*; Deste Foundation, Athens, Greece
1998 *Sightings*; ICA, London, United Kingdom
1999 *Objects in the rear of the mirror may appear closer than they are*; Galerie Max Hetzler, Berlin, Germany
1999 *Children of Berlin*; PS 1, Long Island City, New York
1999 *Modern Starts: People, Places, Things*; Museum of Modern Art, New York, New York
1999 *The Citibank Private Bank Photography Prize*; The Photographers' Gallery, London, United Kingdom
2000 *Breathless! Photography and Time*; Victoria and Albert Museum, London, United Kingdom
2000 *How You Look at It: Twentieth-Century Photography*; Sprengel Museum, Hannover, Germany
2001 *From the Low Countries—Reality and Art 1960–2001*; Charlottenborg Exhibition Hall, Copenhagen Denmark
2001 *Uniform—Order and Disorder*; PS 1, Long Island City, New York
2002 *Performing Bodies*; Moderna Museet, Stockholm, Sweden
2002 *Remix: Contemporary Art and Pop*; Tate Liverpool, Liverpool, United Kingdom
2002 *Moving Pictures*; Solomon R. Guggenheim Museum, New York, New York
2003 *Cruel and Tender: The Real in the Twentieth-Century Photograph*; Tate Modern, London, United Kingdom
2003 *Witness*; Barbican Centre, London, United Kingdom
2003 *Just Love Me: Post Feminisic Art of the 1990s*; Bergen Kunstmuseum, Bergen, Norway
2003 *Strangers: The First ICP Triennial of Photography and Video*; International Center of Photography, New York, New York

Selected Works

Hilton Head Island, South Carolina, USA, June 24, 1992
Kolobrzeg, Poland, July 26, 1992
Saskia, Harderwijk, Netherlands, March 16, 1994
Tecla, Amsterdam, Netherlands, May 16, 1994
Annemiek, February 11, 1997 (video still)
Montemor, Portugal, May 1, 1994

Further Reading

Barthes, Roland. *La Chambre Claire*. France: Editions du Seuil, 1980; as *Camera Lucida*, USA: Hill and Wang, 1981; UK: Jonathan Cape, 1982.
Durden, Mark. "Painful Exposure: Rineke Dijkstra." *Portfolio Magazine* no. 27 (June 1998).
Fletcher, Jane. "Maternal Bodies of Work." *British Journal of Photography* 12 (March 2003).
Fletcher, Jane. "Sweet Liberties: Narratives of Resistance and Desire in Photographs of Women." In *Masquerade: Women's Contemporary Portrait Photography*. Newton, Kate and Rolph, Christine, eds. Wales: Fotogallery, 2003.
Morgan, Jessica, ed. *Rineke Dijkstra: Portraits*. Boston: Institute of Contemporary Art, 2001.
Roodenburg, Linda, ed. *PhotoWork(s) in Progress/Constructing Identity*. Netherlands: Snoeck-Ducaju & Zoon, Gent (B) and Nederlands Foto Instituut, 1997.

DISCURSIVE SPACES

The discussion of discursive spaces in photography must deal with the ambiguity resulting from the mixing of heterogeneous families of concepts, namely the textual and the visual. This ambiguity is inherent to the concept of a discursive space in itself: is it the space created by a form of discourse or is it the space in which a form of discourse is created? The concept of discursive spaces in photography thus contains two angles, as the discourse *on* photography and the discourse *of* photography. Of course the discourse (as meaning or message) *of* photography is always framed by the place attributed to photography as a signifying practice, that is, by the discourse (as conceptualization) *on* photography.

A major shift in the conceptualization of photography between the nineteenth and the twentieth century happened because of an artistic interest in what had been so far a scientific curiosity. Conceptualized as a tool of scientific investigation because of its mechanical and physical (or *indexical*, in the taxonomy of the American philosopher Charles Sanders Peirce) relationship to its subject, photography is a door toward spaces that can then be inventoried and archived according to the logic of scientific discourse. Conceptualized as the expression of an "artist's" vision, the photograph becomes the site, the space of artistic creation functioning within the values of an aesthetic discourse. In a chapter entitled "Photography's Discursive Spaces" in her book *The Originality of the Avant-Garde and other Modernist Myths* (1985), Rosalind Krauss points out the tension between these two discourses in which photography keeps moving. She denounces an effort in the twentieth century to reinscribe photography within the paradigms invented by the discourses of art and its history and to eliminate the purely archival sphere to which nineteenth century photography belonged.

The fact is that photography always participates in a multitude of discourses. Roland Barthes described the photograph as "a message without a code" (as opposed to a textual message, which is an entirely coded way of communication), since it is a perfect analog of the object presented and one does not need an interpretation, a relay, that is a code, to understand it. As an "image without a code," the photograph becomes the receptacle for a variety of codes as it enters the discourses of many different domains, be it art, sociology, psychoanalysis, anthropology, etc. These discourses with their own jargon, methodology, and scope recuperate the photograph for their own purposes and define it in their own languages. With its cross-disciplinary vocation, the photographic image is thus the postmodern representation *par excellence*.

As an object, a physical space in itself, the flat surface of the photograph follows the vicissitudes of the varying degrees of importance attributed to the cultural concept of depth. The twentieth century opened with the Freudian revolution and the discovery of the unconscious. Any surface became suspect and pregnant with underlying signification. Entering into the modern age of introspection, depth became the warrant of truth as opposed to the deceptiveness of appearances. The belief in the possibility of access to a latent layer of meaning slowly dwindled in the course of the twentieth century. New psychoanalytic frameworks, like Jacques Lacan's reinterpretation of Freud, while recognizing the existence of an unconscious and even the evidence of its structure, denied its readability. Postmodern thinkers like Jean Baudrillard brought the attention back to the surface of things, including images, by searching for working strategies rather than for truth: what works is what is true, and appearances are what we work with. Similarly, the photograph as a space of signification, a place from which meanings are inferred, oscillates between conceptions of it as a flat space or as a deep-layered space. A photograph as a layered space becomes a place of interpretation, of discovery, a space where not only the subject but also the subjectivity of the photographer can be seen, a place of meaning readable like a text. Freudian critics like Victor Burgin see the photograph as being all text, to be deciphered. As a flat surface, the photograph is just a silent reflection and a critic like Roland Barthes tries to see it as just that, all image, purely denotative. Both approaches always recognize the limitation of their angles and acknowledge the paradox of photography as a silent discourse or a visual text.

The fascination with photography as a discursive space, a locus of meaning, comes from its direct physical link to the reality it represents. It is the presence of the real without being the real itself. Any other type of representation filters the real through conventions and styles; photography frames and reduces the real without changing it. There is always the possibility for the beholder to see something in a photograph that the photographers themselves have not seen. Photographs always function as a window onto a piece of reality, an ever searchable space.

The privileged link to the real bestowed on photographic representation also carries the unique capability of stopping time. A photograph is always a moment of the past extended into the present of the beholder. These two characteristics account for a fascinating and well documented relationship between photography and literature. The art of narrative is, indeed, constantly reworking its treatment of time and space, which are, in a way, always its primary subjects. Photography as the raw space for a variety of discourses receives here, probably, its most extensive exploration. Indeed, literature addresses photography in a number of ways, as an element both external to the text and inherent to it. Photography can be an archival source of inspiration used as a precursor to the text. The French naturalist writer Emile Zola thought that things are not truly seen before they are photographed. The photograph can also become a more intimate part of the text while still not being reproduced in the text. One can conceive of a narration stemming from specific uses of photography: technical achievements like the decomposition of movement, or social practices like photo displays and photo albums can become models for the organization of a narrative. A text then acquires photographic qualities because it borrows practices attributed to or reminiscent of a photograph.

]Narrative texts also add new dimensions to the photographic concept by reinventing or extending its possibilities. Marguerite Duras's best known novel *The Lover* (1984) is organized around a photograph that does not exist but that could have been taken, had one then understood its photographic importance: the photographic moment emblematizes the workings of memory, and photography becomes pure discourse, the space of writing itself. Rarely does one see actual photographs included in a narrative without being reduced to the rank of illustration, that is, an addition rather than a necessity. An equilibrium between photograph and text in the creation of a narrative is arguably impossible to achieve. Few narrations have been made that necessitate the collaboration of the accompanying photographs. A most famous one in the history of literature is possibly *Nadja* (1928) by the leader of the surrealist movement, André Breton. But, in this case, the use of photographs in the book stems from a desire to annihilate language and literature; the book is therefore staging the heterogeneity of the mediums rather than creating a collaborative space. A narrative discourse that tips the balance in favor of the photographs would be the photo-novel, a genre still striving for respectability. In the only extensive study on this genre, Jan Baetens hopes for the development of a narration in photographs increasingly free of text and for a re-education of the reader. Here again we read the malaise in front of mixed media created by the opposition between text and photograph. To become their own narrative space with a fairly consistent reading, the photographs in a photo-novel need to make concessions, such as being inscribed in a codified layout, and softening their time and space referentiality since the referent is replaced by a staging serving the narrative. The photographs' own discourse possibilities are silenced for the purpose of the narrative since the codes of the expected or recognized staging replace the immediacy of the photographic message.

Any discursive practice in which the photograph seems to inscribe itself as an interpretable text tends as a rule to obscure the photograph. Writing about the uses of photography in discourse will always easily be unfair to the visual hence irreducible and immediate quality of the photograph. Expository prose is by nature nonvisual; it explains rather than it shows. One needs to be aware of all the limitations inherent to treating photographs as texts. If we carefully consider the metaphors we live by, such as "you see what I mean," we realize that the plea for visualization is actually an acknowledgement of one's incapacity to explain. The "image" to be seen, as a metaphor for global intuitive comprehension, is supposed to stand for the text, the explanation that should advantageously replace it. The image, thus, only serves as a fix when the formulation proves difficult. Expository prose in the same logic shuns images since they are crutches when the art of elucidation fails. A text is a site of manipulations that one endeavors to disentangle as one deciphers a code. On the other hand, the image is a site of possible illusions and it functions outside of the mechanisms of comprehension, outside of a text; one can see an image without necessarily making anything out of it. In other words, the image does not explain but opens to explanations.

The theoretical discourse on photography keeps re-articulating the terms in which a photograph enters any type of discourse. W.J.T. Mitchell semi-irritatedly introduces his essay on "pictorial texts" in *Picture Theory* reflecting on the fact that the interpretation of images happens through the medium of different forms of verbal discourse but the interpretation of text is never done by means of pictures (p. 209). Rosalind Krauss, in her preface to *Le Photographique, pour une théorie des écarts* (1990) (a collection of articles written between 1977 and 1984 and only published here as a body, in their French translations with an introduction by Hubert Damish) denies that photography can possibly be, or ever has been, an object of research *per se*. It always becomes an access to something else, a kind of grid or filter through which one can organize the data of another field. She finishes this analysis by peremptorily stating that there is nothing to say, at least on photography, a position which explains her title, *Pour une Théorie des écarts* [for a theory of discrepancies/displacements]. The *on* of "on photography" has more and more become an object of reconsideration since Susan Sontag's celebrated essay, *On Photography* (1977). The foreword of Abigail Solomon-Godeau's *Photography at the Dock* (1991) presents the scope of this collection of essays on photographs as a displacement similar to the one advocated by Krauss. It is a sort of metacriticism that "focuses for the most part not on the photographs themselves but on the discourse of photography as it has been constructed in recent past" (p. xiv). In the discursive space of theory, metacriticism or metalanguage, photography seems to be literally always the thing "next to" which there is something to say. The theoretical discourse on photography, a discourse that tries to conceptualize the place and the essence of photography independently from, but also within, all the other discourses (of history, art history, science, sociology, psychology, anthropology, literature, literary criticism) is the only discourse that repeatedly places photography outside of its scope, outside of the realm of the text, but enacting then in the texts that it produces the very paradox that it seems to denounce. W.J.T. Mitchell who wants to find a way out of the pure image concept or the pure language which both appear at the same time lacking and irreducible comes to this solution in *Picture Theory* (1994): "What if the only adequate formulation of the relation of photography and language was a paradox: photography both is and is not a language" (pp. 281–283). The paradox is however an acceptable state of being when you value appearances, surfaces, strategies above the search for a latent explanation for all things.

Discoursing *with* photography resembles the excitement and vitality of staging a combat. The creation of oppositions and paradoxes fuels the energy of their own discourses. As Baudrillard points out in *Les Stratégies Fatales* (1983), oppositions never resolve themselves, they call each other *ad infinitum*. The discursive spaces of photography are thus ever expanding.

Yves-Antoine Clemmen

See also: **Barthes, Roland; Burgin, Victor; Conceptual Photography; Deconstruction; Krauss, Rosalind; Postmodernism; Representation; Semiotics; Sontag, Susan**

Further Reading

Baetens, Jan. *Du roman-photo*. Paris: les impressions nouvelles, 1992.

Barthes, Roland. *L'obvie et l'obtus*. Paris: Editions du Seuil, 1982.

Mitchell, W.J.T. *Picture Theory*. Chicago: University of Chicago Press, 1994.

Mitchell, W.J.T., ed. *The Language of Images*. Chicago: University of Chicago Press, 1980.

Rabb, Jane M., ed. *Literature and Photography, Interactions 1840–1990*. Albuquerque: University of New Mexico Press.

Krauss, Rosalind E. *Le Photographique: pour une théorie des écarts*. Paris: Macula, 1990.

———. *The Originality of the Avant-Garde and Other Modernist Myths*. Cambridge, Massachussetts: The MIT Press, 1985.

Price, Mary. *The Photograph, a Strange Confined Space*. Stanford, California: Stanford University Press, 1994.

DOCUMENTARY PHOTOGRAPHY

Photography's inclination for documentation was recognized since—or even before—its inception, and even though documentary photography as a genre originated at the end of the nineteenth-century, the term was first widely applied in the 1930s when it in fact dominated the photographic scene. Developed mainly in the United States during the second half of the decade, the style was influenced by the emergence of documentary cinema and several government-sponsored projects, most centrally the Farm Security Administration (FSA), which engendered a style that then became widely imitated. As most of those projects were socially oriented, this contributed to the misconception that documentary photography necessarily embraced a social aspect as a basic precept.

Most literature on the topic also deals with the work of this period and introduces a variety of classifications in an attempt to conceptualize the genre based on the peculiarities of this historical moment. Nevertheless documentary photography did evolve throughout the twentieth century, as did its definition, which today involves a broader sense and direction than mere recording of life with the aim of objectivity in order to educate others or elucidate a truth.

Despite being perceived early on as a tool to explain different cultures, until the end of the nineteenth century photography was most frequently used to simply respond to an interest in the picturesque. Those images were common idealizations composed in tableaux-like scenes with backdrops, often presented on a *cartes-de-visite* form—a sort of predecessor of the postcard. Displaying laborers, street people, and views of distant foreign lands, they served mostly as souvenirs. Some long-term projects were initiated and even though they cannot be truly called documentary, they can be seen as establishing the tenets of its traditional approach. Among them are David Octavius Hill's and Robert Adamson's fishermen images from 1845 made in Newhaven, Scotland; Henry Mayhew's and Richard Beard's *London Labour and London Poor* (1851–1864); Mathew Brady's photographs of the American Civil War (1861–1865); Timothy O'Sullivan's and William Henry Jackson's geographical and geological surveys of the American West in the 1870s, and John Thompson's *Illustration of China and Its People*, from the same decade.

With the coming of the twentieth century, photographers became more concerned in capturing vanishing customs as well as in tracing a parallel between past and present, embodied in numerous projects carried out in the United States that focused on Native Americans. Edward Curtis's project, begun in 1900, consumed 30 years of his life with trips throughout the United States to Indian settlements. Yet his work is controversial in terms of documentation both for romanticizing the Indians as the "other" as well as for staging his photographs to capture aspects, such as the costumes or ceremonies, of these communities that were long gone at the point that he photographed them.

In 1889, the *British Journal of Photography* stated that a comprehensive photographic archive of the world should be created for its valuable future as documents. Historically seen as evidence and a means of investigation, fused with a growing social reform movement in the late 1800s, photography became an essential element in these campaigns, which were often played out in the fast growing arena of the illustrated press. Its development as a tool for social reform, however, was directly related to its technical evolution. As drawings and wood engravings were not realistic enough, the urgency for further and inexpensive advances of photo reproduction resulted in the invention of halftone printing in the 1880s. The invention of the hand-held camera and their increasing availability in 1870–1880 enabled the capturing of candid photographs; from then on photography gradually integrated the printed media.

The Danish immigrant Jacob Riis was one of the first in the United States to put photography at the service for social betterment. Disturbed by the living conditions of immigrants in the 1879s in New York, Riis, a police news reporter, wrote long and detailed articles. Accused of exaggeration, he started to use photography as proof of his claims and as a way to influence public opinion. Yet to reproduce these photographs, photogravures had to be made, and the "documents," still appearing to be drawings, were received with the same skepticism. It was only when Riis used his photographs in slide projector lectures and his publication *How the Other Half Lives: Studies Among the Tenements of New York* (1890) came out—in which 17 of the images were halftones—that he convinced Americans to take action. Even though Riis was a photojournalist, his work can be considered social documentary as he developed a straightforward and methodical, recording of a subject with humanitarian concern.

Especially famous for photographing immigrants in the beginning of the twentieth century, specifically children and youths put to backbreaking labor, Lewis Hine began his involvement in photography when teaching natural science at a New York school. It quickly became clear to Hine that photography could be a powerful tool to fight prejudice against immigrants. In 1904, he began his first documentation on the immigrants of Ellis Islands. Three years later and for a decade he concentrated his efforts on child labor; his celebrated images of children, often dirty and with forlorn expressions on their faces, standing close to machinery generated, through their sense of scale, a feeling that they were indeed very young. Hine called his images "photo-interpretations" referring to his creative decisions and to the dual aim to inform and move the viewer. Published as "human documents" and widely distributed in pamphlets, magazines, and books, as well as shown in slide projections and exhibitions, Hine's photographs in fact achieved the institution of federal legislation regulating child labor. Riis and Hine together are considered the pioneers of social documentary photography.

The photographic scene was dominated by Pictorialism from the end of the nineteenth century until the first years of the 1920s, a movement that produced highly manipulated images intended as fine art. Some photographers, largely overlooked at the time but who took exception to this style, later became emblematic documentarians. After brilliantly documenting his homeland of Hungary during World War I, André Kertész moved to Paris in 1925, where he joined the artistic community and began a photojournalistic career. He then relocated to New York in 1936 where he worked for the next 25 years as a commercial photographer. Kertész's contemporary reputation is mostly as a street photographer, since he never stopped documenting the ordinary in street life during his spare time, and it is for this work he is one of the most admired photographers of the twentieth century. Eugène Atget's life is little known but his oeuvre is legendary. His records of the streets, shop windows, and historical buildings of Paris were initially sold as "*documents pour artistes*" (documents for artists) to painters who used them as guidelines for their work. When discovered by the Surrealists—who saw his images as fragments of reality free of cultural intentions and thus open to subjective interpretations—Atget saw a few of his images published in 1926 in *La Révolution Surrealiste* magazine. A year later, when he died, the American photographer Berenice Abbott bought his complete work, introducing and promoting it in the United States in the 1930s. In 1968, it was purchased by the Museum of Modern Art of New York (MoMA), and finally, in the 1980s, Atget was definitively established as a leading master of photography.

The German August Sander, a commercial studio photographer, had already started, in the very beginning of the 1920s, his ambitious project *Menschen des 20 Jahrhunderts*. This self-assigned project consisted of documenting people of all classes and occupations, and including some of his early commissioned portraits dating from the 1910s when he first developed the idea. Yet acknowledgment of his achievement came much later with the publication of his book *Antlitz der Zeit* (Face of Our Time) in 1929. A selection of 60 portraits, it inspired enthusiastic critics who ranked him at the top of documentary photography. Influential philosopher Walter Benjamin for one regarded Sander's photographs highly and wrote about them in his *Kleine Geschichte der Photographie* (1931), a milestone for photography theory.

In the 1920s, as the dominance of Pictorialism began to fade, photographic practice in general moved closer to the idea of document, denying manipulation, soft focus, or retouching, and seeking to explore the purity of the medium. As modernism spread around the world, a straightforward approach in photography became the rule, but not without engendering contradictory interpretations.

Influenced by the Russian Constructivists, the Hungarian-born László Moholy-Nagy, then teaching at the Bauhaus in Weiner, Germany, in the late 1920s, theorized in his book *Von Material zu Architecktur* (1929, translated as the *The New Vision* 1932), which would expand and free human perception through pure photography. The recommended wide angles, innovative perspectives, and innovative use of materials, however, did not inspire a documentary, but a more experimental outlook. The *Neue Sachlichkeit* (New Objectivity) of the German avant-garde, as exemplified by Albert Renger-Patzch, and the American "straight photography" of Paul Strand, Alfred Stieglitz, Edward Steichen, and Edward Weston, among others, tried to rediscover simplicity and austerity as a descriptive tendency. Renger-Patzch, already known for his book *Die Welt ist Schön* (1928)—

extremely sharp close-ups of natural and man-made things of beauty—received recognition and became the new model of the serious photographer for his apparently impersonal description of the world. At the same time, some American straight photography was shown in the seminal *Film und Foto* exhibition of 1929 in Stuttgart, allowing German critics to project the aspiration of objectivity onto this work as well. In fact, several years earlier, the ideals of directness and simplicity had already been pointed out in European journals as an American issue; many American photographers had been turning away from artifice and creating simpler forms of expression based on sharpness and elegant geometry as evidenced by the publication of Paul Strand's photographs as early as 1916 in Stieglitz's influential journal *Camera Work*. This journal, which had been a proponent of Pictorialism for many years and had in fact helped spread this style worldwide, now helped disseminate the notion that "straight photography" was the new, modern mode.

Although none of the achievements of the practitioners of this new style had at that time been thought of as documentary, later many were, like Weston's Mexican folk art images, and their importance remains as a significant step in the direction of documentary photography. The discovery and wider distribution of Atget's oeuvre in the second half of the 1920s and, a bit later, of Sander's, also worked to question existing photographic ideology.

Another factor decisive for the establishment and growth of the documentary form was the launching of documentary films. *Nanook of the North* (1922), a diary of the lives of Canadian Eskimos by the American filmmaker Robert Flaherty, encountered great success, motivating the big studios to produce films of this kind. Soviet Dziga Vertov, creator of *Man with a Movie Camera* (1929), stated that he was the "film-eye," suggesting that his films showed what and how the eyes see, that is, life as it is. The term "documentary" as a definition of a genre appeared in 1926 in a review on Flaherty's *Moana* (1926) written by the British theorist and filmmaker John Grierson. Similar usage of the term in photography was first applied in 1928 in France and Germany, as affirmed by the French historian Olivier Lugon in his meticulous book *Le Style Documentaire: D'August Sander à Walker Evans—1920–1945* (2001), and around 1930 in the United States.

"Documentary" in fact became a tendency in diverse fields such as the social sciences, literature, and art throughout this era as one legitimated the other. Gisèle Freund asserts in her classic book *Photographie et Societé* (1974) that although the official recognition and public announcement of photography was in January of 1839, this was thirteen years after Joseph Nicéphore Niépce's development of a primitive photographic process. She argues it was only then that photography met a "social element," that theretofore had been absent, which allowed its successful reception; in other words, it was when society was ready to accept it that photography was "invented." It can be argued that the 1930s were the equivalent moment for documentary photography, meeting its social element in the form of the economic disaster of 1929 known as the Great Depression.

As part of President Franklin Roosevelt's New Deal, the Resettlement Administration (RA), later named Farm Security Administration (FSA), was founded in 1935. Its Historical Unit, a small photographic group, had the aim of providing visual documentation that justified the Government's relief and make-work programs and helped the urban public to understand the poverty and difficulties of the rural populations. Roy Stryker, a former economics teacher with little experience of photography, was named director of the project. Although Stryker wrote "scripts" directing what he expected the assignments to achieve, the FSA photographers including Walker Evans, Dorothea Lange, Ben Shahn, Russell Lee, and Arthur Rothstein, had a great deal of freedom in the manner in which they photographed. Evans and Lange, who have been pointed out by historian John Szarkowski as being responsible in great part for FSA's success, used the agency structure to develop their own projects and documentary ideals. Lange's work was clearly humanitarian, centered on people's presence and emotional expressions, which she believed could be socially and politically useful. Evans used the opposite tack with his highly impersonal style to document ordinary things and when he did photograph people, they were presented as anonymous and interchangeable.

Walker Evans's style came to dominate the idea of what documentary photography should be, as "purist" ideas began to dominate photography circles and extend the prohibitions on manipulation of the photographic image to the act of shooting the photographic image. After a short stay in Europe, Evans returned to New York in 1929 willing to employ the experimental precepts of the New Vision, but soon after, influenced by Atget's work, he took up a simpler aesthetic. He concentrated on vernacular architecture, first independently and then by commission, the results comprising the first solo photography exhibition mounted at MoMA in 1933, and in 1938 a selection from it was integrated into his

American Photographs book and exhibition, also at MoMA. Hired by the FSA in 1935, Evans pursued his idea of documenting American society through the everyday environment that gave evidence of but showed no human interaction, like shop windows, advertising signs, and the vernacular architecture.

Evans's work, along with Sander's, thus constitutes a distinct style within documentary photography, presenting images as "types" meant to evoke larger thought rather than inviting the viewer to concentrate on particularities and develop empathy for the individual or circumstance depicted. Evans himself considered the term "documentary" deceiving and suggested in the 1970s that the right term should be "documentary style." By presenting an aesthetic frequently identified as "anti-aesthetic," these bodies of work set up their own theoretical concepts. Embodying the ideals of neutrality and "straight photography's" formal qualities, such as frontality, emphasis on sharpness and brightness, presentation of static elements and balanced compositions with each detail of equal importance to another, the ability of the image to stand on its own without captions or explanations, and presentation of images in series, Evans and Sander created a documentary approach that perhaps too closely mimics actual photo documents. For example, they have been accused of creating works with no more quality than passport pictures. John Grierson clarified, albeit in relation to film, that "documentary was from the beginning...an 'anti-aesthetic' movement...what confuses the history is that we had always the good sense to use the aesthetes. ...We mastered the techniques necessary for our unaesthetic purposes."

As John Szarkowski, whose vision of what photography should be powerfully shaped the postwar aesthetic, wrote "pictures that would look ingenuous and free of guile, that would seem not merely honest but artless...[were] of course an aesthetic choice and an artistic strategy." While the photo document has a strict informational value that was long used to deny that these sorts of photographs could be art, often by the photographers themselves, the documentary style embodies the idea of documentary photography having different possibilities of use and interpretation. Atget's work is a common example of this attitude, even though it is almost certain he was not aware of its potential as an artistic expression and captured his Parisian images because he felt they would not be available for him to enjoy in person as the years passed and progress inevitably changed the face of the city he so loved.

Yet the notions of what constitute a "documentary style" or aesthetic in the realm of fine-arts photography are not necessarily what documentary photography signifies to the larger public, nor were the finer points of the debate of particular interest as photographs continued to be exponentially consumed by society. In mid-century, it was commonly held that all photographs tell the "truth" and some photographs tell stories, and that the stories as presented in the photographs were in fact accurate and fair, a covenant of faith that was developed by the social documentarians early in the century. After Lange and Evans left the FSA, in 1940 and 1937, respectively, they continued documenting their own projects. While Lange worked on the unjust internment of Japanese-Americans in camps following the attack on Pearl Harbor, Evans embarked on a project with the writer James Agee that resulted in the notorious book *Let Us Now Praise Famous Men* (1941). A study of Alabama tenant farmers, this project became a basic text of the civil rights movement later in the century. The FSA project continued to produce the most comprehensive documentation of America to date, despite its propagandistic intentions, contributing to the establishment of documentary photography as a genre and inspiring countless other projects.

Whereas initially documentary photography called up images of rural life, the urban scene was being documented concurrently by Berenice Abbott and the photographers of New York's The Photo League. Abbot, who had a commercial studio in Paris, returned to New York in 1927, initially shooting, as did Evans, under the influence of the New Vision. Later she adopted Atget's path, and attempted to do in New York what Atget did in Paris. The resulting *Changing New York, 1935–1939* was developed under the auspices of the Art Project of the Works Progress Administration.

The Film and Photo League was formed in 1930, and reorganized in 1936 as The Photo League. A group of politically committed photographers who idealized Lewis Hine joined together in order to support working-class rights—an extension of the German worker photography movement—through the documentation of the life and everyday struggles of the common man. Its board of directors included luminaries such as Berenice Abbott, Paul Strand, W. Eugene Smith, and Nancy and Beaumont Newhall. One of its most extensive projects was The Harlem Document, photographed by various Photo League members under the direction of Aaron Siskind between 1932 and 1940 that captured life in this changing African-American neighborhood. In the 1940s, when there was a general tendency toward a personalized approach, the themes considered acceptable to the goals of The Photo League broadened and subjects with greater aesthetic appeal were incorporated, attracting photographers known for their advanced fine-art aesthetics like Ansel Adams and Edward Weston. In 1947, The Photo League was harassed as a subversive Communist organization, and was disbanded in 1951.

In Germany as the political situation in the Weimar Republic grew more complex, the admiration of American straight photography transformed, in the eyes of some, a figure such as Renger-Patzch into someone who had sold out and adopted a foreign tendency. The conservatives, who idealized the representation of an authentic German "soul," criticized the New Objectivity movement for being modernist and internationalist. The leftists decried the same movement as superficial and reflecting bourgeois triviality and called for more socially relevant photographic work. At the end of the 1920s, Renger-Patzch turned to documenting open views of industrial landscapes. This more systematic approach that demonstrated a greater distance from the subject with the idea of thus being more "objective" struck a receptive chord. A peculiarly German style of documentary photography was emerging. Sander surfaced as its epithet in early 1930. Atget's oeuvre was, as in America, pointed out as a model.

The rise of the Nazis in 1933 immobilized free debate and artistic expression with its pernicious ideology and its adaptation of an exaggerated documentary style as propaganda (Socialist Realism). The development of the documentary genre was not completely stopped, however. Roman Vishniac, exiled in Berlin from the Soviet Union, documented the Jewish Ghettos of Poland. Sander, who saw his book *Antlitz der Zeit* removed from the market and his plates destroyed, persisted with the documentation of landscapes.

In the 1920s and 1930s, leftist European and Russian photographers concerned with their countries' economic-political scenes and inspired by the "documentary truth" or agitprop of Alexander Rodchenko and El Lissitzky photomontages, turned to urban documentation. In an attempt to make the working classes aware of their deprived conditions and political power, they formed the worker photography movement, which operated in countries like the Netherlands, Belgium, and England in a diversity of styles. This movement was particularly successful in England and is known as the Mass Observation project (MO), which had the intention of producing anthropological-like documentaries. In the 1930s, the British photographer Bill Brandt, despite not taking part in the MO movement and having been involved with Surrealism, effectively documented the contrasts among classes and the lives of mine workers.

During this same period, Mexico's capital was an international center for artistic and intellectual exchange, benefiting from the political turmoil in Europe by welcoming its artists, writers, and intellectuals. Encouraged by governmental support and the presence of Edward Weston, Paul Strand, and Tina Modotti, a number of photographers embarked on a series of documentary projects in the modernist style. Mexico's most famous photographer, Manuel Álvarez Bravo, at the beginning of his career in the 1920s, had experimented with abstraction. During the 1930s, he created Modernist images and documented Mexican life, religious culture, and landscapes. Bravo's photographic journey was duplicated by others all over the world. In Olivier Lugon's words, the "growing dominance of the genre was an institutionalized form of political and social reaction."

During the 1930s and 1940s, the definitions of documentary approach were malleable and varied according to personal or cultural tendencies and interests of the moment, and at times were even contradictory. Documentary photography was thought to be impartial and simply instructive yet able to convince and move the viewer. After moving toward a cooler, nonauthoritative approach, it was supposed to become more emotional and personal, preferably compassionate and humanistic; when capturing social conditions it first was meant to focus on its hardships and later on its positive aspects; it shifted also from presentation with no supporting text to an almost compulsory pairing of image with text, as documentary photography began to be merged with the notion of the photo essay, coming closer to photojournalism and progressively losing its dominance. The rising demand for photojournalistic-based projects fueled by the flourishing of magazines such as *Life* and the decline of governmental sponsorship and commissioning of documentary projects in the 1940s forced many documentarians to shift to news photography. Documentary photography receded in production and importance throughout the 1940s and 1950s.

There remains a common misunderstanding about what divides documentary photography and photojournalism. Both produce documents in a historical sense and are based on existing ("real") circumstances and issues. Photojournalism, however, is basically factual and has supposed testimonial status as a matter of its own ethics while the documentary image can also be allegorical and not limited to an informative function. As the name indicates, photojournalistic images are made to fulfill the visual needs of the news, and are severely restricted by time and space restraints. Photojournalists tend to work under short deadlines, having little opportunity to become familiar with, never mind truly understand, their subject matter, and as the flow of information has radically increased with the advent of the internet, these deadlines are virtually instantaneous, with photojournalists downloading images almost literally as they are shot. Documentarians typically spend a great deal of time, even when commissioned, methodically researching, observing, and photographing the chosen theme in order to achieve an in-depth depiction. As FSA Chief Roy Stryker said, "the job is to know enough about the subject matter to find its significance in itself and in relation to its surroundings, its time, and its function."

Another difference is that photojournalism always relies on words, and often presents only one image that is subjectively judged to best summarize the story. When a photo-essay is presented, its storytelling approach dictates the choice of photographs to tell the best story-in-pictures, but not necessarily the most accurate or in-depth story on the topic. Documentarians' work is not necessarily accompanied by text or captions, being generally presented as lengthy series. This does not mean, however, that individual photographers cannot be simultaneously photojournalist and documentarian. An example is W. Eugene Smith. Expected to take only weeks, his *Life* magazine assignment *Spanish Village* (1951) took several months to complete and resulted in a revolutionary work as it eliminated the traditional subordination of pictures to words.

Despite its lack of economic viability in the postwar era, documentary photography continued to evolve in America and around the world. Disturbed by growing Americanization, Latin American photographers directed their creativity towards the construction of a visual identity and the exposure of social injustices. Cuban Raúl Colares, for example, documented the evolution of the 1959 Cuban Revolution. A great number of photographers focused on the indigenous peoples of South America, like Brazilian Claudia Andujar who documented the Karajá people in the 1950s and began in the 1970s her Yanomami project. Spanish-born Pedro Mayer and Mexican Graciela Iturbide, among others, photographed Mexican folk rituals and culture, respectively, in the 1960s, and in the 1970s to 1980s.

Japanese photographers, as well, were questioning their identity after defeat in the war. Themes related to devastation surfaced in works such as Shomei Tomatsu's and Ken Domon's *Hiroshima-Nagasaki Document* (1961). Influenced by Harry Callahan, the 1960s street photographs of the American-naturalized-Japanese Yasuhiro Ishimoto transmit the sensation of self-delusion and frivolousness. In Africa, the cameras were often pointed toward political causes. South African Ernest Cole and Peter Magubane exhaustively documented the struggles of apartheid and Ricardo Rangel, from Mozambique, documented Maputo's nightlife during guerrilla resistance against colonization in the 1960s. In the same decade, Czech photographer Josef Koudelka composed a major documentary on the gypsies of Slovakia.

One of the best-known and highly influential postwar documentary projects, Robert Frank's *The Americans*, had no overt political or social aspiration. It was amassed by the Swiss-born Frank who traversed the United States documenting various mundane aspects of American society living off a Guggenheim Fellowship he'd received in 1955. The "American dream," which had been institutionalized during immediate postwar years as a reward for the sacrifices of World War II and used in advertising and other cultural messages to fuel the engines of postwar economic recovery, was not depicted positively. Frank's images, which featured harsh lighting and scenes dense with grain and evidence of their making, also harshly pointed out a nation alienated in its own rampant consumerism. His resulting book, *The Americans* (1958), was shocking to critics and the American public alike and received an overwhelming negative response. Yet his snapshot aesthetic and critical vision opened a new path for younger generations.

William Klein's 1954–1955 *Life is Good and Good for You in New York* (1956) was another highly influential private documentary project that found little initial support. An expatriate American living in France with a background in painting, Klein returned to his homeland and started frenetic camerawork throughout the streets of Manhattan. Disregarding the traditional ideals of sharpness, brightness, and composition, Klein produced highly contrasted and grainy images, with obvious blurring due to movement, and radical cropping in his attempt to represent the anxieties of modernity. Although Klein's achievement was recognized in Europe, it took a very long time for it to be appreciated in America. In different ways, Frank and Klein launched a more subjective and corrosive manner of depicting society that remains a powerful force in both documentary and fine-arts photography.

The 1960s was the decade during which documentary photography regained strength and achieved a wider distribution. In 1962, Edward Steichen, still curator of photography at MoMA, organized *The Bitter Years 1935–1941: Rural America Seen by the Photographers of the FSA*, introducing this work to a whole new generation. John Szarkowski, who replaced Steichen that same year, quickly demonstrated his predilection for a subjective kind of documentary photography. One of the milestones of the documentary revival was his 1967 exhibition *New Documents*, which showcased the works of Diane Arbus, Garry Winogrand, and Lee Friedlander. According to Szarkowski, their similarity resided in the blending of street documentary photography and psychological investigation. This tendency is at its most dramatic in the photographs of Diane Arbus. Producing most of her work in the 1950s and 1960s, Arbus's large oeuvre did not obey any thematic structure, but is remembered mostly for her images of subcultures considered odd by traditional society, like transvestites, homosexuals, and dwarfs. Inspired by Weegee and with a nod to Brassaï, Arbus projected her own internal conflicts through her images by choosing subjects that were opposed to the institutionalized glamour of those decades. She, like Frank and Klein before her, enhanced her expression through technical means by use of hard flash. Although personal and subjective, her portraits at the same time captured certain cultural behaviors.

Greatly influenced by Robert Frank's work, Lee Friedlander's imagery was seen as a "merciless mirror" of American society. His television photographs, juxtapositions, and self-portraits—mostly presented by shadows and reflections—transmit a feeling of displacement, reflecting the distancing and anonymity of modern time. On the other hand, the inclusion of his own representation was meant to remind the viewer that a photograph is a constructed image. Garry Winogrand considered a photograph to be a new fact in the world, not a mere restatement of an existing fact. Also admiring Frank's *The Americans* and making wide use of the snapshot aesthetic, Winogrand shaped, through a massive project of recording of seemingly insignificant moments and ordinary subjects, a psychologically complex oeuvre that goes a long way toward capturing the intangibles of culture.

The depiction of subtle ambiences and ordinary people or situations in a casual, almost sterile way so championed by Szarkowski, had been defined earlier in 1967 in an exhibition at the Rose Art Museum, Brandeis University in Waltham, Massachusetts, *12 Photographers of the American Social Landscape* and the George Eastman House, Rochester, New York 1966 exhibition *Toward a Social Landscape*, which included Lee Friedlander, among others. "Social landscape" derived from the idea of "private realities," a highly subjective approach toward social issues that is present in the street documentations of Harry Callahan of the 1940s, and was quickly codified as a new documentary approach by which the individual projected his or her own psychological reality onto society, finding resonances between private and public that were valuable to others seeking to understand their own relationship to society.

In the 1970s, the capturing of "social landscape" evolved into an impersonal documentation of the suburbia landscape in a sort of modern echo of nineteenth century American West imagery. This tendency was presented at Eastman House's influential 1975 exhibition *New Topographics—Photographs of a Man-Altered Landscape*. As demonstrated by the works of Lewis Baltz, Frank Gohlke, and Robert Adams, among others, this tendency connected documentary photography to Conceptual Art. The genre was further expanded by William Eggleston. Inspired by Friedlander and Winogrand, Eggleston used color photography, long considered the realm of the amateur or the advertising image, to capture banal images of everyday life and represent, among other things, the loss of identity of American cities. His MoMA exhibition in 1976 strengthened the style and affirmed color photography's potential in the documentary realm.

A totally diverse kind of documentary photography that utilized snapshot-family photography-like images appeared in the 1970s and 1980s in what were literally private pictures with no claim on the part of their makers to connect private with public in an instructive manner. Including graphic violence and sexual imagery, Larry Clark's book *Tulsa* (1973), a portrait of drug-addicted teenagers among whom were friends, acquaintances, and those with whom he had grown up, and Nan Goldin's slide show, *The Ballad of Sexual Dependency* (1986) of her friends, lovers, and her own troubled relationships, after initially shocking became cult items and later mainstream classics.

Social documentary also gained in the 1960s with new sources of governmental funding, especially the National Endowment for the Arts, founded in 1965. Increasing foundation and private support and a larger involvement by photojournalists, who proceeded on their own to develop projects that sometimes they started covering for the press continued to expand the field. Danny Lyon and Bruce Davidson, for example, recorded the civil rights movements of the 1960s on assignment and continued independently to document related subjects. Lyon concentrated on the lives of those excluded from mainstream society, as in *The Bikeriders* (1968) a study of the Chicago Outlaw Motorcycle Club to which he belonged, and *Conversations with the Dead* (1971), which depicted the inmates of the Texas State Prison. Davidson transited through different aspects of society, notably Black life as captured in *East 100th Street* (1966–1970), the peculiarities of "underground life" in *Subway* (1986), and *Central Park* (1995), which explored open space within urban life.

Yet independently of the financial or social circumstances, certain photojournalists will always seek to develop their work to a greater extent and depth than allowed by news photography. Americans Gordon Parks and Eugene Richards, British Philip Jones Griffiths, Czech Antonin Kratochvil, French Henri Cartier-Bresson and Raymond Depardon, Russian Georgi Pinkasov, and Indian Raghubir Singh, are some other remarkable photojournalists and documentarians, who engendered numerous self-motivated projects. The Brazilian Sebastião Salgado, one of the most renowned contemporary photographers, first received international distinction through his dramatic news shot of the attempted assassination of President Ronald Reagan in 1981. Salgado is primarily, however, a social documentarian very much in the tradition of Riis and Hine who exhaustively documents what he believes to be the great

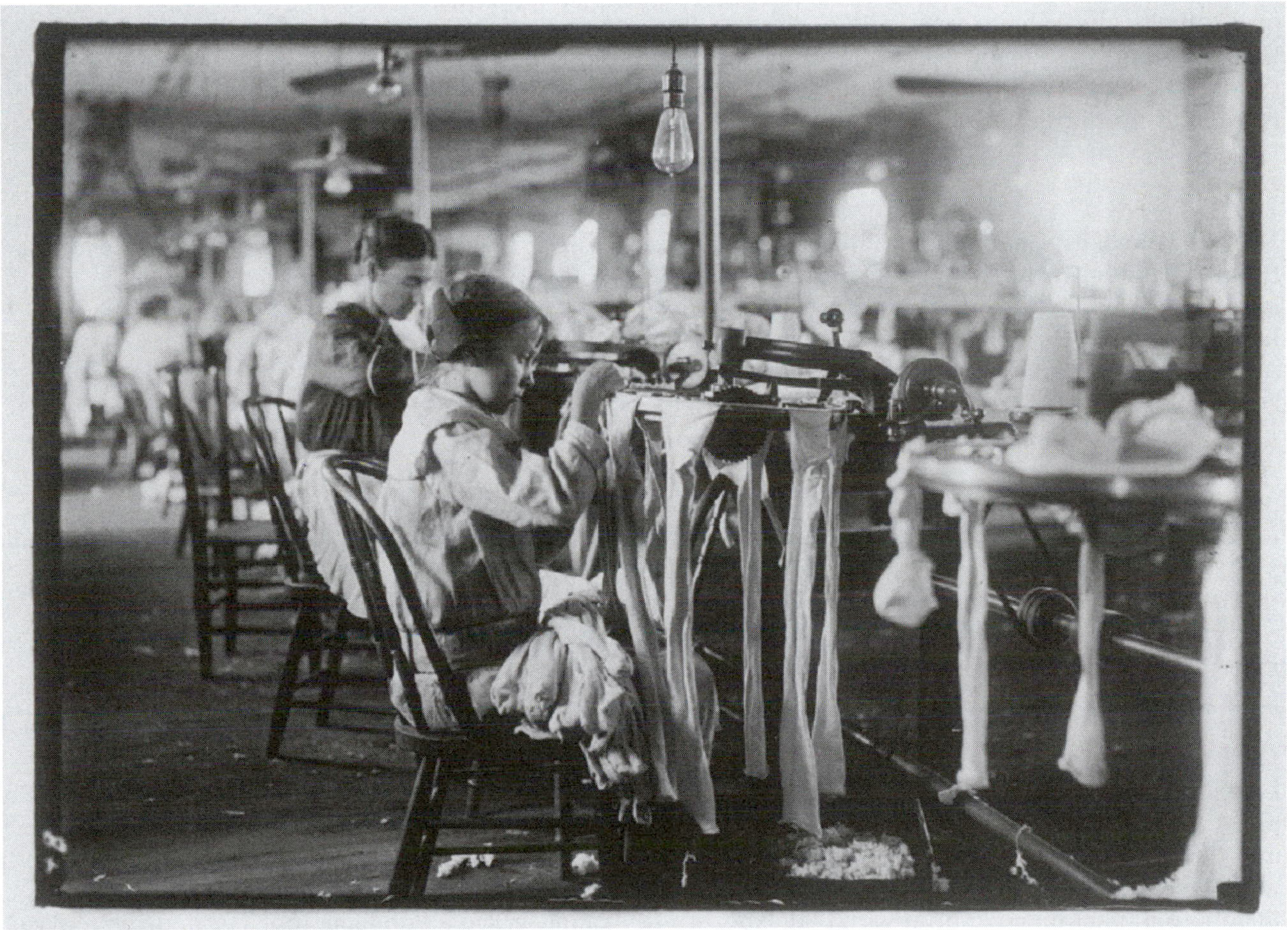

Lewis Wickes Hine, Young knitter in Tennessee knitting mills, 1912, gelatin silver print, 12.6 × 17.7 cm., Gift of the Photo Leaugue, New York: ex-collection Lewis Wickes Hine.
[*Photograph courtesy of George Eastman House*]

problems of the twentieth century—the ravages of war, the brutality of life in poorly-developed countries, and the plight of children.

Today, documentary photography's definition comprises a multiplicity of directions ranging from portraiture to landscape, factual to allegorical, clearly sharp to darkly grainy, social to psychological, neutral to authorial, with major implications for Conceptual Photography and other contemporary art forms. This is particularly demonstrated by the acceptance of certain photographers in the realm of contemporary art that supersedes their reputations within the world of photography. Examples include the Germans Bernd and Hilla Becher with their cool industrial photographs (and who were included in the *New Topgraphics* exhibition in 1975) or Thomas Struth's clinical urban landscapes. What is common in all trends and a basic tenet of the genre is the figurative and systematic recording of a subject through reality-found images that yet are not reduced as proof or absolute truth.

DANIELLA GEO

See also: **Bauhaus; Conceptual Photography; Farm Security Administration; Life Magazine; Modernism; Photographic "Truth"; Portraiture; Representation; Stryker, Roy; The Photo League; Visual Anthropology; Worker Photography; Works Progress Administration**

Further Reading

Editors of Time-Life Books, *Documentary Photography*, New York: Time-Life Books, 1972.

Davenport, Alma. *The History of Photography: An Overview*. Boston and London: Focal Press, 1991; Albuquerque: University of New Mexico Press, 1992, 1999.

Lugon, Olivier. *Le style documentaire – D'August Sander à Walker Evans 1920–1945*. Paris: Macula, 2001.

Marien, Mary Warner. *Photography: A Cultural History*. London: Laurence King Publishing, 2002.

Mora, Gilles. *Photo Speak – A Guide to the Ideas, Movements, and Techniques, 1839 to the Present*. New York: Abbeville Press, 1990.

Newhall, Beaumont. *The History of Photography, from 1839 to the Present Day*. New York: Museum of Modern Art, 1964, 1982; London: Secker & Warburg, 1972.

Rosenblum, Naomi. *A World History of Photography*. New York, London and Paris: Abbeville Press, 1984, 1989, 1997.

Rothstein, Arthur. *Documentary Photography*. Boston and London: Focal Press, 1986.

Stange, Maren. *Symbols of Ideal Life: Social Documentary Photography in America, 1890–1950*. Cambridge: Cambridge University Press, 1989.

Stott, William. *Documentary Expression and Thirties America*. New York: Oxford University Press, 1973, 1986.

Szarkowski, John. *Photography Until Now*. New York: Museum of Modern Art, 1989, 1990, 1999.

Wright, Terence. *The Photography Handbook*. London and New York: Routledge, 2000.

DODGING

Dodging is a technique employed by photographers to fine-tune the tone and highlights of prints in the darkroom. After using a test strip to establish what the overall exposure of the image should be, the photographer makes a print with that exposure time. After the print is developed, however, there might still be one or more small areas in the image that the photographer wishes were lighter than the rest of the print. Dodging is a way of reducing the amount of light a certain area of the print receives, in order to make that area lighter.

It is important to remember that dodging occurs during the overall exposure of the print—the photographer wants to reduce the amount of light received by a specific area of the image, and so must be able to selectively reduce light in one area while still allowing the rest of the photographic paper to be exposed. Dodging is usually accomplished with a small tool, simply called a "dodging tool." A dodging tool can be any small piece of opaque board attached to a thin, stiff wire handle. The photographer uses the handle to move the tool rapidly back and forth between the light and the easel, causing a shadow to fall onto the paper. He should direct this shadow to fall on the place that needs less light, and should continue to move the tool back and forth for the duration of the dodging time to "feather" the light, or prevent hard-edged lines from appearing on the print where the edges of the shadow fall. The thin wire handle allows the photographer to dodge anywhere on the image—even in the center—without creating a thick shadow that falls to the edge and obstructs more of the image than the photographer intends. The dodging tool can be held closer to the light, which will create a bigger shadow, or closer to the easel, which will create a smaller shadow, depending on the photographer's needs. Dodging tools can be created specific to each print, but a few dodging tools with various-sized pieces of board will generally suffice for any dodging needs.

Dodging is often done to increase the amount of detail seen in dark or shadowed areas of a print or to reduce the darkness of an area of the print. Too much dodging, however, can make an area too light, too grey, or murky. In black and white printing, over-dodging turns black into grey, which can decrease the contrast and make the overall print less appealing. Dodging requires practice, and the dodging time is different with each print.

Once a photographer has decided that an area in a print needs to be dodged, he places an unexposed piece of photographic paper into the easel and exposes the negative again, this time using his dodging tool to block the light in the area that needs dodging for a portion of the overall exposure time. The print is then developed as usual. Dodging often takes more than one try to figure out exactly what portion of the overall exposure time needs to be reduced from the dodged area. One way to make the trial-and-error of dodging easier is to make a test strip only in the area that needs to be dodged, making educated guesses as to what the exposure time in that area would be based on the overall exposure time. If, for instance, a photographer figures out that while his overall exposure time is 16 seconds, the area in question only needs to be exposed for 12 seconds, the photographer would then set his timer for 16 seconds and then simply use a dodging tool to cover the area for four of those seconds. Dodging can be done at the beginning, the end, or in the middle of the exposure time.

The technique of dodging can be used for darkroom effects other than simply fine-tuning a print. If a photographer is double-printing, or blending two negatives into one print, he might use dodging techniques to lighten an area on one negative so that the information on the second negative will show through in that area. Or, if a photographer is printing half of one negative and half of another on the same print, he might use his hand to shade half of the image and create a soft, light border where the other image will overlap. Dodging can also be used to create haloes, if, for instance, the photographer dodges a thin outline and then feathers it outward from a subject in the image.

In most digital image manipulation software, there is a variable-sized dodging tool that can be moved across the image to a similar effect as the dodging tool used in the darkroom. The digital dodging tool will lighten parts of the image, but often results in quickly de-saturating or "washing out" the color in those areas. Even in black and white digital images, the dodging tool often results in turning areas a dull grey. Like its use in the darkroom, the digital dodging tool should be used limitedly, and in small areas.

Generally, the photographer intends that the dodged area blend in with the rest of the image—it is for this reason that it is so important to have continuous movement with the dodging tool, so that a line does not appear at the edge of the shadow. Dodging can be a very useful technique to decrease harsh shadows and increase the amount of information that translates from the negative to the print in dark areas. Dodging is also useful when working with thin or uneven negatives to even out tones in the final print.

JENNY ALLRED REDMANN

See also: **Burning-In; Darkroom; Enlarger; Exposure; Manipulation; Multiple Exposures and Printing**

Further Reading

Horder, Alan, ed. *The Manual of Photography*. New York: Chilton Book Co. (Focal Press Ltd.), 1971.

International Center for Photography: Encyclopedia of Photography. New York: Pound Press (Crown Publishers Inc.), 1984.

McDarrah, Gloria S., Fred W. McDarrah, and Timothy S. McDarrah. *The Photography Encyclopedia*. New York: Schirmer Books, 1999.

Swedland, Charles. *Photography: A Handbook of History, Materials, and Processes*. Atlanta: Holt, Rinehard and Winston, Inc., 1974.

ROBERT DOISNEAU

French

Despite a career in commercial photography that included a wide range of industrial, advertising, fashion, and reportage work, Robert Doisneau's true subject was the life of ordinary people on the streets of Paris. About this work he said:

> If you're going to work in a life teeming with people you must have a few rock-hard principles to anchor you and you mustn't dissipate your efforts. So I decided to stick to ordinary, everyday life for my source material and steer clear of picturesque effects. When I had to choose between a member of some lunatic sect and a French polisher, I'd choose the French polisher.
>
> (Doisneau, *Three Seconds of Eternity* 1979 & 1990; Paris: Contrejour)

Doisneau held the popular Parisian view that Paris is a theatre. He was a *flaneur*, someone who walks and observes. His method was to immerse himself in street life, strolling and waiting for the photograph to happen. He said that he worked instinctively and was motivated by a desire to share the visual delights he experienced. He knew Paris intimately and for him the streets were full of familiar pleasures.

> I only feel at home in the sort of streets where you come across an old-age pensioner with a little white dog, a flower lady, a kid on roller skates, and a fat man, all at the same time' he said. 'I shall always be the last person left sauntering in the street.

However, the Paris he immortalised is the Paris of the popular imagination, and one which had largely disappeared by the end of Doisneau's life. This vision of Paris lives on as a romantic dream in his imagery, which is widely used in advertising and is sold in postcard and poster form. As a result, Doisneau is arguably the most popular and best known of French photographers.

Doisneau was born in Gentilly, a banlieue (suburb) of Paris. His father was a plumber. On leaving school at 13 he studied lithography and engraving at L'Ecole Estienne in Paris and his decision to take up photography was, in part at least, a reaction to the outdated techniques and repressive academicism of the school. It also helped him find his subject matter; he later said he would willingly have swapped the whole cupboardful of Roman Emperors he was expected to draw at the school for the chestnut seller in the Place d'Italie who was real and alive.

From the beginning Doisneau combined a career in photography with following his own photographic interests independently. He learned photography both through working for an advertising studio and as an assistant and by buying a Rolleiflex and taking photographs of the Paris streets on Sundays and in time taken off work. Later he commented that initially no-one was interested in this work. In 1934, he became an industrial photographer at the huge Renault factory in Billancourt where, for five years, he worked taking photographs with a large format camera and a magnesium flash. The pleasure he derived from his work would seem to have come as much from entertaining the workers with the magnesium flash as from the photographs. At the same time he was experimenting with his own secret colour print process in his kitchen at home, which he dreamed might make him independent of the factory. However, it was his frequent lateness, for which he was sacked, which achieved this dream. He began a career as a reportage photographer or photojournalist, signing with Rapho Photo Agency; it was interrupted by the outbreak of World War II in 1939. After military service he returned to occupied Paris where it was difficult for him to work as a photographer, although using the engraving skills he had learned at L'Ecole Estienne he forged documents for the French resistance and eventually photographed the liberation of Paris.

After the war Doisneau was able to take up reportage again. He briefly joined the Alliance photo agency then re-joined Rapho in 1946 and stayed with them despite an invitation from Henri Cartier-Bresson to join Magnum Photos. In this period his photographs were published in magazines which included *Le Point*, *Action*, *Regards*, *Life*, and *Vogue*. He worked for *Vogue* for several years but was uncomfortable with the world of fashion photography. The support of the writer, Blaise Cendrars, whom he had met in a barber's shop in Aix-en-Provence, helped Doisneau get his first book of photographs published in 1949. In 1950, his most famous image, *Baiser de l'Hotel du Ville* (Kiss in front of City Hall), was published in *Life* magazine as part of a spread on young lovers in Paris and marks the beginning of a period of international recognition with exhibitions in New York and Chicago. This was followed by a more difficult time with the decline of the illustrated magazines in the 1960s, and he returned to commercial photography.

By the early 1980s, however, his work was being introduced to a new generation, mostly through posters and postcards, which caught the contemporary mood of nostalgia for the romance of Paris. This popularity also caused problems for Doisneau since, under French law, an individual owns the rights to their own image and he was sued for damages on more than one occasion by people claiming to be the subjects of his photographs. As a result Doisneau had to admit to using both models and friends in his work and that not all his photographs were as spontaneous or uncontrived as they initially appear.

Doisneau's work was part of a move away from pictorialism; he was influenced by the modernist and surrealist movements current in Paris in the early twentieth century. He was also influenced by his admiration for Brassaï, his friendships with other Paris-based photographers including Willy Ronis, Izis, and Cartier-Bresson and by working with writers like Blaise Cendrars and the poet Jacques Prevert. Doisneau said that it was Prevert who taught him to have confidence in photographing the everyday scenes that most people ignored.

His work is both an affectionate portrait of Paris, particularly its suburbs, and about those very ordinary moments in life which, once caught on film, allow space for the viewer's imagination to augment the story. His images capture the beauty and absurdity of life. Reputedly a shy and modest man, Doisneau had a subversive sense of humour and a sharp perception of the ridiculous but his satire is affectionate, never condemnatory. Although he was politically left-wing, and both his politics and his background shaped his interest in working class life, his view is of the love and humour, which make life pleasureable in the most adverse of circumstances rather than the bleakness of poverty. In this it is true to its period and, although Doisneau is frequently accused of sentimentality, this writer would argue that his work is an insider's view of a disappearing place and time and stands as one of the classic documentations of twentieth century photography.

Shirley Read

See also: **Brassaï, Izis; Cartier-Bresson, Henri; Life Magazine; Magnum Photos; Photography in France; Street Photography**

Biography

Born Gentilly, Paris, April 14, 1912. Father a plumber. Studied engraving and lithography, L'Ecole Estienne 1925–1929. Worked at Atelier Ullmann, 1930. Assistant to advertising photographer, Andre Vigneau, 1931. First magazine story, 1932. Industrial photographer for Renault, 1934–1939. Freelance reportage, submitted work to Rapho Photo Agency, 1939. Continued to photograph and forged documents for the Resistance, 1939–1945. Commissioned by Maximilian Vox to illustrate *Les nouveaux destins de l'intelligence francaise*, 1942. Joined Alliance Photo press agency, 1945. Returned to Rapho, 1946. Won the Prix Kodak, 1947. Worked for *Vogue*, 1949–1952. Worked with Maurice Basquet on a book project, 1949–1951. *La Banlieue de Paris*, text by Blaise Cendrars, 1949. Prix Niépce, 1956. Photographed in USA, 1960. Consultant to Expo '67, Canada, 1967. Photographed in Soviet Union, 1968. Toured French regional museums, 1971. Film *Le Paris de Robert Doisneau*, 1973. Rencontre d'Arles, 1975. Film *Trois Jours, Trois Photographies*, 1979. Grand Prix National de la Photographie, 1983. Chevalier of the Legion of Honour, 1984. Film *Bonjour, Monsieur Doisneau*, 1992. Died, 1994.

Individual Exhibitions

1951 *Le Monde des Spectacles*; La Fontaine des Quatre Saisons, Paris
1968 *Robert Doisneau*; Bibliothèque nationale, Paris
1972 *Robert Doisneau*; George Eastman House, Rochester, New York
1974 *Robert Doisneau*; Galerie municipale du Château-d'Eau, Toulouse, France
Robert Doisneau; Nelson Gallery, University of California, Davis, California
1975 *Robert Doisneau*; Musée des Arts Decoratifs, Nantes, France
Robert Doisneau; Musée Reattu, Arles, France
Robert Doisneau; Witkin Gallery, New York
1976 *Robert Doisneau*; Hotel de Ville, Dieppe, France
1978 *Robert Doisneau*; Galerie Agathe, Gaillard, Paris
Robert Doisneau; Musée Nicéphore Niépce, Chalon-sur-Saône, France
1979 *Robert Doisneau*; Musée Eugène Boudin, Honfleur, France
Les Passants qui Passent; Musée national d'Art Moderne, Centre Georges Pompidou, Paris
1980 *The Imaginery Photo Museum*; Kunsthalle, Cologne
1982 *Portraits*; Fondation Nationale pour la Photographie, Lyon, France, and travelled to Services Culturels de l'Ambassade de France, New York
1986 *Un Certain Robert Doisneau*; Crédit Foncier de France, Paris, France
Portraits d'Ecrivains; Paris: Maison de Balzac
1987 *St Denis*; Musée de St-Denis
Kyoto: The National Museum of Modern Art, Kyoto
1988 *A Homage to Robert Doisneau*; Villa Medicis, Rome
1989 *Doisneau-Renault*; Grande Halle de la Villette, Paris
1990 *La Science de Doisneau*; Le Jardin des Plantes, Paris
1992 *Robert Doisneau: A Retrospective*; Museum of Modern Art and travelling, Oxford, England
1995 *A Homage to Robert Doisneau*; Galerie Municipale du Château-d'Eau, Toulouse, France

Doisneau 40/44 Robert Doisneau ou la desobeissance; Centre d'Histoire de la Resistance et de la Deportation de Lyon, France
1996 *Robert Doisneau*; Montpelier Photo-Visions, Galerie Municipale de la Photographie and touring Japan
2002 *Robert Doisneau's Paris*; Portland Museum of Art, Portland, Oregon

Group Exhibitions

1947 Bibliothèque nationale; Paris
1951 Museum of Modern Art; New York
1965 *Six Photographes et Paris*; Musée des Arts Decoratifs, Paris
Trois Photographes Francais; Musée Reattu, Arles

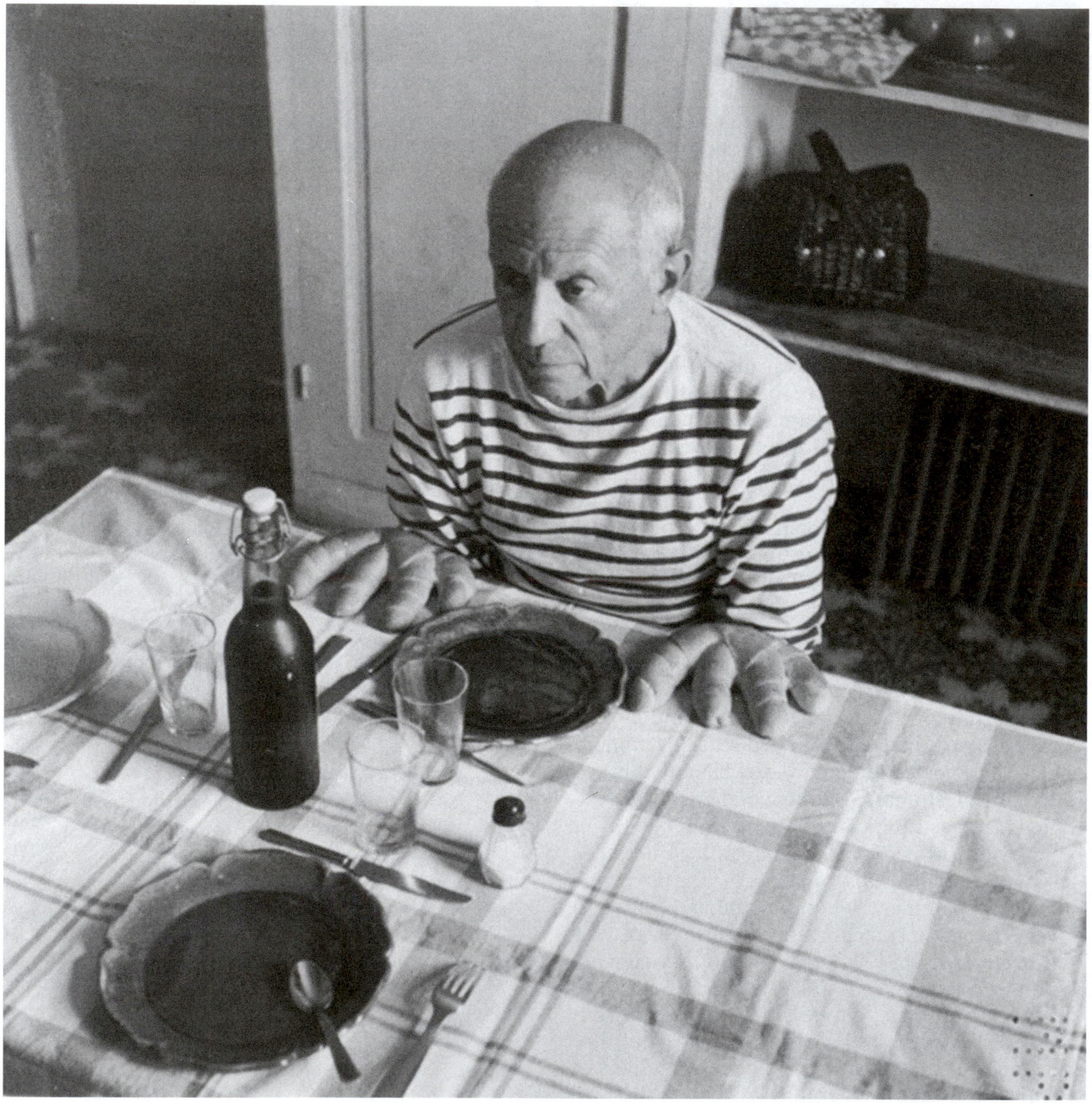

Robert Doisneau, Picasso at the table, 1952.
[*Réunion des Musées Nationaux/Art Resource, New York,* © *Agence Rapho*]

1968 *L'Oeil Objectif*; Musée Cantini, Marseille
1972 *Boubat/Brassaï /Cartier-Bresson/Douisneau/Izis/Ronis*; French Embassy, Moscow
1975 *Le Mobilier Urbain*; Bibliotheque Historique de la Ville de Paris, Paris
1977 *Six Photographes en Quete de Banlieu*; Pompidou Centre, Paris
1982 *Counterparts: Form and Emotion in Photographs*; Metropolitan Museum of Art, New York and traveling
1986 *De Vogue a femme*; Rencontres Internationales de la Photographie, Arles

Selected Works

Two Children Fetching the Milk, Gentilly, 1932
The Brothers, 1937
In the Strictest Intimacy, Montrouge, 1945
Sidelong Glance, 1948
Waltzing on Bastille Day, Paris, 1949
The Kiss at City Hall, 1950
Mademoiselle Anita at La Boule Rouge, 1951
The Accordionist, Rue Mouffetard, 1951
Picasso at the Table, 1952
Kids at the Place Herbert, 1957

Further Reading

Cendrars, Blaise. *La banlieue de Paris*. Paris: Editions Pierre Seghers, 1949.
Doisneau, Robert. *Robert Doisneau: Photographs*. London: Gordon Fraser Gallery, 1980.
Hamilton, Peter. *Robert Doisneau: A Photographers Life*. New York, London and Paris: Abbeville Press, 1995.
Hamilton, Peter. *Robert Doisneau: Retrospective*. London: Cartago, 1992 and Paris: Paris Musées, 1995.
Routmette, Sylvain. *Robert Doisneau*. Paris: Centre nationale de Photographie, 1983; London: Thames & Hudson, 1991.
Trois Secondes d'eternite (Three Seconds of Eternity). Paris: Contrejour, 1979 and 1990.

KEN DOMON

Japanese

One of the most influential and respected Japanese photographers, Ken Domon worked from the 1940s, photographing Japanese military activities for the government, to the 1960s, capturing vivid images of contemporary social issues. Throughout his career, Domon pursued several motifs, as he called them, including children, Buddhist statues, and portraits. Although Domon is most famous for advocating "realism photography," the significance and range of his work and influence extend well beyond this call, manifesting his preeminent stature in the larger sphere of photographic history.

Born in 1909 in Sakata-city, located in the northern part of the Japanese archipelago, Domon dreamt about becoming a painter when he was young. However, after seeing works by Gu Kaizhi, a Chinese literary painter, Gomon realized the limitations of his talent in that medium. On his mother's suggestion, in 1933 Domon apprenticed with a prominent commercial photo studio in Tokyo. During this two-year apprenticeship Domon learned basic techniques of photography and availed himself of the numerous journals stacked in the back of the studio. He was fascinated by images by László Moholy-Nagy and other artists of the Modernist era. Domon's position as an apprentice at a commercial portrait studio and his taste for artistic and journalistic photography presented him with a dilemma that he could not resolve, and he decided to leave studio practice.

In 1935, Domon joined *Nihon Kôbô*, a photographic agency led by Natori Yônosuke, an editor known for his difficult personality. Although Natori constantly confronted Domon with harsh criticisms and engaged in accusatory emotional dramas, the experience with their publication *Nippon*, an English magazine designed to promote Japanese culture abroad, equipped Domon with new skills and experience as a photographer. Around this time, Domon began using a 35 mm Leica camera, instead of a medium format view camera. In 1939, Domon left Nihon Kôbô over a dispute with Natori and began working for the International Association for the Promotion of Culture, a government-sponsored agency. The trip to Murou-ji temple in Nara at the end of 1939 with the art historian Muzusawa Sumio started Domon's lifelong pursuit of a motif—Buddhist statues and temples—and the fruit of his passionate and contemplative approach is evident in numerous publications, such as *Koten Junrei* and *Nihon no Tera*.

In 1940, Domon joined a group from Nihon Mingei Kyôkai (Association of Japanese Folk Art) led by the founder of the "folk movement," Yanagi Muneyoshi, on a visit to Okinawa. During their two-week stay, his group commented that the imposition of "standard" Japanese language on the Okinawan people was a gesture of disrespect toward Okinawan culture. This caused political friction with their sponsoring officials in an incident that came to be known as "Hôgen ronsô" (controversy of dialect).

During the Pacific War, Domon photographed *bunraku*, traditional Japanese puppet theater, Buddhist statues, and created portraits of Japanese intellectuals. The compilation of these portraits was published in the magazine *Shashin bunka* in 1943, (later published as *Fubo* in 1953), and he won the first Arusu Photographic Culture award for this work.

After the war, Domon served on the jury for photographic contests that targeted amateur and emerging photographers sponsored by the international magazine *Camera*, and in 1949 he published his famous essay "on being a jury member for the contest" as introductory remarks for those submitting their works. As a result of this experience, Domon devoted increasingly more time writing criticism and corresponding with amateur photographers. The publication of this essay, in which he brought attention to the concept of "realism photography," had an enormous impact not only on the works submitted to the contests and Domon's own work, but also on the ways that both amateur and professional photographers thought about their work. Controversy followed Domon's call for "realism photography."

According to Domon, realism photography is an attitude toward practicing photography and is not to be defined by abstract concepts or a particular style of photograph. To achieve it, he encouraged photographers to establish a "direct connection" between the motif and the camera, by "listening to the voice that the motif shouts and control the camera in accord with it." He further contended that "when the camera is moved as directed by the motif, there exists a direct connection between the motif and the camera." Domon wrote another essay entitled "Realism photography that takes absolutely non-directed absolute snap as a basic method," in 1953. This essay signals a shift toward more social and political motifs in Domon's own work. Domon stated that "realism photography stares directly at actuality and is a manifestation of a spirit of revolt to change actuality to a correct direction." Furthermore, the absolutely non-directed absolute snap "emerges from the body of photographers who attack wholeheartedly social actuality" and "is the solo creative method to add something to society as an artist." One of the projects that resulted from the exploration and articulation of "realism photography" is *Hiroshima* (1958), and its sequel *Living Hiroshima* (1978), in which Domon illustrated the profound presence of the atomic bomb as an on-going, complicit part of reality in contemporary Hiroshima, refuting the popular tendency to regard Hiroshima as a historical event. Domon suffered a stroke in 1960 that left his right hand paralyzed. This forced him to give up the use of 35 mm cameras, and he turned to the large format view camera, which allowed him to continue photographing Buddhist statues and temples. Domon died in 1990.

Throughout his career, Domon published numerous essays and gave speeches on photography and being a photographer to a wide audience. His often didactic and passionate approach was evident most clearly among the amateur photographers and photographs submitted for contests. Domon also wrote numerous short essays accompanying his photographic images in publications, and his powerful and energetic writings testify to his dedication to the profession and the medium. In 1983, the Ken Domon Museum opened in his birthplace of Sakata, the first museum dedicated solely to the work of one photographer in Japan.

MAKI FUKUOKA

See also: **Moholy-Nagy, László; Photography in Japan**

Biography

Born in Sakata City, Yamagata prefecture, 25 October 1909. Became apprentice to Miyauchi Kotaro at a portrait studio, 1933; worked at *Nippon Kobo* as a photographer in Tokyo, 1935–1939; became an associated photographer of Association of International Cultural Promotion, 1939; A jury to photography contest for a magazine *Camera*, 1950, with Kimura Ihei, 1952, alternately with Kimura, 1953; jury for *Photoart* magazine 1956–1963. ARS Photographic Culture Prize, 1943; Association of Photographers, Koro-Award, 1955; Mainichi Book Prize for the publication of *Murou-ji*, 1955; Mainichi Photography Award, 1958; The Photographer of the Year Award of Japan Photo Critics Association, 1958; The Minister of Education Awards of Arts, 1959; East Berlin International Photojournalism Award, 1960; Photographic Society of Japan Award, 1960; Japan Journalists Congress Award, 1960; Mainichi Award for Arts for *Tsukuhô no kodomotachi*, and *Rumie-chan ha otôsan ga shinda*, 1961; Kikuchi Kan Award for *Koji Junrei*, 1971; Purple Ribbon Medal, 1973; Asahi Award, 1979. Died in Tokyo, 15 September 1990.

Individual Exhibitions

1955 *Kotôno Kodomotachi* (Children of Downtown Tokyo); Nihonbashi Takashimaya Department Store, Tokyo, Japan
1960 *Chikuhô no Kodomotachi* (Children of Chikuhô Cold Mines); Fuji Photo Salon, Tokyo, Japan
1968 *Zoo to Shitui no Hibi-Hiroshima wa tsuzuiteiru* (Days of Hatred and Disapointment-Hiroshima); Ginza Nikon Salon, Tokyo, Japan
1971 *Butsuzô Henreki* (Pilgrimages to Ancient Temples); Shinjuku Nikon Salon, Tokyo, Japan
1972 *Koji Junrei* (Pilgrimages to Ancient Temples); Odakyû Department Store, Tokyo, Japan, and traveled to Osaka, Nagoya, Okayama, and Sakata, Japan
1973 *Bunraku*; Wako, Tokyo, Japan
1974 *Bunraku to Domon Ken*; Odakyû Department Store, Tokyo, Japan, and traveled to Kobe, Kyoto, Osaka, and Sakata, Japan
Koyou Henreki; Fuji Photo Salon, Tokyo, Japan
1975 *Murou ji*; Shinjuku Odakyû Department Store, Tokyo traveled to Nigata, Nagano, Japan
1979 *Gendai Chôkoku Shashinten*; Ginza Mitsukoshi Department Store, Tokyo, Japan
1983 *Domon Ken Zen Shashin*; Seibu Department Store, Tokyo, Japan
1987 *Domon Ken no zenbô*; Sogo Museum of Art, Yokohama, Japan
1991 *Domon Ken no Subete*; Takashimaya Department Store, Tokyo, Japan
1994 *Domon Ken Shashin ten-Koji Junrei*; Fukuoka Municipal Museum of Art, Fukuoka, Japan, and traveling
1995 *Koji Junrei- Domon Ken ten*; Iwaki Municipal Museum of Art, and traveling
Domon Ken no Nihon; Tenmanya, Okayama, Japan and traveling
2000 *Domon Ken—Nihon no Chôkoku*; Daimaru Museum, Kobe, Japan, and traveling

Group Exhibitions

1974 *New Japanese Photography*; Museum of Modern Art, New York, New York
1979 *Japanese Photography Today and Its Origin*; Galleria d'Arte Moderna, Bologna, Italy, and traveling

Selected Works

Ryûzaburô Umehara, 1940 (reproduced in Iizawa, Kotarô, Domon Ken pl. 12)
Detail (left hand) of the Sitting Image of Buddha Shakamuni in the Hall of Miroku, the Murô-ji, 1942–1943
Blind Twins, 1957 from series *Hiroshima*

Further Reading

Iizawa Kôtaro. *Domon Ken*. Tokyo: Iwanami shoten, 1998.
Ikeda Mao, Kishi Tetsuo, Naitô Yutaka, Miki Jun, and Watanabe Yoshiaki, eds. *Domon Ken no Subete*. Tokyo: Kyodotsûshin sha, Domon Ken kinenkan, 1991.
Mainichi Shinbunsha, Domon Ken kinenkan, eds. *Domon Ken no tsutaetakatta Nihon*. Tokyo: Mainichi shinbun sha, 2000.
Putzer, Edward. "The Reality of Domon Ken." *Japan Quarterly* (July 1994): 308–322.
Szarkowski, John, and Shoji Yamagichi, eds. *New Japanese Photography*. New York: Museum of Modern Art, 1974.
Yasushi, Mishima. *Kimura Ihe to Domon Ken*. Tokyo: Heibonsha, 1995.

FRANTIŠEK DRTIKOL

Czech

When František Drtikol arrived in Munich in the year 1901 to study photography, it was apparent that the practice of photography in his native Bohemia and its capital, Prague was inferior, technically backward, and artistically insignificant. It was oriented toward conventional styles of portrait photography; innovation was a foreign word. Drtikol became an innovator of Czech photography and one of the most important pictorialist photographers. Efforts, as for instance those of the British photography circle The Linked Ring Brotherhood or the Vienna Camera Club, to professionalize the practice of photography and lift it to the level of fine art did not find an echo in Prague.

František Drtikol was born in March, 1883 in Príbram (southwest of Prague) in Bohemia. After a short training in one photographic studio in Príbram, he was admitted for a study at the just-opened *Lehr- und Versuchsanstalt für Photographie* in Munich. He left with honor after two years of study. Possible employment as a photographer in Germany or in Switzerland failed. Back in his hometown, in 1907 he created his own studio, which went bankrupt in 1910. Drtikol moved to Prague and opened his own studio in the center of the city. His outstanding portraits attracted first the clientele from the Prague art circles, soon afterwards Drtikol—with his partner Augustin Škarda (1879–1937)—became the premiere portrait photographer in Prague.

Drtikol is considered to be the founder of the modern Czech photography—in addition to Karel Novák (1882–1952) and Vladimír Jindřich Bufka (1887–1916)—whose works mark an end of the general stagnation of the photography in Bohemia. Drtikol developed a specific form of pictorialist photography, the goal of which was to lift to the level of art by depicting "noble" subject matter (such as allegorical scenes, drama tableaux, nature scenes, and architectural ruins) in complex compositions. However, Drtikol was not of the opinion that photography should move into the proximity of painting. His procedure of the oil, pigment, or rubber prints—used until the late 1920s—served rather in his portrait photography to underline the character of the photographed person as clearly as possible. In nude photography, he wanted to show not only the body but also the soul. In order to elicit more clearly this idea, which had to be inherent—according to his opinion—in each artistic photograph, he worked on his negatives by painting whole picture portions or retouching them, manufacturing cutouts, and using different lighting effects, in order to express his visions.

Drtikol began to work on his series of nude pictures. They made him famous before World War I: The complicated noble prints (bromoil, coal, multicolor pigment prints) belong in their elegance, refinement of lines, and expression of strength of the female body to the most important pictorialist pictures and can easily compete with the work of Constantin Puyo or Robert Demachy, leading members of the Linked Ring Brotherhood.

Drtikol entered consciously into the pictorial tradition of the Photo Secession: his nudes mirrored the themes of the paintings of his countryman and famous painter of the Art Nouveau movement Alphonse Mucha, the Belgian Symbolists Fernand Khnopff and Félicien Rops: *Femme fatale*, *Salome*, *Judith*, and *Cleopatra* were the pictorialist contributions to one of the predominant topics of the *fin de siècle*. Drtikol's participation in the large exhibition in London (International Exhibition of the Salon of London of Photography, 1913) announced the beginning of his international career.

In 1920, under the influence of "straight photography," Drtikol's concept of nude photography changed. Gradually he gave up the complicated noble print, of which he was the undisputed master in Prague, and devoted himself above all to the pigment print. Drtikol placed and lit his nudes in front of geometrically arranged window blinds in such a way that the body forms were emphasized. This placement stressed—in contrast to the preceding period, in which the flatness of the noble prints underlined the two-dimensionality and in which space structure was suppressed—the depth and the special light direction characteristic of this second period. Between 1920 and 1925, Drtikol still worked on many photographs with painting and retouching. His 1921 pigmented print *The Bow* emphasized the formal qualities of the nude female form by way of a moody abstraction.

In a manifesto, which he wrote by the end of the 1920s together with Jaromír Funke (1896–1945), Drtikol stressed the primacy of the staging of the photographic picture that was developed before as an "interior (inner) vision":

> We photograph our "inner visions"; although we photograph in such a way as all others, there are only by us composed, arranged subjects, which we take up. We are directors of those subjects, the interiors of which we create by ourselves....Photography is for us an expression of the own and individual aspect.

Under the influence of his wife, the dancer Ervína Kupferová, who practiced free expression dance according to Emile J. Dalcroz (1865–1950) who postulated rhythm and movement as original values of free dance, Drtikol's photographs gained dynamics. Around 1925, he gave up the static conception of the picture, and movement and light direction now stood in the foreground. The female body also was taken up fragmentarily, in order to underline the space structure or the rhythm of movement. Those prints were internationally highly esteemed and sold at expensive prices.

Drtikol's landscape, portrait, and nude photography formed a unit from the beginning. With care and precision, as he had learned in Munich, he worked out every negative. His nude photographs taken between 1910 and 1930 were considered to be revolutionary, sensitive, and absolutely modern. Drtikol was also an outstanding landscape and portrait photographer; his photographs of important personalities of the 1920s and 1930s (Leoš Janáček, Paul Valéry, Rabindranath Tagore, Thomas Garrigue Masaryk, or Josef Čapek) belong to the best of portrait art at this time:

> Every person requires another illumination, in order to recognize his character. Not only that everyone has to recognize himself—but he has to do it at first sight. Nevertheless it is difficult to recognize a human being on the street, whom we had met for the first time in

nocturnal light. The lighting, which the portrait photographer selects, must underline all the characteristic face particularities, which one can suppress neither as daily nor as night lighting—they are not to be excluded from the nature of his face.

His art was based not only on an extraordinary sensibility for the light, but also on its tendency to integrate the theosophical knowledge (which was based on his study of eastern philosophy and book translations) into his photographic work. Drtikol wanted to "write" himself into the soul of human beings with his work.

At the beginning of 1931 the Czechoslovakian Republic fell into a deep economic depression. Drtikol had to give photography and painting lessons in order to survive. Since he could not afford to have models (or only rarely), he cut out—quite schematically—from paper or cardboard a silhouetted female body, which however he idealized very strongly. The dynamics, which had distinguished the second period, were lost. Drtikol needed the participation of the living model. This dialogue between the photographer and the model was one of the sources of the originality of his nude photography.

In 1935, he sold his studio, moved from the center of Prague into a peripheral area, and gave up photography; from then on painting and eastern philosophy were his great interests.

Drtikol's modernity consists of successful integration of elements of the Cubo-Futurism into his work; particularly to integrate them into his nude photography, without submitting himself to the prevailing modes. The price for this persistence on his own style, the origins of which were in the painting of the symbolism of the nineteenth century, was isolation and the decades-long forgetting of his great photographic achievements. When he died on 13 January 1961 in complete isolation, only a few of his friends knew that one of the most important photographers of the twentieth century had left them. Not a single exhibition in Czechoslovakia of Drtikol's work occurred during his lifetime.

Milan Chlumsky

Biography

Born in Příbram (Bohemia), on March 3, 1883. Apprenticeship with Antonín Mattas on October 1, 1898. From autumn 1901 at School of Apprentice and Laboratory for Photography in Munich, graduating with honors and a first prize during the exhibition in July 1903 in the Munich Old City. 1904–1907 military service. 1908–1909 own studio in Příbram. After financial failure, removal to Prague in February 1910. Publications *Doly příbramské* (Coalpot in Příbram, 1910) and *Z dvorů a dvorečků staré Prahy* (From yards and backyards of the old Prague, 1911). Drtikol starts work in 1912 with nude photography. From 1913 he made portraits of important personalities of Czech and international culture (Paul Valéry, Nobel Price Winner R. Tagore, etc.). 1914 Drtikol entered the Austrian-Hungarian army, is sent into war where he is blinded in one eye. His studio in Prague continues to operate, led by Jaroslav Roessler and by his partner, Augustin Škarda. 1921 Drtikol separates from Škarda because of financial discrepancies. 1922 patents procedure of photo lithography, which shows also half-tones. 1925 his nude photographs of the dynamic components—under the influence of the expression-dance of E. Dalcroz—were being extended by movement, cutout, and special lighting effects (light modulation). 1929 appear *Les nus de Drtikol* (Préface Claude de Santuel) in Librairie des Arts décoratifs in Paris. Because of the economic crisis 1929 Drtikol turned to teaching his craft. 1935 he sold his studio, giving his photographs and all documents to the Museum of Arts and Crafts in Prague. 1938 a last publication *Žena ve světle* (Woman in the light). He moves from the center to the periphery of Prague, dedicates himself to painting and philosophy. Died on 13 January 1961 in Prague.

Individual Exhibitions

1928 Cleveland Photographic Society; Cleveland, Ohio
1929 Towarzystwo Milownikow Fotografii; Warsaw, Poland
1930 Kodak Camera Club; Rochester, New York
The Royal Photographic Society; London, England
Cambridge University; Cambridge, England
The London Camera Club; London, England
Brooklyn Institute of Art; Brooklyn, New York
1932 Museum of Fine Arts of Houston; Houston, Texas
Club of the Photo Amateurs; (With Alois Zych), Olomouc, Czech Republic
1936 City Art Galery; Durban, South Africa
Arts Hall; Port Elizabeth, South Africa

Group Exhibitions

1903 International Exhibition for Photography and Graphic Arts; Mainz, Germany
1911 *Výstava Českého klubu fotografů amatérů v Praze* (Exhibition of the Czech Amateur Club of the Photographers); Lucerna, Prague, Czech Republic
1913 International Exhibition of the London Salon of Photography; London, England
1914–1915 *Výstava fotografií*; (Photography exhibition); Rudolfinum, Prague, Czech Republic
1922 Annual Exhibition of the Royal Photographic Society of Great Britain; London, England
1923 *I° Exposizione Internationale di Fotografia*; Ottica, Torino, Italy
1924 *Salon international de Photographie*; Société Française de Photographie, Paris, France
International Salon of Photography; Camera Pictorialists of Los Angeles, Los Angeles, California
1925 International Exhibition of Professional Photography; London, England
Exposition des Arts Décoratifs; Paris, France
Mostra internazionale depression Arti Decorative; Monza, Italy

1926 Annual Pittsburgh Salon of Photographic Art; Pittsburgh, Pennsylvania
1927 International Exhibiton of Pictorial Photography, Pictorial Photographic Society of San Francisco; San Francisco, California
1927 International Circle of Pictorial Photographers; Liverpool, England
Hundert Jahre Lichtbild-Gewerbe (100 years of phototrade); Museum Basel, Basel, Switzerland
1928 Preston Scientific Society—International Exhibition of Photographic Art; Preston, England
Výstava soudobé kultury CSR (Exhibition of the contemporary art in the Czechoslovakian republic); Zemské výstaviště, Brno, Czech Republic
First Rochester Photography; Rochester, New York
International salon of the Pictorial Photographers of America; New York, New York
International Invitation Salon of the Camera Club New York; New York, New York
International Exhibition "*Das Lichtbild*"; Munich, Germany
První celostátní výstava fotografů z povolání; (First national exhibition of the professional photographers); Zemské výstaviste, Brno, Czech Republic
Premier salon international du nu photographique; Paris, France. *mezinárodní fotograficky salón* (II. international photography salon); Mánes, Prague, Czech Republic
Výstava fotografických obrazů Františka Drtikola a ing. Zycha z Prahy (Exhibition of photographic pictures of František Drtikol and Ing. Zych); Olomouc, Czech Republic
International photo exhibition; Berlin, Germany
Exposition internationale de la photographie contemporaine; Paris, France
Tanec v čsl. umení výtvarném a fotografii (Dance in the Czechoslovakian art and in the photography); Mánes, Prague, Czech Republic
100 let české photographie (100 years Czech photography); Umeleckoprůmyslové muzeum, Prague, Czech Republic

Selected Works

Nude study, c. 1929
Composition, 1929
The Bow, 1921

Further Readings

Birgus, Vladimír. *The Photographer František Drtikol*. Prague: KANT, 2001.
Birgus, Vladimír. *Fotograf František Drtikol* (Photographer František Drtikol). Prague: Prostor, 1994.
Birgus, Vladimír *František Drtikol*. Prague: Kant, 2000.
Drtikol, František. Text of K. Klaricová. In *Mezinárodní fotografie* (International photography) No. 7., Pressphoto Prague, 1982. Photography 1918–1938. Cologne: Photokina Cologne, 1982.
Drtikol, František. *Photographe des Art Déco*. Text by Alena Fárová. Munich: Schirmer/Mosel, 1986.
Drtikol, František. Text by V. Birgus and A. Braný, ed. Prague: Odeon, 1988.
Drtikol, František. Text by K. Klaricová and Jirí Masín. *Panorama, photographic personalities*. No. 4, Prague, 1989.
Drtikol, František. *Fotograf, malír, mystik* (Photographer, Painter, Mystic). Text by František Doležal, Anna Fárová, Petr Nedoma. Exhibition catalogue. Prague: Galerie Rudolfinum, 1998.

DAVID DOUGLAS DUNCAN

American

David Douglas Duncan, one of the twentieth century's most accomplished photojournalists, photographed every major war from World War II to Vietnam. Duncan's career is characterized by his strong-willed commitment to photojournalistic clarity, his insightful portraits of war, and his limitless curiosity, which led to images and publications on diverse subjects ranging from the legendary artist Picasso to sunflowers to the treasures of the Kremlin.

Born in 1916 in Kansas City, Missouri, David Douglas Duncan began his photographic career at age 18. Duncan had been studying archeology at the University of Arizona in 1934; he had recently received a camera as a birthday present. When Tucson's largest hotel caught fire, he made some snapshots. It turned out, however, that the man he photographed running out of the hotel with a suitcase in hand was gangster John Dillinger, America's Public Enemy No. 1. This was the beginning of a lifetime of capturing significant moments on film. Duncan soon transferred to the University of

Miami in Florida where he studied marine zoology and deep-sea diving. After college, Duncan freelanced and was published in a variety of publications including *National Geographic* magazine and worked on several projects in Latin America.

In 1943, Duncan entered the Marine Corps and served as a combat photographer in the South Pacific. On the Solomon Islands, Duncan covered Fijian guerrilla warfare, (*Fijian Guerilla, 1944*) and after witnessing deadly ambushes in Bougainville, he was transferred to Okinawa where he photographed combat aviation. This experience of war forged Duncan's close-up and direct style of photography, which so effectively portrays the human aspects of war. Duncan achieved the rank of Lieutenant Colonel and received the Legion of Merit, Distinguished Flying Cross, Air Medal, and a Purple Heart.

In 1946, Duncan was hired by legendary *Life* magazine editor Wilson Hicks as a staff photographer, a major accomplishment for photojournalists at the time. Duncan spent 10 years at *Life* magazine and saw his images published as cover stories, including photographs of GIs that have become contemporary icons. Duncan's coverage of the Korean War in 1950 with the First Division Marines was featured in a famous *Life* spread titled "This is War!". The poignancy and thus power of Duncan's images frequently lies in the eyes of his subjects. The *Life* story, for example, included striking and intimate images of Captain Ike Fenton and Corporal Leonard Hayworth; the haunted yet guarded look in the men's eyes powerfully communicates the horror of war (*Captain Ike Fenton, Baker Company Commanding Officer, receives report of dwindling supplies during the battle to secure "no-name" ridge*, 1950 and *Corporal Hayworth*, 1950).

Duncan's motto for shooting war photographs was "Be close—be fast—be Lucky, Easy, always remember—be humane, never close-ups of the dead, war is in the eyes" (*Photo Nomad*, 2003, 151). In 1951, Duncan published *This is War: A Photo-Narrative*, a book of these haunting images of the Korean War. Years later a 22 cent U.S. stamp was made to honor those who fought in Korea; "Veterans Korea," based on one of Duncan's images. The stamp, however, crops Duncan's original image, *North Korea, 1950*, so that the dead bodies on the ground below the soldiers could not be seen. Duncan's *Life* images were also technologically pioneering in that they were taken with the newly introduced Nikon lens, which he used on a Leica camera. The positive response to the quality of these images contributed significantly to the popularity of the previously unknown Nikon brand.

Duncan's life as a photojournalist also included trips to Saudi Arabia, where he produced *Riyadh*, 1947, and Turkey, capturing *General "Black Avni" Mizrak commanding Turkish cavalry, guarding wintertime Russian frontier*, 1948. He also covered Iran, Palestine, Bulgaria, India, and the Far East, producing stories that include both remarkable portraits and breathtaking landscapes. Other *Life* assignments of the late 1940s and 1950s include the departure of King Farouk from Egypt, the end of the British Raj in India, and Ava Gardner in Rome filming "The Barefoot Contessa."

Duncan resigned from *Life* magazine in 1956 and became a freelance photographer. His travels included trips to the Middle East and the former Soviet Union, where despite Cold War tensions, he was allowed to extensively document the Kremlin treasures.

Throughout his career, Duncan has been very conscious of staying in control of his images and refused to compromise his photographs for political reasons. His 1953 "Indochina All But Lost" *Life* photoessay provoked conflict with Henry Luce, the magazine's founder and editor-in-chief. Luce considered the story "defeatist and therefore wrong" (*Photo Nomad*, 221). For Duncan, the story was the way he saw things; in fact, he correctly foresaw the fall of Dien Bien Phu in 1954, which led to the division of Viet Nam and America's eventual involvement. Remaining faithful to his convictions, in most of his 24 books, he was responsible for all elements of the publications.

Duncan's work was first exhibited in Edward Steichen's *Memorable Life Photographs* exhibition at the Museum of Modern Art in New York in 1951. His work was also featured in another of Steichen's exhibitions in 1951 titled *Korea* as well as in the seminal 1955 exhibition *The Family of Man*.

The mid-1950s was also the beginning of a long friendship between Duncan and Pablo Picasso. The two men, both masters of their respective visual forms, shared a deep passion for work and life. Duncan gained unprecedented access to the great artist and spent several years photographing Picasso, eventually publishing seven books featuring images of Picasso at work and at play. The works are intimate and charming, frequently focusing on Picasso's intense and expressive dark eyes (*Picasso*, 1957).

Undoubtedly influenced by Picasso, Duncan began experimentation with cameras during the 1960s, using the special effects of prismatic lenses. Duncan states in his book, *Prismatics: Exploring a New World*, 1972, "I wanted to fragment then reassemble the subjects before me, limited only by my imagination and ability to fulfill it—sometimes ending with fresh images of very old and tired models" (Foreword, 1). One of his many images of "prismatic" Paris is *The Lido*, 1962/1967.

As the Vietnam War unfolded in the 1960s, the legendary war photographer returned to the battlefield for *Life* and ABC News. Duncan's coverage produced harrowing images of what he quickly came to see as a tragedy, notably the siege of Khe Sanh (*The Snipers of Khe Sanh, 1968*). His "war trilogy" that started with *This is War: A Photo-Narrative* was soon complete with two new books, *I Protest!* (1968) and *War without Heroes* (1970), questioning the role of the American government in Vietnam. In *I Protest!*, he wrote:

> I am no kook, hippie, or dove. I am just a veteran combat photographer and foreign correspondent who cares intensely about my country and the role we are playing—and assigning ourselves—in the world of today. And I want to shout a loud protest at what has happened at Khe Sanh and in all of Vietnam.

Duncan's commitment to accurately recording the story coupled with his human insight and fine composition skills have created a captivating and rich photojournalistic *oeuvre* with many creative and original images to complement the drama of his renowned war photographs. Duncan's 2003 photo-autobiography, *Photo Nomad*, presents a thorough picture of the evolution of his critical eye. Today, the Harry Ransom Humanities Research Center at the University of Texas at Austin now preserves Duncan's legacy as one of the finest photojournalists of his time.

KRISTEN GRESH

See also: **History of Photography: Postwar Era; Life Magazine; Museum of Modern Art; National Geographic; War Photography**

Biography

Born in Kansas City, Missouri, 23 January 1916. Studied archaeology at University of Arizona, 1935; studied marine zoology and deep-sea diving at University of Miami, 1935–1938, B.A., 1938; self-taught in photography. Combat photographer in United States Marine Corps, South Pacific, 1943–1946; Lieutenant Colonel; Legion of Merit, Distinguished Flying Cross, Air Medal, and Purple Heart. Official cameraman, Michael Lerner Chile/Peru expedition, American Museum of Natural History, New York, 1940–1941; photographer and Chile/Peru coordinator, Office of Inter-American Affairs, Washington, D.C., 1941–1942; staff photographer, *Life* magazine, assigned to Korea, Iran, Palestine, Saudi Arabia, India, Europe, and Far East, 1946–1956; freelance photographer and foreign press correspondent since 1956; published 24 books since 1951. Received Gold Medal, *U.S. Camera*, 1950; Overseas Press Club Award, 1951; Robert Capa Gold Medal, 1968; Photographer of the Year Award, American Society of Magazine Photographers, 1968; Honorary Khan of the Qashqui Tribe, Iran. Lives in Castellaras, France.

Individual Exhibitions

1971 *Retrospective*; William Rockhill Nelson Gallery, Kansas City, Missouri
1972 Whitney Museum of American Art, New York
1981 *250 Photographs of Picasso*; Sidney Janis Gallery, New York
1996 *Alone with Picasso*; Jan Krugier Gallery, New York
1999 *Photography of David Douglas Duncan*; Lyndon B. Johnson Library, University of Texas at Austin, Austin, Texas
2001 *Picasso's Studio: David Douglas Duncan's Photographs*; Cleveland Museum of Art, Cleveland, Ohio
2001 *Picasso: The Artist's Studio*; Wadsworth Athenaeum, Hartford, Connecticut

Group Exhibitions

1951 *Memorable Life Photographs*; Museum of Modern Art, New York
1952 *Korea*; Museum of Modern Art, New York
1955 *The Family of Man*; Museum of Modern Art, New York
1964 *The Painter and the Photograph: From Delacroix to Warhol*; University of New Mexico, Albuquerque
1967 *Photographs in the Twentieth Century*; National Gallery of Canada, Ottawa and traveling
1977 *Documenta 6*; Kassel, West Germany
1980 *Photography of the 50s*; International Center of Photography, New York and traveling
1983 *Il Reportage Fotografico nelle Guerre Contemporanee*; Palazzo Fortuny, Venice, Italy

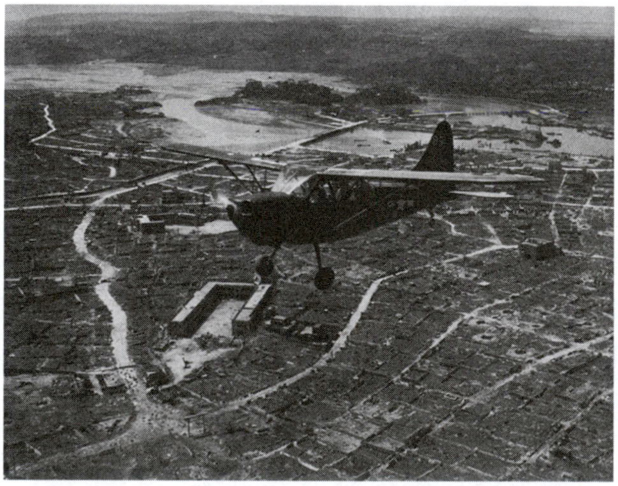

David Douglas Duncan, Marine Observation Plane Over Okinawa.
[© *CORBIS*]

Selected Works

Fijian Guerilla, 1944
Riyadh, 1947
General "Black Avni" Mizrak commanding Turkish cavalry, guarding wintertime Russian frontier, 1948
Captain Ike Fenton, Baker Company Commanding Officer, receives report of dwindling supplies during the battle to secure "no-name" ridge, 1950
Corporal Hayworth, 1950
North Korea, 1950
Picasso, 1957
The Lido, 1962/1967
Marine in Trench at Con Thien, Vietnam, 1967
The Snipers of Khe Sanh, 1968

Further Reading

Duncan, David Douglas. *I Protest!*; New York: Signet Broadside, 1968.
Duncan, David Douglas. *Photo Nomad*. New York: W.W. Norton & Co., Inc., 2003.
Duncan, David Douglas. *The Private World of Pablo Picasso*. New York: Ridge Press, 1958.
Duncan, David Douglas. *Prismatics: Exploring a New World*. New York: Harper & Row Publishers, 1972.
Duncan, David Douglas. *This is War: A Photo-Narrative*. New York: Harper & Brothers, 1951.
Duncan, David Douglas. *War without Heroes*. New York: Harper & Row Publishers, 1970.
Duncan, David Douglas. *Yankee Nomad, A Photographic Odyssey*. New York: Holt, Rinehart & Winston, 1966.
Gee, Helen. *Photography of the 50s: An American Perspective*. Tucson: Center for Creative Photography, University of Arizona, 1980.
Hicks, Wilson. *Words and Pictures: An Introduction to Photojournalism*. New York: Harper & Brothers, 1952.
Maloney, T.J., ed. "Korea: David Douglas Duncan." *U.S. Camera Annual 1951*. New York: U.S. Camera Publishing Corp., 1950.
Porter, Allan. "Living Masters of Photography." *Camera* Lucerne (June 1974).
Rayfield, Stanley, ed. *How Life Gets the Story: Behind the Scenes in Photo-Journalism*. Garden City: Doubleday & Co., 1955.

DYE TRANSFER

A photographic process capable of making color prints of the highest quality, dye transfer was principally used for commercial work. The quality arises from the fact that the final picture is layered onto and absorbed into archival quality paper from four separate color images, creating a subtle and stable color photograph. The dye transfer process, invented by the Eastman Kodak Company, first came on the market in 1945. Kodak discontinued making materials for dye transfer in 1993, effectively ending the practice at both commercial labs and for the few practitioners of the complicated and expensive process.

Basic Process

The dye transfer process is based on principles of color separation discovered in the mid-nineteenth century. To make a set of dye transfer separations, a color transparency is exposed using filters—red, green, and blue—onto three different black and white film sheets. The exposure through the red filter creates a negative separation of the cyan (blue) image. The green filter creates the negative separation for the magenta (red) image; the blue creates the negative separation for yellow. The separations are then each exposed onto another black and white film called matrix film to create a positive (which can be enlarged to the desired size). The separation made with the red filter will then, when reversed, be used to print the cyan image; the green will print the magenta image; the blue will print the yellow. The matrix film has a dimensionally stable plastic base coated with a thick layer of silver halide emulsion suspended in a medium of gelatin yellow dye. This dye serves to control the penetration of the light used during the exposure, allowing less exposure in areas of the thick matrix and more in thinner areas.

When the silver has been reduced in the development process, the gelatin hardens adjacent to points on the image where the silver has turned black. Excess gelatin and yellow dye are then removed with repeated baths of hot water, leaving a relief image in gelatin. This process is repeated for each matrix, resulting in a set of three positive matrices each with a gelatin relief image that is thicker where that color will be darker.

In the presence of acetic acid, gelatin absorbs dye. Each matrix is soaked in its proper color, cyan, magenta, or yellow, then rinsed and rolled individually onto wet paper treated with a gelatin layer and a mordant to hold the dye and to prevent it from bleeding when it hits the paper. Because the paper is much less acid than the dye, the dye migrates from acid to base, transferring from the gelatin on the matrix to the gelatin on the paper. The matrix is peeled away and the next color is rolled down while the paper is still wet. After all three colors are applied, the print is dried and flattened. Because each color is applied separately, precise registration of the matrices is essential.

Manipulating the Process

The contrast range of a transparency is greater than that of a print. Once the separations have been made, masks can be used to control contrast and shadow. Primary masks can be used to lower the contrast in making separations and matrices. Using special lithographic film, several additional sets of three black and white images can be made to mask highlights. These highlight masks can be placed on top of the separations during part or all of the exposure of the matrices, resulting in a brightening of the lighter parts of the print and control of the colors in the highlights. With highlight masks, the highlights can be controlled separately from the midtones and shadows. Contrast reducing masks enable the printer to control the density and color of shadows. Additional shadow separations can add contrast to the shadows, and by exposing a sheet of matrix film through all three shadow masks at once, the black parts of the image can be isolated and printed separately. Thus each print can depend on at least fifteen black and white sheets of film used as separations and masks. Because a variation in any one of these can make a print unusable, the developers and trays must be kept within a quarter of a degree of the proper temperature. Moreover, the printer must understand the unique characteristics of the different types of black and white film used to make separations, highlight masks, and contrast reducing masks.

Burning and dodging, the common techniques used in printing black and white photographs, are considerably more difficult with dye transfer because the alterations would have to be repeated exactly for each of the three separations or matrices. For dye transfer, dodging effects are achieved by painting with a dye called Crocein scarlet on clear film sheets that are placed on top of the separations and masks. Crocein blocks light and can be painted where it is needed. For effects similar to burning, windows can be cut from Amberlith or Rubylith, translucent graphic arts materials that are orange or red. These block the blue light to which the matrix film is sensitive.

Practical Application

Despite its difficulty, dye transfer has distinct advantages as a process for making color prints. Because each color is developed and applied separately, minute alterations can be made to individual colors, resulting in precise control of the final image. The prints have a unique richness and depth, since the dyes actually soak into the fibers of the paper instead of resting on a plastic coating on the surface of the paper. Most important, the prints are archivally stable. Recent research has shown that in dark storage, dye transfer prints would show little deterioration in six hundred years, if properly cared for. Although computer-based digital techniques have replaced the use of dye transfer for commercial photography and only a small handful of art photographers still use the process, existing dye transfer photographs may someday be regarded as some of the most beautiful and enduring color images from our age.

Kirsten A. Hoving

See also: **Emulsion; Non-Silver Processes; Print Processes**

Further Reading

Beede, Mindy. *Dye Transfer Made Easy*. New York: Amphoto Books, 1981.

Doubley, David A. *The Dye Transfer Process*. (published privately), 1984.

Kodak Dye Transfer Process. Rochester: Eastman Kodak Co., 1951.

Powell, Luke. "The Dye Transfer Process," unpublished technical notes.

Wilhelm, Henry. *The Permanence and Care of Color Photographs*. Grinnell, Iowa: Preservation Publishing Co., 1993.

E

EASTMAN KODAK COMPANY

The Eastman Kodak Company was founded in 1892, 12 years after George Eastman, an amateur photographer with barely an elementary school education, invented a machine that put forth pre-coated dry plates and formed a succession of business ventures focused on the new field of consumer photography. The development of this company reflected relentless technical innovation undertaken by Eastman and others, including Thomas Edison. In 1879, Eastman had traveled to London, the intersection of business and photography, and acquired a patent for his new product. By the following year, Eastman began to commercially manufacture pre-coated dry plates in a rented space in Rochester, New York. Successful in this venture, in 1881, Eastman formed a partnership with businessman Henry A. Strong to form the Eastman Dry Plate Company. However, in 1884 this firm evolved into the Eastman Dry Plate and Film Company, with a total of 14 shareholders. Eastman also invented the first transparent roll of film.

From the somewhat unlikely location of Rochester, New York, in the western part of the state, the Eastman Kodak Company ushered in amateur photography, constantly innovating and seeking to keep the price of its products low enough to allow widespread use. The word "Kodak" was first registered as a trademark in 1888, coined as an easy-to-remember, vigorous word by Eastman himself. The first product aimed at the consumer market was a Kodak camera, unveiled in 1888 and priced at $25. This camera appeared as a small, handheld structure that contained a roll of film with 100 exposures and cost $10 to develop at the laboratories in Rochester. Eastman coined the slogan, "you press the button, we do the rest," when he introduced the Kodak camera and within a year, it had became a well-known phrase.

Prior to Eastman's discovery in 1880, photographers had worked laboriously, applying fresh chemicals to a metal plate in order to take a single picture. Kodak's point-and-click novelty not only transformed photography from a complex, artistic method into a common, everyday practice, but it also moved the center of photographic commerce to New York from London. The creation of low-cost mass production combined with international distribution, extensive advertising—Kodak products were advertised in leading papers and periodicals of the day with ads written by Eastman himself—and a focus on the customer were four principles that served as the foundation of the Eastman Kodak Company. In 1896, 100,000 Kodak cameras had been manufactured, signaling a milestone in the evolution of mass photography. However, Eastman was determined to make the camera even more convenient and introduced the Brownie in 1900 which sold for $1.00 and consisted of separate removable containers.

Eastman, moreover, sought to bring amateur photography to the world market. The first sales office of Kodak cameras had opened in London five years after the establishment of the Eastman Dry Plate and Film Company. Amateur photography began to flourish world wide, and in 1889 the Eastman Photographic Materials Company, Limited, was incorporated in London and became the main distributor of Kodak products to countries outside of the United States. Two years later, in 1891, the Eastman Kodak Company constructed a factory in Harrow, England, that was second to Rochester in the manufacture and development of camera film. The word "Kodak" was shown in an electric sign in London's Trafalgar Square in 1897, in one of the first uses of such signs for advertising. Kodak rented booths at the great world expositions so popular around the turn of the twentieth century, and developed the trademark "Kodak Girl," whose clothing styles changed every year along with the camera she carried. By 1900, additional distribution centers appeared throughout Europe, in countries such as France, Germany, and Italy.

The entrepreneurial discoveries of George Eastman had a big influence in the invention of the motion picture. After the first transparent roll of film was introduced to the commercial market in 1889, Thomas Edison created the first motion picture camera in 1891. According to Eastman Kodak, all Oscar-winning "Best Pictures" have been shot on Kodak film. Additionally, the company has won a total of eight Academy Awards in the areas of scientific and technical excellence. In 1929, when Eastman Kodak discovered a way to create film that could record sound, the silent movie that had dominated much of popular culture during the early twentieth century immediately became an artifact of history.

The Kodak, despite its emphasis on consumer photography, also became a center for scientific photography inventions. X-rays were first isolated by William Roentgen in 1895; by the next year, Kodak designed paper that would capture X-ray images, revolutionizing medicine. The Eastman Kodak Company was one of the first to set up an industrial research center in the United States, hiring scientists as early as 1912.

The vast technological advancements made by the Eastman Kodak Company did not occur without incident. In 1921, the U.S. government charged that Kodak was a monopoly that controlled the sale of cameras and photographic supplies. As a result Kodak was required to sell all film as "Kodak" through retail outlets that had previously used different brand names. Later in 1954, Eastman Kodak was charged with bundling the sale of its own film with its photofinishing services, thereby prohibiting the growth of independent photographic laboratories. However, because Kodak no longer maintained an unfair dominance within the exchange of photographic services, the U.S. District Court of Appeals terminated both the 1921 and 1954 decrees in August 1994.

During much of the 1950s, color photography dominated the mass media and later experienced a surge in demand from the amateur and commercial markets. Kodak's earliest form of color film, known as Kodachrome, initially appeared in 1930 and consisted of a color-reversal film that was produced in the form of 35 mm slides, which could be viewed through projection. In 1941, Kodak's Minicolor Print allowed paper prints to be made from these transparencies. A color-negative film, called Kodacolor, was introduced in 1942, and by the latter half of 1955, the color print process was simplified with the invention of Ektacolor paper, also known as "Type C." Color prints previously involved a lengthy three-step process, but this new advancement reduced the production of color prints to 45 minutes.

However, in addition to the commercial and amateur markets, the Eastman Kodak Company has also made exceptional contributions to the areas of medicine, science, and technology. After William Roentgen isolated the X-ray in 1895, Kodak designed a particular kind of paper in 1896 that was devised to capture the X-ray image. As the atomic bomb was developed during World War II, Kodak introduced films that detected radiation exposure. Kodak also brought the first microfilm to the market in 1928, used primarily by the government, insurance agencies, libraries, and transportation agencies. Kodak was also a leader in space photography. In the 1960s, NASA launched five Lunar Orbiter spacecraft that used Kodak film to photograph the moon's surface. As the first American to orbit the moon, John Glenn's reactions were also documented with Kodak film as he traveled through space at 17,400 miles per hour. Beyond medicine and science, Kodak developed new display technology in the late 1980s called Organic Light Emitting Diode (OLED) that contained self-luminous pixels. OLED technology appears in everyday utilities such as digital cameras and mobile phones. Currently the Eastman Kodak Company is focused on the enhancement of info-imaging technologies, which combine images with information in order to improve both interpersonal and business communications.

JILL CONNER

Further Reading

Coe, Brian. *Kodak Cameras: The First Hundred Years*. Hove: Hove Foto, 1988.

Delly, John Gustav. *Photography Through the Microscope*. Rochester: Photographic Products Group, Eastman Kodak Co., c. 1988.

Eastman Kodak Company. *A Brief History of the Contributions of the Eastman Kodak Company to Photographic Progress*. Rochester: Eastman Kodak Co., 1938.

Ford, Colin. *The Story of Popular Photography*. North Pomfret, VT: Trafalgar Square Publications, 1989.

Kodak Museum of Photography. *The Kodak Museum: A Permanent Exhibition Illustrating the History of Photography and Some of Its Applications in Science, Art and Industry*. Wealdstone, Harrow, Middlesex: Kodak, 1947.

Schmidt, Dana M. *Patents at Eastman Kodak*. Rochester: Eastman Kodak Co., c. 1987.

West, Nancy Martha. *Kodak and the Lens of Nostalgia*. Charlottesville: University Press of Virginia, 2000.

HAROLD EDGERTON

American

Harold E. Edgerton is credited with inventing ultra high speed, stroboscopic, and stop-action photography. He was the first to photograph the invisible and the elusive, events that occurred too fast for the human eye to see, from the stroke of a hummingbird's wings to the detonation of an atomic bomb to action that occurs too slowly to notice, such as the movement of sea urchins. Capturing some events with exposures as short as a hundred-millionth of a second, Edgerton patented innovations that greatly advanced the technology of science, industry, and the arts. As an educator, engineer, and explorer, Edgerton's many inventions further developed and aided the diverse fields of photography, medicine, athletics, journalism, espionage, moviemaking, underwater exploration, sonar, and nuclear research. His inventions and innovations have advanced scientific research and have greatly enlarged the parameters of photography, producing classic images that have become part of the visual culture.

Edgerton was born in 1903 in Fremont, Nebraska. During high school, Edgerton learned photography basics from an uncle and built a home darkroom. In 1925, he received a B.S. in electrical engineering from the University of Nebraska in Lincoln. After working both in Nebraska and New York for power generating companies, Edgerton entered the Massachusetts Institute of Technology (MIT) in 1926. In his graduate studies there, Edgerton first used the strobe light to see whirling engine rotors. He received his M.S. in 1927 and later his doctorate in electrical engineering from MIT, where he became a faculty member and was eventually named Institute Professor, MIT's highest honor.

By synchronizing strobe flashes with the motion of the spinning engine rotors, then taking a series of photos through an open shutter at the rate of many flashes per second, Edgerton effectively had invented ultra-high-speed flash and stop-action photography in 1931. In 1932, Edgerton, ever an entrepreneur, developed and perfected the stroboscope for use in both ultra-high-speed and still photography applications, in partnership with former student Kenneth J. Germeshausen, an MIT research affiliate. Later, Herbert E. Grier, another former MIT student, joined the partnership, which was formally incorporated as EG&G in 1947. The team began a long series of experiments documenting familiar events and activities that moved at speeds beyond the ability of the human eye to perceive with the newly-perfected high-speed photography using a stroboscope. The stroboscope was a glass tube filled with exotic gases and excited with an electric jolt that would freeze the action of any moving thing onto continuously moving film. The threesome made their first stroboscope patent application in 1933, the first of 45 patents applied for by Edgerton and his team in the next 35 years. EG&G also developed high-powered strobe lights for commercial use in apparatus ranging from lighthouses to copying machines.

Edgerton's first foray into exhibiting his photographs was at the London Royal Photographic Society's annual exhibition in 1933. The next year, 10 of the photographs made with the stroboscope were exhibited, and Edgerton, Germeshausen, and Grier received their first photography award, a bronze medal, from the Society for the revolutionary new imaging. It was during this time that his achievements first received recognition as fine-arts photography: the photograph *Coronet* (the famous drop of milk frozen in midair splash) was chosen by Beaumont Newhall for inclusion in the Museum of Modern Art's initial exhibition of photography in New York City in 1937.

Edgerton's first book, *Flash! Seeing the Unseen by Ultra High Speed Photography*, co-authored with James R. Killian, Jr., was published in 1939. For the popular audience it was a revelation. E.F. Hall, reviewing *Flash!* in the *New York Times*, wrote, "This whole book...covering the fields of nature, sport, and industry, is a compilation of magic and of things undreamed, calculated to excite the most sluggish mind." Edgerton subsequently published three more books that featured the results of his discoveries.

Always driven to put his inventions to practical use, Edgerton perfected multiflash photography of athletes in action and tried to sell the concept of electronic flash to major U.S. camera manufacturers, but was received with limited interest. He then offered sports photographers his services and equipment. Soon, sports photography was allowing the camera to capture high-speed motion and preserve an unprecedented degree of detail, revolutionizing how sports were portrayed through photography. Electronic flash photographs of sports events were regularly published in major newspapers after 1940.

As World War II broke out in Europe, Edgerton briefly worked for the film industry in Hollywood. At MGM Studios he collaborated on the Academy Award-winning short, *Quicker Than a Wink* (1940), which featured his high-speed photography techniques. Following the United States' entry into the war, the U.S. Army Air Force commissioned Edgerton to design and deliver strobe lamps powerful enough to be used for nighttime aerial photography, and he served in Europe as their technical representative. He directed the use of the strobes, enabling intelligence about troop movements in enemy territory to be collected that had not been obtainable through other means. In the European theater, Edgerton's strobes were used on the nights immediately preceding the D-day invasion of Normandy and during the Battle of Monte Cassino; they were also applied in campaigns in the Far East. Edgerton received the Medal of Freedom from the War Department in recognition of these achievements.

In 1947, Edgerton, through EG&G Inc., began work toward specialized electronic technology. As a prime contractor for the Atomic Energy Commission, EG&G designed and operated systems that timed and fired U.S. nuclear bomb tests. They also invented a camera (the Rapatronic) capable of photographing nuclear explosions from a distance of seven miles.

Edgerton was also important to the development of nature photography. His work reached a wide public through the pages of *National Geographic* magazine, the first of his many articles appearing in 1947. Typical of these is *Hummingbirds in Action*, containing high-speed photographs that for the first time captured the tiny birds' intricate movements.

Edgerton was also a pioneer in the area of underwater photography. Among his innovations were the first undersea time-lapse images and sonar and sounding devices that helped place underwater cameras. He had begun his association with French underwater explorer and fellow inventor Jacques-Yves Cousteau in 1953 and together they explored and photographed a wide variety of sea beds. To position his cameras, he developed a device he dubbed a "pinger" to attach to the submerged camera. The pinger emitted sound waves that bounced off the ocean floor and returned as echoes, indicating the camera's distance to the bottom. He also developed a "thumper" device, which was capable of sub-bottom penetration of the sea floor. Although this was not a photographic technique, the thumper was used to locate ancient rocks from the deepest layers of the earth's crust, advancing scientific research in the arena of geology. Later, Edgerton designed the "boomer," a sonar device useful for continuous seismic profiling of the bottom of the sea.

Using these and other sonar tools, Edgerton pioneered "photo excavation" for the underwater Greek city of Helice, located the sunken warships *Mary Rose*, and the Civil War battleship USS *Monitor*. Later, in 1987, he used the Edgerton-Benthos underwater camera to photograph the sunken RMS *Titanic*, discovered earlier off the coast of Nova Scotia. Edgerton also participated in an inconclusive search for the Loch Ness monster.

Edgerton aimed his camera everywhere. He developed elapsed-time to photograph slow events, such as the movement of sand dollars and sea urchins. He entered the human body to take motion pictures of capillary blood flow and pointed his cameras to the skies to record solar eclipses.

In the 1960s and 1970s, Edgerton continued teaching and directing research at MIT, and earned the affectionate nickname "Doc" from his students. One of his best-known photographs dates from this period. *Shooting the Apple*, 1964, shows the instant a bullet tears through a bright red apple. Edgerton used this image to illustrate the laws of physics in a popular lecture he titled "How to Make Applesauce at MIT." During this period he also continued his many research projects and wide travels. In 1971, the Harold E. Edgerton Laboratory (ERL) in the New England Aquarium in Boston, a center for basic and applied science, was dedicated, honoring aquarium trustee Harold Edgerton. In 1975, he ended his daily association with EG&G, Inc., and became the company's emeritus chairman of the board.

To ensure his pioneering legacy, some of his camera strobe equipment and photographs are installed at the Plainsman Museum in Aurora, Nebraska. The MIT Sea Grant research vessel, a seagoing laboratory and classroom, was commissioned and named *Edgerton*. In 1983, MIT dedicated "Strobe Alley" an 80-foot corridor museum at MIT of Edgerton's photographs and equipment, as well as artifacts recovered on various voyages. MIT also created and dedicated the EG&G Education Center at MIT, a teaching and conference facility built with gifts from EG&G, Inc. and its three founding partners.

Edgerton remained active, however; in 1985, at age 82 he again accompanied Cousteau aboard *Calypso* on an expedition off Matanzas Harbor, near Havana, Cuba, in search of Spanish shipwrecks. Later that year the PBS Nova series aired "Edgerton and His Incredible Seeing Machines," a program based on a film originally produced by Nebraska Educational Television that explored the career and inventions of Edgerton and documents the development of stroboscopic photography.

On January 4, 1990, after lunch at the MIT Faculty Club, Harold E. "Doc" Edgerton died at age 86. Edgerton's inventive genius and his long career allowed all mankind's eyes to observe and record events never before seen. To solidify his legacy and propagate his love for learning, the Harold E. Edgerton Educational Center (renamed Edgerton Explorit Center) opened in 1995 in Aurora, Nebraska, his childhood home. Although his impetus was at base a scientific one, his photographs are today widely appreciated, exhibited, and collected for their formal beauty and aesthetic qualities. A number of his best-known images were printed as dye-transfers in the 1980s and have been collected by museums around the world.

Grant Warren

See also: **National Geographic; Underwater Photography**

Biography

Born April 6, 1903, Fremont, Nebraska. Enrolled at the University of Nebraska, Lincoln, 1921. B.S. in Electrical Engineering, 1925. Enrolled at Massachusetts Institute of Technology (MIT), studied rotating engines using a strobe light, 1926. M.S. in Electrical Engineering from MIT, 1927; joined faculty; married Esther May Garrett, 1928. Announced stroboscope and its use in both ultra high speed and still (or stop-motion) photography; formed partnership with former student Kenneth J. Germeshausen; D. Sc. in electrical engineering from MIT, 1931. First stroboscope-taken photographs appeared in publications, 1932. Applied for U.S. patents for the stroboscope; photographs included in the Royal Photographic Society's annual exhibition in London (first Edgerton exhibition), 1933. Herbert E. Grier joined the partnership of Edgerton and Germeshausen; partnership received its first photography award, the Royal Photographic Society's Bronze Medal, 1934. Designed a strobe lamp for night aerial photography for the U.S. Army Air Force; co-authored first book, *Flash!*, 1939. Served in Europe as technical representative for the U.S. Army Air Force, 1944. War Department Medal of Freedom, 1946. Begins association with underwater explorer Jacques-Yves Cousteau, develops pinger and side-scan sonar, 1953. Photographs ocean floor using thumper, 1960. Designs boomer for seismic profiling of sea floor, 1961. Appointed Institute Professor at MIT, 1966. First slow-motion photographs, 1968. Receives U.S. National Medal of Science, awarded by President Richard M. Nixon; MIT establishes the Edgerton Fund, 1973. Named "New England Inventor of the Year," 1982. "Strobe Alley" and EG&G Education Center, (both at MIT) dedicated, 1983. "Edgerton and His Incredible Seeing Machines" aired by PBS on "Nova," 1985. Inducted into the National Inventors Hall of Fame by the United States Patent and Trademark Office. Died, 1990. Harold E. Edgerton Educational Center (renamed Edgerton Explorit Center) opened, 1995.

Selected Works

Wes Fesler Kicking a Football, 1934
Densmore Shute Bends the Shaft, 1938
Fanning the Cards, 1940
Milkdrop Coronet, 1957
Self-Portrait with Balloon and Bullet, 1959
Shooting the Apple, 1964

Individual Exhibitions

1934 *Harold Edgerton*; Royal Academy of Photography, London, England

1995 *Harold Edgerton*; James Danziger Gallery, New York, New York
1997 *Seeing the Unseen: Dr. Harold E. Edgerton and the Wonders of Strobe Alley*; University of California Riverside, Riverside, California Museum of Photography, and traveling to Norton Museum of Art, West Palm Beach, Florida
1998 *Flashes of Inspiration: The Work of Harold Edgerton*; MIT Museum, Cambridge, Massachusetts
2001 *Harold Edgerton: Faster than a Speeding Bullet (Studies in Motion)*; Jane Corkin Gallery, Toronto, Canada
2002 *Harold Edgerton: Seeing the Unseen*; MIT Museum, Cambridge, Massachusetts, and traveling

Further Reading

Bruce, Roger. *Seeing the Unseen: Dr. Harold Edgerton and the Wonders of Strobe Alley*. Cambridge, MA: MIT Press, 1998.

Edgerton, Harold E., and James R. Killian, Jr. *Flash! Seeing the Unseen by Ultra High-Speed Photograph*. Boston: Hale, Cushman & Flint, 1939; 2d ed. Boston: Charles T Branford, 1954.

Edgerton, Harold E. *Electronic Flash, Strobe*. New York: McGraw-Hill, 1970; 2d ed. Cambridge, MA: MIT Press, 1979.

Edgerton, Harold. *Sonar Images*. Englewood Cliffs, NJ: Prentice Hall, 1986.

Kayafas, Gus, ed. Foreward by Harold Edgerton. *Stopping Time: The Photographs of Harold Edgerton*. Cambridge, MA: MIT Press, 1987.

Killian, James R. Jr. *Moments of Vision: The Stroboscopic Revolution in Photography by Harold E. Edgerton*. Cambridge, MA: MIT Press, 1979.

Sheldon, James. *Exploring the Art and Science of Stopping Time, A CD-ROM based on the Life and Work of Harold Edgerton*. Cambridge, MA: MIT Press, 1999.

WILLIAM EGGLESTON

American

Often called the "father of color photography," William Eggleston is credited with helping establish the basic lexicon of contemporary color photography as art. One of several artists to begin working with color photography in the late 1960s, he was the first of this group to have a major museum exhibition of his color work, *Photographs by William Eggleston*, which was held at the Museum of Modern Art (MoMA), New York, in 1976. Eggleston's subject matter is ordinary life, often presented in simple, centrally organized compositions in a style much like casual snaphots. The similarities of his work to vernacular photography were not lost on his critics, who decried his work following the 1976 exhibition. Nevertheless, Eggleston very quickly became renowned for his deft use of color as an integral element of composition, as well as his unusual perspectives and uncanny ability to monumentalize the minutiae of mundane life.

Eggleston was born in Memphis, Tennessee in 1939. He grew up on a former cotton plantation in Tallahatchie County, Mississippi. At the age of 10, he first toyed with photography using a Brownie Hawkeye. The following year, his father died, leaving his grandfather, a hobbyist photographer, a prominent role in Eggleston's life. As a student at Vanderbilt University in Nashville, Tennessee in 1957, Eggleston bought a Canon rangefinder and began to experiment with photography. After leaving Vanderbilt, he attended Delta State College in Cleveland, Mississippi, and the University of Mississippi, Oxford. During this time, he studied photography independently, seeking out published resources.

Eggleston became an independent photographer in 1962, after the work of Henri Cartier-Bresson, a Magnum photographer, first caught his attention. The painterly quality of Cartier-Bresson's photographs, which bore clear evidence of the influence of artists such as Edgar Degas and Henri de Toulouse-Lautrec, appealed to Eggleston's personal interest in painting theory. The unusual perspectives, so different from the direct, head-on viewpoint typical of photography prior to the 1960s, gave Eggleston new insight into the creative possibilities of photography.

In 1965, Eggleston began experimenting with color photography. He was working exclusively in color by 1966, when color photography was not yet considered a legitimate art form; prior to 1970 color was accepted only for amateur and commercial photography. The 1959 proclamation of revered American photographer Walker Evans, "Color-photography is vulgar," reflected a persistent, widespread perception of color photography as cheap, common, and not artistic. Color photography seemed to distort compositions, exaggerating contrasts, emphasizing certain colors and de-emphasizing others that, in black and white photography, would have held the same visual weight. Color photography necessitates careful consideration of formal elements in more complex terms than those demanded by traditional black and white photography.

Eggleston's earliest color photographs illustrate surroundings familiar to him: friends, family, homes, and neighborhoods, as well as more trivial details from daily life, such as a light fixture on a ceiling, a pile of trash bags leaning against a building, or the inside of an empty oven. As he branched out to less familiar territory, he continued to focus on typically unremarkable visions from daily life, such as the interior of a frosted-over freezer filled with food; a shower stall with a mint green tub and tiles, gleaming stainless hardware, and stained grout; or a shot of shoes, a dime, and a gilt-framed mirror stashed beneath a bed. He is especially well known for his interiors, abandoned landscapes, and lone, centrally-placed figures. Of his photographs, Eggleston says, "I like to think of them as parts of a novel I'm doing" (Knape 1999, unpaginated).

Eggleston's color photographs of trivial images from mundane life sparked considerable controversy following his MoMA exhibition, the first solo exhibition of an artist using color photography at the museum. *Photographs by William Eggleston* presented 75 dye transfer prints, all shot on transparency film between 1969 and 1971. The snapshot-quality of the images, with commonplace subjects and informal, seemingly offhand compositions, left audiences wondering how the images were different from those taken by any amateur photographer. The stigma against color photographs exacerbated the issue. Harsh critical reviews of the show criticized Eggleston's "snapshot chic" as boring, banal, and unacceptable.

Exhibition curator John Szarkowski, then Director of the Department of Photographs at the MoMA, had first met Eggleston in 1967 at the suggestion of mutual friends Garry Winogrand, Diane Arbus, and Lee Friedlander. Szarkowski immediately liked Eggleston's work, but was unable to secure exhibition funding for several years at least partly because of the historical bias against color photography. According to Szarkowski, color photography prior to the 1970s had "failed" in two ways: either photographers neglected to consider color as an integral element of the composition, or they focused solely on color as a formal element separate from other aspects of a composition. In neither case did artists consider color holistically. Eggleston's holistic approach to his photographs is what, according to Szarkowski, separated his work from that of other photographers, professional and amateur alike.

The central compositions of Eggleston's photographs also seemed to relate them to amateur photography, in which the casual photographer centers each subject perfectly in the frame. On closer inspection, Eggleston's compositions are complex and highly ordered. As Alfred Barr noted in 1972, Eggleston's compositions seem to radiate from a central point like a wheel, as in *Southern Environs of Memphis*, 1971. Eggleston acknowledged this recurring design and explained it as mimicking the Confederate flag (a comparison for which he has received much criticism).

The apparent simplicity of his compositions belies their complex sources of inspiration: the *ukiyo-e* viewpoint ("pictures of the floating world") of Japanese art mediated through the work of Post-Impressionist painters and printmakers such as Degas and Toulouse-Lautrec. Whether shot from above or below the subject, Eggleston's photographs are not taken from typical eye level. Regarding his photograph *Untitled* (Tricycle), c. 1970, in which the extremely low perspective angle makes a child's tricycle appear monumental, Eggleston said:

> Sometimes I like the idea of making a picture that does not look like a human picture. Humans make pictures which tend to be about five feet above the ground looking out horizontally. I like very fast flying insects moving all over and I wonder what their view is from moment to moment. I have made a few pictures which show that physical viewpoint. The tricycle is similar. It is an insect's view or it could be a child's view.
>
> (Holborn 1992, 23–24)

By subverting the viewer's usual viewpoint, Eggleston confers new depth to the mundane subjects individuals take for granted every day.

Following Eggleston's MoMA exhibition, critic Janet Malcolm suggested that such snapshot-style photographs had become acceptable material for an exhibition at MoMA because of the work of the Photorealists of the 1960s and 1970s, who painted large-scale, often mundane subjects with photographic precision. She called photographers such as Eggleston "photo-Photo-Realists." Subsequent critics have refuted her claim of a connection, but the pervasiveness of trivial objects in the art of both groups is surely significant.

Eggleston had spent time in New York in the 1970s with Pop artist Andy Warhol and his circle of friends at the Chelsea Hotel. Eggleston's realist images, full of rust and decay, counter the Pop images Warhol produced—clean, bright images of commercial products and popular icons. As Warhol's images are about production, Eggleston's are about consumption; as Warhol's images present popular icons of American life, Eggleston presents ordinary, nameless Americans. Eggleston shows the grittier, real-life side of the idealized world Warhol presented.

The creation of iconic imagery attracted Eggleston to Walker Evans, whose work Eggleston praised for "elevating the casual, the everyday and the literal into specific, permanent symbols" (Holborn 1992, 12). Eggleston shared Evans's goal of glorifying the commonplace. Eggleston also points out where their interests diverge: Evans, like most photographers of the mid-twentieth century, used a square-on, perfectly frontal shot, which Eggleston avoids religiously.

The unusual perspectives and angles of Eggleston's photographs work with his uninhabited, stark scenes to create a sense of unease in many of his images. His frequent depictions of neglected buildings, rusty signs, and dirty streets further the sense of a darkness lurking beneath his colorful surfaces, as in *The Louisiana Project*, 1980. In photographs such as *Untitled* (Toilet), 1970, the low perspective, seen as though lying on the floor, casts a menacing shadow on the scene. The harsh juxtaposition of the eerie pool of red light glowing beyond the green wall intensifies the sickly, ominous atmosphere.

The power of color in *Untitled* (Toilet) points to the additional experiences that black and white photography cannot suggest. Color intensifies the emotional dimension of his works—sinister or beautiful—and infuses his photographs with a sense of immediacy: his scenes seem familiar, more directly connected to our own lives than scenes in black and white, which divorce color from content and emphasize the separation between art and reality.

Eggleston is especially well-known for his use of the dye transfer process of color printing, which he first encountered while teaching at Harvard University in 1973–1974. The dye transfer process creates intense, saturated colors on a rich surface created with layers of dyes. Not only does this layering of colors create a luscious, tactile surface, it also allows the artist to adjust each color independent of the others, permitting greater variation of emphasis and subordination in the overall color scheme. Publishing his first portfolio of dye transfer prints, *14 Pictures*, in 1974, Eggleston was one of the earliest photographers to use the dye transfer process for non-commercial purposes.

Also in 1974, Eggleston completed his project *Los Alamos*. He had taken the series of more than 2,000 photographs over the period of 1967–1974, during travels across the United States, from Memphis to New Orleans, Southern California, Las Vegas, and New Mexico. The vast series was named after stopping at the nuclear research site Los Alamos, New Mexico.

Although Eggleston has lived his entire life in the South, he hastens to avoid being dubbed a "Southern" artist. On his extensive travels, which help shield him from the "Southern" label, he has photographed throughout the United States as well as in Austria, the Caribbean, China, England, Egypt, Germany, Japan, Kenya, Poland, Spain, and South Africa. His goal is to treat his photographs as independent of place: to approach images from his native South in the same way as pictures from Poland or Kenya. He purposefully tries to eliminate elements of his photographs that tie them too closely to a place, including elements that characterize his work as "Southern."

Self-imposed constraints are common in Eggleston's oeuvre. In his series *Wedgwood Blue*, Eggleston photographed the sky with the restriction of only directing his camera straight up. This limited viewpoint captured perfectly ordinary but frequently beautiful scenes, including wispy clouds, fragments of tree branches, and portions of power lines, but avoided the more banal photographic subject of the horizon. This unexpected approach to the ordinary is typical of Eggleston's work.

He used a similar limitation when photographing on commission from AT&T in 1978, when he took pictures along the 32nd parallel. The artist removed himself from the process of content selection; instead, he randomly regimented the process by photographing at timed intervals. Two years earlier, Eggleston had further removed himself from the process by shooting pictures without peering through the camera's viewfinder. He would aim and shoot, sensing the angle he desired rather than precisely arranging his composition before his lens. He felt that working away from the viewfinder allowed him to look more intensely at his surroundings.

The Democratic Forest (1989), a project documented by a book of the same name, included over 10,000 prints created "democratically," without respect to the academic hierarchy of subject matter. The "democratic camera" captures each subject with the assumption that everything—whether a person or a clump of grass—is equally valid subject matter, thereby upending traditional hierarchies of subject matter.

Writer Mark Holborn traces the roots of this idea of the democratic camera to Eggleston's experimentation with video, begun in 1973 and continuing in 1978, when Eggleston's friend Ricky

Leacock, a pioneer of video, invited him to work at the Massachusetts Institute of Technology exploring the possibilities of portable color video. His work in video may have inspired Eggleston's increasing reliance on nontraditional subject matter through the 1970s. In the same way that unedited video moves from one focal point to another, documenting the transitory space between intended subjects, Eggleston's democratic camera captures any fleeting, momentary scene and creates a subject deemed equal in importance to more traditional subjects, such as figures or landscapes.

Eggleston is an extremely prolific photographer. He has produced tens of thousands of prints, shooting each composition only once, as he prefers to eliminate the option of choosing between different versions of similar shots. Although he feels that anything can be a legitimate subject Eggleston edits his production ruthlessly; only a small portion of the tens of thousands of prints he has made have ever been shown.

Eggleston once claimed that his subject matter was secondary to his photographs (Szarkowski 1976, 9). Such a formalist declaration on one hand explains his democratic photography and his glorification of the trivial, and on the other shortchanges his work by reducing his photographs to purely aesthetic objects. His own statement, "I am at war with the obvious," points out the much deeper issues at stake in his work: the public's expectations of photography and the artist's independence and authority in establishing standards of legitimate content and modes of presentation.

Rachel Keith

See also: **Evans, Walker; Museum of Modern Art; Photography in the United States: the South; Szarkowski, John; Vernacular Photography**

Biography

Born in Memphis, Tennessee, 27 July 1939. Studied at Vanderbilt University, Memphis, Tennessee; Delta State College, Cleveland, Mississippi; and the University of Mississippi, Oxford. Begins taking photographs in 1957. Becomes an independent photographer in 1962; begins working in color in 1966. Lecturer in Visual and Environmental Studies at Harvard University, Cambridge, Massachusetts, 1974. Researcher in color video at the Massachusetts Institute of Technology, Cambridge, Massachusetts, 1978–1979. John Simon Guggenheim Memorial Fellowship, 1974, National Endowment for the Arts (NEA) Photographer's Fellowship, 1975, and NEA survey grant, 1978, for a survey of Mississippi cotton farms using photography and color video. Hasselblad Foundation International Award in Photography, 1998. Resides in Memphis, Tennessee.

Selected Individual Exhibitions

1974 Jefferson Place Gallery; Washington, DC
1976 *Photographs by William Eggleston*; The Museum of Modern Art, New York, New York, and traveling
1977 *Election Eve*; Corcoran Gallery of Art, Washington, DC and traveling
1983 *William Eggleston: Color Photographs from the American South*; Victoria and Albert Museum, London, England, and traveling
1984 *Elvis at Brooks: The Graceland. Photographs of William Eggleston*; Memphis Art Museum, Memphis, Tennessee
1984 *Graceland and the South*; Art Institute of Chicago, Chicago, Illinois
1985 *Bill Eggleston*; Victoria and Albert Museum, London, England
1985 *Bill Eggleston: New Orleans Projects*; Memphis Brooks Museum of Art, Memphis, Tennessee
1987 *Eggleston's Egypt*; Memphis Brooks Museum of Art, Memphis, Tennessee
1990–1991 *William Eggleston: The Democratic Forest*; Corcoran Gallery of Art, Washington, DC
1992 *Ancient and Modern*; Barbican Art Gallery, London, England, and traveling
1999 *William Eggleston; 1998 Hasselblad Award Winner*; Hasselblad Center, Göteborg, Sweden

Selected Group Exhibitions

1972 *Photography Workshop International*; Corcoran Gallery of Art, Washington, DC
1974 *Straight Color*; Rochester Institute of Technology, Rochester, New York
1975 *Color Photography: Inventors and Innovators 1850–1975*; Yale University Art Gallery, New Haven, Connecticut
1977 *The Contemporary South*; a United States Information Agency traveling exhibition organized by the New Orleans Museum of Art, New Orleans, Louisiana
1978 *Mirrors and Windows: American Photography since 1960*; The Museum of Modern Art, New York, New York, and traveling

Selected Works

Lunch, 1963
Untitled (Toilet), 1970
Untitled (Tricycle), c. 1970, printed later
Greenwood, Mississippi (Red ceiling), 1973
Memphis (Green shower), early 1970s
14 Pictures (Shoes under bed), 1974
Troubled Waters (Food in freezer), 1980
The Louisiana Project (House), 1980

Further Reading

Eauclaire, Sally. *The New Color Photography*. New York: Abbeville, 1981.
Eggleston, William. *William Eggleston*: Ancient and Modern. Introduction by Mark Holborn. New York: Random House, 1992.
Knape, Gunilla, ed. *The Hasselblad Award Winner 1998: William Eggleston*. Göteborg, Sweden: Hasselblad Center, 1999.

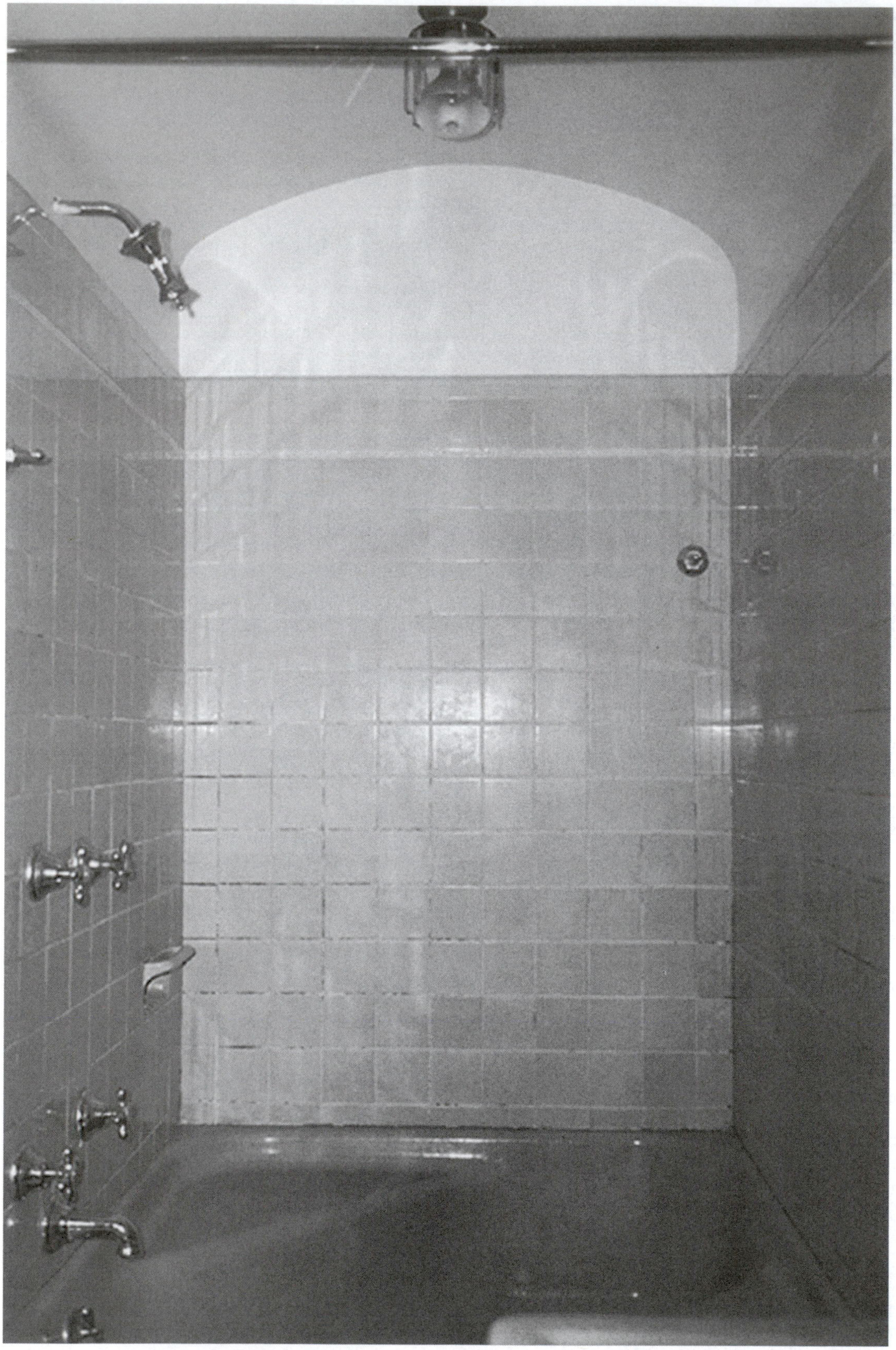

William Eggleston, Untitled (Memphis, Green Shower), Circa 1972, Dye transfer print, 20 × 16″, 50.8 × 40.6 cm, Ed. 20.
[*Courtesy Cheim & Read, New York*]

Kozloff, Max. "To Mystify Color Photography." *Artforum* 15 (3) (November 1976): 50–51.
Szarkowski, John. *William Eggleston's Guide*. New York: Museum of Modern Art, 1976 (reprinted 2002).
William Eggleston. Exhibition catalogue from Fondation Cartier pour l'art contemporain. New York: Thames and Hudson, 2002.

ALFRED EISENSTAEDT

Polish-American

Alfred Eisenstaedt, the man behind the camera that fixed itself on some of the most enduring images of modern history, was a great popular photographer of the twentieth century. He was a preeminent photojournalist of his time, a time that spans eight decades, and he has been frequently called "the father of photojournalism." Until the last years of a life that spanned nearly the entire twentieth century, "Eisie," as he was known, was still shooting and adding to an inventory that included hundreds of thousands of negatives.

His final working days would start at nine in the morning when his sister-in-law, Lulu Kaye, escorted him the five blocks from his apartment to the Time-Life Building. Looking natty in suspenders and often a bow-tie, he answered letters and phone calls long before others had arrived. His days were filled supervising the printing of his photographs for the next exhibit or book project. His five-foot-four frame maneuvered agilely in an office crammed with books and papers and tidy yellow cardboard boxes of prints. His filing system was perhaps inefficiently simple: the boxes marked only "Germany," "Great Americans," "Great Englishmen," "Musicians," and "Miscellaneous." He had no trouble locating pictures, however. His memory was photographic.

Eisie's last project, *95 for 95*, which gathered 95 images in a show for his 95th birthday, was exhibited nationwide in 1993.

Alfred Eisenstaedt was born December 6, 1898, in Dirschau, West Prussia (now part of Poland), one of three sons of Regina and Joseph Eisenstaedt, a merchant. The family moved to Berlin when Alfred was eight, and remained there until Hitler came to power. He may well have followed in his father's footsteps, were it not for an uncle who, when Eisenstaedt was 14, gave the boy an Eastman Kodak no. 3 folding camera in 1912.

Interrupting his studies at the University of Berlin, Eisenstaedt was drafted into the German army in 1916 during World War I, serving at the front until April 1918, when gunfire crippled both his legs. During the year-long recovery, he became fascinated by the local art museums, studying the paintings of the masters.

Although he became a belt-and-button salesman by trade in 1922, with the money he was able to save, he bought photographic equipment. Developing the pictures in his bathroom, Eisenstaedt had yet to learn there was such a thing as an enlarger. In 1927, while vacationing with his parents in Czechoslovakia, he photographed a woman playing tennis. Taken from a hillside 50 yards away, the photo captured the long shadow the woman cast on the tennis court. He wrote:

> I took one picture of the scene with a Zeiss Ideal Camera, 9 × 12 with glass plates. I was rather satisfied when I showed it to a friend of mine. 'Why don't you enlarge it?' he asked. And he showed me a contraption of a wooden box with a frosted light bulb inside attached to a 9 × 12 camera, same as mine....When I saw that one could enlarge and eliminate unnecessary details, the photo bug bit me and I saw enormous possibilities.
>
> (Eisenstaedt 1985)

Those possibilities included making a living with his pictures. In 1927, Eisenstaedt sold his first photograph of that tennis player to *Der Weltspiegel* for three marks, about 12 dollars at the time. By age 31, in 1929 he had quit the belt-and-button business to become a full time photographer. In doing so, he would come to define the profession. As a pioneer in his field, Eisenstaedt had few rules to follow. He looked to the work of Martin Munkasci and Dr. Erich Salomon, with whom he had the opportunity to work.

As a freelancer Eisenstaedt worked for Pacific and Atlantic Photos Berlin office in 1928, which would become part of the Associated Press in 1931. At that time Eisenstaedt began working with the innovative Leica 35 mm camera, which had been developed four years prior. His assignments included portraits of statesmen and famous artists, as well as social events such as the winter season in St. Moritz. In 1933, he was sent to Italy to shoot the first meeting of fascist leaders Hitler and Mussolini. His aggressive yet invisible style of working allowed him to come within arm's reach of the two dictators.

Despite his success in Europe, Eisenstaedt had heard that the greatest opportunity for photojournalists was now in the United States. Two years after Hitler took power, Eisenstaedt immigrated to America in 1935. He sailed from Le Havre on the *Ile de France*, arriving in New York at the end of November, with a portfolio overflowing with photographs of European politicians, entertainers, and royalty including Hitler, Mussolini, Marlene Dietrich, Gloria Swanson, Bernard Shaw, Charlie Chaplin, Arturo Toscanini, and Sergei Rachmaninoff. Among the impressive variety of photographs in his portfolio was a photo essay Eisenstaedt had made aboard the Graf Zeppelin in 1933, which impressed the editor most.

In New York he was soon hired with three other photographers—Margaret Bourke-White, Thomas McAvoy, and Peter Stackpole—by *Time* magazine founder Henry Luce, for a secret start-up known only as PROJECT X. After six months of testing the mystery venture, it premiered as *Life* magazine on November 23, 1936.

The first 10-cent issue featured five pages of Eisenstaedt's pictures. The second week Eisenstaedt—now dubbed "Eisie" by his peers—had his photo of West Point military academy on the cover. Other early assignments included the recovery of America as the country pulled out of the Depression. He traveled his new homeland sending back images of shacks and abandoned cars in Oregon, skid row derelicts in Los Angeles, and signs advertising beer for a nickel. Because he was not yet a citizen, Eisenstaedt could not be sent to cover the war, and so landed a good deal of celebrity assignments instead.

In 1942, Eisenstaedt at last became a U.S. citizen and was able finally to travel overseas to document the effects of the war. In Japan in 1945 he accompanied Emperor Hirohito on tours to see the destruction caused by the dropping of the atomic bomb on the cities of Hiroshima and Naogasaki. He recalls a particularly memorable experience in Hiroshima.

> A mother and child were looking at some green vegetables they had raised from seeds and planted in the ruins. When I asked the woman if I could take her picture, she bowed deeply and posed for me. Her expression was one of bewilderment, anguish and resignation...all I could do, after I had taken her picture, was to bow very deeply before her.

To capture what has become perhaps his most reproduced image, and one of the iconic images of the twentieth century, popularly known as *The Kiss in Times Square on V-J Day*, of 1945. Eisenstaedt had been following the sailor who was

> running along the street grabbing any and every girl in sight. Whether she was a grandmother, stout, thin, old, didn't make any difference. None of the pictures that were possible pleased me. Then, suddenly in a flash, I saw something white being grabbed. I turned around and clicked the moment the sailor kissed the nurse.

In 1991, he told a *New York Times* reporter, "Although I am 92, my brain is 30 years old." To prove it, he recalled that to shoot that victory kiss he used 1/125-second exposure, aperture between 5.6 and 8, on Kodak super Double X film.

But this image, he said, was not his personal favorite. That honor goes to a photo of a young woman in a box seat at La Scala opera, 1933. Editors at *Die Dame*, who had assigned Eisie to the opera, did not feel similarly. They never printed the picture.

In 1949, he married Kathy Kaye, a South African whom he met in New York. The 1950s took him to Korea with the American troops, to Italy to show the plight of the poor there, and to England, where Winston Churchill would sit for him. Portrait assignments such as this one often made Eisenstaedt privy to little-known secrets about his subjects.

For *Life*'s Fourth of July issue in 1952, actor Charles Laughton was asked to choose his favorite American writing to be read aloud. Eisenstaedt illustrated these verses by traveling across the country—to Minnehaha Falls for Henry Wadsworth Longfellow's *The Song of Hiawatha*, to the Hudson Valley for Washington Irving's *Rip Van Winkle*, and on a riverboat for Mark Twain's *Life on the Mississippi.*

He documented the lighter side of life with no less earnest an approach. "You learn something from every picture you take," he said after shooting a story on women's underwear for *Life*. In total, he shot nearly 92 covers for the magazine and some 2,500 assignments, amassing some 10,000 prints.

Portraiture remained a constant: Marlene Dietrich smoldering in top hat and tails; Marilyn Monroe vamping in her backyard; John F. Kennedy clowning with his little daughter Caroline; Albert Einstein lecturing to a class of physicists at Princeton; Sophia Loren—Eisie's favorite model—wearing a negligee in a cover shot that caused some *Life* readers to cancel their subscriptions. No matter how famous or notorious the subject, Eisenstaedt was at ease with them. "In 1938 our picture editor, Wilson Hicks, told me, 'Alfred, I'm sending you to Hollywood. Don't be afraid and in awe of these queens—you are a king in your profession.' I've never forgotten that."

He did, however, allow himself to ask for a few autographs, and treasured a collection that includes notes from artist Norman Rockwell, Secretary of State Henry Kissinger, and actress Lillian Gish.

In 1979, at age 81, Eisenstaedt returned to Germany for the first time. An exhibition of 93 photographs of German life from the 1930s through that year traveled through Europe and the United States. Remarkably, Eisenstaedt's first major retrospective did not come until 1986 at age 88 when the International Center of Photography in New York presented 125 of his prints.

Eisenstaedt has received numerous awards for his work including the National Medal of the Arts, the International Understanding Award for Outstanding Achievement, the Photographic Society of America Achievement Award, and Photographer of the Year, Encyclopedia Britannica. *Time* heralded Eisenstaedt's *V-J Day, Times Square, 1945* as one of the 10 greatest images in the history of photojournalism.

The city of New York named an Alfred Eisenstaedt Day in his honor and the International Center for Photography (ICP) recognized Eisenstaedt with its Master of Photography award in 1988. President George H. W. Bush bestowed on him the National Medal of Arts in 1989. Far from resting on his laurels, Eisie continued to take commissions: when President Clinton vacationed on Martha's Vineyard in Massachusetts in 1994 where Eisie made his home, he was there to photograph the first family, and to present them with their choice of his prints as a gift. Bill Clinton chose *Drum Major at the University of Michigan* of 1951, and his daughter Chelsea picked *Future Ballerinas of the American Ballet Theatre* of 1936.

At the opening of his shows, photographers who looked up to Eisie would ask to take their pictures with him, and perhaps to get some advice. Modestly, Eisie would say, "When the young photographers come...I ask them questions. They know more about the modern cameras than I do."

In 1994, *Life* and *Vanity Fair* ran portraits of Eisie on the Brooklyn Bridge by Annie Leibovitz. "He was telling me what to do during the entire shoot," recalled Leibovitz. "But then he'd say this is your picture, do whatever you want." Eisie did choose the location, though, "because I am still younger than the Brooklyn Bridge," he told the *New York Times*.

A fellow photographer and later *Life*'s director of photography, John Loengard, explained Eisenstaedt's enduring success: "He never tries to please editors. He only makes pictures that please him." For some 60 years, *Life* readers were the beneficiaries of those pictures, a life's work that was also his pleasure. Alfred Eisenstaedt died in Martha's Vineyard, Massachusetts, on August 23, 1995. His photographs are in the permanent collections of the Royal Photographic Society, London; the International Center of Photography, New York; the International Museum of Photography and Film, George Eastman House, Rochester, New York; and the National Gallery of Canada, Ottawa.

Suvash Kumer Barman

See also: **History of Photography: Twentieth-Century Pioneers; Life Magazine; Portraiture**

Biography

Born in Dirschau, West Prussia (now part of Poland), 6 December 1898. At the age of 14, received an Eastman Kodak no. 3 folding camera. Attended Hohenzollern Gymnasium, Berlin, 1906–1912; University of Berlin, 1913–1916. Drafted in to the German army, 1916, serving at the front until 9 April 1918. Belt and button salesman 1922. Sold his first photo to *Der Weltspiegel*, 1927. Worked as a freelancer for Pacific and Atlantic Photo, 1929; Associated Press, 1931. Sent to Italy to shoot the first meeting of Hitler and Mussolini, 1933. Emigrated to the United States and became one of the four original photographers at *Life*, 1935. Photographed in Hollywood, 1938. Became a U.S. citizen and traveled overseas to document the effects of the war, 1942. Marriage to Kathy Kaye, 1949. Traveled to Korea with American troops, 1950, and went on to Italy and England. Returned to Germany, 1979. International Center of Photography (ICP) Master of Photography award, 1988. National Medal of the Arts, 1989. Died in Martha's Vineyard, Massachusetts, 23 August 1995.

Individual Exhibitions

1954 *Alfred Eisenstaedt*; George Eastman House, Rochester, New York

1966 *Witness to Our Time*; Time-Life Building; New York, New York and Smithsonian Institution, Washington, D.C.

1979 *Alfred Eisenstaedt: German Life*; U.S. and traveling

1986 *Alfred Eisenstaedt*; International Center of Photography, New York, New York
Museum of Modern Art, New York, New York
The Whitney Museum of American Art, New York, New York
The Philadelphia College of Art, Philadelphia, Pennsylvania
1994 *95 for 95*; Alfred Eisenstaedt's 95th Birthday Exhibition, U.S. and traveling

Group Exhibitions

1951 *Memorable Life Photographs*; Museum of Modern Art, New York, New York
1959 *Undert Jahre Photographie 1939–1939*; Museum Folkwang, Essen, Germany, and traveling
1967 *Photography in the Twentieth Century*; National Gallery of Canada, Ottawa, Canada, and traveling
1980 *The Imaginary Photo Museum*; Kunsthalle, Cologne, Germany

Selected Works

Ice Skating Waiter, St. Moritz, 1932
Graf Zeppelin, 1933
Joseph Goebbels, 1933
Future Ballerinas of the American Ballet Theatre, 1936
V-J Day, Times Square, 1945
Drum Major at the University of Michigan, 1951
Marilyn Monroe, Hollywood, 1953

Further Reading

Eisenstaedt, Alfred. *The Eye of Eisenstaedt*, New York: Studio Books, 1971. 1969.
———. *Eisenstaedt: People*, 1973.
———. *Eisenstaedt's Album*, New York: Studio Books, 1971. 1976.
Holme, Bryan, Doris C. O'Neil, Alfred Eisenstaedt, and Barbara Baker Burrows. *Eisenstaedt: Remembrances*, Boston: Bulfinch Press. 1990.
Loengard, John. *Life Photographers: What They Saw*. Boston: Bulfinch Press, 1998.
Eisenstaedt, Alfred. *Witness to Our Time*, New York: Viking Penguin, 1966.
———. *Eisenstaedt: Guide to Photography*. New York: Viking Penguin, 1978.
———. *Eisenstaedt: Germany*, New York: Harry N. Abrams, 1981.
———. *Eisenstaedt: Aberdeen: Portrait of a City*. Louisiana State University Press, 1984.
———. *Eisenstaedt on Eisenstaedt: A Self-Portrait*. New York: Abbeville Press, 1985.

ED VAN DER ELSKEN

Dutch

Ed van der Elsken was not only an influential Dutch photographer, but also a first-rank filmmaker. At the age of 30 in 1955, he had already gained some international recognition, mainly in the United States. Hot-tempered, van der Elsken stubbornly lived for photography and developed his creative path: on the one hand self-centered, on the other highly diversified geographically and thematically speaking. Although his interests drove him to record the lives of outcasts worldwide, he was never restricted to the subject. Other themes, approached with much empathy and irony, were documented by his joyful, but truly inquisitive personality:

> I look at you. How lovely you are. How lovely you were. All your fun. All your misery. I picture. There are things I got to tell you. I prod you in the ribs. I grab you by the arm. I yank your coat-tails. I say, d'you see that? Dammit! Fabulous! Unbelievable! Super! Or. Filthy bastards! Dirty dogs! What a lousy squirt! They should pass a law...D'you see that! Look at them! Jesus, I'm alive.
>
> (van der Elsken 1966)

Born in Amsterdam in 1925, van der Elsken lived and grew up there until 1944. As he wanted to become a sculptor, he attended the Institute for Applied Arts Education (1943). For fear he would be sent to Germany to work, he fled to the south of the Netherlands, where he hid. After the City of Arnhem had been freed, he joined the allied forces until the war ended.

His formative years (1945–1950) were characterized by an early recognition by his peers. Whilst attending a film operator's preparatory course, he thought he might support himself as a photographer. For this, he took a correspondence course provided by the School of Professional Photography in The Hague. The fact that he failed the exams did not prevent him from absorbing his lessons, as he was also assisting professional photographers such as Ad Windig in Amsterdam. Van der Elsken also took pictures of his hometown and of a trip from Paris to Marseille (1949). Through such early photographic achievements, he joined, that same year, the GKf, the leading Dutch photographers' organization at which point he also benefited from Kryn Taconis's support. Taconis belonged to the GKf and was associated with Magnum Photos in Paris.

When van der Elsken decided to go to Paris in the summer of 1950, he arrived with Taconis's letter of introduction in hand. Pierre Gassman, the addressee, headed Pictorial Service, a leading photo laboratory that worked for Magnum Photos, and employed him. There he met Ada Kando, a photographer, whom he married in 1954. After six months, however, he left Pictorial Service and started photographing the lives of some of the people he had met. This group of young Bohemians was not the only subject he recorded; many images echoed Parisian street life, comic urban scenes, and his daily life in Sèvres with Ada and her children (1950–1954).

However, this group was the main theme of his first book, *Love on the Left Bank* (1956), published with Edward Steichen's strong encouragement. He had met Steichen in 1953. Steichen, the head of the photography department at the Museum of Modern Art (MoMA) in New York also showed his pictures in two important exhibitions of the time: *Post-war European Photography* (1953) and *The Family of Man* (1955). For *Love on the Left Bank*, van der Elsken composed a love story between Ann and Manuel using short texts followed by a series of images with varying dimensions, which added rhythm to the sequence. Among the last photographs of this visual narration, Vali Myers, alias Ann, lavishly kisses a mirror: van der Elsken knew how to picture sensuality well.

After van der Elsken had come back to Amsterdam and divorced from Ada (1955), he began a life of intense travel while working on photo books and reportages for *Vrij Nederland*, *De Volkskrant*, *Het Parool*. Amsterdam, its neighborhoods and musical life was not neglected. In *Jazz* (1959), his *Chet Baker in Concertgebouw* illustrates how van der Elsken obtained very dark, contrasted, and coarse-grained images. It also shows his shift towards the use of a 35 mm Leica camera equipped with a telephoto lens.

Van der Elsken traveled with Gerda van der Veen whom he married in 1957. Soon after, he accepted the invitation of Gerda's brother, an anthropologist, to come to a small village, Banda, located in French Equatorial Africa. His photographs showing communal life were published in *Bagara* (1958). He and his wife also traveled around the world for 14 months (1959–1960). They went to Sierra Leone, South Africa, Malaysia, Singapore, The Philippines, Japan, Mexico, and the United States. The book, *Sweet Life* (1966), includes his images and comments about each place. In these images van der Elsken demonstrates how his photographs are able to create an emotional link for the viewer with his subjects. In *Durban* (1959), in which a bench "for Whites only" is shown, van der Elsken reveals another ability: his cunning way of denouncing how absurd a situation can be by utilizing visual irony. As *Sweet Life* took a long time to be published and disappointed by the difficulties in moving this project forward, van der Elsken renounced photography after 1962 for five years and concentrated on filmmaking, an activity he had first taken up in 1955.

A new shift in his career followed his moving in 1971 from Amsterdam to the more rural Edam where he lived with his family on a farm. As the 1971 prizewinning film *De Verliefde Camera* testified, van der Elsken had been working on a private record of his country life both in film and photography in the 1970s. Photographs of his son, *Daan* (1975), or of his horses, *Pravda and Fidelito* (1978), illustrate such interests. His taste for intimacy was also exemplified by the slide exhibition *Eye Love You* (1977). Published in color, the exhibition catalogue was a celebration of love, all kinds of love: images of couples, love scenes, or of pregnant women mingled. These personal works were supported by his intense activity as a photojournalist: van der Elsken published photo reportages in *Avenue*, between 1967 and 1980, and in other Dutch periodicals (e.g., *Margriet*). This led him to travel once again to Africa, South-East Asia, and South Asia. In South Asia he reported on the terrible floods, which had taken place in Bangladesh in 1974. Published in 1975 in *Avenue*, his treatment of the tragedy, was an exception to his established way of photographing: for the first time he engaged the viewer with a clear vision of sorrow.

Between 1979 and 1990, van der Elsken concentrated on editing and publishing books using the photographs he had been taking throughout his life, both in the Netherlands and abroad. *De ontdekking van Japan* (1988) was a special case. It emphasized his fascination for the country that from his international travels had impressed him the most. Another South-East Asian experience, in *Korea* (1988), was short-lived, because he was diagnosed with cancer. This would become the main subject of his last film *Bye* (1990) in which he filmed his illness. His last film illustrated another strand of his work from the 1980s: a focus on photographing and filming his own life, his farm life (see *Avonturen op het land*), and his revived love with Anneke Hilhorst whom he had married in 1984. Thus Ed van der Elsken followed until the end his motto: "Laat zien wie je bent!" (show us who you are!).

PHILIPPE JARJAT

Biography

Born in Amsterdam, 10 March 1925. Attended for one year the Institute for Applied Arts Education in Amsterdam, 1943; attended a film operator's preparatory course; followed a correspondence course with the School of Professional Photography in The Hague, 1944–1947. Joined the GKf, 1949. Dutch National Film Award, 1971; Dutch Ministry of Culture Grant, 1987. Died in Edam, 28 December 1990.

Individual Exhibitions

1955 Art Institute of Chicago; Chicago, Illinois
1955 Walker Art Center; Minneapolis, Minnesota
1959 *Foto's Ed van der Elsken*; Gröninger Museum voor Stad en Land, Gröningen, The Netherlands
1966 *Hee... zie je dat?*; Stedelijk Museum, Amsterdam, The Netherlands
1968 *Sweet Life*; De Vishal, Haarlem, The Netherlands
1977 *Eye Love You*; Stedelijk Museum, Amsterdam, The Netherlands
1981 *Paris of the Fifties*; Canon Photo Gallery, Amsterdam, The Netherlands
1983 *Een liefdesgeschiedenis in Saint Germain des Prés*; Stedelijk Museum, Amsterdam, The Netherlands
1984 *Amsterdam!*; Amsterdams Historisch Museum, Amsterdam, The Netherlands
1986 *Une histoire d'amour à Saint-Germain-des-Prés*; Institut néerlandais, Paris, France
1987 *Jong Nederland*; Canon Photo Gallery, Amsterdam, The Netherlands
1988 *De ontdekking van Japan: Foto's van Ed van der Elsken 1961–1988*; Canon Image Center, Amsterdam, The Netherlands
1991 *Once upon a Time*; Stedelijk Museum, Amsterdam, The Netherlands, and traveling to Bunkamura Gallery, Tokyo, Japan; Daimaru Department Store, Osaka, Japan; Fotomuseum, Winterthur, Switzerland
1996 *Ed van der Elsken: L'Amour! Foto's 1950–1990*; Kunsthal, Rotterdam, The Netherlands
Love on the Left Bank; The Photographers' Gallery, London, England
1997 *Ed van der Elsken: Hong Kong*; Nederlands fotoinstituut, Rotterdam, The Netherlands
2000 *Ed van der Elsken: Sweet Life. Fotografie + Film 1949–1990*; Kunstmuseum, Wolfsburg, Germany, and traveling to Fundació "La Caixa," Barcelona, Spain
Eye Love You. Ed van der Elsken 1925–1990. Foto's dia's film s en video; De Beyerd, Breda, The Netherlands
2001 *Ed van der Elsken. Eye Love You. Fotografies + films (1949–1970)*; Barcelona, Centre Cultural de la Fundació "la Caixa", Spain
Ed van der Elsken; The Photographers' Gallery, London, England
Modena per la Fotografia 2001; Galleria Civica, Modena, Italy

Group Exhibitions

1953 Bibliothèque nationale de France; Paris, France
Nederlandse Fotografie 1953; Kunstzaalen De Jong-Bergers, Maastricht, The Netherlands
Post-war European Photography; Museum of Modern Art, New York, New York
1954 *Subjektive Fotografie 2*; Staatliche Schule für Kunst und Handwerke, Saarbrücken, Germany
1955 *The Family of Man*; Museum of Modern Art, New York, New York
1958 *Foto's GKf*; Prentenkabinett der Rijksuniversiteit Leiden, Leiden, The Netherlands
1960 Stedelijk Museum; Amsterdam, The Netherlands
1967 *The Camera As Witness*; International Exhibition of Photography Expo '67, Montreal, Quebec, Canada
1973 *Groepfoto (GKf)*; Stedelijk Museum, Amsterdam, The Netherlands
Five Masters of European Photography; The Photographers' Gallery, London, England
1978 *Fotografie in Nederland 1940–1975*; Stedelijk Museum, Amsterdam, The Netherlands
1980 *Het Portret*; Canon Photo Gallery, Amsterdam, The Netherlands
1982 *Veranderingen in de fotojournalistiek 1960–1980*; Stedelijk Museum, Amsterdam, The Netherlands
1988 *Roots & Turns: 20th Century Photography in the Netherlands*; Sarah Campbell Blaffer Gallery, Houston, Texas
1996 *Karel Appel*; Cobramuseum, Amstelveen, The Netherlands
1997 *Documenta X*; Kassel, Germany
2001 *Dutchdelight*, foam, Amsterdam, The Netherlands
2002 *Het bedrijfsfotoboek 1945–1965. Professionalisering van fotografen in Nederland*; Museum Boijmans van Beuningen, Rotterdam, The Netherlands
2003 *Fotomanifestatie Noorderlicht 2003, De Hommage*; Groningen, The Netherlands
Panorama Amsterdam 1862–2003; Foam Amsterdam, The Netherlands

Selected Works

Untitled (Vali Myers as Ann), 1950–1954
Chet Baker in Concertgebouw, Amsterdam, 1955
Durban, 1959
Daan, 1975
Pravda and Fidelito, 1978

Further Reading

Aletti, Vince. "Café Noir." *Artforum International* (March 2000): 99–107.
Ed van der Elsken. Amsterdam: Stedelijk Museum, 1966.
Ed van der Elsken: Sweet Life. Fotografie + Film 1949–1990. Wolfsburg: Kunstmuseum Wolfsburg, 2000.
Regt, Evelyn de. "Ed van der Elsken." In Ingeborg Th. Leijerzapf, editor, *Geschiedenis van de Nederlandse fotografie in monografieën en thema-artikelen*. vol. 16, Alphen aan den Rijn: Samsom.
Regt, Evelyn de, ed. *Once upon a Time*. Amsterdam: Fragment, 1991.
Sinderen, Wim van. *Fotografen in Nederland: een anthologie 1852–2002*.
Amsterdam and Gent: Ludion; The Hague: Fotomuseum Den Haag, 2002.
Visser, Hripsimé. *Ed van der Elsken*. London: Phaidon, 2001.
Vroege, Bas, Anneke van der Elsken-Hilhorst, and Flip Bool. *Ed van der Elsken: Leve ik!*. Edam: Paradox, 1997.

EMULSION

Photographic materials consist mainly of a support base coated with one or more layers of photosensitive material. In silver gelatin photography, this photosensitive material is customarily called an "emulsion." This term is a misnomer, but is commonly used to refer to the light-sensitive material coated on various substrates including glass plates, flexible films, or papers. However, it is also applied broadly to film and paper products.

Manufacturers and photographers pay great attention to the characteristics of emulsions and sensitized materials because their choice has great influence on the effect and quality of the photographs obtained. Some emulsions are designed to form negative images, and others, positive images. One kind of positive emulsion is designed for reversal processing, where, during processing, a negative image is formed first and then chemically reversed to form a final positive image. The other kind of positive emulsion is the direct positive emulsion, where conventional exposure and processing yield a final positive image. Negative emulsions form negative images, where highlights are rendered dark and shadows light. Negative images are usually printed on another negative material such as printing paper to make final positive images. This is called a negative–positive system.

Photographic speeds of emulsions, that is, sensitivity to light and thus how long the material needs to be exposed to create an acceptable image, vary widely. Contact printing papers are very slow to provide comfortable exposure time in contact printing frames. Enlarging (projection printing) papers are much faster than contact printing papers but much slower than negative emulsions for in-camera use. Document films and duplicating films usually fall between enlarging emulsions and negative emulsions in speed.

Emulsions also vary in contrast. Pictorial photography produces what are called continuous tone reproduction of the original image, consisting of black, white, and many shades of gray; while graphic art processes and reproduction of documents generally use extremely high contrast to produce images of black and white with no gray. In a pictorial negative–positive system, negative films have low contrast to register the subject's wide gradation range, while print emulsions have high contrast to make final prints of normal contrast images. This system provides wide exposure latitude at the time of in-camera exposure, while allowing precise control of image darkness and contrast in the darkroom. In reversal and direct positive systems, the films have higher contrast than negative films because the in-camera film forms the final positive image. Exposure accuracy of these materials is more stringent and has narrow latitudes because of the inherently high contrast of the films and the lack of ability to adjust the contrast in the darkroom.

Most emulsions are of "developing out" type, where light exposure forms a latent image, which is made visible through the development process. The other emulsions are of "printing out" type, where prolonged exposure to intense light forms a visible image without the development process. Printing out papers (POP) were in common use in the early years of photography to make contact prints from large-format glass negatives, but are still used by photographers. Along with silver-gelatin-based POP, there are salted papers and other non-silver-based printing techniques such as platinum printing. These materials have inherently low contrast and therefore the original negatives were made rather high contrast to make the final prints have normal contrast.

Silver-gelatin emulsion consists of light sensitive silver halide crystals in a binding medium. An emulsion is made from soluble silver (silver nitrate) and soluble halides (e.g., potassium bromide) in the presence of a protective colloid, such as aqueous dispersion of gelatin. These agents are mixed in a highly controlled way, using a process called precipitation. Crystals thus prepared are physically ripened to desired sizes, chemically digested to increase the light sensitivity, and stabilized to ensure photographic performance of the film and paper until its specified expiration date.

After film or paper is exposed to light, exposed crystals bear tiny specks of metallic silver, called latent image, which renders the entire crystal developable in the developer solution, while crystals without a latent image are not developable. Thus the emulsion registers light exposure by means of latent image from as little as a few metallic silver atoms among several billion silver halide molecules in a single crystal, and this invisibly registered latent image is chemically amplified by the developer to make a metallic silver grain, which forms the visible image.

Most primitive emulsions are sensitive to blue and ultraviolet light. This is because green and red light do not have sufficient energy to create a latent image on silver halide crystals. Many photographic applications require sensitivity to green or red light, and therefore the spectral sensitivity is extended by sensitizing dyes. Sensitizing dyes allow light of lower energy (longer wavelengths than blue) to form latent images. For example, a sensitizing dye for all visible colors (panchromatic) is used for black-and-white camera negative films so that a natural grayscale is obtained from colored objects.

Enhanced sensitivity is obtained by various means, including optimizing ripening and digestion steps, incorporation of very small amounts of dopants, and use of suitable sensitizing dyes. Optimal formulation improves the efficiency with which the latent image forms upon exposure to light, the stability of the latent image, and the developability of the crystals with latent images. In the past, one could increase photographic speed of emulsion only at the cost of shortening the emulsion's shelf life. This is because chemical reaction will slowly progress in coated, dried materials, until they are for all intents and purposes processed. This appears as elevated fog level, decreased speed, decreased contrast, or a combination of these. Today's high-speed emulsions have excellent photographic properties and long shelf life due to improved technology in sensitization as well as stabilization.

The silver-gelatin process was invented by amateur photographer R. L. Maddox in 1871, in the form of "silver gelatinobromide" plates to be used as in-camera negatives. Maddox's plates were photographically inferior to then-existing wet collodion plates, but within a few years of his publication of the process, other photographers made important contributions to the field. The silver-gelatin process is thus evolved through continued experiments by scientists and application by engineers and photographers. That is, the silver-gelatin process is a form of applied science that enabled various branches of photography that were previously impossible. Indeed, its influence went beyond photography-related fields; the photographic industry motivated and drove early research on dye chemistry, gelatin chemistry, and other branches of physics and chemistry.

RYUJI SUZUKI

See also: **Contact Printing; Film; Non-Silver Processes**

Further Reading

Carroll, B. H. "The Preparation of Photographic Emulsions." *Journal of Chemical Education* 8 (1931) 2341–2367.

Duffin, G. F. *Photographic Emulsion Chemistry*. London: Focal Press, 1966.

Hill, T. T. Laboratory-scale Photographic Emulsion Technique. *Journal of Chemical Education* 43 (1966) 492–498.

Keller, K. *Science and Technology of Photography*. VCH, 1993.

Mueller, F. W. H. "The Photographic Emulsion." In Neblette's *Handbook of Photography and Reprography: Materials, Processes, and Systems*, New York: Van Nostrand Reinhold, 1977.

Sturmer, D. M. and A. P. Marchetti. "Silver Halide Imaging." In J. Sturge, V. Walworth, and A. Shepp, eds., *Imaging Processes and Materials*: Neblette's eighth edition, New York: Van Nostrand Reinhold, 1989.

Zelikman, V. L. and S. M. Levi. *Making and Coating Photographic Emulsions*. London: Focal Press, 1964.

ENLARGER

An enlarger is a device used to project negatives onto light-sensitive materials, most usually photographic paper, which are then processed in appropriate chemistry so that the latent image appears visible. An enlarger can be used to make the image either smaller or larger than the negative itself, though it is most often used (as the name would suggest) to enlarge negatives. Enlargers are generally set up so that they project the image downward onto a base, though some enlargers can pivot so that they project the image straight ahead. These enlargers are often utilized when the size of the projected image warrants a greater distance between the lens of the enlarger and the receptive surface than is manageable with an enlarger that projects downward.

An enlarger's lamphouse contains the light source used to make the exposure. Various enlargers employ different types of light sources, including tungsten, quartz-halogen, and fluorescent. Color printing requires that the light source be accessible to color filtration. There are some enlargers that are specially designed for color printing, and have dial-in color and density combinations made available through built-in gelatin or dichronic filters. A few color enlargers employ three differently-colored light sources to make three separate exposures onto the paper: one in red, one in blue, and one in green. In any enlarger, the light source is directed through either a condenser lens or a diffusion screen onto the negative, which is held in place by some type of negative carrier.

The negative carrier is generally one of two types: dustless or glass-sandwich. The dustless type of negative carrier is two plates of either metal or plastic with holes cut for the particular size of film negative being used. The plates hold the negative in position by its edges. Dustless negative carriers are available for film sizes ranging from subminiature to large-format, though are most often used for 4 × 5-inch and smaller negatives. Glass-sandwich negative carriers are made of two solid plates of glass, which press the negative flat. These negative carriers are most often used for large-format negatives, which tend to sag or droop in the center if not properly supported.

The light from the lamphouse is distributed evenly across the negative, which leads to equal distribution across the surface of the photo-sensitive material. After passing through the negative, the light enters a bellows and lens, where the photographer may control the focus of the image onto the photo-sensitive material. The bellows should be capable of being opened to twice the focal length of the lens, which will allow for 1:1 reproductions of the negative. If a print smaller than the size of the negative is desired, a longer focal-length lens or a special reducing attachment is required.

Degrees of enlargement of a negative are restricted by the structure of the enlarger and the size of the paper. Occasionally, a photographer might be interested in making a print larger than is possible with the fixed space between his enlarger's lens and baseboard. There are ways around this limit, including removing the baseboard and affixing the enlarger to something stable, as a table or bench, and then projecting the image onto the floor (which should greatly increase the distance between lens and photo-sensitive material). Some enlargers allow for the possibility of the head being turned around 180° (which would also facilitate projecting the image onto the floor or some other lower-than-baseboard-height base); these should be stabilized with something heavy to offset the weight of the head, which is suddenly insufficiently supported by the vertical column or girder assembly. Others come equipped with heads that pivot so that the lens is parallel to a vertical surface (such as a wall); the negative is then projected horizontally onto this vertical surface. The enlarger can be moved farther away or closer to the wall to achieve the desired enlargement size.

There are also practical considerations of enlargement: after a certain point, even the most well-developed and high-grade negatives will begin to show grain when enlarged overly much. If enlarged full-frame, 35 mm negatives begin to show grain and look out-of-focus when enlarged much more than 8 × 10 inches, and 120 film negatives begin to show grain and look out-of-focus when enlarged much more than 16 × 20 inches. If only a small area of a negative is enlarged, considerations should be made as to the maximum size of possible enlargement that will still maintain crisp focus. Even so, the graininess that results from over-enlargement of negatives can be appealing to some photographers.

Most enlargers have both rough- and fine-focus controls. The rough-focusing control moves the whole enlarger head (which is comprised of the lamphouse, the negative carrier, the bellows, and the lens) up or down the vertical column or girder assembly that supports the head. Rough-focusing allows the photographer to determine the size of the projected image on the enlarger's baseboard. Some enlargers have automatic rough-focusing controls that allow the photographer to move the head of the enlarger with the press of a button rather than by manually turning a crank.

Focusing the negative takes place before the photo-sensitive material is placed underneath the lens of the enlarger, as it requires the photographer to turn on the enlarger light. The rough-focus is determined without a focusing aid, and is used to ensure that the enlarged negative is not larger than the area available on the light-sensitive material. The rough-focus also allows the photographer to get the negative as close to focused as possible before relying on the fine-focus control. Once the rough-focus control is set, the photographer uses a focusing aid to complete the focusing with the fine-focus control. The fine-focus control actually moves the bellows between the negative and the lens to achieve clear focus.

Focusing aids magnify a small section of the projected negative, which helps the photographer adjust the fine-focus control to achieve as clear focus as is possible from his negative. There are several types of focusing aids, one of which is known as a grain finder. Grain finders come in various powers of magnification, and allow the photographer to see individual grains on the projected image rather than relying on a whole section. They are particularly useful for printing images that might not be in sharp focus themselves: as long as the photographer has fine-focused the grains, he can be assured that any areas of soft-focus that occur on his final print come not from the focusing of the projected negative, but are faithful representations of areas of soft-focus on the negative itself.

The projected image from the enlarger falls directly under the lens onto the enlarger's base (unless, of course, the image is being projected horizontally). The photo-sensitive material being exposed is, in the case of photographic paper, generally held in an easel. The easel is comprised of an opaque base and a metal or plastic frame, which is either a fixed-size or adjustable. The frame holds down the edges of the photographic paper to ensure a flat surface for the negative to be projected onto. When focusing the negative, it is prudent to use a piece of the same-thickness paper to focus onto (often the back of a previously developed print works well) so that your focus will not change when you insert the unprocessed photographic paper into the easel before you make your timed exposure.

Enlargers are generally separated into two types: condenser and diffusion. In condenser enlargers, the light from the light source is concentrated and directed straight through the negative by one or more condensing lenses. Condenser enlargers create images that are more sharply focused and show more contrast than images from diffusion enlargers. Scratches and defects on a negative are more difficult to disguise when using a condenser enlarger. Diffusion enlargers employ the use of a diffusion screen or diffusing surface between the light source and the negative. Rather than concentrating the light rays straight down through the negative, diffusion screens, or reflected light from diffusion surfaces, scatter the light so that it is not traveling in parallel rays when it hits the negative. Diffusion enlargers create an overall softening of the focus of the image and help to mask defects on the negative. While much black-and-white printing is done with condenser enlargers, color printing and black-and-white portraiture are often done with diffusion enlargers.

Enlargers come in various sizes to accommodate various sizes of negatives. Also, interchangeable lenses are available so that the same enlarger can be used to print 35 mm and medium-format 120 film. In general, printing 35 mm negatives requires a 50 mm lens, 120 film requires a 75–105 mm lens, and 4 × 5-inch film requires a 135–150 mm lens.

Enlarger lenses are intended to work at close range and on a flat field, but are generally like camera lenses. Although the photographer cannot control shutter speed because there is no shutter on enlarger lenses, he can control the size of the aperture with *f*-stops like those on his camera. The adjustment of shutter speed that would be made on a camera is replaced by the adjustment of exposure time on an enlarger. Usually, an external timer is employed to ensure consistent exposure time. Some timers, connected directly to the enlarger, automatically turn on and off the enlarger light, though a photographer can also choose to work with a foot pedal that controls the light.

Some enlargers can accommodate below-the-lens filter holders, while others can take above-the-lens filters. Filters are used to achieve a variety of effects; for example, the contrast of black-and-white negatives can be amplified or reduced with graded yellow and magenta filters. Using filters from the yellow end of the spectrum accomplishes a reduction in contrast in a print; this can be useful if the print seems to be overly-contrasted, often from harsh lighting conditions at the time that the film was shot. Filters that are more densely magenta-colored succeed in adding contrast to an image, and are often used if the film was shot on a grey day or is underexposed.

Enlargers are useful not only because they allow for darkroom manipulation of color or contrast of a negative, but because they provide ample opportunity for other darkroom manipulations, such as dodging or burning-in areas on a print. Multiple enlargers (or switching negatives in the same enlarger) can be used to expose multiple images onto one piece of photographic paper before it is processed. Without an enlarger, a photographer is restricted to making contact prints, where the size of the final print is determined by the size of the negative. With an enlarger, the photographer can make final prints of almost any size, regardless of the size of his negative.

Jenny Allred Redmann

See also: **Burning-In; Contact Printing; Darkroom; Dodging; Filters; Lens; Manipulation; Multiple Exposures and Printing**

Further Reading

International Center for Photography Encyclopedia of Photography. New York: Crown Publishers, Inc., 1984.

HUGO ERFURTH

German

Hugo Erfurth was the most influential German portrait photographer of the first half of the twentieth century. Based in Dresden, then Cologne, Erfurth specialized in portraits of leading artists, writers, and dancers. By the 1920s, the photographer, then middle-aged, became closely associated with many of the leading figures of German avant-garde painting. His ability to capture their personalities, using a minimum of props or special lighting, gave him the reputation of being a "modernist." In his printing procedures, however, Erfurth ignored contemporary trends, remaining loyal throughout his career to "painterly" Pictorialist techniques that by 1920 were already considered old-fashioned. An experimenter in many photographic genres, Erfurth is known today almost exclusively as a portraitist, due in part to the uneven survival of his oeuvre during the destruction of World War II.

Born in the Saxon city of Halle in 1874, Erfurth by 1884 was sent to school in Dresden, the old capital of the kingdom of Saxony. Between 1892 and 1896 he studied painting at the Kunstakademie in Dresden, an experience that was to have a significant effect on his aesthetics as a photographer. At the same time, Erfurth was learning photographic techniques with the Dresden court photographer Wilhelm Höffert. In 1896 he took over the J.S. Schröder photographic studio, moving his home and studio in 1906 to the larger and more fashionable Palais Lüttichau.

Though Erfurth was making studio portraits by the late 1890s, his early photographic practice was quite diversified. By 1893 he began exhibiting with societies of amateur photographers, showing staged genre scenes of Thuringian peasants in traditional costume. In Stuttgart in 1899, Erfurth submitted five works: a genre scene, two nudes, a landscape, and a still life (locations unknown). He exhibited no portraits. Among Erfurth's first photographs used as book illustrations were several studio female nudes, as well as outdoor nude studies of children and adolescents for a popular book on pediatrics, Dr. Carl Heinrich Stratz's *Der Körper deines Kindes* (Stuttgart, 1903).

In his earliest surviving works, Erfurth was already committed to the Pictorialist aesthetic that swept through European photography by the turn of the twentieth century. Both his landscapes and portraits were often executed as gum bichromate or oil pigment prints, techniques providing loose, atmospheric depictions and emphasizing volumes over detail. Within a few years he began to favor another "painterly" new process, bromoil printing, and he experimented with Louis Lumière's autochromes, the first commercially viable process for color photography. Throughout his career, however, Erfurth also made gelatin silver prints for portraits of a documentary nature, such as *Otto Dix Teaching a Class in Figure Painting* (1929).

Initially Erfurth's studio portraits of male artists and intellectuals depicted the subjects against a dark background, often with attributes of their professions, such as a paintbrush, easel, or book. By 1920 Erfurth more often used a light background, eliminating all props and concentrating on the face and upper body. Although Erfurth's compositions looked back to the traditions of nineteenth-century German portrait painting, the avant-garde considered the photographer "modern" in his ability to record definitively the personal essence of his sitters. Thus Oskar Kokoschka, the youthful-looking creator of the lithographic series *The Dreaming Boys*, turns from the camera with a faraway expression. By contrast, another Expressionist painter, Max Beckmann, glowers balefully and frontally at the camera, filling the picture space in a forceful image. Unlike his contemporary, August Sander, who systematically photographed all German social types, Erfurth had no explicit program. During the 1920s he thought of creating a *Gallery of Portrait Heads of My Time*, but he did not pursue the idea consistently.

By 1908 Erfurth had also begun to take some of the earliest photographs of dancers in motion. Concentrating on modern dance, Erfurth, over the next two decades, photographed more than 20 dancers, all female, some famous, like Mary Wigman, others little remembered today. His goal was to produce a sense of natural movement, even if blurred, using artificial lighting. These images, rare today, influenced younger dance photographers, including Erfurth's pupil, Charlotte Rudolph. Erfurth also photographed leading opera and theater performers during this period.

Erfurth was probably the best-known portrait photographer in Germany by the late 1920s; he was the subject of an extensive critical literature and even of a 1927 film that showed him planning, executing, and printing a portrait commission. Possessing strong organizational skills, Erfurth curated a major photography exhibition in Dresden as early as 1904, and he later operated an art gallery in his studio, presenting prints and drawings by the most talented younger German artists. Erfurth also published art criticism, writing for example about the Scottish photographer David Octavius Hill (1802–1870), whom Erfurth admired for suppressing unnecessary detail in his portraits. In 1919, he was a cofounder of an exhibiting group, the Society of German Photographic Artists (GDL), in which he played a dominant role for 20 years. Erfurth continued to have an experimental attitude, producing a series of abstract photograms in the mid-1920s.

In 1934, Erfurth relocated from Dresden to Cologne, evidently seeking new portrait commissions from that city's business elite. Unlike many of his artist subjects, who emigrated soon after the advent of the Hitler government in 1933, Erfurth remained in Germany, where he continued to accumulate honors and awards. His attitude toward the new regime is difficult to determine. Erfurth exhibited and published portraits of Nazi storm trooper (SA) soldiers that were widely noted; he had, however, occasionally portrayed military officers in uniform earlier in his career.

In 1943 an Allied air raid destroyed Erfurth's Cologne studio and part of his photographic archives, though not his portraits. He then moved to Gaienhofen am Bodensee in southernmost Germany, where he maintained a photographic studio until his death in 1948. In 1947, he was honored with a large retrospective exhibition in nearby Constance, Switzerland. His work has continued to be exhibited widely, particularly in Germany, where it forms a virtual history of the country's artistic and intellectual movements during Erfurth's time.

Donald Rosenthal

See also: **Photogram; Photography in Germany and Austria; Pictorialism; Sander, August**

Biography

Born in Halle, Germany, 14 October 1874. In Dresden, studied painting at the Kunstakademie and photography in the studio of Wilhelm Höffert. Active professional photographer, principally as a studio portraitist, from 1896 but also exhibited work in other genres. Taught photography privately, and at the Akademie für Buchgewerbe und Graphische Künste in Leipzig, Germany's leading city for book publication, 1929. Curator of Photographic Section, Internationale Kunst-Ausstellung, Dresden, 1904. Operated gallery showing prints and drawings by younger German artists in his Dresden studio in the early 1920s. From this time, frequent contacts with leading avant-garde painters; subject of portraits by Otto Dix and others. Published numerous albums of his own portrait photographs and some articles about other photographers. From 1919, cofounder and jury chairman of the Society of German Photographic Artists. Awarded bronze medal, Stuttgart, 1899; silver medal (first prize), Photographic Exhibition, Düsseldorf, 1902; achievement award, "Day of German Handicrafts," Frankfurt am Main, 1939. Relocated studio in 1934 to Cologne and in 1943 to Gaienhofen am Bodensee; died there 14 February 1948.

Individual Exhibitions

1907 *Photographische Bildnisse*: Kunstsalon Emil Richter, Dresden, Germany
1909 *Einzelausstellung Hugo Erfurths*: Grossherzoglichen Museums für Kunst und Kunstgewerbe, Weimar, Germany
1926 *Bildnisphotographien*; Palais Lüttichau, Dresden, Germany
1930 *Lichtbildnisse*; Kunstsalon Maria Kunde, Hamburg, Germany
1947 *Bildnisse aus dem XX. Jahrhundert*; Wessenberghaus, Constance, Switzerland
1951 *Photokina*; Cologne, Germany
1961 *Bildnisse Hugo Erfurth*; Museum Folkwang, Essen, Germany
1982 *Hugo Erfurth: Between Tradition and the Avant-Garde*; International Center of Photography, New York, New York
1986 *Hugo Erfurth*; Rudolf Kicken Galerie, Cologne, Germany
1989 *Hugo Erfurth*; Bayer-Kulturabteilung, Leverkusen, Germany
1992 *Hugo Erfurth 1874–1948*; Agfa Foto-Historama, Cologne, Germany, and traveling

Group Exhibitions

1893 *Internationale Ausstellung von Amateur-Photographien*; Dresden, Germany
1899 *IV Ausstellung des Süddeutschen Photographen-Vereins*; Stuttgart, Germany
1909 *Internationale Photographische Ausstellung*; Dresden, Germany
1929 *Film und Foto: Internationale Ausstellung des Deutschen Werkbundes*; Stuttgart, Germany, and traveling
1933 *Die Kamera*; Berlin, Germany
1977 *Documenta 6*; Kassel, Germany
1989 *Photography Until Now*; Museum of Modern Art, New York, New York, and traveling
1989 *On the Art of Fixing a Shadow*; National Gallery of Art, Washington, D.C., and traveling
1997 *Deutsche Fotografie: Macht eines Mediums 1870–1970*; Kunst-und-Ausstellungshalle der Bundesrepublik Deutschland, Bonn, Germany

Selected Works

Genre Scene with Thuringian Peasants, 1893
Vanity (Female Nude Holding a Mirror), c. 1900
Archer (Male Nude Study), c. 1905

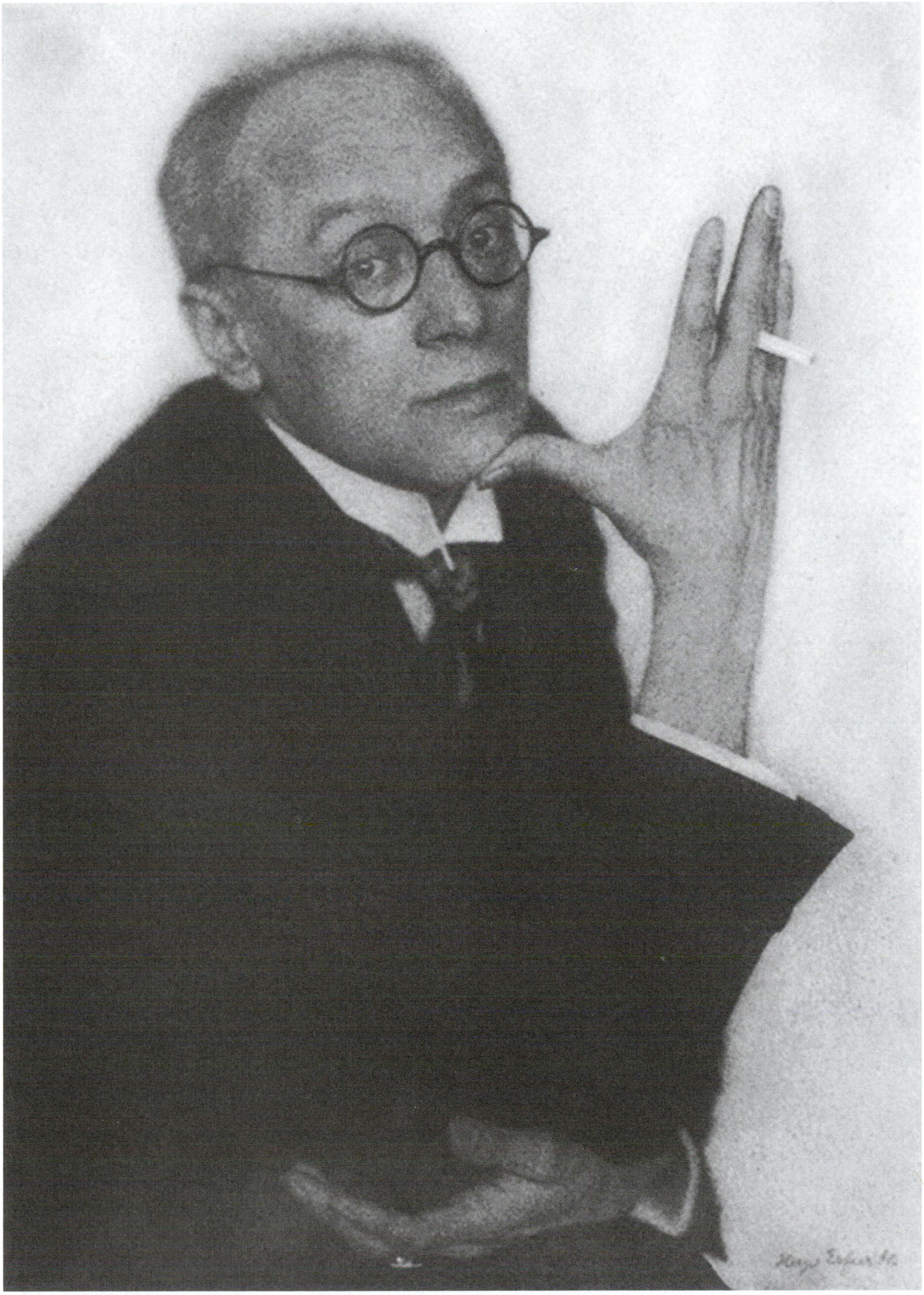

Hugo Erfurth, Frans Blei, 1928, oil pigment, 22.2 × 16 cm (8 ¾ × 6 5/16″).
[*The J. Paul Getty Museum, Los Angeles*]

Wilhelm Klaus, 1908
Mary Wigman, 1914
Oskar Kokoschka, 1919
Otto Dix, 1925
Photogram, 1926
Frans Blei, 1928
Max Beckmann, 1928
Otto Dix Instructing a Class in Figure Painting, 1929
Gerhart Hauptmann Holding a Book, 1944

Further Reading

Dewitz, Bodo von. *Hugo Erfurth: Menschenbild und Prominentenportrait 1902–1936*. Cologne: Wienand, 1989.

Dewitz, Bodo von, and Karin Schuller-Procopovici. *Hugo Erfurth 1874–1948: Photograph zwischen Tradition und Moderne*. Cologne: Wienand, 1992.

"Erfurth, Hugo." *International Center of Photography Encyclopedia of Photography*. New York: Crown Publishers, Inc, 1984.

Erfurth, Hugo. *Kamerabildnisse*. Dresden: Erfurth, 1907.

"Zur Entwicklung der modernen Bildnis-Photographie." In *Wort und Bild*. Dresden: Internationale Photographische Ausstellung, 1909.

"*Bildnisse*." Dresden: Erfurth, 1928.

Kämpf, Tobias. "Erfurth, Hugo." *Saur Allgemeines Künstler-Lexikon* vol. 34, Munich/Leipzig: Saur, 2002.

Loescher, Fritz. "Zu Hugo Erfurths Bildern." *Photographische Mitteilungen* 40 (1903).

Lohse, Bernd. *Hugo Erfurth 1874–1948: Der Fotograf der Goldenen Zwanziger Jahre*. Seebruck am Chiemsee: Heering, 1977.

Misselbeck, Reinhold. "Erfurth, Hugo." *Dictionary of Art* vol. 10. New York: Grove, 1996.

Schöppe, Wilhelm. *Meister der Kamera Erzählen wie sie Wurden und wie sie Arbeiten: Hugo Erfurth, Franz Fiedler, Franz Grainer [u.a.]*, Halle-Salle: Knappe, 1935.

Steinert, Otto. *Hugo Erfurth: Bildnisse*. Gütersloh: Sigbert Mohn, 1961.

EROTIC PHOTOGRAPHY

Erotic art is the art of sexuality. Webster's dictionary defines "erotic," in part, as: "Pertaining to or prompted by sexual feelings or desire." Photographer Peter Barry wrote in 1983 that eroticism must express desire and excitement. Some state that erotic art is sexual but not explicit, while others attempt to define it by its demeanor or attitude toward sex. These artists and critics typically define erotic as possessing a sense of humor. Where pornography is blatant and obvious, eroticism, they claim, is intelligent and witty. What eroticism is or should consist of has been a topic of debate for philosophers, historians, and artists for countless ages. Erotic imagery in photography is as old as the medium itself with known provocative and nude Daguerreotypes being made at least as early as 1840.

In modern times, erotic imagery in high-art has gone hand-in-hand with the avant-garde. Photography, as a medium, lends itself quite well to the production of evocative imagery by virtue of the medium's perceived "truthfulness." According to philosopher Michel Foucault (1926–1984), sexuality and truth are linked in their relationships to society and communication. Erotic art is best when it communicates truthfulness in an intimate but universal manner. For Foucault, this is the communication of experience and wisdom and is best typified in the erotic pictorial traditions of Eastern civilization. The Western reaction to Eroticism has been defined by shame, constriction, and a need to control its production and dissemination. In French *fin de siécle* society sexuality was linked very closely to what Foucault termed "pornography of the morbid," where non-procreative sex was sinful, destructive, and deadly. These attitudes would influence social-political reactions to erotic photography in the twentieth century in France, just as lingering Victorian prudishness in the United Kingdom would determine social and legal positions on erotic photography in England well into the late twentieth century.

The production and exhibition of erotic photography in the United States and Great Britain is greatly constrained by the social moralism of the various eras in which it was made. In the early 1900s, puritanical values reigned over the social consciousness of potential art viewers and markets. The production of erotic art existed, but only to the chagrin of the governments and moral conservatives of these nations. Britain was particularly prudish in its laws governing decency and remained so until after 1918. It was the nightmare of the First World War and the terror of a million British dead that effectively shocked British society loose from their tightly grasped tenants of morality. Literature and the visual arts reacted immediately with a new sense of sexual liberalism. Earlier English publications of erotic photos included magazines such as *Photo Bits*, which became *Photo Fun* in 1906. Magazines such as these couched the nude in socially acceptable naturalistic settings, romanticizing and idealizing the nude form.

During the 1920s, shifting moral values allowed increased sexual liberation and photography of this time put nude imagery firmly into commercial culture. Shorter skirts and haircuts for women at this time became not just acceptable, but fashionable. Burlesque shows of the 1920s and 1930s provided venues for those looking for erotic entertainment. *Ziegfeld's Follies*, *George White's Scandals*, and *Earl Carroll's Vanities* kept nudity and racy content in the paying public's eye and served to legitimize the increasing liberalism of popular culture. Printed photo postcards from these shows not only promoted the careers of the young stage actors, but provided a source of cheap, racy photos readymade for mass consumption. Hollywood began promoting its young starlets with magazines like *Film Fun* providing the public with perhaps the first "pin-ups" as early as the 1920s. Although photos of nude women were very common during this era, artists who did not wish to be discredited or arrested still had to originate their subjects in contrived narrative poses usually imitative of Greek or Roman statuary. Doing so made the images more palatable to the public by making them more "artsy" and less realistic. Implied or even direct eroticism was deemed allowable by virtue of a photo's art-historic context.

It was the advent of the "pin-up" that really brought erotic photography to the general public in the United States and abroad. The term "pin-up" was invented during World War II and applied to the thousands of glossy photos of beautiful women distributed to American soldiers in order to "elevate morale." As a general rule the Second World War pin-up was pretty and her pose suggestive, but she was still innocent and almost never nude. Pin-ups are erotic photography mass produced for commercial distribution, as opposed to thoughtfully crafted, high-art erotic photography with perhaps more specifically aesthetic or conceptual intentions.

Just as the first few decades after the First World War brought radical liberation and changes to social ideas of morality, so too did the first few decades after World War II see sweeping changes in social attitudes towards erotic imagery. The 1950s through the 1970s are often referred to as "the permissive years" in erotic and commercial photography. The 1950s gave birth to a golden age of erotic art, typified by the glossy, well-produced magazine spread found in such men's publications as *Playboy* (first issue published in 1953). The pictorial influence of this magazine's pin-up aesthetic has directly influenced the production of erotic art, fashion photography, and popular advertising up to the present day. *Playboy's* format is probably the most publicly accessible (and arguably the most publicly acceptable) form of erotic photography to date. Noted photographers from *Playboy* include: Peter Gowland, J. Frederick Smith, and later Milton H. Green and Barry O'Rourke. In Britain, a master of post-war erotic photography is George Harrison Marks. His work is pure eroticism with no pretense of aestheticism. He provided naked girls for boys to look at, offering sex for sale with no qualms.

Even with the sexual revolution and rapidly changing social morality of the 1960s and 1970s, any photographs explicitly depicting pubic hair were by and large considered obscene until well into the 1970s. This is even given the earlier legal battles of English photographer Horace Narbeth (known professionally as Roye) who successfully defended his photographic depiction of pubic hair in 1958 by citing issues of artistic integrity. One of the most influential photographers of the 1960s was the Englishman Bill Brandt (1904–1983), whose book *Perspective of Nudes* (1961) was innovative and influential in bringing acceptance of nudity and eroticism to fine art photography.

The inherent problem of defining erotic photography is finding a concise way in which to differentiate the erotic from its more pervasive cousin, pornography. Many commercial and fashion photos are undeniably erotic, ranging from subtly provocative to sexually cliché to startlingly overt. Subjectivity is a problem for the student of any genre of photography trying to find a true interpretation of the image. The intrinsic biases found in the interpretation of sexual art are complicated further by the way and place in which an image is viewed. As artist Rod Ashford wrote in 1998:

> However subtle the erotic motif, when viewed in an inappropriate context, even images that have the power to excite can appear crude, obscene, alarming, or even bland. Similarly, a sophisticated erotic image viewed in the testosterone bravado of an all male environment is more likely to be passed over in favor of something more explicit—an immediate image which seeks to objectify its female subject.
>
> (Ashford, "Prurience and Perfection" 1998, 16.)

As noted by photo-historian Robert Sobieszek, erotic photography can be seen as having two potential approaches in its treatment of subject matter. An iconic approach places the substance of an image's erotic content on the figure itself. Typically "straight" in its formalism and unaltered surface, this approach embodies and signifies the erotic in itself. In photography of this mode, the subject carries the meaning of the photo. The other approach is narrative, which is an extension of nineteenth century pictorialism. Erotic photography that is staged, or relies on props or composition to convey its erotic content and meaning is narrative. All erotic art, however, is emotional, meaning that it connects to the viewer in an expressive way. An erotic image can disturb or delight. A photograph by its nature distances the viewer in space and time, but it also draws in the viewer to a space that is real and personal, mentally and physically. Erotic photography may shock, dismay, arouse, or amuse but it will not fail to be noticed. In this way, it can be argued that an erotic photograph can never be purely formal, but must always be considered expressive.

Erotic imagery in photography typically is subjugated by the traditional male-dominated gaze; that is, a gaze preferring to see women as the object of erotic poses. The male nude in art in general and in erotic art in particular poses a variety of problems for artists, mainly socially and in extreme cases, legally. Though the subject matter of these photos is what is ultimately cited as the spark of controversy, many critics agree that the real cause of social uproar lies more in what erotic photographs of men communicate about the artist or perhaps even the viewer. This is to say that negative public reaction is based on a feeling of discomfort with viewing art produced outside conventional norms of communication. The male nude in photographic art has been dealt with successfully, though often still controversially, by artists such as Robert Mapplethorpe and George Dureau (1930–). Equally controversial, for many of the same reasons, is erotic art produced by women artists. Whether photographing women or men, female photographers find themselves under a great deal of scrutiny due to their denial of the traditionally male-defined sense of sexuality. Many of these images are undeniably erotic, while still ascribing to high-art standards of formalist excellence. In this way artists such as Mapplethorpe can claim artistic validity by virtue of their technical and formal artistic standards, notwithstanding the controversy of the subject matter.

Controversy breeds censorship, and nowhere is this more true than with sexually themed photography. Governments across the world have tried to differentiate what is erotic, and presumably acceptable from what is pornography, and by extension unacceptable. Lawmakers are not always successful in making distinctions clear or guidelines easy to follow. Typically laws define what is erotic as being any sexual art that is not pornographic under legal definition. This kind of definition is problematic because it attempts to define a thing by defining what it is not. Many government-sponsored commissions such as the United States' Attorney General's Commission on Pornography in 1986, usually sweep anything sexual into the same category and attempt to make broad-based judgments founded on prevailing moral and political attitudes as opposed to an attempt to make aesthetic judgments on the works at hand.

The subjective nature of erotic art as discussed above makes any kind of censorship or regulation intrinsically difficult for the reason that censoring agencies typically make the assumption that all representation has equal value to all viewers. Most decency laws also do not allow works to be considered in their proper context.

Whether humorous or disturbing, erotic photography will always have sexuality at the core of its subject. Erotic does not necessarily mean photos of nude people. An erotic photograph can be one of a subject fully or partially clothed. The gaze of the subject can be directed within the picture plane or outward, in direct engagement with the viewer (a typical motif in pin-up photography). An erotic photograph need not show an entire person's body or even a person at all. Eroticism is defined by attitude and context; because of this, erotic photography will always be subjective and reliant upon the very personal reactions of the viewer. The fact that eroticism in photography is as popular and ubiquitous as it is, testifies to the success of artists' universal communication of intimate truths as described by Foucault. The incorporation of erotic photography into commercial, mass culture is indicative of just how universal these truths are, controversial or not.

Erin Schwartz

See also: **Brandt, Bill; Mapplethorpe, Robert; Nude Photography; Pin-Up Photography**

Further Reading

Ashford, Rod. "Prurience and Perfection," *The British Journal of Photography: The Body Issue*, no. 715 (1998).
Barry, Peter. *The Art of Erotic Photography*. New York: Crescent Books, 1983.
Brandt, Bill. *Perspective of Nudes*. New York: Amphoto, 1961.

Corinne, Tee A. *Intimacies*. San Francisco: Last Gasp of San Francisco, 2001.

Davis, Melody D. *The Male Nude in Contemporary Photography*. Philadelphia: Temple University Press, 1991.

Ellis, John. "Photography/Pornography/Art/Pornography." *Society for Education in Film and Television*, 21, no. 1 (1980).

Foucault, Michel. *Histoire de la sexualité;* as *The History of Sexuality, Volume I: An Introduction*. Translated by Robert Hurley. New York: Pantheon, 1978.

Gracyk, Theodore A. "Pornography as Representation: Aesthetic Considerations." *Journal of Aesthetic Education*, 21, no. 4 (1987).

Lewinski, Jorge. *The Naked and the Nude: A History of the Nude in Photography*. New York: Harmony Books, 1987.

Lucie-Smith, Edward. *Sexuality in Western Art*. London: Thames and Hudson, 1991.

Maddon, Ben. "Nude in a Social Landscape." In *Nude: Photographs 1850–1980*. New York: Harper and Row, 1980.

Olley, Michelle. *Blonde: Masterpieces of Erotic Photography*. New York: Thunder's Mouth Press, 2002.

Olley, Michelle. *Homme: Masterpieces of Erotic Photography*. London: Carlton, 1999.

Pearson, Jennifer H. "Erotic and Pornographic Photography Selected Bibliography." *History of Photography*, 18, (1994).

Sobieszek, Robert. "Addressing the Erotic: Reflections on Nude Photography." In *Nude: Photographs 1850–1980*. New York: Harper and Row, 1980.

Stein, Ralph. *The Pin-Up from 1852 to Today*. New York: Crescent Books, 1984.

Sullivan, Constance, ed. *Nude: Photographs 1850–1980*, New York: Harper and Row, 1980.

Vance, Carole S. "The Pleasures of Looking: The Attorney General's Commission on Pornography versus Visual Images." *The Critical Image: Essays on Contemporary Photography*, Seattle: Bay Press, 1990.

ELLIOTT ERWITT

American

Elio Romano Erwitt was born in Paris of Russian parents in 1928. His first name was later Americanized to Elliott. The family spent some time in Milan and Rome before returning to Paris after his Jewish father, Boris, who had a doctorate in architectural engineering and was a partner in a management consulting firm, had offended the fascist regime. On 1 September 1939 they escaped the new European war by emigrating to New York. After a few years there, he and his father moved to California, the marriage having disintegrated. He had begun teaching himself photography as a teenager while living alone after his father moved to New Orleans. After graduating from Hollywood High School, he held exhibits of his work in Los Angeles and New Orleans. His photographic work had been part of a series of odd jobs he had tried in order to support himself. He studied photography at Los Angeles City College (1942–1944) and moved to New York in 1948 when he came to the attention of Edward Steichen and several other notables in photography. He was hired by Roy Stryker to work on a project about Pittsburgh for the Mellon Foundation. After Robert Capa viewed his photographs in 1951 and he subsequently was drafted into the Army, he was invited to join Magnum Photos in 1953.

Erwitt proved himself to be a master photojournalist, adept at handling a wide variety of equipment and assignments, often requiring imagination and quick, intuitive responses to stories rapidly unfolding before his eyes. He began doing documentary photography and news stories. One of his most famous early series, while on assignment for Westinghouse in 1959, recorded the "kitchen cabinet debate" between President Richard Nixon and Soviet Premier Nikita Khrushchev in Moscow. He photographed around the world for *Holiday* and other magazines and produced advertising and commercial photographs as well. From 1950 to 1952, Erwitt was a freelance photographer for *Collier's*, *Look*, *Life*, and *Holiday*. He became a Magnum associate in 1953 and a full member in 1954. Erwitt has shot journalistic essays throughout the world and numerous commercial assignments for Air France, KLM, and Chase Manhattan Bank, among many others.

Erwitt has made a good living with advertising and commercial photography, but he has always done his personal work in tandem with it, his personal photographs in large measure having been made possible by his globe-trotting journalistic and commercial assignments. Something of a purist as a candid photographer, he almost always uses black-and-white film, composes in the viewfinder, seldom crops, and demands unposed subjects. Although his magazine and advertising work dried to a trickle by the late 1980s, his career rebounded with his retrospective exhibition and book, *Personal Exposures*, which kindled renewed interest in his work.

Erwitt is one of the great masters of humor and irony in photography, including what might be called visual puns. Such puns match his in-person verbal style. Usually the humor is gentle, but it can also be biting. His whimsical, story-telling pictures are in the tradition of Robert Doisneau, as well as being grounded in the "decisive moment" aesthetic of Henri Cartier-Bresson. He has been a prolific publisher of books of his photographs, with an emphasis on his humorous views, including the massive, definitive if self-consciously artless *Snaps*. It should be noted, however, that he has frequently recycled some of the same familiar images from book to book. Indeed, some of his "personal" images have even been recycled into his advertising work. A humorous image from one of his nudist series was used as a Barney's advertisement in 1990, and a 1955 picture of a happy couple reflected in a car mirror was used for a Mitsubishi advertisement in 1998. Even a 1950 photograph of two men in suits, hats, and overcoats having a fistfight on a New York street served as an advertisement in the 1990s. He has devoted special attention to the animal world, especially dogs, resulting in two compilations of canine humor, *Dog/Dogs* and *Son of Bitch*. A great devotee of the single story-telling image, Erwitt has a keen sense of when something interesting is about to unfold before his camera. His innate sense of the absurd drives his interest in recording strange or humorous juxtapositions. Ralph Hattersley wrote of Erwitt, "He made the human comedy easier to bear."

Not all of his photographs are humorous. One of his earliest photographs starkly portrays the reality of segregation at "White" and "Colored" drinking fountains. He has made tender photographs of mothers with their infants (especially his own wife and child), and poignant records of other intensely human moments. His photograph of Jaqueline Kennedy at President John F. Kennedy's funeral in 1963 is one of the most memorable records of that national ordeal; earlier he had portrayed Robert Capa's mother weeping over his grave. A young couple dancing in a kitchen in Valencia, Spain (1952) has great warmth of feeling. Thanks to his own notoriety as a photographer, he has had access to many other famous people in his career, including politicians from Kennedy and Lyndon Johnson to Fidel Castro and Khrushchev, actors Humphrey Bogart, Marilyn Monroe, and Grace Kelly, and writer Jack Kerouac.

His professional work includes magazine and advertising photography. After working for *Holiday* magazine, he deftly shifted to advertising photography when Magnum began receiving such assignments in the mid-1950s. He worked for the French, Jamaican, and Australian governments' tourism campaigns, airlines, and Chase Manhattan Bank, among others, as well as accounts for industrial giants such as IBM, General Electric, Allied Chemical, Eli Lilly, and General Dynamics.

Beginning in the 1970s, Erwitt channeled much of his energy into movies, putting his early film school training to use. His feature films, television commercials, and documentaries include *Beauty Knows No Pain* (1971), *Red, White and Bluegrass* (1973), and the prize-winning *Glassmakers of Herat, Afghanistan* (1977). Other documentaries are imbued with his ironic and humorous viewpoint. He created short documentaries about the making of the Arthur Penn film, *Little Big Man*, and another about the training of football game half-time entertainers, *Beauty Knows No Pain* (1971). He worked briefly as director of photography for the feature film, *Paper Lion*. There is a link between his films and his photographs, however, as some of them form short sequences.

In the late 1990s and early years of the new century, Erwitt was again active in advertising photography and television commercials.

David Haberstich

Biography

Born in Paris of Russian parents, 26 July 1928. Family moved to Milan, Italy, returned to Paris; to New York, 1939; to Los Angeles, California, 1940, graduated from Hollywood High School; took courses at Los Angeles City College (1942–1944) while working in a photographic laboratory. To New Orleans, 1947, where he had an exhibition in an artists' club on Pirates Alley. To New York, 1948, where he began taking filmmaking courses in the Film School of the New School for Social Research in exchange for taking photographs for the school (1948–1950). Began making portraits of authors for Alfred Knopf book jackets, 1949. Assistant to commercial photographer Valentino Sarra; a documentarian for Standard Oil Company project. Drafted into the Army in 1951 posted to Germany and France, where he showed his work to Robert Capa. Joined Magnum Photos after being discharged from services, 1953. Began working for *Holiday* magazine, 1953. President of Magnum, 1966. Living in New York City.

Selected Works

New York (Fight), 1950
North Carolina (Segregated drinking fountains), 1950
Jack Kerouac, New York, 1953

New York, 1953
Robert Capa's Mother, Julia, Armronk, New York, 1954
California (Laughing lovers in car mirror), 1955
Marilyn Monroe, New York, 1956
Nixon and Khrushchev, Moscow, 1959
On the set of "The Misfits," Reno, Nevada, 1960
Jackie Kennedy, 1963
Havana, Cuba, 1964
Kent, England (*Nudists*), 1968

Individual Exhibitions

1970 *Photographs and Anti-Photographs*; National Museum of History and Technology, Smithsonian Institution, Washington, D.C.
1989 *Elliott Erwitt: Personal Exposures*; Benteler-Morgan Galleries, Houston, Texas
1989 *Elliott Erwitt: Place Lagane*; Galérie Municipale du Château d'Eau, Toulouse, France

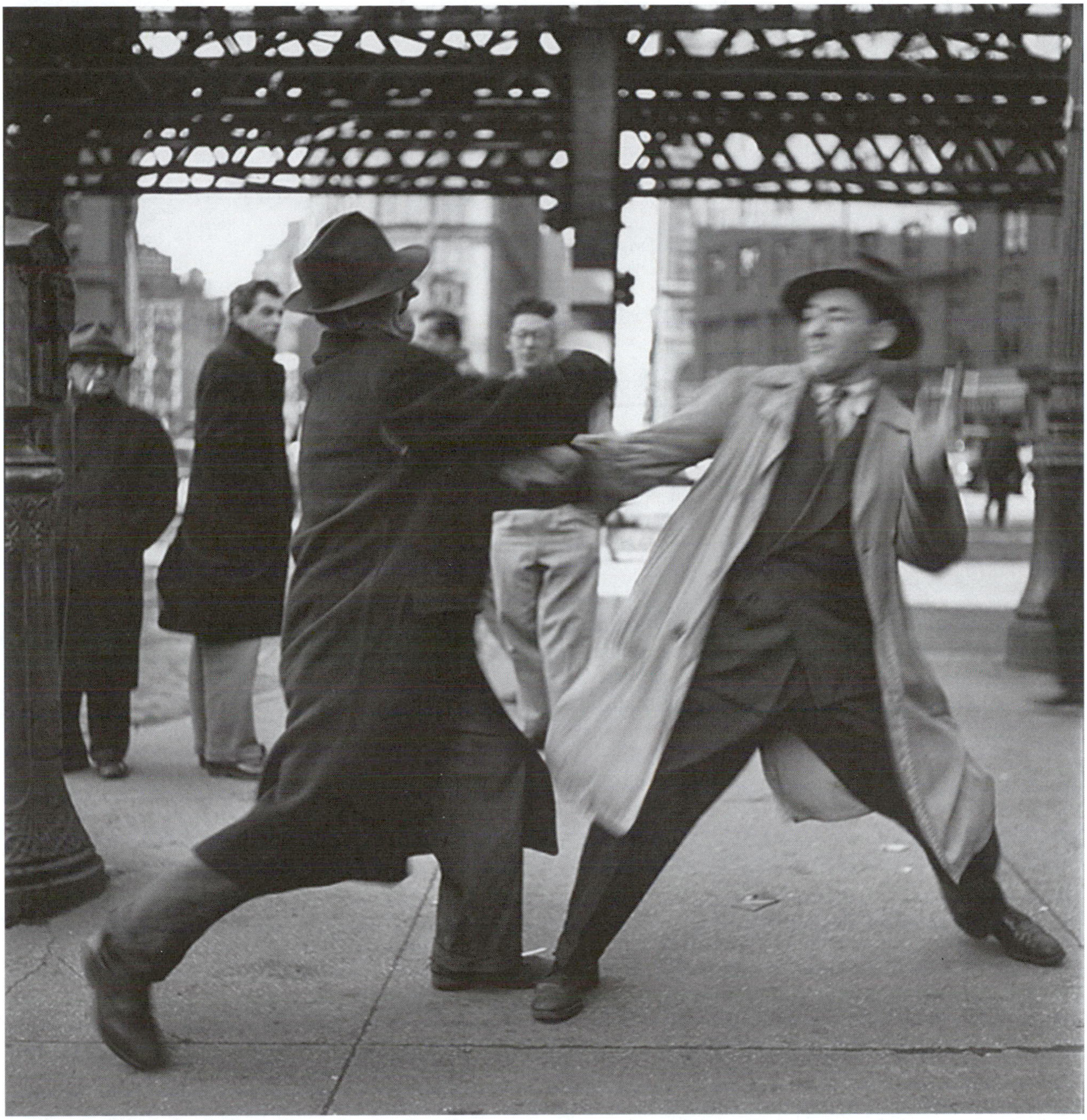

Elliot Erwitt, New York [fight], 1950.
[© *Elliot Erwitt/Magnum Photos*]

1992 A Gallery for Fine Photography; New Orleans, Louisiana
1995 *Between the Sexes*; Fahey/Klein Gallery, Los Angeles, California
2000 *Elliott Erwitt: Photographs from the Hofstra Museum Collection*; Hofstra University, Hempstead, New York
2004 *Elliott Erwitt's Hand Work*; The JCC in Manhattan, New York, New York

Group Exhibitions

1955 *The Family of Man*; Museum of Modern Art, New York, New York
2004 *The New York Subway: A Centennial Celebration*; Lower Level Dining Concourse, East and West Pullman Cars, New York, New York
2004 *Magnum New Yorkers*; The Museum of the City of New York, New York, New York

Further Reading

Bunnell, Peter C. *Degrees of Guidance: Essays on Twentieth-Century American Photography*. Cambridge; New York: Cambridge University Press, 1993.

Callahan, Sean. *The Private Experience, Elliott Erwitt*. London: Thames + Hudson, 1974.

Danziger, James. *Interviews with Master Photographers*. New York: Paddington Press, distributed by Grosset & Dunlap, 1977.

Erwitt, Elliott. *Photographs and Anti-Photographs*. Essay by Sam Holmes, introd. by John Szarkowski. Greenwich, CT; New York Graphic Society, 1972.

———. *Son of Bitch*. Unleashed by P. G. Wodehouse. New York: Grossman Publishers, 1974.

———. *Recent Developments: Photographs*. Introd. by Wilfrid Sheed. New York: Simon and Schuster, 1978.

———. *Personal Exposures*. New York: W.W. Norton, 1988.

———. *Elliott Erwitt*. Milano: Idea Books, 1989.

———. *Between the Sexes*. New York: W.W. Norton, 1994.

———. *Dog / dogs*. London: Phaidon, 1998.

———. *Museum Watching / Elliott Erwitt*. London: Phaidon, 1999.

———. *Elliott Erwitt Snaps*. Text by Murray Sayle. London and New York: Phaidon, 2001.

ETHICS AND PHOTOGRAPHY

Although a comprehensive examination of the ethics of photography has yet to be written, there have been sustained investigations into specific genres within photography, including photojournalism, portraiture, and—to a lesser extent—documentary and street photography in which the question of ethics naturally arises, given the specific intent of the genre.

Photojournalism

The photojournalistic context is that in which the photographer makes a photograph with the aim of informing the public by publication of the image in a newspaper, magazine, or other mass-circulation medium. Famous examples include Eddie Adams's image of the summary execution of a Viet Cong prisoner, and Robert Capa's images made during the Spanish Civil War, particularly that known as "Falling Soldier" (*Loyalist Militiaman at the Moment of Death, Cerro Muriano, September 5, 1936*) and the D-Day invasion at Normandy.

A central ethical consideration in photojournalism is connected with questions about the kind of understanding that such images can engender. At least since Plato's canonical discussion in Book X of the *Republic*, it has been argued that images are incapable of fostering the kind of understanding that is required for knowledge. The contrast is with words, which can provide the sort of narrative that is required for ethical evaluation, or for what Susan Sontag in her essay "In Plato's Cave" calls "ethical or political knowledge."

Consider the example of Adams's photograph of the summary execution. The image itself enables the viewer to know at most that an individual was killed in a deliberate way by means of a pistol shot to the head. But such limited knowledge falls far short of what the viewer needs to know in order to ethically evaluate the act. For such evaluation further knowledge is required concerning such things as the events leading up to the killing and the mental states of the persons involved. The viewer needs to know, for example, whether the executed man himself has in the past committed some deliberate act of killing, or whether the executioner believes that by carrying out the execution in summary fashion he will prevent acts of killing in the future. None of this knowledge can be acquired by means of a photograph. Words, by way of contrast, can easily provide such knowledge. They can, for example, inform the reader of heinous acts committed by the victim prior to the execution. Indeed, in the months after this image was widely circulated in the American press, Adams learned that the executed man had hours before murdered an entire family, a discovery that led Adams to lifelong remorse for the damage the image did to the reputation of the executioner. Such limitations in the kind of meanings photographs (and images generally) can convey lead Sontag to conclude that photojournalistic images can serve only to "goad conscience," and that the effect such images can have will amount to no more than "some kind of sentimentalism."

In her 2003 work, *Regarding the Pain of Others*, Sontag acknowledges some positive ethical dimensions of photojournalism. For one thing, such images can cause viewers to remember past atrocities, and remembering of this sort is for Sontag an intrinsically positive ethical act. As well, photojournalistic images can help keep the suffering of those who are geographically distant in the minds of viewers, and in this way make it more difficult for that suffering simply to be ignored. But Sontag remains steadfast in her lack of optimism with regard to the potential for photographs to foster comprehensive understanding.

A second and increasingly pressing ethical dimension associated with photojournalism arises from the advent of digital technology. Prior to the widespread use of such technology it was difficult to alter a photograph in an undetectable way. As a result, viewers of photojournalistic images developed an implicit trust that the beliefs they formed as a result of viewing such images were generally true, and that they had good reason for believing those beliefs to be true. As Barbara Savedoff notes in her book *Transforming Images: How Photography Complicates the Picture*, such trust has carried over into the digital era, and can be taken advantage of by those who avail themselves of digital techniques. A seamlessly altered image, presented to a trusting audience, can engender radically false beliefs, even while the viewers believe that they have good reason for thinking those beliefs to be true. Concern that such trust will be taken advantage of in this way has led newspapers to deal harshly with photojournalists who succumb to the temptation. There is at least one instance of a photographer for the *Los Angeles Times* being fired for submitting a digitally altered photograph that was run on the front page.

Photojournalists themselves have been active and vocal regarding photojournalistic ethics. The founders and members of such professional groups at Magnum Photos codified many aspects of what is considered ethical practice in the late 1950s and 1960s. Earlier in the twentieth century, the use of photographic images in overtly propagandistic contexts, even those obviously highly manipulated, such as the montages and collages of John Heartfield or Hannah Höch in the 1920s and 1930s, provided a lexicon for use of images for social goals. The viewer was afforded the opportunity to be educated about the nature of the image itself as well as its purpose and thus be empowered to judge better the ethical issues that arose.

Portraiture

The portraiture context is one in which the photographer creates an image of her subject with the subject's willing participation. Commercial instances in which the subject hires the photographer to make an image that is pleasing to the subject—weddings, graduation photographs, department-store portraits—are ethically unproblematic, as in such situations it is understood that the photographer will use her technical expertise to render an image that is flattering in exchange for a certain sum.

Matters are more complicated, however, in contexts where the portraitist has not been hired by the subject, and is expected to make an image that is interpretive. Examples of this sort include images by a diverse range of photographers including Diane Arbus, Richard Avedon, Annie Leibovitz, Robert Mapplethorpe, and Alfred Stieglitz.

A sustained investigation of the ethical dimensions of such portraiture occurs in Arthur Danto's essay "The Naked Truth." Danto's discussion begins with the observation that it is an important aspect of being human that we care about how we appear to others. Unlike non-human animals, with the onset of adolescence, human beings normally become highly conscious of the image they project to those they encounter. Given the centrality of such concern, Danto suggests that we ought to have a right to control over our appearance, a right that can be thought of as akin to our right to control over our bodies. In the same way that it is wrong to do violence to the body of another (including medical procedures absent informed consent) it is arguably wrong to do violence to the image of another.

And since the interpretive portraitist has the power to present via his photographs an image of the subject that is in conflict with the image that that subject desires to project, an ethically problematic situation arises.

Danto illustrates his claim by discussing two portraits of the Warhol-orbit transvestite Candy Darling, one made by Richard Avedon and the other by Peter Hujar. Candy Darling desired to project the image of a glamourous, female, Hollywood film star, notwithstanding her biological maleness. To do so she dressed in the attire, arranged her hair, and exhibited body language and patterns of speech evocative of Lana Turner or Kim Novak. However, when Avedon invited Warhol and members of the Factory to his studio for a group portrait he apparently asked Candy Darling (and several others) to disrobe, so that in the portrait Candy Darling is naked—her penis fully in view—thus presenting an image of her radically at odds with the one she desired to project. Hujar's portrait, by way of contrast, made in a hospital room in the period before Candy Darling's death, shows his subject fully in character, playing out the role of a participant in a glamourous death. Danto is highly critical of Avedon for his "morally bruising" treatment of Candy Darling's desired image, and praises Hujar for having "submerged his artistic will to that of the subject."

The plausibility of Danto's ethical judgment hinges on whether it is desirable to construe the role of the interpretive portraitist so that she is always constrained by a respect for the desired self-image of her subject. While in many instances we may laud a portraitist for submerging her artistic will in this way (certainly this is the case with Hujar's portrait of Candy Darling), there are at least as many instances imaginable in which we feel that the subject's desired self-image is problematic in some respect (inappropriate, vain, inflated, etc.), and that the portraitist is doing all parties involved a favor by violating it. An example might be the portrait made by Diane Arbus of Norman Mailer (*Author Norman Mailer in His Brooklyn Home*, 1963). At the time she made the portrait, Mailer's public image as the embodiment of virile manliness was at its peak, and yet Arbus produced an image that suggests Mailer is physically underendowed. It is arguable that such treatment, notwithstanding the "moral bruising" of Mailer's image it perhaps involved, was appropriate at that time. Given this possibility, in order to complete his examination of the moral structure of such images, Danto will need to provide some guidance regarding when—and when not—it is appropriate for the portraitist to impose her artistic will.

A related debate arose with the publication of a series of photographs taken by Diane Arbus in the early 1970s of residents of homes for the mentally handicapped (Diane Arbus, *Untitled*, Aperture, 1995). In an article published in the *New York Observer*, the photography critic A.D. Coleman harshly condemned Arbus's daughter Doon for allowing such publication. His central claim was that such images constitute "a fundamental violation of human rights," presumably because they project images of subjects who could not have provided the kind of informed consent in the use of their images that Danto's position apparently requires.

In her essay "Aristocrats," Janet Malcolm takes a much more positive attitude towards the Arbus publication. She argues that the subjects are portrayed in a very positive light, reflecting Arbus's attitude that those born with their traumas are society's true aristocrats—they have (in Arbus's words) "already passed their test in life." As well, Malcolm suggests that the images can benefit current residents of homes for the mentally handicapped by presenting images that convey such nobility. These positive consequences, Malcolm seems to suggest, override any concerns we should have about violations of individual rights.

It is difficult—perhaps impossible—to resolve the debate between Coleman and Malcolm. They emphasize different axioms of ethical thinking, axioms that are inherently in conflict. Coleman places a premium on concerns about violations of human rights, concerns that are not lessened by observing that such violations can have positive consequences. Malcolm, by way of contrast, is apparently willing to forgo concerns about human rights if the benefits of doing so are great enough. The difference between the two positions is thus an instance of the traditional philosophical conflict between deontological and teleological approaches to ethics.

Street Photography

The street-photography context involves a photographer making non-photojournalistic images of human subjects in public locations typically without their permission and often without their knowledge. Classic examples of this sort include images by Bill Brandt, Manuel Álvarez Bravo, Henri Cartier-Bresson, Robert Frank, Helen Levitt, and Garry Winogrand.

The legal status of such activity is clear. The general rule is that in the United States photographers are free to publish images of any person who was located in a public venue, whereas in Quebec and parts of Europe the subject's consent must be obtained before an image is circulated.

The ethical dimensions are less clear and have not been discussed in a systematic way. However, it is likely that many of the issues Danto raises in his discussion of portraiture apply in this context as well. If we assume that persons have a right to control over their appearance in the same way that they have a right to control over their bodies, then it follows that a subject's informed consent should be obtained before their image is published. Informed consent embodies two requirements: (i) the subject must be told how their image will be used and, (ii) the subject must understand the possible consequences of such use. However, placing the burden of obtaining such informed consent on a street photographer would render the activity practically impossible. For one thing, such photography often takes place in crowded and fast-moving public spaces, making the apprehension of individuals to sign consent forms impossible. And even if such consent could be obtained, it is unlikely that it would be obtained with the subject's full understanding of the possible consequences of the publication of the image (often even the photographer is unaware of these).

Thus if we take Danto's concerns seriously it may be that street photography is intrinsically unethical. Many will resist this conclusion, objecting that there must be something wrong with an argument that labels unethical many of the best photographic collections of the twentieth century, including Robert Frank's *The Americans*, and Henri Cartier-Bresson's *The Decisive Moment*. The matter remains unresolved and is ripe for sustained investigation.

Documentary Photography

Much like street photography, documentary photography captures images of individuals often, but not always, without their consent. Further, these images are presented as being objective, speaking to some higher "truth" that justifies the use of individuals' images, often rendering those portrayed as anonymous, as in Dorothea Lange's famous *Migrant Mother, Nipomo, California*, 1936. While photographing a person on the street presents little opportunity to identify that individual, Lange clearly was capable of identifying her subject and in fact the title contains the specifics of the place in which the photograph was made, raising the inevitable question of manipulation of the subject in an attempt to structure a more dramatic emotional reaction to the image. Likewise, August Sander's portraits of German "types," which in order to create a social document purposefully avoided allowing individual identity, are often cited as ethically ill-conceived, while simultaneously admired as striking and important photographs.

The rapid rise of social documentary photography with the Works Progress Administration and Farm Security Administration and the illustrated magazines that promulgated these images, such as *Life* or *Look*, combined to produce questions about the ethical behavior of the photographers. A famous example was that of Arthur Rothstein, who was accused of faking his striking image of a skull baking in the wasteland of the Dust Bowl, and stage-directing a shot of a farmer walking through a dust storm with his young children. Rothstein admitted to moving the skull and framing pictures to delete or include points of reference in order to make a more dramatic shot, a common practice in documentary image-making, yet the controversy around this incident seemed to arise more from a clash of political ideologies rather than photographic ones, a not uncommon occurrence. Also of concern was the government's goal of obtaining images to promote social programs, leading some to denounce the entire WPA/FSA project as propaganda.

SCOTT WALDEN

See also: **Adams, Eddie; Alvarez Bravo, Manuel; Arbus, Diane; Brandt, Bill; Capa, Robert; Cartier-Bresson, Henri; Censorship; Digital Photography; Documentary Photography; Farm Security Administration; Frank, Robert; Heartfield, John; Höch, Hannah; Image Theory: Ideology; Klein, William; Lange, Dorothea; Leibovitz, Annie; Levitt, Helen; Magnum Photos; Nude Photography; Portraiture; Propaganda; Rothstein, Arthur; Sander, August; Sontag, Susan; Street Photography; War Photography; Winogrand, Garry; Works Progress Administration**

Further Reading

Coleman, A.D., "Why I'm Saying No to This New Arbus Book." *New York Observer*.

Levinson, Jerrold, ed. *Aesthetics and Ethics: Essays at the Intersection*. Cambridge, MA: Cambridge University Press, 1998.

Malcolm, Janet. "Aristocrats," in *Diana and Nikon: Essays on Photography*. New York: Aperture, 1997.

Savedoff, Barbara. *Transforming Images: How Photography Complicates the Picture*. Ithaca: Cornell University Press, 2000.

Sontag, Susan. *On Photography*. New York: Doubleday, Anchor Books, 1989.

Sontag, Susan. *Regarding the Pain of Others*. New York: Farrar, Straus, and Giroux, 2003.

PHOTOGRAPHY IN EUROPE: AN OVERVIEW

As the birthplace of photography in 1939, Europe has had the medium's longest development and many of its most significant achievements. In the twentieth century, however, an overriding characteristic of photography was that it had become a true worldwide phenomenon. Yet in many spheres, European photography was innovative and continued to lead the world. The period between the two world wars was perhaps the most fertile in photographic history, in experimental fine arts photography, in the development of equipment and other technical advances, as well as in popular forms, particularly the use of propaganda and the development of the illustrated press. Yet during other eras, Europe lost ground. In the manufacture of equipment, the center in the postwar era shifted to Japan and the United States; in scientific advances the United States, though the Eastman Kodak and Polaroid Companies predominated.

The individual countries of Europe each have their unique histories, and regional histories can also be traced. Photography in Europe overall has become a true topic along with the development of contemporary art photography in the last three decades of the century. And even within the realms of contemporary photography, there are very various, different, and equal tendencies, and it would be extremely foolish for example, to reject *libre expression* photography in the name of documentary photography or vice versa.

The most important and erudite essay on photography in Europe was written in the first issue of the magazine *European Photography* (1980) by Jean-Claude Lemagny, curator of contemporary photography at the Bibliothèque nationale de France in Paris. He introduced a model of an aesthetic clock that served as a means for an original as well as conclusive analysis of photography. It was a proposal for the classification of the contemporary tendencies in the medium of photography with great attention to the survey of photography as a whole and thereby tried to explain the different, interrelated processes without neglecting their differences and correlations. In 1991, he did an update and took a second look at his clock.

In his first classification of creative photography in Europe, he started with 236 extremely varied pictures in slide form and laid them out in a circle. He let himself be guided solely by the visual relations that spontaneously developed among the pictures without assigning them a definite place a priori. He noticed that the main points of the circle could be characterized by a few fundamental approaches toward photography. At 12 o'clock stood the conceptual picture, the photo as pure idea; at 6 o'clock, the photo as material object, as chemical-physical matter; at 3 o'clock, the photo as relation to external reality, as reportage; and at 9 o'clock, the photo as relation to inner reality, as surrealism—including, of course, all the transitions between the hours.

If we use this model for the classification of photography in Europe at the end of the century, what would be seen?

What was most conspicuous to Lemagny was the significance of the 9 o'clock pole: photography as a picture of the internal world, as staging. It is undisputed today that photography simultaneously can be a medium for projecting an idea and a medium for recording reality, and the shock generated by this insight has sent a wave along the entire circle.

At the 12-o'clock pole, the significance of photography as an instrument of the conceptual artist has weakened: the mighty impulse from 9 o'clock has covered this pole and almost strives to unite itself with the photo as pure representation (3 o'clock). It is this powerful drive that unites the internal picture (9 o'clock) with photography as social criticism, together with theoretical reflection (Victor Burgin) and post-modern practice. It is currently in the process of overcoming the contradictions between the subjectivity of the artist as an intellectual on the one hand and his duty as an observer of social conditions and their inadequacies on the other.

At 6 o'clock the tendency toward an abstract, geometrizing photography has disappeared in favor of an intensive and multiform search for the substance of photography, for its means of expression: that which Lemagny called the "resurrection of the flesh," in turn driven by the "return of the gods" coming from 9 o'clock and its "theatre of reality."

The pure reportage or photojournalism at 3 o'clock does not seem to have reawakened. Interest in it has further declined in favor of a reflection upon society that comes from the "north" and a formalistic (in a positive sense) attribute that comes from the "south" and is expressed in the pictures of Joseph Koudelka or in documentary commissions (François Hers's DATAR-projects in France).

Thus, according to the most recent state of affairs, the 9 o'clock pole has proven to be the shining victor. Its protagonists were Paul de Nooijer and the Dutch School and elsewhere (in France, Georges Rousse and Bernard Faucon) have become numerous. By way of the intermediate stages of social conception in photography (as the team of Magnum Photos) this pole tends almost to supersede traditional reportage. And by way of the exploration of the material possibilities of photographic production, the movement leads to the "direct" photograph. For no thinking photographer today forgets—regardless of how strongly he may reject any subsequent manipulation of the picture—that the print which he produces is nothing other than the sum of its tactile value.

All these movements first take form and make sense in the long view. We should always remember that contemporary art—in contrast to science—does not advance more quickly than the arts of the past. We notice that from 1930 to 1950 the central pole lay approximately at 3 o'clock (Brassaï, Henri Cartier-Bresson), while today it is located on the opposite side (at 9 o'clock). And that in the 1970s, the liveliest points were likewise opposite each other: 12 o'clock (conceptual artists, Christian Boltanski) and 6 o'clock (Pierre Cordier, Jean-Pierre Sudre). The 9 o'clock pole stood at the beginning of its ascent: Michael Szulc Krzyzanowski and others were still lonely exceptions. And a certain dynamic definitely emanated from the 3 o'clock pole: Gilles Caron, Gilles Peress, Carl De Keyzer, David Hurn, Martin Parr, and many others. The dynamic proceeded "south" (toward 6 o'clock) with William Klein, and "north" (toward 12 o'clock) with Robert Frank, who finally tipped the balance.

Studying the contemporary photography you can conclude that both—two major currents—the "southern" and the "northern" supremacies today.

Photographers such as Suzanne Lafont, Craigie Horsfield, Dirk Braeckman, Pentti Sammallahti, Sophie Calle, Thomas Struth, Andreas Gursky, Anselm Kiefer, David Hockney, Thomas Ruff, Joan Fontcuberta, Andreas Müller-Pohle, Annette Messager, Peter Fischli and David Weiss, Wolfgang Tillmans, Bernard Faucon, Rineke Dijkstra, Pierre et Gilles are to be the truly great artists of our time, representing the United Kingdom, Germany, Belgium, the Netherlands, France, Spain, and Finland.

But more than in other art forms, the subversive and revolutionary strength of photography lies in the muteness of the forms, and the conceptual photography of the 1970s lost significance to the extent that it failed to pose the relevant questions and denied the material qualities of the work, because the true artist's only problems are technical problems.

As for the future, it appears that it lies at 6 o'clock, in a photography that is supported by the objective reality of its material forms, after having forgotten for a moment that in art there are only material forms. But the philosophical point of view (12 o'clock) is also lively. At first sight philosophy and photography appear to be closely linked, until one checks which philosophers have written an essay on the topic. Apart from the major exceptions of Roland Barthes and Walter Benjamin, hardly any have. This is quite astonishing, but then again it is not. It is not, because philosophy reflects; it is a re-view that looks back at what has occurred, and photography is too recent an event already to be part of the question of the essence of humankind. This is because photography displays a similar ambiguity to philosophy. Both show something and are therefore knowing, but also put a question and are therefore unknowing. In the Merleau-Ponty vein, philosophy is an unknowing knowing. And ambiguity is a central element of philosophy. This was formulated somewhat more emphatically by Samuel Ijsseling, when he sought to define philosophy in two opposing statements:

> Philosophy is a body of well-founded affirmations and justifiable denials which altogether display a certain coherence; it is in other words a "science." Philosophy is a body of questions which again and again question what has already been stated (the entirety of affirmations and denials); this means it is an un-knowing.

Photography is equally ambiguous. It shows something, a fragment of reality framed by the camera or in the darkroom which, considering the objectivity of the process, can lay significant claim to factual knowledge. Each one also asks a question: what is the reality-value of an image? And how is the objective de-objectified by the subjectivity of the maker and the viewer, augmented by the contextual influences on both? This ambiguity has been called the "paradox of photography." Could it be more philosophical? It is Barthes in particular who opposes the "doxa." The "doxa" is the view that derives its strength from power in the broadest sense of the word: public opinion, the view of the silent majority, the narrow-minded view, everything that is so-called "natural," the violence of prejudice, that which one maintains *is* so because it *is* so. The metaphorical sense of the word "para" in Greek is "against." *Para tein doxan* means "against expectations." This last word at the same time makes the link with psychology, which assumes that our perception is determined by expectation. The paradox starts us thinking, in order to adjust our expectation to the actual situation. If not we are "dogmatic," a word with the same stem as "doxa," which refers to the unwillingness to change one's opinion. Barthes argues for paradoxical thinking. Photography states this paradox most acutely. Every photo is a "doxa": it is reality the way it is, in many cases even with demonstrative force.

However, every photo is a paradox: it is a picture of reality, or in other words, it is a way of seeing. And that should not be taken too simply, as no more than a relativization by accentuating the fact that it is a way of looking, coupled with the conviction that it actually is reality. Its "image-dom" implies that it is not reality, that it is a way of representation, that in our pan-photographic culture we have learnt that this reality as such cannot say anything with any certainty that we do not know from other sources of information, such as direct observation or verbal explanation.

A philosophy of European photography is part of cultural philosophy when photography is considered as a mass-culture phenomenon, and part of art philosophy when "art photography" is concerned. In my opinion it would at this point be wrong to make a major distinction, on the basis of either philosophy or photography. Art philosophy may be considered part of cultural philosophy. In the case of photography one might ask oneself whether the desire to be art is important. Perhaps photography should just be photography. In addition to this there is the postmodern phenomenon of the blurring boundaries between art and mass culture. The latter is becoming the object of or source of inspiration for the former. And in its outdated modernism art is becoming kitsch.

This is why a philosophy of the history of photography comes down to asking the classic questions: "What are its characteristics? How can one interpret it? What is its value? How does it function and within which systems? How is meaning produced? All this makes a contribution to the fundamental philosophical question: what is photography?"

In Europe we see that the ambivalence between photography's reference to reality and its openness for the imaginary is especially interesting for artists who are investigating how place and the perception of it can be represented. Contemporary photographers are mainly concerned with conceptual reflections on the seamless transition between the presentation and the representation of a place, the documentation of an active, artistic re-arrangement of a location or the construction of space, using diverse media and thus crossing the border of two-dimensional photography.

The field of hybrid rhetoric paradoxically unites the diverse European countries that continue to enjoy the differences of their collective experience. Leaving the 1990s, when "visualism" was at stake, the contemporary photographic practices of Nordic and Eastern countries draw closer to the South and Western aspiration to transgress medium-bound, traditional art photography and move toward critical reflections.

Perhaps we can end with a statement of the man who offers us the red thread in our overview, Jean-Claude Lemagny: "It is certainly clear that in the eternal struggle between reality and the idea of it that one constructs, reality must conquer the idea and only that which Zarathustra calls 'the sense of the earth' deserves to triumph."

Johan Swinnen

See also: **Barthes, Roland; Boltanski, Christian; Brassaï; Calle, Sophie; Cartier-Bresson, Henri; Conceptual Photography; Dijkstra, Rineke; et Gilles, Pierre; Faucon, Bernard; Fischli, Peter and Weiss, David; Frank, Robert; Gursky, Andreas; Hers, Françios; History of Photography: Interwar Years; Klein, William; Koudelka, Joseph; Magnum Photos; Messager, Annette; Museums: Europe; Parr, Martin; Peress, Gilles; Propaganda; Ruff, Thomas; Struth, Thomas; Tillmans, Wolfgang**

FREDERICK H. EVANS

British

Known for his extraordinary interior photographs of churches and portraiture, Frederick Henry Evans went against the prevailing winds of his era in photography to produce startling modern, historically important photographs at the turn of the nineteenth to the twentieth centuries. Despite his international renown in midlife, Evans's early years are largely unknown. Born in 1853, Evans was self-educated, and in the 1870s, he was a bank clerk. In his early 20s, because of poor health, he visited Boston and lived with his aunt for a year. Health was also the reason for visiting England's Lake District, where the scenery made a deep impression.

In keeping with the scientific era, Evans bought a microscope in the 1880s, and then took up photography to record the images. The Royal Photographic Society, in 1887, awarded him a medal for his photomicrographs of shells. In the 1880s, he left clerking and became a partner, and later, sole owner of a London bookstore. The book shop attracted a remarkable clientele, which included George Bernard Shaw whose writing on Ibsen Evans recommended to appropriate customers. In addition to a considerable literary background, Evans also acquired a connoisseur's appreciation of art, and he collected drawings, prints, and Japanese artifacts. Evans recognized the artistic talent of the 18-year-old Aubrey Beardsley, a frequent browser in the store, and it was Evans who recommended this young artist to the publisher J. M. Dent.

Evans's photography included portraiture, and Beardsley proved one of his best subjects in a photograph showing him in profile, his long hands supporting his chin. The pose of this young artist of the Decadence referred to a gargoyle on Notre Dame de Paris.

While running his unusual bookstore, Evans pursued photography in his spare time, and in 1894, he photographed York Minster, where he would return in 1902 to make *In Sure and Certain Hope*, whose title comes from The Book of Common Prayer.

Typically, Evans would visit a cathedral town for days so he could experience the sacred building under many different conditions. If necessary to achieve the right effect, he would pressure church officials to remove furniture and even gas lighting fixtures.

He usually used a 4 × 5-inch camera and occasionally an 8 × 10 camera. Double-coated Cristoid films were used so that shadows and highlights would be recorded on fast and slow emulsions to assure maximum detail. A battery of lenses up to 19 inches in focal length was used to get the desired coverage and perspective. Typically, exposures ranged from several seconds to hours at f/32. The negatives were always printed on platinum paper, which yielded an especially subtle range of middle tones.

Health forced Evans to retire from book selling, and he moved to Epping in 1898, but this allowed him to pursue photography full time. In 1892, some photographers seceded from the London Photographic Society (after 1894, The Royal Photographic Society of Great Britain) and formed the Linked Ring, a select international group open to women and featuring the annual Photographic Salon. Evans was invited to join the Linked Ring in 1900, where he was a leading advocate for the Purist faction as opposed to the Pictorialists or Impressionists, who advocated using manipulative techniques.

As designer and installer of the Linked Ring's Photographic Salon exhibitions at the Dudley Gallery in London from 1902–1905, Evans showed skill and imagination in transforming a somber space and usual hanging methods into a well lit area with photographs arranged to emphasize visual statements. These ideas spread to the Little Galleries of the Photo-Secession. Evans corresponded extensively with Alfred Stieglitz, leader of the Photo-Secession in New York and publisher of *Camera Work*, where Evans's work and ideas were well represented.

Without training in traditional art media, Evans could not practice the manipulative techniques others used to emulate fine art. Consequently, he championed straight or pure photography and wrote frequently in journals such as *Amateur Photographer* and *Photography*, where he championed his beliefs about photographic art. While praising the gum bichromate works by Robert Demachy and other outstanding artists using manipulative techniques, he did not wish to call such images photography. Evans believed photography could achieve the level of art through the medium's limitations rather than with hybrid imitations. While he sometimes resorted to retouching and other corrective measures, he staunchly maintained there should be no tampering with the negative or print.

Such perfectionism was not an end in itself, and Evans aimed for what he called "cathedral picture-making" in which the result would give the viewer an emotional experience equivalent to what might be felt at the actual site. He pursued this aesthetic in all aspects of his photography, including landscapes where trees were photographed for their architectural resemblances. This idea of art through a limited medium was extended to his other passion, the pianola, and though critics derided him, Shaw, another pianola enthusiast, defended him.

Evans was influenced by J. M. W. Turner's architectural watercolors, as well as by Odilon Redon's contemporary Symbolist prints, which he collected. In addition, he steeped himself in the theology of correspondences of the eighteenth century mystic Emanuel Swedenborg as interpreted in the writings of James John Garth Wilkinson. The metaphoric title, *A Sea of Steps* (1903), showing the stone, wave-like steps to the Wells Cathedral Chapter House, would seem to suggest Evans's interest in Swedenborgian thinking as well as in the Symbolist movement.

The purist approach also suggests influences from critic John Ruskin's emphasis on depicting facts and those Pre-Raphaelites who aimed for "photographic" detail. Evans was not a social activist like William Morris, though he shared the Arts and Crafts leader's views on work, and in 1896, he photographed Morris's Kelmscott Manor.

Evans reached a wider audience when *Country Life* published his work on English churches in 1904–1905. This magazine then offered him an open commission, so he chose to photograph mostly chateaux and small churches in France from 1906–1907. Around World War I, Evans concentrated on photographing works of art, which were then privately published in platinotype editions. Never one to compromise, he could not accept silver-based papers, which were replacing platinum paper. So, he stopped photographing.

When he died in London on 24 June 1943, few were familiar with his achievements. The Royal Photographic Society reawakened interest in his work through a memorial exhibition in 1944.

John Fuller

See also: **Architectural Photography; Coburn, Alvin Langdon; History of Photography: Nineteenth-Century Foundations; Linked Ring; Portraiture; Royal Photographic Society; Stieglitz, Alfred**

Biography

Born 26 June 1853. Little known of his early years, but in 1870s was a clerk in a London clearing house. Around 1873, went to Boston for a year because of health. Purchased camera in 1883, made photomicrographs. Bookstore operator in London in 1880s. Became friends with George Bernard Shaw, helped launch Aubrey Beardsley's career. Photographed cathedrals, landscapes, and portraits. Retired from bookstore in 1898, and moved to Epping. Elected to Linked Ring in 1900, from 1902–1905 in charge of London Photographic Salon. Featured in *Camera Work* 4 (October 1903). Photographed English parish churches for *Country Life*, 1905. In 1906–1907 photographed French chateaux and churches for *Country Life*. Joined London Secession, 1908. Landscapes reproduced in George Meredith Memorial Edition, 19 09–1911. Membership in the London Salon Club, 1910. Interior photographs of Westminster Abbey for *Country Life*, 1911. From 1912–1919, privately published editions of platinum prints of artist's works. Made Honorary Fellow of The Royal Photographic Society, 1928. Died 24 June 1943.

Individual Exhibitions

1899 Architectural Club, Boston, Massachusetts
1900 Royal Photographic Society, London, England
1904 Camera Club, London, England
1913 Amateur Photographer's "Little Gallery," London, England
1917 Hampshire House, London, England
1919 Westminster Abbey photographs at Royal Photographic Society, London, England
1922 Royal Photographic Society, London, England
1932 Photographic Society, London, England
1933 Manchester Amateur Photographic Society, Manchester, England
1944 *Memorial Exhibition*; Royal Photographic Society, London, England

Group Exhibitions

1890 Royal Photographic Society Annual Exhibition, London, England
1891 *At Home Portraits*; The Photographic Society, London, England
1892 *Invitation Exhibition*; Camera Club, London, England
1894 Photographic Salon, London, England
1899 American Institute, New York, New York
1901 London Photographic Salon, London, England
1903 F. Holland Day Studio, Boston, Massachusetts
1906 Little Galleries of the Photo-Secession, New York, New York
1910 *International Exhibition of Pictorial Photography*; Albright Gallery, Buffalo, New York

Selected Works

Kelmscott Manor: Attics, c. 1897
Portrait of Alvin Langdon Coburn in Eastern Costume, 1901
In Sure and Certain Hope, York Minster, 1902
A Sea of Steps, Wells Cathedral: Stairs to Chapter House, 1903
Stairs to St. Catherine's Well, Winchelsea, c. 1905
A Fifteenth Century Doorway, Ely, 1903

Further Reading

Camera Work: A Photographic Quarterly, 1903–1917. Reprint, New York: Kraus Reprints, 1969.

Fuller, John. "Frederick H. Evans as Late Victorian." *Afterimage* vol. 4, no. 4 (October 1976): 6–7, 18.

Hammond, Anne. *Frederick H. Evans: Selected Texts and Bibliography*. Boston: G. K. Hall, 1992.

Hammond, Anne. "Frederick Evans—The Spiritual Harmonies of Architecture." In *British Photography in the Nineteenth Century*. Edited by Mike Weaver. New York and Cambridge: Cambridge University Press, 1989.

Hammond, Anne. "Frederick Evans's Parish Churches for Country Life." *History of Photography* vol. 16, no. 1 (Spring 1992): 9–17.

Naef, Weston J. *The Collection of Alfred Stieglitz*. New York: Viking Press, 1978.

Newhall, Beaumont. *Frederick H. Evans*. Millerton, NY: Aperture, 1973.

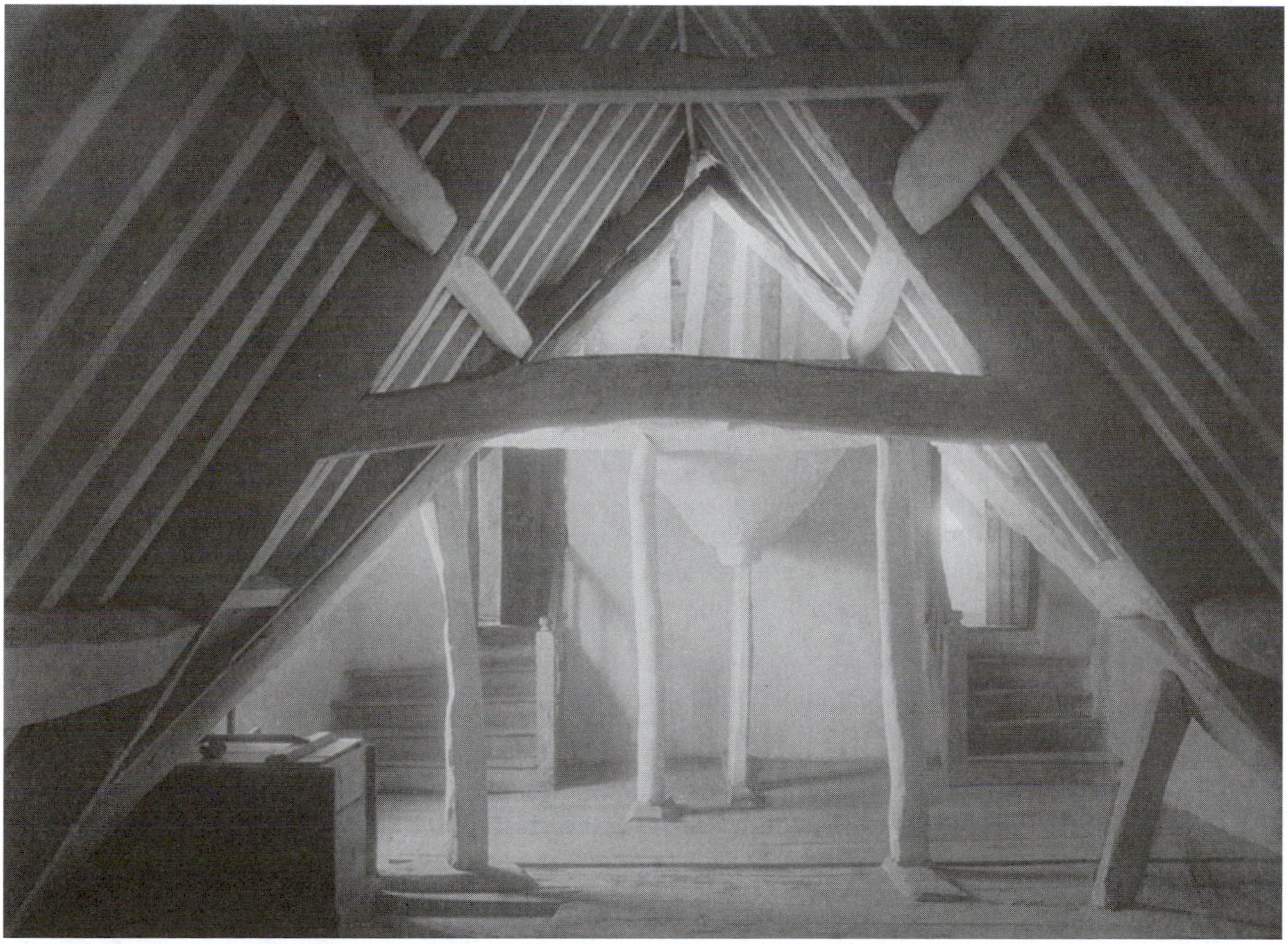

Frederick H. Evans, Kelmscott Manor: Attics, ca. 1897, platinum print, 15.6 × 20.2 cm, Museum Purchase: ex-collection Gordon Conn.
[*Photograph courtesy of George Eastman House, permission supplied by Janet Stenner*]

WALKER EVANS

American

Walker Evans's photographs helped define, document, (and sometimes invent) both the cultural and physical landscape of America in the twentieth century. More than any other photographer before him, Evans relished the anonymity of his camera and its reflective, detached quality, and his subjects, from tenant farmers in Alabama to domestic exteriors throughout America, are simply allowed to exist as themselves, never sentimentalized or celebrated. Walker Evans was as exacting and meticulous as the images he documented, calling his photographs "reflective rather than tendentious and, in a certain way, disinterested" (Hill 1982, 151). Though he worked independently for magazines such as *Time* and *Fortune*, Evans is probably best known for his collaboration with fellow journalist (and poet/novelist) James Agee in a sprawling documentary of tenant farmers in Alabama, *Let Us Now Praise Famous Men*. Originally ignored in its initial publication in 1941, *Famous Men* was re-discovered in the early 1960s, and heralded as a masterpiece by many critics, and Evans's reputation as a documentary photographer enjoyed a rebirth and re-evaluation that continues to this day.

Though born in St. Louis in 1903, Evans spent much of his boyhood in Toledo, Ohio, Chicago, and New York City because of his father's relocations as an advertising director. Evans's family was fairly affluent, sending young Walker off to Phillips Academy in Andover, Massachusetts. After his graduation in 1922, he enrolled in Williams College, Williamstown, Massachusetts, and began studying literature. His love of writing and literature eventually sent him to Paris, where he studied briefly at the Sorbonne, hoping to become a writer himself.

It wasn't until around 1928 that Evans first began to experiment with photography, taking a few shots with a basic, handheld camera and sharing them with his friends. But it was his love of literature (especially European modernists like Pound, Joyce, and T.S. Eliot) that inspired Evans's early photographs and theories about art. His first published photographs of the Brooklyn Bridge (for Hart Crane's epic poem *The Bridge*) were mere shapes, close-ups of the latticework and structure in heavy definition, like the disjointed, cubist canvases of Pablo Picasso.

Around this time, Evans became interested in documentary photography, spending his days on the streets of New York snapping pictures of its architecture and people. His own style began to emerge as a mixture of realism and objectivism, where the subjects or the images became the central focus of the work, non-dramatic, non-posed, and the author's presence was minimized. His friendship with Lincoln Kirstein, the son of a wealthy Boston socialite, allowed him the opportunity to create his first series of domestic exteriors of Victorian houses throughout New England, which would later become his first solo exhibition at the Museum of Modern Art in 1933, and two years earlier, his first group exhibition at the John Becker Gallery in New York put him in the company of up-and-coming photographers Ralph Steiner and Margaret Bourke-White.

Evans's trip to Havana (to provide pictures for Carleton Beals's book) brought the first of Evans's documentary photographs that would later define his style. Evans's photographs in *The Crime of Cuba* were studies of the people of Havana, of the poor families living on the streets, or the ubiquitous beggars fanning out across the town. But Evans stopped short of making any political statement with his camera, observing the ironies of Cuban life remotely. Unlike other documentary photographers, Evans hungered after the non-posed, non-dramatic, simple subjects. His photographs were observant, anonymous, and sequential studies that fit together rather than individual images that stood on their own, and the Cuba series, published in 1933 gave Evans the exposure that propelled him into his next two jobs, as a staff photographer at *Fortune* magazine, and, perhaps most importantly as a documentary photographer under Roy Stryker in the Resettlement Administration (later the Farm Security Administration [FSA]).

But Evans's best-known photographs were most likely taken during a break in his duties with the Resettlement Administration (RA) during a brief stay in Hale County, Alabama, with novelist and friend James Agee. Agee had initially been commissioned by *Fortune* magazine in 1936 to do an article on the plight of the Southern tenant farmer and was assigned a staff photographer. He insisted that *Fortune* get him Evans, and the publishers negotiated a deal wherein Evans would be able to leave the RA, but his photographs would still be in the public domain. There may not have been a more unlikely partnership: Agee was a romantic, obsessed with the superficiality of documenting lives plainly with himself in-frame; Evans was clinically out-of-frame, an anonymous, bodiless eye, recording and observing. The resulting "article" was both too long and too confusing to be anything *Fortune* could publish, and eventually, Agee and Evans published it as a phototext (along the lines of Caldwell and Bourke-White's *You Have Seen Their Faces*).

When *Let Us Now Praise Famous Men* was published in 1941, Walker Evans's 31 photographs were the preliminary "book" to Agee's. The photographs and words were co-equal representations and commentary on the lives of the farmers they lived with. The book was revolutionary, a massive indictment against documentary efforts to represent any life absolutely, and also a re-appropriation of the genre of photo-text itself. But America's period of intense introspection was passing, and Evans and Agee's angry book garnered little comment; it would not be until nearly 20 years later that *Let Us Now Praise Famous Men* would receive the proper attention it deserved. What makes Evans's photographs in *Famous Men* so powerful is their unflinching and clinical attachment to detail and subject. When pictures were framed wrong or focused incorrectly, Evans simply cut out the negatives, physically cropping and editing his pictures to a more faithful representation of what he observed and wished to convey.

Unlike many of the photographers working for the RA, Evans's pictures were lucid, candid; the opposite of the propaganda he was hired to produce. Though the RA was peppered with stellar photographers, some of whom would go on to have important careers, Evans's pictures are the most well-known and the most memorable. They quickly became icons of the period he was documenting and have remained epitomes of both 1930s' photography as well as of the powerfully influential notion that the photographer can be both vitally engaged yet removed and anonymous that results in a sort of transcendence of both subject matter and maker.

His style of anonymity allowed Evans the opportunity to photograph truly anonymous subjects, to observe and reproduce clear images without the burden of heavy commentary and superficial drama that he felt distracted the viewer from the actual topic. This is best demonstrated in Evans's next project after being released from the RA, a portrait series of New York City subway riders. Evans concealed his camera under his coat to snap these pictures in an extreme example of his desire for anonymity, where Evans acted virtually as a voyeur to attempt more realistic, unrehearsed pictures. Indeed, these photographs have a random, detached quality, creating a connection between anonymous photographer and subject.

The simplicity of Evans's subjects and style belies a very complex and focused eye; he attempted to translate what he knew about literature, modern art, and popular culture into a visual reflection. If one is amazed by the clearness of Evans's eye, it must also be considered that such clarity only deepens the difficulty of interpretation. Above all else, Walker Evans did not want his photographs to tell stories, follow moods, and create drama: they resist simple assimilation and understanding. Recently, Evans's pictures of signs and advertisements have come into critical scrutiny, and through them, one can glean not only the documentation of America and its popular culture, but also a real and palpable borrowing of such modern art techniques as collage, found art, and *trompe l'oeil*. His vision and style, crystal clear, uncompromising, makes his photographs some of the most recognizable in the history of American twentieth century photography, and the arbiter and documenter of a peculiarly introspective American decade, the 1930s.

Andy Crank

See also: **Bourke-White, Margaret; Documentary Photography; Farm Security Administration; History of Photography: Interwar Years; Museum of Modern Art; Photography in the United States: South; Propaganda; Representation and Gender**

Biography

Born in St. Louis, Missouri, 3 November 1903. Attends Phillips Academy in Andover, Massachusetts, graduating 1922, and Williams College, Williamstown, Massachusetts for a year. First photographs appear in Hart Crane's *The Bridge*, 1930; Begins documentation of nineteenth century Victorian houses, 1930; Havana pictures published in Carlton Beals's *The Crime of Cuba*, 1933; becomes staff photographer at *Fortune* magazine, 1934; appointed to photograph rural America with the Resettlement Administration (Farm Security Administration), 1935; photographs antebellum architecture; collaborates with author James Agee in Alabama for eventual book, *Let Us Now Praise Famous Men*, 1936; John Simon Guggenheim Memorial Fellowship, 1940; becomes critic-reviewer for *Time* magazine, 1943–1945; promoted to Special Photographic Editor at *Fortune*, 1948–1965; Elected Member of Century Association, 1954; Second Guggenheim Fellowship, 1959; Professor at Yale University's School of Art and Architecture, 1965–1972; Elected fellow in American Academy of Arts and Letters, 1968; Artist in Residence at Dartmouth College, 1972–1973; Distinguished Service Award from the American Academy Institute, 1974; Dies in New Haven, Connecticut, 10 April 1975.

Selected Individual Exhibitions

1933 *Walker Evans: Photographs of Nineteenth-Century Houses*; Museum of Modern Art, New York, New York
1935 *Photographs of African Negro Art by Walker Evans*; Museum of Modern Art, New York, New York, and traveling
1938 *Walker Evans: American Photographs*; Museum of Modern Art, New York, New York
1947 *Walker Evans Retrospective*; Art Institute of Chicago, Chicago, Illinois
1966 *Walker Evans Subway*; Museum of Modern Art, New York, New York
1967 *Walker Evans*; Robert Schoelkopf Gallery, New York, New York
1970 *Walker Evans: Painting and Photographs*; The Century Association, New York, New York
1971 *Walker Evans*; Museum of Modern Art, New York, New York, and traveled to Corcoran Gallery, Washington, D.C.; Museum of Modern Art, San Francisco, California; Museum of Fine Arts, St. Petersburg, Florida; City Art Museum, St. Louis, Missouri; University of Michigan Museum of Art, Ann Arbor, Michigan; Art Institute of Chicago, Chicago, Illinois; Museum of Fine Arts, Boston, Massachusetts
1972 *Walker Evans: Forty Years*; Yale University Art Gallery, New Haven, Connecticut
1973 *Walker Evans: Photographs from the "Let Us Now Praise Famous Men" Project*; Michener Galleries, University of Texas, Austin, Texas
1974 *Walker Evans: Vintage Photographs, 1928–1972*; Lunn Gallery/Graphics International, Ltd., Washington, D.C.
1977 *Walker Evans at "Fortune," 1945–1965*; Jewett Arts Center, Wellesley, Massachusetts
1978 *Walker Evans: Lost and Found*; Drink Hall, New York, New York
1981 *Walker Evans Retrospective*; Comfort Gallery, Haverford, Pennsylvania
1985 *The Sunny South: Depression Era Photographs by Walker Evans*; High Museum of Art, Atlanta, Georgia
1990 *Walker Evans: Havana 1933*; PhotoFest, Houston, Texas
1991 *Walker Evans Subways and Streets*; National Gallery of Art, Washington, D.C.
1992 *Walker Evans: An Alabama Record*; J. Paul Getty Museum, Malibu, California
1993 *Walker Evans: Polaroids 1973–1974*; 292 Gallery, New York, New York
1998 *Walker Evans: Simple Secrets*; International Center of Photography Uptown, New York, New York

Selected Group Exhibitions

1931 *Photographs by Three Americans*; John Becker Gallery, New York, New York
1931 *Modern Photographs by Walker Evans and George Platt Lynes*; Julien Levy Gallery, New York, New York
Documentary and Anti-Graphic: Photographs by Manuel Alvarez-Bravo, Henri Cartier-Bresson and Walker Evans; Julien Levy Gallery, New York, New York
1943 *Masters of Photography*; Museum of Modern Art, New York, New York
1951 *Twelve Photographers*; Museum of Modern Art, New York, New York
1955 *Contemporary American Photography*; Museum of Modern Art, New York, New York, and traveling
Farm Security Administration Photography; Brooklyn Museum of Art, Brooklyn, New York
1962 *The Bitter Years, 1935–1941*; Museum of Modern Art, New York, New York
1964 *The Photographer's Eye*; Museum of Modern Art, New York, New York
1965 *Contemporary Art at Yale I*; Yale University Art Gallery, New Haven, Connecticut
1968 *Just Before the War: Urban America from 1935 to 1941, As Seen by Photographers of the Farm Security Administration*; Newport Beach Art Museum, Newport Beach, California
1969 *The Descriptive Condition–Seven Photographers*; Boston University, Boston, Massachusetts
1976 *Photography in America*; Whitney Museum of American Art, New York, New York
1977 *America Observed: Etchings by Edward Hopper, Photographs by Walker Evans*; California Palace of the Legion of Honor, San Francisco, California
1978 *Roy Stryker: The Humane Propagandist*; Photographic Archives, University of Louisville, Kentucky
1979 *Two Classic Documentary Photographers: Marion Post Wolcott and Walker Evans*; Nova Gallery, Vancouver, B. C., Canada
William Carlos Williams and the American Scene, 1920–1940; Whitney Museum of American Art, New York, New York
1981 *Cubism in American Photography, 1910–1950*; Sterling & Francine Clark Art Institute, Williamstown, Massachusetts
1982 *Three Generations: Walker Evans, Robert Frank, Tod Papageorge*; University Art
1983 Galleries, University of New Hampshire, Durham, New Hampshire
1987 *The Machine Age in America, 1918–1941*; Brooklyn Museum of Art, Brooklyn, New York
The Viewer as Voyeur; Whitney Museum of American Art, New York, New York
1991 *Walker Evans and Jane Ninas in New Orleans, 1935–1936*; Historic New Orleans Collections, New Orleans, Louisiana
1997 *Someone Else with My Fingerprints*; David Zwirner Gallery, New York, New York
2001 *About Faces*; C&M Arts, New York, New York

Selected Works

The Crime of Cuba, 1933
American Photographs, 1938; reissued 1962
Let Us Now Praise Famous Men: Three Tenant Families, 1941; reissued 1960
Many Are Called, 1966
Message From the Interior, 1966
First and Last, 1978

Further Reading

Baier, Lesily K. *Walker Evans at* Fortune*, 1945–1965*. Wellesley, MA: Wellesley College Museum, 1977.

Keller, Judith. *Walker Evans: The Getty Museum Collection*. Malibu, CA: J. Paul Getty Museum, 1995.

Maddox, Jerold C. *Walker Evans: Photographs for the Farm Security Administration: 1935–1938*. New York: Da Capo Press, 1973.

Mellow, James R. *Walker Evans*. New York: Basic Books, 1999.

Mora, Gilles. *Walker Evans: Havana 1933*. New York: Pantheon, 1989.

———. Mora, Gilles, and John T. Hill. *Walker Evans: The Hungry Eye*. New York: Harry Abrams, 1993.

Papageorge, Tod. *Walker Evans and Robert Frank: An Essay on Influence*. New Haven: Yale University Art Gallery, 1981.

Rathbone, Belinda. *Walker Evans: A Biography*. New York: Houghton Mifflin, 1995.

Stott, William. *Documentary Expressions and Thirties America*. New York and London: Oxford.

Thompson, Jerry. *The Last Years of Walker Evans*. New York: Thames & Hudson, 1997.

———. Thompson, Jerry. *Walker Evans at Work*. New York: Harper & Row, 1982.

Ward, J. A. *American Silences: The Realism of James Agee, Walker Evans, and Edward Hopper*. Baton Rouge and London: Louisiana State University Press, 1985.

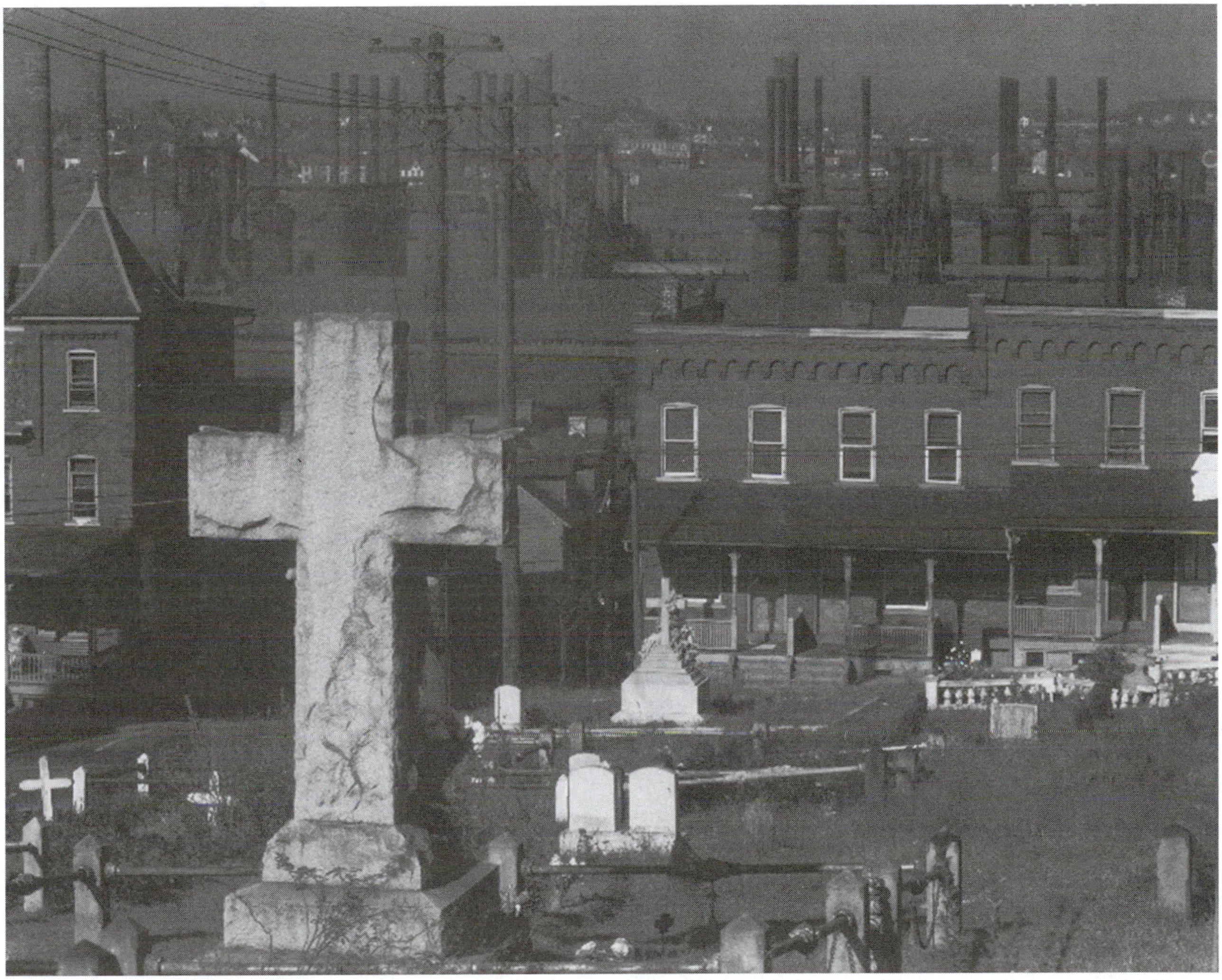

Walker Evans, A Graveyard and Steel Mill in Bethlehem, Pennsylvania, 1935, Gelatin-silver print, 7 ⅞ × 9 ⅝″.
[*Digital Image © The Museum of Modern Art/Licensed by SCALA/Art Resource, New York*]

VALIE EXPORT

Austrian

Valie Export is a leading European figure in the experimental, restless mix of artistic media that characterized late twentieth-century contemporary art practice. She has done drawings, texts, films, video, and performances documented through photographs that explore feminist topics, especially the power relationships between men and women and female sexuality. Binding all of Export's work is a concern with puncturing or deconstructing media representations that shape the viewer's perceptions. Although Export came of age as an artist during the heyday of the *Wiener Aktionismus* (Vienna Actionism) group and Body Art, her status as a woman set her apart from the particular activities of these artists who used their bodies as an extended medium to create transgressive actions meant to question the status quo and shock the public. Arising from the societal upheavals caused by and following World War II, and dealing openly with sex, aggression, and destruction, the Actionists inspired Export to delve into these difficult subjects.

Early in her career Export, rebelling against traditional forms in cinema that she believed were mercenary, helped define the concept of "expanded cinema." Her concept re-examined the processes of shooting, film editing, and projecting film in works featuring numerous screens and installations with mirrors that allowed the illusion of duplication, as in *Abstract Film n°1*, 1967, or *Split Screen Solipsismus* from 1968. The theory of expanded cinema also included interactive works that went beyond passive viewing. Export's *Tapp und Tast Kino* (*Tap and Touch Cinema*) is such a work. A film performance, the artist strolled through the streets of Vienna, her chest covered by a box fitted with curtains. Her frequent artistic partner Peter Wiebel invited passersby to reach through the curtain into the box and touch the artist's breasts, the artist remaining indifferent to men's touches. Export also realized more playful works like *Ping Pong, Ein Film Zum Spielen*. The viewer is invited to play a Ping Pong game in which the opponent is a television screen, emphasizing the split in the reality of contemporary life by presenting both a real and virtual ball and the power relationships between the media (artist-filmmaker) and the consumer (player).

Export's involvement in a wide variety of artistic media can perhaps be explained by her first artistic act in which she took the name by which she is known. Born Waltraud Lehner in Linz, Austria, in 1940, she attended a convent school and then studied at the Textilfachschule (Technical School for Textile Industry) in Vienna. She married, became a mother, divorced, and then completed her studies in 1964, with a specialization in textile design. In 1967, she created her pseudonym, Valie being the diminutive of Waltraud, and Export being an excerpt from the popular Austrian cigarette brand AustriaExport. In taking this pseudonym, Export created a reflection on consumerist ideology and grounded her artistic identity in photography and graphic design. Export prefers that her name be printed in capital letters, emphasizing it as a brand name. In 1970, she created the black-and-white photographic work *Valie Export Smart Export*, where her face is partially hidden by a pack of cigarettes where the AustriaExport logo is replaced with a close-up of her face encircled by the words "*Semper and Ubique, Immer und Uberall*,"—"always and everywhere." She aggressively thrusts the cigarette pack forward toward the viewer, her face frozen into a defiant mask with closed eyes and a lit cigarette between her lips. This appropriation of masculine codes remained at the center of her subsequent works.

Export's impact of photography has been significant in its manifestation as preserving a documentary trace of performances realized in public area. One of her best-known actions, the tattooing of a garter fastener on her thigh in 1970, is known chiefly by its photographic documentation. From her 1969 action *Aktionshose: Gentitalpanik* (*Action Pants: Genital Panic*), for example, there are only a few pictures, posters, and text that remain. This action consisted of walking the aisles in an art movie house wearing pants in which the crotch area had been cut out, exposing her genitals, radically reversing the conventional relationship of the female sex to consumers of movies. During 1968, she created her three *Identitätstransfer* (*Identity transfer*) works, where she presented herself adorned with attributes associated with men, such as a chain bracelet or a chain hanging down an open shirt. The photograph commemorating one of these actions shows her hair ruffled, wearing a leather jacket, tight jeans, and with a gun in one hand. Export plays with posture, spreading her legs so that her sex is obvious, revisiting the codified image of the rebel and proposing a feminist version of male chauvinism. The artist does not play with dressing-up, so cherished by artists like Marcel Duchamp, but presents herself as a woman who assimilates the criteria defining masculinity. In her male garments, masculine posture, and with the ultimate masculine fetish, the gun, as an accessory, she presents her female sex like a weapon in order to explode the cultural taboos about "unladylike" behavior of spreading the legs wide as well as to invoke Freudian theories about fetishism.

From 1972 to 1982, Export conceived perhaps her best-known photographic works, the series *Körperkonfigurationen* (*Body Configuration*) in which she considered the relationships between her body, architectural elements, and geometry. In these images, she lays herself in various configurations out in the urban landscape to both accentuate the architectural space and serve as a constraint to it. In *Aus dem Geometrischen Humanoiden Skizzenbuch der natur* (*From the Geometric Humanoid Sketchbook of Nature*) of 1974 she positions her hand to "hold" the landscape. In these pictures, the body is not always charged with a political message, but suggests its inability to submit to and thus adapt to the architecture, by extension, its inability to submit and adapt to the social and political architecture that shapes society. In 1989, she realized her first digital photographic works, and has continued experimentation with this medium.

THOMAS CYRIL

See also: **Body Art; Feminist Photography; Photography in Germany and Austria; Wiener Aktionismus**

Biography

Born Waltraud Lehner Höllinger, Linz, Austria. Student at Kunstgewerbeschule (School of Decorative Arts) in Textile Department, Linz, 1955–1958. Realizes first paintings and photographic self-portraits: *Metamorphosen der Identität* (*Identity Metamorphose*). Creates name *Valie Export*, 1967; launches "expanded cinema." Founding member Austrian Filmmakers Cooperative; member Wiener Institut für direkte Kunst, founded in Vienna by Günter Brus and Otto Mühl. Awarded prize from City of Vienna for the encouragement of cinematic art, 1969. Signs Women's Art manifesto at the MAGNA exhibition, 1972; conceives and organizes exhibition MAGNA, *Feminismus: Kunst and Kreativität* at the Galerie nächst St. Stephan, Vienna (St. Stephen's Cathedral Gallery). Represents Austria (with Maria Lassng) at the Austrian Pavillion,Venice Biennale, 1980. Appointed professor at the Hochschule der Künste, (Academy of Arts) in Berlin, 1991–1995. Professor of multimedia and performance art at the Kunsthochschule für Medien, (Academy of Media Art), in Cologne, 1995. Oskar Kokoschka Prize, 2000. Living in Vienna and Cologne.

Individual Exhibitions

1971 *Bedeutungsveränderugen*; Gallery Klewan, Vienna, Austria
1975 *VALIE EXPORT, Works from 1968–1975*; Musée d'art moderne de la ville de Paris, Paris, France
1977 *Körpersplitter aus dem hippokratiischen Gesicht der Gegenwart*; Galerie nächst St. Stephan, Vienna, Austria
1980 *Video, Projekte, Fotographien*; Stedelijk Museum, Amsterdam, the Netherlands
VALIE EXPORT; Biennale di Venezia, Pavillon of the Federal Republic of Austria, Venice, Italy
1986 *Body Works*; Eubie Blake Museum, Baltimore, Maryland
1992 *Fotodokumentation: Entwûrfe zu Videoinstallationen und skulpturen der 70er Jahre*; Freie Künstlergruppe, Fribourg, Germany
1993 *Alltagsgeschichten OBJECTIV gesehen Brechtlaus*; Berlin, Germany
1997 *Split Reality: VALIE EXPORT*; Museum moderner Kunst Stiftung Ludwig Wien, 20er Haus, Vienna, Austria
1998 *VALIE EXPORT editionen 1971–1998*; Gallery Olivier Schweden, Munich, Germany
VALIE EXPORT: Werkschau III; Wien Fotogalerie, Vienna, Austria
1999 *Medial Anagrams III*; Museum of Modern Art, New York, New York
VALIE EXPORT, Konzeptuelle Fotographie der 70er Jahre; Gallery Wilma Tolksdorf, Frankfurt, Germany
2000 *VALIE EXPORT, Body Configuration 1972–1976*; Klemens Gasser & Tanja Grunert, Inc., New York, New York
2001 *Ob/De+Con(Struction)*; Santa Monica Museum of Art, Santa Monica, California
VALIE EXPORT; Dum umeni mesta Brna, Brno, Czech Republic
2003 *VALIE EXPORT*; Centre national de la photographie, Paris, France

Group Exhibitions

1996 *Féminin-masculin, le sexe dans l'art*; Centre Georges Pompidou, Paris, France
1989 *Out of Actions—Aktionismus, Body Art & Performance, 1949–1979*; MAK, Vienna, Austria; Museum of Contemporary Art, Los Angeles, California, and traveling to Museu d'Art Contemporani, Barcelona, Spain; and Museum of Contemporary Art, Tokyo, Japan
2000 *Hypermental-Wahnhafte Wirklichkeit, 1955–2000 von Salvador Dali bis Jeff Koons*; Kunsthaus Zürich, Zurich, Switzerland
Art in Central Europe, 1949–1999; Fundación Joan Miró, Barcelona, Spain
2003 *The Last Picture Show: Artists Using Photography, 1960–1982*; Walker Art Center, Minneapolis, Minnesota

Selected Works

VALIE EXPORT-SMART EXPORT, 1967
Cutting, 1967–1968

Ping Pong, Ein Film Zum Spielen-Ein Spielfilm, 1968
Body Sign Action, 1970
Touching, Body Poem, 1970
Split Reality, 1970
Einarmung (Embraced Inwards), 1972, from the series *Körperkonfiguration (Body Configuration)*
Einkreisung (Encirclement) 1976, from the series *Körperkonfiguration (Body Configuration)*
Elongation, 1976, from the series *Körperkonfiguration (Body Configuration)*
Space Seeing-Space Hearing, 1973–1974
Ontologisher Sprung, 1974
I (beat{it})II, 1980
Bilder der Berührungen, 1998
Heads-Aphärese, 2002

Further Reading

Askey, Ruth. "Ein Interview mit Valie Export." *High Performance* vol. 4 no. 1, Frùhjar (1981).
Gentile, Mary C. *Film Feminisms*. Greenwood, CT: Greenwood Press, 1985.
Juna A. and Vale E. *Research Publication 13: Angry Women*. San Francisco, Research Publication, 1991.
Mayne, Judith. *The Women at the Keyhole*. Indianapolis: Indiana University Press, 1990.
Mueller, Roswitha. *Valie Export: Fragments of Imagination*. Bloomington and Indianapolis: Indiana University Press, 1994.
Nesweda, P. "In Her Own Image: VALIE EXPORT, Artist and Feminist." *Arts Magazine* (May 1991).
Stiles, Kristine. "Corporia Vilia, Valie Exports's Body." *Valie Export Ob/De + Con(Struction)*. Philadelphia, PA: Moore College of Art and Design, 1999.
Zell, Andrea. *VALIE EXPORT: Inszenierung von Schmerz Selbstverletzung in den frühen Aktionen*. Berlin: Reimer, 2000.

EXPOSURE

Making an exposure is the first step in making an image permanent. Once an exposure is made, the film is developed, and the image is created. In the case of digital imaging, the exposure is recorded directly to the light-sensitive device. The amount of exposure is determined by how much light strikes the film or light-sensitive device. In negative films, for example, an increase in exposure results in an increase in density on film. Exposure controls include aperture (f/stop) and shutter speeds that are set based on recommendations of the in-camera light meter.

Getting the correct amount of exposure on film is important for capturing all of the detail in the original scene. For example, if the film does not receive enough exposure (underexposure), the shadow areas of the original scene will not record, and the midtones and highlights will seem dark. If a film is given too much exposure (overexposure), the highlight details will be lost.

The amount of exposure needed is based on varying factors. The amount of light in the scene, the film's speed (sensitivity), and the reflective characteristics of the subject are the contributing factors in determining the correct amount of exposure. Other aspects include lens focal length, the distance from the lens elements to the film (bellows extension), and any filters or supplementary lenses that could be used.

Exposure Measurement

The amount of light needed to properly expose film is measured by a light meter. A light meter can either be internal or handheld, and makes its measurements in the context of a given scene. The light meter also needs to be set for the ISO of the film being used; this determines the actual amount of light needed for a "good" exposure based on the film's light sensitivity. The outcome of this measurement is usually in the form of aperture and shutter speed settings, though many meters can also determine the number of EVs (exposure values) for a given scene. All meters render the light or subject they are measuring to a middle grey value, also known as 18% grey. This value is based on the "average" scene, containing an equal amount of highlights, midtones, and shadows. Since not all scenes fall into this "average" standard, the meter can give inaccurate readings for particular scenes. For this reason, it is important to understand how to interpret and modify "suggested" exposure readings so that the proper exposure for a given scene is recorded on film.

Exposure Settings

Aperture and shutters speeds are incremental in the amount of the exposure they give on film. The settings for aperture directly complement shutter speeds, and vice versa. Each step in both settings either doubles or halves the amount of light reaching the film. These settings, known as stops, allow the photographer to add more or less exposure in even, predictable terms. For example, a shutter speed of ½ second delivers twice as much light as ¼ of a second, but ½ second is half as much as 1 second, the next shutter speed up.

1 sec. 1/2 1/4 1/8 1/15 1/30 1/60 1/25 1/250 1/500 1/1000

Common shutter speed settings. Moving left, each number doubles the amount of light reaching the film. Moving right, each number halves the amount of light reaching the film.

Aperture settings, or f/stops, work in an identical fashion. Aperture works by closing metal blades in the lens to create larger or smaller openings. Each f/stop number is based on the diameter of the aperture blades in relation to the focal length of the lens. Therefore, an aperture setting of f/22 represents a very small opening, and an aperture of f/2.8 is considered to be "wide-open." For each increase in aperture size, twice the amount of light strikes the film. For each decrease, the amount of light is cut in half, just as with shutter speeds.

f/2.0 f/2.8 f/4 f/5.6 f/8 f/11 f/16 f/22 f/32 f/45 f/64

Common aperture settings. Moving left, each number doubles the amount of light reaching the film. Moving right, each number halves the amount of light reaching the film.

Each stop change, whether aperture or shutter speeds, represents either a halving or a doubling of the amount of light striking the film. For this reason, photographers may use any number of combinations of aperture and shutter speed to get the same amount of exposure on film. This is called the law of reciprocity. This law states that the amount of exposure is the same, regardless of the rate at which it is given. The classic analogy for this law is the bucket analogy. If a full bucket represents a good exposure, it does not matter if you fill that bucket slowly, drop by drop, or quickly, with great volume. The analogy to the amount of time represents the shutter speed, and the amount of water allowed to leave the faucet represents the aperture.

Because of the law of reciprocity, a metered exposure is given an infinite number of possibilities. For example, a photographer can choose to use a smaller aperture, provided that they compensate the loss of light of the smaller opening with a greater amount of time in their shutter speed. By the same token, if the photographer wishes to use a longer shutter speed, they must close down their aperture an equal amount to compensate and still achieve proper exposure. This is called reciprocal exposure, or equivalent exposure.

f/22@2 sec.	
f/16@1 sec.	
f/11@1/2 sec.	
	f/8@1/4th
Metered Exposure	**f/5.6@1/8th**
	f/4@1/15th
	f/2.8@1/30th
	f/2.0@1/60th

Equivalent exposure. Each setting will give the exact same amunt of exposure on film as the metered exposure.

Bracketing is the term used to refer to deliberately over- and underexposing the film, especially if the photographer is unsure of the meter's accuracy for a particular scene. A typical bracketing method is to overexpose by one stop (twice the amount of light), and underexpose by one stop (half the amount of light) from the meter's recommendation. Because of equivalent exposure, this can be accomplished either with change in aperture settings or by changing the shutter speed.

Minus one stop	**f/8@1/8th OR f/5.6@1/15th**
Metered Exposure	**f/5.6@1/8th**
Plus one stop	**f/4@1/8th OR f/5.6@1/4th**

Bracketing. Subtracting one stop of light will have the amount of light striking the film, resulting in underexposure. Adding one stop will double the amount of light striking the film, resulting in overexposure.

The exception to the law of reciprocity on film is when the exposure is very long or very short.

The film experiences a loss of film speed in these cases, which in turn causes underexposure. Reciprocity law failure is typically encountered with exposures greater than 2 seconds, but varies from film to film.

Exposure and Its Effects on Film

Exposure is directly responsible for the amount of detail captured on film, ultimately determining the quality of the image on film. A film that is able to maintain a great amount of detail, despite some over- or underexposure, is thought to have wide exposure latitude. Black and white films are considered to have good exposure latitude, due to the fact that they are forgiving in the amount of exposure they need to produce a quality image. Color slide films are considered to have very narrow exposure latitude, meaning the exposure needs to be very exact to render detail.

The greater the amount of exposure, the greater the recorded density will be on negative film. Increased density on a negative corresponds to the highlights of a scene in a final print. Conversely, shadow areas correspond to areas of less exposure on a negative. For this reason, shadow detail tends to be the first thing lost when the image is underexposed. Because the amount of light in the shadows of a scene is so low, they are not given the amount of time needed to record on film in underexposure. The highlights in an underexposed image never achieve the proper amount of density to allow them to appear as light as they were in the original scene. Instead of appearing white, the highlights may instead appear grey. The result of an underexposed image is one with lowered contrast and little to no shadow detail. The result on positive (slide) film is identical, though it happens even more quickly given slide film's narrow exposure latitude.

Overexposure on film will cause details in the highlight region of a scene to disappear. Film is not able to handle an infinite amount of exposure. Once maximum density is reached, film characteristically begins to level off. If even more exposure is given, the already overexposed light-sensitive particles in film will begin to grow larger, causing an obliteration of highlight detail. This phenomenon is known as a "blocking up" of the highlight detail.

Film's response to both exposure and development can be graphed in the form of a characteristic curve. A characteristic curve plots exposure versus density in a chart that can be compared in terms of that film's contrast and exposure latitude.

Christye Sisson

Further Reading

Adams, Ansel. *The Negative (Book 2)*. Boston and New York: Little Brown & Co, 1995.

Adams, Ansel. *The Camera (Book 1)*. Boston and New York: Little Brown & Co, 1995.

Langford, Michael. *Basic Photography*. New York: Focal Press, 2000.

London, Barbara and John Upton. *Photography*. 7th ed. Upper Saddle River, New Jersey: Prentice Hall, 1998.

Meehan, Joseph. *The Photographer's Guide to Using Filters*. Amphoto, 1999.

Schaefer, John. *An Ansel Adams Guide: Basic Techniques of Photography, Book 1*. Boston and New York: Little Brown & Co, 1992.

Stroebel, Leslie D., ed. *Basic Photographic Materials and Processes*. New York: Focal Press, 2000.

F

FAMILY PHOTOGRAPHY

Twentieth-century family photography was a collage of technologies and practices, some dating to the advent of the medium, others incorporating social and scientific advances emblematic of the times. Studio portraiture, for instance, whether practiced by highly regarded artists, storefront entrepreneurs, or street or itinerant photographers, remained an essential source of family images. The street photographer was even mechanized in 1928 with the introduction of automatic photography booths ("photo-mats"). And, as in the nineteenth century, family photography could also be understood to include the constant stream of photojournalism, advertising, and other forms of commercial photography that flooded into the home.

Important as these practices were, what distinguished twentieth-century family photography was the preponderance of nonprofessionals producing personal images. The making of photographs became a consumer project with the photographic industry constantly expanding and retooling to meet the consumer's needs. The century's largest single photographic enterprise, Kodak, invented and sustained itself by providing the means for family imagery. Major innovations in photographic technology—if not originally conceived for the family market—came to be adapted for it. The facility and growing sophistication of even the most basic cameras made personal images into the building blocks of lifelong visual narratives. As a result, the practices that constituted family were discussed as part of a larger understanding of change in twentieth-century culture, art, and history.

Technology

The technology of twentieth-century family photography was irrevocably shaped by George Eastman's 1888 Kodak camera and its promise of "you take the picture and we do the rest." Eastman took full advantage of advances such as dry plate photography, roll film, daylight loading cartridge, industrial-scale photo processing, and earlier roll cameras. By 1900, the success of the Kodak camera and industrial processing of its film had resulted in Eastman's marketing of another eight models. These, like all Kodak products, were promoted by Kodak's aggressive advertising campaigns as well as by the company's pressure on merchants to sign exclusive marketing agreements. At the turn of the century, Kodak enjoyed a leadership role in the new home photography industry that included a half million dollars in annual camera sales.

With the introduction of the first Brownie camera in 1900, the final ingredient in the marketing of mass photography fell into place: that is, photography's affordability to unprecedented numbers of middle and working class people. Priced at $1.00 per camera plus $0.15 for the six exposure roll, the Brownie sold some 100,000 units in the United States and Britain during its first year on the market.

While Kodak, from the 1890s to the end of the twentieth century, dominated family photography, it was not entirely free of competition. Its chief American rival was the long established Anthony & Scovill Company (Ansco after 1907) that introduced its own roll film camera in 1905—for which it was promptly sued by Kodak for patent infringement. In Britain, Ilford Ltd., from the mid-1890s, the most successful manufacturer of gelatin dry plates outside the United States, turned to the production of cameras and, in 1912, roll film. The German corporation, Agfa (The Analine Manufacturing Corporation), a commercial dye manufacturer, began producing film in 1908 and cameras in 1928. In Japan, the Cherry portable camera was first manufactured in 1903 by Knoishi Honten, the forerunner of the Konica Corporation.[i]

These, like the majority of large photography companies in the twentieth century, would continue to follow Kodak's lead in developing point-and-shoot cameras as well as the film stocks and industrial processing facilities to support them. Kodak produced 125 models of the Brownie camera between 1900 and 1970. While some of these went so far as to offer bellows lens mounts, stereo exposures and, later in the century, flash attachments, Kodak never lost sight of the parameters of need and accessibility with which the original model was designed. Even as the company diversified, it was careful to maintain its dominance of the family photography market. In 1963, with the introduction of the Instamatic line, Kodak once again emphasized simplicity of use, selling more than 50 million units prior to 1970.

The Instamatic was typical of second generation point-and-shoot cameras in that it incorporated artificial illumination and was designed to use color film. Flashbulbs, first marketed in 1930, were commonplace in home photography in the post-World War II period with 400 million sold in 1951 alone. The Instamatic generation brought an even more practical means for low light photography through the integration of permanent flash units. Home use of color film had become practical, though expensive, with the Kodachrome and Agfacolor stocks introduced in 1936. It wasn't until after the Second World War with the coming of Kodacolor, Ansco-color, Ektachrome, and Fuji-color that color film not only worked well in point-and-shoot cameras but could be processed at competitive prices. By the mid-1960s color had overtaken black and white as a standard for family photography, a trend that continued with the subsequent introduction of ever-faster color stocks.

Other innovations in second generation point-and-shoot cameras owed their origin to the redesign and popularization of 35 mm photography by a number of Japanese companies beginning in the mid-1950s. The Japanese researchers used 35 mm as the platform on which features such as the single lens reflex optics, automatic exposure control, automatic focusing, motorized zoom lenses, and motorized film advance were adapted for general use—including, by the 1960s, use in less expensive family formats.[ii] By the 1980s, cartridge-loaded 35 mm cameras with these features were being sold to family photographers as slightly upscale versions of point-and-shoot cameras.

Other alternatives to the basic family camera proved less successful. The Polaroid Land camera, with its self-developing film, was introduced in 1947. The first Polaroids were relatively expensive, complicated, and produced prints that compared badly to those of conventional cameras. Polaroid improved its technology, introducing color with its Swinger camera in 1962. Its 1972 SX-70 system provided an integrated electronic flash, simplified focusing, and multi-exposure film packs. In the 1990s, Polaroid introduced smaller, less expensive cameras aimed at a youth market. It also emphasized the visual record keeping function of its technology. However, Polaroid's family photography division suffered from the spread of one-hour photo processing labs in the 1970s, disposable cameras in the 1980s, and digital photography in the last decade of the century.

Towards the end of the twentieth century, these last two innovations looked to both the past and the future in their contributions to the reinvention of family photography. Fuji's "utsurundesu" (film with lens), the single use (or disposable) camera, introduced in 1986, reiterated Kodak's 1888 idea of returning the camera to the processor along with its film. These small cardboard box cameras, only marginally more expensive than the roll of color film they contained, were soon available wherever film was sold. Fuji's sale of a million single use cameras in six months led to the rapid development of other manufacturers' models. Single use cameras were soon available with built in flash, panoramic lens, telephoto lenses, or with plastic shells that allowed them to be used underwater. The cardboard box could be printed with custom designs and promotional messages or simply decorated for particular occasions. By 1996, a decade after their introduction, single use cameras were selling at a rate of 80 million annually in Japan alone.

It was not until the very end of the twentieth century that the cost of digital photography was lowered to the point where it became affordable for most families. However, the development of electronic family photography had begun much earlier in the form of home video. Sony's 1965 portable, black and white video camera wired to a separate reel-to-reel half-inch video recorder was a relatively crude and expensive downscaling of professional television cameras and video recorders. By the early 1980s, it had been replaced by color camcorders making use of half inch and, in the 1990s, 8 mm video cassettes. A third generation of home video, in the form of the digital video camcorder, was introduced by Sony in 1982. By the mid-1990s, digital video camcorders, often no larger than conventional still cameras, could be fed into home computers, their footage edited by increasingly sophisticated software. The potential of this domestic version of television-computer convergence, as well as the continually decreasing price of both analogue and digital home video made it, by century's end, the most widely used domestic alternative to silver-based photography.

Digital still photography, as a mass marketed consumer format, was introduced in tandem with the digital video cameras. While digital imaging on computers was first demonstrated in 1979 and marketed by Sony in 1982, the cameras were prohibitively expensive for home use. It was not until 1994 and 1995, respectively, that Kodak and Casio broke the US$1,000 price barrier. The following year, 20 other models of relatively low-cost digital cameras were introduced by Japanese electronics companies and one million units were sold. By decade's end, sales of digital cameras had increased to approximately four million per year with prices of some models falling well below $500.

Digital tools also contributed to changes in chemical-based family photography. After 1990, commercial photo developers could return digital prints of conventional film on Kodak's photo CD, a device that also allowed for in-store and home computer editing of those prints. In 1996, Kodak, with more than 40% of the world photography market, and Fuji, with an additional third of it, together introduced their Advanced Photography System. This hybrid technology was based on magnetically striped cartridge film imprinted by the camera with information used subsequently to set the parameters of digital developers and editing equipment.

At the end of the twentieth century, it remained to be seen whether Kodak and Fuji succeeded in creating anything more than a transitional technology. The exponential growth in home computers, computer speed, and computer memory as well as the increased accessibility of peripherals associated with digital photography (photo editing software, ink jet printers, scanners) offered the family photographer more options for less cost. Digital images could be produced by scanning conventional images or shot directly with digital cameras. Home darkrooms, while greatly facilitated throughout the century by downscaled commercial equipment, and improvements in pre-mixed chemicals and prepared papers, could not match the options available in even the basic photography software distributed with printers and scanners. More advanced software, most notably Adobe Photoshop, offered professional photo finishing on home computers. Finished photographs could be viewed on screen or printed as hard copy on a variety of photo papers. Digital images could be stored in password-protected virtual albums, transmitted to any number of recipients anywhere in the world via e-mail or mounted for universal viewing on the World Wide Web.

Practice

From their first advertising campaigns, Kodak and its competitors went to some length to demonstrate that point-and-shoot cameras could be used by anyone, including women and children. The Kodak "girl" in her striped Edwardian dress was introduced in 1910 to become a mainstay of the company's promotional material until 1940. In North America and Europe, Kodak sponsored photography clubs in schools and youth organizations while publishing photo manuals and other camera literature aimed at children. In 1930, the company went so far as to give away a half million Brownies worldwide to children turning twelve that year.

One result of the proliferation of family photography was common loathing of the ubiquitous "camera fiend." By 1900, the dignified act of sitting for a photographic portrait in the privacy of a studio became far less common than daily encounters with ordinary people photographing each other in public. Bill Jay points out that the aggression associated with photojournalists was first reported with shock and dismay as early as the 1890s in relation to family photographers. In what Henisch and Henisch refer to as "the trivialization of travel," the great monuments and vistas of the world, previously photographed by professionals with great respect and artistry, now shared the frame with grinning spouses and line-ups of reluctantly posed children. Worse still, citizens feared being photographed against their will and did so to the extent that some pressed for, and occasionally obtained, legislation prohibiting the practice.

As the popularity of point-and-shoot photography continued to grow, the "camera fiend" became the more innocuous "shutterbug" and, finally, an entirely assimilated participant in public behavior. Conversely, the importance of public places and events were to some extent signified by the numbers of people taking pictures. Cameras and film were sold at historical sites and monuments, recreational areas, sports arenas, theme parks, zoos, and museums. From at least the 1963 Zapruder home movie of the Kennedy assassination, images, particularly videos taken by non-professionals, were integrated into professional photojournalism.

Throughout the century, families were inundated with these self-generated images. Photographs not consigned to shoeboxes, envelopes, or desk drawers were placed in redesigned family albums—albums differing significantly from their nineteenth-century predecessors. Earlier albums contained ornate pages with slots into which *cartes-de-visite* and cabinet cards were placed. These portraits of family members shared the album with images of illustrious persons or places with which the family wished to be associated. The overall effect was that of a record, often compared to the record keeping pages of the family bible.

Twentieth-century family albums were characteristically composed of blank pages onto which various sized photographs could be attached in an infinite variety of layouts and collages. With this physical change came a change in the tone and purpose of the albums. The illustrious persons and places were phased out as was the nineteenth-century practice of post-mortem photography. Family albums became less a pictorial record of family members than visual narratives of personal triumph: births, children's parties, first days at school, graduations, weddings, anniversaries, other ceremonies and special events. The family displayed its possessions (homes, cars, pets) and, in its travel photos, its possession of the world's most desirable locales. Unlike nineteenth-century portraiture, almost everyone looking at the camera—that is, looking at another member of the family or a friend photographing them—smiled.

Most family photographic albums were arranged in a roughly chronological order that continued in volume after volume. However, as Langford demonstrates, albums could be arranged thematically or could focus on single events or experiences, some of which were not entirely pleasant. The family photographs could be augmented by postcard and studio photographs of family members. Entire albums of professional photographs—most notably the wedding album—were professionally photographed and arranged in a highly ritualized manner. It was also possible for the creation of the album itself to be a ritual, classmates giving each other photographs for graduation albums or, in the 1990s, Japanese school girls assembling "passports to heaven," albums filled with photographs of their good deeds. Albums might even be reduced to a set of wallet-sized images bound together in plastic sleeves.

The visual narrative of the family album was usually accompanied by a verbal narrative, either through elaborate captions or the verbal accompaniment of a family member. Verbal narration also accompanied the presentation of family images as transparencies which, thanks to the electric slide projector, were second only to albums as a means of storing and presenting family images. Verbal narration was also a part of home movies. Kodak's 16 mm home movie system, introduced in 1923, its 8 mm system put on the market in 1932 (re-introduced as the Brownie movie camera in 1946), and its super-8 mm film and equipment, introduced in 1965, produced silent movies over which the film-maker or others were expected to speak.[iii] When these formats gave way to the video recorder, images of family activities became "self-narrating," long takes of synchronized sound activities very much in the manner of the "*cinema verite*" films released by documentary filmmakers. The more edited narration of family video, including music and voice over, came with the appearance of professionally produced wedding tapes and, at the end of the century, with home computer-based digital video editing.

These narrative practices of family photography (sometimes referred to as "vernacular" photography) had, by the latter part of the century, generated some academic commentary. The most frequently quoted work, Roland Barthes' *Camera Lucida*, was a meditation on the manner by which a photograph of his mother functioned as means of focusing his memory. Barthes' work is expanded upon in a more feminist ideological context in work such as Annette Kuhn's *Family Secrets* and Marianne Hirsch's *Family Frames*. Martha Langford's *Suspended Conversations* pursues the idea of narrative in family albums while Linda Haverty

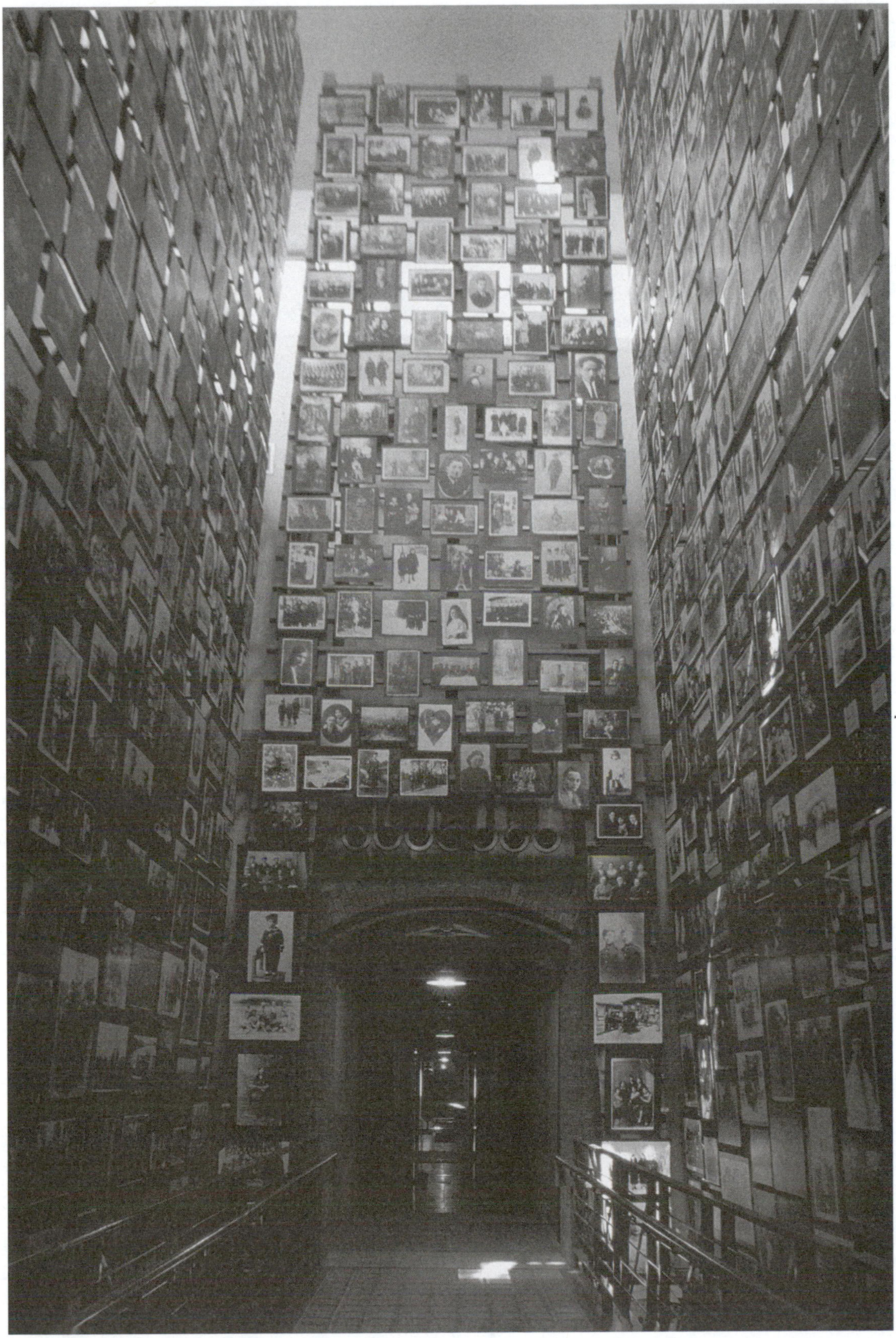

Yaffa Eliach, Tower of Faces.
[© *United States Holocaust Memorial Museum*]

Rugg's *Picturing Ourselves* is a study of the shaping of our perception of four historical figures by the informal photographs taken of them.

Family photography has also been of considerable interest to twentieth-century artistic photographers. The snapshot aesthetic—a rejection of formal aesthetics in favor of the spontaneity and naïveté of amateur photography—has been cited as a sensibility linking the work of fine art photographers from Walker Evans to Garry Winogrand. Home movie formats were essential to the practice of experimental filmmaking. From the 1970s, the art photographer most visibly concerned with family photography has been Jo Spence, particularly in her exhibition, *The Family Album, 1939–1979* (1979) and her 1986 book *Putting Myself in the Picture*. The family photograph has also been the basis for especially striking monumental sculpture. Perhaps the most noted example of this was Yaffa Eliach's *Tower of Faces* in the United States Holocaust Memorial Museum. A three story space whose walls and ceiling are covered with more than 1600 studio portraits and enlarged snapshots, the tower is a visual reincarnation of a single village's holocaust victims.

Eliach's *Tower* effectively summarizes the place of family photography in the twentieth century. It mirrors the expectation of visual identity—everyone, as it turned out, had their picture taken. And that they did so, mattered. For, in Barbie Zelizer's phrase, "the mechanics of visual history and historical record" have, in effect, helped dictate the monumental role of the quotidian.

Renate Wickens-Feldman

See also: **Brownie; Camera: An Overview; Camera: Instant; Camera: Point and Shoot; Eastman Kodak Company; Spence, Jo; Vernacular Photography**

Further Reading

Barthes, Roland. *Camera Lucida; Reflections on Photography*. Translated by Richard Howard. New York: Hill and Wang, 1981.

Eliach, Yaffa. *There Once was a World*. New York: Little, Brown and Company, 1998.

Henisch, Heinz K. and Bridget D. Henisch. *The Photographic Experience, 1839–1914, Images and Attitudes*. University Park: The Pennsylvania State University Press, 1993.

Hirsch, Marianne. *Family Frames; Photography, Narrative and Postmemory*. Cambridge, MA: Harvard University Press, 1997.

Holland, Patricia. "'Sweet it is to scan...': personal photographs and popular photography" in *Photography: A Critical Introduction*. Edited by Liz Wells. London: Routledge, 1997.

Jay, Bill. "The Photographer as Aggressor" in *Observations; Essays on Documentary Photography*. Edited by David Featherstone. Carmel, CA: The Friends of Photography, 1984.

Kuhn, Annette. *Family Secrets; Acts of Memory and Imagination*. London: Verso, 1995.

Langford, Martha. *Suspended Conversations; The Afterlife of Memory in Photographic Albums*. Montreal: McGill-Queen's University Press, 2001.

Lewis, Brian, and Colin Harding, eds. *Kept in a Shoebox: the Popular Experience of Photography*. Castleford: Yorkshire Art Circus, 1992.

Lister, Martin, ed. *Family Snaps; The Meaning of Domestic Photography*. London: Virago, 1994.

Rugg, Linda Haverty. *Picturing Ourselves; Photography and Autobiography*. Chicago: The University of Chicago Press, 1997.

Zelizer, Barbie. *Remembering to Forget; Holocaust Memory Through the Camera's Eye*. Chicago: University of Chicago Press, 1998.

[i] Other Japanese camera companies can trace their origins to the first third of the twentieth century, though none would become major forces in the international market until at least the 1950s.

[ii] In 1981, the sale of 35 mm cameras manufactured by Japanese companies peaked at more than seven and a half million units.

[iii] After 1973, Super-8 was available with magnetic striped film that offered a limited sound on film potential. This was of less interest to family filmmaking than it was to low budget documentary.

ROTIMI FANI-KAYODE

Nigerian

As an African artist whose work engages issues of diaspora and projects multiple subject positions, Rotimi Fani-Kayode often described himself as an outsider in three distinct ways; within his African family, which navigated modern Britain with a traditional spiritual identity; as a gay man in an intolerant black community; and as a black artist in a racist society:

> My identity has been constructed from my own sense of otherness, whether cultural, racial, or sexual. The three aspects are not separate within me. Photography is the tool by which I feel most confident in expressing myself. It is photography, therefore—Black, African, homosexual photography—which I must use not just as an instrument, but as a weapon if I am to resist attacks on my integrity and, indeed, my existence on my own terms.

Rotimi Fani-Kayode was born to a prominent Yoruba family in Lagos, Nigeria in 1955. His father, Chief Remi Fani-Kayode, was a respected high priest and notable politician. Indeed, the Kayode family was well regarded for their spiritual responsibilities in their hometown of Ife, a sacred city in southwestern Nigeria regarded as the spiritual center of Yoruba culture. But when a military coup and civil war threw Nigeria into turmoil in 1966, Fani-Kayode and his family moved to England and settled in the seaside resort town of Brighton. He continued his education there until the age of 21, when he traveled to the United States to further his academic career. While his desire was to study fine arts, he compromised with his parents' wishes for him and also studied economics. After receiving a B.A. from Georgetown University in Washington D.C. in 1980, Fani-Kayode moved to New York and completed an M.F.A. in fine art and photography at the Pratt Institute in 1983.

It was during his graduate studies that Fani-Kayode began making iconic and dramatic color portrait photographs of himself and other black men, nude or dressed in traditional Yoruba clothing. Such images laid the important formal and critical framework for his later photographic works, which explored issues of race, masculinity, homoeroticism, and nationality, often involving a sophisticated and ambiguous mix of African and Western iconography. Upon his return to England after completing his graduate studies in 1983, Fani-Kayode met his partner photographer/filmmaker Alex Hirst, and began an important personal and collaborative relationship. The two moved to London, and Fani-Kayode continued his focus on part-autobiographical and mythical portraits; pursuing the theme of the male black body as a subject of desire.

Although his work is sometimes regarded as similar to the early 1980s work of American photographer Robert Mapplethorpe, in truth Fani-Kayode's work pushes beyond simple references to gay iconography. Indeed, many of his photographs say as much about postcolonial issues and racism in contemporary British society as they do about gay sexuality. In this regard, it is useful to remember that Fani-Kayode's career in the 1980s coincided with the years of political leadership by Prime Minister Margaret Thatcher, a conservative tenure that witnessed several race riots in Britain. In response to his personal experience and social environment, in 1987 Fani-Kayode co-founded the London-based organization Autograph, The Association of Black Photographers, a group that remains vibrant and active to this day.

In the same year, Fani-Kayode published his first book, *Black Male/White Male* (1987), a collection of photographs consisting of intimate portraits made in the early to the mid-1980s, including an image of American writer Essex Hemphill, and accompanied by text by Hirst. The photographs explored formal aesthetics of color photography in a dynamic manner and also challenged stereotypical views on race, interracial relationships, and sexuality. Photographs from this period also recognize the photographer's own spiritual background as an integral part of this investigation. In "Bronze Head" (1987), the bust of a Yoruba god, customarily seen as signifying an artist's spirit, is portrayed in an image of sodomy. In trying to reconcile the notion that the traditions of his Yoruba culture reject homosexuality, Fani-Kayode attempted to create images that rejected profanity and instead provoked contemplation of sexual desire and the act of creation as positive, beautiful concepts.

Another example of Fani-Kayode's complex postmodern style can be acknowledged in the part-autobiographical image "White Bouquet" (1987). Here, a standing white man presents a bouquet of white flowers to his black lover, who lies on a white chaise longue. Both men are nude and anonymous; their faces are unseen. The lighting is soft, setting a sensual tone within an ambiguous scene, which points to the powerful rhetoric of much of Fani-Kayode's work. He presents an intimate moment that can be interpreted several ways, as a homoerotic encounter or a subversive comment on the racial power relationship associated with colonialism. Additionally, in its conceptual reference to Edouard Manet's painting *Olympia* (1863), the image highlights the artist's sophisticated knowledge of European art history. Images from the *Communion* series (1989) display a similar sensitivity and theoretical subtlety in the treatment of the male nude, in what Kobena Mercer has characterized as an exploration of the relationship between erotic fantasy and ancestral death. *Communion* is a group of photographs that appear to have been a very personal and final collaboration between Fani-Kayode and Hirst, which were never exhibited while they were both alive. Fani-Kayode died from AIDS in 1989; Hirst died from HIV-related illness three years later.

Although his six-year professional career may be regarded as brief, Fani-Kayode's art-making was intensely personal and politically engaged. The significance of his work was consistently overlooked during his lifetime, probably due in part to the controversial nature of his chosen subject matter, but also because of debate about the authorship of several of his photographs, despite consideration of the genuine spirit of collaboration he and Alex Hirst shared. Discussion of Fani-Kayode's work in Hall and Sealy's *Different* (2001), and the inclusion of his photographs in exhibitions like the 50th Venice Biennale in 2003, point to recently renewed interest in the Nigerian's work by curators and historians who understand his significant role in having helped shaped various critical discourses in British photography of the late twentieth century.

SARA-JAYNE PARSONS

See also: **History of Photography: the 1980s; Photography in Africa: An Overview; Postmodernism; Representation and Race; Robert Mapplethorpe**

Biography

Born Oluwarotimi Adebiyi Wahab Fani-Kayode in Lagos, Nigeria, 1955. Georgetown University, Washington, DC., B.A. Economics and Fine Art, 1980; Pratt Institute, Brooklyn, New York, M.F.A. Fine Art and Photography, 1983. Founding member and first chair of Autograph: The Association of Black Photographers, London, 1987. Died in London, 21 December 1989.

Individual Exhibitions

1985 B&J Gallery; Lagos, Nigeria
1986 *Yoruba Light for Modern Living*; Riverside Studios, London
1989 Submarine Gallery; London
1989 *Rotimi Fani-Kayode, Photographer (1955–1989): Retrospective*; 198 Gallery, London
1996 *Communion—Selected Works*; Impressions Gallery, York
1999 *Communion—Selected Works*; Café Gallery, London

Group Exhibitions

1984 Art Show Gallery; London
1985 *No Comment*; Brixton Arts Gallery, London
1985 *Sacred and Profane Love*; South West Arts, London
1986 *Same Difference*; Camerawork, London
1987 *Misfits*; Oval House Gallery; London
1989 *Bodies of Experience: Stories About Living with HIV*; Camerawork, London
1990 *Ecstatic Antibodies*; Battersea Arts Centre, London
1992 *Foto Fest*; Houston, Texas
1994 *Significant Losses: Artists who have died from AIDS*; The Art Gallery, University of Maryland; College Park, Maryland
1996 *In/Sight African Photographers, 1940 to the Present*; Solomon R. Guggenheim Museum, New York
1996 *The Other Story*; Kunst Halle Krems, Austria
1998 *Eye Africa*; The Castle of Good Hope, Cape Town
2000 *Portrait Africa. A Century of Photographic Standpoints*; House of World Cultures, Berlin
2000 *Mardi Gras Arts Festival*; E1 Gallery, London
2003 *Dreams & Conflicts the Dictatorship of the Viewer; African Pavilion*, 50th Venice Biennale; Venice
2004 *Staged Realities: Exposing the soul in African photography 1870–2004*; Michael Stevenson Contemporary; Cape Town

Selected Works

Sonponnoi, 1987
White Bouquet, 1987
Bronze Head, 1987
Nothing to Lose XII (Bodies of Experience series), 1989
*Every Moment Counts (*from *Ecstatic Antibodies)*, 1989
Tom Peeping, 1989
Communion series, 1989

Further Reading

Bailey, David A., and Stuart Hall, eds. *Ten.8—Critical Decade: Black British Photography in the 80's*, 3, no. 3 (1992).

Bianchi, Paolo. "Bruchlinien – Kunst uas Afrika." *Kunstforum International*, no. 166 (August/October 2003).

Boffin, Tess and Sunil Gupta, editors, *Ecstatic Antibodies: Resisting the AIDS Mythology*, London: Rivers Oram Press, 1990.

Bright, Deborah, ed. *The Passionate Camera: Photography and Bodies of Desire*. London: Routledge, 1998.

Doy, Gen. Black *Visual Culture: modernity and postmodernity*. London and New York: I.B. Tauris, 2000.

"Exposure." *British Journal of Photography* 132 (January 11, 1985).

Fani-Kayode, Rotimi. *Communion*. London: Autograph, 1996.

Fani-Kayode, Rotimi. *Black Male/White Male*. London: Gay Men's Press, 1987.

Fani-Kayode, Rotimi. "Traces of Ecstasy." *Ten-8*, no. 28 (1988).

Hall, Charles. "198 Gallery, London." *Arts Review*, 43, (January 25, 1991).

Hall, Stuart, and Mark Sealy. *Different*. London: Phaidon Press, 2001.

Mercer, Kobena. *Welcome to the jungle: new positions in Black cultural studies*. New York: Routledge, 1994.

Mercer, Kobena. "Mortal Coil: Eros and Diaspora in the Photographs of Rotimi Fani-Kayode." In *OverExposed: Essays on Contemporary Photography*. Carol Squires, ed. New Press: New York, 1999.

Oguibe, Olu. "A Man Without: Tribute to the Photographer Rotimi Fani-Kayode." *West Africa*, (July 15, 1991).

Oguibe, Olu. "Finding a place: Nigerian artists in the contemporary art world." *Art Journal*, 58, no. 2 (Summer 1999).

Pollack, Barbara. "The Newest Avant-Garde." *ArtNews* (April 2001). *Rotimi Fani-Kayode, Photographer (1955–1989): Retrospective*. London: 198 Gallery, 1990.

Sealy, Mark, and Jean Loup Pivin, eds. *Rotimi Fani-Kayode and Alex Hirst*. Paris: Editions Revue Noire, 1997.

Tawadros, Gilane, and Sarah Campbell. *Fault Lines: Contemporary African Art and Shifting Landscapes*. London: inIVA Books, 2003.

Zaya, Octavio. "On Three Counts I Am an Outsider: The Work of Rotimi Fani-Kayode." *NKA: Journal of Contemporary African Art*, no. 4, (Summer 1996).

FARM SECURITY ADMINISTRATION

The Farm Security Administration (FSA) was the eventual name given to a series of programs designed as a part of Franklin D. Roosevelt's "New Deal" that were meant to bring relief to struggling farmers during the years of the depression. Its existence is important to photography because of the founding of its Historical Section. This section advocated a photographic documenting of both the administration's work as well as the rural areas of America that the programs were supposed to aid. During its ten-year existence, the Farm Security Administration's Historical Section under Roy Stryker helped to both provide work to out-of-work photographers and solidify the careers of a number of the leading American photographers of the era, including Esther Bubley, John Collier, Jack Delano, Fred Driscoll, Walker Evans, Dorothea Lange, Russell Lee, Carl Mydans, Gordon Parks, Arthur Rothstein, John Vachon, Marion Post Wolcott, as well as muralist/photographer Ben Shahn.

The beginning years of the 1930s saw an increase in poverty affecting America's rural populations, including a rise in sharecropping. The economic devastation, known as The Great Depression called for decisive government action. Elected president in 1933, Roosevelt established a series of programs designed to boost America's sluggish economy and help those suffering in America's farmlands. Termed the New Deal, Roosevelt's programs offered jobs to those suffering from unemployment, as well as relief for farmers. The Agricultural Adjustment Administration (AAA) was Roosevelt's first attempt to bring aid to farmers, though it did little to help smaller farmers and sharecroppers. In 1935, Roosevelt created the broader Resettlement Administration (RA) headed by Rexford G. Tugwell, Columbia University economics professor and part of Roosevelt's "brain trust," whose mission, among others, was to document the agency's work through photography. Tugwell chose as the head of this Historical Section his former student, Roy Stryker.

Stryker's vision for the Historical Section was grand. He wanted to attempt to document not only the work of the RA but also the conditions in which rural Americans lived. Within the first year of its founding, the Historical Section of the Resettlement Administration had already employed close to fifteen American photographers. Although Stryker's vision was aligned with the government's goal of not only documenting conditions, but using the photographs as a kind of propaganda for Roosevelt's programs, to the point of writing "scripts" his photographers were to follow. With such independent photographers as Walker Evans in the RA's employ, however, the focus of the branch shifted from government work to pure documentation of rural America, or what Stryker would later call, "introducing America to Americans." One of the first photographers to be appointed to the Historical Section, Arthur Rothstein, an employee of Stryker's at Columbia, developed a preliminary series of principles to guide the work of photographers. In 1936, Stryker also went after a series of higher profile photographers whose work he admired. Carl Mydans, Walker Evans, and Dorothea Lange were all hired in the first year of the section's existence.

By 1937, a number of changes occurred to the Resettlement Administration. It had been swallowed by the larger Department of Agriculture, the head officer Tugwell had resigned, and the agency was renamed the Farm Security Administration by which it is best known. As FSA's photographers fanned out over the Midwest, South, and Southwest to document the conditions of the rural American poor, they created some of the most memorable and famous images of not only the 1930s, but of the twentieth century. As Arthur Rothstein's documentation of the Shenandoah National Park in Virginia, Carl Mydans's images of West Virginia coal miners, or Dorothea Lange's poignant photographs of California migrant workers, were published in various magazines and newspapers, Americans became fascinated with the plight of their rural neighbors.

Walker Evans, in 1936, on leave from the RA/FAS, traveled to Hale County, Alabama, where he and poet-novelist James Agee collaborated on what eventually was published, in 1941, as *Let Us Now Praise Famous Men.* Walker's negatives, though commissioned by *Fortune* magazine, were negotiated to remain in the public domain, as were the negatives of all the government-employed photographers, and this project is often thought of as the epitome of what FSA photographers were able to accomplish. Evans's detached and introspective style contrasted sharply with other FSA photographers such as Dorothea Lange, whose pictures are dramatic events that often offer the structure of a story. Taken in early1936, Lange's *Migrant Mother*, perhaps the most famous of her career, shows a woman and her two children in Nipomo, California. The mother is seated, eyes focused in the distance, while her two children stand in contra posto, each with their backs to the camera. The scene is striking and dramatic with its dark, charcoally blacks and brilliant whites, and the positioning of the figures conveys a clear emotional message. Evans's infrequent portrait photographs, such as those of the Burroughs family in Alabama, offer none of the straightforward emotion of Lange's. In Evans's works, the story of the subject rests just beyond the image, with meaning hinted at but never offered.

Stryker's bold and sometimes argumentative personality caused conflicts with many photographers, most of whom were interested in remaining on the project to produce authentic social documentation that also expressed their creativity and individual viewpoints, not mere propaganda. Internal instability notwithstanding, as the 1930s drew to a close, the FSA's documentation seemed less imperative. America's increasing national introspection was shattered by a European war that, after the attack on Pearl Harbor, turned increasingly threatening. By the time America entered the Second World War in December 1941, the urgent program of "introducing America to Americans" was curtailed, along with many of the various New Deal programs. Stryker's FSA was subsumed into the new Office of War Information, a centralized information agency established in June 1942 as part of the Office of Emergency Management and was dissolved a year later. Though accused of suppression and heavy editing, Stryker managed to protect the catalogue of nearly 270,000 negatives by placing them in the Library of Congress, Washington, D.C.

The FSA had not only documented the impact of government programs on rural America, but had also produced the very image of the Depression in a collective American memory. Their images, varying in style, form, and subject captured the essence of what the Depression meant for hundreds of thousands of America's poor. Lange's photographs of migrant workers helped to inspire John Steinbeck's novel *The Grapes of Wrath*, which proved to be an instrumental text that exposed the corrosion of American ideals in the face of crippling poverty. Evans's detached landscapes and portraits were the first book of the experimental and influential

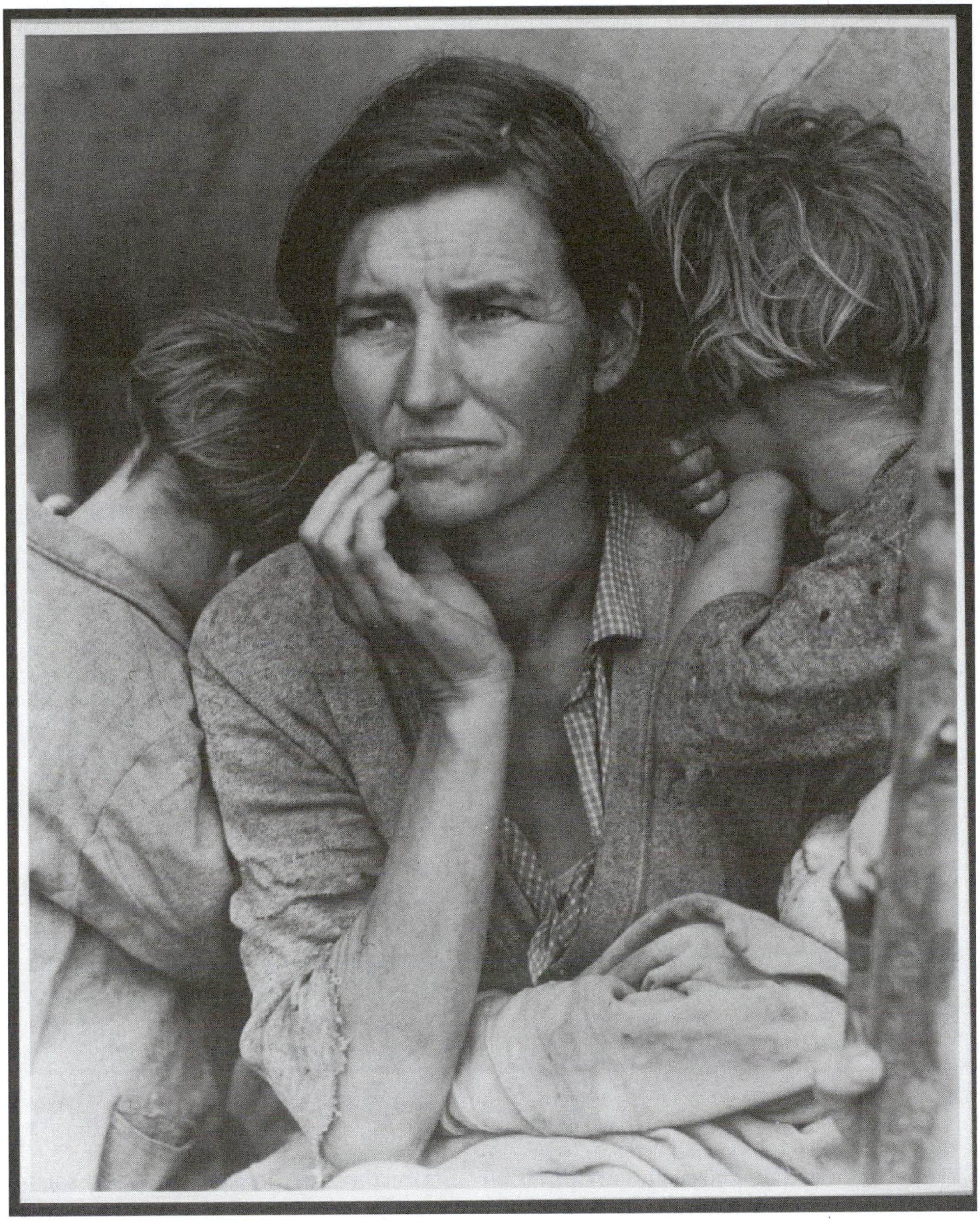

Dorothea Lange, Migrant Mother, Nipoma, California, 1936/printed later, gelatin silver print, 22.1 × 17.7 cm, Gift of Robert Doherty.
[*Photograph courtesy of George Eastman House*]

Let Us Now Praise Famous Men, which argued for the humanity of sharecroppers and tenant farmers and rejected the use of their images for aesthetic purposes. Although there is disagreement as to how effective the FSA was at aiding the broader economic relief efforts of the Roosevelt administration, there is no doubt that it quickly became a program through which America embraced its art and artists. The FSA's legacy, which can be seen at both the Library of Congress or at the website *http://memory.loc.gov/ammem/fsowhome.html*, helped to emblaze the decade of the 1930s onto the American national memory that still reverberates. Numerous exhibitions have been mounted featuring the FSA photographers in anthologies and monographic presentations, including the influential Museum of Modern Art exhibition organized by Edward Steichen, *The Bitter Years 1935–1941: Rural America as Seen by the Photographers of the Farm Security Administration.*

ANDY CRANK

See also: **Delano, Jack; Documentary Photography; Evans, Walker; History of Photography: Interwar Years; Lange, Dorothea; Lee, Russell; Rothstein, Arthur; Shahn, Ben; Social Representation; Stryker, Roy; Works Progress Administration**

Further Reading

Carlebach, Michael and Eugene F. Provenzo, Jr. *Farm Security Administration Photographs of Florida*. Gainesville: University Press of Florida, 1993.

Daniel, Pete, et al. *Official Images: New Deal Photography*. Washington, DC: Smithsonian Institution Press, 1987.

Fleischhauer, Carl, and Beverly Brannan, eds. *Documenting America: 1935–1943*. Berkeley, CA: University of California Press, 1988.

Hurley, F. Jack. *Portrait of a Decade: Roy Stryker and the Development of Documentary Photography in the Thirties*. New York: Da Capo Press, Inc., 1972.

Just Before the War: Urban America from 1935 to 1941 as seen by Photographers of the Farm Security Administration. New York: October House, 1968.

O'Neal, Hank. *A Vision Shared: a Classic Portrait of America and Its People, 1935–1943*. New York: St. Martin's Press, 1976.

Steichen, Edward, ed. *The Bitter Years 1935–1941: Rural America as Seen by the Photographers of the Farm Security Administration*. New York: The Museum of Modern Art, 1962.

The Years of Bitterness and Pride: Farm Security Administration Photographs, 1935–1943. New York: McGraw-Hill, 1975.

FASHION PHOTOGRAPHY

Fashion photography occupies a unique position in the world of photography. It commands the attention of almost everyone. Fashion photography answers the need for what the current image of femininity is in our society. It appears to be easy to do; above all, ever so glamorous, yet fashion photography is amongst the most difficult to practice. As a result, fashion photographers rank at the top of the profession in terms of respect, name recognition, and income. Fashion photography historically has been considered within a nexus of commercial practice including so-called beauty photography and glamour photography. These distinctions are important in the overall field: beauty photography is a commercial pursuit intended to sell cosmetics, hairstyles, physical fitness products, and increasingly, health and food products. Glamour photography historically has implied creating an overall effect accentuating the desirability of the sitter and has been most associated with the photographing of movie stars and other celebrities whose physical appearance is their stock-in-trade.

The photography of fashion began shortly after the invention of the medium in 1839. While it was difficult at first to make portraits due to the long exposures required, gradually film speeds increased and the making of portraits became possible. In many ways the first portraits can be thought of as fashion statements since the sitters almost always wore their best and fanciest clothes. But these photographs were limited in distribution, generally only seen by the immediate family and friends, and were not created for advertising or other commercial purposes. The half-tone process, invented in the early 1890s, made the direct reproduction of a photograph possible. Prior to this advance the lithographic process was used to reproduce photographs, requiring the hand of an artist to transfer the image from photograph to the metal plate or wood block. The half-tone process reduced the continuous tone of a photo into a series of small and large dots on a printing plate. The realism of the photograph was thus brought to the mass circulation media, and everyone who could afford to buy a magazine could discover the latest fashion trends.

History

The first fashion photographer to achieve that distinction was Baron Adolph de Meyer (1868–1946). His first photographic work appeared in 1894 in various exhibitions in London, Paris, New York, and Brussels, where it was noted that he was a dedicated amateur. The term "amateur" was used at this time to denote someone of considerable artistic and intellectual abilities as opposed to commercial practice. He married Olga Caracciolo in 1896 or 1897 and the marriage provided him with entree to fashionable social circles as well as the title Baron. Practising the soft-focus Pictorialist style in ascendancy during the era, de Meyer became a member of the Linked Ring Brotherhood, the Royal Photographic Society, and the Photo-Secessionists in 1908. During these years de Meyer acquired a strong reputation as a portrait photographer particularly of high society and the artistic circles. His fashion career began in 1914 when he signed a contract with Condé Nast to be the first full-time photographer for *Vogue* and *Vanity Fair* magazines.

There were numerous instances where de Meyer provided not only the photography, but also contributed his skills as an accomplished writer and layout artist in the form of complete articles for these magazines. In 1921, he accepted an offer from William Randolph Hearst to work for *Harper's Bazaar* magazine, where he gained even greater editorial control. He continued working for *Harper's Bazaar* until 1929 when his contract was not renewed and the magazine officially changed its name to *Harper's Bazaar*. Following the death of his wife Olga in 1931 he traveled throughout Europe. He made a permanent move to Hollywood, California, in 1939 under the threat of Hitler's advances in Europe. While he continued to make a few society portraits, his success was largely forgotten and he died in relative obscurity of coronary thrombosis in 1946 in Los Angeles.

Baron de Meyer was a technically and visually brilliant photographer. He often used back or side lighting of his subjects, a technique that is not often used today. His models were largely drawn from the ranks of high society or from the theatre world, a practice that has continued. Towards the end of his career as fashion photographer he was strongly influenced by Modernism in the arts, principally Dada and Surrealism, and he began to increasingly photograph his subjects in profile. The best examples of his work in these new directions were a series of advertisements he produced for the Elizabeth Arden Cosmetics Company in which his models became increasingly stylized and unnatural, a newly constructed style of femininity.

American born Man Ray (1890–1976) lived and worked in France during most of his adult life. His work as a fashion photographer was far reaching in terms of its visual impact and influence on other photographers, but has been overshadowed by his work as a painter, film maker, inventor, and sculptor. He arrived in Paris in 1921 and a year later his first rayographs were published in *Vanity Fair*. Man Ray's photographs were extensions of his artistic development and visions, and often highly experimental and like his peer Francis Bruguiere integrated Surrealist and Dada effects.

Another baron, Baron George Hoyningen-Huene, who was born in Russia, followed Baron de Meyer. He fled to Paris in 1921 and along with Man Ray, became the chief photographer in 1926 for *Vogue*. His style of work was quite similar to that of Baron de Meyer, using back and side lighting of his subjects. Visually his subjects became Greek sculptures, his lighting revealed texture and volume, and garments became the center point of all of his photographs.

Horst P. Horst was born in 1906 in Germany and was trained as an architect. At age 24 Le Corbusier accepted him as an apprentice in his Paris office. During his stay in Paris he met Baron George Hoyningen-Huene and traveled with him that winter to England to meet with Cecil Beaton, the British *Vogue* photographer, whose elaborate costuming and set design and decoration reflected his theatrical and briefly influential vision. Early in 1931 Horst was hired by *Vogue*, initially to do design and layout work, but late that year his first photographs were published in the magazine. His visual style was again similar to that of de Meyer and Huene using elements of Greek mythology as the main symbolism in the photographs. But the design and architectural tendencies Horst expressed added unusual surprises to his pictures. He was able to strike the right balance between the model, the garment, and the architectural surroundings. Horst was able to direct and capture a pose that under other circumstances would have looked forced and unnatural, infused with an elegance of design to make his photographs memorable masterpieces.

Horst was also a master of studio lighting, sometimes working three days on a single set-up. He was not afraid to use numerous lights in his set-ups to create the dramatic effects that he felt his photographs needed. One of his most timeless photographs, *Mainbocher's Pink Satin Corset*, published in American *Vogue* in 1939, was also the subject of a video by Madonna, making it an enduring icon.

Louise Dahl-Wolfe was the first woman fashion photographer to reach prominence in the 1930s and is known for her long tenure with *Harper's Bazaar*. Dahl-Wolfe took fashion out into the open and used deserts, beaches, and various exotic locations as her backdrops. While other fashion photographers had sometimes photographed the out-of-doors, notably Heune's *Swimwear by Izod* (also known as *Divers*) of 1930, Louise Dahl-Wolfe raised to it into a new art form, sweeping away the "Greek statue" genre of fashion photography. Another female practitioner, although working in a less distinctive style, was the Berlin-based Germaine Krull. American Lee Miller, whose notoriety as a model overshadowed her work behind the camera, was another fashion photographer based in Europe during this period.

Hungarian Martin Munkacsi, New York's leading fashion photographer during the 1930s and 1940s, left Germany and immigrated to the United States in 1934. That year, he signed an exclusive contract with *Harper's Bazaar*, which under Carmel Snow's editorship and Alexey Brodovitch's art direction established itself as the most sophisticated fashion magazine of the era. He too promoted the highly active style that showed models and clothes in motion, often out on the street, inspiring the upcoming generation of American photographers. Other important practitioners of fashion photography between the wars, working out of Paris and New York, are Brassai, Erwin Blumenfeld, Arnold Genthe, George Platt Lynes, John Rawlings, Edward Steichen, and Maurice Tabard.

Irving Penn and Richard Avedon emerged into prominence following World War II. Richard Avedon was born in 1923, graduated from Columbia University in 1941, and studied with Alexey Brodovitch at the New School for Social Research from 1944 until 1950. He was hired at *Harper's Bazaar* as a staff photographer in 1945, and held that position for twenty years. He also photographed the French collections in Paris for both *Harper's Bazaar* and *Vogue* from 1947 until 1984. He photographed his subjects in sparse settings, stripping away all extraneous elements so that the viewer would concentrate only on the sitter. One of his many books, *In the American West*, published in 1985, exemplifies this principle. All of his subjects were photographed against a clean white background and the visual focus was completely on the sitter.

Irving Penn was born in 1917 in Plainfield, New Jersey, and following his education in public schools enrolled at the Philadelphia Museum School of Art at age 18. He studied advertising design with Alexey Brodovitch and his first job, working for Alexander Lieberman at *Vogue*, was to suggest covers for the magazine. His first photographic cover was published in the October 1943 issue of the magazine and he continues to contribute work. His photographic work covers not only fashion and portraiture, but also still lifes and nudes. His work shows a similar sparseness of backgrounds as Avedon's, but with some important departures. Early in Penn's career he started to use large moveable walls, which he placed at right angles to each other. Into this corner he placed his subjects, giving them and us, a sense of tight space. He discovered a different form of tight space when he rented a local photographer's studio in the Andes Mountains following a fashion assignment in 1948. The studio had a large north-light window as the sole source of illumination and a plain backdrop with a non-descript floor in which he photographed the villagers. During the next few years he constructed a tent with a similar lighting scheme that traveled with him on overseas trips. The book *Worlds in a Small Room* was the result of these travels.

The major shift in fashion photography that came with both of these photographers was the elimination of the sumptuous settings—glamorous drawing rooms, or theatre locations—and sense of aristocracy, which had been greatly eroded by the work of Munkacsi and by that of William Klein and Louis Faurer, who practiced grainy, blurred styles emphasizing personal expression during the waning years of World War II and in the immediate postwar era. Toni Frissell, who had apprenticed with Cecil Beaton, practiced a casual, straightforward style capturing active, vital women. German-born Herman Landshof also made youthful, active women his signature, showing his photographs mainly in magazines such as *Mademoiselle* aimed at a younger audience. This shift also signaled the decline of Paris as the center of high couture and the development of New York, London, and Milan as fashion centers.

Exemplary of another new style, that of the highly eroticized fashion image, Helmut Newton was born in Berlin in 1920. He studied with the leading photographer Yva, left Germany before World War II, and enlisted in the Australian Army. In 1957, he moved to Paris, where he became a regular contributor to *Vogue, Elle, Playboy*, and *Marie Claire* magazines. Helmut Newton was the first photographer to overtly inject sexuality into fashion photographs. From the beginning, sensuality had been an undercurrent in fashion photographs. Almost every photographer working in the area also made nude photographs, and although occasionally a discreet nude was published in the mainstream magazine as a fashion illustration, most of this work was published as a fine arts effort. With Helmut Newton the models were absolutely certain of their sexuality and thrust it into the foreground. In his highly sexualized images, showing nude and partially nude women, Helmut Newton invited the viewer to be a voyeur and in doing so, he opened a window into a previously forbidden world.

Guy Bourdin, born as Guy Louis Babares in Paris (1928), learned the basics of photography during his service in the military from 1948–1949. He was employed at different times as a salesman for a Paris department store and a messenger for the U.S. Embassy. He started working for *Vogue* magazine in 1954, and his first editorial work was published in the magazine the following year. Twelve years later he started to photograph the advertising campaigns for the Jourdan Shoe Company, while continuing his work for various fashion magazines. Bourdin followed the trail blazed by Helmut Newton, but also carved his own niche in the fashion world. His photographs often have a sadomasochistic touch, sometimes humorous, and always provocative. While Newton almost always worked on location, Bourdin created his realities in the studio.

At the end of the century the field had expanded greatly, with numerous top fashion photographers making substantial contributions to the field, experimenting with color, lighting, extreme locations, computer manipulations, and other digital techniques. A substantial number of women have successfully entered the field, including Deborah Turbeville, whose murky, languid style of color work initially was considered unappealing. Ellen Von Unwerth made the transition from model to photographer, as did the British Sarah Moon, who creates highly manipulated images that hark back to the elaborate style of Cecil Beaton and Baron de Meyer. American Sheila Metzner has photographed in some of the most extreme locales on earth, and the Dutch-born Inez Van Lamsweerde has moved between a career as a fashion photographer and a respected contemporary artist utilizing digital manipulation of her images. French-born Patrick Demarchellier, who works primarily in color; East-German born Peter Lindbergh, known for his black-and-white, retro-styled image of supermodels; Chicago-based Victor Skrebneski, known for his starkly light studio works featuring muscular models; Hiro, whose lush work in color signaled a shift from the predominance of black-and-white; Herb Ritts; Bruce Weber; and numerous others continue to make the photographs that exemplify style and luxurious living.

What Is Fashion Photography?

Fashion photography occupies a unique position in the medium; it is the one type of photography that captures, at one point or another, almost everyone's attention. Fashion photographers, particularly those at the top of the profession, most easily cross the line between fine art and commercial work. It is the one arena where art and commerce can exist in an easy and productive relationship. For some photographers, the line dividing art and commerce is indistinguishable; for others there is a sharp line separating the two. Sheila Metzner and Sarah Moon are two photographers who make no distinction, while Irving Penn and Richard Avedon keep their artistic projects apart from their commercial work. Yet, there is no denying that their artistic work informs the fashion pictures and gives their work a distinctive edge.

As the goal of fashion photography is to project an ideal world that is irresistible to the consumer, it demands an extreme amount of attention to detail, and thus is perhaps the least forgiving of all of photographic genres. The tiniest detail that is overlooked may become a major flaw in the finished photograph making it useless.

As is photography itself, fashion is an illusion. The clothes that we wear and the facades they can create are statements about our identity, both to ourselves and the larger world. In creating its illusion photography shows only two dimensions in place of the reality of three dimensions existing within time. Yet this reduction of reality into a two-dimensional image can create a compelling whole; this is particularly true in fashion photography. Fashion photography does so by concentrating on the best and most perfect parts of both the "real world" and photographic practice. In photography, the choice of the right equipment, the correct angle of the shot, lighting, film, and even the studio or location environment creates a compelling image. In the arena of fashion there are additional requirements: it is the choice of the model, the make-up, hairstyling, the costume, and precisely what part of the garment is to appear in the final photo in addition to the inherent photographic requirements that determine a successful image. It is not enough for the photographer to be a masterful observer, he or she must also be a director of sorts, creating the image as it is captured.

The world of fashion is in a constant state of flux. A successful fashion photographer must learn to live with change (which ironically he or she may have introduced only to see it be abandoned as "last-year's-style") and adapt to it. Despite the achievements of towering figures in the field and the ideals they exemplify, there are no formulas to adopt. Constant reevaluation and searching for new ways to look at a familiar subject is required, thus experimentation is the constant companion of the fashion photographer. But experimentation can bring success as well as failure. Success will mean travel into new territories; failure will mean starting over again. For this reason many fashion photographers experiment through their fine art work, with successes translated back into their commercial work and failures left behind. The result is both artistic growth and exciting new images for consumption in the fashion industry.

The twentieth century has seen the shift in fashion photography from the selling of a specific product to the adaptation of a lifestyle. Baron de Meyer's photographs depicted a garment and a setting that the reader of fashion magazines could aspire to, but seldom achieve. Few could afford the clothing the haute couture designers created. Following World War II, the direction of fashion changed in perceptible ways. Ready-to-wear was featured along with couture creations; movie stars and other celebrities continued to be used as models, but more "average" women were also featured in fashion layouts. Athletic models in motion, exemplified by Lisa Fonnsagrives became more popular. In the latter decades of the twentieth century, the feminist movement that demanded equality in rights and income, the mass marketing techniques of such companies as the Gap or Ralph Lauren, and the sudden rise of the Internet as an avenue of commerce and information, all contributed to the change in the point of view of the fashion photographer. Designer labels became available in discount department stores, and magazines regularly feature the side-by-side comparisons of the couture design and the affordable knock-off. The growth of new fashion magazines, art, music, and the increasing emphasis on youth culture were signaled by a new form of fashion photography. The new fashion photography delves deeply into narrative, telling stories that are not necessarily glamorous, including the anxieties and fears and realities of everyday life. In some ways the pictures of Juergen Teller with their "flash-on-camera" look, are closer to the average snapshot that the reader of the magazines have made themselves. Similarly, California-based Larry Sultan's photographs for designer Kate Spade of fictitious families visiting various locales, including New York, have become the family snapshot album of this century. Philip-Lorca diCorcia also uses this technique, blurring the lines between fashion and documentary photography. These approaches infused new authenticity to fashion photography by mimicking vernacular styles and promoting lifestyle over a focus on items to be acquired.

The Business of Fashion Photography

There are two major segments to fashion and beauty photography. One is the advertising side, the other is often referred to as editorial work. The difference between the two can be stated in one word—control. In advertising photographs it is the client, the art director, or the agency that controls the final content of the photograph. The photographer is often chosen based on who can most closely interpret the style and content of the ad or the ad campaign. While the photographer can suggest, it is the client who decides.

In editorial work it is the collaborative work between the magazine editor and the photographer that produces the end result. In editorial photography, the selection of who will be the photographer often depends on who can best interpret the editorial viewpoint of the magazine, offering a certain amount of artistic freedom.

The business of headshots and model composites is another major element of fashion photography, and studios producing this kind photography can be found in almost every town in America. The typical headshot for fashion modeling is almost always done with large light sources such as umbrellas or soft boxes. This approach minimizes any skin blemishes and tends to flatten the perspective. The skillful application of make-up can open up the eyes or emphasize or reduce the prominence of other facial features. Before any application of make-up starts, it must be determined whether the final photograph is going to be in color or black and white. Make-up for black and white should be somewhat stronger than that used for color photographs.

Most photographers will use either 35 mm or medium format camera equipment, and the choice of lenses is usually a medium telephoto lens in order to flatten the perspective. Headshots for other purposes such as theater or publicity stills often utilize somewhat stronger lighting in order to add a sense of drama.

Model composites are an essential part of what a model needs for her or his business success. The composite or "comp card" contains from three to six photographs as well as the physical statistics of the model and the agency with which she or he is associated. The photographs include a headshot, usually on the cover, followed by several partial or full-length photographs. The basic use of the comp is to allow an art or casting director to select the model type needed for a particular assignment. This is generally followed by a casting call or a "look-see" for a more detailed evaluation of the models. A model's comp must be up to date since many decisions are made from the comp card. A change in hairstyle or color requires a new card.

The fashion model is of course an inextricable aspect of fashion photography. When Baron de Meyer started making fashion photographs, he used as his models the people he was acquainted with, namely the high society women in his and his wife's social circles. Occasionally, he would employ an actress from the stage or a ballet dancer. But the reputation of this latter group of models was mostly unsavory. One indication of this was that he would credit the high society women in the title of the picture with their name, but not the actresses. This practice continued for several decades. As women became emancipated in the early part of the twentieth century, the social and moral strictures altered. In the late 1920s, John Robert Powers started the first modeling school and talent agency in New York and the professional model became a reality. Young women were trained in proper etiquette as well as what was expected of a fashion model. The first professional model to achieve celebrity was Lisa Fonssagrives. Born in Sweden, she moved to Paris in the 1930s to train as a ballet dancer. She was discovered by Horst and became famous for her grace and poise. She worked extensively in Europe in the 1930s and 1940s and married the photographer Irving Penn. Following her move to the United States she was in great demand in New York until the late 1950s. Suzie Parker and her sister Dorian Leigh, and Dovima (who appeared in the classic Avedon image with chained elephants) joined Fonnsagrives as top models of the 1950s. The 1970s saw the "super model" phenomenon epitomized by Cindy Crawford's emergence in the 1980s as a major celebrity due to her work as a fashion model.

Hollywood Glamour Photography

In the world of photography there is one category that stands by itself, namely Hollywood glamour photography. It is neither the standard portrait photograph, nor is it the fashion photograph of that era, nor the production stills that were part of the making of a motion picture. It is a category by itself, and while there have been many practitioners of this type of image making, one name stands out above all, George Hurrell (1904–1992) He singularly invented the category and was part of the golden age of Hollywood glamour photography from 1925 to 1950.

From almost the very beginning of motion pictures, the still photograph of either the production highlights or the headshot of the stars, was an integral part of it. The portraits of the stars were mass-produced and were displayed in the theatre lobbies. The format of choice for these pictures was the 8×10-inch camera, because contact prints could be rapidly reproduced in quantities. Every studio in Hollywood employed a staff photographer to make these portraits. Clarence Sinclair Bull was one of the early photographers who defined the visual language of the genre, while Ruth Harriet Louise was the first female head of the MGM portrait studio from 1925 until 1930. Others included Virgil Apger, Eugene Robert Richee, and Ernest Bachrach. In Chicago, Maurice Seymour was the glamour photographer from the early 1930s through the 1960s.

George Edward Hurrell was born in Covington, Kentucky in 1904. He attended the Art Institute in Chicago as a painter, and was hired by Eugene Hutchinson, a prominent Chicago portrait photographer. Under Hutchinson's tutelage, he learned darkroom work as well as retouching, airbrushing, and hand coloring. In 1925 he moved to Laguna Beach, California, with Edgar Payne, another painter. He quickly learned that the making of photographs was more profitable than the painting of the seascape oils he favored at that time. Most of the portraits he produced during the next two years were done outdoors, and he became exceptionally skilled at using sunlight to produce a pleasing portrait. In 1927, he moved to Los Angeles and opened a photography studio in the Granada Building. The following year he received a visit from the legendary photographer, Edward Steichen, who needed a darkroom to process some of his film. Steichen disclosed that he was charging his client $1500 for similar work for which Hurrell was charging $50. Shortly after that the opportunity came for Hurrell to photograph the star Ramon Novarro and Hurrell made a series of portraits that not only pleased Novarro, but also stood out from the usual studio portraits. By then he had acquired two arc lights so that his portraits could be done indoors at any time of the day or night.

Norma Shearer, who was married to Irving Thalberg, head of MGM Studios, was put in touch with Hurrell by the same person who had introduced him to Novarro. Hurrell made a series of indoor portraits of her that were startlingly different from the standard studio portraits. The difference was in the lighting scheme.

The standard equipment of the studio portrait photographer was the 8 × 10-inch view camera. Most studios used a Kodak Portrait lens, which had purposely several chromatic defects. The visible effect of this was the halos that formed around the highlights when the lens was used at a wide open, f-4 aperture. It must also be remembered that using a lens at its widest aperture produces very shallow depth of field and the result is a picture that is sharp in only one plane, but out of focus in all other areas. This "soft focus" effect was actually sought after by the studios since it gave the portraits a dreamlike and romantic quality. But as important was the fact that this method produced fewer skin flaws and reduced the amount of retouching needed. The method of lighting the portrait followed the conventions of centuries of painting. A large light source was placed at eye level, a hair light was set behind the subject aimed in order to separate the subject from the background and finally, a light was aimed at the background to provide even greater separation. This lighting scheme and the use of the soft focus lens satisfied the portrait buying public. This scene was ready for a revolutionary change by a bored and restless George Hurrell.

When Hurrell did Novarro's portrait, he started by placing his main light on a boom directly above his subject. This placement has a tendency to create strong shadows in the eye sockets as well as a deep shadow under the nose and chin. He opened these shadows with his second light set at face level. There were two other tools that Hurrell used. He owned a Wollensak Verito soft focus lens, but for the Novarro portrait he closed the lens down to an aperture of f-22, thus defeating the purpose of the soft focus lens. The result was sharpness across the entire picture plane. Finally, Hurrell used orthochromatic film for his portraits. The effect on skin tones with this film was to give the sitter a tan, which translated into an exotic look. These three parts added up to a greater whole. It provided Hollywood with a new and glamorous way to portray its treasure of stars. It turned the stars into idealized icons.

With the success of the Norma Shearer's portraits, he was hired as the chief photographer at the MGM Studios in 1930. But his interest was in operating his own studio and in 1932, he left MGM. He was quickly imitated, not only in Hollywood, but all over the country, and his style lives on in many studios.

Peter Le Grand

See also: **Beaton, Cecil; Blumenfeld, Erwin; Dada; de Meyer, Baron Adolphe; diCorcia, Philip-Lorca; Erotic Photography; Faurer, Louis; Hiro; Horst, Horst P.; Hoyningen-Huene, George; Hurrell, George; Klein, William; Krull, Germaine; Liberman, Alexander; Lighting and Lighting Equipment; Miller, Lee; Munkacsi, Martin; Nast, Condé; Newton, Helmut; Penn, Irving; Ray, Man; Ritts, Herb; Surrealism; Turbeville, Deborah; Weber, Bruce**

Further Reading

Aucoin, Kevin. *Making Faces*. New York: Little, Brown and Company, 1997.

Avedon, Richard. *In the American West*. New York: Harry N. Abrams, 1996.

Bourdin, Guy. *Bourdin: Exhibit A*. With text by Samuel Bourdin and Fernando Delgado. New York: Little, Brown and Company, 2001.

Buttolph, Angela, et al. *The Fashion Book*. London: Phaidon Press Ltd., 1998.

De l'Ecotais, Emmanuelle, and Alain Sayag. *Man Ray, Photography and its Double*. Corte Madera, CA: Ginko Press, Inc., 1998.

De Meyer, Baron Adolph. *A Singular Elegance*. With text by Anne Ehrenkranz, New York: International Center of Photography, 1994.

Horst, Richard J. and Lothar Schirmer, eds. *Horst: Sixty Years of Photography*. New York: Universe Publishing, 1996.

Kismaric, Suzan. *Fashioning Fiction in Photography Since 1990*. New York: Museum of Modern Art, 2004.

Martin, Richard. *Fashion and Surrealism*. New York: Rizzoli International Publications, Inc., 1987.

Metzner, Sheila. *Form and Fashion*. Santa Fe, NM: Arena Editions, 2001.

Newton, Helmut and Alice Springs. *Us and Them*. Zurich: Scalo, 1999.

Newton, Helmut. *Pola Woman*. Edited by June Newton. Munich: Schirmer/Mosel, 1995.

Penn, Irving. *Worlds in a Small Room*. New York: Viking Press, 1980.

Penrose, Roland. *Man Ray*. London: Thames and Hudson, 1989.

BERNARD FAUCON

French

Discovered in the early 1980s, the work of Bernard Faucon is presently linked to "*mise en scène*" photography, staged or fabricated photographs. With colorful, elaborately constructed images that blend reality and fiction, he has created an original, poetic world.

Present in the world's most important public and private collections, Bernard Faucon is one of the rare French contemporary photographers to have achieved international recognition. His fame in particular throughout Japan and in the United States is vast, reflecting a body of work at once modern and romantic, and anchored in universal issues.

Born in 1950, Bernard Faucon spent the first 20 years of his life in Apt, a small town in the south of France, where his parents set up a summer house. In 1967, his grandmother offered him his first camera, a Semflex, with which he photographed those closest to him as well as his first landscapes.

In 1971, Bernard Faucon settled in Paris, where he studied philosophy at the Sorbonne. There, he was deeply affected by the thinking of the eminent Thomist philosopher Jacques Maritain, with whom he became friendly, and who had a great influence on him. From 1965 on, he began to paint, making pictures in relief. But it was in 1976 that he purchased a Hasselblad camera and decided to dedicate himself to photography, then producing his first photographic "*mises en scène*." Using mannequins he collected like ready-mades; he reconstructed powerful moments in an idealized childhood. His mannequins became veritable characters in fables that at times he mingled with real children. Among his various themes, he favored the natural elements: water, fire, snow; as well as the essential rituals of this young age, such as snack time, games, and parties.

The titles of his photographs: *L'enfant qui vole*, *La neige qui brûle*, *La comète*, *L'enterrement des jouets*, (the child who flies, the burning show, the comet, the toy burial) evoke a magical world halfway between dream and reality.

Discovered in 1979 in two exhibitions, the first in Paris (at the Agathe Gaillard gallery) and the second in New York (at Castelli Graphics), he very quickly achieved international recognition.

He abandoned the use of mannequins in 1981, however, putting them aside to concentrate on landscapes and interiors containing the mere traces of a presence that has already vanished. A glass of water abandoned on a side table under the full moon; a lavender field where brilliantly colored pieces of laundry hang out to dry under a clothesline; a party in the shadowy half-darkness in which one can distinguish lights only from afar. He has also photographed fires that set nature ablaze. As in Giorgio de Chirico's paintings, Bernard Faucon has created a strange, beautiful, metaphysical atmosphere in his work. Little by little, his work structured itself around several important series that evoke the passage of time, the fragility of the moment, and the fleeting quality of happiness.

Simultaneously a scenic designer, stylist, decorator, wardrobe artist, accessory specialist, and lighting designer, Bernard Faucon has produced rigorously composed images that require weeks of preparation.

> I think of works in series...after a very abstract phase, I reconstruct the image from details, objects, situations.... Everything is lighted, brightened, even on the outside, but no effects are added on film. I don't use filters. If I need something to be out of focus, I create a light smoke. I photograph what I want, and even if it lasts only for the moment of shooting the picture, I can believe I saw it.
>
> (From an interview by Hervé Guibert, *Le Monde* 14/01/1981)

He produced only several dozen photographs per year, always in color, and using an ancient technique, that of the Fresson print, which produces a patina similar to that of painting. Following the series *Les Grandes Vacances* (1975–1977) and *Evolution probable du temps* (1981–1984), he invented *Les Chambres d'Amour* (1984–1987). In empty rooms, embers smolder, wild grasses overtake the ground, an expanse of cold milk seeps out like a lake. Ice, straw, dried flowers, an unmade bed make up his poetic furnishings, the last refuges of his intimacy, in which the artist's romantic interrogations and concerns are reflected, as if in a mirror.

In 1987, Bernard Faucon discovered Asia and, thrilled by the golden light of gods and temples, created *Les Chambres d'Or* (1987–1989). Gold leaf applied to walls, landscapes, and bodies sublimates and transforms a reality in which material and spiritual, oriental and occidental, clash violently.

Then followed a more radical series, *Les idoles et les sacrifices* (1989–1991), which juxtaposes 12 portraits of adolescents transfixed in a golden light with a series of 12 landscapes crossed with a blood-red wound.

Bernard Faucon first showed his work at the Yvon Lambert gallery in Paris, at a moment when the Espace Photographique de Paris was also exhibiting a retrospective of his work. He published several books at that time, notably in Japan, and began to travel in Asia and the Middle East.

Les Ecritures (1991–1993), phrases inscribed in the landscape, marked a real turning point in his work. For the series, he wrote text by hand, enlarged it, produced the letters in plywood, covered the letters with reflective tape, then installed them in spaces he had chosen. Artificial lighting revealed the text. But Bernard Faucon created not installations, but photographs. Although his work could easily be categorized within the field of contemporary art installations, he remained faithful to Fresson prints, whose largest formats do not surpass 60 × 60 cm. After having inscribed the words in the landscape, he then started inscribing them onto bodies, even onto skin itself.

A last series, entitled *La fin de l'image* (1993–1995), marked the end of his photographic activity. Fifty-one small-format photographs framed in black unfold like a film. On each, one can read short phrases: "*tout pour un baiser et la vie avec*," "*tu me caches le monde*," "*j'étais aimé*" (all for a kiss and life with it; you hide the world from me; I was loved)... and on the last, simply the word "*fin*" (end) appeared.

In 1997, Bernard Faucon decided to suspend production of his photographic images. Conscious of having said everything he could with the medium, he thus turned toward writing. "Even the greatest do not know how to stop time," he asserts. "Either I regenerate myself dramatically, or I go on to something else. One thing is certain, the history of the image is coming to an end (in an interview with Michel Guerrin, *Le Monde*, June 10, 1995)."

From 1997 to 2000, he developed a vast project in 20 countries, entitled *Le plus beau jour de ma jeunesse*. Aided by a young writer, Antonin Potoski, he invited 100 young people in each country, armed with instant cameras, to a party, and asked them to photograph those they loved and moments of happiness. Selected by and then shown for the first time together at the Maison Européenne de la Photographie, Paris, in November 2000, these images toured the world, accompanied by a book about the project. In 1999, he published his first collection of texts without images, *La peur du voyage*.

JEAN-LUC MONTEROSSO

See also: **Constructed Reality; Photography in Europe: France**

Biography

Born in Apt in Provence, September 12, 1950. Educated at the Lycée d'Apt, 1962–1969. Studied at the Sorbonne, Paris, 1969–1973. Master's Degree in Philosophy, 1973. Painter from 1966 to 1976. Photographic settings since 1977. Recipient: Prix du premier livre de photo de la Ville de Paris, 1979; Grand Prix National, 1989; Prix Léonard de Vinci, 1991.

Individual Exhibitions

1977 Galerie Lop Lop, Paris, France
Fotomania, Barcelona, Spain
1979 Galerie Agathe Gaillard, Paris, France
Castelli Graphics, New York, New York
1980 Galerie Venster, Museum of Rotterdam, The Netherlands
Galerie Canon, Geneva, Switzerland
1981 Galerie Junod, Lausanne, Switzerland
1982 Centre Georges Pompidou, "In situ," Paris, France
1983 Espace Niçois d'art et de culture, "Peindre et photographier," Nice, France
1984 Nouveau Musée, Villeurbanne, Lyon, France
1985 Musée Nicéphore Niépce, Chalon-sur-Saône, France
1986 Houston Center for Photography, Houston, Texas
1988 Espace Photo de la Ville de Paris, "Rétrospective," Paris, France
Interform Gallery, Osaka, Japan
Maison Descartes, "Retrospective," Amsterdam, The Netherlands
1989 Zeit Foto Salon, Tokyo, Japan
Centre Fotografic Visor, Valencia, Spain
1990 Duta Fine Arts Foundation, Jakarta, Indonesia
Institut Français, Freiburg, Germany
1993 Aberdeen Art Gallery, Aberdeen Museum, Aberdeen Scotland
1994 Rebecca Hossack Gallery, London, England
1995 Nun Gallery, Seoul, South Korea
1996 The Photographers' Gallery, London, England
1998 Casa del Cultura Nuevo Leon, Monterrey, Mexico
Le plus beau paysage du monde; Institut Français de Marrakech, Marrakech, Morocco, and traveling
1999 *La fête des anges*; Gallery of Silpakorn University, Bangkok, Thailand
La Isla mas querida del mundo; Centro Wifredo Lam, Havana, Cuba
Le plus beau crépuscule....; Stadt Museum, Göteburg, Sweden
La plus belle promenade...; Kunstverein, Heidelberg, Germany
2000 *The Bernard Faucon Collection*; Utsunomiya Museum of Art, Japan

Group Exhibitions

1980 *Invented images*; U.C.S.B. Art Museum, Santa Barbara, California, and traveling
1982 *Invented images*; Musée d'Art Moderne de la ville de Paris, and traveling
Staged photo events; Lijnbaancentrum, Rotterdam Kunstichting, and traveling
1984 *Images imagines*; Musée Rimbaud, Charleville, and traveling
Contemporary Photographs, towards new developments; Fukuoa Art Museum, Japan
A Contemporary Focus; Hirshhorn Museum and Sculpture Garden, Washington, D.C.
La Puissance de la Photographie; Forum Stadtpark, Graz, Austria
1986 *Constructions et Fictions, 12 artistes Français et L'image Photographique*; Fondazione Scientifica Quérini Stampalia, Venice, Italy, and traveling

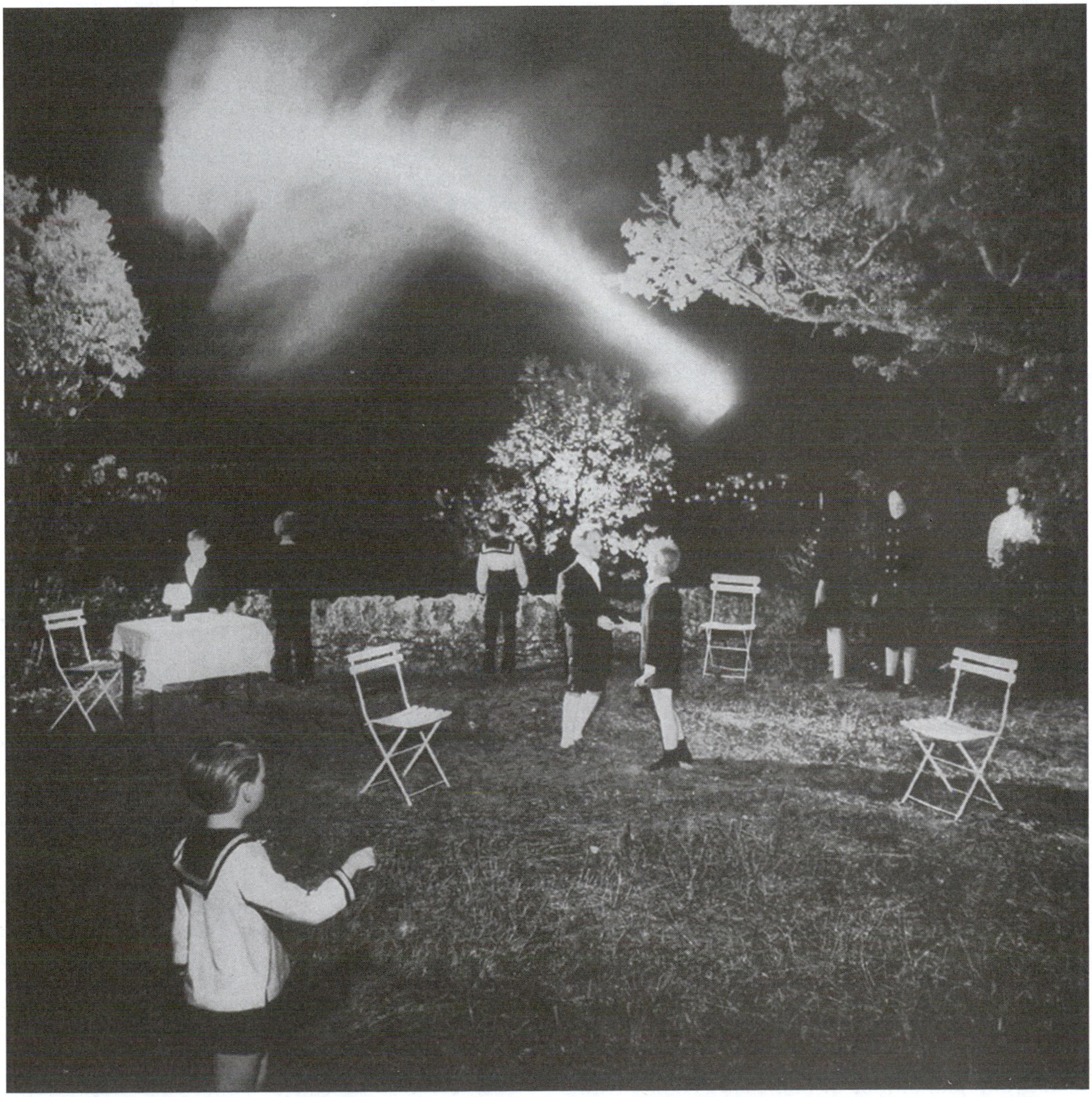

Bernard Faucon, The Comet, 1982.
[*CNAC/MNAM/Dist. Réunion des Musées Nationaux/Art Resource, New York*]

Photography as performance; The Photographers' Gallery, London, England
Angle of Vision, French Artists Today; Solomon R. Guggenheim Museum, New York, New York
1987 *True Stories and Photofictions*; The Ffotogallery, Cardiff, Wales, and traveling
1989 *20 ans de Photographie créative en France*; Musée Ludwig, Cologne, Germany, and traveling
1991 *Contempory French Photography*; International Center of Photography Midtown, New York, New York
1992 *Invented images*; Tokyo Metropolitan Museum of Photography, Tokyo, Japan
1994 *La vie, l'amour, la mort*; FNAC, France, and traveling
1995 *Invented images*; Centro Cultural, Arte Contemporaneo, Mexico
Beyond Recognition; National Gallery of Australia, and traveling
Gommes et pigments; Centre Georges Pompidou, Paris, France
1996 *Invented images*; Aperture's Burden Gallery, New York, New York, and traveling
1998, *La collection Yvon Lambert*; Yokohama Museum of Art, Yokohama, Japan
2000 *Kinder des 20. Jahrhunderts*; Galerie der Stadt, Aschaffenburg & Mittelrhein-Museum, Koblenz
2001 *Invented images*; Matsuzakaya, Tokyo, Japan
Sonne, Mond und Sterne; Staatsgalerie Stuttgart, Germany
Desire; Galeria d'Arte Moderna, Bologna, Italy & Ursula Blickle Stiftung, Kraichtal, Austria

Further Reading

Borhan, Pierre. *Bernard Faucon, "Les grands photographes."* Paris: Belfond, 1988.
Faucon, Bernard. *Les Grandes Vacances*. Paris: Herscher, 1980.
———. Faucon, Bernard. *Summer Camp*. New York: Xavier Moreau, 1980.
———. Faucon, Bernard. *La Part du Calcul dans la Grâce*. Bordeaux: William Blake and Co., 1985.
———. Faucon, Bernard. *Les papiers qui volent*, Paris/Parco, Tokyo: Hazan, 1986.
———. Faucon, Bernard. *Les chambres d'amour*, William Blake and Co., Bordeaux 1987.
———. Faucon, Bernard. *Chambres d'amour, Chambres d'or*. Bordeaux, William Blake and Co., 1989.
———. Faucon, Bernard. *Tables d'amis*. Bordeaux: William Blake and Co., 1991.
Jours d'image. Tokyo: Tréville, 1995.
———. *12 Menus-Paysages*. Sets de Table. Paris: Maison Européenne de la Photographie, 1996.
———. *La peur du Voyage - Visions et Légendes*. Bordeaux: William Blake and Co., 1999.
———. *Le plus beau jour de ma jeunesse*. Paris: Éditions de L'imprimeur, 2000.
Faucon, Bernard, and Antonin Potoski. *La plus belle route du monde*. Paris: POL, 2000.

LOUIS FAURER

American

Louis Faurer emerged in the 1940s as a talented photographer on the basis of both his personal and commercial work. He is best known for his artistic photography: gritty black-and-white emotionally charged photographs that capture the great bustling crowds of New York City streets and the isolated, haunted figures that roam them. His subject matter, raw style, disregard for the "rules" of photography, and his involvement with commercial magazine photography place him in what is now known as the New York School of Street Photography. Although Faurer was included in seminal group exhibitions at mid-century, only within the last few decades has his work regained significant recognition.

Born on August 28, 1916 to Polish immigrant parents in South Philadelphia, Faurer displayed an early predilection towards drawing; he attended Philadelphia's School of Commercial Art and Lettering, and worked as an advertising painter and commercial letterer before turning to photography in 1937. His early photographic education primarily consisted of pouring through Farm Security Administration publications. Faurer particularly admired Walker Evans's photographs, but his own work never had quite the same objective, social documentary style. Not long after picking up a camera, Faurer won the "Photo of the Week" award in a local paper and soon found his preferred subject matter—city streets that alternately teemed with crowds and featured lone figures. Work completed while he was in Philadelphia displays a strong interest in street vendors and beggars. In *Market St., Philadelphia, PA*, 1937, the limbs, cane, sign, and pencil box of a blind man jut out into the picture frame in sharp focus amidst the blurry figures of rushed pedestrians.

In 1946, Faurer began commuting to New York in search of commercial photography work and found a position at Hearst publications' *Junior Bazaar*. He met Walker Evans in the offices of *Fortune* and Robert Frank at *Harper's*. Frank and Faurer became friends, and they admired and influenced each other's work. Frank offered Faurer the use of his studio; Faurer worked both there and in the studio of Sol Mednick (whom he knew from Philadelphia) until moving to New York in 1948. He also met *Harper's Bazaar's* legendary art director Alexey Brodovitch, and attended several classes at Brodovitch's Design Laboratory while he remained primarily self-taught. The utilization of motion, blur, and large grain in Faurer's fashion photography during this period, however, reflect Brodovitch's predilection for dynamism and novelty.

Between 1947 and 1951, Faurer worked prolifically, creating a distinct and haunting body of personal work possessing great emotional impact while maintaining his career as a commercial photographer. He acted as the great roaming eye of the city, wandering its streets and peering out of its windows. Everywhere in the photographs people are looking—at times looking back at the photographer, but most often looking at the surrounding sights of the city. His images capture the bustling energy of postwar America, as in *Broadway, New York, NY*, 1949–1950, which shows laughing young women in a convertible barreling down a street of lighted marquees. Most often, however, his work conveys a sense of underlying isolation and disillusionment. He is particularly drawn to the social outcasts and loners: the retarded man holding a flower in *Eddie, New York, NY*, 1948, the eerie twins in *5th Ave., New York, NY*, c. 1948, or the woman smoking a joint, oblivious to the men behind her in *Barnum & Bailey Circus Performers, Madison Square Garden*, 1950. Faurer, however, always approached these subjects with empathy, never criticism. With themes such as the individual versus metropolis, along with general mood and style, many of Faurer's works from this period display an affinity with cinema's *film noir*.

Faurer was particularly attracted to Times Square at night. His photographs capture the area at its post-war zenith, before it became a seedy center of vice. Graphically bold images of lighted signage, such as *New York, NY*, 1948, capture the dynamism of city life and attest to his continued interest in commercial lettering. Working primarily at night provided technical challenges. Using a 35 mm camera (most often a Leica), the most sensitive films of the time, wide-aperture settings, and slow shutter speed, he primarily relied on intuition and experience, not light meters, to achieve proper film exposure. Many of Faurer's photographs possess a dreamlike quality, owing to his use of multiple exposure and spliced negatives or his seeking out of reflections [see Multiple Exposures and Printing]. In "Accident," 1949–52, Faurer capitalizes upon having accidentally exposed the film in his camera twice, creating a haunting print that eerily combines a wedding with a shivering boy at the scene of an accident.

At mid-century, the Museum of Modern Art included him in many important group exhibitions, including *In and Out of Focus*, 1948, and *The Family of Man*, 1955. In 1949, he became a staff photographer for the short-lived but extravagantly produced *Flair*, which in 1950 published his photo essay, *The Eight Million*. Faurer relocated to Europe in 1968 for reasons described variously as a desire to pursue commercial work, emotional distress, marriage problems, and trouble with the IRS. He returned to New York in 1974, just as photography was gaining greater recognition in the art world with more venues for its display. Faurer began to seek recognition for his artistic work, an endeavor helped after meeting William Eggleston and curator Walter Hopps. During the last decades of his life, he secured exhibitions, taught photography courses, and printed earlier negatives while continuing to photograph; however, his work lacked his former intensity. Faurer also supervised color printing of 35 mm transparencies dating to mid-century. He died in Manhattan on March 2, 2001.

Faurer is often noted as filling a gap in the history of American photography between Walker Evans and Robert Frank, both of whom he knew and admired. His work is far more emotionally wrought and offhanded than Evans's but without the extremely expressive potential and strong sense of composition of Frank's. Faurer's renewed reputation, however, rests less on historiographical convenience than on the intrinsic merits of his strong personal vision of America expressed in works from the forties and fifties.

Amanda Brown

See also: **Eggleston, William; Evans, Walker; Farm Security Administration; Frank, Robert; History of Photography: Postwar Era; Multiple Exposures and Printing; Street Photography**

Biography

Born in Philadelphia, Pennsylvania, August 28, 1916. Attended School of Commercial Art and Lettering, Philadelphia, 1934–37. Civilian Photographer, U.S. Signal Corps, Philadelphia, 1941–45; commercial photographer for *Flair, Glamour, Harper's Bazaar, Junior Bazaar, Seventeen, Mademoiselle, Look, Vogue*, 1946–1967; photographs illustrate Truman Capote's book, *Local Color*, 1950; on-set photographer for the films *Walk on the Wild Side* and *Five Finger Exercise*, 1960. Instructor at Parsons School of Design, New York, 1975–1983; lectured at State University of New York, Stockton State College, New Jersey, and the University of Maryland, College Park, 1981; lectured at Yale University, New Haven and University of Virginia, Charlottesville, 1983; taught Thesis Class in Photography at the School of Visual Arts, New York, 1985–86. Creative Artists Public Service Fellowship Grant, New York State Council for the Arts, 1977–78; National Endowment for the Arts Grant, 1978; John Simon Guggenheim Memorial Fellowship, 1979. Died in New York, New York, March 2, 2001.

Individual Exhibitions

1959 *Louis Faurer: Photographs*; Limelight Gallery; New York, New York
1977 *Louis Faurer: Photographs*, 1937–1966; Marlborough Gallery; New York, New York
1981 *Louis Faurer: Photographs from Philadelphia and New York*; Art Gallery, University of Maryland; College Park, Maryland
Louis Faurer: Photographs; Light Gallery; New York, New York
1986 *Louis Faurer: Photographs;* Davison Art Center, Wesleyan University; Middletown, Connecticut
1987 *Louis Faurer: Vintage Photographs*; Laurence Miller Gallery; New York, New York
1990 *Louis Faurer*; Espace Colbert, Bibliothèque nationale; Paris, France
Louis Faurer; Kathleen Ewing Gallery; Washington, D.C.
1991 *Louis Faurer: Photographs*; Zelda Cheatle Gallery, London
1992 *Louis Faurer*; Centre nationale de la photographie, Palais de Tokyo; Paris, France
1994 *Louis Faurer: Photographs*; Photo Gallery International; Tokyo, Japan
1998 *Louis Faurer, USA*; Zentrum für Fotograpfie; Berlin, Germany
1999 *Louis Faurer*; Casa dos Crivos, Encontros de Imagem, Association de Fotografia e Cinemade; Braga, Portugal
2002 *Louis Faurer Retrospective*; Museum of Fine Arts; Houston, Texas

Selected Group Exhibitions

1948 *In and Out of Focus: A Survey of Today's Photographers*; Museum of Modern Art; New York, New York
1950 *Photography, Mid-Century*; Los Angeles County Museum of Art; Los Angeles, California
Photographs by 15 American Photographers; Museum of Modern Art; New York, New York
1951 *Abstraction in Photography*; Museum of Modern Art; New York, New York
1952 *Then and Now*; Museum of Modern Art; New York, New York
1955 *The Family of Man*; Museum of Modern Art; New York, New York
1958 *Photographs from the Museum Collection*; Museum of Modern Art; New York, New York
1983 *Phototypes: The Development of Photography in New York City*; Whitney Museum of American Art, Downtown Branch; New York, New York
1984 *Automobile and Culture*; Museum of Contemporary Art; Los Angeles, California
1985 *The New York School, 1935–1963: Part I; Part II; Part III*; Corcoran Gallery of Art; Washington, D.C.
1989 *Night Light: A Survey of 20th Century Night Photography, An Exhibition From the Hallmark Photographic Collection;* Nelson-Atkins Museum; Kansas City, Missouri
1991 *Appearances: Fashion Photography Since 1945*; Victoria and Albert Museum; London, England
1995 *American Photography 1890-1965*; Staatliche Museen zu Berlin; Berlin, Germany
1999 *The American Century: Art & Culture 1900–2000, Part I, 1900-1950*; Whitney Museum of American Art; New York, New York
2002 *Visions from America: Photographs from Whitney Museum of American Art 1940-2001*; Whitney Museum of American Art; New York, New York

Selected Works

Market St., Philadelphia, PA, 1937
Eddie, New York, NY, 1948
5th Ave., New York, N.Y. , c. 1948
New York, N.Y., 1948
Broadway, New York, N.Y., 1949–1950
Accident, 1949-52
Family Time Square, 1949–1950
Barnum & Bailey Circus Performers, Madison Square Garden, 1950

Further Reading

Harrison, Martin, and Stuart Alexander. *Louis Faurer*. Collection Photo Poche, Paris: Centre national de la photographie, 1992.
Liebman, Lisa. "People and Ideas: Louis Faurer." *Aperture*, 88 (1982).
Livingston, Jane. *The New York School: Photographs, 1936–1963*. New York: Stewart, Tabori, and Chang, Inc., 1992.
Tonelli, Edith A., and John Gossage, eds. *Louis Faurer: Photographs from Philadelphia and New York*. College Park, Maryland: University of Maryland Art Gallery, 1981.
Tucker, Anne Wilkes. *Louis Faurer*. London: Merrel, 2002.

ANDREAS FEININGER

American

A photographer for *Life* magazine for 20 years, Andreas Feininger created some of the most iconic images of modern America. His view of Coney Island on the July Fourth holiday (1949) congested with a sea of celebrants and a photograph of the car- and pedestrian-clogged Fifth Avenue in Manhattan (1950) conveyed the kinetic and chaotic life of city dwellers in the mid-twentieth century. The 1951 picture of photojournalist Dennis Stock holding a camera in front of his face has become a symbol of the unique marriage between camera and photographer. Building upon themes explored first at *Life*, Feininger focused his later work on nature, in particular on the geometric structures and patterns common among forms such as leaf veins, shell spirals, and forest growth.

Born in Paris in 1906 to American artist Lyonel Feininger, Andreas and his younger brother T(heodore) Lux Feininger (a painter and photographer) traced their early artistic influences to the Bauhaus in Germany, where Lyonel taught in the 1920s. At the avant-garde institution, Feininger studied cabinetmaking and took a photography class from Walter Peterhans, yet he recalled teaching himself how to experiment with form, technique, and subject matter, no doubt inspired by László Moholy-Nagy who lived in the same duplex as his family. By the late 1920s, Feininger published photographs through the Dephot photo agency, and he had several photos included in the landmark 1929 exhibition *Film und Foto* at the Deutsche Werkbund in Stuttgart, Germany.

After acquiring a degree in architecture from the Anhaltische Bauschule zu Zerbst in 1928, Feininger worked as an architect for firms in Dessau and Hamburg until 1932, when his American citizenship prohibited him from legal employment in Germany. He briefly worked for the architect Le Corbusier in Paris, then moved to Stockholm where he found employment as a photographer for architectural businesses. There he married Gertrud Wysse Hägg, with whom he had one son, Tomas, born in 1935. While in Sweden Feininger published a few photography books, including *Stockholm* (1936), which featured images of ships and barges in the city's port, and *New Paths in Photography* (published in English, 1939), which presented some experimental work.

Increasingly challenged to find work, by 1939 Feininger moved his family to New York, where he quickly secured commission assignments from the Black Star photo agency and *Life* magazine. In 1942 the U.S. Office of War Information hired Feininger to shoot a series on the country's factories producing weapons and instruments for the war. The next year *Life* magazine hired Feininger as a staff photographer—a position he held until 1962. At *Life*, Feininger completed more than 340 assignments, many of which he initiated himself. With a straightforward, realistic style, Feininger captured the dynamism of New York, the abstract beauty of factories and manmade landscapes, and the fascinating world of insects. The Dennis Stock image was part of a photo essay on working people and their equipment, such as a welder with a protective helmet or a diver with a face mask.

In addition to his work for *Life*, Feininger wrote articles on technique and aesthetics for *Popular Photography* (1949–1950) and *Modern Photography* (1957–1969 and 1969–1972). He published several books and was included in a number of exhibitions, notably *The Family of Man* at the Museum of Modern Art (1955) as well as a one-person exhibition titled *The Anatomy of Nature* at the American Museum of Natural History (1957).

Feininger's nature subjects became his obsession. After quitting *Life* in 1962, Feininger devoted himself to creating photography books intended to inspire appreciation and environmental action on the part of the reader. Thus *Trees* (1968), *Shells* (1972), and *Leaves* (1984) promote the beauty and variety of species and *Forms of Nature and Life* (1966), *Nature Close Up* (1977), and *In a Grain of Sand* (1986) explore the interrelatedness of natural forms, from a snake's skeleton to mineral deposits in a rock specimen. He typically shot inanimate objects in his studio at home, with minimal background and usually in close-up. In the landscape, Feininger took non-sentimental photos of trees, tightly cropped images of bark, and gripping shots of insects devouring each other. Feininger worked with color photography as early at the 1950s, and he published a few Cibachrome close-ups of butterfly scales and leaf veins in his last book *Nature in Miniature* (1989).

Regardless of subject matter (pine cones or freight ships, feathers or assembly lines), Feininger emphasized formal characteristics in his photographs that he also espoused in his articles. Such qualities included clarity, contrast, pattern, outline, texture, and detail. He credited this approach to his educational background:

> As long as I can remember, I have been interested in the forms of rocks and plants and animals. I have studied them, not with the eye of an artist, but with the eye of the architect and engineer, who is primarily interested in structure, construction, and function.
>
> (*Anatomy* 1956, 8)

Feininger's analytical style posits his photographs somewhere between the clinical work of *Neue Sachlichkeit* (New Objectivity) German artists such as Karl Blossfeldt and Albert Renger-Patzsch and the sensual imagery of American straight photographers Edward Weston and Imogen Cunningham (all of whom Feininger exhibited with at various points in his career). Compared to fellow *Life* photographer Margaret Bourke-White, Feininger lacked drama, both in terms of his photography and his public persona, yet he maintained a consistency in quality and aesthetics.

His imagery and dedication to the field were rewarded by numerous exhibitions and awards. The International Center of Photography organized a traveling retrospective in 1976, and his photographs have been collected by several major museums including the International Museum of Photography and Film, George Eastman House in Rochester, New York, and the Center for Creative Photography, University of Arizona, Tuscon, which also houses his archives. He received a Gold Medal Award for Editorial Design from the Art Directors Club of Metropolitan Washington in 1965 and a Robert Leavitt Award from the American Society of Magazine Photographers in 1966. He died in New York at the age of 92.

N. Elizabeth Schlatter

See also: **Bauhaus; Black Star; Feininger, T. Lux; Modern Photography; Moholy-Nagy, László; Office of War Information; Peterhans, Walter; Popular Photography**

Biography

Born in Paris, France, 22 December 1906 to American parents. Studied at Bauhaus in both Weimar and Dessau, Germany but essentially self-educated in photography, 1919–1928; received degree in architecture from the Anhaltische Bauschule zu Zerbst, near Dessau, Germany, 1928. Worked for architect Le Corbusier in Paris, 1932; in Stockholm worked as photographer for architectural firms, published first book on photography, 1933–1939; worked as freelance photographer for Black Star photo agency, 1940; commissioned by U.S. Office of War Information, Photographic Section, to photograph factories throughout the country, 1942; 20-year career as a staff photographer for *Life* magazine, 1943–1962. Received Gold Medal Award from the Art Directors Club of Metropolitan Washington, 1965; Robert Leavitt Award from the American Society of Magazine Photographers, 1966. Died in New York 18 February 1999.

Individual Exhibitions

1957 *The Anatomy of Nature*; The American Museum of Natural History; New York, and traveling
1963 *The World Through My Eyes*; Smithsonian Institution; Washington, D.C.
1965 *New York in Farbe*; Deutsche Gesellshaft für Photographie; Germany
1968 The Heckscher Museum; Huntington, New York
1970 The Oakland Museum; California
1972 *Shells*; The American Museum of Natural History; New York
1976 *Andreas Feininger: A Retrospective*; International Center of Photography; New York
1978 *New York in the Forties*; New York Historical Society; New York
1981 Center for Creative Photography, University of Arizona; Tucson
1982, 1985 Daniel Wolf Gallery; New York
1995, 1997 Bonni Benrubi Gallery; New York
2002 *Structures of Nature: Photographs by Andreas Feininger*; University of Richmond Museums, Virginia, and traveling
2003 *Andreas Feininger*; Frances Lehman Loeb Art Center, Vassar University, Poughkeepsie, New York

Group Exhibitions

1929 *Film und Foto*; Deutsche Werkbund, Stuttgart, Germany
1948 *50 Photographs by 50 Photographers*; Museum of Modern Art, New York
1948 *In and Out of Focus*; Museum of Modern Art, New York
1955 *The Family of Man*; Museum of Modern Art, New York
1957 *Faces in American Art*; Metropolitan Museum of Art, New York
1958 *Seventy Photographers Look at New York*; Museum of Modern Art, New York
1959 *Photography at Mid-Century*; George Eastman House, Rochester, New York
1960 *The Best of Life—Photographer's Choice*; American Federation of Arts, traveling
1960 *Photography in Fine Arts*; Metropolitan Museum of Art, New York (also 1963, 1964, and 1967)

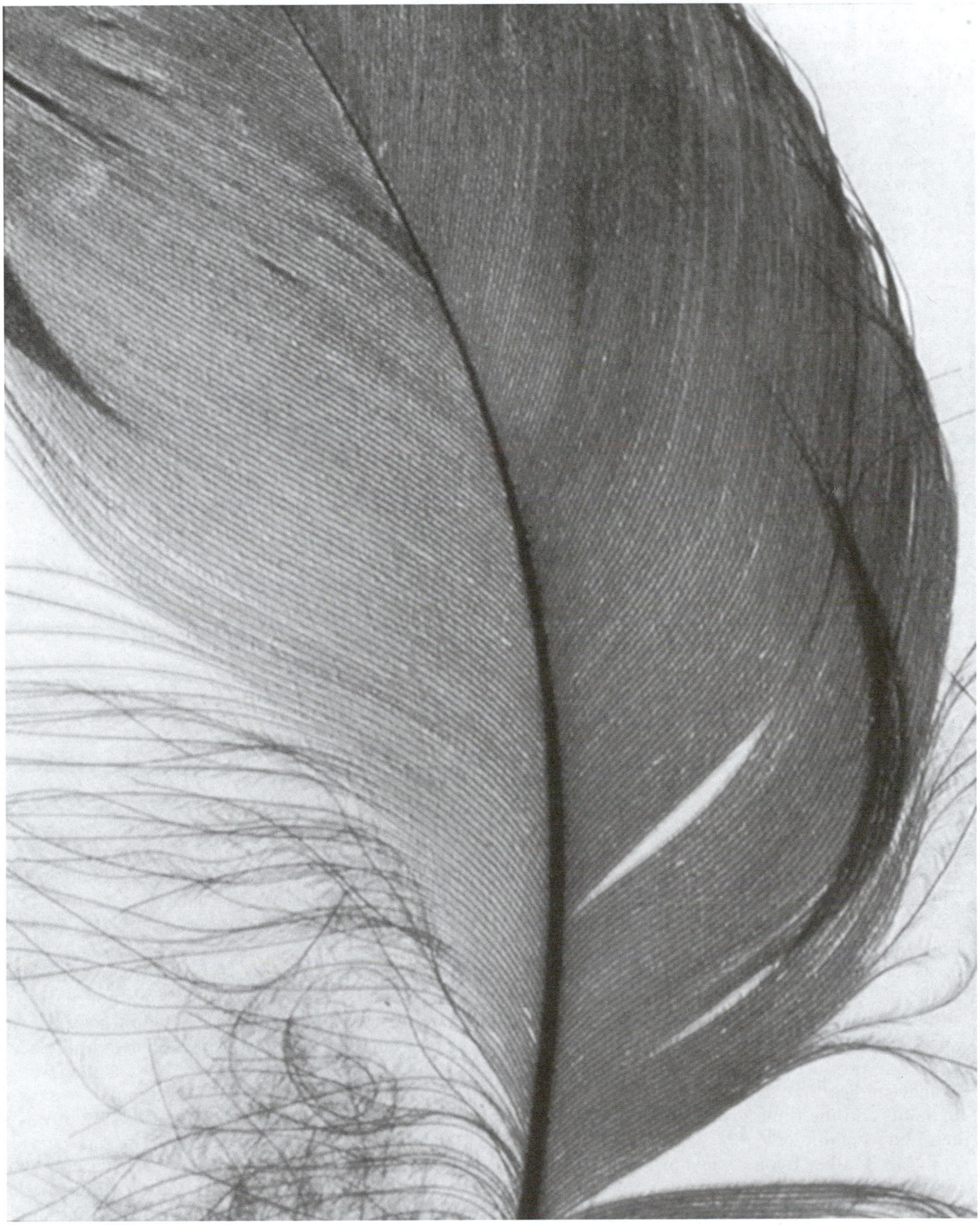

Andreas Feininger, Feather, circa 1956, Gelatin silver print, image: 12½ × 10".
[© *Estate of Andreas Feininger, courtesy, Bonni Benrubi Gallery, New York City*]

1960 *Photography, a Creative Form in Art*; Newark Museum, Newark, New Jersey
1967 *An Exhibition of Works by Lyonel Feininger, T. Lux Feininger, Andreas Feininger, and Laurence Feininger*; Austin Arts Center, Trinity College, Hartford, Connecticut
1967 *Once Invisible*; Museum of Modern Art, New York
1968 *Two Generations, Two Visions*—an Exhibition of Photographs by Andreas Feininger from his book *Forms of Nature and Life*, and paintings by Lyonel Feininger from the Museum of Modern Art exhibit *The Ruin by the Sea*; The Heckscher Museum, Huntington, New York
1971 *Photo Eye of the 20's*; George Eastman House, Rochester, New York and Museum of Modern Art, New York
1973 *Landscape/Cityscape*; Metropolitan Museum of Art, New York
1974 *Manhattan Now*; New York Historical Society, New York

Selected Works

Self-Portrait, Dessau, Germany, 1927
Reed Stalk, 1935
Coney Island Beach on the Fourth of July, 1949, 1949
Helicopter During Take-off, New Jersey, 1949
Traffic on Fifth Avenue, 1950
Photojournalist Dennis Stock, 1951
Feather, c. 1956

Further Reading

Alexander, Stuart. "Andreas Feininger: Early Work." *The Archive* Center for Creative Photography, University of Arizona. no. 17 (March 1983): 4–14.
Andreas Feininger: A Retrospective. New York: International Center of Photography, 1976.
Berkley, Miriam. "The Quiet Man." *American Photographer* (March 1987): 50–59.
Cameron, Franklin. "Meet the Masters." *PhotoGraphic* (March 1987): 38–40.
———. "Relativity." *Photographic* (October 1988): 26–30.
Hattersley, Ralph. *Andreas Feininger*. Dobbs Ferry, NY: Morgan & Morgan, Inc., 1973.
Feininger, Andreas. *The Anatomy of Nature*. New York: Dover Publications, Inc., 1956.
———. *Andreas Feininger: Photographer*. New York: Harry N. Abrams, Inc., 1986.
———. *Shells*. New York: The Viking Press, 1972.
Schlatter, N. Elizabeth. *Structures of Nature: Photographs of Andreas Feininger*. Richmond: University of Richmond Museums, 2001.
Smith, Joel. *Andreas Feininger*. Poughkeepsie, NY: Frances Lehman Loeb Art Center, Vassar University, 2003.

T. LUX FEININGER

German

The youngest of three sons born to caricaturist and painter Lyonel Feininger and Julia Berg, Theodore Lucas Feininger was also one of the youngest students ever enrolled in Germany's Bauhaus Institute of Architecture and Design. Although he would later insist that he was a painter, not a photographer, during his brief photographic career Feininger produced playful candid snapshots and formal studies that described everyday life at the Bauhaus and the waning years of Germany's "golden" interregnum era.

T. Lux's father Lyonel was born in New York to German immigrant parents, and in 1871 he returned to Germany; he studied visual arts in Hamburg, Berlin, and Paris. After 14 years working as a caricaturist and draftsman, on the eve of World War I, Lyonel was appointed a "master" at the Bauhaus in Dessau, where two of his sons were later enrolled. Despite the fact that the elder Feininger was directly opposed to the implementation of formal photographic study at the Bauhaus, all of the Feininger boys experimented with the medium and freelanced as professional photojournalists at one time or another. T. Lux's eldest brother, Andreas Feininger, trained as an architect but became well known as a photographer in the United States, publishing more than 350 photographic essays in *Life* magazine between 1943 and 1962. But it was T. Lux who first took an interest in photography when, as a teenager, he discovered his grandmother's Kodak box camera in the attic of the family's home in Weimar. Within a year, he had purchased a 9 × 12 inch plate camera and, with Andreas's assistance, set up a darkroom in their home in Dessau.

Despite six years of undergraduate and postgraduate study at the Dessau Bauhaus, Feininger nevertheless describes himself as a "self-taught" photographer. Though his formal education in aesthetics no doubt influenced his photographic style, it is also true that the experimental photography for which the Bauhaus is now so well known was not formally implemented into its curriculum until 1929. Though many Bauhäuslers dabbled with the modern *Neue Sehen* or "New Vision" aesthetic in the mid-twenties, photography was widely regarded as a peripheral pursuit by instructors more dedicated to functionalist architecture and design. Feininger himself noted that he did not study photographic literature or theory until well after his emigration to America in 1936. It is perhaps precisely this lack of formal critical thinking about photography that lent such a fresh, unmediated character to Feininger's photographs.

Counting Russian film and German photographers Umbo and Walter Peterhans among his influences, Feininger has been careful to note the distinctions between their approaches and his own. Peterhans, he observed, was a still-life photographer, whereas Feininger preferred to capture movement and human subjects. Feininger's body of work is characterized by two distinct styles—candid snapshots of Bauhaus student life and architecture exploiting the "New Vision" preference for extreme points of view; and an exploration of the spatial relationships between humans and architecture, and more carefully posed formal documents of Oskar Schlemmer's Bauhaus theater workshops and performances. Photos like "Sport at the Bauhaus" (c. 1927) employ a stylistic spontaneity of pose, angle, and shutter speed that reiterates the creative spontaneity for which the school was so well known. In this photograph, two young Bauhaus athletes are suspended in a mid-air, back-to-back collision above a backdrop depicting the school's architectural campus. Their central positioning in the composition over the five-story "Prellerhaus" student studio building coupled with the photographer's worm's-eye view creates a clever distortion of scale that earned the photo the alternative title "Jump over the Bauhaus." This kind of dynamic point of view and playful humor are likewise evident in the mischievous smirks and clowning poses adopted by members of the Bauhaus jazz band, whose ranks Feininger photographed with equal enthusiasm. It is important to note, however, that Feininger's satirical wit extended beyond youthful musing to include a more serious critique of the ideological conflicts at the school. Both students and "masters" were divided between the strict dialectical materialist approach of architects like Walter Gropius and Hannes Meyer and what Feininger described as a more "intuitive" approach of the painter Paul Klee and theater master Oskar Schlemmer. Feininger's critique of Gropius' approach included pictures like *Das Flache Dach (The Flat Roof)*, which called attention to the failure of "functional" architecture by documenting the tendency of the flat roofs to flood and leak.

Feininger's more formal images of the masks, costumes, stage sets, and choreography of the theater workshop are no less dramatic than his candid snapshots, but their drama is conjured more by careful spatial arrangement and lighting than by extreme or oblique points of view. His 1928–1929 studies of masks, for example, are carefully composed still lifes that emphasize the plasticity of the subject through the photographer's use of deep shadows punctuated by well-placed highlights. Taken together, Feininger's body of work functions as much like a thoughtfully constructed family album as it does a documentary record of this famous school's legendary aesthetic ideologies.

Contrary to his own professed lack of interest in professional photographic practice, in 1927 Feininger sent two portfolios of photographs to Alfred Barr, then chief curator of fine arts at New York's Museum of Modern Art (MoMA). Barr, who had visited László Moholy-Nagy at the Bauhaus earlier that year, loaned 16 of these photographs to the Bauhaus Exhibition held at the Harvard Society of Contemporary Art in 1931, and two were officially purchased by MoMA that same year. In 1928, Feininger published his first photographs as a freelance photographer for the Dephot photographic agency, which placed his photographs in a broad range of publications like *Die Woche, Die Dame, Der Arbeiter Fotograf*, and *Das Illustriete Blatt* over the next few years. And in 1929, he had seven photographs accepted into the internationally influential *Film und Foto* exhibition in Stuttgart.

Despite this early success, by the early 1930s Feininger turned his interests to painting, exhibiting two works at Berlin's 1930 Kunstblatt Ausstellung under the name "Theodore Lux," perhaps dropping his last name in an attempt to avoid comparison with his famous father. Just prior to the ascension of Hitler's National Socialist regime, Feininger traveled to Paris, Sweden, and Switzerland before emigrating to New York City in 1936. Branded as a "degenerate artist" by Hitler's cultural ministry due to his association with the Bauhaus and his wife's Jewish heritage, Lyonel Feininger also emigrated to New York the following year. Having left the bulk of his negatives and most of his paintings behind, the youngest Feininger would not resume his photographic practice until 1946, after three years of service in World War II with the U.S. Army. Though he did not publish or exhibit his work during this period, Feininger describes the years between 1946 and 1952 as a time when he "worked the most intensely and consciously at the problems of photography" that led to "a fruitful interchange [between his] photography and painting" (Feininger, *T. Lux Feininger: Photographs of the Twenties and Thirties*, unpaginated preface).

In the years following 1952, Feininger once more left photography behind in order to pursue painting and to work as a teacher at Sarah Lawrence College, Harvard, and finally at the Boston Museum School of Fine Arts from 1962 to 1975. He has since enjoyed a successful career as a painter but will be forever regarded as an important practitioner of the modern New Vision style of photography popularized in Germany in the late 1920s.

LEESA RITTELMANN

See also: **Feininger, Andreas; History of Photography: Interwar Years; Moholy-Nagy, László; Peterhans, Walter; Photography in Europe: Germany and Austria**

Biography

Born Theodore Lucas Feininger in Berlin, Germany, 11 June 1910. Studied at Bauhaus Institute for Architecture and Design, Dessau, Germany, 1926–1929, and undertook post-graduate studies at the Bauhaus, 1929–1932. Freelance photojournalist for Dephot, 1928–1929; participated in Stuttgart *Film und Foto* exhibition, 1929; emigrated to New York City, 1936. Served in the United States Army during World War II, 1942–1945. Design Instructor, Sarah Lawrence College, 1950–1952; Lecturer in Drawing and Painting at Harvard University, Cambridge, MA, 1953–1961; Instructor in Drawing and Painting, Boston Museum of Fine Arts School, 1962–1975.

Individual Exhibitions

1930 *Theodor Lux*; Berlin, Germany
1931 *T. Lux Feininger*; Kunstverein; Erfurt, Germany
1935 *T. Lux Feininger*; Nierendorf Gallery; New York, New York (with subsequent solo exhibitions in 1936 and 1937)
1945 Stuart Art Gallery; Boston, Massachusetts
1947 *T. Lux Feininger*; Julien Levy Gallery; New York, New York
1949 United Nations Club; Washington, D.C.
1950 Edwin Hewitt Gallery; New York, New York
1955 Behn-Moore Gallery, Cambridge, Massachusetts
1956 Cambridge Art Association; Cambridge, Massachusetts (subsequent solo exhibition in 1971)
1958 Design Corporation; Boston, Massachusetts (with subsequent solo exhibition in 1959)
1962 *T. Lux Feininger Retrospective*; Busche-Reisinger Museum, Harvard University Art Museums, Cambridge, Massachusetts
1973 Wheaton College; Northhampton, Massachusetts
1980 Prakapas Gallery; New York, New York
1982 Sacramento Street Gallery; Cambridge, Massachusetts
1988 Gallery on the Green; Lexington, Massachusetts (with subsequent solo exhibitions in 1990 and 1992)

Group Exhibitions

1929 *Film und Foto: Internationale Ausstellung des Deutschen Werkbundes*, Ausstellungshallen und Königbaulichtspiele; Stuttgart, Germany (traveled throughout Germany for two years)
1930 *Kunstblatt*; Reckendorfhaus, Berlin, Germany
1931 *Bauhaus Exhibition*; Harvard Society for Contemporary Art, Cambridge, Massachusetts
1931 *Juryfreie Sonderausstellung*; Berlin, Germany
1931 *T. Lux Feininger and Clemens Röseler*; Bauhaus, Dessau, Germany
1932 Ferdinand Möller Gallery; Berlin, Germany
1933 *Carnegie International*; Carnegie Museum of Art; Pittsburgh, Pensylvania (included 1933–1936, 1939, 1943, 1946–49)
1940 *T. Lux Feininger and Ben Shahn*; Julien Levy Gallery; New York, New York
1943 *American Realists and Magic Realists*; Museum of Modern Art; New York, New York
1951 *Whitney Museum Annual*; Whitney Museum of American Art; New York, New York
1951 *Revolution and Tradition in Modern American Art*; Brooklyn Museum; New York, New York
1954 *Four American Painters*; Massachusetts Institute of Technology; Boston, Massachusetts
1954 *Reality and Fantasy*; Walker Art Center; Minneapolis, Minnesota
1956 *Feininger Family*; Mint Museum of Art; Charlotte, North Carolina
1964 *Annual Exhibition*; Westport Art Group; Wesport, Massachusetts (participates annually 1964–1995)
1967 *Feininger Family—three generations*; Cambridge Art Association; Cambridge, Massachusetts and traveling to Trinity College, Hartford, Connecticut
1979 *Film und Foto*; Stuttgart, Germany (50th Anniversary recreation of original 1929 exhibition)

Selected Works

Bauhaus Jazz Band, 1927
Sport am Bauhaus (*Sport at the Bauhaus*, alternatively titled *Jump over the Bauhaus*), c. 1927
Clemens Röseler, c. 1928
Stabetanz (Dance of the Staves, alternatively titled *Black-White*), 1928
Mask for the Bauhaus Theater, c. 1928
Das Flache Dach (The Flat Roof), 1928–1929
Self-Portrait as Chaplin, c. 1929

Further Reading

Büche Wolfgang, ed. *T. Lux Feininger. Von Dessau nach Amerika. Der Weg eines Bauhäuslers*. Moritzburg Halle: Staatliche Galerie, 1998.

"Feininger and Sons." in *Life*, Nov. 12, (1951): 89–98.

Fiedler, Jeannine. "T. Lux Feininger: 'I am a painter, not a photographer!,'" translated by Louis Kaplan and Jeannine Fiedler. In *Photography at the Bauhaus*. Cambridge, MA: M.I.T. Press, 1990, 44–53.

Feininger, T. Lux. *Photographs of the Twenties and Thirties*. New York: Prakapas Gallery, 1980.

Feininger, T. Lux. "Aus meiner Frühzeit." In Ute Eskildsen, Jan Christopher Horak (ed.), *Film und Foto der zwanziger Jahre*. Stuttgart: Württ. Kunstverein, 1979.

Feininger, T. Lux. "The Bauhaus—Evolution of an Idea." *Criticis*., Wayne State University Press, vol. II, no. 3, 1960. Reprinted as "Das Bauhaus: Fortentwicklung einer Idee," in Eckhard Neumann (ed.), *Bauhaus und Bauhäusler*. Cologne, 1985.

Feininger, T. Lux. "Essay on Modern Art," *Harvard Journal*, 1. 1966, no. 1.

Feininger, T. Lux. "Vater und Söhne." In *Feininger. Eine Künstlerfamilie*. Stadt Karlsruhe, Städtische Galerie: Hatje Cantz Verlag, 2001.

Graaf, Vera. "'Mein Vater hat einen Fehler gemacht' Vera Graaf—Interview mit T. Lux Feininger 1986." *Du. Die Zeitschrift für Kunst und Kultur*, H. 5, (1986).

Schardt, Alois J. "Zum Schaffen Feiningers." *Das Kunstblatt* 15. Jg., (1931): 215–220.

T. Lux Feininger. *Fotografien 1927–1950*. Essen: Museum Folkwang, 1981.

HANS-PETER FELDMANN

German

Born in 1941, Hans-Peter Feldmann is one of the most enigmatic personalities of the art world to emerge after 1960. As much as his photographic images seem to center on the everyday, his pursuit of an artistic career is unconventional. By 1989, when the comprehensive catalogue *Hans-Peter Feldmann: Das Museum im Kopf* was published and a retrospective was established in Frankfurt and a year later in Düsseldorf, Feldmann had stopped his artistic activities, preferring to run a shop for accessories and crafts, later a mail-order operation for thimbles, and then a business for selling toys made of tin. After 1980, he destroyed all works in his possession and had a seemingly farewell exhibition at the Museum van Hedendaagse Kunst in Ghent, Belgium and then avoided the art world. His rediscovery in 1990 not only focused on the reception of his artistic works but also was guided by an important aspect of 1970s art: the confrontation with mass media and especially with the social, political, and aesthetic function of photography. This important function of the photograph was first described in "The Work of Art in the Age of Mechanical Reproduction," Walter Benjamin's highly influential 1931 essay, which Feldmann has consistently acknowleged.

Feldmann's oeuvre reflects the collective cosmos of images that condition perception and reality in the late twentieth-century, the millions upon millions of private, press, and advertising images that are often anonymous, banal, and seemingly worthless and yet form the most important archive of the twentieth century.

Just as East Germany-born painter Gerhard Richter, to whom Feldmann offers the highest praise, began to collect these images which surround us daily for his *Atlas* shortly after immigrating to the West in 1961, Feldmann collected illustrations, advertising photographs, postcards, placards, and photo albums that he obtained from their owners or from flea markets, and expanded the work of these found images with his own photographs. Though Richter also thought his collection worthy to exhibit, he mainly used it as the basis and point of departure for his paintings. Feldmann, on the other hand, never hesitated to exhibit his seemingly artless, mass-produced product, relying on the art context to transform it while retaining an aspect of originality.

Although he studied as a painter, he abandoned this medium in 1968. After 1968, Feldmann began to categorize (as Richter did in his own way) the daily flood of haphazard images with which he was inundated into small booklets arranged according to subjects, such as chairs, mountains, bicyclists, swimmers, trees, and sailboats, and these serializations closely suggested the works of Bernd and Hilla Becher. He self-published these booklets as simple stapled brochures in various sizes as black-and-white offset publications with no annotation or commentary on what was being presented. The covers were gray cardboard, the title was stamped in blue, and they were not signed; the maximum print run was one thousand.

Feldman's first booklet was *12 Bilder* (12 Images; 1968). For these 12 images of airplanes in the sky, he took more than 100 photos and edited them down to a dozen. He had also published booklets that feature just one image. Most characteristically, however, Feldmann errs on the side of excess. For example, to ridicule normative aesthetics and the interchangeability of images, he collects his series of subjects from calendars, books, and postcards or from amateur and professional photographers, often choosing the most banal and hackneyed sorts of imagery and presenting often over 100 images. Feldmann preferred that the average number of objects and photographic representations mirror each other. The number of publications per year varied; in 1968 there were two, and in 1972 there were seven. In one instance, in *3 Bilder* (1976), he substitutes the images with descriptions, which made clear how close his work is to conceptual art. (In a reverse strategy, he once answered interview questions by providing photographic images.) The exhibitions of these booklets are as unpretentious as the booklets themselves; in museums and galleries they are tethered by cords from the ceiling or lie on tables that the visitors may handle them.

In 1977, Feldmann showed his *Bilderfundus* (Fund of Images), which he described as a "copy of the world," in the Folkwang-Museum in Essen, Germany. The museum exhibition of these materials as well as their display in booklets raised questions about the traditional concept of art and work: photos are trivial, and these are readymades and reproductions. In the age of mass media the artistic original has become, for Feldmann, a dubious category.

Before 1968, under the influence of Konrad Klapheck, who like Ritcher was a professor at the Kunstakademie Dusseldorf, Feldmann painted precise representations of simple objects, avoiding any of the individual style that would later emerge. According to an often-circulated anecdote, he created his large-format photographs that are difficult to transport to demonstrate to gallery workers how the reproduction replaces the original. The ensuing departure from painting and the general breakup of the concept of art have their origins in the political, social, and cultural movements of the 1960s, in which the power of mass-media images was evident: when millions of people followed their television screens for the moon landing, the Vietnam War, the student protests, and the civil rights demonstrations and media theorist Marshall McLuhan became a cult figure. Reactions in art abounded: at the 1972 Documenta 5 in Kassel, Germany there was an exhibition of title pages of the German weekly newsmagazine *Der Spiegel* from 1960 to 1972.

Although Feldmann has often been portrayed as an artistic maverick, his work joins that of many other American and European artists reacting to the disruptions of the 1960s. Feldman himself has pointed to an intellectal closeness of his work especially to Belgian conceptualist Marcel Broodthaers, Gilbert & George, and French conceptual painter Daniel Buren. His work has many affinities to that of Ed Ruscha, who also created booklets of collections of images. Like the French artist Christian Boltanski, Feldmann creates archives from the massive archive of vernacular photography, family snapshots, and other images that are often overlooked. Although his work was not as well known as these figures in the 1960s and 1970s, he later was recognized as having a seminal role in the development of conceptual photography in the 1980s, and has even been identified as an early example of appropriation as an artistic strategy.

Feldmann also created books, which were essentially collections of his brochures, where he displayed comprehensive photo series, interconnections of the media, and documentations of periods of time. Many remain unpublished; others accompanied exhibitions, such as *Eine Stadt: Essen* from 1977. Because it thematized German left-wing terrorism, very much like Gerhard Richter's cycle on the Red Army faction, *18 Oktober 1977*, Feldmann's self-published book *Die Toten [The Dead], 1967–1993* (1998) caused a sensation, with its 95 photographs of terrorists and their victims culled from the news media. Feldmann's contribution to the end of the century was *100 Jahre*, photographs of 101 people from his circle of family and friends, beginning with an eight-week-old baby and ending with a 100 year old woman.

As a logical consequence of his work, Feldmann also used the media itself as a platform. Without securing the cooperation of the publishers, he managed to have photos placed in feature and business sections of Cologne newspapers that had no relationship to the text and no caption. He smuggled them in many times, some having no comment or indication that they were Feldmann's artistic contributions. They confirm that we accept empty formulaic images as documents and organize them in stereotypically defined categories. Another kind of action in newspapers occurred in 1975, when he placed colorations on one page of the feminist *Emma*. In his *Zeit-Serien* (Time Series) he took 36 photographs of a scene, the number of images on a standard roll of film, documenting various everyday situations or scenes, such as pictures of a car radio while music that he enjoyed was playing. In 1995 he founded the magazine *OHIO*.

Many of Feldmann's projects are postcard series and placard-like prints. For the yearly exhibition in Vienna called Das Plakat, he created toward the end of 1994 and the beginning of 1995, 3,000 public placard partitions, on which he arranged family photos of his own and of strangers in black and white on a blue background. In his subversive mimicry, Feldmann is active in all media he can copy.

BRIGITTE HAUSMANN

See also: **Appropriation; Artists' Books; Conceptual Photography; Family Photography; Gilbert & George; Photography in Europe: Germany and Austria; Vernacular Photography**

Biography

Born 1941 in Düsseldorf; studied at the Düsseldorfer Kunstakademie; Gustav Klimt-Preis, 1995; Camera Austria-Preis der Stadt Graz für internationale zeitgenössische Fotografie, 1999; lives in Düsseldorf.

Individual Exhibitions

1972 *Hans-Peter Feldmann*; Daner Galleriet; Copenhagen, Denmark
1973 *Hans-Peter Feldmann*; Galleria Sperone; Turin, Italy
1974 *Hans-Peter Feldmann*; Kunstbibliothek; Copenhagen, Denmark
1975 *Hans-Peter Feldmann*; Kunstraum; Munich, Germany
1977 *Hans-Peter Feldmann*; Museum Folkwang; Essen, Germany
1979 *Hans-Peter Feldmann*; Ink, Halle für internationale Kunst; Zurich, Switzerland
1988 *Hans-Peter Feldmann*; Galerie Paul Maenz; Cologne, Germany
1989 *Hans-Peter Feldmann*; Portikus; Frankfurt am Main, Germany
1990 *Hans-Peter Feldmann. Retrospektive*; Kunstverein für die Rheinlande und Westfalen; Düsseldorf, Germany
Hans-Peter Feldmann: Die Toten; Galerie Barbara Wien; Berlin, Germany
1999 *Hans-Peter Feldmann: Bücher*; Neues Museum Weserburg; Bremen, Germany
2001 *Hans-Peter Feldmann*; Kunstverein Graz; Graz, Austria
2001 *Inter-Archiv*; Kunstraum der Universität Lüneburg; Lüneburg, Germany

Group Exhibitions

1972 *Documenta 5*; Kassel, Germany
1974 *Projekt '74*; Wallraf-Richartz-Museum, Kunsthalle Köln, Kölnischer Kunstverein; Cologne, Germany
1976 *Documenta 6*; Kassel, Germany
1977 *Malerei und Photographie im Dialog*; Kunsthaus Zürich; Zurich, Switzerland
1979 *Schlaglichter*; Rheinisches Landesmuseum; Bonn, Germany
1980 *Kunst na '68...in Europa*; Museum van hedendaagse Kunst; Ghent, Switzerland
1983 *Kunst mit Photographie*; Neue Nationalgalerie; Berlin, Germany, and traveling
1988 *Zwischen Schwarz & Weiss*; Neuer Berliner Kunstverein; Berlin, Germany
1993 *Romantik in der Kunst der Gegenwart*; Ludwig Forum; Aachen, Germany
1994 *Aura: Die Realität des Kunstwerks zwischen Autonomie, Reproduktion und Kontext*; Wiener Secession; Vienna, Austria
1994 *Das Archiv*; Forum Stadtpark; Graz, Austria
1995 *Dicht am Leben. 3. Internationale Foto-Triennale*; Villa Merkel; Esslingen, Germany
1995 *Take Me (I'm Yours)*; Serpentine Gallery; London and Kunsthalle Nürnberg; Nürnberg, Germany
1999 *Stadtluft—Der urbane Raum als Medium der Macht*; Hamburger Kunstverein; Hamburg, Germany
1999 *Moving Images: Film-Reflexionen in der zeitgenössischen Kunst*; Galerie für zeitgenössische Kunst Leipzig; Leipzig, Germany

Selected Works

Artists' Books

12 Bilder, 1968 (Airplanes)
11 Bilder, 1969 (Knees)
1 Bilder, 1970 (Coat)
152 Bilder, 1971 (Portraits of women)
6 Bilder, 1971 (Soccer players)
6 Bilder, 1974 (Hedges)

Books

Der Überfall, Cologne: Wolfgang Hake Verlag, 1975
Ein Leben, unpublished, 1978
Telefonbuch, Dudweiler: AQ-Verlag, 1980
Enzyklopädie, vols. 1 and 2, Düsseldorf: Feldmann Verlag, 1994
Porträt, Munich: Schirmer/Mosel, 1994
Die Tote,. 1967–1993, Düsseldorf: Feldmann Verlag, 1998
Feldmann, Hans-Peter, and Christian Konrad, *Die Johanneskirche in Düsseldorf*, Düsseldorf: Feldmann Verlag, 1999
100 Jahre, Munich: Schirmer/Mosel, 2001

Magazines-Articles

Zeitschrift *EXTRA*, Cologne, 1975, no. 5, 8 (Nudes)
Zeitschrift *Salon*, Cologne/Düsseldorf 1977–1983, nos. 1–11 (Title pages)
Zeitschrift *Image*, Zurich 1979
Zeitschrift *Profil*, Vienna 2000, no. 6

Postcard Series und Posters

Alle Kleider einer Frau, 72 b/w-photos, 1974
Zeitabläufe, more than 500 b/w-photos, various series, 1971–1973
Sonntagsmotive, 21 Posters, offset prints, silk screens, b/w, various formats, 1976–1977
Familienphotos, Posters, Vienna 1994–1995

Further Reading

Feldman, Hans-Peter. *Billeder of Feldmann*. Copenhagen: Sommersko Verlag, 1973.
———. *Hans-Peter Feldman: Bilder/Pictures*. Munich: Kunstraum. München, 1975.
Thomas, Karin, and Gerd de Vries. *Künstlerlexikon von 1945 bis zur Gegenwart*. Cologne: Dumont, 1977.
Lippert, Werner. *Hans-Peter Feldmann: Das Museum im Kopf*. Cologne: Verlag der Buchhandlung Walther König, 1989.

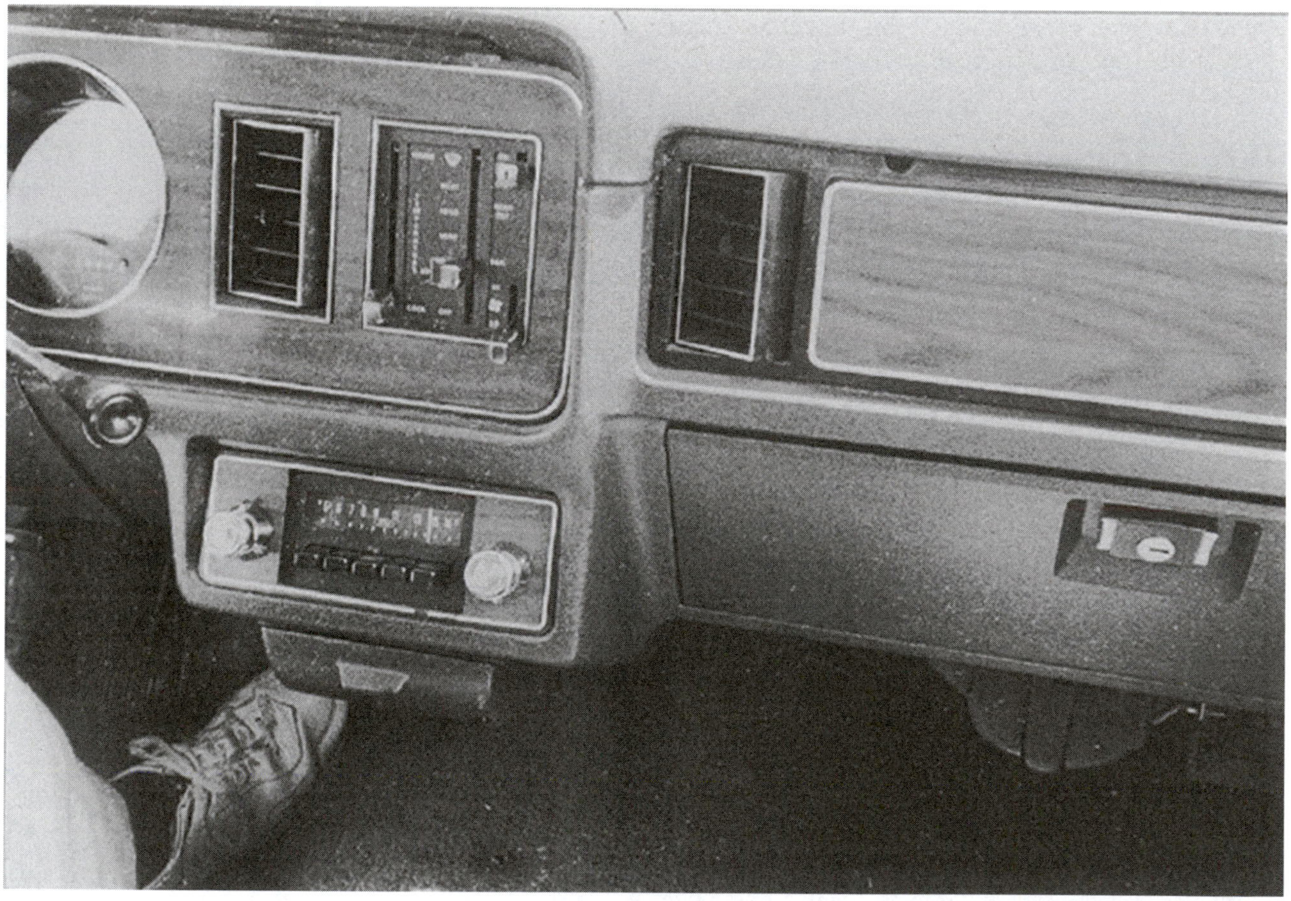

Hans-Peter Feldmann, Car radio while it is playing good music.
[*Courtesy of the artist*]

FEMINIST PHOTOGRAPHY

Twentieth-century feminism has been a richly diverse, multifarious, and hotly contested terrain. Feminist artists, activists, and historians continue to negotiate the terms of the debate, often with widely different positions. There is no one definition of feminism, but a web of occasionally conflicting theories and practices emanating from changeable cultural conceptions of sexuality and gender. Attempting to categorize feminist photography is, therefore, an even more slippery task. Suffice it to say that in the wake of feminist political action in the 1960s and 1970s, a newfound interest in women's photography—both contemporary and historical—was spreading. Mirroring developments in the emerging fields of women's history and women's studies, those working in this first wave of feminist investment in photography began by re-situating and rescuing. Their assignment was to re-situate the work of women photographers within the history of photography and rescue those women photographers who had disappeared from the historical record. They also worked in photographic images, publications, and exhibitions, to present new ways of thinking about and looking at representations of women. On the heels of this initial interest in the idea of women and photography, a new generation of feminist artists and photographers began to emerge in the 1970s and early 1980s. Although evolving at the same historical moment as the first group of photographers, what set this group apart was an active engagement with feminist political and theoretical debates and the fact that their enterprise was immersed in the developing fields of postmodern and feminist theory. The work of this second generation of feminist photographers, particularly their keen examination of power, privilege, and the formation of identities in contemporary culture, set the tone for a growing number of women who entered the photography scene in the late 1980s and 1990s, women from backgrounds and orientations that had been previously underrepresented. Composed primarily of women artists of color and lesbian artists, this third generation of feminist photographers often challenged the tenets of what they perceived to be the prevailing mainstream, White, middle-class, straight feminist orthodoxy.

The Women's Movement, 1970s

Two early traveling exhibitions in the United States demonstrate the emerging overlap between feminism and photography in the 1970s. On the West Coast in 1975, the San Francisco Museum of Modern Art launched the exhibition and catalogue organized by Margery Mann and Anne Noggle titled *Women of Photography: An Historical Survey*. This exhibition surveyed the work of 50 women photographers; the catalog remains a significant source on the work of women in photography. In New York in 1979, the International Center of Photography sponsored Margaretta Mitchell's traveling exhibition with accompanying catalog titled *Recollections: Ten Women of Photography*. Mitchell received a National Endowment for the Arts grant in 1978–1979 to develop the project, thus demonstrating the topical nature of such projects for the art community and the nation in the late 1970s.

As these exhibitions traveled across the country, a group of young women photographers including Bea Nettles, Wendy Snyder MacNeil, Judith Golden, Anne Noggle, and Judy Dater were gaining significant exposure for their own photographic work that consistently explored women's issues. Bea Nettles has created mixed-media photographic pieces dealing with domesticity and women's identity since 1970. Snyder MacNeil and Golden both started in the early 1970s by photographing themselves and their own personal relationships. These very subjects—domesticity, family, and issues of personal identity—were key areas of inquiry for those participating in the feminist movement in the 1970s (and after), yet women photographers of the time rarely used the term "feminist" in connection with their work. Dater and Noggle became known for their direct, psychologically evocative portraits, mostly of female sitters. The strong and self-assuredly sexy women typically photographed by Dater, such as her portrait of *Laura Mae* (1973), seemed to typify the newly defined liberated, young, American female. In contrast, Noggle, who came to photography as a return college student in her early 40s, turned her lens to less fashionable and not-so-sexy middle-aged subjects, including a series of self-portraits from 1975 of the artist recovering from a face-lift. Like most women photographers of their generation, both Dater and Noggle not only used their female subjects as substitutes for themselves, they also produced self-portraits throughout their photographic careers. This interest in female subjects in photography established an exploration of female identity that would pervade feminist photography for the remainder of the twentieth century. As their imagery reveals, the impetus for their work was often rooted in their own personal history. Unlike later feminist photographers such as Cindy Sherman and Barbara Kruger, the photographic projects in this first generation of feminist photography were not yet specifically conceived of or discussed as political or cultural critique. In fact, Dater and other women photographers of the time were often quite ambivalent about politics and feminism in particular. These women worked at being considered photographers in their own right, not "women" photographers per se. Although their work focused on women's identity, their public attitude was that gender itself was not the primary issue. In stark contrast, the next generation of feminist photographers would construct their work around the very issue of gender.

A somewhat similar early history can be traced in Great Britain, although from the start feminist photography in Britain was a clearly political, feminist enterprise. This was primarily due to its roots in the social documentary tradition, originating with the 1972 exhibition *Women on Women,* a collective documentary project initiated by the Half Moon Gallery in Whitechapel. The exhibition featured women photojournalists photographing women subjects and led to the formation of the socialist, feminist group the Hackney Flashers in 1974. One of the major forces behind the group was the photographer Jo Spence, who wrote and exhibited extensively before her death in 1992 and became a significant figure in the development of twentieth-century feminist photography in Europe and the United States. Rooted in a straight documentary photography tradition, Spence's early work in the 1970s and 1980s consisted mostly of social documentary projects focusing on women, work, and the domestic sphere. Diagnosed with breast cancer in 1982, Spence, in collaboration with Rosy Martin, developed "photo therapy," a healing technique, realized through a series of self-portraits. Spence has become a major inspiration for breast cancer survivors and a generation of British women photographers, including the Irish born Angela Kelly. Now living and working in the United States, Kelly's work, while focusing on the problems of growing up female in a male-dominated society, also reexamines the social documentary tradition itself, questioning the nature of realism and representation.

Gender Discourse, 1970s–1980s

Thoroughly immersed in the new wave of ideological investment in Freudian psychoanalytic, feminist film, and predominantly French critical theoretical models, the next generation of feminist photographers working in the 1970s and 1980s grappled with the nature of representation and issues of sexual difference in their photographic work. Often coming to photography from a conceptual art, fine art, film, video, or commercial art background, artists including Sarah Charlesworth, Martha Rosler, Mary Kelly, Barbara Kruger, and Cindy Sherman, examined the construction and perpetuation of cultural myths and stereotypes through visual images and the mass media. These artists used photography as one tool in their creative repertoire. Sarah Charlesworth, for example, came from a conceptual art background to investigate photography as a subject in itself. From her *Modern History* project in the late 1970s to her *Objects of Desire* and *Doubleworld* projects in the 1990s, Charlesworth explores how photography functions as a play of symbols in our culture—symbols that affect us individually and collectively. Straddling the first generation of feminist photography and the second, Martha Rosler has worked in video, photography, performance, and installation since the late 1960s, creating politically motivated works that challenge cultural and political biases. Rosler's engagement with media images came directly out of her involvement in anti-war protests and the women's liberation movement. Her *Bringing the War Home* series from 1967–1972, was a response to the artist's frustrations with media portrayals of the U.S. military involvement in Vietnam. Rosler used photographs from mainstream American magazines to create photomontages that juxtaposed images from the war in Vietnam with scenes of American domestic interiors, creating a startling contrast. Rosler's well-known photo/text project, *The Bowery in Two Inadequate Descriptive Systems* from the mid-1970s, used text and images in order to rethink the documentary photography tradition and demonstrate the limitations of both pictures and words as vehicles to reveal social realities. In her video and performance work of the time, such as her *Semiotics of the Kitchen*, 1975, Rosler commented more directly on women's issues. Mary Kelly inserted psychoanalysis and semiotics in art practice and agitated the London art scene when she first exhibited her now renowned *Post-Partum Document* (1973–1979) at the Institute of Contemporary Art in 1979. Commenting on psychoanalytic discourses of gender and motherhood, Kelly's complex multiple section, mixed media work used literary, scientific, psychoanalytic, linguistic, and archaeological modes of representation to document the artist's relationship to her son in his early stages of development. *Post-Partum Document* was radical not only because it took on the tabooed conjunction of motherhood and desire, but also because it presented an analysis of language and sexuality as socially determined. This kind of statement was novel at the end of the 1970s, although it would become the foundation of the emerging discourse on sexual difference in the next decades. Like many feminist artists of their generation and after, both Rosler and Kelly were quite articulate about their work and successfully negotiated the crossover from artist to critic and vice versa.

Inspired by this developing feminist critique of photography's role in the perpetuation of gender stereotypes, media-savvy artists such as Barbara Kruger and Cindy Sherman created imagery that worked against such stereotypes and undermined the authority of the male gaze. In reaction to the objectification of women in the art, advertising, and Hollywood film industries, both Kruger and Sherman adopted the very same strategies used in those industries in order to subvert their power and harness it for their own critique. After working for several years as an art director and photo editor for fashion magazines, Kruger began in the 1970s to create image and word pieces, culminating in what have become her signature style photo/text montages banded with red striped slogans. Her untitled series of images, including *Untitled (Your Body is a Battleground)*, 1989, appropriates the look of the mass media in order to comment on its pervasive power in our culture and its disembodied authorial voice. This piece, and others in the series, also implies a specific political agenda, as Kruger takes on the pro-choice/abortion debate with the slogan "Your body is a battleground." Kruger's work became more politically engaged over the next decades as she gained exposure through a variety of international public art projects and poster campaigns.

The significance of the female body as a site for political action and resistance, as seen in Kruger's work, was further developed in the work of Cindy Sherman and would ultimately become the backbone of feminist photography for the rest of the century. With her black and white *Untitled Film Stills* series from the late 1970s and early 1980s, Sherman expanded the gender discourse to focus on the instability of identity, the social constructions of gender, and the idea of femininity as masquerade. In these photographs, as in almost all of her work, Sherman posed herself as the model in a series of narratives that mimic classic Hollywood film stills, although these images do not directly reference any original film or story; they are completely made-up. Sherman's photographs emphasize the voyeurism of film, as the viewer often peers in at the woman through a doorway, or a window, or from below. By using herself to create a seemingly unlimited cast of female characters, Sherman not only forces us to confront our inability to fix or locate her own identity, they point to the precariousness and fluidity of female identity, and femininity, overall. In her later color work, Sherman moved away from typically glamorous representations of women and pursued darker more ambiguous images of femininity, images that involved violence, eating disorders, and the sex industry. For a series of images produced in the 1990s, Sherman used various sex toys, dolls, and other paraphernalia to create rather horrifying large-scale "still-life" photographs in intense color. Although harshly criticized for this work, with these images Sherman was portraying the other, overlooked side of the glamour and sex industries, the side that sustains violence against women and urges them to binge and purge in order to maintain an artificial standard of female beauty.

Sherman's employment of the body, specifically her own body, as a vehicle for social and cultural critique, can be linked to a group of feminist performance/body artists and their photographic production. Feminist artists including Americans Hannah Wilke, and Dorit Cypis and Cuban-born Ana Mendieta, for example, all used themselves as a subject in order to address issues of personal and public identity. Ranging from studio pieces, to earthworks, to mixed media installations, Wilke, Mendieta, and Cypis use their own bodies to create representations about the female body where they implicate the viewer as a participant in their potentially voyeuristic and narcissistic projects. In photographs made from the early 1970s until her death in 1993, Wilke, the most prominent of this group, played with notions of narcissism, masquerade, and female objectification. In her *S.O.S.—Starification Object Series*, 1974–1979, Wilke photographed herself using various poses and props, her body covered with small rolled-up pieces of chewing gum shaped like female genitalia. Through this performative piece, Wilke participated in, constructed, and controlled her own objectification, thereby invoking and destabilizing the power of the male gaze. Condemned by feminist critics as narcissistic and exploitative of her own beauty, Wilke's final series of photographs served as a chilling response to those critics. In her *Intra-Venus* series from 1992–1993, Wilke (with Donald Goddard) produced photographs of her body while undergoing treatment for cancer. These images, much like Cindy Sherman's later color works, force the viewer to confront their expectations of the female body and female beauty. In comparison, American photographer Jeanne Dunning has taken up the human body as subject, mingling notions of the body and the grotesque, in a series of photographs of bodies and food. Since the 1990s, Dunning has created vibrant large-scale color photographs of bodies covered in ambiguous puddings and liquids, with messy, oozing flesh. Although Dunning's work is about the actual body itself, not representations of the body per se, again like Sherman and Wilke she encourages the viewer to look at something that is considered taboo in our society. The following generation of feminist photographers will take up this concern, picturing bodies that have been consistently overlooked.

Other Voices, 1980s–1990s and After

In the late 1980s and 1990s, a plenitude of racially and sexually defined women artists gained recognition for their photographic work that looked to represent their identity in contrast to Western, White, heterosexual standards of femininity. It is, essentially, a bit misleading to isolate these women here as the third generation of feminist photographers, for much of their work overlaps with or fits into categories of feminist art production already discussed in this essay. However, for continuity and clarity, I have chosen to discuss these women as a group. An impressive list of feminist artists beginning with veterans Clarissa Sligh, Pat Ward Williams, Lorraine O'Grady, Carrie Mae Weems, Lorna Simpson, and Deborah Bright, carrying over to a younger generation of women including Catherine Opie, Laura Aguilar, Kaucyila Brooke, Jolene Rickard, Korean-born Young Soon-Min, the Australian Tracey Moffatt, and others, worked to identify their own discourses of identity and representation. Although richly diverse in ethnicity and ideology, much of the work of these women artists is rooted in notions of family and community, and stems from their own personal histories. Clarissa Sligh and Carrie Mae Weems, for example, initially photographed, or used photographs, of their own families in their works. In her *Reading Dick and Jane with Me* book project from the 1980s, Sligh reconstructs the standard American public school reader published between 1935 and 1965, with images from her own family album. Within and among the images, Sligh interjects her commentary on the differences between the upper middle class happy White family depicted in the readers and her own experience as a poor black child growing up in the American south. Carrie Mae Weems began photographing her *Family Pictures and Stories* series, 1978–1984, where she uses text and images to tell her own family story, when she was a college student in California. In this series, Weems presents an intimate yet complex portrayal of her family where she, as the photographer, functions as an insider and an outsider. Weems returned to photograph her working-class family as an educated black woman. Although emerging out of their unique personal histories, Weems and Sligh create imagery that resonates with the African American community and has relevance to all members of families. In her *Untitled Kitchen Table Series* from the 1990s, Weems uses herself as the model in a series of domestic narratives that circulate around a kitchen table. Combined with poetic text, the images in this series, much like Cindy Sherman's *Untitled Film Stills*, are less about Weems's experiences and more engaged with constructions of femininity and domesticity in American culture. Even photographer Tracey Moffatt's fictional photo-narratives, where she also uses herself as the model, stem from her background growing up female and aboriginal in a predominantly White, working class Australian suburb.

In photographing the members of their communities, Catherine Opie and Laura Aguilar also use photography as a way of representing their own identities. Located in Los Angeles, Opie and Aguilar picture different lesbian communities. In her *Latina Lesbians* series, an ongoing photographic project begun in 1986, Aguilar combines black and white images of lesbian women set in mostly domestic interiors with handwritten descriptive captions written by the sitters themselves. In contrast, Opie's *Being and Having* and *Portraits* series from 1991 present large-scale vibrantly colored studio portraits of her friends within the local lesbian and S-M communities; communities that remain relatively unseen in our culture. In *Being and Having,* Opie photographs her lesbian friends in masculine drag, whereas *Portraits* sympathetically depicts transsexuals, cross-dressers, tattooed dominatrixes, drag kings, and other subjects. Aguilar started in the late 1990s to produce startling nude self-portraits, and Opie included herself in her *Portraits* series. Artists from Sligh and Weems, to Opie and Aguilar have returned at the end of the twentieth century to practice a feminist photography rooted in personal experience—much like Dater, Noggle, and the women of the first generation of feminist work in photography—thereby signaling once again that the personal is indeed the political. Moreover, through their work, the women in this third generation not only broadened the scope of the feminist debate, they also intensified and improved it, pointing to the limitations of traditional Western feminist orthodoxy in its refusal to confront questions of race and gender. Further, they truly opened up feminism, proving it to be a completely heterogeneous discourse at the end of the twentieth century.

STACEY MCCARROLL

See also: **Conceptual Photography; Deconstruction; History of Photography: 1980s; Postmodernism; Representation and Gender; Semiotics; Sherman, Cindy; Simpson, Lorna; Spence, Jo; Structuralism; Weems, Carrie Mae**

Further Reading

Frueh, Joanna, Cassandra L. Langer, and Arlene Raven, eds. *New Feminist Criticism: Art, Identity, Action*. New York: HarperCollins, 1994.

Jobling, Paul. *Bodies of Experience: Gender and Identity in Women's Photography Since 1970*. London: Scarlet Press, 1997.

Mann, Margery and Anne Noggle. *Women of Photography: An Historical Survey*. San Francisco: San Francisco Museum of Modern Art, 1975.

Mitchell, Margaretta K. *Recollections: Ten Women of Photography*. New York: Viking, 1979.

Neumaier, Diane, ed. *Reframings: New American Feminist Photographies*. Philadelphia: Temple University Press, 1995.

Rosenblum, Naomi. *A History of Women Photographers*. New York: Abbeville Press, 1994.

Solomon-Godeau, Abigail. *Photography at the Dock: Essays on Photographic History, Institutions and Practices*. Minneapolis: University of Minnesota Press, 1991.

Williams, Val. *Women Photographers: The Other Observers 1900 to the Present*. London: Virago, 1986.

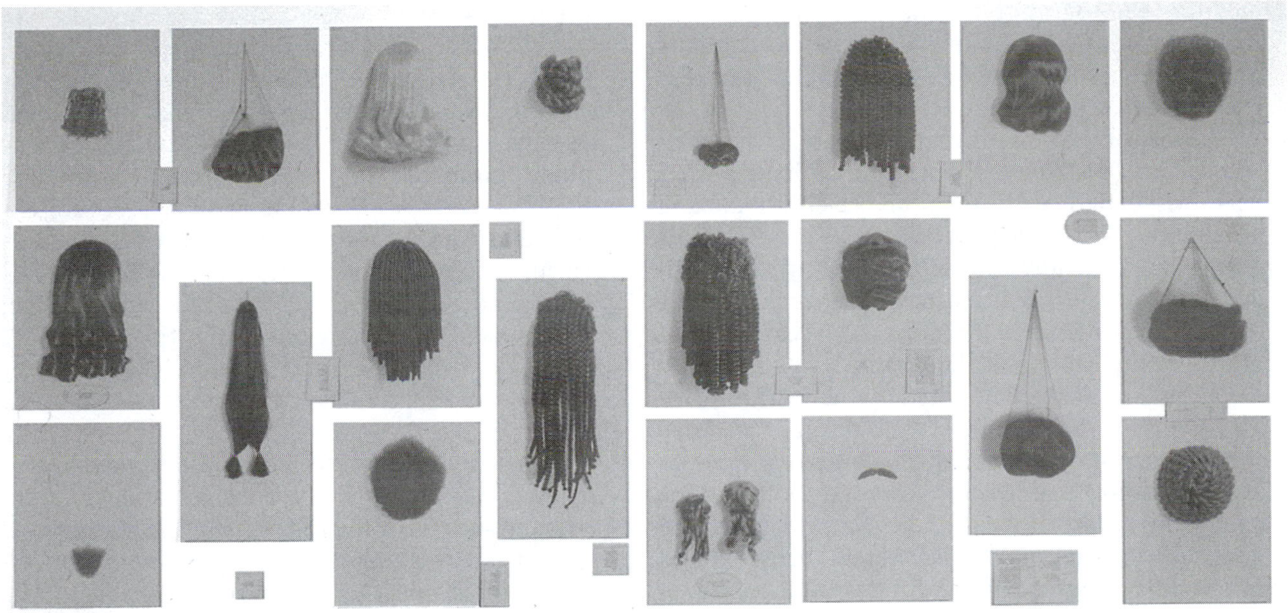

Lorna Simpson, Wigs (Portfolio), 1994, Waterless lithograph on felt, 72 × 162 ½" (182.9 × 412.8 cm), Collection Museum of Contemporary Art, Chicago, gift of Rhona Hoffman Gallery and the artist.
[*Photograph © Museum of Contemporary Art, Chicago, Courtesy: Sean Kelly Gallery, New York*]

FESTIVALS

Proliferating widely in the last quarter of the twentieth century, photography festivals are now an intrinsic part of both the exhibition of photography and the growth and development of the medium. The festivals serve as meeting places for a community of photographers, critics, collectors, and photographic enthusiasts. Festival curators, in selecting works and designing programs around specific themes, help to identify current and emerging issues as well as acknowledge new talent and previously unrecognized bodies of work. Speakers, forums, publications, and other educational activities further the work of photographic history, criticism, and theory. By publishing catalogues, archiving exhibitions, and providing both face-to-face and online access to these holdings, photography festivals contribute significantly to the study of the medium. Photography festivals also play a central role in the establishment of a global network linking photographers to academic, professional, and general audiences.

The history of photography festivals parallels that of arts festivals. While the arts have always been associated with religious celebrations and other recurrent public gatherings, the idea of events designed specifically to celebrate the arts is a product of nineteenth century arts societies and academies presenting annual salons and seasons. For photography, this took the form of events such as the annual print show initiated by the British Royal Photographic Society in 1858. As the academy shows sparked oppositional *salons des refuses*, public exhibitions became sites of contestation over the ownership of art and taste. At the same time, the arts, both official and oppositional, were featured in a series of international exhibitions that began in the latter half of the nineteenth century. Photography was on display at the first of the major events of this kind, the *Great Exhibition of 1851*.

In 1895, the launch of the *Venice Biennale* marked the beginning of the international arts festival as we know it. The *Biennale*, like the Olympics founded contemporaneously with it, invited national delegations to compete for prizes awarded according to commonly held standards of excellence. In the twentieth century, events such as Emile Jaques-Dalcroze's *Hellaru Festival* (founded 1910) and Max Reinhardt's *Salzburg Festival* (founded 1921) helped redefine the nature of performing arts by acting as showcases for avant-garde work. In 1932, the *Venice Biennale* established an *Esposizione d'Arte Cinematografica*—what was to become the first of the large international film festivals. It was followed in 1946 by the *Cannes Film Festival*, an event that placed the international competition for artistic excellence within a commercial context.

Despite the success of international arts festivals focused on other art forms, the first such festival dedicated to photography was not founded until 1969. In that year, Lucien Clergue organized the *Recontres d'Arles* in Arles, France, a general arts festival with a significant photography component. *Recontres d'Arles* remained a relatively obscure event until 1974 when Clergue persuaded both Ansel Adams and Brassaï to attend as featured speakers. Attracting major figures to the festival—in a manner similar to the way film festivals use the star system—gave the *Recontres de Arles* photography festival an international prominence. Photographers such as Yousef Karsh, André Kertész, and Aaron Siskind were featured by the festival in succeeding years. The festival continued to grow and, in 2004, the 35th *Recontres d'Arles* mounted 40 simultaneous exhibits, published a 300-page catalogue, and offered 21 workshops and two conferences as well as presenting five *Rencontres d'Arles* Awards.

In his introduction to the 2002 *Recontres d'Arles* catalogue, Artistic Director François Hébel argues that the success of the festival and the many photography festivals that have succeeded it derives from a need on the part of photography's audience, like cinema's audience, to develop standards of taste in a medium where the difference between "master and clone" is often difficult to discern. Hébel suggests that the pursuit of this taste-building exercise has taken place at three different types of events: the city-based "month of photography" festival; the smaller, specialized festival; and events designed for professionals working in the medium.

The original and pre-eminent "month of photography" event—arguably photography's equivalent of the *Cannes Film Festival*—has, since 1980, been the biennial Paris *Mois de la Photo*. It was Paris that developed the model for incorporating a large number of the city's exhibition spaces into a single event. These spaces include major museums (which in the 2004 Paris *Mois de la Photo* featured the Louvre, the Pompidou Centre, the Jeu de Paume, and the Musée d'Orsay) as well as smaller museums and commercial galleries. The Paris *Mois de la Photo* also incorporates exhibitions in foreign embassies and cultural agencies, once again evoking the idea of nation-based representation within a global event. In general, the individual exhibits can be divided into three categories: historical retrospectives; exhibits organized around contemporary genres, artists, and practices; and more idiosyncratic exhibits in which curators provide a subjective view of contemporary photography.

From the beginning, Paris established that the scheduling of the festival for an entire month is intended to do more than just allow the time to find and view shows mounted at dispersed venues. It is also a means of asserting photography's cultural eminence within the city's cultural calendar.

In the 25 years that followed the launch of *Mois de la Photo,* cities as diverse as Berlin, Bratislava, Cape Town, Krakow, Mexico City, Moscow, and Stockholm have declared their own "month of photography." Festivals such as Buenos Aires' *Encuentros Abiertos*, Madrid's *PHotoEspaña*, Rome's *FotoGraphia*, and *Fotografie Biënnale Rotterdam* while not using the "month of photography" phrase have borrowed from the French model. Houston's *FotoFest* was the first North American Biennial "month of photography" in 1986 and in the scope of its festival and inter-festival programs is now second only to the Paris event. In Canada, Montreal's *Mois de la Photo* and Toronto's rapidly growing *Contact* are building on the success of their cities' major film festivals. Brazil hosts *Foto Arte*, a major festival in Brasilia, as well as festivals in Sao Paolo and Rio de Janeiro. China has located its international photography festival in the ancient city of Pingyao while Denmark's major photography festival, the *Odense Foto Triennial*, takes place in galleries on the island of Fyn.

As the "month of photography" festivals mature, they incorporate a variety of functions including speakers, conferences, workshops, and portfolio reviews. Some offer adjunct mini-festivals of photography-based new media or festivals within festivals featuring films by and about photographers. Increasingly, these various activities have been organized around themes that curators cite as being especially pertinent to the medium today. Montreal's *Mois de la Photo*, having declared itself "a cohesive, single themed festival," labeled its 2003 theme: "Now. Images of Present Time." In 2004, *PHotoEspaña* organized its 170 presentations under the general theme of "new documentary languages" while in the same year the Paris *Mois de la Photo* highlighted a program entitled, "HiStories—from documentary to fiction."

Many of the festivals have also organized programs to take place between their main events. These include programs of speakers, conferences, and the publication of journals. Houston's *FotoFest* operates a classroom education program, "Literacy Through Photography," which utilizes photography to enhance writing skills, visual literacy, and cognitive learning in grade school students. But perhaps the most important function of the festivals between events is their archiving of the work they show. The Paris *Mois de la Photo* has amassed a collection of more than 15,000 works while *PHotoEspaña* gets two million hits per year on its Internet archive.

Events comprising the second of François Hébel's categories, the festivals in smaller centers and specialized festivals, can be every bit as ambitious as the larger "months of photography." The *Noorderlicht Photofestival*, for instance, an annual collaboration between the Dutch cities of Groningen and Leeuwarden, constructed a website featuring all 950 photographers who participated in the event. In Germany, the festivals staged by *Das BildForum* in Herten and Mannheim function as eclectic gatherings of professional and amateur photographers with a wide range of exhibitions and workshops. *Encontro da Imagem*, a photography festival in the Northern Portuguese city of Braga, engaged visiting photographers in an ongoing visual documentation of the city.

Other festivals have earned reputations as high profile specialized events. Photojournalism is the sole focus of both *Visa pour l'image* in Perpignan, France, and *ClickArt*, a festival held in conjunction with the Singapore trade show, *Photo & Imaging Asia*. *Foto & Photo*, hosted by the Italian city of Cesano Maderno, is known for its exhibition of experimental photography. The French seaside resort of Biarritz hosts *Terre d'Images*, a festival of travel photography. Thousands of amateur photographers compete for awards offered by the *Togher International Festival of Amateur Photography* in Cork, Ireland.

Smaller festivals have also been used to enable the emergence of local photography. This is particularly true of festivals in two of the poorest nations on earth. In 2000, Bangladesh staged *Chobi Mela* which, in addition to its exhibition of foreign work, mounted a retrospective of photographs taken during the nation's 1974 war of independence. The Bamako (Mali) *African Encounter with Photography* combines international exhibitions with a unique perspective on the work of African photographers.

Hébel's third category of photography festival, events for professionals, encompasses both the production and collection of photographs. *Photolucida* in Portland, Oregon, and the *Rhubarb-Rhubard Festival* in Birmingham, England, both display the work of internationally recognized photographers but are primarily designed for mid-career photographers wishing to enhance their professional abilities through portfolio reviews and workshops. *Fotonoviembre*, in the Canary Island capital of Tenerife (Spain), offers exhibitions and workshops for an audience of photography scholars, conservation experts, critics, and journalists.

An entirely different sort of festival is the photography fair organized for photography dealers and buyers. These range from small events organized by local collectors clubs to regional and national gatherings at which sellers display both photographs and photography equipment. Other events, such as the *Daguerreian Society Symposium and Trade Fair*, serve a more specialized group of dealers and buyers. On the international level, two events dominate the photography trade fair circuit: the Association of International Photography Art Dealers (AIPAD) *Photography Show* and *Paris Photo*. The Washington-based AIPAD, organized in 1979 to aid and regulate dealers in art photography, held the first of its annual *Photography Shows* the following year. The annual *Paris Photo*, founded in 1997, bills itself as "the global reference for the market in 19th century, modern, and contemporary photos" and, each year, highlights the work of photographers from a designated nation. In 2004, a third annual event, *photo-london*, was established as a meeting place for galleries and dealers of historic and contemporary photographs as well as film and video.

In the first years of the twenty-first century, photography festivals work towards increased cooperation and globalization. Increasingly, festivals coordinate the use of traveling exhibitions and events, often across international borders. *The San Antonio Photography Festival*, for instance, has mounted a cross border exhibition in conjunction with the *Fotoseptiembre* festival staged by Mexico's *Centro de la Imagen*. In 2005, Paris's *Mois de la Photo* went a step further by working with festivals in Vienna and Berlin to mount the first *European Month of Photography*. The idea will be expanded in future festivals to include other cities such as Rome, Bratislava, and Moscow. In announcing that its Europeanization of the month of photography "draws its inspiration from the collective values and references that provide the foundations of today's Europe," the Paris *Mois de la Photo* harkens back to François Hébel's definition of the photography festival as an instrument for the pursuit of common taste.

Perhaps the most ambitious collaborative effort among photography festivals is the *Festival of Light*, a joint initiative by 22 photography festivals in 16 European, North American, and South American countries. From the mid-1990s, annual meetings have facilitated international exchanges of exhibits while the Festival's website is a useful portal to its members' events. In its mission statement, the *Festival of Light* reflects a growing sensibility among photography festivals when it proposes a permanent "pathway of photography around the world."

Renate Wickens

See also: **Professional Organizations; Royal Photographic Society**

WEBSITES

(Accessed May 8, 2005)

Association of International Photography Art Dealers (AIPAD) Photography Show *http://www.photoshow.com/tps.html*

Berlin Photography Festival *http://www.berlin-photography-festival.de/en/*

Cape Town Month of Photography *http://www.photocentre.org.za/festival_body.htm*

Chobi Mela (Bangladesh) *http://www.chobimela.org/2000/*

ClickArt (Singapore) *http://www.photoimagingasia.com/ClickArt/*

Contact (Toronto) *http://www.contactphoto.com/*

Daguerreian Society Symposium *http://www.daguerre.org/society/sympos.html*

Das BildForum (Germany) *http://www.dasbildforum.de/index.htm*

Festival of Light *http://www.festivaloflight.org/*

Foto & Photo (Cesano Maderno, Italy) *http://www.cesano-fotoephoto.it/english/home.htm*

Foto Biënnale Rotterdam *http://www.nfi.nl/fbr/fbr2003.html*

FotoFest (Houston) *http://www.fotofest.org/about.htm*

Fotoseptiembre (Mexico City) *http://www.conaculta.gob.mx/cimagen/fotosep.html*

Fotonoviembre (Tenerife) *http://www.fotonoviembre.com/*

Mesiac Fotografi (Bratislava) *http://www.fotofo.sk/*

Miesiac Fotographi w Krakowie (Karkow) *http://www.photomonth.com/index.php?lang=en*

Le Mois de la Photo (Paris) *http://www.mep-fr.org/us/default_test_ok.htm*

Le Mois de la Photo à Montréal *http://www.moisdelaphoto.com/index.html*

Moscow House of Photography Photobiennale *http://www.mdf.ru/english/festivals/fotobiennale/*

Noorderlicht Photofestival (Holland) *http://www.noorderlicht.com/index.html*
Odense Foto Triennial *http://www.brandts.dk/oft/sidereng/eintroduction.htm*
Paris Photo *http://www.parisphoto-online.com/PP04/ENG/PP-introduction.html*
photo-london *http://www.photo-london.com/*
Photolucida (Portland, Oregon) *http://www.photolucida.org/default.aspx*
PHotoEspaña (Madrid) *www.phedigital.com*
Pingyao International Photography Festival (PIP) *http://www.pipfestival.com/pysy1.aspx*
Recontres d'Arles *http://www.rip-arles.org/*
Rhubarb-Rhubarb (Birmingham) *http://www.rhubarb-rhubarb.net/00-home.asp*
San Antonio Photography Festival *http://www.safotofestival.com/about.html*
Terre d'Images (Biarritz) *http://www.terredimages.com/*
Togher International Festival of Amateur Photography (Cork, Ireland) *http://homepage.eircom.net/~togherfest/index.html*
Visa pour l'image (Perpignan, France) *http://www.visapourlimage.com/francais/index.php3*
Xposeptember (Stockholm) *http://www.xposeptember.se/index.asp*

FILM

Photography literally means "drawing with light." If light is the pen, then film is the canvas on which the artistry unfolds. Before film, events were "captured" over time and with an artist's pen, subject to the bias of memory and drama of the artist. Events in history, faces of the famous and of loved ones, faraway places; all could be brought quite literally and realistically to the viewer's doorstep. The invention of flexible roll film, allowing cameras to be lighter and more portable, meant that photographers could now capture events more dynamically, no longer restricted to the confines of a tripod.

Film is made up of a light-sensitive emulsion supported on a flexible base, and must remain in complete darkness until the image is to be made. Compounds in the film react as they are struck with photons of light, creating a microscopic chain reaction within the film's emulsion. This reaction is then amplified by development, and made permanent with fixing. Without both of these steps, the image captured by exposure to light would be fleeting, destroyed by the light needed to view it. The concept of film as a sensitized material has remained remarkably unchanged since the origins of photography.

History

The *camera obscura* ("dark room" in Latin) was an early device dating back to ancient times that allowed artists to literally draw from life via a darkened room and a well-placed hole in a shaded window or wall facing a scene. The artist could set his subject outside this room in front of the hole, hang a canvas or paper from the opposite wall, and sketch the upside-down image of the subject projected there. This device was later modernized and made portable with the help of lenses and mirrors. The camera obscura was a boon for artists struggling for the realism of proper perspective and proportion, but took some time to execute.

The Daguerreotype

In 1826, a Frenchman by the name of Joseph-Nicéphore Niépce was experimenting with a novel way of making the images projected with the camera obscura permanent without the help of an artist's pen. Using the basis of a graphic process known as lithography, Niépce captured the first known photograph outside the window of his country home. Grainy and lacking in fine detail, this image required an exposure of eight hours in bright sunlight.

Louis-Jacques-Mandé Daguerre was also experimenting with light-sensitive materials when he heard of Niépce's accomplishments. Daguerre contacted Niépce in 1829, and soon after, they became partners. Together, they found that by using silver iodide compounds that were known to react to light by turning black in color, they could capture a transient image. Their process involved the sensitization of a copper plate. By exposing the plate to iodine vapor, a coating of the light-sensitive silver iodide would form on the plate. They then used this plate in place of the canvas or paper in the camera obscura, and would expose it for a period of time to the chosen scene. The difficult part, Daguerre found, was making that image permanent so that it could be viewed under the same light that created it. He discovered that he could develop the image by using heated mercury. The mercury vapors would cling to the areas that had been previously exposed. The greater the amount of exposure in a given area, the greater the concentration of mercury would be. The image was then made permanent or fixed in a solution of sodium thiosulfate, known historically as hyposulfite of soda, the derivation of the darkroom term "hypo."

The resulting product, called a daguerreotype, was an image of stunning quality and detail. The silvered image was at once positive and negative, depending on how it caught the light. While more sensitive than Niépce's original emulsion of bitumen of Judea and lavender oil, daguerreotype still required that the subject remain motionless for several minutes. In addition, the process was incredibly difficult and inherently hazardous. Despite these factors, the popularity of daguerreotypes grew to staggering proportions, particularly for portraiture.

The Calotype

At the same time, an Englishman by the name of William Henry Fox Talbot was working on his own technique. Instead of a metal plate, Fox Talbot sensitized paper by saturating it alternately with common salt (sodium chloride) and silver nitrate, producing silver chloride. This compound gained density in direct proportion with the amount of light striking it. The resulting negative images were also fixed in a hypo solution. Fox Talbot then took these paper negatives and placed them on top of another piece of sensitized paper, and exposed the negative sandwich to bright sunlight. The second paper was then developed and fixed, resulting in a positive image called a calotype. Unlike the daguerreotype, multiple identical images could be created from the same negative. However, the nature of the paper was such that the images lacked the clarity and detail of daguerreotypes.

Wet Collodion

The next advance in photographic materials was in 1851 with the wet collodion process. Fredrick Scott Archer, also of England, made use of collodion, a substance that suspended the light-sensitive particles within a sticky emulsion that could be poured over a glass plate. When dry, the emulsion became a tough transparent suspension for the latent exposed image, which was then developed in pyrogallic acid or iron sulfate. The plate was then fixed, washed, and dried. The resulting negative on a transparent base provided the ability to make multiple positives of the images, like Fox Talbot's calotype. However, the image also had the clarity of the daguerreotype. Soon, the wet collodion process would replace both the calotype and the daguerreotype as the dominant photographic process.

The disadvantage of the wet collodion process was that the plate was only sensitive while the emulsion was still wet. That meant the photographer would need a veritable darkroom wherever he was going to take the picture. Despite this drawback, the process was used widely in some of the first examples of photojournalism during the American Civil War. War photographer Mathew Brady documented never-before-seen images of war with a traveling darkroom inside a horse-drawn wagon.

Color Films

Meanwhile, avenues for reproducing the colors of reality on film were being pursued. James Clerk Maxwell, a Scottish physicist, demonstrated that all colors could be represented through combinations of the three additive primaries (red, green, and blue). It was not until 1907, however, that practical commercial color photography was achieved by brothers Auguste and Louis Lumière. The duo were inventors of the autochrome process, which involved the integration of several layers of dyed starch grains (red, green, and blue) with a coating of photographic emulsion over a glass plate. The results were impressionistic, with pointillism-like dots of color.

Kodachrome was the product of two research scientists associated with the Eastman Kodak Company. Using a subtractive process, Leopold Mannes and Leopold Godowsky came up with a way to manufacture an emulsion containing layers sensitive to each primary color (red, green, and blue). The result was the first example of realistic color in photography when Kodachrome was introduced in 1935.

Film's Evolution

In 1871, R.L. Maddox, an English photographer, pioneered the dry plate process. This process made photography considerably more convenient, as the photographer was now free to photograph without a portable darkroom in tow. In addition, emulsions became more sensitive, allowing exposures in fractions of a second instead of minutes. The camera was now truly a portable device, and the snapshot was born.

The final steps in the evolution of film came with the invention of gelatin in the 1880s, a thin flexible material in which the emulsion could be suspended and coated onto virtually any surface. The ideal surface came a few years later with the use of a thin, flexible cellulose. By coating gelatin emulsion onto this new, flexible base, photographers were no longer restricted to large view cameras or the limitation of only shooting one image, then needing to reload the film. The new flexible film could be made into rolls, allowing images to be photographed quickly and in sequence. George Eastman of Eastman Kodak was at the forefront of this photographic revolution, manufacturing some of the first pre-loaded consumer-based cameras. Once the roll was exposed, the camera was sent back to the company for processing. Kodak's famous slogan, "You take the picture, we'll do the rest," outlined the new convenience roll film afforded the world of photography.

Modern Film

Modern film comes in many types, depending on what the photographer wants as a final outcome. Black and white films result in images made up of thousands of tones of gray. Color films are designed to reproduce the most realistic color possible in a given situation. There are special application color films as well, designed to render a pastel version or even a highly saturated version of the original scene.

Negative films, available in both color and black and white, most often are used if a photographic print is the intended final outcome. Slide film, (most often color) also called reversal film, produces positive transparencies of the image. Color slide film comes in different color balances, daylight balanced, and tungsten balanced. Each film most realistically represents color in the scene when photographed using those light sources.

Other considerations when choosing film include film size. Roll film, used in most consumer cameras, includes 35 mm, medium format film (120 mm and 220 mm), APS (Advanced Photo System) and miniaturized formats, such as disc film and 110-cartridge film. Sheet film, typically used in view cameras, is most commonly found as 4 × 5-inch film, but can come in sheets as large as 8 × 10-inches.

Films for specialized applications include instant film, popularized by the Polaroid Company. This film contains the processing chemistry within its structure, allowing the film to be processed almost immediately after exposure. High contrast film, sometimes known as graphic arts or lithographic film, produces monochromatic images using only black and white, with no shades of gray in between.

Film Speed

Film sensitivity, or the amount of light needed to make a proper exposure, is determined by the film's speed. Film speed is denoted by its ISO (International Standards Organization), which is based on testing done by the manufacturer. ASA (American Standards Association) is an older notation that uses the same numerical system of determining a film's speed.

The film speed determines how sensitive that film is to light. The more sensitive the film is to light, the higher the film speed, and the "faster" the film. The less sensitive the film is (the more light it needs), the lower the film speed number; lower numbers are considered "slower" films. For example, a film with an (ISO) speed of 400 is very sensitive to light and is considered to be fast. Part of the reason for this terminology relates to how these films are used. Since an ISO 400 film needs very little light to make an exposure, this allows the photographer to shoot in low-light situations. It also allows for the freezing of motion, since the film allows for smaller and smaller fractions of seconds to be used. In contrast, a slower film, such as ISO 100, needs a greater amount of light to make a proper exposure.

ISO numbers correspond directly to the sensitivity of the film.

Film Speed	Amount of light needed
ISO 100	****
ISO 200	**
ISO 400	*

ISO 100 film needs twice the amount of light to make an exposure as ISO 200 film, which needs twice as much as ISO 400 film. Respectively, ISO 400 speed film requires half the amount of light to make an exposure as ISO 200. For every doubling of ISO numbers, the amount of light needed is cut in half.

Grain

As film speed increases, so does the grain of that film. The grain of a faster film needs to be physically larger to provide more light-gathering surface area. While the advantage is greater sensitivity, the larger grain is more visible in the final image, particularly as it is enlarged. Larger grain tends to interfere with overall sharpness and contrast in an image. Theoretically, one should use the slowest speed (lowest ISO) film that is permissible in a given situation. A slower film will produce a smoother, more uniform distribution of detail, resulting in a sharper, higher contrast image. However, extremely large grain, such as that found in 1000+ ISO films, can be used to achieve an intentional effect.

In recent years, manufacturers have worked to reduce grain by increasing the efficiency of the light-sensitive portions of the emulsion. The result is greater sensitivity with relatively smaller grain. An example of this technology is Kodak TMAX, which provides a smaller grain size than films of the same speed.

Developer/film combinations can also be used to try and reduce the size of the grain in the final image. Fine-grain developers are manufactured for this express purpose.

Storage and Handling

Film should be kept in a cool, dry place, out of direct light, when not in use. Even a short-term exposure to heat can affect the film adversely. Heat can "fog" the film; add exposure to the film that is non-image forming. The result can be streaks, total film density, or partial fog, which can cause resulting images to look dull and have low contrast. Heat can cause color films to shift color responses, resulting in unpredictable color reproduction.

For long-term storage, film should be kept in a refrigerator or freezer (instant film, such as Polaroid, should not be frozen). Before using, film that is stored in either a refrigerator or freezer should be allowed to reach room temperature before using. Failure to do so can result in condensation that can image on the film, as well as potentially damage the internal chamber of a camera.

Roll film should always be loaded out of direct sunlight. Sheet film is loaded into special holders in complete darkness.

Note the film's expiration date, usually printed on the film box. If kept at room temperature, film quality decreases steadily after this date. If frozen or refrigerated, a film's "life span" can be extended significantly.

X-rays, such as those used in airport security machines, can potentially affect and fog faster ISO films. Precautionary measures include specialty lead-lined film bags and request for hand inspections.

How an Image Is Recorded

Structure

Film is constructed of several layers on a polyester or acetate base. The top-most layer is the scratch-resistant coating. Directly beneath this layer is the emulsion, which holds all the light-sensitive and image-forming components of the film suspended in gelatin. Beneath the emulsion is an adhesive layer to provide extra support between the emulsion and the plastic base. Beneath the base is another layer of adhesive, which mounts the final layer, the anti-halation coating. This layer is used to reduce the amount of potential reflection of light coming back through the film off of the back of the camera, resulting in a higher contrast image with greater detail.

Response to Light

Within the film's emulsion are compounds responsible for the film's sensitivity to light. These compounds, known as silver halide crystals, are made up of silver and a halogen, such as bromine, iodine, or chlorine. If this combination resulted in a perfect structure, the crystal would not be sensitive to light. Because of flaws and irregularities in the crystal, free-floating silver ions are also present.

When light strikes the silver crystal, it results in the excitation of electrons within the matrix, which in turn attracts these free floating silver ions. The result is a small clump of silver ions, their size ultimately determined by the amount of exposure on the film. The exposure must achieve a minimum threshold to provide at least four atoms of silver to this clump to make it developable. At this point, the film has recorded a latent image, chemical in nature but not viewable on film.

The Formation of an Image

After film has been exposed, the resulting latent image needs to be developed to be visible. Development accomplishes several goals. The first is amplification of the latent image to silver metals to produce a physical image. The second is to neutralize the film's light sensitivity so that viewing light does not destroy the intended image. Finally, the image needs to be "fixed" making it permanent.

The first step in processing any type of film is development of the latent image. This is usually accomplished by providing a chemical reducer (developing agent) to the silver halide. The exposed silver halide compounds are converted to metallic silver, leaving the unexposed crystals unchanged. The developer also contains an alkali, often known as the accelerator, to provide the pH of 7 or higher needed for the developing agent to function. Other components of modern developer include agents that reduce the amount of development that could potentially take place in unexposed areas (known as chemical fog). Preservatives may also be added to reduce the reaction of developing agents to air, resulting in oxidation (rust).

Once the image is formed, the next step is to neutralize the non-exposed silver's sensitivity to light and make the image permanent. These two things are accomplished by fixing the film in a fixing bath. The fixer, usually a sodium thiosulfate, converts the unexposed remaining silver halides into a soluble compound that can be washed away. By getting rid of any silver that could react later to light (the developed image no longer has that capability), fixing accomplishes both goals. What is left behind is the developed image.

Chromogenic (most often color) films are slightly different in structure in that they contain dye couplers as well as silver halides. The same reaction takes place during exposure, but development of these films yields the formation of dye clusters as opposed to silver. The remaining silver is bleached out, leaving only the dye layers intact on the film.

Density and Exposure

The resulting density on film is directly proportional to the amount of exposure the film received. The more light that strikes the film, the more silver will form, and the resulting density will increase. In a negative process, this means that greater density will occur in areas of highlight, and lesser density will form in shadows. The response of film in this way can be diagrammed in the form of a characteristic curve.

If one plots increasing negative density on the x-axis, and increasing exposure on the y-axis, the result is a curve that outlines the film's response to light. The lower portion of the curve, the toe, is indicative of the shadow portions of the negative. The straight-line portion is representative of the film's midtones. The shoulder, or upper portion of the curve, where exposure and density are at their highest, represents the highlights recorded on film. This curve shows that density does not increase in direct proportion to the amount of exposure the film receives. In the shoulder and toe portions, increase in exposure results in a smaller increase in density than does the straight-line portions. The straight-line portions show a proportionate increase in density as exposure increases. Therefore, the tonal separation of the midtones in the negative will most accurately represent the original tones in the scene.

Characteristic curves vary with the contrast of the film. The higher the contrast of the film, the more quickly it will record greater density. The result is a characteristic curve with a very steep slope, with very little straight-line portion. Since this type of film is generally lacking in midtones, this portion of the curve is very limited.

Exposure has a direct affect on the appearance of the film's characteristic curve, and therefore, the film's contrast. For example, if a film is underexposed, the tones move toward the toe of the curve. As a result, shadow areas are near to non-existent, and midtones lack the density they need to provide sufficient contrast. Highlights are recorded on the straight-line portion, and represent the only tones in the negative that will reproduce a sufficient amount of detail.

Overexposed film will result in a shift toward the shoulder portion of the curve. While shadows will be well represented, midtones and highlight areas of the negative will contain too much silver, resulting in a loss of detail.

Spectral Sensitivity

Films react differently to light than the human eye does. Human vision is sensitive only to the visible spectrum, which contains wavelengths from 400 (violet) to approximately 700 nm (red). The human eye peak sensitivity is at approximately 500 nm, which is green.

Panchromatic film, the most common type of black and white films, has a sensitivity that extends from outside the visible spectrum (300 nm) in the ultraviolet range to about 650 nm (red). The result is an increased sensitivity to blues and violets appearing in a scene. For this reason, a clear blue sky will appear lighter on the final black and white image than it did in the scene.

Orthochromatic film is more sensitive to blues and greens, but does not respond at all to reds. It is most often used in graphic arts applications. Because it does not record light falling inside the red wavelength, orthochromatic film can typically be handled under a safelight without fear of fogging.

Infrared films, usually created with the incorporation of dyes, are able to record wavelengths far outside the visible spectrum. The resulting image is capable of showing details invisible to the human eye.

CHRISTYE SISSON

Further Reading

Adams, Ansel. *The Negative (Book 2)*. Boston: Little Brown & Co., 1995.

American Museum of Photography. *Resources: A Primer on Process. http://www.photographymuseum.com/primer.html* (accessed May 8, 2005).

Encyclopedia Britannica Intermediate. *Photography. http://search.ebi.eb.com/ebi/article/0,6101,36467,00.html* (accessed May 8, 2005).

Greenspun, Phillip, for Photo.Net. *History of Photography Timeline. http://www.photo.net/history/timeline* (accessed May 8, 2005).

Langford, Michael. *Basic Photography*. New York: Focal Press, 2000.

Leggat, Robert, Ph.D. *A History of Photography: From its Beginnings until the 1920s. http://www.rleggat.com/photohistory/index.html* (accessed May 8, 2005).

London, Barbara and John Upton. *Photography*. 6th ed. Longman Addison-Wesley, 1998.

PBS Online: The American Experience. *Wizards of Photography. Eastman Kodak Introduces Full Color Photography. http://www.pbs.org/wgbh/amex/eastman/peopleevents/pande19.html* (accessed May 8, 2005).

Schaefer, John. *An Ansel Adams Guide: Basic Techniques of Photography, Book 1*. Boston: Little Brown & Co., 1992.

Stroebel, Leslie. *Basic Photographic Materials and Processes*. New York: Focal Press, 2000.

FILM: HIGH-CONTRAST

High contrast films are marketed for various specialized application. Depending on the particular nature of the process, there are different requirements for the film in terms of contrast, maximum density, speed, spectral sensitivity, processing chemicals, and dimensional stability with their own specified processing chemistries. Because of stringent technical requirements for each application, there are subdivided categories of films. This article will describe high contrast films and their processing in general terms.

Line photography and halftone photography are two major parts of graphic arts process photography. Reproduction of line drawings begins with originals in solid black-and-white with no intermediate gray tones. Line films have high maximum density and high contrast (gradient of 5 to 10). However, line films must be dimensionally very stable, of high resolution and provide high fidelity of reproduction.

Several other high contrast films are often similar in photographic characteristics to line films. These include document films, copy films, phototypesetting films, and image-setting films. Different applications have their own requirements in terms of film size, base material, packaging, and life expectancy.

Halftone photography is used to convert continuous tone originals (e.g., pictorial photographs) to halftone images, an optical illusion in which the tones are represented by solid dots of equal spacing and density but varying area. Very high contrast lith films are employed, and films are exposed twice, one with overall flashing, and another imagewise, detail exposure. Originals are photographed onto lith films with a contact screen, a crossline screen, or other means of screening, and processed in a special lith developer, which gives rise to lith effect and extremely high gradient (greater than 10) to render solid dots of sharp edges.

Line films and lith films differ in terms of developer solutions in which they are processed. Line films as well as other non-lith films are typically processed in rapid access developers that produce a high contrast image of good resolution. This type of developer can be used in automated processing machines with replenishment.

Lith films are processed in lith developers (e.g., Kodak D–85), consisting of hydroquinone as the sole developing agent, a small amount of free sulfite, a bromide, and an alkaline agent. The free sulfite level is often maintained by a sodium formaldehyde bisulfite system. In lith developers, well exposed grains in the emulsion are developed first. Chemical reaction products of this development influence the subsequent development of nearby grains in two ways: the products enhance development of well exposed grains, and they suppress that of poorly exposed grains. This autocatalytic mechanism enhances the image contrast and contributes to the very sharply edged halftone dots, called hard dots. One peculiarity of lith development is that, unlike conventional development, the contrast peaks at certain development times and further development will lower contrast and degrade the dot quality. Also, lith development tends to render fine clear lines to be filled in, and for black lines to be broadened, distorting fine details of the originals, thereby making it unsuitable for line type applications.

One major shortcoming of the classic lith development is the instability and short life of the working developer solution. Development is manually performed in trays, and factors such as agitation can significantly alter the results. Therefore, newer generations of lith films were designed for new types of lith developers. They use nucleating agents and nucleating accelerators in films and developers so that extremely high contrasts and lith effects are obtained with more stable processing chemistry. In this type of system, interaction between neighboring grains are stronger than in classic lith development in the sense that the development products can render unexposed nearby grains developable, called infectious development.

Another kind of high contrast photography is used for scientific imaging such as microscope photography. Techniques vary widely among researchers, from high contrast technical films developed in medium contrast developers (e.g., Kodak Technical Pan processed in HC-110) to low contrast pictorial films developed in high contrast developers (e.g., Ilford HP5 Plus processed in D–19). Higher contrast is desired in these applications because the original specimens are often of low contrasts. The resulting images are of continuous tone nature with enhanced details.

Some photographers use high contrast technical or document films to record continuous tone pictorial images. Such films are developed in extremely low contrast developers (such as Kodak Technidol Liquid and POTA formula) to produce negatives of pictorial quality. These techniques offer higher resolution but often with inferior tonal rendition than those obtained with pictorial materials, especially with subjects of wide luminance ranges. As described above, there are many different products for high contrast imaging. Such a range of products attain desired contrasts and other photographic properties by a variety of techniques in formulation of emulsion and the processing chemicals. The photographic properties of these films vary greatly when processed in low contrast developers for pictorial applications.

RYUJI SUZUKI

See also: **Camera: An Overview: Developing Processes; Film**

Further Reading

Bruno, M. H. "Imaging for graphic arts." In *Imaging Processes and Materials*. Edited by Sturge, J., Walworth, V., and Shepp, A. New York: Van Nostrand Reinhold, 1989.

Haist, G. *Modern Photographic Processing*. vol. 1, New York: John Wiley and Sons, 1979; 484–507.

Lazaridis, C. N. "Hydroquinone oxidation in lithographic developers." *Photographic Science and Engineering* 20 (1976) 20–23.

Yamada, K., Kawato, K., Hirano, S. and Katoh, K. "The development of new nucleating agents for the low-pH graphic arts system." *Journal of Imaging Science and Technology* 43 (1999) 103–110.

Yule, J. A. C. "Formaldehyde-hydroquinone developers and infectious development." *Journal of the Franklin Institute* 239 (1945) 221–230.

Zwicky, H. "The mechanism of lith development." *The Journal of Photographic Science* 33 (1985) 36–40.

FILM: INFRARED

In a rainbow we see the decomposition of sunlight in its visible components, however, there are parts of this light not detectable by human vision. Beyond violet rays are ultraviolet rays to which photographic film is also sensitive, below red rays there are infrared rays. Photographic films thus make it possible to "see" more of the electromagnetic spectrum, and infrared film makes it possible to photograph within wavelengths between 730 and 900 nanometers (nm—one-millionth of a millimeter). This film is used for various scientific applications as well as by fine arts photographers for its aesthetic appeal.

For the purposes of photography, the wavelengths of 730 to 900 nm are called the near infrared, and cannot normally be perceived in any way. Far infrared, which can be felt as heat, is 900 nm and beyond, some people define the end of this spectrum at 1200, others at 1400. "Normal" film is aimed towards reproducing, as close as possible, the spectrum of human vision, with the exception of early photographic emulsions, which were sensitive only to the ultraviolet and blue parts of the spectrum. Light sources other than the sun produce different spectrums. Tungsten light has a spectrum leaning more in the yellow and red part of the spectrum, and is high on infrared radiation. Discontinuous light sources, such as fluorescent, neon, and sodium vapor lamps produce little or no infrared light.

Infrared film was designed to photograph in the near infrared part of the spectrum; the expected uses were scientific and military. With this film it is possible to photograph scenes illuminated by infrared rays that would not be visible by the subject. Differences invisible to "the naked eye," could be captured by infrared film "illuminated" with infrared radiation. Although designed to photograph in the infrared part of the spectrum, most infrared films are also sensitive to visible light. Each of the commercially manufactured black and white infrared films, however, has its own particular characteristics: Kodak Infrared High Speed film (Kodak HIE) is the more widely available; it also has the highest sensitivity in the infrared part of the spectrum. It produces the soft and grainy images characteristic of pictorial infrared photography, is available in 35 mm and wider rolls for use in aerial photography. Sheet film formats are only available by special order. The Konica Infrared 750 has a name describing its sensitivity peak at 750 nm; its sensitivity falls sharply beyond that point. In the visible part of the spectrum it is sensitive to blue light. It is slower in speed, with higher contrast and finer grain than Kodak. It is available in 35 mm and in 120 formats. Ilford SFX 200 addresses itself to the pictorial uses of infrared. Its infrared sensitivity is not too wide and is promoted as a "special effects" film, not as an infrared one. The newest comer is Maco 820; the number 820 describes its sensitivity limit. Users report it to have characteristics close to the Konica Film; produced by a small German company it is not widely available.

The only available color slide infrared film is Ektachrome Professional Infrared, and it is sensitive to infrared in the 700 to 900 nm region, providing false colors, with infrared reflecting objects appearing with red or magenta tones. Like infrared black and white film, it requires filtering for best results.

All these films require special care while loading and unloading the camera. The Kodak films even require all handling operations to be made in complete darkness. Other special care should be taken when using infrared films: Some modern cameras have infrared devices for loading and frame counting; these devices will, in most cameras, fog a part of the film frame. Infrared light may focus at a different point than visible light, thus some lenses are marked with an infrared focusing mark, while some Konica Hexar models had their autofocus systems with two infrared focusing programs. For Kodak and Konica films, however, the easiest way of dealing with infrared focus shift is to use a wide angle lens with a small lens aperture to get more depth of field. Another difficulty related to the use of infrared film is the fact that exposure meters are not reliable on setting infrared exposure. Testing is the only way to set infrared exposures, and the best starting point is on film manufacturer's tables.

As infrared films are also sensitive to visible parts of the spectrum they are used with filters to block that visible light. The most common is the red #25, which still allows the passage of enough visible light to use the viewfinder of a SLR camera. Yellow and orange filters can also be used, even if with a slighter effect. A #29 dark red filter will give a stronger effect than the #25, however, there are filters like the #87 and the #89 that are opaque to visible light, giving the strongest effect. As only infrared light is recorded on film, these are not widely used in pictorial photography.

The typical look of an infrared photograph lies in the facts that the objects reflect infrared light in a different way than they do in visible light. Skies are rendered very dark with white clouds, foliage is much lighter than it appears to the eye. Fair skin tones and lips appear lighter, but eyes appear very dark in black and white infrared photography. With Kodak Infrared, highlights will appear with great halos or flares due to the lack of anti-halation backing on the film. There is a popular idea that some kinds of cloth will appear transparent to infrared radiation but a picture where a dressed person appears to be undressed has yet to be made.

Color infrared film is easily recognizable by its artificial colors. The use of yellow and orange filters is advised, and infrared reflecting objects will be rendered as red or magenta.

Some electronic image equipment seems to have no difficulties dealing with infrared, and some video cameras and digital still cameras are capable of producing images in the infrared part of the spectrum. They are now used as preview devices or to produce a final image. They are able to take away some of the unpredictability of infrared photography. However this unpredictability is part of the fun in photographing the invisible.

NUNO PINHEIRO

See also: **Astrophotography; Film; Filters; Infrared Photography; Light Meter**

Further Reading

Paduano, Joseph. *Infrared Nude Photography*. Buffalo: Amherst, 1994.

White, Laurie. *Infrared Photography Handbook*. Buffalo: Amherst, 1995.

FILTERS

A filter is a transparent, often colored piece of glass or plastic that is placed over a camera lens to produce a particular effect. Filters function as a barrier in front of the film, changing the characteristics of the light passing through it.

Filters are used in photography for a wide variety of reasons, including contrast control and color correction, as well as special effects and applications. Larger filters are also used in other ways, such as to provide safelight illumination or to otherwise change the color and intensity of a light source. Filters are also used to produce special effects as well as enhance the effects of certain wavelengths on film.

The Behavior of Light

Light is composed of three colors: red, green and blue. These are known as the additive primaries. The combination of these primaries produces all the variations of color.

Light that strikes the surface of an object can be reflected, absorbed, or transmitted. Objects appear to be certain colors due to their transmission or reflection of different wavelengths of light, producing color. Black objects non-selectively absorb most of the light falling upon them, while light and white objects reflect the majority of the light falling on their surface.

Filters work by reflecting, absorbing, or removing part of the light entering the camera lens. Filters cannot add anything to the incident light; in order for a green filter to transmit green light, the green wavelength must be present in the light to start with.

Types of Filters

Filters can be classified by how they remove or reflect radiation. In the case of color filters, the wavelength is removed selectively. For example, a green filter absorbs red and blue, but transmits the green wavelengths of light. This selective transmission is what causes the filter to appear green to the eye.

Other filters remove light non-selectively by wavelength. These filters, known as neutral density filters, remove an equal portion of all wavelengths, reducing the amount of light being transmitted through the filter in general.

Other filters, called polarizers, remove light according to its angle of polarization, or vibration. These filters are used to reduce reflections and capture patterns of refraction as color.

Another method of categorization of filters is through how transmission of light is accomplished. Transmission filters absorb other wavelengths, while generally transmitting a category of wavelength through the filter. These filters can be plastic or glass, and have the common distinction of being the color that they transmit. Transmission filters are the most common type of filters, since the wavelength transmitted can remain fairly general, i.e., green or ultraviolet radiation. They can be made of gelatin, plastic, or glass, and come in several sizes and shapes, from screw-mount filters designed to attach to the front of a camera lens to large acetate filters used to change the color of a light source.

Other filters reflect the wavelengths of light not transmitted. These filters, known as interference or barrier filters, can be made to be much more selective in terms of the final transmitted wavelength. For example, instead of transmitting all greens, an interference filter can be made to transmit only from 400–410 nm. This specificity makes these filters an ideal choice for scientific and medical applications where more precise narrow-band transmission is needed. Interference filters often are made of glass and have a mirrored appearance. The color of the wavelength band is only apparent on an interference filter if it is held to a light source.

Special application filters include soft-focus filters, which scatter light across the filter, creating a softened, pastel effect, and cross-screen filters, which produce a "starburst" effect around lights.

Uses of Filters

By absorbing (or reflecting) certain wavelengths, color filters can create contrast effects, particularly on black and white film. A color filter will lighten colors adjacent to its color on the color wheel, and darken colors opposite, also known as complementary colors. If a green filter is used on a scene of apples on a green background, for example, the apple will appear darker in tone while the background will render lighter on black and white film. This is due to the filter's absorption of red light, making the apples very dark, and the transmission of green, lightening that part of the subject.

This method of using filters to enhance or change contrast on black and white films can also be used to overcome film's inherent blue sensitivity. Black and white films are more sensitive to colors in the blue and ultraviolet wavelengths than the human eye, and therefore, render these areas lighter on film than we see them. As a result, images that include sky often render as bright white, even if it's a blue sky on a cloudless day. A popular technique to darken the sky on black and white film is to use one of blue's complements (yellow, orange, or red).

Color correction filters, more subtly colored than contrast filters, are designed to correct film's response under certain light sources. For example, a magenta-toned filter is used to correct for the green cast that accompanies photography under fluorescent illumination.

Neutral density filters, which remove light equally from all wavelengths, are used in a variety of applications. Most commonly, neutral density is used when it is important to reduce the amount of light striking the film without altering the color. For example, if photographing a busy city street at high noon, there may be too much light to use an appropriately slow shutter speed to blur the action of the fast-moving cars and pedestrians. A neutral density filter could be used to reduce the amount of light, thereby allowing the photographer to use an exposure of several minutes if desired.

Polarizing filters remove light according to the angle it enters the filter. The effect is one of reducing reflections, increasing contrast and saturation, and darkening skies. Since much of these factors involve the scattering of light, polarizing filters effectively remove the glare created.

Filters are used in infrared and ultraviolet photography to absorb all wavelengths except those intended to reach the film. Since these wavelengths are outside the human visible spectrum, the resulting images are often unusual. Often, infrared and ultraviolet photography is used in the sciences to record information not readily seen with the human eye.

Filter Factors

By their nature, filters reduce the amount of light striking the film. For the purposes of exposure compensation, many manufacturers publish filter factors for each filter, which determine how much light is lost. Filter factors are measured in powers of two, corresponding to stops of light needed to compensate for the light loss (see figure). Filter factors can vary with the light source being used.

CHRISTYE SISSON

Filter Factor	Stops lost
1	0
2	1
4	2
8	3
16	4
32	5
64	6

See also: **Adams, Ansel; Camera 1: Overview; Camera 2: 35 mm; Color Theory; Exposure; Film; Film: Infrared; Infrared Photography**

Further Reading

Adams, Ansel. *The Negative (Book 2)*. Boston: Little Brown & Co., 1995.
Eastman Kodak. *Kodak Photographic Filters Handbook*. Saunders, 1996.
Eastman Kodak. *Using Filters (The Kodak Workshop Series)*. Sterling, 1996.
Kingslake, Rudolf. *Optics in Photography*. SPIE (International Society for Optical Engineers), 2000.
Langford, Michael. *Basic Photography*. New York: Focal Press, 2000.
London, Barbara and John Upton. *Photography*. 6th ed. Longman Addison-Wesley, 1998.
Meehan, Joseph. *The Photographer's Guide to Using Filters*. Amphoto, 1999.
Schaefer, John. *An Ansel Adams Guide: Basic Techniques of Photography, Book 1*. Boston: Little Brown & Co., 1992.
Stroebel, Leslie D. *Basic Photographic Materials and Processes*. 7th ed. Butterworth-Heinemann, 2000.
White, Laurie. *Infrared Photography Handbook*. Amherst Media, 1995.

FINE ARTS PRESSES

Throughout the twentieth century, publishing houses and independent entrepreneurs established fine arts presses around the world, publishing art anthologies, art history books, artists' books, broadsides, catalogues raisonnés, editioned prints, exhibition catalogues, monographs, multiples, and photographic essays. In the production of such works, each press defined itself through the unique reproduction, printing, and distribution methods chosen for a project. The diversity and reach of these presses grew in tandem with the receptivity of the general readership to visual books and limited editions. Hundreds of commercial and private presses, along with museums, universities, foundations, and ateliers began creating book lists and imprints specifically for photographically illustrated works. The art publishing niche expanded as imported and exported books, predominantly between the United States and Europe, brought international exposure to artists and publishers.

New avenues of artistic and critical dialogues arose as photo-books proliferated, influencing art photographers, collectors, curators, and historians. The book format offered both a portable viewing venue and a level of mass exposure for photographers that would presumably eclipse that of a single gallery or museum exhibition. A partnership between publisher and artist, leading to the creation of an art book, often represented both a united creative vision and the desire for either a wider or more exclusive audience. The resulting work alternately was considered a stand-alone art object, or as French art historian André Malraux famously wrote in his 1953 book *The Voices of Silence*, "a museum without walls."

The photo-book held special appeal for artists, art collectors, bibliophiles, curators, gallerists, and print-houses. Photographers now had an entirely new set of creative possibilities in architecting a book—from its physical structure, paper quality, and image sequencing to its text, typography, and graphic design. The images selected for a book could be read as iterations of the original works, with the associated differences in size, tonal quality, texture, sequencing, and presentation. Alternatively, a book could serve as the original, sole manifestation of an artist's photography-based work. In the seminal essay *The Work of Art in the Age of Mechanical Reproduction* (1936), German critic Walter Benjamin explored the theoretical implications of image reproduction on art and society.

In 1900, when acclaimed French photographer and novelist Adrien Gaspard-Félix Tournachon, known as Nadar, published *Quandj'etaisphotographe (When I was a Photographer)* (Paris: Flammarion), there was already a well-established history of photographic images appearing in book form. In 1844, London publisher Longman, Brown, Green, and Longmans released the first volume of William Henry Fox Talbot's *The Pencil of Nature.* Bound with 24 original salted paper prints made from calotype negatives, it is widely considered the first commercially sold photographic book. British botanist and photographer Anna Atkins is credited as the first person to publish a book consisting only of photographic illustrations. Atkins self-published the scientific reference work *Photographs of British Algae: Cyanotype Impressions* in 1841.

The tradition of the fine art book became firmly established in the early part of the century, fueled by patrons specifically interested in handcrafted, limited editions. In the United States alone, the annual tally of fine arts editions tripled, from nearly 200 in 1900 to about 600 in 1919. Print houses generally produced each new book as an edition of 100, 250, 500, and sometimes 1000 copies. Whether a publisher limited the number of available copies or released a short-run first edition, the value of each book was greater than a mass-market version because of its high-quality printing and inherent scarcity. Limited edition art books also were usually signed by the artist or author, which created another layer of desirability around the work.

In America, Alfred Stieglitz began publishing his renowned periodical *Camera Work* in 1903, featuring the work of photographers from around the world as photogravure images. Though the last issue of *Camera Work* appeared in 1917, the journal was a forerunner for similar publications, which focused more on exposure to like-minded peers than profitability. In 1919, Weyhe Gallery in New York, headed by Carl Zigrosser, published *The Weyhe Portfolio: Twelve Prints by Contemporary Artists.* Considered a groundbreaking model of fine art publishing, the portfolio successfully promoted the artists it featured as well as the gallery's name. Edward Weyhe's press later went on to create the first Eugène Atget monograph, *Atget Photographe de Paris* (1930), which was co-published in Paris and Leipzig by Henri Jonquières.

A flurry of inventions in commercial printing that made photomechanical reproduction possible had begun after Richard M. Hoe of New York patented the rotary press in 1847. Printers who acquired the machinery were able to produce larger editions in a more reliable, less labor-intensive way. In the early 1900s, art presses welcomed the mechanization of photogravure production, which became known as rotogravure. From its early stages, gravure printing for photographic reproductions was more popular in Europe than the United States. After esteemed Los Angeles photo-book publisher Twin Palms and Twelve Trees Press started business in 1980, gravure printing for its new titles was outsourced to Nissha Printing Company of Kyoto, Japan. Overall, the photogravure exhibited seamlessness in tonal range and compatibility with inks and papers that made it a favorite among art presses, until the less expensive letterpress halftone and photo-offset lithograph competed for attention in the years to follow.

Across the Atlantic, small private presses in western Europe also were experimenting with the photographic image in print. In London, a press known as The Studio published *Colour Photography and Other Recent Developments of the Art of the Camera* (1908), with simultaneous editions in Paris and New York. Editor Charles Holme compiled 98 monochrome and 18 color plates for the book, which was regarded as the first color anthology of major photographers. Contributors included Frances Allen, James Craig Annan, Alvin Langdon Coburn, and Baron Adolph de Meyer. Holme selected multicolored plates for the work, which were reproductions of autochrome originals. The autochrome, a three-color print process patented by Auguste and Louis Lumière in 1904, gained popularity among photographers as soon as it entered the marketplace in 1907.

As photography began to saturate new magazines and newspapers in America, the cultural cachet of the fine art book became more publicly visible, especially in large metropolitan areas. A burgeoning interest in fine book buying sparked the establishment of organizations such as the Limited Edition Club in 1929. Exhibitions of books-as-art were held at the New York Public Library in 1919, The Grolier Club in 1921, and The Metropolitan Museum of Art in 1924. Contemporary art museums also began commissioning private presses to publish exhibition catalogues, monographs, and art history books.

Legendary photographer Edward Steichen, then director of the Museum of Modern Art's photography department, curated *The Family of Man* in 1955. All 503 images from the exhibition—the most successful photography show of the twentieth century—were reproduced in the catalogue as black-and-white photogravures. Maco Publishing, a magazine printing company, produced MoMA's first edition, which went on to sell hundreds of thousands of copies worldwide. By 1961, ten editions later, MoMA had sold more than one million copies of the work, making it the single most successful photography publication in the twentieth century.

During the Great Depression of the 1930s and leading up to World War II, the market for fine editions shrank considerably, attracting only those who could afford what was generally considered a luxury item. The so-called paperback revolution of the 1930s and 1940s, exemplified by the stream of inexpensive books entering the marketplace, drew more readers into bookstores than ever before. While mass-market paperbacks gained popularity, the fine art book maintained its connotations of prestige, aesthetic value, and collectability.

Within the first half of the twentieth century, the comparatively labor-intensive techniques of the hand-made calotype, photogravure, and woodcut illustration gave way to the machine-made halftone, rotogravure, and photo-offset lithograph. Later in the century, as computers entered publishing and print houses, digital offset computer-to-plate technologies yielded further photo-reproduction options for art presses. In considering all art presses in existence at any given time, the range of printing methods used was as varied as the methods available at that time. As the variety of approaches to high-grade art printing grew, large commercial print houses tended to favor methods that would accommodate longer print runs and shorter production timelines.

The arrival of the new and improved halftone screen was viewed as a great leap forward in production efficiency, as printers could now place a photographic image next to lead type, then transfer both to the same printing plate. In the late 1800s and early 1900s, brothers Louis and Max Levy of Philadelphia developed and refined the press equipment used to create halftones. The "Levy screen" came into widespread commercial use, offering printers better control over the replication of photographic tonal range. Walker Evans's book *American Photographs* (1938), published by MoMA, was considered the highly successful result of a marriage between his black and white photographs and the letterpress halftone printing technique.

Alongside developments in the halftone process of photographic reproduction, many publishing houses began exploring the advantages of offset printing. In 1903, American printer Ira Washington Rubel and German lithographer Caspar Hermann independently invented and unveiled offset presses to the commercial publishing industry. Through continuous improvements in the 1930s and 1940s, photo-offset lithography offered economy and speed that was comparable to and increasingly better than letterpress. As color film types and color print processing options multiplied in the 1950s and 1960s, photo-offset lithography became the process of choice for the high-quality tonal subtleties yielded by its four-color separations.

In the postwar arena of fine art publishing, the fluctuating dynamics of international production and distribution were widely attributed to the acquisitions and mergers that would dominate industry news through the end of the century. The path of Abrams Books is a prime example. Established in 1949 by Harry Abrams of New York, Harry N. Abrams, Inc., was considered the first company in the United States to focus entirely on art book publishing and distribution. Initially, most of the Abrams book list consisted of imports from European publishing houses. By the 1960s, Abrams had begun championing emerging American artists through its *Contemporary Artists* series and by exporting titles to Europe. In 1966, the Times-Mirror Company in Los Angeles acquired the company, which was later sold to La Martinière Groupe of France in 1997. Through such changes, Abrams retained its size, and after purchasing the Stewart, Tabori & Chang imprint in 2000, its catalog diversified to include such areas as cooking, fashion, and interior design.

Larger publishing houses, particularly subsidiaries of corporate conglomerates, assessed the profitability of a single new title or series against the production costs of long print runs. By using the sales channels already in place and extending print runs further, many large presses were able to lower the per-copy price of each book to meet an even broader audience. Publishers who owned world rights could distribute their books internationally and release co-editions elsewhere. In 1991, Callaway Editions published seven simultaneous co-editions of Irving Penn's *Passage*, which won the prestigious Prix Nadar. The award, given by the *Bibliothèque nationale de France*, honors the best photographic book published in France or in the French language each year.

Many print houses, such as independent press David R. Godine of Boston, relied on reprint programs to flesh out their offerings. With the necessary legal rights and permissions, a publisher could reprint or re-release a work using their own production techniques and design approach, often with a new introduction by an author, critic, curator, or art historian. More than 25 years after Random House subsidiary Pantheon Books published the internationally successful trade edition of *Wisconsin Death Trip* (1973) by Michael Lesy, the University of New Mexico Press released its own version as a paperback reprint edition in 2000. Many other successful works, in contrast, did not extend their availability via a second edition. Henri Cartier-Bresson's *The Decisive Moment* (1952) was published simultaneously by Simon & Schuster, New York, and Éditions Verve, a Paris-based art press run by Stratis Eleftheriadis, known as Tériade. After its immense impact on twentieth century photography, the book sold out and did not reappear as a new edition.

Along with reprints and co-editions, the procession of rare art books perpetually re-entering the art market lengthened through each decade. *The North American Indian*, a 20-volume photographic and narrative series by Edward Sheriff Curtis, was published from 1907 to 1930 with financial backing from John Pierpont Morgan. John Andrew & Son and the Suffolk Engraving Company hand-pressed 2276 bound and portfolio photogravure prints for each of the nearly 300 editions produced. By the time The Plimpton Press of Norwood, Massachusetts, published the final volume in the set, the unprecedented publishing feat went largely unnoticed by book patrons in the 1930s. In the 1970s, collectors and auction houses began to express a surge of interest in Curtis's work, and by the turn of the century, each volume sold for prices ranging from $7,500 to $20,000.

As smaller art presses produced more short-run books of the highest production quality each year, many sought to enhance distribution opportunities and marketability to potential collectors. From its first year in 1952, New York-based Aperture was known for its influential photography magazine of the same name, led by Minor White. In 1965, when Michael Hoffman came on board as editor after White's departure, Aperture created a book publishing program. Released that same year, the Edward Weston monograph *The Flame of Recognition*, edited by Nancy Newhall, became one of the best-selling photography books of the century. In 1968, Hoffman partnered with publisher Jonathan Williams to establish The Book Organization, a cooperative endeavor designed to strengthen bookstore sales for a group of small art presses. As Aperture's publishing operations expanded under the Aperture Foundation umbrella, publications like the *Masters of Photography* series and the landmark monograph *Diane Arbus* (1972), published in association with MoMA, brought the press its greatest visibility and successes yet.

In 1979, photo-eye of Santa Fe, New Mexico, created *Booklist*, a quarterly international guide to photography book publishing. Photo-eye developed *Booklist*, deemed the only publication of its kind, alongside its own imprint, photo-eye Books. Within 20 years, photo-eye became the largest independent photography bookstore in the United States. When New York-based Distributed Art Publishers, known as DAP, was established in 1990, it soon became the largest international distributor of contemporary fine art books. The DAP catalog includes titles from independent presses such as Actar of Barcelona, Spain; Steidl of Gottingen, Germany; and Hatje Cantz Verlag of Ostfildern, Germany. Publications from museums such as the Solomon R. Guggenheim Museum, New York; the Art Institute of Chicago, the Walker Art Center, Minneapolis; the San Francisco Museum of Modern Art; and the Museum of Fine Arts, Boston; rounded out the catalogue.

From the 1970s onward, dozens of small presses specializing in photography books debuted, as demand for such works grew along with their affordability as mass-produced art objects. In New York, photographer Ralph Gibson started his own art press, Lustrum, in 1969. The following year, Gibson self-published the highly acclaimed book *The Somnambulist*, and in 1971, Larry Clark's groundbreaking *Tulsa*. Gibson later produced more than 30 monographs that established him as both a photographer and book artist.

In 1984, Benedikt Taschen began publishing photography under his Taschen Books imprint, based in Cologne, Germany. Over the next 15 years, the press established its reputation through the lush, high-quality printing of its photo-book line. Each title was produced in mass quantities and sold at relatively low prices in large bookshops. In 1999, Taschen published a 464-page photo-book by Helmut Newton called *Sumo*. Measuring 31 × 32 inches and weighing in at 66 pounds, it was the biggest and most expensive book published in the twentieth century. Taschen released a limited edition of 10,000 signed and numbered copies, with each one accompanied by its own display stand.

In 1991, Walter Keller and George Reinhart founded Scalo in Zurich, Switzerland, with an additional office and gallery in New York. The definitive Robert Frank book *The Americans*, first published by renowned French press Robert Delpire in 1958, joined the Scalo edition list in 1998. Phaidon Press, founded in 1923 by Bela Horovitz and Ludwig Goldscheider of Vienna, Austria, became of the most widely recognized imprints worldwide, opening offices in London, Paris, Berlin, and New York. In 1993, Phaidon published *Workers* by Sebastião Salgado, a book of black and white photographs that won best book of the year prizes from the *Rencontres Internationales de la photographie Arles* (Arles International Festival) and the International Center of Photography, New York. Five years later, Phaidon published *Cream: Contemporary Art in Culture (1998)*, a successful book-as-exhibition showcasing the work of 100 emerging artists chosen by an international group of critics.

London-based Thames & Hudson is another art publisher that expanded internationally, opening offices in Paris and New York, as well as subsidiaries in Melbourne and Singapore. Since its inception in 1949, Thames & Hudson became one of the largest illustrated book publishers in the world, producing nearly 200 hardcover and paperback titles annually. In 2000, another large art publisher, Rizzoli International Publications, became even larger as its Milan-based parent company, RCS Libri, acquired French house Flammarion and its Italian counterpart Skira. Rizzoli maintained the art publishing operations of Rizzoli New York, along with the imprint's flagship bookstore.

Unlike the larger multinational houses with booklists spanning several art media, many of the new, smaller presses tended to build and streamline their catalogues solely around photo-books. PowerHouse Books in New York debuted in 1995 under the leadership of Daniel Power, a co-founder of DAP. Other prominent publishers such as Schirmer-Mosel Verlag of Munich, Germany; Schaden of Cologne, Germany; and Umbrage Editions of New York also focus primarily on photography book publishing. In 2000, Nazraeli Press in Tucson, Arizona, published the first of its well-received *One Picture Book* series of artist's photo-books, limiting each new edition to 500 signed and numbered copies. Each book contains an original print by the artist commissioned for each project in the series.

As the demand for art and photography books continued on into the next century, new and well-established presses were dealing with many of the same questions as their predecessors, namely about project funding, production values, distribution goals, and printing innovations. While independently addressing such variables, each fine arts press aspired to a perfect result that would appear tangibly in print, and as each one defined it.

KELLY XINTARIS

See also: **Artists' Books; Atget, Eugène; Bibliothèque nationale de France; Cartier-Bresson, Henri; Clark, Larry; de Meyer, Baron Adolph; Evans, Walker; Frank, Robert; Gibson, Ralph; Museum of Modern Art; Newton, Helmut; Penn, Irving; Salgado, Sebastião; Steichen, Edward; Stieglitz, Alfred; Weston, Edward; White, Minor**

Further Reading

Benton, Megan L. *Beauty and the Book: Fine Editions and Cultural Distinction in America.* London and New Haven, Connecticut: Yale University Press, 2000.

Cave, Roderick. *The Private Press.* London: Faber and Faber, 1971; 2nd ed. New York: R.R. Bowker Company, 1983.

Cravens, Richard H. *Photography Past Forward: Aperture at 50.* New York: Aperture Foundation, Inc., 2002.

Frizot, Michel. *A New History of Photography.* Cologne: Könemann, 1998.

Lehmann-Haupt, Hellmut. *The Book in America: A History of the Making and Selling of Books in the United States.* New York: R. R. Bowker Company, 1952.

Newhall, Beaumont. *The History of Photography From 1839 to the Present.* New York: Museum of Modern Art, Revised Edition, 1982.

Rosenblum, Naomi. *A World History of Photography.* New York, London, and Paris: Abbeville Press, 1984; 2nd ed., 1989; 3rd ed., 1997.

Roth, Andrew, ed. *The Book of 101 Books: Seminal Photographic Books of the Twentieth Century.* New York: PPP Editions in association with Roth Horowitz LLC, 2001.

Schiffrin, Andre. *The Business of Books: How International Conglomerates Took Over Publishing and Changed the Way We Read.* London and New York: Verso, 2000.

Taft, Robert. *Photography and the American Scene.* New York: Macmillan Company, 1938; and New York: Dover Publications, Inc., 1964.

Tomkinson, Geoffrey S. *A Select Bibliography of the Principal Modern Presses Public and Private in Great Britain and Ireland.* London: J. Curwen and Sons Limited, 1928.

Weitenkampf, Frank. *The Illustrated Book.* Cambridge, MA: Harvard University Press, 1938.

HANS FINSLER

German

Hans Finsler is a leading representative of the movement *Neue Sehen* (New Vision) or *Neue Fotografie* of the 1920s. He was an art historian, photographer, educator, and, for a while, a librarian. One of his greatest merits is to have driven commercial photography towards artistic representation in a decisive way. His photographic œuvre consists almost exclusively of arranged objects which seem to come out of the picture like sculptures. Evident in his images is the influence of the extraordinary design of the *Neue Sachlichkeit* (New Objectivity): perspective of the camera, focus, concentration on details, and an emphasis on diagonals. The two groups in this movement stressed either the experimental, process-related focus, or focus on the object; Finsler belonged to the latter group. He dedicated himself to questions of design, light, and the arrangement of special structures in his pictures.

Born in 1891 in Heilbronn as the son of a Swiss merchant, Hans Finsler studied architecture in Munich and Stuttgart as well as art history with Heinrich Wölfflin and Paul Frankl at Munich University. In 1921, he moved to Halle (Saale) to complete his Ph.D. under the supervision of Paul Frankl. During this time, he earned his living by working as a librarian and teacher of art history at the school of commercial arts *Burg Giebichenstein*. Here, he started using photography as a means to collect demonstrative material for his courses and to document the works of the school and its artists. Soon this developed into the first course of photography at a German art school. In 1929, the magistrate sanctioned the establishment of a new department for modern artistic photography at the art school, with Hans Finsler as its head. Finsler led this photography course until 1932.

In addition to his teaching assignments, Finsler worked for municipal institutions and firms in and outside Germany, as, for example, a chocolate producer in Halle, the "United Factories" in Düsseldorf and Munich, the *Werkbund* and North German Lloyd, by supplying advertising photographs. In 1928, Finsler had his first solo exhibition in Halle; the year after, he participated with numerous photographs in the *Fifo* (film and photography exhibition) at Stuttgart. The pictures taken during the decade in Halle—probably around 2000—are considered the most important part of his photographic œuvre. Finsler's work and the activities of his students found high acclaim in Halle and beyond. He published in various journals and took part in exhibitions in Berlin, Munich, Zurich, Stuttgart, Paris, and London. The city of Halle repeatedly hired him for advertising and documentary photography; Finsler studied the interplay of architecture and landscape in the industrial town, and the recording of the city's appearance was one of his important concerns.

Thus, the years in Halle were a fulfilling time for him and led him to attain artistic maturity as a photographer. He soon found his photographic language, his "optical grammar." The functional context of objects, their characteristic use, and productive qualities figured prominently in his pictures. Some of his most impressive shots are those of ocean steamers of the Lloyd, taken from an oblique bottom position. A striking feature of his experiments in creating an abstract image through photographing objects is Finsler's predilection for geometrical structures that are achieved through calculated arrangements. Finsler was also a master of architectural photography, his photographs capturing the plasticity and materiality of buildings and cityscapes through his choice of perspective, composition, and play of light. As did other exponents of the Neue Fotografie, Finsler also favoured eggs as still life subjects: a series of these pictures, consisting of 22 pictures, was probably produced in the beginning of 1929.

In 1931, the city of Zurich offered Finsler a teaching position in photography at the commercial arts department of the school of commerce. Finsler accepted "for reasons of health and family" and remained there as head of the department until his retirement in 1958. Among his pupils were Werner Bischof, Amil Schulthess, Ernst Scheidegger, and René Burri. He was active publishing articles on photography for *Camera, Du*, and other journals. In Switzerland, Finsler also found a circle of clients highly appreciative of his work, among them the modern furnishing house of Switzerland, *Wohnbedarf AG*. At the end of the 1930s, Finsler increasingly committed himself to his work for the *Schweizerischer Werkbund*, and he acted as its chairman from 1946 to 1955. In 1969, he showed a selection of his works of the 1920s, which he published two years later, with his own comments, under the title *Mein Weg zur Fotografie* (My Way to Photography). Finsler died in 1972 in Zurich.

FRANZISKA SCHMIDT

Biography

Swiss, Born in Zurich, 7 December 1891. Studied architecture at the *Technische Hochschule*, Munich, 1909–1914; studied art history in Munich by Heinrich Wölfflin und Paul Frankl, 1914–1918; married Lita Schmidt, a study colleague, 1921; Librarian and Professor in Art History at the *Kunstgewerbeschule Burg Giebichenstein*, Halle, Germany, 1922–1932. Autodidact in photography, from 1922; founded first class for "object photography" at the *Burg Giebichenstein*, 1927–1932; taught photography at the *Kunstgewerbeschule*, Zurich, 1932–1958. President, Swiss *Werkbund*, Zurich, 1932. Died in Zurich, 1972.

Individual Exhibitions

1928 *Neue Wege der Photographie*; Museum Moritzburg, Ausstellungsraum Roter Turm: Halle an der Saale, Germany (Hans Finsler and his students)
1969 *Mein Weg zur Fotografie*; galerie 58; Rapperswil, Switzerland, and traveling
1991 *Hans Finsler. Neue Wege der Photographie*; Staatliche Galerie Moritzburg; Halle an der Saale, Germany, and traveling

Selected Group Exhibitions

1929 *Photographie der Gegenwart*; Museum Folkwang; Essen, Germany
Film und Foto; International Exhibition of "Deutscher Werkbund"; Stuttgart, Germany, and traveling
Gesellschaft Deutscher Lichtbildner; Eisenach, Germany
Altonaer Kunstverein; Hamburg, Germany
1930 Kunstgewerbeverein Erfurt; Erfurt, Germany
German Advertising Photographs; Camera Club; London, Great Britain
II. Internationale Hygiene-Ausstellung; Deutsches Hygienemuseum; Dresden, Germany
1931 *Die Neue Fotografie*; International Travelling Exhibitions of the "Deutscher Werkbund" and "Münchner Bund"; Gewerbemuseum; Basel, Switzerland
Das Lichtbild; Museum Folkwang; Essen, Germany
1932 *Die neue Fotografie in der Schweiz*; Schweizerischer Werkbund; St. Gallen, Switzerland, and traveling
1937 *Exposition Internationale des Arts et Techniques dans la Vie Moderne*; Paris, France
1952 *Subjektive Fotografie*; Staatliche Schule für Kunst und Handwerk; Saarbrücken, Germany
1974 *Photographs Suisses depuis 1840 à nos Jours*; Kunsthaus Zurich; Zurich, Switzerland
1977 *Medium Fotografie*; Staatliche Galerie Moritzburg; Halle an der Saale, Germany
1978 *Das Experimentelle Photo in Deutschland 1918–1940*; Galleria del Levante; Munich, Germany
1979 *Photographie als Kunst 1879–1979/ Kunst als Photographie 1949–1979*; Tiroler Landesmuseum Ferdinandeum; Innsbruck, Austria, and traveling
1980 *Avant-Garde Photography in Germany 1919–1939*; San Francisco Museum of Modern Art; California, and traveling
1983 *Die fotografische Sammlung*; Museum Folkwang; Essen, Germany
1984 *Subjektive Fotografie: Images of the 50s*; San Francisco Museum of Modern Art; California, and traveling

Further Reading

Finsler, Hans. *Mein Weg zur Fotografie*. 1970.
Finsler, Hans. *30 Aufnahmen aus den 20er Jahren*. Zurich, 1971.
Roh, Franz, and Jan Tschichold. *Foto-Auge/Oil et photo/ Photo-Eye: 76 Fotos der Zeit*. Stuttgart, 1929.
Schmidt, Georg, and Peter Meye., *Die neue Fotografie in der Schweiz*. Exh. cat. Zurich, 1932.
Gasser, Manuel, Hugo Loetscher, Walter Binder, and Rosellina Burri-Bischof. *Photographes Suisses depuis 1840 à nos Jours*. (Exhibition catalogue) Zurich, 1974.
Gasser, Manuel. "Hans Finsler 1891–1972." In *Photographie in der Schweiz von 1840 bis heute*. Niederteufen, 1974.
Syberberg, Hans-Jürgen. *Fotografie der 30er Jahre: Eine Anthologie*. Munich, 1977.
Schmied, Wieland, and Ute Eskildsen. *Neue Sachlichkeit and German Realism of the Twenties*. (Exhibition catalogue) London, 1978.
Mellor, David. *Germany: The New Photography 1927-33*. London, 1978.
Bertonatie, Emilio. *Das Experimentelle Photo in Deutschland 1918-1940*. Munich, 1978.
Eskildsen, Ute, and Jan Christopher Horak. *Film und Foto der 20er Jahre*. Stuttgart, 1979.
Kempe, Fritz, Bernd Lohse, et al. *Fotografie 1919–1979, Made in Germany: Die GDL-Fotografen*. Frankfurt, 1979.
Weiermair, Peter. *Photographie als Kunst 1879–1979/ Kunst als Photographie 1949–1979*. Exh. cat. Innsbruck, 1979.
Steinorth, Karl. "Hans Finsler." In *Photographen der 20er Jahre*. Munich, 1979.
Steinorth, Karl, ed. *Internationale Ausstellung des Deutschen Werkbundes "Film und Foto" 1929*. Facsimile reprint, Munich, 1979.
Coke, Van Deren, Ute Eskildsen, and Bernd Lohse. *Avant-Garde Photography in Germany 1919–1939*. Exh. cat. San Francisco: San Franciso Museum of Modern Art, 1980.
Gruber, L. Fritz and Renate Gruber. *The Imaginary Photo Museum*. Cologne, 1981, London 1982.
Eskildsen, Ute, Manfred Schmalriede, and Dorothy Martinson. *Subjektive Fotografie: Images of the 50s*. Exh. cat. Essen, 1984.
Göltz, Klaus E., Theo Immisch, Peter Romanus, and Axel Wendelberger. *Hans Finsler. Neue Wege der Photographie*. (Exhibition catalogue) Leipzig, 1991.

ARNO FISCHER

German

Arno Fischer and Evelyn Richter are the most prominent names of the older generation of the former German Democratic Republic (East Germany) photographers. Arno Fischer is today seen as the outstanding East German photographer personality and as "the most well-known of the unknown German photographers." Even to the present, Fischer devotes himself to photography in two ways: as a photographer and teacher. In both fields he has been very influential on generations of younger photographers.

Born in 1927 in Berlin-Wedding, Arno Fischer soon had the idea of becoming a press photographer, but ultimately decided to undergo an apprenticeship in carpentry. His parents died early, and he was raised by relatives. His uncle, a dedicated amateur photographer, inspired him to make his first photographs in 1941. After his military service and imprisonment in England, he returned to Berlin in 1946 and started to study drawing and sculpture at the *Käthe-Kollwitz-Kunstschule* in West Berlin in 1947–1948. After the closing of that school, he continued his studies of sculpture at the *Hochschule für Angewandte Kunst* at Berlin-Charlottenburg; he broke off his studies in 1953 when he was denied a scholarship for having previously studied in the east. It was for solely financial reasons that he moved into the eastern part of the city with his wife and started working as a photolab technician. In 1956, he obtained an assignment at the picture archive of the *Hochschule für Bildende und Angewandte Kunst* in Berlin-Weißensee. There he became first assistant of the graphic artist Klaus Wittkugel and freelance photography teacher. Since 1962, he worked as a photographer for the fashion and culture magazine *Sibylle*. From the middle of the 1960s, he shot picture reports in other socialist countries and worked for various magazines and newspapers like *Freie Welt, Wochenpost, Sonntag*. In 1971, Fischer resigned from Weißensee and continued as a freelance photographer. He traveled to Africa on behalf of his clients and published several illustrated volumes on cities. In 1974, he took a two-year teaching fellowship at the *Hochschule für Grafik und Buchkunst* (HGB) in Leipzig. In the 1970s and 1980s, he undertook several trips to the USSR, France, Great Britain, The Netherlands, and the United States.

Together with others, Fischer founded the work group *Fotografie* in the *Verband Bildender Künstler* of the GDR. In 1983, he obtained an assignment at the HGB in Leipzig as a professor of artistic photography. Besides this, he taught press journalism at the *Fachhochschule* in Dortmund, West Germany, from 1991 until 2000; in 1993, he had to leave the HGB.

Arno Fischer always looked for a direct confrontation with reality, and was a committed proponent of subjective social photography. He tried to convey a familiar feeling for life, and to express his political convictions in a symbolic way. From 1952 onwards, Fischer concentrated on photography as his medium. His experience as a student of sculpture made him stress the presentation of plastic bodies in his pictures. "One of my strong points in sculpture was relief, and that consists mainly of composition for me. That is, I see the world already as something composed when I look at it." Nevertheless his style is narrative and does not depict a posed reality. Even if some pictures look as if they have been staged, they are never more than sometimes intensely awaited moments of real events—'the decisive moment.' His commercial photographs also were imbued with considerable artistry, seeking to rise above mere illustration and to raise important existential questions.

Fischer habitually worked with single images, although at times he later arranged many into a series. The most important among these series are photographs from divided Berlin of the 1950s. The pictures were meant to document what was happening in Berlin, the focal point of the German division that had taken on a distinct shape by then: the social, political, and economical polarisation of the city had become an unmistakable fact. Fischer's doubts about the West and sympathy for the East are conspicuous. Fischer did not focus on the symbolic interpretation of ruins or the architectonic destruction of Berlin; his interest was rather to gain insight into social structures and the encounters and gestures of human beings. The strong impact of his photographs was due to a photographic language that was uncommon and both aesthetically and formally well-calculated: it went counter to contemporary clichés. The publisher *Edition Leipzig* wanted to publish this series under the title *Situation Berlin*. The evaluation of his experiences of the West were more or less in conformity with GDR authorities, but not his aesthetics; and the building of the Wall in 1961 became a pretext for banning the book. The series reappeared 40 years later, following the wall's dismantling.

An often quoted, important experience for Fischer was his encounter with Robert Frank's works, and especially his book *The Americans* of 1958. Frank's passionate photographic language and his conception of street photography encouraged Fischer to continue in this vein. He felt supported in his approach to search for the symbolic aspects in the fleeting nature of everyday situations. A further inspiration for Fischer and some of his colleagues was René Burri's book *Die Deutschen*, published in 1962, which was conceptually similar to Frank's works.

It was by accident that Fischer joined the fashion and cultural magazine *Sibylle* in 1962. Until 1985, he published photographs in its pages which formally qualified as fashion photography, although he never saw himself as a fashion photographer. Partly due to his and Thea Melis's work, the appearance of the magazine changed radically in the 1960s. Through a new concept and altered imagery of fashion photography, it wanted to establish a more realistic self-representation of society, and traditional "puppet poses" were abolished. Elements of live photography were adapted to the presentation of fashion photography: moments of movement, background as authentic environment, withdrawn depiction of fashion. These features were nothing new internationally, but gave a completely different appearance to fashion photography in the GDR. For a long time, *Sibylle* remained a forum for the otherwise hardly conceivable publication of such photography in the GDR.

Arno Fischer, always conceiving of photography in social and cultural terms, also saw himself as a teacher and mediator of photography. Especially in this context, his charisma has fully revealed itself: during all these years he has constantly had a circle of pupils and admirers around him. His lectures on photography resemble conversations about this medium. It is one of his greatest talents to mobilise the energies and trigger the independent artistic development of others. In this way, he has become an example to many photographers.

FRANZISKA SCHMIDT

See also: **Burri, René; Frank, Robert; Photography in Europe: Germany and Austria; The Decisive Moment**

Biography

Born in Berlin, Germany, 14 April 1927; Apprenticeship in carpentry. Study of sculpure in East and West Berlin, Artschool *Berlin-Weißensee* and *Hochschule der Künste* in Berlin-Charlottenburg, 1948–1953; work as a photolab technican. Decision for photography, Berlin, 1947–1953; assistant to Klaus Wittkugel at the art school in Berlin-Weißensee, 1956; first assistant with lectureship, 1957–1971; Fischer's book *Situation Berlin* was not published because the wall was built, 1961. Worked as photographer and publicist for the magazine *Sibylle*, Berlin, 1961; founded together with other photographers the group *Direkt*, in the mid-1960s; assignment at the *Hochschule für Grafik und Buchkunst* in Leipzig (HGB), 1972–1974; founded the work group *Fotografie* in the *Verband Bildender Künstler* of the GDR, 1981; lectureship at the HGB, Leipzig, 1983–1985; professor for artistic photography, HGB Leipzig, 1985–1992; individual exhibition at the "Recontres Internationales de la Photogaphie" in Arles, France, 1987; teacher and artistic director of the class *Fotografie* at the HGB Leipzig, 1992–1993; assignment for press journalism at the *Fachhochschule Dortmund*, 1990–2000; award Dr. Erich Salomon of the Deutschen Gesellschaft für Photographie (DGPh), 2000; living and working in Gransee near Berlin.

Individual Exhibitions

1958 Warszawa, Poland (together with Evelyn Richter)
1967 *Am Wege*; Fotogalerie, Bratislava, CSSR
1978 Kunstmuseum Vienna, Austria
1979 Galerie Berlin; East Berlin, Germany
1983 *Indien*; Club der Kulturschaffenden der DDR, East Berlin, Germany
Alt *Delhi-Neu Delhi*; Galerie Sophienstraße 8, East Berlin, Germany
1985 *Fotografien aus vier Jahrzehnten*; Fotogalerie am Helsingforser Platz, East Berlin, Germany
1987 Recontres Internationales de la Photographie, Arles, France
1988 Akademie der Künste, East Berlin, Germany
1989 Braga, Portugal
1991 Almeria, Spain
1991 Galerie im Margarethenhof, Königswinter, Germany (together with Ulrich Wüst)
1993 Omes da Fotografia, Lisbon, Portugal
1995 Laurence Miller Gallery, New York, United States
1996 *Arno Fischer und Schüler*; Galerie GAFF, Rotenburg/Wümme, Germany
1997 *Arno Fischer. Photographien*; 4. Internationale Fototage Herten, Germany, and traveling

1997/98 *Arno Fischer. Photographien*; Staatliche Galerie Moritzburg Halle, Halle an der Saale, Germany, and traveling
1998 *Arno Fischer. Ost-West-Berlin und andere Photographien 1943–1990*; Galerie Zimmer, Düsseldorf, Germany
2000 Exhibition on the occasion of the award *Dr. Erich-Salomon* of the DGPh, Martin-Luther-Universität Halle-Wittenberg, Halle an der Saale, Germany
2000 *Arno Fischer. Photographien 1943–1989*; Haus der Fotografie Hannover, Hannover, Germany

Selected Group Exhibitions

1977 *Medium Fotografie*; Staatliche Galerie Moritzburg, Halle, Germany
1979 *DDR Fotografie*; Galerie Gurzenich, Cologne, Germany
1981 *II. Porträtfotoausstellung*; Fucik Hallen, Dresden, Germany
1982 *9. Kunstausstellung* DDR; Fucik Hallen, Dresden, Germany
1985 *Photographs Contemporains en R.D.A.*; Cherbourg, France, and traveling
10 Fotografen aus der DDR; Graz, Austria, and traveling
Begegnungen; Altes Museum, East Berlin, Germany
1992 *Nichts ist so einfach wie es scheint. Ostdeutsche Photographie 1945–1989*; Berlinische Galerie, Landesmuseum für Moderne Kunst, Photographie und Architektur, Berlin, Germany
1996 *Arno Fischer and His Students*; Galerie GAFF, Rotenburg/Wümme
1997 *Positionen künstlerischer Photographie in Deutschland seit 1945*; Berlinische Galerie, Landesmuseum für Moderne Kunst, Photographie und Architektur, Berlin, Germany
1998 *Zwischen Abstraktion und Wirklichkeit. Fotografien der 50er Jahre*; Kunstverein Ludwigshafen, Germany
1998 *Signaturen des Sichtbaren. Ein Jahrhundert der Fotografie in Deutschland*; Galerie am Fischmarkt, Erfurt, Germany
1999 *Macht eines Mediums. Deutsche Fotografie von 1870 bis 1970*; Kunst-und Ausstellungshalle, Bonn, Germany

Selected Works

Situation Berlin, 1953–1960
New York, 1980
East Berlin, 1956

Further Reading

Auer, Barbara, ed. *Zwischen Abstraktion und Wirklichkeit. Fotografien der 50er Jahre*. Ludwigshafen: Kunstverein, 1998.

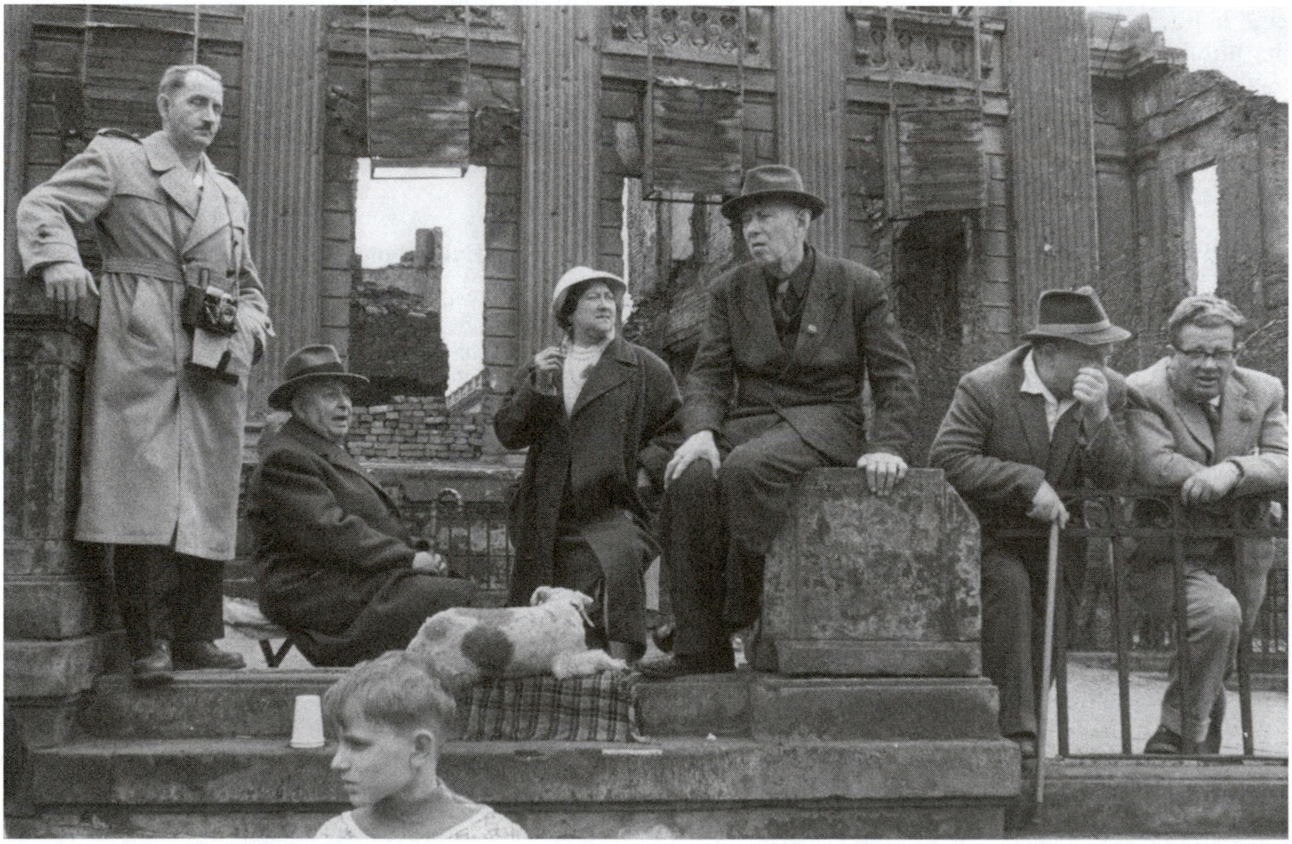

Arno Fischer, East Berlin, 1956.
[*Courtesy Gallery argus Fotokunst, Berlin*]

Centre Regional de la Photographie Nord Pas-de-Calais. Exhibition catalogue. Douchy-les-Mines, 1990.
Domröse, Ulrich, ed. *Nichts ist so einfach wie es scheint. Ostdeutsche Photographie 1945–1989.* Exh. cat. Berlin: Berlinische Galerie, Landesmuseum für Moderne Kunst, Photographie und Architektur, 1992.
Domröse, Ulrich, ed. *Positionen künstlerischer Photographie in Deutschland seit 1945.* Berlin: Berlinische Galerie, Landesmuseum für Moderne Kunst, Photographie und Architektur, 1997.
Domröse, Ulrich, ed. *Arno Fischer: Situation Berlin, Fotografien 1953–1960.* Berlin: Nicolai Verlag, 2001.
Fischer, Arno. *Cleopatra das kluge Kind.* Text Heinz Kahlow, Zeichnungen Heinz Bormann, Berlin: Das Neue Berlin, 1960.
———. *Schläft ein Lied in allen Dingen. Romantische Gedichte.* Auswahl Klaus Friedrich Köpp, Berlin: Ruetten & Loening, 1970.
———. *Polens Hauptstädte. Poznan, Krakow, Warszawa.* Text Rolf Schneider. Berlin: Volk und Welt, 1974.
———. *Leningrad. Erinnerungen und Entdeckungen.* Text Daniil Granin. Berlin: Volk und Welt, 1981.
———. *Alt-Delhi, Neu-Delhi. Zwischen Affenstadt und Rotem Fort.* Text Richard Christ. Berlin: und Welt, 1983.
———. *Gruppe "Direkt". Redaktionsgespräch.* In *Bildende Kunst* Nr. 4, 1984.
———. *Arno Fischer. Fotografien aus 4 Jahrzehnten.* Ausst. Kat., Fotogalerie Berlin-Friedrichshain, 1985.
———. *New York. Ansichten.* Text Heiner Müller. Berlin: Volk und Welt, 1988.
———. *Berlin 1943–1990.* Douchy-les-Mines: Centre Regional de la Photographie Nord Pas-de-Calais, 1990.
Frühe Bilder. Eine Ausstellung zur Geschichte der Fotografie in der DDR, Exh. cat. Leipzig 1985.
Gernot Kuehn, Karl ed. *Caught: The Art of Photography in the German Democratic Republik.* Los Angeles, Berkeley, London: 1997.
Gundlach, F.C. and Ulli Richter, eds. *Berlin en vogue. Berliner Mode in der Photographie.* Exh. cat. Berlin: Martin-Gropius-Bau, 1993.
Ich brauche Leute um mich herum, am liebsten junge. Ein Gespräch mit Arno Fischer. In *Photonews* no. 9 (2001).
Immisch, T.O., and Klaus Göltz, eds. *Arno Fischer. Photographien.* Leipzig: Connewitzer Verlagsbuchhandlung, 1997.
Leipziger Schule. Fotografie, Arbeiten von Absolventen und Studenten 1980–1993. Exh. cat. Leipzig: Hochschule für Grafik und Buchkunst, 1993.
Leipzig trifft Dortmund in Berlin. Studenten der Fotografie von Arno Fischer. Exh cat. Berlin: Neue Galerie der Bildenden Künste, 1993.
Melis, Dorothea, ed. *Sibylle. Modefotografie aus drei Jahrzehnten DDR.* Berlin: Schwartzkopf & Schwartzkopf, 1998.
Signatur des Sichtbaren. Ein Jahrhundert der Fotografie in Deutschland. Exh. cat. Erfurt: Galerie am Fischmarkt, 1998.
'Zustandsberichte'. Deutsche Fotografie der 50er bis 60er Jahre in Ost und West. Exh. cat. Stuttgart: Institut für Auslandsbeziehungen, 1992.

PETER FISCHLI AND DAVID WEISS

Swiss

Collaborating since the late 1970s, Swiss artists Peter Fischli and David Weiss work in various media, including sculpture, film, installation, text, photography, and video. In their aesthetic practices and public life, the two artists have taken great pains to circumnavigate their individual personas, forging instead a rigorously collaborative identity. As such, precious little is known about them beyond the most basic biographical data.

While the work of Fischli and Weiss reflects a definite relationship to pop art and conceptual art, their fixation on seemingly banal objects and images breaks with Warholian detachment, suggesting that the stuff of everyday life may carry potential philosophical and spiritual consequence. This longstanding preoccupation with the quotidian is a constant in their work, evident in their first collaboration, *Wurstserie* (Sausage Series), 1979. In the 10 color photographs, a variety of sausages and meat products are posed in scenes with alternately generic and specific titles, including *In den Bergen* (In the Mountains) and *Titantic*. The most widely circulated image from the series is *Der Unfall* (The Accident), a two-car sausagemobile collision against a backdrop of roughly carved cardboard high-rises, with cigarette butts, in lieu of human bodies, posed in the scene as both onlookers and casualties. The image bears a timbre common to all of the work of Fischli and Weiss: it is at once ludic, with a childlike sense of inventiveness, and bothered, with a trace of agitation.

For the five years following *Wurstserie*, Fischli and Weiss abandoned the camera in favor of the unfired clay of *Plötzlich diese Übersicht* (Suddenly this Overview), 1981; and the polyurethane, cloth, and paint of their three subsequent projects. While many of their collaborations do away with the camera altogether, it seems that the possibilities and practices associated with photographic technologies are always at work in the output of Fischli and Weiss. Like the sausage-animated images of their debut collaboration, their practices in other media of the same period show a commitment to the commonplace, and an exploration of the promise and thresholds of archival practices and the positivist systems of modernity—every image captured with a camera begs the viewing subject to wonder how many other images might have been missed. With their return to the camera in *Stiller Nachmittag* (Quiet Afternoon), 1984–1985, the pair produced a series of black-and-white and color photographs of contraptions devised out of food and kitchen gadgets. These still images of contrivances anticipate the best-known work of Fischli and Weiss, *Der Lauf der Dinge* (The Way Things Go) 1985–1987.

A half hour of color footage shot on 16 millimeter film, *Der Lauf der Dinge* follows a chain reaction, from a rotating trash bag which sets a tire in motion through a series of other events, to the ultimate overflow of a foamy substance and its subsequent ignition. En route, there are a number of spills, unravelings, eruptions, explosions, and rotations. Frequently characterized as a Rube Goldberg, the events shown in *Der Lauf der Dinge* are fundamentally different from the zany contraptions invented by Goldberg, who illustrated them to amuse his readers. A Rube Goldberg device entails, per definition, an obsessively elaborate design, ultimately yielding the completion of a very simple task, such as juicing an orange or shutting a window. Goldberg's inventions were a playful critique of Taylorist fantasies of efficiency, but nothing happens at the end of *Der Lauf der Dinge*; it is utterly non-teleological. In spite of this apparent aimlessness, or perhaps because of it, the footage is absolutely compelling and uneasy. Arthur Danto has suggested that the uncanny quality of the piece may be attributed to its visual quality and the materials used in the contraption, suggestive of an interrogation space and various implements of torture. 2003 saw renewed interest in *Der Lauf der Dinge* when Fischli and Weiss publicly considered legal action against Honda in response to a car commercial which clearly references their work, giving rise to provocative debates around questions of intellectual property.

In the years devoted to the realization of *Der Lauf der Dinge*, Fischli and Weiss also produced a number of cast rubber works before returning to the photographic medium with *Airports* in 1988. The series of cibachrome images taken around the world show commercial jets of variously relevant global import on runways, surrounded by cargo, truckloads of luggage, and the occasional worker, shot against a range of landscapes, including mountain ranges, bleak industrial surroundings, and lush flora. The images are aggressively generic; one could easily imagine them on the pages of an inflight children's activity book. The strategically artless photographs have an undercurrent of anxiety; even in a pre-9/11 world, airplanes and all of the trappings of air travel connote the threat of contamination from afar, and the dangers of hijackers, mechanical malfunctions, and crashes. If *Airports* evokes the nervousness of departure, then the next Fischli and Weiss project addresses the anticipation of arrivals. The 1991 *Bilder, Ansichten* (Pictures, Opinions) is a series of color photographs including the most clichéd images of Paris, Giza, Stonehenge, Sydney, and Rome, as well as snow-capped mountains, butterflies and flowers, goldfish, children, and a kitten. Without question, the artists maintain their attention to the seemingly banal in still photographs, and in their video work this inevitably stands in the foreground of issues of temporality and duration.

In the early nineties, Fischli and Weiss completed a number of color videotape projects, explicitly confronting questions of the archive and the limits of spectatorship. The most epic of these projects is the untitled video installation mounted at the Swiss Pavilion of the 1995 Venice Biennale, consisting of 30 color videotapes containing 80 hours of footage of the artists' journeys, from little local drives to intercontinental trips. The artists installed the video in Venice on 12 monitors, making it impossible to watch everything at once. Throughout the 1990s,

Fischli and Weiss maintained their commitment to everyday objects and the nature of contemplation in a range of media practices.

Their first major work of the new millennium distills many of the key concerns so characteristic to their oeuvre. *Món Visible* (Visible World), 2000, consists of 14 massive light box tables lined up end to end in a dark room, displaying 2,800 slides shot by Fischli and Weiss over the course of 13 years, including many images seen in their previous collaborations. The sheer volume of images places a particular set of demands on the viewer, and the subject matter and exhibition method suggest that Fischli and Weiss will continue to repeat the same set of concerns in their work: the pleasure of banality, the status of the artwork, and the limits of positivism.

RONI SHAPIRA

See also: **Conceptual Photography**

Biography

Peter Fischli: Born in Zurich, Switzerland, 1952. Attended the Accademia di Belle Arti, Urbino,1975–1976 and the Accademia di Belle Arti, Bologna, 1976–1977.
David Weiss: Born in Zurich, Switzerland, 1946. Attended the Kunstgewerbeschule, Zurich,1963–1964 and the Kunstgewerbeschule, Basel, 1964–1965.
The artists live in Zurich, where they have been working collaboratively since 1979.

Individual Exhibitions

1981 *Plötzlich diese Übersicht*; Galerie Stähli, Zurich, Switzerland
1983 *Fieber*; Monika Sprüth Gallery, Cologne, Germany
1985 *Stiller Nachmittag*; Monika Sprüth Gallery, Cologne, Germany
Peter Fischli/David Weiss; Kunsthalle Basel, Basel, Switzerland
Groninger Museum; Groningen, Netherlands
Centre Culture Suisse; Paris, France
Produzentengalerie; Hamburg, Germany
Kölnischer Kunstverein; Cologne, Germany
1986 Sonnabend Gallery; New York
The Corridor; Reykjavik, Iceland
1987 Monika Sprüth Gallery; Cologne, Germany
List Visual Arts Center, Massachusetts
Renaissance Society; Chicago, Illinois
Institute for Art and Urban Resources, P.S. 1; New York
Museum of Contemporary Art; Los Angeles, California
Dallas Museum of Art; Dallas, Texas
Berkeley Art Museum; Berkeley, California
1988 ICA Art Gallery; London, England
Third Eye Center; Glasgow, Scotland
Musée de peinture et de sculpture; Grenoble, France
Interim Art; London, England
Centre d'Art Contemporain; Geneva, Switzerland
Portikus; Frankfurt am Main, Germany
1989 University of South Florida; Tampa, Florida
Sonnabend Gallery; New York
Monika Sprüth Gallery; Cologne, Germany
Le Case d'Arte; Milan, Italy
Galerie Susan Wyss; Zurich, Switzerland
Akhenaton Gallery; Cairo, Egypt
1990 Galerie Hussenot; Paris, France
Kunstverein München; Munich, Germany
Galerie Marga Paz; Madrid, Spain
1991 Kunstverein der Rheinlande und Westfalen; Düsseldorf, Germany
Wiener Secession; Vienna, Austria
Galerie Achenbach; Frankfurt am Main, Germany
Galleria Bonomo; Rome, Italy
1992 Galerie Walcheturm; Zurich, Switzerland
Galleria Locus Solus; Genoa, Italy
Galerie Francesca Pia; Bern, Switzerland
Musée national d'Art Moderne, (Centre Georges Pompidou); Paris, France
1993 Kunsthalle Zurich; Zurich, Switzerland
Le Case d'Arte; Milan, Italy
Musée d'Art et d'Histoire; Geneva, Switzerland
1994 Sonnabend Gallery; New York
1995 *Swiss Pavillon*; XLVI Biennale Venice; Venice, Italy
Monika Sprüth Gallery; Cologne, Germany
1996 *In a Restless World*; Walker Art Center, Minneapolis, Minnesota
Serpentine Gallery; London, England
Kunsthaus Zurich; Zurich, Switzerland
1997 Institute of Contemporary Art; Philadelphia, Pennsylvania
Wexner Center for the Arts; Columbus, Ohio
Museum of Modern Art; San Francisco, California
Centre de Saint-Gervais; Geneva, Switzerland
1998 Monika Sprüth Gallery; Cologne, Germany
White Cube; London, England
Galerie Hauser & Wirth & Presenhuber; Zurich, Switzerland
Institute of Contemporary Art; Boston, Massachusetts
Kunstmuseum Wolfsburg; Wolfsburg, Germany
1999 Matthew Marks Gallery; New York
ARC Musée d'Art Moderne de la Ville de Paris; Paris, France
2000 *Sichtbare Welt, Plötzlich diese Übersicht, Grosse Fragen-Kleine Fragen*; Museum für Gegenwartskunst, Basel, Switzerland
El mon visible; Museu d'Art Contemporani de Barcelona, Barcelona, Spain
ARC Musée d'Art Moderne de la Ville de Paris, Paris, France
2001 *Busi (Kitty)*; Matthew Marks Gallery, New York
Fischli & Weiss. Mundo visivel; Serralves Museum of Contemporary Art, Porto, Portugal
Airports; Monika Sprüth/Philomene Magers, Munich, Germany
2002 *Fragen Projektionen*; Museum Ludwig, Cologne, Germany
Matthew Marks Gallery, New York
2003 Museum Boijmans Van Beuningen; Rotterdam, Netherlands
Hunde (Dogs); Matthew Marks Gallery, New York-Galerie Barbara Wien, Berlin
Galerie Sprüth & Magers, Köln

Selected Group Exhibtions

1984 *An International Survey of Recent Painting and Sculpture*; Museum of Modern Art, New York
1989 *Comic Iconoclasm*; ICA Gallery, London, England
1991 *Metropolis*; Martin-Gropius-Bau; Berlin, Germany
1997 *documenta X*; Kassel, Germany

2002 *Moving Pictures*; Solomon R. Guggenheim Museum, New York
2003 *Traveling: Towards the Border*; The National Museum of Modern Art, Tokyo, Japan

Selected Works

Der Lauf der Dinge (The Way Things Go) 1985–1987
Airports, 1988
Bilder, Ansichten, 1991
Món Visible (Visible World), 2000

Further Reading

Armstrong, Elizabeth, ed. *Peter Fischli and David Weiss: In a Restless World*. Minneapolis: Walker Art Center, 1996.
Cameron, Dan. "Through the Looking Glass, Darkly: Fischli/Weiss." *Artforum International*, v. 31 (September 1992).
Tiravanija, Rirkrit. "Real Time Travel: Rirkrit Tiravanija talks with Fischli and Weiss." *Artforum International*, v. 34 (Summer 1996).

ROBERT JOSEPH FLAHERTY

American

Robert J. Flaherty has been widely acknowledged as "the inventor of documentary film." Although primarily known as a film director and a cameraman (for the films *Nanook*, *Moana*, *Man of Aran*, *The Land*), he was also a still photographer, capable of lyrical images with an ethnographer's perspective. Born in Iron Mountain, in Michigan's Upper Peninsula, on February 16, 1884, he was the eldest of seven children of an Irish Protestant father and German Catholic mother; his paternal grandfather had lived in Quebec City, Canada. His father was a mining engineer and an iron ore explorer, and the young Flaherty was more often in the northern woods with his father, looking for iron ore, than in school.

In the employ of a railroad company exploring the eastern coast of the Hudson Bay, the great indent in the frozen north of Canada between 1910 and 1912, Flaherty made several expeditions to the Nastapoka Islands, Fort George, Great Whale Island, and across the Ungava Peninsula. He took many still photographs and became acquainted with the native Inuit. His striking body of photographs from these expeditions are held largely in the collection of the Thunder Bay Historical Museum Society. These photographs included images from Fort George, Baffin Island, the Ungava Peninsula, and Fort Chimo, and they depict the Natives of Northern Quebec, including the Nasakapi of the Nastapoka Islands with their distinctive headgear and clothing, and the Inuit. He captured portraits of men, women, children, candid and posed; and images of their dogs, dwellings, and boats, as well as daily life in Port Arthur, today's Thunder Bay. On all of his trips, Flaherty had heard tales of the Belcher Islands, and he was determined to explore them; for a trip launched in August, 1913 with this goal in mind, Flaherty was carrying a hand-cranked Bell and Howell movie-camera. The weather, however, prevented his success, and he returned to the United States for his marriage in 1914 to Frances Hubbard, who was to become as well his collaborator on future projects. Flaherty gave to friends some of the photographs that he made; they found them fascinating in their depiction of a people and culture of which they had little knowledge. Further motivated, Flaherty returned to explore the Belchers from 1914 until 1916, shooting about 70,000 feet of film footage—mostly of the Inuit pursuing their prey, but also of the landscape and wild life. The title of this first effort was to be *Innuit* (*Eskimo*), roughly edited in 1917. But disaster struck when the highly flammable film stock in use at the time caught fire while Flaherty was working with the negative; the only copy seems to be lost.

Unsatisfied by his first experience with motion pictures (and badly burned by the fire of the nitrate celluloid), Flaherty returned to the Canadian North on exploration assignments, always accompanied by his movie camera. In 1919, with the financial help of the French fur company, Révillon Frères, Flaherty again shot the Inuit with the idea of telling a story instead of merely juxtaposing images and short scenes. This effort, *Nanook of the North* (1922), becomes his first real movie and the one that earned him enduring fame—a silent film made with an Inuit family living in Inukjuaq (also known as Inukjuak, or Port Harrison), on the east coast of the Hudson Bay, in northern Québec. It showed the everyday life of an engaging Inuit named Nanook ("The Bear"), with scenes such as his hunting a walrus, participating in the building of an igloo, and a surprising scene of the whole family sleeping together side-by-side, naked. The enjoyment of modern, Western culture, such as listening to a record played on a gramophone, was also captured. *Nanook of the North* was later reedited with a soundtrack; thus, two versions of the film remain today. The film was a huge success worldwide, although some critics condemned Flaherty for showing an exotic side of the Inuit doing things that they had left behind, such as wearing traditional clothing (which was made especially for the film) or hunting using primitive harpoons. Later critics also point out that Nanook was more or less "hired" to be the lead in the film, as he served as Flaherty's main assistant, coordinating transportation, taking care of the equipment, and even suggesting scenarios, thus creating a work of fiction more than that of a dispassionate ethnographic documentary. Flaherty's technical innovations were considerable as well; shooting in the frigid conditions of the north provided endless challenges; the use of graphite as a lubricant was one important innovation.

Nevertheless, by contemporary accounts, the audience that most enjoyed the movie was the Inuit themselves. Tragically, as the film was entrancing audiences worldwide, the Inuits were facing exceedingly harsh conditions; Nanook died of starvation not long after filming was complete.

For his still photographs made in the Canadian north from 1910 onwards, Flaherty utilized a 5 × 4-inch Eastman plate (or view) camera and a 4 × 5-inch Graflex roll-film camera to take photographs of Inuit groups. Although the Inuit people were by no means entirely isolated, when Flaherty showed photographs to Nanook for the first time in his life, the Inuit did not understand what he saw and could not grasp what the images represented. As Flaherty explained later:

> My task is to make Nanook understand what I intended to do. My first difficulty was that he didn't even know how to read a picture. The first pictures I showed him meant no more to him than so many curious marks. It was only when I showed him some photographs of himself which I had made as tests—I had him look at himself in the mirror, and then at the photographs—that I got him to understand what a picture meant.
>
> (Flaherty [1934], quoted in Christopher, 1998: 187)

Although Flaherty is widely credited with coming up with the first film documentary and his device of shooting footage with the idea of constructing a narrative was pioneering and has proven to be enduring, according to filmmaker Dennis Doros Flaherty had in fact been influenced by previous films such as Edward S. Curtis's film, *In the Land of the Head Hunters* (aka *In the Land of the War Canoes*, 1914), and Herbert Ponting's *90 Degrees South: with Scott to the Antarctic*.

Flaherty went on to make a number of other films, including *Moana: A Story of the South Seas* (1926), about the Samoan people, with whom Flaherty and his wife lived for almost three years. *Moana* was innovative: Flaherty pioneered the use and development of panchromatic black-and-white film. When Flaherty's friend, the British producer (and later founder of the National Film Board of Canada), John Grierson saw *Moana*, he coined a new term, namely "documentary," to describe his innovative style, combining an ethnographic approach with poetic images. Although his documentaries were successful, Flaherty's career as a filmmaker was difficult. Often at odds with those interested in the commercial exploitation of his films, or with his producers or collaborators, his only other great success was *Man of Aran* (1934). Invited by his old friend John Gierson to England to live in 1933, Flaherty shot for over a year off Ireland's Galway coast, on the island of Aran, creating an epic without dialogue, which showed the rude life of fishermen, who re-enacted for the camera some fishing practices that were long abandoned.

After other setbacks, including work on a big-budget production in India of Rudyard Kipling's *Elephant Boy*, Flaherty returned to the United States. There, he made *The Land* (1942) for the U.S. Department of Agriculture, and *Louisiana Story* (1948), funded by corporate support.

Robert J. Flaherty died of a thrombosis on July 23, 1951, in Dummerston, Vermont. The Annual Robert Flaherty Film Seminar, an international event, has been held every year since 1954, having been inaugurated by Flaherty's widow. The Robert Flaherty Foundation was established in New York City in 1953; it moved to Brattleboro, Vermont, the following year. Canada also remembered Flaherty's presence as an explorer; today, one of the Belcher Islands in Hudson Bay is named after him. The Robert Flaherty Papers are housed at the Butler Library of Columbia University, New York.

Yves Laberge

See also: **Photography in Canada**

Biography

Born Robert Joseph Flaherty in Iron Mountain, Michigan, 16 February 1884. Studied in various primary schools in Michigan. Between 1896 and 1989; lived with his father, a mine manager, in Port Arthur (now Thunder Bay). From 1899–1890, sent to board at the Upper Canada College in Toronto; returned to US in 1900. From 1902 to 1903, studied for a short period at the Michigan College of Mines, in Houghton, but abandoned formal education after being expelled. Worked as a prospector north of Lake Huron, between 1907 and 1910. In August 1910, hired by Sir William Mackenzie, a builder of the first Canadian railroad, to explore the eastern coast of the Hudson Bay. Made three journeys on the Hudson Bay between 1910 and 1913. Studied motion picture photography and movie-camera technique for a month, in 1913 at the Eastman Company in Rochester, New York. Married Frances Hubbard (1883–1972), who studied with him at the Michigan College of Mines, on November 12, 1914, in New York City. Fourth expedition in the Canadian North 1915. Began to shoot the Inuit again in 1919. Released first film, *Nanook of the North*, as director, cameraman, and producer, 1922. Wrote his impressions about life in the Canadian North, *My Eskimo Friends*, in 1922–1924. After living three years in the South Seas, released his film *Moana*, 1926. Lived in U.K. between 1931 and 1939. Received the "Best Film" Award at the 1934 Venice Film Festival. Returned to the U.S. in 1939, until his death. In 1948, his film *Louisiana Story* received a British Film Academy award. Honorary Ph. D. awarded by the University of Michigan, 1950. Died of a thrombosis on July 23, 1951, at his home, in Dummerston, Vermont.

Further Reading

Christopher, Robert J. "Through Canada's Northland: The Arctic Photography of Robert J. Flaherty." In King, J. C.H., and Henrietta Lidchi, eds. *Imaging the Arctic*. Seattle and Vancouver: University of Washington Press and UBC Press, 1998, 181–189.

Flaherty, Robert J. "How I Filmed 'Nanook of the North'." *World's Work* October 1922: 632–640.

Hubbard Flaherty, Frances. *The Odyssey of a Film-Maker: Robert Flaherty's Story*. Urbana, Illinois: Beta Phi Mu, 1960.

Hubbard Flaherty, Frances. *Picturing Paradise: Colonial Photography of Samoa, 1875 to 1925*. Daytona Beach, FL: Southeast Museum of Photography, with the Daytona Beach Community College, 1995.

Murphy, William T. *Robert J. Flaherty: A Guide to References and Resources*. Boston: G.K. Hall & Co, 1978.

Rotha, Paul. *Robert J. Flaherty: A Biography*. Jay Ruby, ed. Philadelphia: University of Pennsylvania Press, 1983.

The Robert Flaherty Papers, housed at the Butler Library of Columbia University, New York.

VILÉM FLUSSER

Czech

Vilém Flusser, an important philosopher in the arena of the new communications media and their cultural function, was a representative of a Czech intellectual tradition that included writers like Franz Kafka and Franz Werfel and philosophers like Edmund Husserl. Flusser was also influenced by the language philosophy of Ludwig Wittgenstein and by many aspects of Walter Benjamin's writings on art, technology, and history. While he wrote on a number of topics related by the theme of globalization, including technology, emigration, and nationalism, his ideas about the nature of photography and the photograph have made him an important influence on image theory in the 1980s to the present day. In contrast to the analytical modernist thinking, focused on the depth of the signified and represented by theorists like Karl Marx or Sigmund Freud, Flusser directed his main interest to the "surfaces" of the signifier and their equivalence. He emphasized the creative possibilities of communication, and especially of artificially created worlds.

Flusser was born in 1920 in Prague into a German Jewish family. He began studying philosophy at Charles University in Prague in 1939 but fled Nazi occupation to England in 1939. He continued on to Brazil in 1941. There, Flusser enrolled at the University of Sao Paolo. He managed an electronic transformer factory while establishing himself as a philosopher. In 1963, he was appointed a Professor of the philosophy of communication at the University of Sao Paolo. In 1976, he settled in France and taught in Aix-en-Provence and Arles, while giving lectures and serving as a visiting professor at various European and American universities. He died in 1991 in a car crash near the Czech-German border after delivering his first public lecture in Prague.

Flusser tried to conceptualize the semiotic, communicational, and aesthetic implications of the photographic medium by focusing on its technical specificity. Nevertheless, a photograph is not for him "a message without a code," as Roland Barthes put it, nor a transparent image of an objective reality. Rather, it is defined as a way of transcoding, that is, re-writing, the scientific formulas which made possible technological progress and, therefore, photography itself.

According to Flusser, the transition from the prehistorical to the historical period was parallel to the substitution of magical thinking, dominated by images, by rational or linear thinking. Flusser believed that in the late twentieth century humans entered a transitional period between historical and post-historical thinking. Linear thinking—based on writing and essential to history—is about to be put aside by a new form of thinking that is much more complex: thinking which is multi-dimensional and visual, based on algorithms, and inspired by system and chaos theory.

In that sense, traditional images are pre-historical and technological images post-historical; the former signify visual phenomena, the latter the scientific concepts which made them possible. Photography, by transforming linear equations to images, re-injects magical thinking into modern societies, introducing the postmodern era. Flusser's questioning of contemporary culture joins in that point the necessity, expressed by Walter Benjamin, of a dialectical form capable of linking together the modernist rationalization of the culture and the simultaneous revival of magical or mythical models of behavior.

Flusser was intensely interested in the potential of virtual reality to enable human beings to create and manipulate their environments. In the cultural logic of post-modern societies, the technological potential available to humans brings about a rupture with the humanist traditions of the past and the forms of subjectivity associated with them. The autonomous subject has been decentred and transformed into a product of his own creation, a fairly consistent theme in postmodern thinking.

Flusser postulated that the invention of photography was the starting point of a technological and cultural process in which the mechanical structures introduced by industrial revolution give place to cybernetic ones, based on algorithms. In this context, the increasing dominance of electronic means of communication is the most distinctive feature of post-industrial societies. Photography is thus regarded as the last step before the complete dematerialization of the image and its transformation to pure information. What is important in a photograph is not the object itself but the information of which it is the vehicle. In Flusser's perspective, there could be no such a thing as an "original photography."

The extreme mobility and general equivalence of information make photographic images volatile, nomadic, and uncertain, easy to manipulate: their final meaning depends much more on their context than on the images themselves. For Flusser, visual images, unlike verbal information, are multidimensional symbolic structures open to interpretation. Through a feed-back effect, photographic reproductions of reality influence and transform reality itself, attempting to conform it to pre-programmed and standardized stereotypes. In that way, photography tends to generalize its own range of technical possibilities to the large scale of social exchange. As Flusser observes, the operating model of photographic vision is not one of causal but of functional thinking. The difference is that in the latter, the result is programmed in advance and not analytically deduced. In that way, Flusser considers the social implications of photography as an integral part of its meaning.

Electronic media of communication and their imagery absorb and recycle their objects, dissolving the historical dimension of reality in a series of redundant reproductions. As artist Alfredo Jaar puts it: "Images have an advanced religion. They bury history." For Flusser, no meaningful distinction can be drawn between reality and representation, for they differ only in degree of probability, not in essence.

Like the French philosopher Jean Baudrillard, Flusser addressed media images as representations of a radically new kind, calling not for the traditional aesthetics of production but for a historically relevant aesthetics of reception. Such aesthetics should be capable to understand the postmodern inversion of the supposedly stable relation between subject and object of representation, as well as its historical and cultural implications and perversions. Thus, photography, rather than being just a new entry in the lexicon of visual history, calls for the revision and re-consideration of traditional aesthetic categories.

During the course of his life, Flusser published numerous essays on a wide range of topics and many books, writing in German and Portuguese. Among them, *Für eine Philosophie der Fotografie* ("Towards a philosophy of photography"), 1983, explores the implications for human society of the transition from writing culture to image-culture. *Die Schrift* ("Writing"), 1989, asks what is lost if the alphanumeric code of writing is superseded. In 1992, Flusser's "philosophical autobiography" was published under the title *Bodenlos* ("Bottomless"). *Nachgeschichte* ("Post-History"), 1993, considers the different implications of "the end of history" in the post-industrial world.

VANGELIS ATHANASSOPOULOS

See also: **Barthes, Roland; Image Theory: Ideology; Photographic "Truth"; Postmodernism; Representation; Semiotics**

Biography

Born in Prague, Czechoslovakia, 1920. Studied philosophy at Charles University, Prague, 1939. Fled Czechoslovakia to England, 1939–1940; immigrated to Sao Paulo, Brazil, 1941. Completed education at University of Sao Paolo. Member of the Brazilian Institute of Philosophy, 1962; appointed Professor of Philosophy of Communications, at FAAP (School of Communications and Humanities) University of Sao Paolo, 1963; co-editor of the *Brazilian Philosophical Review*, 1964. Special delegate of the Brazilian Ministry for Foreign Affairs for cultural cooperation with the United States and Europe, 1966. Relocated to Italy, 1972; France in 1976. Professor of Philosophy, University of Aix-en-Provence; visiting professor at various European and American Universities. Died in Prague, Czechoslovakia, 1991.

Selected Works

Von der Freiheit des Migranten: Einsprüche gegen den Nationalismus, 1994, *The freedom of the migrant: objections to nationalism*, translated by Kenneth Kronenberg, 2003
Schriften, 1993, *Writings: Selections*, edited by Andreas Ströhl, translated by Erik Eisel, 2002
Für eine Philosophie der Fotografie, 1983, *Towards a philosophy of photography*, translated by Anthony Mathews, 2000
Die Schrift: hat Schreiben Zukunft?, 1989
Gesten: Versuch einer Phänomenologie, 1991
Ende der Geschichte, Ende der Stadt?, 1992
Bodenlos : eine philosophische Autobiographie, 1992
Vom Stand der Dinge : eine kleine Philosophie des Design, 1993, *The shape of things: a philosophy of design*, 1999
Nachgeschichte: eine korrigierte Geschichtsschreibung, 1993
Kommunikologie, 1996
Medienkultur, 1997

Further Reading

Sander, Klaus, ed. *Vilém Flusser, Zwiegespräche: Interviews 1967–1991.* Göttingen: European Photography, 1996.

FORMALISM

Formalism in the visual arts is a philosophy of aesthetics first formulated in its modern form in the early part of the twentieth century by such British Bloomsbury Group writers as Clive Bell and Roger Fry. Bell's and Fry's theories had arisen from the consideration of painting, but the basic notions of formalism could be applied to other two-dimensional forms, and were soon being used to examine and understand photography.

The basis for the theories of Bell and Fry was simply that representation was irrelevant to paintings' value as an art form, that is, what the work depicted was not what made a work of art great. Applying his ideas to the whole of art history in his

1914 work, *Art*, Bell considers very few artists actually great. For Clive Bell the essential quality of any artwork was its ability to provoke an aesthetic emotion. Aesthetic emotion is obtainable only through the presence of what Bell termed "significant form."

Bell does not deny that art can contain representational forms and still be considered art, but he asserts that artistic value can only be measured through significant form, which although it can be pointed out by a critic, an object is not art until it has independently provoked this response from the viewer. By Bell's own admission all art experiences are thus entirely subjective. While representational imagery can be amusing or intellectually challenging, it is often not aesthetic. Its nature is often more documentary. Bell compares the history of art to the history of religion and finds a common motive for both. The aesthetic and the divine are both roads for people to exchange mundane reality for ecstasy. Aesthetic and religious rapture are very similar as described by Bell, and at their best both are completely independent of historic facts or contrived dogmas.

A contemporary of Bell, Roger Fry published his major writing on art in 1920, called *Vision and Design*. While Bell was dismissive of the relatively new tendency in painting, Impressionism, Fry cites the movement as the beginning of a new revolution in art. Impressionist artists removed art from the arena of strict representation and placed it firmly in the realm of structural design and harmony. More technical than Bell, Fry identified five emotional elements of design in all forms of art: rhythm or gesture, mass, space, light and shade, and color.

According to Fry, art stimulates emotion by using the emotional elements of design, and combined with sympathy within the viewer for the artist, and the purpose of the thing, thereby creates a feeling of unity and harmony in the viewer. These are what indicate a successful work of art. Following from Kant, Fry believed distinguishing art from natural beauty is the consciousness and the intent of the artist.

The contemporary painter-theorist in Poland, Stanislaw Ignacy Witkiewicz, deserves mention for his 1919 work *Nowe Formy w Malarstwie (New Forms in Painting)*. His Formalist theory was very similar to Bell's argument. He identified that the essence of art lies in its form and that a successful artist strove to create a multi-structured unity of forms. He acknowledged that all art comes from an understanding of life, and because of this art may or even must contain referents to the real world, but that the evaluation of any work of art must be dependant on aesthetic qualities not related to the real world referents on which that work may be based.

In 1904, American photographer Sadakichi Hartman wrote essays strongly objecting to painterliness in photography, a basic tenet of the overriding photographic style of the day, Pictorialism. He referred to over-manipulated negatives and allegorical sentimentality and the inferiority of these to pure photography relying on nothing more than an artistic eye and technical skill. The straight photography movements in the early part of the century included such American artists as Alfred Stieglitz, Paul Strand, and Edward Weston. In Russia the Constructivist photographers had many of the same aims as the straight photographers did, and was epitomized by the work of Alexander Rodchenko. These movements addressed the tension between the concepts of objectivity and subjectivity. The important matter for these artists was not the object being captured, but rather the mind that directs the capturing. Photography of the 1920s and 1930s made such a visual impact that its effects were seen in the works of painters around the world. Despite this, aesthetic theorists of the era, like Bell and Fry, largely ignored photography in favor of painting, sculpture, and architecture.

Perhaps art history's best-known straight photographer was Alfred Stieglitz, who was very interested in Formalist composition. For Stieglitz, form was the main concern of the photographer, whatever narrative or moral or allegorical interpretations might come from the final image was irrelevant to the production of the image. Perhaps Stieglitz's most famous photo, *The Steerage* (1907), is potentially a cold, documentary criticism of class divisions in a democratic society, but for the artist and for the Formalist it is a composition in form consisting of round and triangular shapes, diagonals, and light areas juxtaposed with dark masses. In order to reach his lofty formalistic goals without provoking confusion about potentially meaningful subject matter, Stieglitz and others in his group began photographing ordinary objects. The epitome of his efforts was the production of a series called the *Equivalents* and his *Dreaming Trees* series. The *Equivalents* began in 1923 with cropped studies of clouds. They were documentary, but also evocative and beautiful. These works have a connection to Bell's theories as they use significant form without narrative or even pictorial context to invoke an aesthetic emotion. He moved the documentary out of mundane life and into the realm of high art. The images are still works of straight photography, but as documents, they have no function.

Stieglitz had a direct effect on Edward Weston's work. Straight, simple, pure form was his hallmark. Weston's studies of a toilet, including *Excusado* (1925), are completely devoid of irony or cultural criticism and stand as a document of pure form divorced from reference to Duchamp's *Fountain* of 1917, an actual urinal displayed as a "ready-made" sculpture. The primary distinction between Formalist and documentary photography lies with Formalism's core reliance on the technical skill of the photographer, whereas documentary photography is interested in the subjective meanings of the people and things being depicted. Imogen Cunningham's 1923 nude study *Triangles* also exemplifies the Formalist approach, in which the highly loaded subject of female flesh is reduced to a series of volumes and shapes, sensual in its gradations of light and tone rather than in its representation of the nude female body.

Bell's and Fry's theory of Formalism contained logical flaws. Bell's terms, aesthetic emotion and significant form, are inseparably linked and he can offer no definition of one without implying the definition of the other. This, of course, leads to circular reasoning. Also, he can provide no adequate criterion for differentiation on what emotions are aesthetic and which are not. Another flaw in Bell's approach is his inability to completely dismiss the historic importance of subject matter as it is opposed to form. Bell's logic defines criteria for what an artwork is by first finding a common denominator for all art. Not all art is Expressive; many artists have strived to remove any emotive content from their works. Not all art is representational. But it seems all art has form, therefore a thing is not art unless it has form. Some would argue, however, that everything has form, so Bell qualifies himself, and says art is that which has significant form. This, critics maintain, does little to differentiate fine art from a mathematic theorem. In response, the formalist cites a theory of function. A mathematical theorem does not have the primary function of displaying its significant form. It may be more eloquent with form, but it is still a valid and accepted theorem without form. Art, to be art, must have the primary function of displaying its form. Yet this argument is also flawed because it ignores the very real possibility that art may have no primary function unique to itself. This point of criticism, with the mathematical comparison, is eloquently explained in *The Routledge Companion to Aesthetics* (2001).

An essential modern theorist whose Formalism radically changed painting after World War II was the American Clement Greenberg. Greenberg differs most radically from Fry and Bell in the Marxist bent of his writings. This is seen in his idea of dialectical conversion, which is a phenomenon that occurs when one pushes a concept to its extreme and finds oneself proceeding in the opposite direction. An example is the painting movement Cubism of the early years of the twentieth century. Cubism's pursuit of naturalism by depicting objects and figures in the world from multiple viewpoints and planes, ends in utterly flat abstraction. In this way, Greenberg, like Bell, considers abstract, non-representational art as continuous with representational forms; indeed they are a natural evolution of art towards unity.

Greenberg reduces art to formal elements but is much more extreme than his predecessors. An artist must exploit the characteristic methods of his media to embed the art in its area of expertise. Painting must therefore exhibit only the characteristics of paintings, not sculptures or photographs, and so on. In the 1950s and 1960s he championed pure painting as he contrasted it with the painterliness of Abstract Expressionism. He applauded the openness of artists such as Clifford Still, Barnett Newman, and Mark Rothko.

In Greenberg's thought art was in danger of becoming kitsch, entertainment. To avoid this art must purge itself of uncharacteristic elements and become literal and purely self-referent, but most of all, abstract. Essential to his abstraction is the complete absence of any illusionist space. Greenberg believed, as did Fry, in art-for-art's sake. Art was outside reality and morality; it stood as a refuge from the chaos of ordinary life.

Formalism as it developed in the latter half of the twentieth century is relatively easy to understand but difficult to apply with any consistency. Many critics acknowledge that there are two basic camps of Formalist thought. Hard or Extreme Formalism, which is absolute in its assertion that art is only that which evokes aesthetic emotion through significant form, meaning that all aesthetic properties are formal properties; and Soft or Moderate Formalism, which allows that the historic nature of subject matter may be considered in the value of some works. This mode of Formalism allows that many aesthetic properties of art are formal, while many are not formal.

Moderate Formalism addresses the critique of the theory that points out that much of what is currently and openly accepted as art does not have the primary function of displaying significant form. Some art, like Dadaist ready-mades, have no created aesthetic form at all. Such pieces are made to provoke intellectual consideration. For a Hard

Formalist a ready-made sculpture or even a public monument cannot be art, but a Moderate Formalist can still accept these items as art, conditionally. The condition allows that even though one may require considerable knowledge of history or of the formal properties of previous works to properly judge the aesthetic merits of a particular piece, it stipulates that the judgment or emotion provoked once arrived upon, given previous experience, is itself independent of that history or those previous works. The artist's intention in creating the work is not relevant to its value, neither are issues of originality. DuChamp's *Fountain* (1917) may be *best* understood in the context of its history and intent, but it does not necessarily follow that it can *only* be so understood. It can be formalistically appreciated outside of context, on its own merits.

Formalism as an aesthetic concept in photography has been linked to and at times confused with the medium's inherent strengths as a medium of document. Photography's immediate referent to reality and—representationalism has made it difficult for some artists and critics to define photographic images in purely aesthetic, Formalist terms. However, from the very beginning of the twentieth century, photographers have fought against the notion of narrative in their works and have pushed for an interpretation of Formal or straight photography.

One of the most powerful recent voices in Formalist photographic criticism was John Szarkowski who served as Director of the Department of Photography at the Museum of Modern Art from 1962 to 1991. Szarkowski championed straight photography and agreed in large part with the judgments of Clement Greenberg. He promoted that the meaning of a photo lies in the medium itself, that is: form follows function. In the 1960s, exhibitions at the Museum of Modern Art under Szarkowski promoted highly formalistic readings of artists such as Stieglitz. Szarkowski sought to remove any metaphoric interpretations from contemporary photography. He identified five formal properties of photography: the thing itself, the detail, the frame, the time, and the vantage point.

Postmodern theory stands in opposition to modern Formalist arguments. The postmodern stance often holds that photography has no inherent context and therefore no inherent historic unity. A photographic image, for these critics, has no meaning unto itself as an aesthetic object. A photo is inseparably tied to its use or function as an object in a context outside of itself.

From a radical and new way of appreciating and evaluating what art should be, to an interesting but not as widely believed tenet of historical aesthetics, Formalism has developed throughout the twentieth century, and in its course has had a profound effect on all arts, particularly the visual and musical. Bell's Formalism contained a Romantic ideal of the artist-savior, who could move an individual to catharsis by the use of significant form in painting. Roger Fry was more pragmatic than Bell and preferred that form be an indication of aesthetic beauty and not necessarily moral obligation. In the latter part of the century theorists like Greenberg strove to remove subjectivism from the visual arts. His calling for a purely abstract and flat art that contained referents only to itself was an extension of Fry's theory with a markedly political bent. John Szarkowski, during his years at the Museum of Modern Art shaped the way contemporary photography was evaluated and interpreted showing that despite the obvious connection photography had to the real world, it too could be a Formalist medium. At the heart of any of these writers' works is the notion that a work of art need not be evaluated against the subjective, social-political structure in which it was created. For the Formalist, an artwork is the fullest expression of the characteristics of its medium so produced to create an aesthetic response that is unique to that one work and utterly devoid of meaning in a real world sense.

Erin Schwartz

See also: **Cunningham, Imogen; Image Theory: Ideology; Stieglitz, Alfred; Strand, Paul; Weston, Edward; Witkiewicz, Stanislaw Ignacy**

Further Reading

Batchen, Geoffry. *Burning with Desire: The Conception of Photography*. Cambridge, MA: MIT Press, 1997.
Bell, Clive. *Art*. London: Chanto and Windus, 1914.
Curtin, Deane W. "Varieties of Aesthetic Formalism." *Journal of Aesthetics and Art Criticism*, 40 (1982).
Daval, Jean-Luc. *Photography: History of an Art*. New York: Rizzoli, 1982.
Dziemidok, Bohdan. "Artistic Formalism: Its Achievements and Weaknesses." *Journal of Aesthetics and Art Criticism*, 51, no. 2 (1993).
Eisinger, Joel. *Trace and Transformation: American Criticism of Photography in the Modernist Period*. Albuquerque, NM: University of New Mexico Press, 1995. Friday, Jonathan. *Aesthetics and Photography*. Burlington, VT: Ashgate, 2002.
Fry, Roger. *Vision and Design*. New York: Meridian, 1956.
Gaut, Berys and Dominic McIver Lopes, eds. *The Routledge Companion to Aesthetics*. London and New York: Routledge, 2001.
Greenberg, Clement. "Toward a Newer Laocoön." *Partisan Review*, VII, no. 4 (1940).
Greenberg, Clement. *Art and Culture*. Boston: Beacon, 1961.

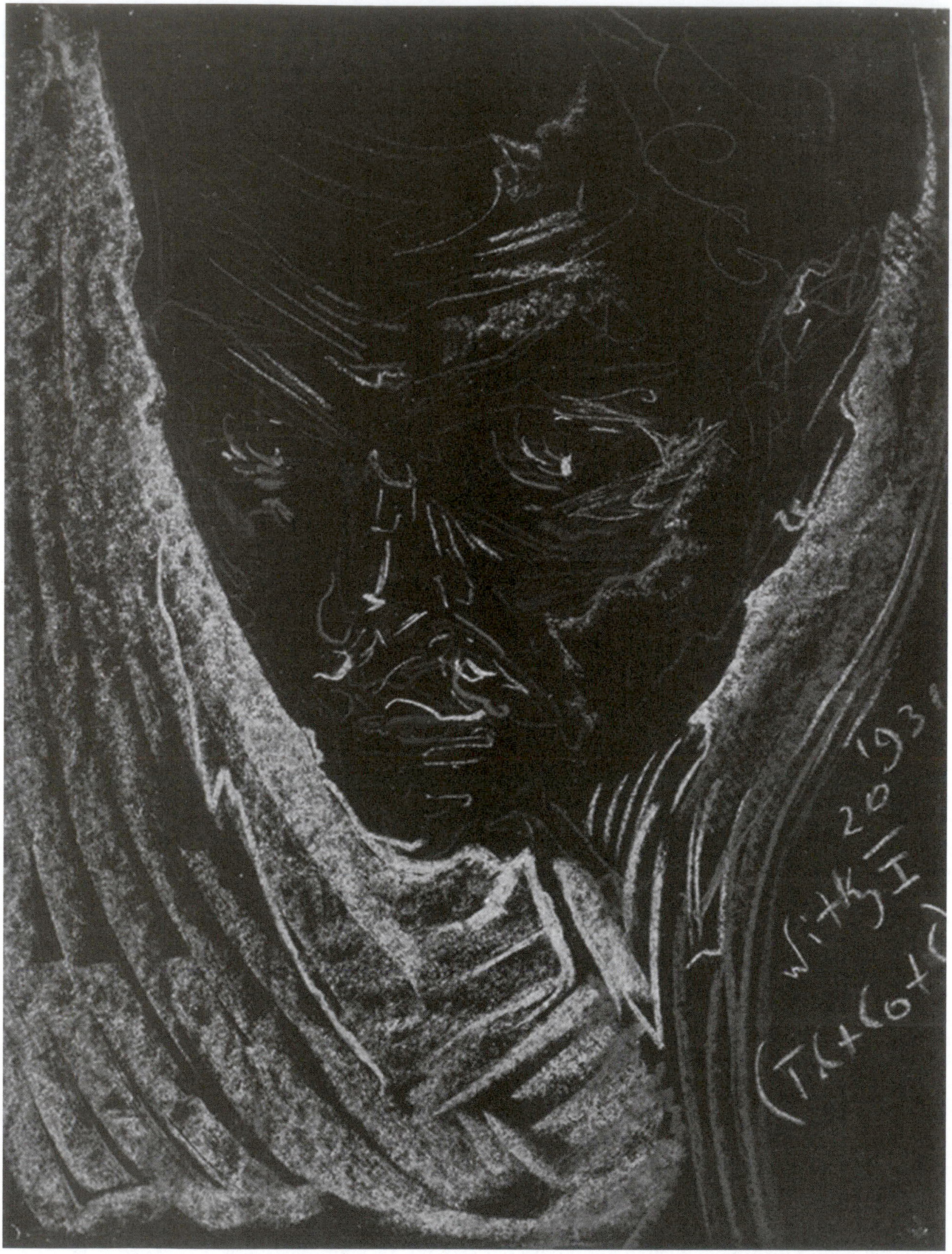

Witkiewicz, Stanislaw, Portrait Type C, attributed title "Portrait of Czeslaw Blachninski," 1931, Photo: Christian Bahier and Philippe Migeat.
[*CNAC/MNAM/Dist. Réunion des Musées Nationaux/Art Resource, New York*]

Hartman, Sadakichi. *American Amateur Photographer*. 16 (1904).
Lemagny, Jean-Claude, and André Rouillé, eds. *A History of Photography*. Translated by Janet Lloyd. New York: Cambridge University Press, 1986.
Manns, James W. *Aesthetics*. Armonk, NY, and London: M.E. Sharpe, 1998. Szarkowski, John. *The Photographers' Eye*. New York: Museum of Modern Art, 1966.
Witkiewicz, S.I. *Nowe Formy w Malarstwie. Szkice Estetyczne. Teatr*. Warsaw: PWN, 1974.
Zangwill, Nick. "Defusing Anti-Formalist Arguments." *British Journal of Aesthetics*, 40, no. 3 (2000).
Zangwill, Nick. "In Defense of Moderate Formalism." *The Philosophical Quarterly*, 50, no. 201 (2000).

SAMUEL FOSSO

Nigerian/Cameroonian

The photographs of Samuel Fosso have often been exhibited with the work of his West African compatriots Malick Sidibé and Seydou Keïta, but Fosso's work is unparalleled in Africa. Although Fosso worked as a commercial studio photographer like Sidibé and Keïta, it is not his portraits of locals but his intriguing self-portraits that have excited great interest in Africa, Europe, and the United States. His self-portraits have incited frequent comparisons to the American photographer Cindy Sherman in their presentation of different identities through clothing and props that remain ambiguous in their intentionality. Although this comparison may be superficially apt, it must be noted that Fosso created his portraits in the 1970s in relative isolation, inspired by highlife music and American singer James Brown, and without knowing that his portraits would eventually be exhibited. Fosso's self-portraits must also be contextualized within Central African Republic's (CAR) history and politics. The ambiguous roles that Fosso's identities perform against the backdrop of political unrest in CAR accomplish a socio-political critique of conventional society's restrictions, while subtly pointing to the grotesque self-reinventions of CAR's dictator, "Emperor" Jean-Bedel Bokassa.

Born in Cameroon to a Nigerian mother and Cameroonian father, Samuel Fosso belongs to the Ibo tribe. According to his own story, he was paralyzed until age three, but was cured when a healer rolled him off of the roof of a house. Fosso's grandfather, who was also a healer and village chief, had arranged for this curing of his grandson. Fosso's recent color photographic series *le rêve de mon grand-père* (2003) refers to this event, showing Fosso painted as a healer and dressed as a chief. According to Fosso, "It's a staging of the way of life I experienced as a child, a way of life that has since often haunted my dreams....I did it to pay homage to my grandfather and to honour him" (Bonetti and Schlinkert 2004, 25). Fosso's mother died by the time he was five, near the time the Biafran civil war broke out in Nigeria, endangering the lives of many Ibos. Fosso's village fled to the forest to escape the fighting and survived there for several years. At age ten, Fosso went to live with his uncle in Bangui, the capital of the Central African Republic.

Two commercial photographers worked in Bangui when Fosso arrived, one from Cameroon and one from Nigeria. Disliking the long, hard hours of work in his uncle's shoe factory, Fosso asked his uncle if he could apprentice with the Nigerian photographer, and by the age of 13 he opened his own studio, which went through a series of name changes: Studio Photo Gentil, Studio Hoberau, Studio Convenance, and Studio Photo Nationale. Fosso's black-and-white studio practice followed the conventions of many West African commercial photographers. He was in the business of making people appear as their best and ideal selves; in effect, making people look as beautiful as possible. The slogan in his shop read, "With Studio Photo Nationale you will be beautiful, chic, elegant and easy to recognize" (Bonetti and Schlinkert 2004, 97).

Fosso began making self-portraits after shop hours, originally to send to his grandmother in Nigeria to show he was doing well in his new life; but the impetus to take his own picture became a pleasure in itself. Fosso says: "It was fun...It was beautiful. I was liberated from the past, from the suffering" (Bonetti and Schlinkert 2004, 33). A teenager impressed by 1970s youth culture imported from the West, Fosso had a local tailor sew fashionable bell-bottoms and tight shirts from pictures on record covers like the ones by African rock star Prince Nico Mbarga. As Manthia Diawara has noted, such clothing was a sign of youthful rebellion against traditional society, a way of both dissolving ethnic friction and avoiding the strictures of elders. Fosso's black-and-white self-portraits androgynously celebrate the young man's handsome and sexy persona; he mimics rock stars and 1970s dandies. He kept these photographs to himself; public dissemination of certain photographs which border on the erotic, with Fosso posing gracefully in white underwear or wearing nothing but a tight, striped swimsuit and rubber kitchen gloves, could have gotten him into trouble.

Formally, many of Fosso's early black-and-white self-portraits consistently include a checkerboard or diamond-patterned floor, a low, patterned stage running the length of the studio horizon line, and a backdrop, sometimes with patterned cloth curtains. Often the backs of studio lights appear at the sides of the photograph, glamorously framing the subject. Some photographs include Fosso with a friend dressed the same as he. In an appropriation of advertising or record cover aesthetics, Fosso also added text in the form of adhesive letters to some of his photographs, using proverbs that he copied from books such as "Life is liberty."

Fosso began to gain international fame after his self-portraits were exhibited in the first photography biennale in Bamako in 1994, *Rencontres de la Photographie Africaine*. Two years later his works were included in the landmark African photography exhibition *In/sight: African Photographers, 1940 to the Present* at the Guggenheim Museum in New York. After Fosso entered the international art world, his style changed. Fosso was commissioned to shoot a series for the Parisian department store Magasins Tati, associated with Africa because it traditionally served the immigrant Algerian community. For this work, Fosso had access to different props and costumes, and worked with the help of assistants. The color photographs from this series continue Fosso's investigation into different identities, including a lifeguard, an African chief, a "liberated American woman," and a golf player. The roles Fosso plays are more clearly designated than in his earlier self-portraits, although ambiguity remains in the strangeness of the identities Fosso chose. In a more serious vein, the recent black-and-white series, *Mémoire d'un ami* (2000), refers to the murder of a good friend by the police just outside of Fosso's studio. Metaphorical memorials, these self-portraits depict uneasiness, anxiety, and vulnerability.

Allison Moore

See also: **Keïta, Seydou; Photography in Africa: An Overview; Photography in Africa: Central and West; Portraiture**

Biography

Born in Kumba, Cameroon, 1962. Apprenticed to studio photographer in Bangui, Central African Republic in 1975. Opened own studio in September, 1975. Received "Afrique en creation" Award in 1995; "DAK'ART" first prize for photography in 2000; Prince Claus Award of the Prince Claus Fund for Culture and Development, The Hague in 2001. Lives in Bangui, Central African Republic. Married with children, Fosso continues to live in Bangui while exhibiting internationally.

Individual Exhibitions

1995 Centre national de la photographie, Paris
1996 Galerie du Théâtre,Gap, Hautes Alpes, France
1997 *Samuel Fosso. Photographs*, greengrassi, London
1999 Galerie Maï Ollivier, Paris, France
2003 *Samuel Fosso Autorretratos*, "PhotoEspaña 2003. Nos Otros," Madrid, Spain
2003 Jack Shainman Gallery, New York
2004 *Sameul Fosso*, Centro Internazionale di Fotografia Scavi Scaligeri, Verona, Rome

Group Exhibitions

1994 *Autoportaits*, "Premières Rencontres de la Photographie Africaine," Bamako, Mali
1995 *Photographes Africains*, FNAC, Forum des Halles, Paris
1995 *Festival Africa 95*, Photographers' Gallery, London
1996 *In/sight: African Photographers, 1940 to the Present*, Solomon R. Guggenheim Museum, New York, New York
1997 *Studio Photo. 50 ans des Magasins Tati*, Paris
1998 *L'Afrique par elle-même*, Maison Européenne de la Photographie, Paris
1999 *Africa by Africa: a Photographic View*, Barbican Art Gallery, London
2000 "DAK'ART, Exposition Internationale d'Art Contemporain Africain," Dakar, Senegal
Portrait Afrika: Photographische Positionen eines Jahrhunderts, Haus der Kulturen der Welt, Berlin

2000–2001 *Africa Inside*, "Noorderlicht Photo Festival," Fries Museum, Leeuwarden, The Netherlands
2001 "Troisièmes rencontres de la Photographie Africaine," Bamako, Mali
2001–2002 *The Short Century: Independence and Liberation Movements in Africa 1945–1994*, Villa Stuck, Munich/Haus der Kulturen der Welt im Martin-Gropius-Bau, Berlin, Museum of Contemporary Art, Chicago, P.S. 1 Contemporary Art Center and The Museum of Modern Art, Long Island City, New York
2002–2003 *Samuel Fosso. Seydou Keita. Malick Sidibe. Portraits of Pride*, "Xpo September-Stockholm Fotofestival," Moderna Museet c/o Enkehuset, Stockholm, Bildens Hus, Sundsvall, Norskt Fotomuseum, Oslo, Norway
2003 *Make life Beautiful! The Dandy in Photography*, Brighton Museum & Art Gallery, Brighton
2003 *Geometry of the Face*, Det Nationale Fotomuseum-Det Kongelige Bibliotek, Copenhagen, Denmark
2004 *Africa Remix, Zeitgenossiche Kunst eines Kontinents*, Museum Kunst Palast, Dusseldorf, Germany Hayward

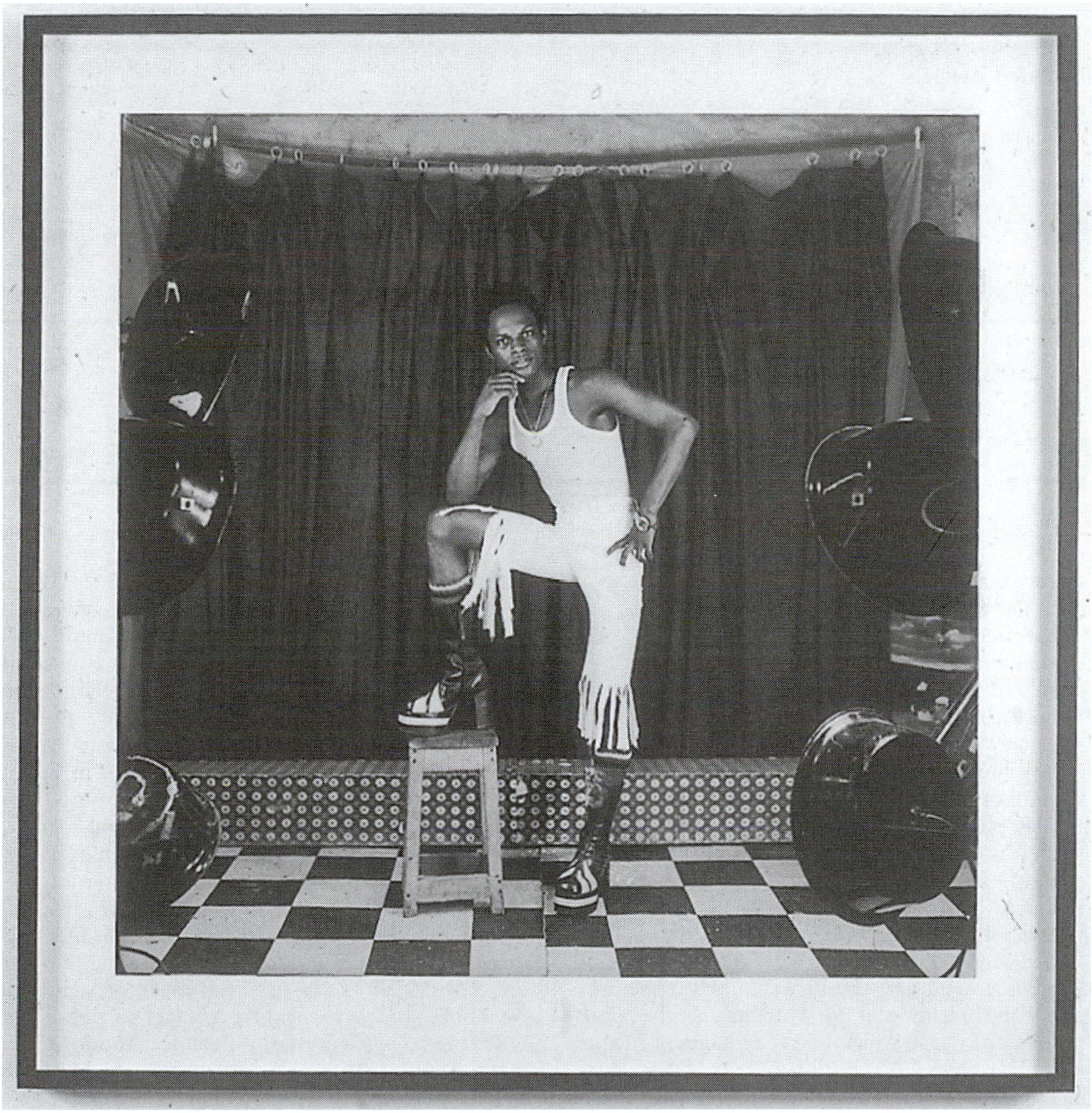

Samuel Fosso, Self Portrait (Prince Nico), 1977, gelatin silver print.
[*Courtesy of Jack Shainman Gallery, New York*]

Gallery, London, Georges Pompidou Centre, Paris, Mori Art Museum, Tokyo

Selected Works

Untitled self-portraits, 1975–1977
La vie c'est la liberté, Self Portrait (Life is liberty), 1977
La femme liberée américaine dans les années 70s (The liberated American woman in the 1970s), 1997
The Lifeguard, 1997
Le Chef (The Chief), 1997
Mémoire d'un ami (Memory of a Friend), 2000
Le rêve de mon Grand Père (My Grandfather's Dream), 2003

Further Reading

Bell, Clare, Okwui Enwezor, Danielle Tilkin, Octavio Zaya and Olu Oguibe. *In/sight: African Photographers, 1940 to the Present*. New York: Guggenheim Museum,1996.
Bonetti, Maria Francesca, and Guido Schlinkert. *Samuel Fosso*. Milan: 5 Continents Editions srl, 2004.
Cotter, Holland. "When the I Is the Subject, and It's Always Changing." *The New York Times*. (September 12, 2003).
Deitcher, David. "Samuel Fosso." *Time Out New York*. (October 2–9, 2003).
Fall, N'goné and Pascal Martin Saint Léon, eds. *Anthology of African and Indian Ocean Photography*. Paris, France: Éditions Revue Noire, 1998: 166–7.
Kelsey, John. "Samuel Fosso." *Artforum* v. 42, no. 4 (December 2003):147.
Noorderlicht Photo Festival. *Africa Inside*. Groningen, The Netherlands: Aurora Borealis, 2000.
Vine, Richard. "Report from Madrid: Our Photos, Our Selves." *Art in America* v. 92, no. 1 (January 2004): 30–1, 33, 35.
Xpo September. *Samuel Fosso. Seydou Keita. Malick Sidibe. Portraits of Pride*. Stockholm Fotofestival in collaboration with Rencontres de la photographie africaine, 2002.

PHOTOGRAPHY IN FRANCE

France was a major locus of photographic activity until the mid-twentieth century. For the better part of the second half of the century, it was, however, characterized by a relative lag in institutional presence, which kept photography in its status as a minor art. The situation changed in the years 1980–2000 with a popular, scholarly, and artistic establishment of the medium. Yet, significantly, at the end of the century there no scholarly history of French photography available (Nori 1988 is an illustrated popular outline), and the only two French general histories of photography (Rouillé & Lemagny and Frizot) were written essentially from the perspective of American photography.

If French Pictorialism was indistinguishable from others, the early century should be remembered for the invention of the Autochrome, the photographs of Eugène Atget, and the images of Jacques Henri Lartigue.

The Autochrome, appearing in 1907, was the result of a long train of research to produce direct color images. As the first stable commercial color emulsion, it was adopted by artists (such as Alfred Stieglitz) and reporters (such as the operators commissioned by financier Albert Khan). Although it remained mostly confined to France, it raised "crucial questions about the relationship between photography and painting." But it excluded at the same time "the possibility of manipulation of the final image" (Frizot in Frizot 423), thus pushing the medium further away from pictorialism and into a more autonomous form.

Eugène Atget (1857–1927) can be seen as a link between the nineteenth and twentieth centuries (Nesbit in Frizot 399). Beyond the documentary value of his pictures of Paris, he illustrates the "discovery" that later spectators, and especially other photographers and artists, can make of images, a symbol of the permanent recycling of photography. "Invented," as it were, by Berenice Abbott in the late twenties, Atget was also reinvented by much more contemporary photographers and critics as a "precursor of modernism" and a "mystery" in the history of photography.

Jacques Henri Lartigue (1894–1986), as scion of the upper class, started taking pictures in 1902 and did so throughout his life. Experimenting more or less consciously with forms, formats, and subjects, he kept a visual diary of a changing world at the same time as he explored the language of the medium. Celebrated towards the end of his life, he was one of the first French photographers to be canonized by the museums in the 1970s. His images should be placed alongside the growing reservoir of personnel documents on artists (see Elvire Perigo, "Intimate moments and secret gardens," in Frizot) and their vision (Loti, Zola, Bonnard, etc.), and of family albums which have helped reassess the history of the medium since the 1980s.

Paris was undoubtedly one of the high places of avant-garde or modernist photography in the interwar years. A great many of the most interesting modernist experimental photographers, many of them central Europeans, met and worked there for a few years. Not always connecting formally with pictorial avant-gardes yet keeping a close contact with the "document" through their commercial activity, photographers such as Hungarian André Kertész, American expatriate Man Ray, Jacques-André Boiffart, Maurice Tabard, or Emmanuel Sougez expanded the field of photographic vision, questioning the power of the eye to invent the world. Women were numerous and particularly creative in both form and content of images (Germaine Krull, Florence Henri and the modern city, the strange and innovative Claude Cahun).

The other avant-garde was Surrealism. Although the work of another Hungarian immigrant, Brassaï, can be connected to that influence, it is certainly best characterized by Man Ray, Dora Maar, Raoul Ubac, and Hans Bellmer. Maurice Tabard (1897–1984), who remained active for the better part of the century from the 1930s to the 1960s, is an interesting case in point, combining surrealist images with more formal work such as photograms *à la* Man Ray.

The interwar years also experienced the expansion of ethnographic photography, in keeping with a nineteenth-century tradition. The Mission Dakar-Djibouti (1931–1933), collecting artifacts and images for the Musée du Trocadéro, was a particularly remarkable instance which perfected Marcel Griaude's investigative method based on a system of reconstitution ("staging"). Photography does not seem, however, to have caught with French ethnographers, in any case less than with their American colleagues, at least until the 1960s, when a new form of study and intervention appeared.

World War II brought an end to this most creative moment of the history of French photography. In Vichy France, while still seen as secondary to radio and cinema, photography was enlisted in propaganda, and all agencies were placed under direct control of the Ministry of Information and Propaganda. The Central Service of Photography (SCP), despite its modest size, became a tool for the massive dissemination of images participating in the cult of Marshal Petain. But the creative photographers of the prewar years either left the country or did not collaborate with the Vichy regime and the Nazis, and most of the propaganda remained relatively mediocre compared to what happened in other countries (Germany, Italy, and the Soviet Union, and for that matter, in a different context, the United States) (Denoyelle 11–17).

However, for humanistic photography, the major movement of French photography, the war was simply a parenthesis (de Thézy). Defined loosely as a type of approach centered on man and proposing an ode to human life, humanistic photography aims at revealing the hidden beauty of the world. Between art and reportage, it was less experimental than the extraordinary avant-garde that preceded it, but was nonetheless its inheritor, if only with the idea that photography was a mode of expression in its own right. After its disappearance in the 1960s, it would form the inspirational basis for "creative photography," a practice that affirmed the inventiveness and autonomy of the photographic medium. Marked by a great classicism of composition and framing, always preferring the greatest clarity (with a medium format Rolleiflex), finding its inspiration most of the time in the streets of Paris and its suburbs (although other cities and the country were not forgotten), humanistic photography created a type of visual imagination that was to bloom in the culture of the immediate post war, in the cinema, and in literature in the form of "poetic realism." Although they never formed a school per se, the common characteristics of humanistic photographers' practices are strong enough to mark them as a movement: the street, the workshop or factory, the working class home, and of course the *bistrot* or the *guinguette* and night life. Among the best-known artists were Pierre Boucher, Marcel Bovis, Brassaï, Yvonne Chevallier, Pierre Jahan, André Kertész, François Kolla, Willy Ronis, Emmanuel Sougez and, in the next generation, Jean-Philippe Charbonnier (1921–2004), and Edouard Boubat (1923–1999), whose subtle and efficient modernism makes him much more than simply a "humanistic photographer."

Robert Doisneau seems the archetypal French humanistic photographer, and his public reputation has soared since the 1980s with massive publications of his images in albums, books, postcards, and calendars. His *Baiser de l'hôtel de ville* has become a popular icon, very comparable to the fame of American painter Edward Hopper's *Nighthawks*. Most of these photographers learned photography as a trade, and they kept practicing it, for a living, as craftsmen. With the complete absence of any photographic market for prints in France until the 1970s, their major medium and source of income was the printed page. They worked for the most part with the expanding illustrated press (*Miroir du monde, Marianne, Voilà, Détective, Paris-Match, Vu* and *Regards*) without forgetting the professional press (industry and medicine), and they published their images in the growing number of illustrated books—travel, arts, and even fashion, advertising and the cinema. A few important "livres d'auteur" were published, such as Brassaï's 1933 *Paris de nuit;* or Izis's 1950 *Paris des rêves; Instantanés de Paris* by Doisneau of 1955, and Cartier-Bresson's famous *Images à la sauvette* of 1952, which combined photographs and texts by famous writers, and sometimes illustrated literary works.

A particular place should be made for Henri Cartier-Bresson, not only the most famous and influential French photographer of the second half of the century, but also as the perfect representative of the French touch, or *qualité à la française*. Cartier-Bresson began as a modernist formalist (as evidenced in his pre-war images, see Galassi) and developed, after the war, a more humanistic philosophy of the person that he celebrated in his famous "geometrical eye," placing on a same line the "subject" and the "heart of the photographer." His exceptional body of work should be seen in the context of several others, in between such photographers as Robert Capa and Chim (David Seymour), Kertész and Willy Ronis, as well as his younger *alter ego*, Marc Riboud (1923–). Blending geometry and morals, a theory that he justified with references to both French seventeenth-century classicism and Eastern philosophy, Cartier-Bresson formulated photography as an ethic and an aesthetic based on "the decisive moment," a manner of visual climax or epiphany only existing in framing, when the world suddenly *makes sense* and reveals itself.

Cartier-Bresson was also the co-founder of Magnum Photos, which had a great influence on the emergence of a practice of photo-reportage, both concerned with and highly conscious of form, which combined sensitivity to events with personal expression.

For a while indeed, Paris was the capital of photographic agencies (Gamma, Sigma, Sipa) created in the wake of the movement of May 1968 (Guy Le Querrec, Gilles Caron, Martine Frank, Hervé Gloaguen, Claude-Raymond Dityvon). Raymond Depardon, who is also a documentary filmmaker, is a case in point and a survivor in a world which has destroyed much of the "concerned photography," combining assignment with personal expression, and an investigating and tender look at human situations with powerful and yet simple visual forms. Paradoxically, one could place in the same category Jean-Loup Sieff, Jean-François Bauret, and Guy Bourdin, whose pioneering work in fashion photography in the 1970s provides examples of freedom of creation within a highly constrained field; their imaginative iconography (Bourdin's fantasies and Sieff's ultra-wide-angle shots and black-and-white landscapes) has now become common place.

Despite the magnitude of Cartier-Bresson as an influence, most French photography between the 1950s and the 1980s was of a different kind, indirectly claiming an American lineage, and marking its dependence on American inspiration. The "naturalists" such as Denis Brihat, Lucien Clergue, Jean-Paul Gautrand, and Jean-Pierre Sudre (Nori 99) took natural forms as their source of poetic inspiration and treated photographs as objects like paintings in a manner not unlike Edward Weston's. They were also active in fostering an institutional recognition of photography. The "subjective realists" could be seen as the heirs of the Swiss-born American Robert Frank, whose seminal book *The Americans* was first published in France, combining wandering and the practice of the narrative exploration of the series. Bernard Plossu is the paradigmatic example of this widely present trend, as well as Arnaud Claass, who teaches at the Ecole nationale de la Photographie in Arles. An important figure of the period is the critic and exhibition curator (and sometimes photographer) Gilles Mora (1945–). Typically combining a background in French literature (which he teaches) and a fascination for American culture of the 50s and 60s (literary and musical), Mora gathered many creative talents in photography in the late 70s and founded the *Cahiers de la photographie*. He also curated exhibitions and edited several books, among which is a reference monograph on Walker Evans. Common to many of these players is the concept of "photographic act," which aimed at defining photography as index (as opposed to emblem or sign), rooting it, and its analysis, in the act which produces it.

In the 1990s, the demise of press photography definitely drew photography towards art. The most interesting pursued a direction inaugurated by Christian Boltanski, using photo albums, toys, and personal memories to construct a questioning of memory and figuration in complex installations; and by Denis Roche, poet and author, member of group Tel Quel, who writes aesthetic and metaphorical analyses of photography, while composing visual fictions about himself (self-portraits and reflexive images). Commissions by private and public sponsors has also led to new forms of documentary. Marc Pataut photographs the French poor while Jean-Luc Moulène, in a more formalist approach, reworks daily objects and places in the language of conceptual art to foster their reversibility and ambiguity (Poivert 184) changing the role and nature of the spectator. They may constitute a revival of the social documentary tradition, through the medium of contemporary art. More original—but no less ambiguous—is the work of the many photographers who in the wake of the huge commission by the national planning agency DATAR (1983–1989) studied the changing landscapes of France under the general title of *The Territories of the French*. Inspired by the photographic myth of the Farm Security Administration and the memory of the Mission Héliographique of 1851, the DATAR hired photographers to document—visually and aesthetically, but not sociologically—the changing environment of the country and to educate viewers to its perception. It chose to contract with artists and, once selected, to leave them a fairly free hand as to the way they handled the subject.

Although the project was conducted under the intellectual supervision of photographer François Hers and critic Jean-François Chevrier, whose able introduction to the published book tried to inscribe the survey in the history of art, it was little seen outside the photographic world, and its results varied greatly in quality and relevance (Doisneau's and Depardon's are among the miscast). The project inaugurated a spate of similar smaller ones, often conducted without much thought and evaluation given to it, and in a somewhat repetitive manner. The reason might have been that although much poetical thinking about photography was available in the 1980s and 1990s, there was a relative paucity of serious scholarly historical tradition in the field. Very different was a project conducted by three photographers commissioned by the Plan urbain to "accompany" the urban development of three towns in La Réunion, a French "departement" in the Indian Ocean. Based on a long collaboration with the population (1989–1994) and a permanent evaluation of their work by outside sociologists, anthropologists, and critics, the BKL project is an original and pioneering example of the revival of a photographic practice combining the individual and the group, the photographer and the community, art and action, creation and testimony.

The interest in landscape photography has been relatively less marked in France than in the United States, despite the influence of the New Topographics group on a younger generation tired of human interest photography (Jean-Louis Garnell). Results have often mimicked some of the best American photography without really opening new vistas, except for Eric Dessert.

Despite its apparently varied practices, contemporary practice is marked by its autobiographic and often egoistic tendencies, and a particular attention to the phenomenon of memory (Poivert 64), paradoxically leading to its great homogeneity and repetitive nature.

With the democratization of the photographic process in the 1920s, photo-clubs, or photo societies, which had existed since the nineteenth century, took a great importance in the development of photographic practice among amateurs. Until the 1970s, in the absence of structured teaching and exhibiting of photography, they offered the only "photographic community," especially in the Provinces (every city has a photo club affiliated to the French Federation of Photography). They were deeply influenced by the movement for popular education in working class environments, although most major French photographers of the second half of the century came to photography from an art background, and many were from a bourgeois milieu often with independent means, when their immediate predecessors ("The Humanists") had gone through the trades.

Le Rectangle (created by Emmanuel Sougez in 1937) was a professional and overtly nationalistic—if not slightly xenophobic—reaction against what was perceived, with the increasing availability of equipment, as an amateuristic shift of the practice, and the dangerous competition of Germans and Central Europeans, who stifled French photographers (de Thiry 66). It defined itself as "an association of French advertising and illustration photographers...of faultless technician." (de Thiry 66). It was followed by the *Groupe des XV* (1946–1957), an association based on much of the same principles as the former one but with a more experimental and intellectual turn.

Among the clubs, the *Photo-club des 30 × 40* (created in 1951 by Roger Deloy) was particularly innovative and welcoming to new trends in contemporary photography, as was the *Groupe Libre Expression* (founded in 1963 by Jean-Claude Gautrand, Jean Dieuzaide, Pierre Riehl), which formed the avant-garde of a renaissance of creation. Of a somewhat hybrid kind, the *Gens d'Images* association, created by Albert Plécy in 1954, includes photographers, graphic designers, printers and journalists, and gives out two important awards: the Niépce Award to a young photographer wanting to become a professional, and the Nadar Award to the best photobook of the year. As for the *Société française de photographie*, created in 1851 and owning a rich collection of images, it spent most of the century as a slumbering belle, before being revived in the 1990s by a group of young scholars who now publish the respected *Etudes photographiques*, a French equivalent of *History of Photography*.

The real new start of French photography took place in the 1970s with the simultaneous expansion of exhibitions, teaching, collection, and writing about photography, while teaching remained modest until the 1980s, and, one could even argue, the 1990s. The American model was very important (see Kempf) in this change, as young Frenchmen and aspiring photographers discovered in the United States not only a photographic form but also a country where photography was taken seriously by powerful cultural and educational institutions. In a country that had introduced the cinema in the university and invented the nouvelle vogue, they longed for similar recognition. Museums created and expanded their collections of photography, thus forming a base for recognition and a market for prints. The Rencontres Internationales de la Photographie (RIP), founded in Arles in 1970, functioned as a series of American-style workshops for almost a decade before turning into a mini Cannes festival of photography. Festivals, with the biennale *Mois de la Photo* (Month of Photography) in Paris (begun in1980), multiplied in the provinces as well, as did houses of photography and photography museums (including the Centre national de la photographie in 1982; Maison européenne de la photographie following Paris-Audiovisuel of 1977, created by Jean-Louis Monterosso; and the Centre photographique du Nord-Pas-de-Calais founded by Pierre Denain). Many public and semi-public institutions (DATAR, Fondation de France) commissioned or supported photographers and photographic projects, developed collections, produced exhibitions and books, stimulating at least the market, and making it possible for a sizeable number of photographers to earn a living outside the press, whose market had shrunk considerably in the 90s. Contrejour, founded by Claude Nori (born in 1949) in 1975, as both a publishing house and a meeting place for contemporary photography until its folding in the 1990s, helped disseminate contemporary French photography through various short-lived but influential publications, exhibitions, and low-cost books. Interestingly, as photography finally achieved a broader status, almost all trace of an industry of photographic equipment and material had disappeared, with the acquisition of the Lumière company by Ciba and its successive merging with Ilford (1961–1976) and narrowing of activity, and that of the camera and lens makers SOM and OPL (and their famous Foca). Only Kodak remained in Paris.

Teaching has always remained the poor relation of photography. Because of a lack of means, universities have never managed to launch comprehensive Bachelor of Fine Arts/Master of Fine Arts programs in photography, so common in the postwar era in the United States. The notable exceptions of Paris 8 and Paris 1, and the existence of seminars and workshops in other universities and especially fine arts schools (where photography is now a fashionable and necessary part of the curriculum) should not hide the dearth of technical means, which often limits teaching to theory, a fact that the recent development of computer graphics and digital photography has managed to hide. Only two institutions actually tackled the problem of the specialized and comprehensive curriculum: the old lycée Lumière, whose orientation is the training of technicians in photography and the cinema; and the Ecole Nationale de la Photographie (ENP) in Arles (1982), which, under the able leadership of its first director, Alain Desvergnes, became a model school training "image people."

This theoretical slant is mirrored in the written production on photography. With the exception of Pierre Bourdieu and his *Un art moyen*, a sociology of photographic practice, French photographic writing has been essentially of a theoretical or aesthetic nature, and in any case very limited. The paradigm has been—and to a great extent remains in contemporary studies—philosophical (more in fact than semiological, despite a few pieces by Roland Barthes and lesser-known scholars) and literary, often mixing the two in the Blanchot tradition (Denis Roche, Régis Durand, Jean-Marie Shaeffer). The archetypal work by Barthes, *Camera Lucida*, seems a case in point where theoretical concepts solidify in formulas as they coalesce through a rambling autobiographical meditation and sensitive readings of images. Newspapers only began running columns on photography in the 1980s (mostly *Le Monde* with Serge Guibert).

The history of photography has long been an underdeveloped discipline, one essentially based on the nineteenth century. Although two histories of photography (Rouillé et Frizot) were published, their editors had to rely on many foreign scholars in the absence of specialized French historians. The field is now undergoing a revival after the pioneering work of nineteenth-century historian André Rouillé, with MA and PhD students doing original research under the guidance of a younger generation of scholars trained in many different disciplines, making the study of "the photographic image" an exciting transdisciplinary field (Brunet, Frizot, Gunthert, Poivert).

France was both early and late in institutionalizing photography. Just as the newly born photographic process was immediately taken within the field of the law through the patent—in that respect differing from what happened in Great Britain and the United States (Brunet, *L'histoire de l'idée de photographie*)—photography was included in official collections as early as the nineteenth century. Because of the *dépôt légal* law, requesting that all printed matter be registered at the Bibliothèque nationale de Paris (National Library), the Cabinet des estampes (Prints Division) received pictures as early as 1851, on the grounds that they were "paper editions." It remained, however, an archival and haphazard process until the mid-40s and early 50s, when young librarians started an active policy of collecting images, not from the point of view of illustration and information (organized by subject matter) but from that of authorship (organization by author). In the 1970s, Jean-Claude Lemagny, the head librarian for photography at the Cabinet des estampes, furthered the process, making the Cabinet des estampes a central player in the field. However, in the early 1980s, creative photography of the first half of the twentieth century and especially of the interwar years was still virtually absent from public collections. A policy of acquisitions and gifts (against tax exemption) allowed such institutions as the Bibliothèque nationale, the Musée national d'art moderne, and the Ministry of Culture (since 1975) to acquire such archives as those of Lartigue (1979/1986), Ronis (1983), Kertész (1984), Kollar (1987), and René-Jacques (1990). Various museums in the Regions also developed their photographic collections, such as the Musée Nicéphore Niépce (Châlons-sur-Saône), the Réattu (Arles), and the Museums of Marseille. Almost independently, the Municipal gallery of the Château d'eau in Toulouse, created by Jean Dieuzaide (1974), ran many important exhibitions. Eventually, the Fonds National d'Art Contemporain, which started to collect photography in 1980, and its regional branches, FRAC, especially FRAC-Aquitaine, began large collections of mostly contemporary photography and commissioned works as well.

Jean Kempf

See also: **Abbott, Berenice; André; Atget, Eugène; Barthes, Roland; Bellmer, Hans; Bibliothèque nationale de Paris; Boltanski, Christian; Brassaï; Cahun, Claude; Capa, Robert; Cartier-Bresson, Henri; Centre national de la photographie; David "Chim"; Digital Photography; Doisneau, Robert; Festivals; Frank, Martine; Frank, Robert; Henri, Florence; Hers, François; History of Photography: Interwar Years; History of Photography: Postwar Era; Kertész; Krull, Germaine; Lartigue, Jacques Henri; Lemagny, Jean-Claude; Maar, Dora; Magnum Photos; Maison européenne de la photographie; Photogram; Photography in Europe: An Overview; Pictorialism; Plossu, Bernard; Propaganda; Ray, Man; Riboud, Marc; Semiotics; Seymour; Surrealism; Tabard, Maurice; Ubac, Raoul**

Further Reading

BKL. *Trwa Kartié. Entre mythologies et pratiques.* Lyon: La Martinière, 1994.

Bouqueret, Christian. *Les Femmes photographes de la Nouvelle Vision en France 1920–1940.* Paris: Marval, 1998.

Bourdieu, Pierre. *Un art moyen*, Paris: Minuit, 1965; *Photography, a middle-brow art.* Translated by Shaun Whiteside. Stanford, Calif.: Stanford University Press, 1990.

Brunet, François. *La Naissance de l'idée de photographie.* Paris: PUF, 2000.

Durand, Régis. *Le temps de l'image: essai sur les conditions d'une histoire des formes photographiques.* Paris: la Différence, 1995.

Etudes photographiques. 1996. (http://etudesphotographiques.revues.org, http://www.sfp.photographie.com)

Galassi, Peter. *Henri Cartier-Bresson: The Early Work.* New York: Museum of Modern Art, 1987.

Kempf, Jean. "American Photography in France since World War II: Was France Liberated by the United States." In *American Photographs in Europe.* David Nye and Mick Gidley, eds. Amsterdam: Vu University Press, 1994.

Krauss, Rosalind, and Jane Livingston. *L'amour fou: photography and surrealism.* Washington, D.C.: Corcoran Gallery of Art; New York: Abbeville Press, 1985.

Les Cahiers de la photographie 1979–1993.

Mora, Gilles, and Claude Nori. *L'Été dernier: manifeste photobiographique.* Paris: Éditions de l'Étoile, 1983.

Nesbit, Molly. *Atget's Seven Albums.* New Haven: Yale University Press, 1992.

Paysages Photographies en France les années 80. Paris: Hazan, 1989.

Poivert, Michel. *La Photographie contemporaine*. Paris: Flammarion, 2002.
Roche, Denis. *La disparition des lucioles (réflexions sur l'acte photographique)*. Paris: Editions de l'étoile, 1982.
Barthes, Roland. *La Chambre claire. Notes sur la photographie*. Paris: Editions de l'étoile, Gallimard Seuil, 1980. (*Camera Lucida: Reflections on Photography*, New York: Hill & Wang, 1981.).
Schaeffer, Jean-Marie. *L'Image précaire: du dispositif photographique*. Paris: Seuil, 1987.

MARTINE FRANCK

Belgian

One of only five women photographers to be full members of Magnum Photos, Martine Franck has placed her mark on photography through her compassion and commitment to the profession. Her consistent strength in image-making is evidenced through the visual telling of diverse stories in her images. Yet Franck has resisted any attempt by others to label her work with any specific gendered viewpoint, commenting that photography is a language through which reality is made understandable, regardless of gender.

Born on 2 April 1938 in Antwerp, Franck was educated in the United States, primarily in New York and Arizona, before finishing her childhood education at the Heathfield School in Ascot, England in 1954. From 1956–1957 she studied at the University of Madrid and then from 1958–1963 at the Ecole du Louvre in Paris. Saying the camera gave her a "function," Franck's early interest in photography came from her grandfather and her first forays into photography began with trips to China, Japan, and India in 1963. The following year she took a job as the photographic assistant to Eliot Elisofon and Gjon Mili at the Time-Life Photo Laboratories in Paris and in 1965 Franck began freelancing for *Life*, *Fortune*, *Sports Illustrated*, *New York Times*, and *Vogue*.

Since the 1960s, Franck has been photographing with a discipline and drive to create documentary images that become more than mere records. Therefore, her work ranges from being aesthetically forceful to socially relevant, depending upon the project she has chosen. Cool with a graphic vigor, *Le Luberon, Alpes-de-Haute, Provence, France, 1976*, the high contrast landscape pushes towards the viewer as if the land is an ocean of undulating, metallic strips. In other images, subtle irony plays an underlying element in what seems to be straightforward documentary. In a photograph dated 1972, a well-dressed woman leans over to read the wall text accompanying a painting by Paul Delvaux, not noticing how her action plays into the Delvaux's painted nude woman walking towards her. Other times, such as is the case with the Théâtre du Solei work, the extended series seems like a labor of love threaded into the lens of her camera. Through her friend, Ariane Mnouchkine, in 1965, she began her association with the newly founded Théâtre du Soleil cooperative. In the years since then, Franck has shown how her work and the company have matured to a high level of professionalism and acclaim.

During the 1970s Franck began exploring the possibilities of film by being the director of *Music at Aspen* and *What has happened to the American Indian?* This interest continued with *Contre l'oubli: Lettre a Mamadou Mauritania* (1991) and the production of filmed stills with Robert Delpire of *Ariane & Co. Théâtre du Soleil* (1995).

After becoming a member of the Vu photographers agency from 1970 to 1971, in 1972 she became one of the seven founders of the photography agency Agence Viva, an organization seeking more social goals beyond straight documentary image-making. After Viva closed in 1979, Franck became an associate member of the Magnum Photos cooperative agency the following year. In 1983 she became a full member of the agency. Throughout her career in photography, Franck's interest in the human face has led her to create some of most remarkable and telling portraits. In her book and exhibit, *Le Temps de Viellier*, her subjects become portraits of old age, a reality in which oftentimes the physical shell houses a youthful mind. This is exemplified in the 1975 image, *Hospice at Ivry-sur-Seine, Val-de-Marne* where an elderly woman mimics Franck's act of photographing. The woman's face scrunches up and her eyes twinkle. Other portraits of the elderly convey their loneliness and dejected feelings as life closes in around them, even during the momentary joy of holidays shared with the Les Petits Frères des Pauvres. Capturing the private moments of well-known people in the arts is another important portion of Franck's portraits. Lili Brik, companion of the Soviet poet and playwright Vladimir Mayakovsky and sister of Elsa Triolet, reclines pensively in her sumptuous chair in a Paris hotel in 1976. Brik's dramatically made-up eyes avert away from the camera's perspective. Yet in another image dated 1993, a casually posed Curator-in-Chief Pierre Rosenberg smiles proudly in front of one of his favorite paintings by Rubens at the Musée du Louvre. In a portrait dated 1978, Michel Foucault's intense gaze, doubled by the light reflections on his glasses and the gesture of his finger held across his lips, makes us uncomfortable, much like his thought-provoking theories. Many of these portraits have become telling documents of a particular moment in time.

The same sensitive handling of the human face is expressed in Franck's images of children and the innocence of childhood, or in some cases lack of, found in the most unusual circumstances. The expressions and gestures of the three boys amidst the rusted junk cars in *Graveyard for stolen cars, Darndale (on the outskirts of Dublin), Ireland, 1993* are disturbing and serve as contrast to the anxious young faces of the ballerinas in *Petits rats (young dancers) of the Paris Opera in the foyer of the Opera Garnier, Paris, France, 1979*. The concrete sided staircase wraps around and carries the curious faces of little children up to the very top in the 1965 photo, *Children's library built by the Atelier de Montrouge, Clamart*.

Whenever the human element is the subject of Franck's camera, compassion links all. This compassion has caused her to form long-term associations with several organizations, such as Théâtre du Solei and Les Petits Frères des Pauvres. Her work in the 1990s with this latter organization was part of a photo project on exclusion in Europe with Franck's most notable contribution being of Tory Island, off the Donegal coast of Ireland, from 1993 to 1997. A rugged, desolate place with a population of only 130 people, the Irish government sought to transplant the people from what is perceived as an impractical way of life. Without actively intervening in their lives, Franck managed to document the tight-knit community where all are subtly intertwined in a timeless way apart from the fast moving global economy. The circle of life expressed in the joyful image, *The wedding of Tory Islander Pauline Doohan to Brian Gallagher, 1996*, corresponds to the portrait of *Francis McAteer, replacement parish priest of Tory Island, 1993*, who oversees the joys and sorrows of the village. Thirty-five of these images were part of the exhibit, *Magnum's Women Photographers*, at the National Galleries of Scotland in Edinburgh in 1999.

In the 1990s, Franck became interested in the cause of the displaced Tibetan Buddhist people living in Nepal and India. This project specifically addresses the life of the "Tulkus," the young reincarnations of great Tibetan lamas. Her images tell a story and yet also are making a difference by illustrating the continuation of traditions and rituals outside of their sacred homeland. Young boys are photographed being playful with their tutor or merely sleeping on their thrones surrounded by the tributes of the Tibetan New Year celebration. Her sharp eye seeking the socially marginalized, the devoted amidst desolation, and the displaced continues, becoming part of the diverse body of work Franck has created since 1963.

Married to Henri Cartier-Bresson since 1970, Franck was one of the few permitted to photograph the reticent photographer. She and their daughter, Melanie, worked together to create the Fondation Henri Cartier-Bresson in Paris.

SUSAN TODD-RAQUE

See also: **Cartier-Bresson, Henri; Life; Photography in Europe: France; Portraiture**

Biography

Born in Antwerp, Belgium, 2 April 1938. Studied at the University of Madrid and Ecole du Louvre, Paris (1956–1963). Began photographing in 1963. Assistant to Eliot Eliosofon and Gjon Mili of Time-Life Photo Laboratories, Paris, 1964. Freelance photographer for *Life, Fortune, Sports Illustrated, New York Times, Vogue*, and others since 1965. Photographer for the Théâtre du Solei cooperative in Paris since 1965. Member of Vu Photographers Agency 1970–1971; Founding member of Agence Viva, 1972–1979; Associate Member, 1980, and Member since 1983 of Magnum Photos cooperative agency. In 1995 worked on film, *Ariane et compagnie: le Théâtre du Soleil*, with Robert Delpire. Married to Henri Cartier-Bresson since 1970. One daughter, Melanie.

Individual Exhibitions

1971 Le Théâtre du Soleil, Galerie Rencontre, Paris
1974 *La Paroisse St. Pierre de Chaillot*, Chaillot-Galliera, Paris
1976 Marches et Foires, Les Amis des Arts, Reillanne, Provence

Le Quartier Beaubourg, Centre Georges Pompidou, Paris
1978 Carlton Gallery, New York
1979 Pentax Gallery, Tokyo
Northern Images, Side Gallery, Newcastle-upon-Tyne, United Kingdom
Photo-Galerie Portfolio, Lausanne, Switzerland
1981 *Le Temps de vieillir*, Musée Nicéphore Niépce, Chalon-sur-Saône, France
1982 Galerie municipale du Château d'Eau, Toulouse, France
1983 *Des Femmes et la Création*, Maison de la Culture, Le Havre
1984 Maison Descartes, Amsterdam
Le Temps de vieillir, Konsthall Malmö, Malmö, Sweden
1985 *Vingt contemporains vus par Martine Franck*, Centre Georges Pompidou, Paris
1986 Galerie A.R.P.A., Bordeaux, Paris
Centre d'Art Contemporain, Forcalquier, France
1987 Centro Culturale Pier Paolo Pasolini, Agrigento, Italy
1988 *65 Portraits*, Maison de la Culture, Amiens
Le Théâtre du Soleil, Centre Culturel Français, Berlin
1989 *De Temps en Temps*, Centre National de la Photographie, Paris
1992 Museo d'Arte Contemporaneo, Santiago, Chile
1994 Le College de France, FNAC, Paris
1998 *D'Un jour l'autre*, Maison Européenne de la Photographie, Paris and traveling
Tory Island, The Gallery of Photography, Dublin

Group Exhibitions

1973 *Viva: Familles en France*, Galleria Il Diaframme, Milan and traveling
1974 *There Is No Female Eye*, Neikrug Galleries, New York and traveling
1976 *French Photography*, French Consulate, New York and traveling
1977 *Le Photojournalisme*, Musée Galliera, Paris
1979 *Paris 1979: Les Parisiens*, Salon de la Photo, Paris
1980 *La Jeunesse a 20 ans*, Centre Georges Pompidou-B.P.I., Paris
Jeune Photographie, Fondation Nationale de la Photographie, Lyons
1981 *Four French Photographers*, Friends of Photography, Carmel, California
1982 *Photographier le Théâtre*, Maison Jean Vilar, Avignon
Handicaps sans Frontières, FNAC Forum, Paris and traveling
Contrastes humains, Galerie Zahno, Moutier, Switzerland
1983 Galerie Paule Pia, Antwerp, Belgium
1984 *Six photographes chez Le Corbusier*, Centre Georges Pompidou, Paris
Théâtre du Soleil: Shakespeare, Los Angeles
1985 *Magnum Concert*, Musée d'art et d'Histoire, Fribourg, Switzerland
1988 *C'etait 68*, FNAC Forum des Halles, Paris
1989 *De Temps en Temps*, Centre National de la Photographie, Paris
1991 *130 Photographies*, Taipei Fine Arts Museum, Taiwan and traveling
1997 Paris Photo, Eric Franck Fine Arts, Paris
1999 *Magna Brava: Magnum's Women Photographers*, National Galleries of Scotland, Edinburgh

Selected Works

Painting by Paul Delvaux in an exhibition of Belgian Surrealists and Symbolists at the Grand Palais, Paris, France, 1972
Suburbs of Newcastle upon Tyne, Tyne and Wear, England, 1977
Michel Foucault at home in Paris, France, 1978
Fisherman's Family, Amagansett, Long Island, New York, USA, 1983
Meal after the Christmas Mass, organized by the Little Brothers of the Poor, Palais des Congres, Paris, France
Tibetan New Year at the monastery of Sonada, near Darjeeling, India; Tulku Kalou
Rinpoche sleeping on his throne, 1993
Tory Island, County Donegal, Ireland, 1995
Tulku Khentrol Lodro Rabsel with his tutor Llagyel in the Shechen monastery, Bodnath, Nepal, 1996

Books

Etienne Martin, sculpteur. Text by Michel Ragon. Brussels: Edition La Connaissance, 1970
La Sculpture de Cardenas. Text by Jose Pierre. Brussels: Edition La Connaissance, 1971
Le Théâtre du Soleil: 1789. Paris: Théâtre Ouvert – Stock, 1971
Le Théâtre du Soleil: 1793. Paris: Théâtre Ouvert – Stock, 1976
Martine Franck. Preface by Ariane Mnouchkine. Paris: Contrejour, 1976
Les Luberons. Text by Yves Berger. Paris: Chene, 1976
Le Temps de Vieillir. Introduction by Robert Doisneau. Paris: Denoel-Filpacchi, 1980
Martine Franck. Introduction by Jean Dieuzaide. Toulouse: Galerie municipale du Château d'Eau, 1982
Martine Franck. Text by Vera Feyder and Attila Colombo. I Grandi Fotografi Series. Milan: Gruppo Editoriale Fabbri, 1982
Martine Franck: Des Femmes et la Création. Introduction by Vera Feyder. Le Havre: Maison de la Culture du Havre, 1983
Le B.I.P. en toute liberte. Paris: Editions du Centre Pompidou/BIP, 1986
Martine Franck. Introduction by Giuliana Scime. Agrigento, Italy: Centro Culturale Editorale Pier Paolo Pasolini, 1987
De Temps en temps. Preface by Claude Roy. Postface by Michel Christolhomme. Paris: Les Petits Frères des Pauvres, 1988
Portraits. Text by Yves Bonnefoy. Amiens, France: Editions Trois Cailloux, 1988
Le College de France. Paris: Imprimerie Nationale, 1994
The Man Who Planted Trees. Text by Jean Giono. New York: The Limited Editions Club, 1995
From One Day to the Next. Introduction by John Berger. London: Thames & Hudson, 1998
Martine Franck: Tory Island. Dublin, Ireland: Wolfhound Press, 1998
Henri Cartier Bresson photographie par Martine Franck. Text by Ferdinando Scianna. Milan: Franco Sciardelli, 1998
Magna Brava: Magnum's Women Photographers. Introductions by Isabella Rossellini, Christiane Amanpour, and Sheena McDonald. Essay by Sara Stevenson. Munich: Prestel-Verlag, 1999

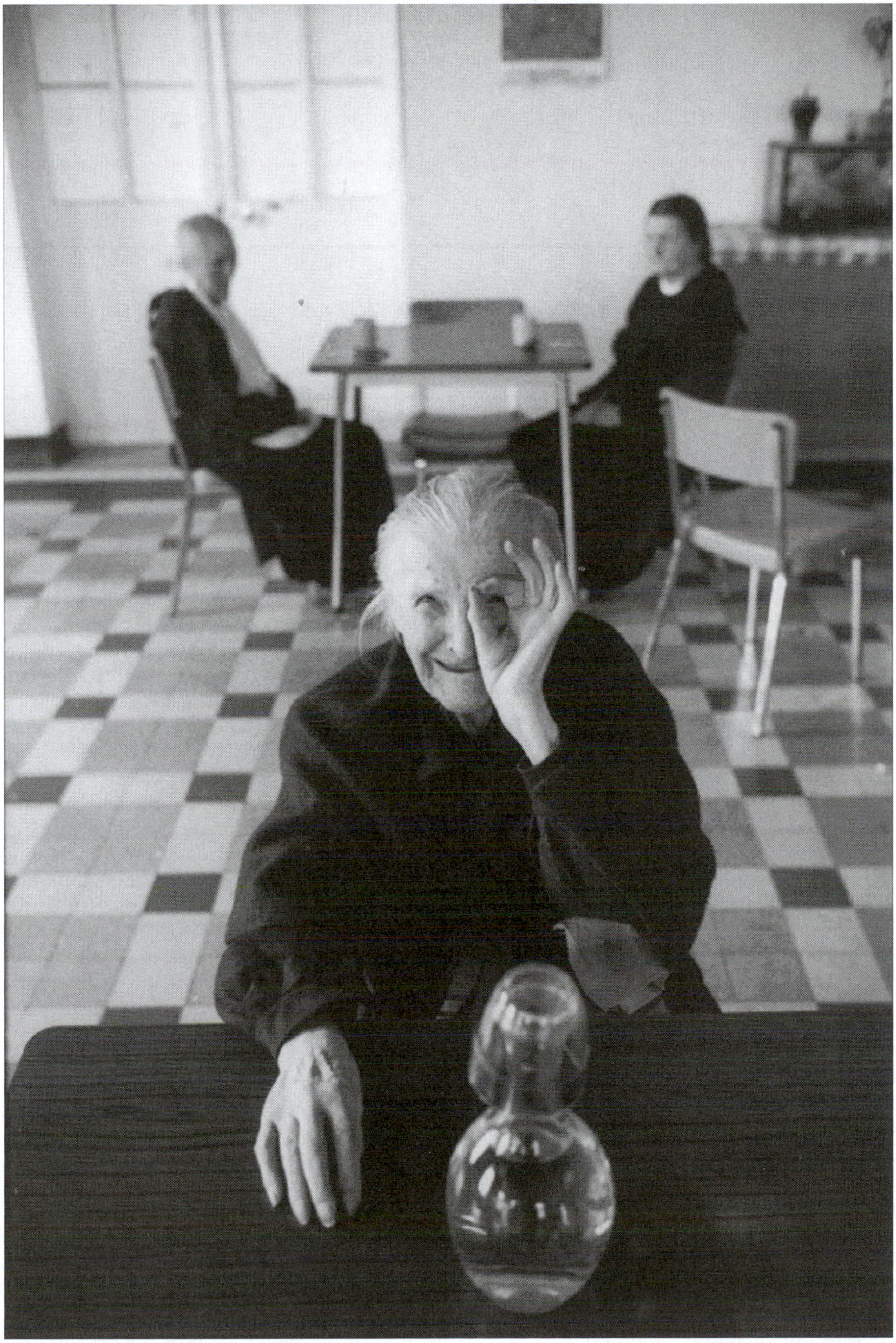

Martine Franck, Hospice at Ivry-sur-Seine, Val-de-Marne, France, 1975.
[© *Martine Franck/Magnum Photos*]

Further Reading

Arnold, Eve. "Eve Arnold on Martine Franck." *Aperture* 151 (Spring 1998): 4–13.

di Folco, John. "The Magna Brava Exhibition and Symposium." *History of Photography*. Vol. 25. Issue 1. (Spring 2001): 110–114.

Loke, Margarett. "About Man and Nature, Both at War and at Peace." *New York Times* Vol. 149 Issue 51309, final ed., sec. Op: E42.

ROBERT FRANK

Swiss-American

One of the most-cited figures in twentieth century photography, Frank's contribution to the postwar era lies with his revelatory book, *The Americans*, which was not only a seminal work of photography, but a prickly social document that called into question the rosy picture of American life widely accepted during the Eisenhower years. Although Frank's career has spanned more than 50 years, he has always worked, to some extent, in the long shadow cast by *The Americans*. Frank expressed his frustration with the legendary status of his early work thus: "I wished my photographs (the old ones) would move—or talk—to be a little more alive"; and much of his subsequent work has been more of this nature: varied, experimental, and multimedia, embracing film, video, text, poetry, and performance. A peer of Henri Cartier-Bresson, who occupies a similar legendary status with photographs that capture the mood of the street and the alienation of the individual in society, Frank's philosophy is in fact diametrically opposed to that of the French photographer. "There is no 'decisive' moment," Frank has famously said. "You have to create it. I have to do everything necessary for it to appear in my viewfinder" (*Conversations in Vermont* [film] quoted in *Bild für Bild Cinema*, Zurich, 1984). The bulk of his work, aside from *The Americans*, is in fact autobiographical, even confessional in nature.

Robert Frank was born on November 9, 1924 in Zurich, Switzerland to Hermann Frank and Rosa Zucker, a Jewish couple. He attended primary and secondary schools in Zurich, and upon his graduation, apprenticed with graphic designer and photographer Hermann Segesser between 1941 and 1942. Although Jews were being exterminated all across Europe, in the safety of neutral Switzerland, the Franks were able to go about their lives relatively undisturbed. As a German immigrant, however, in 1941, Hermann Frank, along with his sons Robert and Manfred, was forced to apply for Swiss citizenship. Robert Frank was finally granted official Swiss citizenship in 1945. During this unsettled period, he had continued his study of photography, working as a still photographer on a film, and at the film and photography studio of Michael Wolgensinger. Wolgensinger had studied with Hans Finsler, who had trained at the Bauhaus, and he taught Frank about large format cameras, instilling by example classical and experimental techniques. Frank briefly was assistant to a photographer in Geneva, and he was impressed by the work of the leading Swiss photographer of the day, Jakob Tuggener, who documented the street, architecture, and social life in Switzerland in a straightforward and unsentimental way.

After military training in 1945, Frank relocated to Basel to work at the Hermann Eidenbenz studio, a graphic design firm, at which time he produced his first book, a unique volume of original prints called *40 Fotos* (street photographs taken with 6 × 6 Rolleiflex), and he traveled with his family to Paris and Milan. Frank's desire, however, was to leave Switzerland and go to America, which he achieved in 1947, arriving in New York in February of that year. He found employment as a junior photographer at *Harper's Bazaar* magazine under the tutelage of legendary art director Alexey Brodovitch. This association was short-lived, however, for by the fall he had quit to work as a freelance photographer, completing assignments, including fashion shoots, for a variety of publications, including magazines and newspapers, including the picture magazines *Life* and *Look*, and *The New York Times*. Purchasing a 35 mm rangefinder Leica, Frank began a series of travels, notably to Peru and Bolivia, he arranged these series, using original prints, in book form. He met his future wife, Mary Lockspeiser, in the late 1940s as well; they married in 1950. Mary Frank, from whom Robert separated in 1969, went on to become a well-known artist working primarily in ceramics. The year 1950 marked his introduction as an exhibiting photographer when he was included in the seminal group exhibition at the Museum of Modern Art (MoMA), New York, *51 American Photographers*.

Following the birth of their first child, Pablo, in 1951, the Frank family relocated to Paris. Frank traveled to the United Kingdom, where he photographed in London and later Wales (1953). In England, Frank came to know and admire the work of Bill Brandt, and somewhat under his aesthetic influence, made a series of pictures of coalminers. These early works from London and Wales were reissued in book form in 2003. Back in Paris in 1952, he met Edward Steichen, in Europe to research photographers for exhibitions at MoMA, including *The Family of Man*, which was mounted in 1955. Traveling extensively during this period of his life, Frank returned to New York in 1953, where he became friends with Walker Evans and with whom he later worked as an assistant. Evans's book, *American Photographs*, was also highly influential on Frank's rapidly developing ideas about the sequencing of photographs. His second child, Andrea, was born in 1954, and he met poet Allen Ginsberg, who was to become a important influence and collaborator. He also took his first photograph for what would become *The Americans* at a Fourth of July event in Upstate New York (*Fourth of July—Jay, New York*). Frank's restless desire to travel was facilitated in 1955 when he received a John Simon Guggenheim Memorial Foundation fellowship, the first European to receive such a grant. With this grant and its extension in 1956, he crisscrossed the United States, photographing in New Jersey, Chicago, Detroit, North and South Carolina, Hollywood, the western states of Montana, Idaho, Nevada, and Nebraska, the southwest in Arizona and New Mexico, especially along Route 66, at that time the main artery across the nation, along the Mississippi River in the deep south, and Texas. After photographing the inauguration of Dwight D. Eisenhower for his second term in 1957, Frank selected and printed the works for his envisioned book.

While attempting to find a publisher, he worked on his first film, a 16 mm short shot in Florida with beat writer Jack Kerouac, whom he'd asked to write an introduction for his book. Later, commentators note that Frank was reacting to the massive project which he had assisted on (and was included in, both with his own works and in a portrait of him and his wife by Louis Fauer), Steichen's *The Family of Man*. Kerouac's introduction is diametrically opposed to the humanistic, often romantically idealistic language of Carl Sandburg's introduction to *Family*. Frank shared with Kerouac, whom he'd met in New York, a more realistic image—some might even say it was cynical—of postwar America, and its social structures, including the rampant segregation, the vast divide between rich and poor, the dark fears aroused by the Cold War, and the constant threat of nuclear holocaust, the alienation of youth exemplified by the emerging "beatnik" culture that Kerouac so brilliantly chronicled. That he couldn't find an American publisher was not entirely unexpected, as frustrating as it was. This would change with a trip back to Paris, and the embracing of the project by visionary publisher Robert Delpire. The book, first published in 1958, has never been out of print.

Opening with a now-classic image of two figures standing at windows of a ordinary brick structure, the American flag streaming across the center top of the picture (*Parade—Hoboken, New Jersey*), 82 images follow, showing, in gritty, dense tonalities, a panoply of American life. Politicians in top hats contrast with African Americans attending a funeral in their fedoras and straw boaters (*Funeral—St. Helena, South Carolina*). A glamorous Hollywood starlet (*Movie Premiere—Hollywood*) contrasts a Hollywood counter waitress (*Ranch Market—Hollywood*). The works are exquisitely selected and presented, forming rhythms and meanings that interweave throughout the book. The "great themes" of *The Family of Man* are likewise presented, yet they speak quietly, without the stage-managing of emotions of that project. Death is juxtaposed poignantly with the joy of living through the sequencing of a picture of an exuberantly smiling African American woman sitting in a chair against the setting sun of a weedy field (*Beaufort, South Carolina*) and a funeral view on the next page that shows an elderly African American in his coffin, formally attired men passing respectfully by (*Funeral—St. Helena, South Carolina*). The "exotic" is found in a cowboy leaning against a waste can in an urban setting (*Rodeo—New York City*), the personal in the book's final image of Frank's own car, within it his sleeping wife and child (*U.S. 90, en route to Del Rio, Texas*). Yet the individual images hold up as works of art: among the best known are of a Black nurse holding a baby so preternaturally White it seems to glow (*Charleston, South Carolina*) and a tuba player at a political rally, his face completely blocked by the giant circle of the tuba's horn (*Political Rally—Chicago*).

Although the process of shooting for the classic images that make up *The Americans* was a solitary, peripatetic activity, Frank's more common process is one of collaboration. His well-known 16mm film, *Pull My Daisy* (1959) was realized with New York painter Alfred Leslie and is a free interpretation of an act from Jack Kerouac's play *The Beat Generation*. Frank went on to make more than 20 films, including *Me and My Brother* (1965–1968), *Cocksucker Blues* (1972), featuring Mick Jagger and Keith Richard of the rock group The Rolling Stones, and *This Song for Jack* (1985), featuring Beat poets and writers Gregory Caruso, Allen Ginsberg, and William S. Burroughs, and dedicated to Jack Kerouac. Frank also produced the music videos Run for New Order (1989) and *Summer Cannibals* for Patti Smith (1996).

His works subsequent to *The American*, are filled with family, friends, and places that reflect the fabric of his life. In the 1960s, he concentrated primarily on making films, although he was beginning to have some success with his photographs: his first solo museum exhibition was held in 1961 at the Art Institute of Chicago, and the George Eastman House purchased 25 images from *The Americans* in 1965. Photographs that made up his next publication, *The Lines of My Hand*, began to be amassed. Published in 1972, this book looks inward, at Frank's own life and what it means to be an artist.

In 1970, Frank, his marriage to Mary over, had become involved with artist June Leaf, and together they purchased property in the desolate, often extreme climate of Mabou, Nova Scotia, where they built a studio and resided part of the year, and which was to be the setting for and subject of many photographs. The 1970s were full of personal difficulties for the photographer; his daughter Andrea, only 20, died in an airplane crash in Guatemala in 1974. His close friend and frequent collaborator on films, Daniel Seymour, disappeared and was presumed dead. His father died in 1976. His son, Pablo, who would eventually commit suicide, was becoming increasingly troubled by mental illness, and Frank unflinchingly confronted these tragedies with his camera, often in montaged sequences of snapshot-like images that are difficult to read in that they are fractured, shot at extreme angles, and inscribed with texts, some written into the film's emulsion. Rather than the fluid narrative line achieved by *The Americans*, the works of *The Lines of My Hand* are disjointed and resist easy interpretation. Many are clearly expressions of grief and are often painful to become involved in, such as *Monument for my Daughter Andrea, April 21, 1954/December 28, 1974*, which consists of Polaroids presented on a photo album page, or *Sick of Goodby's*, 1978.

In 1990, on the occasion of a major retrospective mounted by the National Gallery of Art, America's most prestigious museum, the Robert Frank Collection was founded. Consisting of negatives, contact sheets, work, and exhibition prints, it is a fitting tribute for the Swiss-born artist who helped reveal America to itself. Yet Frank's work can be best summed up by the work *Hold Still—Keep Moving* of 1989, used as the title for his 2000 retrospective at the Museum Folkwang in Essen, Germany. A photograph is seized from a flow of life; it holds life still, yet all the photographer, or the viewer, for that matter, can do is to keep moving.

Lynne Warren

See also: **Evans, Walker; Fauer, Louis; History of Photography: Twentieth-Century Pioneers; Museum of Modern Art; Street Photography**

Biography

Born Zurich, Switzerland, 9 November 1924. Apprenticed to and worked for various photographers and photo studios, including Hermann Segesser and Michael Wolgensinger Studio, Zurich, and Victor Bouverat, Geneva, 1941–1945. Employed by Hermann Eidenbenz graphic design studio, Basel, 1946. Began extensive period of traveling and photographing with trip to Paris and Milan, 1946. Moved to New York, February 1947, employed as a junior photographer, *Harper's Bazaar* magazine. Freelance photographer, 1947–1958. Traveled to South America, 1948. Married to Mary Lockspieser, 1950. Co-founder, group "New American Cinema," with Jonas Mekas, Shirley Clarke, Peter Bogdanovich, and others, 1960. Involvement with artist June Leaf (marriage 1975) and purchase of residence in Mabou, Nova Scotia, Canada, 1970. Death of daughter Andrea in plane crash, 1974. Death of son, Pablo, 1994. Taught in filmmaking: Visual Studies Workshop, Rochester, New York, 1971; Nova Scotia College of Art and Design, Halifax, 1972; University of California, Davis, 1973. Extensive travels in 1990s, including Italy, Spain, Egypt, Russia, and Japan. Awards include: Erich Salamon Award of the Deutsche Gesellschaft für Photographie, Berlin, 1985; Peer Award for Distinguished Career in Photography, Friends of Photography, San Francisco,

1987; International Photography Award, Hasselblad Foundation, 1996; Cornell Capa Award, International Center of Photography, New York, 2000. Honorary doctorate, University of Göteborg, Sweden. Founds Andrea Frank Foundation in New York, 1995 in memory of his daughter. Lives in Mabou, Nova Scotia, Canada and New York.

Individual Exhibitions

1961 *Robert Frank, Photographer*; Art Institute of Chicago; Chicago, Illinois
1969 *Robert Frank*; Philadelphia Museum of Art; Philadelphia, Pennsylvania
1976 *Robert Frank*; Photo-Galerie, Kunsthaus Zurich; Zurich, Switzerland
1978 *Robert Frank*; The Photo Gallery, National Film Board of Canada; Ottawa, Ontario, Canada
Robert Frank: An Exhibition of Photography and Films 1945–1977; Mary Porter Sesnon Art Gallery, University of California at Santa Cruz; Santa Cruz, California
1980 *The New American Filmmaker Series: Robert Frank*; Whitney Museum of American Art; New York, New York
1985 *Robert Frank: Fotografias/Films 1948–1984*; Sala Parpalló, Institució Alfons e Magnánim; Valencia, Spain
Visions of Hope and Despair: Robert Frank's Black-and-White Photographs; Stanford University Museum of Art; Stanford, California
1986 *Robert Frank: New York to Nova Scotia*; Museum of Fine Arts, Houston, Texas and traveling to Museum Folkwang, Essen, Germany
Robert Frank: Etats d'urgence; Centre national de photographie, Palais de Tokyo; Paris, France
Robert Frank and American Politics; Akron Art Museum; Akron, Ohio
1988 *In the Margins of Fiction: The Film of Robert Frank*; American Film Institute, John F. Kennedy Center for the Performing Arts; Washington, D.C.
The Lines of My Hand; Museum für Gestaltung; Zurich, Switzerland
1994 *Robert Frank: Moving Out;* National Gallery of Art; Washington, D.C. and traveling to Yokohama museum of Art, Yokohama, Japan, Kunsthaus Zurich, Zurich, Switzerland, Stedelijk Museum, Amsterdam, Netherlands, Lannan Foundation, Los Angeles, California
1997 *Robert Frank: Les Américains*; Maison Euopéenne de la Photographie; Paris, France
2000 *Hold Still—Keep Going*; Museum Folkwang; Essen, Germany and Museo Nacional Centro de Arte, Reina Sofia; Madrid, Spain

Group Exhibitions

1950 *51 American Photographers*; Museum of Modern Art; New York, New York
1953 *Post-War European Photography*; Museum of Modern Art; New York, New York
1955 *The Family of Man*; Museum of Modern Art; New York, New York
1962 *Photographs by Harry Callahan and Robert Frank*; Museum of Modern Art; New York, New York
1967 *12 Photographers of the American Social Landscape*; Rose Art Museum, Brandeis University; Waltham, Massachusetts
1974 *Photographie in der Schweiz—1840 bis heute*; Kunsthaus Zurich; Zurich, Switzerland
1981 *Walker Evans and Robert Frank: An Essay on Influence*; Yale University Art Gallery; New Haven, Connecticut

Selected Works

Park Avenue Rolls Royce, 1948
Beaufort, South Carolina, 1955 (from *The Americans*)
Charleston, South Carolina, 1955 (from *The Americans*)
Funeral—St. Helena, South Carolina, 1955 (from *The Americans*)
Parade—Hoboken, New Jersey, 1955 (from *The Americans*)
Political Rally—Chicago, 1956 (also known as "Chicago Convention," from *The Americans*)
U.S. 285, New Mexico, 1956 (from *The Americans*)
Pull My Daisy, 1959 (film)
William Buckley, 1962
Monument for my Daughter Andrea, April 21, 1954/December 28, 1974, 1974
Sick of Goodby's, 1978
Los Angeles–February 4th–I wake up turn on T.V., 1979
Mabou, 1981
Hold Still—Keep Moving, 1989
St. Rita's Hospital #401, Sidney, Nova Scotia, January 20, 1991

Further Reading

Alexander, Stuart. *Robert Frank: A Bibliography, Filmography, and Exhibition Chronology 1946–1985*. Tuscon, AZ: Center for Creative Photography, 1986.
Bennett, Edna. "Black and White Are the Colors of Robert Frank." *Aperture*, 9 1961:
Eskildsen, Ute, ed. *Hold Still—Keep Going*. Zurich: Scalo, 2001.
Frank, Robert. *Les Américain*. Paris: Robert Delpire, 1958. lst American edition: *The Americans*, preface by Jack Kerouac, New York: Grove Press, 1959; reprinted Zurich: Scalo, 2000.
———. Frank, Robert. *The Lines of My Hand*. Zurich: Parkett/Der Alltag, 1989. (revised and enlarged edition)
———. Frank, Robert. *Robert Frank*. Paris: Centre national de la photographie, 1983.
Greenough, Sarah, and Philip Brookman. *Robert Frank*. Washington, D.C.: National Gallery of Art, 1994.
Tucker, Anne, and Philip Brookman. *Robert Frank: New York to Nova Scotia*. Houston: Museum of Fine Arts, 1986.
Wurlitzer, Rudolph. *Robert Frank, Aperture History of Photography Series*. Millerton, NY: Aperture, 1976.

GISÈLE FREUND

French

Gisèle Freund's portrait of Virginia Woolf (1939), taken a few weeks before the novelist's suicide, captures the patient attention and poignant sincerity that characterizes her photographic eye. It is interesting, then, that Freund's decision to become a photographer arose out of economic necessity. Her portraits of some of modernism's most celebrated figures have become canonical images, despite the fact that Freund purposely downplayed her aesthetic role, having always considered herself a documenter rather than an artist. Because of her fascination with everyday human experience, Freund's oeuvre includes such wide-ranging work as travel reportage, documentation of poverty and political life, and even a study of mediums and palm readers. Arguably, the color portraits taken in the 1930s and 1940s are Freund's most striking work. Her experimentation with Kodachrome and 35 mm Agfacolor, combined with her uniquely candid portraiture style, would help distinguish her work from the era's other proficient photographers and guarantee her role as an invaluable witness to and recorder of a most creative and productive generation.

As a Jew and a Socialist, Freund was forced to flee Germany in 1933 as the Nazi violence she was documenting had become a threat to her personal safety. Freund arrived in Paris with an incomplete dissertation and the Leica her father had given her when she was 15. Befriending Adrienne Monnier, the proprietress of *La Maison des Amis des Livres* bookshop, was personally and professionally transformative for Freund, as Monnier would eventually publish the completed dissertation and introduce Freund to the artists and writers who would prove her most captivating subjects. Monnier would remain a lifelong mentor and companion.

While completing her doctorate in sociology at the Sorbonne, Freund was steadily establishing herself as an adept photographer. Her views from Notre Dame (1933) and the publication of a photo-essay in the first year of *Life* magazine (1936) were the beginning of a formidable career in documentary and portrait photography. Because no French magazine could process color, *Life*'s publication of Freund's piece on poverty in northern England was a singular opportunity that would turn into a lifelong collaborative alliance. Her first official assignment, given to her by the director of the Bibliothèque nationale de France, was to photograph all the libraries in Paris for the 1937 World's Fair. *Vu* magazine featured this commission, whose affectionate analysis of the eccentric library patrons was just the beginning of Freund's characteristic scrutiny of her subjects' bodies, clothing, and posture.

Freund's unwillingness to retouch photographs led her to focus upon artists and writers, whom she assumed were less concerned with physical perfection. Though many were apparently quite disappointed with their portraits, Freund continued to photograph the era's most celebrated artists and writers, including Jean Cocteau, Marcel Duchamp, Henri Matisse, André Gide, Simone de Beauvoir, Samuel Beckett, Jean-Paul Sartre, Colette, and Walter Benjamin. Her photographs for the dust-jacket of André Malraux's *Man's Fate* (1939) and James Joyce's *Finnegan's Wake* (1939) were among her most prestigious commissions. Freund's precise composition and traditionally posed subjects offer an interesting counterpoint to the work's intense intimacy and technologically advanced use of color. The result of this implicit tension is a gallery of faces whose graphically featured skin tones and eye color create pictures quite distinct from the more widely reproduced black and white photographs of her contemporaries.

Freund fled France in 1941 and eventually traveled to Buenos Aires where she would remain for the duration of the war. In South America, Freund worked as an assistant film producer and a photojournalist, completing assignments in Argentina, Chile, Ecuador, and Uruguay.

Returning to Europe for a brief time in 1946, Freund, like many other photographers, visited the post-liberation concentration camps. Once there, however, Freund felt that she could best serve the efforts by identifying the bodies of former acquaintances rather than by documenting Nazi atrocities.

In 1948, Freund joined Magnum Photos, Robert Capa's photographers' collaborative, for which she would become the Latin American contributor. It was during her six years associated with Magum that Freund produced her well-known *Life* spread on Eva Peron, wife of Argentinean dictator Juan Peron, then at the height of notoriety. Her portraits of Mexican muralist Diego Rivera and of his wife, painter Frida Kahlo with her dogs were also taken during this extraordinarily productive period. Because of her friendship with post-revolutionary writers and artists, Freund was denied entry into the United States and placed on the McCarthy blacklist. For this, Capa dismissed her from Magnum.

Throughout her career, Freund remained committed to the productive intersection of sociology and photography and to the social history of her medium. In numerous interviews and essays she explained her love of portraiture as arising directly out of a fascination with the human face's profoundly expressive quality. Freund's prodigious writings articulate her interest in photography's transformative capacity, particularly what she explained as its ability both to democratize and transform artistic production and representation. In this assessment, she also remained sharply critical of photography's availability to further an unethical agenda in which manipulation and persuasion often play upon a viewer's emotions. In her photographs and critical essays, Freund consistently demonstrates such sensitivity, insisting in one interview that love of humanity is essential to good photojournalism.

Even after she ceased photographing in the 1980s, Freund remained passionate about the various ingredients that constitute her craft. The bond between photographer and sitter, the complex nuances of the human face, and the relative merits of various photographic equipment were equally important components in Freund's approach to a subject. In *Photography and Society*, her well-known study of photography's social history, Freund expresses a modest pride in her influence upon fellow photographers, claiming that she legitimized the more versatile and modern Leica camera. Indeed, the dynamic quality of much of her work illustrates the Leica's revolutionary impact on photography.

Upon returning from Mexico in 1954, Freund established permanent residence in Paris, where she lived until her death in 2000. Though no longer a photographer, Freund continued her dedication to photography by giving lectures, exhibiting her work, and writing—a practice she at one point claimed was her real love. In 1977, Freund became president of the French Federation of Creative Photographers and was awarded a doctor *honoris* from the National Museum of Photography at Bradford University. Ironically, one of her most widely reproduced images is seldom recognized as part of her body of work. Taken at the 1981 inauguration, Freund's picture of François Mitterand became his official presidential photograph, a staple image found in official buildings throughout France.

Annalisa Zox-Weaver

See also: **Life; Magnum Photos; Modernism**

Biography

Born in Berlin, Germany, 19 December 1912; emigrated to France in 1933; naturalized in 1936. Studied sociology and art history at Albert-Ludwigs-Universtadt Freiburg, Breisgau, Germany, 1931; at the Institute for Social Sciences, University of Frankfurt, 1932–1933; and at the Sorbonne, Paris, 1933–1936, receiving a Ph.D. in sociology and art in 1936. Freelance journalist and writer in Paris for *Life, Weekly Illustrated, Vu, Picture Post, Paris-Match, Du*, and others, 1935–1940, 1946–1950, and from 1953 on; photographer and assistant film producer for Louis Jouvet Theater Company in Argentina and Chile, 1943–1944; worked for France Libre in Argentina, 1944–1945; member of Magnum Photos in Paris, 1947–1954. Kulturpreis, Deutsche Gesellschaft fiir Photographie, 1978; Grand Nx National des Arts, France, 1980; Officier des Arts et Lettres and Chevalier de la Légion d'Honeur, 1980. Died in Paris, France, 31 March 2000.

Individual Exhibitions

1939 *Ecrivains célèbres*; Galerie Adrienne Monnier; Paris; and Peggy Guggenheim Jeune Gallery; London
1946 *Amérique Latine*; Maison de I' Amérique Latine; Paris, France
1968 *Au Pays des Visages* 1938–1968, Musée d'Art Modeme de la Ville de Paris, France
1973 Musée d'Art et d'Histoire; Nimes, France
1975 Robert Schoelkopf Gallery; New York, New York
1977 *Gisèle Freund: Retrospective*; Fotoforum der Gesamthochschule; Kassel, Germany
1978 Musée Reattu; Arles, France
1979 Sidney Janis Gallery; New York, New York
1981 Axiom Gallery; Melbourne, Australia
1984 Fotografie Forum International; Frankfurt, Germany
1992 Itinéraires; Centre Georges Pompidou and Musée d'Art Moderne de la Ville de Paris, France
1993 Anita Neugebauer Galerie; Basel, Switzerland
1995 Museum für Modeme Kunst; Frankfurt, Germany
1996 Goethe Institut; Paris,
Galerie nationale du Jeu de Paume; Paris
1998 *Gisèle Freund: Photographs*; Ton Peek Gallery; Utrecht, Netherlands
2000 Fotografisk Center; Copenhagen, Denmark
2001 Centre de Cultura Contemporania; Barcelona, Spain

Group Exhibitions

1951 *Memorable Life Photographs*; Museum of Modern Art; New York, New York

1961 Salon Internationale de la Photographie; Bibliothèque nationale de France, Paris
1965 *Femmes Photographes*; Les 30/40; Paris, France
1966 *Commemoration Joyce*; Centre Culturel Americain; Paris, France
1972 *Photographes Français*; Moscow Museum
1975 *Women of Photography*; San Francisco Museum of Art; San Francisco, California, and traveling
1977 *Photographes Français*; Centre Beauborg; Paris, France
1981 *Les Réalismes*; Centre Beauborg; Paris, France
1982 *Color as Form*; International Museum of Photography at George Eastman House; Rochester, New York
1997 *A History of Women Photographers*; Akron Museum of Art; Akron, Ohio
2000 *Working Cultures*; Carreau de Forbach; Forbach, France
2001 *Frida Kahlo Unmasked*; Mexican Fine Arts Center Museum; Chicago, Illinois

Selected Works

"La Photographie en France au XlXe siècle, essai de sociologique at d'aesthetétique," Ph.D. diss., Sorbonne, 1936
Mexique Précolumbien, 1954
James Joyce in Paris: His Final Years, 1965
Le Monde et Ma Camera, 1970; as *The World in My Camera*, translated by June Guicharnaud, 1974
Photographie et Société, 1974; as *Photography and Society*, translated by David R. Godine, 1980
Memoires de l'Oeil, 1977
Trois Jours avec Joyce, 1982
Itineraires, 1985; as *Gisèle Freund, Photographer*, translated by John Shepley, 1993 *Gisèle Freund: Photographer* 1985 with Rauda Jamis, *Gisèle Freund Portrait*, 1991

Further Reading

High Heels and Broken Glass. Videotape. Written and Produced by Deborah lrmas and Klaus Homef, editor. *Gisèle Freund: Fotografien, 1932–1977*. Bonn: Rheinisches Landesmuseum, and Cologne: Rheinland-Verlag, 1977.
Hopkinson, Amanda. "Photographic Perception." *British Journal of Photography* 139, no. 6862 (1992).
Mann, Margery, ed. *Women of Photography*. San Francisco: San Francisco Museum of Art, 1975.
North, Ian. *International Photography 1920–1980*. Canberra: Australia National Gallery, 1982.

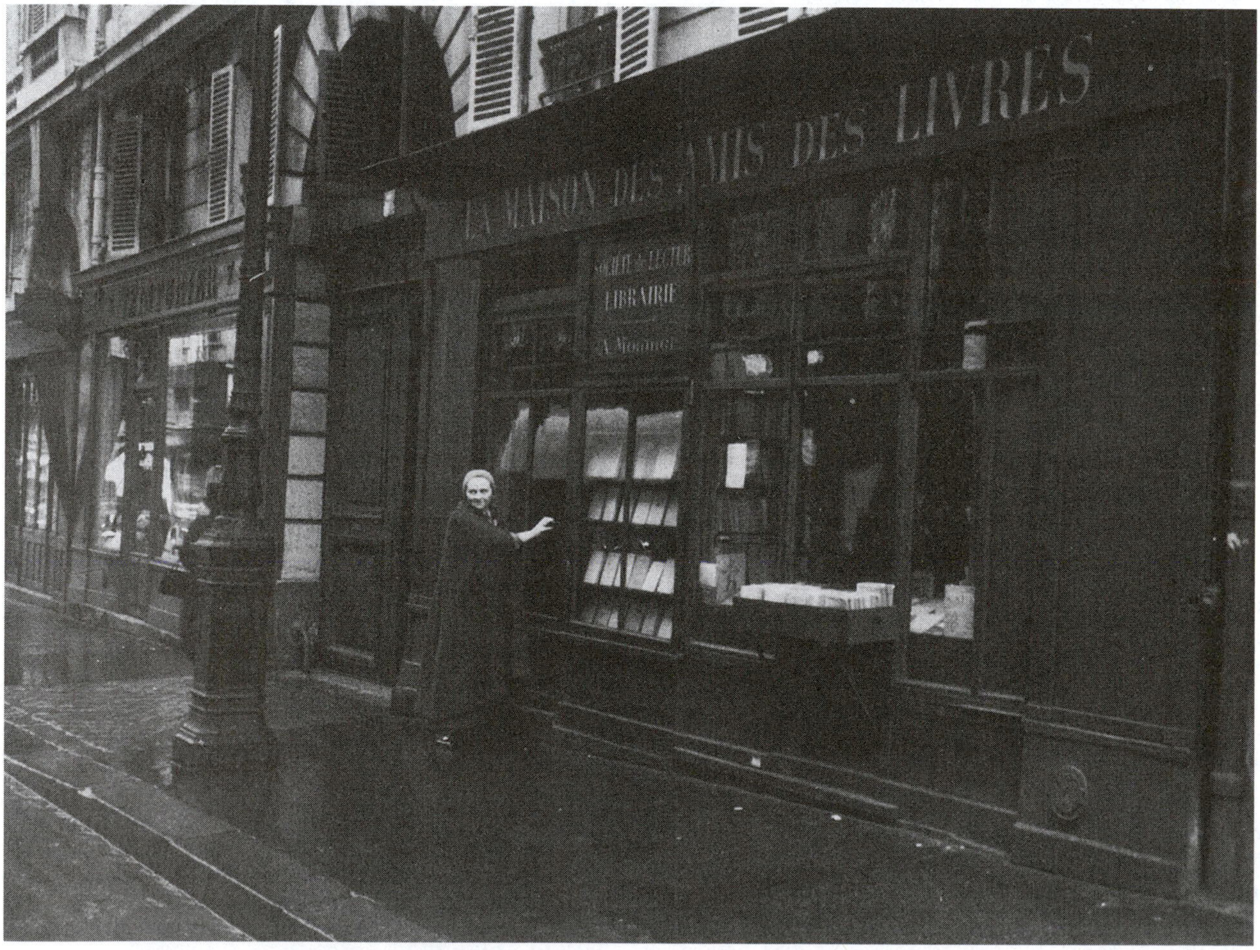

Gisèle Freund, Adrienne Monnier in front of the Bookstore Maison des Amis des Livres, 1937.
[© *Gisèle Freund/Agence Nina Beskow*]

Paris Was a Woman. Videotape. Directed by Greta Scmier and Hans Puttnies, editor, New York: Zeitgeist Films, 1996.
Catalogue de l'oeuvre photographique Gisèle Freund, Paris: Editions du Centre Pompidou, 1991.
Rosenblum, Naomi. *A History of Women Photographers*. New York: Abbeville Press, 1994.
Steichen, Edward. *Memorable Life Photographs*. New York: Museum of Modem Art, 1951.
Weiss, Andrea. *Paris Was a Woman*. San Francisco: Harper San Francisco, 1995.

FRIENDS OF PHOTOGRAPHY

The Friends of Photography was a group of photographers, photo historians, and photo enthusiasts who were dedicated to the promotion of creative photography through exhibitions, publications, workshops, and community outreach programs in the greater San Francisco area. For nearly 34 years the group supported the medium of photography and its practitioners through active and varied community programs.

The Friends of Photography was officially established when a core group of 12 individuals met at the home of Virginia and Ansel Adams in Carmel, California, on January 1, 1967. The Founding Group included Arthur Connell, photographers Morely Baer, Wynn Bullock, Gerald Robinson, Gerry Shape, and Cole Weston, writer and photographer Liliane DeCock Morgan, architect Edgar Bissantz, musician Rosario Mazzeo, and photo historians Nancy and Beaumont Newhall. Ansel Adams was elected President and Brett Weston was named Vice President. The diverse makeup of this initial group, which included people engaged with photography on varied levels, established the group's unique perspective. Created at that time was the first Board of Trustees, consisting of 18 Trustees; the position of Honorary Trustee was established in 1985. An Advisory Committee was elected and those people were formally designated as Advisory Trustees in 1974.

For the first three years operations were handled by volunteer committees led by members of the Board of Trustees. In 1972, as The Friends became more established, a full-time, professional and paid staff was hired to operate the organization's growing program. Membership revenue was the largest single income source for The Friends, which was augmented by wholesale and retail sale of books as well as special offers of fine prints and books to members.

Exhibitions were a significant component of The Friends of Photography's program, offering a venue for audiences to explore and be inspired by all styles and generations of creative photography. The work of Adams, Wynn Bullock, Imogen Cunningham, Dorothea Lange, Brett Weston, Edward Weston, and Minor White comprised the first exhibition of The Friends of Photography, which was held in the historic Sunset Center in Carmel, California, from June 23 through July 30, 1967. Later in 1969, a second gallery was opened in the same complex allowing simultaneous exhibitions until 1976 when all exhibitions were on view in the Sunset Center's main gallery. That first year, The Friends held four additional exhibitions that included the work of Eugène Atget, Ruth-Marion Baruch, Bruce Davidson, Pirkle Jones, W. Eugene Smith, and Paul Strand.

The exhibition program continued through 2001, rotating monthly or bi-monthly, and included the work of Berenice Abbott, Manuel Álvarez Bravo, Paul Caponigro, Harry Callahan, Judy Dater, Emmett Gowin, Robert Heinecken, Anthony Hernandez, Lewis Hine, Harold Jones, Barbara Morgan, Marion Palfi, Robert Rauschenberg, Edmund Teske, Jerry N. Uelsmann, Todd Walker, and Adam Clark Vroman, to name only a sampling. Also mounted were thematic exhibitions such as *Ten Top European Photographers, East and West* (1971), *Classics of Documentary Photography* (1976), *The Photograph as Artifice* (1978), *Dyed Images: Recent Work in Dye Transfer* (1982), *Narrative Images/Post-Documentary Photography* (1987), *Proof: LA Art and The Photograph 1960–1980* (1993), and *Landscapes of War: The American Civil War in Photographs* (1997). Over the years, there were ten exhibitions that featured the work of the members of The Friends of Photography. During the early years (1967–1972) exhibitions were organized by a committee headed by Wynn Bullock. With the formation of a paid staff, the position of curator was established and made responsible for organizing all exhibitions or inviting special guest curators.

As the organization grew, so did its breadth of publications. As an early form of communicating news to members, mimeographed newsletters were sent out to members (eight between 1970 and 1972). Beginning in January 1978 and running until December 1986 a monthly publication titled *The Newsletter of The Friends of Photography* was mailed to its members. From January 1987 through spring 2001, *Review, Newsletter of The Friends of Photography* was distributed to members monthly. In 1972, The Friends of Photography released its *Untitled* series; over the subsequent 22 years, 58 issues were published and beginning in the late 1970s, each issue focused on one artist or theme with a unique design to complement the content. Each member received a copy of *Untitled* and individual titles were also available for sale. Beginning in autumn 1994, and running until spring, 1996 The Friends published for their members *see: a journal of visual culture*, which included photography, creative writing, and criticism.

With the death of Ansel Adams in 1984, The Friends of Photography began a search for a new location in San Francisco. Named the Ansel Adams Center, this facility opened in 1989, and was first located on Pier 1 at Fort Mason before relocating to the Yerba Buena Center, where it had five exhibition spaces and an extensive photography bookstore. The final location was 655 Mission Street in San Francisco.

Conceived of as a living and growing educational force, education through, The Friends had a tremendous impact on the whole community from children to seniors. Beginning in 1969 The Friends held educational seminars and workshops focused on practical photography skills. Over the history of the group, educators involved included Adams, Morley Baer, photo historians and critics Peter Bunnell and Andy Grundberg, Linda Conner, Imogen Cunningham, Robert Dawson, Rod Dresser, Lee Friedlander, Emmet Gowin, Michael Kenna, Mark Klett, Annie Leibovitz, Ellen Manchester, Sally Mann, Richard Misrach, Lisette Model, Wright Morris, Olivia Parker, Meridel Rubenstein, John Sexton, Ruth Thorne-Thompsen, Al Weber, and Jack Welpott.

Specific goals of the education and outreach program included the promotion of visual literacy and the implementation of innovative programs that used photography to increase involvement with local communities. Some of the programs sponsored by The Friends included: The Look Again! program that promoted museum/school collaboration; Hands on History of Photography aimed at familiarizing high school students with the history of the medium; Workshops for Educators were one-day sessions aimed at primary and secondary teachers accompanied by Resources for Educators, which provided hands-on educational materials free of charge; designed for grades 4–8 was Ansel Adams' Curriculum Resource for Teachers focused on Adams' accomplishments in photography. In the late 1990s, The Friends offered free photography classes for children, youth, and adults through Community Partnerships with Bayview Opera House, Ruth Williams Memorial Theater, and Horace Mann Academic Middle School.

On October 31, 2001, due to rising rent costs in San Francisco and budgetary deficiencies, The Friends of Photography closed all operations and exhibitions. All of the group's assets were distributed among other organizations. The San Francisco Art Institute received the 3,000-volume library, the archives and records were given to the University of Arizona's Center for Creative Photography, and The Oakland Museum of California adopted the education program operating with funds from The Friends of Photography Education Endowment.

Rebecca Morse

See also: **Abbott, Berenice; Adams, Ansel; Alvarez Bravo, Manuel; Atget, Eugène; Callahan, Harry; Caponigro, Paul; Center for Creative Photography; Cunningham, Imogen; Davidson, Bruce; Gowin, Emmett; Heinecken, Robert; Hine, Lewis; Jones, Harold; Jones, Pirkle; Lange, Dorothea; Leibovitz, Annie; Morris, Wright; Newhall, Beaumont; Rauschenberg, Robert; Strand, Paul; Teske, Edmund; Uelsmann, Jerry N.; Welpott, Jack; Weston, Edward; White, Minor**

Further Reading

Alinder, James G., ed. *Light Years: The Friends of Photography 1967–1987*. Carmel, California: Untitled 43, The Friends of Photography, 1987. http://www.friendsofphotography.org (accessed May 8, 2005).

Baker, Ken. "Influential Photo Group Dissolved." *San Francisco Chronicle*, 2 March 2004.

Newhall, Nancy. Introduction to *Portfolio I: The Persistence of Beauty*. Carmel, California: The Friends of Photography, 1969.

MASAHISA FUKASE

Japanese

Masahisa Fukase's career, which came to an abrupt halt in 1992 from a fall and subsequent brain damage, points to his obsessive need to confront and seek his changing self. Fukase's insistence on photographing his life events and his immediate surroundings often result in images that provoke unease, yet they also affirm his existence reciprocally. His works hold a unique place in postwar Japanese photography. In a culture where public displays of private emotion have often been found distasteful, Fukase's work has been provocative, while the photographer himself has developed a persona of mystery.

Born in 1934 into a family who owned a photographic studio in Bifuka-cho, Hokkaido, Fukase acquired skills of developing film and making prints as a child, assisting his father. Later in his life, Fukase commented that his enmity for photography probably emerged from the experience during youth when he washed prints continuously at his father's studio despite his wish to go and play with his friends.

His relationship to photography, based on "enmity" grew stronger and more complicated throughout his career. In a sense, his body of work testifies not only to his changing self, but also to the changing nature of his relationship to photography. He once noted that "I work and photograph while hoping to stop everything. In that sense, my work may be some kind of revenge drama about living now. And this is what I like the most." Photography, in Fukase's mind, serves both as the enmity against and as the necessary means with which to explore and express himself.

Fukase planned to take over his father's portrait studio after his graduation from university with a bachelor's degree in photography. However, because he began living with a woman immediately after his graduation in 1956, he remained in Tokyo and took a job as a photographer for an advertisement agency. The miscarriage by this woman in 1961 and her sudden disappearance in 1962 with a newborn baby left Fukase emotionally distraught. Although Fukase began photographing in slaughterhouses in 1961 for a series called "*Kill the Pigs!*" his visit to the slaughterhouse in Shibaura became almost a ritual after her departure. He took the earliest train there and photographed all day, everyday, for a year. He continued to visit the location after he met Kanibe Yôko, his future wife, juxtaposing the stale and cold conditions of the slaughterhouse with the unmistakable and expressive human existence of Yôko.

His life with Yôko played a central and decisive role in his career from 1963 on. Series such as *Yôko* (published in 1978) and *Ravens* (published in 1986) attest to their transformative and challenging relationship through intensely symbolic and emotional representations. Particularly after their separation in 1975, Fukase traveled to his hometown in Hokkaido more frequently, while photographing ravens in various places out of his train windows. The images included in the series *Ravens* are often printed with overtly visible grains, and the silvering eyes of the ravens as well as their shadowy existence create a weary mood of detachment and darkness. For Fukase, ravens became an appropriate projection of his own feelings and living conditions. As he noted at the third installment of the series, "I did not care a bit about ravens. I assumed a defiant attitude that I myself was a raven." Fukase exhibited the series *Ravens* in four installments in galleries, and for the last "chapter," he revisited the town housing project where he and Yôko spent their married life. On this occasion he stated, "I felt scary, something like a crime offender going back to the crime scene...The desire to photograph grew larger and larger, and various images of tombstones kept spreading in front of me." The result from the interaction among Fukase's effort to reconcile with the unrepeatable past, his completely changed life after Yôko, and his enmity toward photography construct a powerful personal journey that sustained Fukase and his relationship with photography for a decade.

During these trips home, Fukase continued to work on another series of photographs entitled *Family*, using a large-format view camera that his father used in his portrait studio. For about 20 years, Fukase photographed his family portrait in similar compositions. Photography, for Fukase, is not merely an expressive medium of choice, but also an unbreakable tie back to his father and his family business. Quiet and composed postures and expressions of family portraits contrast dramatically with his *Ravens* series. In *Family*, his camera calmly captures his family members who continue to belong to his world. If *Ravens* is a meditation on the past he tries to forget and his struggle with forgetting, *Family* serves as a reminder of the past that is present and remains. This series came to an end when his father died in 1987, and Fukase used the photograph of his father at the funeral as the last image. In the same year, he selected and exhibited a series *Memories of my Father*, which was shown in Tokyo and Israel. His relationship with photography changed through this project, and Fukase began including his own body in photographs around this time.

In 1990, Fukase published and exhibited the first section of *Shikei* (private scenes) series, which include his travel shots from various places as well as self-portraits in a bath tub using an underwater camera. In these images, Fukase composes the image by including a part of his body, pictorially asserting his existence. In a number of images entitled "*bukubuku*," which mimics the sound of air bubbles from underwater, Fukase stares directly at the camera, confronting his enmity of photography from childhood as if to enact his final revenge drama. The tension between Fukase's reliance on and vengeance toward photography seems to be an unmediated confrontation for the first time in these images. Before he could further explore his new relationship to his photography, an unexpected fall prevented Fukase from continuing this dialogue.

MAKI FUKUOKA

Biography

Born in Bifuka-cho, Hokkaido, 25 February 1934. Attended Nihon University Department of Fine Art, 1952–1956. Worked as a photographer for advertisement and publishing companies 1956–1968; Freelance photographer 1968–1992. Ina Nobuo Award 1976. Ina Nobuo Special Award 1992; The 8th Higashikawa Special Prize 1992. Fell from stairs near his favorite bar, and stopped photographing 20 June 1992.

Individual Exhibitions

1960 *Seiyujo no Sora* (Sky over an Oil Refinary) Konishisoku Gallery; Tokyo, Japan
1961 *Buta wo Korose!* (A Slaughterhouse); Ginza Gallery; Tokyo, Japan
1976 *Tori*; Ginza Nikon Salon and traveled to Shinjuku Nikon Salon; Tokyo and Nikon Salon; Osaka, Japan
1978 *Yôko*; Nikon Salon; Tokyo, Japan
1979 *Karasu 1979*; Ginza Nikon Salon; Tokyo and traveled to Shinjuku Nikon Salon; Tokyo and Nikon Salon, Osaka, Japan
1981 *Karasu Tokyo hen*; Ginza Nikon Salon; Tokyo and traveled to Nikon Salon; Osaka, Japan
1982 *Karasu Shûshô*: Ginza Nikon Salon; Tokyo, Japan
1983 *Arukume 1* (Walking Eyes/Part 1); Ginza Nikon Salon; Tokyo, Japan
Arukume 2 (Walking Eyes/Part2); Shinjuku Nikon Salon; Tokyo, Japan
1985 *Irohanihoheto* (ABC...); Ginza Nikon Salon; Tokyo, Japan
Karasu kei (Ravens Scene); Polaroid Gallery; Tokyo, Japan
1987 *Ravens*; Zait Photo Salon; Tokyo, Japan
Chichi no Kioku (Memories of Father); Ginza Nikon Salon; Tokyo, Japan
1990 *Shikei Tabi no Tayori* (Private Scenes—Letters from Journeys); Ginza Nikon Salon; Tokyo, Japan
1992 *Shikei '92* (Private Scenes); Ginza Nikon Salon, Tokyo, Japan
The Solitude of Ravens; Stephen Wirtz Gallery; San Francisco, California, and Robert Mann Gallery; New York, New York

Group Exhibitions

1974 *New Japanese Photography*; Museum of Modern Art, New York, New York
1975 *Fifteen Photographers*; Museum of Modern Art, Tokyo, Japan
1976 *Juninin no Shashinka ni yoru Jisen Sakuhinten*; Shiseidô The Ginza, Tokyo, New York
Neue Fotografie aus Japan; Graz Municipal Museum of Art, Graz, Austria
1979 *Japan: A Self-Portrait*; International Center of Photography; New York, New York, and traveling
Japanese Photography and its Origin, Callaria d'Arte Moderna; Bologna and traveled to Palozzo Reale; Milan, Palais des Beaux-Arts; Brussels, and the Institute of Contemporary Arts; London
1984 *Six Contemporary Photographers*; Seibu Art Forum; Tokyo, Japan
1985 *Black Sun: The Eyes of Four*; Oxford Museum of Modern Art, Oxford, England, and traveled to The Philadelphia Museum of Art; Philadelphia, Pennsylvania
Paris, New York, Tokyo; Tsukuba Museum of Photography, Tsukuba, Japan
1988 *Revenge of Memories*; Forum Stadtpark; Graz, Austria
1989 *Juichinin no 1965–75* (1965–75 by Eleven Photographers); Yamaguchi Prefectural Museum; Yamaguchi, Japan
1989 *Photography Now*; Victoria and Albert Museum; London, England
1990 *New Documents '90*; Toyama Prefectural Museum of Modern Art; Toyama
1996 *By Night*; Foundation Cartier pour L'Art Contemporain; Paris

Selected Works

Shibaura, 1963
Kudan Kyokai, 1964
Hakodate, 1975 (from the series "The Solitude of Ravens")
Kanazawa, 1977 (from the series "The Solitude of Ravens")
London, 1989

Further Reading

Breicha, Otto, Ben Watanabe, and John Szarkowski. *Neue Fotografie aus Japan*. Graz and Vienna: Museum des 20. Jahrhunderts, 1977.
Colombo, Attilio, and Isabella Doniselli. *Japanese Photography Today and its Origin*. Bologna: 1979.
Holborn, Mark. *Black Sun: The Eyes of Four*. Millerton, NY: Aperture, 1986.
Iizawa, Kôtaro. *Fukase Masahisa*. Tokyo: Iwanamishoten, 1998.
Ollman, Arthur. *The Model Wife*. Boston: Bulfinch Press, 1999.
Szarkowski, John, and Shoji Yamagishi. *New Japanese Photography*. New York: Museum of Modern Art, 1974.
Yamagishi, Koko. "A Photographer's Quest for Himself." In *La Photographie Traversée*. Arles, Actes Sud (2000): 188–190.
Yamagishi, Shoji, Capa Cornell, and Taeko Tomioka. *Japan: A Self-Portrait*. New York: International Center of Photography, 1979.

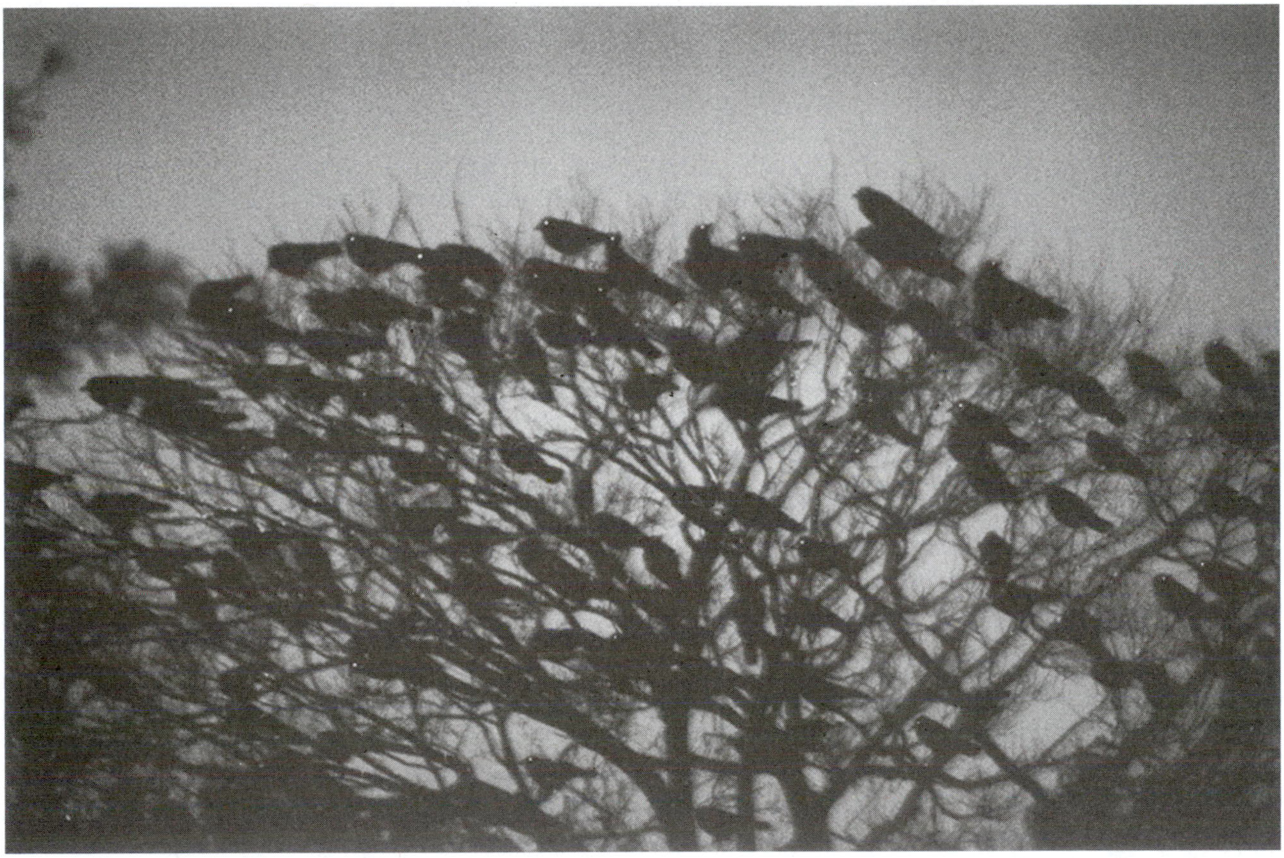

Masahisa Fukase, Kanazawa, 1977.
[© *Masahisa Fukase Estate. Courtesy Robert Mann Gallery*]

MIRAN FUKUDA

Japanese

Exemplary of the young generation of Japanese artists emerging at the end of the century, Miran Fukuda is known as a multi-media artist who often deals with issues of authorship, authenticity, and the coding of visual information, and the relationships among photography, painting, and consumer culture. While she does not create photographs in any traditional manner, in her art Fukuda often deals with her senses developed through photography, the history of art, and the digital culture, and she expands upon the experiments of the conceptual photographers of the 1970s and 1980s, including figures such as Gilbert & George, Robert Heinecken, and Richard Prince.

Fukuda was born into a family of artists; her maternal grandfather was an illustrator of children's books, and her father, Shigeo Fukuda, is perhaps Japan's best-known graphic designer of the post-World War II era. She grew up in a family home where prints by American Pop Artists Roy Lichtenstein and Andy Warhol were hung, and it was not surprising that Fukuda began considering an artistic career at age 15.

Upon completing a master's degree in oil painting at the prestigious Tokyo University of Fine Art and Music in 1987, Fukuda started receiving attention from Japan's art world and received numerous awards, including the 32nd (1989) Yasui Prize (created in honor of Sotaro Yasui, a Japanese modernist painter) for her still life painting *Wednesday* as the youngest recipient in the history of the award, which was given annually until 1996 to an artist of excellence younger than age 50 pursuing representational painting. Soon, she started showing internationally, including the traveling exhibition *Photography and Beyond* in Japan (1995), where she showed six photo-based works, including *Tablecloth* (1990), acrylic paint and commercially photo-printed plastic on panel; *Still Life: Apple, Pears, Cake Boxes and Pot* (1992), color photograph; and *The Princess Margarita as Seen by Doña Maria Augustina* (1992), acrylic on board) that demonstrated her unique conceptual interplay between photography and painting mediums.

To Fukuda, art is a means of expression through which she challenges viewers on conventional recognition and concepts of art, and through which she proposes new ways of looking and thinking. Further, Fukuda believes that her work, a realized manifestation of her thoughts and values, is effective only if it is transmitted to a viewer as a clear opinion, as if it were an excellent writing piece. Desiring her paintings not to be the paintings of the past, while acknowledging they are like paintings from the past, and desiring her work to be revolutionary, Fukuda has investigated and challenged the issue of "subjectivity" in the work of art, which, she believes, has been a core element of historical painting. Fukuda has attempted to construct art through "coded" visual information, using well-known existing images and icons such as master European and Japanese paintings and Disney characters to minimize subjectivity in her work, presenting it as ready made and reproducible. Her investigation of the photographic medium, particularly newspaper photography, is related to this interest. Perhaps her best-known works dealing with this issue are *Gilbert & George and I* (2001) and *Frank Stella and I* (2001), both painted with acrylic on panel. Both paintings are based on enlarged snapshots in which Fukuda posed with well-known artists. She investigates whether snapshots, which usually exist as recorded evidence (i.e., I was there with the artists) rather than as art works, thus perhaps lacking "subjectivity" as art, can be turned into works of art. With respect to "authenticity," since 1996, Fukuda has been making a series of works, composed simply of a newspaper page which shows reproduction of her work (e.g., an exhibition review), titling it with a name of the newspaper and the date of publication, and giving it an edition number based upon a number of the newspaper printed. In this series, Fukuda focuses on the commercial practice of and market for reproductions of paintings, whether by her or a historical master painter, which reduces them to mere commodities, suggesting that there may be no conceptual (and perhaps no production value) difference between such fine arts reproductions and a newspaper reproduction. This critical approach is evident in Fukuda's installation *Mainichi Shimbun Newspaper, April 30, 2000* (2000). This work consists of a page from a newspaper showing an art review, including photographs of excited viewers at a Vermeer exhibition in Osaka, Japan, in which one photograph from the newspaper is enlarged to the extent that the Vermeer painting therein, *Girl with the Blue Turban*, is displayed in its original dimensions. Impressed with the high quality of reproduction available in newspaper printing and excited about the fact that the painting reproduced in the newspaper can be viewed as an original by dint of her re-contextualizing it, Fukuda placed a color reproduction of the painting over the photocopied painting in the enlarged newspaper photograph. Fukuda also used newspaper reproductions in earlier works, such as *Metrocard* (1995) by placing on one side of the Tokyo subway prepaid transit Metrocard well-known photo images from newspapers, covering the notorious 1995 Tokyo sarin attack by Aum cultists that killed and injured a number of subway passengers. Such images include casualties rescued on a subway station platform, heavily gas-masked and uniformed hazardous materials works decontaminating the subway, and one of the attackers presenting an innocent demeanor while being interviewed. These images, have become signature images of the attack and thus coded into the public's memory.

YASUFUMI NAKAMORA

See also: **Conceptual Photography; Gilbert & George; Photography in Japan; Vernacular Photography**

Biography

Born in Tokyo in 1963. In 1985, received BFA (in painting) from Tokyo National University of Fine Arts and Music. In 1987, received MFA from Tokyo National University of Fine Arts and Music and received Honorable Mention at *The 18th Contemporary Art Exhibition of Japan*. In 1989, received The Yasui Prize at *The 32nd Yasui Prize Exhibition*. In 1991, received the Triennale International Prize, the *VII Triennale India*

Selected Solo Exhibitions

1990 Tokyo Gallery, Tokyo
1992 *Hara Documents: Miran Fukuda* (Hara Museum of Contemporary Art)
1994 Nabisu Gallery, Tokyo
1995 Tokyo Gallery, Tokyo
1996 *One day One show*, Gallery 360°, Tokyo
2000 *Takumi Na Takurami (Ingenious Schemes), Miran Fukuda & Traditional Craftsmen* (Sumida Riverside Hall Gallery, Tokyo)
2001 *Shigeo Fukuda, Miran Fukuda* (Setagaya Art Museum, Tokyo)
2002 *Yurinso. Fukuda Miran. Ohara Museum of Art* (Yurinso, Ohara Museum of Art, Okayama, Japan)

Selected Group Exhibitions

1988 *The 17th International Art Exhibition of Japan*, Tokyo Metropolitan Art Museum and The Kyoto Municipal Museum of Art
1991 *VII Triennale India* (awarded International Award), New Delhi, India
1993 *The 1st Asia-Pacific Triennial Exhibition of Contemporary Art*, Queensland Art Gallery, Brisbane, Australia
The Return of the Exquisite Corpse, Drawing Center, New York, New York
1994 *Shinjyuku Shonen Art Exhibition*, on the streets, Kabukicho, Shinjuku, Japan
1994 *The 7th Busan Biennial*, Busan Culture Center, Busan, Korea
1995 *Make Believe*, Royal College of Art, London, England
The "VOCA" Exhibition, The Ueno Royal Museum, Tokyo
Photography and Beyond in Japan, Hara Museum of Contemporary Art, Tokyo, traveling to museums in North America including Corcoran Gallery of Art, Washington, D.C. and Los Angeles County Museum
1997 *The First Steps: Emerging Artists from Japan*, Grey Art Gallery, New York University, New York
Cities on the Move, Vienna Secession, Vienna, Austria and traveling to six museums including P.S. 1 Contemporary Art Center, Long Island City, New York
2000 *The 5th Biennial of Lyon*, the hall Tony Garnier, Lyon, France
2002 *New Acquisitions*, Hiroshima City Museum of Contemporary Art, Japan
2003 *Masterpieces of Contemporary "Japanese Paintings [Nihonga]"*, The Contemporary Art Museum, Kumamoto, Japan
2004 *20th Anniversary Exhibition: The Copy Age – From Duchamp through Warhol to Morimura*, The Museum of Modern Art, Shiga, Japan

Selected Works

Tablecloth, 1990
3D-waterfall, 1990
The Forge of Vulcan, 1992
Metrocard, 1995
Mainichi Shimbun Newspaper, April 30, 2000, 2000
Gilbert & George and I, 2001
Frank Stella and I, 2001

Further Reading

Conceptual Photography; History of Photography: 8: the 1990s; Photography in Japan; *Vernacular Photography*; Gilbert & George.

Picturesque, Miran Fukuda 1992–1998 (1998), Asahi Shimbun, Tokyo, Japan; *Miran Fukuda* (2001), Setagaya Art Museum, Tokyo, Japan.

JAROMÍR FUNKE

Czech

In the history of Czech photography Jaromír Funke (1896–1945) is considered both a pioneer of the modern view of photography in the 1920s and 1930s, as well as one of the most influential intellectuals and pedagogues. Next to Karel Teige, concerning his journalistic activities, and Josef Sudek, concerning his photographic work, he is without any doubt one of the most important personalities of the left cultural scene of those years.

Funke, from a wealthy family, photographed since his twelfth year. In his first self portrait he selected a photograph in the mirror, as if he wanted to point out that not only the photographed one is of importance, but also the way in which the photo was composed.

His study of medicine (which he had probably begun in 1915, in order to escape war service) he gave up in 1919 and then studied law at his father's request. His first painting and graphic attempts (which he sent for evaluation to Karel Teige) showed him that talent was lacking. Later he spoke of the fact that an internal need to express himself "in pictures" led him to choose photography.

In 1922, Funke discontinued his law studies without any exams. He decided to dedicate himself mainly to photography. His first photographic attempts, which he sent to the magazine "*Fotografický obzor*" (Photographic Review), and which are reminiscent of the work of Jacques Henri Lartigue, were not published. It was only in 1924 that the Swiss magazine *Camera* printed—along with his articles on photography—his photographs. This was Funke's breakthrough in the Czech photographic circles. Invitations to exhibitions Paris and Toronto followed.

Against the generally prevailing pictorialist trend, Funke regarded the brightness and the accuracy of the photograph as its most important characteristic: He called it "photoingenuity," which can only be achieved by the lens of the camera. He defined modern photography as precise, with sharpness, eschewing manipulation or retouching of both the negative and positive. According to Funke, the photographer can achieve great success within the documentary and artistic traditions, if he avoids the prevailing "impressionistic" style. With his articles Funke commented on his own development, which had begun with the arranged experimental series "*Still life,*" done in 1923.

In his studio work, Funke photographed plates, glasses, phials, and transparent geometrical objects in elegant arrangements; these materials were supplemented (1924) by pasteboard or cardboard geometric forms. Style screen means were thereby the shade, which delineated the forms by exact light direction. Thus in the photograph "*Spirála*" (Spiral) shades of gray are embodied in the area of a triangle form as a result of the lighting. Funke began in 1925 to experiment with photographic abstraction using patterns of light and shade created by objects off-camera rather than the objects themselves. Funke saw therein a further confirmation of his thesis of "photoingenuity," by which it additionally wins more autonomy: Those "light-abstractions" confirm the "essence of the photography, which is developed by light and not by objects."

In one article in "*Fotografický obzor*" (Photographic Review, 1927) Funke dissociated himself from the Rayograms of Man Ray. For him a photograph is possible only as shot through the camera, and every photographic "product" that is created without it is not authentic:

> Those photographic specialities are not any more photographs. It finds neither a release act (of an interaction between successful shot and successful development, which expresses in consequence perfectly the creative idea M.Ch.) nor a gesture of release and still less the solution itself of a taken over task.

This criticism, which Funke employed on the illustrations of the surrealistic book of "*Les champs délicieux*" by Man Ray, he repeated again in a manifesto project, which he addressed together with František Drtikol to the artist union "*Umělecká beseda*" (Artist Federation) in Prague. Both photographers rejected pictorialism and suggested a new modern direction. Funke and Drtikol began to experiment at the same time with the conscious integration of light and shadow into the photographic picture shot. For Drtikol this technique served to underscore the decorative quality of the picture, particularly in his nudes; Funke used it in order to create abstract forms.

Along with Funke's fine arts efforts, he produced a large number of commercial works, including architecture, advertising, landscape photography, and portraiture. At the end of the 1920s Funke was considered one of the most progressive photographers in Czechoslovakia, whose works received attention everywhere and whose critical contributions in different magazines were often discussed. Now, as before, most of his texts could be read as explanations or additions to his photographic intentions. Thus Funke extended for example his theses over the "photoingenuity" by terms of the integration and visualisation of the emotions, which he formulated (1929) on the occasion of the second member exhibition of the *Czech Photographic Society* (Česká fotografická společnost) in Prague 1929: "For us the photographic purism [that is, "photoingenuity"] is fundamental, to which two substantial components belong: Feeling and arrangement."

He shared these opinions with another well known Czech photographer, Josef Sudek, who also lived in Kolín and who was of the same age. The two took up the industrialization of the city—so that it is difficult sometimes to differentiate between the two. It was Sudek, who convinced Funke to participate further in international exhibitions although both were excluded from all Czech photographic circles either because of their criticism of the pictorialism, which was still in vogue. During their excursions they were joined by the photographer Eugen Wiškovský, who—contrary to Funke—was always interested in practical applications reflected theoretically upon the point of view of the "*Gestalt*"—psychology over the medium. Wiškovský propagated the *Neue Sachlichkeit* (New Objectivity) in the Czech Republic, particularly after the legendary *Film und Foto* exhibition of 1929 in Stuttgart. The cooperation at the magazine published by Karel Teige "*ReD*" (Revue Devětsilu) in 1929 began after his acquaintance with Anna Kellerová, later his wife. She was active in the communist movement and her father was one of the initial members of the Czech communist party. She probably arranged the contact with the poet František Halas, who drew Teige's attention to Funke. In "*Red III,*" No. 1 some photographs of Funke appeared. He was also invited to supply his photographs for the magazine "*Index,*" published in Moravian Brno. At the end of 1929 he contributed slides that reproduced abstract photographs to a new form of scenery in the Brno City Theatre.

At the beginning of the 1930s, the exhibition "*Nová fotographie*" (New photography) presented the Czech avant-garde photography in its breadth for the first time. Funke took part both organizationally and with his own work. In the summer of that same year he was in Brno, where he was to cooperate in an advertising film, but without success. Instead he took photographs of newer buildings of Czech avant-garde architects, among them from Bohuslav Fuchs. These works, which appeared in Fuchs' self-edition, have been lost.

Funke's interest in socially engaged photography continued to grow while he at the same time turned down an offer to teach at the Bauhaus in Dessau with Walter Peterhans because Peterhans's aesthetic contradicted his own. Instead he accepted the offer to teach at the Slowakian "*Učňovské Škole Fotografické*" (Slowakian Apprentice School on Photography, 1931–1934) and at the *Škole uměleckých řemesel* (School of Applied Arts, starting from school year 1931–1932 to 1934). A stay in Bratislava, which compared with Prague was a city pregnant with social differences, and his journeys through Slovakia and finally through that part of the Ukraine (Subcarpathian Ruthenia), which belonged to the Czechoslovakian Republic, shocked Funke in such a way that he reported photographically the poverty (cycle *Špatné bydlení*, Bad living, 1930–1931).

In the 1930s Funke created some of his most well-known works, including the series *Čas trvá* (Time Persists). He also published the folios *Nová architektura* (New Architecture, 1931), *Fotografie vidí povrch* (Photography Sees the Surface, 1935), and he was particularly busy with teaching. He sketched (1933) guidelines for photography instruction at higher commercial schools, which were immediately applied at the "*Státní grafická kola*" (State School of Graphic Arts) in Prague. At the end of 1934 Funke asked for a transfer from Bratislava to Prague, and on February 1, 1935 his request was approved.

His articles, lectures, and photographs witness the variety of his interests, making Funke one of the most demanded personalities of cultural life in Prague. In 1936, he became a member of the most important group of artists in Czechoslovakia at that time—*Mánes.* He prepared numerous publications (or worked on them), in which his photographs (and those of his colleagues) were featured. He also took part in organizing—and contributing to—the new photo section *Mánes* (February–April). Because teaching at the *Státní grafická Škola* in Prague took up five to eight hours daily, Funke's public engagements were reduced considerably in order to have the time for other work.

By the outbreak of World War II in 1939, travel possibilities were limited. Funke photographed nevertheless in the area of Louny (symbolically the origin of the Czech nation), photographed churches and monuments in Prague (the fear that they could be destroyed by the war was not groundless), and returned occasionally to Kolín to photograph there also.

In Kolín he survived an immense bombing of the city in August 1944 but fear accompanied him constantly. On March 22, 1945, Jaromír Funke died suddenly because an emergency operation, needed because of an intestine perforation, could not be carried out due to a four-hour air raid alarm.

MILAN CHLUMSKY

See also: **Abstraction, Photogram; Drtikol, Frantisek; Man Ray; Pictorialism; Sudek, Josef; Teige, Karel**

Biography

Born in Skuteč (Bohemia) on 1 August 1896. Childhood in Kolín, there attending High School. 1914 admission at the "French Lyzeum" (Secondary School) in Grenoble. 1915 "Abitur" at the High School in Kolín. 1915 Funke studied medicine in Prague. 1919 changed to study law. Between 1919 and 1922 also attended lectures on philosophy and history of art at the Philosophical Faculty. 1920 began intensively to dedicate himself to photography. Met Josef Sudek in Kolín, with whom he maintained a lifelong friendship. Photography publications in the Swiss magazine *Camera*, first participation in exhibitions (Toronto, Paris). Member of the *Photo Club Prague* (March 1924). In January 1925 co-founded the *Czech Photographic Society*. In 1927 gave first public lectures on photography. 1929 exclusion of Funke (and Sudek) from the *Czech Photographic Society*. 1929 the beginning of his cooperation at the magazines *Red* and *Index*. In April 1930 participated in the legendary exhibition "*New Photography*" in the Mansarde of the Aventinum (Aventinská Mansarda). From September 1931 lectured at "*Škola umeleckých remesiel*" in Bratislava (School of Applied Arts in Bratislava) and the "*Učňovské Škole Fotografické*" (Apprentice School of Photography, in Bratislava). From March 1932 photographs for the monthly magazine "*Nová Bratislava*" (New Bratislava). At the beginning of 1933 prepared guidelines for photography instruction used in the school year 1933–1934 at *Státní Grafická Škola* v Praze (State School of Graphic Arts in Prague). In May 1933 external professor to this SSGA in Prague. 1.9. 1934 regular professor for photography in Bratislava. 1.2. 1935 appointment as regular professor for photography at SSGA in Prague. Apart from teaching, worked on several photographic cycles, notably on "*Čas trvá*" (Time Persists). Beside numerous portraits of well-known artists, Funke took photographs of Bohemian churches, monuments, and landscapes: After the outbreak of the war he intensified this personal "Mission héliographique" both in Prague as well as in the environment (Kolín, Karltejn, Louny, Poděbrady). During the war cooperated at numerous photo publications, among them the Portfolio *Moderní česká fotografie* (Modern Czech Photography, Prague, 1943). Numerous lectures on photographic techniques and esthetic problems of the photography. Died March 22, 1945.

Individual Exhibitions

1931 *Kolín ve fotografi* (The city of Kolín in the photography), Kolín
1935 *Krásná jizba* (Nice Living), Prague (also shown in Bratislava 1936)
1941 *Louny ve fotografii* (The city of Louny in the photography), Louny
1943 *Chrám sv. Bartoloměje v Kolíně ve fotografii Professora Funkeho* (The Cathedral of St. Bartholomeus in Kolín in the Photography of Professor Funke), Kolín
1946–1947 *Professor Jaromír Funke*, Kolín
1953 *Krásný Kolín v umělecké fotografii Professora Jaromíra Funkeho* (A nice city of Kolín in the artistic photography of Professor Jaromír Funke), Kolín
1958 *Kabinet Jaromíra Funkeho* (The photographic cabinet of Jaromír Funke), Brno, (The same exhibition in Kolín, 1960)
1965 Jar*omír Funke, fotografie z let 1924–1944* (Jaromír Funke, The Photography from 1924–1944), Gallery Vincenc Kramář, Prague
1976 *J.F.: Fotografie* (J.F.: Photography), District Museum, Kolín nad Labem, and traveled in Aachen, 1976, Bochum, 1977, West Berlin, 1978, Paris,1979
1979 *Kabinet Jaromíra Funkeho* (The photographic cabinett of Jaromír Funke), Brno, and traveled in Prakapas Gallery, NewYork 1982
1984 *Jaromír Funke, Surface of the Reality*, Gallerie Rudolf Kicken, Cologne and Basel
1986 *Jaromír Funke, Vintage prints*, Robert Koch Gallery, San Francisco
1986 Sudek, Funke, Old City Hall in Prague
1993 *Funkeho Louny* (The city of Louny in Photography of Funke), District Museum, Louny
1993 *Funke, Výstava fotografií ze sbírky lounského muzea* (Funke, Photographic Exhibition from the Collection of Museum of Louny), Dobrá Gallery, Prague
1993 *Jaromír Funke- Fotografie* (Jaromír Funke- Photography), Funke Photography Festival in Kolín, District Museum, Kolín
1993 *Lounský cyklus* (Photographic Studies on the city of Louny), Louny
1995 *Jaromír Funke. Fotografie 1919–1943.* Věci skleněné a obyčejné (Jaromír Funke. Photography 1919–1943. Objects from glass, banal objects), Prague House of Photography
1996 *Jaromír Funke. Svatovítský cyklus* (Jaromír Funke, Photographic Studies on the Cathedral of St.Veit in Prague)

Selected Group Exhibitions

1923 *Druhá výstava ČKFA v Českých Budějovicích* (Second Exhibition of the Czech Club of Photographers Amateurs), City Center Museum in České Budějovice
1924 *I. Výstava Svazu ČKFA v Praze* (Ist Exhibition of the Czech Club of Photographers Amateurs in Prague)

1924 *19° Salon International de Photographie*, Paris
1924 *33. Toronto Salon of Photography*, Toronto
1925 *2nd Midland Salon of Photography*, Birmingham, England
1925 *The Northern Photography Exhibition*, Bradford, England
1925 *Salon International d'Art Photographique*, Calais, France
1925 *International Exhibition of Pictorial Photography*, New Westminster, Canada
1925 *20° Salon international de Photographie*, Paris
1925 *30th Annual Exhibition of Pictorial Photography*, London
1925–1926 *Primo Salon Italiano d'Arte Fotografica Internazionale*, Torino, Italy
1926 *7th Annual Salon of Photography*, Buffalo Camera Club, The Albright Art Gallery, Buffalo, New York
1926 *Foersta Internationella Fotografiska Salongen*, Stockholm, Sweden
1926 *Zealand Salon of Photography*, Dunedin, New Zealand
1926 *II. Salon International*, Zaragoza, Spain
1926 *13th Annual Pittsburgh Salon of Photographic Art*, Pittsburgh, Pennsylvania
1984 *Czech Photography 1918–1938*, Museum Folkwang, Essen, Germany

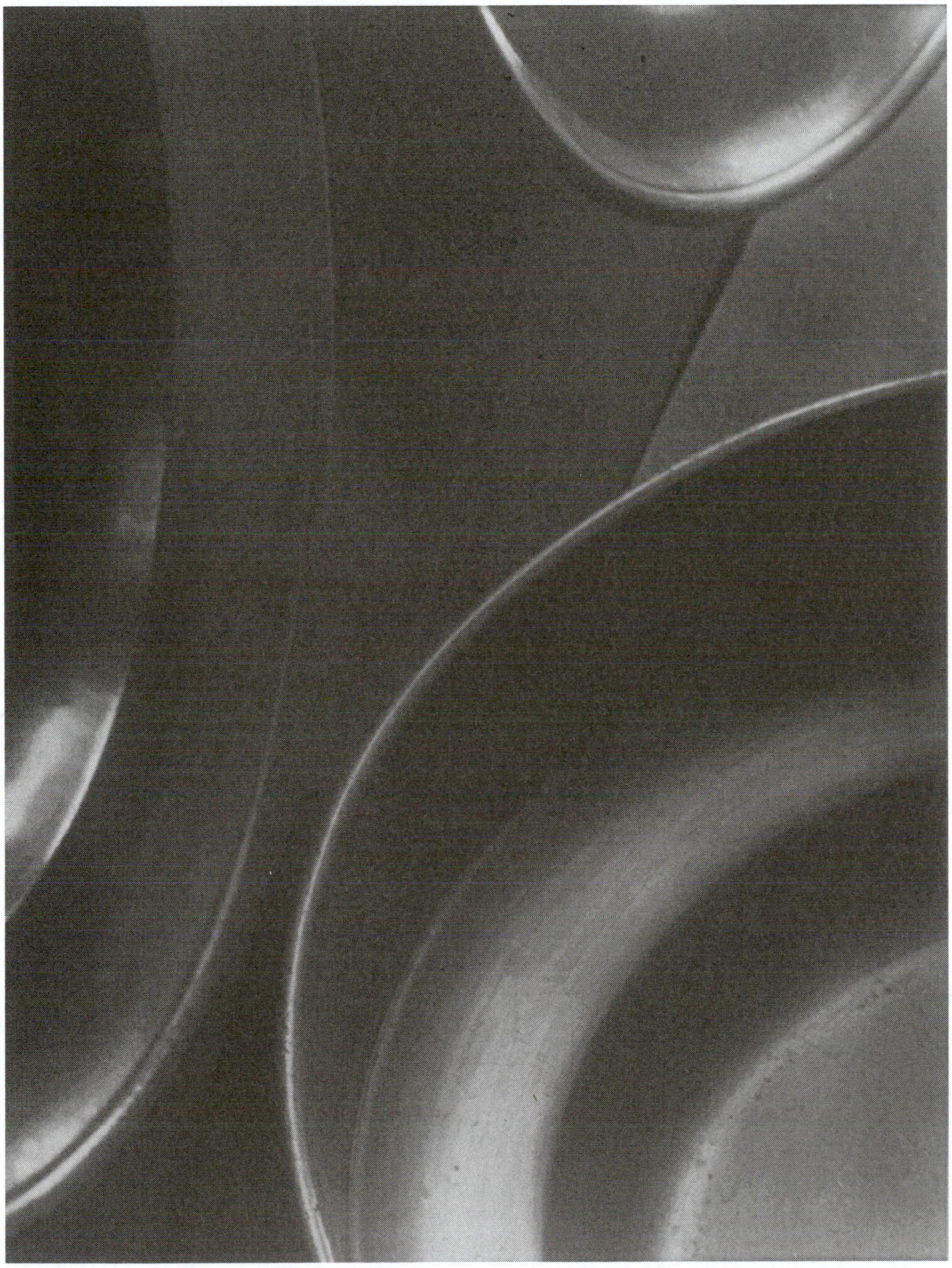

Jaromír Funke, Still life (plates), 1923, Photo: Jean-Claude Planchet.
[*CNAC/MNAM/Dist. Réunion des Musées Nationaux/Art Resource, New York*]

1986 *Facets of Modernism: Photographs from the San Francisco Museum of Modern Art*, San Francisco Museum of Modern Art, San Francisco, California
1989–1990 *Czech Modernism: 1900–1945*, Museum of Fine Arts, Houston, Texas and traveling
1990 *Les avantgardes techèques*, Arles, Texas
1994 *Czech and Slovak Photography from Between the Wars to the Present*, Fitchburg Art Museum, Fitchburg, Massachusetts

Further Reading

Coke, Van Deren, and Diana Dupont. *Facets of Modernism: Photographs from the San Francisco Museum of Modern Art*. New York: Hudson Hills, 1986.
Tucker, Anne. *Czech Modernism: 1900–1945*. Houston: Fine Arts Museum, 1989.
Dufek, Antonin. *Jaromír Funke (1896–1945), Pioneering Avant-Garde Photography*. Moravian Gallery, 1996.

SEIICHI FURUYA

Japanese

During his early studies in architecture, Seiichi Furuya began photographing the everyday aspects of life in Tokyo. This relationship with his camera led to him giving up architecture and devoting himself entirely to the study and practice of photography. But it was not until he left Japan for Vienna, Austria that his professional life in photography began. From the mid-1970s through today, Furuya has developed work that ranges from the deeply personal, evolving images of his wife, family, and home, to the changing political and environmental landscapes that surrounded him in Eastern Europe. Furuya's work captures notions of living both geographically and emotionally on life's borders, and is punctuated by the moment the Berlin Wall fell. He continues to engage viewers with photographic insights about home, memory, and the ways of revisiting and interpreting the divisions of space and ethos.

Born in Japan, Furuya moved to Vienna after his photography studies in 1973. After two years in Vienna, he moved to Graz, Austria, where he met Christine Gössler, who immediately became the subject of many of his photographs. They wed in 1978, during Furuya's first return to Japan since his departure. Upon their return to Graz, Furuya became more involved with other artists and in seeking exhibition possibilities. In 1980, photographs of Gössler were published in the magazine *Camera Austria*. That same year, Furuya spent time in Amsterdam, where he documented the coexistence of families and strangers, often distressed or displaced on the city's streets. Although a more distant view of the conflict between the simultaneous closeness and isolation involved in relationships, these photographs paralleled the resolution Furuya may have sought in his images of Gössler. Following Amsterdam, Furuya relocated to Vienna, where he and Gössler had a son, Komyo Klaus, in 1981.

While establishing himself in the Austrian and European worlds of photography, Furuya also remained committed to the work of other Japanese photographers, and encouraged their involvement in the European art world. He introduced such figures as Nobuyoshi Araki, Daido Moriyama, and Shomei Tomatsu to the exhibition and publishing practices in which he was flourishing. During this time, Furuya continued to photograph Gössler while carrying on with his own journey as a Japanese foreign national living and working in Cold War Eastern Europe. Mental and physical borders and boundaries appear in his 1981–1983 works entitled *National Frontier*. For this work, Furuya used the idea of himself as the traveling, displaced photographic eye to capture a story about the borders between Austria, Czechoslovakia, Hungary, and Yugoslavia. The story consists not only of the physical evidence of division and boundaries, but of the human response of inhabiting a space that is constantly divided, questioning whether an identifiable place exists at all. Furuya's own interactions with the fractured physical and mental spaces consist of his written responses to those images.

In 1984, Furuya accepted a job as a translator for a Japanese construction company, and he and his family moved to Dresden. Gössler's severe depression eventually led to hospitalization, and the family decided to move to East Berlin. Gössler, ill and less frequently photographed, nevertheless remained Furuya's consistent and beloved subject. In 1985, Gössler committed suicide by jumping to her death. Furuya photographed the traces of the tragedy: her neatly placed shoes left behind, her body lying on the ground, the police approaching the scene. These were his final images of Gössler, and even then the camera proved its power as a connecting force between the couple.

Furuya did not exhibit photographs of his wife until 1989, four years after her death. That year, Furuya developed the first of two *Mémoires* exhibitions, which consisted predominantly of images of Gössler, and centered around the themes of life and death. Revisiting a life through the memorial of the photograph was something that Furuya chose to do both privately and publicly, just as he had done in his earlier years while documenting Gössler. It was in preparation for exhibiting loss that Furuya publicly presented Gössler's images to the world. In the book accompanying this 1989 exhibition, Furuya did not arrange Gössler's images in a chronological replay of their life together. Instead, he pursued the ways in which his memories were shifting, altering, and reconciling a loss of love and life with an attempt to organize the photographs of a living memory.

In 1995, Furuya developed a second *Mémoires* series, again visiting the past and the need to resituate his photographic memories. For the 1995 series, Furuya included photographs of both Gössler and their son. This reinterpretation of his work led to critical success and a second accompanying publication. By rearranging his memories again in 1995, Furuya enacted both the role of photographer/author, the one who is in control of the arrangement, and also the viewer/spectator, who begins looking and remembering differently during this later phase of life and work. An exercise in dealing with death through visual representations and photographic communication, Furuya's work adheres to the varying roles of engaging with an image. Themes of loss and emptiness are also evident in the photographs without Gössler: the moment Furuya isolates an urban street scene or rural landscape, the image is often cut or bound by some event or person out of range.

The Model Wife exhibition in 2000 placed Furuya's work alongside several prominent photographers, including Baron Adolph de Meyer, Alfred Stieglitz, Edward Weston, Harry Callahan, Emmet Gowin, Lee Friedlander, Masahisa Fukasse, and Nicholas Nixon. The exhibition focused on the enduring complex relationship between husband and wife when the two are photographer and subject. In 2004, Furuya's *alive* exhibition in Vienna marked a transitional moment in the artist's process of remembering with a collection of works from 1970 to 2002. These photographs remain untitled, but each offers a date and location, arranged according to Furuya's evolving memories.

HEATHER BLAHA

Biography

Born in Izu, Japan, 1950. Studied architecture in Numazu, 1966–1969. Studied photography at the Tokyo Polytechnic University, 1970–1972; co-founded photo magazine *Camera Austria*, 1980; published *AMS* by *Camera Austria*, 1980–1981; co-founded the Austrian Photo Archive, 1983; co-curated and co-edited exhibitions and catalogues for: *Daido Moriyama*, Graz, 1980, *Shomei Tomatsu: Japan 1952–1981*, Graz, 1984, *Araki. Akt Tokyo. 1971–1991*, Graz, 1984, and *Keep in Touch. Positions In Japanese Photography*, Graz, 2003. Received the Camera Austria Award for Contemporary Photography, Graz, 1993; Rupertinum Photography Award, Salzburg, 2000; Ina Nobuo Prize, Tokyo, 2002. Lives with his son, Komyo Klaus in Graz, 1987–present.

Individual Exhibitions

1975 *199 Fotos;* Fotogalerie im Schillerhof, Graz, Austria
1975 *Seiichi Furuya*; Fotogalerie Focus, Ljubljana, Slovenia
1978 *Seiichi Furuya*; Galerie im Taxispalais, Innsbruck, Austria
1980 *Portraits von Christine*; Forum Stadtpark, Graz Austria
1981 *AMS*; Forum Stadtpark, Graz, Austria
1982 *AMS*; Nagase Photo Salon, Tokyo, Japan *AMS*; Canon Photo Gallery, Amsterdam, Netherlands
1983 *Mythos und Ritual*; steirischer herbst '83, Kulturhaus Graz, Graz, Austria
1989 *Mémoires*; Neue Galerie am Landesmuseum Joanneum, Graz, Austria
1990 *Mémoires*; Museum moderner Kunst, Vienna, Austria
1991 *Staatsgrenze*; The Brno House of Arts, Brno, Czech Republic
Mémoires; Parco Gallery, Tokyo, Japan
Mémoires; exposure, Tokyo, Japan
1994 *Zu Hause in Berlin-Ost*; Forum Stadtpark, Graz, Austria
Vertreiben–Flüchten; Zeit-Foto Salon, Tokyo, Japan
Border/Borderless; Galerie Fotohof, Salzburg, Austria
1995 *Mémoires*; Fotomuseum Winterthur, Winterthur, Switzerland
1997 *Christine Furuya-Gössler 1978–1985*; Past Rays Gallery, Yokohama, Japan and traveling throughout Japan
1998 *Mémoires*; Museum für Photographie, Braunschweig, Germany
Christine Furuya-Gössler 1978–1985; Nikon Salon, Osaka, Japan
2000 *Portrait*; Rencontres Internationales de la photographie, Arles, France
Berlin-Ost 1985–1987; La Camera, Tokyo, Japan
2001 *Portrait*; Scalo Gallery, Zurich, Switzerland

2002 *Last Trip to Venice*; Shinjuku Nikon Salon, Tokyo/ Osaka Nikon Salon, Osaka, Japan
2003 *Seiichi Furuya*; Scalo Gallery, Zurich, Switzerland *Seiichi Furuya;* Wekstadt Graz, Graz, Austria

Group Exhibitions

1979 *5 Jahre Fotogalerie im Forum Stadtpark*; Graz, Austria
1980 *Europäische Fotografen, Teil I: Steiermark*; steirischer herbst '80, Forum Stadtpark, Graz, Austria
1981 *Erweiterte Fotografie/Extended Photography*; Wiener Secession, Vienna, Austria
Neue Fotografie aus Österreich; Forum Stadtpark, Graz, Austria and traveling
1982 *Lichtbildnisse*; Rheinisches Landesmuseum, Bonn, Germany
1983 *Portraits*; Fotogaleria Forum, Tarragona, Spain *Geschichte der Fotografie in Österreich*; Museum des 20. Jahrhunderts, Vienna, Austria
1988 *Die Rache der Erinnerung/The Revenge of Recollection*; steirischer herbst '88, Forum Stadtpark, Graz, Austria *Stadtpark eins*; Villette in Cham, Zug, Switzerland
1990 *Zeichen im Fluss*; Museum des 20. Jahrhunderts, Vienna, Austria
1992 *Zeitgenössische Photographie aus der Sammlung des Museums moderner Kunst in Wien*; National Gallery of Slovakia, Bratislava, Slovakia
1993 *Border/Borderless*; Tokyo Metropolitan Museum of Photography, Tokyo, Japan
1994 *Zu Hause in Berlin-Ost*; Galeria Mesta Bratislavy, Bratislava, Slovakia
Vertreiben–Flüchten; Nederlands Fotomuseum, Rotterdam, Netherlands
1995 *Antagonismes*; Musée de l'Elysée, Lausanne, Switzerland*Antagonismes*; Centre national de la photographie, Paris, France *New Japanese Photography*; Civic Art Gallery, Yokohama, Japan
1997 *The Artist & An Urban Environment*; Art Gallery Slovenj Gradec, Slovenj Gradec, Slovenia
1998 *Love's Body*; Tokyo Metropolitan Museum of Photography, Tokyo, Japan and traveling
2000 *The Model Wife*; Museum of Photographic Arts, San Diego, California and traveling
2001 *Open Ends*; Museum of Modern Art, New York, New York

Selected Works

Izu (Japan), 1978
Portrait of Christine, Graz and Vienna, (series) 1978–1984
Mémoires, 1989

Further Reading

Honnef, Klaus. *AMS*. Graz: Edition Camera Austria, 1981.
Faber, Monika, Werner Fenz, Christine Frisinghelli, and Wilfried Skreiner. *Mémoires*. Graz: Edition Camera Austria/Neue Galeria am Landesmuseum Joanneum, 1989.
Stahel, Urs, and Toshiharu Ito. *Seiichi Furuya, Mémoires 1995*. Zurich: Scalo, 1995.
Furuya, Seiichi. *Christine Furuya-Gössler: Mémoires, 1978–1985*. Kyoto: Korinsha Press, 1997.
Faber, Monika. *Portrait*. Salzburg: Edition Fotohof, 2000.
Faber, Monika. *alive: Seiichi Furuya*. Vienna: Scalo, 2004.

ADAM FUSS

British

In a time when sophisticated single-lens-reflex (SLR) cameras are being increasingly challenged by rapid advances in the resolution and color quality of digital cameras, Adam Fuss stands apart in his commitment to photographic images made without the use of a camera. Mechanically if not conceptually aligning himself with the earliest photographers William Henry Fox Talbot, Louis Jacques Mandé Daguerre, and Joseph Nicéphore Niépce, Fuss works almost exclusively with paper exposed directly to light. His images are made with pinhole cameras, large-format photograms, and silver-plated daguerreotypes. But unlike his nineteenth-century predecessors, Fuss is less interested in the objective nature of such direct representations—the sheer fact of being able to capture the effect of light bouncing off objects in the world onto a sensitized medium—than he is in the metaphorical qualities that arise from direct exposures. Metaphorical associations abound quite naturally from the timeless, fundamental simplicity of his chosen subject matter: flora and fauna of the natural world as exemplified by sunflowers, swans, snakes, and eviscerated rabbits, and elemental icons of pure energy such as water, smoke, skulls, and newborn babies. While today we take the photomechanical nature of photography for granted, Fuss's anachronistic rejection of the camera invites us to reexamine the kinds of imagery possible with the simplest of photographic means. When compounded by the open symbolism of his subject matter, the images create a profound sense of magic and loss, fluctuating between the wonder of life and the inevitable cessation of death.

As a child Fuss moved back and forth between the countryside of southeast England and southeast Australia, where his mother's family lived. Because of his father's illness and early death due to a stroke and the frequent relocations as a consequence, Fuss's childhood years were riddled with uncertainty. The only constant for the young artist seems to have been his connection to nature, a relationship that has obvious vestiges in his adult artistic preoccupations. Fuss became invested in photography while still a teenager, primarily interested in the gadgetry of the camera and photo processing. After boarding school in West Sussex, England, Fuss once again returned to Australia to work as an assistant in a photo studio where for the first time he was exposed to the history of photography and the concomitant theoretical issues. In 1982, Fuss moved to New York, working at the Metropolitan Museum, where roaming the sculpture halls at night he got the idea to take pinhole photographs of the classical figurative sculptures. Using a handmade pinhole camera affixed with an 8 × 10-inch photo back, Fuss created dramatic black-and-white images of the figures in space, the forms centralized in the photos by the encroaching circles of darkness and the focus fall-off so typical of pinhole photography. He devoted the next two years to shooting this first extended series of work, in part motivated in reaction against the consumerist, technological slant of commercial and art photography he saw elsewhere in the culture.

Fuss's focus on the photogram, for which he is perhaps best known, came about as the result of an accident. While shooting sculpture in a museum in Washington, D.C., he forgot to take the cover off the hole of his makeshift pinhole camera, but because light leaked within the box, when he developed the photograph he witnessed the image of dust floating within the interior of the camera recorded on the paper, essentially creating his first photogram. This revelation of what he could do without the camera led to an intense period of experimentation, during which Fuss happened upon many of the themes and sources that continue to today: large-headed sunflowers pressed en masse against photosensitive paper, seeming to grow and decay before our eyes; spirals of light created by swinging a suspended flashlight over Cibachrome paper; splashes and droplets of water caught in frozen motion, alternating chaotic and cataclysmic or serenely geometric; snakes writhing through talcum powder and swimming through water; young babies blotting out their own shadow against hyperpigmented fields of yellow. The water pictures are made by submerging photographic paper in a shallow pan filled with water, in which a splash is made, a snake released, a child lain down, the movement caught in brief flashes of light. Despite the static nature of the still images they exude a palpable energy, an immediate aftershock of the material presence of the subjects to their own representation. The artist describes his move from sophisticated SLR cameras to low-tech pinhole photography to cameraless photograms as a process of internalization, both in terms of photographic methodology and in psychological, personal terms. As he has brought the source closer and closer to direct contact with the surface of his media he has turned further and further inside himself for motivation and meaning. Both choices wrestle the image from a space of darkness, the one literally, the other metaphorically.

Two major series exist in Fuss's oeuvre: *Details of Love* and *My Ghost*. In the hotly colored Cibachrome photograms of *Details of Love* rabbits pair off facing one another, the cute and cuddly silhouettes suggesting all the solace and communion of romantic love. But their iconic bodies are in sharp contrast to the mass of entrails spread out from mouth to anus linking them in a visceral tangle of real and symbolic connections. Intensifying the photomechanical, photochemical nature of the images, the acids of the internal organs in contact with the paper shift the resulting color chemistry. In comparison, the color palette of *My Ghost* is a subtle range of a daguerreotype's silver blues and the graphic blacks, whites, and smokey grays of silver gelatin photograms. True to the title, all the images are ghostly and ethereal: sheer, see-through structures of old-fashioned children's nightdresses, swirls of smoke bellowing up across the picture plane, frantic birds caught in mid flight, silvery embossed swans spreading out their wings, stark figures of women hunched over in despair. Collectively they evoke a story of sadness and mourning, potent images of a childhood rendered indecipherable and abstract with age and memories strangely recollected through the photographic, creative process. Fuss's ability to render the literal metaphorical is at the heart of his production.

JAN ESTEP

See also: **Camera: Pinhole; Photogram**

Biography

Born in London, England, 1961. Living in New York, New York.

Individual Exhibitions

1985, 1988, 1989 Massimo Audiello Gallery; New York, New York
1990 Robert Miller Gallery; New York, New York
Massimo Audiello Gallery; New York, New York
Thomas Soloman's Garage; Los Angeles, California
1992 Fraenkel Gallery; San Francisco, California
Robert Miller Gallery, New York, New York
Thomas Soloman's Garage; Los Angeles, California
Akron Art Museum; Akron, Ohio
National Gallery of Victoria; Melbourne, Australia
1993 *Details of Love*; Robert Miller Gallery; New York, New York
1994 Fraenkel Gallery; San Francisco, California
In Between; Laura Carpenter; Santa Fe, New Mexico
Galerie Ghislaine Hussenot; Paris, France
1995 Robert Miller Gallery; New York, New York
Galerie Charlotte Lund; Stockholm, Sweden
1996 *Mary and Love Machine*; Rhona Hoffman Gallery; Chicago, Illinois
Pinhole Photographs; Baumgartner Galleries; Washington, D.C.
1997 *Adam Fuss: Fotogramme*; Galerie Sabine Knust; Munich, Germany
Maximillian Verlag; Munich, Germany
My Ghost; Galerie Charlotte Lund; Stockholm, Sweden
1998 *Pinhole Photographs*; Fay Gold Gallery; Atlanta, Georgia
Snake Powder, Spore and Mucus Prints; Fraenkel Gallery; San Francisco, California
Glenn Horowitz Booksellers, East Hampton, New York
1999 *Adam Fuss*; Fotomuseum Winterthur; Germany (traveled to Umea, Sweden)
My Ghost; Cheim & Read Gallery, New York, New York
Details of Love; Xavier Hufkens; Brussels, Belgium
2000 Galerie Karsten Greve; Milan, Italy
Martin Browne Gallery; Sydney, Australia
My Ghost; Galerie Charlotte Lund; Stockholm, Sweden
2001 *Adam Fuss: My Ghosts*; Fraenkel Gallery; San Francisco, California
Adam Fuss: My Ghost: Viewing Room, Yotsuya/Yumiko Chiba Associates; Shinjuku-ku, Tokyo, Japan
Galerie Karsten Greve; Cologne, Germany, and Paris France
2002 *Circular Forms*; Fraenkel Gallery; San Francisco, California
Adam Fuss: My Ghost; Xavier Hufkens; Brussels, Belgium
2003 *Adam Fuss*; Museum of Fine Arts; Boston, Massachusetts (traveled to Kunsthalle Bielefeld, Germany)
Adam Fuss: New Work Cheim & Read Gallery; New York, New York

Selected Group Exhibitions

1985 Alternative Museum; New York, New York
1986 Stux Gallery; Boston, Massachusetts
1987 *Adam Fuss, Mark Morrisroe, and The Starn Twins*; Massimo Audiello Gallery; New York, New York
Fine Arts Museum of Long Island; New York, New York (traveled)
1989 *Photography: Recent Acquisitions*; Australian National Gallery; Canberra, Australia
Frankfurter Kunstverein; Frankfurt, Germany
The Photography of Invention: American Pictures of the 1980s; National Museum of American Art, Smithsonian Institution; Washington, D.C.
1990 *Javier Baldeon and Adam Fuss*; Fundacio Caixa de Pensions; Barcelona, Spain
1991 *Whitney Biennial*; Whitney Museum of American Art; New York, New York
Circle; Queens Museum; Flushing, New York
The Interrupted Life; The New Museum of Contemporary Art; New York, New York
1992 *Healing*; Wooster Gardens; New York, New York
Skulpturen-Fragmente: The Vienna Secession; Vienna, Austria
1993 Robert Miller Gallery; New York, New York
The Language of Flowers: Paul Kasmin Gallery; New York, New York
1994 *Experimental Vision: The Evolution of the Photogram Since 1919*: Denver Art Museum; Denver, Colorado
The Abstract Urge: Recent Photographs Beyond Description: Ansel Adams Center for Photography; San Francisco, California
The Light Fantastic; Laguna Gloria Museum; Austin, Texas
Shooting Blind; Wesleyan University; Middletown, Connecticut
1995 *Silhouettes: Elliott Puckette, Adam Fuss, Christopher Bucklow*; Paul Kasmin Gallery; New York, New York
Abstract Photographs: Baltimore Museum of Art; Baltimore, Maryland
1996 *Under the Sun*; Fraenkel Gallery; San Francisco, California
Prospect 96; Frankfurt, Germany
Into the Deep Surface; PaceWildensteinMacGill; New York, New York
The Quiet in the Land: Everyday Life, Contemporary Art and The Shakers; Sabbathday Lake Shaker Museum; the Shaker Community, Sabbathday Lake, New Gloucester, Maine
1997 *Lynda Benglis, Adam Fuss, David Salle and Serge Spitzer*; Cheim & Read Gallery; New York, New York
Hope Photographs; National Arts Club; New York, New York
1998 *Still Life 1900–1998*; Marlborough Gallery; New York, New York
In Site '98—Mysterious Voyages: Exploring the Subject of Photography: The Contemporary Museum; Baltimore, Maryland
Tension; Robert Miller Gallery; New York, New York
Color; Edwynn Houk Gallery; New York, New York
1999 Pace Gallery; New York, New York (traveled to University Art Gallery; University of California at San Diego, San Diego, California; Bayly Art Museum, University of Virginia, Charlottesville, Virginia; George Eastman House, Rochester, New York)
Evoking Myths, Evoking Dreams; Alan Koppel Gallery; Chicago, Illinois
2000 *Tomorrow Land*; Alan Koppel Gallery; Chicago, Illinois
Now! Modern Photographs from the Permanent Collection; The Metropolitan Museum of Art; New York, New York.
Grace; curated by Bill Hunt of Rucco/Maresca; The Center for Photography at Woodstock; Woodstock, New York
Couples; Cheim & Read Gallery; New York, New York
2001 *Chorus of Lights: Photographs from the Collection of Sir Elton John*; High Museum of Art; Atlanta, Georgia

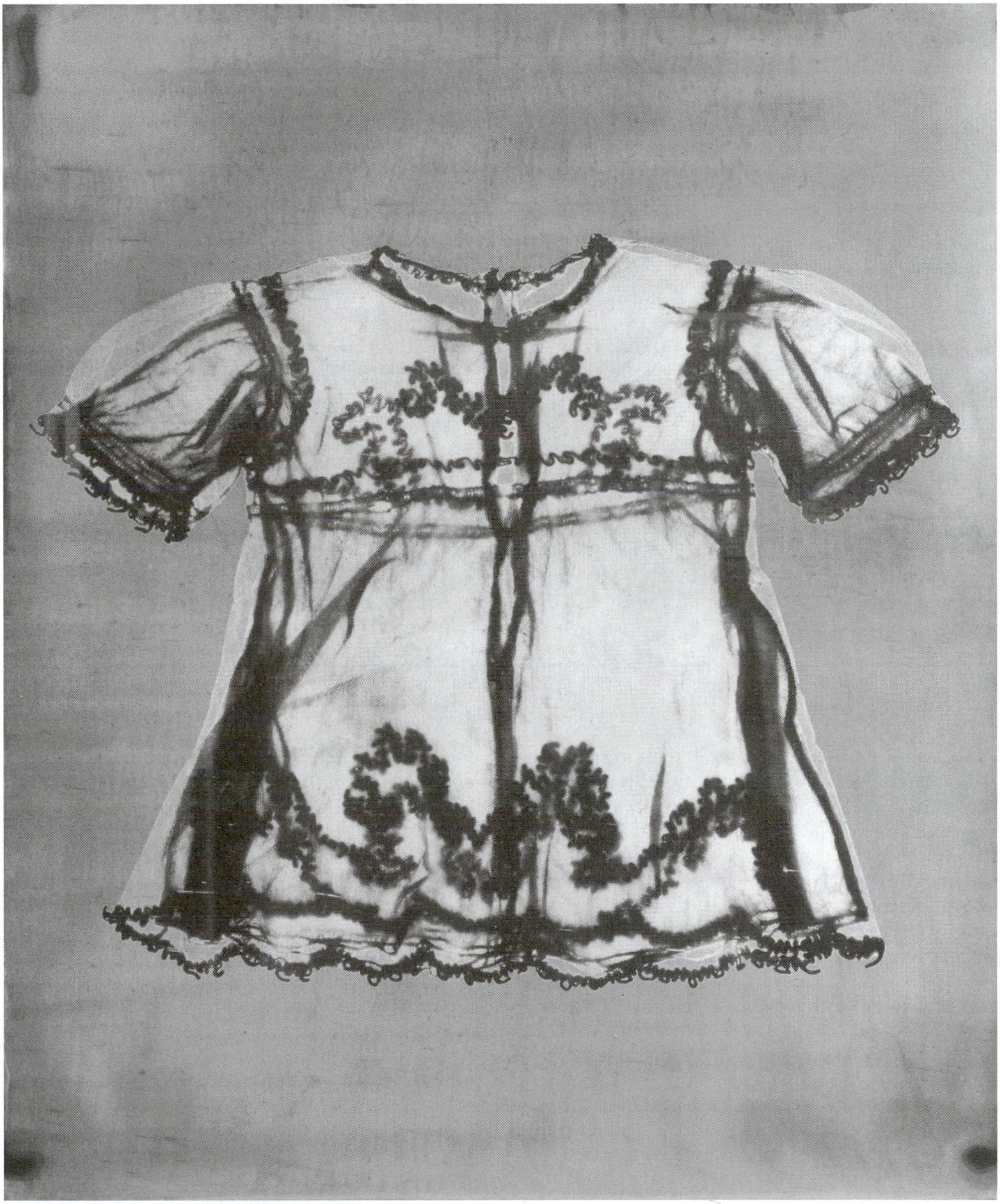

Adam Fuss, From the Series "My Ghost," 1999, Daguerreotype, 23 ½ × 19 ½".
59.7 × 49.5 cm, AF# D19.1, Unique.
[*Courtesy Cheim & Read, New York*]

Liquid Properties; Cheim & Read Gallery; New York, New York

Selected Works

Untitled (Ark), 1988 (description of image: black and white photogram of water drop with perfect circle ripple)
Invocation, 1992 (cibachrome photogram of baby in water against yellow)
Love, 1992 (cibachrome photogram of rabbits and entrails)
From the Series My Ghost, 2001 (black and white photograms, daguerreotypes, 2 or 3 from here: child's dress, swan, birds, smoke)
Untitled, 1990 (color photogram of sunflower in full bloom centered on paper)
Untitled, 1998 (color photogram of snake moving in water)

Further Reading

Fuss, Adam. "Behind the Scenes with Adam Fuss." *Art on Paper* 68–73, September–October (2002).
Fuss, Adam, Thomas Kellein, and David Galloway. *Adam Fuss*. New York: Distributed Art Publishers, 2003.
Fuss, Adam, and Jerry Kelly. *Adam Fuss: My Ghost*. Santa Fe, NM: Twin Palms Publishers, 2002.
Fuss, Adam, and Andrew Roth. *What is Man*. East Hampton, NY: Glen Horowitz, 1998.
Fuss, Adam, Andrew Roth, and Jerry Kelly. *My Ghost, Daguerreotypes from the Series*. East Hampton, NY: Roth Horowitz, 1999.
Fuss, Adam, and Constance Sullivan, eds. *Pinhole Photographs, Adam Fuss Photographers at Work, A Smithsonian Series*. Washington, DC, and London: Smithsonian Institution Press, 1996.
Grundberg, Andy, and Jerry Saltz. *Abstraction in Contemporary Photography*. Clinton, NY: Emerson Gallery, Hamilton College, 1989.
Hay Halpert, Peter. "Adam Fuss, Light and Darkness." *Art Press*, E13-E15, month (1993).
Parry, Eugenia, and Adam Fuss. *Adam Fuss*. Santa Fe, NM: Arena Editions, 1997.
Sand, Michael. "Adam Fuss." *Aperture* no. 133, 2, 44–53, Fall (1993).
Tannenbaum, Barbara. *Adam Fuss: Photograms*. Akron, OH: Akron Art Museum, 1992.

FUTURISM

Futurism is a movement of the Italian avant-garde that emerged in the early years of the century and exerted a strong influence on all aspects of Italian art, architecture and design, and literature. While having the greatest impact on the cultural life of Italy, Futurism was one of many movements that swept the European continent advocating revolutionary change and issuing a call to arms to artists, writers, and musicians of all types to rise up against the status quo and adopt modern forms and modern technologies with the intent of improving society. In photography this movement produced highly experimental works by numerous figures from the 1910s to the 1940s.

On February 20, 1909, the Parisian newspaper *Le Figaro* published the first futurist manifesto by Filippo Tommaso Marinetti, who explained his conceptual innovations for poetry. Thereafter, the Italian painters Umberto Boccioni, Giacomo Balla, Gino Severini, Carlo Carrà, and Luigi Russolo, among others, gathered around Marinetti and drew up *Manifesto dei pittori futuristi* (Manifesto for Futurist Painting), published in February 1910, and then *La pittura futurista: Manifesto tecnico* (Futurist Painting: Technical Manifesto), published in April of the same year. Later they created manifestos on other subjects, such as sculpture, music, architecture, clothes, and food.

The painters committed themselves, in the words of the French philosopher Henri Bergson, to the goal of representing the inner, subjective perception of a body's movement in flux and presenting its apparent transposition with other bodies and its dematerialization. At the same time in Rome, Anton Giulio Bragaglia and his brother Arturo were conducting their first experiments with motion photography, which they called photo dynamism. Following the futurists' manifestos, Anton Giulio Bragaglia came to appreciate the simultaneous perception of successive movements of a body and represented these in photography through a synthesis of long and multiple exposures; he captured the traces of movement and recorded in a single picture a body in motion overlapping multiple times. The results of Bragaglia's work contrast with the series of analytic images from motion studies by nineteenth century figures such as those of photographic innovator Eadweard Muybridge and the time photography of physician and physiologist Étienne-Jules Marey. Marinetti endorsed Bragaglia's investigations and exhibited all of his photodynamic images. Bragaglia also commented on them in lectures and in his published essay *Fotodinamismo futurista* (Rome: Nalato, 1911). Afterward, an initiative by Boccioni in 1913 officially banned Bragaglia's photographic experiments from the futurist movement. Boccioni rejected photography as a potentially creative medium for the intuition of the artist and feared that futurist paintings would be seen as based in motion-study photography. Bragaglia dedicated himself from that time on to making film. In the futurist movement, photography was then used only to make portraits of individual members and of group gatherings. During the 1920s outside of Italy, countless experiments were conducted with multiple and long exposures, photo collages, and montages, as well as photograms. These were undertaken by such people as Ilse Bing, Anton Stankowski, László Moholy-Nagy, and Heinz Hajek-Halke in Germany, many of these figures associated with the Bauhaus; Maurice Tabard and Man Ray in France, who were associated with Surrealism; and Alexandr Rodchenko and El Lissitzky in the Soviet Union, associated with Constructivism. At this time Italian photographers and artists also began once again to experiment with photography. The photography of the European avant-garde was exhibited from May to July 1929 at the exhibition *Film und Foto* in Stuttgart.

The second generation of Italian futurism, as Enrico Crispolti first called it in 1958, is characterized by an intensive engagement with new technologies. This included a fascination with speed, the automobile, and the internal mechanisms of machines. In September 1929, Marinetti published his first theoretical writings about *aeropittura*, painting that represents the visions and emotions experienced while flying and thematizes the conquering of space—a notion developed by many futurist artists, such as Giacomo Balla, Benedetta Cappa, Tullio Crali, Enrico Prampolini, and Tato. In November of the same year, Vinicio Paladini published an essay on photomontage, which originated in Germany with László Moholy-Nagy and Hannah Höch. In 1930, Tato (pseudonym of Guglielmo Sansoni) and Marinetti published *Il manifesto della fotografia futurista* (Manifesto of Futurist Photography). In this work they called for the art of photography to explore many things: the drama of the static and moving object; the effect of surprise; the transformation of objects; the inversion of the reality effect; the optical fusion of bodies and objects; the perspective from heights to depths and from depths to heights; and photographing characteristics of people or bodies with extreme close-ups or psychological and satirical combinations with other bodies that suggest an inner psychological state. In the sixteen points listed in his manifesto "The Art of Transforming Objects," Marinetti, whose creative work was influenced by a passion for war, includes, though it seems unconnected, the art of war camouflage, which aims to elude observation from the air.

Between 1930 and 1933 many amateur and professional photographers exhibited futurist photography in Turin, Milan, Rome, and Trieste. Filippo Masoero presented views of flight, *Aerofotografia*, that recorded distorted images of cities from the perspective of an airplane. In 1915, Fortunato Depero created staged self-portraits that Giovanni Lista describes as the first futurist photo performance. Like Ivo Pannaggi and Marcello Nizzoli, Paladini created collages, such as the series "Olympic Games" (1934), made from photographs, images printed with type, and colored paper, which were similar to Dadaist works. In the second and third decades of the twentieth century, Arturo Bragaglia created many-headed portraits and extended time exposures of everyday body movements, such as *The Smoker* (1913) and *The Slap* (1912). Tato, Ferruccio A. Demanins, and Wanda Wulz stand out with their sandwich-board portraits. These portraits represent how the overlapping of memory and the impressions of the present in an individual's consciousness affect perception. They were also intended to represent characterizations of people and their inner psychological state. In this way, artists play with symbols and with combinations of the ironic and serious, as in the self-portrait of Wanda Wulz *Ich + Katze* (1932) and in the portrait by Tato of the writer Mino Somenzi—whose piercing gaze is shown simultaneously from various directions, with a central symbol of futurism, the propeller, transposed over it. Tato combined different objects under extreme lighting to create new and strange figurations. He calls attention to these optical effects in his naming of the images, for example, in the ironic photographs titled the *Perfect Citizen* (1930) and *Shepherd with Little Ass* (1930). He constructs the scenes from paper figures and so deconstructs, very much like Giulio Parisio, the claim to reality that is generally imposed on photography, leading the viewer through the same medium but to a subjective reality of fantasy and dream. Different from Tato, Gianni Croce, Mario Bellusi, and Giorgio Riccardo Carmelich compose from various everyday objects abstract still-life constructs that they pose in harshly contrasting light to bring out the drama between objects.

Around 1933, the artists Bruno Munari, Tullio D'Albissola (pseudonym of Tullio Spartaco Mazzotti), and Luigi Veronesi began creating photograms. In general, they directed the content of futurist photography to the themes of dance, sport, flying, psychological portraits, the still life, the city, and machines. Giovanni Lista collected, studied, and published many works of futurist photography that are now in various private and public photography collections, such as the George Eastman House in Rochester, New York; the Metropolitan Museum of Art in New York; the J. Paul Getty Museum in Los Angeles; Museo di Storia della Fotografia Fratelli Alinari in Florence, Italy; and Museo d'Arte Moderna e Contemporanea di Trento e Rovereto in Trento, Italy.

KATHARINA HAUSEL

See also: **Abstraction; Aerial Photography; Bauhaus; Bragaglia, Antonin Giulio; Dada; Hajek-Halke, Heinz; Lissitzky, El; Man Ray; Moholy-Nagy, László; Montage; Multiple Exposures and Printing; Photogram; Surrealism**

Further Reading

Apollonio, Umbro. *Futurist Manifestos.* London: Thames and Hudson, 1973.

Bozzolla, Angelo, and Caroline Tisdall. *Futurism.* London: Thames and Hudson, 1989.

Hulten, Pontus, ed. *Futurismo + Futurismi.* Milan: Bompiani, 1986; 2nd ed., 1992.

Lista, Giovanni. *Futurismo e fotografia.* Milan: Multhipla, 1979.

Lista, Giovanni. *Photographie futuriste italienne.* Paris: Musée d'Art Moderne de la Ville de Paris, 1981.

Lista, Giovanni. "Futurist Photography." *Art Journal* (Winter 1981).

Lista, Giovanni, and Yolanda Trincere. *Futurism & Photography.* New York: Hillwood Art Gallery, 1984.

Lista, Giovanni. *Futurism & Photography.* London: Merell Publishers in association with Estorick Collection of Modern Italian Art, 2001.

Nobis, Norbert, ed., and Enrico Crispolti, Francesca Talpo, Massimo Carrà, Michael Erlhoff, Christoph Hoch, Mario Pasi, Giovanni Lista, and Juan Allende-Blin. *Der Lärm der Strasse: Italienischer Futurismus, 1909–1918.* Milan: Mazzotta, 2001.

Sanzin, Giordano Bruno. *Mostra fotografica nazionale futurista.* Trieste: 1932, 2nd ed., Gorizia: Edizioni della Laguna, 1986.

INDEX

A

Abbott, Berenice, 1–6, 56
  accomplishments, 1
  Alfred Stieglitz and, 3
  American High School Biology, 2
  appearance of on television, 3
  biography, 4
  Changing New York, 2
  endorsements by, 3
  Eugène Atget and, 1, 3
  Federal Arts Project and, 2
  Greenwich Village: Today & Yesterday, 3
  group exhibitions, 4
  The House of Photography incorporated by, 2
  individual exhibitions, 4
  Man Ray and, 1
  New York photographs, 2
  periods of photography, 3
  Physics, 3
  selected works, 4
  studies in Paris, 1
  subjects dramatized by, 2
  work for *Vogue*, 1
  youth, 1
Abstract manipulation, origins of, 7
Abstraction, 6–9
  evolution of, 6–9
  further reading, 9
  modernist, 7
  movement and blurredness, 7
  origins of, 6
  paradox of discussions of, 6
ACP, *see* Australian Centre for Photography
Actionism movement, Vienna, 144
Adams, Ansel, 9–14
  American, 9–11
  approach to photography, 11
  Basic Photo Series, 11
  biography, 11
  books of photographs, 13
  Born Free and Equal, 11
  Camera Craft, 10
  Center for Creative Photography and, 253
  Clearing Winter Storm, 10
  conception of subject, 9
  experimentation by, 10
  first individual exhibition, 10
  Friends of Photography, 11
  further reading, 14
  group exhibitions, 12
  individual exhibitions, 12
  Lodgepole Pines, 9
  Making a Photograph, 10
  Minor White and, 1682
  Moon and Half Dome, 10
  Moonrise, Hernandez, New Mexico, 10
  Mount Conness, 10
  Mount Williamson, 10
  Parmelian Prints of the High Sierras, 9
  Paul Caponigro and, 241
  Portfolio 1: In Memory of Alfred Stieglitz, 11
  Portfolio 2: The National Parks and Monuments, 11
  Portfolio 3: Yosemite Valley, 11
  reputation, 10
  Ruth Bernhard and, 124
  selected works, 12, 13
  Sierra Nevada: The John Muir Trail, 10
  studies, 9
  technical books, 13, 14
  Tenya Lake, 10
  toning and, 1547
  Unknown Ansel Adams, 11
  Winter Sunrise, 10
  Zone System, 10, 11, 1620
Adams, Eddie, 14, 15
  Barnstorm: the Eddie Adams Workshop, 15
  biography, 15
  The Boat of No Smiles, 14
  further reading, 15
  most significant photograph, 14
  Parade magazine, 15
  photographic essay of South Vietnamese refugees by, 14
  Pulitzer Prize winning photograph, 14
  selected works, 15
  Truth to Power: Human Rights Defenders Changing Our World, 15
  war photography and, 1642
Adams, Robert, 16–20
  American, 16, 17
  biography, 17
  documentary-style images of, 16
  education, 16
  From the Missouri West, 17
  further reading, 18–20
  group exhibitions, 18
  hopes, 17
  individual exhibitions, 17, 18
  inspirations, 17
  New Topographics: Photographs of a Man-Altered Landscape, 16
  The New West: Landscapes Along the Colorado Front Range, 17

Adams, Robert (*Continued*)
selected works, 18
social concerns, 16
Summer Nights, 17
To Make it Home: Photographs of the American West, 17
West from the Columbia, 17
White Churches of the Plains, 17
ADC, *see* Analog-to-digital converter
Aerial photography, 7, 20–22
"Changing the Earth" series, 22
"Earth from Above" series, 21
American Civil War, 20
Canadian government, 233
conception of, 20
days of Sumer, 20
development during Cold War, 21
digital technology, 22
ecological and conservation efforts, 21
fine-arts photography and, 22
further reading, 22
geometric disciplines and, 20
historical and research purposes, 21
history, 20
improvements, 20, 21
kite, 22
Middle Eastern archeological sites, 21
Midwest United States, 1590
nature photographers, 22
prime innovators, 21
relation between photographs and maps, 20
remote sensing, 22
satellite imagery, 21
scientific realm, 21
vantage points offered by skyscrapers, 22
war and, 20
Africa, Central and West, 27–30
anthropological studies, 27
"civilized" vs. "savage", 28
colonial ethnography, 28
Congo expeditions, 28
contemporary artists, 28
Drum magazine, 28
European counterparts, 27
further reading, 28–30
government-sponsored projects, 28
growing middle class, 27
independent mass-media, 28
means of distributing ethnographic images, 28
national independence, 27
outdoor photography, 27
portrait photography, 27
postcards, 28
self-portraits, 27
spread of commercial studios, 27
surface adornment, 28
Africa, East Africa and Indian Ocean islands, 30–32
contributions of South Asian photographers, 31
daguerreotype, 31
early commercial studios, 31
exotic animal life, 30
famine of Ethiopia, 30
formal images for life passages, 31
further reading, 31, 32
history of photographic practices, 30
hunting with camera, 30
identity photographs, 31
important studio photographers, 31
Madagascar's first indigenous photographer, 31
Nairobi's Camerapix agency, 30
official photography agencies, 31
photosafaris, 30
political role of photography, 30
racially-based distinctions between populations, 31
royal court photographers, 31
safaris and disasters, 30
wish fulfillment, 31
Africa, North, 32, 34
archives, 32
body at birth and death, 33
colonization, 32
commercial studios, 32
direct color autochrome plates, 33
dirty war, 32
further reading, 33–34
golden age for commercial photography, 32
image of Algerian women, 33
Koranic injunction against realistic images, 32
L'AlgÕrie Artistique et Pittoresque, 33
Madonna of Benthala, 32
Orientalist picturesque, 32
photographic history, 32
photojournalism of Algeria's conflicts, 32
postcards, 33
Second World War, 33
surveillance images from secret police files, 32
tourism, 32
Africa, overview of, 23–26
affordability of photography, 25
agency photographers, 25
apartheid, 24
art world interest in African photography, 23
black South African life, 24
censorship, 25
colonialist life documented by Europeans, 23
Congo Free State, 24
cultural generalization, 23
documentation of political process, 25
Drum, 24
establishment of colonial rule, 24
European racism, 24
evolution of Pan-African sensibility, 24
feminist methodologies to analyze photographs, 24
further reading, 25, 26
government assertion of authenticity, 25
history of photography in, 23
In/sight: African Photographers, 1940 to the Present, 23
incorporation of photography into religious rituals, 23
inherited studio, 25
need for identity photos, 25
Nka: A Journal of Contemporary African Art, 23
participation in image creation, 25
photographies, 23
portrait photography, 24
public attention in the West, 24
regional photographic practices, 25
The Short Century, 23, 24
South Africa's best known photographers, 23
studio portraits, 25
"tribal" Africans, 23
use of box cameras, 25

Africa, South and Southern, 34–37
apartheid, 35
archetype of pristine native life, 35
"bantu homelands", 35
The Bantu Tribes of Southern Africa (1928–1954), 35
Beyond the Barricades, 36
The Black Photo Album/Look At Me 1890–1950, 35
Boer War, 34
daguerreotypes, 34
De Beers Consolidated Mines, 35
democratic elections, 36
documentation of Afrikaners, 35, 36
Drum magazine, 35
ethnographic photography, 35
exoticism, 34
experimental photographic techniques, 36
exposure of atrocities, 36
foreign domination, 34
further reading, 36
illegal drinking establishments, 35
images of amaZulu, 35
middle class family portraits, 35
native stereotypes, 34
"natural" separation of races, 35
partition of African continent, 34
paternalistic fantasy, 34, 35
political rallies, 36
problems of overcrowding and urban blight, 36
propaganda for missionaries, 34
racial classification, 34
Sallo Epstein and Company, 34
social activism, 36
South Africa: *The Cordoned Heart*, 36
Staffrider, 36
tension regarding subject matter, 36
tourism, 34
tourist colony, 35
trauma of industrialization, 34
use of press photography by State, 36
workshop atmosphere, 36
African Arts, 27
Afterimage: The Journal of Media Arts and Cultural Criticism, 38, 39
criticism of institutional understanding of photography, 39
cultural diversity and, 38
editor of, 39
essays, 38, 39
focus of, 38
further reading, 39
list of exhibitions, 39
political stance of, 38
publication of, 39
questions motivating founding of, 38
questioning of photography's aesthetics, 39
revisionist art history and, 38
socio-political critiques of photographic representation, 38
social issues, 39
topical issues, 39
vernacular photography, 39
Visual Culture Studies and, 38
Agitprop, 39–42
aim of, 39
Arbeiter Illustrierte Zeitung, 40
capitalist "degeneracy" and, 40
communist revolution and, 39, 40
Electrification of the Entire Country, 40
generation of class-conscious photographs, 40
German mass media empire, 40
legitimizing function of, 40
Marxist-Leninist ideology and, 39
The Meaning of the Hitler Salute, 42
photomontage, 40, 42
political circumstances, 39, 40
redefinition of, 42
role of photography in culture of, 40
Stalin's Five-Year Plans, 40
USSR in Construction, 40
Worker-Photographer, 40
Air cable release, 196
Albers, Josef, homage to the square paintings, 104
Alpert, Max, 42–44
biography, 44
denunciation of nonrepresentational works, 43
Exhibition of Works by the Masters of Soviet Photo Art, 43
First All-Union Exhibition of Photo Art, 43
images of family life, 43
life, 42
magazine photography of, 42
photo stories, 43
propagandist, 42
Red Army, 42
Red Proletarian factory, 43
selected works, 44
Ambrotypes, 34
American Revolutionary Popular Alliance (APRA), 262
American western landscape, Ansel Adams and, 9
Analog-to-digital converter (ADC), 218
An American Place, 10, 44–46
Ansel Adams and, 45
contact with Stieglitz, 45
Equivalents, 45
final decade of, 45
funds from, 45
lack of promotion of, 45
limited season of, 45
opening of, 45
photographers exhibiting at, 45
retrospective, 45
solo exhibition, 45
Anderson Galleries, 44
Ansel Adams Gallery, 10
Anthropological photography, 33
Apartheid, 24
Aperture magazine, 149
Aperture, 212, 216
Aperture, shutter speed and, 216
Appropriation, 46–48
After Walker Evans, 46
artists, 46
Barbara Kruger and, 47, 48
digital replication and, 47
diminished power and influence of, 47
distortion of photographs, 47
feminist critique, 47
film clips, 46
Harry Callahan and, 205
market support, 46, 47
mimicked look of Hollywood films, 46
New York East Village painter, 47
Pop Art movement, 46

Appropriation (*Continued*)
Postmodernist territory, 46
readymades, 46
rephotography and, 235
response to cultural surroundings, 47
return to painting, 47
shift in practice, 46
slogans, 47
Untitled Film Stills, 46
use of found objects, 46
Victor Burgin and, 179
APRA, *see* American Revolutionary Popular Alliance
Araki, Nobuyoshi, 49–51
artificiality, 49
biography, 50
camera, 49
censorship, 49
Cibachrome, 49
Edo period painting, 50
erotic imagery, 49
fashion photography, 50
flower studies, 50
following, 50
further reading, 51
group exhibitions, 50
individual exhibitions, 50
interest in urban areas, 50
Japanese, 49
kinbaku, 50
paradoxical work of, 49
photo-diarists, 50
photo-maniac, 49
preoccupation with female sexuality, 49
selected works, 50, 51
Taschen, 50
Tokyo Love, 50
worldwide notoriety, 49
Arbus, Diane, 51–56
American, 51–54
August Sander and, 52
biography, 54
ceremonies, 53
commercial career, 52
Diane Arbus Revelations, 52
discontent with prevailing photographic conventions, 51
emphasis on portraiture, 52
Esquire magazine, 52
famous subjects, 52
fine art aesthetics, 51
first commissioned photo essay, 52
further reading, 54–56
gap between intention and effect, 52
group exhibitions, 54
Guggenheim Grant, 53
Harper's Bazaar, 53
home for mentally retarded, 53
iconic images of 1960s, 51
individual exhibitions, 54
interest in subcultures, 53
Jasper Johns and, 53
portable 35 mm cameras, 51
printing with borders, 53
prosaic subjects, 52
selected works, 54
self-conscious creativity, 51
self-produced portfolio, 53
shift in documentary approach, 52
shocking portraits, 51
snapshot aesthetic, 51
social landscape, 51
suicide of, 53
symptoms and moments, 53
typologies influencing, 52
voyeuristic iconography, 53
Archaeological photography, 33
Architectural photography, 56–63
academy professorship, 61
accentuation of building, 57
adaptation by commercial photography studios, 59
architects-in-training and, 56
architecture as propaganda tool, 59
Arts-and-Crafts movement, 57, 58
Beaux Arts architect, 57
Becher class, 61
bird's eye views of urban places, 61
Charles Rennie Mackintosh and, 57
city scape as subject, 60
collaborations among photographers and architects, 60
commercial application, 56
competition, 61
Concept Art groups, 60
concept, 61
Conceptual Art and, 61
conventions about depicting modern architecture, 58
criticism of politics, 56
cross-fertilization, 58
cross-over artists in, 60
definition of, 56
destruction of Hiroshima and Nagasaki, 59
destruction of World War II, 59
Deutsche Werkbund, 58
dissemination of ideas, 58
as documentation, 57
emergence of Nazi regime, 59
Eugene Atget and, 56
European architects, 58
fame of architect and, 62
further reading, 62
Gerhard Richter and, 61
German *fotoform* group, 60
German painting movement, 58
Global Architecture magazine, 61
Henry Hobson Richardson and, 57
historic buildings, 60
incorporation of into curricula, 62
inventories of buildings, 60
Julius Shulman and, 60
modernism and, 59
need for in magazines, 62
panoramas of motorway crossings, 61
Parisian avant-gardists, 56
Pop Art and, 61
postwar reconstruction, 60
profession of, 57
propagandists, 57
Prussian health insurance, 57
as reference for manufacturing industries, 56
small format cameras, 57
social activism and, 59
straight photography as fine art, 58

Architectural photography (*Continued*)
surveillance units, 59
The International Style, 59
urbanism, 61
use of infra-red photography, 59
vernacular architecture, 56
Virtual Reality and, 62
Walker Evans and, 56
Walter Gropius and, 58, 59
whole human philosophy, 59, 60
works influencing, 60
Architectural Record, 2
Archives, 64–68
aesthetic object, 65
anonymous daguerreotypes, 64
archival theory, 65
archival, library, and museum traditions, 64, 65
Art Institute of Chicago, 66
artifact archives, 67, 68
artificial collections, 65
attempts to maintain order, 65
Center for Creative Photography, 66
container list, 64
Corbis, 67
cultural artifact, 65
distinction between curators and archivists, 67
Eastman House, 67
emphasis in art museum, 64
features, 65
finding aid, 64
further reading, 68
genre sustaining donor interest, 67
historical evidence, 67
Hulton Archive, 67
item-level access, 65
layers of meaning of photographs, 65
library collections, 68
library special collections, 66
Machine Readable Cataloguing, 66
manuscript collections, 67
Margery S. Long and, 65
motion pictures, 67
museum collections, 67
non-profit historical organizations, 66
organization methodology, 64
original order of photographs, 66
PABIR slogan, 67
parallel between library and archival practice, 64
photographers' archives, 66, 67
photographs as primary source materials, 68
photographs in archives, 65, 66
primary source materials, 68
processing of, 64
professional staff, 64
research collection, 66
respect for original order, 64
Society of American Archivists, 65
Special Media Archives Services Division, 66
true archives, 64
U.S. government, 66
unit to be identified, 64
Women in Photography International Archive, 67
Arnold, Eve, 68–71
American, 68, 69
biography, 69–71
female insight, 69
further reading, 71
Hollywood stars, 69
human condition, 68
individual exhibitions, 71
Magnum Photos, 68, 69
Marilyn Monroe, 69, 70
photojournalism, 68
portraiture, 69
relocation to England, 69
Rolleicord camera, 69
selected works, 71
unpredictability of photography, 68
use of color, 69
vision, 68
words accompanying pictures, 69
Art Institute of Chicago, 71–73
archives of, 66
Association of Arts and Industries, 71
competition with European product design, 71
contemporary photography shows, 72
curatorial departments, 71
establishment of photography as art form, 72
exhibitions by photographers early in their careers, 72
further reading, 73
graduate program in photography, 71, 72
Hugh Edwards and, 72
Illinois Institute of Technology, 71
influential curator of photography, 72
Institute of design's contribution to American photography, 72
Julien Levy Collection, 72
New Bauhaus: American School of Design, 71
president of, 72
School of the Art Institute, 71
series of evolutions, 71
size of, 71
Society of Amateur Photographers, 72
Art Nouveau, Herbert Bayer and, 105
Art photography, 104
Artists' books, 73–76
altered books, 73
art fairs, 74
art movements and, 73
binding of, 73
book forms excluded, 73
Carnegie Mellon Libraries, 74
Constructivism, 73, 74
containers of information, 73
Dadaism, 73, 74
desk-top publishing, 74
Dieter Roth and, 74
digital technological changes and, 74
Expressionism, 73, 74
Franklin Furnace, 74
funds for production of, 74
further reading, 76
Grolier Club, 73
limited editions, 73
literary sausages, 74
livre d'artist books, 73
mass-production of books, 73
National Endowment for the Arts funding, 74
Printer Matter Bookstore, 74
Robert Heinecken and, 73
rubberstamping, 74

Artists' books (*Continued*)
Russian Futurism, 73
Surrealism, 73, 74
technology changes and, 73
Visual Studies Workshop, 74
Walker Evans and, 74
World Wide Web, 73
Associated Press, 15
Astrophotography, 76–78
ability to track stars, 78
autoguided photography, 78
camera and tripod, 78
camera in space, 77
charge-coupled device, 77
color, 77
Daguerreotype, 76
dry emulsions, 76, 77
fleeting image of celestial body, 76
Frederick Scott-Archer and, 76
further reading, 78
George Eastman and, 77
Hasselblad cameras, 77
Hubble Space Telescope, 77
invention of celluloid-based photographic film, 77
Kodak 103a spectroscopic films, 77
Louis Daguerre and, 76
lunar calendars, 76
marketing of Kodachrome process, 77
Mars Pathfinder mission, 77
most accessible type of, 78
night sky movements, 76
Palomar Observatory, 77
piggyback photography, 78
professional observatories, 77
Ritchey-Chretien telescope, 77
spectroscopy, 76
Warren de la Rue and, 76
wet Collodion process, 76
wet plate process, 76
Atget, Eugène, 56, 78–82
Andrè Calmettes and, 78, 82
Avenue des Gobelins, 80, 81
Berenice Abbott and, 78, 79
biography, 82
collections purchased, 82
contradictions of Paris, 80
customers, 79
dislike of commissions, 79
faulty technique, 80
French, 78–82
further reading, 82
habits, 80
Hausmannizaton, 79
intriguing aspect of photos, 79
La Revue des Beaux-Arts, 79
life reconstructed, 78
Man Ray and, 78, 80
natural images, 79
objet trouvé, 80
paper selection, 80
photographic style, 80
photographs of Old Paris, 79
reason for lack of recognition, 80
recording of landmarks before destruction, 79
Salvador Dali and, 82
selected works, 82
self-taught photographer, 79
straight photographer, 80
subject matter, 80
Surrealists and, 80
typology and, 1563
unknown at death, 78, 82
use of rapid rectilinear lens, 80
works at Bibliothèque Nationale de France, 129
Auerbach, Ellen, 82–86
Abyssinian war, 84
American, 82–84
baby photographer, 84
biography, 84
carbo printing process, 84
commissions, 84
confusion between living model and manikin, 83
creative interplay, 83
education, 83
experimentation, 83
financial independence, 83
further reading, 84
Grete Stern and, 82
group exhibitions, 84–86
Hitler's rise to power and, 82, 83
immigration to United States, 84
individual exhibitions, 84
Ishon, 83
Jewish National Fund, 83
montage, 83
Mounting Tension, 84
Neue Sehen, 83
New York School circles, 84
object as cultural study, 83
pioneering woman-run photography studio, 82
ringl + pit, 83, 85
study of sculpture, 83
third eye, 83
Willem de Kooning and, 84
Women's International Zionist Organization, 83
work in Palestine, 83–84
Australia, 86–91
advent of New Media, 90
appropriate of imagery from various sources, 89
Art Gallery of New South Wales, 88
Australasian Photo-Review, 87
Australian Centre for Contemporary Photography, 88
Australian National Gallery, 88
Axel Poignant, 88
best-known photo-journalist, 88
Bicentennial, 89
B-grade films, 89
Brotherhood of the Linked Ring, 87
camera as aesthetic tool, 88
Carol Jerrems, 88
collaborative approach in documentary work, 88
corpse of photography, 90
diversity in photography, 89
Documentary photography, 88
Documentary style, 87
Felix H. Man Memorial Prize, 90
first professional Aboriginal photographer, 88
free settler population, 86
George Goodman, 86
Harold Cazneaux, 86

Australia (*Continued*)
humanistic approach of Documentary work
impact of counter-culture politics, 88–89
important source of inspiration, 88
imported magazines, 87
indigenous artists, 90
influence of Postmodernism, 89
institutional funding with Labour government, 88
introduction of photography, 86
John Grierson, 87
John Kauffman, 86
location of, 86
Max Dupain, 87
Max Pam, 88
National Gallery of Victoria, 88
Olive Cotton, 87
outlets for documentary work, 88
Persona and Shadow, 89
photo-essays, 89
Photofile, 89
photograms, 90
Pictorialism, 86, 87
prolific photographer of, 87
publications of art and social histories, 89
questioning of objectivity of medium, 89
raiding of visual language of popular culture, 89
revitalization of society following World War One, 87
re-working of traditional processes, 90
settlement of, 86
significant trends of 1990s, 90
Sir Ernest Shackleton's expeditions to Antarctica, 87
Sunshine School, 87
surge of interest in photography, 88
theatrical images, 88
Tracey Moffatt, 89, 90, 92
Wolfgang Sievers, 88
Australian Centre for Photography (ACP), 91, 92
accusations of elitism, 91, 92
American museum-based formalism, 92
art school graduates, 92
broadening of, 92
constituency, 91
David Moore and, 91
digital media and, 92
director, 92
foundation for photography, 91
funding, 91
gallery/museum model, 91
interest in photography as creative art, 91
museum professionalism in gallery, 92
opening of, 91
photo ghetto, 92
Photofile, 91, 92
photographic retrospective, 92
photography boom, 91
psychological phenomenon, 92
Austria, *see* Germany and Austria
Auto focus lenses, 211
Auto-exposure, point-and-shot cameras and, 227
Auto-focus systems, 227
Autoguided photography, 78
Automatic bracketing, 156
Avant-gardism, 3, 7
Avant-gardists, treasure trove of architecture photography discovered by, 56

B

Baby photographer, 84
Ballen, Roger, 93–95
apartheid, 93
biography, 95
Boyhood, 93
democratic election in South Africa, 94
Dorps: Small Towns of South Africa, 93
economic deprivation, 95
extracting of essence, 93
founding of Photography House, 93
government of South Africa, 94
graffiti, 95
horrible era, 95
ironic archetypes of alienation and immobility, 94, 95
irony, 95
mixed relationships, 95
Nelson Mandela, 94
opposition political parties, 94
Outland, 95
Platteland: Images from Rural South Africa, 93, 94
poverty, 93, 95
search of boyhood, 93
South Africa's psychosis, 93, 94
South African, 93–95
subjects, 95
tension in rural areas, 94
universal and metaphorical scenarios, 95
use of hard flash, 95
Balloon reconnaissance, 20, 21
Baltz, Lewis, 95–99
alienating effects of commercial development, 96
American, 95–97
biography, 97
Canadian Centre for Architecture, 97
cultural theorists and, 96
Deaths in Newport, 96
digital photography, 95
farmland transformed into real estate, 96
further reading, 98, 99
George Eastman House, 96
group exhibitions, 97, 98
iconography of realism, 95
individual exhibitions, 97
influence of commercial development, 96
isolation of details, 96
minimalist structures, 95
New Industrial Parks, Irvine California, 97
New Topography movement and, 95, 96
reflection of destruction of natural landscape, 95
resistance to categorization, 96
selected works, 97
social documentary, 96
urban planning, 96
Barnstorm: the Eddie Adams Workshop, 15
Barr, Jr., Alfred H., 99–101
Abby Rockefeller and, 99
adamantine ladies and, 99
America, 99, 100
art historical training, 99
Barnes Foundation of Pennsylvania, 99
Bauhaus and, 99
biography, 100
contribution to modern art, 100

Barr, Jr., Alfred H. (*Continued*)
criticism of abstract art, 99
further reading, 101
Harvard museum course, 99
Lillie P. Bliss and, 99
Machine Art, 100
May Quinn Sullivan and, 99
Modern Architecture: International Exhibition, 100
MoMA biographer, 100
MoMA director, 99
MoMA as laboratory, 100
MoMA librarian, 100
Nelson A. Rockefeller, 100
relationship between modern and contemporary art, 100
salary, 99
spellbinders, 99
stock market crash of 1929, 99, 100
summer reading lists for trustees, 100
Vanity Fair magazine, 99
Barthes, Roland, 101–103, 120
analysis of structure of communication, 101
biography, 102
Camera Lucida, 102
continuous message, 101
drawing's message, 102
French, 101, 102
further reading, 103
images used in advertising, 101
message without code, 101
most controversial critique, 102
photography's noeme, 102
poststructuralist, 101
professional writing career, 101
punctum, 102
selected works, 102–103
Sergei Eisenstein, 102
signification, 102
signifier, 101
stability of linguistic structures, 101
structural methodology, 101
studium, 102
The Photographic Message, 101
The Third Meaning, 102
uncoded message, 102
vernacular photography and, 1611
Winter Garden photograph, 102
Bataille, George, famous notion of unformed, 1567
Batchen, Geoffrey, vernacular photography and, 1610
Bauhaus, 103–105
abstractions of commonplace objects, 104
Alfred H. Barr, Jr., and, 99
art photography, 104
Chicago manifestations of, 106
closure of by Nazis, 104
director of, 103
economic realities of capitalism, 103
famous Bauhausbucher series, 103
founding of, 103
furniture, 103
further reading, 105
Herbert Bayer and, 104
identifiable, experimental method, 103
integration among arts, 103
introduction of photography to school, 103
Josef Albers and, 104
Karel Teige and, 1532
legacy of, 105
light graphics, 104
Metallmobel design exhibition, 104
Moholy-Nagy's Institute of Design, 105
New Objectivity, 104
self-referential art, 103
typography master, 104
use of technology to create designs, 104
Walter Gropius and, 103
Bayer grid, 218
Bayer, Herbert, 104–107
aesthetic philosophies, 105
archives of work, 106
Art Nouveau and, 105
Austrian, 105–106
Bauhaus and, 106
Bauhaus-Manifest and, 105
biography, 106
contributions to world of art, 106
design consultant, 106
fotoplastiken, 105, 106
group exhibitions, 107
immigration to United States, 106
individual exhibitions, 106, 107
Man and Dream, 106
Metamorphosis, 106
selected works, 107
training, 105
universal typestyle, 105
Vogue magazine, 106
Beaton, Cecil, 108–110
abstractions of destruction, 109
chronicle of women, 108
Edith Sitwell and, 108
fashion photography, 109
Film and Foto exhibition, 108
Kodak No. 3A Autographic camera, 108
new realism, 109
portraitist, 108
restrained scenarios, 109
Royal Air Force and, 109
set and costume designs, 108, 109
society women and, 108
Sotheby's London, 109
style of, 108
variety of roles, 109
Vogue magazine, 108, 109
Wallis Simpson and, 109
war correspondent, 109
Beaux Arts school, 57
Becher, Bernd and Hilla, 111–115
Artforum, 113
Becheresque visual language, 111
beginning of collaboration, 111
biography, 113
buildings threatened with destruction, 112
camera as aid in creating paintings, 111
categories of structures, 112
centered viewpoint, 111
Documenta 5, 113
documentary works, 111
flat lighting, 111
framing of individual typologies, 113
further reading, 114

Becher, Bernd and Hilla (*Continued*)
German, 111–113
ground-breaking exhibition, 113
group exhibitions, 114
individual exhibitions, 113, 114
industrial relics, 112
influence of, 113
minimal and conceptual art, 112
photo-herbarium, 112
precursor of work, 112
sculptural presence, 113
selected works, 114
SK-Stiftung Kultur, 113
Spurensicherung, 113
typological serialization of photos, 112
Typologien, 111, 113
unique approach, 112
unique collaboration, 111
vanishing industrial architecture, 111
vernacular architecture, 112
Walter Eichgru and, 111
Bellmer, Hans, 116–119
anagram, 117
biography, 117
fascination with figure, 116
first constructed doll, 116
further reading, 119
gene technologies, 117
German, 116, 117
graphic art, 117
group exhibitions, 119
hopeless artificiality, 116
individual exhibitions, 117, 118
meanings of sexual signs, 117
objects of bad taste, 116
opposition to rise of Nazism, 116
panorama of female torso, 116
prose poem, 116
sculptures, 117
selected works, 117
sense of metamorphosis, 116
Surrealist exhibitions, 117
Berger, John, 119–121
A Fortunate Man, 120
ambiguity, 120
Another Way of Telling, 119
art of photograph, 120
biography, 121
British, 119–121
collaboration, 120
criticism of photography, 120
existential testimony, 120
further reading, 121
Kitchen Sink School, 119
Marxist-oriented critic, 119
The New Statesman, 119
photomontages, 120
quotation of reality, 120
reputation as critic of photography, 120
university umbrella, 119
visual grammar, 120
Why We Look at Photographs, 120
working-class realism, 119
Berlinische Galerie, 121–123
Art Nouveau prints, 122
August Sander, 123
Berlin as fashion center, 123
East-Berlin collection, 123
Eberhard Roters and, 121
financial problems, 121
fledgling museum, 121
founding director, 121
further reading, 123
future of, 123
history of photography, 122
initial goals, 122
Lapidarium, 122
Lotte Jacobi, 123
Martin-Gropius Bau, 121
operation of, 121
overall collection, 122
photograms, 121
photographic collection, 122
photographic history of East Germany, 123
photo-montages, 122
portrait daguerreotypes, 122
Pushkin Museum, 122
recorder of levels of society, 123
vision, 121
Volk und Welt magazine, 123
Zwischenspiel, 122
Bernhard, Ruth, 123–125
Ansel Adams and, 124
avant-garde photographers, 123
biography, 124
bisexuality, 124
Classic Torso, 124
complex aesthetic, 124
Edward Weston and, 124
first published image, 123
further reading, 125
German, 123–124
group exhibitions, 124
Imogen Cunningham and, 124
individual exhibitions, 124
Machine Art Exhibition, 123
Price Rice and, 124
radiant photographs of female nudes, 123
turning point, 124
Women's Land Army, 124
Beuys, Joseph, 125–128
Actions, 126
aesthetic ideology, 125, 126
biography, 126, 127
co-founder of Green Party, 125
documentary authority of photography, 126
Enterprise, 126
expanded concept of art, 126
Fluxus, 126
further reading, 128
German military, 125
German Student Party, 125
German, 125, 126
group exhibitions, 128
hospital records, 125
individual exhibitions, 127, 128
instant recognition, 125
isolated moments, 126
Luftwaffe, 125
Organization for Direct Democracy through Referendum, 125

Beuys, Joseph (*Continued*)
performance artist, 126
personal iconography, 125, 126
political organizations established by, 125
question-and-answer sessions, 126
sculpture, 126
selected works, 128
self-determination, 125
Social Sculpture, 125
Bibliothèque Nationale de France (BnF), 128–130
Bibliothèque François-Mitterrand, 129
Cabinet Photography, 129
consultation, 129
Curator of Photography, 129
departments, 129
expansion of library, 129
French Revolution, 128
further reading, 130
legal deposit, 129
national repository of international work, 128
Prints and Photographs department, 129
Richelieu library, 129
royal collections, 128
SAFARA, 129
source of images for major exhibitions, 130
special collections, 129
transient collection, 128
works by Atget, 129
works exhibited at National Museum of Modern Art and, 130
works exhibited at Pavilion des Arts, 130
Bidermanas, Israel, *see* Izis
Billingham, Richard, 130–133
Anthony Reynolds Gallery, 130
auto-exposure camera, 130
Barbican Art Gallery, 130
biography, 131
British, 130–131
controversial family pictures, 130, 131
critique of social documentary practices, 130
father's alcoholism, 130
first book of photographs, 130
first major commissioned work, 131
Fishtank, 131
formal concerns of pattern, 131
further reading, 132
group exhibitions, 132
Ikon Gallery, 131
individual exhibitions, 131, 132
landscape aesthetic, 131
New Pictures, 131
Playstation, 131
Ray's a Laugh, 130
selected works, 132
snapshot aesthetic, 130
spontaneous images, 130
Turner Prize, 131
use of gaudy color, 130
Who's Looking at the Family?, 130
Biography
Abbott, Berenice, 4
Adams, Ansel, 11
Adams, Eddie, 15
Adams, Robert, 17
Alpert, Max, 44
Araki, Nobuyoshi, 50
Arbus, Diane, 54
Arnold, Eve, 69–71
Atget, Eugène, 82
Auerbach, Ellen, 84
Ballen, Roger, 95
Baltz, Lewis, 97
Barr, Jr., Alfred H., 100
Barthes, Roland, 102
Bayer, Herbert, 106
Becher, Bernd and Hilla, 113
Bellmer, Hans, 117
Berger, John, 121
Bernhard, Ruth, 124
Beuys, Joseph, 126, 127
Billingham, Richard, 131
Bischof, Werner, 134, 135
Blossfeldt, Karl, 139
Blumenfeld, Erwin, 143
Boltanski, Christian, 147
Bourdeau, Robert, 151
Bourke-White, Margaret, 154
Bragaglia, Anton Giulio, 159
Brandt, Bill, 162
Brassaï, 164
Bravo, Manuel Álvarez, 168
Breitenbach, Josef, 172
Bruguière, Francis Joseph, 177
Burgin, Victor, 179
Burri, Renè, 184
Burrows, Larry, 187
Burson, Nancy, 190
Cadieux, Geneviève, 198
Cahun, Claude, 202
Callahan, Harry, 206
Calle, Sophie, 208
Capa, Robert, 239
Caponigro, Paul, 242
Carrillo, Manuel, 246
Cartier-Bresson, Henri, 249
Chambi, Martín, 263
Chargesheimer, 266
Christenberry, William, 281
Clark, Larry, 287
Close, Chuck, 289
Coburn, Alvin Langdon, 291
Cohen, Lynne, 295
Coke, Van Deren, 298
Connor, Linda, 312
Coplans, John, 330
Crewdson, Gregory, 342, 343
Cunningham, Imogen, 350
Dahl-Wolfe, Louise, 357
Dater, Judy, 362–363
Davidson, Bruce, 365
de Meyer, Baron Adolph, 368
Deakin, John, 370
DeCarava, Roy, 373
Delano, Jack, 382
diCorcia, Philip-Lorca, 390
Dijkstra, Rineke, 398
Doisneau, Robert, 413
Domon, Ken, 416, 417
Drtikol, František, 419
Duncan, David Douglas, 422
Edgerton, Harold, 429

Biography (*Continued*)
Eggleston, William, 433
Eisenstaedt, Alfred, 437
Elsken, Ed van der, 440
Erfurth, Hugo, 446
Erwitt, Elliott, 452, 453
Evans, Frederick, 462
Evans, Walker, 465, 466
Export, Valie, 469
Fani-Kayode, Rotimi, 480
Faucon, Bernard, 492
Faurer, Louis, 497
Feininger, Andreas, 499, 500
Feininger, T. Lux, 503
Feldmann, Hans-Peter, 506
Finsler, Hans, 532
Fischer, Arno, 534
Fischli, Peter, and David Weiss, 538
Flaherty, Robert Joseph, 540, 541
Flusser, Vilém, 542, 543
Fosso, Samuel, 550
Franck, Martine, 558
Frank, Robert, 563
Freund, Gisèle, 566
Fukase, Masahisa, 570
Fukuda, Miran, 573
Funke, Jaromír, 576
Furuya, Seiichi, 579
Fuss, Adam, 582
Gelpke, André, 591
Gerz, Jochen, 600, 601
Giacomelli, Mario, 604
Gibson, Ralph, 606
Gidal, N. Tim, 609
Gilbert & George, 612
Gilpin, Laura, 615, 616
Gloaguen, Hervé, 618
Gohlke, Frank, 620
Goldin, Nan, 623
Gowin, Emmet, 626
Graham, Dan, 628
Graham, Paul, 632
Grossman, Sid, 635
Gursky, Andreas, 644
Gutmann, John, 647
Haas, Ernst, 650, 651
Hahn, Betty, 654
Hajek-Halke, Heinz, 658
Halsman, Philippe, 661
Hamaya, Hiroshi, 664–666
Hammarskiöld, Hans, 668
Hartmann, Erich, 672
Heartfield, John, 675
Heath, David Martin, 679
Heinecken, Robert, 682
Hellebrand, Nancy, 685, 686
Henderson, Nigel, 688
Henri, Florence, 692
Hers, François, 695
Hilliard, John, 696
Hine, Lewis, 699
Hiro, 702
Höch, Hannah, 753, 754
Horst, Horst P., 757
Hosoe, Eikoh, 761
Hoyningen-Huene, George, 764–766
Hurrell, George, 768
Hütte, Axel, 770
Ishimoto, Yasuhiro, 807, 808
Iturbide, Graciela, 810
Izis (Israel Bidermanas), 812
Jacobi, Lotte, 820
Janah, Sunil, 823
Jones, Harold, 832
Jones, Pirkle, 835
Josephson, Kenneth, 839
Karsh, Yousuf, 843
Käsebier, Gertrude, 845
Kawada, Kikuji, 849
Keetman, Peter, 852
Keïta, Seydou, 855
Kertész, André, 859
Kessels, Willy, 862
Kesting, Edmund, 864
Khaldei, Yevgeny, 868
Killip, Chris, 870
Klein, Aart, 873
Klein, Astrid, 876
Klein, William, 879
Klett, Mark, 882
Koudelka, Josef, 887
Kozloff, Max, 890
Krauss, Rosalind, 892
Kruger, Barbara, 894
Krull, Germaine, 898
Lange, Dorothea, 904
Lartigue, Jacques Henri, 908
Laughlin, Clarence John, 913–915
Lebeck, Robert, 916
Lee, Russell, 919
Leibovitz, Annie, 921
Lemagny, Jean-Claude, 923
Lerski, Helmar, 927
Levinthal, David, 930
Lèvi-Strauss, Claude, 934, 935
Levitt, Helen, 936
Liberman, Alexander, 942
Liebling, Jerome, 950
Link, O. Winston, 961
List, Herbert, 965, 966
Long, Richard, 969
Lüthi, Urs, 976
Lynes, George Platt, 978
Lyons, Nathan, 984
Maar, Dora, 988–990
Madame d'Ora, 992
Man Ray, 1002
Man, Felix H., 1005
Mapplethorpe, Robert, 1009
Mark, Mary Ellen, 1013
McBean, Angus, 1017, 10183
Meatyard, Ralph Eugene, 1020
Meiselas, Susan, 1024
Messager, Annette, 1027
Metzker, Ray K., 1031
Meyerowitz, Joel, 1041, 1042
Michals, Duane, 1044, 1045
Mikhailov, Boris, 1047
Miller, Lee, 1050
Misrach, Richard, 1053

Biography (*Continued*)
Model, Lisette, 1057
Modotti, Tina, 1066
Moholy-Nagy, László, 1070, 1071
Morath, Inge, 1079, 1080
Morimura, Yasumasa, 1082
Morris, Wright, 1085
Moses, Stefan, 1088, 1089
Mulas, Ugo, 1092–1093
Muniz, Vik, 1096
Munkacsi, Martin, 1099
Namuth, Hans, 1143
Newhall, Beaumont, 1154
Newman, Arnold, 1156
Newton, Helmut, 1159
Nixon, Nicholas, 1163
Novak, Lorie, 1171
Olson, Lennart, 1183
Outerbridge Jr., Paul, 1189
Owens, Bill, 1191
Parr, Martin, 1196
Penn, Irving, 1200
Peress, Gilles, 1203–1204
Peterhans, Walter, 1218
Pfahl, John, 1221
Pierre et Gilles, 1269
Plossu, Bernard, 1275
Plowden, David, 1279
Porter, Eliot, 1285
Prince, Richard, 1298
Rainer, Arnulf, 1318–1319
Rauschenberg, Robert, 1322
Ray-Jones, Tony, 1324
Renger-Patzsch, Albert, 1327
Riboud, Marc, 1339–1340
Rice, Leland, 1343
Riefenstahl, Leni, 1345–1346
Riis, Jacob, 1349
Ritts, Herb, 1350
Roh, Franz, 1355
Rosler, Martha, 1357
Rothstein, Arthur, 1360
Rubinstein, Eva, 1365
Ruff, Thomas, 1367
Salgado, Sebastião, 1380
Salomon, Erich, 1382
Sander, August, 1385
Schadeberg, Jürgen, 1392
Schmidt, Michael, 1395
Schneiders, Toni, 1398
Sekula, Alan, 1401
Serrano, Andres, 1406–1407
Seymour, David "Chim", 1410
Shahn, Ben, 1412–1413
Shaikhet, Arkadii, 1415
Sheeler, Charles, 1418
Sherman, Cindy, 1420
Shibata, Toshio, 1424
Shore, Stephen, 1426–1427
Simpson, Lorna, 1429
Singh, Raghubir, 1434
Siskind, Aaron, 1437
Skoglund, Sandy, 1440
Snow, Michael, 1443
Snowdon (Anthony Armstrong-Jones), 1446–1447
Solomon-Godeau, Abigail, 1462
Sommer, Frederick, 1464
Sontag, Susan, 1467
Spence, Jo, 1479, 1480
Starn, Doug and Mike, 1482
Steichen, Edward, 1487, 1488
Steiner, André, 1490
Stettner, Louis, 1493
Stieglitz, Alfred, 1495, 1496
Stone, Sasha, 1499
Strand, Paul, 1502
Struth, Thomas, 1509
Stryker, Roy, 1513
Sudek, Josef, 1515
Sugimoto, Hiroshi, 1518
Szabo, Steve, 1523
Szarkowski, John, 1525
Szilasi, Gabor, 1527
Tabard, Maurice, 1530
Teige, Karel, 1533
Teske, Edmund, 1535–1537
Tice, George, 1539
Tillmans, Wolfgang, 1542
Tosani, Patrick, 1549
Toscani, Oliviero, 1552
Traub, Charles, 1556
Tseng Kwong Chi, 1558
Turbeville, Deborah, 1561
Ubac, Raoul, 1568, 1569
Uelsmann, Jerry, 1572
Ulmann, Doris, 1575
Umbo (Otto Umbehr), 1579
Uzzle, Burt, 1602
Van Vechten, Carl, 1606
VanDerZee, James, 1609
Virilio, Paul, 1619
Vishniac, Roman, 1625
Wall, Jeff, 1633, 1634
Watanabe, Yoshio, 1646
Webb, Boyd, 1648
Weber, Bruce, 1652
Weber, Wolfgang, 1654
Weegee, 1660
Weems, Carrie Mae, 1664, 1665
Wegman, William, 1668
Welpott, Jack, 1673
Weston, Edward, 1676–1678
White, Clarence, 1680
White, Minor, 1683
Willis-Kennedy, Deborah, 1689
Winogrand, Garry, 1692
Witkiewicz (Witkacy), Stanislaw Ignacy, 1696, 1697
Witkin, Joel-Peter, 1699
Wojnecki, Stefan, 1702
Woodman, Francesca, 1705
Zwart, Piet, 1719
Bischof, Werner, 133–136
Allianz, 133
avoidance of dramatic effects, 134
biography, 134, 135
Famine in Bihar, 134
fashion photography, 133
further reading, 136
group exhibitions, 136
individual exhibitions, 135

Bischof, Werner (*Continued*)
interior designer, 133
internalized effects of war, 133
international press, 134
Life magazine, 134
most famous reportage, 134
most well-known pictures, 133
New Vision school, 133
painting, 133
photo essays, 133
photoessays, 134
post-World war II photojournalists, 133
poverty of Indian people, 134
primary subject, 133
selected works, 136
Swiss National Exposition, 133
Swiss, 133, 134
symbolic communication, 134
technically-oriented photography, 133
technique, 134
tranquil compositions, 134
Winter Olympics, 134
Black Star, 136–138
America's first large-format picture magazine, 137
appetite of magazines for photographs, 137
corporate business and, 137
Deutscher Verlag, 137
founders, 137
further reading, 138
Henry Luce and, 137
importance of in history of twentieth-century photography, 137
Life magazine, 137
mid-1930s photojournalism, 136
Mike Cowles and, 137
Nazi news agency, 137
noncredited press images, 136
origins, 137
proliferation of photographically-illustrated magazines, 137
public support for newspapers, 136
Blossfeldt, Karl, 138–141
apprenticeship, 138
Berlin gallerist, 139
Berlin School of Arts and Crafts, 139
biography, 139
flower documents, 138
further reading, 141
group exhibitions, 139
ideas, 138
individual exhibitions, 139
industrial designs, 139
intention to publish teaching methods, 138
Karl Nierendorf, 139
Kunstgewerbeschule, 138, 139
Moritz Meurer, 139
photo-herbarium, 112
plant photography, 138
reorientation, 139
sculpture, 138
selected works, 141
similarity to avant-garde art, 139
size of negative format, 138
still life painters, 138
systematically photographed plants, 139
task in beginners' classes, 139
vision, 138
Wundergarten der Natur, 139
Blumenfeld, Erwin, 141–143
American, 141, 142
apprenticeship, 141
Askanisches Gymnasium, 141
biography, 143
bourgeois life, 141
Dada founder, 141
Der Sturm, 141, 142
establishment as Dada artist, 142
fashion photographer, 142
father's mental deterioration, 141
first camera, 141
first portfolio, 142
founding members of Berlin Dada movement, 142
Fox Leather Company, 142
further reading, 143
group exhibitions, 143
Harper's Bazaar, 142
Hebrew Aid Society, 142
individual exhibitions, 143
Kaiser Friedrich Museum, 141
Photographie, 142
recurrent theme, 141
selected works, 143
Tristan Tzara, 141
Verve, 142
Vogue magazine, 142
works published posthumously, 142
BnF, *see* Bibliothèque Nationale de France
Body art, 143–146
Abstract Expressionism and, 143
American Happenings artist, 143
arrangement of photographs into tableau, 145
Azione sentimentale, 145
bodies as instruments of artistic work, 143
Chris Burden, 144, 145
coining of term body works, 144
Conversion II, 145
differences in practitioners, 143
Doorway to Heaven, 145
Fountain, 144
freezing of flow of time, 145
French Art Informel figures, 143
Hannah Wilke, 145
icon of postwar contemporary art, 144
Jackson Pollock, 143
Life-Video-Performance, 145
Marcel Duchamp, 144
Marina Abramovic, 144
photography documenting, 144
scatological actions, 144
Self-Portrait as a Fountain, 144
spectrum of photography, 145
Super 8 film, 145
Through the Night Softly, 145
variations of, 144
Vienna Actionism movement, 144
Vito Acconci, 144
Boltanski, Christian, 146–149
biography, 147
French, 146, 147
further reading, 149
group exhibitions, 148

Boltanski, Christian (*Continued*)
  individual exhibitions, 147, 148
  selected works, 148, 149
Books of photographs, Ansel Adams, 13
Borrowed images, 47
Bourdeau, Robert, 149–152
  abandoned industrial sites, 150
  Advertising & Design Club of Canada Award, 151
  all-consuming landscape, 150
  Aperture magazine, 149
  biography, 151
  camera work, 149
  Canada Council grants, 150
  Canadian, 149–151
  elegiac quality, 150
  experience of photographing, 150
  feeling state, 149
  further reading, 151, 152
  group exhibitions, 151
  humanity, 149
  individual exhibitions, 151
  inspiration, 149
  KodakMaster View, 150
  National Film Board, 149
  photography dealer, 149
  pictorialism, 149
  print quality, 150
  relationship with Paul Strand, 149
  selected works, 151
  station point, 150
  subject, 150
  Windowsill Daydreaming, 149
Bourke-White, Margaret, 152–155
  American Economic Life, 154
  American, 152–154
  autobiography, 154
  avant-garde vocabulary, 153
  biography, 154
  career, 152
  chaos of patterns, 152
  commercial practice, 152
  day in the life of representative character, 154
  Dust Bowl, 153
  elevated consumption, 154
  first major clients, 153
  free-lancing for *Life* magazine, 153
  further reading, 155
  group exhibitions, 154, 155
  idealized picture, 152
  image as woman, 152
  imperial views, 153
  individual exhibitions, 154
  language of pristine Pictorialism, 153
  manipulation by agents, 154
  marketable hit, 152
  mood-inducing atmosphere, 152
  most famous image of 1930s, 153
  multiple exposures, 152
  national byline, 152
  national publicity campaign, 153
  private scenarios, 152
  promise of ideal American way, 153
  publicity shots, 152
  risk taking, 152
  selected works, 155
  Tonalism, 153
  war assignments, 154
Bracketing, 155–157
  automatic, 156
  consistent ISO, 156
  correct exposure, 155
  digital photography, 156
  disadvantage of, 156
  incorrect exposure, 155
  insurance for photographer, 157
  manipulation of images in software program, 156
  multiple exposures, 157
  shutter speed, 156
  stopping motion, 156
  wasting of film, 156
Brady, Mathew, 3
Bragaglia, Anton Giulio, 157–159
  biography, 159
  Boccioni's view of photodynamics, 158
  Casa d'Arte Bragaglia, 159
  Change of Position, 158
  chronophotographs, 157
  deforming of visual world, 158
  dematerialization, 158
  document of avant-garde performance, 159
  European avant-garde approaches, 157
  exhibition promotion, 159
  first modern revolution in photography, 157
  Fotodinamismo, 157–159
  further reading, 159
  Futurist plastic dynamism, 158
  Futurist ringleader, 157
  group exhibitions, 159
  influence of Bergson's theories on, 158
  intuition over rationalized thought, 158
  Italian, 157–159
  liberation of photography, 157
  Luigi Russolo and, 157
  metaphysical predilections of imagery, 157
  method of vitalist expression, 157
  negative element, 158
  Nuova archaeologia romana, 158
  selected works, 159
  shared epithet, 157
  shared use of camera, 158
  theoretical tracts on theater, 159
  The Typist, 158
Brandt, Bill, 160–162
  biography, 162
  British, 160, 161
  Camera in London, 160, 161
  distortion of female form, 161
  empathy for working class subjects, 160
  exploration of new processes, 161
  extreme formalism, 161
  further reading, 162
  genres followed, 160
  important theme, 160
  individual exhibitions, 162
  influence of artistic avant-garde, 160
  influence of *Citizen Kane*, 161
  innovations in night photography, 161
  Lilliput magazine, 161
  mystery, 160
  photographic language, 160

Brandt, Bill (*Continued*)
portrait commissions, 161
reality and surrealism, 160
social documentary photographer, 160
social interaction of classes, 160
stylistic grit, 340
subjects, 161
Surrealists and, 160
three-dimensional collages, 161
vision, 161
World War II London at night, 160
Brassaï, 162–166
biography, 164
bracketing of reference to reality, 162, 163
diverse character of social relationships, 162
drawing, 164
fascination with built environment, 163
further reading, 165
graffiti and, 164
group exhibitions, 165
Harper's Bazaar and, 163
Henri Matisse and, 164
Henry Miller and, 162
Hungarian-French, 162–164
image of rebellious bohemian, 163
individual exhibitions, 164, 165
interest in physical world, 164
journalism career, 163
landscapes of nighttime monuments, 162
magazine assignments, 163
magazines legers, 163
Nazi occupation, 164
nickname, 162
photography as illustration, 163
Picasso and, 163, 164
Proust's interest in photography and, 164
pursuit of imaginative resemblance, 163
selected works, 165
sources of income, 163
style, 162
The Secret Paris of the 30s, 163
Transmutations series, 163
Trente dessins, 164
Bravo, Manuel Álvarez, 167–170
acknowledgement of innate capacity, 167
biography, 168
bonsai, 167
esthetic strategy, 167
further reading, 170
group exhibitions, 168–170
individual exhibitions, 168
influence of on Mexican photography, 168
international art forms, 167
interviews with, 170
La mamá del bolero y el bolero, 168
Mexican revolution, 167
Mexico's otherness, 167
modest imagery of, 168
politics of, 168
recurrent imagery of maguey cactus, 168
rejection of official nationalism, 168
respect, 167
Sand and Pines, 167
search for *mexicanidad*, 167
selected works, 170
Sepor de Papantla, 167
understated esthetic, 168
Breitenbach, Josef, 170–172
apprenticeship, 170
association with Social Democratic party, 171
biography, 172
bleaching, 171
bureaucratic hurdles, 171
desperation of exile, 170
expatriate list, 171
family business, 170
flight from National Socialism, 172
forfeiture of German citizenship, 171
Fortune magazine, 172
Free German Art, 171
further reading, 172
German-American, 170–172
group exhibitions, 172
hand-coloring, 171
individual exhibitions, 172
multiple printing solarization, 171
National Socialist government, 171
other Germany, 170, 171
poetic photographs, 170
portraiture, 171
recognition of contribution, 170
refugee artists and, 170
Royal Photographic Society of London, 171
selected works, 172
Social Democratic Association, 170
stage photographer, 171
thorough individual specialist training, 171
Walker Evans and, 172
Brotherhood of the Linked Ring, 87
Brownell, Frank A., 173
Brownie, 173–175
advertisements, 174
aesthetic potential of, 175
amateur snapshot photography, 173
ANSCO, 174
Baby 174
competing line of cameras, 174
cost, 173
description, 174
detective camera, 173
Eastman Company slogan, 173
Eastman Dry Plate, 173
element of everyday, 175
embellishments, 174
emphasis of initial advertisements, 175
first, 174
Frank A. Brownell and, 173
George Eastman and, 173
Jack Welpott's use of, 1672
Kodak Girls, 174
marketing of camera to children, 173
marketing of camera to women, 174
Minor White's use of, 1682
No. 1 Scout, 174
original packaging, 174
preloaded Kodak camera, 173
snapshot as subject of scholarly attention, 175
use of by George Tice, 1538
vernacular photography and, 1613
viewfinder, 173, 174

Brownie (*Continued*)
Walter Dorwin Teague and, 174
William Christenberry's use of, 279, 280
Bruguière, Francis Joseph, 175–177
Alfred Stieglitz's Photo-Secession, 175
American, 175, 176
avant-garde photography experiments, 175
Beyond this Point, 176
biography, 177
collaborations, 175, 176
Few Are Chosen, 176
film-noir-esque lighting, 176
fourth dimension, 176
Frank Eugene and, 175
further reading, 177
group exhibitions, 177
individual exhibitions, 177
legacy, 176
modern aesthetic, 176
Panama-Pacific Exposition, 176
photography as art form, 175
Photo-Secessionists, 176
selected works, 177
solarization, 176
variations on photographic processes, 176
vision, 175
Bullock, Wynn, Center for Creative Photography and, 253
Burgin, Victor, 178–181
appropriation and, 179
Between, 179
biography, 179
class consciousness of Karl Marx, 178
colonial imagery, 179
contemporary society, 178
denaturalizing photography, 178
England, 178–179
feminism, 178
film theory, 178
group exhibitions, 179–181
individual exhibitions, 179
motivating preoccupations, 179
multi-threaded videos, 179
open-ended narratives, 179
Performative Narrative, 178
Possession, 178
postmodernism, 178
selected publications, 181
selected works, 181
Sigmund Freund and, 178
Some Cities, 179
text narratives, 178
theme of migration, 179
When Attitudes Become Form, 178
Burning-in, 181, 182
addition of light, 181
artificial vignetted-edged effect, 182
burning-in tool, 182
changing burning time, 182
contact printing and, 326
digital image manipulation software, 182
exposure length, 181
foot pedal, 182
further reading, 182
muddied colors, 182
obviousness of, 182
overuse of, 181
practice, 182
purpose, 181
re-exposure, 182
technique, 181
Burri, Renè, 183–186
aerial cityscapes, 184
biography, 184
black and white work, 184
Die Deutschen, 183
documentary photography, 183
films for advertisement, 184
first book, 183
further reading, 185, 186
group exhibitions, 184, 185
human nature, 183
individual exhibitions, 184
international contracts, 184
Leica camera, 183
live photography, 183
Magnum Photos, 183
national identities, 184
portraits of artists, 183
selected works, 185
Swiss, 183, 184
war zones, 184
Burrows, Larry, 186–188
The Air War, 187
apprenticeship, 186
biography, 187
British, 186, 187
courage of, 187
freelance photography, 186
further reading, 188
group exhibitions, 187, 188
Home Guard, 186
individual exhibitions, 187
Keystone Photographic Agency, 186
Life magazine, 186
One Ride with Yankee Papa 13, 187
photo essays, 186, 187
press photographers in Vietnam, 187
selected works, 188
sensitivity to pictorial composition, 186
soldier's emotional journey, 187
Vietnam: A Degree of Disillusion, 187
vision of Vietnam war, 186
Burson, Nancy, 188–193
aged photographs, 189
The Age Machine, 189
American, 188–190
biography, 190
children with Apert Syndrome, 189
color Polaroids of faith healers, 188
composite image, 188
computer-generated portrait, 188
Diana camera and, 190, 217
The Difference Between Love and Anger, 190
DNA images, 190
faces with blurred features, 190
further reading, 193
genetic deformities, 189
group exhibitions, 191–193
history of physiognomy, 189
The Human Race Machine, 188

Burson, Nancy (*Continued*)
individual exhibitions, 190, 191
interactive ageing machine, 188
investigations into science and technology, 190
patent, 189
perception of visual reality, 188
phases of oeuvre, 188
preconceived notions about subjects, 189
seeing equated with believing, 189
selected works, 193
similarities of works, 188
snapshot images, 190
special faces, 188
startling ways of reflecting ideas, 190
straight portraits, 189
use of digital technology, 189
voyeuristic composites, 189
Warhead I, 188
warmth of images, 190

C

CAAD visualizations, architectural photography and, 62
Cable release, 195–196
air bulb, 195
air, 196
applications, 195
cable lengths, 195
camera selection, 196
camera shutter and, 195
elaborate lighting setups and, 196
electronic, 196
hands-off device, 195
homemade, 196
macro-photography, 196
mechanical, 196
nature photography, 195
plunger, 196
relaxed subject and, 195
remote camera activation with, 195
straightforward, 196
studio photographer's use of, 195
trip wires, 195
variation, 195
CAD, *see* Computer Aided Design
Cadieux, Geneviève, 196–200
archives, 197
attraction and alienation, 198
biography, 198
Canadian, 196–198
classical genres, 197
Family Portrait, 198
fascination for body, 198
force of work, 196
formal features of work, 197
further reading, 200
group exhibitions, 198–199
implicit damage, 197
individual exhibitions, 198
influence of father's repertory cinema, 196
La Fõlure, au choeur des corps, 197
labeling of work, 197
most well-known works, 198
Paramour, 197
portrait statements, 198
quotation in Braille, 197
selected works, 199, 200
serial forms, 197
Storyville Portraits, 197
use of blown-up scars, 197
Venice Biennale, 197
works likened to pornography, 198
Cahun, Claude, 200–204
ambiguity of gender, 200, 201
Aveux non avenus, 201
Bifur, 201
biography, 202
central works, 200
collaboration with Malherbe, 201
collaboration with surrealists, 202
Communist International aesthetic conflict, 201
Contre-Attaque, 202
doubling montage, 201
ever-changing roles, 200
feminist theory, 200
formal portraits, 201
French, 200–202
frontal portraits, 201
further reading, 204
gender and identity debates, 200
group exhibitions, 202
imprisonment, 202
individual exhibitions, 202
L'Association des crivains et Artistes Revolutionnaires, 201
lesbian Jew, 201
most important book, 201
Nazi occupation of France, 202
Parisian avant-garde, 200
personal identity, 200
photographic tableaux, 202
postmodern strategies of self-production, 200
selected works, 202
Spanish Civil War, 202
surrealist journal, 201
unsettling effect of portraits, 201
warning of blind party loyalty, 201, 202
California School of Fine Arts (CSFA), 1682
Callahan, Harry, 204–207
American, 204–206
appropriation and, 205
art curators and, 204
articulated goal, 205
Bauhaus curriculum, 205
biography, 206
Center for Creative Photography and, 253
Detroit Photo Guild workshop, 204
double-exposure images, 206
European Modernism and, 205
formative period, 205
further reading, 207
General Motors Corporation photo lab, 204
Graham Foundation, 206
group exhibitions, 206, 207
image scavenging, 205
individual exhibitions, 206
influence of travels, 206
Institute of Design in Chicago, 204
international exhibition, 206
magazines, 206

Callahan, Harry (*Continued*)
mass media, 205
New Bauhaus, 204
personal fellowship, 204
personal innovations, 205
photographs infused with emotion, 204
popular culture, 205
portraits of wife, 205
retrospective at MoMA, 206
Rhode Island School of Design, 205
role model for students, 205
selected works, 207
workshop taught by Ansel Adams, 204
Calle, Sophie, 207–210
biography, 208
clandestine photographs, 207
feature-length video, 208
French, 207, 208
further reading, 210
group exhibitions, 210
hallmark of creative approach, 207
hallucination, 208
idiosyncratic works, 207
individual exhibitions, 208–210
Last Seen, 208
Libèration, 207
merging of fact and fiction, 208
Palestinian struggles, 207
Paul Auster and, 208
physical absence with verbal description, 208
politics of late 1960s, 207
Pop Art, 207
private detectives, 208
selected works, 210
social and personal contexts, 208
spying on participants, 208
stunts, 207
The Blind, 207, 208
The Sleepers, 207
unfinished work, 208
Venetian Suite, 207
visual records of financial transactions, 208
Camera(s)
Amphibious Nikonos-type, 1583
auto-exposure, 130
box, 25
box, vernacular photography and, 1613
built-in light meter, 154
Contax, 239
Deardorff view, 280
detective, 173
digital, 299
DX-code enabled, 216
first functioning roll film, 227
folding, 223
format, today's most popular, 210
Hasselblad, 77
Holga, 217
hunting with, 30
Kodak No. 3A Autographic, 108
KodakMaster View, 150
-less imagery, 7
Mamiyaflex, 53
Nikon 35 mm, 52
portable 35 mm, 51
prototype for modern, 225
real-time maps created by, 20
Rolleicord, 69
Rolleiflex, 238
roll-film, 215
selection, cable release and, 196
telephoto disposable, 221
type, most common, 215
wide-angle Rolleiflex, 53
without film, 224
world's first self-contained underwater, 1582
Camera, 35 mm, 210–213
camera components, 211–213
accessories, 213
body, 211
exposure, 212
filters, 213
flashes, 213
lens, 211, 212
lens types, 212
metering systems, 212, 213
tripods, 213
film size, 210
f/stop range, 211
further reading, 213
lens, 210
light-tight body, 210
main parts, 210
number of U.S. households owning, 210
point-and-shoot cameras, 210
shutter speeds, 211
technical challenges of, 227
types, 210
viewfinder, 210
Camera, Diana, 217, 218
blurred images, 217
early milestones, 217
fine art, 217
further reading, 218
Great Wall Plastic Factory, 217
idiosyncrasies of, 217, 218
manufacture of, 217
names marketed under, 217
Nancy Burson's use of, 190, 217
photojournalism, 217
plastic toy, 217
popular successors, 217
portraiture, 217
Camera, digital, 218–220
analog-to-digital converter, 218
astronomy and, 219
Bayer grid, 218
benefits of, 219
Charge-Coupled Device, 218
Color Filter Arrays, 218
Complementary Metal Oxide Semiconductor, 218
demosaicing, 218
digital film, 218
functioning of, 218
further reading, 220
Junction Field Effect Transistor, 218
Logitech Fotoman, 219
Mavica, 219
memory, 219
Microdrive, 219

Camera, digital (*Continued*)
  photojournalism, 219
  pixel, 218
  Secure Digital card, 219
  sensor array, 219
  still video camera, 219
  studio cameras, 219
Camera, disposable, 220, 221
  35 mm film in, 220
  APS format, 221
  basic concept, 220
  black and white, 221
  children's use of, 220
  environmental consciousness and, 220
  first, 220
  Fuji Quick-Snap, 220
  further reading, 221
  Konica, 221
  low price of, 220
  main concerns of consumers, 220
  marketing, 220
  panoramic format, 221
  pseudo-panoramic, 220
  reduction of film frame, 221
  success of in other markets, 221
  telephoto, 221
  use of in harsh environment, 220
  user re-loadable, 221
Camera, instant or Polaroid, 221–223
  art photographers, 223
  Captiva/Vision series, 223
  cheaper plastic bodied models, 222
  children/youth market, 223
  competition, 223
  Edwin Land and, 222
  electronic shutter, 222
  film speed ISO 640, 223
  fine art photography, 221
  first films, 222
  first integral film system, 222
  focus system, 223
  folding cameras, 223
  further reading, 223
  history of instant photography, 221
  I zone, 223
  Joycam, 223
  Konica auto-focus camera, 222
  lawsuits, 223
  mechanical process, 221
  one-step photography, 222
  Onestep, 222
  Polaroid's difficult situation, 223
  Popshots, 223
  Quintic lens, 223
  second generation of cameras, 222
  Spectra/Image cameras, 223
  success of, 222
  SX702, 222
Camera, overview, 213–216
  camera obscura, 214
  further reading, 216
  light control, 215, 216
    exposure, 215
    light meters, 215, 216
    shutter and aperture, 216
  pinhole camera, 214
  rangefinder cameras, 215
  simple camera, 214
  single lens reflex, 215
  twin lens reflex, 215
  view cameras, 214–215
Camera, pinhole, 214, 225, 226
  ambient light, 225
  Andre Kertzenblatz, 225
  angle of view, 226
  camera obscura, 225
  chaotic quality of light, 226
  coining of, 226
  depth of field, 226
  exposure times, 226
  further reading, 226
  historical activity in art world, 226
  history, 226
  Jeff Guess, 225
  mouth as, 225
  multiple exposures, 226
  Patricia Gabas, 225
  pinhole cabin, 225
  pinhole photography as well-published topic, 226
  qualities to pinhole photographs, 226
  scientific activity, 226
  Sir David Brewster, 226
Camera, point and shoot, 227, 228
  active system, 227
  assist beam, 227
  auto-focus systems, 227
  available film speeds, 228
  backlit subjects, 228
  first functioning roll film camera, 227
  fixed lens, 228
  Kodak Brownie, 227
  light meter sensors, 228
  miniaturization, 227
  mousetraps, 227
  night mode, 228
  passive system, 227
  rangefinder cameras and, 227
  slow sync flash, 228
  spot meters, 228
  technical challenge of 35 mm cameras, 227
  warning lights, 228
Camera obscura, 214, 224, 225
  camera without film, 224
  coining of phrase, 224
  Della Porta accused of sorcery, 224
  development of tiny versions, 224
  first account of, 224
  first recorded observations of, 224
  forms, 224
  further readings, 225
  Jan Vermeer, 225
  Johann Kepler and, 224
  Leonardo da Vinci and, 224
  Magiae Naturalis, 224
  naturally occurring phenomenon, 224
  Nicèphore Nièpce, 225
  oculus artificialis, 224
  prototype for modern, 225
  recorder of truth, 225
  replication of human vision, 225

Camera obscura (*Continued*)
true descendant, 225
walk-in, 225
William Henry Fox Talbot, 225
Canada, 228–236
Aboriginal nations, 230
aerial photography by provincial governments, 233
America's dominance, 229
appropriation, 235
artistic possibilities of photography, 234
Authorization, 234
Before the Flood, 234
books showing the Canadian landscape, 233
Canadian monuments, 229
Canadian Museum of Contemporary Photography, 232
Canadian North, 229
Canadian Press Photo Archives, 234
catalogues, 236
celebrity portraits, 230
Chow Dong Hoy, 230
Cinéma direct, 232
Claudel Huot, 233
colonial point of view, 229
colorized photographs, 230
contrasting seasons, 228
The Convent Series, 234
Copy Art, 235
Edward Burtynsky, 234
Emergence from the Shadow: First Peoples' Photographic Perspectives, 232
environmental photographer, 234
Eugen Kedl, 233
exhibition catalogues, 233
exploring history through archival photography, 234
famous experimental photographer abroad, 234
Fernand Nathan, 233
fine-arts concerns, 231
foreign photographers and perception of Canada, 231
Fotoflash, 235
francophones, 229
further reading, 236
General Idea, 307
George Johnston, 232
government portraits, 231
Henri Cartier-Bresson montage, 231
history of Canadian photography, 229
holography, 235
illustrated books, 234
immigrant photographers, 230
international trends, 235
John Max, 231
La Province de QuÒbec, 233
laboratory of photographers in Quèbec City, 230
Land Art movement, 233
Lida Moser, 231
Malak, 231
Manifestation, 234
Michael Snow, 234
Michel Brault's aesthetic innovation, 232
most original contribution from Canadian filmmakers, 232
National Archives, 231
National Association for Photographic Art, 235
National Film Board of Canada, 232
Native and Inuit photographers, 232
Native women photographers, 232
Niagara Falls, 229
Nova Scotia College of Art and Design, 235
official photographers, 229
photo clubs, 236
photographers of importance, 231
Photographic Guild of Nova Scotia, 235–236
Pinsonneault family studios, 230
population of, 228
regeneration, 235
renowned Canadian photographer, 230
rephotography, 235
respected photographer, 230, 231
Roloff Beny, 231
Sam Tata, 231
Sidney Carter, 230
social documentary photography, 231
sports, 233
St. Lawrence Valley photographers, 229
stereoscopy, 229
stereotypes, 229
Studios Livernois collaborators, 230
tintype, 229
uniting of, 228
Vogue magazine, 231
war photography, 233
workaday professionals, 229
worker photography, 234
World Heritage List, 229
Xerography, 235
Yousuf Karsh, 230
Yukon Field Force, 233
Canadian Centre for Architecture, 97
Capa, Robert, 237–241
Allied landing at Omaha Beach, 238
American citizenship, 239
Andrè Kertèsz and, 237
The Battle of Waterloo Bridge, 238
biography, 239
close-range candid photo-reportage, 237
Contax camera, 239
David Szymin and, 237
Dephot, 237
Der Welt Spiegel, 237
emergency replacement photographer, 239
exiled revolutionary Leon Trotsky, 237
further reading, 241
Gerda Taro and, 238
group exhibitions, 240
Henri Cartier-Bresson and, 237
Hungarian-American, 237–239
Illustrated, 239
individual exhibitions, 240
Japanese invasion of China, 238
Life magazine, 238
Magnum Photos, 239
miscellaneous assignments, 238
orphanages, 238
Overseas Press Club, 239
political activism, 237
professional contacts, 237
rise to power of Adolph Hitler, 237
Robert Capa Gold Medal Award, 239
Robert Capa-David Seymour Photographic Foundation, 239
Rolleiflex camera, 238
selected works, 240, 241

Capa, Robert (*Continued*)
Slightly Out of Focus, 239
Spanish civil war, 238
Tour de France bicycle race, 238
Vu magazine, 237
war photography and, 1639
war photography, 237
Werner Bischof-Robert Capa-David Seymour Photographic Memorial Fund, 239
World War II iconic photographs, 238
Capitalist Realism, 47
Caponigro, Paul, 241–244
American, 241, 242
Ansel Adams, 241
biography, 242
close-ups, 241
craftsmanship, 241
darkroom technique, 241
distinctive strength, 241
Eastern brush painting, 242
elusive image of nature's subtle realms, 241
enduring influences on, 241
further reading, 244
language of photography, 241
monographs, 242–244
Native American art, 242
photographs with most meaning, 241
power of natural landscape, 241
ritual objects, 242
selected exhibitions, 242
selected works, 244
sensitivity to place, 241
spiritual dimensions of landscape, 241, 242
survey of material world, 242
Carbo printing process, 84
Carrillo, Manuel, 244–246
artistic legacy, 245
biography, 246
choice of subject matter, 245
Club Fotográfico de Mèxico, 244
criticism of work as sentimental, 245
developing and printing, 245
emaciated street dogs, 245
further reading, 246
greatest regret, 244
group exhibitions, 246
individual exhibitions, 246
international exhibitions, 245
Los Inseparables, 245
Mamiyaflex camera, 245
Mexican film industry, 244
Mexican, 244, 245
Mi Pueblo, 244, 245
odd jobs, 244
Photozoom magazine, 245
private collections, 245
publication of photographs in foreign magazines, 245
reputation as artistic genius, 244
Saturday Review photograph competition, 244, 245
selected works, 246
trophy, 244
well-known photograph, 244
Cartes-de-visite, 34
Cartier-Bresson, Henri, 246–250
abstraction of real world, 247
archetype of itinerant photojournalist, 246
biography, 249
Brownie camera, 247
cooperative photo agency, 248
decisive moments captured, 248
Far Eastern assignments, 248
French, 246–249
further reading, 250
German invasion of France, 247
group exhibitions, 249
Henri Cartier-Bresson Foundation, 248
individual exhibitions, 249
international travel, 248
introduction to medium, 247
Magnum Photos, 248
Man and Machine, 248
member of Resistance, 247, 248
Museum of Modern Art retrospective, 248
New York Times, 246
philosophy, 247
pre-visualization of images, 247
prisoner-of-war camps, 247
rise as international photojournalist, 248
selected works, 249
seminal figure in postwar era, 246
sympathy for oppressed classes, 247
the decisive moment, 247
vision, 247
CCD, *see* Charge-coupled device
CCP, *see* Center for Creative Photography
Censorship, 250–252
Alice Sims, 252
anti-Catholic photograph, 251
anti-religious themes, 251
Associated Press, 250
Bauhaus and Nazism in Germany, 251
blacklisting, 251
Chinese government control, 251
communistic tendencies in modern art, 251
Corcoran Gallery of Art cancellation, 251
danger of photography, 250
Eastman Kodak private censorship operation, 250
further reading, 252
government view of conflict, 250
Jock Sturges, 252
military censors, 250
Minor White's omitted references to homosexuality, 251
multiplicity of agendas and, 250
National Endowment for the Arts, 252
outcry against photographs deemed to be obscene, 251
Photo Notes, 251
power of control, 250
prevalence of, 250
Sally Mann, 252
selection process for government grants, 252
self-censoring artist, 251
sexual censoring, 251
Sleeping Venus, 250
times of war, 250
United States government, 250
use of, 250
volatile censorship battle, 251
Works Progress Administration, 251
Center for Creative Photography (CCP), 66, 252–254
Ansel Adams Research Fellowship, 254

Center for Creative Photography (CCP) (*Continued*)
Center for Creative Photography, 253
copyright, 254
department of rights and reproductions, 254
exhibitions hosted by, 252
exhibitions, 253
founding archives, 253
founding of, 252
further reading, 254
Harold Jones, 253
Light Gallery, 253
location of, 252
manuscript collections, 253
print collection, 253
publications circulated by, 252
publishing record, 253
scholarly bibliographies, 253
traveling exhibitions, 253
Central Africa, *see* Africa, Central and West
Central America, 254–260
aesthetic, 255
arrival of photography, 254
Barbados, 259
Caribbean countries, 254
colonialist market, 255
Coloquio Latinoamericano de Fotografia, 256
comment by Fidel Castro, 255
communication structure, 257
contemporary reality, 256
Corcoran College of Art and Design, 259
Costa Rica, 259
countries, 254
criticism of Hecho colloquia, 256
Cuba, 257
decline in sponsorship of documentary photography, 256
dictatorships, 256
distinctive aura to Latin American work, 256
documentation by journalists, 255
Dominican Republic, 259
El Salvador, 258, 259
Fidel Castro's official photographer, 258
Fotofest, 257
Fotogrupo, 259
further reading, 260
Guatemala, 258
Guerrillero Heroica, 258
Honduras, 258
hoping for social change, 257
identity, 255
Images of Silence, 255, 257
In the Eye of the Beholder, 259
itinerate photographers, 255
Jamaica, 259
Jueves 68, 259
lack of available information, 257
leftist orientation, 256
mobile business of photography, 255
Museum of Contemporary Hispanic Art, 258
mythical interpretations, 256
Nicaragua, 258
Nicaraguan Institute of Film, 258
Panama, 258
perspectives, 255
photography competition, 256
photojournalism, 258
pioneer photographers, 254
Popular Culture Association, 259
Portobelo, 258
praise for *Hecho en Latinoamerica*, 257
Puerto Rico, 259
recent paths of photography, 257
Revolucion, 258
revolutionary importance, 258
scarcity of information, 255
sources of information, 255
struggles for political stability, 255
studio portraiture, 255
surprise visit by Fidel Castro, 256
three-dimensional works, 258
unified projects, 256
violent national agenda, 259
web galleries, 259
Windows on Latin American, 255
Zonezero, 259
Zurich exhibition, 257
Centre Nationale de la Photographie (CNP), 260, 261
American Farm Securities Administration photography project, 261
audiovisual productions, 261
audiovisual productions, 261
biennial exhibition, 260
contact sheet, 261
creation of, 260
cultural services, 261
first director, 261
Grand Prix International Henri-Cartier Bresson Award, 261
One Minute for One Image, 261
Palais de Tokyo, 260
Photo Poche, 260
Printemps du Cahors, 261
publication, 260
Regis Durand and, 261
role of, 261
solo exhibitions, 260
vision for, 261
works of unknown photographers, 260
world's largest exhibition space, 260
CF form factor, *see* CompactFlash form factor
CFAs, *see* Color Filter Arrays
Chambi, Martín, 262–264
American Revolutionary Popular Alliance, 262
appreciation of indigenous culture, 262–263
apprenticeship, 262
artistic legacy, 262
biography, 263
cultural identity, 263
dignity of individuals, 262
Earthwatch Foundation, 263
Edward Ranney and, 263
further reading, 264
group exhibitions, 263
Inca culture, 262
individual exhibitions, 263
Indo America, 262
Machu Picchu, 263, 264
most productive years, 263
newly rich clients, 262
outdoor work, 262
Peruvian, 262, 263
political indifference, 262, 263

Chambi, Martín (*Continued*)
selected works, 263–264
singular chiaroscuro, 263
technical achievements, 263
Charge-coupled device (CCD), 77, 218, 299
Chargesheimer, 265–268
adoption of artist's name, 265
articles published about, 266
biography, 266
close-up portrayals of stars, 265
Cologne Intime, 266
darkroom experiments, 266
description of approach, 265
early photography, 265
further reading, 268
German, 265, 266
group exhibitions, 266–268
individual exhibitions, 266
influence of *Art Informel*, 265
Museum Ludwig, 265
photo-essay books, 265
photographic theater, 265
Photo-Kino exhibition, 265
portraits, 265
post-war photography of, 265
reevaluated negatives, 266
selected works, 268
Stadtsbrger, 266
Subjective Photography, 265
theater designer, 265
Wolfgang Vollmer, 266
Chemical experimentation, 7
China and Taiwan, 268–279
ambitious photo album, 273
anti-imperialist movement, 269
arrival of photography in China, 268
Chang Tsai, 273, 274
Chen Changfen, 271
Chen Chieh-jen, 277
Chen Lingyang, 272
Chen Shun-chu, 277
Chen Wanli, 269
Cheng Shang-his, 276
Cheng Yin-jen, 276
Chin dynasty, 269
China Photographic Society, 270
China Pictorial, 270
China Reconstructs, 270
Chinese painting principles, 275
Chinese Photography Association, 274
Community Party and, 270
contemporary photography after mid-1990s, 271–273
contemporary photography in connection with digital technology in 1990s, 276, 277
contemporary photography in Taiwan, 277
Cultural Revolution, 271
cyber culture, 277
Dafengji, 269
Darwin's theory of evolution, 277
documentary photography in China after 1911, 269, 270
documentary photography in late 1980s, 271
dominance of realist style, 274
Donald Mennie, 269
Duplicated Me Photo Shop, 273
Echo magazine, 276
Felice Beato, 269
female photographers, 276
fine-arts expression in People's Republic, 271
first photographs made, 269
Forbidden City, 269
Four Beauties, 271
further reading, 277
Gao Shin-jiang, 276
Guang Association, 269
"High Class Photographer," 268
historical motifs, 272
Hong Lei, 272
Hou Bo, 270
Hu Boxiang, 270
Hu Yung, 275
Huang Baohui, 270
increasing affluence, 271
intentional photography and modern photography in 1960s and 1970s, 275
Jang Jao-tang, 275
Jang Jao-tung, 276
Jang Shr-shian, 276
Judgement, 277
Ke Shi-jie, 275
landscape photography of Great Wall, 271
landscape photography, 271
leading exponent of theories on photography in China, 269
Lee Ming-diao, 273, 274
Lin Tsao, 273
Liu Bannong, 269
Liu Zheng's series, 271
locust symbol, 271
Long Chin-san, 269
Long Chin-san, 274
Man and Land, 276
May 30th Movement, 269
Mee Cheung, 268
Milton Miller's motifs, 268
montage pictorial photography after World War II, 274, 275
montage pictorial photography, 274
National Geographic Society, 269
Orchid Island aboriginals, 276
Origin, 277
Peng Ruei-lin's experimentalism, 273
Photo Century, 275
Photographers, 276
photography from 1895 to 1948 during Taiwan's colonial period under Japanese occupation, 273, 274
photography in China, 268, 269
photography in Taiwan, 273
portraits of Communist leaders, 270
process of Western modernization, 271
propaganda tools, 270
Renjian, 276
reportage photography from 1970s to 1990s, 275, 276
Rong Rong, 272
Shr Chiang, 273
significant moment in PRC history, 270
Sino-Japanese War, 273
social documentary during anti-Japanese war and civil war in 1930s, 270, 271
symbolism of wartime patriotic struggle, 271
Taiwan forced out of United Nations, 275
Taiwan Photographic Society, 274
Talking about Photography, 269

China and Taiwan (*Continued*)
tea ladies, 274
Teng Nan-kuang, 273
Teng Nan-kuang's best-known work, 274
The Sino-Japanese Hostilities, 268
traditional Chinese aesthetic, 269
training, 268
Twelve Moon Flowers, 272
urban development, 272
V-10, 275
violent events, 277
Wall Straddle, 272
Wang Xhin, 276
Weng Fen, 272
Western photographers, 268, 269
Wulsin Expedition to Northwest China, 269
Xu Xiaobing, 270
Yang Yong, 272
Yang Zhenzhong, 273
Yao Jui-chung, 277
Zhang Huan, 273
Zhuang Hui, 272
Christenberry, William, 279–284
Abstract Expressionists, 279
accidental introduction to photography, 279
American, 279–281
Arshile Gorky and, 279
biography, 281
Brownie prints, 280
childhood experiences, 280
Deardorff view camera, 280
desire to possess subjects, 281
direct compositions, 280
dolls, 281
Fortune, 280
further reading, 283
group exhibitions, 282, 283
iconography, 281
incorporation of signage into work, 279
individual exhibitions, 282
Kodak Brownie, 279
Ku Klux Klan, 281
kudzu, 281
Let Us Now Praise Famous Men, 280
life cycles, 281
losses of past, 280
paintings, 281
Pop artists, 279
portraits of American Deep South, 280
post-World War II color photographer, 279
sculptures, 281
selected works, 283
seminal moment, 280
Southern roots, 281
stereotypes, 281
subject matter, 280
Walker Evans and, 280
Willem de Kooning and, 279
Chronophotography, 6, 157
Cibachrome, 49
Cinéma direct, Canadian, 232
Citroen, Paul, Umbo and, 1578
Civic responsibilities, photography fulfilling, 3
Clarence H. White School of Photography, 7
Clark, Larry, 284–287
American, 284–287
Another Day in Paradise, 285
baby portrait photographer, 285
biography, 287
Bully, 285
coming-of-age story, 285
conventions of documentary, 284
expression of subconscious emotional responses, 287
first feature film, 285
further reading, 287
graphic photographs, 284
group exhibitions, 287
heroin users, 285
individual exhibitions, 287
influence of mass media on teenagers, 285
intimate situations, 284
montage, 284
National Endowment for the Arts, 285
Ralph Gibson's Lustrum fine arts press, 285
selected works, 287
self-destruction, 285
sexualized violence, 287
Teenage Lust, 285
themes, 284
Tulsa, 284, 285
voyeuristic fascination with potential for violence, 284
Class Seven, 1617
Close, Chuck, 287–290
American, 287–289
biography, 289
classmates, 288
confrontational portraits, 288
A Couple of Ways of Doing Something, 288
differentiation between illusion and reality, 289
digital IRIS prints, 288
enormous scale, 288
found photographs, 288
further reading, 289–290
group exhibitions, 289
iconic portraits, 287
individual exhibitions, 289
knitting, 287
Pace/MacGill Gallery, 288
Photorealists, 288
Polaroid format, 287, 288
post-war American art, 288
recognition as painter, 287
selected works, 289
sense of overallness, 288
subject matter, 288
truth behind realism, 289
updating of daguerreotype process, 288
use of photography to answer questions, 288
Yale University School of Art, 288
CMOS, *see* Complementary Metal Oxide Semiconductor
CMY primaries, 301
CNP, *see* Centre Nationale de la Photographie
Coburn, Alvin Langdon, 290–293
Arts and Crafts' ideals of craftsmanship, 291
association with Photo-Secession, 290
biography, 291
bookmaking, 291
British, born American, 290, 291
camps straddled, 290
complex career, 290

Coburn, Alvin Langdon (*Continued*)
Composition, 290
experimenting in photography, 291
further reading, 293
George Bernard Shaw, 290
group exhibitions, 291–293
individual exhibitions, 291
Linked Ring Brotherhood, 290
Little Galleries of the Photo-Secession, 290
Metropolitan Magazine, 290
naturalized British citizen, 291
New School of American Photography, 290
nickname, 290
non-objective photography, 291
Pictorial photography's soft tone, 291
portrait studio, 290
selected works, 293
spiritual concerns, 291
Symbolist leanings, 291
Vorticist movement, 291
Vortographs, 291
Cohen, Lynne, 293–296
artist residencies, 295
biography, 295
black and white work, 294
Canadian, 293–295
desire for directness, 294
early influences, 294
evolution of subject matter, 293
Formica, 294
found places, 294
framing of photographs, 295
Front and Back, 294
further reading, 296
group exhibitions, 295, 296
individual exhibitions, 295
Minimalism, 294
modern human experience, 295
New Topographic photographers, 293
No Man's Land, 294
Pop Art, 294
printmaking projects, 294
selected works, 296
signature impassive style, 293
social landscape, 293
stand-ins for bodies, 294
view camera, 294
Coke, Van Deren, 297–299
American, 297, 298
biography, 298
Cibachromes, 298
control of Eastman House, 297
court enigma, 298
Edward Weston and, 298, 299
essence of art, 298
first American exhibition by contemporary German artists, 297
flashing prints, 298
further reading, 299
group exhibitions, 298
individual exhibitions, 298
means philosophic communication, 297
rejection of art history topic, 297
San Francisco Museum of Modern Art, 297
selected works, 298, 299
self-expression, 297
surreal photographs, 298
Cold War, aerial imagery during, 21
Colonial ethnography, 28
Color correction filters, 213
Color Filter Arrays (CFAs), 218
Color temperature, 299, 300
CCD sensors, 299
daylight film, 299
definition of, 299
digital cameras, 299
filters, 299
fluorescent light, 300
further reading, 300
improper color balance, 300
magenta filter, 300
natural daylight, 300
photo floodlight, 299
tungsten film, 299
tungsten light bulb, 299
types of film, 299
white balancing, 299
Color theory, natural and synthetic, 300–303
achievement of color balance, 302
Adobe PhotoShop, 302
analogous hues, 303
brightness, 300
Cibachrome, 302
CMY primaries, 301
CMYK mode, 302
color balance in digital imaging, 302
color contrast, 303
color elements, 300
color transparency film, 301
color wheel, 301
cool colors, 303
dye diffusion, 302
dye sublimation prints, 302
early color experimentation, 301
graininess and fast film, 302
hue, 300
Ilfachrome, 302
Kodachrome film, 301
overexposure of slide film, 301
perceived difference in adjacent colors, 303
photo multiplier tubes, 302
photographic color theory, 300
process color, 302
process popular for advertising, 301
purposes of color photography, 303
RGB colors, 301
saturation, 300
subtractive color process, 301, 302
value, 300
warm colors, 303
Communication, picture as means of, 1
Communication, symbolic, 134
CompactFlash (CF) form factor, 219
Complementary Metal Oxide Semiconductor (CMOS), 218
Composition, 303–305
balance, 304–305
basic building blocks of image, 304
contrast, 304
emotional response, 304, 305
focus, 304
framing, 304

Composition (*Continued*)
further reading, 305
gaze, 304
impact of image, 305
lighting, 304
lines, 303–304
perspective, 304
planes, 304
responses to image, 303
rule of thirds, 303
scale, 304
shape, 304
vantage point, 304
Computer Aided Design (CAD), 1623
Concept Art groups, architectural photography and, 60
Conceptual Art, architectural photography and, 61
Conceptual photography, 305–308
After Walker Evans, 306
AIDS crisis, 307
Andy Warhol, 305
architectural forms and, 305
artists' books genre, 305
Auditions, 307
auditions, 307, 308
characteristics of, 305
dematerialized image, 305
documentation of performance, 307
Duchamp's radical use of ready-made, 306
Ed Ruscha's photo-based books, 305
Eight Student Nurses, 306
emphasis of, 305
exploration of identity, 306
feminist theory and, 306
flourishing of in 1960s, 305
further reading, 308
gay subcultures, 307
General Idea, 307
histories, 308
impact of cinema, 306
message conveyed by photographic image, 305
method of documentation, 305
montage work, 306
philosophical principle, 305
photographic image as cultural text, 306
photographic lightboxes, 306
photographic reproductions, 305
photography as typology, 305
political issues, 307
popular culture, 307
poststructuralist philosophy, 306
reinterpretations, 308
rephotographing, 306
rigorously aesthetic composition, 307
Robert Rauschenberg, 305
sequential presentation, 307
sexual identity, 307
Stretch, 306
Condé Nast, 308–310
Advance Publications, Inc., 310
approval of photographs, 309
archive, 310
audience, 309
avant-garde approaches to portraiture, 309
Collier's Weekly, 308
commissioned photography, 309
consumer magazine publishing, 308
editorial themes, 309
further reading, 310
fusion of color photography and glossy magazine pages, 309
generous contract, 309
The History of Fashion Photography, 309, 310
Internet publication, 310
launching of photographers' careers, 308
publishing empire, 308
stylistic preference, 309
Vanity Fair, 308, 309
Vogue art director, 309
Vogue editor-in-chief, 309
Vogue fashion editor, 309
Vogue, 308
W magazine, 310
Connor, Linda, 310–315
American, 310–312
anthropological notations, 311
best-known image, 311
biography, 312
conservationist sympathies, 310
cosmic relationships, 312
Critical Mass, 311
definition of self in nature, 311
depictions of landscape, 310
desert environments, 311
dream-like vignettes, 311
duplication of platinum print, 311
Earthworks, 310
enlightenment, 312
further reading, 313–314
group exhibitions, 312–313
The Heavens, 312
individual exhibitions, 312
lunar solar eclipses, 312
manifest destiny, 310
modern traveler in search of religious grounding, 312
Native American spiritual sites, 311
New Topographics, 311
oblique portrait, 311
overtaking of nature for corporate development, 311
prints of astronomical occurrences, 312
religious longings, 312
romantic leanings of work, 312
selected works, 313
Spiral Jetty, 310
spiritual energy, 311
spiritual interests, 312
summation, 312
symbiotic mythology, 311
tourist attraction, 310
Conservation, 315–320
acid free papers, 317
acid free tissue, 319
CD-ROM, 319
cellulose acetate film, 318
chemical changes, 317
cold storage, 316, 318
color photographs and negatives, 318
commonplace photography, 315
conservation papers, 317
digital media, 319

Conservation (*Continued*)
disrespect for photographs, 315
emulsion, 316
environmental problems, 317
exposure to light, 316
film based negatives, 318
further reading, 319, 320
handling, 317
heat and moisture, 316, 317
housekeeping, 317
invention of cellulose nitrate film base, 318
layers of photographs, 316
light levels in museum settings, 316
memory cards, 319
most overlooked aspect of preservation, 317
mounts and albums, 319
new image carrying devices, 319
nitrate film stock, 318, 319
overlooked methods of preserving images, 315
photographic materials, 315
pHoton, 317
physical and chemical structures, 315
physical damage, 317
plastic coated prints, 316
polyester film and rainbow effect, 318
polyester, 317
prevention of deterioration, 315, 317
problems, 316
relative humidity, 316, 318
removal of surface dirt, 319
restoration services, 316
retouching of vintage prints, 319
safety film, 319
Silversafe, 317
storage, 317, 318
storing negatives, 318
strain of emulsion, 317
sunlight, 316
vinegar syndrome, 318
wet cleaning processes, 319
Constructed reality, 320–324
The Accident, 322
ambiguous imagery, 321
challenge to photographic realism, 321
conversion of actual into photographic, 323
Dadaists, 321
decisive moment, 320
devised fauna and flora, 322
directorial photography, 320
dismantling of constructions, 324
Excavations, 322
fabricated imagery, 320
Fading Away, 320
female stereotypes from B-movies, 322
Fox Games, 322
further reading, 324
historical precedents, 320
importance of fabricated pieces, 323
Julia Margaret Cameron, 320
Man Ray, 321
manipulation of photographic elements, 323
mockumentary, 322
notion about nuclear energy, 322
Notman studios, 320
Oscar Gustave Rejlander, 320, 323
photograms, 321
photographic truth, 321
photographic use within scientific circles, 322
photomontage, 320
picture perfect images, 322
preconceived idea of final image, 320
Rayographs, 321
representational codes, 323
Russian Constructivist, 321
set *in situ*, 323
set-up photography, 320
social concerns, 321
staged photography, 320, 321
tableaux photography, 320, 322
Tourism series, 322
types of, 320
Untangling, 322
Constructivism, 73, 74
Constructivist preoccupation, photogram processes and, 7
Constructivists, 43
Consumer-level cameras, first, 215
Contact printing, 324–326
advantages of proof sheets, 325
alternative processes, 326
burning-in, 326
common uses, 325, 326
cropping, 326
dodging, 326
drawback with paper-negative, 326
Emmet Gowin, 325
emulsion-to-emulsion contact, 324
experimentation with loss of detail, 325
f/64 group, 325
final photographic prints, 325
fixing of test strip, 325
further reading, 326
generations, 324
gum bichromate prints, 326
handling of paper, 324
limitations, 326
manipulation of photograph, 325
negative-and-paper stack, 324
negative-holding sheets, 325
Ortho-on-Ortho, 326
paper negatives, 324, 325
positive print, 325
printing frame easel, 324
printing frames, 324
Sally Mann, 325
test strips, 324, 325
Contax camera, 239
Contrast, 327–328
changing of filters, 327
darkroom techniques, 327
density range of negative, 327
enlarger light source, 327
film speed, 327
finding style, 328
negative, 327
photographic print paper, 327
positive versus negative space, 327
presence or absence of, 328
print, 327
range, 327
salvage procedures, 327

Contrast (*Continued*)
shadows, 328
tonality of print, 328
variable contrast papers, 327, 328
Coplans, John, 328–332
Andy Warhol and, 329
Artforum, 328, 329
biography, 330
British, 328–330
career as writer, 328
commonality of human form, 330
Constantin Brancusi's photographs, 329
dialogue magazine, 328, 329
Ed Ruscha and, 329
exhibitions of photomontages, 329
further reading, 332
group exhibitions, 330–332
humankind in most primal sense, 330
individual exhibitions, 330
Judy Chicago and, 329
monographs on contemporary artists, 329
need to establish forums for artists, 329
neglect of West Coast art scene, 329
perspective of Weegee's photography, 329
Roy Lichtenstein and, 329
selected works, 332
self-portraits, 328
shared genetics, 330
social reactions to age, 330
sublime understanding of humanity, 328
Swahili, 328
Tate Gallery, 329
technique to de-emphasize youth, 330
timeless subject, 329
Copy Art, Canadian, 235
Corbis, 67
Corbis/Bettmann, 332–336
Bettmann Archive, 334
celebrity archive, 334
center of European book trade, 333
dissertation, 333
enthusiasm for collecting images, 333
film footage, 334
first commission, 333
flourishing business, 334
forward migration, 335
further reading, 336
gelatin, 335
Gendreau Collection of Americana, 334
grand plan, 333
hand-made art book, 333
Henry Wilhelm and, 335
Hitler's rise to power, 333
image bank, 334
images appropriate for clients' needs, 335
immigration to America, 333
intelligentsia of Leipzig, 332
interest in academics, 333
Microsoft Corporation, 334
New York Public Library, 333
newsworthy images, 335
original intent, 335
Outline, 334
photographic conservation expert, 335
photo-journalist archives, 334
pounding the pavement, 333
Prussian State Art Library, 333
rare books, 334
repository of imagery, 333
Reuters, 334
royalty-free imagery, 334
sub-zero vault, 335
The History of the World in Pictures, 333
transporting of archive, 335
United Press International, 334
Web site, 335
world's largest underground storage facility, 335
Coronet, 2
Corporate collections, 336–339
art consultants and, 336
auctioned, 339
Baron James de Rothchild, 336
best-known, 336
building adornment, 338–339
commissioned photographs, 336
contemporary artists, 337
David Rockefeller, 337
digital prints, 338
first, 336
further reading, 339
Gillman Paper Company collection, 337
Hallmark photographic collection, 337
Henry Fox Talbot, 337
historical works, 337
Institute of Design, 337
insurance company, 338
International Museum of Photography and Film, 336
JP Morgan Chase collection, 337
Kodak company, 336
LaSalle National Bank collection, 337, 338
Metropolitan Museum of Art, 337
Microsoft collection, 338
museum exhibitions, 336
photo transfers, 338
Polaroid collection, 338
post-war photographers, 338
Safeco collection, 338
Seagram collection, 338, 339
7-Eleven collection, 336
Sotheby's New York, 336
Southland Corporation, 336
testing of instant films, 338
traveling exhibitions, 337
vintage works, 337
Walker Evans, 337, 339
Weegee, 339
Creative camera, 339–341
The Arts Council of Great Britain, 340
Bill Brandt, 340
British reconstruction, 339
camera club alliances, 339
changes in social politics, 340
changing opinion, 341
Colin Osman's editorial voice, 339
Coo Press Limited, 339
distribution of, 339
DPICT magazine, 341
editorial influences, 339
end of funding reliance, 341
France's Cinema Veritè, 340

Creative camera (*Continued*)
funding, 340
further reading, 341
gallery guide, 339
international debate, 339
mail-order section, 339
Mansfield Books International, 339
Mass Observation project, 339, 340
MoMA closing exhibition, 340
photography critic, 341
photography's progression since World War II, 339
public projects, 339, 340
Realist Movement, 340
separation between articles and photographs, 340
stylistic grit, 340
subscription base, 341
Thinking Photography, 340
three-dimensional presence, 339
Victoria and Albert Museum, 341
Crewdson, Gregory, 341–344
aesthetic technique, 342
aesthetic vision, 342
ambiguous narrative, 342
American vernacular landscape, 342
American, 341, 342
Aperture magazine, 341, 342
biography, 342, 343
Cindy Sherman, 342
controlled lighting, 342
description of photography, 341
Diane Arbus, 341
documentary photography with staged elements, 342
fictional worlds, 341
further reading, 344
group exhibitions, 344
individual exhibitions, 343
influential films, 342
Natural Wonder series, 342
selected works, 344
suburbia, 341
Twilight series, 342
uncanny aspect of photograph, 342
use of narrative in photography, 341
Vertigo, 342
Crime photography, 344–346
abuse, 345
autopsy record, 345
common sub-area, 344
crime victims, 345
Federal Bureau of Investigation, 345
further reading, 345
J. Edgar Hoover's philosophy of overkill, 345
John Wilkes Booth, 344
later investigation and, 344
murder scenes, 345
national legitimacy of, 344
philosophy, 345
photograph analysis, 344
reconstruction of crime scenes, 344
shocking photographs, 345
stakeout, 345
thoroughness, 345
types of, 344
Wanted posters, 344
Cropping, 346–348
Adobe Acrobat, 347
clip art catalogue, 347
contact printing and, 326
definition of, 346
freeform, 347
general principle for use of space, 347
golden triangle, 347
images eliminated, 346
importance of background, 347
journalism and, 346
layout and design, 346
means of, 347
Microsoft Picture IQ, 347
one-click, 347
Patrick Tosani and, 1548
Photo-Channel Networks Inc., 347
PhotoIQ, 347
virtual correction, 347
CSFA, *see* School of Fine Arts
Culture wars, 38
Cunningham, Imogen, 348–352
After Ninety, 350
American, 348–350
Aperture magazine, 350
avant-garde culture, 348, 349
Berkeley Art Museum, 349
biography, 350
Camera Work, 348
celebrity, 350
commercial portraiture, 349
conservatism of Victorian era, 348
double-exposures, 349
Duchamp's famous Dada painting, 349
fellowship, 348
Film und Foto exhibition, 349
first portraits, 348
first solo exhibition, 349
further reading, 351, 352
group exhibitions, 351
Group f/64, 349
Guggenheim Fellowship, 350
Harper's Bazaar, 349
individual exhibitions, 350
Lisette Model and, 349
nude photography, 348
portrait studio, 348
portraits in last series, 350
portraits of diverse personalities, 348
re-photography, 350
risks taken early in career, 348
search for reality, 348
selected works, 351
street photographs, 349
studies of mother and child, 348
The Craftsman, 348
thesis, 348

D

Dada, 353–355
cameraless images, 353
constructed reality and, 321

Dada (*Continued*)
founder, 141
further reading, 355
movement, founding members of Berlin, 142
Dadaism, 73, 74
Dadaist preoccupation, photogram processes and, 7
Daguerre, Louis, 76
Daguerreotype(s), 31
African, 34
anonymous, 64
astrophotography and, 76
Berlinische Galerie, 122
Dahl-Wolfe, Louise, 355–358
America, 355–357
biography, 357
further reading, 358
group exhibitions, 357
individual exhibitions, 357
selected works, 357, 358
Dali, Salvador, 82
Darkroom, 358–361
experimentation, 7
film processing, 358, 359
further reading, 361
print processing, 359–361
Date/time imprinting, 211
Dater, Judy, 361–363
American, 361, 362
biography, 362, 363
further reading, 363
group exhibitions, 363
individual exhibitions, 363
selected works, 363
Davidson, Bruce, 364–366
American, 364, 365
biography, 365
further reading, 366
group exhibitions, 365, 366
individual exhibitions, 365
selected works, 366
Daylight film, 299
de Meyer, Baron Adolph, 367–369
American, born France, 367, 368
biography, 368
further reading, 369
group exhibitions, 368
individual exhibitions, 368
selected works, 369
Deakin, John, 369, 370
biography, 370
British, 369, 370
further reading, 370
individual exhibitions, 370
DeCarava, Roy, 371–374
American, 371, 372
biography, 373
further reading, 373, 374
group exhibitions, 373
individual exhibitions, 373
selected works, 373
Decisive moment, 374, 375
Cartier-Bresson and, 247
constructed reality and, 320
further reading, 375
Deconstruction, 375–380
Baudrillard, 379
Derrida, 377, 378
further reading, 380
photographic text, 376
punctum, 378, 379
variety of postmodernism, 376, 377
Delano, Jack, 380–382
American, 380, 381
biography, 382
further reading, 382
group exhibitions, 382
individual exhibitions, 382
selected works, 382
Democratic medium, photography as, 1613
Demosaicing, 218
Depth of field, 383, 384
Deutscher Verlag, 137
Developing processes, 384–389
Diana Camera, *see* Camera, Diana
diCorcia, Philip-Lorca, 389–391
American, 389, 390
biography, 390
further reading, 391
group exhibitions, 391
individual exhibitions, 390
selected works, 391
Digital film, 218
Digital image manipulation software, 182
Digital media, conservation of, 319
Digital photography, 95, 391–396
bracketing with, 156
concerns raised, 395, 396
further reading, 396
history, 393–395
Digital replication, 47
Digital technology, Nancy Burson and, 189
Dijkstra, Rineke, 396–398
biography, 398
Dutch, 386–398
further reading, 398
group exhibitions, 398
individual exhibitions, 398
selected works, 398
Direct color autochrome plates, 33
Discursive spaces, 399–401
Documentary content, champion of, 3
Documentary photography, 402–410
Australia, 88
empathic, 1638
further reading, 410
Renè Burri and, 183
use of as tool for social change, 161
Dodging, 10, 410, 411
contact printing and, 326
further reading, 411
Doisneau, Robert, 412–415
biography, 413
French, 412, 413
further reading, 415
group exhibitions, 414, 415
individual exhibitions, 413, 414
selected works, 415
Domon, Ken, 415–417
biography, 416, 417
further reading, 417

Domon, Ken (*Continued*)
group exhibitions, 417
individual exhibitions, 417
Japanese, 415, 416
selected works, 417
Drtikol, František, 417–420
biography, 419
Czech, 417–419
further reading, 420
group exhibitions, 419, 420
individual exhibitions, 419
selected works, 420
Drum magazine, 24, 28
Duchamp, Marcel, readymades, 46
Duncan, David Douglas, 420–423
American, 420–422
biography, 422
further reading, 423
group exhibitions, 422
individual exhibitions, 422
selected works, 422
Dupain, Max, 87
DX-code enabled camera, 216
Dye transfer, 423, 424
basic process, 423, 424
further reading, 424
manipulation of process, 424
practical application, 424

E

Eakins, Thomas, 6
Earthworks, 310
East Africa, *see* Africa, East Africa and Indian Ocean islands
Eastern Europe, *see* Russia and Eastern Europe
Eastman, George, 77, 173
Eastman Dry Plate, 173
Eastman Kodak Company, 425–427
further reading, 427
invention of cellulose nitrate film base by, 318
private censorship operation, 250
rangefinder cameras developed by, 215
Edgerton, Harold, 427–430
American, 427–429
biography, 429
further reading, 430
individual exhibitions, 429, 430
selected works, 429
Edwards, Hugh, 72
Eggleston, William, 430–435
American, 430–433
biography, 433
further reading, 433–435
group exhibitions, 433
individual exhibitions, 433
selected works, 433
Eisenstaedt, Alfred, 435–438
biography, 437
further reading, 438
group exhibitions, 438
individual exhibitions, 437, 438
Polish-American, 435–437
selected works, 438
Eisenstein, Sergei, 102
Elsken, Ed van der, 438–440
biography, 440
Dutch, 438–440
further reading, 440
group exhibitions, 440
individual exhibitions, 440
selected works, 440
Emulsion, 441, 442
Enlarger, 442–444
further reading, 444
light source, contrast and, 327
Erfurth, Hugo, 445–448
biography, 446
further reading, 448
German, 445, 446
group exhibitions, 446
individual exhibitions, 446
selected works, 446–448
Erotic imagery, 49
Erotic photography, 448–451
Erwitt, Elliott, 451–454
American, 451, 452
biography, 452, 453
further reading, 454
group exhibitions, 454
individual exhibitions, 454
selected works, 453, 454
Esquire magazine, 52
Ethics and photography, 454–458
documentary photography, 457
further reading, 457, 458
photojournalism, 454, 455
portraiture, 455, 456
street photography, 456, 457
Ethiopia, famine of, 30
Ethnographic photography, 28
Ethnographic photography, African, 35
Eugene, Frank, 175
Europe, overview, 458–461
Evans, Frederick, 461–464
biography, 462
British, 461, 462
further reading, 463
group exhibitions, 462, 463
individual exhibitions, 462
selected works, 463
Evans, Walker, 56, 74, 464–467
American, 464, 465
biography, 465, 466
corporate collections, 337, 339
further reading, 467
group exhibitions, 466
individual exhibitions, 466
Josef Breitenbach and, 172
selected works, 466
William Christenberry and, 280
Export, Valie, 468–470
Austria, 468, 469
biography, 469
further reading, 470
group exhibitions, 469
individual exhibitions, 469
selected works, 469, 470

Exposure, 470–472
  effects on film, 471, 472
  further reading, 472
  incorrect, 155
  measurement, 470, 471
  settings, 471
Expressionism, 73, 74
Extreme formalism, Brandt's, 161
The Eye of Paris, 162

F

Family life, images of, 43
Family photography, 473–478
  further reading, 478
  practice, 475–478
  technology, 473–475
Fani-Kayode, Rotimi, 479–481
  biography, 480
  further reading, 481
  group exhibitions, 480
  individual exhibitions, 480
  Nigerian, 479, 480
  selected works, 480
FAP, *see* Federal Arts Project
Farm Security Administration (FSA), 481–484, 1588
  further reading, 484
  Library of Congress FSA-OWI collection, 1643
  the South and, 1593
  survey team, 1586, 1587
Fashion photography, 484–490
  business of, 488, 489
  definition of, 487, 488
  further reading, 490
  Hollywood glamour photography, 489, 490
Faucon, Bernard, 491–495
  biography, 492
  films, 495
  French, 491, 492
  group exhibitions, 493–495
  individual exhibitions, 492, 493
Faurer, Louis, 496–498
  American, 496, 497
  biography, 497
  further reading, 498
  group exhibitions, 497, 498
  individual exhibitions, 497
  selected works, 498
FBI, *see* Federal Bureau of Investigation
Federal Arts Project (FAP), 2
Federal Bureau of Investigation (FBI), 345
Feininger, Andreas, 498–501
  American, 498, 499
  biography, 499, 500
  further reading, 500
  group exhibitions, 500
  individual exhibitions, 500
  selected works, 500
Feininger, T. Lux, 502–504
  biography, 503
  further reading, 504
  German, 502–503
  group exhibitions, 504
  individual exhibitions, 503–504
  selected works, 504
Feldmann, Hans-Peter, 504–508
  biography, 506
  further reading, 508
  German, 504–506
  group exhibitions, 506, 507
  individual exhibitions, 506
  selected works, 507
Felix H. Man Memorial Prize, 90
Feminist photography, 508–513
  further reading, 512, 513
  gender discourse of 1970s–1980s, 509–511
  other voices of 1980s and after, 511, 512
  women's movement of 1970s, 508, 509
Feminist theory, Claude Cahun and, 200
Festivals, 513–516
Festivals, websites, 515, 516
Film(s), 516–521
  bracketing and wasting of, 156
  calotype, 517
  celluloid-based photographic film, invention of, 77
  cellulose acetate, 318
  color films, 517, 518
  color transparency, 301
  daguerreotype, 516, 517
  daylight, 299
  digital, 218
  film speed, 518, 519
  film's evolution, 518
  further reading, 521
  grain, 519
  graininess and, 302
  high-contrast, 521, 522
  history, 516
  how image is recorded, 519–521
    density and exposure, 520
    formation of image, 519, 520
    response to light, 519
    spectral sensitivity, 520, 521
    structure, 519
  infrared, 523, 524
  Kodachrome, 301
  Kodak 103a spectroscopic, 77
  modern film, 518
  Polaroid, 214
  safety, 319
  sensitivity, 215
  sheet, 214
  speed(s)
    contrast and, 327
    point-and-shoot cameras, 228
    shutter speed and, 212
  storage and handling, 519
  SX70/Time Zero, 222
  tungsten, 299
  wet collodion, 517
Filters, 213, 524–526
  behavior of light, 524
  contrast and, 327
  filter factors, 525, 526
  further reading, 526
  magenta, 300
  types of, 524, 525
  uses of, 525

Fine art, photography as, 44
Fine arts presses, 526–530
Finsler, Hans, 531, 532
  biography, 532
  further reading, 532
  German, 531, 532
  group exhibitions, 532
  individual exhibitions, 532
Fischer, Arno, 533–536
  biography, 534
  further reading, 535–536
  German, 533, 534
  group exhibitions, 535
  individual exhibitions, 534, 535
  selected works, 535
Fischli, Peter, and David Weiss, 536–538
  biography, 538
  further reading, 538
  group exhibitions, 538
  individual exhibitions, 538
  selected works, 538
  Swiss, 536–537
Five Year Plans, Stalin's, 42
Flaherty, Robert Joseph, 539–541
  American, 539, 540
  biography, 540, 541
  further reading, 541
Flashes, hot shoe, 213
Fluorescent light, 300
Flusser, Vilèm, 541–543
  biography, 542, 543
  Czech, 541, 542
  further reading, 543
  selected works, 543
Fluxus movement, 46
Focal plane shutters, 216
Formalism, 543–547
Fortune, 2
Forward migration, 335
Fosso, Samuel, 29, 547–550
  biography, 550
  further reading, 550
  group exhibitions, 550
  individual exhibitions, 550
  Nigerian/Cameroonian, 547–549
  selected works, 550
France, 551–556
Franck, Martine, 556–560
  Belgian, 556–558
  biography, 558
  books, 560
  further reading, 560
  group exhibitions, 558–560
  individual exhibitions, 558
  selected works, 560
Frank, Robert, 560–564
  biography, 563
  further reading, 564
  group exhibitions, 563, 564
  individual exhibitions, 563
  selected works, 564
  Swiss-American, 560–563
Franklin Furnace, 74
Freeform cropping, 347
Freund, Gisèle, 564–567
  biography, 566
  French, 564–566
  further reading, 567
  group exhibitions, 567
  individual exhibitions, 566, 567
  selected works, 567
Friendly interpreter, 2
Friends of Photography, 11, 567–569
FSA, *see* Farm Security Administration
f/stops, 216
Fuji film corporation, CCD developed by, 218
Fuji Quick-Snap, 220
Fukase, Masahisa, 569–572
  biography, 570
  further reading, 572
  group exhibitions, 571
  individual exhibitions, 570, 571
  Japanese, 569, 570
  selected works, 572
Fukuda, Miran, 572–574
  biography, 573
  further reading, 574
  group exhibitions, 573, 574
  individual exhibitions, 573
  Japanese, 572, 573
  selected works, 574
Funke, Jaromír, 574–578
  biography, 576
  Czech, 574–576
  further reading, 578
  group exhibitions, 577, 578
  individual exhibitions, 576, 577
Furuya, Seiichi, 578–580
  biography, 579
  further reading, 580
  group exhibitions, 580
  individual exhibitions, 579, 580
  Japanese, 578, 579
  selected works, 580
Fuss, Adam, 580–584
  biography, 582
  British, 580–582
  further reading, 584
  group exhibitions, 582–584
  individual exhibitions, 582
  selected works, 584
Futurism, 584–586
  further reading, 586
  Italian, 6
Futurist plastic dynamism, 158

G

Galleries, 587–590
Gallery 291, 290
GEH, *see* George Eastman House
Gelpke, Andrè, 590–592
  biography, 591
  further reading, 592
  German, 590–591
  group exhibitions, 591
  individual exhibitions, 591
  selected works, 591
General Idea, Canadian collective, 307

Geographic Information Systems (GIS), 21
Geometric disciplines, aerial photography and, 20
George Eastman House (GEH), 96, 1683
  corporate collection, 336
  International Museum of Photography, 16, 38, 297
  Minor White on staff at, 1683
German mass media empire, 40
German photographers, kineticism of, 7
Germany and Austria, 592–599
Gerz, Jochen, 599–602
  biography, 600, 601
  further reading, 602
  German, 599, 600
  group exhibitions, 601, 602
  individual exhibitions, 601
  selected works, 602
Giacomelli, Mario, 602–605
  biography, 604
  further reading, 605
  group exhibitions, 604
  individual exhibitions, 604
  Italian, 602–604
  selected works, 604, 605
Gibson, Ralph, 605–607
  American, 605, 606
  biography, 606
  further reading, 607
  group exhibitions, 607
  individual exhibitions, 606, 607
  selected works, 607
Gidal, N. Tim, 607–610
  biography, 609
  further reading, 610
  German, 607–609
  group exhibitions, 609
  individual exhibitions, 609
  selected works, 609, 610
Gilbert & George, 610–614
  biography, 612
  further reading, 614
  group exhibitions, 613, 614
  individual exhibitions, 612, 613
  Italian/British, 610–612
  selected works, 614
Gilpin, Laura, 614–616
  American, 614, 615
  biography, 615, 615
  further reading, 616
  group exhibitions, 616
  individual exhibitions, 616
  selected publications, 616
  selected works, 616
GIS, *see* Geographic Information Systems
Gloaguen, Hervè, 616–618
  biography, 618
  French, 616–618
  further reading, 618
  group exhibitions, 618
  individual exhibitions, 618
  selected works, 618
Global Architecture magazine, 61
Gohlke, Frank, 619–621
  American, 619, 620
  biography, 620
  further reading, 621
  group exhibitions, 621
  individual exhibitions, 620
  selected works, 621
Goldin, Nan, 621–624
  American, 621–623
  biography, 623
  further reading, 624
  group exhibitions, 624
  individual exhibitions, 623, 624
  selected slide shows, 623
  selected works, 623
Gowin, Emmet, 624–627
  American, 624–626
  biography, 626
  further reading, 627
  group exhibitions, 626
  individual exhibitions, 626
  selected works, 626
Graffiti, 47, 164
Graham, Dan, 627–630
  American, 627–628
  biography, 628
  further reading, 630
  group exhibitions, 630
  individual exhibitions, 628–630
  selected works, 630
Graham, Paul, 630–634
  biography, 632
  British, 630–632
  further reading, 634
  group exhibitions, 632–633
  individual exhibitions, 632
  selected works, 634
Graham Foundation, 206
Grain, 7
Great Depression, 44
Green Party, Joseph Beuys and, 125
Grolier Club, 73
Gropius, Martin, 121
Gropius, Walter, 58, 59
  Bauhaus and, 103
  Bauhaus-Manifest and, 105
Grossman, Sid, 634–637
  American, 634–635
  biography, 635
  further reading, 636
  group exhibitions, 636
  individual exhibitions, 636
  selected works, 636
Group exhibitions
  Abbott, Berenice, 4
  Adams, Ansel, 12
  Adams, Robert, 18
  Araki, Nobuyoshi, 50
  Arbus, Diane, 54
  Auerbach, Ellen, 84–86
  Baltz, Lewis, 97, 98
  Bayer, Herbert, 107
  Becher, Bernd and Hilla, 114
  Bellmer, Hans, 119
  Bernhard, Ruth, 124
  Beuys, Joseph, 128
  Billingham, Richard, 132
  Bischof, Werner, 136
  Blossfeldt, Karl, 139

Group exhibitions (*Continued*)
Blumenfeld, Erwin, 143
Boltanski, Christian, 148
Bourdeau, Robert, 151
Bourke-White, Margaret, 154, 155
Bragaglia, Anton Giulio, 159
Brassaï, 165
Bravo, Manuel Álvarez, 168–170
Breitenbach, Josef, 172
Bruguière, Francis Joseph, 177
Burgin, Victor, 181
Burri, Renè, 184, 185
Burrows, Larry, 187, 188
Burson, Nancy, 191–193
Cadieux, Geneviève, 198, 199
Cahun, Claude, 202
Callahan, Harry, 206, 207
Calle, Sophie, 210
Capa, Robert, 240
Carrillo, Manuel, 246
Cartier-Bresson, Henri, 249
Chambi, Martín, 263
Chargesheimer, 266–268
Christenberry, William, 283
Clark, Larry, 287
Close, Chuck, 289
Coburn, Alvin Langdon, 291–293
Cohen, Lynne, 295, 296
Coke, Van Deren, 298
Connor, Linda, 312, 313
Coplans, John, 330–332
Crewdson, Gregory, 344
Cunningham, Imogen, 351
Dahl-Wolfe, Louise, 357
Dater, Judy, 363
Davidson, Bruce, 365, 366
de Meyer, Baron Adolph, 368
DeCarava, Roy, 373
Delano, Jack, 382
diCorcia, Philip-Lorca, 391
Dijkstra, Rineke, 398
Doisneau, Robert, 414, 415
Domon, Ken, 417
Drtikol, František, 419, 420
Duncan, David Douglas, 422
Eggleston, William, 433
Eisenstaedt, Alfred, 438
Elsken, Ed van der, 440
Erfurth, Hugo, 446
Erwitt, Elliott, 454
Evans, Frederick, 462, 463
Evans, Walker, 466
Export, Valie, 469
Fani-Kayode, Rotimi, 480
Faucon, Bernard, 493–495
Faurer, Louis, 497, 498
Feininger, Andreas, 500
Feininger, T. Lux, 504
Feldmann, Hans-Peter, 506, 507
Finsler, Hans, 532
Fischer, Arno, 535
Fischli, Peter, and David Weiss, 538
Fosso, Samuel, 550
Franck, Martine, 558–560
Frank, Robert, 563, 564
Freund, Gisèle, 567
Fukase, Masahisa, 571
Fukuda, Miran, 573, 574
Funke, Jaromír, 577, 578
Furuya, Seiichi, 580
Fuss, Adam, 582–584
Gelpke, André, 591
Gerz, Jochen, 601, 602
Giacomelli, Mario, 604
Gibson, Ralph, 607
Gidal, N. Tim, 609
Gilbert & George, 613, 614
Gilpin, Laura, 616
Gloaguen, Hervé, 618
Gohlke, Frank, 621
Goldin, Nan, 624
Gowin, Emmet, 626
Graham, Dan, 630
Graham, Paul, 632, 633
Grossman, Sid, 636
Gursky, Andreas, 644, 645
Gutmann, John, 647, 648
Haas, Ernst, 651
Hahn, Betty, 654, 655
Hajek-Halke, Heinz, 658
Halsman, Philippe, 661–663
Hamaya, Hiroshi, 666
Hammarskiöld, Hans, 668
Hartmann, Erich, 672
Heartfield, John, 676
Heath, David Martin, 679, 680
Heinecken, Robert, 683, 684
Hellebrand, Nancy, 686
Henderson, Nigel, 688–690
Henri, Florence, 693
Hers, François, 695
Hilliard, John, 697
Hiro, 703
Höch, Hannah, 754
Horst, Horst P., 757–758
Hosoe, Eikoh, 762
Hoyningen-Huene, George, 766
Hurrell, George, 768
Hütte, Axel, 770
Ishimoto, Yasuhiro, 808
Iturbide, Graciela, 810, 811
Izis (Israel Bidermanas), 814
Jacobi, Lotte, 820
Janah, Sunil, 823
Jones, Harold, 833
Jones, Pirkle, 836
Josephson, Kenneth, 839, 840
Karsh, Yousuf, 843
Käsebier, Gertrude, 847
Kawada, Kikuji, 849–851
Keetman, Peter, 852, 853
Keïta, Seydou, 855, 856
Kertész, André, 860
Kessels, Willy, 862
Kesting, Edmund, 865
Killip, Chris, 870, 871
Klein, Aart, 873, 874
Klein, Astrid, 876
Klein, William, 879
Klett, Mark, 882, 883

Group exhibitions (*Continued*)
Koudelka, Josef, 887
Kozloff, Max, 890
Kruger, Barbara, 894
Krull, Germaine, 898
Lange, Dorothea, 905
Lartigue, Jacques Henri, 909
Laughlin, Clarence John, 915
Lebeck, Robert, 916
Leibovitz, Annie, 921
Lerski, Helmar, 927, 928
Levinthal, David, 931
Levitt, Helen, 936, 937
Liebling, Jerome, 951, 952
Link, O. Winston, 962
List, Herbert, 967
Long, Richard, 971
Lüthi, Urs, 975
Lynes, George Platt, 979
Lyons, Nathan, 984, 985
Maar, Dora, 990
Man Ray, 1002
Man, Felix H., 1005
Mapplethorpe, Robert, 1009, 1011
Meatyard, Ralph Eugene, 1021
Meiselas, Susan, 1024, 1025
Messager, Annette, 1029
Metzker, Ray K., 1031
Meyerowitz, Joel, 1042, 1043
Michals, Duane, 1045
Mikhailov, Boris, 1048
Miller, Lee, 1051
Misrach, Richard, 1054
Model, Lisette, 1058
Modotti, Tina, 1067
Moholy-Nagy, László, 1071
Morath, Inge, 1080
Morimura, Yasumasa, 1082, 1083
Moses, Stefan, 1089, 1090
Mulas, Ugo, 1093
Muniz, Vik, 1097
Namuth, Hans, 1143
Newman, Arnold, 1157
Newton, Helmut, 1159, 1160
Nixon, Nicholas, 1163, 1164
Novak, Lorie, 1171–1173
Olson, Lennart, 1184
Outerbridge Jr., Paul, 1189
Owens, Bill, 1191, 1192
Parr, Martin, 1197
Penn, Irving, 1200, 1201
Peress, Gilles, 1204
Peterhans, Walter, 1219
Pfahl, John, 1222–1224
Pierre et Gilles, 1270, 1271
Plossu, Bernard, 1275
Porter, Eliot, 1286
Prince, Richard, 1298, 1299
Rainer, Arnulf, 1319
Ray-Jones, Tony, 1324
Renger-Patzsch, Albert, 1327, 1328
Riboud, Marc, 1340
Rice, Leland, 1343
Roh, Franz, 1355
Rosler, Martha, 1357, 1358
Rothstein, Arthur, 1360
Rubinstein, Eva, 1365
Ruff, Thomas, 1367, 1368
Salomon, Erich, 1383
Sander, August, 1385
Schadeberg, Jürgen, 1393
Schmidt, Michael, 1395, 1396
Schneiders, Toni, 1398
Sekula, Alan, 1402, 1403
Serrano, Andres, 1407, 1408
Seymour, David "Chim", 1410
Shahn, Ben, 1413
Shaikhet, Arkadii, 1416
Sheeler, Charles, 1418
Sherman, Cindy, 1421, 1422
Shibata, Toshio, 1424, 1425
Shore, Stephen, 1427
Simpson, Lorna, 1430, 1431
Siskind, Aaron, 1438
Skoglund, Sandy, 1440, 1441
Snow, Michael, 1443–1445
Sommer, Frederick, 1465
Spence, Jo, 1480
Starn, Doug and Mike, 1482, 1483
Steichen, Edward, 1488
Steiner, Andrè, 1491
Stettner, Louis, 1493
Stieglitz, Alfred, 1496
Stone, Sasha, 1500
Struth, Thomas, 1510
Sudek, Josef, 1516
Sugimoto, Hiroshi, 1519
Szilasi, Gabor, 1527, 1528
Tabard, Maurice, 1530
Teske, Edmund, 1537
Tice, George, 1539, 1540
Tillmans, Wolfgang, 1542, 1543
Tosani, Patrick, 1550
Traub, Charles, 1556
Tseng Kwong Chi, 1558, 1559
Turbeville, Deborah, 1562
Ubac, Raoul, 1569, 1570
Uelsmann, Jerry, 1572–1574
Ulmann, Doris, 1575–1577
Umbo (Otto Umbehr), 1579
Uzzle, Burt, 1602, 1603
Van Vechten, Carl, 1607
VanDerZee, James, 1609
Vishniac, Roman, 1625
Wall, Jeff, 1634, 1635
Watanabe, Yoshio, 1647
Webb, Boyd, 1649
Weber, Bruce, 1652
Weber, Wolfgang, 1654
Weegee, 1661
Weems, Carrie Mae, 1665, 1666
Wegman, William, 1668–1672
Welpott, Jack, 1674
Weston, Edward, 1678
White, Minor, 1684
Willis-Kennedy, Deborah, 1689
Winogrand, Garry, 1693, 1694
Witkin, Joel-Peter, 1699, 1700
Wojnecki, Stefan, 1703
Woodman, Francesca, 1705

Group f/64, 10, 638–642
characteristics of photographs, 638
dissolution and legacy, 641
further reading, 642
Imogen Cunningham and, 349
precedents and background, 638, 639
relationship to pictorialism, 639, 640
straight photography and Great Depression, 640, 641
Guess, Jeff, pinhole camera and, 225
Guggenheim Fellowship, 11
Gursky, Andreas, 643–645
biography, 644
further reading, 645
German, 643, 644
group exhibitions, 644, 645
individual exhibitions, 644
selected works, 645
Gutmann, John, 645–648
American, 645–647
biography, 647
further reading, 648
group exhibitions, 647, 648
individual exhibitions, 647
selected works, 648

H

Haas, Ernst, 649–653
Austrian, 649, 650
biography, 650, 651
further reading, 651–653
group exhibitions, 651
individual exhibitions, 651
selected works, 651
Hahn, Betty, 653–655
American, 653, 654
biography, 654
further reading, 655
group exhibitions, 654, 655
individual exhibitions, 654
selected works, 654
Hajek-Halke, Heinz, 656–660
biography, 658
further reading, 658–660
German, 656–658
group exhibitions, 658
individual exhibitions, 658
selected works, 658
Halftone screen process, African, 34
Halsman, Philippe, 660–663
American, 660, 661
biography, 661
further reading, 663
group exhibitions, 661–663
individual exhibitions, 661
selected works, 663
Hamaya, Hiroshi, 663–666
biography, 664–666
further reading, 666
group exhibitions, 666
individual exhibitions, 666
Japanese, 663, 664
selected works, 666
Hammarskiöld, Hans, 666–669
biography, 668
further reading, 669
group exhibitions, 668
individual exhibitions, 668
selected works, 668–669
Swedish, 666–668
Hand coloring and hand toning, 669, 670
Harlem Renaissance, 1605
Harper's Bazaar, 53, 163
Hartmann, Erich, 670–674
American, 670–672
biography, 672
further reading, 672–674
group exhibitions, 672
individual exhibitions, 672
selected works, 672
Hasselblad cameras, 77
Hausmannizaton, 79
Heartfield, John, 674–677
biography, 675
further reading, 676
German, 674, 675
group exhibitions, 676
individual exhibitions, 675, 676
selected works, 676
Heath, David Martin, 678–680
biography, 679
Canadian, born United States, 678, 679
further reading, 680
group exhibitions, 679, 680
individual exhibitions, 679
selected works, 679
Heinecken, Robert, 73, 681–684
American, 681, 682
biography, 682
further reading, 684
group exhibitions, 683, 684
individual exhibitions, 682, 683
selected works, 682
Hellebrand, Nancy, 684–687
American, 684, 685
biography, 685, 686
further reading, 686, 687
group exhibitions, 686
individual exhibitions, 686
selected works, 686
Henderson, Nigel, 687–690
biography, 688
British, 687–688
further reading, 690
group exhibitions, 688–690
individual exhibitions, 688
selected works, 690
Henri, Florence, 690–693
biography, 692
further reading, 693
group exhibitions, 693
individual exhibitions, 692
Swiss, 690–692
Hers, François, 693–695
Belgian, 693–695
biography, 695
further reading, 695
group exhibitions, 695
individual exhibitions, 695

Hilliard, John, 695–697
biography, 696
British, 695, 696
further reading, 697
group exhibitions, 697
individual exhibitions, 696, 697
selected works, 697
Hine, Lewis, 697–701
American, 697–699
biography, 699
further reading, 701
individual exhibitions, 699–701
selected works, 701
Hiro, 701–703
biography, 702
further reading, 703
group exhibitions, 703
individual exhibitions, 702
selected works, 703
Historical evidence, 67
Historical organizations, archives of, 66
Historical periodicals, *see* Periodicals, historical
History
1980s, 744–752
nineteenth-century foundations, 703–713
postwar era, 737–744
History, interwar years, 731–737
circulation, 731–732
cultural revolution in Europe, 732, 733
effect of technique, 736
further reading, 736–737
human condition, 735, 736
History, twentieth-century developments, 713–722
color, 718, 719
contemporary photography, 720
documentary photography, 715, 716
fashion photography and portraiture, 717, 718
further reading, 721
influence of avant-garde art, 715
institutionalizing photography, 720, 721
photojournalism, 716, 717
post-war photography, 719, 720
science and technology, 718
straight photography, 714, 715
History, twentieth-century pioneers, 723–731
definition of documentary, 726, 727
further reading, 730, 731
home and nation, 729
late century pioneers, 730
motion and color, 728, 729
photojournalists, 727, 728
pioneering fashion and portrait photographers, 725, 726
provocation, 729, 730
stylistic pioneers, 723–725
war photographers, 727
Höch, Hannah, 752–755
biography, 753, 754
further reading, 754, 755
German, 752, 753
group exhibitions, 754
individual exhibitions, 754
selected works, 754
Holga camera, 217
Holography, Canadian, 235
Homage to the square paintings, Albers's, 104
Horst, Horst P., 756–759
American, 756, 757
biography, 757
further reading, 758
group exhibitions, 757, 758
individual exhibitions, 757
selected works, 758
Hosoe, Eikoh, 760–763
biography, 761
further reading, 763
group exhibitions, 762
individual exhibitions, 761, 762
Japanese, 760, 761
selected works, 762, 763
Hot shoe, 213
The House of Photography, 2
Hoyningen-Huene, George, 763–766
American, 763, 764
biography, 764–766
further reading, 766
group exhibitions, 766
individual exhibitions, 766
selected works, 766
Hurrell, George, 766–769
American, 766, 767
biography, 768
further reading, 769
group exhibitions, 768
individual exhibitions, 768
selected works, 768
Hütte, Axel, 769–771
biography, 770
further reading, 770
German, 769, 770
group exhibitions, 770
individual exhibitions, 770
selected works, 770

I

ID, *see* Institute of Design
Ikon Gallery, 131
Image
construction, perspective, 773–775
focusing, 215
theory, ideology, 775–777
Impressionism, 778–781
Indian Ocean Islands, *see* Africa, East Africa and Indian Ocean islands
Individual exhibitions
Abbott, Berenice, 4
Adams, Ansel, 12
Adams, Robert, 17, 18
Araki, Nobuyoshi, 50
Arbus, Diane, 54
Arnold, Eve, 71
Auerbach, Ellen, 84
Baltz, Lewis, 97
Bayer, Herbert, 106, 107
Becher, Bernd and Hilla, 113, 114
Bellmer, Hans, 117, 118
Bernhard, Ruth, 124
Beuys, Joseph, 127, 128
Billingham, Richard, 131, 132

Individual exhibitions (*Continued*)
Bischof, Werner, 135
Blossfeldt, Karl, 139
Blumenfeld, Erwin, 143
Boltanski, Christian, 147, 148
Bourdeau, Robert, 151
Bourke-White, Margaret, 154
Brandt, Bill, 162
Brassaï, 164, 165
Bravo, Manuel Álvarez, 168
Breitenbach, Josef, 172
Bruguière, Francis Joseph, 177
Burgin, Victor, 179
Burri, René, 184
Burrows, Larry, 187
Burson, Nancy, 190, 191
Cadieux, Geneviève, 198
Cahun, Claude, 202
Callahan, Harry, 206
Calle, Sophie, 208–210
Capa, Robert, 240
Carrillo, Manuel, 246
Cartier-Bresson, Henri, 249
Chambi, Martín, 263
Chargesheimer, 266
Christenberry, William, 282
Clark, Larry, 287
Close, Chuck, 289
Coburn, Alvin Langdon, 291
Cohen, Lynne, 295
Coke, Van Deren, 298
Connor, Linda, 312
Coplans, John, 330
Crewdson, Gregory, 343
Cunningham, Imogen, 350
Dahl-Wolfe, Louise, 357
Dater, Judy, 363
Davidson, Bruce, 365
de Meyer, Baron Adolph, 368
Deakin, John, 370
DeCarava, Roy, 373
Delano, Jack, 382
diCorcia, Philip-Lorca, 390
Dijkstra, Rineke, 398
Doisneau, Robert, 413, 414
Domon, Ken, 417
Drtikol, František, 419
Duncan, David Douglas, 422
Edgerton, Harold, 429, 430
Eggleston, William, 433
Eisenstaedt, Alfred, 437, 438
Elsken, Ed van der, 440
Erfurth, Hugo, 446
Erwitt, Elliott, 454
Evans, Frederick, 462
Evans, Walker, 466
Export, Valie, 469
Fani-Kayode, Rotimi, 480
Faucon, Bernard, 492, 493
Faurer, Louis, 497
Feininger, Andreas, 500
Feininger, T. Lux, 503, 504
Feldmann, Hans-Peter, 506
Finsler, Hans, 532
Fischer, Arno, 534, 535
Fischli, Peter, and David Weiss, 538
Fosso, Samuel, 550
Franck, Martine, 558
Frank, Robert, 563
Freund, Gisèle, 566–567
Fukase, Masahisa, 570, 571
Fukuda, Miran, 573
Funke, Jaromír, 576, 577
Furuya, Seiichi, 579, 580
Fuss, Adam, 582
Gelpke, André, 591
Gerz, Jochen, 601
Giacomelli, Mario, 604
Gibson, Ralph, 606, 607
Gidal, N. Tim, 609
Gilbert & George, 612, 613
Gilpin, Laura, 616
Gloaguen, Hervé, 618
Gohlke, Frank, 620
Goldin, Nan, 623, 624
Gowin, Emmet, 626
Graham, Dan, 628–630
Graham, Paul, 632
Grossman, Sid, 636
Gursky, Andreas, 644
Gutmann, John, 647
Haas, Ernst, 651
Hahn, Betty, 654
Hajek-Halke, Heinz, 658
Halsman, Philippe, 661
Hamaya, Hiroshi, 666
Hammarskiöld, Hans, 668
Hartmann, Erich, 672
Heartfield, John, 675, 676
Heath, David Martin, 679
Heinecken, Robert, 682, 683
Hellebrand, Nancy, 686
Henderson, Nigel, 688
Henri, Florence, 692
Hers, François, 695
Hilliard, John, 696, 697
Hine, Lewis, 699–701
Hiro, 702
Höch, Hannah, 754
Horst, Horst P., 757
Hosoe, Eikoh, 761, 762
Hoyningen-Huene, George, 766
Hurrell, George, 768
Hütte, Axel, 770
Ishimoto, Yasuhiro, 808
Iturbide, Graciela, 810
Izis (Israel Bidermanas), 812–814
Jacobi, Lotte, 820
Janah, Sunil, 823
Jones, Harold, 832, 833
Jones, Pirkle, 835, 836
Josephson, Kenneth, 839
Karsh, Yousuf, 843
Käsebier, Gertrude, 845–847
Kawada, Kikuji, 849
Keetman, Peter, 852
Keïta, Seydou, 855
Kertész, André, 859, 860
Kessels, Willy, 862
Kesting, Edmund, 864, 865

Individual exhibitions (*Continued*)
Killip, Chris, 870
Klein, Aart, 873
Klein, Astrid, 876
Klein, William, 879
Klett, Mark, 882
Koudelka, Josef, 887
Kozloff, Max, 890
Kruger, Barbara, 894
Krull, Germaine, 898
Lange, Dorothea, 904
Lartigue, Jacques Henri, 908, 909
Laughlin, Clarence John, 915
Lebeck, Robert, 916
Leibovitz, Annie, 921
Lerski, Helmar, 927
Levinthal, David, 930, 931
Levitt, Helen, 936
Liberman, Alexander, 942
Liebling, Jerome, 950, 951
Link, O. Winston, 961, 962
List, Herbert, 966, 967
Long, Richard, 969–971
Lüthi, Urs, 975
Lynes, George Platt, 978, 979
Lyons, Nathan, 984
Maar, Dora, 990
Man Ray, 1002
Man, Felix H., 1005
Mapplethorpe, Robert, 1009
Mark, Mary Ellen, 1013, 1014
McBean, Angus, 1018
Meatyard, Ralph Eugene, 1020, 1021
Meiselas, Susan, 1024
Messager, Annette, 1027
Metzker, Ray K., 1031
Meyerowitz, Joel, 1042
Michals, Duane, 1045
Mikhailov, Boris, 1047, 1048
Miller, Lee, 1050, 1051
Misrach, Richard, 1053, 1054
Model, Lisette, 1057, 1058
Modotti, Tina, 1066, 1067
Moholy-Nagy, Lászlò, 1071
Morath, Inge, 1080
Morimura, Yasumasa, 1082
Morris, Wright, 1085
Moses, Stefan, 1089
Mulas, Ugo, 1093
Muniz, Vik, 1096, 1097
Namuth, Hans, 1143
Newman, Arnold, 1156, 1157
Newton, Helmut, 1159
Nixon, Nicholas, 1163
Novak, Lorie, 1171
Olson, Lennart, 1183
Outerbridge Jr., Paul, 1189
Owens, Bill, 1191
Parr, Martin, 1196, 1197
Penn, Irving, 1200
Peress, Gilles, 1204
Peterhans, Walter, 1218
Pfahl, John, 1221, 1222
Pierre et Gilles, 1269, 1270
Plossu, Bernard, 1275
Porter, Eliot, 1285, 1286
Prince, Richard, 1298
Rainer, Arnulf, 1319
Ray-Jones, Tony, 1324
Renger-Patzsch, Albert, 1327
Riboud, Marc, 1340
Rice, Leland, 1343
Ritts, Herb, 1350–1352
Rosler, Martha, 1357
Rothstein, Arthur, 1360
Rubinstein, Eva, 1365
Ruff, Thomas, 1367
Salgado, Sebastião, 1380, 1381
Salomon, Erich, 1382
Sander, August, 1385
Schadeberg, Jürgen, 1393
Schmidt, Michael, 1395
Schneiders, Toni, 1398
Sekula, Alan, 1401, 1402
Serrano, Andres, 1407
Seymour, David "Chim", 1410
Shahn, Ben, 1413
Shaikhet, Arkadii, 1415
Sheeler, Charles, 1418
Sherman, Cindy, 1420, 1421
Shibata, Toshio, 1424
Shore, Stephen, 1427
Simpson, Lorna, 1429
Siskind, Aaron, 1437, 1438
Skoglund, Sandy, 1440
Snow, Michael, 1443
Sommer, Frederick, 1464, 1465
Spence, Jo, 1480
Starn, Doug and Mike, 1482
Steichen, Edward, 1488
Steiner, André, 1490
Stettner, Louis, 1493
Stieglitz, Alfred, 1496
Stone, Sasha, 1499
Struth, Thomas, 1509, 1510
Sudek, Josef, 1516
Sugimoto, Hiroshi, 1518, 1519
Szilasi, Gabor, 1527
Tabard, Maurice, 1530
Teske, Edmund, 1537
Tice, George, 1539
Tillmans, Wolfgang, 1542
Tosani, Patrick, 1549, 1550
Traub, Charles, 1552, 1553
Traub, Charles, 1556
Tseng Kwong Chi, 1558
Turbeville, Deborah, 1561, 1562
Ubac, Raoul, 1569
Uelsmann, Jerry, 1572
Ulmann, Doris, 1575
Umbo (Otto Umbehr), 1579
Uzzle, Burt, 1602
Van Vechten, Carl, 1606, 1607
VanDerZee, James, 1609
Vishniac, Roman, 1625
Wall, Jeff, 1634
Watanabe, Yoshio, 1646
Webb, Boyd, 1648, 1649
Weber, Bruce, 1652
Weber, Wolfgang, 1654

Individual exhibitions (*Continued*)
Weegee, 1661
Weems, Carrie Mae, 1665
Wegman, William, 1668
Welpott, Jack, 1673
Weston, Edward, 1678
White, Minor, 1683, 1684
Willis-Kennedy, Deborah, 1689
Winogrand, Garry, 1692, 1693
Witkiewicz (Witkacy), Stanislaw Ignacy, 1697
Witkin, Joel-Peter, 1699
Wojnecki, Stefan, 1702, 1703
Woodman, Francesca, 1705
Industrial photography, 781–787
1900–1920, 782, 783
1920–1930, 783, 784
1930–1940, 784, 785
after 1940, 785
further reading, 787
Infrared photography, 787–789
exposure, 788
further reading, 789
infrared film, 788
infrared light and lenses, 788, 789
light spectrum, 788
processing and handling, 789
reason for using infrared films, 789
Instant photography, 789–792
Institute of Design (ID), 204, 793–799
1937–1946, 793–795
1946–1961, 795–797
1961–1978, 797–799
Bauhaus curriculum, 205
Charles Traub and, 1554
corporate collections, 337
Department of Photography, 1588
Edmund Teske and, 1534
further reading, 799
graduates from, 1588
Harry Callahan and, 204
instructors, 1589
International Report Photographers Society (IRP), 1645
International Standards Organization (ISO), 212, 215
Internet, 800–803
Condè Nast publications, 310
Corbis/Bettmann web site, 335
further reading, 802
Lorie Novak's web project, 1616
museum websites, 1112
virtual reality and, 1622
websites, 802, 803
Interpretation, 803–806
The Intimate Gallery, 44
IRP, *see* International Report Photographers Society
Ishimoto, Yasuhiro, 806–808
American, Japanese, 806, 807
biography, 807, 808
further reading, 808
group exhibitions, 808
individual exhibitions, 808
selected works, 808
ISO, *see* International Standards Organization
Italian futurism, 6
Iturbide, Graciela, 809–811
biography, 810
further reading, 811
group exhibitions, 810, 811
individual exhibitions, 810
Mexican, 809, 810
selected works, 811
Izis (Israel Bidermanas), 811–814
biography, 812
French of Lithuanian birth, 811, 812
further reading, 814
group exhibitions, 814
individual exhibitions, 812–814
selected works, 814

J

Jacobi, Lotte, 818–821
American, 818–820
biography, 820
further reading, 821
group exhibitions, 820
individual exhibitions, 820
selected works, 820, 821
Janah, Sunil, 821–824
biography, 823
further reading, 823, 824
group exhibitions, 823
Indian, 821–823
individual exhibitions, 823
Japan, 824–831
Jewish National Fund (KKL), 83
JFET, *see* Junction Field Effect Transistor
Johns, Jasper, 53
Jones, Harold, 831–833
American, 831, 832
biography, 832
further reading, 833
group exhibitions, 833
individual exhibitions, 832–833
selected works, 833
Jones, Pirkle, 833–837
American, 833–835
biography, 835
further reading, 837
group exhibitions, 836
individual exhibitions, 835, 836
selected works, 836
Josephson, Kenneth, 837–840
American, 837–839
biography, 839
further reading, 840
group exhibitions, 839, 840
individual exhibitions, 839
selected works, 840
Joycam, 223
J. Paul Getty Museum, 815–818
Carrie Mae Weems and, 1663
further reading, 818
Junction Field Effect Transistor (JFET), 218

K

Kandinsky, Vasily, 6
Karsh, Yousuf, 230, 841–843
biography, 843

Karsh, Yousuf (*Continued*)
Canadian, 841, 842
further reading, 843
group exhibitions, 843
individual exhibitions, 843
selected works, 843
Käsebier, Gertrude, 844–847
American, 844, 845
biography, 845
further reading, 847
group exhibitions, 847
individual exhibitions, 845–847
selected works, 847
Kawada, Kikuji, 848–851
biography, 849
further reading, 851
group exhibitions, 849–851
individual exhibitions, 849
Japanese, 848, 849
selected works, 851
Keetman, Peter, 851–853
biography, 852
further reading, 853
German, 851, 852
group exhibitions, 852, 853
individual exhibitions, 852
selected works, 853
Keïta, Seydou, 854–856
biography, 855
further reading, 856
group exhibitions, 855, 856
individual exhibitions, 855
Mali, 854, 855
selected works, 856
Kertész, André, 856–860
American, born in Hungary, 856–859
biography, 859
further reading, 860
group exhibitions, 860
individual exhibitions, 859, 860
selected works, 860
Kessels, Willy, 860–862
Belgian, 860–862
biography, 862
further reading, 862
group exhibitions, 862
individual exhibitions, 862
selected books, 862
selected works, 862
Kesting, Edmund, 863–866
biography, 864
further reading, 865, 866
German, 863, 864
group exhibitions, 865
individual exhibitions, 864, 865
selected works, 865
Khaldei, Yevgeny, 866–868
biography, 868
further reading, 868
selected works, 868
Ukrainian, 866–868
Killip, Chris, 868–871
biography, 870
British, 868–870
further reading, 871
group exhibitions, 870, 871
individual exhibitions, 870
selected works, 871
Kineticism, of German photographers, 7
Kitchen Sink School, 119
Kite aerial photography, 22
KKL, *see* Jewish National Fund
Klein, Aart, 871–874
biography, 873
Dutch, 871, 872
further reading, 874
group exhibitions, 873, 874
individual exhibitions, 873
selected works, 874
Klein, Astrid, 874–877
biography, 876
further reading, 876, 877
German, 874, 875
group exhibitions, 876
individual exhibitions, 876
Klein, Astrid, selected works, 876
Klein, William, 877–880
American, 877–879
biography, 879
further reading, 879, 880
group exhibitions, 879
individual exhibitions, 879
selected works, 879
Klett, Mark, 880–884
American, 880, 881
biography, 882
further reading, 883, 884
group exhibitions, 882, 883
individual exhibitions, 882
selected works, 883
Knitting, 287
Kodachrome film, 77, 301
Kodak company
corporate collection, 336
Kodak Girls, 174
marketing breakthrough, 1613
spectroscopic films, 77
Konica
auto-focus camera, 222
disposable cameras and, 221
Korea, 884, 885
Koudelka, Josef, 886–889
biography, 887
Czechoslovakian, 886, 887
further reading, 887–889
group exhibitions, 887
individual exhibitions, 887
Kozloff, Max, 889, 890
American, 889, 890
biography, 890
further reading, 890
group exhibitions, 890
individual exhibitions, 890
Krauss, Rosalind, 891, 892
American, 891, 892
biography, 892
further reading, 892
selected works, 892
Kruger, Barbara, 47, 48, 892–896
American, 892–894

Kruger, Barbara (*Continued*)
biography, 894
further reading, 896
group exhibitions, 894
individual exhibitions, 894
selected works, 894, 895
Krull, Germaine, 896–899
biography, 898
Dutch, born German, 896–898
further reading, 899
group exhibitions, 898
individual exhibitions, 898
selected works, 898

L

Land, Edwin, 222
Land Art movement, 233
Lange, Dorothea, 901–905
American, 901–903
biography, 904
further reading, 905
group exhibitions, 905
individual exhibitions, 904
selected works, 905
Lartigue, Jacques Henri, 905–909
biography, 908
French, 905–907
further reading, 909
group exhibitions, 909
individual exhibitions, 908, 909
selected works, 909
Latin America, overview, 909–912
Cuban Revolution, 911
Cuzco School, 910
diversity of works, 909
First Colloquium of Latin American Photographers, 912
further reading, 912
horrors of war, 910
sincere photographs, 911
women involved in photography, 911
Laughlin, Clarence John, 913–915
American, 913, 914
biography, 914, 915
further reading, 815
group exhibitions, 915
individual exhibitions, 915
selected works, 915
Lebeck, Robert, 916, 917
biography, 917
further reading, 917
German, 916, 917
group exhibitions, 917
individual exhibitions, 917
Lee, Russell, 918, 919
American, 918, 919
biography, 919
exhibitions, 919
further reading, 919
Leibovitz, Annie, 920, 921
American, 920, 921
biography, 921
further reading, 921
group exhibitions, 921
individual exhibitions, 921
selected works, 921
Leica, Van Vechten's use of, 1606
Lemagny, Jean-Claude, 922, 923
biography, 923
France, 922, 923
further reading, 923
selected works, 923
Lens(es), 923–925
fixed, 228
further reading, 925
macro, 212
purpose of, 211
types, 212
zoom, 211, 212
Lerski, Helmar, 925–928
biography, 927
films, 928
further reading, 928
group exhibitions, 927, 928
individual exhibitions, 927
selected works, 928
Swiss-Polish, 925–927
writings, 928
Levinthal, David, 929–933
American, 929, 930
biography, 930
further reading, 933
group exhibitions, 931
individual exhibitions, 930, 931
selected works, 931
Lèvi-Strauss, Claude, 933–935
biography, 934, 935
French, 933, 934
selected works, 935
Levitt, Helen, 935–937
American, 935, 936
biography, 936
further reading, 937
group exhibitions, 936, 937
individual exhibitions, 936
selected works, 937
Levy, Julien, 938–940
American, 938–940
further reading, 940
Liberman, Alexander, 940–943
American, 940, 941
biography, 942
further reading, 942, 943
individual exhibitions, 942
selected works, 942
Library of Congress, 943–948
access, 947, 948
collections, 945–947
FSA-OWI collection, 1643
further reading, 948
Lichtenstein, Roy, John Coplans and, 329
Liebling, Jerome, 949–952
American, 949, 950
biography, 950
further reading, 952
group exhibitions, 951, 952
individual exhibitions, 950, 951
selected works, 952

Life magazine, 2, 10, 952–955
Bischof's assignment for, 134
Black Star and, 137
further reading, 955
Larry Burrows and, 186
Margaret Bourke-White and, 153
Robert Capa and, 238
Life-Video-Performance, 145
Light
manipulation of, 7
most damaging type of, 316
Light control, 215, 216
exposure, 215
light meters, 215, 216
shutter and aperture, 216
Light graphics, 104
Light meters, 212, 215, 956, 957
different meters for different scenes, 957
further reading, 957
metering systems, 957
middle gray, 956, 957
sensors, 228
types, 856
Lighting and lighting equipment, 958, 959
direction of light, 959
key method of lighting, 959
light modifiers, 959
size of light source, 958, 959
Link, O. Winston, 960–962
American, 960, 961
biography, 961
further reading, 962
group exhibitions, 962
individual exhibitions, 961, 962
selected works, 962
Linked Ring, 290, 962–964
Clarence White and, 1679
further reading, 964
List, Herbert, 964–967
biography, 965, 966
further reading, 967
German, 964, 965
group exhibitions, 967
individual exhibitions, 966, 967
selected works, 967
Lithographic prints, African, 34
The Little Galleries of the Photo-Secession, 44
Live photography, important representatives of, 183
Logitech Fotoman, 219
Long, Richard, 967–971
biography, 969
British, 967–969
further reading, 971
group exhibitions, 971
individual exhibitions, 969–971
selected works, 971
Look magazine, 971–973
Lüthi, Urs, 973–976
biography, 976
further reading, 976
group exhibitions, 975
individual exhibitions, 975
selected works, 975, 976
Swiss, 973–975
Lynes, George Platt, 977–980
American, 977, 978
biography, 978
further reading, 980
group exhibitions, 979
individual exhibitions, 978, 979
selected works, 978
Lyon, Danny, 980–982
American, 980–982
further reading, 982
Lyons, Nathan, 982–985
American, 982–984
biography, 984
further reading, 985
group exhibitions, 984, 985
individual exhibitions, 984
selected works, 985

M

Maar, Dora, 987–990
biography, 988–990
French, 987, 988
further reading, 990
group exhibitions, 990
individual exhibitions, 990
Machine Readable Cataloguing (MARC), 66
Mackintosh, Charles Rennie, 56
Macro lenses, 212
Macro-photography, cable release and, 196
Madame d'Ora, 990–993
Austrian, 990–992
biography, 992
exhibitions, 992
further reading, 992
selected works, 992
Magenta filter, 300
Magnetic Video Camera (Mavica), 219
Magnum Photos, 994–999
Eve Arnold and, 68, 69
exhibitions, 998
further reading, 998, 999
Henri Cartier-Bresson and, 248
members, 998
René Burri and, 183
Robert Capa and, 239
war photography and, 1639
Maison Européenne de la Photographie, 999, 1000
collection, 999
films and videos, 1000
other activities, 1000
Romèo Martinez Library, 999, 1000
Mamiyaflex camera, 53
Man Ray, 56, 78, 80, 1000–1003
American, 1000, 1001
Berenice Abbott and, 1
biography, 1002
constructed reality and, 321
further reading, 1002
group exhibitions, 1002
individual exhibitions, 1002
Maurice Tabard and, 1530
Raoul Ubac and, 1567
selected works, 1002
virtual reality and, 1621

Man, Felix H., 1004, 1005
  biography, 1005
  books, 1005
  further reading, 1005
  German, 1004, 1005
  group exhibitions, 1005
  individual exhibitions, 1005
Manipulation, 1006, 1007
Mapplethorpe, Robert, 1007–1011
  American, 1007–1009
  biography, 1009
  further reading, 1011
  group exhibitions, 1009–1011
  individual exhibitions, 1009
  selected works, 1011
MARC, *see* Machine Readable Cataloguing
Mark, Mary Ellen, 1011–1014
  American, 1011, 1012
  biography, 1013
  individual exhibitions, 1013, 1014
Market Photography Workshop, African, 36
Mars Pathfinder mission, 77
Martin-Gropius Bau, 121
Marxist-Leninist ideology, 39
Masking, 1014–1016
Mass media, influence of on teenagers, 285
Mass Observation project, 339, 340
Massachusetts Institute of Technology (MIT), 1683
Mavica, *see* Magnetic Video Camera
McBean, Angus, 1016–1018
  biography, 1017, 10183
  further reading, 1018
  individual exhibitions, 1018
  selected works, 1018
  Welsh, 1016, 1017
Meatyard, Ralph Eugene, 1019–1022
  American, 1019, 1020
  biography, 1020
  further reading, 1021, 1022
  group exhibitions, 1021
  individual exhibitions, 1020, 1021
  selected works, 1021
Meatyard, Ralph, virtual reality and, 1621, 1622
Meiselas, Susan, 1023–1025
  American, 1023, 1024
  biography, 1024
  further reading, 1025
  group exhibitions, 1024, 1025
  individual exhibitions, 1024
  selected works, 1025
Messager, Annette, 1026–1029
  biography, 1027
  French, 1026, 1027
  further reading, 1029
  group exhibitions, 1029
  individual exhibitions, 1027
  selected works, 1029
Metering system, most common, 212
Metering systems, 212, 213
Metzker, Ray K., 1029–1032
  American, 1029–1031
  biography, 1031
  further reading, 1032
  group exhibitions, 1031
  individual exhibitions, 1031
  selected works, 1031, 1032
Mexican film industry, 244
Mexico, 1033–1040
Mexico, further reading, 1040
Meyerowitz, Joel, 1040–1043
  American, 1040, 1041
  biography, 1041, 1042
  further reading, 1043
  group exhibitions, 1042, 1043
  individual exhibitions, 1042
  selected works, 1043
Michals, Duane, 1043–1046
  American, 1043, 1044
  biography, 1044, 1045
  further reading, 1046
  group exhibitions, 1045
  individual exhibitions, 1045
  selected works, 1045
Microdrive, 219
Microsoft Corporation
  Corbis, 67
  Corbis/Bettmann, 334
  corporate collection, 338
Mikhailov, Boris, 1046–1049
  biography, 1047
  further reading, 1049
  group exhibitions, 1048
  individual exhibitions, 1047, 1048
  selected works, 1048
  Ukrainian, 1046, 1047
Miller, Lee, 1049–1051
  American, 1049, 1050
  biography, 1050
  further reading, 1051
  group exhibitions, 1051
  individual exhibitions, 1050, 1051
  selected works, 1051
Miller, Milton
  motifs, 268
  portraits, 268
Misrach, Richard, 1052–1055
  American, 1052, 1053
  biography, 1053
  further reading, 1054, 1055
  group exhibitions, 1054
  individual exhibitions, 1053, 1054
  selected works, 1054
MIT, *see* Massachusetts Institute of Technology
Mockumentary, 322
Model, Lisette, 1056–1058
  American, 1056, 1057
  biography, 1057
  further reading, 1058
  group exhibitions, 1058
  Imogen Cunningham and, 349
  individual exhibitions, 1057, 1058
  selected works, 1058
Moderna Museet, 1059–1062
  further reading, 1062
  library, 1061
Modernism, 1062–1064
  architecture and, 59
  Edward Weston and, 1675
  further reading, 1064
  history of photography converging with, 6

Modernist abstraction, 7
Modotti, Tina, 1065–1068
  biography, 1066
  further reading, 1068
  group exhibitions, 1067
  individual exhibitions, 1066, 1067
  Italian, 1065, 1066
  selected works, 1067, 1068
Modern photography, 1058, 1059
Moholy-Nagy, László, 1068–1073
  biography, 1070, 1071
  Foundations Program, 1587
  further reading, 1071–1073
  group exhibitions, 1071
  Hungarian-American, 1068–1070
  individual exhibitions, 1071
  Institute of Design, 105
  selected works, 1071
MoMA, *see* Museum of Modern Art
Montage, 1073–1077
  Ellen Auerbach and, 83
  further reading, 1077
  Larry Clark and, 284
  negative, 1621
Moore, David, 88, 91
Morath, Inge, 1078–1080
  biography, 1079, 1080
  further reading, 1080
  German, 1078, 1079
  group exhibitions, 1080
  individual exhibitions, 1080
  selected works, 1080
Morimura, Yasumasa, 1080–1084
  biography, 1082
  further reading, 1083, 1084
  group exhibitions, 1082, 1083
  individual exhibitions, 1082
  Japanese, 1080–1082
  selected works, 1083
Morris, Wright, 1084–1087
  American, 1084, 1085
  biography, 1085
  further reading, 1085–1087
  individual exhibitions, 1085
  selected works, 1085
Moses, Stefan, 1087–1090
  biography, 1088, 1089
  further reading, 1090
  German, 1087, 1088
  group exhibitions, 1089, 1090
  individual exhibitions, 1089
  selected works, 1090
Motif(s)
  Chen Changfen, 271
  Milton Miller's, 268
  use of architecture as, 58
Mousetraps, 227
Mulas, Ugo, 1090–1093
  biography, 1092, 1093
  further reading, 1093
  group exhibitions, 1093
  individual exhibitions, 1093
  Italian, 1090–1092
  selected works, 1093
Multiple exposures and printing, 1093–1095
Muniz, Vik, 1095–1098
  biography, 1096
  Brazilian, 1095, 1096
  further reading, 1098
  group exhibitions, 1097
  individual exhibitions, 1096, 1097
  selected works, 1097
Munkacsi, Martin, 1098–1100
  biography, 1099
  exhibitions, 1099, 1100
  further reading, 1100
  Hungarian, 1098, 1099
  selected works, 1100
Museum Folkwang, 1100–1102
Museum of Modern Art (MoMA), 10, 16, 45, 1102–1109
  before MoMA, 1103
  biographer, 100
  Creative Camera and, 340
  department of photography under Beaumont Newhall, 1104, 1105
  department of photography under Edward Steichen, 1105, 1106
  department of photography under John Szarkowski, 1106, 1107
  department of photography under Peter Galassi, 1107, 1108
  further reading, 1109
  Garry Winogrand works shown at, 1690, 1691
  Harry Callahan and, 204, 206
  inaugural exhibitions at, 100
  influence of MoMA on photography, 1108, 1109
  influence of photography on MoMA, 1108
  as laboratory, 100
  librarian, 100
  Machine Art Exhibition, 123
  Minor White and, 1682
  MoMA before department of photography, 1103, 1104
  solo show of George Tice, 1538
  Weegee photographs acquired by, 1658
Museums, 1110, 1112
  catalogues and art books, 1111
  further reading, 1112
  new technologies and their impact on museums, 1112
  new wave of museums, 1111, 1112
  photography as narrative, 1111
  role of museum in acceptance of photography, 1110, 1111
  two families of museums, 1110
  websites, 1112
Museums, Canada, 1112–1118
  Art Gallery of Greater Victoria, 1113, 1114
  Art Gallery of Hamilton, 1113
  Art Gallery of Newfoundland and Labrador, 1113
  Art Gallery of Nova Scotia, 1114
  Art Gallery of Ontario, 1114
  Canadian Centre for Architecture, 1114, 1115
  Canadian Museum of Contemporary Photography, 1115
  Edmonton Art Gallery, 1115
  further reading, 1118
  Glenbow Museum, 1115, 1116
  Library and Archives Canada, 1116
  MacKenzie Art Gallery, 1116
  McCord Museum of Canadian History, 1116
  Montreal Museum of Fine Arts, 1116, 1117
  National Gallery of Canada, 1117
  Vancouver Art Gallery, 1117
  Winnipeg Art Gallery, 1117, 1118
Museums, Europe, 1118–1131
  Austria, 1118, 1119
  Belgium, 1119

Museums, Europe (*Continued*)
Croatia, 1119
Czech Republic, 1119, 1120
Denmark, 1120
Finland, 1120
France, 1120–1122
Germany, 1122, 1123
Great Britain, 1123–1125
Hungary, 1125, 1126
Ireland, 1126
Italy, 1126
Latvia, 1126
Netherlands, 1127
Norway, 1127
Poland, 1127, 1128
Portugal, 1128
Spain, 1128, 1129
Sweden, 1129–1131
Switzerland, 1131
Museums, United States, 1131–1139
Art Institute of Chicago, 1137
Center for Creative Photography, 1137
further reading, 1139
International Center of Photography, 1137
International Museum of Film and Photography at George Eastman House, 1137, 1138
J. Paul Getty Museum, 1137
Library of Congress, 1138
Metropolitan Museum of Art, 1138
Museum of Contemporary Photography, 1138
Museum of Modern Art, 1138
Museum of Photographic Arts, 1138, 1139
museums and their collections, 1136, 1137
Sand Francisco Museum of Modern Art, 1139
Whitney Museum of American Art, 1139

N

Nairobi, Camerapix agency, 30
Namuth, Hans, 1141–1144
biography, 1143
further reading, 1143, 1144
German, 1141–1143
group exhibitions, 1143
individual exhibitions, 1143
selected works, 1143
NAPA, *see* National Association for Photographic Art
National Association for Photographic Art (NAPA), 235
National Endowment for the Arts (NEA), 252, 1697
National Film Board of Canada (NFB), 232
National Geographic magazine, 21, 1145–1149
further reading, 1148, 1149
underwater photography and, 1582
visual anthropology and, 1627
National Geographic Society, 269
Nature
honest representation of, 9
photography, cable release and, 195
Nazi news agency, 137
Nazi regime, architecture photography and, 59
NEA, *see* National Endowment for the Arts
Negative contrast, 327
Neo-expressionism, 47
Netherlands, 1149–1151
New Bauhaus, 204
Newhall, Beaumont, 1151–1154
American, 1151–1153
biography, 1154
further reading, 1154
selected works, 1154
Newman, Arnold, 1154–1157
American, 1154–1156
biography, 1156
further reading, 1157
group exhibitions, 1157
individual exhibitions, 1156, 1157
selected works, 1157
New Media, advent of in Australia, 90
New Objectivity, 104
New School for Social research, 2
Newton, Helmut, 1158–1160
biography, 1159
further reading, 1160
German, 1158, 1159
group exhibitions, 1159, 1160
individual exhibitions, 1159
selected works, 1160
New topographic photographers, 16
New Topography movement
iconography of realism, 95
Lewis Baltz and, 95, 96
New Vision school, German, 133
New York Times, 2
NFB, *see* National Film Board of Canada
Night photography, innovations in, 161
Nitrate film stock, 318
Nixon, Nicholas, 1160–1165
American, 1160–1163
biography, 1163
further reading, 1164, 1165
group exhibitions, 1163, 1164
individual exhibitions, 1163
selected works, 1164
Non-silver processes, 1165–1169
North Africa, *see* Africa, North
Novak, Lorie, 1169–1173
American, 1169–1171
biography, 1171
further reading, 1173
group exhibitions, 1171–1173
individual exhibitions, 1171
selected works, 1173
Nude photography, 1173–1178
further reading, 1178
Bernhard's photographs of female, 123
Imogen Cunningham, 348

O

Office of War Information (OWI), 1179–1182, 1588
Olson, Lennart, 1182–1184
biography, 1183
further reading, 1184
group exhibitions, 1184
individual exhibitions, 1183
selected works, 1184
Swedish, 1182, 1183
O'Keefe, Georgia, 44

Optics, 1184–1187
Other, vision of North Africa as exotic, 33
Outerbridge Jr., Paul, 1187–1190
  American, 1187–1189
  biography, 1189
  further reading, 1189, 1190
  group exhibitions, 1189
  individual exhibitions, 1189
  selected works, 1189
Owens, Bill, 1190–1192
  American, 1190, 1191
  biography, 1191
  further reading, 1192
  group exhibitions, 1191, 1192
  individual exhibitions, 1191
  selected works, 1192
OWI, *see* Office of War Information

P

PABIR, *see* Photographic archives belong in Rochester
Painting, *see* Photography and painting
Panoramic photography, 1193–1195
Parr, Martin, 1195–1198
  biography, 1196
  British, 1195, 1196
  further reading, 1197
  group exhibitions, 1197
  individual exhibitions, 1196, 1197
  selected works, 1197
Penn, Irving, 1198–1202
  American, 1198–1200
  biography, 1200
  further reading, 1201
  group exhibitions, 1200, 1201
  individual exhibitions, 1200
  selected works, 1201
Peress, Gilles, 1202–1205
  biography, 1203, 1204
  French, 1202, 1203
  further reading, 1204, 1205
  group exhibitions, 1204
  individual exhibitions, 1204
  selected works, 1204
Performance artist, Beuys as, 126
Periodicals, historical, 1205–1210
  camera clubs and photographic societies, 1206
  fashion magazines, 1208, 1209
  further reading, 1209, 1210
  illustrated newsmagazines, 1206, 1207
  modern weekly, 1207, 1208
  photographers' periodicals, 1209
  reprint series, 1209
Periodicals, professional, 1210–1213
Perspective, 1213–1216
Peterhans, Walter, 1217–1219
  American, born Germany, 1217, 1218
  biography, 1218
  further reading, 1219
  group exhibitions, 1219
  individual exhibitions, 1218
  writings, 1219
Pfahl, John, 1220–1224
  American, 1220, 1221
  biography, 1221
  further reading, 1224
  group exhibitions, 1222–1224
  individual exhibitions, 1221, 1222
  selected works, 1224
Photo agencies, 1224–1226
Photo-diarists, 50
Photo floodlight, 299
Photogenic drawings, 6
Photo ghetto, 92
Photogram(s), 7, 1238–1244
  avant-garde experiments, 1239–1242
  Berlinische Galerie and, 121
  constructed reality and, 321
  contemporary photograms, 1242
  further reading, 1244
  historical beginnings, 1239
  Umbo and, 1578
Photographer(s)
  Aboriginal, 88
  agency, African, 25
  content vs. style, 43
  England's most British, 160
  nature, aerial photography and, 22
  new topographic, 16
  straight, 80
  western, 16
Photographic archives belong in Rochester (PABIR), 67
Photographic theory, 1249–1255
  academic period, 1253–1255
  further reading, 1255
  pre-academic period, 1249–1253
  recent developments, 1255
Photographic "truth", 1245–1248
Photography
  aerial, 7
  autoguided, 78
  boom, ACP and, 91
  denaturalizing, 178
  documentary authority of, 126
  ethnographic, 28
  graduate program in, 71, 72
  live, important representatives of, 183
  one-step, 222
  painting and, 1255–1259
  piggyback, 78
  plant, 138
  sculpture and, 1259–1262
  set-up, 320, 321
  social landscape, 51
  Socialist Realist, 42
  straight, 7, 10
  truth-value of, 14
  use of cable release, 195
  visual and tactile qualities of, 7
  worker, 234
Photography House, founding of, 93
Photojournalism
  of Algeria's conflicts, 32
  mid-1930s, 136
  pioneer of modern, 1653
Photo League, 1227–1229
Photomontage(s), 40
  constructed reality and, 320
  John Berger and, 120

Photomontage(s) (*Continued*)
virtual reality and, 1621
Photo multiplier tubes (PMT), 302
Photosafaris, 30
Photo-Secession, 1229–1233
"American Pictorial Photography Arranged by the 'Photo-Secession'", 1230
Camera Work, 1231
Clarence White and, 1678
demise of organization, 1231, 1232
further reading, 1232
Little Galleries of, 290, 1231
origins, 1229, 1230
principles, organization, and goals, 1230, 1231
Photo-Secessionists, 1234–1238
Carl Van Vechten and, 1606
Francis Joseph Bruguière and, 176
further reading, 1238
Physical Science Study Committee of Educational Services (PSSCES), 3
Pictorialism, 86, 87, 1262–1266
Clarence White and, 1678
further reading, 1264–1266
language of, billboards with slogans, 153
Robert Bourdeau and, 149
Picture Post, 1266–1268
Pierre et Gilles, 1268–1271
biography, 1269
French, 1268, 1269
further reading, 1271
group exhibitions, 1270, 1271
individual exhibitions, 1269, 1270
Piggyback photography, 78
Pinhole camera, 214
Pin-up photography, 1271–1273
Pixel, 218
Plate glass images, African, 34
Plossu, Bernard, 1273–1276
biography, 1275
French, 1273–1275
further reading, 1275
group exhibitions, 1275
individual exhibitions, 1275
selected works, 1275
Plowden, David, 1277–1279
American, 1277–1278
biography, 1279
books, 1279
further reading, 1279
PMT, *see* Photo multiplier tubes
Point-and-shoot cameras, 210, 211
Polaroid Corporation, 1279–1282
Ansel Adams Research Fellowship, 254
corporate collection, 338
film, 214
further reading, 1282
Pollock, Jackson, 143
Polyvinyl chloride (PVC), 317
Pop Art
architectural photography and, 61
movement, 46
Popular photography, 1282–1283
Popular Photography, 2
Porter, Eliot, 1283–1288
American, 1283–1285
biography, 1285
further reading, 1288
group exhibitions, 1286
individual exhibitions, 1285, 1286
selected publications, 1286–1288
Portraiture, 1288–1292
African, 24
contribution of Berenice Abbott to, 1
Eve Arnold and, 69
further reading, 1292
Portugal, *see* Spain and Portugal
Posterization, 1292–1294
Postmodernism, 1294–1296
characteristic style, 1295
deconstruction and, 376, 377
further reading, 1296
influence of on Australian photography, 89
postmodernism and photography, 1295, 1296
sociohistorical age, 1294, 1295
Pound, Ezra, 6
Pravda, 42
Pre-Civil War American buildings, recording of, 3
Prince, Richard, 1296–1299
American, 1296, 1297
biography, 1298
further reading, 1299
group exhibitions, 1298, 1299
individual exhibitions, 1298
selected works, 1299
Print contrast, 327
Printer Matter Bookstore, 74
Printing frame easel, 324
Print processes, 1299–1304
further reading, 1303
monochromatic iron processes, 1301
monochromatic pigment processes, 1301, 1302
monochromatic silver processes, 1299–1301
subtractive color processes, 1302, 1303
Private collections, 1305–1307
Process color, 302
Professional organizations, 1308–1310
Professional periodicals, *see* Periodicals, professional
Proof sheets, advantages of, 325
Propaganda, 1310–1313
African missionaries and, 34
further reading, 1313
propagandists, 42, 57
tool, architecture as, 59
Provincetown Playhouse, 1
PSSCES, *see* Physical Science Study Committee of Educational Services
Public art photography, 1313–1316
Pure photographic aesthetic, 6
Pushkin Museum, 122
PVC, *see* Polyvinyl chloride

R

Rainer, Arnulf, 1317–1320
Austrian, 1317, 1318
biography, 1318, 1319
further reading, 1319, 1320
group exhibitions, 1319
individual exhibitions, 1319

Rainer, Arnulf (*Continued*)
selected works, 1319
Rangefinder cameras, 210, 215
Rauschenberg, Robert, 1321–1323
American, 1321, 1322
biography, 1322
further reading, 1323
selected works, 1322, 1323
Ray-Jones, Tony, 1323, 1324
biography, 1324
British, 1323, 1324
further reading, 1324
group exhibitions, 1324
individual exhibitions, 1324
selected works, 1324
Rayographs, 321
RCA, *see* Royal Canadian Academy of Arts
Realist Movement, *Creative camera* and, 340
Red-eye reduction, 211
Red, green, and blue (RGB), 218, 301
Relative humidity (RH), 316, 318
Remote sensing, aerial photography and, 22
Renger-Patzsch, Albert, 1325–1330
biography, 1327
books, 1328
further reading, 1328–1330
German, 1325–1327
group exhibitions, 1327, 1328
individual exhibitions, 1327
selected works, 1328
Rephotography, 235, 350
Representation, 1330, 1331
from tokens to trueness of items, 1330
further reading, 1331
gender and, 1332–1335
race and, 1335–1338
to create, 1331
to imitate, 1330, 1331
Resettlement Administration, 3
RGB, *see* Red, green, and blue
RH, *see* Relative humidity
Rhode Island School of Design (RISD), 205
Riboud, Marc, 1338–1341
biography, 1339, 1340
French, 1338, 1339
further reading, 1341
group exhibitions, 1340
individual exhibitions, 1340
selected works, 1340, 1341
Rice, Leland, 1341–1343
American, 1341, 1342
biography, 1343
further reading, 1343
group exhibitions, 1343
individual exhibitions, 1343
selected works, 1343
Riefenstahl, Leni, 1343–1346
biography, 1345, 1346
further reading, 1346
German, 1343–1345
selected works, 1346
Riis, Jacob, 1346–1349
American, 1346–1347
biography, 1349
further reading, 1349
selected works, 1349
RISD, *see* Rhode Island School of Design
RIT, *see* Rochester Institute of Technology
Ritchey-Chretien telescope, 77
Ritts, Herb, 1349–1352
American, 1349, 1350
biography, 1350
further reading, 1352
individual exhibitions, 1350–1352
selected works, 1352
Rochester Institute of Technology (RIT), 1683
Roh, Franz, 1352–1355
biography, 1355
further reading, 1355
German, 1352, 1353
group exhibitions, 1355
Rolleicord camera, 69
Rolleiflex camera, 53, 238, 1624
Roll-film cameras, 215
ROPF, *see* Union of Russian Proletarian Photographers
Rosler, Martha, 1355–1358
American, 1355–1357
biography, 1357
further reading, 1358
group exhibitions, 1357, 1358
individual exhibitions, 1357
selected works, 1358
Rothstein, Arthur, 1358–1362
American, 1358–1360
biography, 1360
further reading, 1362
group exhibitions, 1360
individual exhibitions, 1360
selected works, 1360
Royal Canadian Academy of Arts (RCA), 150
Royal Photographic Society, 1362, 1363
Rubberstamping, 74
Rubinstein, Eva, 1364, 1365
American, 1364
biography, 1365
further reading, 1365
group exhibitions, 1365
individual exhibitions, 1365
selected works, 1365
Ruff, Thomas, 1365–1368
biography, 1367
further reading, 1368
German, 1365–1367
group exhibitions, 1367, 1368
individual exhibitions, 1367
selected works, 1368
Ruscha, Ed, typology and, 1563
Russia and Eastern Europe, 1368–1375
Russian Futurism, 73

S

Safelight, 1377, 1378
Safety film, 319
Salgado, Sebastião, 1379–1381
biography, 1380
Brazilian, 1379, 1380
further reading, 1381
individual exhibitions, 1380, 1381

Salomon, Erich, 1381–1383
biography, 1382
further reading, 1383
German, 1381, 1382
group exhibitions, 1383
individual exhibitions, 1382
selected works, 1383
Sander, August, 52, 1383–1387
Berlinische Galerie and, 123
biography, 1385
further reading, 1385–1387
German, 1383–1385
group exhibitions, 1385
individual exhibitions, 1385
selected works, 1385
typology and, 1563
Sandwiched negatives, 1387, 1388
San Francisco Art Institute, Minor White and, 1682
Satellite imagery, 21
Scanning, 1388–1390
dot control, 1389
further reading, 1390
guidelines for scanning halftone and continuous tone art, 1390
resolution, 1389
Schadeberg, Jürgen, 1390–1393
biography, 1392
group exhibitions, 1393
individual exhibitions, 1393
selected works, 1393
South African, 1390, 1391
Schmidt, Michael, 1393–1396
biography, 1395
further reading, 1396
German, 1393–1395
group exhibitions, 1395, 1396
individual exhibitions, 1395
selected works, 1396
Schneiders, Toni, 1396–1399
biography, 1398
further reading, 1398
German, 1396–1398
group exhibitions, 1398
individual exhibitions, 1398
Science Illustrated, 2
Science photography, contribution of Berenice Abbott to, 1, 2
Scott-Archer, Frederick, 76
Sculpture, *see* Photography and sculpture
SD, *see* Secure Digital card
Secure Digital card (SD), 219
Sekula, Alan, 1400–1403
American, 1400, 1401
biography, 1401
further reading, 1403
group exhibitions, 1402, 1403
individual exhibitions, 1401, 1402
selected works, 1403
Selected works
Abbott, Berenice, 4
Adams, Ansel, 12, 13
Adams, Eddie, 15
Adams, Robert, 18
Alpert, Max, 44
Araki, Nobuyoshi, 50, 51
Arbus, Diane, 54
Arnold, Eve, 71
Atget, Eugène, 82
Baltz, Lewis, 98
Barthes, Roland, 102, 103
Bayer, Herbert, 107
Becher, Bernd and Hilla, 114
Bellmer, Hans, 117
Beuys, Joseph, 128
Billingham, Richard, 132
Bischof, Werner, 136
Blossfeldt, Karl, 141
Blumenfeld, Erwin, 143
Boltanski, Christian, 148, 149
Bourdeau, Robert, 151
Bourke-White, Margaret, 155
Bragaglia, Anton Giulio, 159
Brassaï, 165
Bravo, Manuel Álvarez, 170
Breitenbach, Josef, 172
Bruguière, Francis Joseph, 177
Burgin, Victor, 181
Burri, René, 185
Burrows, Larry, 188
Burson, Nancy, 193
Cadieux, Geneviève, 199, 200
Cahun, Claude, 202
Callahan, Harry, 207
Calle, Sophie, 210
Capa, Robert, 240, 241
Carrillo, Manuel, 246
Cartier-Bresson, Henri, 249
Chambi, Martín, 263–264
Chargesheimer, 268
Christenberry, William, 283
Clark, Larry, 287
Close, Chuck, 289
Coburn, Alvin Langdon, 293
Cohen, Lynne, 296
Coke, Van Deren, 298, 299
Connor, Linda, 313
Coplans, John, 332
Crewdson, Gregory, 344
Cunningham, Imogen, 351
Dahl-Wolfe, Louise, 357, 358
Dater, Judy, 363
Davidson, Bruce, 366
de Meyer, Baron Adolph, 369
DeCarava, Roy, 373
Delano, Jack, 382
diCorcia, Philip-Lorca, 391
Dijkstra, Rineke, 398
Doisneau, Robert, 415
Domon, Ken, 417
Drtikol, František, 420
Duncan, David Douglas, 422
Edgerton, Harold, 429
Eggleston, William, 433
Eisenstaedt, Alfred, 438
Erfurth, Hugo, 446–448
Erwitt, Elliott, 453, 454
Evans, Frederick, 463
Evans, Walker, 466
Export, Valie, 469, 470
Fani-Kayode, Rotimi, 480
Faurer, Louis, 498
Feininger, Andreas, 500

Selected works (*Continued*)
Feininger, T. Lux, 504
Feldmann, Hans-Peter, 507
Fischer, Arno, 535
Fischli, Peter, and David Weiss, 538
Flusser, Vilém, 543
Fosso, Samuel, 550
Franck, Martine, 560
Frank, Robert, 564
Freund, Gisèle, 567
Fukase, Masahisa, 572
Fukuda, Miran, 574
Furuya, Seiichi, 580
Fuss, Adam, 584
Gelpke, André, 591
Gerz, Jochen, 602
Giacomelli, Mario, 604, 605
Gibson, Ralph, 607
Gidal, N. Tim, 609, 610
Gilbert & George, 614
Gilpin, Laura, 616
Gloaguen, Hervé, 618
Gohlke, Frank, 621
Goldin, Nan, 623
Gowin, Emmet, 626
Graham, Dan, 630
Graham, Paul, 634
Grossman, Sid, 636
Gutmann, John, 648
Haas, Ernst, 651
Hahn, Betty, 654
Hajek-Halke, Heinz, 658
Halsman, Philippe, 663
Hamaya, Hiroshi, 666
Hammarskiöld, Hans, 668, 669
Hartmann, Erich, 672
Heartfield, John, 676
Heath, David Martin, 679
Heinecken, Robert, 682
Hellebrand, Nancy, 686
Henderson, Nigel, 690
Hilliard, John, 697
Hine, Lewis, 701
Hiro, 703
Höch, Hannah, 754
Horst, Horst P., 758
Hosoe, Eikoh, 762, 763
Hoyningen-Huene, George, 766
Hurrell, George, 768
Hütte, Axel, 770
Ishimoto, Yasuhiro, 808
Iturbide, Graciela, 811
Izis (Israel Bidermanas), 814
Jacobi, Lotte, 820, 821
Jones, Harold, 833
Jones, Pirkle, 836
Josephson, Kenneth, 840
Karsh, Yousuf, 843
Käsebier, Gertrude, 847
Kawada, Kikuji, 851
Keetman, Peter, 853
Keïta, Seydou, 856
Kertész, André, 860
Kessels, Willy, 862
Kesting, Edmund, 865
Khaldei, Yevgeny, 868
Killip, Chris, 871
Klein, Aart, 874
Klein, Astrid, 876
Klein, William, 879
Klett, Mark, 883
Krauss, Rosalind, 892
Kruger, Barbara, 894, 895
Krull, Germaine, 898
Lange, Dorothea, 905
Lartigue, Jacques Henri, 909
Laughlin, Clarence John, 915
Leibovitz, Annie, 921
Lemagny, Jean-Claude, 923
Lerski, Helmar, 928
Levinthal, David, 931
Lèvi-Strauss, Claude, 935
Levitt, Helen, 937
Liberman, Alexander, 942
Liebling, Jerome, 952
Link, O. Winston, 962
List, Herbert, 967
Long, Richard, 971
Lüthi, Urs, 975, 976
Lynes, George Platt, 978
Lyons, Nathan, 985
Madame d'Ora, 992
Man Ray, 1002
Mapplethorpe, Robert, 1011
McBean, Angus, 1018
Meatyard, Ralph Eugene, 1021
Meiselas, Susan, 1025
Messager, Annette, 1029
Metzker, Ray K., 1031, 1032
Meyerowitz, Joel, 1043
Michals, Duane, 1045
Mikhailov, Boris, 1048
Miller, Lee, 1051
Misrach, Richard, 1054
Model, Lisette, 1058
Modotti, Tina, 1067, 1068
Moholy-Nagy, László, 1071
Morath, Inge, 1080
Morimura, Yasumasa, 1083
Morris, Wright, 1085
Moses, Stefan, 1090
Mulas, Ugo, 1093
Muniz, Vik, 1097
Munkacsi, Martin, 1100
Namuth, Hans, 1143
Newhall, Beaumont, 1154
Newman, Arnold, 1157
Newton, Helmut, 1160
Nixon, Nicholas, 1164
Novak, Lorie, 1173
Olson, Lennart, 1184
Outerbridge Jr., Paul, 1189
Owens, Bill, 1192
Parr, Martin, 1197
Penn, Irving, 1201
Peress, Gilles, 1204
Pfahl, John, 1224
Plossu, Bernard, 1275
Prince, Richard, 1299
Rainer, Arnulf, 1319

Selected works (*Continued*)
Rauschenberg, Robert, 1322, 1323
Ray-Jones, Tony, 1324
Renger-Patzsch, Albert, 1328
Riboud, Marc, 1340, 1341
Rice, Leland, 1343
Riefenstahl, Leni, 1346
Riis, Jacob, 1349
Ritts, Herb, 1352
Rosler, Martha, 1358
Rubinstein, Eva, 1365
Ruff, Thomas, 1368
Salomon, Erich, 1383
Sander, August, 1385
Schadeberg, Jürgen, 1393
Schmidt, Michael, 1396
Sekula, Alan, 1403
Serrano, Andres, 1408
Seymour, David "Chim", 1410
Shahn, Ben, 1413
Shaikhet, Arkadii, 1416
Sheeler, Charles, 1418
Sherman, Cindy, 1422
Shibata, Toshio, 1425
Shore, Stephen, 1427
Simpson, Lorna, 1431
Singh, Raghubir, 1434
Siskind, Aaron, 1438
Skoglund, Sandy, 1441
Snow, Michael, 1445
Sommer, Frederick, 1465, 1466
Spence, Jo, 1480
Starn, Doug and Mike, 1483
Steichen, Edward, 1488
Steiner, André, 1491
Stettner, Louis, 1493
Stieglitz, Alfred, 1496
Stone, Sasha, 1500
Strand, Paul, 1503
Struth, Thomas, 1510, 1511
Sudek, Josef, 1516
Sugimoto, Hiroshi, 1519
Szarkowski, John, 1525
Szilasi, Gabor, 1528
Tabard, Maurice, 1530
Teske, Edmund, 1537
Tice, George, 1540
Tillmans, Wolfgang, 1543
Tosani, Patrick, 1550
Traub, Charles, 1556
Tseng Kwong Chi, 1560
Turbeville, Deborah, 1562
Ubac, Raoul, 1570
Ulmann, Doris, 1577
Umbo (Otto Umbehr), 1579
Uzzle, Burt, 1603
Van Vechten, Carl, 1607
VanDerZee, James, 1609
Virilio, Paul, 1619
Vishniac, Roman, 1625
Wall, Jeff, 1635, 1636
Watanabe, Yoshio, 1647
Webb, Boyd, 1649
Weber, Bruce, 1652
Weegee, 1661
Weems, Carrie Mae, 1666
Wegman, William, 1672
Welpott, Jack, 1674
Weston, Edward, 1678
White, Clarence, 1680
White, Minor, 1684
Winogrand, Garry, 1694
Witkin, Joel-Peter, 1700, 1701
Wojnecki, Stefan, 1703
Woodman, Francesca, 1705
Zwart, Piet, 1719
Self-portraits, Central and West African, 27
Self-production, Claude Cahun and, 200
Semiotics, 1403–1405
further reading, 1405
history of semiotics of photography, 1404, 1405
semiotics and photography, 1404
Serrano, Andres, 1405–1408
American, 1405, 1406
biography, 1406, 1407
further reading, 1408
group exhibitions, 1407, 1408
individual exhibitions, 1407
selected works, 1408
Seymour, David "Chim", 1408–1411
American, born in Poland, 1408–1410
biography, 1410
further reading, 1410, 1411
group exhibitions, 1410
individual exhibitions, 1410
selected works, 1410
Shahn, Ben, 1411–1413
American, 1411, 1412
biography, 1412, 1413
further reading, 1413
group exhibitions, 1413
individual exhibitions, 1413
selected works, 1413
Shaikhet, Arkadii, 1414–1416
biography, 1415
further reading, 1416
group exhibitions, 1416
individual exhibitions, 1415
Russian, 141–1415
selected works, 1416
Sheeler, Charles, 58, 1416–1419
American, 1416–1418
biography, 1418
further reading, 1418, 1419
group exhibitions, 1418
individual exhibitions, 1418
selected works, 1418
Sheet film, 214
Sherman, Cindy, 1419–1422
American, 1419, 1420
biography, 1420
further reading, 1422
Gregory Crewdson and, 342
group exhibitions, 1421, 1422
individual exhibitions, 1420, 1421
selected works, 1422
Shibata, Toshio, 1423–1425
biography, 1424
further reading, 1425
group exhibitions, 1424, 1425

Shibata, Toshio (*Continued*)
individual exhibitions, 1424
Japanese, 1423, 1424
selected works, 1425
Shore, Stephen, 1425–1428
American, 1425, 1426
biography, 1426, 1427
further reading, 1428
group exhibitions, 1427
individual exhibitions, 1427
selected works, 1427
Shutter(s)
definition of, 211
focal plane, 216
ultra-fast miniaturized, 1701
Shutter speed(s), 211
aperture and, 216
film speed and, 212
long, 211
time exposure and, 1544
Sierra Club, Ansel Adams and, 9
Simple camera, 214
Simpson, Lorna, 1428–1431
American, 1428, 1429
biography, 1429
further reading, 1431
group exhibitions, 1430, 1431
individual exhibitions, 1429
selected works, 1431
Singh, Raghubir, 1431–1434
biography, 1434
further reading, 1434
Indian, 1431–1434
selected works, 1434
Single-lens-reflex (SLR), 210, 211, 215, 219
advantage of over point-and-shoot cameras, 211
folding, 222
incorporated viewfinder, 211
integrated motor drive, 211
metering choices, 213
point-and-shoot cameras and, 227
Siskind, Aaron, 1434–1438
American, 1434–1437
biography, 1437
Center for Creative Photography and, 253
further reading, 1438
group exhibitions, 1438
individual exhibitions, 1437, 1438
selected works, 1438
Skoglund, Sandy, 1439–1441
American, 1439, 1440
biography, 1440
further reading, 1441
group exhibitions, 1440, 1441
individual exhibitions, 1440
selected works, 1441
Skyscrapers, vantage points offered by, 22
Slide film, overexposure of, 301
SLR, *see* Single-lens-reflex
Snapshot aesthetic, 51
Snow, Michael, 1441–1445
biography, 1443
Canadian, 1441–1443
further reading, 1445
group exhibitions, 1443–1445
individual exhibitions, 1443
selected works, 1445
Snowdon (Anthony Armstrong-Jones), 1445–1447
biography, 1446, 1447
British, 1445, 1446
further reading, 1447
Social activism, architectural photography and, 59
Socialist photography, 1452–1458
aesthetic and ideological conflicts, 1454–1456
codification of socialist realism, 1456–1458
further reading, 1458
Socialist Realist photography, 42
Social landscape photography, 51
Social representation, 1447–1451
Social Sculpture, Joseph Beuys and, 125
Society of American Archivists, 65
Solarization, 1459, 1460
Edmund Teske and, 1535
Francis Joseph Bruguière and, 176
further reading, 1460
virtual reality and, 1621
Solomon-Godeau, Abigail, 1461, 1462
American, 1461, 1462
biography, 1462
further reading, 1462
Sommer, Frederick, 1463–1466
American, 1463, 1464
biography, 1464
Center for Creative Photography and, 253
further reading, 1466
group exhibitions, 1465
individual exhibitions, 1464, 1465
selected works, 1465, 1466
Sontag, Susan, 1466, 1467
American, 1466, 1467
biography, 1467
further reading, 1467
South Africa, *see* Africa, South and Southern
South America, 1468–1473
Argentina, 1469
Bolivia, 1469, 1470
Brazil, 1470
Chile, 1470, 1471
Colombia, 1471
Ecuador, 1471
further reading, 1473
Perú, 1471, 1472
Uruguay, 1472
Venezuela, 1472–1374
websites, 1473
Southern Africa, *see* Africa, South and Southern
Soviet industry and ideology, record of, 42
Space, cubist diffraction of, 6
Spain and Portugal, 1474–1477
further reading, 1478
Portugal, 1476–1478
Spain, 1474–1476
Spectroscopy, 76
Spence, Jo, 1478–1480
biography, 1479, 1480
British, 1478, 1479
further reading, 1480
group exhibitions, 1480
individual exhibitions, 1480
selected works, 1480

Stalin's Five-Year Plans, 40
Starn, Doug and Mike, 1481–1483
  American, 1481, 1482
  biography, 1482
  further reading, 1483
  group exhibitions, 1482, 1483
  individual exhibitions, 1482
  selected works, 1483
State Pushkin Museum, Moscow, 43
Station point, 150
Stedelijk Museum, 1483–1485
Steichen, Edward, 1485–1489
  American, 1485–1487
  biography, 1487, 1488
  further reading, 1488, 1489
  group exhibitions, 1488
  individual exhibitions, 1488
  selected works, 1488
Steiner, André, 1489–1491
  biography, 1490
  French, 1489, 1490
  further reading, 1491
  group exhibitions, 1491
  individual exhibitions, 1490
  selected works, 1491
Stettner, Louis, 1491–1493
  American, 1491–1493
  biography, 1493
  further reading, 1493
  group exhibitions, 1493
  individual exhibitions, 1493
  selected works, 1493
Stieglitz, Alfred, 1494–1497
  abstraction and, 6
  American, 1494–1495
  anti-commercial philosophy of, 1679
  biography, 1495, 1496
  corporate collections, 337
  further reading, 1496, 1497
  group exhibitions, 1496
  individual exhibitions, 1496
  Photo-Secession, 175
  selected works, 1496
Stone, Sasha, 1497–1500
  biography, 1499
  further reading, 1500
  group exhibitions, 1500
  individual exhibitions, 1499
  Russian, 1497–1499
  selected works, 1500
  Umbo and, 1577
Straight photography, 7, 10
  aesthetic, 6
  beginnings of as fine art, 58
  Eugène Atget and, 80
Strand, Paul, 9, 58, 1500–1503
  American, 1500–1502
  biography, 1502
  exhibitions, 1502, 1503
  further reading, 1503
  Robert Bourdeau and, 149
  selected works, 1503
Street photography, 1503–1508
  further reading, 1508
  Imogen Cunningham and, 349
Strobe light
  time exposure and, 1544
  underwater photography and, 1583
Struth, Thomas, 1508–1511
  biography, 1509
  further reading, 1511
  German, 1508, 1509
  group exhibitions, 1510
  individual exhibitions, 1509, 1510
  selected works, 1510, 1511
Stryker, Roy, 153, 1511–1514
  American, 1511–1513
  biography, 1513
  further reading, 1513, 1514
Studio cameras, digital, 219
Subjective Photography, Chargesheimer and, 265
Sudek, Josef, 1514, 1517
  biography, 1515
  Czechoslovakian, 1514, 1515
  further reading, 1516, 1517
  group exhibitions, 1516
  individual exhibitions, 1516
  selected works, 1516
Sugimoto, Hiroshi, 1517, 1519
  biography, 1518
  further reading, 1519
  group exhibitions, 1519
  individual exhibitions, 1518, 1519
  Japanese, 1517, 1518
  selected works, 1519
Super 8 film, body art and, 145
Surrealism, 7, 73, 74, 1519–1522
  further reading, 1521, 1522
  Joel-Peter Witkin and, 1697
  Raoul Ubac and, 1568
  typical role of female artist in, 201
Surrealists
  Bill Brandt and, 160
  Eugène Atget and, 80
  postulate of, 1533
Surveillance satellite, first, 21
Szabo, Steve, 1522, 1523
  American, 1522, 1523
  biography, 1523
  further reading, 1523
Szarkowski, John, 1523–1525
  American, 1523–1525
  biography, 1525
  further reading, 1525
  selected works, 1525
Szilasi, Gabor, 1526–1528
  biography, 1527
  Canadian, 1526, 1527
  further reading, 1528
  group exhibitions, 1527, 1528
  individual exhibitions, 1527
  selected works, 1528

T

Tabard, Maurice, 1529–1531
  altered realities, 1529
  avant-garde photography, 1530
  biography, 1530

Tabard, Maurice (*Continued*)
Composition with Guitars, 1529
fashion magazines, 1530
French, 1529, 1530
French Motion Picture Service, 1530
further reading, 1530
group exhibitions, 1530
individual exhibitions, 1530
Man Ray and, 1530
Marie-Claire, 1530
Photographer's Association of America, 1530
reversals of tones, 1529
selected works, 1530
simultaneous impressions, 1529
solarization, 1529
Taiwan, *see* China and Taiwan
Talbot, William Henry Fox, 6
TASS news agency, 43
Technical books, Ansel Adams, 13, 14
Teige, Karel, 1532–1534
anti-bourgeoise art, 1532
architecture lectures at Bauhaus, 1532
art-theoretical activities, 1533
aura of the original, 1532
biography, 1533
Czech, 1532, 1533
Erotic revue, 1532
exhibitions, 1534
free photo assembly, 1532
further reading, 1534
interpretation of dreams, 1532
nude fragments, 1533
opposition to Surrealist manifestos, 1532
photo-assembled book cover, 1532
photo-collage, 1532, 1533
poetic anthology, 1532
poetic function, 1533
postulate of the Surrealists, 1533
psychoanalysis, 1532
renouveau, 1532
selected publications, 1533, 1534
unconsciousness of internal model, 1533
water color paintings, 1533
would-be artist, 1532
Telephoto disposable camera, 221
Teske, Edmund, 1534–1537
American, 1534, 1535
biography, 1535–1537
documentary style, 1535
emotion and intuition, 1534
experimental filmmaker and, 1535
experimentation, 1535
Federal Arts Project, 1534
Frank Lloyd Wright's Taliesin, 1534
further reading, 1537
group exhibitions, 1537
homoerotic imagery, 1535
Huttle Art Studio, 1534
individual exhibitions, 1537
initial inspiration, 1534
Institute of Design, 1534
Lust for Life, 1535
purpose in life, 1534
romantic tradition, 1534
selected works, 1537
solarization process, 1535
Vogue magazine, 1535
Tice, George, 1537–1541
American, 1537–1539
Amish Portfolio: Twelve Original Photographs, 1538
biography, 1539
books, 1540, 1541
connection to sense of place, 1537
cradle of American industry, 1538
documenting of American landscape, 1537
further reading, 1541
group exhibitions, 1539, 1540
individual exhibitions, 1539
Kodak Baby Brownie camera, 1538
large format camera, 1537
MoMA solo show, 1538
monumental in commonplace, 1537
most personal project, 1538, 1539
Petit Mobil Station, 1538
selected works, 1540
solitude of image, 1538
Ticetown, 1538, 1539
Urban Romantic, 1538
View Camera, 1538
workshops taught by, 1539
Tillmans, Wolfgang, 1541–1453
abstracted nature of photograph, 1542
Arts Institute of Bournemouth, 1541
beauty of the mundane, 1542
biography, 1542
British Turner Prize, 1542
chronicler of a generation, 1541
contradiction in work, 1541
early photographs, 1541
first monograph, 1541
further reading, 1543
German, 1541, 1542
group exhibitions, 1542, 1543
individual exhibitions, 1542
magazine photography, 1541
painterly photographs, 1542
Parkett, 1542
Purple magazine, 1542
selected works, 1543
Time exposure, 1543, 1544
camera's built-in meter, 1543
control of shutter speed, 1544
definition of, 1543
dragging effect to light, 1544
extension of pre-set limitations of camera, 1543
further reading, 1544
handheld light meters, 1543
large-format cameras, 1543
popular destination to photograph, 1544
scientific applications, 1544
shakiness, 1544
strobe lighting, 1544
Tokyo Metropolitan Museum of Photography, 1544–1546
blockbuster exhibitions, 1545
closing of, 1546
collection, 1545
financer, 1544
first municipal art museum in Japan, 1544
focus of, 1545
history of Japanese documentary photography, 1545, 1546

Tokyo Metropolitan Museum of Photography (*Continued*)
Image & Technology Gallery, 1545
inaugural exhibition, 1545
one-person exhibitions, 1546
opening of, 1546
Ordinance of, 1544
retrospectives, 1545
Shashin-Geijyutsu-Sha, 1545
size of, 1545
W. Eugene Smith photographs, 1545, 1546
Tomb of Tutankhamen, discoverers of, 33
Toning, 1546, 1547
archival qualities of, 1547
direct toners, 1547
further reading, 1547
gelatin silver papers, 1546
gold chloride, 1546
idealistic Impressionism, 1547
image bleaching, 1547
methods of, 1546, 1547
multiple toning, 1547
nostalgia, 1546
Orotone process, 1546, 1547
photographers who popularized toning, 1547
photogravure, 1546
romanticism, 1547
silver prints, 1546
straight photography, 1547
Tosani, Patrick, 1548–1550
biography, 1549
blow-ups, 1548
body pictures, 1549
Braille, 1548
creation of fictional narrative, 1548
cropped framing, 1548
French, 1548, 1549
further reading, 1550
group exhibitions, 1550
individual exhibitions, 1549, 1550
inherent paradoxes of photographic image, 1548
Les masques, 1549
model's identity, 1548, 1549
Niveaux, 1548
Portraits, 1548
rain as sculpture, 1548
reflections about appearance and surfaces, 1548
selected works, 1550
serial practice, 1548
Têtes, 1548
white background, 1549
Toscani, Oliviero, 1550–1553
advertising campaigns, 1550
agency images from Magnum and Sygma, 1551
awards, 1552
biography, 1552
Colors, 1552
Contrasts in Black & White, 1551
ethical messages, 1551
Fabrica, 1552
fashion photographer, 1550
international exhibition of contemporary art, 1552
Italian, 1550–1552
lifestyle advertising, 1552
political meaning, 1551
prejudices, 1551
spare presentation, 1550
United Colors of Benetton, 1551
volatile topics, 1551
world-wide reputation, 1550
Traub, Charles, 1554–1556
abstraction, 1554
absurdities of everyday life, 1555
Beach photographs, 1554
biography, 1556
chance encounters, 1554
enduring legacy, 1555
fly on the wall quality, 1555
further reading, 1556
group exhibitions, 1556
individual exhibitions, 1556
Institute of Design, 1554
intrusion of camera, 1554
juxtaposition of photographic image and text, 1555
magazines, 1555
selected works, 1556
technology-based writings, 1555
verbal-visual poetry, 1555
voyeuristic implications, 1554
Tripods, 213
Tseng Kwong Chi, 1557–1560
American, 1557, 1558
artist's identity as foreigner, 1558
biography, 1558
Disneyland, California, 1557
documenting chalk drawings, 1557, 1558
East Meets West, 1557
The Expeditionary Series, 1558
further reading, 1560
group exhibitions, 1558, 1559
individual exhibitions, 1558
international travel, 1557
Keith Haring and, 1557, 1558
Maoist uniform, 1558
mature artistic identity, 1557
national identity, 1558
order and control of characters, 1557
selected works, 1560
self-portraiture, 1557
SLUTFORART, 1557
Whitney Biennial, 1558
Tungsten film, 299
Turbeville, Deborah, 1560–1562
American, 1560, 1561
biography, 1561
books published, 1561
camera choices, 1560
Claus von Bulow book review, 1561
controversial fashion images, 1560
creation of mood, 1560
experimentation, 1560
Fulbright scholarship, 1561
further reading, 1562
group exhibitions, 1562
images out of focus, 1560
individual exhibitions, 1561, 1562
Jacqueline Onassis and, 1561
Maquillage, 1561
narrative inspiration, 1560
selected works, 1562
unorthodox exhibitions, 1561

Turbeville, Deborah (*Continued*)
Unseen Versailles, 1561
Wallflower, 1561
Turner Prize, Billingham's nomination for, 131
Twin lens reflex, 215
Two-dimensional patterns, formalism of, 7
Typestyle, universal, 105
Typography master, 104
Typology, 1562–1565
archive, 1565
August Sander and, 1563
characteristics, 1565
definition of, 1562
Eugène Atget and, 1563
examples and parallels, 1563–1565
further reading, 1565
George Eastman House exhibition, 1563
image-making approach, 1562
Jungian psychology and, 1562
lack of luminosity, 1565
new objectivity, 1562
New Topographics approach, 1563–1565
often-cited model, 1563
origins and precedents, 1563
people inhabiting Weimar Germany, 1562
personality assessment and, 1562
predominance of subject matter, 1562
premise, 1562
use of term within photography, 1562
Tzara, Tristan, 141

U

Ubac, Raoul, 1567–1570
Belgian, 1567, 1568
billboard campaign, 1568
biography, 1568, 1569
choosing French naturalization, 1567
experimental style, 1567
first significant series of works, 1567
fossils, 1568
further reading, 1570
group exhibitions, 1569, 1570
individual exhibitions, 1569
L'invention collective, 1568
Man Ray and, 1567
Messages group, 1568
Minotaure, 1568
Montparnasse Studios, 1567
Nazi occupation, 1568
selected works, 1570
Stones of Dalmacy, 1567
Surrealist movement, 1567
Uelsmann, Jerry, 1570–1574
American, 1570–1572
biography, 1572
combination printing, 1571
digital images, 1571
Friends of Photography, 1571
further reading, 1574
group exhibitions, 1572–1574
Guggenheim Fellowship, 1571
illogical landscapes, 1571
individual exhibitions, 1572
juxtapositions of nature to geometrical elements, 1571
merging of reality and fantasy, 1570
psychological emphasis, 1571
reprints, 1571
subconscious, 1570
Surrealist ideology about dreams, 1570
teaching style, 1571
themes, 1571
virtual reality and, 1621, 1622
work as metaphors for ideas, 1570
Ulmann, Doris, 1574–1577
American, 1574–1575
Appalachian photographs, 1575
biography, 1575
camera used, 1574
contact prints, 1575
further reading, 1577
group exhibitions, 1575–1577
Gullah culture, 1575
individual exhibitions, 1575
Pictorial Photographers of America, 1574
Portrait of a Child, 1574
portraits of celebrities, 1575
Roll, Jordan, Roll, 1575
selected works, 1577
Shaker and Mennonite communities, 1575
vanishing customs, 1574
Umbo (Otto Umbehr), 1577–1581
Bauhaus stay, 1577
biography, 1579
close-up-effect, 1578
DEPHOT, 1578
designs for billboards, 1577
experimenting with perspectives, 1578
further reading, 1579–1581
German, 1577, 1578
group exhibitions, 1579
individual exhibitions, 1579
Life in Dead Things, 1578
lighting and principles of formation, 1578
photo montages, 1577, 1578
photograms, 1578
selected works, 1579
self-taught photographer, 1577
visually staging spontaneously found objects, 1578
work with Sasha Stone, 1577, 1578
Underwater photography, 1581–1584
advantage of housing systems, 1582
amphibious Nikonos-type cameras, 1583
atmospheric pressure, 1582
backscattering, 1583
behavior of light in water, 1583
Calypsophot, 1583
color affected by water, 1583
color distortion, 1583
diving and, 1584
Eadweard Muybridge and, 1581
experiments in, 1581
first true underwater photograph, 1581
floatation device, 1581
further reading, 1584
invention of flash, 1582
Jacques-Yves Cousteau, 1582
Louis Boutan, 1581
National Geographic, 1582

Underwater photography (*Continued*)
popularity of, 1581
scarcity of light, 1582
Sea & *see* Motormarine, 1583
strength of light, 1583
strobe light, 1583
watertight box, 1581
world's first self-contained underwater camera, 1582
UNESCO, World Heritage List, 229
Union of Russian Proletarian Photographers (ROPF), 43
United Nations, Taiwan forced out of, 275
United Press International (UPI), 334
United States, Midwest, 1584–1591
1910s, 1584, 1585
1920s, 1582–1586
1930s, 1586, 1587
1940s onward, 1587–1589
1960s and 1970s, 1589
1980s onward, 1589–1591
abstract compositions, 1585
aerial photographs, 1590
America's heartland, 1584
auto-making, 1585
black and white studies of industrial landscape, 1590
built environment, 1584
Charles Sheeler, 1585
Chicago School, 1584
Chicago's A Century of Progress International Exposition, 1585
Clarence H. White, 1584
community, 1591
decline of sales of Model T, 1585
digital alterations, 1590
documenting of building types, 1586
emotional attachments, 1591
Estée Lauder's first national advertising campaign, 1589
ethnological displays, 1585
everyman images, 1589
family album of humanity, 1591
family album quality photographs, 1586
first major figure, 1584
FSA survey team, 1586, 1587
further readings, 1591
glamorous advertising photography, 1589
Harry Callahan, 1584
Hedrich-Blessing photography collection, 1586
hobby photographer, 1587
inhabited prairie, 1590
institutional spaces, 1590
Jessie Tarbox Beals, 1585
Kansas Album, 1591
landscape photographers, 1590
lower culture grades of people, 1585
mind of architect, 1586
Moholy-Nagy's Foundations Program, 1587
New Bauhaus, 1587
photojournalists and 1904 World's Fair, 1585
plight of farmers, 1586
portraits of machinery, 1585
portraits of prairie grasses, 1590
precisionist artist, 1585
Print Study Room, 1589
Resettlement Administration, 1587
the Rouge, 1585
Rural Electrification Act, 1587
Tom Arndt's black-and-white images, 1589
trade exhibitions, 1585
trends, 1584
working-class values, 1589
United States, South, 1591–1600
African American photographers, 1592
Appalachian Mountains, 1593
Baptists church, 1598
changing ethnicity, 1598
Civil War reenactments, 1598
color photography, 1595
combination printing, 1595
Confederate icons, 1595
Cuban exiles, 1598
Depression Era views, 1593
DoubleTake, 1598
Edgerton Garvin, 1592
Emmet Gowin's aesthetic approach, 1596
environmental issues, 1598
feminist issues, 1599
first museum devoted to photography, 1597
folklorist, 1596
further reading, 1600
George Washington Carver, 1592
Gory, 1599
identity, 1591
illuminated photographs, 1597
influx of Hispanic artists, 1598
jazz, 1594
Juke Joints, 1596
literary renaissance, 1592
lost in time Southern places, 1594
mail order magazines, 1592
MANUAL, 1599
Mojo music, 1596
narrative voice, 1591
National Child Labor Committee, 1592
New Contemporary South, 1597
New Orleans, 1593
New South, 1595
Nexus, 1595, 1596
nonprofit organization, 1597
Old South, 1595
Olympics, 1597
oral traditions, 1592
outsider' artists, 1598
painting on photographs, 1599
The Picture Man, 1596
Pinky/MM Bass, 1600
prisons, 1598
Sahara of the Beaux Arts, 1592
service-oriented age, 1598
sites of leisure, 1598
social landscape photographer, 1594
The Southern Ethic Show, 1595
South of popular imagination, 1593
spiritual truths, 1598
superhighways, 1595
Tenants of the Allmighty, 1593
Tuskegee Institute, 1592
Walker Evans, 1595
ways photographer could earn living, 1591, 1592
William Christenberry, 1595
Works Progress Administration, 1593
writers and photographic arts, 1592
UPI, *see* United Press International

Urbanism, 61
U.S. Balloon Corps, 20
U.S. Camera, 2
User re-loadable cameras, 221
USSR in Construction, 40
Uzzle, Burt, 1600–1603
American, 1600–1602
Americanness, 1601
biography, 1602
everyday Americans, 1600
Florida's Daytona Bike Week, 1601
further reading, 1603
group exhibitions, 1602, 1603
individual exhibitions, 1602
Leslie Fry and, 1602
National Endowment for the Arts Photography Fellowship, 1601
Newsweek, 1602
panoramic typologies of shredded papers, 1602
portraits, 1601
preference for wandering freely, 1601
selected works, 1603
subjects, 1601
visual music, 1602

V

V&A, *see* Victoria and Albert Museum
VanDerZee, James, 1608–1610
American, 1608, 1609
artistic portraits, 1607
biography, 1609
contrived settings, 1607
controversial exhibition, 1607
first solo retrospective, 1608
further reading, 1609, 1610
ghost image of child, 1607
group exhibitions, 1609
Guarantee Photo Studio, 1607
Harlem Renaissance, 1607
individual exhibitions, 1609
outdates portraits, 1607
painted backdrops, 1608
portraits, 1607
selected works, 1609
UNIA's military-style events, 1607
Wedding Portrait: 'Future Expectations', 1607
Vanity Fair, 2, 308, 309
Van Vechten, Carl, 1605–1607
American, 1605, 1606
avant-garde opera, 1605
back-and-white portraits, 1605
biography, 1606
Chicago American, 1605
dance critic, 1605
further reading, 1607
group exhibitions, 1607
Harlem Renaissance, 1605
individual exhibitions, 1606, 1607
literary criticism, 1606
Photo-Secessionists and, 1606
post-impressionist painting, 1605
preserving the personalities of African-American culture, 1606
selected works, 1607
Vernacular photography, 39, 1610–1616
aesthetic merit, 1615
aesthetic value, 1610
Andy Warhol and, 1615
Antiques Roadshow, 1615
Arts in Modern American Civilization, 1610, 1611
box camera, 1613
Brownie camera and, 1613
characterizations of, 1612
Collected Visions, 1616
collecting vernacular photographs, 1615
contesting of definition of, 1610
culture of, 1616
daguerreotype portraits, 1611
definition of snapshot, 1612
early daguerreotypey, 1613
everyday life, 1610
further reading, 1616
genre codes, 1610
Geoffrey Batchen and, 1610
good taste, 1610
images used against the grain, 1610
instincts, 1612
Kodaking, 1613
Kodak's influence on snapshot genre, 1613
Kodak's marketing of inexpensive cameras, 161
legibility over style, 1611
Lorie Novak's web project, 1616
morphology of, 1614
negative construction, 1610
neoprint photo-sticker machines, 1614
new breed of photographers, 1613
newspaper clippings, 1611
Nikki S. Lee, 1615
non-aesthetic genres, 1610
nostalgia, 1611
origin of snapshot, 1613
other vernacular forms, 1614, 1615
paradoxical nature, 1611, 1616
parts series, 1615, 1616
Patricia Holland's anthology, 1611
photographic hegemony, 1612
photography as democratic medium, 1613
Photography: A Middle Brow Art, 1612
photo-objects, 1614
Pop Photographica exhibition, 1614
portable daguerreotypes, 1614
practically-oriented approach, 1610
private contexts, 1611
production of, 1612
qualities signifying value, 1615
Roland Barthes and, 1611
Snapshot Versions of Life, 1611
snapshot, 1612–1614
that-has-been, 1612
time capsules, 1615
vernacular photography as fine art, 1615, 1616
virtual reality and, 1620
visual codes, 1612
visual rhetoric, 1611
wedding portraits, 1614
Victoria and Albert Museum (V&A), 1616, 1617
Class Seven, 1617
Creative camera and, 341
first acquisitions of photographic art, 1617

Victoria and Albert Museum (V&A) (*Continued*)
further reading, 1617
genre concentrations, 1617
international collection, 1617
museum as research institution, 1617
Photographic Society of London, 1617
reference collection of publications, 1617
Vienna Actionism, *see* Wiener Aktionismus
View cameras, 214, 215
Vinegar syndrome, 318
Virilio, Paul, 1618, 1619
Aesthetics of Disappearance, 1618
apprehension for the future, 1619
Architecture Principe, 1618
art critic of technology, 1618
biography, 1619
Claude Parent and, 1618
criticism of contemporary art, 1619
dromology, 1618
French, 1618, 1619
further reading, 1619
Howard Hughes, 1619
influential ideas, 1619
nostalgia, 1619
oblique function, 1618
primary interest, 1618
selected works, 1619
September 11, 2001, and, 1618
violence of speed, 1618
Virtual reality (VR), 1620–1623
altering of images, 1620
Ansel Adams' Zone System, 1620
architectural photography and, 62
basis of film, 1620
Computer Aided Design, 1623
definition of, 1620
digital imagery and, 1623
fashion photography, 1620
further reading, 1623
hand-coloured photomontages, 1622
images from television shows, 1622
Internet and, 1622
Jerry Uelsman and, 1621, 1622
Joel-Peter, 1620
magazine ads, 1621
Man Ray and, 1621
method of darkroom alteration, 1621
models decorated with, 1621
movie-like, 1622
music groups, 1622
negative montage, 1621
oldest method of achieving effects, 1620
Pablo Picasso and, 1621
photomontage, 1621
Pop artists, 1621
Ralph Meatyard and, 1621, 1622
semi-robotic figures, 1622
sensual experience and, 1623
Shanghai stock exchange, 1623
simulation games, 1622
solarization and, 1621
staging and, 1620
suspension of disbelief, 1620
switching roles of stage and reality, 1620
technical media, 1620
vernacular photography and, 1620
William Wegman and, 1622
Vishniac, Roman, 1623–1626
biography, 1625
business of discovery, 1625
color microphotographic images, 1623
concentration camp, 1624
documents of time and place, 1623
Edward Steichen, 1623
fascination with nature, 1623
favorite portrait, 1625
fugitive Jews, 1623
further reading, 1625
German political climate, 1624
group exhibitions, 1625
hidden camera, 1624
Holocaust, 1623
idea, 1625
individual exhibitions, 1625
jewels in the mud, 1625
march in Nazi uniform, 1624
political protests, 1624
portrait photography, 1624
Rolleiflex camera, 1624
Russian Revolution, 1624
Russian, 1623–1625
selected works, 1625
sensitivity toward life, 1625
threatened, 1624
ultimate concerned photographer, 1623
Visual Anthropology, 27
Visual anthropology, 1626–1629
art world as system of power relations, 1627
control of camera, 1626
definition of, 1626
deployment of camera in research situations, 1626
didacticism and display, 1627
fading of modernist paradigm, 1626, 1627
feminist scholarship, 1628
found way of structuring world, 1627
fugitive testimony, 1626
functional display of objects, 1628
further reading, 1628, 1629
international communication, 1627
Margaret Mead and, 1626, 1628
memorial museums, 1628
National Geographic, 1627
NEThing Company, 1627
objectivity of knowledge, 1627
pioneer in, 1626
Pitt Rivers Museum, 1628
Portfolio of Piles, 1627
relationship between visual and verbal signs, 1628
self-critique, 1627, 1628
staged cibachrome dramas, 1628
subjects, 1627
unequal looking relations, 1627
Visual documentary, contribution of Berenice Abbott to, 1
Visual grammar, 120
Visual music, 1602
Visual Studies Workshop (VSW), 38, 74
Book Bus, 38
overall goals of, 38
Vogue magazine, 1, 308
art director, 309

Vogue magazine (*Continued*)
Blumenfeld and, 142
Cecil Beaton and, 108, 109
editor-in-chief, 309
fashion editor, 309
Herbert Bayer and, 106
Vorticism movement, 6
Vortographies, 6
Voyeuristic iconography, Arbus's, 53
VR, *see* Virtual reality
VSW, *see* Visual Studies Workshop

W

Wall, Jeff, 1631–1636
back-lit Cibachrome transparencies, 1632
biography, 1633, 1634
Canadian, 1631–1633
computer-aided imagery, 1632
Conceptual art and, 1631
Courtauld Institute of Art, 1631
Dead Troops Talk, 1633
digital manipulation, 1631
Double Self-Portrait, 1632
Faking Death, 1632
further reading, 1636
group exhibitions, 1634, 1635
imagined truths, 1631
individual exhibitions, 1634
interest in cinema, 1631
large-scale color transparencies, 1631
lightbox photographs, 1632
philosophical comedy, 1633
Picture for Women, 1632
preoccupations, 1633
prestigious honor, 1633
selected works, 1635, 1636
The Stumbling Block, 1632
visual anthropology and, 1628
War
aerial photography and, 20
internalized effects of, 133
photographer, greatest, 237
Warhol, Andy
John Coplans and, 329
landmark photo silkscreens, 46
War photography, 1636–1644
Abu Ghraib prison, 1641
aesthetic surplus, 1640
alternate form of engaged 1639
archive of World War II pictures, 1638
authenticity, 1639
Canadian, 233
Cold War, 1641
concerned, 1642
crimes against humanity, 1641
death camps, 1641
destruction of European Jewry, 1640
Dwight D. Eisenhower, 1638
Eddie Adams, 1642
embedded reporting, 1643
empathic documentary photography, 1638
further reading, 1644
gruesomeness of soldiers' experiences, 1637
Hiroshima-Nagasaki '61, 1640
human costs of war, 1637
illustrated battlefield tour guides, 1637
indictment of way, 1639
Life's portrayal of war, 1638
Magnum Photos, 1639
mediated records, 1636
Middle East conflicts, 1643
modern warfare, 1636
mushroom cloud, 1640
Nazi genocide, 1641
Nazi propaganda magazine, 1638
negative epiphany, 1640
Normandy invasion, 1639
photographs censored by military, 1637, 1638
photography of atrocity, 1641
popular memory, 1638
private cameras of anonymous soldiers, 1637
professional, 1643
propaganda ministry, 1640
Pulitzer Prize winning photographs, 1642
risks and values of, 14
Robert Capa and, 1639
Shoah, 1640
Signal, 1638
Soviet photographers, 1639
Susan Sontag, 1640
technologically advanced weapons, 1636
television coverage, 1642
Text offensive, 1643
twentieth-century death tools, 1636
U.S. postwar hegemony, 1641
Vietnam, 1642
Vietnamese nationalist resistance, 1643
visual culture, 1636, 1637
Watanabe, Yoshio, 1645–1647
ancient Shinto Shrine, 1645
authentic depiction, 1643
avante-garde, 1645
awards, 1646
biography, 1646
Camera Works, 1645
further reading, 1647
group exhibitions, 1647
individual exhibitions, 1646
International Report Photographers Society, 1645
Ise Shrine, 1645
Japanese, 1645, 1646
Library of Congress FSA-OWI collection, 1643
New Objectivity, 1645
Photographic Society of Japan, 1646
Photo-Times, 1645
sacred ceremony, 1646
selected works, 1647
spiritual dialogue between human being and divine spirits, 1645, 1646
Tokyo Metropolitan Museum of Photography, 1645
War on Terrorism, 1643
Webb, Boyd, 1647–1650
best-known images, 1648
biography, 1648
clash between nature and technology, 1648
computer-manipulated photographs, 1647
digital manipulation, 1648
diptychs, 1647

Webb, Boyd (*Continued*)
expatriate artist, 1647
further reading, 1649
group exhibitions, 1649
individual exhibitions, 1648, 1649
interest in human biology, 1648
New Zealand, 1647, 1648
River Crossing, 1648
Robert Self Gallery, 1647
satire, 1647
science fictional work, 1647
selected works, 1649
tableaux, 1648
Zygote, 1648
Weber, Bruce, 1651–1653
Abercrombie and Fitch, 1651, 1652
accusations, 1651
American, 1651, 1652
biography, 1652
black and white photographs, 1651
Calvin Klein advertisements, 1651
film career, 1652
further reading, 1653
group exhibitions, 1652
individual exhibitions, 1652
influences on, 1651
intimate lifestyle-like settings, 1651
Let's Get Lost, 1652
portraiture, 1651
Roadside America, 1652
selected works, 1652
technically acute work, 1651
videos, 1652
Weber, Wolfgang, 1653–1655
author, 1653
biography, 1654
*Das Gesicht der Stä*dte, 1653
estate, 1654
further reading, 1654, 1655
German, 1653, 1654
group exhibitions, 1654
individual exhibitions, 1654
magazine work, 1653, 1654
pioneer of modern photojournalism, 1653
political personalities, 1654
television, 1654
Ullstein Verlag, 1653
Wedding photography, 1655–1658
challenges to industry, 1656
commercial cabinet photographs, 1655
difficulties in, 1656
digital processes, 1656
further reading, 1656–1658
history, 1655
locations, 1656
loss of quality, 1655
non-western cultures, 1655
photojournalistic, 1655
poses, 1655
predominant styles, 1655
professional organizations, 1655
proofs, 1656
sociological levels, 1656
trade terms, 1655
traditional, 1655
variety in albums, 1656
Wedding Video Exposition, 1656
Weegee, 1658–1662
ACME News Pictures, 1658
Action Photography exhibition, 1658
American, 1658–1660
biography, 1660
books published, 1659
camera used, 1658
connection with subjects, 1660
corporate collections, 339
The Critic, 1658
further reading, 1660
group exhibitions, 1661
individual exhibitions, 1661
innovations, 1658
John Coplans and, 329
most famous image, 1658
naiveté of images, 1659
Naked Hollywood, 1659
photo-caricatures, 1659
photographs acquired by MoMA, 1658
police emergency calls, 1659
poor man's Stork Club, 1660
press photographer, 1659
Rembrandt light, 1659
rise to celebrity status, 1659
seedy New York City, 1658
selected works, 1661
Squeegie Boy, 1658
trademark, 1660
trust by subjects, 1658
Weems, Carrie Mae, 1597, 1663–1667
activism, 1663
Alpert Award in the Arts, 1664
alternative to the feminist gaze theories, 1664
American, 1663, 1664
anthropology, 1663
biography, 1664, 1665
challenge to herself and audience, 1663
civil rights, 1663
deconstruction issues, 1664
documentary foundations, 1663
Family Pictures and Stories, 1663
further reading, 1666, 1667
group exhibitions, 1665, 1666
individual exhibitions, 1665
interest in African-American folklore, 1663
J. Paul Getty Museum commission, 1663
National Museum of Women in the Arts, 1664
Pleasures and Terrors of Domestic Comfort, 1663
reproaching of popular culture, 1664
room-sized installations, 1664
selected works, 1666
Wegman, William, 1667–1672
American, 1667, 1668
biography, 1668
conceptual investigations, 1667
Family Combinations, 1667
further reading, 1672
genres, 1667
group exhibitions, 1668–1672
humor, 1668
incorporation of found objects, 1667
individual exhibitions, 1668

Wegman, William (*Continued*)
large-format Polaroids, 1668
Man Ray, 1668
pathetic irony, 1668
puns, 1668
selected works, 1672
seriousness of conceptual art, 1668
virtual reality and, 1622
works with Weimaraner dogs, 1667
Weiss, David, *see* Fischli, Peter, and David Weiss
Welpott, Jack, 1672–1674
American, 1672, 1673
biography, 1673
Brownie camera, 1672
cityscape photographs, 1673
formal problems, 1673
further reading, 1674
G.I. Bill, 1672
group exhibitions, 1674
Henry Holmes Smith and, 1672
individual exhibitions, 1673
interest in psychology, 1672
landscapes, 1673
painting, 1673
pioneer in photographic education, 1672
selected works, 1674
subjects, 1673
winding down of Beat Generation, 1673
West Africa, *see* Africa, Central and West
Western photographers, 16
Weston, Edward, 1674–1678
American, 1674–1676
ARMCO photographs, 1675
artists shaping aesthetic, 1675
biography, 1676–1678
break with pictorialism, 1675
competitions, 1675
first monograph, 1676
further reading, 1678
group exhibitions, 1678
Guggenheim Fellowship, 1676
individual exhibitions, 1678
Kodak Bulls-Eye #2 camera, 1674
Limited Editions Club, 1676
Modernism, 1675
nudes, 1675
Photo-Secession movement, 1674
postcard camera, 1674
posthumous showings, 1676
purists, 1674
selected works, 1678
straight prints, 1674
toning and, 1547
White, Clarence, 1678–1681
American, 1678–1680
anti-commercial philosophy of Stieglitz, 1679
biography, 1680
Camera Work, 1679
commercial photography, 1679
election to Linked Ring Brotherhood, 1679
further reading, 1680
London Salon, 1679
Morning, 1679
Photo-Secession and, 1678
Pictorialism, 1678
Premo view camera, 1679
selected works, 1680
Socialism, 1679
White School of Photography, 1679
White, Minor, 1682–1685
American, 1682, 1683
Ansel Adams and, 1682
biography, 1683
bold vision, 1682
contribution to photography, 1682
further reading, 1684
George Eastman House staff, 1683
group exhibitions, 1684
individual exhibitions, 1683, 1684
innocence of vision, 1682
Jerry Uelsmann and, 1570
manuscript, 1682
MoMA photographer, 1682
Oregon Art Project, 1682
People's Power League, 1682
selected publications, 1684
selected works, 1684
spiritual aspects of photography, 1682
statement of philosophy, 1683
student of photomicrography, 1682
teaching at Rochester Institute of Technology, 1683
theater techniques introduced by, 1682
U.S. Army Intelligence Corps, 1682
visiting professor at Massachusetts Institute of Technology, 1683
Zen meditation, 1682
White balancing, 299
Wiener Aktionismus, 1686, 1687
alchemy, 1687
communal life, 1686
deliberately extreme actions, 1687
documenting of actions, 1687
Festival of Psycho-Physical Naturalism, 1686
further reading, 1687
Gunter Brus, 1686
Herman Nitsch's life work, 1686
notoriety of, 1686
performance artists, 1686
Post-war Modernism, 1687
ritualistic statement, 1686
shock-artists, 1687
Viennese expressionism, 1686
work ignored by critics, 1687
Wildlife photo books, African, 30
Wilhelm, Henry, Corbis/Bettmann and, 335
Willis-Kennedy, Deborah, 1687–1689
African American photographic history, 1687
American, 1687, 1688
biography, 1689
fine art exhibitions, 1687
further reading, 1689
groundbreaking work, 1687
group exhibitions, 1689
identity of new negro, 1688
important themes in exhibits, 1688
individual exhibitions, 1689
MacArthur Foundation Grant, 1687
neutral stance of critics, 1688
notable national exhibits, 1688
research positions, 1688

Winogrand, Garry, 1690–1695
abrupt character, 1691
aggressive approach to photographing public life, 1690
American, 1690–1692
archive, 1690
biography, 1692
complexity of photographs, 1691
comprehensive source of information on, 1692
compulsive photographing of women, 1691
esthetic self-absorption, 1691
explanation of photographs, 1691
further reading, 1694, 1695
group exhibitions, 1693, 1694
individual exhibitions, 1692, 1693
influences on work, 1691
last few thousand rolls, 1692
legacy, 1692
MoMA exhibition, 1690, 1691
partial precursors, 1690
scale of backlog, 1692
selected works, 1694
Unfinished Work, 1692
Winter Garden photograph, 102
Witkiewicz (Witkacy), Stanislaw Ignacy, 1695–1697
avant-garde modernist artist, 1695
biography, 1696–1697
discovery of experiments, 1695
final period, 1696
further reading, 1697
individual exhibitions, 1697
Life Theater, 1696
Metaphysical Feeling of the Strangeness of Existence, 1696
Multiple self-portrait, 1696
novel, 1695
permanent exhibition, 1697
philosophy, 1696
Polish, 1695, 1696
seminal influences on, 1695
style of portrait photography, 1696
Witkin, Joel-Peter, 1697–1701
acclaim from National Endowment for the Arts, 1697
American, 1697–1699
biography, 1699
exaggerated peculiar in photographs, 1698
Feast of Fools, 1698
first experience with the macabre, 1698
further reading, 1701
group exhibitions, 1699, 1700
human anomalies, 1697
individual exhibitions, 1699
interest in religious dogma, 1698
memento mori, 1697
physical prodigies, 1698
selected works, 1700, 1701
Surrealism of 1930s, 1697
WIZO, *see* Women's International Zionist Organization
W magazine, 310
Wojnecki, Stefan, 1701–1703
biography, 1702
digital manipulation, 1702
Duogrammes series, 1701
further reading, 1703
group exhibitions, 1703
Hyperphotography, 1702
individual exhibitions, 1702, 1703
locked perception of viewer, 1702
new artistic practices, 1701
Polish, 1701, 1702
political vision, 1701
post-media photography concept, 1702
Profile, 1701
research about photographic medium, 1702
selected works, 1703
technical characteristics of material, 1701
ultra-fast miniaturized shutter, 1701
Woman-run photography studio, pioneering, 82
Women's International Zionist Organization (WIZO), 83
Woodman, Francesca, 1703–1705
American, 1703–1705
Beyond Photography 80, 1704
biography, 1705
further reading, 1705
group exhibitions, 1705
individual exhibitions, 1705
selected works, 1705
willingness to entrust viewer, 1703
Worker photography, 1706–1708
founding of Arbeiter-Fotograf, 1707
further reading, 1707, 1708
impact of, 1707
Willi Münzenberg and AIZ, 1706, 1707
Works Progress Administration (WPA), 251, 1593, 1709–1711
further reading, 1711
Oregon Art Project, 1682
World War II, documentation of destruction of, 59
World Wide Web, artists books circulated on, 73
WPA, *see* Works Progress Administration

X

Xerography, 1713–1715
Canadian, 235
further reading, 1715
Xerox photo albums, 49

Z

Zero-61 group, 1717, 1718
Zone System
development of, 10, 11
popularity of, 11
Zoom lens, 211, 212
Zwart, Piet, 1718, 1719
biography, 1719
Dutch, 1718, 1719
further reading, 1719
selected works, 1719